THE APOCALYPSE

THE

Apocalypse

LECTURES ON THE
BOOK OF
REVELATION

J. A. Seiss

Zondervan Publishing House
GRAND RAPIDS, MICHIGAN

FIFTH REPRINT EDITION 1964
SIXTH REPRINT EDITION 1966
SEVENTH REPRINT EDITION . . . 1967

Printed in the United States of America

PREFACE

THERE is a widespread prejudice against the study of the Apocalypse. Though it is the great prophetic Book of the New Testament, the last of all the writings of Inspiration, a special message from the ascended Saviour to His Churches on earth, and pressed upon every one's attention with uncommon urgency, there are religious guides, sworn to teach " the whole counsel of God," who make a merit of not understanding it, and of not wishing to occupy themselves with it. If such treatment of an acknowledged part of the Sacred Canon is compatible with ministerial fidelity and Christian duty, the author of these Lectures is very much mistaken in his understanding of Christ's commands, as well as in his estimate of the purposes for which a Divine Revelation has been given.

It is also manifest, if the Apocalypse is to be comprehended by Christians, and made to serve them as a writing from God worthy of the Holy Ghost, that a new style of dealing with it must be inaugurated, and a different class of books made to take the place of the prevailing literature on the subject. Indeed, there is no part of Biblical exposition in which real guides are so scarce, or fresh effort so much needed.

Whether the work here offered is of the class to be desired, is to be determined by the character of its contents. Candid readers will hardly deny to it the merit of honesty of purpose, straightforwardness in the treatment of Divine things, simplicity and consistency in the application of what the rapt Seer narrates, direct leaning on the Sacred Word over against the stilted theories and rationalistic systems of men, and a self-evidencing force and satisfactoriness not generally found in attempts at Apocalyptical interpretation.

The theological stand-point of the author is that of Protestant orthodoxy. He claims to be in thorough accord with the great Confessions of the early Church and of the Reformation. Contrary to these he has nothing to teach, though he is quite convinced that they have not, in every direction, altogether exhausted the contents of the Scriptures. Their Eschatology, particularly, is very summary, rendering further inquiry and clearer illustration desirable. These Confessions themselves also legitimate and provide for such further investigation of the Divine Oracles. It is contrary both to them and the Scriptures, to undertake to warn off from the study of anything which God has caused to be written for us, provided that no part of settled Christian faith be contravened. Not *against* that whereunto the Church has hitherto attained, but *on the basis of* it, it is the vocation of Christians to go on exploring for the full truth which God has given for their learning and profit. And if anything is encountered in these Lectures, beyond what has been commonly thought, let it not be rejected too hastily, but dispassionately weighed, in the fear of God, and in just regard for His infallible Word.

A " Revised Text " has been printed at the heads of the Lectures. It is not offered as a substitute for the common English Version ; though the received text of the Apocalypse is in a worse condition than that of any other book of the New Testament. The object of the author's " Revised Text " is simply to present, in connected form, the best results of modern textual criticism, as developed by Tischendorf, Tregelles, Hengstenberg, Alford, Trench, Wordsworth, and other able and laborious investigators, together with an original collation of the lately discovered and highly to be prized *Codex Sinaiticus.* The value of such a " Revised Text," in more fully representing the idiom of the inspired record, in exhibiting what certainly belongs to the most ancient copies, and in assisting the verification of the expositions given, will not be disputed by scholars, nor lightly esteemed by the common reader. As Tregelles has said of his version of the Apocalypse, translated from the Ancient Greek text, so it may be said of this, and now with greater certainty, that " the reader may rest satisfied, that he has here a version of a Text, of which every word rests on competent evidence of twelve hundred years old at least ; and almost all on consenting evidence of fourteen hundred years old ; indeed, including the evidence of the Versions, ALL has authority of at least this antiquity." And as to the translation, nothing has been given which has not the concurrent sanction of eminent masters of the Greek tongue in general, and of the Greek of the New Testament in particular.

The Lectures themselves have been composed and delivered at different intervals of time, as occasion rendered convenient. From the interest manifested in them at their delivery, and at the urgent solicitation of many who listened to them, their publication has been commenced before the completion of the course.

*   *   *   *   *   *

From the beginning, the author of these Lectures was led to take the inspired title of this Book as the proper key to its contents, and to that he has adhered throughout. " *The Apocalypse of Jesus Christ*," does not mean a communicated message, but the *coming, appearing, manifestation, uncovering, presentation, of* JESUS CHRIST in person. Dr. Ebrard remarks in his Commentary, that the word *apokalupsis* should be translated *enthüllung, unveiling, uncovering*. Dr. Bleek admits, in his Lectures on the Apocalypse, that " the genitive after *apokalupsis* stands in the New Testament (even in this combination with *Christou*, I Cor. I : 7 ; 2 Thess. I : 7 ; Pet. I : 7–13), as a genitive of the object of what comes forth, as being revealed." Here Jesus Christ is the genitive of object. The *Apocalypse* would therefore be the coming, revealing, appearing, or manifestation of *Himself*, the Revelation *of* Him, not *to* Him. Dr. Lücke, in his work on the Apocalypse, for the same grammatical reasons, considers that " The Apocalypse of Jesus Christ," means " the unveiling of Christ in His majesty, as His glorious appearing." So also Dr. Heinrichs. And there is every reason for the conclusion that the great theme and subject of this Book is the Coming of Christ, the Apocalypse of Himself, His own personal manifestation and unveiling in the scenes and administrations of the great Day of the Lord. When men speak of " the *death* of Jesus Christ," their language inevitably conveys the idea that it is Christ who experiences the death affirmed ; and so when the Holy Ghost speaks of " The *Apocalypse* of Jesus Christ," by the same necessity of language the only admissible idea is, that it is Christ who experiences or undergoes the Apocalypse affirmed. The only *Apocalypses* of Jesus Christ that we read of in the New Testament, are personal manifestations of Himself. And it is thus against all the laws of speech, and against the whole *usus loquendi* of the sacred writers, to understand the inspired title of this Book as referring to anything but the revelation, or personal manifestation, of Jesus Christ in the great Day of Judgment, as everywhere foretold in the holy Scriptures.

So the Book's own description of its subject-matter pronounces, and to this every succeeding vision accords when taken in the plain straightforward sense of the record. It is thus unmistakably proven that we have here a portrayal, not of a few dim outlines of the fortunes of the Church in its march through this present world, but a scenic account of the actual occurrences of that period " when the Lord Jesus shall be revealed (ἐν τῇ ἀποκαλύψει τοῦ κυρίου—*in the Apocalypse of the Lord Jesus*) from heaven with His mighty Angels, in flaming fire, taking vengeance on them that know not God, and that obey not the Gospel ; who shall be punished with everlasting destruction *from the presence of the Lord, and from the glory of His power;* when He shall come to be glorified in His saints, and to be admired in all them that believe in that day." (2 Thess. I : 7–10.) This is *The Apocalypse of Jesus Christ*, expressly so called in the passage ; and this it is that John was made to see, and commanded to write, that all might learn exactly how things are then to be ordered.

A tremendous Revelation is therefore brought before men in this Book. And if any one would fully profit by it, let him bear with him this one vital and all-conditioning thought, that he is here dealing with Christ's own infallible foreshowings of the style, manner, and succession of events in which the Apocalypse awarded to Him by the Father is to take place. He who fails in this, misses the kernel of the Book, and must fail of the blessing of those who read, hear, and observe the things which are written in it.

*   *   *   *   *   *

By the goodness of that God from whose providence that urgency came, and in despite of all discouragements, hindrances, interruptions, and delays, the original purpose has been carried through to completion. And if what has now been produced shall serve to clear and edify the minds of others to the extent that these studies have served to instruct and satisfy the writer on a profoundly important but much-abused and much-misunderstood subject, ample will be the reason to thank God that the labour was begun, and that strength was given to finish it.

And now, earnestly praying the Divine Blessing upon what has been written, and upon all who read the same, the author devoutly commits the results of his labours to the care and direction of that good and wise Providence which has enabled him to complete the work, and to the serious attention of all who take pleasure in learning about what must shortly come to pass.

CONTENTS

ix

CONTENTS

CONTENTS

THE APOCALYPSE

LECTURE FIRST

THE SPIRIT IN WHICH THE SUBJECT IS TAKEN UP—THE PREFACE—THE SCOPE AND CONTENTS OF THE BOOK—WHAT THE REVELATION OF CHRIST IS—JOHN IN THE DAY OF THE LORD—THE DERIVATION OF THE APOCALYPSE—THE VALUE AND PRECIOUSNESS OF THIS BOOK—OUR SPECIAL STUDY DEMANDED.

REV. CHAP. I : 1–3 (Revised Text).—The Revelation of Jesus Christ, which God gave unto him, to show unto his servants that which must come to pass speedily ; and he signified [it] sending by his angel to his servant John ; who attested the word of God, and the testimony of Jesus Christ, what things soever he saw. Blessed he who readeth, and those who hear the words of the prophecy, and observe the things which are written in it : for the time [is] near.

IT has been upon my mind, and in my heart, for a long time, to deliver a series of special discourses upon this remarkable portion of the Holy Scriptures ; not from a conceit of superior wisdom or spiritual gifts ;—not with the vain ambition of making all mysteries plain,—nor yet out of mere curious desire to pry into the things of the future ; but out of solemn reverence for all that God has caused to be written for our learning, with a view conscientiously to declare the whole counsel of God, and with an earnest desire to secure for myself and those who hear me that special benediction which is pronounced upon them that read, hear, and keep what is written in this prophecy.

I have delayed the commencement of this work till now, partly on account of the bodily infirmities under which I have laboured for the past two years, and partly because I desired first to qualify myself better by ampler investigation, and by a more thorough mastery of the difficulties which have hindered the success of other attempts to explain this book. And, for the same reasons, I am unable, even now, to promise the continuation of these discourses, except at irregular intervals. So far, however, as God shall give me strength, I shall pursue them to their end.

I am also very sure, as God has promised his Spirit to them that ask him, and directed those who lack wisdom to seek for it at his hands, and pronounced all inspired writings to be " for our learning " and comfort, that it will be profitable for all of us, in humble dependence upon Divine grace and guidance, carefully to review what this book was meant to teach.

And may I not ask you, to give me your attention, as I proceed with these expositions, and to unite with me in earnestly invoking God's helpful illuminations, that we may rightly understand his solemn message to his people.

The words which I have announced for our present consideration, give us the Divine Preface or superscription to this book. They are meant to advise the reader as to that with which he is about to deal, and to prepare him to appreciate what is to follow. They relate to three leading points :

    I. THE SUBJECT AND CONTENTS OF THE BOOK.
    II. ITS DERIVATION AND AUTHORSHIP.
    III. ITS VALUE AND PRECIOUSNESS.

Let us look briefly at these several particulars.

What concerns the subject and contents of this book, I find for the most part in the name which it gives itself. It is the common rule with Scripture names, to express the substance of the things to which they are applied. The name of God expresses what God is ; so the names of the Lord Jesus Christ, and all the leading names found in the Bible. Even those which the Church has given, are often wonderfully expressive and significant. *Genesis* is the generation of things ; *Exodus*, the going forth from bondage ; *The Gospel*, the very heart and substance of all God's gracious communications—the good news. And when God himself designates this book *The Revelation of Jesus Christ*, we may rest assured, that it is the very substance and kernel of the book that is expressed in this title.

What, then, are we to understand by " *The Apocalypse of Jesus Christ ?* " There are certain books (adopted and held sacred by the Church of Rome, which we, however, receive only as human productions), which have a name somewhat similar to this in sound. You find them in some Bibles, between the Old and New Testaments, bearing the name of *Apocrypha*. But *Apocrypha* is just the opposite of *Apocalypse*. *Apocrypha* means something that is concealed, not set forth, not authentic ; *Apocalypse* means something revealed, disclosed, manifested, shown. The verb αποκαλύπτω, means *to reveal, to make manifest, to uncover to view*. The noun αποκαλυψις, means *a revelation, a disclosure, an appearing, a making manifest*. The Apocalypse, or Revelation of Jesus Christ, must therefore be the revealment, manifestation, appearing, of Jesus Christ.

Some accept the words as if they were meant to express the revealment of the Revelation. This I take to be a mistake, and a vital mistake, as regards any right interpretation of this book. It is not the Apocalypse which is the subject of the disclosure. This book is not the Apocalypse of the Apocalypse, but THE APOCALYPSE OF JESUS CHRIST.

And this is the key to the whole book. It is a book of which Christ is the great subject and centre, particularly in that period of his administrations and glory designated as the day of his uncovering, the day of his appearing. It is not a mere prediction of divine judgments upon the wicked, and of the final triumph of the righteous, made known *by* Christ ; but a book of the revelation *of* Christ, in his own person, offices, and future administrations, when he shall be *seen* coming from heaven, as he was once seen going into heaven. If " The Revelation of Jesus Christ " meant nothing more than certain communications made known by Christ, I can see no significance or propriety in affixing this title to this book, rather than to any other books of holy Scripture. Are they not all alike the revelation of Jesus Christ, in this sense ? Does not Peter say of the inspired writers in general, that they were moved by the Spirit of Christ which was in them ? Why then single out this particular book as " The Revelation of Jesus Christ," when it is no more the gift of Jesus than any other inspired book ? Besides, it would be particularly strange, that this book should be so specially designated " The Revelation of Jesus Christ " in the sense of revelation *by* Christ, when the book itself declares that it was not received from Christ, but from *an angel* or messenger of Christ. These considerations alone ought to satisfy us that there is something more distinctive and characteristic in this title than is embraced in its ordinary acceptation. For my own part, I am perfectly convinced, from a review of the places in which the word occurs in the New Testament, as well as from all the contents of this particular part of it, that *The Apocalypse*, or Revelation of Jesus Christ, means Jesus Christ *revealed*, and uncovered to mortal view ; and not merely Jesus Christ *revealing*, and making known hidden things to be recorded for our learning. Let me refer to a few passages bearing upon the case.

Paul, in his first letter to the Corinthians (i : 7), speaks of them as enriched in every spiritual gift, confirmed in the testimony of Christ, and " waiting for *the Apocalypse* (την αποκάλυψιν) *the coming* of our Lord Jesus Christ." The original word here is exactly the same as that in the text ; the structure of the sentence is also much the same ; but no one mistakes its meaning for a moment. All agree that it refers to Christ in his revelation from heaven, when he shall come in the clouds with power and great glory. And if such is its unmistakable meaning here, why not take it in the same sense in the text? So in Thessalonians (1: 6–10) he refers his readers to a time of rest, "when the Lord Jesus shall be revealed from heaven (εν τη αποκαλυψει του Κυρίου, literally, *at the Apocalypse of the Lord*), with his mighty angels, in flaming fire, taking vengeance on them that know not God ;—*when he shall come* to be glorified in his saints, and to be admired in all them that believe." No one misunderstands what The Apocalypse of the Lord Jesus is in this passage. Paul himself explains it to be His *coming*, in just such administrations as were shown John in this book.

So again in 1 Peter 1: 7, where that apostle speaks of his brethren as " in heaviness through manifold temptations," that the trial of their faith, " being much more precious than of gold that perisheth, though it be tried, with fire, might be found unto praise and honour and glory *at the Apocalypse* (εν αποκαλύψεν), *appearing* of Jesus Christ." Also in verse 13, where he exhorts his readers to " be sober, and hope to the end for the grace that is to be brought unto them at *the Apocalypse* (εν αποκαλύψει), *the revelation* of Jesus Christ." All understand the reference in these passages to be to the coming of Christ in the glory of his second advent, when " every eye shall see him, and they which pierced him." We all feel that it would be a wilful perversion of the word of God to make *the Apocalypse of Christ*, in these passages, mean anything else than his *personal appearing*. And the same is the fixed meaning of this phrase in every other passage in which it is used. Even in that from Galatians (1: 12), which might seem to assign it a different signification, the idea is not simply that of a revealer, but of one revealed by personal manifestation. Paul there avers, that the gospel he preached was not of man ; " for," says he, " I neither received it of man, neither was I taught it, but by *the Apocalypse* (δι αποκαλυψεως) *through the revelation* of Jesus Christ," that is, by Christ's personal *appearance* to him, as the succeeding verses show ; for he straightway proceeds to narrate that marvellous affair on the way to Damascus. What that Apocalypse was, he on various occasions described. Before Agrippa, he said,—" As I went to Damascus with authority and commission from the chief priests, at midday, O King, I saw in the way a light from heaven, above the brightness of the sun, shining round about me and them which journeyed with me. And when we were all fallen to the earth, I heard a voice speaking unto me, and saying in a Hebrew tongue, Saul, Saul, why persecutest thou me ? And I said, Who art thou, Lord ? And he said, I am Jesus whom thou persecutest, but rise, and stand upon thy feet ; for I have *appeared unto thee* for this purpose, to make thee a minister and a witness both of these things which thou *hast seen*, and of those things in which *I will appear unto thee*." Hence his appeal in vindication of his apostleship. " Am I not an apostle ? Have I not *seen Jesus Christ* our Lord ? " (1 Cor. 9: 1.) All this shows, as conclusively as may be, that the Apocalypse of Christ, through which he obtained at once his office and his text, was a *personal appearance*, as every real Apocalypse predicted of a person must be.

With the meaning of this word thus established, what can that book be, of which it is descriptive, but an account of the revelation of Christ in his personal forthcoming from his present invisible estate, to receive his Bride, judge the wicked, and set up his eternal kingdom on the earth.

With this also agrees the statement of John as to the circumstances under which he came to the knowledge of the things which he narrates. He says he " *was in Spirit in the Lord's day*," in which he beheld what he afterwards wrote. What is meant by this *Lord's day* ? Some answer, *Sunday*—the first day of the week ; but I am not satisfied with this explanation. Sunday belongs indeed to the Lord, but the Scriptures nowhere call it " the Lord's day." None of the Christian writings, for 100 years after Christ, ever call it

" the Lord's day." But there is a " *Day of the Lord* " largely treated of by prophets, apostles, and fathers, the meaning of which is abundantly clear and settled. It is that day in which, Isaiah says, men shall hide in the rocks for fear of the Lord, and for the glory of his majesty ;—the day which Joel describes as the day of destruction from the Almighty, when the Lord shall roar out of Zion, and utter his voice from Jerusalem, and the heavens and the earth shall shake ;—the day to which the closing chapter of Malachi refers as the day that shall burn as an oven, and in which the Sun of Righteousness shall arise with healing in his wings ;—the day which Paul proclaimed from Mars' Hill as that in which God will judge the world, concerning which he so earnestly exhorted the Thessalonians, and which was not to come until after a great apostasy from the faith, and the ripening of the wicked for destruction ;—the day in the which, Peter says, the heavens shall be changed, the elements melt, the earth burn, and all present orders of things give way to new heavens and a new earth ;—even " the day for which all other days were made." And in that day I understand John to say, he in some sense was. In the mysteries of prophetic rapport, which the Scriptures describe as " *in Spirit,*" and which Paul declared inexplicable, he was caught out of himself, and out of his proper place and time, and stationed amid the stupendous scenes of the great day of God, and made to see the actors in them, and to look upon them transpiring before his eyes, that he might write what he saw, and give it to the Churches.

This is what I understand by his being " in Spirit in the Lord's day."* I can see no essential difference between ἡ Κυριακη ἡμερα—*the Lord's day,*— and ἡ ἡμερα Κυριου—*the day of the Lord.* They are simply the two forms for signifying the same relations of the same things.† And if John was thus mystically down among the scenes of the last day, and has written only what he says he has written, that is " *things that he saw ;* " it cannot be otherwise but that in dealing with the contents of this book we are dealing with what relates pre-eminently to the great Apocalypse and Epiphany of our Lord, when he cometh to judge the world in righteousness.

And when we come to consider the actual contents of this book, we find them harmonizing exactly with this understanding of its title. It takes as its chief and unmistakable themes what other portions of the Scriptures assign to the great day of the Lord. It is nothing but Apocalypse from beginning to end. First we have the Apocalypse of Christ in his relation to the earthly Churches, and his judgment of them ; then the Apocalypse of his relation to the glorified Church, and the marshalling of them for his forthcoming to judge the world ; then the Apocalypse of his relation to the scenes of the judgment, as they are manifested on earth under the opening of the seals, the prophesying of the witnesses, and the fall of Babylon ; then the Apocalypse of his actual manifestation to the world in the battle of the great day of God Almighty, the establishment of his kingdom, and the investiture of the saints in their future sovereignties ; and finally the Apocalypse of his relation to the final act of judgment, the destruction of death and the grave, and the introduction of the final estate of a perfected Redemption. What, indeed, is all this, but just what was foretold by all the prophets, by Christ himself, and by all his apostles, as pertaining to THE

---

* And so Wetstein, Züllig, Dr. S. R. Maitland, Dr. Todd, and B. W. Newton.

† Our English Translators have frequently used both these modes of expressing the genitive case of the same noun, both in Hebrew and Greek. Compare Gen. 28 : 17 and Gen. 28 : 22, where " House of God " and " God's house " mean precisely the same. So " Lord's law," Ex. 13 : 9, and " Law *of* the Lord," 2 Chron. 12 : 1 ;—" The Lord's people," 1 Sam. 2 : 24, and " People *of* the Lord," Judges 5 : 11. In all these instances the Septuagint presents the same forms as the original. So in the New Testament we have the same variety of expression to signify exactly the same relations. In 1 Cor. 10 : 21, for the same grammatical form in Greek, we have " Lord's table," and " Table *of* devils " ; in 2 Cor. 2 : 12, " Christ's Gospel " for " Gospel *of* Christ " ; in 2 Pet. 4 : 13, " Christ's sufferings," and in 1 Pet. 5 : 1, " Sufferings *of* Christ." The same may be seen in Rev. 11 : 15, where the kingdoms *of* the world become our *Lord's* and his *Christ's* kingdoms.

DAY OF THE LORD ? Verily, this book is but the rehearsal, in another and ampler manner, of what all the Scriptures tell us about the last day and the eternal judgment. It is pre-eminently The Apocalypse and Epiphany of Jesus Christ.*

II. Notice now *its derivation and authorship.* The text represents it as the gift of God to Christ. It is called " The Apocalypse of Jesus Christ, which God gave unto him." Some understand this gift in the sense of *signified, made known to ;* and so put themselves under the necessity of explaining how this could be without compromising our Lord's Divinity. This is the first difficulty engendered by the departure from the proper scriptural meaning of the word Apocalypse. People take it as denoting a piece of information, and so represent Christ in a state of ignorance respecting the sublimest results of his mediatorship until after his ascension into heaven. The incongruities of such an acceptation should teach men better. The Apocalyps of Christ is the future reappearance of Christ, clothed with the honours and crowned with the triumphs which are to characterize that forthcoming, and not the mere knowledge or description of these things. And it is that Apocalypse, with all its glorious concomitants and results, that God has, in covenant, given to Christ ;—given to him as the crowning reward of his mediatorial work, as the Scriptures everywhere teach.

The promise of the victory of the woman's seed involved this gift. Hannah's song speaks of it as strength and exaltation which the Lord bestoweth upon his anointed. God's promise to David of a son whose kingdom is to be established forever embraces it. It is the great theme of the second Psalm, where God says to his son : " I shall give thee the heathen for thine inheritance, and the uttermost parts of the earth for thy possession—thou shalt break them with a rod of iron ; thou shalt dash them in pieces like a potter's vessel." It is in Isaiah's pictures of Messiah, in Jeremiah's prophecies, in the words of the annunciation to Mary, in Christ's own parables, and in all the writings of the Apostles. *Because* Christ " made himself of no reputation, and took upon him the form of a servant, and was made in the likeness of men, and humbled himself, and became obedient unto death, even the death of the cross, God hath highly exalted him, and given him a name which is above every name, that at the name of Jesus every knee should bow, of things in heaven, and things in earth, and things under the earth, and that every tongue should confess that Jesus Christ is Lord, to the glory of God the Father." We are told that there was joy set before Christ as the reward of his sufferings and death, and that it was " *for* the joy that was set before him, he endured the cross, despising the shame." And whatever else may be included in that exaltation or that joy, highest and greatest of all is a future Apocalypse, when " the Son of man shall come in his glory, and all the holy angels with him, and he shall sit upon the throne of his glory." This, then, is what God " gave to Jesus Christ," in promise, when he commenced his work, in its earnest, when he raised him from the dead and received him into glory ; and *thus gave* what constitutes the substance of this book.

But as the full manifestation of this endowment of Christ is still future, and it is important for his followers to be well informed concerning it, the blessed Saviour, after his ascension, took measures to have the facts becomingly communicated to his servants on earth. " *And he sent and signified [the same] by his angel.*" In stating who this angel was, I do not venture to be specific. His own account of himself to John, was, " I am thy

---

* " This divine book, let others call it what they please, is an admirable prophecy, directed wholly to the times, immediate upon the coming of the Lord. In which are announced all the principal matters which shall immediately precede ; in which is announced in a manner the most magnificent the very coming of the Lord in glory and majesty ; in which are announced the admirable and stupendous events which shall accompany that coming, and which shall follow it. The title of the book shows well to what it is all directed ; what is its argument, and what its determinate end : *The Apocalypse—Revelation of Jesus Christ.*"
—Emanuel Lacunza, " *Coming of Messiah,*" p. 200.

fellow-servant, and of thy brethren the prophets, and of them which keep the sayings of this book " (Rev. 22 : 9). From this, it has been thought, that he was one of the old prophets, or some one standing in a closer relation to Christ and the Church than can be affirmed of angels proper. It is also somewhat confirmative of this view, that whilst the angels are called " ministering spirits " (Heb. 1 : 14), they are not called " God's servants," nor fellows of the prophets and apostles, as in the case before us. Let it suffice, however, for us to know, that it was some heavenly messenger, commissioned by the Lord Jesus in glory, to come and make known these apocalyptic wonders.

Some have found difficulty in tracing the agency of this angel in the book itself. " It is remarkable," says one, " that this angel does not appear as the imparter of the visions until chapter seventeen." This would imply, that what God here says about the derivation of this book is only true with respect to a very small fraction of it. I cannot agree thus to stint and stultify the words of the Almighty. The proper explanation of the office of the angel is to be found in the words *signified* and *saw*. The word rendered *signified*, taken in connection with the fact that the things signified were matters of contemplation by means of the eyes, can denote nothing else than an actual picturing of those scenes—a making of them pass before the view the same as if they were really transpiring. The office of the angel, then, as I take it, was, to form the connection between John's senses or imagination and the things which he was to describe, making to pass in review before him what was only afterwards to take place in fact. How this was done, I cannot say : but as the devil could take Jesus to a high mountain, and show him at one view " all the kingdoms of the world, and the glory of them," I am sure that it falls sufficiently within the sphere of angelic natures thus to picture things to man ; and that when commissioned of the Lord for the purpose, no good angel is wanting in ability to be the instrument in making John *see* whatever visions he describes in this book. And when God himself tells me that what is here set forth *was* thus signified to John, I will persist in referring every one of the visions, with all that he says he saw and heard, to the intervention of this angelic agent, and believe that in all sacred things we are vastly more dependent upon angelic ministrations than we know or can understand. " *Are they not all ministering spirits, sent forth to minister for them who shall be heirs of salvation ?* " (Heb. 1 : 14.)

But there is still another link in the chain of agencies through which the great things of this book have been made known to men. Given of God, sent by Christ, signified by an angel, they were finally recorded by John, and by him communicated to the Churches.

Nor need we be in doubt as to what John this is. The text describes him as that " John, who attested the word of God, and the testimony of Jesus Christ." And who is it that the Churches from the beginning have known as the attestor of the *Logos*, or Word of God, and of the testimony which Christ gave, but John the Apostle, the beloved disciple ? Turn to the Gospel by John, and see whether it be not wholly taken up with exactly these things. The first chapter gives the only full account which the Scriptures contain respecting the pre-existence of the *Logos*, or Word, in the Godhead, and the sameness of that Word with him who was born of Mary, tabernacled in the flesh, and was called Jesus of Nazareth. Was not this bearing " record of the Word of God ? " Do we not find another summary of the same testimony in the first chapter of his first epistle ? What else does he mean by the account which he gives of his testimony, when he says, " That which was from the beginning, which we have heard, which we have seen with our eyes, which we have looked upon, and our hands have handled of the Word of life, declare we unto you ? " Are not both his first and second epistles but arguments, against various evil spirits which were gone abroad, that Jesus is the Word of God, the only Christ, the Son of God, and that all who deny this are liars and Antichrist ? And in reference to the great body of his Gospel, does he not himself say, " These things are written, that ye might believe that Jesus is the Christ, the Son of God, and that believing ye might have life through his name ? " Does not all this make out for John a particular distinction as the apostle " who attested the Word of God, and the testimony of Jesus Christ ? "

Some say that it was not John the Apostle who wrote this book, but another John, contemporaneous with the apostle. But it is not yet conclusively proven that there was such a John other than the apostle ; and, if there even was, there is not the first tittle of evidence that he had ever distinguished himself for his record concerning the Logos, or concerning the testimonies, which he himself saw, by which Christ announced himself as the Messiah and the Son of God. I conclude, therefore, upon the solid basis of God's own identification of the author of this book, that it was the Apostle John who wrote it.

Such also has been the conviction of the best portions of the Church from the beginning. For the first two centuries the universal Christian testimony ascribed the Apocalypse to the pen of " that disciple whom Jesus loved." In the third century, out of a desire to get rid of its authority for certain unpalatable doctrines, there were some who ascribed it to Cerinthus, a reputed heretic of the first century. But, " if the common consent of all antiquity is to overturn the heady rashness of well-meaning but inconsiderate men of evil name ; then we have the most satisfactory evidence that this book was written by John the Apostle, and believed by the Church to be most fully inspired. Justin Martyr, Irenæus, Tertullian, Clemens Alexandrinus, Origen, Jerome, Augustine, and a continued stream of Orthodox authority to our day, from the age next to that in which it was written, concur in the reception, the admiration, and the observance of this book."*

Such, then, is the exalted source and derivation of this wonderful production. It takes its origin in God's covenant gift to Jesus Christ as the reward of triumph and glory for his humiliation and obedience unto death. It was sent by the loving Saviour from heaven, in the charge of an angelic messenger, to be shown to John. And by the hands of " that disciple whom Jesus loved," thus visited in his lonely exile—emblem of that consolation in distress with which this book has ever irradiated the dark and gloomy days of the Church,—

* Irving *in loc.* Some have sought to make a great deal of certain alleged discrepancies between the style and modes of expression used in the Apocalypse, and those contained in John's Gospel and Epistles. But Alford has very well observed, that " there are at the same time striking notes of similarity in expression and cast of thought," and that " we are not in a position to take into account the effect of a totally different subject and totally different circumstances upon one, who though knowing and speaking Greek, was yet a Hebrew by birth."—*Greek Test. Prol. Rev.*

And one of our ablest linguists and critics, " after an examination successively renewed through many years," says, " I have never been able to satisfy myself, that what has been the common belief of the Churches in all ages respecting the authorship of the Apocalypse, is not sustained by more and better grounds than any other opinion."—*Stuart on Apoc.*, I, 285.

" There is scarcely a book in the whole Bible whose genuineness and inspiration were more strongly attested on its first appearance than the Apocalypse. No doubts whatever seem to have been entertained on these points. Suffice it now to say, that Papias, Justin Martyr, Irenæus, Melito,—that is, eminent teachers in the Church, in the next age to that in which it was written—proclaim that its writer was St. John, the beloved disciple of Christ. Such was *then* the voice of the Church."—*Wordsworth on Apoc.*, p. 22.

" So ends our Catena of testimonies to the genuineness and divine inspiration of the Apocalypse traced through the three half centuries that followed after its publication. Alike from East and West, North and South,—from the Churches of the Asiatic province and the Syrian, of Italy and of Gaul, of Egypt and of Africa,—we have heard an unbroken and all but uniform voice of testimony in its favour. And on the whole, and in conclusion, it does appear to me that Augustine and the Latin Council had good reason for their solemn verdict ; and that we may safely and unhesitatingly direct our inquiries into the meaning of the Apocalypse, as into that of a prophecy of the future, revealed to the beloved disciple, by none other than Christ's own divine, eternal, omniscient Spirit."—*Elliott's Horæ Apoc.*, *Prel. Essay.*

was traced out in the language of mortals, and delivered over as Christ's last message to his people on earth.

III. A word or two now as *to the value and preciousness of this book.* A gift which the Great God thinks a befitting honour and compensation to Christ for all his great deeds of love and condescension ; a thing which the blessed Lord in heaven esteemed of sufficient moment to be made known by a special embassage, which holy angels considered it an honour to be permitted to signify, and which the tenderness of the disciple of love so conscientiously recorded for the comfort and admonition of the people of God in every age, certainly is not a thing of trifling significance. If we are interested in the story of the manger and the cross ; if we can draw strength for our prayers and hopes by invoking Christ by the mystery of his incarnation, fasting, temptation, agony, and bloody sweat ; if we find it such a precious treasure to our souls to come into undoubting sympathy with the scenes of his humiliation and grief ; what should be our appreciation of this book, which treats of the fruits of those sufferings, and tells only of that wronged Saviour's glory and triumphs, and shows us our Lord enthroned in majesty, riding prosperously, and scattering to his ransomed ones the crowns and regencies of empire which shall never perish, and celestial blessednesses without number and above all thought !

"All Scripture," indeed, "is profitable, for doctrine, for reproof, for correction and instruction in righteousness, that the man of God may be thoroughly furnished unto all good works ; " but there are some portions more especially significant and precious, and proper attention to which is fraught with particular advantages. Of this sort is this book of the Revelation of Jesus Christ. What saith the text ?—" Blessed is he that readeth, and they that hear the words of this prophecy, and keep those things which are written therein." The same is repeated in chapter 22 : 7,—" Blessed is he that keepeth the sayings of the prophecy of this book." Of course, the more we learn and know of Christ, the better it will be for us, if the spirit of faith and obedience be in our hearts, and this book is pre-eminently the Revelation of Christ. It sets out our blessed Lord, and draws away the veil which hangs between us and him, and lifts us up into the sublimest things of heaven. It shows us how the Son of man has been rewarded by the Father, and what works and offices are assigned unto that meek Lamb. It shows us the history of our Saviour's person, all-glorious and exalted, and his great ministrations in the Church and in the universe, until his coming again from the throne and in the power of the Father, with all the armies of heaven with him. Above all does it dwell upon that great Apocalypse, the condition in which it will find the world, what it will bring to his prepared and waiting saints, what it will inflict upon lukewarm believers, infidels, and evil-doers, and what will be the character and issues of that great day of God Almighty. It tells what the Church will be till Christ comes, what it will be in that period of dreadful trial, what Satan and his children will attempt, and how the Lord Jesus shall trample them down under the glory of his power, raise the dead, renew the world, and set up forever his blessed reign in it. It shows us what will be the final triumphs and rewards of the saints for their present griefs and toils ; what will be the future of our world ; how it is to be renewed, cleansed, beautified, and invested with heavenly excellencies ; and how the light, and knowledge and glory of God is to become its eternal possession.

It is always important for us to be forwarned with regard to the future. It is our nature to be forecasting, and it is one of the necessities of our well-being to be able to anticipate with accuracy, at least with regard to the leading things that shall concern us. He who does not shape the conduct of to-day with reference to some end foreseen or calculated on for some other day, is a mere fool and madman, whether it be in the things of God, or in the things of the world. And in this book we are certified beforehand of what God hath determined concerning the future—what the devout may hope for, what the indifferent and unbelieving have to fear, wherein the true safety and consolation of man is to be found, what tribulations are to come upon the world, and what birth-pangs are yet to be passed through to reach that Golden Age of which prophets and poets of all nations and times have spoken.*

There is also a peculiar efficacy and power in the doctrine of Christ's speedy return. Like a magnet, it lifts the heart of the believer out of the world, and out of his low self, and enables him to stand with Moses on the mount, and transfigures him with the rays of blessed hope and promise which stream upon him in those sublime heights. It is the most animating and most sanctifying subject in the Bible. It is the soul's serenest light amid the darkness and trials of earth. And the great end and aim of this book is to set forth this doctrine. The things of which it treats, are things touching the Apocalypse of Jesus Christ, and which it describes as " things which must shortly come to pass." *The impending Advent* is the theme which pervades it from its commencement to its close. And just in proportion as he who is awake to the great truth of the Saviour's speedy coming, and is engaged in waiting and preparing himself accordingly, is a better man, and in a safer condition, and really more happy, than the half-christian and the lukewarm ;—in that same proportion is he who reads, hears and keeps the words of this prophecy blessed beyond all other people. This book, at least its subject-matter, thus becomes to him an instrument of security and attainment to save him from surprise when his Lord cometh, and from the tribulations which shall try the indifferent ; as well as a passport to admit him to the marriage supper of the Lamb, and to the highest awards of eternity. Precious book ! and happy they who study it !

Nor can I close without remarking how all this plucks up, and crushes to atoms, those erroneous and mischievous notions entertained by many, that there is nothing useful in prophetic studies. To say nothing of the duty of giving heed to what God has thought it important to record, or of the folly of seeing only peril in trying to understand what the Spirit of God has inspired for our learning and consolation, what man is he, who, in the face of this text, and its outspoken benediction, will venture to denounce investigation into sacred prophecy ? What if it is often dark and mysterious ? The darker and more difficult, the greater the reason for earnest examination. Be the obscurity and mystery what it may, God says, " Blessed is he that readeth, and they that hear the words, and keep those things which are written." What if this book of Revelation is the fullest of all of dark things and perplexing mysteries ? It is then a book which above all needs our most solemn and studious attention. Nay, it is concerning this book especially that God pronounces this blessedness upon the devout and obedient inquirer.

Some tell us that what is yet future ought not to be examined into till after it has come to pass. I can hardly realize that this is seriously meant. Yet I have had it argued to me, even in Jerusalem itself. Do such persons not perceive that they thus judge God, and Christ, and the sent angel of Christ, and John the beloved disciple of Christ, and join issue with the God of truth as to the correctness of his utterances ? I find also that those who so argue are prone to insist that the day of death is the same as Christ's coming. Do they then mean that a man is only to study the predictions of that coming after he is dead ? Out upon such doctrine as this ! Away with such presumptuous deprivation of the Church of the precious legacy left her by her ascended Lord ! I will not for a moment regard that as wrong and dangerous which the Lord himself hath pronounced *blessed*. Jesus knew what he was about when he sent this book to be shown unto his servants. He understood his own words when he said and repeated : Blessed is he that reads and he that keeps what is in this book. And I will insist that it is to be studied. As Christ said

---

* " The Apocalypse *completes* the Canon of Scripture ; and with reverence be it said, the sacred Canon would be imperfect without it."—*Wordsworth.*

to the writer of it, so he says to all his ministers, and all his people, in all time : " SEAL NOT THE SAYINGS OF THE PROPHECY OF THIS BOOK." It is an open book, and meant to be ever kept open to the view of the Church from that time forward to the end. Woe, then, to the man who undertakes to draw away God's people from it, or to warn them against looking into it ! He takes from the Church, which has now been these 2000 years among the dashing waves, the chart by which above all Christ meant she should be guided, and wherein she may best see whither she is bearing, what are her perils, and where her course of safety lies ! He undertakes to seal what God has said should not be sealed ! He not only " takes away from the words of the book of this prophecy," (which who does, " God shall take away his part out of the book of life, and out of the holy city, and from the things which are written in this book,") but seeks to take away the book itself !

And the more dangerous and reprehensible is such a course, now that " the time is near." Nearly two thousand years ago, it was said of the things herein written, that they must speedily come to pass. These records were from the first pressed upon the study of the Church by the solemn consideration that the period of their fulfilment was rapidly approaching. But if this argument was of force then, how much more now ?

Standing, then, as we do, upon the very margin of the great Apocalypse, by all the solemnities with which it is to be accompanied, I not only invite and recommend, but conjure Christians, as they hope to be present at the marriage supper of the Lamb, not to put this precious book from them, or to forgo the faithful study of its contents.

The Lord open our hearts to its teachings, and make us partakers of the blessings it foretells !

LECTURE SECOND

JOHN'S SPECIAL INTRODUCTION—CHRISTIANITY COURTEOUS—THE CHURCHES—THE BLESS-
ING IMPLORED UPON THEM—AN EXULTANT ASCRIPTION—THE BASIS AND CHARACTER OF
IT—A SOLEMN PROPHETIC ALLUSION—THE COMING AGAIN OF CHRIST—HOW THE EARLY
CHRISTIANS VIEWED THE SUBJECT—A DEVOUT REFERENCE TO THE SAVIOUR'S TESTIMONY
CONCERNING HIMSELF.

REV. CHAP. I : 4–8 (Revised Text).—John to the seven churches in Asia, Grace unto you
and peace, from Him who is, and who was, and who is to come, and from the seven Spirits
which [are] before his throne, and from Jesus Christ, the Faithful Witness. The First-born
of the dead, and The Prince of the kings of the earth.

Unto Him that loves us, and freed us from our sins by his own blood, and hath made us
a kingdom,—priests unto Him who is his God and Father ; to Him be glory and dominion
unto the ages. Amen.

Behold, he cometh with the clouds, and every eye shall see him, and they which pierced
him, and all the tribes of the land shall mourn about him. Even so ; Amen.

I am Alpha and Omega, saith the Lord God, who is, and who was, and who is to come,
the Almighty.

THERE is not another book of holy scripture which opens with so much
special remark and solemnity. There is everything here to impress the belief,
that there is not another so profoundly important, or meant to be studied with
such particular care and seriousness. We have had before us the impressive
account of itself with which this marvellous book opens. The text is a special
additional preface, by John, which will be quite sufficient to occupy us
to-night. Strictly, it is no part of the Apocalypse. It has proceeded from the
same Spirit, and is in a measure anticipative of its contents ; but it deals
more with the writer's personal feelings, than with any features of the grand
message itself. It is the mere prelude to the piece—the apostolic overture to
the Revelation of Christ. But, it is a magnificent introduction. Though
marked with the frequent sententious abruptness of this apostle's writings,
there is not, in all human literature, a more sublime or appropriate opening.
Separating it into its several parts, I find

   I.   AN AFFECTING SALUTATION ;
   II.   AN EXULTANT ASCRIPTION ;
   III.   A SOLEMN PROPHETIC ALLUSION ;
   IV.   A DEVOUT THEOLOGICAL RECOGNITION.

Having carefully surveyed these, we shall have comprehensively explored
the whole text. May the Lord aid us in the attempt, and fill us with the Spirit
of him whose words we are to consider !

As to the Salutation, we may note first that Christianity is courteous. It
enlivens all kindly feelings, and prompts to every gentle amenity from one to
another. There is no refinement of manner, or polish of feeling and behaviour,
which it does not foster. Coarseness and vulgarity have no place in the domain
of genuine piety. He who speaks in the text was bred in humble life, but,
by the exalting power of the gospel which he preached, he was raised into a
courtliness of tone and temper, as sincere as it was lovely. He does not
venture to deliver his great message to the Churches without first declaring
his own kind wishes towards them. Though a high officer, and addressing
persons of much inferior estate to himself, his loving heart begins with the
pouring out of gracious affection, sympathy and benediction. By apostolic
example, then, as well as by apostolic precept, we are taught to be kindly
affectioned one toward another, and to be courteous to all men.

This gracious Salutation is addressed " to the seven Churches in Asia."
We sometimes speak of " the Church " in its entire collective capacity, as if
it were but one body. And such it really is in its source, head, faith and
sacraments, but not in its earthly organization. We also speak of the Church
of a particular country or denomination ; and not improperly when we wish
to designate clusters of Churches of particular and distinctive type, or regime,
or geographical contiguity. But the Scriptures express themselves differently.
They do not contemplate the Christians of so many countries or confessions,
as so many Churches ; but find a Church in every individual congregation,
having its own minister, elders and deacons, without regard to any corporation other than itself. " Asia " is a large district of country, lying on the
north of the Mediterranean, east of the outlet of the Euxine. It had but one
general government at the time. But the Apocalypse does not speak of the
collective body of Christians on that territory as " the Church of Asia."
They were organized into distinct congregations in the several towns and
cities, and these separate and independent assemblies are spoken of as so
many " Churches." They are addressed singly as " the Churches which are
in Asia," such as " the Church in Ephesus," " the Church in Smyrna," " the
Church in Pergamos," &c. The ecclesiastical unit is, therefore, to be reckoned
from the local assembly under one minister, and such helpers as may be
grouped around him, in the acknowledgment and the administration of the
commands of Christ. These several units, or any number of them, may lawfully join together in other and more general organizations and administrations, but never so as to ignore or supersede the proper churchly character
of each without regard to the rest. The original order of the Church, as the
apostles founded it, and as they addressed and left it, is *congregational*.
And every system which obliterates that order, in so far departs from what
God and his inspired servants have authorized and ordained. John knew of
no Churches but the individual congregations, however they might voluntarily come together for mutual counsel and general edification.

Note also the style and substance of this Salutation. Such addresses were
common in the intercourse of the ancients. Their writers were accustomed to
wish to their readers every good and prosperity. The Egyptian steward
greeted the Hebrew strangers with the words—" Peace be to you." The
Assyrian King headed his royal proclamation with—" Peace be multiplied
unto you." And David sent to Nabal saying : " Peace be to thee, and peace
be to thine house, and peace be unto all that thou hast." The like may be
heard to this day, in the common salutations of the people of those lands.
But never did Jew or Gentile give such a salutation as this. It is not the
ordinary prosperity of the world which is here bespoken, but something
infinitely higher. John wishes the Churches " peace " indeed, but a peace
preceded by, and rooted in " Grace." No one, in his right mind, will despise
the comforts and blessings of this life. They are all good and precious gifts
of God, which are to be thankfully received and devoutly appropriated. But,
what is all this world's prosperity if there be no peace with God, and no
spiritual consolation in the conscience ? Of what avail is it to pass brilliantly
over the stage of time, only to sink forever in the darkness and sorrows of
eternity ! What we sinful beings need is *Grace*, and the peace which has its
root in grace. " By the deeds of the law shall no man living be justified."
There must be some outlet of Divine benignity by which we can be accepted
notwithstanding these disabilities under the law. That outlet has been found
in the Gospel, which publishes absolution and eternal life on the simple
condition of faith. And this is that " Grace " of which the apostle speaks,
and by which Paul declares Christians to be saved. It is God's favour to us
in Christ Jesus, notwithstanding our fallen condition. It is the forgiveness
of sins, the inspiration of a new life, the renewal of the soul to holiness. It is
the removal of God's wrath from us and our purgation from all enmity
towards God, reconciliation and atonement with our Maker, and full partici-

pation in all the blessings of his uninterrupted favour. It is justification, and all the peace with God, and in our own hearts and estate, resulting from justification. In other words, what the apostle here bespeaks upon the Churches is, the entire fulness of the blessing of the Gospel, in all its length and breadth and depth and height of consolation and eternal prosperity.

Notice also the sources from which he implores all this. From man, no such blessings could come ; nor yet only from God as God, or from this or that person in the Godhead alone. The whole Deity in its mysterious and eternal Triunity is concerned in furnishing what is bespoken. It is first of all " *from Him which is, and which was, and which is to come ;* " that is, from the Absolute One, who knows no change, no dependence on time or place, but to whom the present, the past, and the future are one and the same eternal now ; who is, and who was, and who is to be, even the infinite, incomprehensible, unapproachable Father of lights, from whom cometh every good and every perfect gift, and with whom is neither variableness, nor the least shadow of turning. Hence the joyful thanksgiving, " Blessed be the God and Father of our Lord Jesus Christ, which, according to his abundant mercy, hath begotten us again unto a lively hope."

In the next place it is " *from the seven Spirits which are before his throne ;* " that is, from the Holy Ghost, in the full completeness of his office and powers, as sent forth for the illumination, comfort and edification of all the subjects of God's redeeming grace. " Seven " is the number of dispensational fulness and perfection ; and as there are seven Churches, making the one Church, so there are " the seven Spirits of God," making up the completeness of the one gracious administration of the Holy Ghost. " *Before the throne ;* " that is, connected with the throne, and fulfilling the purposes of Him who sits upon the throne. The Holy Ghost is one sent. (Jno. 14 : 26.) He goeth forth from the throne, and serves in behalf of the throne. He is God himself *imparted* to work in his elect the good pleasure of his own will, making his grace availing in them and for them, filling them with " all peace and joy in believing," helping their infirmities, witnessing to their adoption, and carrying into effect all the divine administrations of the kingdom of grace.

But there is a third, from whom these great blessings are implored—" *from Jesus Christ.*" There is neither grace nor peace for man, except through Christ. He is the stone which was set at naught by the builders, who is become the head of the corner. Neither is there salvation in any other ; for there is none other name under heaven given among men whereby we must be saved. (Acts 4 : 11, 12.) If God the Father hath begotten us again to a lively hope, it is only " by the resurrection of Jesus Christ from the dead." If we now have liberty to enter into the holiest, it is only " by the blood of Jesus, by a new and living way, which he hath consecrated for us, through the veil, that is to say, his flesh." (Heb. 10 : 19, 20.) And if there cometh to us peace, it is because " this man is our peace," and standeth and feedeth in the strength of the Lord, and in the majesty of the name of the Lord his God. (Micah 5 : 4, 5.)

And as three titles are given to each of the other sources of grace and peace to the Churches, three are also given to Christ. If the eternal Father is He which is, and which was, and which is to come ; if the Holy Ghost is spirit, sevenfold, and before the throne : Jesus Christ is " *the faithful witness, the first-born of the dead, and the Prince of the kings of the earth.*" Isaiah prophesied of him as " A witness to the peoples : a leader and commander of the peoples." God said of him, " I will make him my first-born, higher than the kings of the earth," and his throne " as a faithful witness in heaven." (Is. 55 : 4 ; Ps. 89 : 27, 37.) And as was predicted, so it has come to pass. " To this end was I born," says he, " and for this cause came I into the world, that I should bear witness unto the truth." Having died a martyr to his testimony, and given his life an offering for sin, he was restored to life again, as all the Scriptures witness, and became " the first fruits of the resurrection," " the first-born from the dead." And having been " faithful unto death," God hath exalted him, far above all principalities and powers, that at his name every knee should bow, and every tongue confess that Jesus Christ is Lord, to the glory of God the Father.

Conceive of these three, then, as one Almighty and ineffable Godhead,—the Father in the absoluteness of his unchanging nature and universal presence, the Spirit in all the completeness of his manifold energies and diversified operations, and the Son in the virtues of his blood-sealed testimony, of the new begotten power of his resurrection, and of the super-royal administrations of his eternal kinghood, each in his place, and all as one, laid under contribution, and unreservedly and irrevocably pledged, for the blessedness of them that believe ;—sound the depths of such a fountain of good ; test the firmness of such a basis of confidence ; survey the strength and majesty of such a refuge for the soul ; weigh the treasures of bliss which are opened up in such a presentation ; and you may begin to form some conception of the resources of the saints, and of the real breadth and joyousness of this apostolic Salutation to the Churches. Is it any wonder that John's heart took fire at the contemplation, or that he should abruptly pass from affectionate greeting to jubilant doxology ? Surely " the name of the Lord is a strong tower : the righteous runneth into it, and is set on high."

II. Let us look, then, for a few moments at this exultant Ascription. He does not even name the object of it. He seems for the time to be so bewildered among the glories of the Godhead as not to distinguish whether but one, or three, are embraced in his joyous adoration. He speaks of One who loves, and one who atones, and one who renders this love and atonement effective to our deliverance and exultation ; and yet includes the three in one, giving glory and dominion forever and ever unto Him that loves us, and freed us from our sins by his own blood, and made us a kingdom, priests unto his Father and his God. But before he completes the sentence, his rapt heart settles upon Him alone whose Apocalypse he is about to unfold. A higher testimony to the proper Deity of Christ could not well be given. He also runs together the present, the past, and the future in the same conception, as in the previous description of God himself. He speaks of an exercise of Divine love, which *now is* (ἀγαπῶντι, *loves ;* not αγαπ ησαντι, *loved*) ; of a cleansing by blood, which *has* taken place ; and of a regency and priestly dignity which remains to be realized in its fulness hereafter. All these are embraced in the grace and peace of which he had just spoken, and each separately, as well as all conjointly, is made the subject of sublime praise to Him from whom it proceeds. Observe the particular specifications.

The ever adorable One " *loves us.*" We are apt to think of the great love of God as past ; as having spent its greatest force, and reached its highest culmination, when he gave his only begotten Son to humiliation and death in our behalf. But in this we are mistaken. That love is *a present love,* and in as full force at this moment as when it delivered up Jesus to the horrors which overwhelmed him on the cross. Nay, the greatest stress and perfection of it is in exercise now, being the more intensified by reason of what was there so meekly endured for us. That was a love for enemies ; what must it then be for friends ? That was for man in his unloveliness and sins ; what must it then be for those who have been washed from their sins, and clothed in all the heavenly beauty of the Saviour's righteousness ? That was a love for the self-ruined and the lost, without claim upon Divine compassion ; what must it then be to the redeemed, who are recommended by all the worth and claims of the sinlessness, and unswerving obedience, and high Divinity of Christ ? Oh, the breadth, the length, the depth, the height, of the love of Christ ! Who shall measure it ? Who can comprehend it ? It encompasses us like a shoreless, bottomless sea. It passeth knowledge. It transcends all thought. And it is in full force *now*, to make us forever blessed. Alas, what Doxology is strong enough adequately to acknowledge it ?

" And freed us from our sins by his own blood."   We are prone to overlook this as an accomplished fact.   As we refer the height of the Divine love and compassion to the past, and so diminish the comfort which belongs to us from it as a present reality ;   so we are too apt to refer our absolution in Christ's blood to some future attainment, and to hold back from the proper appropriation of its virtue except as connected with certain works or experiences of our own.   In both instances we are grievously at fault.   As God's great love, in all its fulness, is a present love ;   so our absolution through the blood of Christ is a *past* absolution.   We have not to wait and work to be forgiven.   The work has long since been done.   The decree went forth, the releasing word was spoken, the forgiveness was declared, when Jesus left his tomb ;   and all that any man has to do on that subject is to believe it, and to appropriate to himself the glorious reprieve.   What saith the Scripture ? " God sent not his Son into the world to condemn the world, but that the world through him might be saved.   He that believeth on him is not con- demned." (Jno. 3 : 17, 18.) What of " the hand-writing of ordinances that was against us, which was contrary to us ? "   Has not Jesus long since entirely disposed of it ?   Does not the apostle testify that He hath blotted it out, and taken it out of the way, nailing it to his cross ? (Col. 2 : 14.) It is not written, that " there is now therefore no condemnation to them which are in Christ Jesus, who walk not after the flesh, but after the Spirit ? " (Rom. 8 : 1.) And in the light of passages like these, I should stultify the message which God has given me to deliver, and detract from the richness of that Gospel which I am ordained to preach, if I did not come to you with the blessed announcement of a pardon already passed, and a complete absolution already spoken, for all your sins, however many or deep-dyed, on the simple condition that you but believe my word, and take the assurance to your souls. And we live beneath our privilege and fail to make the required use of the great expiation which has been wrought, and want in proper appreciation of our Saviour's work, if we do not rise up from our prostration under the law, and cast from us forever the whole burden of its condemnation. Can you not feel, even as I pronounce these words, the starting pulsations of that life of freedom which flows down to us from Calvary's cross ? Can you not this moment look back to that mysterious and all-availing immolation of the Son of God, and believe that it was the taking away of your guilt, even yours ? O my downcast, sorrowing brother, look, look, at that scene of sacred blood- shedding ;   weigh the virtues of that expiation ;   fathom the depths of its power ;   realize the blessedness of its efficacy ;   behold in that day of atone- ment the incoming of thy year of jubilee, breaking thy bonds, returning to thee thy lost estate, restoring thee to thy unfallen friends ;   and see if there be not cause for some Miriam's song of triumph—some reason for thee to join in this joyous doxology.

" And made us a kingdom—priests unto his God and Father."   The glory brightens as the account proceeds.   That we should have a place in the affectionate regard, and tender, effective love of the great Lord, is much. That we should have forgiveness for all our sins, made perfect by his free grace at the cost of his own life's blood, is almost too much for belief.   But, to affection is added honour, and to salvation, official dignities.   We are not only loved, and freed from our sins, but, if indeed we are Christians, we are princes and priests, named and anointed for immortal regencies and eternal priesthoods.   Let men despise and contemn religion as they may, there is empire connecting with lowly discipleship, royalty with penitence and prayers, and sublime priesthood with piety.   Fishermen and taxgatherers, by listening to Jesus, presently find themselves in apostolic thrones, and ministering as priests and rulers of a dispensation, wide as the world, and lasting as time.   Moses, by his faith, rises from Jethro's sheepfold to be the prince of Israel ;   and Daniel, from the den of condemnation and death, to the honour and authority of empire ;   and Luther, from his cell, to dictate to

kings and rule the ages. There is not a believer, however obscure or humble, who may not rejoice in princely blood, who does not already wield a power which the potencies of hell cannot withstand, and who is not on the way to possess eternal priesthood and dominion.

Consider, then, what is embraced in the priestly reign of the saints in the ages to come,—" what untried forms of happy being, what cycles of revolving bliss," are before us in those high spheres,—what sceptres are to be wielded and what altars served amid the sublimities of our immortal destiny,— what streams of ascending influence shall concentrate in those holy adminis- trations, letting forth God to his creatures, and guiding the adoration of realms unknown as yet to the unsearchable bosom of the invisible God ;— and who that believes does not feel his heart stirred to its profoundest depths, and the devout ascription of " glory and dominion forever and ever " rising unbidden to his lips, unto Him who so loved us, and has done such great things for us ? " Oh, that men would praise the Lord for his goodness, and for his wonderful works toward the children of men ! "

III. But we pass to another topic, in which we find a pre-eminently solemn prophetic Allusion. The mention of these kinghoods and priesthoods of the saints, and the glory and eternal dominion of Christ, suggests an occurrence which must precede the full realization of these things, both for Christ and his people. And, with his soul on fire with these sublime contemplations, thirsting for the great consummation, and running over with interest in the tidings which he was about to communicate, the loving apostle seems to have felt as if the grand climacteric of time had come : " Behold he cometh with the clouds ; and every eye shall see him, and they which pierced him : and all tribes of the land shall mourn about him. Even so. Amen."

Again he omits to mention the name of Him of whom he is speaking. There is, however, no room for mistake. This coming One is the same who freed us from our sins by his own blood, and who is to have glory and dominion forever and ever. John was present when that blessed One left the earth. He had heard the angels say : " Ye men of Galilee, this same Jesus, which is taken up from you into heaven, shall so come in like manner as ye have seen him go into heaven." (Acts 1 : 11.) He had seen how " a cloud received him out of their sight," and thenceforward carried in his memory what the words of the angels authorized him to regard as a picture of something in the future to which he ever looked with the profoundest interest. And all the stupendous visions of the Apocalypse did not for one moment disturb that picture, or divert his mind from it. However variously he may have been moved, as scene followed scene in the great exhibition of the Divine purpose, the key- note to which he ever returned was the coming and kingdom of that ascended Lord. Even in all the long course of unending ages, that upon which his thoughts most firmly fastened was, the coming again of the Lord Jesus. With this he begins ; with this he continues ; and with this he ends. But let us separate his words a little, and look at their several implications individually.

" *He cometh.*" Here is the great fact unequivocally stated. Christ has not gone to heaven to stay there. He has gone for his Church's benefit ; and for his Church's benefit he will return again ; not in spirit only, not in providence only, not in the mere removal of men by death, but in his own proper person, as " the Son of man." Few believe this, and still fewer lay it to heart. Many sneer at the very idea, and would fain laugh down the people who are so simple as to entertain it. But it is nevertheless the immutable truth of God, predicted by all his prophets, promised by Christ himself, confirmed by the testimony of angels, proclaimed by all the apostles, believed by all the early Christians, acknowledged in all the Church Creeds, sung of in all the Church Hymn-books, prayed about in all the Church Liturgies, and entering so essentially into the very life and substance of Christianity, that without it there is no Christianity, except a few maimed and mutilated relics too powerless to be worth the trouble or expense of preservation. That religion which does not look for a returning Saviour, or locate its highest hopes and triumphs in the judgment scenes for which the Son of man must reappear, is not the religion of this book, and is without authority to promise salvation to its devotees. And those addresses to the Churches which have no " *Behold he cometh* " pervading or underlying them, have not been indited by " the Seven Spirits of God," nor sent by Him whose Apocalypse is the crown of the inspired Canon. Murmur at it, dispute it, despise it, mock at it, put it aside, hate it, and hide from it, as men may, it is a great fundamental article of the Gospel, that that same blessed Lord, who ascended from Mount Olivet, and is now at the right hand of God the Father Almighty, shall come from thence to judge the quick and the dead, and to stand again on that very summit from which he went up. This is true, as Christ himself is true ; and " he that hath an ear to hear, let him hear." Amen.

" He cometh *with the clouds*." Here is the great characteristic in the manner of his coming. " *With the clouds*," that is, in majesty and glory ;—with the awful pomp and splendour of Him " who maketh the clouds his chariot : who walketh upon the wings of the wind."

" *And every eye shall see him*." Here is the publicity of the sublime event. It is not said that all shall see him at the same time, or in the same scene, or with the same feelings. Other passages teach us that some eyes will see him whilst he is yet to others invisible ; and that he will be manifested to some at one time and place, and to others at other times and places, and in different acts of the wonderful drama. But, somewhere, at some time, in some stage of his judicial administrations, there never has been and never will be that human being who shall not see him. To every one that has lived, and to every one who shall live, he will show himself, and compel every eye to meet his eye. The dead shall be brought to life again, and shall see him, and the living shall see him. The good shall see him, and the wicked shall see him. Some shall see him and shout : " Lo, this is our God ; we have waited for him, and he will save us : this is the LORD ; we have waited for him, we will be glad and rejoice in his salvation ; " and others shall see him and cry to " the mountains and rocks : Fall on us, and hide us from the face of him that sitteth on the throne, and from the wrath of the Lamb ; for the great day of his wrath is come ; and who shall be able to stand ? "

" *And they which pierced him*." Though his manifestation shall be absolutely universal, it has an awful distinction with reference to some. Of all beings who shall then wish to be saved that sight will be those who murdered him. But they shall not escape it. They must each and all some day confront him, and meet his all-penetrating gaze. From the wretched man who betrayed him, down to the soldier who pierced his side, and all who have made common cause with them in wronging, persecuting, wounding and insulting that meek Lamb of God, shall then be compelled to face his judgment-seat, and to look upon him whom they have pierced.

" *And all the tribes of the land shall mourn about him*." Is not this a special word for the Jews ? Is it not an allusion to a wail of penitence which shall be elicited from long apostate Israel, when they shall look upon him whom they have pierced, and doubt of his messiahship no more ? Does it not refer to the fulfilment of Zechariah 12 : 10, where the house of David and the inhabitants of Jerusalem shall mourn for him, as one mourneth for his only son, and shall be in bitterness for him as one is in bitterness for his first-born ? Oh, the intensity of that bitterness ! Brethren, I do not wonder that worldlings and half-Christians have no love for this doctrine, or that they hate to hear about Christ's speedy coming. It is the deathknell of their gaieties and pleasures—the turning of their confidence to consternation—the conversion of their songs to shrieks of horror and despair. There is a day coming, when " the loftiness of man shall be bowed down, and the haughtiness of man shall be made low ; " when there shall be " upon the earth distress of nations, with perplexity ; " when " all the tribes of the earth shall mourn ; " when men shall " go into the holes of the rocks, and into the caves of the earth," " into the clefts of the rocks, and into the tops of the ragged rocks, for fear of the Lord, and for the glory of his majesty ; " when men " shall seek death, and shall not find it ; and shall desire to die, and death shall flee from them." And that day is the day of Christ's coming, and those dismayed ones are such as love not his appearing. Fear and dread shall fall upon the wicked ; trouble and anguish shall make them afraid ; and men's hearts shall fail them for fear, and for looking after those things that are coming on the earth. The saints will then have been caught away to their Lord. From the same field, the same shop, the same bed, one shall have been taken and the other left. And on those remaining ones, who had not watched, neither kept their garments, nor made themselves ready, shall the terrors of judgment fall, and not a family or tribe of all that live shall escape.

" *Even so, Amen.*" Some take this as the seal and ratification of the solemn truths which have just been uttered. If this be the true meaning, what particular stress is to be laid upon these things—how sure to come to pass— how unmistakably certain ! Brethren, it does seem to me, when I look at the Scriptures on this subject, that even the best of us are not half awake. May God arouse us by his Spirit, and not permit us to sleep till the thunders and terrors of the great day are upon us ! But I find another and more natural sense of these words. I find in them John's acquiescence in all that the great day is to bring, and his prayer, as repeated at the end of the book, that the Lord would hasten its coming. Terrible as it will be to the wicked, and the unprepared, and those who refuse the warnings which we give them, it is a precious day to the saints, a day to be coveted, and to be prayed for with all earnestness of desire. The poor faint-hearted Christianity of our times can hardly contemplate it without trembling and annoyance. Many who profess and call themselves Christians would rather not hear about it, and would prefer, if they had their choice, that Christ might never come. It was not so in the days of Christianity's pristine vigour. Then the anxious inquiry of disciples was, " Tell us, when shall these things be ? and what shall be the sign of thy coming, and of the end of the world ? " " Lord, wilt thou at this time restore the Kingdom to Israel ? " Then Christians wrote to each other in joyous congratulation, that their citizenship was in heaven, whence they looked for the coming of the Saviour ; and comforted one another in the assurance that the Lord himself is to descend from heaven with a shout, with the voice of the arch-angel, and with the trump of God ; and, as directed by their Lord, lifted up their heads, and looked up with joyful hope at every turn in human affairs which they could by any means construe into a probable herald of his nearing epiphany. Then the prayer, " Thy Kingdom come," had a depth of meaning and lively anticipation which now has well-nigh been lost.   Then " the appearing of Jesus Christ " had a power over the soul which made it " rejoice with joy unspeakable and full of glory ; " and the most earnest and constant call of apostles and their followers was, " Come, Lord Jesus ; come quickly. Even so. Amen." Nor can the Church ever be her true self, or enter into the true spirit of her faith, or rise to the true sublimity of her hope, where this is not the highest object of her deepest desire. For how, indeed, can we regard ourselves as rightly planted upon the apostolic foundation, if we cannot join with heart and soul in this apostolic prayer ?

IV. To all this, the apostle yet adds a most devout reference to Christ, and to Christ's declaration concerning himself, the further to confirm the solemn truthfulness of his words, and to incite us to lay the more stress upon them.

Great things, and, to human reason, very improbable things, were upon his mind, and about to be submitted to the Churches. Their importance, and the predisposition on the part of men to disregard them, seemed to call for some especial pledge of the likelihood and certainty of their accomplishment. And that pledge he gives by devoutly referring everything to that omniscient, eternal and almighty Being, whose Apocalypse he was commissioned to describe. He invokes the Alpha and the Omega, the beginning and the ending, —He who was, and is, and is to come, the Almighty,—as his judge in these utterances, to whom also he leaves the fulfilment of all that had been given him to write. It was as much as to say, if this was not a faithful and honest declaration of his inmost feelings and belief, and a true account of what he had seen and heard, such is the majesty of the Being who is to deal with him for it ; and that, if there be any unlikelihoods in these things, such is the character of Him from whom he has received them, and to whom he refers for the power to make good his words.

And how sublime is the majesty of our blessed Redeemer as thus set forth ! Never before had he given such an account of himself. He had intimated as much, and permitted his apostles to use language which implied the same. But never till in this Apocalypse had he formally assumed to himself such Divine majesty. He here proclaims Himself to be The Almighty, the very God, the One existing before anything was made, comprehending all things in His own existence, and possessing immensity and eternity. Look a moment at the particulars.

" I am Alpha and Omega." These are the names of the letters which begin and end the Greek alphabet. It is the same as if it were said in English, " I am A and Z." That is, our Saviour claims to be what letters and language were meant to be, namely the expression of truth. He is THE WORD—the embodiment of all Divine verities from first to last.   God is a Spirit—an invisible, incorporeal, intangible, unapproachable Spirit. But that hidden and unsearchable Mind may be expressed, may let itself forth in comprehensible utterance. And that expression, that utterance of invisible Godhead is Jesus Christ— the Divine Wisdom—the only communication from the absolute to the created.

" The beginning, and the ending." This is not found in some of the oldest and best copies of this book. It was, perhaps, introduced merely as an explanation of the clause going before it. It does not seem to convey any additional thought. He is the first, because all things took their beginning from him ; and he is the last, because in him shall all things have their consummation. But what follows is unmistakably genuine.

" Who is, and who was, and who is to come." This sublime form of speech is used to describe the Eternal Father ; but it belongs equally to the Son. He is the I AM, whose being is the same through all reckonings of time. As the Father exists in all the past, present, and future, eternal and unchangeable ; so Christ, who is the express image of the Father, is " the same, yesterday, to-day, and forever." He was with the Father before the world was. He is now at the right hand of the Father. And he is to come in the name and the glory of the Father in those eternal administrations which are the joy and hope of his people.

" The Almighty." Than this there is no higher name. It declares the complete and unqualified subjection of all created things to our Lord Jesus Christ. It leaves nothing which is not put under Him.   Oh, the adorableness and majesty of our Redeemer ! Who could play false in such a presence ? What son of Belial may escape righteous retribution in such hands ? What untruthfulness can there be in such a Being ? What lack for the full performance of all the will and purpose of One with such characteristics ! Rather than give way to doubt and unbelief, let us fall down in lowly adoration at his feet, take His truth, and rejoice in Him as our hope and our everlasting consolation.

But, I must conclude these observations for the present. The Apostolic prelude to this solemn book is sufficiently before us to be made of great spiritual profit. Let us see to it that we do not fail to realize that advantage which it is intended and so well fitted to impart. Here is grace and peace from the Triune God spoken for our acceptance ; let us see to it that we do not receive the inspired salutation in vain. Here is a glorious celebration of an

B

accomplished absolution, an existing love, and sublime endowments, all made ours in Christ Jesus ; let us make sure that our hearts are in tune to the same lofty song. Here is an apostolic admonition to direct our most earnest thoughts to the personal return of our Lord, which is to be so dreadful to the unready and so joyous to them that watch and pray ; let us make it our business to be properly exercised in that " Behold." Here also we are referred to the ineffable greatness and Divinity of our Redeemer and Judge ; and let us beware how we trifle with his word, question his power, or dash ourselves against his Almightiness.

And " unto Him that loves us, and freed us from our sins by his own blood, and hath made us a kingdom—priests unto Him who is his God and Father ; to Him be glory and dominion unto the ages. Amen."

LECTURE THIRD

REV. CHAP. I : 9–17. (Revised Text).—I, John, your brother and copartner in the tribulation, and the kingdom, and the patient waiting, in Jesus Christ, was in the isle that is called Patmos, on account of the word of God and the testimony of Jesus Christ. I became in Spirit in the Lord's day ; and I heard behind me a great voice, as of a trumpet, saying, [" I am Alpha and Omega," &c., is here without due authority] What thou seest, write in a book, and send it to the seven Churches : to Ephesus, and to Smyrna, and to Pergamos, and to Thyatira, and to Sardis, and to Philadelphia, and to Laodicea.

And I turned about to see the voice that was speaking with me, and, being turned, I saw seven candlesticks [lampstands or lamps] of gold ; and in the midst of the seven candlesticks [one] like to the Son of man, clothed in a long garment reaching to the feet, and girt at the breasts with a girdle of gold. His head and his hairs [were] white, as white wool, as snow, and his eyes as a flame of fire, and his feet like fine brass glowing with fire as in a furnace ; and his voice as the voice of many waters ; and he had in his right hand seven stars ; and proceeding out of his mouth a sharp two-edged sword ; and his countenance as the sun shineth in his strength.

And when I saw him, I fell at his feet as dead. And he laid his right hand upon me, saying unto me, Fear not.

WE now approach the Apocalypse proper. Hitherto we have only been considering superscriptions and prefaces. Henceforward we have to deal with the thing itself.

Those acquainted with the contents of this remarkable book are aware that it is made up of several distinct scenes or acts. The first gives us the Apocalypse of Christ in his relation to his Churches on earth, and his judgment of them. The second gives us the Apocalypse of Christ in his relation to the Church in heaven, or his glorified Church, and the scenes into which the saints are introduced after they are caught up from the earth. The third gives us the Apocalypse of Christ in his relation to the world, and his administrations of retribution to the nations. And so on, till we see everything settled in the excellencies of the new heavens and the new earth. We have to do now only with the first, which extends to the close of the third chapter. It consists of two leading parts : first, a magnificent vision of the Saviour, with some circumstantial particulars and explanations, and second, seven epistles, descriptive of character, and how it fares in the solemn judgment. It is the first part of this first act that I propose now to consider ; that is, THE VISION.

    I.   THE CIRCUMSTANCES OF IT ;
    II. THE SUBJECT AND SUBSTANCE OF IT ;
    III. THE RESULTS OF IT.

Lift up your hearts, then, unto the Lord, the giver of light and grace, that He may enable us rightly to conceive of these important matters.

The seer of this vision was *John*. At the time of the vision, he was the only remaining apostle, and perhaps the only survivor of those with whom Christ had personally conversed. He was therefore the most interesting and exalted Christian then living upon the earth—a most reverend and venerable man.

But he was as humble and meek as he was high in place. He gives himself no titles. He says nothing of his sublime official relations. It was enough for him to put himself on a level with the common brotherhood of believers. Whatever may be our gifts and stations, we are all one in Christ Jesus. The high and the low, the rich and poor, the bond and free, those who have known the Saviour after the flesh, and those who have seen him only with the eye of faith, are all brethren together, children of one Father, servants of the same Lord, and fellow-heirs to the same hopes and inheritance. He was the inspired teacher of those to whom he was writing. His words were to be to them a rule of faith and life. But, with all, he calls himself simply their " *brother*, and co-partner in tribulation, and in the kingdom, and in the patient waiting, in Christ Jesus."

And in this statement he brings out what were the chief characteristics of the Christian confession in those days ; namely, a common brotherhood in Christ, a common suffering for Christ, a common royalty and kingship as yet unrevealed, and a common hopeful and patient waiting for the time of blessed coronation, and joyous entrance with the Lord upon the dominion of the world. The same may serve to show in how far our Christianity answers to the Christianity of the Apostles' days, and to assure us that, in so far as these characteristics appear in us, we are the brethren of Apostles, and partakers in the same fellowship with those who saw the miracles, heard the words, and waited about the steps of Him who now reigns in the highest heavens, and are also to reign with Him forever and ever.

John was at the time in exile, upon a lonely and desolate island. But neither seas, nor Alps, nor ages, can sever the bonds by which Christians are united to each other, or to Christ, their Lord. Less than a year ago I passed that island. It is a mere mass of barren rocks, dark in colour and cheerless in form. It lies out in the open sea, near the coast of Western Asia Minor. It has neither trees nor rivers, nor any land for cultivation, except some little nooks between the ledges of rocks. There is still a dingy grotto remaining, in which the aged Apostle is said to have lived, and in which he is said to have had this vision. A chapel covers it, hung with lamps kept burning by the monks. He had been banished to this inhospitable place by the persecuting Roman government, not for crimes, but " for the word of God, and for the testimony of Jesus Christ." He was the acknowledged head of the witnesses of Jesus, and the great promulgator and defender of the truth as it is in Jesus, and for his zeal and prominence in this, he was dealt with as a felon and an outlaw. The unconverted heart always has been, is now, and always will be, at enmity with God, and hence at disagreement with God's truth and people. It cannot endure what is not conformed to its views and tastes, and is full of malice, resentment, and revenge towards everything which holds with God and with Christ. And if the world is at any time at peace, and on good terms with the Church, it is because the Church itself has become debauched, and has descended to a compromise to be at one with the wicked. The nominal Christian and the formalist the world cannot hate, for they are of it, and it will love its own ; but the Johns and Pauls must go into banishment, or give their necks to the stateblock.

But the wrath of the wicked does but bring saints the nearer to the choice favours of God. The Patmos of persecuting Rome is to John the door of sublimest communion with heaven. The chains of resentful power may confine the body, but they cannot bind the soul. The Apostle, doomed to the isle of convicts, soars on the wings of prophetic ecstasy, traverses ages, and moves among the most stupendous administrations of the last day. Circumscribed in his natural life, he is lifted to a higher life. Shut out from this world, and estranged from earthly friends, he becomes conversant with one of spiritual realities, and is made to communicate with celestial orders. In solitude secluded, if not in some dungeon immured, he is thrilled with visions and revelations of the Lord, " whose overpowering splendour that he might endure, whose great variety that he might remember and record, whose various places of representation that he might be transported to," the very conditions of his existence are transformed, as in the case of Ezekiel on Chebar's banks, and as in the case of Paul caught up to Paradise, and hearing unspeakable words, not knowing whether he was in the body or out of the body. In a word, he was (εν πνευματι) IN SPIRIT—in a condition wholly loosened from the earth—transported by means of the Spirit,—(εν τη χυριαχη ημερα) INTO THE LORD'S DAY—stationed as a spectator amid the very scenes of the great judgment itself.*

In this state of prophetic exaltation, the first thing that arrested the Apostle's attention was, " *a great voice as of a trumpet.*" When God revealed himself on Mount Sinai, he broke silence with the " voice of a trumpet, exceeding loud." When the service of the temple began in the morning, and the great door was opened, it was at the sound of the trumpet. When the year of Jubilee came round, it was ushered in by the sounding of the silver trumpet. And so when the silence of the tomb is to be broken, and the scattered children of God gathered for their rewards, it shall be with " the voice of the archangel and the trump of God : " " for the trumpet shall sound, and the dead shall be raised incorruptible, and we shall be changed." And whilst the sounding of the great trumpet in this case was intended to fix the attention of the seer, and assure him of the Divinity of the Speaker and of the importance of what was to follow, and to give him his commission with reference to this whole Apocalypse, I cannot disconnect it from the sounding of that very trump by which the blessed Lord, in the great day, will arouse, and call together his scattered saints, and announce to them their everlasting Jubilee. It summoned the Apostle, and it summons us, to the contemplation of the fact, that the great Apocalypse of our Saviour is to be preceded with the sound of " a great voice as of a trumpet." The godless world may not hear that voice ; but Apostles shall hear it ; and all who have place with them in the blessed brotherhood of suffering and patient waiting for Christ, whom John here represents, shall hear it ; and they shall be transfigured when they hear it ; and mount up with wings like eagles to the open presence of their Lord.

The instant John turned to " see the voice that spake with " him, he " saw seven golden candlesticks (or lampstands), and in the midst of the seven candlesticks one like to the Son of man." From the conclusion of the chapter, we learn that these " seven candlesticks are the seven Churches." In all languages, truth and knowledge are likened to light. The Psalmist speaks of God's word as a lamp to his feet and a light unto his path. And so the Churches are the lampstands, or light-bearers. They have no light in themselves, but they hold forth and diffuse the light which they have from the oil of grace and the fire of the Spirit. Each Christian is a lighted candle. And all God's children are described as " lights in the world, holding forth the word of life." It is therefore a most significant image by which the communities of saints are here set forth. They are as so many lampstands of God's light and truth in a world of darkness ; and as such Christ deals with them.

These lampstands are *gold*—composed of the costliest, the most precious, the most glorious, the royal, the *sacred* metal. A saint is an excellent, a glorious, a royal, in some sense a sacred being ; and a congregation of Christians is altogether the most precious thing on earth. It is the pure gold of the world.

Seven is the number of completeness. It here designates the whole Christian body, of all times and all places.

The " one like unto the Son of man," is Christ himself. He is described in the same way in the Psalms, in the visions of Daniel, and in his own discourses concerning himself. It is a form of speech meant to set forth the essential importance and prominence of the human element of the Saviour's character ; for it is in his human nature that his redemption work is conducted, and his victories achieved. It is as the Son of man that he came, lived, suffered and

* See First Discourse, pp. 20, 21.

died. It was as the Son of man that he rose from the dead, ascended into heaven, and will come again, judge the world, and set up his glorious everlasting rule. But he is not to be conceived of as nothing but a man. He is " one *like* unto the Son of man." This word *like* sets us upon the scent of something higher than humanity, though conditioned as humanity, and having everything in common with it. Thus we read of him as " made in the likeness of men,"—" in all respects made like unto his brethren." This assumption of likeness to man, presupposes some modification of what properly is not human. And so we also read of him as The Word made flesh—God manifested in the flesh—the Son of God condescending to be the Son of man,—not in appearance only, but in literal reality ; not for certain acts of humiliation only, but for glory and dominion as well ; not temporarily only, till a few facts are accomplished, then to return to what he was before the marvellous process began, but forever,—as well throughout the unending duration of the results achieved as in the immediate mysteries of the passion which laid the foundation of these results. It is a mischievous error to suppose that the Son of God's assumption of human nature was only for the immediate private end of redeeming fallen man—a mere phenomenon in Godhead's ever busy administration—a simple act the like of which may have been before, or may be again. It is the abiding miracle of eternity. It is, and was meant to be, a thing of abiding permanence, the eternal continuity of which is as vital to the everlasting future of the redeemed, and the great purposes of God, as the continuity of creative power is to the preservation of the universe. To deny this, is to strip the Gospel of its chief glory, and to start on a path of heretical peril almost sure to end in utter shipwreck of the faith. Christ is " one like unto the Son of man," that is Godhead embodied in humanity, not only for what has transpired in the past, or is going on at present, or is to be enacted at the judgment, but also for the whole eternity of administrations appertaining to the saints, and to the race. And this Divine man is the great subject of this vision, especially in his relation to the Churches. John beholds him " in the midst of the seven candlesticks," and " the seven candlesticks are the seven Churches."

Some have given out that it is simply in his character of *Priest*, that the Saviour appears in this vision. He is indeed a priest, even our great High Priest that has passed into the heavens ; but this is not his only character, nor expressive of his entire relation to the Churches. Neither is it the only or even the chief aspect in which he comes before us in this vision. There is no mitre, no ephod, no breastplate, no censer, no blood. The garment reaching down to the feet is as distinctive of royal dignity as of sacerdotal functions, if not more so. The girdle might appear to be priestly ; but it is *gold*, all gold, indicative of royalty ; whilst the proper priestly girdle was not gold, but simply wrought and interwoven with gold. He also wields a sword, which is another mark of sovereignty and judicial power, which does not belong to the sacerdotal office, albeit that sword proceeds from his mouth. This ought to satisfy us that the character which Christ bears in this vision is something more than a Priest. There is royalty and magistracy, as well as priesthood. We here have to do with the Lord and Judge of the Churches. The throne is yet in the background, but the royal majesty is manifest. As Judge of the world, more is to be shown hereafter ; but here he appears as Judge of the Churches. He is a Priest, but a Priest invested with royal prerogatives, and come forth to pronounce judgment upon the candlesticks which he attends. In a word, as this vision, and the epistles which follow it, have respect to the entire Church from the days of the Apostle on to the resurrection, grasped in a single view, so it is Christ's whole relation to that Church, with special reference to his judgment of it, that is here presented to our contemplation.

Behold, then, O man, thy Lord and Judge.

1. He is " *in the midst of the seven candlesticks*." When he left the world, he said to his disciples, " Lo ! I am with you always, even unto the end of

the world." And lest the promise should be mistaken as belonging to ministers alone, he gave the still further assurance, that where two or three are gathered together in his name, there he is, in the midst of them. I cannot explain to you the method of this presence. Even in things with which we are familiar, there is mystery attaching to what we call *presence*. We speak of a man as present in a room, and of what transpires in that room as taking place in his presence. But how is he present beyond the immediate space occupied by his body ? That his presence extends beyond the few feet marked by the outlines of his physical frame, is a fact which we all feel and realize ; but how it is so, we cannot so easily explain. I am present in this audience-chamber. I am as much present to those in the remotest pews, as to those who are in the nearest. And yet, my body is present only in these few feet within the pulpit. Suppose, then, you were to conceive of me as suddenly exalted into a majesty and glory like that of Jesus. Imagine these walls widened out in corresponding proportion. Fancy everything now on the scale of the earthly and human expanded to the scale of the heavenly and glorified. And it may, aid you somewhat in conceiving how Christ can be present with all his Churches, and yet occupy a definite space in heaven. The whole world is not as great to him as an ordinary room to us. And if my presence can fill this Church, whilst I keep my place in this pulpit, his presence can certainly fill all his Churches, even from his mysterious celestial location at the right hand of the Father. This, however, is certain, that he is, in some sort, in all his Churches. There is not a member which he does not see and know. There is not a Christian service held, of which we are not authorized to say, The Lord is there. He is in his Churches, not only by his word, by his sacraments, by his ministers, by his authority, power and Spirit ; but he is there himself, as the Son of man. He is present as Priest, as Lord, as Judge ; and hence in his own proper person, as the Godman. There is another, nearer, and more manifest presence, to be realized when he shall come again ; but not more true or real than that by which he is even now in the midst of us. Were these dull, dim senses of ours but unlocked and energized, after the style of that transformation for which the saints are taught to look, we would see our Saviour, present to-night, as really as John saw him " walking in the midst of the seven golden candlesticks." It is a solemn and startling thought ; but it is true.

2. " *Clothed with a garment reaching to the feet, and girt at the breasts with a girdle of gold.*" In former times, and to this day in some sections of the world, the long trailing robe is the token of dignity and honour. Thus, in Isaiah's vision of the Lord upon his throne, he speaks of just such a robe, the train or skirts of which filled the temple. Righteousness is indicated by a garment. The priestly dignity was marked by a robe of this kind, though somewhat shorter, and hung around the skirt with pomegranates and bells. The high officer who drew the marks of distinction in Ezekiel's vision of the great slaughter was also similarly attired. One of those mighty personages with whom Daniel dealt in his heavenly visions was clad in this way, and also girded with gold, though about his *loins*, indicative of service, and not about *the breasts*, as indicative of privilege and superior dignity. If, then, we are to take this attire of the Son of man as symbolical, as commentators generally have taken it, it must describe personal qualities, official dignity, and celestial majesty, at which we may well bow down in the deepest reverence.

But why not also take it literally ? There is no such thing as nakedness in heaven. Clothing and raiment enter into all the descriptions we have of the saints in glory. They have robes, they have crowns, they have wedding-garments. Christ is not naked ; and when we see him, it will not be in a state of divesture and nudity. He has his appropriate clothing for every scene of his grand administrations. And when we have this minute account of his attire, why should we strive to explain it away as mere figure and symbol ? Was it not the literal Son of man whom John saw ? Did he not have explained to him what was mystical, leaving this to be taken just as it was seen ?

For my own part, I believe that our blessed Lord is at this moment arrayed just as he is here described, and that this is the dress in which he will deal with the Churches, and be seen of the saints, when the judgment begins. But everything outward in heaven is in exact correspondence with the inward. Official robes are confined to official dignities, and whatever the attire of Christ indicates, that he is. Everything there is reality. The garments are real, and that with which they connect is real. There will be no cloak there for unrighteousness, and no saints in tatters, or kings in rags, or plebeians in royal array. All are in dress what they are in reality. Christ in the priestly robe, is a priest ;—in the royal dress, is a king ;—in judicial attire, is a judge. And in the words before us, we have all these dignities in one, and each contributing to express the sublime power, majesty and glory of that great Lord and Saviour with whom we have to do.

3. And " *his head and his hairs were white like wool, as white as snow*." The Scriptures tell us, that " the hoary head is a crown of glory." The same appears in Daniel's vision of " The Ancient of Days, whose garment was white as snow, and the hair of his head like pure wool." Many have taken these white hairs as symbolic of the Godhead of Christ. Pure, undistributed light certainly is the representative of Deity. Paul also says, " The head of Christ is God." White hairs connect with fatherhood, and patriarchal dignity ; and " with the ancient is wisdom." But I take this peculiarity as I take the robe and the golden girdle. It belongs to the glory and beauty in which our Lord now appears, and will appear to his saints, when he shall call them to himself. It connects indeed with his eternal Deity, but also with his human majesty, and the sublime reverence that appertains to him as a man. He is the everlasting Father, as well as the Prince of Peace. He is the second Adam, with all the patriarchal honour and dignity which would by this time attach to the first, if he had never sinned.

4. " *And his eyes were as a flame of fire*." Here is intelligence ; burning, all-penetrating intelligence. Here is power to read secrets, to bring hidden things to light, to warm and search all hearts at a single glance. And all this is expressed in the very aspect of our Lord. It is given as one of the marks of Cæsar's greatness, that he had fiery eyes—a penetrating, warming, revealing glance—a look which enemies and dissemblers could not stand. Christ is the sublime and the almighty Cæsar of the Church. He trieth the hearts and reins. " His eyes behold, his eyelids try, the children of men." " Neither is there any creature that is not manifest in his sight : but all things are naked and opened unto the eyes of him with whom we have to do." The light of the human eye is from without, and shifts its focal point as the rays happen to fall on it ; but the light in the eye of Christ is from the Divinity within, and streams forth with steady and all-penetrating sharpness, as well in the darkness as in the day, into the soul as well as upon the body. But his sharp look is one of inspiring warmth to the good, as well as of discomfiting and consuming terror to the hypocritical and the godless. Will you believe it, my friends, that this is the look which is upon you, and which is to try you in the great day ! Well may we pray the prayer of David : " Search me, O God, and know my heart ; try me, and know my thoughts ; and see if there be any evil way in me, and lead me in the way everlasting."

5. " *And his feet [were] like unto fine brass, as if they burned in a furnace*." He once said, through Isaiah, " I will make the place of my feet glorious." But here we have the feet themselves, those feet with which he is to tread down the wicked ; and the description corresponds with the rest of the picture. Christ is all-glorious, even to his feet. They are like *glowing brass*— like brass in the fire heated unto whiteness. The glory of this metal, in such a state, is almost insufferable to the human gaze. It presents an image of pureness which is terrible. And it is upon these feet of dreadful holiness that our Lord walks among the Churches, and shall tread down all abominations, and crush Antichrist, and Satan, and all who unhappily set aside his authority

and his claims. Beautiful are those feet to them that love him, but terrible and consuming to those who shall be trodden by them.

6. " *And his voice as the sound of many waters.*" How could it be otherwise, considering how he is speaking and uttering himself throughout all his Churches, and all the world, from the beginning until now, and on to the day of his coming ? Or, leaving this out of the question, how could it be otherwise, considering that the day is approaching when " all that are in the graves shall hear *the voice* of the Son of man, and they that hear shall live ? " But this majesty and power of voice is elsewhere more especially referred to the dreadfulness of Christ toward his faithless servants and enemies. It is particularly characteristic of his rebukes. His word came to Jeremiah, saying, " Say unto them, The Lord shall roar from on high, and utter his voice from his holy habitation ; he shall mightily roar upon his habitation ; he shall give a shout, as they that tread the grapes, against all the inhabitants of the earth. A noise shall come even to the ends of the earth, for the Lord hath a controversy with the nations ; he will plead with all flesh ; he will give them that are wicked to the sword, saith the Lord." But whether for the overthrow of his enemies or the salvation of his people, " The voice of the Lord is powerful ; the voice of the Lord is full of majesty." It scattereth the proud, and it giveth joy and confidence to the lowly.

7. " *And he had in his right hand seven stars.*" " The seven stars are the angels (ministers) of the seven Churches," and, as such, they are distinct from the candlesticks. Christ walks among the candlesticks, but he holds these ministers in his right hand. The democratic idea of Church organization, which makes all power proceed from the members, and makes the ministerial position nothing more than what inheres in every Christian, is thus scattered to the winds. Ministers have relations to Christ and to the Church, which ordinary Church members have not. They partake directly of Christ's authority, and are responsible directly to him, and are upheld by his right hand, beyond the power of men or angels to displace them. What a lesson for ministers, as to the holiness of their office, the solemnity of their responsibilities, the necessity of unswerving fidelity, and the exercise of every confidence in their sacred functions. They are in Christ's hand. If they are unfaithful none can deliver them out of that hand ; but if true to their position, none can touch them, or quench their light. They shall shine as the stars forever and ever. What a lesson for the people as to the authority of those ministrations which they are so prone to despise. Dealing with the regular ministers of the Churches, you are dealing with the jewels on Christ's right hand. And what a lesson for all as to the Divine majesty and glory of our Lord ! The Pauls, and Johns, and Husses, and Luthers, and Cranmers, and Knoxes, and Wesleys, and all the hosts of those who have been teaching and guiding the Churches for these 1800 years, are no more than the rings upon his fingers. But they are jewels to him. He holds them as precious. Disregarded as they may be of men, they are dear to him. He holds them, as a man holds what he most esteems. He holds them, for service now, and for judgment when he cometh. He holds them, for success against the hosts of evil, for glorious honour if they are faithful, and for eternal disgrace if they are not.

8. " *And out of his mouth went a sharp, two-edged sword.*" The sword is the symbol of magistracy and judgment. But this is not a *hand*-sword, but a *word*-sword. Nevertheless, it accords exactly with what Christ has himself said. " He that rejecteth me, and receiveth not my words, hath one that judgeth him : the word that I have spoken, the same shall judge him in the last day." Even now the word of Christ is all the while absolving, or binding under condemnation, every one to whom it is preached. A certain judicial process inheres in every faithful presentation of the Gospel. It is good news— glad tidings ; but there is a sword in it ; a sword of double edge ; and that a sword of judgment. And all the solemn administrations of the last day are

nothing more than the full revelation of this sword-power of Christ's word, cutting asunder the unfaithful servant, and carrying into effect what is now already spoken. The word of God is not an empty utterance. It is " quick and powerful, and sharper than any two-edged sword, piercing even to the dividing asunder of soul and spirit, and of the joints and marrow." And this potency pertains to the matter of punishment, as well as to the matter of conviction. In the beginning, God spake, and it was done ; He commanded, and it stood fast. The word was potent. And so in the Gospel and the final summing up of this word of Christ. It will carry its own sharp execution into the Church and into the world, into the heavens and into the earth. " By the word of God the heavens were of old, . . but the heavens and the earth which are now *by the same word* are kept in store, reserved unto fire against the day of judgment and perdition of ungodly men." It is that word which is described as the instrument of punishment to the impenitent in Pergamos, and to the hosts of the mighty ones whom the great day is to overwhelm in the winepress of the Almighty's wrath. And it is that same word which is the sword that shall be bathed in heaven, when its powers shall be shaken, and its hosts fall. Oh, the majesty of Jesus, and the fearfulness of his judgments ! Vengeance is his ; and he will repay.

9. " *And his countenance was as the sun shineth in his strength.*" The Churches are *lamps ;* the ministers are *stars ;* but Christ is the *sun.* He is to the moral world what the sun is to the natural. But let us not consider the description exhausted by its spiritual significations. Christ has a literal face ; and that face must have a form and expression. He is not a fiction, but a reality—not a spirit, but a man, with all the features of a man, though it be in a glorified condition. He has a countenance, and that countenance is " as the sun shineth in his strength." Something of this was seen in the mount of transfiguration, when " his face did shine as the sun, and his raiment was white as the light." Something of the same was manifest when he appeared to Saul of Tarsus in " a light above the brightness of the sun." And so glorious and pervading is this light which issues from his face, that in the New Jerusalem there will be neither sun, nor moon, nor lamp, nor any other light, and yet rendered so luminous by his presence, that even the nations on the earth walk in the light of it. And so the lightning brilliancy, which is to flash from one end of heaven to the other at the time of his coming, and the glory which is then to invest him and the whole firmament, is simply the uncovering or revelation of that blessed light which streams from his sublime person.

Such, then, is the full-drawn picture of our glorious Lord, as he walks among his Churches, and proceeds to pass his solemn judgment upon them. There have not been wanting some to pronounce it grotesque and intolerable. But I cannot so regard it. If a sublimer conception of Divine and glorified humanity, so true to the Saviour's offices and work, ever entered into the imagination of man, I have never seen it, and never heard of it. And when I recall the magnificent portraiture, the human form, walking majestically amid golden furniture, clothed with the garment of royalty, girded with gold, crowned with flowing locks that reflect the light and purity of heaven, having a glance of electric power, feet glowing with the liquid splendour of melted brass, a voice of majesty at which the earth and the heavens shake, the right hand lit with starry jewels, a mouth whose words carry their own execution in them, and a countenance as glorious as the noonday sun ;— when I survey such majestic lineaments, and such mighty powers, and hear the possessor of them say : " I am the First and the Last, and THE LIVING ONE ; and I was dead, and behold, I am living forever and ever : and I have the keys of death and of hades ; "—I say, when I bring all this before me, and try to realize it in my imagination, I am almost overwhelmed with the sublimity of the picture, and with the goodness, and grace, and power, and might with which the eternal Father hath invested the person of Jesus Christ. In the Gospels even, I see him mostly as a man of sorrows, persecuted unto death, and laid in the grave, though raised again in vindication of his righteous goodness. But here I see him lifted up to the right hand of power, and clothed with all majesty, that creation's knees might bow at his feet, and creation's tongues confess his greatness and proclaim his praise. Here I see Godhead in manhood, unhumbled and unalloyed by the union ; and humanity transformed and exalted to the sphere of the worshipful and Divine ; and all, to give greatness to the lowly, and strength to the feeble, and honour to the despised ; and to bring the lofty neck to obedience, tear away the masks of falsehood, and enforce the rule of heaven on the earth. I do not wonder at the effect the vision produced upon the exiled apostle as it burst upon him in his lonely solitude.

" And when I saw him, I fell at his feet as dead." Had it not been that he was in the Spirit, and sustained by the Spirit, it were hardly too much to suppose that it would have extinguished his life altogether. There is an awe and terror of a spiritual appearance which is indescribable. Job's friend says that when he saw a Spirit, the hair of his flesh stood up. Daniel, who feared not the wrath of a king, nor the lions' den, when he saw the vision, was left without strength in him. So also Ezekiel, and Isaiah, and others of whom we read. God has inwrought into our nature a common reverence for a spiritual world. And there is something fearfully prophetic in these irrepressible instincts. They not only argue the existence of a spiritual world, and that we have deep, mysterious and awful connections with it, but also that the veil which covers it is very thin, and destined some day to be withdrawn ; and that its withdrawal connects with realities which sinful humanity well may dread.

And if John was so overwhelmed with this vision of the Saviour, on whose bosom he leaned, and with whose power he was so familiar, how will it be with those who know him not, how will it be with us, when the startling trump of God shall make these heavens ring with the tidings of that great Saviour's presence, and these eyes of ours shall meet his eyes, and see him in his glory ? Will there be no fainting, falling, swooning, then ? Will there be no sinking in the souls of men, no drying up, as it were, of the very fountains of life at the stupendous Apocalypse ? Do I not hear the anxious inquiry started in many a heart at the mere thought of it : Alas, alas, how can I behold it and live ? But a single utterance made it all right with John ; and with that, if you be indeed a Christian, I would have you comfort yourself in view of that awful moment. Jesus said, " *Fear not.*"

Great and dreadful was the glory, and power, and wonder, and majesty which had suddenly opened upon the seer. The trumpet sound, the scene of splendour, the all-revealing look, the voice of power, the countenance of blazing light, all commingling, were enough to undo humanity. But the word was *Fear not.* Still more awful scenes were coming. The Churches were to be sifted, the saints were to be crowned, the seals of judgment were to be opened, the days of vengeance were to be revealed, the sun was to be darkened, the moon to be turned to blood, the stars to fall, the hills to be overthrown, the islands to be shaken out of their places, the pit to be opened, the hordes of hell to overrun the apostate nations, the angels to shout from the sky, the martyrs to cry from under the altar, unprecedented plagues to overwhelm the world, the battle of the great day of God Almighty to be fought, the winepress of the wrath of God to be trodden, the places of the wicked to be swept with the besom of destruction, and the fowls to be called together unto the supper of the great God, to eat the flesh of kings, and of captains, and of mighty men, and of multitudes of small and great. But the word was *Fear not.* Thrones were to be set, the dead were to be raised, the heavens and the earth were to be changed, death and hell were to be summoned up for destruction, a city was to come down from God out of heaven, and wonders of power and glory were to be enacted as at the going forth of the words which spoke creation into being. But the word was *Fear not.*

The true Christian is forever safe. If you be in the Spirit, and the Spirit be in you, the life that would otherwise fail you will not fail; the fear that would otherwise overwhelm you shall not overwhelm you. In your weakness, Christ will give you strength. In your terror, Christ will be your consolation. In your wild wonderment, his hand will touch, and his gracious words assure you. Only see to it that you are on right terms with him—that you are one of his true people—that you are a brother of John, and a co-partner in the kingdom, and in patient waiting, in Christ Jesus. Having this, you have secured your armour against all the terrors of the Apocalypse. Let us, then, devoutly join in the prayer—

Draw near, O Son of God, draw near,
  Us with thy flaming eye behold ;
Still in thy church vouchsafe to appear,
  And let our candlestick be gold.

Still hold the stars in thy right hand,
  And let them in thy lustre glow,
The lights of a benighted land,
  The angels of thy church below.

Make good their apostolic boast,
  Their high commission let them prove,
Be temples of the Holy Ghost,
  And filled with faith, and hope, and love.

Give them an ear to hear thy word ;
  Thou speakest to the Churches now :
And let all tongues confess their Lord,
  Let every knee to Jesus bow.

LECTURE FOURTH

THE VISION SUPPLEMENTED WITH DECLARATIONS—CHRIST THE FIRST AND THE LAST, THE LIVING ONE, DIED, IS ALIVE, HAS THE KEYS OF DEATH AND HADES—WHAT HE COMMANDED JOHN TO WRITE—THE KEY TO THE ANALYSIS OF THIS BOOK—THE HISTORIC INTERPRETATION —THE MYSTERY OF THE STARS AND CANDLESTICKS—THE WORLD IN WHICH THEY ARE STATIONED.

REV. 1 : 17-20. (Revised Text.)—I am the first and the last, and THE LIVING ONE ; and I became dead, and behold, I am living for the ages of the ages ; and I have the keys of death and of hades. Write therefore what thou sawest, and what they are, and what shall come to pass after these things ; the mystery of the seven stars which thou sawest upon my right hand, and of the seven candlesticks of gold. The seven stars are [the] angels of the seven Churches, and the seven candlesticks are [the] seven Churches.

THERE is much of glory and majesty in Christ which cannot be pictured to the eye. Hence the vision which John had of him is supplemented with titles and descriptions, the further to assure his faith, and to deepen our apprehension of the true nature and sublimity of our great Lord and Judge. Our business this evening will be,

I.   TO TAKE A BRIEF SURVEY OF THESE SUPPLEMENTARY DECLARATIONS ;
II. TO LOOK AT THE DIVINE COMMAND UNDER WHICH THE WRITING OF THE APOCALYPSE WAS ORDERED ;
III. TO INQUIRE A LITTLE MORE DEFINITELY INTO THE MYSTERY WHICH JOHN WAS DIRECTED TO EXPLAIN.

" *I am the First and the Last.*" This is a form of speech often employed by the Almighty, when about to comfort his people, and to assure their faith. We find it three times in Isaiah, and three times in the Apocalypse ; and in every instance used for a like purpose. Its meaning is hardly to be mistaken ; and yet it has been mistaken, by some who wished to avoid the doctrine which it teaches, and by others who did not sufficiently weigh it in all its connections. These take it as if the Saviour had said : " I am He who, being the foremost and first in all honour, became the lowest and last in dishonour, sounding the lowest depths of ignominy and shame." That this is true of Christ may readily be admitted. He was, as Artemonius says, " the most excellent, and the most abject." But this is not the truth meant to be expressed in this formula. It does not fall in with the course of thought, or the end for which it is introduced, in this or in any other connection in which it is found. In Isaiah 41 : 4 ;—45 : 6 ;—48 : 12 ;—and in Rev. 22 : 13 ;—it is plainly intended to express what appertains exclusively to the divine and the eternal ; and it must be so taken here. It is not a mere statement of the extent of Christ's humiliation, from the estate of one first in honour to the estate of one lowest in disgrace ; but a formula which sets forth the eternity of God, and his high superiority to all created things. Creation had a beginning ; but God was first, before creation, without beginning, himself the beginner. All created things are continually changing, and each particular style or order is for some end beyond itself ; but God is last, abiding when all these changes have been wrought, and surviving every consummation, himself the end. As appropriated by Christ, it asserts his proper and eternal Deity, and his real participation in all that is characteristic of Godhead. It assigns him an existence before creation, and after all consummations, himself the beginner and the consummator. Before him none was, for he " was in the beginning with God ; " and after him none shall be. He is the first, in that

45

all things are from him ; and the last, in that all things are to him and for him.
The beginning was made from him, and everything will be consummated by
him and in him. The first motion of the absolute, eternal, unapproachable
Godhead toward outwardness of expression, calling the worlds into existence,
and organizing all created things, was this Christ and Son of God ; and that
to which all creation, providence and grace is ordered and tending, and in
which all is to have, not a cessation of existence, but the fulfilment of its
ultimate purpose and accomplishment, bodying forth all the harmony,
richness, beauty, glory and perfection of every divine thought and intent,
is nothing more nor less than the conformation of all things to, and the setting
out of the unspeakable fulness of, this self-same Christ and Son of God. It is
therefore a formula spanning the nature and philosophy of Godhead, in all
his works, from the unsearchable depths of the eternal past, to the equally
unsearchable depths of the eternal future, showing all to be from Christ, and
by Christ, and to Christ, originating in him, perpetuated through all successions of change by him, and with their final consummation standing in and
embodying his fulness. It is the title which Jehovah takes where he declares
his eternal and universal creatorship, and his infinite superiority over all
other beings : " Hearken unto me, O Judah, and Israel my called ; I am he,
I am the First, I also am the Last. Mine hand hath laid the foundations of
the earth, and my right hand hath spanned the heavens." And when Jesus
appropriates this description to himself, he identifies himself with the eternal
Creator, and with the emphatic, *I*, claims to himself what is distinctive of
Godhead. Nor is he a whit less than God, though he did become man, and is
now joined forever to a human nature.

" AND THE LIVING ONE."* This is another title of Deity. It refers not to
mere manifested life, but to life inherent and underived. The words do not
relate simply to the fact of Christ's having lived in the flesh, but to his
possession of a deeper and self-existing life, of which that was only one manifestation. The life here claimed by Christ is life coeval with the creation of the
world, and which had an eternal subsistence with the Father before the world
was. John tells us that in Christ was life, and that that life was the same
eternal life which was with the Father. (1 Jno. 1 : 1,2.) All mere creatures are
dying ones, except as their being is sustained by him who gave it ; but God
is the Living One, as life in him is self-existent. It needs no other to uphold it.
It came from none, and it is sustained by none, but itself. Immortality may
be imparted to creatures, but God only *hath* it in and of himself. And when
Christ declares himself to be THE LIVING ONE, he claims and asserts a consub-
stantiality with the self-existent God, from whom all things proceed, and on
whom all creatures depend.

And yet he " *became dead.*" It is impossible for our dull powers to penetrate
the depths of these divine mysteries. When the ancient sage was asked to
give a definition of God, he said, God is a circle, whose centre is everywhere,
and whose circumference is nowhere. He had expressed the truth, but under
very contradictory conceptions. God is truly in every particular place, and yet
beyond all place at the same time. He is in every place entire, as a centre,
and yet he is bounded by no lines of limitation. Neither is he diffused, or
scattered in parcels here and there, partly at one place and partly at another.
This is true, but it is very confusing to our feeble comprehension. And we have
like difficulty in explaining how Godhead is to be found, as in the Father, so
in the Son, or how the self-existent and eternal could yet become dead. We
are on safe and sure ground when we assert that God is ever-living, self-
existent, and eternal ; and that the same is true of the Christ and Son of God ;
and yet, it is equally true and certain, that this same Christ and Son of God,
in that manifestation of his eternal life which he lived in human flesh, also

* " 'O ζῶν expresses not so much that He, the Speaker, ' lived,' as that He was ' The
Living One,' the Life (Jno. 1 : 4 ; 14 : 16), αὐτοζωή, having life in Himself, and the
fountain and source of life to others."—*Trench on the Seven Epistles*, p. 70.

died—as we say in the Creed, " *was crucified, dead, and buried.*" He who had life within himself from all eternity, he who was made the depository of all outward life before any creature was formed, became a dead person. All this, indeed, was accomplished in the flesh, in the man Christ Jesus ; but it was that flesh and manhood to which The Living One was conjoined in one person. It is the same *I* who proclaims himself the First and the Last, and The Living One, who says that HE became dead. Some tell us that what was of the Divine substance in Christ withdrew when he died ; this I cannot admit. It was

> — " God the mighty Maker died
> For man the creature's sin."

If it was not so, then I am at loss to know what atoning power there could be in his death more than in that of any martyr to the truth. And yet there was no suspension of the continuity of that which is eternal and ever-living. That there was a certain emptying of himself on the part of Christ in his humiliation and death is taught us. And that there was a certain quitting of the use and claim of his Godhood in his incarnation and submission to death—a certain putting of himself out of self-existing life in order to receive it again from the Father,—we must believe. But we must at the same time hold, that it was somehow The Living One that became dead, and the eternal life that had share in the mysterious immolation, giving virtue to the sacrifice, and imparting itself through it.

But this becoming dead is specially connected, and that with a note of exclamation, with another announcement, that this same who became dead is *alive, and living for the age of the ages.* The state of death was but for an instant, and was succeeded by a resurrection, which put him again in the possession and exercise of the attributes of the ever-living. He laid down his life that he might take it again, and thus gave the more brilliant proof that he is The Living One. The most successfully to show that the distinction belongs to one man to accomplish what no other man can accomplish, is to have the experiment made by each. " So God, in order to prove that Christ, and he alone, is The Living One, doth permit the many to come under the dominion of death ; and having thus proved that no man is The Living One, he then bringeth Christ into the same controversy with death, who, by overcoming it, doth prove himself the Prince of Life, and the Master of Death ; so that he could say, ' I am the Resurrection and the Life.' By being the Resurrection, he is proved to be the Life. He is not the Life in consequence of the resurrection, but in antecedence of it. The resurrection proves him to be that being in whom it had pleased God that it should reside as in an invincible fortress, which was tried and proved to be death-proof."*

Hence the further proclamation, " *and I have the keys of death and of hades.*"† It is hardly possible that the Saviour meant to represent death as a *place.* It is, however, a power, and a fearful power, locking up and holding tight all who come under its sway. What millions have gone down beneath that power, and are now held by it ! Every acre of the earth is full of them, and the bottom of every sea. I have seen their grim skeletons on mountain summits, eight thousand two hundred feet above the level of the sea ; and I have walked upon their ashes more than a thousand feet below that level. And from far deeper depths to still more elevated heights, on all the slopes and hillsides, and in all the fields and valleys of the earth, death's victims lie in fetters of darkness, silence and dust. Even on the life-powers of the Son of God were these manacles made fast. But by him they were also opened ; for he hath the keys of death.

* Irving *in loc.*

† " So all the best MSS. and Versions have it, while the reading of our Translation inverts the natural and logical order ; for it is death which peoples hell or hades ; it is a king of death who makes possible a kingdom of the dead (6 : 8 ; 20 : 13, 14) ; for by hell, or hades, this invisible kingdom or dominion of the dead is intended, and that in all its extent, not merely in one dark province of it, the region assigned to the lost."—Trench *in loc.*

And as death holds the bodies of men, so hades holds their souls. There is an under world, intermediate between death and the resurrection, and the souls of all the dead are in that world, the good in rest and hope, and the wicked in unrest and fearful awaiting of judgment. I know not where it is, nor what it is. I only know that it is Paradise for the righteous, and anything but Paradise to all others—that all who die are retained there, shut in and locked up till the time of the fulfilment of this Apocalypse. It was into this " hell " that the soul of Christ descended when he expired, and where it would be retained till now, had he not been master of the keys, by which he opened its gates, and came forth to make this glorious declaration to his people. But the new cords of the Philistines could not tie down the strength of Samson, nor the gates of Gaza retain him in their custody. Whilst his enemies were shouting against him, the Spirit of the Lord came mightily upon him, and the cords that were upon his arms became as flax when touched with fire, and the doors of the gates that were shut upon him, and their very posts, his shoulders bore away in everlasting triumph.

And those keys and potencies are still in his possession, and wielded by him. He giveth persons to death and hades, and retains them there, as he will, and he brings them forth again at his pleasure, as he did the nobleman's daughter, the widow's son, and Mary's brother. When he arose, he not only brought his own soul forth, and his own body from the grave, but likewise those of other saints, levying tribute on those mysterious realms, as now their conqueror, and henceforth their Lord. And there is no hell so deep but he can open it, and thrust his enemies in, and lock it that they may never more come out. Nor is there any disability of the saints by reason of death or hades, nor any doors or bands locked upon them in their state of separation from the body, but he has the key to turn back the dingy bolts and set all such prisoners free. And as he said of old, " O death, I will be thy plague : O grave, I will be thy destruction ; " the time is coming when he will apply those keys, and leave not a soul or body more in death or hades which shall not be brought forth in the power of his resurrection.

Some tell us that this was all spoken to John in his affright, that he might not be overwhelmed with his fears. But I cannot see how such grand and overpowering declarations of the majesty of Christ could add to the strength and confidence of a man already sinking and next thing to dead on account of the glory he was called to contemplate. It was the " Fear not," and the strength-imparting touch, that were for John's special benefit ; but what is said more than that is the filling out of the picture on which the apostle had just been gazing, and which he could not perhaps have endured to hear from Christ's own lips, but for this " Fear not," and assuring touch. No, no ; let us not thus miss the great meaning of the Scriptures. It was not John's particular comfort, but the world's enlightenment, that was intended by these overwhelming proclamations. What the Saviour here utters in the terrified apostle's ears, the same as what had just passed before the apostle's astonished eyes, relates to the grand portraiture of Christ, as he now stands related to his churches and ministers, and as he will presently come to judge them. He is the First, and the Last, and The Living One. He is the same who died on Calvary's cross a sacrifice for our sins, and descended into hell as the vanquisher of all the dominions of darkness. Though once dead, and an inmate of hades, he is alive now for all the ages of ages. In this eternal life, which he had from all eternity, he walks among his people, locking and unlocking death and hades, disposing of souls and bodies as to him seems best, and keeping them in his own power for that Apocalypse and administration which it is the office of this book to describe. This is the Christ, in those great attributes, acts and offices, on whom the Churches are built, in whom our faith and hopes as Christians stand, and with whom we have to do as our Lord and Judge.

II. Hence the command, not with reference specifically to the apostle's fears, but with reference to the seven Churches, " *Write* (οὖν)* *therefore what thou sawest, and what they are, and what shall come to pass after these things.*"

Here, then, is the great starting-point, and grand foundation of this book, and the key to its true analysis. Assuming all the facts of the Gospel history,—the life, death, resurrection and ascension of Christ,—as accomplished ; the Churches fully organized and equipped ; the new dispensation established and in working order ; the Apocalypse starts with a presentation of the character, titles, and administrations of our risen and glorified Lord in relation to the Churches, and the dispensation as then inaugurated. This first vision, and the proclamations and explanations connected with it, accordingly spans the whole interval from the time John wrote to the end of the dispensation, the outlines of which it sets forth. Christ is not one thing for one age and country, and another thing for another age and country. What he was then, and the characteristics and relations in which he then appeared, are those in which he now is to be contemplated, and in which he will continue until the entire economy reaches its consummation. And what he utters in the seven epistles is his judgment of the Church, his mind and decision with reference to it, not only as it then existed, but in its whole universality, and entire continuity, and multiform membership, from the commencement to the consummation, including the portion assigned to each and all when he comes.

Taking in, then, all that John saw and heard in his first vision, together with what he was commanded to write, we are carried down to the end of the third chapter. Everything to that point is received from one scene of observation, and holds together as belonging to one and the same order of things. From the same standpoint he sees and hears and writes it all. It is the same glorious Saviour that is first seen, then heard in the announcements concerning himself, in the explanations of what had been seen, and in the seven addresses to the seven Churches. From the first sound of the trumpet voice with which the Apocalypse begins, to the last " He that hath an ear, let him hear what the Spirit saith unto the Churches," we find no break, no change, in the speaker, in the position of the seer, in the outlines of the picture, or in the course of the communications made. It is all ONE, cohering in all the parts, touching only the same subjects, and finishing up in a clean and perfect conclusion. What follows introduces us to quite other scenes, other characteristics, and other administrations. There is no coming back again to this after it is once left. We then read no more of the Churches, or of Christ among the candlesticks. There is not anything of the order set forth in this first section after the third chapter. As perfect as the unity of everything up to the conclusion of the seven epistles, is the diverseness from it of everything that comes after.

Whatsoever then is signified by this vision of Christ among the candlesticks, its entire career is embraced. If it means the Church, it is the entire Church to its end in this world. If it is the present dispensation, it is that dispensation to its close. And if it be something else, it is that something to the conclusion of its history. This I consider important, and settled by the facts in the case. The whole character of the vision shows that it is not fragmentary or sectional, but complete. There is much coming after it, but the subject is no longer the same, and all the administrations are of a different order. What it sets forth is, therefore, the whole of it.

And with this point fixed, there is another equally important, which this command makes clear. As this vision embraces the entire career of that to

---

* " It is certainly a piece of carelessness on the part of our translators to have omitted, which none of the previous translators had done, the οὖν (*therefore*), about the right of which to a place in the text no question has ever been made. With what intention the illative particle is used is perhaps best referred to what goes immediately before : Seeing that I am this mighty One, the first and the last, who was dead and am alive, do thou therefore write ; for the things declared by me are all steadfast and sure."—Trench *in loc.*

which it refers, and stretches to the very end of its history, so what follows does not commence till what is signified by this first vision is accomplished. What there is more than was seen and heard in this instance, and in the accompanying explanations, is only to " come to pass *after these things.*" In other words, the things presented are as consecutive in their fulfilment as in John's visions of them. What is contained in the first three chapters must run out and end, before what is contained in the subsequent chapters can begin. So that if we can ascertain what order of things that is which is set forth in the first vision, and whether it has run its course or still holds, we are in a position to know exactly whether what is to " come to pass after these things " is still future or not.

What have we then by which to identify what is contained in the first vision? Fortunately, the Saviour has not left us in uncertainty. His command to John was not only to write what he had seen, but also " *what they are.*" Nor was John unfaithful to the charge. He has written " what they are ; " and we have the explanation in Christ's own words. " *The seven stars are [the] angels of the seven Churches, and the seven candlesticks are [the] seven Churches.*" Do you ask what Churches ? The answer is, the Churches existing at the time of the vision. Not Churches in heaven, but Churches on the earth. Their very names and localities are given. So far, then, we are on solid ground. The vision is that of Christ in relation to his Churches on earth, or that economy of things which we call the Christian dispensation, which had come into full and settled force and sway at the time John wrote, and which·exists now precisely as it existed then. There have been changes, but not in the laws of the dispensation, or in Christ's offices, relations, and administrations under it, or in it. We cannot, therefore, be mistaken. It is *the present Church, or order of things with respect to the Church*, which is the subject of this vision. And as the vision includes the whole course of that to which it relates, the present order, so far as respects the Church on earth, must wind up and close, before one particle of this book, beyond the third chapter, in any full and proper sense, can be fulfilled. And until people come to see and admit this, they will try in vain to understand or interpret this book.

Some maintain that we are now living under the sixth vial, and that nearly everything up to the eighteenth chapter has already been fulfilled. Nor will I dispute that there is a sense, dim and inchoate, in which this is true. Prophecy, in its fulfilment, is made up of several concentric circles, blended in the same general picture. It is said that history is continually repeating itself. Much truer is this of prophecy. But each fulfilment is in a higher fulness, till the last sums up all. There is but one proper and ultimate literal fulfilment of any prophecy ; but, in anticipation of that there are typical and precursory fulfilments—preliminary rehearsals in advance of the grand performance. We can accordingly trace out in history a very interesting but not always distinct correspondence to what is contained in the first eighteen chapters of this book. But if that were the true and only fulfilment, so much learning and acquaintance with history would be necessary in order to track it through the multiplicity and complication of human events, that it must needs remain an uncertain and second-hand thing to the great body of the Lord's people. I look then for another, simpler, more direct and easier understood fulfilment.

It has been said that the way for a missionary to approach a non-christian population is to " carry his Bible in one hand and Gibbon in the other, to show out of the pages of an infidel historian how exactly the prophets have up to the present time been fulfilled." But it will require more evidence than I have yet seen, to convince me that it is necessary to take men through the school of the historian, whether sceptic or not, in order to teach them the truth of Christianity, or the meaning of the prophets. The Scriptures are self-demonstrative and self-explanatory, if men will only read them as they are written, and let them speak for themselves. Valuable as history is, and much as may be made of Gibbon, we need neither of them to get at the true meaning of the Apocalypse. The early Christians had them not, and yet understood this book better than all the hundreds of learned commentators who think to verify their interpretations out of Gibbon and history. In other words, the exclusively historic school of interpreters, as things appear to me, do but darken and obscure this book with learned rubbish, and lend their influence to the mischievous notion that it is a book of wild and grotesque fables, and uncertain riddles, which it is wisdom, greatness and piety in a man never to touch.

Whilst, then, I admit that these predictions may have had a dim, imperfect, but oft scarcely traceable fulfilment in the past, I am firmly convinced that the true and proper fulfilment of everything beyond the third chapter is to take place only after the Church has run its course, completed its history, and received its judgment. We are elsewhere told that "judgment must *begin* at the house of God." (1 Pet. 4 : 17.) If that be true, then the judgment of the world is something subsequent, a judgment which takes place *after* the judgment of the Church. The Seals, Trumpets, and Vials, therefore, must be future, as the judgment of the world is future ; for it is the judgment of the world that they foreshow. Read the Apocalypse in this view, and you will find it a new book to you, luminous and precious, which needs no infidel Gibbon to explain it, or to prove it to be of God.

III. Look we now a little more particularly into the mystery which John was directed to explain, and the explanation given—the mystery of the seven stars upon Christ's right hand, and of the seven candlesticks of gold.

In the language of Scripture, a " mystery " is something which man is capable of knowing, but can only know when it is revealed. So here, it is not beyond the range of our understanding to take in what these stars and candlesticks represent ; but we know what they represent, not from our own wisdom, or searching, but through God's revelation. *He tells us* that " the seven stars are [the] angels of the seven Churches, and the seven candlesticks are [the] seven Churches," and a child at once understands what no sage could otherwise have known.

You will notice also that there is nothing in this vision to which the word *mystery* is applied, but the stars and the candlesticks. Everything else is its own explanation ; that is, it is literal and to be taken as it is written. The stars and candlesticks are symbolic, and stand for something which could not otherwise so well be fitted to the picture ; but only these. We are thus furnished with several very important hints of interpretation. One is, that when the Scriptures employ symbols they tell you so. Another is, that where no indication to the contrary is given, we must interpret according to the letter. Another is, that what is symbolic and mysterious must have the mystery revealed to be correctly understood, and that what is revealed is no longer a mystery. This book, then, is not a book of symbols, as some speak. It is a book of *revelations*, as its own title declares ; and revelations are not mysteries. Mystery and Apocalypse are correlative terms. (Rom. 16 : 25.) The one is the lifting off of the chief peculiarity of the other. We find mysteries or symbols in this book, but only exceptionally, and always accompanied with the proper note of indication, and the necessary αποχαλυψις, or unveiling of what is meant.

The stars are mentioned first and have the most conspicuous place. They are the angels of the Churches. Stars are frequently employed as representative of lordship and authority, if not in its centre, yet in its distributions around the centre. Symbolically they indicate high official place. They here denote the very highest officers of the individual Churches. They are called *angels*, and hence some have argued for an order of superhuman creatures. But the word *angel* is more descriptive of office than of nature. It means a *messenger*, one invested with a special commission. It can apply as well to men as to celestial orders. (Hag. 1 : 13 ; Mal. 2 : 7 ; 3 : 1.) And that it is here meant to apply to *men*, I gather from the delinquencies which are subsequently laid to the charge of some of these angels, and from the utter silence of the Scriptures with reference to any arrangement putting the Churches under the charge and instruction of heavenly beings. Some of the holy angels must be very naughty at times, and the ministers and Churches in very strange ignorance concerning an important part of their allegiance, or these mystic stars are but men of like passions with ourselves,—nothing more nor less than *ministers* in charge of the Churches ; not only of the Churches named, but of all Churches in every age.

They are *stars* because they are illuminators, and because they are heads and leaders of the flocks over which the Holy Ghost hath placed them. They are *angels* or messengers, because God hath sent them, and made them his representatives, the guardians of his Churches, and the stewards of his mysteries. They are ambassadors for Christ, as though God did beseech by them. They are, for the purposes of their office, " in Christ's stead." (2 Cor. 5 : 20.) In Daniel we read of heavenly angels, guardians of *nations*, and communicating with men in God's name ; and here we have earthly angels, guardians of *Churches*, set and authorized to exercise their ministry in the name of Christ.

Nor is it only *bishops*, in the modern sense of that term, as some have argued that we are to understand by these angels. They are *overseers* indeed, but not of sees consisting of many distinct churches. There was just one angel for one Church, not one angel for the seven Churches ; and so each angel was simply the pastor in charge of his particular Church.

Upon the dignity and importance of this office I need not dwell. That is manifest in the fact that it stands foremost in this Revelation of Jesus Christ. " And well is it entitled to that pre-eminence, for without the ordinance to preaching there would be no Church ; and without a Church there would be no Christian kingdom ; and without a Christian Church and kingdom there would be no apostasy, no beast, no false prophet : so that the whole substance of this book, the whole drama of God's providence therein, doth derive itself out of the office of the preacher of the word, the angel, the sent one of Christ, the Christian pastor."*

" *And the seven candlesticks are [the] seven Churches.*" I have already sufficiently remarked upon the aptness of this symbol. If the ministers are *lightgivers*, the congregations are *lightbearers*—the organization for upholding the light. Hence the Church is elsewhere described as " the pillar and ground of the truth." We must have Churches as well as ministers. This is the Divine order and constitution. " God hath set the members every one of them in the body, as it hath pleased him. There are many members, yet but one body. And the eye cannot say unto the hand, I have no need of thee : nor again the head to the feet, I have no need of you. Nay, much more those members of the body, which seem to be more feeble, are necessary." (1 Cor. 12 : 18–22.) Yea, the whole Church, Christ the Head, the stars on his right hand, and the entire membership of believers clustered around them, are but one great mystic candlestick, for setting and holding forth the great light of salvation ; which saves them that believe, and judges and condemns the world that lieth in unbelief and sin.

The number of these angels and Churches is *seven*. I must reserve for another occasion what I have to say upon the meaning of these numbers. There is a sacred arithmetic, as well as sacred persons, places, and times. Numbers in the Scriptures are as significant as words. They are as much a part of the Apocalypse as anything else. And there is as much resting upon them, as upon any other class of particulars contained in this book ; as we shall see when we come to consider them. There were more Churches than these seven in existence when John received this commission ; and some of more prominent standing than several of those named. But the number was

* Irving *in loc.*

fixed at *seven*, no more and no less, and to these particular seven for reasons which will appear in due time.

There is yet one point in this mystery of the stars and candlesticks to which I will refer. It is the realm in which they are stationed, and its characteristics as indicated in the provision made for it. Where you see stars, and need candles, there is darkness. And how dark is that world, that kingdom, that community, that heart, into which the light of Christianity has not effectually penetrated? With all the splendour of its genius, all the glory of its arms, all the brilliancy of its power, how savage, how beastly, how like a sepulchre, full of chilly gloom and festering death! When the Gospel first arose upon the world, in what state did it find mankind? Let the apostle answer: "Given up to uncleanness through the lusts of their own hearts; filled with all unrighteousness, fornication, wickedness, covetousness, maliciousness; full of envy, murder, debate, deceit, malignity; whisperers, backbiters, haters of God, despiteful, proud, boasters, inventors of evil things, disobedient to parents, without understanding, covenant breakers, without natural affection, implacable, unmerciful; doing these things, and having pleasure in them that do them." (Rom. 1 : 22-32.) The same had been true for ages—their governments, fierce beasts and monsters; their morals, selfishness and vainglory; their very gods deified vices and bad passions. And when God's messengers came to them with the light of truth and righteousness, how were they treated? Let the same apostle answer: "Some were tortured; and others had trial of cruel mockings, and scourgings, of bonds and imprisonment: they were stoned, they were sawn asunder, were tempted, were slain with the sword: they wandered about in sheepskins and goatskins, being destitute, afflicted, tormented; compelled to make their homes in deserts, and in mountains, and in dens and caves of the earth." (Heb. 11 : 35-38.) Even the Lord of the covenant was crucified and killed, and all his apostles martyred, and the Church's first age made one continuous baptism of blood by the enthroned malignity of the unsanctified heart. Such is humanity, unreached and unredeemed by the grace of God in Christ Jesus. Such it was, and such it is, and such it always will be, as long as the world stands. And this is the realm in which God has stationed his candlesticks and his angels. Well might the Saviour say: "Behold, I send you forth as lambs among wolves." (Luke 10 : 3.)

Those stars and candlesticks have not been useless. Some hearts, communities and kingdoms have been attracted by the light, and have learned to appreciate its transforming beauty, and are found to a greater or less degree walking and rejoicing in it. But still the world in the main is a dark and wicked world. The light sent of God is " a light that shineth in a dark place," and will so continue " until the day dawn," for the great consummation. Till then, therefore, we must expect to suffer and to fight. While the light will never fail to make itself felt upon the dark world, neither will the depravity and darkness of earth fail to make itself felt upon us. The wheat and the tares, good and evil, Christ and Antichrist, are side by side, each at war with the other, and the conflict ever increasing in intensity, until the Lord of the harvest shall come with his reapers, and make the separation by removing the candlesticks, and giving over what remains to its own proper darkness, and " the blackness of darkness forever." God make us faithful in our work of waiting and witnessing till the silver note from heaven shall sound the signal for our release, and welcome us to the glad home of light and rest ! Amen.

HE COMETH

Watch, fair Spouse ; the heavenly Bridegroom neareth ;
   Soon he comes, his waiting love to claim ;
Quickly, surely, he, thy Lord, appeareth,
   To bestow on thee his own new name.
Watch, in readiness of love, to meet him,
   For his heart once throbb'd out blood for thee,
That thou might'st amid his glory greet him,
   And the King in all his beauty see.

Mourner, wipe the tears thy cheeks bedewing,
   For the Man of Sorrows draweth nigh ;
He has wept, and he, thy struggles viewing,
   Hastes to bid the flowing drops be dry.
Then shall all thy griefs be calm'd forever,
   When thy Saviour clasps thee to his breast,
Whispering that no veil again shall sever
   Thee from God, thy everlasting rest.

Sinner, dread ! for the Avenger bendeth,
   Looking on thy darken'd deeds of sin ;
When his way amid the clouds he wendeth,
   How wilt thou thy Sovereign's mercy win ?
Haste, before that day's terrific dawning,
   Trust the saving blood on Calvary spilt ;
Though the ready gulfs for thee are yawning,
   He can save thee, he can cleanse thy guilt.

Trembler, let his trump thy spirit gladden,
   Lo, it soundeth even now from far !
All the fears which now thy weak heart sadden,
   At his coming shall be chased afar.
Jesus cometh, Saviour, Prince, Creator !
Christian, thy redemption draweth near
Watch we for the glorious Consummator,
   So that we may meet him without fear.

LECTURE FIFTH

THE CHURCH — " ASIA " — EPHESUS — SMYRNA — PERGAMOS — THYATIRA — SARDIS — PHILADELPHIA—LAODICEA—SIGNIFICANCE OF THE SEVEN CHURCHES—MEANING OF NUMBERS—REASONS FOR TAKING THE SEVEN CHURCHES REPRESENTATIVELY AS WELL AS LITERALLY—THE SEVEN AGES OF THE CHURCH—THE SEVEN CLASSES OF CHRISTIANS.

REV. 1 : 20. The seven Churches.

THE word *Church* stands in the English Testament as the equivalent of a compound Greek word (εχχλησια, from εχ and χαλεω), signifying *to call out of* or *from among*. In three instances, our translators have rendered it *assembly*. This is its primary sense, which underlies all its applications in the New Testament, the Septuagint, and the Greek language in general. The heathen Greeks used it to denote the select assemblies of free citizens convened for the transaction of public affairs, in which the common populace, strangers, and such as had forfeited civic rights, had no place. It is used by Stephen to denote the congregation of the children of Israel in the wilderness, who had been called forth from Egypt, and were on their way to the promised land. (Acts 7 : 38.) It is sometimes used to denote the entire community of Christian people, of all nations and ages ; as where the Saviour says : " Upon this Rock will I build my [εχχλησια] Church ; " and where Paul exhorts the elders to " feed the [εχχλησια] Church of God with he hath purchased with His own blood." It is also used to denote the small companies of Christians belonging to one household, as where we read of " Nymphas and the [εχχλησια] Church which is in his house ; " " Priscilla and Aquilla, and the [εχχλησια] Church that is in their house." But its most frequent applica-ion is to denote some particular society of Christians, in the same neighbour-hood or city, organized around a common altar, and statedly coming together in the same services : as we read of " the [εχχλησια] Church which is at Corinth ; " " the [εχχλησια] Church which is at Jerusalem," &c. It means an assembly, convened by authority, and constituted of a specific class, out of, but withdrawn from, the general mass of the population. It therefore most expressively sets forth what a true Church is.

The Gospel everywhere speaks of a calling and an election, and the Church is the organized society of the called and elected. It is the assembly or community of those whom God has called out from the world into a common fellowship of faith, hope, and obedience, and which is preserved and perpe-tuated by means of functions and services included in the call. And wherever there is a company of such as have received and believed the Gospel, organized into one body, in the charge of one authorized minister, and coming together in the same stated services, there is a true Church. And such societies were " the [επτα εχχλησιαι] seven Churches " of the text, concerning which I propose to notice more especially :

    I. THEIR LOCATIONS.
    II. THEIR SIGNIFICANCE.

The locations of these seven Churches are twice given : first, in the general commission which John received ; and second, in the specific directions what to write to each. The command of the trumpet voice was : " What thou seest, write in a book, and send it to the seven Churches : unto Ephesus, and unto Smyrna, and unto Pergamos, and unto Thyatira, and unto Sardis, and unto Philadelphia, and unto Laodicea." And in the succeeding chapters, he was further directed to write " unto the angel of the Church in Ephesus ; unto the angel of the Church in Smyrna ; unto the angel of the Church in Pergamos," &c.

These are not unknown places. They all lie within the scope of a few hundred miles north of the Mediterranean and east of the outlet of the Black Sea. The Churches in these localities are sometimes called " the seven Churches *of Asia ;* " but the " Asia " of which the Scriptures speak is not the great continent of Asia, or even of Asia Minor, but only the western part of Asia Minor, directly south of the Black Sea. The whole of it does not include a larger territory than the single State of Pennsylvania. Less than thirteen months ago, I passed entirely around two sides of it, and visited two of the most noted places to which the text refers.

The first in the list is *Ephesus.* This was once an important and magnificent city—to proconsular Asia, about what Philadelphia is to Pennsylvania. Of the seven, it was the nearest to the point at which John had the vision. It was the centre of trade for a rich and beautiful country, and the seat of its government, learning, art, wealth and religion. It was a place specially consecrated, in the minds of the people, by many myths and legends of gods and goddesses, and by the presence of a temple which was one of the wonders of the world. It was here that Paul lived for two years, and achieved some of his most brilliant missionary successes. Here he wrought many " special miracles," healing the sick and casting out demons, even with " handkerchiefs and aprons " which he had touched. Here he gained that glorious triumph over the exorcists and magicians, for whom Ephesus was famous, who " brought together their books, and burned them before all men," the price of which was " fifty thousand pieces of silver." Here he daily taught and debated the great doctrines of the faith, till " all Asia " had tidings of the truth as it is in Jesus, and the frightened silversmiths began to cry out for their craft, in consequence of the power of his arguments against the alleged divinity of Diana and the worshipfulness of her shrines. Here he wrote his first letter to the Corinthians ; and to the converts here he afterwards sent a masterly epistle, which constitutes an important part of the Christian Scriptures.

Ephesus was also the home of the Apostle John. Here he ministered and subsequently died. The ruins of a church still remain, which are said to mark the spot where he was buried. Here, most likely, the blessed mother of the Saviour had her last home, and laid off her mortal body. Here Apollos was converted to Christ, and first exercised his great gifts in the Gospel's interests. Here, too, the beloved Timothy lived, and discharged the duties of his sacred ministry, and died a victim of mob violence for his protests against the licence and frenzy of the great festival of Artemis. And next to Jerusalem itself, the world, perhaps, has not another spot around which cluster so many holy histories, classic interests, and precious traditions.

But Ephesus is a mere desolation now, altogether waste, without an inhabitant. The great market-place, where the exchanges of a renowned metropolis were once conducted, I saw planted with tobacco, unenclosed, unattended, weedy, and forsaken. The great lizards, as we rode along, darted about in amazement at the sight of man, over fallen columns of porphyry and marble, and splendid cornices and capitals, which were once the admiration of the world. And silence, malaria and death brooded upon what was proudly styled " the first of cities," and embraced the names of some of the greatest in wealth and wisdom, religion and literature, arts and arms. The vast theatre, the largest ever constructed, which once rang with the shouts of the frenzied thousands who, " all with one voice, about the space of two hours, cried out, Great is Diana of the Ephesians ! " still shows its grand outlines of walls and arches ; but old wild bushes are gnarled about its heavy masonry, and the camel was browsing in its forsaken circles as I rode through it. Even the glorious temple of the great mother goddess can no longer be identified with certainty. Two piles of colossal ruins are each claimed as its remains, and I plucked wild berries in both of them. Remnants of cyclopean walls, causeways, temples, streets, and houses, line the plains and hills and mountain-sides of a vast area which once was filled with their glory ; but the whole place is a complete desolation, enveloped in a poisonous atmosphere, and tenanted only by things unclean and vile.

Smyrna is the next in the list, the next nearest to Patmos, and the next in importance. It is the only one of the seven places named which retains anything of its ancient standing. It is finely situated, at the head of a beautiful bay, about forty miles northeast of Ephesus. It is now the commercial centre of the Levant, and is being invested with a system of railroads, sending out their iron arms into the interior, to gather to it the riches and trade of the fertile lands which lie almost desolate behind it. It has a population of about one hundred and twenty thousand, mostly Greeks, but profusely intermingled with people of all nations, languages, complexions, religions and fashions, who live in small, dark houses, strung along narrow, crooked and filthy lanes, dignified with the name of streets. There are a few good, clever buildings ; but it does not appear so much like a city, as a sort of confused convention of the long-severed inhabitants of Babel, with a view to make a city, upon the plan of which they cannot agree. One of its most marked features is the constant coming and going of almost interminable strings of camels and donkeys, which even the railroads have not been able to supersede. The appearance and habits of the people are anything but attractive, and mosquitoes abound almost to suffocation.

Smyrna was originally founded by Alexander, and is stoutly claimed as the birthplace of Homer. It was at first laid out with great regularity and architectural taste, and was considered the most beautiful city in Asia. It was celebrated for its library, its temples, and its sacred festivals and games. There is no allusion to it in the Scriptures, except in the Apocalypse. How and when Christianity was introduced into it, we have no account. The Church there was no doubt founded during Paul's stay at Ephesus. It was the seat of Polycarp's ministrations and martyrdom. It was there that Irenæus studied, and that many Christians in different ages perished on account of their faith. The hillside of Pagus, on which Polycarp was burned, has since been reddened with the blood of fifteen hundred confessors at one time, and eight hundred at another. It is as sacred in Christian annals as it is majestic and conspicuous to the beholder. Remnants of the ancient acropolis still stand on its summit, from which the view is exceedingly attractive. Fancy could hardly paint a more fitting mount for the ascension of the saints who from thence went up to their rest.

Pergamos is the next in the list. This lies directly north of Smyrna, perhaps forty miles distant. It was settled and named by the Æolian Greeks, after the fall of Troy. I was within twenty miles of it, but no nearer. At the time the Apocalypse was written, it was a sumptuous city, the home of rich chiefs, who had adorned it with magnificent residences, temples and groves. It had a library which rivalled that at Alexandria, a great medical school, and was famous for the rites which were there celebrated in honour of Æsculapius. It was not a commercial town, such as Ephesus, but a union of a Pagan Cathedral city, a university seat, and a royal residence, embellished, during a succession of years, by kings and chiefs fond of expenditure and ample in resources. It was a city of heathen temples—a grand Pantheon of Pagan worship—a metropolis of sacred sensuality—and hence " Satan's throne." It is now a mere tomb of former greatness. Half-buried arches, columns prostrate in the sand, and a few thousand Turkish and Greek huts, is about all that remains to mark the luxuriant and sensuous city, where the faithful Antipas suffered, and so much glory reigned.

Twenty or thirty miles to the southeast was *Thyatira*, the fourth in the list, and once a considerable town, founded by Seleucus Nicator. In the time of John, it was mainly inhabited by Macedonians, who had formed themselves into various guilds of potters, tanners, weavers, rope-makers and dyers. Lydia, the seller of purple stuffs, whom Paul met at Philippi, was from this place, and was connected with one of these departments of the industrial activity for which it was distinguished. It was a place of great amalgamation of races and religious observances. It now has about thirty thousand inhabitants, and is full of ruins. The mouths of many of the wells are made of capitals of old columns ; and the streets, in places, are paved with fragments of carved stones—the relics of the ancient city.

From Thyatira, some thirty miles to the southward, we come to *Sardis*, at the foot of Mount Tmolus, on the banks of a rivulet famous for its golden sands. Here the wealthy Crœsus lived and reigned. Here the wise Thales, Cleobulus, and Solon had their homes. And on the plains around it once lay the hosts of Xerxes, on their way to find a sepulchre at Marathon. It was a rich and glorious city when Cyrus conquered it ; and though subsequently destroyed by an earthquake, it obtained considerable distinction under the Romans, in the reign of Tiberias. It is now a scene of melancholy ruins, with a mill and a few shepherds' huts. When Emerson visited it, he says : " There were more varied and vivid remembrances associated with the sight of Sardis, than could possibly be attached to any other spot of earth ; but all were mingled with a feeling of disgust at the littleness of human glory : all— all had passed away ! There were before me the fanes of a dead religion, the tombs of forgotten monarchs, and the palm-tree that waved in the banquet hall of kings ; while the feeling of desolation was doubly heightened by the calm, sweet sky above me, which, in its unfading brightness, shone as purely now as when it beamed upon the golden dreams of Crœsus."

Southeastward, less than forty miles, stood *Philadelphia*, the great wine-market of Phrygia, rocked with oft-recurring earthquakes, and with a population once large and powerful, but never very distinguished. It took its name from the king who founded it. It is still a considerable country town, with a dozen churches or more, but not Christians enough to fill one-fourth of them, and those of a very doubtful sort. In Roman times, it was not of sufficient importance to command law-courts of its own, but belonged to a jurisdiction which had its centre in Sardis. Those who constituted the Church to which John was commanded to write, are supposed to have been poor people, living on the outskirts, and heavily taxed for public purposes.

Laodicea lay some fifty miles still further to the southeast. It was built, or rather rebuilt, by one of the Seleucid monarchs, and received its name in honour of his wife. It was a place of considerable size, trade and wealth. Both under the Romans and under the Turks, it has been the battle-ground of contending parties in Asia Minor. The remains of theatres, temples and other public edifices, still bear testimony to its former greatness. It does not appear that Paul ever visited it in person ; but it was evidently through him that Christianity was there introduced ; and to the believers there he once wrote a letter—which has been lost*—and sent his friendly greetings from his prison at Rome. In subsequent times it became a Christian city of eminence, the see of a bishop, and a meeting-place of Church Councils. It was destroyed by the Mahommedan invaders, and is now a scene of utter desolation. There is a small village in the neighbourhood, the houses of which are built of its ruins. Emerson says it is even more solitary than Ephesus, for the latter has the prospect of the rolling sea, or of a whitening sail, to enliven its decay ; whilst Laodicea sits in widowed loneliness, its walls grass-grown, its temples desolate, its very name perished. He left it in a thunderstorm, preferring to hasten on, through rain and tempest, to delay in that melancholy spot, where everything whispered desolation, and where the very wind that

---

* Col. 4 : 16. It is thought by some that the epistle here referred to has not been lost, but is the same as the Epistle to Philemon, or the First Epistle to Timothy.

swept impetuously through the valley sounded like the fiendish laugh of Time, exulting over the destruction of man and his proudest monuments.

So much, then, for the *locations* of these seven Churches. We pass to the more important matter of their *significance*. This is indicated in the number seven. The earliest commentator on the Apocalypse, whose work has come down to us, was Victorinus, Bishop of Pettau, or Petavium, who died a martyr in the year 303. He was the contemporary of Irenæus, and a man of piety, diligence in setting forth the teachings of the Scriptures, and vigorous in his perceptions of the meaning of the sacred writers. Most of his writings have been lost, except some fragments. His comments on the Apocalypse survive, in a text less pure than we could wish, but sufficiently giving the substance of his views. In his *Scholia in Apocalypsin*, he says that what John addresses to one Church he addresses to all ; that Paul was the first to teach us that *there are seven Churches in the whole world*, and that *the seven Churches named mean the Church Catholic ;* and that John, to observe the same method, has not exceeded the number seven.*

What Victorinus means, is that Paul, in writing to *seven* Churches, and to seven only, intended to have it understood that all the Churches of all time are comprehended in seven ; and that, in the same way, the seven Churches in the Apocalypse are meant to comprise all the Churches in the world : that is, the Church Catholic of all ages. This was also the view of Tichænius, of the fourth century ; Arethas of Cappadocia, and Primasius of Adrumetum, in the sixth ; and Vitringa, Mede, More, Girdlestone, and a large body of divines, of later periods.†

There is a sacred significance in numbers : not cabalistic, not fanciful ; but proceeding from the very nature of things, well settled in the Scriptures, and universally acknowledged in all the highest and deepest systems of human thought and religion.

The unit, *one*, is the source and parent of all numbers. It therefore stands for God, in the most hidden absoluteness of His being, in which the whole Godhead, and all things, stand. " There is one God, and there is none other but He." (Mark 12 : 32.) *One* expresses commencement, and God is the commencement. The unit underlies all continuation, and by God all things

---

* The passage, as it stands in Migne's *Patrologiæ* (tom. 5, col. 320), reads thus : " Istæ septem stellæ sunt septem Ecclesiæ quas nominat in vocabulis suis, et vocat eas ad quas fecit epistolas. Non quia ipsæ solæ sunt Ecclesiæ, aut principes ; sed quod uni dicit, omnibus dicit. Nihil enim differunt, ut ex illa ratione quis paucorum similium majori numero anteponat. *In toto orbe septennatim Ecclesias omnes, septem esse nominatas, et unam esse Catholicam Paulus docuit.* Et primum quidem ut servaret et ipse typum septem Ecclesiarum, non excessit numerum. Sed Scripsit ad Romanos, ad Corinthios, ad Galatas, ad Ephesios, ad Thessalonicenses, ad Philippenses, ad Colossenses. . . . *In his ergo septem Ecclesiis, unius Ecclesiæ Catholicæ, fideles sunt, quia una in septem qualitatem fidei et electionis est.*"

† This view has, indeed, been pronounced " egregious trifling "—" a mere castle in the air "—" the offspring of nothing but imagination "—" mere gratuitous assumption." And if blustering words make it so, there is no doubt that we must so regard it. But the murderers of Victorinus got no credit, in the judgment of truth and heaven, for their work ; and those who seek to overturn his opinion in this particular, may yet find themselves with quite as little for theirs. The author whose language I have just given has so stultified himself by his rejection of the natural and necessary conclusion announced by Victorinus, that, after two large and ponderous volumes on the Apocalypse, he has left it wholly unexplained why seven Churches, and only seven, and these particular seven, were chosen to be the subjects and recipients of these seven epistles. Nay, when he comes to his elaborate exposition of the significance of numbers, he gives the data for his own confutation, and, in effect, establishes what he elsewhere ridicules. " Seven," he says, " is the designation of that which is perfect "—" the perfect number by way of eminence "—" often employed in the sense of a complete, adequate, perfect number "—" the number nearly everywhere employed throughout the book in a symbolic way "—" a number which may stand, as it were, in the place of a representative of all other numbers." Take these conclusions, and apply them to the seven Churches, and to what other result are we brought but exactly that announced by Victorinus—that the seven Churches stand for the entire Church, the complete society of professing Christians, *the Church universal*, in the whole of its member-ship and the entireness of its earthly condition and career ?

consist. And nothing can so well express the absolute First Cause, as the number ONE. It stands for the absolute Unity in heaven, and the abstract individual on earth.

But Godhead, as let forth to the contemplation of rational beings, is a *Trinity*—a One Three and a Three One. Nearly all the leading nations of antiquity, in harmony with revelation, have so represented Him. In this Trinity, the Son is the second. *Two*, therefore, stands for Christ, and is significant of incompletion, or something wanting. It is the first from the one, and reposes on the one, and is necessary to the making up of the first complete complex number, but is not complete in itself. It is the productive number, but it is only complete when the product is added. The Spirit proceeds from the Father and the Son. Man and wife are two-one, but the product of dual unity is needed to complete the family.

Three is the number of individual completion. It is composed of three numbers, each of which is in itself *one*, and which multiplied together still make only *one*. Three, therefore, represents the Trinity, each number of which is God, and yet the Three together are still only One. It is the simplest composite unity, and forms the simplest compound figure in geometry— the equal-sided triangle, which is indivisible, and unresolvable into anything else. It is the first and fixed compound unit of mathematical science. It therefore properly stands for the Trinity and individual completeness. As such, it has been also wrought into all God's works. Man is body, soul, and spirit—three-one. The family is man, and wife, and offspring—three-one. Religion is knowledge, action, and experience—three-one.

> " Matter, and breath, and instinct, unite in all the beasts of the field ;
> Substance, coherence, and weight, fashion the fabrics of the earth ;
> The will, the doing, and the deed, combine to form a fact ;
> The stem, the leaf, and the flower—beginning, middle, and end ;
> Cause, circumstance, consequent : and every three is one.
> Yea, the very breath of man's life consisteth of a trinity of vapours,
> And the noonday light is a compound—the triune shadow of Jehovah."

Four is the worldly number. It proceeds from three, and includes three. And as three represents the Trinity—the highest, and the perfect—four designates that which proceeds from the Trinity, and is dependent thereon : the creation, the universe. Hence, the world resolves itself into four elements : fire, air, earth, and water. The points of the compass are four : north, east, south, west. There are four seasons, four winds, four grand divisions of the earth. The great world-powers of history and prophecy are four. The living beings, supposed to represent the forces of providence, are four. Ezekiel's vision of God's providence in the world revealed four cherubim, four wheels with four sides, four faces, and four wings. The waters in Eden were four. The fourth commandment, and the fourth clause in the Lord's Prayer, refer to the earth. The square and the cube, those important ground-forms of common geometric relations, are fours. And to the Oriental philosophers, four is always the figure of the universe, especially of the world. There is therefore no mistaking of this number.

Five represents progress, but incompleteness. It is the perfect three, with the imperfect two. On the fifth day life was created in the sea, but there was yet no life on land. Five toes, or five fingers, are but half of what pertain to a complete man. Under the fifth seal the martyrs are impatient, but are told to wait yet a season. They are enjoying some of the fruits of their faith, but their crowns are deferred. The fifth vial is poured upon the seat of the beast, but does not destroy it utterly. The virgins were five wise and five foolish, showing that the one class does not include all the saved, nor the other all that fail to enter into the marriage of the Lamb.

Six is the Satanic number. As the darkest hour immediately precedes the dawn, and the darkest years are the last before the millennial Sabbath, so the number immediately preceding the complete seven is the worst of all. The sixth body in the solar system is a shattered one. The sixth epistle to the Churches tells of an hour of universal trial and suffering ; the sixth seal brings destruction and death ; the sixth trumpet destroys the third part of men ; and the sixth vial introduces the unclean spirits who gather the kings of the earth and of the whole world to the war of the great day of God Almighty. Antichrist's number is three sixes : six units, six tens, and six hundreds—666—the individual completion of everything evil. And Christ was crucified on the sixth day, which is still the common execution day, and is popularly regarded as the most unlucky of the seven.

Seven is the number of dispensational fulness. It is the complete in that which is temporary—not the finally complete. It carries with it the idea of sacredness in that which relates to this world. It is the Trinity and the created in contact—the divine Three with the worldly four. Hence, it is always connected with whatever touches the covenant between man and God, worship, and the coming together of the Creator and the creature. Hence the sacred number. " The evidences of this reach back to the very beginning. We meet them first in the hallowing of the seventh day, in pledge and token of the covenant of God with man, as indeed in the binding up of seven in the very word Sabbath."* They are also traceable in the nature and confirmative power of an oath, which is signified by a Hebrew word embracing this number. It is a number which, somehow, occurs in cases of union between God and man ; in representations of the holy in the earthly ; in all expressions of the completeness of any specific sacred order or time. The instances, at any rate, are too numerous to mention. The Bible is full of them. And the Apocalypse, which is the book of the consummation of all God's dispensational dealings with mankind, is, above all, *a book of sevens*. It consists of seven visions, with the sevenfold ascription of glory to God and to the Lamb, and discloses to us the seven Spirits of God, the seven candlesticks, the seven stars, seven lamps of fire, seven seals, seven horns and seven eyes of the Lamb, seven angels with seven trumpets, seven thunders, seven heads of the beast and seven crowns upon those heads, the seven plagues, seven vials, seven mountains, and seven regencies. And it is this book of sevens because it is the book of the fulness of everything of which it treats—the Trinity's consummation of all divine dispensations. It is therefore the number of dispensational fulness. And whatever bears this number, in the divine reckoning, is full, complete, with nothing left out, and nothing of its own kind to be added.

Eight is the number of new beginning and resurrection. The eighth day is the beginning of a new week. The Jewish child was circumcised the eighth day, which was its birth into covenant relations. Noah was " the eighth person," and his family consisted of eight, and they started the new world after the flood. Christ rose from the dead on the eighth day. David was the eighth son of Jesse, and he established a new order for Israel. In the eighth year, the Jews were to sow the ground again as the fresh beginning of a new septenary. The eighth head of the beast was the revival of the seventh. Our Sunday, which celebrates the new creation which began in the Saviour's resurrection, is the eighth day, the first of the new week. And the eternal order of blessedness is to begin with the eighth thousand years from Adam.

Ten is the number of worldly completion, especially in the line of worldly evil. The great beast of worldly power, in its final form, has ten horns. The body of man, in earthly completeness, has ten fingers and ten toes. The moral law, as applicable to man in this world, has ten precepts. The earthly manifestations of Christ after His resurrection were ten. The tribulation spoken of to the Church in Smyrna was for ten days. The lost tribes of Israel are ten. The Church, in its mixed earthly condition and slumbering, is represented by ten virgins. It is the union of the worldly four and the Satanic six ; of the new

---

* Trench on the Seven Epistles.

eight and the incomplete two ; of the individually perfect three and the dispensationally full seven.

Twelve is the number of *final completeness*. Hence the twelve months in the year, the twelve signs in the zodiac, the twelve tribes of Israel, the twelve apostles of the Lamb, the twelve stars in the crown of the woman clothed with the sun, the twelve gates of the New Jerusalem, the twelve fruits of the Tree of Life, &c.

But I will not linger among these numbers. I have said enough to show that they have an important significance, rooted in the nature of things, and acknowledged in the Scriptures and in the common language and thinking of the great mass of mankind. They are not inventions of men, but expressions of God and His works. They also furnish new and forcible evidence of the truthfulness of the estimate of this book which I have given—to wit : that it is the book of the consummation—a divine picture of the fulness and winding up of all God's dispensations in this world. I have given more than was necessary for my purpose, but I thought it best to give the connected list. The text contains but one of these numbers. That number is *seven*. These Churches are *seven*. And if this number has the significance which I have assigned it, and which seems to be admitted by all who have looked into the subject, it gives us the key to the true significance of these Churches. It assigns to them the unmistakable character of *completeness*. As " the seven Spirits which are before the throne " are the *one Holy Spirit*, in all the fulness and completeness of His offices and powers in this dispensation, so " the seven Churches " are the *one Holy Catholic Church*, in all the amplitude and completeness of its being and history, from the time of the vision to the end.

Nor does this conflict with the fact that these were literal historic Churches, existing, at the time the apostle wrote, at the places which I have described. They were Churches of Ephesus, Smyrna, Pergamos, &c., as really as our St. John's is a Church of this present Philadelphia. But there were other Churches then existing, at Collosse, Antioch, Alexandria, Corinth, Rome, and elsewhere, some of them larger and more powerful than some of those named. Why, then, were these not taken into the account ? Did they not need instruction, and rebuke, and encouragement, and warning, as well as the favoured seven ? The only explanation is, that they were somehow included in the seven. They were not specifically and locally addressed, because what concerned their estate, and the mind of Christ with reference to it, are embraced and expressed in the seven. In other words, these seven Churches, in their names, in their graces, in their defects, in their relations to Christ, and in His promises and threatenings to them severally, comprehend everything found in the entire Church, as it then existed, or was to exist. Seven, by common consent, is just the number to express this idea. That it is a mere accident in the composition—a mere grace of rhetoric, the more to interest the reader by the artistic method by which these momentous matters are handled, I cannot admit. That a man with the zeal and fire of the apostle John, standing in the midst of the most stupendous and overwhelming scenes ever to be enacted on earth, should, amid it all, coolly set to work to elaborate a style, and round up his message into graceful sections and harmonious divisions, merely to entertain the taste and please the imagination of his readers, is to me incomprehensible. The idea carries absurdity on its face. And it so sinks the apostle into the poet, and the inspired man of God into the rhetorician, and the direct words of Christ into the fancies of men, that it strips the Apocalypse of that sacredness which it claims for itself ; transmutes it into a mere religious Iliad, or Paradise Lost, or Paradise Regained, and places it before us as a book for æsthetic criticism and rhetorical study, rather than, as it was meant to be, a message from Jesus to regulate our faith, and hope, and life, with reference to the judgment to come, every word and feature of which is from God, and much in the very language of God. I must, therefore, insist that this doctrine of numbers, if we had nothing else, settles upon these seven Churches a representative comprehensiveness which embraces the entire fulness of the Church of all time.*

There are, however, other considerations to corroborate this view. One is found in the seven times repeated admonition : *" He that hath an ear, let him hear what the Spirit saith unto the Churches."* Such language, seven times underlined, as if printed in the largest capitals, has in it an intensity of universality and urgency beyond anything in all the volume of Scripture. Why is this ? The whole Apocalypse is encircled with a special promise of blessing to him that reads and keeps it. We find it in the first verses, and among the last ; and we argue from it that there is something special in this book, calling for our particular attention. And when we find this sevenfold additional admonition affixed to the seven epistles, and in each place made to refer to the whole seven, what are we to gather from it but that, in the mind of Jesus, there is much more in these seven epistles than we find on the surface of them, and that they apply to Christians universally, and concern every man, throughout all Gospel times, in a way which turns the peculiarities of these seven particular Churches into types and images of the Church general in its entireness of membership and history ? Admit that these epistles contain a panoramic outline of the whole visible Church, as that Church and her deeds appear in the light of the throne of God, and this vehemency, the scope and intensity of which cannot be exaggerated, is at once explained. If, in dealing with these epistles, every man, of every age, has a divine thermometer whereby to tell exactly where he or his Church stands in Christ's judgment, and one constructed and delivered to him from Christ himself for this specific purpose, then this fulness and unlimitedness of urgency is comprehensible and fitting ; but on any other assumption, it degenerates into mere poetry and rhetoric. And as I am bound to believe that Christ's words, so solemnly and significantly given, are entitled to all the fulness of meaning of which they are capable, I must conclude, from this sevenfold charge concerning these seven epistles, that these seven Churches of Asia, as here described, were meant to be paradigmatic of the whole Church, every Church, and every member of the Church, and Christ's judgment of them, then and thereafter, up to and inclusive of His final apportionment of rewards and punishments to each.

The same may be argued from the word *mystery*, as applied to these Churches and their angels. It intimates, from the start, that there is something more intended than is seen upon the surface ; and what that something is, we find in the view I have given. And, indeed, the nature of the vision in which John received these epistles, assumes that not these seven Churches alone, but in them the entire Church, is to be contemplated. The angels of other Churches, and other ages, are as much stars in Christ's right hand as these seven, and why should we think to leave them out of the solemn representation ?

---

* " The seven must be regarded as constituting a complex whole—as possessing an ideal completeness. Christ, we feel sure, could not have placed Himself in the relation which He does to them,—as holding in His hand the seven stars, walking among the seven golden candlesticks, these stars being the angels of the Churches, and candlesticks the Churches themselves,—unless they ideally represented and set forth, in some way or other, the universal Church militant here upon earth."—*Trench on the Seven Epistles*, p. 44.

" The number seven is used throughout the Apocalypse in a symbolic sense, and is admitted to be expressive of completeness or perfection. Why should ' the seven Churches ' be an exception to the rule ? Were the seven local Churches, the names of which are given, the only light-bearers or candlesticks ? Did the light entirely cease to shine when these Asiatic Churches ceased to exist ? Let these seven Churches, or candlesticks, be regarded as a sevenfold or perfect representative of the one Church, in its responsibility to Christ as His light-bearer or witness before the world, and we have an interpretation at once consistent with the entire character of the book, and sufficient to account for the selection of seven local Churches, the divers states of which furnish what was needed for this sevenfold or perfect view of the whole professing body."—*Plain Papers*, p. 418.

" The number seven in the Scriptures denotes something universal and complete."— *Luther (see Walch's Luther*, ix. 2063).

These seven Churches, then, besides being literal historical Churches, stand for the entire Christian body, in all periods of its history. But how, or in what respects? Upon this point, let me add a word or two before I close.

In the first place, the seven Churches represent seven phases or periods in the Church's history, stretching from the time of the apostles to the coming again of Christ, the characteristics of which are set forth partly in the names of these Churches, but more fully in the epistles addressed to them. There has been an *Ephesian* period—a period of warmth and love and labour for Christ, dating directly from the apostles, in which defection began by the gradual cooling of the love of some, the false professions of others, and the incoming of undue exaltations of the clergy and Church offices. Then came the *Smyrna* period—the era of martyrdom, and of the sweet savour unto God of faithfulness unto death, but marked with further developments of defection in the establishment of castes and orders, the licence of Judaizing propensities, and consequent departures from the true simplicities of the Gospel. Then followed the *Pergamite* period, in which true faith more and more disappeared from view, and clericalism gradually formed itself into a system, and the Church united with the world, and Babylon began to rear itself aloft. Then came the *Thyatiran* period—the age of purple and glory for the corrupt priesthood, and of darkness for the truth; the age of effeminacy and clerical domination, when the Church usurped the place of Christ, and the witnesses of Jesus were given to dungeons, stakes and inquisitions; the age of the enthronement of the false prophetess, reaching to the days of Luther and the Reformation. Then came the *Sardian* period—the age of separation and return to the rule of Christ; the age of comparative freedom from Balaam and his doctrines, from the Nicolaitans and their tenets, from Jezebel and her fornications; an age of many worthy names, but marked with deadness withal, and having much of which to repent; an age covering the spiritual lethargy of the Protestant centuries before the great evangelical movements of the last hundred years, which brought us the *Philadelphian* era, marked by a closer adherence to the written word, and more fraternity among Christians, but now rapidly giving place to *Laodicean* lukewarmness, self-sufficiency, empty profession, and false peace, in which the day of judgment is to find the unthinking multitude who suppose they are Christians and are not.

The details in these outlines I leave till we come to the more direct exposition of the epistles themselves, but will yet observe, on this point, that everything which marks one of these periods pertains also, in a lower degree, to every period. It is simply the predominance, and greater or less vigour, of one element at one time, which distinguishes the seven eras from each other. The seven periods, in other words, coexist in every period, as well as in succession, only that in one period the one is predominant, and in another the other.

In the next place, the seven Churches represent seven varieties of Christians, both true and false. Every professor of Christianity is either an Ephesian in his religious qualities, a Smyrnaote, a Pergamite, a Thyatiran, a Sardian, a Philadelphian, or a Laodicean. It is of these seven sorts that the whole Church is made up, the several marks and characteristics of each of which will be brought out hereafter.

Nor are we to look for one sort in one period, or in one denomination, only. Every age, every denomination, and nearly every congregation, contains specimens of each. As all the elements of the ocean are to be found, in more or less distinctness, in every drop from the ocean, so every community of Christian professors has some of all the varied classes which make up Christendom at large. One may abound most in Ephesians, another in Smyrnaotes, another in Thyatirans, and others in other kinds; but we shall hardly be at a loss to find all in all. There are Protestant Papists, and Papistical Protestants; sectarian anti-sectarians, and partyists who are not schismatics; holy ones in the midst of abounding defection and apostasy, and unholy ones in the midst of the most earnest and active faith ; light in dark places, and darkness in the midst of light.

I thus find the seven Churches in every Church, giving to these Epistles a directness of application to ourselves, and to professing Christians of every age, of the utmost solemnity and importance. They tell what Christ's judgment of each of us is, and what we each may expect in the great day of His coming. In every age, and in every congregation, Christ is walking among His Churches, with open, flaming eyes ; and these epistles give us His opinion of what His all-revealing glance discovers. And as we would know where we stand, and what we may expect when this Apocalypse is fulfilled, let us carefully examine, and pray God to help us to the true understanding of, these special summaries of what the Spirit saith unto the Churches.

LECTURE SIXTH

THE SEVEN EPISTLES—A DISTINCT AND INVITING DEPARTMENT OF SACRED LITERATURE—STRANGELY NEGLECTED BY THE CHURCH—EACH EMBRACES SEVEN PARTS—THEIR TEACHINGS IN RELATION TO THE PARTICULAR CHURCHES ADDRESSED—CHRIST REMEMBERS HIS PEOPLE—SPEAKS TO THEM THROUGH THEIR MINISTERS—THE MORAL STATE OF THE PRIMITIVE CHURCHES—THE IMPORTANCE ASSIGNED TO THE PRACTICAL IN RELIGION—CHRIST'S USE OF THE DOCTRINE OF THE SECOND ADVENT—THE FUTURE OF THE REDEEMED.

REV. CHAPS. 2–3. (Revised Text.)—To the angel of the Church in Ephesus write : These things saith He that holdeth the seven stars in his right hand, who walketh in the midst of the seven candlesticks of gold : I know thy works, and thy labour, and thy endurance, and that thou canst not bear those who are evil, and hast tried those who say they are apostles and are not, and hast found them false, and hast endurance, and didst bear for my name, and hast not fainted. Nevertheless, I have against thee that thou hast left thy first love. Remember, therefore, whence thou hast fallen, and repent, and do the first works ; otherwise I am coming unto thee, and will remove thy candlestick out of its place, if thou dost not repent. But this thou hast, that thou hatest the deeds of the Nicolaitanes, which I also hate. He that hath an ear, let him hear what the Spirit saith unto the Churches. To him that overcometh will I give to eat of the tree of life, which is in the paradise of my God.

And to the angel of the church in Smyrna write : These things saith the first and the last, who became dead and revived : I know thy tribulation, and thy poverty (nevertheless thou art rich), and [I know] thy reproach from those who say they are Jews and are not, but [are] Satan's synagogue. Fear not the things which thou art about to suffer ; behold, indeed, the devil is about to cast [some] of you into prison, that ye may be tried, and ye shall have tribulation ten days : be faithful unto [the endurance of] death, and I will give thee the crown of life. He that hath an ear, let him hear what the Spirit saith unto the Churches. He that overcometh shall not be hurt of the second death.

And to the angel of the Church in Pergamos write : These things saith He which hath the sharp sword with two edges : I know where thou dwellest, [even] where Satan's throne [is], and thou holdest fast my name, and didst not deny the faith of me, even in the days of Antipas my witness, my faithful one, who was slain among you, where Satan dwelleth. Nevertheless, I have against thee a few things, [that] thou hast there those who hold the teaching of Balaam, who taught Balak to put a stumbling-block (an occasion of sin) before the sons of Israel, to eat things offered to idols, and to commit fornication. So thou thyself also hast those who hold the doctrine of the Nicolaitanes in like manner. Repent, therefore, otherwise I am coming to thee quickly, and will make war with them with the sword of my mouth. He that hath an ear, let him hear what the Spirit saith unto the Churches. To him that overcometh will I give of the hidden manna, and I will give to him a white stone [a bright gem], and on the stone a new name written [engraved], which no one knoweth saving he that receiveth it.

And to the angel of the Church in Thyatira write : These things saith the Son of God, who hath his eyes as a flame of fire, and his feet like unto fine brass : I know thy works, and charity, and faith, and service, and thy endurance, and thy last works [to be] more than the first. Notwithstanding, I have against thee that thou sufferest thy wife Jezebel, who calleth herself a prophetess, and teacheth and leadeth astray my servants to commit fornication, and to eat things sacrificed unto idols. And I gave her time that she should repent, and she is not minded to repent of her fornication. Behold, I cast her into a bed [of sickness, torment or perdition], and those who commit adultery with her into great tribulation, if they do not repent of her works. And her children will I slay with death ; and all the Churches shall know that I am He who searcheth the reins and hearts ; and I will give to every one of you according to your works. But unto you who are the remnant in Thyatira, as many as have not this teaching, who have not known the depths, as they speak, ([depths] of Satan), I put not upon you any other burden ; only that which ye have hold fast till I come. And he that overcometh, and he that keepeth my works unto the end, to him will I give authority over the nations ; and he shall rule them with a rod [sceptre] of iron ; as the vessels of earthenware shall they be broken to shivers ; as I also received from my Father ; and I will give to him the morning star. He that hath an ear, let him hear what the Spirit saith unto the Churches.

And to the angel of the Church in Sardis write : These things saith He that hath the seven Spirits of God, and the seven stars : I know thy works, that thou hast a name that thou livest, and art dead. Be watchful, and strengthen the things that remain, that were about to die ; for I have not found thy works complete in the sight of my God. Remember, therefore, how thou hast received and heardest, and observe and repent. If, therefore, thou dost not watch, I will arrive over thee as a thief, and thou shalt not by any means know at what hour I will arrive over thee. Nevertheless, thou hast a few names in Sardis which have not defiled their garments ; and they shall walk with me in white, for they are worthy. He that overcometh thus, shall be clothed in white raiment, and I will not by any means wipe out his name out of the book of life, and will confess his name in the presence of my Father and in the presence of His angels. He that hath an ear, let him hear what the Spirit saith unto the Churches.

And to the angel of the Church in Philadelphia write : These things saith the Holy [One], the True, He that hath the key of David [of Hades ? comp. 1 : 18], Who openeth and no one shall shut, Who shutteth and no one shall open : I know thy works ; behold, I have given before thee a door opened, which no one is able to shut ; because thou hast a little strength, didst keep my word, and didst not deny my name. Behold, I give [those] of the synagogue of Satan, who say they are Jews and are not, but do lie, behold, I will make them that they shall come and shall do homage before thy feet, and that they may know that I loved thee. Because thou didst keep my word of patient endurance, I also will keep thee out of the hour of temptation [the appointed season of sore trial] which is about to come upon the whole world, to try those who dwell upon the earth. I am coming quickly ; hold fast that which thou hast, that no one take thy crown. He that overcometh, him will I make a pillar in the temple of my God, and he shall go no more out of it ; and I will write upon him the name of my God, and the name of the city of my God, the new Jerusalem which cometh down out of the heaven from my God, and mine own new name. He that hath an ear, let him hear what the Spirit saith unto the Churches.

And to the angel of the Church of Laodiceans write : These things saith the Amen, the faithful and true Witness, the Beginning [Head Prince] of the creation of God : I know thy works, that thou art neither cold nor hot ; would thou wert cold or hot. So then because thou art lukewarm, and neither cold nor hot, I am about to spue thee out of my mouth. Because thou sayest, I am rich, and increased with goods, and have need in nothing, and knowest not that thou art the wretched and the pitiable [one], and poor, and blind, and naked ; I counsel thee to buy from me gold refined out of the fire, that thou mayest be rich ; and white raiment, that thou mayest be clothed, and [that] the shame of thy naked-ness be not made manifest ; and eye-salve to anoint thine eyes, that thou mayest see. As many as I love, I rebuke and chasten ; be zealous, therefore, and repent. Behold, I stand at the door and knock ; if any one hear my voice, and open the door, I will enter in to him, and will sup with him, and he shall sup with me. To him that overcometh will I give to sit with me on my throne, as I also overcame and sat down with my Father on His throne.

I<small>N</small> the second and third chapters of the Apocalypse, upon which we now enter, we find a distinct and unique section of sacred literature, which the learned and devout Dr. Bengel used to commend, above everything, to the study especially of young ministers. We call the contents of these chapters *Epistles ;* but they are not so much messages from an absent Lord as sentences of a present Judge, engaged in the solemn act of inspection and decision.

There is much pertaining to these sentences to recommend them to the particular attention of Christians. They are a prominent and vital part of the Apocalypse, which pronounces special benedictions upon its attentive readers and hearers. Like the parables, they consist exclusively of Christ's own words, and are the very last which we have directly from Him. They are, perhaps, the only unabridged records of His addresses in our possession. They are most impressively introduced, and so directly addressed as to beget the idea that they are something of unusual solemnity and importance. They are also accompanied with a seven times repeated entreaty and command to hear what is said in them. And yet there is not another portion of Scripture, of equal extent and conspicuity, to which so little attention has been paid. Strange to say, the Church has nowhere included these Epistles in the lessons prescribed to be read in the public services, except in a secondary and very remote manner. In the Church of England, Archbishop Trench remarks that it is impossible, if the canons of the Church be followed, for these Epistles ever to be read in the public services.* Though so specifically and urgently

* " It is very much to be regretted, that while every chapter of every other book of the New Testament is set forth to be read in the Church, and, wherever there is daily service, is read in the Church, three times in the year, and some, or portions of some, oftener, while even of the Apocalypse itself two chapters and portions of others have been admitted into the service, *under no circumstances whatever can the second and third chapters ever be heard in the congregation.*"—*Epist. to the Seven Churches.* p. 10.

addressed to the Churches, it would seem as if there had been some general concert to prevent them from being seen or heard.

Exposition is also remarkably barren with respect to these Epistles. Though in every way marked as of equal account with the parables, they have not received a tithe of the attention. We have hundreds of disquisitions on other special discourses of the Saviour, where it would be difficult to find *tens* devoted to these, His last and most solemn, dictated from heaven, super-scribed with His own marvellous attestations, and urged upon all by the sevenfold admonition to hear and ponder what they contain. Even writers on the Apocalypse itself, in very many instances, have passed these Epistles with hardly a word of remark. Erroneously assigning to them nothing but what concerned the particular Churches named, and mistakenly commencing the Apocalypse proper only with the fourth or sixth chapter, writers on prophecy have thought they had no occasion to deal with these divine letters, and have generally passed them by, to the utter discomfiture of their attempts, without them, to understand or expound this book.

I have already indicated the manner in which the seven Churches are to be viewed. They were literal historical Churches, existing at the time John wrote, but, at the same time, representative and comprehensive of all other Churches of all nations, places and ages—a complete sample of the whole body, in the entirety of its character and career. And it is the same with reference to these seven Epistles. They are neither exactly nor only prophetic. They were really messages to these particular Churches, in view of their several conditions, to stir them up to hold fast what was right, and to amend what was wrong, as also all other Churches in like conditions. But as the seven Churches were representative and inclusive of the entire Church, these Epistles also give Christ's judgment of the entire Church, and are necessarily anticipative of its entire history. In other words, they give us, from the beginning, the exact picture of the whole history of the Church, as that history, when finished, shall present itself to the mind of Christ as he contemplates it from the judgment seat, which is really the point from which everything presented in the Apocalypse is viewed. We may therefore read in them what was in the beginning, and what the career of the Church has been since, and will be to the end.

The number of these Epistles is *seven*, corresponding with the number of the Churches. Each one also embraces seven distinct parts : first, an address ; second, a citation of some one or more of the sublime attributes of the Speaker; third, an assertion of His complete knowledge of the sphere, duties and doings of the persons addressed ; fourth, a description of the state of each, with such interspersions of praise and promise, or censure and admonition, as the case required ; fifth, an allusion to His promised coming, and the character it will assume to the persons described ; sixth, a universal command to hear ; and seventh, a special promise to the ultimate victor. In the last four, the order of succession is varied from the first three, and the call to attention is there put *after* the promise " to him that overcometh ; " but in each these seven parts may be distinguished, showing that there is a completeness and fulness about the whole, which will not admit of their being confined in their signification to the few particular congregations to which they were originally addressed.

But without descending into all the particulars, I propose to note briefly some of the teachings of these Epistles, considered—

I.   In relation to the particular Churches addressed.
II.   In relation to the entire Church represented.

1. The first Churches were very obscure assemblies, without badges save their common adherence to Christ and obedience to his Gospel, and their congregation in quiet, if not in secrecy, around the altars of a simple worship. They were unnoticed by the great world, in the midst of which they were planted, or were observed only to be despised. But, neglected or persecuted

on earth, we see from these Epistles that they were considered in heaven, and had the very first place in the blessed Saviour's regard. Wonderful doings among the potencies of this world were about to take place. Seals were to be opened, at which the heavens should shake, the sun be darkened, the stars fall, and mountains and islands move from their places. Trumpets were to be blown, which should turn the very rains to hail, fire and blood, open the pit, and fill the earth with woe. Battles were to be fought, in heaven and on earth, and vials of wrath emptied, and scenes enacted over which heaven should shout hallelujah. But in advance of all, and above all, the mind of the great Judge was on His little companies of believers, and to them He gave His first attention. "Write," said He, "and send to the seven Churches."

2. But when we come to inspect what is written, we find all addressed to the ministers in charge of these Churches. Each Epistle is written to "*the angel* of the Church." What is written we know to be meant not for him alone, for the command is to every one to hear "what the Spirit saith *to the Churches;*" but we thus encounter an item of ecclesiastical order, binding up these congregations very closely with their pastors, and their pastors with them. This is important. It shows that there is a ministry—an official order— in the Christian Church, which assigns one angel to one congregation, and makes him its representative and head. The method by which these officers succeeded to their places, or the precise extent of their functions and authority, is not defined. Neither is it denied, that what pertained preeminently to them also belonged subordinately to the whole company of believers. But a special ministerial appointment is recognized, as part of the sacred economy, the proper life, and the wholesome ongoing of the Church, and which no power on earth may disturb without insurrection against God, and invasion of the dignity of our Lord. This is a doctrine from which, indeed, many deplorable abuses have sprung (of which we will have occasion to take notice), and on account of which some have rejected it as not of God. But it is a true doctrine of our holy religion, and, in its legitimate relations, enters essentially into the system which Christ has himself ordained for the bringing of souls to eternal life.

3. From this peculiarity in these Epistles, we may also trace something of the nature and responsibility of the ministerial office. It is not a lordship, but a service ; not a service to be commanded of man, but of God. It is the business of the angel to hear for the Church, receive for the Church, and to answer for the Church, which has been committed to his care. He is its chief, its guardian, its watchman, the under-shepherd of the flock. He is to receive the word at the mouth of the Lord, and at the hands of His inspired servants, and to present it faithfully to his people, and to see that it is accepted, observed and obeyed according to the true intent of its divine Author. Christ sends His Revelation to these angels above all, and looks to them for the right ordering of His Churches. To them He addresses His judgments, His rebukes, and His directions, as if the whole estate of the Churches were wrapped up in them, and they alone responsible for that estate. And so far as they keep themselves to their true sphere and work, whosoever heareth them heareth Him, and he that despiseth them despiseth Him.

4. But these Epistles show us more particularly what was the moral condition of the primitive Churches. Nor is the exhibition what we would perhaps have expected. Churches founded and instructed by apostles, and ministered unto by those who were the pupils of the apostles, appointed under apostolic supervision, we would think to find models of every excellence, and pure and free from the evils, heresies and defections of later periods. But these Epistles show that the Churches then were much like the Churches now, and of all ages : that is, interminglings of good and bad, and as full of the workings of depravity as of the fruits of a true faith. There was much to commend, but quite as much to censure. There were worthy sons and daughters of the Most

High, whose conversation was in heaven ; but many more whose love had cooled, whose hearts were in the world, who had a name to live but were dead, and esteemed themselves rich, and increased with goods, and needing nothing, not knowing that they were wretched, and miserable, and poor, and blind, and naked. With five out of the seven, Christ finds serious fault ; and in one of these five, He finds nothing whatever to commend. Two alone pass the solemn inspection, and they in contact with elements which He quite condemns.

The first and most distinguished was that of Ephesus. This Church was characterized by strong impulse toward God, earnestness, and zeal, and yet with a giving way in these qualities from what they were at first. This is signified in the word εψεσις, which thus exactly fits to the description. He who holds the seven stars, and walks in the midst of the candlesticks, found in Ephesus works, labour, endurance, steadfast opposition to evil, faithfulness and firmness in discipline, cheerfulness in bearing any burden for Christ's sake, and a just hatred of deeds and practices which Christ also hates. But He found there also this defect, which called for repentance and return to first works, if they would not be unchurched entirely : namely, that they had left their first love. There is such a thing as having and exercising a sharp penetration into the true and the false, a correctness of judgment in sacred things, a zealous and self-sacrificing devotion to the right and true, and an earnest-minded severance from false apostles and all evildoers, and yet being without that warmth and purity of love which is the first impulse in the breast of young disciples, and without which, well cherished and kept in vigorous life, there is unfitness to meet the judgment or to stand in it. And this was the sorry fault of the Church of Ephesus. Of course, it was not the estate of every particular member that is thus described. There were Smyrnaotes and Philadelphians in Ephesus also ; but their number was few, and the prevailing characteristic of the whole together was great zeal for truth and right, with a love in fatal decline.

Smyrna is a word three times translated in the New Testament. (Matt. 2 : 11 ; Mark 15 : 23 ; John 19 : 39.) It signifies *myrrh*, an aromatic exudation from a thorny tree, which furnished one of the ingredients of the holy ointment, and was used by the ancients in embalming the dead. It had associated with it the idea of something grateful to God, and connected also with death and resurrection. It well describes a Church persecuted unto death, and lying embalmed in the precious spices of its sufferings, such as the Church of Smyrna was. It was the Church of Myrrh, or bitterness, and yet agreeable and precious unto the Lord, holy in the midst of its tribulations, and full of blessed hopes for the world to which the resurrection is to bring the saints. Nothing of complaint is said of this Church ; but neither are any special works or achievements enumerated to its praise, whilst the presence of an evil synagogue is affirmed. A poor Church, in the midst of persecution and suffering, cannot be expected to do much. To endure steadfastly is, then, all that can be looked for, and is worthy of highest commendation. From two sources did these troubles spring : from blaspheming Jews, and from intolerant Pagans ; both actuated by the devil. When Polycarp was tried and martyred (whom some regard as the angel of the Church here addressed), we are told that the Jews joined with the heathen in clamouring for the good bishop's destruction, and were the most forward in bringing the fuel for the fire which consumed him. These Jews were blasphemers, in the enmity and contempt which they felt and enacted against Christ and His people ; and they were false Jews, and a mere Satanic synagogue, because of that blasphemy. " For he is not a Jew which is one outwardly ; but he is a Jew who is one inwardly." It was thus a two-horned Antichrist by which this little Church was gored, bereft, oppressed and trampled ; a Church destitute, powerless, crushed, but rich in divine grace, pleasing to God, and comforted with joyous hopes for the world to come, though having nothing but suffering to expect in this.

Pergamos carries in its etymology the idea of a tower, and also of marriage.* It well describes a Church in close proximity to the centre of the kingdom of evil, and yielding itself to sensual alliances. And such was the Church at Pergamos. There was Satan's throne, the darkest centre of Pagan abominations. It had faith, and courage, and endurance, and faithful witnesses to Christ ; but it had also some of the worst of elements. It had those who held to a system of ideas answering to the treacherous teachings of Balaam, by which Israel was seduced to fornication and idolatry. It had also those who held to another system of ideas involving tyrannical lordship over the Church : Nicolaitanes, or people-conquerors. It was a Church with a tower of unrighteous assumption in it, and indulgently compliant with the adulterous solicitations and embraces of worldliness. With all its saintship and fidelity, it had need to repent if it would have the approbation of the Lord. It was a Church of much praiseworthy fidelity, but with wicked pretences to loftiness and power on the part of some, and base alliances with what was earthly and Satanic, on the part of others.

The Church in Thyatira had some of the same excellencies, but conjoined with even worse defects. It was active in services and charities, patient in reliance upon God's promises, and increasingly vigorous in its endeavours ; but it was lacking in proper zeal for the maintenance of godly discipline and doctrine, and was so indulgent toward errors and errorists that falsehood and idolatry permeated, overlaid and modified the whole character of the Church, obscuring the faith, deceiving the saints, and setting up in its very midst the infamous school of Satan himself. With all that is said commendatory of this Church, the idea of effeminacy connects with its whole history and character. The first Christian in Thyatira was a woman. The name, Thyatira, some take as equivalent to *thygatira*, a daughter. If we take it as a compound of θυγατης and τειρω, we get the idea of feminine oppression. The false prophets who first enticed the members of this Church into apostasy were women. And the great fault which Christ finds with these Christians is their toleration of the false pretences, the miserable domination, and the abominable doings, of one whom He designates as " that woman Jezebel," who, like her namesake of old, seems to have borne down what should have been the governing will, set aside the true prophets of God with her falsities, and entirely taken possession of the Church for her own impurities. It was a Church with much activity of faith and love, but lying in the embraces of an adulteress, and, for the most part, completely in her power.

The name of the fifth of these Churches has been variously derived. Some connect it with the precious stone, called *sarda*, which was found about Sardis, and sometimes used as an amulet to drive away fear, give boldness, inspire cheerfulness, sharpen wit, and protect against witchcraft and sorceries. Others have derived it from the Hebrew, and have assigned it the signification of *remnant*, or *an escaped few*. Ebrard finds for it an etymological derivation denoting something new, or renewed. And there is a further explanation which derives it from a word which denotes a builder's rule, or measuring line. These several explanations, though different, are not antagonistic, as applied to the condition of a Church. They can be very well combined in one picture. Courage and boldness imply great conflict and danger. In a great contest, many would be vanquished, but a remnant would escape. Those surviving and escaping would necessarily involve new features of life and *régime*. And in this process of renewal there would appropriately come in the use of the carpenter's rule in fashioning the new edifice. We accordingly see in this Church comparative freedom from the sorceries of the domineering prophetess of Thyatira, and an account of things remaining as though they had with difficulty been saved from some far-reaching and crippling danger, and of some names which had clean escaped from the abounding defilements. The ideas

---

* Donegan gives πυργος, a tower ; γαμος, marriage ; τα πψγαμα signifies things lofty or high.

of newness from old degeneracies, and of the true rule re-given for the new
order, run through the entire description. But with all, the boasted new life
was in many things but name, and not reality. These Sardians had heard and
received that which was right and good ; but they did not properly hold or
improve what had been given them, and became dead in the very forms and
attirements of the new life. Having defied and escaped the sorceress, they
suffered their garments to drag in other defilements. There were some noble
exceptions, whom Christ pronounces worthy, and who are to walk with Him
in white, and whose names He will confess before the Father and His angels,
because they were not ashamed to confess Him, and to stand true to His
pure Gospel in its spirit and life ; but in a large part, the Church of Sardis
was but a drooping plant and a dead carcass. It started fresh and new ; it
had heard and received that to which it is the true life of saints to hold ;
but it soon had more profession than vitality, and more boastfulness than
purity or fruit.

The Church in Philadelphia shows no interminglings of evil, but is addressed
as if embracing only a small exceptional company of acknowledged ones in
the midst of a larger body who are no longer recognized as strictly a part of
Christ's Church. They are spoken of as having kept His word, and not denied
His name : as though many had failed in these particulars, and so lost their
place in the acknowledged Christian body. These Philadelphians were but a
little flock, poor in wordly goods, and of small account in the eyes of men.
They had but little strength, and were greatly oppressed by heretical teachers
and pretenders ; but they held fast to the word of Christ, in patient waiting
for His promise. They were an exceptional band, joined by cords of loving
fraternity, as the meaning of the word is, and they had promises given them of
special exemptions and special triumphs.

Very different was the Church of Laodicea. Here was nothing to commend,
though having in it a few suffering ones whom Christ loves and chastens. Its
name* designates it as the Church of mob rule, *the democratic Church*, in
which everything is swayed and decided by popular opinion, clamour and
voting ; and hence a self-righteous and self-sufficient Church. It is described
as thinking itself the perfection of Churches. It said in its heart, " I am rich,
and increased with goods, and have need in nothing ; " but never was a body
of people so woefully self-deluded. With all this boastfulness, the faithful
and true Witness found nothing which He could abide, and pronounces them
wretched, and pitiable, and poor, and blind, and naked, and about to be
vomited up and cast out.

We thus find all sorts and shades of intermingled or coexistent good and
evil in the Church of that day. Some were priestridden, and on that account
condemned ; and some were mob-ridden, and hence unsatisfactory to Christ.
Some had great zeal for pure doctrine and godly discipline, whilst they failed
in the important element of love and charity ; and others, with much faith
and beneficence, yet permitted the manlier things of doctrine, and the ruling
out of impurity, to be overlaid by the false pretences and dominations of
lewd effeminacy. Some in their sufferings were faultless, but feeble ; and
others in their prosperity were strong, but dead and corrupt. There was true
faith, and false faith, and sometimes no faith. There were schisms, and heresies
and sects, as well as devout works, and noble self-sacrifices, and instances of
fidelity unto death. There were children of the kingdom and children of the
wicked one, wheat and tares, truths and errors, sins and sanctities, then as
now, and as in all intervening ages. The leaven of evil was even then already
working in the woman's meal, and the birds of impurity finding lodgment in
the branches of the springing tree.

5. We may also notice, in this connection, the stress which our blessed
Lord lays upon the practical features of religion. It is upon these that His
commendations and censures turn. What He praises in the Ephesians is

* Λαοδικυα, from λαος, people, and δικη, judgment, or justice.

their labour, their endurance, their resistance of evil, their patience, their courageous perseverance in well doing ; and what He proposed as the remedy for their defects, was that they should return to first *works*. Love, ministries, patience, labours, works : these are the things to which He refers with most delight, as the marks of the true election, and the proper badges of approved saintship. It is in vain to boast of a correct creed, of right theories, of sound doctrine, if there be no practical godliness, no good works, no positive virtues and active charities and labours. Orthodoxy is important, but orthodoxy alone will not do. The most orthodox in this list is depictured as the deadest. Mere ecstasies, pleasant frames, joyous feelings, loud professions, or dreams that we are rich in grace and in the divine favour, will not do ; for the most ecstatic and the best pleased with itself, among these Churches, was the worst. There must be faith, and a true faith ; but also a living, working, bearing, self-denying faith—a faith which shows its life and power by love, by charities, by gracious ministries, by active services and sacrifices for God. Persecutions and sufferings may cut off opportunity for such displays, as winter overlies and locks up the germs and life-powers of nature, and hides them from our view ; but, as spring-time and summer bring those hidden germs to light, and cause them to put forth and fill the face of heaven with joyous freshness, beauty and fruit, so must true piety in the soul show itself in the life, in good deeds, in devoted endeavours, in a loving spirit, and in faithful standing to the truth, whatever might be the cost or storms.

There are, indeed, such things as " dead works ; " works that have no life-connection with piety ; works put on from without, and not brought forth from within ; fruits tied upon the tree, and not the product of its life ; which are not at all characteristics of true religion. There may be prayers, vigils, fasts, temples, altars, priests, rites, ceremonies, worship, and still be no true piety. Heathenism has all these. There may be Christian profession, connection with the Church, observance of the sacraments, where saving religion has never taken root. None of these things alone characterize a Christian. That which distinguishes him, where all other tests fail, is his living, active love to God and man—his CHARITY. If this be lacking, the defect is fatal. All knowledge, all faith, all mastery of tongues, all miraculous powers, cannot atone for such a deficiency. For " pure religion, and undefiled before God and the Father, is this : to visit the fatherless and widows in their affliction, and to keep unspotted from the world."

6. These Epistles further set before us Christ's use of the great doctrine of His return, and the very high place it occupies among the motives to penitence, hope, steadfastness and godly fear. In this respect, the language of the blessed Lord harmonizes exactly with that of His inspired servants. Finding the Ephesians cooling in their love, He enjoined on them a speedy repentance and return to their first works, lest His coming should suddenly overtake them. The suffering Smyrnaotes, though taught to look for naught but tribulation in this world, were exhorted to be faithful in view of the crowns which it is assigned to that day to bring. The Pergamites were plied with it as an object of just dread to them, in consequence of their Balaamite and Nicolaitane doctrines, and as the great incentive to immediate repentance. The believers of Thyatira were referred to it as the motive for holding fast to the faith, and as an event which was to end their struggles and temptations. The Sardians are commanded to remember how they had received and heard, and to hold fast, and repent, and watch, on pain of having their Lord and Judge come upon them as a thief, which is contemplated as the worst of calamities. To the Philadelphians it is announced, as a subject of comfort and hope, that Christ shall quickly come. And to the Laodiceans He is represented as already present, knocking at the door, prepared to bless those ready to receive Him, but about to eject with loathing the lukewarm masses who fail in fervency and timely repentance.

Some tell us that *death* is, to all intents and purposes, the coming of Christ to the individual, and that we are to comfort and exhort men with reference to their mortality. But that is not the method of Christ in these Epistles. With the exception of the one to Smyrna, there is no hint that there was any such thing as death for any of those who really believed. I have my doubts whether the Scriptures warrant any Christian in expecting to die at all. Paul, in several places, has taught us most specifically that there are Christians who shall never die. Such of Christ's waiting and watching people as shall be alive and remaining at the time of Christ's coming, are not to sleep, not to die, but to be suddenly transfigured and caught up to the clouds, to meet the Lord in the air. (I Thess. 4 : 17.) And as Christ may come in any of these passing generations, I cannot see how true Christians of any generation can reconcile it to the Scriptures to count upon dying. Death, to the saint, is not that certainty which it is sometimes represented ; nor is it of a character to impress and comfort as the doctrine of Christ's coming, in power and glory, to give deliverance to His sighing and dying creation, and dominion to His saints. It is to that coming, therefore, and the translation of the watching and faithful without tasting of death, and of the glorious honours into which it is to induct the patient waiters for it, and the fearful disasters which it is to bring upon the unprepared, that the Scriptures everywhere refer us, and upon which the Saviour Himself relies in all His exhortations to the seven Churches.

And if this was the proper method eighteen hundred years ago, when that coming of the coming One was yet so many centuries in the future, how much more is it the proper method now that threescore generations have passed, and that we have come to the very margin of the great occurrence ! People may call it idiosyncrasy in us, that we persist in preaching the near and speedy coming of Christ ; but, after all, we only preach as He did when it would seem to have been less in place than now, and as all His inspired apostles also preached when they were yet eighteen centuries further from the event than we are. And if some will have it a sort of amiable hallucination under which we are labouring, it is sufficient for our consolation that the blessed Saviour has trod this path, " leaving us an example that we should follow His steps."

7. There are also important and most interesting hints in these Epistles, respecting the future life and honours which the coming of Christ is to bring to the redeemed. Each Epistle has a promise to a particular victor. These several promises unitedly give us at least a seven-sided view of the future possessions of the saints. To the Ephesian victor Christ awards " to eat from off the tree of life which is in the midst of the paradise of God." To him who abides faithful amid the Smyrna trials, is awarded " the crown of life, and exemption from the second death." To the victor of Pergamos is awarded " the hidden manna, and a white pebble engraved with a new name which no one knoweth saving he that receiveth it." The victor of Thyatira is to have " authority over the nations, to rule them with a sceptre of iron," and to receive " the morning star." The victor of Sardis is to be " clothed with white raiment, and walk with Christ in white," and have his name continued upon the book of life, and confessed in the presence of the Father and of the holy angels. The victor of Philadelphia is to be made a pillar in the temple of God, never again to go out, and to have the name of God written upon him, and the name of the new Jerusalem, the city of God, and the new name of Christ himself. And to the victor of Laodicea is the highest promise of all,—even to sit with Christ on His throne, as Christ overcame and sitteth with the Father on His throne.

Have we here seven orders of rewards, to seven orders of Christians, succeeding in their triumph through seven orders of surroundings ? Or have we here seven steps or degrees in the rewards of the saints, unto which each one attains ? Or have we really both ? They rise in degree from the first to the last, as do the evils and the adversities over which the victories are achieved. They also seem to have been framed in the light of the whole sweep of God's varied dispensations, from the days of Adam onward, until Christ shall have reinstated His saints in the fruition of all that Adam lost. The first refers to a readmission to a paradise and a tree of life, answering to, if not the very same from which Adam was excluded. The next proclaims a triumph over the afflictions, and an exemption from the death, which pertain to the state of expulsion from paradise and the tree of life. The third throws open the same or like storehouses out of which the pilgrim Hebrews were sustained in the wilderness, and imparts the engraved and shining jewel, as on Aaron's breastplate, which admits as a priest into the presence-chamber of the Lord. The fourth promises authority and judicial administrations upon nations, which find their type in Joshua's and David's and Solomon's victories and reigns, with an addition the exact nature of which I have not been able to penetrate.* And having thus exhausted the range of the dispensations of the past, the next three move forward to things predicted of the future. The promise to the victor of Sardis links itself with the solemnities which are to end this world : with the resurrection, the opening of the books, and the official acknowledgment of those whose names are in the registry of the faithful. The next takes its elements from the setting up of a new kingdom, and a new city, and rights of celestial citizenship, and a temple, not made with hands, eternal in the heavens. Whilst the last conducts to a point of settlement and dominion beyond which there is nothing higher to be imagined or desired : even session with Christ upon His everlasting throne.

But in whatever way we take these promises, they set before us a body of honour, and privilege, and power, and blessedness, greater than eye hath seen, or ear heard, or the heart of man conceived. It has been well observed that these seven promises together, in their twofold aspect, form by far the completest description to be found in all the Word of God, of what good things they are which God has prepared for them that love Him.† They set before us a destiny to which the faithful shall attain, at which the lean, meagre, shallow, shadowy, flimsy thing some present as heaven, sinks into insipidity and contempt. They present us with something fitting and competent to brace up the courage of the Church, to carry her to the pitch of bearing the cross, and crucifying herself with Christ, and actualizing her professed expatriation from this world. They open to us prospects which put upon the common-places of heavenly anticipation the disgrace and shame of scarcely having caught the first syllables of what is laid up for the true saints of God. But we have not time to dwell here, or even to touch sundry other topics suggested by these Epistles, in their relation to the particular Churches addressed. The consideration of these Churches, in their representative and prophetic character, we therefore necessarily must defer to another occasion. Meanwhile, let us think of the standard which the Saviour has here set up for His people, and seek to animate ourselves to the zeal, self-sacrifice and devotion which alone can secure the prize here held out for our attainment.

> Must Jesus bear the cross alone,
>   And all the world go free ?
> No, there's a cross for every one,
>   And there's a cross for me.
>
> How happy are the saints above,
>   Who once were sorrowing here !
> They ever taste unmingled love,
>   And joy without a tear.
>
> The consecrated cross I'll bear,
>   Till Christ shall set me free,
> And then go home, my crown to wear,—
>   For THERE'S A CROWN FOR ME.

---

* I have since thought the promise to refer to the exalted position of those saints who are joined with Christ in the judgment of the world, which heralds and brings the final consummation as the morning-star the day.

† Rev. Wm. Lincoln, " Javelin of Phineas," p. 149.

LECTURE SEVENTH

THE SEVEN EPISTLES PROPHETIC—THE CHURCH TO BE NEVER OTHER THAN A MIXED SOCIETY—
THE CONSTANT CUMULATIVENESS OF ECCLESIASTICAL EVIL—CHRIST'S OPINION OF THE
PROFESSED CHURCH IN ITS VARIOUS PHASES—NICOLAITANISM—BALAAMISM—MARRIAGE
OF THE CHURCH WITH THE WORLD—JEZEBEL—THE REFORMATION—THE REVIVALS OF
THE PAST CENTURY—CHARACTERISTICS OF THE CHURCH IN OUR DAY—THE EXCEEDING
VALUE OF THESE EPISTLES PROPHETICALLY VIEWED.

REV. 3 : 21.—He that hath an ear, let him hear what the Spirit saith unto the Churches.

WE have glanced over the contents of these Epistles, considered in relation
to the particular Churches addressed. But this is not the only nor the chief
aspect in which they are to be viewed. As I have repeatedly affirmed, these
particular Churches have a representative character, comprehending the
entire Church of all places and ages. It is impossible to find an adequate
reason why only these seven were written to in this manner, except upon this
assumption. The number is that significant of dispensational fulness, entire
completeness. The Saviour speaks of them as involving some sort of
" mystery," having significance beyond what appears upon the surface. The
command to hear and consider what is said is given with such urgency and
universality, as to argue something peculiarly significant to all people of all
time. Much of the language is symbolically applied, and fits and receives a
comprehensive lucidness, in a prophetic acceptation, which it is not otherwise found to possess. These seven Epistles are also a very prominent and
vital part of a book which is specifically described as a book of *prophecy*.
(Chap. 1 : 3 ; 22 : 18.) There is also an evident historical consecutiveness
in the several pictures, as well as contemporaneousness ; and such a complete
successive realization of them can be traced in the subsequent history of the
Church, even down to the present, that it seems to me impossible fairly to get
rid of the conclusion, that these seven Churches were selected as affording,
in their respective names, states, wants, and messages, a prefiguration of the
entire Church in it successive phases from the time John wrote to the end of
its history. Joseph Mede has well presented the case, where he says : " If we
consider their number, being seven (which is the number of revolution of
times, and therefore in this book the seals, trumpets and vials also are seven) ;
or if we consider the choice of the Holy Ghost, in that He taketh neither all,
no, nor the most famous Churches then in the world, as Antioch, Alexandria,
Rome, and many others, and such, no doubt, as had need of instruction as
well as those here named ; if these things be well considered, it will seem that
these seven Churches, besides their literal respect, were intended to be as
patterns and types of the several ages of the Catholic Church from the beginning thereof unto the end of the world ; that so these seven Churches should
prophetically sample unto us a sevenfold successive temper and condition of
the whole visible Church, according to the several ages thereof, answering the
pattern of the seven Churches here."*
Receiving this, then, as the truth in the case, I now take up the topic

* Mede's Works, Book V, chap. 10, p. 90. So also Andreas, one of the earliest writers on
the Apocalypse : διὰ τοῦ ἐβδοματικοῦ ἀριθμοῦ τὸ μυστικὸν ἀπανταχῇ ἐκκλησιῶν σημαίνων. So
also Vitringa (*Anac. Apoc.* p. 32) : Omnino igitur existimo Spiritum S. sub typo et
emblemate septem Ecclesiarum Asiæ nobis mystice et prophetice voluisse depingere
septem variantes status Ecclesiæ Christianæ, quibus successive conspiceretur, etc. See
also Augustine, (*Epist.* 49 : 2,) and Cocceius.

deferred when we last had this subject before us, and proceed to note some of the teachings of these Epistles, considered—

II. In relation to the entire Church represented.

And so important and far-reaching is the subject, that it becomes us to approach it with solemn hearts, and to pray God to aid us with His enlightening grace, that we may indeed hear, mark, learn and inwardly digest what the Spirit saith unto the Churches.

1. Viewing these Epistles, then, as descriptive of the entire Church, I find in them this item of fact : that the professed Church, as pronounced upon by Christ himself, is a mixed society, embracing interminglings of good and evil from its beginning to the end. Whether we take the seven Churches as significant of seven successive or as seven coexisting phases, they must needs reach to the end, and so depicture the entire Church. And as there is not one of these Epistles in which the presence of evil is not recognized, so there can be no period in the earthly history of the Church in which it is without bad admixtures. Whether the Ephesian Church extends, as in some sense it must, from the apostolic era to the consummation, or whether it relates mainly to the first period alone, and the Laodicean the last, we still have a vast deal which the Lord and Judge of the Church condemns, stretching its dark image from the commencement to the close. There were fallen ones, and some whose love had cooled, and some whose first works had been abandoned, and some giving place to the base deeds of the Nicolaitanes, and some false ones claiming to be apostles and were not, even among the warm, patient, fervent, enduring and faithful Ephesians. In Smyrna were faithless blasphemers, and those of Satan's synagogue, as well as faithful, suffering ones, and those whom Christ is to crown in heaven. In Pergamos were those who denied the faith, and followed the treacherous teachings of Balaam, and the doctrines of the detested Nicolaitanes, as well as those who held fast the name of Jesus, and witnessed for Him unto death. In Thyatira, we find a debauching and idolatrous Jezebel and her death-worthy children, and multitudes of spiritual adulterers, as well as those whose works, and faith, and charity, and patience are noted with favour, and who had not been drawn into Satan's depths. In Sardis there was incompleteness, deadness, defalcation, need for repentance, and threatened judgment, as well as names of those who had not defiled their garments. In Philadelphia we discover " the synagogue of Satan," falsifiers, those who had settled themselves upon the earth, and such as had not kept Christ's word, as well as such as should be kept from the sifting trial, and advanced to celestial crowns. And in Laodicea there was found disgusting lukewarmness, empty profession, and base self-conceit, with Christ himself excluded.

Never, indeed, has there been a sowing of God on earth, but it has been oversown by Satan ; or a growth for Christ, which the plantings of the wicked one did not mingle with and hinder. God sowed good seed in Paradise ; but when it came to the harvest, the principal product was tares. At earth's first altar appeared the murderer with the saint—Cain with Abel. God had His sons before the flood ; but more numerous were the children of the wicked one. And in all ages and dispensations, the plants of grace have ever found the weeds upspringing by their sides, their roots intertwining, and their stalks and leaves and fruits putting forth together. The Church is not an exception, and never will be, as long as the present dispensation lasts. Even in its first and purest periods, as the Scriptural accounts attest, it was intermixed with what pertained not to it. There was a Judas among its apostles ; an Ananias and a Simon Magus among its first converts ; a Demas and a Diotrephes among its first public servants. And as long as it continues in this world, Christ will have His Antichrist, and the temple of God its men of sin. He who sets out to find a perfect Church, in which there are no unworthy elements and no disfigurations, proposes to himself a hopeless search. Go where he will, worship where he may, in any country, in any age, he will soon find tares among the wheat, sin mixing in with all earthly holiness ; self-deceivers, hypocrites and unchristians in every assembly of saints ; Satan insinuating himself into every gathering of the sons of God to present themselves before the Lord. No preaching, however pure ; no discipline, however strict or prudent ; no watchfulness, however searching and faithful, can ever make it different. Paul told the Thessalonians that the day of the Lord should not come until there came a falling away first, and an extra-ordinary manifestation of sin and guilt in the Church itself ; and assured them that that embodied apostasy was to live and work on until the Lord himself should come and destroy it by the manifestation of His own personal presence. The Saviour himself has taught us, that in the Gospel field wheat and tares are to be found ; that it is forbidden to pluck up the bad, lest the good also be damaged ; and that both are to " grow together until the harvest," which is the end of the economy—the winding up of the present order of things— " the end of this world."

2. But I further ascertain from these Epistles, that, in Christ's judgment of the Church, the evil that is in it is constantly cumulative and growing. The first of nearly everything in the Scriptures is mostly considered the best ; and so the Church was purest at its beginning. As Hegisippus has said, " The virgin purity of the Church was confined to the days of the apostles." The further centuries carry it from its first years, the more of its original excellence does it lose, and the more apostate does it become. It was so before the flood. It was so in the Jewish economy. And it is so in our dispensation. If these seven Churches represent so many phases or states of the Church general, those phases or states must also be successive, as well as coexistent. And if successive, then they must succeed each other in the order in which Christ has put them : the first first, and the last last. The Church in Ephesus thus becomes descriptive of the first phase or period ; that in Smyrna of the second ; that in Pergamos of a third ; that in Thyatira of a fourth ; and so to the end. Viewing them, then, in this order, we can readily identify the growth of evil, from its first incoming, through its various stages, to its final culmination. Indeed, these seven Epistles are so many photographs of apostasy, taken at different periods of its life, from its infancy to its maturity.

In the first Epistle, the Lord puts his finger upon the origin of the mischief. Here is depictured a first and model estate, which is described as that of " *first love.*" From that " first love " the Saviour notes a decline. This is the first picture. It was in the very hearts of Christ's own people that all corrup-tions of Christianity and apostasy began. " *Thou hast left thy first love.*" It is to the heart that Christ traces all evils. And it is according to the estate of the heart that He judges of us. Where love declines, bad practices soon creep in. The Ephesians waned in original fervour, and soon were troubled with those who departed from the simplicities of the Gospel, betook themselves to Jewish and Pagan intermixtures, and began to put forward the ministry as a sort of priestly class, depreciating and setting aside the laity. Of these were Diotrephes, who coveted preeminence ; and those of whom Peter disapproved, as undertaking to be " lords over God's heritage ; " and those whom Paul resisted, as seeking to transfer to Christianity what pertained to the Jewish ritualism and Pagan philosophy. These were the " Nicolaitanes,"* whose " *deeds* " are singled out for reprehension. But so long as the apostles lived, their influence was inconsiderable. At first, they had but few followers and small success. It was not long, however, as Church history shows,† until they gained adherents and force, and laid the foundations of all subsequent defections and troubles. What in the first picture was feeble, and vigorously resisted, and found only in isolated cases, in the second picture has already grown to be a distinguished and influential party, whose utterances are

---

* From νικαω, to vanquish, and λαος, people, or laity.
† See Mosheim's Ecc. Hist., Cent. I, Part II, chap. 5.

heard and felt, and which is now characterized as a " synagogue of Satan."
And in the third picture, what were only " *deeds* " have come to be taken
up as *doctrine*. The false practices now appear in the shape of an article of
faith. What had previously been kept pretty well at bay, is now found
nestled in the very heart of the Church. What in the first picture was hated
and withstood, is now tolerated, and seemingly cherished. And to it is added
another feature, equally condemned by the Saviour, and equally favoured by
many of these Pergamites. To the Nicolaitanes are added Balaamities :
destroyers of the people, as well as vanquishers of them, as the meaning of
the word Balaam is.* The sin of that prophet was, that he counselled with the
enemies of Israel, and advised the drawing of them into forbidden friendships
and adulterous and idolatrous alliances, by means of which " twenty and four
thousand " were destroyed. (Numb. 25 : 9.) The Pergamite Church had those
who counselled like unlawful unions between the Church and its powerful
enemies, thus repeating the apostate prophet, who taught Balak to seduce
Israel to sin. And whatever interpretation of the matter we accept, it bears
the condemnation of Christ, and in His view so unfavourably characterizes
the Pergamites as to furnish a picture of most fearful advances in the inroads
of evil.

And the next view gives us a still further advance in the same disastrous
tendencies. Here is a heathen, impure and bloody woman, exalted to queenly
dominion over God's people, governing them, and domineering over them, and
drawing them away into spiritual harlotry and abomination. She is even
taken to the bosom of the very angel of the Church, and suffered to assume
the prerogatives of a prophetess to the people, though in reality another
Jezebel. Have we not here the plain and indubitable evidences of continuity
and growth in evil, defection, and apostasy? From the gradual decline of
first love we have one steady and onward march, till that line of development
reaches its climax in the scarlet woman.

But now comes a new and reactionary movement. The pure Gospel is
reproduced, once more heard, and largely received. The old and corrupt order
of things is not overthrown or superseded, but a remnant escapes from it,
and starts out upon a career of fresh life in a new order. But notwithstanding
the re-announcement of the Gospel, and the many noble names whom God
enabled to clear their skirts of the abounding and terrific abominations, the
growth of evil, though it took another direction, was not stopped. The renewal
was hindered, and the works of the Sardians did not come to perfection.
Christ does not find them complete before God. What was " received and
heard " was not properly remembered and held. The things which were
preserved were left to droop, ready to fall into the embrace of death. The
new life that had been engendered was soon enfeebled and brought to languish-
ment. And under the name and boast of life, there was death. The old was
not changed, and the new which had escaped out of it was stagnant and
lifeless. Evil had gained a new victory on a new field. Christendom had
completed a new phase, and was one step further in its process of ripening for
ultimate rejection.

Another is described, in which the work of God is revived and thriving in
many hearts, who are drawn together in united efforts and brotherly affection.
An open door of usefulness in the spread of the truth is set before them, which
no one can shut. They show a little strength, and in poverty and self-denial
hold fast to the word and the name of Christ. But they are an exceptional
band of brothers in the Lord. About them are the great multitudes of nominal
Christians, dwelling upon the earth, and comfortably settled down in its good
things, who require the sifting of great trial to bring them to even a tolerable
Christianity. And besides, there is a great herd of errorists and liars, who
wear the profession of Christians, but are really " the synagogue of Satan."

One other picture is added, and it is the worst. In the first four, the progress

---

* From בלע, destruction, and עם, people.

of mischief is in the line of consolidation and concentration of power, with all
its abuses. In the last three, the reverse obtains, and the evil runs in the line
of disintegration, separation, and individualism, until finally each man comes
to be pretty much his own Church. The Laodicean Church is not the Church
in Laodicea, as in the other cases, but " the Church *of Laodiceans*."* It
would seem as if the Church, in its proper character of an elect company, had
quite faded from view, and the world itself had now become the Church. The
confessing body is hardly any longer distinguishable from any other body.
It is neither one thing nor the other—" neither cold nor hot." And yet, in
pride and boastfulness, hypocrisy and self-deception, there never has been
its like. It claims to be rich, and increased with goods, and having need in
nothing, and yet is the wretched and pitiable, and poor, and blind, and naked.
It thinks itself all it ought to be, and appropriates to itself all divine favour and
blessedness ; and yet, the very Lord in whom it professes to trust is denied
a place in it, and is represented as barred out, where He stands and knocks as
His last gracious appeal before giving over the infamous Babylon to the
judgments which are ready to sweep it from the earth. That which started
as a little band of loving, self-sacrificing and persecuted saints, redeemed out
of the world, and no longer of it, comes to be a vast, wide-spread, character-
less, Christless, conceited *thing*, to which Jehovah says, " *I am about to spue
thee out of my mouth*."
    We may trace this continuous growth of ecclesiastical evil, also, in the
varying attitude and conduct of the Saviour toward these several Churches.
To the first, He utters himself in the utmost gentleness. He first commends
with great satisfaction, and then rebukes with great mildness and reluctance.
Much the same tone is maintained in the second Epistle, with a stronger
insinuation with reference to the closer and more potent presence of a body of
Judaizers, whom He denounces as blasphemers. But in the third, His words
gather sharpness, and the angel of the Church of Pergamos is reproved with an
intensity of displeasure and condemnation for the first time seen, and which
heightens with the next. " Thou hast there those who hold the teaching of
Balaam. . . . Thou thyself also hast those who hold the doctrine of the
Nicolaitanes." And in the fourth Epistle, besides the sweeping severity of
His complaints and threatenings, He makes a change in the position of the
admonition of the Spirit to hear. Up to this point, that admonition precedes
the promise ; here, and in the subsequent Epistles, it is put *after* the promise.
In the first three instances, it would seem to be the address of the Spirit from
within the professing body, calling to the world without ; but in the last four,
it would seem that the Spirit itself is without, and that the call is considered
now as having the same relation to the body of the professed Church as to the
world. It is thus intensely significant of prevailing apostasy, which has so
Paganized the professing Church as to make true Christians as exceptional in
the Church as in the world. As the pillar of cloud went up from before the
camp of Israel, and took its place behind it, to sever the Lord's people from
the Egyptians, so this change intimates that the Church, as a body, has
become so blended with the world, that a separation needs to be drawn between
Christ's true people and it, the same as *its* calling was meant to sever it from
the world. Hence, in all the Epistles in which the Spirit's warning takes its
place *after* the promise, the great body of the professed Church, as such, is
treated as apostate, and hopelessly corrupt, whilst at the end the fearful
announcement is made that Christ is about to cast it loathingly from Him.
    And in still another respect does Christ successively alter His attitude
toward these Churches, indicative of growing displeasure on His part, and
gradual ripening for judgment on their part. He required of the Ephesians to
repent of their decline of love, simply referring to the fact that He " will
come." He enjoined upon the Pergamites to repent of their still worse

---

* Ἐκκλησίας Λαοδικέων. Some of the MSS., however, have ἐν Λαοδίκια, the same as in
the other instances.

defections, by the sharper announcement : " Otherwise I am coming to thee quickly." Concerning the Thyatirans, he gives a still more fearful picture of His coming to judgment, and declares that He will cast Jezebel and her paramours into perdition, and slay her children with death. Upon the Sardians he threatens the disaster of arriving over them as a thief, at a moment of supposed security. The liars and errorists of Philadelphia He says He will humble in the utmost degree, and bring upon those settled down in the world an hour of dreadful trial, the same as shall befall the world itself ; and that He is coming quickly, as already in the very act of it. And with reference to the loathsome Laodiceans, He represents himself as already present, appealing to them for the last time, and ready now to spue them out of His mouth.

What, then, does all this mean, but that the Church, as a professing body, pure and excellent as it was at the beginning, and with all the partial revivals that mark different periods of its career, and with all the myriads of saints it has embraced, is yet, in the judgment of the Son of God himself, a subject of gradual and ever-increasing decline and decay, first in one direction, then in another, until it becomes completely apostate, and, as such, is finally and forever rejected ? This will be for many a very sad and startling doctrine. It is a paradox. It crosses many a fond dream. It carries dismay to certain humanitarian theories, which are much preached up. It strikes the death-blow to the doctrine of a temporal millennium, and to the hope of an ecclesiastical renovation of the world. Contrary to much of the thinking which prevails, it shows the professed Church in process of conversion to the world, instead of the world in process of conversion, by its means, to Christ. But I am sure that it is the truth of God. Be the logical consequences what they may, I stand here upon the solid rock of Christ's own presentation of the case, as viewed from the judgment seat.

3. But I further learn from these Epistles, considered in their representative relations, what is equally, if not more, important. They give Christ's own judgment and decision concerning many very grave matters which have agitated, divided, distracted and despoiled the Church in various ages, and some of which are still of the most intense practical moment. In this respect, they differ greatly from most other portions of Scripture. We elsewhere find what, if rightly applied, would give us the same results. But here we have, not only principles, which we in our weakness are to take and apply as facts and circumstances may require, but the facts themselves, under Christ's own eye, and directly and authoritatively pronounced upon by Him ; not only the materials out of which to form our judgment of what Christ is likely to think of particular systems, tendencies or measures in the Church, but those systems, tendencies, and measures themselves, brought before the judgment seat, reviewed by His all-searching intelligence, and their true character declared direct from His own lips.

In view of these Epistles which I have been endeavouring to bring out, we can be at no great loss to know what Nicolaitanism is. If they relate to successive phases of the Church general, there can be no disagreement as to the identity of the Smyrna period with the era of the Pagan persecutions. Smyrna was to have a tribulation of " *ten days ;* " and all ecclesiastical writers agree in enumerating " *ten* " of these persecutions, raging most fearfully during *ten years*, from the decree of Dioclesian in A.D. 303, to the Constantinian edict of Milan in A.D. 313. Even the opponents of the prophetic view of these Epistles agree, that " Smyrna represents excellently well the *ecclesia pressa* in its last and most terrible struggles with heathen Rome."* *The distinctive Pergamite period did not therefore commence before the fourth century*. And as we find these Nicolaitanes in full sway in this period, and giving character to it, it follows unmistakably that they were *not* a primitive sect, of which some have spoken, but of which no one knows anything.

* See Trench on the Sev. Epist., p. 309.

Existing already in the Ephesian era, we find Nicolaitanism stretching through centuries, and exerting an influence so marked, that it is not possible that history should be entirely silent with reference to it, although not known by this name. The truth is, that it figures largely in all Church annals ; and we have only to look at the signification of the name which Christ gives it, and at the characteristic tendencies of the period succeeding the Pagan persecutions, to identify it. We know that it was a thing which started in practice, and afterwards embodied itself in theory, and became a feature of doctrine. We know that it was something which put down the people, superseded them in their rights, and set them aside ; for this is the plain import of the name which Christ gives it, and the names which are divinely given are always exactly descriptive of the things or persons that receive them. We also know, from the Scriptures, and from the common representations of all ecclesiastical historians, that the Church was hardly founded until it began to be troubled with the lordly pretensions and doings of arrogant men, in violation of the common priesthood of believers, and settling upon ministers the attributes and prerogatives of a magisterial order, against which Peter, Paul and John were moved to declare their apostolic condemnation, but which grew nevertheless, and presently became fixed upon the Church as part of its essential system. We know that there is to this day a certain teaching, and claim, and practice, in the largest part of the professed Church, according to which a certain order severs itself entirely from the laity, assumes the rights and titles of priesthood, asserts superiority and authority over the rest in spiritual matters, denies the right of any one, whatever his gifts or graces, to teach or preach in the Church who has not been regularly initiated into the mysterious puissance of its own self-constituted circle, and puts forward its creatures, however glaringly deficient in those heavenly gifts which really make the minister, as Christ's only authorized heralds, before whom every one else must be mute and passive, and whose words and administrations every one must receive, on pain of exclusion from the hope of salvation. We also know that this system of priestly clericalism and prelatical hierarchism claims to have come down from the earliest periods of the Church, and traces for itself a regular succession through the Christian centuries, and appeals to patristic practice as its chief basis, vindication and boast. We know that it first came into effective sway in the period immediately succeeding the Pagan persecutions,* reaching its fullest embodiment in Popery, and has perpetuated itself in the same, and in Laudism, tractarianism, and high-Churchism, even to our day, and to our very doors. And if we would know what the Lord Jesus thinks of it, we have only to recur to these Epistles, in which He lays His hand right on it, and says : " THIS THING I HATE."

Contemporaneous with the flowering of Nicolaitanism, was another influential and characterizing feature manifested in the Church, of which the name of Pergamos itself is significant—a certain *marriage with worldly power*, which the Saviour pronounces adulterous, idolatrous and Balaamitic. Nor can we be in doubt respecting this, any more than the other. Its development is located in the period immediately succeeding the Pagan persecutions, when the Church, according to all historians, sacred and secular, did consent to one of the most marked and marvellous alliances that has occurred in all its history. We know that there was then formed a union between the Church and the empire, which the fall of that empire hardly dissolved, and which has been perpetuated in the union of Church and State, in the greater part of Christendom, down to this very hour. It was an alliance cried up at the time, and by many since, as the realization of the millennium itself, and the great consummating victory of the cross. But Christ here gives His verdict upon it, pronouncing it an idolatrous uncleanness ; Israel joining himself to Baal-

---

* Even Archbishop Cranmer testifies that " the bishops and priests were at one time, and were no two things, but both one office, in the beginning of the Christian religion."— *Burnet's Reform*, App., Book III.

peor ; a fearful and disastrous compromise of Christianity with the world, which disfigured and debauched the Church, and destroyed myriads of souls. Nor can any one dispute the appropriateness of the imagery, or the justness of the sentence. (See also Heb. 12 : 6 ; James 4 : 4 ; 1 John 2 : 15 ; Rev. 18 : 3–9.)

And by means of Nicolaitanism and affiliation with worldly power, by which all sorts of corrupting elements were taken up, the Church soon put on another phase, the distinguishing features of which are most graphically sketched. " For such Protestant expositors," says Trench, " as see the Papacy in the scarlet woman of Babylon, the Jezebel of Thyatira appears exactly at the right time, coincides with the Papacy at its height, yet at the same time with judgment at the door in the great revolt which was even then preparing."* Systematized prelacy, and Balaamism, made the emperor president of the Church Councils and the confirmer of their decrees, brought the community of saints into conjunction with " Satan's throne," and so gave being to that mongrel but mighty thing in which Pagan life was transferred to Christian veins, heathen pomp and ceremony commingled with Christian rites and sacraments, and the professed Bride of Christ transformed into a queenly adulteress, the harlot mother of a harlot household. And in all history there is not another character which so completely represents the Papal system—its character, works and worship—as the unclean wife of Ahab, the Jezebel of these Epistles. She was a heathen, married to a Jew ; and such is the character of the Papal system in its main elements—Paganism joined to an obsolete Judaism. She is described as calling herself a prophetess, and as undertaking to be the teacher of God's servants ; and Popery claims and professes to be heaven's only infallible teacher of God's truth. She is described as having a set of " works," emphatically " *her works*," as distinguished from others which are called *Christ's* " *works ;* " and Popery is a system of works—a religion of ceremonies, penances, fasts, masses, prayers, vigils, abnegations, bodily macerations, purgatory, and supererogatory and meritorious holiness of saints, by which it proposes to save its devotees. She was an adulteress ; and Popery, above all, has been characterized by her unclean dealings with the kings and powers of the earth, lending herself to serve their pleasure, to bring them under her sway, and teaching God's people to accept worldly conformity as a means of Christian victory. She was a persecutor and murderess of God's prophets and witnesses ; and the Papacy is marked by nothing more than its severity toward such as stood out against its impious pretences, and its public and secret tortures and butcheries of the saints. " For in her was found the blood of prophets, and of saints, and of all that were slain upon the earth." According to the most credible reading of these Epistles, this Jezebel is represented as the angel's wife ; and it is characteristic of Popery to enforce celibacy upon the clergy, holding them to be married to the Church, and hence teaching all her sons and daughters to call them " fathers." This Jezebel is also described as having " children," alike with her unsatisfactory to Christ ; and whence but from that unclean source have we those semi-Papal national religious establishments, by which the Church of Jesus is befouled, hindered and disgraced, even in many Protestant countries ? We thus obtain from these Epistles Christ's own direct verdict upon Romanism, both in its more offensive features in the old mother, and in its more modified forms in the daughters.

And so, if we would know how the Reformation stands in the Saviour's estimation, we also find it here. As to the great spiritual leaders in it, His comforting declaration is, that their garments were undefiled ; that their names are held in honour ; and that they shall walk with Him in white ; " for they are worthy." As to the character of the doctrines on which it was based, His command is to remember them, observe them, and watch, as the means of being ready for Him when He comes. And as to the final outcome of

* On the Seven Epistles, p. 310.

the blessed movement, His plain and unmistakable word, on the other side, is, that it was *not complete ;* that its works have not been found perfect in the sight of God ; that the new phase of the Church which resulted from it had not the vitality which it professed ; and that the things which it had taken in hand to conserve, it did too much neglect and leave to droop and wither. Its agents were pure and noble, its principles were right and true ; but its fruits were incomplete, its results were marred, and its achievements fell short of the mark at which it aimed. The Saviour almost names the great-souled men who led in that glorious work, and seems almost to sign with His own hand the Protest of Spire and the Confession of Augsburg, and to reiterate from heaven the great foundation doctrines :

An open Bible man's only law of faith ;
Trust in a crucified Saviour man's only justification ;
The glorified Jesus the only Lord and Master of the Church.

But the working out of these principles in what followed, He as clearly pronounces defective ; and the embodying of them in the life developed upon them, He adjudges to be a thing of " name " more than reality.

Two centuries passed and the Protestant Churches assumed another phase. The times of the Pietists, and the Puritans, and the Methodists came on, and there was a new stir in dead Christendom. Those who had escaped from the dominion of Jezebel began to remember how they had received, and heard, and to observe, and repent, and wake up to a sense of the common brotherhood of man, and especially of believers. Christians began to see and feel that the Gospel is more than orthodoxy, and that living aggressiveness is one of its fundamental features. The era of revivals, and missions, and united efforts for the general conversion of mankind ensued, such as had not been since the primitive ages. Many indeed continued to live on in ease, settled comfortably upon the earth, and but slightly influenced by the new spirit. Great multitudes of false professors, boastful of their claims, and sneering and censorious toward the men of true faith, yet swarmed throughout Christendom. But, upon the whole, there was great revival of life and fraternity among Christians. All this we find depictured in the Sixth Epistle, and verified in the history of the last hundred years. And Christ's estimate of this state of things is also given. The true men of love He declares He loves. As their hearts have been to extend the victories of the cross, He promises them an open door of success which none should be able to shut, notwithstanding the efforts made to silence and hinder them. Because they kept His word in patient waiting on Him and for Him, He promises that they shall be kept out of the sifting trials which He threatens to send upon those dwelling at ease. And as for the rest, they are the " synagogue of Satan," whom He engages to humble at the very feet of His faithful ones.

There is yet one other phase. Shall I say that it is yet future, or that we have already entered it ? Here are still some whom Christ loves,—mostly suffering ones, under the rebukes and chastenings of their gracious Lord. But the body of Christendom is quite apostate, with Christ outside, and knocking for admission into his own professed Church. Paul prophesied of the Church that in the last period, men would be mere " lovers of their own selves, covetous, boasters, proud, blasphemers, disobedient to parents, unthankful, unholy, without natural affection, truce-breakers, false accusers, incontinent, fierce, despisers of those that are good, traitors, heady, high-minded, lovers of pleasures more than lovers of God, *having the form of godliness but denying the power thereof."* (2 Tim. 3 : 1–5.) This is a fearful picture, almost as dark as that which he gave of the heathen world before Christianity touched it. (See Rom. 1 : 26–32.) But it answers precisely to the Saviour's portraiture of the characteristics of the Church in its last phase.

It is *Laodicean,*—conformed in everything to the popular judgment and will,—the extreme opposite of Nicolaitane. Instead of a Church of domineering clericals, it is the Church of the domineering mob, in which nothing may be safely preached except what the people are pleased to hear,—in which the teachings of the pulpit are fashioned to the tastes of the pew, and the feelings of the individual override the enactments of legitimate authority.

It is *lukewarm*,—nothing decided,—partly hot and partly cold,—divided between Christ and the world,—not willing to give up pretension and claim to the heavenly, and yet clinging close to the earthy,—having too much conscience to cast off the name of Christ, and too much love for the world to take a firm and honest stand entirely on His side. There is much religiousness, but very little religion ; much sentiment, but very little of life to correspond ; much profession, but very little faith ; a joining of the ball-room to the communion-table, of the opera with the worship of God, and of the feasting and riot of the world with pretended charity and Christian benevolence.

And it is self-satisfied, boastful, and empty. Having come down to the world's tastes, and gained the world's praise and patronage, the Laodiceans think they are rich, and increased with goods, and have need in nothing. Such splendid churches, and influential and intelligent congregations, and learned, agreeable preachers ! Such admirable worship and music ! Such excellently manned and endowed institutions ! So many missionaries in the field ! So much given for magnificent charities ! Such an array in all the attributes of greatness and power ! What more can be wanted ?

And will it answer to say that all this is not largely and characteristically the state of things at this very hour ? Can any man scrutinize narrowly the professed Church of our day, and say that we have not reached the Laodicean age ? Is it not the voice of this Christendom of ours which says : " I am rich, and increased with goods, and have need in nothing ? " And is it not equally the fact that this selfsame Christendom of ours is " the wretched, and the pitiable, and poor, and blind, and naked ? " Did the " Mene, mene, tekel upharsin " of Belshazzar's palace better fit the ancient heathen than this modern Christian Babylon ? Men talk of it as destined to glorious triumph. They proclaim it commissioned of God to convert the world. They point to its onward march as about to take speedy possession of the race for Christ and heaven. But " The Amen " hath spoken. " The faithful and true Witness " hath given His word : " I AM ABOUT TO SPUE IT OUT OF MY MOUTH."

Friends and brethren, I have not *made* these pictures ; I have *found* them ; and the sevenfold admonition of Almighty God with reference to them is : " He that hath an ear, let him hear." You have listened to my statements ; have you taken in their truths ? If there is any just apprehension of Holy Scriptures in them, these seven Epistles stand out in transcendent interest and value, as they do in the urgency with which they are pressed upon our attention. They are Christ's own history of His Church. They are Christ's own criticisms upon all its characteristic features and doings for nearly two thousand years. They are Christ's own verdict upon all the great questions which have agitated it, and upon all the great influences and tendencies, from within and from without, which have affected its character or destiny in every period of its career. The touches are few, but the marks of their divinity are in them. They are comprehensive, true, and unmistakable to Him who will rightly approach and fairly deal with them.

And if these Epistles really are what I have represented them to be, then we have in them what Christians have so much felt the want of, namely, an authoritative settlement of the great questions between us and prelatists, papists, state-churchists, and false pretenders, errorists and radicals of many sorts. Then also we have in them a final settlement of the question whether the Church, or the returned Saviour, is to carry redemption into successful effect upon earth's depraved and rebellious peoples,—whether there is to be a millennium of peace and universal righteousness wrought by present instrumentalities or not,—whether the tendency of Christendom is toward improvement and perfection, or, like everything else with which fallen man has to do,

earthward, deathward, and hellward,—and whether or not the true flock of
God is ever to be anything else in this dispensation than a feeble, depressed,
and hated minority. All these questions, and many more alike interesting,
important, and vital, are put beyond all reasonable disputation in these
Epistles if the doctrine of their proper prophetic aspect is to be maintained.
And I submit it to you, as you shall answer before the bar of God, whether the
truthfulness of this acceptation of them has not been credibly and conclusively
made out. The key exactly fits the lock, the impression answers to the stamp,
the cast bears the precise outlines of the mould ; and it would seem to me
like trifling with the truth not to admit that, in the mind of Jesus, they
belong together. Let us see to it, then, that we hear as the text commands,
and learn to view the Church's errors, corruptions, mistakes, and sins, as
Christ views them ; to love what He loves, to hate what He hates, and to
hope only as He has given us authority to hope. And to this may Almighty
God grant us His helping grace ! Amen.

> Help, mighty God !
>> The strong man bows himself,
>> The good and wise are few,
>>> The standard-bearers faint,
>>> The enemy prevails.
> Help, God of might,
> In this thy Church's night !

> Help, mighty God !
>> The world is waxing gray,
>> And charity grows chill,
>>> And faith is at its ebb,
>>> And hope is withering !
> Help, God of might,
> Appear in glory bright !

LECTURE EIGHTH

REV. 4: 1. (Revised Text). After these things I saw, and behold, a door set open in the heaven, and the former voice which I heard, as of a trumpet, speaking with me, saying, Come up hither, and I will show thee the things which must take place after these things.

THESE words begin a new vision, which constitutes the second grand section of the Apocalypse. It occupies two chapters. It relates not to things on earth, but to things in heaven, and to things subsequent to the period covered by the seven Churches. As the first vision embraces the entire earthly career of the Church on earth, from its organization under the apostles to the coming of Christ, this gives us the state of things intervening between the removal or rapture of the saints, and the letting forth of judgment upon apostate Christendom. In other words, it is the Apocalypse of Christ in relation to His elect in heaven, after they have been "taken"—"caught up"—miraculously removed from the world to the pavilion cloud,—and previous to the going forth of His visitations upon those not "accounted worthy to escape all these things," and "left."

But before entering upon this sublime disclosure, there are still some things relating to the Church in its earthly career and fate, which it will be important first to clear up more fully.

In applying the seven Epistles to the successive periods in the history of the Church, a succession of pictures of growing apostasy and defection was exhibited, so contrary to current feelings and ideas, that some, perhaps, might be disposed to question the correctness of the interpretation. Some may perhaps think, that if the tendency of the professed Church is ever downward, then the Church must be considered a failure, and the Gospel regarded as inadequate to its purposes. I had not overlooked these bearings of the subject. It is also due to the truth, and to such as are honestly perplexed in adjusting our expositions to the general scheme of Providence and Revelation, that something more should be said.

Observe, then, in the first place, that so far as regards the history of the Church hitherto, it is a simple matter of fact that its course has always been in the line of deterioration ; that mischiefs of different sorts have successively assailed it, and made sad havoc of its faith and life ; and that from no one of them has it ever recovered, or given signs of its ability or destiny to recover. In a recent course of able Lectures on the Ages of Christendom, I find it announced, as the result of a faithful induction of the facts, that "*Ecclesiastical history is, to a large extent, a history of corruptions.*"* That such is the truth, every one may easily ascertain for himself. The very creeds of the Church are just so many protestations against the consuming errors which have invaded and preyed upon it, and which, once introduced, never entirely disappear. Apart, then, from all prophetic interpretation, it is a stubborn fact, which we must dispose of the best way we can, that the power of deterioration has hitherto held vast sway in the professing Church. History thus accords with prophetic foreshowing, and bears upon its unalterable records

* Congregational Lecture for 1855, by John Stoughton, p. 423.

what was already foreseen and foretold from the very beginning. And if we do shut our eyes and ears to what the prophets have said, because the picture is unwelcome and embarrassing, the same stands written where we *must* meet it, and where we *must* deal with it, unrelieved by the convenient resort of referring it to some wild and bewildering theories of prophetic interpretation. It is *fact*, and we must admit it, whether it be in the prophecies or not.

It is, moreover, a very foolish thing for us to attempt to marshal the course of God's providence according to our preconceptions and narrow judgments of what is consistent and right. No human philosophy has ever yet been able to cast its boldest guesses half way to the sublimity of the divine plans and purposes. We have justly been compared with children playing on the sea-shore, now and then picking up a few beautiful pebbles or shells, but with the great ocean of God's thoughts lying all undiscovered before us. We may wonder, and question, and debate ; but all the fabrics of our wisdom are utterly overwhelmed by the first swell from those mysterious depths. People may ask how it is that the great Author of Christianity has permitted the history of its realization to include so much that is painful and revolting ; how it is that He did not keep unpolluted His own sacred institutions—that He did not save the light from being dimmed—that He did not preserve the Church an unblighted garden, a home of unruffled love. We can only answer, that His ways are not as our ways, nor His thoughts as our thoughts. The truth is, that God's universe throughout is a very different realm from what man's wisdom would have made it. The human ideal of what a world should be— of what a system of creation should be—of what an order of moral government should be—of what a revelation from heaven should be—is a frail conceit, dashed to atoms the moment it encounters God's actual world, government or word. And the Church is only a more mysterious and more miraculous part of a grand system of mysteries and miracles, as wide as space, and stretching through eternity. It is therefore the part of piety and true wisdom to accept God's word as it is, and facts as they are, without interposing barriers to the reception of the truth, by our philosophizing and vain imaginings as to how things should be.

It is also to be remarked that the history of the Church, as we have found it projected in the seven Epistles, accords very well with the history of the universe in general. It is only a smaller circle within a larger of the same sort. " God revealed truth and duty to angels in heaven. He did the same to Adam and Eve on earth. They were all at first perfect, according to their nature. The greater Church above was pure and holy—the lesser Church below had on it no taint. Then a part of the celestial *Ecclesia* apostatized ; morning stars fell ; sons of God kept not their first estate. The little terrestrial *Ecclesia*, as a whole, was disobedient ; as its members multiplied, they corrupted religion, accepted shadows for substances, and went fearfully astray. Here, then, we have examples of responsible creatures having before them divine communications full of holiness and love, while they are either in declared hostility to the gracious message and law, or else keeping hollow peace, and paying hypocritical deference. Infinite power and goodness have not prevented such a collision, nor excluded such an alliance. Evil exists in this world and in other worlds. Is it out of harmony with that fact, that evil should be found in Christendom ? The analogy between the corruptions of the Christian religion, and the prior corruptions of reason and conscience— between the introduction of sin among angels, and the appearance of sin among Christians—is obvious enough. There is only this difference : that whereas in the earlier case there was apostasy after *perfection*—a departure from the ideal after a full realization of it—in the latter case there has never been full perfection ; at the beginning, the ideal was not more than partially realized. The first fall was deeper than the second, and far more wonderful. If nature be corrupted, is it so great a marvel that revelation should be perverted ? Amidst the raging of moral disease, is the mystery much increased when we see mortals resisting or misapplying the remedy? How could human sin and folly, prevalent everywhere, be kept out of Christendom, without a miracle very different from, and far greater than, any which the Bible relates?" So Stoughton has well put the case.* Why, then, should we become so disturbed and unsettled at the prophetic portraiture of a continuously corrupting Christendom, down even to the very end of the dispensation? Nay, why should we entertain the idea of an end at all, except upon the underlying assumption, either, as we hold, that it was never meant to be that final and universally effective thing which some have erroneously conceived it to be, or that there has been some disastrous miscarriage in its aim?

Neither does it compromise the perfection or the divinity of Christianity, that so large a part of its history, even to the end, is a history of corruption and apostasy. The ideal of a thing may be perfect, and the realization of it be very different. Crimes argue nothing against the excellence of the laws by which they are condemned and punished. No more is the Gospel responsible for man's perversions of it, or for the defections which it denounces. Nay, these very apostasies help to evidence its divinity. Having foretold, warned against and condemned them from the commencement, their actual occurrence is proof that it is from Him who knew the end of all things from the beginning. The very announcements of the Gospel, and all its original and authoritative records, predicted "a falling away," the coming of "false prophets in sheep's clothing," a "departing from the faith," the bringing in of "damnable heresies," and all varieties and forms of evil with which the Church has hitherto been marred and disgraced. The darkest pages of its history are just what was foreseen.

> Ere it came,
> Its shadow, stretching far and wide, was known,
> And two who looked beyond the visible sphere
> Gave notice of its coming : he who saw
> The Apocalypse, and he of elder time,
> Who, in awful vision of the night,
> Saw the four kingdoms, distant as they were.

Had it not been so, then these sad disasters might weigh to overturn our faith ; but with the whole story of Christendom traced out in advance, in the foretellings of its founders, and the facts in all their details coinciding with the predictions, so contrary to all man's anticipations and ideas, we are assured of the presence of superhuman foresight, and of a wisdom which could only come from God.

Nor does it follow that we must consider the Gospel a failure because of these augmenting defections. If it had been stated in the New Testament that the Gospel was never to be misapprehended or denied by its professors ; that the heavenly gift could never be soiled by earthly touch ; that the circle of the Church should be forever free from Satanic invasion ; that no heresies, schisms, inconsistencies, falsehoods, frauds, hypocrisies or crimes should ever be found in ecclesiastical annals ; and that the career of the Church should be like a pure and peaceful river, unobstructed in its flow, unpolluted in its waters, and ever expanding through the centuries, until the world should be covered with the ocean of its outpoured blessings ; then, indeed, such obscurations of the sunny picture would necessitate the admission that Christianity has failed. But no such things are written in the New Testament. The very reverse is found in every allusion which it makes to the estate of the Church in this world, or to the nature and object of this dispensation. Christ's own miraculous ministry gathered around Him but a "little flock," and one of them was a devil. The highest expectation of Paul in his great labours, was that he "might save some." James declared the object of the offer of God's grace to the Gentiles to be, "to take out of them a people

* "Ages of Christendom," pp. 426-8.

for His name," and that " to this agree the words of the prophets." (Acts 15 : 14, 15.) The very designation of the true subjects of divine grace (εκκλησια) singles them out as exceptional to the general mass ; as elected and chosen ones, in whose high privileges the great multitudes in every age have no part. And he who looks upon the present Gospel, simply as we now have it, as meant, equipped, and ordained, for the conversion of all mankind, and the recovery of the whole world to holiness, believes what the Scriptures do not teach, and is expecting what God has nowhere promised. There is not a respectable creed in all Christendom that embodies any such doctrine. On the contrary, the fundamental Confession of Protestants condemns, as " Jewish notions," all idea " that, prior to the resurrection of the dead, the godly shall get the sovereignty in the world, and the wicked be brought under in every place."* In like manner, the Latter Confession of Helvetia condemns " the Jewish dreams, that before the judgment there shall be a golden world in the earth, and that the godly shall possess the kingdoms of the world, their wicked enemies being trodden under foot ; for the Evangelical truth (Matt. 24 and 25, and Luke 21) and the apostolic doctrine (in the Second Epistle to Timothy, 3 and 4) are found to teach far otherwise."† Luther says : " This is not true, and is really a trick of the devil, that people are led to believe that the whole world shall become Christian. It is the devil's doing, in order to darken sound doctrine, and to prevent it from being rightly understood. . . . Therefore, it is not to be admitted that the whole world and all mankind shall believe on Christ ; for we must perpetually bear the sacred cross, that they are the majority who persecute the saints."‡ Melancthon also puts it forth, as part of the essential faith, that the Church in this life is never to attain a position of universal triumph and prosperity, but is to remain depressed, and subject to afflictions and adversities, until the period of the

* John Conrad Goebel, in his sermons on the Augsburg Confession, interprets this article as repudiating the doctrine of the conversion of the world, and declares that " the idea of a golden age in this world, before the resurrection of the dead, is a mere phantasm, not only contrary to the entire Holy Scripture, but especially contrary to the clear and lucid prophecies of the Lord Jesus Christ and His beloved apostles, where they speak of the times immediately preceding the day of judgment—Matt. 24 : 23 ; 1 Tim. 4 : 1 ; 2 Tim. 3 : 1 ; 2 Pet. 3 : 3 ; and other places, where more may be seen upon the subject. Nothing is there said or predicted of a golden age, but only crosses and tribulations, which touch all the estates of the world. Concerning ecclesiastical affairs, it was predicted that in the last times many false Christs and false prophets shall arise, and shall do great signs and wonders, and deceive, if it were possible, the very elect. Concerning hearers, it was predicted that love should wax cold in the hearts of many, and faith wane to such a degree that Christ himself asks : ' When the Son of Man cometh, shall He find faith on the earth ? ' Will that be a golden age ? Concerning matters of state, it was predicted that unrighteousness shall sway them, and there shall be wars and rumours of wars, nation rising against nation, and kingdom against kingdom. Will that be a golden age ? Concerning the family, it was predicted that the son shall be against the father, the daughter against her mother, and that a man's foes shall be those of his own house. Will that be a golden age ? Concerning common life, it was predicted that there shall be distress of people on earth, and trembling, and fainting for fear, and for looking after the things that are to come upon the earth, and tribulation such as was not from the beginning and never shall be again. Will that be a golden age ? And if we will only consider this matter a little in the fear of God, it will be seen that this fanatical notion contradicts all Scripture, as it is contrary to this article of our common Christianity. . . . Here on earth, while the world lasts, we are in the militant Church, and have to suffer as God wills, waiting patiently for the true golden age, and the kingdom of the adorable Trinity—not in this world here on earth, but in the future kingdom of eternal glory and blessedness."—*Die XXI Art. Aug. Conf. in Predigen Erklärt*, pp. 1256–59.

A recent writer (*Das Tausend järige Reich gehört nicht der Vergangenheit, sondern der Zukunft an : Gütersloh*, 1860) also maintains that this article of the Confession condemns the modern ideas of the universal conversion of the world in the present order of things.

† See Hall's Protestant Confessions, pp. 88, 106.

‡ " Das ist nicht wahr, und hats eigentlich der Teuful zugerichtet, das man gläubt, die ganze Welt werde Christen werden. Der Teufel hats darum gethan, das er die recht-schaffene Lehre verdunkelte, das man sie nimmer recht verstünde. Darum hüte eich dafür. . . . Darum müst ihr es nicht also verstehen, das die ganze Welt und alle Menchen an Christum werden gläuben ; denn wir müssen immer das heilige creuz haben, dass ihr das mehrere Theil sind, die die Christen verfolgen."—*Walch's Luther*, vol. xi, cols. 1082–83.

resurrection of the dead.* All that God has promised concerning His Church in this dispensation, is, that by it the offer of salvation shall be made to mankind in general ; that the preaching of the Gospel shall be effective to the taking out of an elect people for His name ; and that Christ shall have His acknowledged representatives in every generation. No one pretends that there has been any failure in these respects. And as the great apostasies of the past argue no deficiency or miscarriage in these particulars, so, in all time to come, if but here and there a few faithful ones be found, it will be enough to vindicate every promise which the Church has on this side of the day of judgment.

We do not regard the Mosaic dispensation as a failure because the Jews as a body perverted it by their traditions, and crucified Him for whose kingdom it was given as the means of their preparation. It was never intended to supersede voluntary obedience on their part. They had opportunity to become the Lord's ransomed ones and to attain the highest honours of the kingdom. There was not a promise but was yea and amen, if they had been willing to comply with the conditions of it. But, as a people, they would not hearken ; apostatized, and were rejected. But the purposes of the dispensation did not fail. It was competent to do all that it proposed, and did prepare a people for the Lord, and effectually filled its place in the ongoing of the history of God's vast plans of mercy. And what the former dispensation was to the Jewish nation, the Gospel is to Christendom. The Christian Church is only a graft upon the same original stem. It has characteristics of its own, but its aim and underlying substance are essentially the same. Its promises are all conditioned after the same manner as the covenant with the natural posterity of Abraham. The breaking off of the graft cannot therefore be considered any more disastrous to the efficiency of the Gospel, than the breaking off of the " natural branches." The cases are precisely parallel, and the argument can only apply in one case as in the other. The Church of the old covenant apostatized, and was cast away ; but it accomplished God's purposes, which still went on as effectually as if no such defection had occurred. The Church of the new covenant may prove equally faithless, as all the prophecies show that it will ; and God may fulfil His threat also not to spare it ; and still no hindrance come to the progress of His great redemptive administrations. Man's perverseness surely cannot unmake God's purposes, or disarrange the divine plans. The Church will still fill out its place in the chain of the economies of His grace.

It is also distinctly told us, that the devil is the prince and god of this age ; that Christ's ministers in this dispensation are never anything but ambassadors at a foreign court ; that the saints are always mere pilgrims and strangers on the earth ; that the Gospel is ever to be preached only as a witness to the nations ; that when the Son of Man cometh, he shall hardly find faith on the earth ; that the days in which He shall come will be evil days, like the days of Noah before the flood ; and that the judgment will find mankind banded together in grand confederations of unparalleled rebellion and wickedness. And how thinking people can take in these unmistakable statements, and still cling to a theory of Providence which would make the plainly predicted apostasy of Christendom equivalent to a failure of the plans and promises of God, I cannot understand.

But I may not dwell longer upon this topic now. Whatever defections or judgments befall the nominal Church in any age, this is true, and clearly foreshown in these Epistles : that *God is never without His witness upon the earth*. With all the waning love, and false apostles, and Nicolaitane practices of Ephesus, there were some who could not bear those who were evil ; and who endured, laboured and suffered for the name of Jesus, and whose fidelity is to be rewarded with the joys of Paradise. With all the poverty and tribu-

* " Scimus item, quod Ecclesia in hoc vita subjecta sit cruci," etc.—*Mel. Op. Corp. Ref.*, vol. xxvi. p. 361,

lation and reproach of the Smyrnaotes, and the false ones of Satan's synagogue by whom they were afflicted, there were some rich in grace, faithful to the last, and destined to wear the crown of life, unhurt of the second death. With the proximity of the Church of Pergamos to Satan's throne, and the presence in it of the advocates of adulterous alliances, and systematizers of usurpation and evil, it had members who held fast to the Saviour's name, and kept the faith steadfast unto death, who are to receive of the hidden manna, and feast on heavenly bread, and wear the engraved gem of celestial privilege and honour. Even in Thyatira, where Jezebel herself enacted her damning uncleannesses, there was a remnant who kept aloof from Satan's depths, and wrought the deeds of faith and charity, and made good their title to share in the judgment of nations, and to receive the morning star. The deadness of Sardis was not so pervading, but a few names were left which had not defiled their garments, which had received the truth, and taught it, and lived it, and which are to walk with Christ in white, and to be confessed in heaven. The Philadelphians, though but a handful in the midst of false ones, and dwellers among those too much at ease in worldly comfort, are still a band of earnest brothers, on whom the doors cannot be shut, at whose feet Satan's synagogue shall be humbled, and who are to be kept out of the trying hour, transferred to the celestial temple, and adorned with the name of God, and the new Jerusalem, and the new name of Christ himself. And in among the sickening lukewarmness, pride, boasting and emptiness of the Laodiceans, there are some chastened ones whom Jesus loves, and some who hear His voice, and open unto Him, and sup with Him, and whose destiny is to sit with Him on His everlasting throne. And if in these seven pictures the whole length of the Church's history is embraced, the fact stands out, in noonday clearness, that God has His saints in every age.

When we survey the characteristics of our times,—the unrighteousness, the avarice, the lustfulness, the untruthfulness, the hypocrisy, the impiety, the crime, the hollow-heartedness, and the untold hidden iniquities which prevail in all circles of Church, business and State ; when we consider the wickednesses which are perpetrated by people who call themselves Christians, and the shameless worldliness of professors of religion, and the wreck of all distinctive doctrinal belief, and the prostitutions of the house of God and the sacred desk itself to vanity, politics, selfishness, sensuality, and base trickery in the name of Jesus ; when we look at the insubordination which is left to run riot in the great majority of so-called Christian families, and the secret vices and concealed blood-guilty crimes of so-called Christian husbands and wives, and of the utter moral emptiness, headiness and incontinence of the mass of the busiest and noisiest modern religionists ; when we contemplate the goings forth of sin in these days, like Death on the pale horse, with hell following in its train, and come to count up the names of those in our congregations whom we can confidently set down as true and thorough saints of God,—we are sometimes tempted, with the Psalmist, to say, " All men are liars," and to doubt whether God has not resigned His dominion over mankind, and abandoned them to be drifted, by the whirlwinds of their own passions, to irremediable ruin. But, with all the hard things which we are in honesty and fairness compelled to write against the present population of Christendom, God has not left Himself without witnesses, and still has His true people, who have not kissed their hands nor bowed their knees to the reigning idolatry of the times. Earthy and vile as the congest may be, there is gold in it, as there was an Enoch and a Noah in the generation before the flood, and a Lot even in Sodom itself. Amid all Christianity's corruptions, there has always been some standing out against them. The pure ideal has never failed to produce some proximate realization of itself. Dreary as the annals of the Church appear, both in prophetic and historic records, the student of them still finds his path skirted with spiritual verdure ; and in the distant scenery, examples of faith, purity, love, heroism, devotion and obedience, are never once entirely out of view, the loveliest often being found in the by-paths, and encountered where they would be least expected. Even in the darkest eras, imbedded in neglected chronicles, noble names are to be found, sparkling with the radiance of every Christian grace. And by a sort of system of compensation, in nearly every instance, while darkness and death reigned in one place, light and life were vigorous at another. " Contemporary with the waning of piety in Antioch, was its waxing in Milan. When the Churches of Alexandria and Carthage were sinking in the decrepitude of formalism, the Churches of Gaul were battling the vices of imperial civilization, and the rudeness and disorder of barbarism. The era of the early growth of Rome's impious pretensions was the era of Ireland's light and life, holiness and beauty. While Mahomet was God's avenger on Syria and Egypt, the monks of Iona were studying their Bible, and Scotch missionaries were crossing the Anglo-Saxon border and entering the heart of Germany. As Gregory IV was encouraging the sons of the Emperor Lewis in parricidal wars, Claude was preaching the truth at Turin, and adorning it with a holy life. When the pontifical court at Avignon was disgracing the name of religion by luxury and vice, pious men were writing books, and preaching sermons, and practising godly virtue, in Teutonic cities. When the night of superstition and despotism was getting blacker than ever in France, the morning star of the Reformation rose on England. When Italian fields were covered with rotten stubble, Bohemia was whitening to the harvest."* And so, in all the ages, there have never failed some blessed offsets to the ever downward tendency of things. Nor will it ever be, in the darkest and dreadest days of Christendom's apostasy, that there will be none to stand up for God and His pure truth, or that His true prople shall fail from the earth.

Who, then, are they ? And what are their characteristics ? Nowhere in the Scriptures may we find a more direct and satisfactory answer to these inquiries, than is furnished us in these Epistles. Christ himself here looks down with flaming eyes upon His people, and with a certainty infallible points His finger to those whom He acknowledges, and for whom His everlasting rewards are in reserve. The field which thus opens to our survey is full of inviting riches of instruction and Evangelic truth, in which it would be well for us to linger, and to wander back and forth to note each word, and hint, and incident. The merest glance is all that we can now attempt ; but even that will be enough to reveal, in vivid outline, who and what are the saints, and the partakers in the honours of transforming grace.

First of all, they are *Ephesians*—people of warm and kindled hearts, glowing with the impulses of ardent love and zeal toward Christ, as the " chief among ten thousand, and altogether lovely."

> Talk they of morals, O thou bleeding Lamb !
> The best morality is love to Thee.

Love to Jesus is the root of all true Christianity. It is the perfection of faith, and it is the fulfilling of the law. The heart that takes fire at the mention of the Saviour's name,—that swells with sympathetic ardour at the story of His life, and deeds, and death, and triumph ; that looks to Him in His hidden home as the Lord of its affections and the chief joy of its life ; that is bound and drawn, by sweet constraints of living gratitude, to untiring devotion and obedience ; that is not content but in leaning with John upon His breast, or clinging with Mary to His blessed feet ; that thrills with the contemplation of seeing Him as He is, and being with Him forever ; and that pines, and sighs, and ever prays in His absence, " Come, Lord Jesus, come quickly," —is the heart most surely in harmony with heaven, and on which the favour of the Lord of the Church is most unmistakably set. The primal source of all defective saintship, and of all that the Divine Judge censures in any of His professed people, is the wane of love. Let a man be alive in love to God, and

---

* Stoughton's Ages of Christendom, p. 431.

make it his joy to give his whole heart to Jesus, and his title is clear, and his acceptance sure.

And as the fruit of their affection, Christ's true people are further characterized by unswerving and uncompromising devotion to their profession. They have taken Christ for their Lord, and they will know no obedience but obedience to Him. For Him they labour, for Him they endure, and His they count themselves to be, to the full extent of all they have and are. Pledged to stand out unshaken against whatsoever is wrong, they will have no communion with evil ones, and will not fellowship with such as say they are apostles and are not, and hate and loathe the deeds of tyranny which would tread down any in whom God's image is, and are not afraid to speak their condemnation of wrongdoers, whatever may be their pretensions or their place. There is a tendency, in these days, to account that the purest Christianity which has the largest " *charity*," as it is called, and toleration for everybody and everything, and which disdains social differences for opinion's sake, or separations and controversies on account of the faith. But that is not the sort of Christianity which our Lord and Judge commends in these Epistles. Those whom He here approves as His true people, are such as cannot bear those who are evil, such as test men's claims to apostolicity, and expose their falsities, and hate the deeds of the Nicolaitanes, and stand to the truth as they have received it from the Lord, earnestly contending for the faith.

Another characteristic is, that they are poor, and reproached, and tried, and often persecuted unto death. Smyrnaotes, to a greater or less extent, are all the true saints of God. It seems to be one of the unvarying laws of this dispensation, that the absence of censure from heaven conducts through affliction on earth. The richest and most independent man, if he be a true Christian, is quite convinced that he is one of the very poorest and most helpless of God's creatures. He is poor in spirit, and his earthly possessions are no riches to him. And if any would live godly in Christ Jesus, it is useless to think of exemption from trials, reproaches and persecutions. People may serve the devil all their lives ; and if they only manage to do it decently, not a word from the world shall ever be said against them, and not a frown need they fear. But let them start in earnest, honest Christianity, and they are snubbed, and sneered at, and put out of the synagogue, and made to hear of it and feel it at many points. Pious people, somehow, have ever been afflicted people. It seems to be God's plan to make his children ill at ease in this world, that they may the more earnestly long for that which is to come. The mass of them have been martyrs, living martyr lives, if not dying martyr deaths. The holiest men are always suffering men. There is no saintship which is exempt from trial, sorrow, and this world's frowns. Nor may any one be a Christian of the purer and better sort, with whom the world is satisfied, on whom earthly fortune ever smiles, and of whom no spiteful ill is ever said. Woe unto you, when all speak well of you, is the word of Christ himself.

But along with this, we find another feature. Afflicted, poor and persecuted, God's true people cheerfully bear whatever He appoints, and keep Christ's word of patient endurance. The saints of Ephesus did bear for the Saviour's name, and fainted not. Those of Smyrna were faithful to the last, as illustrated in the case of Polycarp, who preferred burning to a compromise of his faith, and found place for songs and thanksgivings amid the flames that consumed him. Those of Pergamos held fast Christ's name, and did not deny the faith of Him, and stood out in glad adherence to the truth, under the very sword of the executioner. Those of Thyatira and Philadelphia are specially commended for their endurance in the midst of falsity and suffering, and held fast in joyous prospect of the speedy coming of their Divine Deliverer. And so it is ever the character of God's saints to choose rather to suffer affliction with the people of God, than to enjoy the pleasures of sin for a season, esteeming the reproach of Christ greater riches than all the treasures in Egypt.

And if there is yet another mark of saintship singled out in these Epistles, it is the profound regard which true believers have for the recompense of the reward at the coming and revelation of Jesus Christ. There is a Paradise of God on which their hopes are set. There is a crown of life at which they aim. There is a heavenly sustenance and gem of celestial privilege and honour, and a sceptre of holy dominion, and an inheritance of the morning star, and an acknowledgment before God and angels, and an enrolment among principalities in the eternal empire, and a session with Jesus on His everlasting throne, on which their hearts are set. They believe that these things exist, and that they are meant for them, and that it is the merciful will of God that they should have them ; and they wait for them, looking not at the things which are seen, but at the things which are not seen. Seeing that Christ has given these promises, they embrace them, and confess that they are strangers and pilgrims on the earth, " looking for that blessed hope, the glorious appearing of God our Saviour."

What, then, is to become of these people ? Many of them have fallen asleep ; and daily one and another of them, in every age, has been consigned to the tomb. Scattered over all the world their wasting ashes lie, whilst the places that once knew them know them no more. But these Epistles take very little account of death. The most that they say of it is that Christ has passed through it and revived, and that He has the keys of both it and Hades. Since then, it is hardly any more accounted death. The addresses to the Churches are given as if those same Churches were to continue through all the ages, and to meet the scenes of the great consummation just as they were living at the time. Hence, the resurrection also is but inferentially embraced. It is, indeed, presupposed in all the seven promises ; but the short hiatus in the lives of individual saints is treated as hardly worth being embraced among the greater things of this vision. The return of Jesus and His Apocalypse to His Church is the master theme ; and the preparation for that, and the rewards then to come to the saints, absorbs everything. And when Christ comes, it will be the same with those faithful ones of His that sleep, as with those who may be still alive and waiting for Him. There will be no advantage to the one class above the other as respects what is to follow. When the Lord himself shall descend from heaven with a shout, with the voice of the archangel and the trump of God, first of all, the saints that sleep in Him shall rise. This is plainly taught us in the apostolic messages. And when they have been thus recalled, whatever is further said is the same with regard to them as to those living saints who shall not have died at all.

One very striking statement concerning them, is that they are to be kept out of the hour of temptation—out of that season of trial which is then to come upon the whole world, to try those who dwell upon the earth instead of cherishing a heavenly citizenship. (See chap. 3 : 10.) How this deliverance is to be wrought, St. Paul explains. The saints, both living and resurrected, are to be miraculously snatched away from earth to heaven, suddenly, and in the twinkling of an eye. His own unmistakable words are : " Then we who are living, who remain, shall be caught up together with them (the resurrected ones) in the clouds, to meet the Lord in the air." (1 Thess. 4 : 17.) The Saviour himself has also given assurances to the same effect, where He says : " I tell you, in that night there shall be two in one bed : the one shall be taken, and the other shall be left. Two women shall be grinding together : the one shall be taken, and the other shall be left. Two shall be in the field : the one shall be taken, and the other left. And they answered and said unto him, Where [or Whither], Lord ? And he said unto them, Wheresoever the Body is, thither will the eagles be gathered together." (Luke 17 : 34-37.) And to this same marvellous occurrence, which Paul speaks of as one of the great mysteries (1 Cor. 15 : 51), do the words at the head of this discourse refer. " I saw," says John, " and behold, a door set open in the heaven, and the former voice which I heard as of a trumpet, speaking with me, saying, *Come up hither.*"

That door opened in heaven is the door of the ascension of the saints. That trumpet voice is the same which Paul describes as recalling the sleepers in Jesus, and to which the Saviour refers as the signal by which His elect are gathered from the four winds, but which we have no reason to suppose shall be heard or understood except by those whom it is meant to summon to the skies. And that " COME UP HITHER " is for every one in John's estate, even the gracious and mighty word of the returning Lord himself, by virtue of which they that wait for Him shall renew their strength, and mount up with wings as eagles. (Is. 40 : 31.) And thus, as the Psalmist sung, the Lord will hide them in the secret place of His presence from the vexation of man, and screen them in a tabernacle from the contradiction of tongues. (Ps. 31 : 19, 20.)

Such, then, is the termination of the earthly career of God's elect, for which the saints of every age have waited, longed and prayed.*

And such is the next great scene which may now be any day expected. I know of nothing in the prophecies of God, unless it should be the mere deepening of the signs that have already appeared, which yet remains to be fulfilled before this sudden summons from the skies : " Come, my people, enter thou into thy chambers, and shut thy doors about thee : hide thyself as it were a little moment, until the indignation be overpast ; for, behold, the Lord cometh out of his place to punish the inhabitants of the earth for their iniquity." (Is. 26 : 20, 21.) Any one of these days or nights, and certainly before many more years have passed, all this shall be accomplished. Some of these days or nights,—while men are busy with the common pursuits and cares of life, and everything is rolling on in its accustomed course,—unheralded, unbelieved, and unknown to the gay world, here one, and there another, shall secretly disappear, " *caught up* " like Enoch, who " was not found because God had translated him." Invisibly, noiselessly, miraculously, they shall vanish from the company and fellowship of those about them, and ascend to their returning Lord. Strange announcements shall be in the morning papers of missing ones. Strange accounts shall be whispered around in the circles of business and society. And for the first time will apostate Christendom, and the slow in heart to believe *all* that the prophets have written, have the truth brought home, that no such half-Christianity as theirs is sufficient to put men among the favourites of the Lord.

Brethren and friends, these are neither dreams nor fables. They are realities, set forth in the infallible truth of God, and as literally true as anything else

---

* " At the voice of the archangel, the dead saints rise from the dust ; the living saints, in a moment—in the twinkling of an eye—are changed ; and both together are rapt up far above the clouds, to meet the Lord in the air, long before He is seen by the inhabitants of the earth."—*Cunningham on Apocalypse*, 3d. ed., p. 491.

" The being taken up to meet the Lord before the time of trial and judgment, would seem to be the manifest import of the promise to the faithful, in the Epistle to the Church at Philadelphia, as also that of our Lord's exhortation in Luke 21 : 36."—*Richard Chester, Vicar of Ballyclough, Mallow.*

" Ere judgment comes on Christendom, the true Church will have been, like Enoch, translated to heaven. . . . We are not comforted by the assurance of our being gathered to the grave in peace, but by the hope of being gathered to meet the Lord in the air, so that, when the judgments come, we shall not be amid the scene on which they are poured, but in the heavens whence they issue."—*Plain Papers*, pp. 94-96.

" It is evident, from 2 Cor. 5 : 4, that we are not to conceive of the transfiguration of the body as taking place at the end and in the general resurrection, for the apostle wishes it for his own person instead of death."—*Auberlen on Dan. and Rev.*, p. 332.

" Daniel appears to be a type of those kept out of the hour of temptation. When all nations, kindreds and people are required to worship the image of the plain of Dura, he is not there."—*Apocalypse Expounded*, vol. i, p. 207.

" John 14 : 1-3, doth absolutely require an assumption from the earth of all the saints, after the same manner as Christ was taken up. And to this great head of doctrine, all those legends of the Catholic Church, concerning the assumption of the blessed Virgin, and other saints, do point. By being taken up, to be clothed upon by our house which is from heaven, I believe that Christ's people will be delivered out of their tribulation."—*Irving on the Apoc.*, vol. ii, p. 1024.

in the inspired Word. And as you value the prize of our high calling in Christ Jesus, and take this holy book as an unfailing guide, be not faithless, but believing. And if you feel yourself unready for such events, do not think of setting them aside by scoffs and sneers. If they are in the purpose of God, as He so plainly says they are, and as I conscientiously believe they are, your unbelief cannot alter them. Better bestir yourself to be prepared, with your loins girded and your lamp trimmed and burning. There is chance for you yet to be among these favoured ones whom God has engaged thus to keep out of the judgment plagues and sorrows ; but that this opportunity shall remain to you for another year, or month, or week, or day, or hour, no living man or angel of heaven is authorized to promise. What you do must be done quickly. To your knees, then, to your Bibles, and to the mercy seat of your God, O man, O woman ! " Rend your heart, and not your garments, and turn unto the Lord your God." Let not another day pass leaving you still in your sins ; " for in such an hour as you think not, the Son of man cometh." And may God in mercy grant us each the grace and diligence to be found of Him in peace, without spot, and blameless.

D

LECTURE NINTH

THE MIRACULOUS TRANSLATION—A HEAVENLY SCENE—RELATES TO A TIME SUBSEQUENT TO THE PRESENT CHURCH-PERIOD—COMES BEFORE THE JUDGMENT OF THE WORLD—IS TRULY PROPHETIC—THE THRONE OF JUDGMENT—THE RAINBOW ENCIRCLING IT—THE SEVEN TORCHES—THE GLASSY SEA—THE TWENTY-FOUR ELDERS—SUCCESSION IN THE GATHERING OF THE SAINTS—THE FOUR LIVING ONES—THE BANNERS OF ISRAEL—THE CHERUBIM—THE HEAVENLY ADMINISTRATORS OF THE NEW ORDER—THE DIGNITIES PROPOSED BY THE GOSPEL—AN APPEAL TO EMBRACE THEM.

REV. 4: 1–11. (Revised Text.) After these things I saw, and behold, a door set open in the heaven, and the former voice which I heard, as of a trumpet, speaking with me, saying, Come up hither, and I will show thee the things which must take place after these things.

Immediately I became in the Spirit, and, behold, a throne was set in the heaven, and upon the throne one sitting; and he that was sitting [was] like in appearance to a jasper and a sardine stone, and a rainbow encircled the throne, in appearance like to an emerald; and around the throne twenty-four thrones, and upon the twenty-four thrones elders sitting, clothed in white garments, and on their heads golden crowns. And out of the throne go forth lightnings, and voices, and thunders; and seven torches of fire burning before the throne, which are the seven Spirits of God : and before [or, the prospect from] the throne as it were a ¡glassy sea, like unto crystal; and amidst the throne, and around the throne, four living ones, full of eyes before and behind; and the living one the first like a lion, and the second living one like a young ox, and the third living one having the face like a man, the fourth living one like a flying eagle. And the four living ones, each one of them had around them six wings apiece, and within they are full of eyes; and they have not rest day and night, saying, Holy, Holy, Holy [repeated eight times in Codex Sinaiticus], Lord God the Almighty, who was, and who is, and who is to come.

And whensoever the living ones give glory, and honour, and thanks to Him that sitteth on the throne, to Him that liveth for the ages of the ages, the twenty-four elders fall down before Him that sitteth on the throne, and worship Him that liveth for the ages of the ages, and cast their crowns before the throne, saying : Thou art worthy, O Lord and our God, to receive the glory, and honour, and the power, because Thou didst create all things, and by Thy will they were, and were created.

I HAVE said that this open door in heaven, and this calling up of the Apocalyptic seer through that door into heaven, indicate to us the manner in which Christ intends to fulfil His promise to keep certain of His saints " out of the hour of temptation ; " and by what means it is that those who " watch and pray always " shall " escape " the dreadful sorrows with which the present world, in its last years, will be visited. Those of them that sleep in their graves, shall be recalled from among the dead ; and those of them who shall be found living at the time, " shall be changed, in a moment, in the twinkling of an eye ; " and both classes " shall be caught up together in the clouds, to meet the Lord in the air." The same voice which John heard, even " the voice as of a trumpet," whether dead or living, they shall hear, saying to them, " COME UP HITHER." And there shall attend it a change and transfer as sudden and miraculous as in his case. And as the seven Epistles show us these faithful ones in their sufferings, conflicts, virtues, and victories on earth, the chapter before us carries us up to the contemplation of their estate and dignities in heaven. It is high and peculiarly holy ground that here rises to our view, and it becomes us to venture upon it with measured and reverent steps. It would seem, indeed, as if it were rather a subject for angels than for men ; but God hath caused it to be written for us, and has pronounced special blessing upon them that read, hear, and keep what has been thus recorded for our learning. " Secret things belong unto the Lord," and we may not trespass on that reserved, mysterious realm ; " but those things which are revealed, belong unto us, and to our children forever ; " and it is our duty, as well as our privilege, humbly to inquire, and to search diligently into what has been prophesied of the grace and the glory which is to come to the saints.

Discarding, then, that false humility, which is the offspring or the cloak of spiritual sloth, let us, in the fear of God, go forward with our investigations, and stir ourselves up to the effort to obtain some distinct ideas of what the blessed Saviour has thought it so important to show to His Church. Happy shall we be if the sublime King but admit us into His court, though He may not now take us into His counsel. We notice :

I.   SOME OF THE SURROUNDINGS AND RELATIONS OF THE VISION.
II. THE PARTICULARS BROUGHT TO VIEW IN IT.

And may Almighty God open our hearts to the subject, and the subject to our hearts !

The scene of this vision is *in heaven ;*—not in the temple, as some have represented. The door which John saw, was an opening " in the heaven." The voice that he heard came from above. It commanded him to " Come up." And it was potent ; for " immediately " he " became in the Spirit." It wrought an instantaneous rapture, so that the next opening of his eyes disclosed his presence in a supernal region. There is no allusion to Jerusalem or to its temple. The whole scene is heavenly, and relates only to what is heavenly. It belongs to a realm above the earth, and above all the sanctuaries of the earth.

The Rabbins dreamed of seven heavens. Paul speaks of three, in the highest of which he " heard unspeakable words, which it is not lawful for a man to utter." But as John was commanded to write what he saw, and to communicate it to the Churches, and Paul was forbidden to describe what he saw and heard, this would seem to be a different heaven from that called " the third." The truth is, that anything above the earth—the upper air, the region of the clouds, as well as the region of the stars, and beyond the stars— the scriptures call " heaven." Other circumstances connected with this subject indicate, that what is here referred to, is simply *the sky.* " The sign of the Son of Man " is to be displayed in the empyrean, no further off from the earth than to be visible to men, yet it is to appear " in heaven." The place where the returning Saviour is to meet His resurrected and translated saints, is, " in the air "—" in the clouds." The heaven of this vision would therefore seem to be, indefinitely, the regions above us—the firmament—the higher portions of the atmosphere which envelops the earth. This, however, I take to be certain, that the location of what John beheld, was not earth, but above the earth, and quite unconnected with the earth.

Whether there was a literal, bodily transportation of the seer from the earth to the regions of space, is not stated, nor inferable from the description. Perhaps the apostle himself was not able to perceive how it was. Paul could not tell whether he was " in the body, or out of the body," when he " was caught up." This only he knew, that he was somehow present in " the third heaven," and that that presence was the same to him as a bodily transportation, equally real, and equally effective. It was the same in John's case. He tells us that he was called by a mighty voice to come up into heaven, and straightway " became *in the Spirit* "—in some mysterious, miraculous, ecstatic state, wrought by the power of God—which was, to all intents and purposes, a complete translation from Patmos to the hidden sky. He was not dead ; he was not in a mere swoon ; he had all his senses entire ; his ears heard ; his eyes saw ; his heart felt ; his capacity to weep and to speak continued with him ; and the thing was, in all respects, the same as a bodily carrying up to the heavenly sphere, where he found what he was commanded to describe.

We notice also, that this vision sets forth what is to be *after* the fulfilment of the vision and letters concerning the Churches. The links of consecutiveness are distinctly expressed, and are by no means to be overlooked. The declared object for which the apostle was called up into the sky, was to be shown—not what existed in heaven at the time, as some have mistakenly thought—but "*the things which must take place* AFTER" what he had already seen and described. The seven Churches, in all the amplitude of their representative significance, were first to run their course, and the order of things to which they belonged was to touch upon its end, before one jot of what is here portrayed was to be realized.* As John was called up just to be shown " the things which must take place *after these things*," of course, all that he saw and heard consequent upon that rapture, can only be referred to the period next following the things of the first vision. That vision, as we have been led to conclude, and as we think must be admitted, embraces the whole continuity of the dispensation under which we are now living, and takes in the entire earthly Church-state, from the time of the apostles to the end of the age ; which is at Christ's coming again to receive His people to himself. That "*end*" we regard as very near ; but so long as it is yet future, the time to which this vision refers is also future. It relates to things which do not exist as yet, and which cannot become reality till that to which they are specifically said to be subsequent is fulfilled. It is therefore a picture of things in the sky, immediately upon the first movement of the Saviour in His coming to judgment, marked by the miraculous seizing away of the saints from their associates on earth to the clouds of heaven.

It is also to be observed, that the things foreshown in this vision, whilst they come after the first interference with the present order, still *precede* the great tribulation, and the scenes of judicial visitation upon the apostate Church and the guilty world. Indeed, it is from what is here depictured, that those inflictions proceed. What John sees, is permanent. It continues through all that comes after, the same as seen at the first. The throne, the Elders, the Living ones, retain their places unchanged, and have direct connection with all that subsequently transpires. Nay, the action of the seals, in chapters six and seven which brings the great tribulation upon the world, and the still remoter action of the trumpets and vials, and the whole catena of judgments described in the afterpart of this book, proceed from, and depend more or less on, the scene of glory and power represented in these two chapters. The realization of what they describe must, therefore, fall intermediately between the first removal of saints from earth, and the forthcoming of the great troubles, and the destruction of Babylon and Antichrist. In other words, it is a scene of things to be manifested in heaven, immediately succeeding the beginning of the judgment of the Church, and preceding the judgment of the world of apostates and sinners. It is a picture of the results of the former, and of the source and instrument of the latter.

There have been writers, I will not call them interpreters, who regard the contents of these two chapters as a mere scenic exordium to the revelations that follow, intended to impress the writer or the reader's mind with the divinity and solemnity of what was to be communicated. Some have even fallen so low as to affirm that it is simply the creation of the writer's own fancy, meant to set forth how deeply he was impressed and pervaded with a sense of God's power and glory, and hence, in how fit a state he was to take in and express the mysteries of the divine purposes. For such bald rationalism I have neither sympathy nor respect. If there is anything divine in the book, and everything in it proves to me that it is divine, the announcement of the object for which John was taken up to heaven to see these sights, must also be divine. It was a trumpet-voice from heaven that made it ; and its effect was instantaneously miraculous, carrying the prophet by some mysterious unlocking of

---

* " From the expression, ' I will show thee what shall be after these things,' we gather, that the facts set out under this vision are subsequent to the facts set out under the former vision ; that all in the former vision which cometh within the condition of time, is anterior to all in this vision which comes within the same condition."—*Irving in loc.*

his inner nature, quite away from earth. And that voice declared that John was thus called and transported to see, not what was to beget seriousness in him, or merely to persuade the reader that there was something of moment to be told, but WHAT MUST TAKE PLACE after the fulfilment of the things pertaining to the Churches. What he was to be shown was not *to prepare for* the prophecy, but was itself the head and front of the prophecy. What he was to see was to become reality ; it was to come to pass ; it was in due time to be history and fact. And to apply this divine affirmation only to what follows these chapters, and not to what these chapters themselves contain, is like undertaking to render the play of Hamlet, with the part of Hamlet left out. No, if there is any sacred prediction in the case, these chapters are a most vital element of it, without which, indeed, the remainder is but imperfectly intelligible. And upon evidences as solid as those which prove the inspiration of this book, I hold, that these two chapters are as substantially prophetic as any other part. They do not relate directly to the earth, but they compass a very grand part of the results of God's gracious doings in the earth for all these ages past, and a very grand part of what is to affect the earth for all the recurring ages of the future.

With these points settled, we are now prepared to look at the particulars which the magnificent picture brings to our contemplation.

The first thing named, and that which is at once the central object of the vision, and of all that follows it, is A THRONE. The Scriptures continually speak of *thrones*, in connection with the sovereignty and majesty of God. They tell us that " the Lord hath prepared His throne in the heavens, and His kingdom ruleth over all." (Ps. 103 : 19.) Among the last words of the preceding chapter, Christ refers to His throne, and the Father's throne. And here the apostle sees *"a throne in the heaven."* No intimations are given of the form of the magnificent object. The throne on which Isaiah saw the Lord, was " high and lifted up ; " and in another vision John saw a throne, " great and white ; " but everywhere we are left to think of the power and authority of which the throne is a symbol, rather than of any particular form or material structure. A visible image was presented to the eye of the seer, but he does not stop to tell us what it was like. It was simply an undescribed, and perhaps indescribable, seat of grandeur, greatness, majesty, and dominion.

Nor was it the eternal throne of the Father, at least not in the position and relations which it occupies anterior to the time to which this vision relates. John sees it, not as long since fixed and settled in this locality and form, but just as it was taking up its rest in this place. It was *being set* as he was looking ; ἰδοὺ, ἔκειτο. The expression is in a tense which denotes unfinished action, reaching its completion at the time of the seeing. Dean Alford objects to the phrase " *was set*," as giving too much the idea that the *placing* of the throne formed part of the vision. But this is just exactly what the original expresses ; and it is important, as showing that this vision refers to a new order of things, which first comes into being at the time to which the vision refers. The apostle's language implies, that the act of the placing of the throne where he saw it, was only being completed at the moment of his looking. That moment was the moment of his being called up from earth into heaven. The rapture of the saints, then, is the point of transition, where the present dispensation begins to end, and another, of which this throne is the centre, takes its commencement. The passage is an exact parallel, both as to subject and phraseology, to Daniel 7 : 9, where the prophet says : " I beheld till the thrones were *set* (not *cast down*, as our version has it), and the Ancient of days did sit, whose throne was like the fiery flame." The vision embraced *the placing* of the throne, as well as the throne itself, and the locality it occupied.*

" *And upon the throne one sitting.*" There is no name mentioned, and no figure described ; but we can be at no loss to distinguish who is meant. John was manifestly filled with mysterious awe, and his words sufficiently

* So agrees also the author of " The Apocalypse Expounded by Scripture," vol. ii, p. 13.

intimate that he was looking upon " the unnameable, indescribable Godhead," in which Father, Son, and Holy Ghost are consubstantial, and the same. And yet there was visible manifestation.

" *He that was sitting* [*was*] *like in appearance to a jasper and a sardine stone ;* "—not as to shape, for Deity has no shape, but in colour and flashing brilliancy. The scriptural representations of the jasper are, that it is " most precious," crystalline, and purple in hue. The sardine, or sardius, is also described as exceedingly precious, and of a beautiful bright, red, carnation colour. It is capable of a particularly high and lasting polish. Uniting the qualities of tint and brilliancy belonging to the purer specimens of these precious gems, we have the appearance of flames, without their smokiness— a pure, purple, fiery, red, crystalline, flashing light. And this was the appearance of the unnameable and indescribable occupant of this equally indescribable throne.

" *And a rainbow encircled the throne, in appearance like to an emerald.*" The rainbow is one of the most beautiful and majestic of earthly appearances. It is the token of God's covenant with all flesh, never again to destroy the earth or its inhabitants, as in the flood. (Gen. 9 : 11, 17). Encircling this throne, the intimation is, that, although a throne of judgment, it is not a throne of destruction, but one of conservation, which bears with it the remembrance and the stability of the ancient promise. From what the apostle subsequently saw go forth from this throne, and the shakings and overturnings in heaven and earth of which it was to be the source and means, fears might naturally arise as to the continuity of the earth as an organized structure for the habitation of God's creatures. But this rainbow around the throne forever scatters such apprehensions. All these ministrations are under the symbol of the Noachian covenant, which standeth forever. The idea that this world, and its creature inhabitants, are to pass into oblivion, is a foolish notion of poets, against which we have the special pledge and covenant of God, rehearsed in nearly every summer shower, and borne aloft as one of the glorious decorations of the judgment throne itself.

And yet, the intimation is, that the fulfilment of that covenant is not to be always in the course of nature, as we now have it. The true iris is around the throne, but there is a change in it now. Its prevailing hue is light *green*— " in appearance like to an emerald,"—which is an appearance having something additional to nature, or nature modified, with one part of its exalted and strengthened beyond its wont. The jasper and the sardine flash terrible glory, but over them is the soft-beaming emerald of promise and hope— mercy remembered in wrath—salvation over-spanning the appearance of consuming fire.

" *And out of the throne go forth lightnings, and voices, and thunders.*" These demonstrate that the throne is one of judgment, and that wrath is about to proceed from it. When God was about to visit Egypt's sins upon her, He " sent thunder [in Heb. ' voices '], and hail, and fire ran along upon the ground." And Pharaoh sent and said, " Intreat the Lord that there be no more voices of God." (Ex. 9 : 23, 28.) When He wished to show Israel the terribleness of His anger with sin, " there were thunders and lightnings, and a thick cloud upon the mount, and the voice of the trumpet exceeding loud." (Ex. 19 : 16.) When He sent forth His wrath upon the Philistines, " the Lord thundered with a great thunder on that day upon the Philistines, and discomfited them, and they were smitten before Israel." (1 Sam. 7 : 10.) So also was His displeasure expressed at Israel's demand for a king. Samuel said, " The Lord shall send thunder and rain [in wheat-harvest], that ye may perceive and see that your wickedness is great, which ye have done in the sight of the Lord, in asking you a king. And the Lord sent thunder and rain that day, and all the people greatly feared." (1 Sam. 12 : 17, 18.) These instances show us, that this is not a throne of grace, but a throne of judgment. These lightnings, thunders, and voices, proceeding from it, tell of justice and wrath to be visited upon transgressors. The river of water of life is gone, and in its place is the terror and fire of judgment and death.

"*And seven torches of fire burning before the throne, which are the seven Spirits of God.*" These are not candlesticks or lamps within doors, but torches borne aloft without, speaking preparation for battle. When Gideon went forth in vengeance against the Midianites, his three hundred men took each a burning torch in his left hand, and a trumpet in his right, " and they cried, THE SWORD OF THE LORD, *and of Gideon.*" (Judges 7 : 16, 20.) So in the prophetic announcement of the going forth of God's wrath upon Nineveh, the destroyer is described as displaying " flaming torches in the day of his preparation." (Nahum 2 : 3, 4.) So the throne which is set for the judgment of the world, hath before it its " torches of fire burning," charged with the fulness of consuming vengeance upon all the enemies of God ; for they are " seven." The Spirit of God, in all His plenitude, is these seven torches. That Spirit descended on Jesus as a dove ; but here He is the " Spirit of judgment, the Spirit of burning." (Is. 4 : 4.) It is not peaceful *light*, but flaming indignation, which is betokened, which at last sets the world on fire, producing that day " that shall burn as an oven, and all the proud, yea, and all that do wickedly, shall be stubble, and it shall burn them up, that it shall leave them neither root nor branch." (Mal. 4 : 1.) The throne speaks vengeance upon the guilty, and the Spirit of God is the spirit of the throne, the spirit of devouring fire.

" *And before* [or, *the prospect from*] *the throne as it were a glassy sea, like unto crystal.*" When Moses, and Aaron, and Nadab, and Abihu, and the seventy elders of Israel, went up unto the Lord on Sinai, " they saw the God of Israel ; and there was under His feet as it were a paved work of a sapphire stone, and as it were the body of heaven in clearness." (Ex. 24 : 10, 11.) And in the vision of Ezekiel, the floor or plain on which the throne of God rested, was " the likeness of the firmament, as the colour of the terrible crystal." (Ezek. 1 : 22.) These several descriptions explain each other. This throne, and all surrounding it, or connected with it, had its place upon a plain, which resembled a wide sea, solid, transparent, and full of inexpressible beauty, splendour, and majesty. Though in the air, it was not hung there. It had a base. There is a pavement, like a sapphire stone, like a clear, cerulean, golden *mer de glace*, on which it, as the whole celestial assemblage, rests ; as we also read of the street of the heavenly city being " pure gold, as it were transparent glass." (Rev. 21 : 21.) Heaven is not a world of mists and shadows, but of substance and beautiful realities.

" *And around the throne, twenty-four thrones ; and upon the twenty-four thrones, Elders sitting, clothed in white garments, and on their heads golden crowns.*" There was more than one throne. In the centre, conspicuous, and majestic beyond description, was the throne of Deity ; but in a wide circle around it were twenty-four other thrones, distinct and glorious, but smaller and lower than that which is, by eminence, called "*The Throne.*" Our translators call them " *seats ;* " but the original word is the same in the case of the twenty-four in the circle, as in that in the centre. They are all " *seats*," certainly ; but a particular kind of seats, *regal* seats, seats of majesty and dominion, seats of royal assessorship with the enthroned One. Nor can we be much at a loss as to the persons who occupy them.

They are not angels, but human beings. This is ascertained by the song they sing, in which they speak of having been gathered out of the tribes and peoples of the earth. (Chap. 5 : 9.)

They are not the patriarchs, Jews, or apostles, only ; for they are from " *every* tribe, and tongue, and people, and nation." (Chap. 5 : 9.)

They are not unfallen beings, but ransomed sinners ; for they give honour to Christ for redeeming them—" *Thou redeemedst* US *by Thy blood.*"* (Chap. 5 : 9.)

---

* Ἠγόρασας ἡμᾶς. Some critics and expositors have rejected this ἡμᾶς (US), for the reason that it is omitted in the Codex Alexandrinus, and in the Ethiopic version ; though the latter is not much more than a loose paraphrase. The Codex Sinaiticus, however,

They are not disembodied spirits of the saints, but glorified subjects of grace ; for they are enthroned, crowned, and robed in white, which is a fruition of blessedness and honour which is everywhere reserved till after the resurrection and the glorifying rapture. Paul tells us that he was to receive his " crown of righteousness," not at his decease, but " *at that day* "— the day of Christ's coming to awake and gather His saints,—and that the same is true of " *all* " who are to be partakers of that crown. (2 Tim. 4 : 8.) The entire scriptural doctrine concerning the state of the dead, forbids the idea that disembodied souls are already crowned and enthroned, although at rest in the bosom of God. Such rewards, Christ is to bring with Him (see chap. 22 : 12 ; 11 : 18 ; Is. 52 : 11) ; hence, no one receives them until He comes, recalls the sleepers, and completes that redemption of power for which all things wait. (See Rom. 8 : 22, 23.) The coronation time, is the resurrection time ; and no one can be crowned until he is either resurrected if dead, or translated if living. Any other doctrine overthrows some of the plainest teachings of the Scriptures, and carries confusion into the whole Christian system. And as John beholds certain subjects of redemption, robed, and crowned, and enthroned, as priests and kings in heaven, we here have (let it be noted) positive demonstration, that, at the time to which this vision relates, a resurrection and a translation *have already taken place*. It will not do to say, that the picture is *anticipative* of the position and triumphs of the Church after the seals, trumpets, and vials have run their course. They occupy these thrones, while yet the closed book, which brings forth the seals and trumpets, lies untouched in the hand of Him that sits upon the throne. They see it there, and they vote the Lamb worthy to open it. They behold Him taking it up, and fall down and worship as He holds it. They are in their places when heaven receives the accession of the multitude which come " out of the great tribulation." (Chap. 7 : 11-14.) They have their own distinct positions when the still later company of the hundred and forty-four thousand gather round the Lamb on Mount Sion. And they are spectators of the judgment of great Babylon, and sing Alleluia in glory as they see her fall. (Chap. 19 : 4.) Instead of *anticipation* of the final result of the great day of the Lord, there is actual *participation* in the processes and administrations by which that result is wrought.

They are " *Elders*," not only with reference to their official places ; for that term is expressive of *time*, rather than of office. The *elder*, is the older man ; and in the original order of human society, he was the ruling man because he was the older man. These enthroned ones are *elders*, not because they are officers, but they are *officers* because they are elders. They are the older ones of the children of the resurrection. They are the first-born from the dead—the first glorified of all the company of the redeemed—the seniors of the celestial assembly ; not indeed with respect to the number of their years on earth, but with respect to the time of their admission into heaven. They have had their resurrection, or their translation, in advance of the judgment-tribulations, and are crowned and officiating as kings and priests in glory, whilst others, less faithful, are still slumbering in their graves, or suffering on the earth. They do not represent, by any means, the whole body of the redeemed, as some have supposed, but are exactly what their name imports—the seniors of them—the first-born of the household—the oldest of the family,—and hence the honoured officials.

which was discovered in 1860, and which is of equal antiquity and authority with the Codex Alexandrinus, contains it. The Codex Basilianus, in the Vatican, contains it. The Latin, Coptic or Memphitic, and Armenian, which are of great value, contain it. And so do *all other MSS. and versions*. And to discredit it, simply and only because it does not appear in that one single Codex of Alexandria, is most unreasonable and unjust to the weight of authority for its retention. Dr. Tregelles, on full examination, was firmly convinced of its right to a place in the text, before the Codex Sinaiticus appeared ; and the presence of this ἡμᾶς in that MS., ought to settle the question of its genuineness forever. The evidences from the context, also argue powerfully for a construction which necessarily embraces it, whether expressed or not. We regard it as indubitably genuine.

There certainly is, as we shall more fully see hereafter, a succession in the order in which the saints are gathered into their final glory. There are some who " *escape* " the tribulation, being taken to heaven before it comes ; there are others who suffer it, and are only taken to heaven out of it. Then, there is a peculiar company of sealed ones, who come in at a still later period ; and a " harvest of the earth," still subsequent to their appearance with the Lamb on Mount Sion, if not a still remoter bringing in of those under Antichrist, who " had not worshipped the beast, neither had received his mark upon their foreheads, or in their hands," all of whom together make up the fulness of " the first resurrection." And of these successive companies and orders, the enthroned ones of this vision are among the first, if not absolutely the first. They are the seniors—" *the Elders.*"

John saw but *twenty-four* of them ; but these were the representatives of many others. There were many priests and Levites under the old economy. The number of those who " were set to forward the work of the house of the Lord, was twenty and four thousand." (1 Chron. 23 : 3, 4.) But they were all arranged in courses of twenty-four (1 Chron. 24 : 3–5), so that never more than twenty-four were found on duty at a time. There were also many prophets appointed to praise God with instruments of song ; but they too were arranged in twenty-four courses, each course with its own individual representative. (1 Chron. 25.) These were not human devices, but things specially directed by the Spirit of the Lord (1 Chron. 18 : 11–13, 19), and meant to be " figures of the true," and " patterns of things in the heavens." (Heb. 9 : 9, 23, 24.) Accordingly, we are to see in these twenty-four royal priests, but one course of as many more courses, all of which together do but represent thousands upon thousands of the same high and privileged class. Heaven is not an empty place, nor is it stinted in the number of its honoured dignitaries.

I find, then, in these enthroned Elders, the highest manifested glory of the risen and glorified saints. They are in heaven. They are around the throne of Deity. They are pure and holy, wearing white, " which is the righteousness of the saints." They are partakers of celestial dominion. They are kings of glory, with golden crowns. They are settled, and at home in their exalted dignities ; not standing and waiting as servants, but seated as royal counsellors of the Almighty. They are assessors of the great Judge of quick and dead, the spectators of all that transpires in heaven and earth, and participants in the judgment of the world for its sins, the Church for its apostasies, Babylon for her impurities, Antichrist for his blasphemies, and that old Serpent and his brood, for their ungodliness and wickednesses during all these weary ages.* They are the Elders of the glorious house of the redeemed, and kings and priests in the temple and palace of the Lord God Almighty, whom all the earth shall obey, and all the ages acknowledge.

And yet, there is another picture in the vision, which some take to be still higher.

" *Amidst the throne and around the throne,*" John saw " *four Living ones,*" unfortunately called " *beasts* " by our translators, " *full of eyes before and behind ; the first like a lion, and the second like a young ox, and the third having the face like a man, and the fourth like a flying eagle. And the four Living ones, each one of them, had around them six wings apiece, and within they are full of eyes ; and they have not rest day and night, saying,* HOLY, HOLY, HOLY, LORD GOD ALMIGHTY, WHO WAS, AND WHO IS, AND WHO IS TO COME.*"

What are we to understand by these ? They sing precisely the same song (chap. 5 : 9, 10) which the Elders sing. They give praise to the Lamb for having died for them, and for redeeming them by His blood " out of every tribe, and tongue, and people, and nation." They say to the Lamb, " Thou *redeemest* us to God by Thy blood." This settles the point that they are also glorified men, not " beasts " at all, nor mere personifications of mute creation

---

* " Do ye not know that *the saints shall judge the world ?* Know ye not that we *shall judge angels ?* " (1 Cor. 6 : 2, 3.)

or nature's forces. The schoolmen, and some of the later Fathers, took them to be the four Evangelists.* Hence, the lion of St. Mark, the eagle of St. John, &c. But this is fancy, and against the record ; for the four Evangelists were Jews, and these Living ones are from all tribes, tongues, peoples, and nations. Some interpret them of the redeemed in general, and as emblematic of the cardinal virtues of the saints ; but this also is quite too indefinite to meet the requirements of the vision. Some take them as representing the several dispensations ; the lion, the patriarchal ; the ox, the Mosaic ; the man, the Christian ; and the eagle, the Millennial ; but we are dealing with living beings, who are all in their places before the Millennial dispensation comes into existence, and actually participating in its introduction. Others explain them as the forces of Providence, which is somewhat nearer the truth, if we understand it, not of Providence in general, but of that economy of things which first comes into being at the resurrection ; and of Providence, not as a mere impersonal thing, but in those personal centres whence the power issues.

Perhaps the easiest and shortest way for us to get at the true explanation of this remarkable manifestation, is to go back to the ancient dispensation, so much of which was copied exactly from these heavenly things. The Jewish writers tell us, that the standard of each tribe of Israel took the colour of the stone which represented it in the high priest's breastplate, and that there was wrought upon each a particular figure—a lion for Judah, a young ox for Ephraim, a man for Reuben, and an eagle for Dan. These were the representative tribes, and all the rest were marshalled under these four standards (Num. 2) ;—Judah, on the east, with Issachar and Zebulon ; Reuben on the south, with Simeon and Gad ; Ephraim on the west, with Manasseh and Benjamin ; and Dan on the north, with Asher and Naphtali. In the centre of this quadrangular encampment was the tabernacle of God, with four divisions of Levites forming an inner encampment around it. It was thus that Israel was marched through the wilderness, under the four banners of the lion, the young ox, the man, and the flying eagle. These were their ensigns, their guards, their coverings, the symbols of powers by which they were protected and guided. They were parts of that divine and heavenly administration which led them forth from bondage, preserved them in the wilderness, and finally settled them in the promised land. Such at any rate was the earthly, outward, material aspect of the case. In Ezekiel's vision of the cherubim, we have the same thing in its more interior and heavenly aspects. (Ezek. 1.)†

---

* So Victorinus, in his *Scholia in Apocalypsin*. And so Adam, of St. Victor, the great hymnologist of the middle ages, taught the Latin Church to sing :

"——Circa thronum magistatis,
Cum spiritibus beatis,
Quatuor diversitatis,
  Adstant animalia.

*　*　*　*

Formæ formant figurarum
Formas evangelistarum ;
Quorum imber doctrinarum,
  Stillat in ecclesia."

† Thus rendered by Milton, in Paradise Lost, Book vi :

——Forth rushed with whirlwind sound
The chariot of paternal Deity,
Flashing thick flames, wheel within wheel undrawn,
Itself instinct with Spirit, but conveyed
By four cherubic shapes ; four faces each
Had wondrous ; as with stars their bodies all,
And wings were set with eyes, with eyes the wheels
Of beryl, and careering fires between ;
Over their heads a crystal firmament,
Whereon a sapphire throne.

To cover and guard, is thought to be the proper signification of the word *cherub*. After the expulsion of our first parents from Eden, cherubim were placed at the east of the garden " to keep the way of the tree of life " (Gen. 3 : 24) ; and the prince of Tyrus is likened to the cherub that covereth. (Ezek. 28 : 14.) A vision of the cherubim, then, is a vision of them that cover, protect, guard, and keep. And in this vision of Israel's protectors and keepers, what did Ezekiel see ? " Above the firmament was the likeness of a throne, as the appearance of a sapphire stone, and the likeness as the appearance of a man above upon it." This was the throne of God. But under the throne, connected with the throne, and instinct with the life of the throne, was " the likeness of four living creatures," who " ran and returned as the appearance of a flash of lightning," and moved with complicated wheels, with high and dreadful rings, full of eyes. It was through them that the Spirit of the throne went forth, every way, whithersoever it would. And these living creatures, the executors of the will of the Spirit of the throne, had the same forms combined in each, which were borne upon the four banners of the children of Israel, the lion, the man, the ox, and the eagle. (Ezek. 1 : 10.) These cherubim were not human beings ; for they were doing service in the Garden of Eden, when yet there were no human beings but Adam and Eve ; and at the time Ezekiel saw them, there were no human beings yet glorified, or, hence, capable of taking such offices. These cherubim were angelic beings. " Of the angels He saith, He maketh His angels spirits, and His ministers a flame of fire." (Heb. 1 : 7.) " He shall give His angels charge concerning thee, and in their hands they shall bear thee up." (Matt. 4 : 6.) And what these cherubim were in the ancient order, these " living ones " are in the order which obtains at the time to which this vision of John refers. They are redeemed men, glorified, and related to the judgment-throne in heaven, and to the interests and affairs of the future kingdom on earth, as the cherubim are related to the throne and kingdom now, and in the former dispensations. They are the cherubim of the new order. They are joined directly to the throne of the new order. They are in the midst of it. They are around it. They are expressions of it. And they take the forms of the lion, the man, the young ox, and the flying eagle, for the reason that they are the heavenly powers who guard and cover the camp of the Lord, which, under them, the entire world is to become. Jesus tells us that " they which shall be accounted worthy to obtain that αἰῶνος, and the resurrection from among the dead, . . . are (ἰσάγγελοι) *equal unto the angels* " (Luke 20 : 35, 36) ; and this is the vision of that declaration fulfilled, showing us certain preeminent classes of the eclectic resurrection and translation, not only angelic as to their form of existence, but in the exact positions which angels held in other dispensations.

Ezekiel saw but *four* cherubim. The number was significant of the scene of their ministrations—the world. But these four included and represented many more ; for " the chariots of God " are " twenty thousand, even many thousands of angels." (Ps. 68 : 17.) And for the same reason John saw but four of these " living ones." This is the worldly number, and denotes that their office has reference to God's providence in the world. But in these four are embraced thousands of glorified ones (see Ezek. 7 : 10.) whose high distinction is to share the throne with their Divine Redeemer, as His ministers, and as executors of His will throughout eternal ages.

They have wings, for they are angelic now ; and more wings than their angelic predecessors, showing how fully they are capacitated for motion, and how much wider is the sphere of their movements. The Israel of old was but one nation, the Israel they do for, is all the nations.

They are full of eyes, before, behind, and within ; which is the symbol of intense intelligence, looking backward into the past, and forward into the future, and inward upon themselves and into the nature of things, and able to direct their ways and administrations with unlimited penetration and discretion.

And they never rest, in the fervency and grandeur of their zeal, perpetually expressing the holiness and glory of the Lord God Almighty, who was, and is, and is to come.

Some have taken them to be the same as the Elders, only in other relations, and in other features of their dignities and blessedness. I cannot so understand it. They have, it is true, the same priestly censers as the Elders, and they sing the same song of a common redemption, kinghood, priesthood, and dominion over the earth. But they have, as a class, an individual distinctness, which is never lost sight of, and never confounded with the eldership. Even on earth, " there are diversities of gifts, and differences of administrations ; " and much rather will there be varieties of place and function in heaven. The Elders have crowns and thrones distinct from the central throne ; but these living ones have for their crown the very throne itself. They are joined to the throne ; they are in the midst of it, and directly express it.* They also lead the Elders in their adorations ; for " whensoever they give glory and honour, and thanks to Him that sitteth on the throne," then it is that " the twenty-four Elders fall down before Him that sitteth on the throne, and worship Him that liveth for the age of the ages, and cast their crowns before the throne," giving glory, honour, and power to the Almighty Maker of heaven and earth. The one class have more the semblance of counsellors, the other, that of executors, and the two together are the closest to God of all the redeemed.

And these, my friends, are the dignities and glories to which you, and I, and all who hear the Gospel of Christ, are called and invited. There is not a prerogative of that celestial eldership—not an office or possession of these living ones—not a song they sing—not an attribute they wear—not a place they fill—which is not this night held out and offered to every one of us. Oh, the grandeur, the blessedness, the sublimity of the overtures of the Gospel of Christ ! And with your eye on these heavenly splendours, these celestial princedoms and priesthoods, these eternal royalties with God and with His Son, Jesus Christ, and with your heart warmed with the contemplation of their unfathomed excellency, I ask you, whether you are willing to despise and cast away this your golden opportunity to obtain them ? I wish to put it to your conscience, O man, O woman, whether, after all this has been put within your reach, you can still hope for clemency, if you wilfully turn a deaf ear, and carelessly let your chance go by ! I wish to have your honest, sober, practical decision on the question, whether you are willing to allow this world's fleeting vanities, and damning sins and follies, to occupy and possess you in preference to these immortal regencies, and eternal principalities and powers ? Believe me, that I am in earnest in this appeal ; for I make it as a messenger of God, ordained to deal with these holy things for your salvation. The Lord fasten it on your soul, and give each of us grace to let go friends, pleasures, comforts, home, country, freedom, life, *everything*, rather than let slip so blessed an opportunity for so great a prize !

* " These four beasts are living emblems and ornaments of the throne, denoting a nearer admission than the twenty-four Elders."—*Bengel's Gnomon in loc.*

LECTURE TENTH

REV. 5 : 1–14. (Revised Text.) And I saw upon the right hand of Him that sitteth upon
the throne, a book [or roll], written on the inside and on the back, fast-sealed with seven
seals. And I saw a mighty angel proclaiming with a great voice : Who is worthy to open
the book, and to loose the seals of it ? And no one was able, in the heaven, nor on the
earth, nor under the earth, to open the book, nor even to look upon it. And I was weeping
much, because no one was found worthy to open the book, nor even to look upon it. And
one from among the elders saith to me : Weep not ; behold the Lion from the tribe of
Judah, the Root of David, overcame [ἐνίκησε, see chap. 3 : 21], to open the book and its
seven seals.

And behold, and amidst the throne and the four living ones, and amidst the elders, a
Lamb, standing, as it had been slain, having seven horns and seven eyes, which are the
seven Spirits of God, sent forth into all the earth. And He came and took [the book] from
the right hand of Him that sitteth upon the throne.

And when He took the book, the four living ones and the twenty-four elders, fell down
before the Lamb, having each a harp and golden bowls full of incenses, which are the prayers
of the saints ; and they sing a new song, saying : Thou art worthy to take the book, and
to open the seals of it ; for Thou wert slain, and redeemedst us to God by thy blood, out
of every tribe and tongue, and people, and nation and, Thou madest us* unto our God,
kings and priests, and we shall reign on the earth.

And I saw and heard a voice of many angels around the throne, and the living ones and
the elders, and the number of them was myriads of myriads, and thousands of thousands,
saying with a loud voice, Worthy is the Lamb which hath been slain to receive the power,
and riches, and wisdom, and might, and honour, and glory, and blessing. And every
creature which is in the heaven, and on the earth, and under the earth, and upon the sea,
and all the things in them, heard I saying, To Him that sitteth upon the throne and to the
Lamb [be] the blessing, and the honour, and the glory, and the dominion for the ages of
the ages. And the four living ones said, Amen ; and the elders fell down and worshipped.

THIS chapter continues the description of the vision last had under consideration. The scene is still in the sky. The throne, the Elders, the Living ones,
are still in view, the same as in the preceding chapter. But there is a making
ready for great things, and hence a disclosure of new items, which now claim
our attention.

Prominent and first among these is a *book*, or *roll*, upon the right hand of
Him that sitteth on the throne, written on the inside and on the back, fast-
sealed with seven seals. It was doubtless there from the very first glance the
seer had of this sublime display ; but it was kept out of his notice, at least
reserved from the particulars of his description, until this point, at which
starts one of the sublimest scenes in heaven, and the occasion of the most
tremendous convulsions and changes on earth. The meaning of it has been
differently represented by different expositors. But the outlying facts, that
it, and it alone, brings upon the scene the prime mover of the new song in
heaven, and the great actor of all the succeeding events of earth ; that He
appears and deals with this book only in the character of the Lamb which

* Some of the best MSS. read " *them* " in place of *us ;* but the sense is not altered by it,
or by reading " *they*," as some MSS. do in the next clause, instead of " *we* " ; for the subject
is settled by the preceding declaration to be the persons uttering the song, namely, by the
phrase " *redeemedst* us ; " the genuineness of which must be considered established since
the discovery of the Codex Synaiticus. See note on page 103.

had been slain ; and that what He does with it is something from which all creation has shrunk back in unworthiness and inability to perform, ought to be sufficient to set us upon the track of the conclusion, that this book has its primary and most essential reference to redemption. It has been very well observed : " If it concerned *creation*, there were no propriety in the Divine order of the piece, for the creation honour is all ascribed already (chap. 4 : 11), without either the presentation of the book or of the Lamb to our view. Nor, if it concerned creation, were there any fitness in presenting Him as a Lamb, and a Lamb slain ; because thus was He not, when He laid the foundation of the earth, and set His compass on the face of the deep. So, likewise, from considerations merely of order, we can perceive that it is *not revelation* [any more than creation], with which this book is concerned ; for to reveal, is proper to Him as the Word, as the Prophet, as the Messenger of the covenant, as the Light between the cherubim, as the Apostle of our profession ; but it is not proper to Him as the Lamb which is slain. To reveal, is proper for Him in the form of a Man, and not in the form of a Lamb ; which Lamb, though it hath horns and eyes, hath not a mouth like the mouth of a man, to speak the glorious things of God, nor speaketh it ever during these visions, and therefore we suspect that this sealed book is not so much the symbol of revelation, as it is the symbol of redemption ; in which conclusion we are altogether confirmed by the song which the Living ones and the elders sung, over the taking of the book, which is altogether a song of redemption."*
And if it is at all admissible that the Seven Epistles cover the entire career of the present dispensation, it is simply impossible, in any direct and proper sense, to accept this sealed book as the book of the fortunes of the Church during these ages ; for the book does not even appear until after the career of the Church is run. Those commentaries, therefore, which undertake to find in the opening of the seals of this book merely the history of the present dispensation, and think to exhaust their meaning in what they find in Gibbon, Alison, and the writers of this world's annals, must all pass for about so much labour lost ; and, so far as touches the proper understanding of these magnificent pictures, they are worse than worthless. They may furnish much that is useful in other directions, and deserve respect for their research and ability, and help to show us how many-sided and multifariously applicable God's great prophecies are, and demonstrate how the images of the mighty things to come are reflected in the histories which precede them ; but as expositions of what is chiefly and properly meant to be foreshown, they are simply mischievous failures. Having myself experienced the unfortunate bewilderment and confusion which they involve, and seen the confessed hesitation and embarrassment which they have ever entailed upon all their authors and adherents, and tested, as I believe, the utter sandiness of the foundations on which they rest, I am satisfied, convinced, and confident, that they are just what I here pronounce them to be, namely, learned blunders, and erudite but by no means harmless mistakes. It is not ecclesiastical history, which this book is introduced to foreshow, but something to which all ecclesiastical history is only the prelude and introduction, and which the Scriptures call " *The redemption of the purchased possession.*"

It may be well here for us to correct a misapprehension which largely obtains in the common conception of what redemption is. When this word is used, most men's minds go back to the birth, life, death, and resurrection of Christ, and think of something already accomplished and complete in the blessed facts of the blessed Saviour's history. This is well enough as far as it goes, and touches indeed, the great central particulars on which redemption reposes. But, viewed as a whole, redemption is a vastly wider and more wondrous thing. It stretches back through a history of six thousand years, and yet its sublimest part is still future. It includes all past dispensations and theophanies, and the coming and achievements of Christ in the flesh ; but it

* Irving *in loc.*

embraces still other dispensations, and more wonderful theophanies, and a more glorious advent of Christ, and vastly more far-reaching achievements, of which His miracles were the symptomatic pre-intimations. There is already much of redemptive power and blessing in the world. The truth is, that everything on earth rests on a mediatorial basis. The world stands, and man exists, only because of Christ and His undertaking to be our Saviour. But for His mediatorship, Adam would have perished the day that he transgressed, and never a human being would have been born. The very ungodliest of the race owe whatever blessings they enjoy to the blood and engagement of Christ. Even the lower animals, and the very grasses of the fields, live and flourish by virtue of the same. Redemption is therefore so far a living force. Like a golden chain, it girdles the world, upholds it from destruction, and sustains, and blesses all the varied and successive generations on its surface. But, all this sea of mediatorial mercies is as nothing, compared with what is yet to come. Redemption has its roots and foundations in the past, but its true realization lies in the future, and connects directly with the period and transactions to which our text relates. The Scriptures everywhere point forward to Christ's Apocalypse, as the time when first the mystery shall be finished, and the long process reach its proper consummation. Jesus talked to His disciples about the signs which were to precede His coming, and said, " When these things begin to come to pass, then look up, and lift up your heads ; for your redemption draweth nigh." (Luke 21 : 28.) In His view, then, redemption proper, or in its true reality, lies far more in the future than in the past ; so much more that the past is hardly to be named apart from what is yet to come. And with all Paul's glorying in the cross, he did not hesitate to say : " If in this life only we have hope in Christ, we are, of all men, most miserable ; " and that " the whole creation groaneth and travaileth in pain together until now ; and not only they, but ourselves also, which have the first fruits of the Spirit, even we ourselves groan within ourselves, waiting for the adoption, to wit, the redemption of the body." (1 Cor. 15 : 19 ; Rom. 8 : 22, 23.) He speaks of Christians as indeed " sealed with the Holy Spirit of promise," which he commends greatly, but which he pronounces the mere " earnest " or pledge-penny of something vastly greater—of an " inheritance " still future, which is only to come at a yet unaccomplished " redemption of the purchased possession." (Eph. 1 : 13, 14.) To him, therefore, redemption is still largely a subject of hope. There is an inheritance pledged, and a possession purchased, but it is not yet redeemed. The action of claiming, disencumbering, and taking possession of it is still future. And it is just this action that is brought to our view in the taking up of this book and the breaking of its seals.

The word *redemption* comes to us, and takes its significance from certain laws and customs of the ancient Jews. Under these laws and customs, it was impossible to alienate estates beyond a given time. Whatever disposition one may have been forced to make of his lands, and whoever might be found in possession of them, the year of Jubilee returned them to the lawful representatives of their former owners. Upon this regulation there was founded another, which made it the right of the nearest of kin to one who, through distress or otherwise, had alienated his inheritance to another party, to step in and redeem it ; that is, to buy it back, and retake it, at any time, or at such times not falling within certain stipulated intervals. When an inheritance was thus disponed away by its rightful possessor, there were two books, or instruments of writing, made of the transaction, the one open, and the other sealed, specifying price and particulars. These books or mortgage-deeds went into the hands of the one to whom the property was thus made over. A sealed book thus became a standing sign of an alienated inheritance, but so held as to be liable to be recovered on the terms specified. And when any one legally representing the original proprietor, was found competent to lift and destroy that sealed instrument, and thus to buy back what had been disponed away, he was called the *goel*, or redeemer, and the inheritance was considered redeemed, so far that he now had full right to dispossess of it whoever might be found on it, and to enter upon its undisturbed fruition.*

From this it will be seen, that the transactions which John witnessed, in regard to this sealed book, accord precisely with this ancient arrangement for the redemption of inheritances. And the coincidence is so complete, and sealed books in Scripture are so much confined to this particular sort of writings,† that I take it as separating this book in God's right hand from all other subjects to the one subject of forfeited inheritances.‡ The idea that it must refer to matters of knowledge, or information to be communicated, is a mere prejudice, derived from modern things, and not at all from any Scriptural allusions to sealed books. It is also incompatible with the intent of God's word, for it to be sealed up, in the literal sense of this passage ; for that word is given for opening, not concealing ; and for treating it as a sealed book, and not opening it to the people, Isaiah prophesied, and Christ himself confirmed fearful judgment upon the doctors of Jerusalem. And to make this book refer to things to be revealed, is also in disagreement with what follows the breaking of the seals ; which was not for the reading of the book, for no reading followed, but only shouts of praise that a worthy Redeemer was found, and the action of judgment and destruction to dispossess usurpers and aliens.

We also know very well, that there has been an inheritance forfeited and disponed away for these thousands of years, and that for all this time the proper heirs have lain out of it, and had no proper possession of it. That inheritance we know to be just τα παντα—*the all things*—in which man, in his first creation, was installed, and which God made good, and sin made evil. Everything testifies that it was a high, holy, and blessed investiture. But, alas, its original possessor sinned, and it passed out of his hands to the disinheritance of all his seed. The sealed book, the title-deeds of its forfeiture and mortgage, are in the hands of God, and strangers and intruders have overrun and debased it. And from the days of Adam until now, those deeds have lain in the Almighty's hands, with no one to take them up or to dispossess the aliens. And even when the saints are caught up to the sky, they will find it still lying there, awaiting this very scene of the text, when the Goel adjudged worthy shall appear and take it up, and destroy the sad testimonial by breaking its seals forever.

" *Seven seals* " are upon this book, indicative of the completeness of those bonds of forfeit which have all this while debarred Adam's seed from their proper inheritance. The original estate is totally gone from man, apart from some competent Redeemer. Just as the final taking of the book, and the breaking of its seals, eventuate in complete redemption, and the full reinstatement of the acknowledged seed into the blessedness which sin forfeited, and the Goel redeemed, so those seals unbroken, set forth the completeness of the alienation, and the thoroughness of the incumbrances which are upon the estate, until that competent Goel has performed his work.

This book was " *written within and on the back.*" This again tends to identify it with these books of forfeited inheritances. Within were the specifications of the forfeiture ; without were the names and attestations of the witnesses ; for this is the manner in which these documents were attested.§

It is in the right hand of God. No literal hand is described ; but, so to speak, it was on the right hand of the undescribed and indescribable One who occupied the throne. This is significant of His high and supreme right to what the sealed instrument binds. Failing from man, it reverted to the

---

* In this connection, see Ruth, chapter 4.
† See Jeremiah 32 : 6–12.   ‡ So also Irving *in loc.*
§ " For the manner of writing the contract, he who was to buy the ground wrote two instruments ; the one to be sealed with his own signet, the other he showed unclosed to the witnesses, that they might subscribe and bear witness of that which was written. *This, the witness did subscribe* UPON THE BACK *of the inclosed instrument.*"—*Weemse on the Judicial Law of Moses*, chapter 30.

original Giver. Sin cannot vitiate any of the rights of God. Satan's possession is a mere usurpation, permitted for the time, but in no way detrimental to the proprietorship of the Almighty. The true right still lives in the hand of God, until the proper Goel comes to redeem it, by paying the price, and ejecting the alien and his seed. The same is significant of the fact that this matter of the book and its seals is the principal subject of the transaction displayed ; and furthermore, that the intensest holiness and sublimest power are required to be able or worthy to approach and take possession of the record ; for to come to the right hand of God, is to come to the highest place of exaltation and authority in the universe.

But, along with the sealed book, appeared a mighty angel, asking with a great voice, if any one was prepared to take the book and break its seals. This further accords with our interpretation of the nature of this book, and shows that the forfeited inheritance was now open for redemption. The description is not as if the privilege to redeem was now first opened. For all that John saw and heard, the proclamation may have been sounding long. But the time had come, when, if a competent Goel was to be found, he should come forward and exercise his right. The way was open before ; but, no one having appeared till now, the great, universal, final call is made, that, if any one is worthy, he should now exercise his power.

The result of the call was, that " *no one was able, in the heaven, nor on the earth, nor under the earth, to open the book, nor even to look upon it.*" Angels shrunk back from it as beyond their qualifications. Heavenly principalities and powers stood mute and downcast as they surveyed the requirements for the work. And yet, it would seem as if somewhere there had been efforts making to achieve it. And what, indeed, have been all the endeavours of unsanctified men, in politics, in science, and in all the arts of civilization, improvement, philosophy, and even religion, but to work out this problem of successful repossession of what was lost in Adam, to attain to that forfeited perfection and supreme good which has ever danced before their imaginations. What, indeed, has been the spring of the activity of the under world, in these ages of seductive effort with mortals, but to persuade men that they can make good the lying promise, " Ye shall be as God," and in spite of the Almighty, and without Him, to realize through human expansion and demoniacal guidance, the dream of a better destiny for the world and the race. It has also been in the plan of God so far, to drop the reins to His rebellious creatures, to permit the experiment to be carried to its utmost, and to give scope for its most conspicuous failure at the last. Varied, and many, and complicated, have been the attempts, all of which, as they always must, have resulted in disastrous failure. Egypt attempted to play the goel for the world, and cringed to the bloodiest tyrannies, bowed to the worship of the basest of creatures, and went down in ignominious ruin. Babylon tried it, and became the world's great symbol of all that is blasphemous in power, impure in life, besotted in affection, and terrible in desolation. Greece tried it, and only consummated her destruction in the marriage of the intellect of heaven with the vices of hell. Rome tried it, and became the iron arm which threshed the world in blood, and then dissolved in the putrefaction which itself had wrought. The spirit of liberty, democratic confederation, and universal communism and enlightenment, uniting largely with elements of infernal origin, is now trying it, and will perpetuate its efforts to the most gigantic and bewitching consummation that the world shall ever have seen, but only to work out the most dreadful failure that has yet occurred. For, as in heaven, so on earth, and under the earth, the ultimate record will be, what is here written : " *no one was able to open the book, nor even to look upon it.*" The lost estate of man, by man, or angel, or spirits of the under world, can never be recovered.

It is a sad and melancholy contemplation. Heaven, itself, seems to grow silent and breathless under it. And the tender and loving heart of John overflows as the picture opens before him. " *I was weeping much, because no one was found worthy to open the book, nor even to look upon it.*"

Some speak of these tears as mere tears of disappointed curiosity. This, indeed, is the common explanation. We are told that the book had unknown revelations in it, which John was very impatient to understand ; and that his much weeping was caused by the prospect of having his personal desire to obtain a knowledge of the future, ungratified. Poor John ! what a silly mortal, to be troubling himself about unrevealed prophecy, and to keep up this crying in heaven because there was no one to open the book for him ! The thing is absurd. It is beneath criticism. And if we cannot get through our interpretations without such left-handed compliments to the " natural emotion " of men " in the Spirit," it seems to me that it would be the part of fairness and honour, to confess frankly that the subject is beyond our comprehension. I am very certain that if John had looked upon these solemn and mighty transactions as some of his commentators have represented them, we would not only never have heard of these tears, but they never would have been shed. What a picture of inspiration, that it should thus strip a venerable and disciplined servant of God of all manly dignity, and make of him a silly and peevish child ! No, no ; John knew by that Spirit in which he was, what that sealed book meant. He knew that if no one was found worthy and able to take it from the hand of God, and to break its seals, that all the promises of the prophets, and all the hopes of the saints, and all the preintimations of a redeemed world, must fail. He understood the office of the Goel, and that if there was failure at this point, " the redemption of the purchased possession " must fail. Could it be possible that this should be ? Had he all this while been hoping, and preaching, and prophesying what should, after all, not be accomplished ? Was the promised inheritance, now at the ripened moment for its recovery, to go by default into eternal alienation ? How could he bear the thought ? Yet such were some of the suggestions of this interval of blankness and awful pause in heaven. And in this view of the case, well might an earnest prophet weep without damage to his meekness or his honour. But in this chief mourner over the unopened book, we may see the state of the Church up to that time,—a widowhood household, weeping before the Lord over the spoliation of its inheritance. Do not His own elect " cry day and night unto Him," to avenge them in this particular ? Do not the sons of the bride-chamber continually weep and fast because the Bridegroom is taken from them, and His house oppressed by the children of the alien ? That book, unlifted and unopened, is the Church's grief and distress. It bespeaks the inheritance unredeemed—the children still estranged from their purchased possession. But that book opened, is the Church's joy and glory. It is the assertion of her reinstatement into what Adam lost—the recovery to her of all of which she has been so long and cruelly deprived by sin. Until, therefore, that book is opened, and its seals broken, the people of God must remain in privation, sorrow, and tears.

But, blessed are they that mourn, for they shall be comforted. Such anxious and tearful longing for the " better country " and the ransomed inheritance, is noticed in heaven, and has many precious assurances from thence. One of the Elders said unto John : " *Weep not ; behold the Lion from the tribe of Judah, the Root of David, overcame to open the book and its seven seals.*" And this is what the Church has been hearing from her elders, and prophets, and apostles, and ministers, in all the ages. It is the very essence of the Gospel, which has been sounding ever since the promise in Eden, that the seed of the woman should bruise the serpent's head. It is what all the ancient types prefigured, what the songs of the prophets foretold, and what the first Christians and their successors went heralding over all the earth. It has been the only comfort of God's children in all these ages of their disinheritance, a comfort which has cheered their pilgrim steps through life, illumined their passage to the grave, and will be the joy of their souls as they stand waiting in heaven for the consummating victory of Him who has thus far been so uniformly triumphant on so many trying fields. Jesus is the Lion sprung from Judah. He is this Root of David—the foundation on which the Davidic hopes repose. He overcame, in the trials of life, in the temptations in the wilderness, in the agonies of the garden, in the terrors of death, and in the bonds of the grave. He hath gone up, leading captivity captive. He is Victor now over law, and sin, and death, and hell. He hath paid the redemption price of the forfeited inheritance. He is the true Goel, who, having so far triumphed and been accepted, will also prove ready and worthy to complete His work, by lifting those long-standing deeds of forfeiture, and breaking their debarring seals. Such is our faith, and hope, and comfort, here re-confirmed to us from heaven. And what we find in the further particulars of this vision, is simply the picture of its accomplishment.

" *And behold, and amidst the throne, and the four Living ones, and amidst the Elders, a Lamb, standing, as it had been slain.*" The description of the location of this Lamb, is of the same sort with that of the Living ones. They were " amidst the throne, and around the throne ; " that is, they were seen everywhere within the bounds of the throne, from centre to circumference, as if the life and being of it, present in every part. And so this Lamb was amidst the throne, the Living ones, and the Elders—visibly omnipresent within these bounds, as if the animating soul of all—the Life of the life of the throne, and of the forms of being and dignity about it.

He who appears here as a Lamb, is the same whom the Elder had just described as a Lion. The two titles might seem to be incongruous. What more opposite than the monarch of the forest, in strength and majesty, inflicting terror and death, and the lamb, in its uncomplaining meekness, in the hands of the sacrificer. But the two pictures do not conflict. They supplement each other, and combine to bring out what could not be otherwise so well portrayed, and yet what the nature of the case required. The opening of the seals, is an act of strength—an exploit of war—a going forth of power to take possession of a kingdom. As one after another is broken, out flies a strong One in fierce assault upon the enemies and usurpers who occupy the earth. There is terror and destruction at every successive movement. And in the accomplishment of this, Christ is a Lion, clothed with power, and majesty, and terribleness. But the character in which He overcame, and became in that respect qualified for this work, and that in which He presents Himself before the throne as a candidate to be adjudged worthy to do it, is that of the sacrificial Lamb, who had innocently and meekly suffered, bearing our sins in His own body, and vanquishing all legal disabilities by His atoning blood. It is in this character of a Lamb that was slain, who overcame by His perfect obedience unto death, and who paid the price of redemption in His meek sufferings, that He is adjudged " worthy to take the book, and to open the seals of it." It is by His sacrifice as a Lamb slain, that He comes to the qualifications for the further office of a Lion, to assert and enforce His supremacy. Both these characters are essential, hence, both appear in the description. " He was led as a *Lamb to the slaughter*, and as a sheep before her shearers is dumb, so He opened not His mouth " (Is. 53 : 7) ; but He is yet to " send forth judgment unto victory." (Matt. 12 : 20.) As the Lamb, He hath " borne our sorrows and carried our iniquities," and stands before the throne in passive humiliation and loyal suffering ; but it is reserved for Him, as Judah's Lion, " in righteousness to judge and make war," and to enforce the indignation of that throne against all who stand out in rebellion against it.

He is here described, not by the ordinary word (αμνος) used to signify a lamb, but by another (αρνιος) more intensely significant of gentleness and domesticity—*a pet lamb*—in sharp contrast with the *wild beasts*, in opposition to whom He is arrayed. This, the more fully brings out His particular mildness and familiar identification with His people, and the utter inexcusableness and guilt of those savage and untamable ones who persist in rejecting, persecuting, and warring against Him. They wrong and injure the gentlest and most inoffensive of beings—they murder the pet Lamb of the family of God.*

You will notice the attitude of this Lamb—" *standing.*" Though He had all the appearances of recent slaughter, He is alive, upon His feet. The resurrection of Christ is not a myth, but a *fact.* The same John who saw Him dead on Calvary, here sees Him alive in heaven—alive in the body, with the marks of slaughter upon Him. We believe not in a dead Christ only. Our faith does not terminate with a sepulchre. It takes in a living Redeemer, who is as much upon His feet as if He never had been dead, and qualified by His having died for what He never could have done, had he not surrendered His life and gone down among the dead. And with these tokens of His slaughter, as the once dead but now living Lamb, He stands before the throne—stands accepted and approved—stands for those who accept Him as their Redeemer—stands for the maintenance of their cause and the fulfilment of their hopes.

" *Having seven horns.*" Here is the intimation that something more than sacrifice and intercession is now to be His business. The horn is the symbol of strength and aggressive power. Moses, in blessing Joseph, says : " His glory is like the firstling of His bullock, and His horns are like the horns of unicorns : with them He shall push the people together to the ends of the earth." (Deut. 33 : 17.) We find the same imagery in Psalms (89 : 17, 24), applied both to Christ and His people, and in both instances connected with strength and conquest. Zechariah (1 : 18, 19), says : " I lifted up mine eyes, and saw, and behold four horns. And I said unto the angel that talked with me : What be these ? And he answered me : These are the horns [that is, the powers], which have scattered Judah, and Israel, and Jerusalem." The horn thus stands for imperial, kingly, and aggressive power. *Seven* is the number of completeness. So that whilst Christ appears here as the sacrificial Lamb, He is at the same time possessed of the fulness of imperial strength and mighty force. He has ability for invincible conquest, as well as meekness for patient suffering.

And with the " seven horns " are " *seven eyes, which are the seven Spirits of God sent forth into all the earth.*" When Isaiah prophesied of the Rod out of the stem of Jesse, he said : " The Spirit of the Lord shall rest upon [have its home in] Him." And he enumerated seven in the blessed fulness of the holy endowment : First, " the spirit of wisdom ; " second, " the spirit of under-standing ; " third, " the spirit of counsel ; " fourth, " the spirit of might ; " fifth, " the spirit of knowledge ; " sixth, " the spirit of the fear of the Lord ; " and seventh, " the spirit of quick understanding in the fear of the Lord." (Is. 11 : 1–3.) Thus has inspired prophecy identified, and described in advance, these very " seven Spirits of God," which here come to view as the " seven eyes " of the Lamb. His horns show His fulness of *imperial* power ; His eyes show His fulness of *intellectual and spiritual* power. His is not a blind force, but an almightiness directed by perfect and all-searching intelligence, and divine understanding. Upon that BRANCH which God was to lay as the chief corner-stone of the mystic temple, were also " seven eyes—eyes of the Lord, which run to and fro through the whole earth." (Zech. 3 : 8, 9 ;

---

* There is a passage in Isaiah (16), with which this description seems also directly to identify itself, and which the more helps to confirm our whole interpretation of this vision. In our version it reads : " Send ye the lamb *to* the ruler of the land from Sela, unto the mount of the daughter of Zion." But neither the original, nor any of the other versions, so give it. The true rendering of the words, in conformity with the Vulgate, Luther, and some other translations, would be : " *Send ye [or I will send] the Lamb, the Ruler of the land,* from Sela of the wilderness unto the mount of the daughter of Zion." It falls in with Hab. 2 : 3. It identifies the Lambhood with future Rulership of the earth. And as He appears in this vision as the Goel, to recover and repossess the inheritance, it is in exact accordance with the character in which He was anciently prophesied of, that He should make His appearance as the Lamb advancing to take the Rulership of the world.

4 : 10.) And this Lamb is that selfsame Branch and Corner-stone ; and these are the selfsame eyes of all-penetrating vision and completeness of spiritual and universal wisdom.

Three grand qualities of the Goel are thus brought to view ;—*first*, sacrificial virtue, to take away sin ; *second*, aggressive strength to conquer and to overcome all foes ; and *third*, perfect and universal intelligence, direct from the indwelling Spirit of God in all its fulness. Such were the qualifications with which He appeared amidst the throne, the Living ones, and the Elders, and advanced to take the book and break its seals. And when it is considered, that no qualifications less than these would answer, we need not wonder that no one else in heaven, earth, or under the earth, was found worthy to open the book, or even to look upon it. Who among the angels of God could show such spotless innocence, maintained amid such trials—such meek and meritorious submission—such victory over the inexorable demands of a violated law—such triumph over the unmutilated power of death—such perfection of aggressive might—such intensity of spirituality, intelligence, wisdom, and Godly comprehension ! Well might the mightiest messenger of God, with the greatest voice, send out through the universe, and all heaven pause in mute and solemn waiting, and not find such another. Brethren, there is but one sun in our system, and there is but one Christ in the universe.

" *And He came and took [the book] from the right hand of Him that sitteth upon the throne.*" This is the sublimest individual act recorded in the Apocalypse. It is the act which includes all that suffering creation, and the disinherited saints of God have been sighing, and crying, and waiting for, for all these long ages—for six thousand years of grief and sorrow. It is the act which carries with it all else that is written in the succeeding part of this glorious revelation. It is the act by virtue of which the world is subdued, Babylon judged, Antichrist destroyed, the dragon vanquished, death overthrown, the curse expunged, the earth made new, and the reign of everlasting blessedness and peace made to cover its hills and illuminate its valleys, and transform it into an unfading paradise of God. It was the lifting of the title-deeds of the alienated inheritance—the legal act of repossession of all that was lost in Adam, and paid for by the blood and tears of the Son of God. Heaven looks on in solemn silence as that act is being performed. The universe is stricken with awe, and grows breathless as it views it. And the Living ones, and Elders, and all the hosts of angels, are filled with adoring wonder and joy, as if another FIAT had gone forth from God for a new creation.

" *And when He took the book,*" there went a thrill through the universal heart of living things. " *The four Living ones, and the twenty-four Elders fell down before the Lamb.*" A song which was never sung before, broke from their lips. John hears the lofty anthem rolling sublime through heaven : " THOU ART WORTHY TO TAKE THE BOOK, AND TO OPEN THE SEALS OF IT ; *for Thou wert slain, and redeemedst us to God by Thy blood, out of every tribe, and tongue, and people, and nation, and Thou madest us unto our God, kings and priests, and we shall reign on the earth.*" Nor they alone were moved to new and intenser adoration ; but " around the throne, and the Living ones, and the Elders," and afar in the depths of space, he " *heard the voice of many angels, and the number of them was myriads of myriads, and thousands of thousands, saying with a loud voice ;* WORTHY IS THE LAMB WHICH HATH BEEN SLAIN TO RECEIVE THE POWER, AND RICHES, AND WISDOM, AND MIGHT, AND HONOUR, AND GLORY, AND BLESSING." And wider, and still wider spread the sympathetic response of adoring rapture. There was not a holy heart unmoved, nor a holy tongue that did not lift up its song. " *Every creature which is in the heaven, and on the earth, and under the earth, and upon the sea, and all things in them,*" John " *heard saying,* TO HIM THAT SITTETH UPON THE THRONE, AND TO THE LAMB, [BE] THE BLESSING, AND THE HONOUR, AND THE GLORY, AND THE DOMINION FOR THE AGES OF THE AGES. *And the four Living ones said,* AMEN ; *and the Elders fell down and worshipped.*"

Now, to take all this sacred pomp, and universal thrill of adoration, as the mere *Proem* to a few chapters of dim and often untraceable outline of the Church's history in this world, I confess to you, looks to me as little less than blasphemy. Not for my right arm, not for my right eye, could I consent so to regard it. Where, in all the revelations of eternity, is there another such a scene ? Where, in all the disclosures of God, and His awful administrations, is there another such a picture, or another such a crisis ? Search the book of inspiration from end to end, and you will find no parallel to it. Even the great voice of the mighty angel would inquire for the like in vain. I must therefore take this act of the Lamb, so far from being the mere fancy work of John, or even of the Holy Ghost, as involving the heading up and highest consummation of the highest things of our faith, and of all the contents of the revelation of God. And as the view which I have given of it, *and that only*, assigns to it a significance commensurate with such awful and universal solemnities, I feel that I am planted on the rock of immutable truth in teaching you so to accept it.

And strikingly confirmative is still another particular in the description, which does not appear until after the Lamb has taken the book. In the preceding chapter, when the Living ones and Elders paid their adoration, it was unto Him that sitteth upon the throne ; and their cry of WORTHY, was to Him who created all things, and by whose will they were, and were created. But here they fall down before the Lamb, and cry their WORTHY, unto Him that was slain, and had redeemed them with His blood. And in connection with their new song to Him who holds the book, they are described as " *having each a harp and golden bowls full of incenses, which are the prayers of the saints.*" I find here nothing of that saint mediatorship with which the Church in some sections and ages has been so much debauched, and the glory of her true Intercessor so much obscured. Christ has just now been acknowledged as the possessor of the ability and the right to enter, with His redeemed ones, upon their inheritance. It is therefore the time for all the prayers of all the saints of all the ages to come into remembrance, that that which has ever been their chief burden may now be answered and fulfilled. " THY KINGDOM COME. THY WILL BE DONE ON EARTH AS IT IS IN HEAVEN." So have all Christians ever prayed. Such is the theme of all true supplication, as it looks out over futurity, and utters the spirit of faith and hope. And who can reckon up the volumes and oceans of such entreaties, which remain to this day unanswered ? But, not one of them is lost. They are all carefully treasured in golden bowls. They are as sweet incenses before God and before the Lamb. And when we come to take our places with our Lord, and He takes the book of forfeiture to break its debarring seals, then will those supplications come into play ; and blessed he who has his bowl full of them. The picture is not that of saints in heaven officiating for saints on earth ; but of saints in heaven holding up to Christ their own prayers, and the prayers of one another, and the prayers of all saints, that now they may be fulfilled to the making of things on earth as they are in heaven—that now the answer which has been so long delayed may be speedily accomplished. And the *harps* bear upon the subject in the same direction. As the incense connects with the priest's office, so the harp connects with the prophet's. Samuel said to Saul : " Thou shalt meet a company of prophets coming down from the high place, with a psaltery, and a tabret, and a pipe, *and a harp before them*, and they shall prophesy." (1 Sam. 10 : 5.) We read of six sons of Jeduthun, " *who prophesied with a harp.*" (1 Chron. 25 : 3.) David says, of his prophetic utterances, " I will open my dark sayings upon the harp." (Ps. 49 : 4.) And the holding up of these incense prayers and prophetic harps together before the Lamb as He takes the book, is that He may now remember and fulfil what all His holy prophets have spoken and sung, as well as what all His saints have prayed. Both combine to assure us, that it is the very summit and consummation of all pious desire, and all sacred prediction and song, that is involved in this taking of the book.

And to the like end is the hopeful and joyous exclamation at the conclusion of the lofty anthem which these Living ones and Elders sing to Him who holds the lifted book. " *And we shall reign on the earth.*" Why express themselves thus, just at this point ? Because this taking up of the book was the pledge and proof that now He was fully invested and ready to redeem the inheritance, and to carry into effect the blessed promises, that " the meek shall inherit the earth," and that " the kingdom, and dominion, and the greatness of the kingdom under the whole heaven, shall be given to the people of the saints of the Most High." (Matt. 5 : 5 ; Dan. 7 : 27.) It was now certain *to sight* that all was about to be literally fulfilled, and that their golden crowns and dignities were not mere empty things, but carrying with them all that such marks import.

Some people tell us that it is quite too low and coarse a thing to think of the earth in connection with the final bliss of the saints. They preach that we do but degrade and pervert the exalted things of holy Scripture, when we hint the declaration of the wise man, that " the earth endureth forever," and that over it the glorious and everlasting kingdom of Christ and His saints, is to be established in literal reality. But if the ransomed in heaven, with golden crowns upon their brows, kneeling at the feet of the Lamb, before the very throne of God, and with the prayers of all saints, and the predictions of all prophets in their hands, could sing of it as one of the elements of their loftiest hopes and joys, I beg to turn a deaf ear to the surly cry of " *carnal* "— " *sensual* "—" *unspiritual* "—with which some would turn me from " the blessed hope." Shall the saints in glory shout : " *We shall reign on the earth,*" and we be accounted heretics for believing that they knew what they were saying ? Is it come to this, that to be orthodox we must believe that these approved and crowned ones kneel before the throne of God with a lie upon their lips ? Shall they, from thrones in heaven, point to earth as the future theatre of their administrations, and give adoring thanks and praises to the Lamb for it, and we be stigmatized as fanatics and Judaizers, for undertaking to pronounce the blessed fact in mortal hearing ? Oh, I wonder, I wonder, how the dear God above us can endure the unbelief with which some men deal with His holy word.

Shall we then keep silence on the subject ?—When the Living ones and Elders fail to sing about it in heaven ; when inspired apostles no longer admit the subject into their holy writings ; then, but not till then, let it be dropped from the discourses of our sanctuaries, and from the inculcations of them that fear God. And woe, woe, to that man who is convinced of its truth, but, for the sake of place or friendship, refrains from confessing it ! Well has it been said of him : " He barters away his kingdom for the applause of men. He eclipseth the glory of Christ to enhance his own." He stultifieth the adoring songs of celestial kings, that he may win a little empty favour by base pandering to the pleasure of an ignorant, unbelieving, and godless world.

LECTURE ELEVENTH

OPENING OF THE SEALS—TO WHAT IT REFERS—NOT THE EARTHLY HISTORY OF THE CHURCH OR ROMAN EMPIRE—DENOTES A NEW ADMINISTRATION AFTER THE PRESENT—IN SOME SENSE EMBRACES THE PRESENT—SHOWS THE PROCEEDING BY WHICH CHRIST JUDICIALLY TAKES POSSESSION OF THE EARTH—PORTION OF THE APOCALYPSE AND OF TIME EMBRACED—DAY OF JUDGMENT MORE THAN TWENTY-FOUR HOURS—FIRST SEAL—UTTERANCE OF THE LIVING ONES—HORSES, EARTHLY IMAGES OF DIVINE POWER—SPECIFIC WORK OF THE FIRST HORSEMAN—A GREAT REFORMATION AMONG CHRISTIANS AFTER THE JUDGMENT BEGINS.

REV. 6 : 1, 2. (Revised Text.) And I saw when the Lamb opened one from among the seven seals, and I heard one from among the four living ones, saying, as the voice of thunder, Go ! [or, *Come !* The words, " *and see,*" are doubtful, and generally rejected by critics.] And I saw, and, behold, a white horse ; and he that sat on him having a bow ; and a crown was given to him : and he went forth conquering, and to conquer.

A NEW turn of the vision which John began to describe in the fourth chapter, now comes before us. The scene and actors are unchanged, but the manifestations all move earthward. The sealed book has been lifted out of the hand of the Sitter on the throne. It is in the possession of Him found worthy to take it, and able to break its seals. The universal thrill of exultation over the fact has subsided. Everything in the heavenly presence has become quiet with reverent expectancy. And the Lifter of the document now proceeds to destroy its seals. May God help us to a right comprehension of the mysterious transaction !

Two things are to be considered,—

I. THE SUBJECT TO WHICH IT REFERS ;
II. THE PARTICULAR OCCURRENCES WHICH IT PORTRAYS.

I. There are many who assume, that what is here treated of under the imagery of the opening of the seven seals, is the continuous fortune of the Christian Church and the Roman world, from the time of John's banishment, or soon thereafter, to the consummation of all things. By this class of interpreters, the opening of the seals was the opening of a prophetic roll, containing an outline of the triumphs of the Gospel, in connection with the great world-powers, down to the coming of Christ, and the introduction of the Millennial reign. That there is truth of some sort underlying this view, we may readily admit ; but that it is exactly of the kind which the advocates of this theory usually describe, we may just as readily question.

The amazing pomp, solemnity, and universal demonstration, with which the opening of these seven seals is approached in the two preceding chapters, forbids the assumption, that nothing more is meant than the disclosure to the Church of a dim epitome of its earthly history. God does not employ so much parade, nor do all the angels and principalities of eternity become so profoundly enthusiastic, over the letting forth of a few scarcely traceable predictions, touching the earthly successes of the Gospel, the reigns of a few Roman Emperors, and the mere mundane fortunes of Christian confessors.

The several particulars in the preliminary description, also, prove that something transcendently higher is intended, than has transpired since the vision was seen, or that ever will transpire within the limits of the present dispensation. The Elders already have their crowns, the giving of which belongs to the resurrection period. (2 Tim. 4 : 8.) The throne comes to its place just at the moment in which John beholds it (chap. 4 : 2), betokening a new administration other than that which had previously been. Christ appears as the Lamb, which is not the character of a Revelator ; but it is the character of the predicted " Ruler of the land " about to take possession of the inheritance. (Is. 16 : 1.)* The question of worthiness and ability, presented a condition wholly unheard of in all the multiplied instances of the giving of sacred predictions. The bringing forward of the prayers of the saints, and the joyous utterances of the prophets, show that more is embraced than a laying open of the course of this world's history ; for prayer and prophecy have quite another burden. The much weeping of John is rendered ridiculous, if referred to a feeling of disappointment at not being able to find out a little more prophecy. The universal and adoring gladness of all the angels, and all holy beings, can find no adequate justification in the mere disclosure to men of the occurrences cited by the historical school as the fulfilment of the seals, trumpets, and vials. The entire absence of any reading of what was written, either on the inside or on the outside of the book, or of any reference to anything supposed to be recorded in it, should lead us to question that the breaking of its seals had reference to the rehearsal of its contents. And the character of the manifestations, along with concurrent explanations, as seal after seal was broken ; besides the numerous cross lights from other parts of Scripture ; all combine to prove, that something else is signified than the history of the present dispensation.

There is also a link of consecution, given in the record itself, which must not be overlooked. We hold it to be out of the question, in all just exegesis, to give an adequate explanation of the vision of the stars and candlesticks, including the seven Epistles, without making it span the entire earthly church state. The objections that have been urged to the contrary, are futile in the extreme, and can be made to weigh as heavily against any scheme of Apocalyptic interpretation, as against this. And if the scope of the first vision stretches to the period of the consummation, it is settled that everything relating to this book and its seals, refers above all, not to things which run parallel with the earthly church state, but to "·the things which must take place AFTER these things " (chap. 4 : 1) ; that is, to another administration.

But, as the coming administration of power is to be the consummation of the present dispensation, and as all its wonderful actings of sovereignty and judgment move in the same line of God's providence with men and nations now ; as a matter of course, an imperfect fulfilment through all the ages of the present order is also embraced. The resurrection of Christ and the distribution of the gifts of the Holy Ghost, was the germ of everything that is to be when the final consummation is complete. The preaching of the Gospel, and its struggles with the world-powers in this dispensation, is the embryo of everything to come. It is the justification of believers, and their anointing to eternal regency and priesthood ; and it is the judgment of the world and of Satan, with prelibations of the doom that awaits them. Only, the thing is not yet consummated, actualized, and manifested. Nor will it be, in the present order, until Christ's coming with power, to enforce, by a new administration, what is now realized in part, but is still mainly prospective. Accordingly, the breaking of the seal of the sepulchre, the outpouring of spiritual power upon the apostles, the visitations upon antagonizing potencies, and all the victories of the Gospel in the course of the earthly church state, are really precursory fulfilments of the opening of these seven seals, and are in some sense included in them.

There is, then, a solid basis on which, within certain limitations, the views of the Preterist, who traces the events under the opening of the seals in the course of history since John's time, and the views of the Futurist, who refers them to the period of the judgment hereafter, may be harmonized, and both accepted, without either one impairing the distinctness or truthfulness of the other. The only prerequisite to the entertainment of both is, that the two

* See Lecture X, p. 116, note.

should be homogeneous, and that the one fulfilment should be regarded as inchoate, and only a sort of preliminary and imperfect rehearsal or earnest of the other. Solid objections may certainly be urged against the doctrine of a double sense of Scripture ; at any rate, against a double sense of such sort that one is of a wholly different nature from the other. But it is not to be doubted or denied, that many sacred prophecies have embraced events of the past, which nevertheless still travail with blessing, and await a further and completer fulfilment. Many of the Old Testament predictions of the coming of the Christ, if not the most of them, embraced at the same time, and without distinction, what was partially fulfilled in his first coming, but is to be much more largely fulfilled at his second coming. Who can question that Haggai 2 : 6, 7, has received some partial illustration in the first advent ? Yet the Holy Ghost, in Heb. 12 : 26, teaches us still to await its complete fulfilment. The inspired Peter informs us that the promise given, in Joel 2 : 28, has, in part, at least, been accomplished. (Acts 2 : 47.) And yet, surely, the word is big with blessed things for the future. Enoch's prophecy (Jude 14, 15) may reasonably be supposed to have had some reference to the flood then impending, whilst its language yet directs us forward to the future coming of the Lord.

Bacon has well observed, that there is a " latitude which is agreeable unto Divine prophecies, being of the nature of the Author, with whom a thousand years are but as one day, and therefore they are not fulfilled punctually at once, but have springing and germinant accomplishments throughout many ages, though the height or fulness of them may refer to some one age."* And it is altogether reasonable, and accordant with the nature of the subject, to agree, that something of this sort is to be found in the instance before us, giving us precursively and imperfectly the same things through the course of centuries, which are to be finally and perfectly consummated in the new administrations which the period of the great judgment is to bring forth.

Without questioning, therefore, that these foreshowings embrace the general spirit and tenor of the Church's history in this world, or that an imperfect and germinant fulfilment of the opening of these seals may be traced through the events of the past, I must yet refer their height and fulness altogether to the future, and assign them their complete fulfilment only in that momentous section of time, which intervenes between the termination of the present order, and the full establishment of the everlasting kingdom and reign of Christ and his saints over all the earth. With a very able and eloquent preacher of the early part of this century, I take the opening of these seals as significant of the Lion-Lamb's entry, by successive stages, upon the right and possession of the earth, and his actings of judicial power and sovereignty whereby he asserts and enforces his claim and title as the victorious kinsman of our fallen race, to the end that all its territory, kingdoms, peoples, and tongues may thenceforward be manifestly and in fact his forever. In other words, it sets before us the Apocalypse of Jesus Christ, in his relation to the world, and his administrations toward the nations, after his elect of the Church have been caught up from their trials and their graves to their heavenly thrones. It is the judicial proceeding of the Almighty *Goel*, to rid " the purchased possession " of the dynasties of wickedness, to cast out the rulers of the darkness of this world, to restore the earth to its proper fertility and peace, and to bring in the empire of righteousness and salvation.

The portion of the Apocalypse covered by these seven seals, includes everything between the fifth and twentieth chapters ; the seventh seal taking in the seven trumpets, and the seventh trumpet, the seven last plagues, with the battle of the great day of God Almighty.

The period of time more directly covered by these seven seals, is that which lies between the assumption of the resurrected and translated saints of the first class, and the full instalment of the millennial order, when Satan is bound,

* Advancement of Learning, Book 2.

the first resurrection completed, and the blessed and holy who have part in it reign with Christ as his kings and priests.

I have several times explained, that the first thing to be looked for in the great and marvellous transactions embraced in the consummation of all things, is the mysterious coming of the Lord Jesus to take those that wait and watch for him, with such of the dead as have fallen asleep in the same attitude. Good people are apt to be thinking of dying, and of being ready for death. But no true Christian has any right to count on dying. There is something that is more certain than death. There are some who will never die. Those who are alive and waiting for Christ when he comes, shall never taste of death. They shall be " *taken* " as Enoch was taken, as Elijah was taken, as Romanists allege that the Virgin Mary was taken, and as some say the Apostle John was taken. The words of Paul upon this point are too plain to be misunderstood. He says, " The Lord himself shall descend from heaven with a shout, . . . and we which are alive and remain shall be caught up . . . in the clouds, to meet the Lord in the air : and so shall we ever be with the Lord." (1 Thess. 4 : 16, 17.) I have no idea that a very large portion of mankind, or even of the professing Church, will be thus taken. The first translation, if I may so speak, will embrace only the select few, who " watch and pray always " that they " may be accounted worthy to escape all these things that shall come to pass, and to stand before the Son of man." (Luke 21 : 36.) " In that night there shall be two in one bed ; the one shall be taken, and the other shall be left. Two shall be grinding together ; the one shall be taken, and the other left. Two shall be in the field ; the one shall be taken, and the other left." (Luke 17 : 34, 36.) The idea is that the great body of the Church even, will be " left." And this assumption of the saints to immortality, which may occur any of these passing days or nights, and certainly is to be devoutly awaited as very near, is the first signal act by which the great period of the consummation is to be introduced.

But it will not, of itself, materially change the ordinary course of earthly things. The world will still stand, with all its wicked populations, and its apostate churches. Indeed, then only will commence the time when evil shall rush unhindered to its highest bloom of daring and blasphemy. That which hindered, being taken away, " then shall that wicked be revealed, . . . whose coming is after the working of Satan with all power and signs and lying wonders, ànd all deceivableness of unrighteousness in them that perish ; because they received not the love of the truth, that they might be saved." (2 Thess. 2 : 7–10.)

What immediately follows the translation of the elect saints, has two aspects : one as it relates to things in heaven, the other as it relates to things on earth. What relates to heaven, we have had described to us in the sublime vision of the Throne, the Living ones, and the Elders. What relates to earth, is set forth under the opening of these seven seals.

The exact number of years covered by what is described under these seals, is not specifically given ; unless, indeed, this should be the mystic seventieth week of Daniel, as generally supposed by the Fathers, and affirmed by many well-deserving modern interpreters. To the latter portion of this period, there *is* a specific duration assigned. A term of " forty and two months "— " a thousand two hundred and threescore days "—" a time, times, and half a time,"—that is, a period of *three years and a half*,—is several times mentioned ; first, in reference to the treading down of the city by the Gentiles ; second, in reference to the prophesying of the witnesses ; third, in reference to the flight of the woman into the wilderness ; and fourth, in reference to the beast's persecuting power. All these appear to be synchronous, and to fall very much, if not entirely, within the same period of time. And as the dominion of the beast ends with the battle of the great day, with which the action of the seals, trumpets, and vials sums up, we have only to date back from that consummation, to find at least three and a half years before the end, through which the opening of these seals is to run.

But it is quite manifest that this is not the entire period embraced. It is only under the seventh seal, and the sixth and seventh trumpets, that these three and a half years come in ; showing that there must be a period preceding them, of not less than equal length for the foregoing six seals. And when we take into account how Daniel's seventieth week is divided, and that it is only the latter half of it that takes in those consummated impieties which mark the beast's reign, it is rendered almost certain, that three and a half years more are to be added before the last three and a half ; thus making full *seven years* in all, as the space covered by these seals, and their included trumpets and vials.

Some have taken these numbers mystically, and so have made out a much longer period. But, I am persuaded, that no such elongation of these dates ever has had, or ever will have, an exact, or anything like a complete fulfilment. They are literal, not symbolic. And when we consider how intensely the number seven pervades this entire book, and connect its notes of time with those given in the book of Daniel, there appears to be sufficient reason to conclude, that just seven literal years are spanned by the transactions set forth under the opening of these seals ; no less, and hardly any more.

An important feature of doctrine is thus brought out, well worthy of notice as we pass. It is this, that the day of judgment, like the day of the Lord, is not a day limited to twenty-four hours, as people often erroneously imagine. All the acts described under these seven seals, are acts of judgment. Every scene is a judgment scene. The throne is a judgment throne. The agencies are all messengers of judicial power. Their operations are all connected with judicial awards. The finished work presents Satan and his world-powers vanquished, the saints in resurrection glory on their thrones, and the kingdoms of this world become the kingdoms of our Lord and of his Christ forever. There is another and final judgment scene, at the end of the thousand years ; but all the elements of that, and more, are found in what is described under these seals, trumpets, and vials. Indeed, that is only the finishing up of what is here so vigorously begun. The one gives us the morning, and the other the evening, of the great day of judgment viewed as a whole. The judgment is not one simple act, but a series of varied administrations, which do not reach all alike, nor all at the same time. It begins at the house of God, before it at all touches the world, except in a mere symptomatic way. And when it comes upon the present world-powers, it takes in many diverse and successive acts, running through the course of years, and finally concludes a thousand years afterward, by the consignment of Satan and all his seed to " the lake of fire," which is " the second death." (Rev. 20 : 14, 15.)

We accordingly have in the events set out under the opening of these seals, the characteristics and leading facts of a grand transition period. A time of judgment is always a time of transition. It is the closing up of one order of things, and the opening of another. And this is eminently the nature of the transactions here described. They show us how the present world-powers, with their Satanic intermixtures, are to terminate, and the exact particulars by and through which another and better order is to be reached ; one which is finally, by still another putting forth of judicial energy, to be resolved and settled into what shall be disturbed no more.

II. With these remarks touching the scope of these seals, we proceed to the particulars described.

The number of the seals is seven, indicative of the completeness of the administrations to which they refer. They are arranged in two distinct groups of four and three. It is the reverse of the order presented in the groupings of the seven Churches. There we had first three, and then four—perfection first and worldly deterioration afterwards. Here we have first four, and then three, intimating advance from worse to better, from earthiness to heavenliness.

The first four seals are mainly distinguished by the part which the four Living ones have in the proceedings, and the appearance of a horseman in connection with each. In all of them, the action goes out from heaven, and proceeds from the enthroned powers on high. The effect, however, is uniformly on earth, or on what relates to the earth. Some of the scenes are exceedingly disastrous and revolutionary. It would sometimes seem as if everything were falling into utter destruction. But, amid all the extraordinary and fearful shaking, upheaval, and commotion, in earth and sky, our planet still continues revolving in its place, and reappears from every scene, however terrible, neither depopulated of its generations, nor stripped of its proper investiture or elements. There is suffering, change, and an accumulation of awful and destructive prodigies ; but there is no missing of our mundane orb, and no interruption to the succession of its seasons, or the continuity of the orders of being with which God has peopled it.

As soon as the first seal was broken, " one from among the four Living ones " *spoke*. Some have said that it was the lion ; but it is not said which it was. Neither does it matter, as all four are equally concerned, and successively speak precisely the same thing.

It is, perhaps, worthy of note, that where the Living ones and Elders speak separately, there is this distinction between them : that when the subject concerns heaven, and matters of instruction, the Elders speak ; and when it concerns earth, and the going forth of power, the Living ones speak.

The speaking in this case was as with " the voice of thunder." It is the tone of terror, majesty, and judgment, in keeping with the character of the throne, and the nature of the proceeding, which is that of judicial administration.

The cry itself is very brief—Ερχου! It may be equally rendered *Go*, or *Come!* Our translators give it about as often one way as the other. It does not alter the sense here whichever way we take it. It is not an address to John, as many have regarded it, and as the questionable addition to the text—" *and see* "—would seem to require. John was already on the spot, beholding all that was transpiring, and did not need to be called any nearer, or to remove any further off. And if his nearer approach or further departure had been needed in the case of the first horseman, it could not have been needed for the succeeding ones. But we find the same command repeated in each successive instance. Neither can we explain why it should be such a voice of thundering power, if it was simply a call to the seer. Critics agree that the words, " *and see*," should be omitted.

Nor is it a call addressed to Christ, as others have supposed. That the Saviour should come, or go forward with his grand redemptive administrations, may well be conceived to be the earnest desire of the Living ones in heaven, as it should be of the saints on earth, and as it is of the whole suffering creation. But the same cry is uttered in the case of the three succeeding horsemen, in neither of which is Christ the rider. The cry is also one of official command, rather than of supplication. The voice of thunder is not the voice of prayer. And, at the time of this cry, Christ is already present. The prayer for his coming is then not properly in place. The expression is really nothing more nor less than a *bid of power*, calling the several horsemen into action.

It is the teaching of Christ and his apostles, that " the saints shall judge the world "—" shall judge angels." (1 Cor. 6 : 2, 3.) They are to share in the administrations of power against the ungodly world, and against the hosts of the wicked one, both human and angelic. And here is where the fulfilment of that teaching, in part at least, comes in. These Living ones are glorified saints. They are connected with the throne of judgment. They express the mind, and enact the will of that throne. Much of its power toward the earth goes out through them. They are enactors of the judicial energy of Him who sits upon the throne. And it is in this capacity that they speak the word " Go ! " And as they speak, so it is. As soon as it is uttered by them in heaven, it is already potent on earth. John hears the command above, and at once he sees it doing execution below.

What, then, does he see ? Mere power is an abstract quality, and not a subject of sight. It must put on shape in order to be seen. Mere effects would not so well, so clearly, and in so summary a manner, display its character and movements. The significance of the command accordingly embodies itself in living forms. John beholds horses, with riders on them. They are not literal horsemen, but symbolic pictures, in which are shown the characteristics and doings of the invisible *Goers*, put into action through the Living ones. They are the powers of the Lion-Lamb, as the Almighty Lord and Judge of all, administered by glorified saints, exalted to participation in his sublime prerogatives. Judgment upon the world has commenced, and here are the symbols of its manifestation.

" *And I saw, and, behold, a white horse ; and he that sat on him having a bow ; and a crown was given to him ; and he went forth conquering, and to conquer.*" It has been a common error, to regard this as a symbol of the success of a preached Gospel. The progress of the truth is indeed included, after the manner that I have explained ; but history furnishes nothing which can be set down as *the* fulfilment of this prophetic picture. The Gospel, as now preached, is not, and in the present order of things never will be, triumphant. This is demonstrated in the seven Epistles, and is the common teaching of the Scriptures on the subject. A leading feature in its entire history is, that it is mostly rejected. It is universally preached " as a witness to all nations," but nations, as such, with all their patronage, have never received it, and have ever been the slayers of its witnesses. The description, again, is not one of progress merely, but of a primary sending forth. The Gospel, as now preached, was sent forth more than half a century before this vision. And the vision itself is prefaced with the statement, that it refers to what was to take place after the seven Churches, and hence after the time of the apostle. Neither is a victorious conqueror on a war-steed a fitting image of " the foolishness of preaching," or the work of beseeching men to be reconciled to God. A sower going forth to sow, or a peaceful ambassador, is the scriptural picture of the preacher. And it is quite out of the spirit and scope of the Apocalypse, to find here the patient and forbearing ministrations of grace, as we now have them. We must, therefore, look for some other meaning. Nor does it lie remote. We need not consult the Roman medals or Gibbon's pages, to find it. Scripture itself is always the best interpreter of Scripture, if we only let it tell its own story.

Who has not felt a check of awe upon his heart, when contemplating that magnificent description in the book of Job ? " Hast thou given the horse strength ? Hast thou clothed his neck with thunder ? Canst thou make him afraid as a grass-hopper ? The glory of his nostrils is terrible. He paweth in the valley, and rejoiceth in his strength. He goeth on to meet the armed men. He mocketh at fear, and is not affrighted ; neither turneth he back from the sword. The quiver rattleth against him, the glittering spear and the shield. He swalloweth the ground with fierceness and rage : neither believeth he that it is the sound of the trumpet. He saith among the trumpets, Ha, ha ; and he smelleth the battle afar off, the thunder of the captains and the shouting." (Job. 39 : 19–25.) Put upon that animal now the rider of the text, crowned with sovereign power, and rushing forth to conquest unceasing ; and say whether this is the sort of picture which represents a Gospel preacher, or the slow working of the message of grace among human hearts, the great mass of which, in every age, reject and despise it.

Zechariah says, " I saw by night, and behold a man riding upon a red horse, and he stood among the myrtle trees that were in the bottom ; and behind him were red horses, speckled, and white. Then said I, O my lord, what are these ? And the angel that talked with me said unto me, I will show thee what these be. And the man that stood among the myrtle trees answered and said, These are they whom the Lord hath sent to walk to and fro through the earth." (Zech. 1 : 8–11.) Were these the ministers of grace and evangelic overture ? Were they not rather the powers of God's providence and government of the world? Hear further : " And I turned, and lifted up mine eyes, and looked, and, behold, there came four chariots out from between two mountains ; and the mountains were mountains of brass. In the first chariot were red horses ; and in the second chariot black horses ; and in the third chariot white horses : and in the fourth chariot grizzled and bay horses. Then I answered and said unto the angel that talked with me, What are these, my lord ? And the angel answered and said unto me, These are the four Spirits of the heavens, which go forth from standing before the Lord of all the earth." (Zech. 6 : 8.) And when Elisha prayed that his servant's eyes might be opened to behold the mighty powers of God, by which he protects his people, and inflicts judgment upon their enemies, what did he see ? Let the sacred word itself tell us : " And the Lord opened the eyes of the young man ; and he saw : and, behold, the mountain was full of horses and chariots of fire round about Elisha," and the hosts of Syria were smitten, and hurled back whence they came. (2 Kings 6 : 15–18.)

Is it difficult then to divine, what horses signify in connection with the Divine government and administrations ? Is not the whole idea that of swift and irresistible power ? What then are we to see in these horsemen, but earthly images of the swift, invisible, resistless power of God, going forth upon the proud, guilty, and unbelieving world ? So far as the preaching of the Gospel is a potent war-power, and an agent of judicial visitation upon the wicked, so far it is included in this symbol of the white horse and his crowned and conquering rider, but no further. Roman Emperors are here quite out of the question.

There is something special, which I have not seen satisfactorily explained, touching the nature of the work accomplished by this first horseman. It is not war and bloodshed between man and man ; for that is the work of the rider of the red horse. It is not famine and scarcity ; for that is the work of the rider on the black horse. Neither is it pestilence and mortality ; for that is the work of the rider on the pale or livid horse. What then is the character of the demonstration by which this crowned rider of the white horse pushes forward the conquest for the heavenly dominion ? That it involves a demonstration of judgment, is an idea which we dare by no means let go. This is rooted in the whole spirit of the scene, and required by the tenor of the transactions along with which this horseman appears. What then was the specific form of judgment unto victory which is here adumbrated ? It is a most interesting and important inquiry, and one which dare not be passed over without some adequate explanation.

Several peculiarities in the description may help us toward the true meaning. Of the four horsemen, only this one has " a crown." His conquests, therefore, are specifically conquests of the crown—achievements augmentative of heavenly dominion. The colour of the horse is " white "—the colour of righteousness, triumph, peace. The picture must then somehow link itself with something righteous and good, though associated with a judicial proceeding. The rider of this horse has " a bow." This is an instrument of war ; but as no literal slaughter connects with this horseman, it cannot refer to the destruction of life, but to a moral effect. Similar imagery is used to denote conquest resulting in salvation. Habakkuk says, " Thou didst ride upon thine horses and thy chariots of salvation. *Thy bow was made quite naked, even thy word.*" (Chap. 3 : 8, 9.) The disclosure and demonstration of the truth by judicial visitations of power, and its triumphant subjugation of those who would not yield to it until thus judicially " made quite naked," would be a legitimate and fitting conception to be associated with this part of the picture. The language employed concerning the career of this horseman, is also suggestive. He goes forth " conquering, and to conquer." There is an idea of continuity in the expression. It describes an ongoing of the work. It is not a past, or mere present success, but a continuous one, resulting, along with what else comes upon the scene, in complete and sovereign dominion.

Is there, then, anything in the declarations of Holy Scripture, or justly inferable from them, touching the period of the judgment, which conforms at all to these intimations? There is; and it is strange that futurist inter-preters have not been more impressed with it. " *When thy judgments are in the earth, the inhabitants of the world will learn righteousness.*" (Is. 26: 9.) " God shall shoot at them [that encourage themselves in an evil speech] with an arrow; suddenly shall they be wounded. And men shall fear, and shall declare the work of God; for they shall wisely consider of his doing." (Ps. 64: 7-9.) " *Thy people shall be willing,*" themselves presenting themselves as living sacrifices, " *in the day of thy power.*" (Ps. 110: 3.) These are all Messianic prophecies. They can be clearly identified as referring to the period of judgment. And they each affirm a mighty moral subjugation to the Lord, as the result of judicial administrations. Daniel also affirms of " the time of the end," that " many shall be purified, and made white, and tried; but the wicked shall do wickedly, and none of the wicked shall understand." (Dan. 12: 8-10.) And after the unwatchful and evil servant shall have been sur-prised by the presence of his lord whom he thought still far away, and after he has been judicially cut off from partaking of the high privileges and rewards of the " faithful and wise servant," THEN the kingdom of heaven shall assume the character of ten virgins going forth with uniform zeal and activity to meet the Bridegroom. (Matt. 24: 42-25: 1.) To locate the state of things represented in this parable, except where the Saviour himself puts it, namely, after the manifest and decisive judgment of the Church has commenced, is to miss more than half its significance. And that it shows a state of conviction, zeal, and general earnestness and anxiety touching the movements of the returning Christ, altogether different and more uniform than was ever witnessed before, no attentive observer can fail to note. It therefore proves to us, that the opening scenes of the judgment include revolutions in the religious views and feelings of men, subduing them into submission to the word and sovereignty of God in unexampled generality and power. To the same effect is the prophecy of Joel, where he connects the great outpouring of the Spirit of God, with the incoming of " the great and terrible day of the Lord." (Joel 2: 28-32.) Paul also refers to the period of the future forthcoming of the Deliverer, as a period of the turning away of unrighteousness, and of favourable change in the convictions and moral condition of multitudes, so marked and vast as to be like " *life from the dead.*" (Rom. 11: 15-26.)*

* " Prophecies foretell that even during an era of great judgments—in one of the very crises of the world's tribulations—the evangelization and salvation of mankind, so far from being arrested, shall proceed and triumph. ' For when thy judgments are in the earth,' saith the prophet Isaiah, ' then the inhabitants of the world will learn righteousness; '— thy heaviest inflictions will subserve thy purposes of mercy in the salvation of mankind."— *The Great Commission*, by J. Harris, D.D., p. 131.

And whence indeed are we to derive that " multitude which no man could number," described in chapter 7: 9-17, if not in part at least from among the living population of the earth after the crowned elders and the living ones have been taken? They are speci-fically described as persons who " come out of the great tribulation." And as they are said to have " washed their robes, and made them white in the blood of the Lamb,"— remedied the deficiency which kept them out of the first translation,—it is legitimate and reasonable to refer this wonderful cleansing to a new impulse which the incoming of that tribulation imparted to the minds and hearts of people who had been so unsanctified in their surroundings before. Bickersteth has properly said, " The return of our Lord Jesus Christ will be accompanied by unprecedented effusions of the Divine Spirit, and this with such enlarged knowledge, that judgment shall dwell in the wilderness, and righteousness in the fruitful field." The wicked will persevere in their perverseness, but understanding shall come to multitudes who would not be instructed till enlightened by the Spirit of judgment, which for ever cuts them off from the first dignities of the kingdom.

We are therefore authorized to expect, that when the great transactions of the coming judgment begin, and the Lord lays bare the literal truthfulness of his word by the marvellous demonstrations then to be made, there will be a conquering of the hearts of men to the sovereignty of Heaven, such as has never been.

Nay, if there be any truth in the doctrine of successive translations of the saints,—a doctrine so necessary to a consistent and satisfactory construction of a great variety of passages,—it is plainly to be foreseen, that great and mighty changes for the better must ensue, wherever there is any moral susceptibility left. The simultaneous disappearance from the churches of so many watching and praying ones, the demonstration thus given of the reality of all these things, and the certain excision of all the rest from the first honours of the kingdom, must needs have an effect upon those that are " left," which none but the hopelessly hardened can fail to feel in their deepest souls. Their eyes will open then, as they never were opened before. Quite naked to them then, will have become God's bow, even his Word. Gone then, will be all their spiritualizing and rationalizing with which they so long and sadly deluded themselves. At one stroke the whole Bible will have become to them a new book, and prophecy an unmistakable reality. And to all shall be added the certainty, not only that they have forever missed the high honours which once were within their reach, but that a few brief years of terror and tribulation, furnish their last hope and chance of being saved at all. How then can it be otherwise, but that there will be a breaking down of hearts in penitence, and a stirring up of souls to religious activity, and an earnestness of seeking unto the Lord ere his eternal judgments go over them, such as has never been in all the period of time !

And this is the sort of conquest and triumph which is set forth by the white horse, and his crowned rider, going forth conquering, and to conquer. It is the bloodless conquest of men to God, by the potencies of a present judgment. It is the first great effective symptom that the earth and its inhabitants are about to become our God's and his Christ's. It is a conquest of Judgment. It is the result of the laying bare of God's word and power by a judicial wound, cutting off from the exalted blessedness to which the Gospel now calls. It is the fruit of a proceeding, not in the line of humble entreaty, but in the line of penal infliction, driving home with resistless demonstration the awakening truth, that the first honours are clean gone, and that stern necessity has come for speedy and thorough work ere the last chariot of salvation shall have gone by forever. It is the knock of Christ at the door of the Church of the lukewarm Laodiceans—the sharp knock of terrifying judgment—in which he makes his last proposal to them, even of so much as to share of his supper.

Let us then learn the truth, and profit by it while we may, that this easy halfway Christianity will not avail. God requires something decisive, earnest, and hearty ;—a religion which truly renounces the devil and all his works, the vanities of the world, and the sinful desires of the flesh ;—a devotion which puts upon us a difference from the world, and marks us in heart and life as citizens of a heavenly country, only sojourning here ;—a sanctification of our earthly investments, as well as an inward looking to Christ to save us. After such a religion let us seek, and such a faith let us endeavour to exemplify ; denying ungodliness and worldly lusts, and living soberly, righteously, and godly in this present world, looking for that blessed hope, and the glorious appearing of our great God and Saviour Jesus Christ, who gave himself for us, that he might redeem us from all iniquity, and purify unto himself a peculiar people, zealous of good works.

E

LECTURE TWELFTH

JUDGMENT OF THE QUICK AND OF THE DEAD—FALSE NOTIONS CORRECTED—THE SEVERAL SEALS PARTIALLY CONTEMPORANEOUS—OPENING OF THE SECOND SEAL—BRINGS WARS AND BLOODY STRIFES—THIRD SEAL—BRINGS SCARCITY AND FAMINE—FOURTH SEAL— BRINGS GOD'S FOUR SORE JUDGMENTS—THE WAY TO ESCAPE THESE DREADFUL CALAMITIES —THE FAITHFUL SERVANTS OF GOD EVER SAFE.

REV. 6 : 3–8. (Revised Text.) And when he opened the second seal, I heard the second living one saying, Go ! And there went forth another, a red horse ; and to him that sat on him—to him was given to take away peace out of the earth, and that [men] shall slay one another : and there was given to him a great sword.

And when he opened the third seal, I heard the third living one saying, Go ! And I saw and behold a black horse, and he that sat on him having a pair of balances in his hand. And I heard as if a voice in the midst of the four living ones, saying, A measure [chœnix] of wheat for a penny [denarius], and three measures [chœnixes] of barley for a penny [denarius] ; and the oil and the wine injure thou not.

And when he opened the fourth seal, I heard [the] voice of the fourth living one saying, Go ! And I saw, and behold a pale-green horse, and he that sat on him [was] named Death, and Hades was following with him, and there was given to them power over the fourth part of the earth, to kill with sword, and with famine, and with pestilence, and by the wild beasts of the earth.

IT must be borne in mind, in dealing with these seal-openings, that we are dealing with the scenes of the judgment. They relate to " the day of the Lord." Anticipatory fulfilments have occurred, but the proper breaking of these seals, and whatever is connected with their opening, belongs to the future, and to that momentous period, now at hand, which is to close up the entire order of things now existing. The whole scene presents the action of the judgment-throne in heaven, toward those then living upon the earth.

There is an important distinction, noted in the Scriptures, and in all the creeds, between the judgment of " *the quick* " and the judgment of " *the dead*." The common idea is, that all men, those that have died, and those who are found living at the time, shall be judged alike, and in one and the same great congregation. It is conceived that the dead will all be simultaneously resurrected, and all the living simultaneously changed, and that only then the judgment will sit for the adjudication of the eternal destiny of each. Painters and poets have outdone themselves in their efforts to portray the overwhelming majesty and terror of so grand and universal an assize. But it is not according to the plain letter of the Scriptures, or of the creed of the Church. If the day of judgment is ever to come, it must find people living upon the earth, who are described as " the quick." They must, therefore, either be judged in the flesh, while still living in their natural life, or they must meet with some miraculous transformation equivalent to the resurrection, by which they lose the distinctive character of " quick." Such a change before the judgment, has also been accepted and affirmed concerning all who shall be living when the day of judgment comes. Thus, Bellarmin teaches, that the breaking in of that day will instantaneously end the natural life of all the living ; that they will all be suddenly struck dead, and by the same stroke transformed into precisely the same state in which the resurrected shall be ; and that then all distinction between " *quick* and *dead* " will have entirely and forever disappeared. And, if we take the doctrine of the simultaneous judgment of all men, we are necessitated to accept some such explanation. But then what becomes of the judgment of " *the quick*," as distinguished from the judgment of " *the dead ?* " There is, in that case, no such judgment. All natural life in the flesh being ended and overpast before any judicial awards are made, the judgment becomes only a judgment of the dead, or rather of immortals ; for there are no subjects of it except those who have ceased from the natural life, and passed into the post-resurrection state. The distinction made by the Scriptures and the creeds, between the judgment of " the quick " and the judgment of " the dead," is thus turned into a distinction without a difference—a mere matter of words, signifying nothing in particular. But the phraseology of Jesus and his inspired apostles, so uniformly employed wherever the subject is touched, is not thus to be slurred over, and stripped of its proper and natural signification. If words have any meaning, " quick " does not mean " dead," and " dead " does not mean " quick ; " and the judgment of the one cannot, therefore, be the judgment of the other. Two distinct classes are unmistakably intended, not only as to that state in which the day of judgment finds them, but also as to that state in which the day of judgment deals with them. If the natural life of " the quick " ends before they are judged, then theirs is not a judgment of the quick any more than of the dead, and one part of the sacred description utterly falls away. We must, therefore, allow a judgment which respects men still living their natural life in the flesh, the awards of which they receive, and have visited upon them in their distinctive character as " quick."

And even as respects the judgment of " the dead," there lurks in the popular idea a mischievous and confusing error. People take the resurrection as a mere preliminary of the judgment, and view the judgment itself as something distinct from the resurrection, and coming after it. The language of the last trump they conceive to be : " Awake, ye dead, and come to judgment." They consider that the dead are to be awakened for the purpose of being judged. It is also true, that not *all* the awards of the judgment are made or go into effect till after the resurrection ; but the resurrection is itself a part of the judgment. The resurrection of the wicked is certainly something different from the resurrection of the saints. It is different both in character and in time. The one is a resurrection " in glory," and the other is a resurrection of " shame and everlasting contempt." The one is " adoption, the redemption of the body," and the other is " the resurrection of condemnation." The one is a " change of our vile body, that it may be fashioned like unto Christ's glorious body," and the other is a mere reversal of the state of death, with all the corrupt fruits of the sowing to the flesh still clinging to him who is the subject of it. (Gal. 6 : 7, 8.) The one is the peculiar privilege of the elect, of those who are Christ's, who rise at Christ's coming, and live and reign with him the thousand years ; the other is subsequent—*εἶτα—afterwards,*—and embraces " the rest of the dead " who live not again until the thousand years are finished. (1 Cor. 15 : 23, 24 ; Rev. 20 : 4, 5.) These distinctions are very plainly drawn, and embrace the very highest things of our faith. Nothing that comes after the realization of them can add anything not already substantially included. The estate and destiny on both sides is thus effectually and irreversibly settled in advance. We accordingly would have the anomaly of the chief work and result of the judgment accomplished and concluded, before the judgment itself sits ! The truth is, that the resurrection, and the changes which pass " in the twinkling of an eye " upon the living, are themselves the fruits and embodiments of antecedent judgment. They are the consequences of adjudications then already made. Strictly speaking, men are neither raised nor translated, in order to come to judgment. Resurrections and translations are products of judgment previously passed, upon the dead as dead, and upon the quick as quick. " The dead in Christ shall rise first," because they are already adjudged to be in Christ ; and the living saints are caught up together with them to the clouds, because they are already adjudged to be saints, and worthy to attain that world. And the rest of the dead live not again until the thousand years are finished, and the rest of " the quick " are " left," by virtue of judicial decisions already had, and of which these things are the results. Whatever, in the line of increased blessedness or enhanced damnation, may come after, is only the further carrying into effect of what was already predecided, before there could be either resurrection or translation. And what so irreversibly fixes the estates of the persons concerned, must necessarily, in the very nature of things, be their judgment. The judgment is not a sham formality, or a solemn farce ; it is something real ; and the substance of it is the award to every man according to his works. And when we see these awards in potent effect in the very life which the dead live again, it is absurd to be thinking of the judgment as only a grand assize to which resurrection and cessation of natural life are only preliminary. And if the true judgment thus precedes, or is already embodied in, the resurrection and translation, it must necessarily take hold of the dead as dead, and the living as living. The language which the Scriptures and the creeds so carefully preserve, is thus found to possess a literal accuracy and depth too generally overlooked. We profess to believe that Christ " shall come to judge the quick and the dead." He does not come first to raise " the dead," and then to judge them, but he judges them as dead, that they may rise in their appointed lot, and share the resurrection of the just. He does not first come to change " the quick " in order to judge them ; but to judge and discriminate between them while yet living, in order that those accounted worthy may be " changed," and caught up together with the resurrected ones, and that those adjudged unworthy of so high a portion may be cut off from it, and made to suffer still other inflic- tions in this world. And it is to these judicial dealings with people " left," and living in the flesh, that the action under these horses refers.

I have shown that horses, in prophetic vision, are images of God's swift, invisible, resistless power for the defence of his people, especially in its going forth upon the proud, guilty, and unbelieving world. It was so in the case of those seen by Elisha's servant, and in the case of those mentioned by Zechariah.

In these four different horses and horsemen, we are to see four different forms of the coming forth of the judicial power of God upon the inhabitants of the earth, looking to the breaking up of the dominion of wickedness, the punishment and casting out of transgression, and the consummation of that long-pending revolution whose accomplishment is at once the fulfilment of all prophecy and all prayer.

We are not to suppose, however, that the action of one ceases entirely, before the other comes into play. They are consecutive in their incoming, in the main stress of them, and in some of their more marked circumstances, but they are all, in a measure, contemporaneous. The action of the first horseman certainly is continuous ; for he goes forth in conquest unto conquest, which terminates only in the complete victory in which the opening of the seals ends. His career, therefore, runs on through that of his three successors, and through all the remaining seals. No such intense continuity is expressed with reference to the action of the other horsemen ; and the nature of their work is such as not likely to extend itself so far. But there is an inner and natural relationship between the things adumbrated, which renders it quite evident that their several careers overlap each other, and that the doings of the one run side by side with the doings of the other.

We have seen that the white horse, and his crowned rider, and bloodless conquests, indicate mighty moral victories for the heavenly Kingdom, wrought by the spirit of judgment. When God's judgments are in the earth, then will the inhabitants thereof learn righteousness. People shall be made willing in the day of His power.

But John beheld a second horse, called into action in like manner as the first,—" a red horse ; and to him that sat on him, was given to take away peace out of the earth, and that [men] shall slay one another : and there was given to him a great sword."

The colour of this horse is *red—fiery—the hue of blood*. This itself is indicative of vengeance and slaughter. The great dragon is " red," and he is " a murderer from the beginning." The mighty Hero of Salvation, travailing in the greatness of his strength, and crushing his enemies beneath his feet, is " red " in his apparel, emblematic of his work of violent destruction. Nor can we be mistaken in regarding this horse and his rider as significant of bloody times. His work is specifically described to be the taking of peace out of the earth. A great and terrible weapon is also put into his hand ; not the ordinary sword of war (ρομφαία), but (μαχαιρα μεγαλη) a great sword of one having the power of life and death. And the result of his presence is war, much taking of life by public executions, and mutual killing among men.

The picture is particularly terrific. It presents not only disturbance of the relation of nations, the rising of nation against nation, and kingdom against kingdom ; but internecine collisions, civil wars, the murderous hate of one portion of citizens exercised against another portion, and bloody commotions all over the face of society, having no issue but wretchedness and depopulation. It is the rampage of human passion raging to all forms of bloodshed, and the authorities of state in vain drawing the sword to put it down.

A small specimen of this state of things was enacted in the days of Asa, when Israel had been " a long season without the true God, and without a teaching priest, and without law ; " in which times " there was no peace to him that went out, nor to him that came in, but great vexations were upon all the inhabitants of the countries. And nation was destroyed of nation, and city of city ; for God did vex them with all adversity." (2 Chron. 15 : 3, 5.)

Another small specimen of the same was realized in those times of which Josephus writes, when " the disorders in all Syria were terrible, and every city was divided into two armies, encamped one against another, and the preservation of the one party was the destruction of the other : so the day-time was spent in the shedding of blood, and the night in fear." And again, when, as he writes, " There were besides disorders and civil wars in every city : and all those that were quiet from the Romans turned their hands one against another. There was also a bitter contest between those that were fond of war, and those that were desirous of peace. At first, this quarrelsome temper caught hold of private families, who could not agree among themselves: after which, those people that were the dearest to one another, broke through all restraints with regard to each other, and every one associated with those of his own opinion, and begun already to stand in opposition to one another, so that seditions arose everywhere, while those that were for innovations, and were desirous of war, by their youth and boldness, were too hard for the aged and the prudent ; and in the first place, all the people of every place betook themselves to rapine : after which they got together in bodies, in order to rob the people of the country, insomuch that for barbarity and iniquity, those of the same nation did no way differ from the Romans ; nay, it seemed a much lighter thing to be ruined by the Romans than by themselves."

Fancy a world which has no peace in it—no concord but that of lawless and selfish passion—no regard for life when it stands in the way of covetousness or ambition—no amity between its nationalities, or internal harmony and toleration between citizens of the same city or state—but every man's sword is against his fellow, and every one's hand rises up against the hand of his neighbour, and international slaughter, civil butchery, and private revenge and murder are the order of the day,—and you have what the earth will be under the judgment power of this red horse and his rider. Of old, already, Jehovah threatened to bring a sword to avenge the quarrel of the covenant ; and to " call for a sword upon all the inhabitants of the earth." (Jer. 25 : 29.) And in this horseman, with his great sword taking peace from the earth, and desolating the world with violence and bloodshed, we have the final fulfilment of that threat. Nor need any one be at a loss to see how everything is already tending to just such a condition of society and the world.

But the breaking of the third seal starts another horse—" a black horse "—at whose appearance the seer is moved to exclamation : " *And I saw, and, behold, a black horse, and he that sat on him having a pair of balances in his hand.*"

More feeling is expressed at the appearance of this power, because a more general and unmanageable plague is the subject of contemplation. Long ago did Jeremiah say : " They that be slain with the sword are better than they that be slain with hunger ; for these pine away, stricken through for want of the fruits of the field." (Lam. 4 : 9.) *Black* is the colour of dearth and famine. When Jeremiah contemplated Judah and his gates " *black* unto the ground," it was a picture " concerning the dearth." (Jer. 14 : 1, 2.) The same prophet says : " Our skin was *black* like an oven, because of the terrible *famine.*" (Lam. 5 : 10.) It is the hue of mourning ; and the rest of the description identifies it as mourning by reason of scarcity.

The rider of this black horse carries a pair of balances in his hand. There is close and careful weighing : and the things weighed are the common articles of food. John also " heard as if a voice in the midst of the four Living ones, saying : A chœnix of wheat for a denarius, and three chœnixes of barley for a denarius." When things are plentiful, exact weight or measure is not regarded. The Spirit, as given to Christ, was given without measure. So, also, in Joseph's gathering of corn, and in David's gathering of copper for the temple. And when corn is abundant, it is sold by gross measure, and no attention is paid to a few hundred grains, one way or the other. But when it becomes high in price and scarce, then it is strictly weighed, and every ounce is taken into account. And, in numerous places in Scripture, the weighing out of the bread to be eaten, is given as one of the marks of great scarcity and want. (Lev. 26 : 20 ; Ez. 4 : 10, 16.)

But the picture is further shown to be one of scarcity, by the prices of provisions which John heard declared. People do not generally suppose that God has much to do with price-lists. They go up and down, and millions higgle over them every day, but no one thinks of anything Divine connected with them. But whether men realize it or not, price-lists are made in heaven. John hears the rates of corn and bread announced by the same heavenly powers by which these mystic horses are called into action. Whatever the weather, the crops, the quantities of money in the country, the extent of speculation in the market, or other subordinate causes may have to do with it, the prime and all-controlling cause is the decree of the throne. It is God, from whom we have our daily bread, and it is by His will that it is plentiful and cheap, or scarce and costly.

The prices here given, are judgment prices, indicative of extreme scarcity and distress.. A *chœnix* is about a pint and a half of our measure, and is the ordinary allowance of wheat to a man for one day's scanty subsistence. A *denarius* was the ordinary wages for a full day's labour. And when a chœnix of wheat costs a denarius, it is as much as a man can do to earn the bread he himself consumes, leaving nothing for his family or for his other wants.

But even at these ruinous rates, there is not wheat enough. People have to betake themselves to barley—the food of horses and beasts of burden. Yet the barley is as difficult of procurement as the wheat. In ordinary times, a denarius would buy twenty-four chœnixes of barley ; but here a denarius will buy but *three*—the scanty allowance for a day's subsistence for a slave. The arrival of things at such a pass, accordingly argues a severity of hard times, distress, and want, almost beyond the power of imagination to depict. Yet, it is but the natural result of the state of things under the red horse. The two are closely connected as cause and effect. Take away peace from the earth, and inaugurate universal wars, civil strifes, and bloody feuds, and terrible scarcity of the means of subsistence must follow.

One mitigation attends this fearful judgment. The command to the invisible messenger is, " The oil and the wine injure thou not." These would naturally be less affected by the diversion of the population from their proper business to their bloody work, than those crops which depend more upon human efforts. Olive trees and vines, when once established, will grow and produce year after year without much attention ; but not wheat and barley. Yet these also depend upon God, and grow and produce only by his command. And it is by his special order that their fruitfulness is preserved in the midst of this reigning scarcity of other things. And it is a matter of grace, that the minister of vengeance is so far restrained.

But the very reservation also reflects the intensity of the famine as respects the ordinary means of subsistence. It carries with it the intimation that, but for the preservation of the oil and wine, it would be impossible for men to find sufficient food on which to keep themselves alive. Nay, though a thing of mercy as regards men's lives, it also bears with it a moral aggravation of the affliction. It is everywhere set forth as one of the characteristics of the last times, that people shall be given to luxurious habits, and inordinate appetency for superfluities of diet. " Eating and drinking," and every extreme of carnal indulgence, is then to mark their modes of life. The staple food of mankind is despised, and every expensive luxury is impatiently pursued. Hence, God shuts them in to their luxuries, partly in mitigation of judgment, but at the same time also in aggravation of it. Just as Israel, lusting after flesh, and no longer satisfied with the bread Jehovah provided, was compelled to live on flesh until it became almost impossible for the people to swallow it (Numbers 11 : 19, 20) ; so God in judgment takes away what men despise, and forces them to live on luxuries made loathsome because there is nothing else, that they may learn the folly of their wisdom, and taste the fearfulness of their guilty hallucination.

But while all this is being experienced, a fourth seal is broken, and out comes another horse, and horseman, still more terrible. This is the last, and the climax of this particular series of terrific images. The first horse is pure white, mighty, but bloodless in his career ; the second is fiery red, blood-coloured, and revengeful ; the third is black, mournful, gloom-shaded ; and when we would think everything dreadful in colour exhausted, another breaks upon the view, more terrible than any that have gone before. A pale, death-green, and cadaverous horse appears. Χλωρος, translated *pale*, denotes a leprous colour. (Lev. 13 : 49 ; 14 : 37.) It properly means *green*, and is several times so translated in the Apocalypse and elsewhere. (Rev. 8 : 7 ; 9 : 4 ; Mark 6 : 39.) There are instances of its use in the classics to denote the wan and deathly expression of the face when overwhelmed with fright or faintness. When applied as here, it can only mean a greenish ghastliness, something like the colour of a corpse or putrefying flesh. It describes this last horse as unspeakably more horrible than either of the others.

But his rider and attendants intensify the awfulness of the picture. That rider is *Death*, and *Hades* follows with him. There is also given to them power over the fourth part of the earth, to kill with sword, and with famine, and with pestilence, and by means of the wild beasts of the earth. The preceding pictures continue, and repeat themselves in this, but with increased intensity and still other additions. The rider of the red horse is War, destroying peace and exciting all manner of strife and bloodshed. The rider of the black horse is Famine, taking away the staff of bread and oppressing the world with terrible scarcity. And the rider of this ghastly-coloured horse carries on the work of his predecessors to still more horrible excesses, and matures their fruits in death-plague and depredations of the animal tribes. The several forms of affliction advance from the lesser to the greater, and one naturally grows out of the other. General war and bloody strife becomes the occasion of famine ; and famine brings pestilence ; and their combined depopulation of the earth encourages the increase and ferocious instincts of wild beasts, and the multiplication of noxious creatures. God does not work miracles where none are needed ; and evils are all so closely related, that it is only necessary to start one, to bring down the whole train. A state of general war and bloody civil strife is terrible enough, but when to it is added scarcity, black hunger, desolating pestilence, and the ravages of depredacious animals—when, as in this instance, Death takes the reins, and the living world is over-run by the legions of the dead—then comes " the great and terrible day of the Lord."

Death is not a being, but the fruit of a power, which operates through many different agencies. It is here personified and represented under the picture of some mighty Cæsar, mounted, and riding forth in fearful triumph.

Hades is not a being ; it is the grave—the dark region of the dead—the realm which remorselessly swallows up all the living. It is here personified under the image of some great voracious monster, stalking after the rider on the ghastly horse, indicating that whither this horseman comes, Hades comes, and the world of the dead takes the place of the world of the living.

The means by which these awful desolations are wrought, are God's " four sore judgments,—the sword, and the famine, and the noisome beast, and the pestilence to cut off man and beast." (Ezek. 14 : 21.) These are the most dreadful plagues with which God usually chastises men. They are not reserved exclusively for the last periods of time. We can trace them under Roman emperors, but also before there were Roman emperors, and since Roman emperors have ceased to be. But the height and fulness of them falls within the period to which these seals relate.

The true sample, as it was in some sort the beginning of the tribulation set forth under these horses, was given in what befell the Jews in the last period of their state. War was there in all its fearfulness. Commotion and strife distracted and distressed the whole land. Wholesale butchery was the order of the day. Whole cities were turned into mere graves, full of dead. Millions of men, women, children, fell by the sword, famine, exposure, fright, and other forms of death. Shut in at last to their holy city by the tight cordon of Rome's legions, the soul sickens over the recitals of the sufferings, oppressions, cruelties, and living death which settled down upon the doomed people. Perishing by houses and families every day, the dead became too numerous for the living to bury ; and the wretchedness was so great that men, and even mothers, forgot their sympathies. Affection died ; all regard for the rights of one another died ; and the glorious city of David and Solomon was turned into a tomb under the prancings of the ghastly horse, whose rider is Death, whose attendant is Hell, and who is yet to dash through the world and trample it in like manner under his dreadful hoofs.

We are not to infer, however, that there is to be an utter extirpation and extinction of the race of mankind under these visitations. Only " the fourth part of the earth " is put under this fourth horseman's sway. There are also other seals to be broken, and other judgment scenes to be enacted, of which men in the flesh, nations and earthly confederations are largely the subjects. We have thus far only the first acts in the terrible drama. We have been contemplating merely the beginning of sorrows, which multiply and grow in fearfulness till the last seal is broken, the last trumpet sounded, and the last bowl of wrath emptied. Other and worse impieties are to come, and still more awful displays of Almighty vengeance upon the enactors of them. The greatest masterpiece of hell yet awaits full development, and the greatest thunders of God's judgment remain for its wreck, and the final ruin of its unsanctified abettors.

I know not, my friends, what degree of credit or thought you may give to these things ; but, as Paul told the assembly on Mars' Hill, so I tell you, that " God hath appointed a day, in the which he will judge the world [*the living world of mankind*] in righteousness, by that man whom he hath ordained; whereof he hath given assurance unto all men, in that he hath raised him from the dead." (Acts 17 : 31.) You may shrink back and exclaim as Balaam did : "Alas, who shall live when God doeth this ! " Like Balaam you may also turn away from it to pursue the wages of unrighteousness. But, I beseech you to beware, lest you procure for yourselves a Balaam's end. The picture may be dark, and awful beyond what you are willing to contemplate ; but it must be filled out in the real world some day, as certainly as God's word is true.

Neither has it been so graphically sketched without a purpose. The Almighty intends that we should look at it, that we should be premonished by the contemplation of it, and that it should have effect upon our hearts and lives. He would have us see and know to what this vain, proud, and guilty world is coming, that we may separate ourselves from it, and secure a better portion. And with all the universal agony in which its presumptuous dominion shall expire, there is this to be added by way of comfort, that there is no necessity that any of us should ever feel it. A way of escape exists. As there was an ark for Noah when the world was drowned, and a Pella for the saints when Jerusalem sunk under God's resentment for the murder of His Son, so there is a place of safety provided for us, where we may view these horsemen, as unharmed by their fearful doings, as was the apostolic seer himself. It was of this the Psalmist sung, when he said : " In the time of trouble he shall hide me in his pavilion : in the secret of his tabernacle shall he hide me." (Ps. 27 : 5.)

Nor is the grave this hiding-place. Should these scenes begin to-night, the refuge is as available and as availing as if they should tarry yet a thousand years. God's pavilion is above the clouds, not under the ground. Not hades, but heaven, is the true centre of the aspirations of the saints. And as Isaiah beheld these desolating judgments about to sweep the earth, he heard a voice of sweetness going before them, saying : " Come, my people, enter thou into thy chambers, and shut thy doors about thee : hide thyself as it were for a little moment, until the indignation be overpast." (Is. 26 : 20.) That voice comes from heaven. It is none other than the loving Saviour's voice. It is a voice addressed to his true people. It is a voice which calls them to where he is. Hence the same prophet adds : " They that wait for the Lord shall renew their strength ; they shall mount up with wings as eagles." (Is. 40 : 31.) Hence the apostle still more plainly declares : " We which are alive and remain shall be caught up . . . in the clouds, to meet the Lord in the air : and so shall we ever be with the Lord." (1 Thess. 4 : 17.) Hence also that admiring song of David : " Oh how great is thy goodness, which thou hast laid up for them that fear thee ; which thou hast wrought for them that trust in thee before the sons of men ! Thou shalt hide them in the secret of thy presence from the pride of man : thou shalt keep them secretly in a pavilion from the strife of tongues." (Ps. 31 : 19, 20.) And the direction of the apostle is, that we " comfort one another with these words." (1 Thess. 4 : 18.)

The only question is, as to how we stand in relation to the Lamb who breaks these seals. Do we accept and rely on him as our hope and salvation ? Are we trusting to his meritorious sacrifice as the satisfaction for our guilt, and to his victorious exaltation to the right hand of the Father, as compassing everything needful to make us forever safe ? Have we truly taken him as our Lord, confessed ourselves to his Gospel, and given our hearts and our all to his service ? Are we making it the great business of our lives to " watch and pray always," and to keep ourselves in fellowship with him, patiently waiting upon him as our all-sufficient portion ? Oh, blessed, blessed, is that servant who, when his Lord cometh, shall be found so doing ! He is safe. His judgment is passed. No dregs of wrath remain for him to drink. Christ will not leave him to suffer with hypocrites and unbelievers. And while these storms of woe are desolating the earth, he shall be rejoicing in a heavenly crown. Yea, and I would be recreant to my commission as a minister of Christ, if I did not declare the Master's readiness this hour to receive and seal every one of you against all dangers of the great day of wrath. Indeed, these pictures of coming woe have been given to awaken us from our false security, to quicken us in the search for the refuge set before us, and to bring us to unreserved consecration to the Lord our Redeemer. Only fall in with his offers, and " salvation will God appoint for walls and for bulwarks." (Is. 26 : 1.) Cleave unto him, and to his unfailing promises, and " ye shall have a song, as in the night when a holy solemnity is kept ; and gladness of heart, as when one goeth with a pipe to come into the mountain of the Lord, to the mighty one of Israel." (Is. 33 : 29.) Rest in Jesus, and do his commandments, and the place which he has gone to prepare is yours ; and before his wrath breaks forth upon the guilty world, he will come again, and receive you to himself, that where he is, there you may be also. (John 14 : 1–3.)

You have read in the Scriptures of the superior favours of " the wise," in relation to the day of judgment. The wise virgins went in with the Bridegroom when the door was shut against their foolish companions. Solomon wrote : " The wise shall inherit glory." But an essential part of that blessed wisdom is, to " observe these things "—to understand this, to consider what the end shall be. " A prudent man foreseeth the evil, and hideth himself." To close our eyes and ears against these foreshowings of God, or to delay earnest and energetic effort in view of their speedy fulfilment, is not wisdom. There must be the wakeful, observant, far-seeing eagle eye, if there is to be a timely and triumphant eagle flight. And if we would " escape all these things that shall come to pass," and find a place of safety in the presence of the Son of man, we must learn to realize that the day of these fearful visitations is approaching, and that we have no time to lose, and no opportunities to be neglected. " The voice of free grace cries escape to the mountain ; " but it is a voice which we have occasion to heed with solemn care and prompt obedience. " For if the word spoken by angels was steadfast, and every transgression and disobedience received a just recompense of reward, how shall we escape if we neglect so great salvation, which, at the first, began to be spoken by the Lord, and was confirmed unto us by them that heard him ; God also bearing them witness, both with signs, and wonders, and divers miracles, and gifts of the Holy Ghost, according to his own will ? " (Heb. 2 : 2–4.)

LECTURE THIRTEENTH

THE CHARACTER OF THE FIFTH SEAL—INDICATES BLOODY PERSECUTION—THE TESTIMONY
FOR WHICH MEN SHALL BE SLAIN IN THE PERIOD OF THIS SEAL—DISEMBODIED SOULS—
THEIR LIVING CONSCIOUSNESS—THEIR PLACE BENEATH THE ALTAR—THEIR CRY TO CHRIST—
THE ANSWER THEY RECEIVE—COMMENTS ON THEIR CASE TOUCHING THE CONSUMMATION.

REV. 6: 9–11. (Revised Text.) And when he opened the fifth seal I saw beneath the
altar the souls of those that had been slain on account of the word of God, and on account
of the testimony which they held fast : and they cried with a great voice, saying : Until
when, thou Master, the holy and true, dost thou not judge and avenge our blood from them
that dwell on the earth ? And there was given to each of them a white robe, and it was said
to them that they should rest yet a little time, until their fellow-servants also, and their
brethren, shall have been completed, who are about to be slain as also they themselves
[had been].

IT is hardly worth while to occupy attention with the diverse and contradictory interpretations that have been given of this seal. Though all are more
or less intermingled with some truth, the principles upon which the Apocalypse
is to be construed, and which have been followed in this exposition, lead us,
with directness and certainty, to conclusions which brush away, as only so
much rubbish, the most that has been written on the subject.

Professor Stuart takes this fifth seal as a mere artistic prelude to certain
very simple results. He refers to Nelson's address to his squadrons, on the
eve of the engagement which yielded England her greatest naval victory,
as an illustration, in real life, of what he supposes John to be attempting in
poetic fancy, as a preparation for the victorious conclusion ; only that the
hosts here are imaginary, and their inspiration, by the cry of the slaughtered
saints, merely a lively poetic conception.

But if the array is mere poetry, we would naturally suppose that the
vengeance and the victory are ideal also ; and so the whole Apocalypse is
turned into artistic fiction ; which is about all it is in the hands of this writer.
With him it is a book everywhere full of wondrously grand beginnings,
exordiums, and proemial marshallings of poetic images ; but when he reduces
the results to literal and solid prose, what crowds John's twenty-two eventful
chapters, might be more clearly stated in twenty-two well-written *lines*. The
least to be said of such exposition is, the less of it the better.

According to an older commentator, " the scope of this seal is not prophetically to point out new events, and to relate to a particular time." But
this is exactly the opposite of the truth. If the text means anything, " new
events " are just what it is intended prophetically to point out, and " a
particular time " is precisely that to which it does relate. As certainly as the
Apocalypse is the book of the consummation of God's providence with this
present world, and as certainly as the action under these seven seals is the
action of judgment upon faithless Christians, usurpers, and rebels, just so
certainly does this fifth seal refer to a particular stage and phase in these
judicial transactions, and to a class of events which only then come to their full
development. As the throne is a judgment throne, and the whole administration
proceeding from it is an administration of judgment, every seal that is
broken must lay open a phase of judgment, in one direction or another. All
the seals, thus far, have been judgment seals ; and the two that follow are
judgment seals ; capable of being identified, as such, from the nature of the
events attending them. The symmetry of the whole would therefore be
interrupted, and an unaccountable break made in the distinctly connected

series, if this fifth in the list were to be taken in any other acceptation. The four horsemen are judgment powers. The earthquake, and the terrific commotions in earth and sky, under the sixth seal, are directly linked with the presence of judgment. The seventh seal, with its seven trumpets and seven last plagues, is nothing but judgment from beginning to end. And whatever peculiarities may attend the breaking of the particular seal now before us, it can be nothing other than judgment also.

The manifestations under the breaking of this seal differ, in some respects, from the four preceding. There is here no expression from the Living ones. There are no horsemen or horses. And the burden of the description is exhibited in the results rather than in the processes. Still, everything turns out as belonging to the same general category of trial and suffering. Under the first seal we have the picture of moral conquest, by means of the arrow of truth, sped by the power of sorrowful judgment. Under the second, we have war, disorder, strife, and bloodshed. Under the third, we have famine and distressing scarcity. Under the fourth, we have the combined fruit of all these,—pestilence, death-plague, and the living world largely overrun with the regions of the dead. And, under this fifth seal, we have added, bloody persecution of those who hold and testify to the truth. The entire population of the earth, at that period, being alike rejected from the company of those accounted worthy to escape these evil times, is alike made to feel the stripes of judgment. The good as well as the bad suffer the hour of trial. And though there shall be multitudes then brought to the knowledge of the truth, they will all be such as had failed to improve their more favourable opportunities in the preceding days of Divine long-suffering and forbearance ; and hence, by way of judgment for their previous folly, their piety, at this late hour, becomes a thing of sore cost. Having been unbelieving, worldly-minded, and hypocritical, when they might have walked with God without serious risk, they now find the way of salvation judicially become a way of torture and of death. Evil and depravity will hold the sovereignty and power in this world unto the last. And it would be strange if the bad passions, which then are to reach their most aggravated intensity, should not also develop particular violence in the direction from which the Church, in every age, has suffered more or less.

Hence, this fifth seal is the picture of Persecution and Martyrdom. As soon as it was opened, John saw souls of people " slain on account of the word of God, and on account of the testimony which they held fast." It sets before us the solemn fact, that people who will not give their hearts to God now, when once these judgment times set in, if they ever get to heaven at all, will be compelled to go there through fire and blood.

There are no voices of command from heaven under this seal, and no messengers despatched from the throne ; for the reason, that bloody persecutions of God's servants come from beneath—not from above. It is the devil who is the murderer from the beginning, and by him, and his seed, has all martyr-blood been made to flow that ever has flowed or ever will. It is the Dragon that makes war with the saints. Celestial powers are concerned in it no further than to permit the malignant butchery. It is not flashed forth from the sky, like the calamities with which the wicked and rebellious are overwhelmed ; but it is left to develop itself from Satan's reign and domination in the hearts of his children, unmoved by any direct agency from heaven. The Living ones do not say, *Go !* for they are neither directly nor indirectly concerned in bringing suffering upon God's servants for their fidelity to the truth. No horses dash out upon the scene, because no Divine powers are employed in martyring the saints. The entire earthly part of the proceeding enacts itself by the powers already in sway among depraved mortals, and John beholds only the results. The seal opens, and the invisible world has a vast accession of souls of martyrs, slain on account of the word of God, and on account of the testimony which they held fast. They are not the martyrs of the past ages, for those, by this time, already have their crowns, and are seated on their heavenly thrones, and are with Christ in glorified form, as we saw in chapters 4 and 5. These are, therefore, martyrs of this particular period—martyrs who suffer the great tribulation which all preceding saints and martyrs escape—martyrs of the judgment times, who lose their lives for their faithful testimony during the sharp and troublous era in which God's judgments are in the earth.

In treating of them more particularly, we may notice,

I. THE CAUSE OF THEIR MARTYRDOM ;
II. THEIR ESTATE AS JOHN BEHOLDS THEM ;
III. THE CRY THEY UTTER ;
IV. THE ANSWER THEY RECEIVE.

It is an old maxim : *Non est mors, sed causa mortis quæ facit martyrem.* " It is not death, but the cause in which death is incurred, which constitutes a martyr." Millions upon millions perish under the preceding seals, but they are not therefore martyrs. The cause for which the persons mentioned here were slain, constitute them true martyrs. They " had been slain *on account of the word of God, and on account of the testimony which they held fast.*" However sceptical, rationalistic, or unbelieving they may have been previous to the setting in of the judgment, the occurrences under the first four seals had quite cured them of their erroneous thinking and indifference. What they once held only in the coldness of mere speculative faith, or received only with much subtle refining, and rasping down to a materialistic philosophy, or disbelieved altogether, they had now learned, to their sorrow, to have been the literal and infallible word of God. The Bible they now read with new eyes, and received and obeyed with a new heart. Its literal teachings they now were brought to understand, appreciate, live, and proclaim as the unmistakable Revelation of the Lord God Almighty. There will still be plenty of unbelief, scepticism, and utter rejection of the Scriptures ; and the dominant spirit of the times will be the spirit of rebellion against the Lord, and of contempt for his word. But that spirit will now have been quite cast out of the persons brought to view in this vision. Having learned to deny themselves, to crucify their self-seeking, to cease from their confidence in their own fancies, and to accept, live, and testify to the true will and word of God, they will have come to be genuine servants of the Most High. And this is one of the procuring causes of the world's hatred of them, and wish to have them put out of the way.

But there is something more special entering into the cause of their martyrdom. In addition to their close adherence to the Divine word, and as one of the most marked fruits of it, there was a particular " testimony which they held fast ; " and on account of which, more directly, the world could not abide them. Many have regarded their whole testimony as nothing different from the common testimony of good and faithful men in every age. John says that he " was in the isle that is called Patmos, for the word of God, and for the testimony of Jesus Christ ; " and the testimony of these martyrs is considered to be the same for which John was banished. But the phraseology is not the same, and seems to indicate something personal to these martyrs themselves. It was not the testimony of Jesus in general ; but " τὴν μαρτυρίαν—THAT *testimony, which they held fast* "—some particular testimony specially in question in their times, and specially obnoxious to the then reigning spirit. And when we consider the character of the period in which they were called to testify ; what it was that had operated to bring them into this attitude of zeal for the Divine word ; what would naturally be uppermost in a mind enlightened as to the times on which they had fallen, and what would be most offensive to an unbeliever in those times, we can be at no loss to have suggested to us what the particular character of that testimony was. It was necessarily a testimony touching the judgment already begun ; a testimony which interpreted all the plagues, disorders, and horrors around them, as the veritable inflictions of the Almighty, now risen up to pay off all the long-accumulating arrearages of his wrath upon transgressors ; a testimony that the true elect had already been received up into glory, and that, in a few short years more, the whole mystery of God should be finished, and all his enemies cast down to irretrievable perdition ; a testimony that swift and utter destruction now impended over all the governments, fabrics, powers, and hopes of this world ; that the fires were then already burning which should never more be extinguished or repressed till everything of this world, and all its devotees, should be consumed from root to leaf ; that Christ, the angry Judge, was then present in the clouds, ready to be revealed in all the terrors of his consuming power ; that the day of grace was in its last darkening twilight of departure, after which nothing should remain but everlasting discomfiture and death ; a testimony that the world was then already trembling in the agonies of its dissolution, and that the last hope of salvation was flickering in its socket, ready to expire.

In a modified degree, this is ever the testimony of the true people and ministers of God ; but, at such a time, and in such surroundings as these martyrs testified, there would needs be an intensity, a certainty, and a pressing urgency in their convictions and utterances, such as had never before appeared. People who had been cool, complacent, and philosophic in their religion before, will then have been awakened to a state of warmth, and earnestness, and excitement, and zeal, a thousandfold more irrepressible and energetic than what they had previously regarded as sheer fanaticism, and piety run mad. Oh, there will be fervour then, and outspoken testifying for God then, and warnings with tears and entreaties then, and striking exposi-tions of the prophecies then, and appeals and outpourings from the men of God more thrilling than the cries of Jonah in the streets of Nineveh ! It will be more than the hardened hearts of scorning unbelievers can bear. And because of being besieged and pressed by the resistless arguments and fervency which then shall be brought to bear upon them, they will seize the witnesses of the truth, and punish them, and resort to all sorts of murderous violence, to silence them, and put them out of the world. Thus, then, because their days of indifference toward the Divine predictions have passed away, and because they now are faithful in standing to the truth as to what God has said, and as to what times they have fallen upon, and because they will no more keep silence touching the awful perdition about to break forth upon the guilty world, they are massacred and slain.

II. THEIR ESTATE AS JOHN BEHOLDS THEM.

They are " souls "—disembodied souls—souls in that state which ensues as the result of corporeal death.

Their slaying, then, is not the end of them. It is not the total interruption of their being in all respects. It makes them invisible to men in the flesh, in the natural state ; but it does not hinder their living on as souls, or their being visible to heavenly eyes, or to the eyes of John in his supernatural and prophetic exaltation. The holy Apocalyptist tells us that he " saw " them, although they " had been slain ; " and heard them speaking with loud voices, though their material tongues had been burnt to ashes, and their corporeal organs of speech had been stiffened in death.

It is altogether a wrong interpretation of the Scriptures which represents the dead in a state of non-existence, unconsciousness, or oblivion. I am not among those who think that " they which are fallen asleep in Christ are perished," either forever, or for a limited time. There is such a thing as an intermediate state between death and the resurrection ; but it is not a state of utter dilapidation and cessation of being. It is an abnormal and unsatis-factory state, far below what is to be gained by the resurrection ; but it is not a state of vacancy and nothingness. However strongly the ruinous character and evil of death may be stated in some Old Testament passages, there are others in the Scriptures which, by all just and fair exegesis, prove and demonstrate that mental and psychical life continues under it, and continues in wakeful consciousness. And if any one has doubts upon this point, let him candidly consult and determine the positive meaning of the following texts :

Matt. 10 : 28 : " *Fear not them which kill the body, but are not able to kill the soul ; but rather fear Him which is able to destroy both soul and body in hell.*" The argument from this text is plain, unanswerable, and conclusive. If the soul dies, or goes into oblivion, when the body dies, then he that kills the body would, with the same stroke, kill the soul too. But our Saviour tells us that those who kill the body cannot kill the soul. And if it be said that this is meant only of the utter destruction of the soul, God having promised a resurrection to life again, then our Saviour might as well have denied that it is in the power of man to kill the body, because God certainly will raise it again at the last day. But our blessed Lord grants that the body may be killed by man, in the same sense wherein he denies that the soul can be ; and therefore he is not speaking with reference to the resurrection at all. There is, then, a life which the death of the body cannot touch.*

Luke 20 : 38 : " *He [the God of Abraham, Isaac, and Jacob] is not the God of the dead, but of the living : for all live unto him.*" So far as the righteous are concerned, we are here assured that, although they " sleep in Jesus," as regards the body, and are " absent from the body," as regards the soul, they still " ALL LIVE UNTO GOD." This the Saviour quotes from the Old Testament, where " Moses calleth the Lord the God of Abraham, and the God of Isaac, and the God of Jacob ; for He is not a God of the dead, but of the living : for all live unto Him." The argument assumed is, that a negation of existence dissolves all covenant relations. God cannot be called the God of beings who no longer exist, or the continuity of whose existence has been interrupted by a blank. Whatever else He may be, it is no property of His to be a God of nonentities. " HE IS NOT A GOD OF THE DEAD, BUT OF THE LIVING." But Abraham, Isaac, and Jacob were dead, and had been dead for centuries ; and yet He proclaims Himself " the God of Abraham, Isaac, and Jacob." The conclusion is thus deduced by the Saviour, that though Abraham, Isaac, and Jacob were dead, as to their bodies, they were still, in some sense, *living unto God.*

Very pertinent, also, was this argument to the question of the resurrection, in support of which it was produced. Abraham, Isaac, and Jacob, being still *alive unto God*, though corporeally dead, God's covenant with them still held—held because both parties were still in being ; and because it still held, the promises which it included had yet to be fulfilled, which could only be in the resurrected state. In this text we accordingly have existence and life predicated of the righteous dead, and that existence and life put forward as the basis of the continued validity of the covenant, which covenant necessitates a resurrection, that its promises may not fail. And though this passage specifically refers to but one class of the dead, yet, by disproving the non-existence, and establishing the continued life of departed believers, it overthrows the doctrine of the oblivion of the dead in the abstract, and fastens very strong unlikelihood upon its truth in any case.

Luke 16 : 19-31 : the case of the rich man and Lazarus. In this startling parable, if parable such an unveiling of the invisible world may be called (it is not called a parable in the Scriptures), we have not only principles on which to argue the non-oblivion of the dead, but literal instances and illustrations of the continued life and consciousness of departed souls of both classes—good and bad. That the scene of this narrative is laid in the state

---

* The attempts of Whately, McCausland, and Courteney to answer this argument, are really mere evasions ; and there is nothing in all the literature on the subject that at all meets it.

immediately succeeding death, and anterior to the resurrection, is indisputable. Hades is to be destroyed at the final resurrection ; and it is not in Hades that the wicked are to have their ultimate portion. That is the Abyss, the lake of fire, the second death. (See Rev. 20 : 14.) But this rich man was in Hades—" *in Hades* (εν τω ἁδη) he lifted up his eyes, and seeth Abraham and Lazarus." And at the very time he is suffering in Hades, he still has relatives *living in the flesh*, whom he wishes to have warned, that they may not encounter similar sufferings. " He said, I pray thee, therefore, father, that thou wouldst send Lazarus to my father's house, for *I have five brethren*, that he may testify unto them, *lest they also come into this place of torment.*" Either, then, there will be probation after the general judgment, and godless men living in the flesh upon the earth after the wicked are adjudged to their final punishment, or this picture must relate to the state intermediate between death and the resurrection. The first alternative is as unscriptural as it is absurd. The latter, then, must be the fact, and the whole scene necessarily fixes itself to the period immediately succeeding the death of the body. All the terms and relations of the narrative require this location of it. The received belief of the orthodox Jews was such that they could not otherwise understand it. And there is no show of right to accept the picture in any other relation.

Taking it, then, as we are in reason bound to take it, we have it settled, by Christ himself, that wicked souls have a life and consciousness which death does not interrupt, and that there is still a form of being for both good and bad between death and the resurrection.*

Luke 23 : 43 : " *Verily I say unto you, To-day thou shalt be with me in Paradise.*" Language more clear and precise, as to the life and conscious happiness of a saved soul immediately after death, cannot be framed. All that Psychopannychists have been able to do with it on their theory, is, to say that the case of the penitent thief is so " peculiar," that we cannot infer from it what will be the lot of other men. But it concerned the dying *Christ* as well as the dying thief ; and He certainly died as deep a death as any of His saints. And as both died that day, so they both went that day, and before the resurrection of either, into Paradise. Be that Paradise what it may, Christ and the thief were not yet in it while they lived on their crosses, and yet were in it before the day ended, and while their bodies yet hung upon those stakes. It was not a state of non-existence or oblivion, for it was the subject

---

* Whately and Courteney think that the torturing " flames " spoken of, argue the presence of the body, and so the craved water and the parched tongue. But it is assuming too much to affirm of the soul in Hades, that it is altogether disrobed of sensitive and vehicular clothing—that it is a mere thought-principle, a substance without parts, extension, or circumspection—a mere nobody. Such is not our doctrine, nor that of the Scriptures. Man is a trinity. The apostle assigns to his composition a *body*, a *soul*, and a *spirit*. (1 Thess. 5 : 23.) There is such a thing as the " dividing asunder of soul and spirit " (Heb. 4 : 12), but there is nothing to show that death can do this, or that anything of the sort occurs at death. And why may not the soul serve to give the mental principle a locality and a sensibility to outward impressions in the state after death, somewhat as the body serves the soul in this life ? Besides, as the world in which the scene is depicted is spiritual, which the whole narrative assumes, what right have we to condition its flames by the laws which apply only in the natural world ? The torments which the rich man suffered were, of course, of a sort answering to the character of the world in which he felt them, and of a nature to take effect on the sort of existence in which the scene is laid. Leaving the earth, the flames are no longer to be considered flames of earthly fire, or the thirst as earthly thirst, or the water desired as earthly water, or the pain as earthly pain. All is of a class with the new state and character of things. It is not figurative, as some have been willing to claim, but neither is it corporeal, as these men would assume. And if it were, we have no proof that material fire can affect a resurrected body any more than a disembodied soul. It is precisely of the nature of Hades, and of the nature of man's form of being in Hades, that all this is affirmed. So the narrative alleges, and in no other way is it allowable to argue with reference to these flames or sufferings. At any rate, Hades is specifically indicated as *the place and state*, and the lifetime of his " five brethren " in the flesh is noted as *the time*, in which these conscious pains and anxieties were experienced by this godless deceased worldling. Hence, if Christ is to be accepted as authority, wicked souls are alive and conscious between death and the resurrection.

of consoling hope and promise, and the declaration embraced the idea of conscious presence and fellowship with each other, on reaching the blessed place. *Being* is affirmed—ἔση, *thou* SHALT BE. *Communion* is affirmed—μετ᾽ εμου, WITH ME. *Conscious happiness* is affirmed—ἐν τῳ παραδεισῳ IN PARADISE. *Time* is specified, not the time of the resurrection, or after a long and indefinite period of nothingness, but σημερον, THIS DAY—the very day they hung side by side on Calvary, and before the setting of the sun then sinking beyond the sea.*

The case of Paul (Phil. 1 : 2) is also in point. If ever son of Adam lived a noble life on earth, it was this great apostle. To him to live was an unspeakable blessing to the Church, and to himself a zeal, and joy, and divinest fellowship with the Father, and His Son Jesus Christ. *To him to live was Christ.* And yet he adds, " TO ME TO DIE IS GAIN,"—gain even upon such a life. " Then, surely," as William Arthur puts it, " it was not to enter into nothingness, and to continue in nothingness while the world stands. From the life of an apostle to a state of torpor, is progress, not from glory to glory, but from glory to death—not gain, but blank and benumbing *loss*. Though his life here had many burdens, Paul proclaimed its joys to all ; yet he had a desire to depart and be with Christ, which is far better. He does not mean that the resurrection life is better, for it would not be delayed a day by his staying to profit the churches here, nor hastened by his departing. The better state he had in view is manifestly one which is postponed while he remains in the body, but which will open so soon as he goes hence. Is it, then, better to be nothing than to be an apostle ? to miss days and years, than to improve them ? to be as inanimate as water spilled upon the ground, than to be communing with God and serving man ? Had Paul expected that, in departing, he would become inanimate, surely he would have regarded each moment added to his holy labours, not as a delay of a far better life, but as so much golden time rescued from emptiness. Who can reconcile to his heart the notion of Christ's great ambassador desiring to depart and be a blank ? And, at last, that great soul stands on life's extremest verge, crying, ' I have finished my course.' A moment, and it is gone ! And what now is it in its new dwelling ? A dark and vacant thing, mere emptiness ? " Then nothingness is gain on apostolic usefulness, and communion with God ! Then to lie in oblivious death, is better than to hope, and pray, and praise, and live Christ Himself ! Who can believe it for a moment !

Consider also the experiences of dying believers, and the consciousness which they sometimes manifest in their last moments, of the presence of a world which they, then, for the first time, see, and among the bright dwellers in which they feel themselves going to take their places as earth " recedes and disappears." Shall we say that these visions of a new-dawning life, and bliss, and conscious fellowship, is all hallucination, the mere fantasies of an outgoing being, the delusions of the holy soul bidding farewell to the universe and God, until the archangel's trump shall sound ? Shall we draw the black line through all these cherished testimonies of those saints of God who have gone from us, and account them all meaningless, eccentric sparks of scattering existence, as it sinks to dark oblivion ? Believe it who wishes ; I have not so learned Christ, or the portion of His saints.†

* Some have proposed to change the punctuation of the passage, so as to make the σημερον refer to the time of the utterance of the promise, and not to the time of its fulfilment. But whence the reason for so solemnly asserting that he said it *that day*, when it was evident that he was speaking it *that day*, and not on some other day ? Well has Dean Alford observed: " This attempt, considering that it not only violates common sense, but destroys the force of the Lord's promise, is surely something worse than silly." And every interpretation of these words which cuts out of them the recognition of the conscious life and blessedness of righteous souls between death and the resurrection, so far as we have seen, does but put an equivoke in those holy lips, otherwise as guileless as the heavens.

† Refer also to 1 Peter 3 : 19, 20, which, grammatically and literally interpreted, proves not only the conscious activity of Christ's own soul, in the interval between his death and resurrection, but also the consciousness of those human spirits to whom he went and

Nor ought it to be necessary for any one to go beyond the text itself, to be assured of the fact, that the death of the body is not the death of the soul. These martyrs were " slain," and yet John sees and hears them in living and speaking sensibility between their death and their resurrection. It will not answer to say that the whole thing is only a vision. It was a vision of *the reality*—a miraculous view, in advance of the facts, indeed, but of *the facts themselves*, as they are actually to transpire. The slaying of these martyrs was, likewise, nothing but a vision ; but no one thinks of assuming that no literal martyrdom is in contemplation. Why then suppose that the asserted continuation of their soul-life, after their corporeal death, is not to be understood as equally a matter of literal reality? When an author gives us a thing as a matter of fact, that has occurred in his own experience, we must either accept what he says as true, or impeach his credibility or his competency. And when John tells us that he *saw and heard* " *the souls of those that had been slain*," either he is not to be believed, or he saw what had no manner of existence, or the souls of dead saints *do live, and act, and speak*, in a state of separation from the body.

John saw the souls of these martyrs " *beneath the altar*." Many regard this as " simply symbolical ; " but I am not clear that it is so to be taken. No earthly altar is meant, for none such existed at the time of the vision, or shall exist at the time of its fulfilment ; at any rate, none acknowledged of God. Nor is it exactly a material altar, as we are conversant with material things. It is something heavenly, and partaking of the same heavenly and spiritual nature of the scene out of which all these proceedings issue, and from which they are contemplated. There is a heavenly Temple, and everything that related to the earthly one, was patterned after the celestial one. There is a " true tabernacle, which the Lord pitched, and not man," of which that which Moses built was the material picture and copy. (Heb. 8 : 1–5 ; 9 : 21–24.) And this altar pertains to that heavenly sanctuary whence the " pattern " of the earthly was taken. It was at the altar of burnt-offerings that all bloody sacrifices were made. Under it there was a deep excavation in the solid rock, into which the blood of the slain victims was poured. The law commanded the officiating priest to " pour all the blood of the bullock at the bottom of the altar of the burnt-offering, which is at the door of the tabernacle of the congregation." (Lev. 4 : 7.) The ancient arrangement for the reception of this blood is still visible. I have myself stood in the opening, under the rock, on which the altar had its place, and stamped my foot upon the marble slab which closes the mouth of the vast receptacle, and satisfied myself, from the detonations, that the excavated space is very deep and large. And as the life of the animal was in its blood, this vast subterranean cavity was, naturally enough, regarded as the receptacle of the lives of the victims which there were slain. The Mahommedans, to this day, as I was told on the spot, regard it as the place where spirits are detained until the day of judgment. They call it *The well of spirits*. It is in the centre of the Mosque of Omar, whose interior had, for ages, been most rigidly guarded from the visits or eyes of any but Moslems, but, by firman from the government, can now be seen. And as the deep cavern under the earthly altar was the appointed receptacle of the lives of the animal sacrifices, so the souls of God's witnesses, who fall in His service, are received into a corresponding receptacle beneath the heavenly altar.

Some describe that altar as Christ, under whose protection and shade the souls of the martyrs are preserved, free from all perils and evils, till their recall, in renewed bodies, by the resurrection. It denotes a near and holy relation to God ; a place of sacred rest under the protection of Christ and

preached in the unseen world. Consider, too, the facts and doctrines concerning *demons*, and the desires of these beings to be incorporated with living bodily organisms, and the laws and scriptural prohibitions of necromancy and communion with the souls of the dead. Was this all superstition ? And did God legislate against intercourse with nonentities ?

His sacrifice, and a state of blessedness, to which, however, higher stages are to come.   The idea of sacrifice also pervades the language of Scripture in general, respecting eminent devotion in the Divine service, especially when life is jeoparded or lost in consequence of it.   Hence our bodies are to be offered a willing sacrifice unto the Lord.   Hence Paul spoke of his sufferings for Christ, and of his approaching martyrdom, as an offering in the sacrificial sense.   All martyrs are contemplated as sacrifices to God.   And as sacrifices to the heavenly altar, their souls pass into the sacred receptacle beneath that altar.   It is precisely the place where we would most naturally expect them to be, and where they are most sacredly kept, waiting for the adoption, to wit, the redemption of the body.*

III.   THE CRY THEY UTTER.

It is not a mere metaphorical cry, like that of the blood of Abel from the ground ;   but a literal cry of visible and conscious existences—an articulate cry, the voice of which is heard, and the utterances of which are in literal words.   " *Until when, Thou Master, the holy and true, dost thou not judge and avenge our blood from them that dwell on the earth ?* "   It appears, from this, that their murderers are then still living.   Consequently these crying ones are a specific class of martyrs, who had then very recently been slain.   It is another item to fix the vision to this particular time.

The cry is addressed to the throne.   It is not a vindictive cry, although it looks to the avenging of their blood.   If the whole scene did not relate to the judgment period, it would be difficult to avoid attaching the idea of intense vindictiveness to this utterance.   Such a cry would be out of season, except in this place.   But it is the time of judgment.   The judgment throne is set.   The judgment proceedings have commenced.   The years have come in which God had long ago promised that the principles of His righteous government should be enforced, to the recompense of His people, the vindication of their wrongs, and the overthrow of evil.   They had every assurance that such was the Divine intention, and that this was the period for its fulfilment.   They could not, therefore, understand why there should be delay.   The thing had begun, why was it not at once carried to its consummation ?   They had sacrificed their lives to this particular testimony, and everything had appeared to them in the very article of the long-predicted fulfilment ;   how was it, then, that it now tarried ?   Even the titles by which they address the Lord, show that this was the feeling and spirit of their inquiry.   It was not so much impatience that their blood was not avenged, as their perplexity about the hesitation which seemed to retard the ongoing of what they knew had commenced.   They do not address Christ as the *Saviour*, but as ὁ Δεσπότης—the centre of irresistible power already in force—the holy and true DESPOT, now on His judicial throne.   Their hearts are set, as they were in life, on the glorious consummation begun before they were slain.   They had died for their testi- mony that the time for that consummation had come.   And as it still delayed, and could only be realized in the visitation of vengeance upon the wicked hosts who had murdered them, they cry to the great and holy Avenger, to know why it tarried, and how long the suspense was to last.   It was an utterance from the world of disembodied saints, somewhat akin, in feeling and meaning, to that which John the Baptist sent from his prison to the Saviour.   (Matt. 11 : 2–10.)   It shows us that the intermediate state is still an imperfect state, and that the proper hope of saints is connected with the resurrection of the body.   Bede has remarked upon this passage, that " those souls which offered themselves a living sacrifice to God, pray eternally for His

---

* " The souls of Martyrs repose in peace under the Altar, and cherish a spirit of patience (patientiam pascunt) until others are admitted to fill up their company of glory."— *Tertullian*, Scorpiace, c. 12.

" The souls of the departed go to the place assigned them by God, and there abide until the Resurrection, when they will be reunited with their bodies ;   and then the saints, both in soul and body, will come into the presence of God."—*Irenæus*, Grabe, v. 31.

coming to judgment ; not from any vindictive feeling against their enemies, but in a spirit of zeal and love for God's glory and justice, and for the coming of that day, when sin, which is rebellion against Him, will be destroyed, and their own bodies raised."

IV. THE ANSWER THEY RECEIVE.

Jehovah does not disdain to lend an ear to the cry of His faithful servants. He is concerned for their rest, comfort, and right information, even while they lie disembodied beneath His altar. The prayers of His people are always precious before Him, and their peace He will ever consult. He heard the appeal of His slain ones, and came to minister to their souls the requisite comfort. Living or dead, if we are faithful to God and His word, we shall not want any merciful grace and help appropriate to us. The Lord remembers us in our sufferings and trials on earth, and He will not fail to come to us under the altar, to comfort and establish us concerning His purposes and ways. He will not forget or disregard us when dead, any more than when living ; and our necessities, apart from the body, are as graciously cared for as those in the flesh. Indeed, His promises overspan every possible contingency of our existence, in the body or out of the body, in time or in eternity. His word to us is, that He will *never* leave nor forsake us.

" *There was given to each of them a white robe.*" Can lifeless shades and non-existences receive white robes ? Can spilled blood, dead and absorbed in the earth, wear the livery of heaven ? Yet these souls of slain ones received each the celestial stola, even while their resurrection delayed. And that stola was the symbol of their justification—the Divine assurance of the truth and acceptableness of their testimony—the cheering token from the throne that they were approved, and precious, and near to their Lord, and blessed with his favour, notwithstanding that what they hoped and testified was still deferred. White robes, in such connections, are always the emblems of Divine approval and blessed relationship with God. And the giving of them to these zealous and anxious souls under the altar, was the cheering proof of their preciousness in the Master's sight.

" *And it was said to them* "— . . . Mark ; how could dead ashes hear and understand ? Where was the use and meaning of speaking promises to unconscious dust, which knows not anything ? Where is the sense or intelligibility of such a converse, if no living and wakeful beings are concerned ? God does not speak his comforts and promises to nothings. And yet it was said to these souls of martyrs, in advance of their resurrection, " *that they should rest yet a little time.*" This implies that they had been resting, and that their state was one of blessed repose and quiet, though imperfect. The dead in the Lord are not wandering, melancholy ghosts. They are experiencing the meaning of that sweetest word of our language—*rest.* And over their ashes, at least, we may confidently sing :

> Happy the dead ! they peacefully rest them,
> From burdens that galled, from cares that oppressed them ;
> From the yoke of the world, and from tyranny,
> The grave, the grave hath set them free,
> The grave hath set them free.

But, after this rest, comes a brighter day, and a sublimer station. " Yet a little time," these slain ones are told, and then that day will come. The reason for the delay is also explained to them. Their number is not yet full, and the world is not yet quite ripe for its doom. Hence it was said to them, " that they should rest yet a little time, *until their fellow-servants also, and their brethren, shall have been completed, who are about to be slain, as also they themselves [had been]*.*" John is made to hear these words, because they are a prophecy for the Church on earth, as well as an explanation to the souls waiting in heaven. They tell of continued persecution and bloody sufferings for God's witnesses among men. Many good people are wont to think the days for killing men, on account of their religious principles, have long since passed, never to return. They flatter themselves that the world has become too enlightened, too humane, too civilized, too much pervaded with a reasonable and forbearing spirit, ever to repeat such scenes as were enacted by Pagan rule, or in the dark ages of Christendom. But they are entirely mistaken. We may think the world has changed, but it still has that ancient murderer for its god and prince, and its malignity towards the Lord's people, especially when they come to be sifted out from their present adulterous intimacy with the world, will again head up into an intensity to which there has been no parallel in the past. This fifth seal is a revelation of nothing but slaughter for the saints, as regards this world, and the times to which it relates. It shows us slaughtered saints in heaven, and tells of the slaughter of many more. And elsewhere, in this book, we are advised of coming times, when an idol shall be the object of the world's adoration, and as many as will not worship it shall be killed. (Rev. 13 : 15.)

This might seem to be but poor consolation to these resting souls ; and yet, a real consolation it was. It assured them that they were not alone in the sufferings they had experienced ; that theirs was but the common lot of all faithful ones in those trying times ; that, though they were dead, the cause in which they died still had representatives, who would stand to it unto death, as they had done ; and that, though the consummation was delayed yet for a little while, *their* sufferings were over, and there was a flood of sorrow still to deluge the earth from which *they* now were free.

But, above all, was the assurance, pervading and implied in each particular, that what they had hoped and testified, was presently to be accomplished. Those white robes were the earnest of a sublimer life. Their martyrdom for their steadfast maintenance of the truth, was duly remembered, and, in a little while, should be fully requited to them, and to the godless hosts who had inflicted it. Their blood was not long to remain unavenged from them that dwell on the earth. The years of waiting and of suffering were now on the margin of their close. Yet a little time, and the consummation should be complete. Yet a little while, and the wicked should not be : yea, they should diligently consider his place, and it should not be. The thrones were already set ; the work was really in progress ; the time of the end had verily come ; and, after a short space more, they would be able to say : " I have seen the wicked in great power, and spreading himself like a green bay-tree ; yet he passed away, and lo, he was not : yea, I sought him, but he could not be found." (Ps. 37 : 35, 36.)

Striking and impressive is the fact here brought to view, that that which the saints of all ages have been " looking for," and which has been their " blessed hope " in every time of earthly trial and adversity, even " the glorious appearing of our great God and Saviour Jesus Christ " (Tit. 2 : 13, 14), is also the chief comfort and stay of the pious dead in their heavenly rest. " Until when, Thou Master, the holy and true, dost thou not judge and avenge our blood from them that dwell on the earth ? " is the cry which they utter " with a great voice " from beneath the altar. They rest, but their desire for the end still rises, and glows, and pleads. And the chief element of the consolation which they receive is, that that consummation cometh.

And if the holy martyrs, in their white robes under the heavenly altar, make so much of it, and find their chief comfort in the contemplation of its nearness, how unreasonable and unjust that we should be accounted enthusiasts and fanatics, for pointing to it as our hope and joy amid these earthly tribulations ? Why should it be branded as lunacy, when we wish and pray, with departed saints, that sin's long war against the majesty of heaven were over—that the rending strife of spiritual evil, which has so long torn God's world, should come to an end—that the vast train of wrongs, with which Satan has been oppressing Heaven's sons and beautiful creations, should be done away ? Would it really be for the peace, and piety, and consolation of the Church, that all such interest should cease, and that all such testimony should be silenced? Would it really be God's kingdom come, and His will done on earth as it is in heaven, if all prayer and prophecy of coming and nearing judgment were to be hushed from such a world as ours? Or, should we not rather be grateful that there are on earth, and will be, even in its darkest times, some to echo the spirit which thrills in the hearts of departed souls, testifying to an evil and adulterous generation, of a coming vengeance, in order to a completed redemption? Let men scowl, and mutter their ill-timed reproaches, if they will, and persecute, even unto death, those who hold it fast, there is in this theme what constitutes the true hope of the saints, whether suffering in the flesh or resting in heaven, and on account of which we may well ever

> Thank God, there's still a vanguard
>   Fighting for the right!
> Though the throng flock to rearward,
>   Lifting, ashen-white
> Flags of truce to sin and error,
> Clasping hands, mute with terror,
> Thank God, there's still a vanguard
>   Fighting for the right!
>
> Through the wilderness advancing,
>   Hewers of the way,
> Forward! far their spears are glancing,
>   Flashing back the day.
> "Back!" the leaders cry, who fear them;
> "Back!" from all the army near them;
> They, with steady step advancing,
>   Cleave their certain way.
>
> *Slay them!* From each drop that falleth
>   Springs a hero armed.
> Where the martyr's fire appalleth,
>   Lo, they pass unharmed.
> Crushed beneath thy wheel, oppression,
> Bold, their spirit holds possession,
> Loud the dross-purged voice out-calleth
>   By the death-throes warmed.
>
> Thank God, there's still a vanguard
>   Fighting for the right!
> Error's legions know their standard,
>   Floating in the light.
> When the league of sin rejoices,
> Quick outring the rallying voices:
> "Thank God, there's still a vanguard
>   Fighting for the right!"

LECTURE FOURTEENTH

THE SIXTH SEAL—WRONG APPLICATIONS OF IT—DESCRIBES FEARFUL PRODIGIES IN NATURE—GENERAL CONVULSION—DARKENING OF SUN AND MOON—FALLING OF THE STARS—RECOIL OF THE HEAVENS—MOVING OF MOUNTAINS AND ISLANDS—STATE OF SOCIETY WHEN THESE THINGS COME—THE DISMAY THEY OCCASION—HOW PEOPLE WILL INTERPRET THEM—THE ABSURDITIES TO WHICH THEY WILL DRIVE MEN.

REV. 6 : 12–17. (Revised Text.) And I saw when he had opened the sixth seal, and there was a great shaking ; and the sun became black as sackcloth of hair, and the whole moon became as blood ; and the stars of the heaven fell to the earth, as a fig-tree sheddeth her untimely [or winter] figs when shaken by a great wind. And the heaven recoiled as a book [or scroll] rolling itself together ; and every mountain and island were moved out of their places. And the kings of the earth, and the great men, and the captains of thousands, and the rich, and the mighty, and every slave, and every freedman, hid themselves in the caves and the rocks of the mountains. And they say to the mountains and to the rocks, Fall on us, and hide us from the face of Him that sitteth on the throne, and from the wrath of the Lamb : because the great day of His [or, as some MSS., their] wrath is come, and who is able to stand !

WE have here a sublime and startling description. Some think that it refers to the destruction of Jerusalem ; others, to the persecutions under Diocletian; still more, to the victories of the Church under Constantine ; and some, to the final judgment and the end of all things. But neither of these applications of this vision, as I am constrained to take it, is the true one.

The evidence is sufficiently conclusive that John wrote years after the fall of the Jewish state, whilst he is particular to tell us that all these visions refer to things to come subsequent to the time of his writing. It is also plain that the terrors described are not such as pertain to Christians, however fiercely persecuted. And the theory which applies it to the age of Constantine, besides other objections which it cannot satisfactorily solve, labours under the fatal embarrassment of having to adapt a picture of sheer disaster and calamity to events which were not only, for the most part, terrorless, but whose chief characteristics were peaceful and prosperous. Had John beheld the sun bursting forth, with new lustre, from an eclipse of darkness, and the moon coming out from under a bloody obscuration, to shine with silver light, and the stars taking their places serenely in the heavens, there might be some show of adapting the description to the events marking the Constantinian period. But he saw no such things. He saw the very reverse, with not a relieving ray from first to last. Nor were all kings, rulers, and great men, then driven from their thrones and palaces to seek shelter in the rocks and mountains. With all the changes, Pagans were still permitted to enjoy full religious liberty, and did not answer at all to the terrified and conscience-stricken masses of high and low, whom we here behold confessing the power and majesty of God and the Lamb, and seeking for death to conceal them from the fearfulness of avenging wrath. And whatever secondary and imperfect fulfilments this opening of the sixth seal may have had in the history of the past, it is impossible for any one to look at it attentively without feeling that the day of judgment itself must come in order to exhaust the description, and that it belongs properly and only to those great events which immediately precede and usher in the great consummation.

And yet it does not refer to the last acts of that terrible drama. It is only the *sixth* seal, while there is yet a seventh to follow it. With all its terrors, it is only one link in the chain of judicial wonders which the great day will bring. Much of the language employed, and the descriptions which follow, show that we still have to do with the present order of things, although in its last stages. The action of all the seals is the action of judgment, after the saints have been taken to their Lord in the sky ; and we here have the sixth in the series, whilst the final catastrophe is still deferred. Neither Titus, nor Diocletian, nor Constantine, has anything whatever to do with it ; but only those people who shall be living upon the earth in " the time of the end."

The words before us present two classes of facts—

I. FEARFUL PHYSICAL PRODIGIES ;
II. THE EFFECTS OF THEM UPON MANKIND.

We will consider them in the order in which they are narrated, looking to God to enlighten and bless us in the attempt.

1. *Great commotion in the fabric of nature.* " I saw when he had opened the sixth seal, and there was a great shaking." The common version says *earthquake*, but the original word (σεισμὸς) is not so limited and specific. Though usually rendered *earthquake*, it denotes quakings in general, and is often used for any sudden and violent shaking in any part of the world. In the following verse it is applied to the shaking of the fig-tree. Matthew employs it to express tempestuous commotion of the air and sea (8 : 24) ; and in the Greek translation of Joel (2 : 10), it is used to denote violent disturbances in the heavens. In the form of a verb, it signifies to shake, toss, jolt, agitate,— whether the things shaken be the earth, the air, the sea, the sky, or anything else. It here includes a general shaking of the earth, as is plainly manifest from the context ; but there is the same reason for extending it beyond the earth to the atmosphere, sky, and heavenly regions. The whole system of the world is implicated in the vastness and violence of the commotion.

In very many places, great convulsions of nature are spoken of in connection with special manifestations of Deity, particularly when those manifestations are of a judicial character. When God gave the law, which was for the restraint and condemnation of sin, " Mount Sinai was altogether on a smoke, because the Lord descended upon it in fire, and the smoke thereof ascended as the smoke of a great furnace, and the whole mount quaked greatly." (Ex. 19 : 18.) When Elijah made complaint unto the Lord that Israel had shed the blood of His prophets, and trembled for his own safety, " The Lord passed by, and a great and strong wind rent the mountains, and brake in pieces the rocks ; and after the wind an earthquake." (1 Kings 19 : 11.) When Jesus was murdered, " the veil of the temple was rent in twain from the top to the bottom ; and the earth did quake, and the rocks rent." (Matt. 27 : 50, 51.) And when Paul and Silas were beaten, imprisoned, and put into the stocks, and appealed unto the Lord in songs and prayers, " suddenly there was a great earthquake, so that the foundations of the prison were shaken, and all the doors were opened, and every one's bands were loosed." (Acts 16 : 26.)

Especially are such convulsions prophesied of in connection with the judgment, and the approach and consummation of the end of this world. Jesus has plainly told us that " famines, and pestilences, and *earthquakes*," are more and more to characterize the coming of the end. (Matt. 24 : 7–9.) In the preceding visions we have had the famines, pestilences, and persecutions, and here we behold the commotions of nature. Haggai has prophesied : " Thus saith the Lord of Hosts, Yet once, it is a little while, and *I will shake the heavens, and the earth, and the sea, and the dry land* " (2 : 6) ; and all this in specified connection with the coming of the Desire of nations. Paul, commenting upon this and like ancient predictions, speaks of a shaking of the earth and of the heaven, and connects this shaking with the coming administrations which are to determine and end the dispensation. (Heb. 12 : 26–28.)

We know something of earthquakes—how they overturn and change the surfaces of countries, sink the hills, alter the courses of rivers, overwhelm vast populations, dry up lakes, set the mountains to vomiting fire, and agitate the mightiest seas. But, in the time to come, when God shall judge the nations for their iniquities, there shall be enlargements and intensifications of such convulsions. The commotions are to be "*great*," and they are to extend to the whole system of our world, and to involve the very heavens.

2. To the general convulsion is added *the darkening of the sun.* "And the sun became black as sackcloth of hair." I take all this literally. There is neither reason nor piety in undertaking to explain away the plain terms of Scripture, where there is no necessity for departure from their common meaning. When the Lord came down on Sinai the mountain was shrouded in darkening smokiness. When Jesus hung upon the cross, "There was darkness over all the earth until the ninth hour. And *the sun was darkened.*" (Luke 23 : 44, 45.) When the judgment of God was upon Egypt, "There was a thick darkness in all the land three days." (Ex. 10 : 22.) By Isaiah (33 : 9, 10) the word came forth : "Behold, the day of the Lord cometh, cruel both with wrath and fierce anger, to lay the earth desolate : and he shall destroy the sinners thereof out of it. *The sun shall be darkened in his going forth.*" The same was repeated by Joel (3 : 9-15). And the blessed Saviour himself has told us, that "immediately after the tribulation of those days," and soon before the appearance of the sign of the Son of Man in heaven, "*shall the sun be darkened.*" (Matt. 24 : 29, 30.)

In what manner this darkening is to be produced, is nowhere told us. It may be by some natural eclipse, or it may be by some extraordinary putting forth of the power of God for the purpose. We cannot explain the three days' darkness sent upon the Egyptians, nor the darkness which prevailed during the Saviour's crucifixion. It is easy enough for Omnipotence, either by natural or miraculous causes, to fulfil His own word. Extraordinary obscurations of the sun have more than once happened, and they can just as readily be made to happen again, if God so wills, and in a still more marvellous degree of intensity. On the 19th of May, 1780, a wonderfully dark day was experienced throughout the northeastern portion of this country. The witnesses of it have described it as supernatural and unaccountable. It was not an ordinary eclipse, for the moon was nearly at the full. It was not owing to a clouded condition of the atmosphere, for the stars were visible. Yet it was so dark from nine o'clock in the morning throughout the usual hours of sunshine, that work had to be suspended, houses had to be lit with candles, the beasts and fowls went to their rest as in the night-time. And though the sun was visible, it had the appearance of being shorn of all its power of illumination. Connect such an occurrence with the general convulsions which have just been described, extend it over the world, intensify it according to the description of the text, and you may form some conception of this feature of what the opening of the sixth seal shall bring, when the sun shall be dull and rayless as the hair cloth of a Bedouin's tent.

3. A further particular is *the ensanguined appearance of the moon.* "And the whole moon became as blood." A writer on the Apocalypse has said : "The further I advance in the exposition of this book of prophecy, the more convinced I feel that the key to its interpretation is to be found in the great outline of things which shall be hereafter sketched out by our Lord Jesus Christ in His prophecy on the Mount of Olives." Recurring to that "outline," we find this lunar phenomenon distinctly referred to. As the sun is to be darkened, so also "*the moon shall not give her light.*" (Matt. 24 : 29.) The nature of the portentous obscuration is also described. With the privation of its usual effulgence, the moon is to be converted into an object of horror. In place of the genial silver disc, men shall behold, as it were, an orb of blood—dark, dim, sickly, and portentous. The same is spoken of in other prophecies. In Joel (2 : 30) we read, that before the consummation of "the great and terrible day of the Lord," not only "the sun shall be turned into darkness," but also "the moon into blood." Anticipations and foreshadows of this have, in like manner, occurred. Great convulsions in the earth and

atmosphere often produce such appearances of the sun and moon. When the earth is shaken by the wrath of God, the heavenly luminaries sympathize with the general commotion ; and along with this " *great shaking*," a shaking, not of the earth only, but of heaven also, we might well expect the sun to put on blackness, and the full moon to appear as if deluged in blood. Whatever the specific details of the manifestation may be, by whatever means produced, or however long continued, the general character of it will be sufficiently marked and terrific to correspond with the awfulness of the occasion to which it relates. Similar language may have applied to other scenes, but it will then be realized with a fulness and literalness which have never yet been, and on a scale altogether unprecedented.

4. Then comes *the falling of stars.*—" And the stars of the heaven fell to the earth, as a fig-tree sheddeth her untimely [or winter] figs, when shaken by a great wind." Some see in this an impossibility in the way of accepting this description as literal. But they are thinking only of the great and unknown bodies which shine in the vast fields of immensity. It remains to be proven, however, that the apostle had his eye upon stars of that character. Those heavenly orbs, of which astronomy tells, are not the only objects to which, in common language, the word *stars* literally applies. Even science speaks of " shooting stars," and " falling stars," which are not worlds at all, but *meteors*, visible only while they fall, and leaving no discoverable remains where they seem to alight. It used to be thought that they were generated in our atmosphere, but learned men now regard them as incandescent fragments of matter, detached perhaps from their proper places, and set on fire and consumed by contact with the atmosphere of the earth. Such a convulsion as the text describes, would naturally multiply the number of such loose particles, which, precipitated into our atmosphere, and ignited by contact with it, would not only fill it with moving incandescent points, such as we call shooting or falling *stars*, but also fulfil the image to which the apostle likens the falling. Conceiving of the physical universe as a great fig-tree, he beholds it terrifically shaken, but in no way blown down or destroyed. Only its unseasonable fruit, which winter has overtaken, and incongenial weather has rendered ready to drop, is made to fall.

There is also something peculiar in the apostle's designation of these falling stars, which does not appear in the common version, but which is worth notice. He calls them " *the stars of the heaven*." Not simply " the stars," as if there could be no mistake as to the objects intended—nor yet " the stars of the heavens " generally considered—but " the stars *of the heaven ;* " some particular stars of some particular heaven. And when we call to mind that the word *heaven* is often used to denote the air, the atmosphere which surrounds the earth, the region in which the clouds move, it becomes more than probable that he is here referring to objects which pertain to this particular region alone. The stars proper are certainly still found in their places after the fulfilment of this vision. (See chap. 8 : 12.) And remembering that the Scriptures speak in the common language of men, without reference to the distinctions of science, and that even science itself still popularly speaks of " falling stars," when it means simply meteoric phenomena, it appears but reasonable that we should understand the apostle to be speaking of something of the same sort. Professor Stuart agrees that the meaning of the words is sufficiently met by such an interpretation, and that the reference most likely is to some meteoric manifestation, the like of which has once in a while happened, and which we find spoken of, among the people and in the books, under the name of *falling stars*.

A most marvellous meteoric shower of this class was witnessed on the night of the 13th of November, 1833. It is perhaps remembered by many now present. During the three hours of its continuance, hundreds and thousands of people, of all classes, were thrown into the utmost consternation, and filled with the belief that the very scene described in this text, was actually transpiring. Fiery balls, as luminous and as numerous as the stars, came darting after each other from the sky, with vivid streaks of light trailing in the track of each. They were of various sizes and degrees of splendour, flashing as they fell, and so bright as to awaken people from their sleep. It seemed as if every star in the firmament had suddenly shot from its sphere, and was falling to the earth. And all who saw it will bear witness that it was a most terrific spectacle.

Conceive, then, of a repetition of that scene, intensified and extended according to the spirit of this vision, with stunning explosions added to the general commotion, and the alarming rush of hissing balls of fire, darting like rain-drops from the sky, and you have exactly what John foresaw in this part of his vision of the opening of the sixth seal.

5. " *And the heaven recoiled as a scroll rolling itself together.*" We have here the same particular heaven. With the prodigies already named, the sky folds upon itself. The fastenings which held it outstretched, are loosed in the general convulsion, and it rolls up.   Great, massive, rotary motion in the whole visible expanse, is signified, as if it were folding itself up to pass away forever. Some tell us that this never can literally happen, and that we are not therefore to expect it to be fulfilled in any physical fact. But why not ? Does not Peter, in a plainly literal passage, tell us of just such commotions in the aerial heavens ? Does he not say, in so many words, that they shall be *loosed* ($\lambda\upsilon\theta\eta\sigma\sigma\nu\tau\alpha\iota$), and move with a noisy rushing, after the manner of a tempest ?* And so significant and awful is to be the nature of the fact, that nearly all the prophets have taken notice of it, and foretell the same in language which we must monstrously pervert to understand in any other than a literal sense. We may not be able to describe it in the language of modern science, and philosophers may laugh at the unsophisticated descriptions of God's prophets ; but, everything that relates to the coming of Christ, and the day of judgment, has upon it the same disability. And if the literal truthfulness of the record will not hold in one case, I cannot see by what reason we can insist upon it in another. God certainly is able to fulfil literally all that he has spoken, and here John tells us that he really *saw* what Peter and other prophets have said shall come to pass.

6. And all this is further attended with *fearful changes in the configuration of the earth*. " And every mountain and island were moved out of their places." These are but the natural effects of the terrible convulsions that shake everything. On a smaller scale, the same has often happened. Within the space of a month past, the world has been astounded with accounts of an earthquake along the Pacific coast of South America, by which cities and villages by the score have been blotted from the earth, islands moved in their places, mountains shaken, vast districts of shore engulfed in the sea, thousands and thousands of lives lost, and hundreds of millions of treasure destroyed. Extend the same to every country and every sea ; let all the dwellers on earth be made to feel such a shock, intensified so as to hurl the mountains from their seats, and wrench the islands from their roots, and convulse each ocean from centre to circumference ; let the hills exchange places with the waters, and all the consequences of such vast and sudden transformations be spread over the face of the world, with their natural effects upon its cities, its traffic, and its thronging populations, and you may have some idea of the dreadfulness of what John beheld as ordained to come to pass under the opening of this seal.

Such, then, are the physical prodigies here foreshown. Let us now look at the impression they make upon those who witness them.

" And the kings of the earth, and the great men [nobles, lords, princes], and the captains of thousands, and the rich, and the mighty, and every slave, and every freedman, hid themselves in the caves, and the rocks of the mountains ; and they say to the mountains and to the rocks, Fall on us, and hide

---

* $\rho'\circ\iota\zeta\eta\delta\circ\nu\ \pi\alpha\rho\epsilon\lambda\epsilon\upsilon\sigma\circ\nu\tau\alpha\iota$.   See 2 Pet. 3. 10–12.

us from the face of Him that sitteth on the throne, and from the wrath of the Lamb : because the great day of His wrath is come, and who is able to stand ! "

1. We have here a glimpse of the constitution and general condition of society at the time these prodigies befall the world. Some believe and teach, that free institutions are destined to become universal, and that monarchy is doomed to fall before the march of modern civilization. We here see that such hopes will not be realized. Kings are still on their thrones, and princes and orders of nobility remain, till the judgment comes. Some are looking for a blessed time of peace and prosperity in this world, when all wars shall cease, all armies be disbanded, all nations transmute their implements of destruction into instruments of husbandry, and the clash of arms be hushed forever. We here see that there will still be soldiers and military commanders pursuing their bloody profession up to the time of the end. Some will have it that universal emancipation has but a few more battles to fight, and that human slavery is as good as at an end. We here see that the day of judgment still finds slaves in the world, as well as men who have but recently been freed, and all the present distinctions of class and fortune unchanged. Suppose that the sixth seal were to be opened to-night ; what would it find ? Kings and emperors on their thrones ; princes, nobles, dukes, and lords, securely priding themselves in the prerogatives of their caste and station ; standing armies at rest and in action, and military commanders with swords upon their sides ; rich people wallowing in wealth and luxury ; men and women in high places and in low, working the wires that fashion events ; slaves toiling at their tasks, and freedmen just out of their bondage ; and evidences everywhere of a depraved and disordered state of things. This is what the judgment would find if it came to-night. And this, John tells us, is what it finds when it does come in reality. Let political reformers and theologians then say to the contrary what they please, human society as it is, and as it has been for these ages, with all its burdens, disorders, and inequalities, will continue the same, till Christ himself shall come to judge it for its sins.

2. There is one thing, however, which shall be very different under the opening of the sixth seal, from what it is now. The self-security and composure with which godless people live, will then be driven to the winds. Though all the judgments under preceding seals may have failed to appal or arouse them, they will not be able to maintain their equanimity under what this shall bring forth.

I have said, that we know something of the dreadfulness of earthquakes. And yet, we, who know them only by descriptions, cannot at all enter into the feeling of alarm and horror which they produce. A gentleman who has had some experience on the subject, says : " Although I am not a man to cry out or play the fool on such occasions, yet I do fairly own that these earthquakes are very awful, and must be felt to be understood. Before we hear the sound, or, at least, are fully conscious of hearing it, we are made sensible, I do not know how, that something uncommon is going to happen. Everything seems to change colour. Our world appears to be in disorder. All nature looks different to what it was wont to do. And we feel quite subdued and overwhelmed by some invisible power, beyond human control or comprehension. Then comes the terrible sound, distinctly heard ; and immediately the solid earth is all in motion, waving to and fro like the surface of the sea. Depend upon it, a severe earthquake is enough to shake the firmest mind. No custom can teach any one to witness it without the deepest emotion of terror." But when this seal opens, not only the earth here and there, but everywhere, and the sea, and the air, and the heavens, shall shake, as for their final dissolution. And with the sun turned to blackness, and the moon to blood, and the mountains toppling from their bases, and the whole framework of nature jarring and creaking like a wrecking ship, there will come over the hearts of men a discomfiting consternation, such as they never felt or imagined.

We know something of the alarm and terror which the meteoric shower of 1833 struck into the hearts and minds of men. People now laugh at the strange demonstrations which were then enacted, and wonder how it was possible that intelligent and reflecting men could become so terrified, or act so contrary to all that had ever distinguished them before. But the truth is, that it is a good deal easier to play brave toward such things after they are over, than when they are upon us with all their solemn sublimity. And when to the falling of the stars is added the rocking of the earth, the loosening of the mountains, the darkening of sun and moon, and the tempestuous collapse of the firmament, men may think they can muster the nerve to stand it, but they will fail.

Nor does it matter who or what men may be, they will be alike overwhelmed with inexpressible dismay and horror. Kings, princes, nobles, men used to the shocks of battle, the rich, the great, the wise, the bond, the free, high and low, without exception, become the victims of their fears, and tremble, and howl, and pray, and rush to the fields, to the cellars, to the caves of the rocks, to the clefts in the mountains, to every place where shelter and concealment is dreamed of amid the general desperation. So John foresaw the scene, and so it will be. Self-possession, unshaken courage, dignified composure, philosophic thinking, hopefulness, assurance, and the last remains of the stern intrepidity and statue-like imperturbability which characterize some men now, will then have vanished from humanity. That day will destroy them utterly.

3. We notice, also, the correct interpretation which mankind will then put upon the terrific disturbances of nature around them. Storms, earthquakes, eclipses, and unusual phenomena in the heavens, are natural symbols of Divine wrath.   The ancients regarded them as auguring and embodying the destroying power and wrath of Deity. They are always and everywhere precursors and prophecies of the forthcoming judgment of God. They are so presented in the Scriptures, and accordingly inwrought with all inspired diction. There is also an instinct to the same effect, which has ever lingered with the race, and which cannot be entirely suppressed. Modern science calls it superstition. Savants of earthly wisdom propose to explain all upon philosophic principles, and think to prove to us that neither God, nor His anger, nor His judgments, have aught to do with it. People also have become so enlightened nowadays, as to be above alarm at strange commotions in the elements, or signs in the sky. They have learned better. These things may all be naturally accounted for. Why, a little care might give us tables of them for a thousand years to come, with the days, and hours, and minutes noted. Indeed, men have become so knowing about Nature and her laws, that they do not see much necessity any more for a God at all, much less for any judgment or interference of His in the affairs of the universe. This is the spirit of much that men call science,—a spirit which is working itself into the popular mind, and, sad to say, largely affecting even the theological thinking and teaching of the day. But when the vision of the text comes to be realized, woe to the materialistic, pantheistic, and atheistic philosophies with which men suppose they have rid themselves of the superstitions of antiquity ! One flash from the judgment throne will confound them utterly. When the sixth seal breaks, and the vibrations of it are upon the universe, turning sun and moon to darkness and blood, convulsing the firmament, shaking down the stars, and moving mountains and islands from their places, not the ignorant only, but the philosophic and the learned—kings and magnates of science and state, and all classes and kinds of men together, rush from their dwellings, strike for the caverns, cry out like terrified babes, confess to the presence of a Divine Power whose existence their superior learning had put down as a fable, and with one accord now preach and proclaim the advent of a day which they had pronounced impossible ! Why this consternation—this change in their way of regarding and treating these advent doctrines—this preaching of the judgment—this trepidation and horror about the day of wrath now ? This

is not the way they used to deal with this subject. There is a mighty shaking indeed ; but earthquakes are all from natural causes ! Rather remarkable eclipses truly ; but such things are easily explicable on natural principles ! An extraordinary star-shower ; but these are innocent periodic things which belong to the natural ongoing of the universe ! Unusual storms and atmospheric commotions ; but they are the results of natural causes ! Why, then, this dismay at the sublime activities of nature, which a philosophic understanding should be able calmly to contemplate and really enjoy ? Cowardly fools ! shall we call them, to break down in the conclusions of their superior intelligence, amid such splendid opportunities for enjoyable scientific observation ? Alas, alas, the old superstition is too strong for the modern wisdom ! The horror-stricken world—kings, savants, heroes—with strained eyeballs and bloodless lips, fall prostrate and confess that these beautiful activities of nature and her laws, are, after all, somehow linked in with the wrath and judgment of God and the Lamb !

4. Nor is it so much the physical prodigies, as what they argue, that renders the dismay so unsupportable. If there were nothing but the convulsions of the body of nature, terrific as they are, there would be a chance for some to endure them without becoming so thoroughly unmanned. But the chief consternation arises, not simply from the outward facts, but from the unwelcome conclusions which they force upon the soul. The physical manifestations may be in the line of physical laws, and in no way contrary to them ; but whether miraculous or not, they are so terrific and Divine, that they compel the most atheistic to see in them the hands, and arms, and utterances of a Being transcendently greater still, and to feel the demonstration in their souls that He has verily risen up in the fierceness of just indignation against long neglect and defiance of His authority. It is not that nature has ceased to be herself, or that the principles of her activities have been repealed, that overwhelms them, but the resistless proof that all her awful potencies, now in such terrific motion, are God's direct powers, aroused and inflamed with His dreadful anger, and charged as heralds and executioners of His almighty wrath. It is not the shaking, the obscured sun, the bloody moon, the falling stars, the recoiling heavens, the moving mountains, so much as the moral truths they flash into the spirit, to wit, that God is on the throne, that sin is a reality, that judgment is come, and that every guilty one must now face an angry Creator. It is not nature's bewildering commotions, for they would willingly have the falling mountains cover them, if that would shelter them from what is much more in their view, and far more dreadful to them. What they speak of is, God upon the throne, the fear of His face, the day of reckoning, and the wrath of the Lamb. These are more than all the horrors of a universe in convulsions. These are the daggers in their hearts—the thunderbolts that rend and rive their souls—the fires that kindle the flames of hell within them.

5. And how pitiable and absurd the expedients to which they are driven ! Many an opportunity for prayer had they neglected. Always had they contemned such humiliating employment. It did not suit their ideas of dignity, or their theories. But now they pray, and have a grand concert of prayer, in which kings and mighty ones join with the meanest and lowest. They had often laughed and sneered at praying men ; but now they all pray. Some prostrate in the dust, some on their knees in dens and caves, some clinging to the trees, and all shrieking out in unison their terror-moved entreaties. O, imbecile people ! When prayer would have been availing, they scorned and detested it as mean and useless ; and now, that it is futile, they go at it with a will.

Still more absurd is the direction in which they address their prayers. Once they considered it folly that man should call on the living God ; but now they pray to dead rocks ! Once they thought it philosophic to deny that He who made the ear could hear prayers, or that He with whom is the Spirit, and whose is the power, could answer them ; but now they supplicate the deaf and helpless mountains !

And yet weaker and more insane is the import of their prayers and efforts. Beautifully has the Psalmist sung : " Whither shall I go from thy Spirit ? or whither shall I flee from thy presence ? If I ascend up into heaven, thou art there. If I make my bed in hell, behold, thou art there. If I take the wings of the morning, and dwell in the uttermost parts of the sea ; even there shall thy hand lead me, and thy right hand shall hold me. If I say, Surely the darkness shall cover me ; even the night shall be light about me. Yea, the darkness hideth not from thee ; but the night shineth as the day : the darkness and the light are both alike to thee." (Ps. 139 : 7–13.) Omniscience and omnipresence are among the natural attributes of God. The very things before these people's eyes should have been enough to teach them this. And yet, philosophers as they are, their proposal is to conceal themselves from the Almighty, and so elude His wrath ! Often had shelter and peaceful security been offered them in the mercies of the loving Saviour, and as often had they despised and rejected them ; but now the silly souls would take the miserable rocks for saviours ! O, the foolishness of men who think it folly to serve God ! " He that fleeth of them, shall not flee away, and he that escapeth of them, shall not be delivered. Though they dig into hell," saith the Lord, " thence shall mine hand take them ; though they climb up to heaven, thence will I bring them down ; and though they hide themselves in the top of Carmel, I will search and take them out thence." (Amos. 9 : 1–3.)

These kings and mighty ones of the earth had highly estimated the terrors of death, and tried to restrain and terrify. men with fears of them. As shown in the preceding seal, they had been persecutors of the saints, and shed their blood to silence their testimony. Yet, what they then thought so awful, they are now themselves willing and anxious to suffer ; yea, and to go down into everlasting nothingness, as a happy alternative to what they find coming upon them. " They say to the mountains and to the rocks, Fall on us, and hide us from the face of Him that sitteth on the throne, and from the wrath of the Lamb ! " O, miserable extremity to which guilt brings men at last ! There are those whom these judgments shall not thus overwhelm. Hid in Jesus, and His sheltering grace, they are secure against all such dismay. But " the day of the Lord of Hosts shall be upon every one that is proud and lofty, and upon every one that is lifted up ; and he shall be brought low." (Isa. 2 : 12.)

Friends and brethren, what a mercy that that day is not yet upon us ! There is a Rock to which we still may fly and pray, with hope of security in its wide-open clefts. It is the Rock of Ages. There are mountains to which we may yet betake ourselves, and be forever safe from all the dread convulsions which await the world. They are the mountains of salvation in Christ Jesus. I believe that I am addressing some who have betaken themselves to them. Brethren, " hold fast the profession of your faith without wavering ; for He is faithful that promised." (Heb. 10 : 23.) But others are still lingering in the plains of Sodom, who need to take this warning to heart as they never yet have done. O ye travellers to the judgment, seek ye the Lord while He may be found, and call upon Him while He is near ! And may God in His mercy hide us all from the condemnation that awaits an unbelieving world !

> Jesus, lover of my soul,
>   Let me to thy bosom fly ;
> While the billows near me roll,
>   While the tempest still is high ;
> Hide me, O my Saviour, hide,
>   Till the storm of life be past,
> Safe into the haven guide,
>   Oh, receive my soul at last !

LECTURE FIFTEENTH

THE SEALING OF THE 144,000—MERCY IN THE MIDST OF JUDGMENT—ARE JEWISH PEOPLE—
ARE DESCRIBED BY THEIR TRIBAL NAMES—THE NUMBER OF THEM—THE NATURE OF
THEIR SEALING—NOT A MERE ARBITRARY OR EXTERNAL WORK—THE AGENT PERFORMING
IT—AN IMPARTATION OF THE HOLY GHOST—HOW MANIFESTED IN THESE SEALED ONES—
THE INTENT AND EFFECT OF THIS SEALING—GOD NOT YET DONE WITH THE JEWS—OUR
CALLING.

REV. 7 : 1–8. (Revised Text.) After this I saw four angels standing over the four corners of the earth, holding the four winds of the earth, that wind might not blow upon the earth, nor upon the sea, nor upon any tree.

And I saw another angel going up from the sun-rising, having a seal of the living God ; and he was crying with a great voice to the four angels to whom it was given to injure the earth and the sea, saying : Injure ye not the earth, nor the sea, nor the trees, until we have sealed the servants of our God upon their foreheads.

And I heard the number of the sealed : a hundred and forty-four thousand [were] sealed, out of every tribe of the children [rather, *sons*] of Israel ; out of the tribe of Juda, twelve thousand [were] sealed ; out of the tribe of Reuben, twelve thousand ; out of the tribe of Gad, twelve thousand ; out of the tribe of Aser, twelve thousand ; out of the tribe of Nepthalim, twelve thousand ; out of the tribe of Manasses, twelve thousand ; out of the tribe of Simeon, twelve thousand ; out of the tribe of Levi, twelve thousand ; out of the tribe of Issachar, twelve thousand ; out of the tribe of Zabulon, twelve thousand ; out of the tribe of Joseph, twelve thousand ; out of the tribe of Benjamin, twelve thousand [were] sealed.

THESE words describe the continuation of the action and course of events signified by the breaking of the sixth seal. It is, therefore, still the period of the judgment with which we here have to do. But in the midst of wrath, God remembers mercy. With all the fearful physical prodigies which mark the first shock under this seal, and the terror and dismay of mankind in general in view of those prodigies, the material universe remains, the earth continues in its place, and gracious operations still go on among its remaining populations. Though the heavens and the earth are terrifically shaken, and the whole system of nature is thrown into commotion, as if on the verge of utter ruin, there is a lull in the storm ; the angels who have charge of the disturbing blasts are commanded to hold them back for a season ; and a scene of calm, and of gracious manifestation to certain of the children of men, ensues, before the great and terrible day of the Lord advances to its meridian. The judgment has begun, and has progressed through a number of its most important stages, but still Divine compassion lingers, grace has not entirely departed, and the merciful act of the sealing of the 144,000 has to be completed before another step in the succession of judicial wonders can occur. And this sealing, it is, which is to occupy our attention this evening. We may consider,

    I.   THE SUBJECTS OF IT ;
    II. THE NATURE OF IT ;
    III. THE EFFECTS OF IT.

And to this end, may God help us with the illumination and guidance of his Holy Spirit !

I. *Who, then, are these* 144,000 *sealed ones ?* This is a vital question, in the right interpretation of this part of holy writ. But very conflicting and uncertain have been the answers generally given to it. Many writers are so perplexed and confounded with it, that they scarcely presume to answer it, and seek to quiet inquiry by saying that the subject is too difficult for man to handle. Did people only keep themselves to the plain reading of the words as they are, without subjecting them to chemical treatment to bring them into affinity with radically false conceptions of the Apocalypse, they would save themselves much perplexity, and their readers much confusion.

So long as men will keep thinking of the present Church, and the location of these events in the past, or in what is now transpiring ; just so long they will remain bewildered in the fog, and fail to find any solid way through these wonderful revelations. If we only take to heart, that, when John writes *" children of Israel,"* he means " children of Israel "—the blood descendants of the patriarch Jacob,—and that, when he mentions " the tribe of Juda," " the tribe of Reuben," " the tribe of Gad," " the tribe of Aser," " the tribe of Nepthalim," " the tribe of Manasses," " the tribe of Simeon," " the tribe of Levi," " the tribe of Issachar," " the tribe of Zabulon," " the tribe of Joseph," and " the tribe of Benjamin," he verily means what he says, we will at once have the subjects of this apocalyptic sealing unmistakably identified. But many are so morbidly prejudiced against everything Jewish, that it is concluded in advance, that anything merciful, referring to the Israelitish race, must needs be understood some other way than as the words are written. Though all the prophets were Jews, and Jesus was a Jew, and the writer of this Apocalypse was a Jew, and all the Apostles were Jews, and salvation itself is of the Jews, and the Jews as a distinct people are everywhere spoken of as destined to continue to the world's end, it is regarded as the next thing to apostasy from the faith, to apply anything hopeful, that God has said, to this particular race. Though Paul says, that, to his " kinsmen according to the flesh," " the promises " pertain ; that " God hath not cast away His people which He foreknew ; " " that blindness in part is happened to Israel, until the fulness of the Gentiles be come in," but only " in part," and only until then ; and that God's unchanging covenant still has something favourable for them in reserve ; even many otherwise enlightened Christians become impatient, and will not at all hear us, when we presume to pronounce God's own words as if He really meant what He has said.

No wonder, therefore, that they cannot find a consistent interpretation of a vision of grace which is predicated of Jacob's literal seed, in contradistinction from all others. Nor is there a vice or device of sacred hermeneutics, which so beclouds the Scriptures, and so unsettles the faith of men, as this constant attempt to read *Church* for *Israel*, and Christian peoples for Jewish tribes. As I read the Bible, when God says " *children of Israel*," I do not understand Him to mean any but people of Jewish blood, be they Christians or not ; and when He speaks of the twelve tribes of the sons of Jacob, and gives the names of the tribes, it is impossible for me to believe that He means the Gentiles, in any sense or degree, whether they be believers or not. And this would seem to be so plain and self-evident a rule of interpretation, that I can conceive of no legitimate variation from it, except in such case as the Holy Ghost Himself may explain to the contrary.

There is a sense in which a man may be a Jew outwardly, and yet not be one according to the spiritual calling of the Jews ; and there is a sense in which even Gentiles, if they be true believers, are " Abraham's seed ; " but I know of no instance in which the descendants of the twelve tribes of Israel include the Gentiles, or in which, what is discoursed specifically of persons out of the tribes of Juda, Reuben, Gad, Aser, Nepthalim, Manasses, Simeon, Levi, Issachar, Zabulon, Joseph, and Benjamin, is to be understood only of " the blessed company of *all* faithful people, gathered together from all parts of the world, and constituting the Church universal." Above all, would such a way of interpreting the Scriptures be out of place in a book in which more is said about " the church," strictly as such, than in any other sacred book, and in which it is particularly shown that the Church's judgment has begun, and to a large extent already gone into effect, before what is thus written of the tribes of the sons of Jacob takes place.

F

It is also to be remembered, that the crowned Elders and the Living ones are a part, and a very conspicuous part, of " the glorified company of the whole Church ; " yet, in chap. 14 : 3, they appear in connection with the 144,000, but as a wholly distinct body. The sealed ones are one company, complete in itself ; and the Elders and Living ones are another company complete in itself. John beholds them both at the same time, the one in the presence of the other, but each with its own separate place, character, and blessedness. The 144,000 therefore can by no possibility " represent the glorified company of the whole church." There is no proof that they represent any body but themselves, or that they are at all a part of the Church, properly so called. Everything shows that they are a class of the saved, separate and distinct from all others.

They are also described as being " the first fruits unto God and the Lamb." But they cannot be the first fruits of all saints ; for the Elders and Living ones are glorified, and have received their golden crowns, *before* these 144,000 have even been sealed on earth. They must therefore be the first fruits of another calling and order, after the present period of the Church, strictly so called, has run its course.

And when we take along with us the apostolic commentary upon the ancient covenants, to wit : that, after the fulness of the Gentiles is come in, the scales are to drop from the eyes of Israel's blinded descendants, and a fresh current of salvation is to set in towards them ; the argument seems to me conclusive and overwhelming, that these 144,000 are just what John says they are—*Jews*, descendants of the sons of Israel—the first fruits of that new return of God to deal mercifully with the children of His ancient people for their father's sakes.

If we look a little further on in the chapter, we find another company described, whose nationalities are also distinctly given. They are " out of every nation, and [of all] tribes, and peoples, and tongues." Literal nationalities are therefore an important element in the whole chapter. And as those said to be out of all nations, tribes, peoples, and tongues cannot be Jews only, so those said to be out of the twelve tribes of the children of Israel cannot be Jews and Gentiles indiscriminately.

Some have inferred the necessity of taking these Jewish tribes in a mystic sense, from the omission of the names of Dan and Ephraim, and the substitution of the names of Levi and Joseph in their stead. But these are circumstances from which I infer the exact contrary. If it were the common body of all believers that is meant, the proper symbol would be the complement of the common twelve tribes, as historically known. But here is a new enumeration, and quite a different order developed, so far as respects this sealing. It is, therefore, a new and original thing to itself, in which one of the historical tribes appears to be omitted altogether, and a double number taken out of another. Besides, if we are to take these tribes mystically of the whole Church, it is impossible to find anything to correspond to it in all the history of the Church, past, present, or to come. On that theory, the vision has never been and cannot be explained. Hence, we are driven back upon the literal sense, which was the accepted sense in the time of Irenæus, and which introduces no such embarrassing difficulty. The tribes mentioned by name, are the tribes meant. So, at any rate, I read the sacred account ; and if I err, I err with " many," and err on the side of the most direct and plainest sense of the word, as God has caused it to be written. Nor have I ever yet seen the argument for any other acceptation, which does not seem to me to torture and browbeat all the records that bear upon the case, set aside all safe laws of exegesis, and bring the whole Apocalypse into inextricable confusion.*

* Alford remarks on the passage : " By many, and even by the most recent commentator, Düsterdieck, these sealed ones are taken to represent Jewish believers ; the chosen out of the actual children of Israel." Among these we may note Irenæus, Bullinger, Grotius, Bossuet, Bengel, Eichorn, Heinrichs, Maitland, Züllig, Hoffman, B. W. Newtton, Kelly, " Matheetees," and others.

But these 144,000 are not simply Jews, for there are many of Jewish blood, and even of the saved among them, who are not of this number. They are Jews of a particular class, singled out from the Israelitish populations on account of spiritual attainments and character not found in the rest. They are not only descendants of the Hebrew patriarchs, living in the time of the judgment, but such of those descendants as shall then correspond in their characteristics to the signification of the several tribal names by which they are designated.

In Genesis 5, we have the names of the antediluvian patriarchs, from Adam to Noah. In the meaning of those names, taken in the order in which they stand, we have a singular epitome of the history of the race, and of the principal teachings of holy Scripture from first to last. Taking these tribal names of the 144,000 in the same way, we also find a very striking indication of their personal character, on the ground of which their peculiar honours are based. All Jewish names are significant, and the meaning of those which here are given, is not hard to trace. Juda means *confession* or *praise of God ;* Reuben, *viewing the Son ;* Gad, *a company ;* Aser, *blessed ;* Nepthalim, *a wrestler* or *striving with ;* Manasses, *forgetfulness ;* Simeon, *hearing and obeying ;* Levi, *joining* or *cleaving to ;* Issachar, *reward,* or *what is given by way of reward ;* Zabulon, *a home* or *dwelling-place ;* Joseph, *added* or *an addition ;* Benjamin, *a son of the right hand, a son of old age.* Now put these several things together in their order, and we have described to us : Confessors or praisers of God, looking upon the Son, a band of blessed ones, wrestling with forgetfulness, hearing and obeying the word, cleaving unto the reward of a shelter and home, an addition, sons of the day of God's right hand, begotten in the extremity of the age.

This certainly is very remarkable, and cannot be taken as mere accident, particularly as the order of the names, and some of the names themselves, are changed from the enumerations of the twelve tribes found in other places. The same will also account for the omission of the names of Dan and Ephraim, and the substitution of the names of Levi and Joseph in their stead. Those names are not of the right import to describe these 144,000. Dan means *judging,* or *the exercise of judicial prerogatives ;* but these 144,000 are not judges, and never become such. Ephraim means *increase, growth by multiplication ;* but these 144,000 are a fixed company, with none of the same class going before them, and none of the same class ever to come after them. The idea of increase or multiplication is altogether foreign to them. " They are virgins." These names are therefore unsuitable, and are superseded by others better adapted to describe the parties to whom they are applied.

These 144,000, then, are Israelites, living in the period of the judgment, who are only then brought to be confessors and praisers of God, whilst the most of their kindred continue in unbelief and rebellion. Viewing the Son, as their fathers never would view Him, they acknowledge Him as their Messiah and Judge. As Jews, they thus constitute a distinct company to themselves, and are blessed. As the result of their conversion, they are also very active in practical righteousness. They strive and wrestle against their own and their nation's long obliviousness to the truth as it is in Jesus, hearing and obeying now the voice of the Lord, cleaving unto the shelter and heavenly home promised by the prophets as the portion of those who call upon the name of the Lord even at that late hour. They are not of the Church proper ; for their repentance comes too late for that. They are a superaddition to the Church—a supplementary body—near and precious to Christ, but made up after the proper Church has finished its course. As Paul in his apostleship was like one born out of due time, so they are in the position of children belated in their birth ;—sons of God indeed, and destined to follow the Lamb whithersoever He goeth ; but sons begotten in the day of God's right hand, in the period of His power and judgment, in the last extremity of this age. All this comes out naturally and distinctly, without the least straining of a single word.

As to the number of this company, there could not be a clearer or more definite announcement than that which is given. John says : " *I heard the number of the sealed : a hundred and forty-four thousand,*"—twelve thousand out of each of the twelve tribes named,—twelve times twelve,—not a unit more, nor a unit less.

Owing to the fact that most of our expositors suppose this company to embrace all the saved of all the natural children of Jacob, or the whole Israel of God both Jewish and Gentile, they have generally taken these numbers as mystical—a definite number for an indefinite. Unwilling to believe, as they well might be, that only 144,000 of all the children of men, or of all the children of Abraham, are finally saved, they propose to understand a much greater number than the figures give. But such views of this body of sealed ones are thoroughly erroneous. These 144,000 are not all the saved, either from among the Jews and Gentiles together, or from among the Jews alone. They are a particular class of the saved, gathered up from among the seed of Jacob in and during the period of the Judgment. And with this made out, as I think it is most conclusively, every reason for taking these numbers in any but a literal sense entirely disappears. John heard the number of them announced as twelve times twelve thousand ; and I know not by what right they are to be accounted any more or any less.

II. We come, then, to inquire into the nature of the sealing of which these 144,000 are the subjects.

1. It is manifest that the transaction takes place on earth, and in the case of people contemporaneously living in the flesh. It does not run co-ordinately with the entire Christian dispensation, for it only begins after the Judgment has begun, and has progressed beyond the opening of the sixth seal. It is also completed and finished before the opening of the seventh seal ; for the opening of the seventh seal, with its trumpets and vials, is the letting loose of the four hurtful blasts which are commanded to be held back until the sealing is done. Under the sounding of the fifth trumpet particularly, we find these sealed ones living and moving among those upon whom the plague falls, and exempted from it by reason of their having been sealed. The sealing has therefore been finished before that time.

2. This sealing involved the impartation of a conspicuous and observable mark. A sealing is necessarily a marking of some sort. It is a common thing in God's administrations to have some fixed and understood token by which His people are distinguished. Under the Old Testament He set a visible mark in the flesh of His chosen. When He visited Egypt with death, He exempted the children of Israel by a mark which He commanded to be put upon their dwellings. When Jericho fell, He saved Rahab by the mark of the scarlet line which she was directed to bind about her window. Antichrist, in his mimicry of Christ, causes a mark to be put upon the right hand or forehead of his people, and will not permit any one to buy or sell who has not the mark. And we hence infer, that this sealing also involves the impressment of some manifest sign upon those who are the subjects of it.

Ezekiel describes a similar transaction, under similar circumstances, in which reference may be to precisely the same thing beheld in this vision. In the one case the executioners of vengeance appear with slaughter weapons in their hands, in place of the four angels with their hurtful blasts in this instance. But in that description also, a single sealer appears, who is sent out before the slaughterers, to " set a mark upon the foreheads of the men that sigh and that cry for the abominations," on account of which judgment impends. That mark was to be a visible means of identifying those who receive it, and of securing their safety in the midst of general destruction. And so these 144,000 have impressed upon them some manifest token, at least as conspicuous and prominent as a physical inscription upon their foreheads, if not, indeed, a physical mark. It is described as a sealing " in their foreheads," and as the " Father's name written in their foreheads." (Rev.

9 : 4 ; 14 : 1), and it cannot be otherwise than something particularly distinguishing.

3. It is something Divine. The seal with which the sealing is done, is " a seal of the living God." The affixing of a seal of God can only be by Divine authority and appointment. It is so intensely an official act, and connects so fully with the direct administrations and government of God, that it must needs be done by the hand or ordination of the Almighty himself. It so pledges Him, and to Him, that it must be regarded as His own act.

4. The office of this sealing is in the hands of an Angel, who comes forth from the sun-rising. He is a high officer of God. He carries a seal of the miracle-working God, and He gives commands to the angels of judgment. Many take Him to be the Lord Jesus himself. There is much to sustain this view. The star which heralded His nativity came from the East. He is himself called " the bright and morning star." Ezekiel beheld the Shekinah returning to the deserted temple from the East. His second coming is referred to as the lightning which shines from the East even unto the West. The promise to the Jews with reference to the judgment time is : " Unto you that fear my name shall the Sun of Righteousness arise ; " which involves a going up from the East. And He is the sender of the Holy Ghost. With these representations the vision of this Angel well harmonizes. We may, therefore, readily regard this Sealer as verily the Jehovah-Angel, even the Lord Jesus Christ himself, who comes forth, invisibly it may be, for the sealing of the 144,000. That He appears as an Angel, that He speaks of God as *his* God, and that He alludes to the sealing as if other agencies were associated with Him in the work, does not at all interfere with this conclusion. Like language is found in the lips of Jesus in other portions of the Scriptures ; and one of His most characteristic titles represents Him as the Messenger from God—the Angel of the Lord. He is here also very particularly distinguished from, and assigned an authority over, the four angels of judgment. It really does not alter the character of the matter whether this Sealer from the sun-rising be Christ in person or not. It is, at any rate, a high officer of God who has charge of the work ; and what he does proceeds from Christ's mediatorial achievements.

5. This sealing was moreover a moral, and not a mere arbitrary or external thing. Those who receive it are described as " the servants of our God," as contradistinguished from other classes of men. And from what is said of them in the fourteenth chapter, they are very eminently and very peculiarly God's servants. They are there described as having been entirely free from the adulterous and idolatrous defilements of mankind in general. " In their mouth was found no guile." And they finally come up faultless before the throne. The whole spirit of the record shows, that this their extraordinary sealing is connected with, and based upon, their extraordinary spiritual characteristics. This was also the case in the parallel instance in the ninth of Ezekiel. It was the men who sighed and who cried for the abominations that were done, upon whom the mark was set. And it is the common law of the Divine proceedings, that His special honours are never otherwise conferred than in connection with special dutifulness and fidelity under very special trials and difficulties. Every branch that bringeth forth fruit he purgeth, that it may bring forth more fruit ; and he who doth not profit by the talents bestowed, from him shall be taken away even that which he hath. These were people who had humbled themselves under the mighty hand of God. They had learned rightly to interpret the signs of judgment enacting about them in the heavens above and in the earth beneath. They had learned, and effectually taken to heart, the true character of the times in which they were living, what God was doing in their day, and what place they occupied in the ongoing of the Divine purposes. And the fruit of all was a vigour of faith, confession, and holy consecration seldom attained among the children of men. All their idolatries, and sensualities, and unbeliefs, they had most solemnly abjured. They had now given up to know nothing but God and

His service, in the most unfaltering trust in that Lion of the tribe of Judah under whose wondrous power the whole earth was trembling and smarting, as if in the agonies of dissolution. And because of this thorough spiritual transformation, and their holy sighing and crying for the abominations that cover the world, " the Angel of the covenant " comes up from the quarter of grace to honour their devotions, and to set apart and seal them for a peculiar destiny of favour and exaltation.

6. And from this we are enabled to get a still deeper glance into the nature of this peculiar sealing. The seal of God is the Spirit of God, particularly in His more unusual gifts. Thus Christ himself was *sealed* by the Father, when the Holy Ghost descended upon Him from heaven, marking Him out, and endowing Him for His wonderful career. (John 6 : 27.) Thus, also, Paul wrote to the Ephesians (1 : 13) : " After that ye believed, ye were *sealed* with that holy Spirit of promise, which is the earnest of our inheritance ; " and besought them : " Grieve not the holy Spirit of God, whereby ye are *sealed* unto the day of redemption." (Eph. 4 : 30 ; also, 2 Cor. 1 : 22.) We may, therefore, conceive of this sealing of the 144,000 as a special and extraordinary impartation of the Holy Ghost ; which again connects this vision with particular Old Testament promises. By the mouth of Joel, the Lord said to Israel : " I will pour out my Spirit upon all flesh." This was indeed a general promise, but with it was coupled another, which is not so general, but particularly to Israel : " And *your* sons and *your* daughters [O Jews] shall prophesy, *your* old men shall dream dreams, *your* young men shall see visions, and also upon the servants and upon the handmaidens in those days will I pour out my Spirit." Peter tells us that this began to be fulfilled in the miracle of Pentecost ; but the fulfilment did not end there. There are also particulars in the passage which were not fulfilled upon the primitive Church—particulars which refer to the judgment times, and connect directly with the scenes to which this sealing of the 144,000 is related. " Wonders in heaven and earth, blood, and fire, and pillars of smoke," are spoken of ; and the turning of the sun into darkness, and the moon into blood ; and all, directly on the eve of " the great and terrible day of the Lord." In this we distinctly recognize the occurrences under the red horseman of the second seal, the physical prodigies of the sixth seal, and the exact manifestations under the first and fifth trumpets. And in connection with these wonders, " Whosoever shall call on the name of the Lord shall be delivered ; for in Mount Zion and in Jerusalem shall be deliverance, as the Lord hath said, and in the remnant whom the Lord shall call." (Joel 2 : 28–32.) Pre-eminent among this " remnant " are these 144,000. In them, therefore, is fulfilled above all what is foreshown of mercy and grace thus mixed up with the terrors of the judgment. They are the sons and daughters of the people whom the prophet addressed. They are the ones who, above others of their time, call upon the name of the Lord. They are related to Mount Zion and Jerusalem as none of the Gentiles are. And it is not too much to say, that their peculiar sealing at least embraces this self-same miraculous endowment with the Spirit of God, which is so often referred to as the seal of God. They shall be made to dream God-begotten dreams, and to see God-shown visions. The Pentecostal Baptism from heaven shall be renewed in them with its original vigour. All the fruits and manifestations of the Holy Ghost, which characterized the apostles and early Christians at the beginning, shall reappear in them, perhaps with augmented power. And whether particular ceremonies connect with the thing or not, this is the chief element and essence of this sealing with " a seal of the living God." At any rate, those sealed, by virtue of their sealing, have the Father's name in them ; and *so* in them, as to mark and distinguish them as though a visible inscription stood written upon their foreheads. And those who are so eminently and peculiarly the bearers of the Father's name, must needs be partakers, in very extraordinary degree, of the gifts and powers of the Holy Ghost. Besides, the title of " the living God "

is seldom, if ever, used except in connection with some display of His power in the sphere of the miraculous.

7. Very various and diverse, hence would also be, the outward manifestations of this mark. It would show itself in the doctrines professed by the sealed ones, in the power with which they announce and defend them, perhaps in miraculous works wrought in proof of them, in a particularly holy, prayerful, and self-denying life, in a bravery and fearlessness before gainsayers which no earthly powers can daunt, and in a wisdom and heavenliness of demeanour, making them appear like beings from another world, and lighting up their very faces, perhaps, like the face of Moses when he came down from the mount, or like the face of Stephen in the midst of his murderers.

III. We come, now, to the intent and effect of this marvellous sealing.

It is agreed, on all hands, that it is a merciful and gracious act. Its first effect is to stay the blasts of judgment, and to produce a lull in the work of vengeance. Four angels, stationed over the earth at the four points of the compass, have already received power to hurt the earth and the sea. These four agents seem to be the same that act in connection with the first four trumpets, under which the whole system of the world is so fiercely smitten. Hail and fire, mingled with blood, there fall upon the earth, and the third part of what grows in the fields is destroyed. A great burning mountain is cast into the sea, and a burning star upon the rivers and fountains, turning the waters into blood or bitterness, and making havoc with all forms of life, both in the deep and on the land. Portentous and afflictive manifestations are also wrought in sun, moon, and stars. All these would seem to be, at least included in, the blasts with which these four angels had received power to blow upon the earth, the sea, and the trees. But the sealing Angel, with a great voice, commands them to hold back their blasts, until these servants of God are sealed.

And so it is ever. God's people are the salt of the earth. But for them, and God's gracious purposes toward them, judgment and ruin would instantly break over the globe. It is only for the elect's sake that the world stands, that the sun shines, that the fields yield their increase, and that men's greatest blessings are not at once turned into curses. It is only because God has his servants in the world, and saints preparing for glory, and children among earth's populations who sigh and cry for the abominations that are done, that the chariots of destruction do not rush over all that is. Governments stand, society exists, the waters flow, the trees live, the sea retains its salubrity, the grasses grow upon the earth, and the death-blasts of the destroying angels are restrained, only because the Lord is engaged taking out from among the nations a people for His name, the number of which must first be made up. Ten righteous persons in Sodom would have put off the ruin of that sink of sin ; and even when the terrific scenes of the great day have begun, and advanced to the very margin of their culmination, the whole process is made to delay till the 144,000 servants of God are sealed. O the compassion and forbearance of Jehovah, and the intensity of His faithfulness to them that call upon Him ! Nor do the proud and haughty ones of this world begin to comprehend, neither can it be measured, how much they owe to those meek children of obscurity, whose faith, devotions, and concern about the judgment, they so often ridicule, and so much despise.

But this sealing was more particularly for the comfort, assurance, and security of the sealed ones themselves. In the parallel passages in Ezekiel and Joel, the preservation of the marked ones, and the deliverance of those who call upon the name of the Lord, are specifically asserted. Here also, in the general commission of the agents of destruction and torment against men in general, there is a reservation in favour of those who have the seal of God in their foreheads. (Chap. 9 : 4.) The nature of the sealing itself is such as to forewarn and empower those who receive it against the impending evils. The restraint upon the blasts until this sealing is completed, also shows a relation of this sealing to those blasts, implying securement against them. And all such Divine markings in every other case had protection and deliverance for their object. It was so in the case of the children of Israel in Egypt. It was so in the case of Rahab. And it is so in the case of Baptism now. Hence, as remarked by Wordsworth, " this action of sealing with the sea or signet of God, is equivalent to a declaration, that they, who are so sealed, appertain to God, and are distinguished as such from others who do not thus belong to Him, and are assured by Him of His protection against all evil." As the gift of the Holy Ghost certified and assured the apostles, of the Divinity of the cause they had espoused, of their acceptance as God's acknowledged ambassadors, of the certain fulfilment unto them of all that their Lord had promised, and of their everlasting life, triumph, and glory, no matter what men might do unto them, or what might happen ; so this sealing with the seal of the living God certified and assured these 144,000 of the unmistakable character of their faith, of their election as a first fruits of incoming new administrations, and guaranteed unto them, not only security amid the blasts of heightening judgment upon earth, but also a peculiar and blessed portion with Jesus in His glory. And as the Baptism of the Spirit secured the safety of the primitive Christians when Jerusalem was overwhelmed, so this sealing secures the safety of the sealed ones as the judgment of the great day goes over the nations. They trust in the Lord, and wait patiently for Him ; and the Psalmist's words are fulfilled unto them : " *When the wicked are cut off, thou shalt see it.*"

From this, then, we see, that God is not yet done with the Jews. Their national restoration is not necessarily involved in this text ; though such a restoration in advance of this sealing, would admirably agree with the vision, and with other predictions relating to the same transactions. But it *is* involved that the Jews shall remain a distinct people upon earth up to the day of judgment ; and that, before the final consummation, God will again turn Himself toward them, and begin to deal with them once more in mercy, as in the days that He brought them up out of the land of Egypt. Edom, and those who disbelieve with Edom in Jacob's birthright, may sneeringly ask : " Watchman, what of the night ? " But, there is a morning coming. A stormy morning it may be ; but a morning nevertheless, and not without its sunshine and its rays of blessing. They err who tell us that all God's promises to Israel as a race are dead, never again to be revived. The Giver of them does not so speak. His inspired Apostle, even after Jerusalem had fallen, wrote, with regard to this very subject, that " the gifts and calling of God are without repentance ; " and that for the self-same Israel which has fallen, and been cast down, and broken off, there is a coming fulness, recovery, and grafting in again, when the Deliverer shall come. (See Rom. 11.) And the visible pledge of something special yet in reserve for this marvellous race, is written in all their history, from the fall of Jerusalem to this hour. Else why the unparalleled preservation of this people, with such unwaning and ever-active life-energy, " against such overwhelming odds, through the storms of so many centuries, the vicissitudes and perils of so many generations, and amid the wrecks of so many buried empires ? " Else why that undying presentiment, which throbs in the universal Jewish heart, and which no adversity can quench or prosperity entirely charm into quiet, of some future return to the high estate of their fathers ? The very land itself, in its perpetual refusal to give peaceful and secure home to any of the Gentiles who have overrun it, throughout all its sad desolations, gives out its plaints and prayers that Jehovah would not forget his covenant with the house of Israel, and utters from every hill and valley, shore and sea, the prophecy of some future of hope and blessing which cannot be delayed forever. What that hope is, we need not here inquire. But linked in with it is the sealing of 144,000 out of the twelve tribes of the children of Jacob, to stand as God's servants and witnesses upon earth amid the ongoings of the judgment, and finally to take their places with the Lamb on the Mount Zion, amid the Halleluias and harpings of heaven, and to sing there a song, never sung before, and never to be sung by any but themselves.

Friends and brethren, it is not for us to be a part of this 144,000. But we have our calling also, and a much superior one. The Jehovah Angel from the sun-rising is even now at work throughout the world, marking and sealing men for kinghoods and priesthoods far sublimer than all the honours of these 144,000. His proposal is made alike to all, whether Jew or Gentile, male or female, bond or free : and that proposal is, by His word, sacraments and Spirit, to set a seal upon each of us, not only for our safety in the day of judgment, but for our admission into the royalties of heavenly empire. And it is only to allow time for the making up of the full number to reign with Him forever, that the blasts of vengeance are restrained, and the day of judgment tarries. Child of Adam, hast thou, then, the mark ? Hast thou been set apart to God, and sealed with that Holy Spirit of promise ?

I am addressing some who hope they have the seal of God. Baptized into His name, enrolled among His professing people, communing punctually at His table, lifting oft their hearts and voices unto Him as their stay and strength amid earth's trials, believing with all their soul in Jesus as their salvation, and with the desire ever burning in their breasts to be found of Him in peace, they promise well to be among the first-born in heaven. But, " Let him that thinketh he standeth take heed lest he fall." (1 Cor. 10 : 12.) No one of us is out of danger yet ; and the word of the Master is : " Hold fast that which thou hast, that no man take thy crown." (Rev. 3 : 11.)

But I am addressing others who have forfeited their right to any such hope. Though baptized, it is the same as if they had not been, except that they have vows upon them which they do not fulfil. Though outwardly grafted into the Church, no life-connection has been formed, and to-night they are mere dead branches, leafless, fruitless, unsightly, and ready for the burning. They are witnesses against themselves that they have chosen them the Lord to serve Him ; but they have not done it. O ye backsliding children, remember whence ye are fallen, and repent, and do the first works, lest your Lord come in an hour when ye think not, and assign you place with hypocrites and unbelievers. Though you may never have run to the same excess of riot with many around you, if you have lived forgetful and neglectful of God and duty, it would be blasphemy for you to say that you are ready for the judgment. Up, then, and be doing ; for your opportunities will soon be past.

And yet others are listening to me who have not so much as been baptized ; whose names are nowhere on the records of the pious ; who have hitherto been living without God and without hope in the world ; and who are conscious that no saving mark is on their foreheads. Prayerless and careless, they have passed the precious hours in which they might have become the sons of God, and are to-night on the road to everlasting death. O sinful, self-deceiving mortal, to thee, once more, is the word of this salvation sent !

> Jesus ready stands to save thee,
> Full of pity joined with power.

With the seal of the living God in hand, He waits consent to stamp its saving impress on thy brow. Ask, and it shall be given ; seek, and thou shalt find. But let not another day or hour be lost, lest there should be no more hope for thee.

LECTURE SIXTEENTH

THE VISION OF THE PALM-BEARING MULTITUDE—UNCERTAINTY OF COMMENTATORS AS TO WHO THEY ARE—NOT FIRST CLASS SAINTS—NOT THE SEALED ONES—NOT THE CHURCH GENERAL—HARDLY ANY RESURRECTED ONES AMONG THEM—ARE RANSOMED MEN— PEOPLE WHO LIVED IN THE JUDGMENT TIME—THE "LEFT" WHEN THE CHURCH WAS TAKEN—THEIR CONVERSION AND FINAL BLESSEDNESS—HIGHER BLESSINGS THAN THEIRS.

REV. 7: 9–17. (Revised Text.) After these things I saw, and behold, a great multitude which no one could number, out of every nation, and [of all] tribes, and peoples, and tongues, standing before the throne and before the Lamb, clothed in white robes, and palm-branches in their hands ; and they cry with a great voice, saying, The salvation [be ascribed] to our God who sitteth on the throne, and to the Lamb. And all the angels were standing around the throne, and the elders, and the four living ones, and they fell before the throne on their faces and worshipped God, saying, Amen, the blessing, and the glory, and the wisdom, and the thanksgiving, and the honour, and the power, and the might, be to our God unto the ages of the ages. Amen.

And one of the elders answered, saying unto me, These that are arrayed in the white robes, who are they ? and whence came they ? And I said unto him, My lord, thou knowest. And he said (to me), These are they that come out of the tribulation, the great [one] ; and they have washed their robes and made them white in the blood of the Lamb. On this account they are before the throne of God, and serve him day and night in his temple ; and he that sitteth on the throne [Codex Sinaiticus : *knows them*] shall tabernacle over them. They shall not hunger any more, nor yet thirst any more ; neither shall the sunlight on them, no, nor any scorching heat : because the Lamb which is in the midst of the throne is their shepherd, and shall lead them to fountains of waters of life, and God shall wipe away every tear out of their eyes.

THREE visions are embraced in the results of the breaking of the sixth seal : first, the prodigious commotions which fill the world with consternation ; second, the sealing of the 144,000 ; and here, the multitude of palm-bearers before the throne. The first two of this particular series relate to the earth and to people in the flesh ; the one which we are now to consider relates to heaven and to people in heaven. What it presents is subsequent in time, both to the great shaking and the gracious sealing. The great and terrible Day of the Lord is not one ordinary day of twelve or twenty-four hours. All these seals, and the varied occurrences under them, belong to that day ; but it is very manifest that each of them covers a continuous period of months and years. The vision now before us refers to one section in a series of successive judicial wonders.

The rapt apostle is in heaven. He was called thither at a very early stage of these successive visions, and from thence he contemplates all that he narrates after the beginning of the fourth chapter. It was from heaven that he beheld the shaking and the sealing ; and from the same point of observation he sees this company of palm-bearers. They stand before the throne, and before the Lamb. They shout and praise God for their redemption. The angels form a grand circle around them ; the throne, with the Living ones and the Elders, as described in the fourth chapter, being in the centre. They are arrayed in bright robes, are acknowledged as servants of God, and pronounced forever free from tribulation, and from whatever might distress them or interfere with their blessedness.

The picture would seem to be a very plain one, and one easy to be understood. There was also such a particular announcement of the history and character of the multitude in view, that there would appear to be no room for difficulty in this regard. And yet, on all the prevalent systems of Apocalyptic interpretation, the question of the Elder : *" Who are they ? and whence came they ?* " is still the great question to be decided. Indeed, there is scarcely one point with reference to these palm-bearers upon which expositors are agreed. It is generally acknowledged that they are, or represent, children of men, who had a deal of trouble in their day, and are some way related to the family of the redeemed ; but whether people in the flesh on earth, or disembodied spirits in the intermediate state, or risen and glorified saints in their heavenly home, is matter of mere dreamy opinion, indifferently debated, and in no way settled. And from what I have seen upon the subject, I would take it as a crucial point to try the consistency of any proposed method of interpreting the Apocalypse, whether it has capacity satisfactorily to dispose of this palm-bearing multitude.

Some have taken these palm-bearers to be the early Christians, victorious over the sorrows and persecutions which afflicted the Church in the first ages. Others see in them a symbol of the prosperity which came to the Church by the conversion of the Emperor Constantine ; or of the vast accessions which were made to the Church under his and subsequent reigns ; or of the exalted and happy state of the Church in a fancied millennium yet to be realized in this world. Others take these palm-bearers to be the spirits of the redeemed, anterior to the resurrection ; others, the 144,000 sealed ones of the preceding vision, exalted to their final glory ; others, the whole body of the Church of all ages ; others, the Church of the Gentiles ; some the Church on earth ; some the Church in resurrection glory ; some the Church in some ceremony of recognition by Christ in heaven ; and some a mere poetic adumbration of victory for the Gospel, without definite significance or application. A greater chaos of opinions and fancies is scarcely to be found on any other distinct subject presented in the Scriptures, than that which exists upon this. There is no alternative, therefore, if we would at all ascertain the truth, but to go back to first principles, and find out some method of explaining this whole Book, which will take in these palm-bearers, in the place at which they appear, in harmony with all the statements given concerning them, and with all that goes before and follows after.

On the plain and simple principles upon which we have conducted this exposition thus far, we cannot well fail to reach results of a definite and solid character, needing no far-fetched and doubtful substructure to bring us to them, and so direct that the plainest understanding may judge of their worthiness to be accepted as the real truth meant to be set forth.

It is sometimes profitable to consider questions negatively. It serves to narrow the inquiry, and to free and clear the subject for more direct solution and settlement. And this method seems to be called for in this case. In order, therefore, to decide rightly who these palm-bearers are, I will first show *who they are not.*

1. Evidently they are not the first and highest class of redeemed men. As we have seen in the fourth and fifth chapters, there is a body of ransomed ones, glorified, crowned, and promoted to pre-eminent dignity in heaven, where the apostle beheld and heard them before the book was taken, and hence in advance of all the judgment plagues developed under the seals. These are the Elders and the Living ones, redeemed out of every kindred, and tongue, and people, and nation—the seniors in glory, and highest of all the saints— crowned with golden crowns, and related to the throne as none others. No sooner had John seen the judgment throne set, than he also saw other thrones around it, and these princely Elders seated on them, ready to take part in the solemn adjudications about to be visited upon the earth ; and also Living ones conjoined with the throne, and sharing in the administration of its decrees. These same Elders and Living ones appear again in the vision before us, occupying the same nearness to the throne and the same royal dignity in which the seer first beheld them. They are distinguished in various particulars from the palm-bearing multitude. They *sit ;* the palm-bearers *stand.* They have crowns and thrones ; the palm-bearers have neither. They

appeared in their places and received their rewards before the sorrows of judgment began ; the palm-bearers only come to their place before the throne *after* the judgment has progressed to the sixth seal. The Elders were in heaven before " the hour of trial " came, being " accounted worthy to escape all these things ; " the palm-bearers were *in* that " trial," and only reach heaven " out of the tribulation, the great one." The Elders and Living ones are " Kings and Priests ; " the palm-bearers are connected with the same general company, but only in the capacity of servants. It is therefore, a great mistake to confound these palm-bearers with the highest order of saints.

2. Equally erroneous is it, to identify these palm-bearers with the sealed ones of the preceding vision. The sealed ones consist of a definite and ascertained number ; but these palm-bearers are uncounted and numberless. The sealed ones are all Israelites, blood-descendants of the patriarch Jacob ; but these palm-bearers are described as " *out of every nation, and [of all] tribes, and peoples, and tongues.*" The sealing of the sealed ones had reference to their preservation through storms of judgment upon men on earth, which storms are only let loose under the seventh seal ; but these palm-bearers are already in heaven before the seventh seal is touched. Besides, in a subsequent vision, in chap. 14, we find this particular 144,000 again, in their own distinct character, and only then, at that late period, introduced into their glorified estate. It is, therefore, most unreasonable, and forever irreconcilable with the record, to take these palm-bearers and the 144,000 sealed ones as one and the same body. They are as different as time, place, and characterizing circumstances can make two classes of people.

3. Neither do these palm-bearers represent the Church universal at the end of the great tribulation. We have that in the 20th chapter, in its own proper place, and including all these several separate classes of the redeemed. I have seen it put forth by an otherwise creditable writer, and upon the authority of the vision now before us, that there is no such thing as a rapture of the Church before the great tribulation ; that these palm-bearers show us the Church in final salvation ; and that they all pass under the great tribulation, and only come to glory through it. But he is sadly mistaken in every point of this statement. Where do the gold-crowned Elders and Living ones come from, if there is no rapture of the Church before the great tribulation ? They are glorified saints, clearly identified as such, in chapters 4 and 5 ; and they are glorified and crowned before the great judgment tribulation begins, being saved from that " hour of trial." And where is the proof that these palm-bearers represent the Church at all ? They are not called the Church, or any part of it. The Church—the *Ecclesia*—in its proper New Testament acceptation, ends its earthly course with what was represented by " the seven churches," and is never heard of again in all the Apocalypse, after the third chapter, except as it appears in the Elders and Living ones in glory. There still are believers, saints, and witnesses for God, who subsequently attain to high and glorious places in the Divine Kingdom ; but they are not " the Church of the *first-born*,"—the only proper Church,—which receives its judgment, and whose true members are apportioned their heavenly dignities, before a single seal is broken, and hence some time before this palm-bearing multitude appears before the throne.

Besides, if there is no rapture of the Church until the final termination of the judgment troubles, and all the saints together only then are introduced into glory, how shall we account for John's mental questionings and uncertainties with reference to these palm-bearers ? If they represent the finally complete Church, did he not know that the Church was to be thus exalted and glorified ? Was he so ignorant of the character and destiny of that chosen body of which he was an apostle and a chief, as not to know it, or whence it came, upon encountering it in heaven ? Would it not be a sorry impeachment of his apostolic character and enlightenment, besides very stupid and unreasonable, to proceed on such an assumption, or on anything which involves it ? The manifest fact that he was perplexed and in doubt with reference to these palm-bearers, and that the Elder interfered to solve his questionings, proves that they are not the Church proper, but the Church of the *after-born*, if of the Church at all ; that is, a body of saved ones, with a history and place peculiarly their own, and not as yet exactly understood by the apostle.

Still further, it is a false gloss upon the Elder's words, to understand them as if these palm-bearers had passed through the entire duration of the judgment troubles before reaching the position in which John beholds them. The language corresponds with the order of succession in these several visions, and suggests, if it does not imply, that these palm-bearers cease to be in the great tribulation before its final termination. It is not said that they *pass through it*, but that they *come out of it*, thus leaving it behind them to run on after they are gone.

Some argue, indeed, that " the great tribulation " is realized only under the seventh seal, during the murderous domination of the Beast and the False Prophet ; and that as these palm-bearers " come out of the tribulation, the great one," we must necessarily throw this vision forward, and nearer to the extremity at which all tribulation ends. But this also is a mistake. That which the Scriptures describe as " the great tribulation," though inseparably linked with the Judgment, is made up of more than one blast. There is a tide in it, dividing it into sections. There was a prelibation of it in the destruction of Jerusalem and the Jewish state, as that was also a prelibation of the Judgment itself. And though the highest stress and fulness of the great tribulation are realized under the seventh seal with its trumpets and vials, we have the testimony of Christ himself, that mighty gusts of its power are expended before the opening of the sixth seal. The darkening of the sun, the obscuration of the moon, the falling of the stars, and the shaking of the whole system of nature, described in Matthew 24 : 29, and Mark 13 : 24, are precisely identical with the great physical prodigies which John beheld at the opening of the sixth seal, and are the great characteristics of the sixth seal. And yet, in both instances, these occurrences are located by the Saviour " *after* " and " immediately after," very sore and awful tribulation, which is necessarily embraced in, though it does not exhaust, that " great tribulation, such as was not since the beginning of the world to this time, no, nor ever shall be." (Matt. 24 : 21.)* We thus have it scripturally ascertained, that " the tribulation, the great one," partly precedes, as well as partly succeeds, the breaking of the sixth seal. These palm-bearers could therefore be *in it* and *come out of it*, and still be transferred to heaven before the last dregs of it are poured out upon the guilty world.

Referring back to the second, third, fourth, and fifth seals—to the red horseman, taking peace from the earth and filling it with strife, havoc, and bloodshed—to the black horse of scarcity and famine—to the livid horse, with death-plague on his back and greedy hell at his heels, overrunning the

---

* It is manifest that the great and unequalled tribulation here described, is not viewed by the Saviour as finally ended before the occurrences of verse 20. This is proven from what is said in verse 30 ; for there he tells us that " *then* "—after the physical commotions of verse 29—" *shall all the tribes of the earth mourn.*" This universal mourning is certainly a part of what is summarily referred to in verse 21 ; but it is specifically said to come *after* the events which are confessedly coincident with the sixth seal. The manner in which Mark gives the same things, seems also distincly to imply, that the tribulation preceding the disturbances in sun, moon, and stars, is only a part or section of *the one* great time of trouble. He represents the Saviour as saying, " after *that* tribulation, the sun shall be darkened," &c., implying some *other* or *further* tribulation, which the record in Matt. 24 : 30, and the trumpets and vials of the Revelation show to be subsequent to these marked commotions, just as the first was before them.

It is quite untenable to assign the unequalled tribulation of Matt. 24 : 21 to the fall of Jerusalem, and the subsequent afflictions of the Jewish people, in any sense except as preliminary first fruits—a mere sample in advance ; for in Daniel 12: 1, this unparalleled time is unmistakably connected with *the deliverance*, not with the destruction, of that people. Properly, therefore, it relates to the *ending* of the times of the Gentiles, not to the beginning of them, as some have erroneously insisted.

world—and to the persecution and butchery of men for their faithful testimony for God under the fifth seal—we behold an accumulation of sufferings and horrors which, if they belong not to the Great Tribulation of the judgment times, I know not how to place or what to call. And as these palm-bearers do not appear upon the heavenly scene until after the opening of the sixth seal, they must needs have been partakers in these dreadful trials, and hence are rightly described as coming *out of* " the tribulation, the great one," though translated and in heaven before its last blasts smite the guilty world.

Our position thus stands firm, that these palm-bearers do not represent the Church general at the end of all tribulation, or anywhere else.

4. It is doubtful, even, whether there are any resurrected people at all among this multitude. There may be such, but there is no proof to that effect. There is nothing said about resurrection, and nothing which necessarily involves it. A rapture or translation, like that of Enoch or Elijah, is implied ; for these people are in heaven, and have received their places and rewards ; but it is not intimated that any of them had ever died. They are to hunger and thirst no more ; but it is not added that they shall die no more. To those under the fifth seal, who had lost their lives for Christ, the word was that they must rest as disembodied souls under the altar, until others of their brethren should be slain as they had been. But we read of no more such slaying of witnesses for the truth before the opening of the seventh seal. This would seem to imply that no resurrection occurs between the fifth and the seventh seals. It is but a remote implication, and cannot be regarded as conclusive ; but if correct, it precludes the possibility of any resurrected ones being among this palm-bearing multitude. At any rate, as all of them come " out of the tribulation, the great one," there can be no resurrected ones included, except such as died during the great tribulation time.

We thus find our inquiry greatly narrowed, and ourselves far on the way to a satisfactory understanding of the whole matter. I therefore proceed to state more positively who these palm-bearers are, and whence they come.

1. They are ransomed human beings. They were once sinners and sufferers on the earth, and members of its tribes and peoples. They were cleansed and sanctified by the blood of Jesus. They ascribe their salvation to God and to the Lamb. Whether they be rated with the Church proper, or not, they are by nature of the stock of Adam, and by grace of the family of the redeemed.

2. They are people who were living on the earth in the period of the Judgment. The great tribulation times are everywhere inseparably linked with the judgment times (see Dan. 12, Matt. 24, Mark 13, Rev. 1: 7) ; and this whole multitude is made up of those who come *out of the great tribulation.* This is positively stated by the hierophant Elder, and so recorded by John. It is therefore true, and no man is at liberty to question it. There are other saved ones, of several classes, who subsequently come out of the afterparts of this great tribulation—the 144,000, for instance, the two witnesses, and those which refuse to worship the Beast or to receive his mark—but they are not of this particular company.

Some make a great deal of the allusion to *the number* of these palm-bearers, and might perhaps bring this forward against their being contemporaries in one particular period of the world's history. But Dr. Hengstenberg has well observed that, " this magnifying of the numbers here to something beyond all bounds," is not legitimate. The Jews constitute a very small fraction of the people now living, or that will be living when the judgment comes. And yet, the few elect and sealed from among them, as beheld in the preceding vision, make up a multitude which the Apostle did not pretend to count. He " *heard* the number " of them ; otherwise, even that company would have been numberless to him. And if we add to that number, in proportion as all nations, peoples, kindreds, and tongues exceed the Jewish population, we will necessarily have a body sufficiently large to answer all the terms of the description before us. When John speaks of these palm-bearers as " a great multitude which no one could number," he speaks relatively, not absolutely. (Compare his language in John 21 : 25.) And if we add to the number of the sealed ones, but twenty-five for one, we will have more than 4,000,000 of people, who, if viewed in one congregation, as in this vision, would be vastly in excess of the capacity of one man to count, and hence " a great multitude which no one could number." And when we consider the import of the opening of the first seal, the moral and spiritual revolution which it sets forth in vast masses of mankind, and the continuous ongoing of these conquests, judgment-aided, under all the subsequent seals, there certainly is no just reason for hesitating to believe, that by the time the end of the sixth seal is reached, there will be people enough, won from the half-christianity, lukewarmness, unbelief, and sins in which the beginning of the judgment found them, to make up even " a great multitude which no man could number." At any rate, we are not to allow reasonings of our own, upon expressions altogether indefinite, to stand against the clear and positive Divine statement, that all these palm-bearers come *out of the great tribulation*, and hence must of necessity have lived upon the earth contemporaneously in the judgment time.

3. They are people whom the judgment found unprepared, and who consequently were " left " when the rapture of the Church took place. The Scriptures are everywhere very particular in forewarning us that the day of the Lord shall come as a thief in the night—that it will come as a snare on all them that dwell on the earth—that the great mass of men, and even of the professing Church, shall be overtaken by it unawares—and that, " in that night, there shall be two in one bed," one of whom " shall be taken, and the other left ; " and " two grinding at the mill," one of whom " shall be taken, and the other left ; " and two in the field, one of whom " shall be taken, and the other left." The representations are also very clear, that great will be the number of those who will thus be " *left*." Indeed, the intimations are, that so few will be found ready, and waiting for their Lord, that their removal will cause no very noticeable depletion in the population of the earth. The great body of the professed Church of that day will be " left," as well as the entire community not of the Church ; for " when the Son of man cometh, shall he find faith on the earth ? " And to all that are then found unready, and are " left," gone forever will be the privileges and honours of " the Church of the first-born ! " Gone, the crowns, the thrones, the princedoms of eternity, which are now so freely offered to every hearer of the Gospel ! Gone, to return no more, all hope and opportunity of regaining the lost prize of immortal kingship and dominion ! Grovelling worldlings, profane blasphemers, blinded sceptics, may not understand it, and, for the most part, go on in their sins ; but, for millions upon millions, " there shall be weeping and gnashing of teeth." In place of invitations to heavenly rulership, will be judgment pangs; and in place of the joyous day of God's long-suffering, will be the dark waves of the great tribulation.

But, even then, not yet everything will be lost. The crown will be gone, but salvation may still be attained. There will then be no more heavenly thrones to be distributed, but there will still be palms to be secured. The pains of the great tribulation will then have to be endured, but there will remain a possibility of coming out of it, before it culminates in eternal perdition. And many, whose repentance comes, alas, too late for eternity's higher glories, will turn themselves in sorrowful earnestness to that Saviour whose sublimer offers they let slip for this paltry and perishing world. " For when God's judgments are in the earth, the inhabitants of the world will learn righteousness." (Is. 16 : 9.)

Not by any means all, who are " left " when the Church is translated, will thus turn unto the Lord. The corrupt world will continue to be the same base and God-defiant world, until the waves of hell go over it forever. " Many shall be purified, and made white, and tried ; but the wicked shall do wickedly." (Dan. 12 : 10.) As the calamities thicken and deepen, evil will become more out-breaking, and rush with giant strides to its final consummation. But, amid much painful disappointment, regretful tears, and great tribulation, Laodiceans, who thought they were rich, and increased in goods, and had need of nothing, will discover how wretched, miserable, poor, blind, and naked they were the while, and repent, and profit by their chastenings, and find salvation, though having lost their crowns ; and many more, who would not give themselves to Jesus in order to be eternal Kings, will learn to think themselves happy to follow him in the fires of judgment, if they may only be servants in the kingdom of heaven. And these are they whom John here beholds " standing before the throne and before the Lamb, clothed in white robes, and palms in their hands."

All this is latently contained in what is recorded of these palm-bearers. " These are they that come out of the tribulation, the great one ; and they have washed their robes and made them white in the blood of the Lamb. On this account they are before the throne of God, and serve him day and night in his temple." Having been " left " when the elect were " taken," John would naturally be surprised to find them in heaven. Having come under the judgment pains, he would naturally infer that heaven was not for them. Hence his silent astonishment at beholding so large a company of after-comers exalted into the presence of God ; and hence the special explanation of the Elder.

It is one of Christ's messages from heaven to his people on earth : " Behold, I come as a thief. Blessed is he that watcheth, and keepeth his garments." (Rev. 16 : 15.) The implication of the Elder's words is, that these people had failed to comply with these conditions, while the judgment delayed ; but were worldly in their temper, had their " garments spotted by the flesh," and so were without right to the promises. Making themselves at home in the ways, and thinking, and emoluments of this world, of course they had no claim on heaven. The Apostle was, therefore, justly surprised to see them in heaven. But the Elder explains it. Having been cut off from the Church of the first-born, and made to feel their failure by the fierceness of judgment sorrows, they came to a better mind. Their spotted garments they washed in the blood of the Lamb. Their false philosophizing they gave up for the simplicities of the faith ; and the truths they once accounted fanaticism, they found to their sorrow and at length confessed to be realities. And by the depths of their penitence, amid the pains of the great tribulation, and by the sorrowful earnestness of their seeking unto Jesus in the last extremities, they obtained forgiveness, and were recovered from their sins. " On this account," the Elder says, they are saved, though out of the fires of judgment ;—admitted into heaven, even though they have lost their places among the crowned ones ;—permitted to stand " before the throne of God," though they have no thrones for themselves ;—made servants in God's house, though not of the high order of royal sons.

Having, then, ascertained who these Palm-bearers are, the next point to be considered is *their blessedness*. We have not the time now for such a discussion of it as it deserves ; but a few observations are demanded, before dismissing the subject.

1. *They are in heaven.* This is a great thing to say of any one. It is to be in the enjoyment of an estate, by the side of which all the exaltation, honour and glory this world can bestow, shrinks into utter nothingness. Lazarus in heaven, is a far sublimer picture than that of any rich man on earth, however royally clad, or sumptuously luxuriant in worldly possessions. " Oh, if I can only get to heaven ! " is often the highest ejaculation of the noblest and purest hearts. And this goal of pious longing, these Palm-bearers have reached. They are where the gold-crowned Elders and the glorious Living ones are. They are where the holy angels stand round them in serried ranks of glory upon glory. They are where the Almighty's throne is located, where God is, and where the Lamb shows Himself in all His sublime benignity and power.

They are where the pure worship ascends forever in the presence of eternal Godhead, and the *Amens* to every strain of adoration come in from principalities and powers. They are in Heaven ! True, they have no crowns, no thrones, no dominion. True, they stand while some others sit, and serve while others reign. True, they come in after all the royal places of the first-born are filled. But still, *they are in Heaven !*—bright, beautiful, lovely, untainted, imperishable, HEAVEN !

2. *They are " before the throne of God,"*—that throne which John saw set in heaven, encircled with an iris of emerald, and filled by Him whose appearance is like crystalline and smokeless flame ; that throne around which all other thrones are stationed, and out of which go forth the lightnings, and voices, and thunders of the eternal forces. They are not joined to the throne, as the Living ones ; nor associated with its Occupant in subregencies, like the Elders ; but they are in the presence of it, before it, near it ;—nearer even than the angels. To be admitted into the presence of the King, to be permitted to stand before the throne when the King is there in the majesty and state of His eternal dominion, and to be allowed to remain in such a station permanently, is an honour not be despised. It was the high distinction of David to stand before King Saul, after that victory over Goliath. It is a privilege which is awarded to none but those who find favour in the King's sight. And these Palm-bearers " stand before the throne, and before the Lamb."

3. *They are " clothed in white robes."* They wear the garments of saints—they are attired in unspotted righteousness and faultless splendour, acquired through the Saviour's blood. They were sinners once, but they are holy now. They were naked once, but they are clothed now ; and their clothing is the pure and shining raiment of heaven. To be free from sin !—to be sure that our hearts are clean !—to be released forever from the soils of earth and its corruptions !—to be clothed with the unsullied purity of the spiritually perfect !—is the deepest, greatest, heaviest sigh of every child of God ! But these Palm-bearers realize what it is to have these yearnings satisfied. They have robes ; and those robes are spotless bright, having been washed and whited in the blood of the Lamb.

4. *They have " palm branches in their hands."* The joy of the feast of tabernacles is theirs. God ordained for his ancient people that, after the harvest was gathered, they should take the branches of palm trees, and dwell in booths, and rejoice before Him, as the Lord that brought them up out of Egypt. And so we read in Nehemiah, that " all the congregation of them that were come again out of the captivity," as they found written in the law, fetched olive-branches, and palm-branches, and branches of thick trees, to make booths, and sat under the booths, " *and there was very great gladness.*" These seasons were the most joyous, exultant and bright, observed by the Israelitish people. They were times when everything glittered and thrilled with deep, pure, and lively joy. And these palm-branches in the hands of this white-robed multitude connect with the ancient feast of tabernacles, and bespeak gladdest exultation over their deliverance. To this also answers the further description, which represents them as " crying with a great voice, saying, The Salvation [be ascribed] to our God who sitteth upon the throne, and to the Lamb ; " whilst angels, and Elders, and Living ones fall down on their faces in reverent adoration, and answer : " Amen, the blessing, and the glory, and the wisdom, and the thanksgiving, and the honour, and the power, and the might, be to our God, unto the ages of the ages. Amen."

5. *They serve day and night in the temple of God.* This shows them to be no longer subject to the clogs and weariness of mortal life, but glorified, and in the immortal state. John saw no temple in the New Jerusalem ; but the New Jerusalem is not all of heaven. There is a celestial temple as well as an earthly one. Jesus, in this very Apocalypse, gives the promise : " Him that over-

cometh will I make a pillar in the temple of my God, and he shall go no more out." (Chap. 3 : 12.) And in that temple these Palm-bearers serve continually. In what their services consist, is not told us ; but they are services befitting saints and the glory of heaven, and such as give ample exercise to all their glorified capacities and powers.

6. Nor are they without God's distinct and favourable acknowledgment. " He that sitteth on the throne knows them ; " or, as in other copies of the text, He " shall spread his tent upon them," " tabernacle over them." As the Shekinah brooded over the pilgrim Hebrews by day and by night, the glorious symbol of the Divine presence, protection, and favour, so these Palm-bearers abide under the shadow of the Almighty. As in the final consummation the tabernacle of God shall be with men, and he shall tabernacle with them, and they shall be his people, and God Himself shall be with them as their God ; so shall His pavilion cover these Palm-bearers, and they shall be His people, and He will be their God.

7. " They shall not hunger any more, nor yet thirst any more ; neither shall the sun light on them, no, nor any scorching heat." Oh, to be delivered from the straits, and wants, and painful necessities of mortal life !—to be released from these earthly burdens, vicissitudes, and deaths !—to find some blessed homestead, where these aching, wasting, dying natures may once know what it is to have abiding rest ! Man's anguished spirit knows no intenser hunger and thirst then this. But what we all thus yearn for, is the everlasting possession of these saints. Once they felt the weight of famine, the plague of drought, the fires of trial, and the burdens of toil ; but, gone forever, now, are all " the burdens that galled, and the cares that oppressed them."

And the reason why they fare so happily, as stated by the Elder, is, " because the Lamb which is in the midst of the throne is their shepherd, and shall lead them to fountains of waters of life, and God shall wipe away every tear out of their eyes."

O the blessedness, the peace, the comfort, the everlasting satisfaction, which is the portion of these Palm-bearers ! Our souls thrill with the mere contemplation of it ! What must it then be to possess it—to feel it to be our own—to enjoy it without let or hindrance forever ! A home so happy, a rest so glorious, a place so high, a bliss so exquisite and enduring, would not be too dearly purchased at a cost of all the pains of the great tribulation. It is verily the very mount of transfiguration to which we are carried by this theme. We feel ourselves overshadowed with the cloud of brightness. We cannot open even our drowsy eyes to the scene, but our lips mutter : " Lord, it is good for us to be here." Fain would we set up our tabernacles where we might ever contemplate the blaze of living glory. Here we would sit forever viewing bliss so great, so true, so high. This glorious Lamb ! This glorious throne ! These glorious ones with their glorious crowns ! This effulgence of gracious Godhead ! These sinless splendours ! These eternal consolations ! These holy services ! These smiles of favour beaming from the King ! These never-withering palms ! These ever-shining robes ! These ever-thrilling songs ! These ever-flowing springs of never-failing life ! These joy-speaking eyes which never weep, and singing lips which never thirst, and uplifted hands which never tire, and comforts from God as a mother would comfort the child she loves, and sorrow and sighing forever fled away ! O blessed, blessed, blessed contemplation !

And yet, this is only an inferior part of Heaven. There are higher dignities and sublimer joys. " It doth not yet appear what we shall be ; " but, as golden crowns exceed palm-branches, and kings are above servants, and the possession of a throne is more than to stand before one, even by so much is the heavenly estate held out to us greater than that of these Palm-bearers.

I know not, O I know not,
  What royal joys are there !
What radiancy of glory,
  What light beyond compare !

And when I fain would sing them,
  My spirit fails and faints ;
And vainly would it image
  The possessions of the saints.

But, from these high scenes, we must go down again into the common world, where tears, sin and death still hold dominion. Duties, and pains, and trials await us there ; and often we may grow faint and weary under them. Let us, then, go to them, humbler, wiser, and better men, determined to do, and bear, and wait, and watch, till the Master says, It is enough. But, let us not omit to carry with us the strengthening, quickening, and purifying inspiration of what we have seen and learned this night. These Palm-bearers reached their blessedness through the pains of the great tribulation ; but to us is offered a better and higher portion than theirs, and without the judgment sorrows which they were made to feel. If we will but keep our garments, and the word of Christ's patience, and work, and watch, and pray, as He has given command, His word is out to keep us from the hour of trial which shall come upon the lukewarm, the worldly-minded, and the unbelieving in that day, now so near at hand. Let us then know and improve our privileges, and ever press toward the mark for the prize of our high calling ; remembering the words of the Lord Jesus, how he said : " Behold, I come quickly ; hold fast that thou hast, that no man take thy crown."

LECTURE SEVENTEENTH

Rev. Chap. 8: 1–5. (Revised Text.)—And when he opened the seventh seal, there followed a silence in the heaven, as it were half an hour.

And I saw the seven angels who stand in the presence of God ; and to them were given seven trumpets.

And another angel came and stood over the altar, having a golden censer ; and there was given to him many incenses, that he might offer [them] for [or *with*] the prayers of all the saints on the altar of gold before the throne. And the smoke of the incenses went up for [or *with*] the prayers of the saints, out of the hand of the angel, in the presence of God. And the angel took the censer and filled it out of the fire of the altar, and cast into the earth ; and there followed thunderings, and lightnings, and voices, and an earthquake.

THERE has been a somewhat protracted silence in the continuity of these lectures. In breaking that silence this evening, we come upon another silence —a silence in heaven. The rapt apostle is still in heaven. What he describes is viewed altogether from a heavenly point of observation. The subject is still the ongoing of the judgment. The roll, which was taken up amid thrills of celestial adoration, is still in the hands of the Lamb. He has broken six of its seals, and the action resulting we have considered. The breaking of the only remaining one, and the most momentous of them all, now comes before us. It will occupy us for some time before it is finally disposed of. Even the seven trumpets and the seven vials come under it. The immediate sequences of the breaking of it, we have in the text, in which we observe

    I.   A MYSTERIOUS SILENCE IN HEAVEN.
   II. SEVEN ANGELS OF THE DIVINE PRESENCE.
  III. ANOTHER ANGEL offering THE PRAYERS OF THE SAINTS.

To God, then, let us look for grace to understand these things according to the intent of the record, giving praise to His holy Name forever and ever.

When the first seal was broken, a voice like thunder was heard, saying, Go ! It was the same at the opening of the three succeeding ones. At the breaking of the fifth, there was a great cry from beneath the altar. And when the sixth was broken, a fearful tremor ran through the whole frame of nature, filling the earth with consternation. But, at the opening of the seventh, not a voice is heard ; not a motion is seen ; an awful pause ensues, and all heaven is silent. A little while ago everything was ringing with triumphant exultation over the multitude which no man could number, but now silence takes the place of songs, and everything is mute and motionless.

This silence, nevertheless, has made a good deal of noise in the world, especially among commentators. It would be difficult to find another point upon which there have been so many different and discordant voices. Indeed, Hengstenberg gives it as the general rule, that when expositors come to this silence they break out into all sorts of contradictory conjecture. Though the marks of historic continuity are as distinct as it is possible to make them, some take this silence as a full stop to the chain of apocalyptic predictions, and so treat what follows as a mere rehearsal, in another form, of what had preceded. Others regard it as a blank, leaving everything belonging to the seventh seal unrevealed, so that its action can only be known when we come to the immortal life. Some pronounce it a mere poetic invention to heighten the dramatic effect, but having no particular significance. Others treat it as a prophetic symbol of scenes and experiences in the earthly history of man ; some, as the suspension of divine wrath in the destruction of Jerusalem ; some, as the freedom granted to the Church under the reign of Constantine ; some, as the interval of repose enjoyed by Christians between the persecutions by Dioclesian and Galerius in A.D. 311, and the beginning of the civil wars toward the end of the same year ; some, as the disappearance of human strivings against God and his Christ ; others, as a lull in earthly revolt and persecution, equivalent to a jubilee for the truth among men ; others, as the millennium of peace and righteousness to be induced by the triumphs of evangelic effort and the progress of liberty ; and yet others, as the everlasting rest of the saints. And yet there is not a word in the record about the Church, nor about the earth. The whole thing is distinctly located " *in heaven*," and its duration is specifically limited to " *about half an hour*."

Others find in this silence a mystic connection with Jewish rites, and the silent prayers commonly joined with the incense oblation. This is the more insisted on, as there is a subsequent reference to an incense offering. Even if such a connection could be made out, it is difficult to see what is thereby to be gained for an interpretation. But it cannot be made out. The facts prove that there is no such connection. The Jewish silent prayers occurred while the offering was in the act of being made ; but here the silence occurs before the offering, and before ever the angel that makes it appears or takes his station at the altar. Nay, there is a distinct and separate vision intervening between this silence and the offering by the angel. It is also plain that this silence is connected with the breaking of the seal, and is the direct result of that act, whilst the incense offering connects with the series of actions by which the stillness is interrupted. It is impossible, therefore, for this silence to be a part of the ceremony of the offering by the angel, or that it should mean any of the things to which reference has been made. Nor can we but wonder that such wild and far-fetched conjectures should ever have found place in men's minds. The language is all simple and plain, and means exactly what is written. There is silence. It is in heaven. It lasts for about half an hour. It is a silence of intense interest and awful expectancy with reference to the results of the breaking of the seventh seal. And this is the whole of it.

We read in Acts of " *a great silence*," induced by Paul, as he waved his hand to his boisterous accusers, from the stairs of the castle at Jerusalem, and began to speak to them in their sacred tongue. It was the silence of surprise, wonder, and interest to catch what was being said. It is written in the Psalms : " Praise waiteth—*is silent*—for thee, O God, in Zion." It was the silence of adoring expectancy waiting for the manifestations of the Divine presence. When Numa was made King of Rome, and the august ceremony had reached the moment that he was to look for the birds by which the gods were expected to foreshow his fate, the priest's hand was laid devoutly on his head, and " *an incredible silence reigned among the people*." It was the silence of anxious expectation. It was the result of an intense interest and awe, with reference to what the gods had decreed, and were about to reveal, concerning the destiny of their new king. And so here. The Lion-Lamb of God has been engaged breaking the seals of the mysterious roll, which He only was worthy to touch or look upon. Six of those seals had been broken, enacting events of the most stupendous moment. But one more remained— the last in the series—and involving the final consummation of the great mystery of God. And as that seal is broken, an interest and awful expectancy rises in the hearts of the celestial orders, which renders them as silent as the grave. All heaven becomes mute and breathless. Saints and angels hush their songs to look and wait for the results. And even the Almighty pauses before the action proceeds.

It is not figure—not symbol—not extravagant rhetoric—not mere poetic delineation of something else. It is history—the literal narration of literal fact ;—for fact it was to John in the vision. It is the natural expression of the deep sympathy of all-glorified existence with the momentousness of the occasion—a voiceless utterance more powerful than words, of the yearning awe of heaven at the arrival of the climacteric of the ages, and the forthcoming events which characterize it. Hence a motionless stillness, more awful, and fuller of thrilling import, than that overwhelming wave of adoration which went over the universe of holy beings when the Lamb first took the book.

"*As it were half an hour*," this solemn stillness lasted. A half-hour is not long in itself ; but time is longer or shorter according to what is transpiring, or what the circumstances are. Moments of agonizing suspense stretch out into hours and days, in comparison with moments of ordinary life. Two minutes of delay, when a man is drowning, is an awful period to have to wait. A stoppage of ten minutes between the words I am speaking, would be an intolerable interval. When on the margin of the realization of great expectations, or interrupted in the midst of what has been absorbing the intensest interest of the soul, every instant of delay expands into hours, and even ages. And when we consider the circumstances of this case—the world in which this pause occurs—the sort of occupations which it interrupts—the kind and number of beings it affects—the nature of the feelings, interests, and expectations which it holds in suspense—and the awfulness of the stillness itself—there is everything to make this half-hour a thing so tremendous that we may be sure there never was the like before, and never will be again thereafter. Nor is the length of it the least remarkable of its features.

II. After this awful pause, the action of the throne is resumed. A company of angels make their appearance on the heavenly arena. They are seven in number. They are of particular rank and distinction, for not all angels are of the same dignity and office. Paul enumerates " dominions, principalities, and powers " among the celestial orders. Daniel speaks of some chief princes. Paul and Jude refer to archangels. Angelic beings are not, therefore, of one and the same grade. The sons of God, in general, come before him only at appointed times (Job. 1 : 6), but the Saviour speaks of some angels who " do always behold the face of the Father which is in heaven." (Matt. 18 : 10.) And the sublime agents which John beheld after the opening of the seventh seal, are described as " *the seven angels who stand in the presence of God.*"

The Jews were familiar with seven angels of this particular class. Gabriel is one of them, as he himself said to Zacharias : " I am Gabriel, that stand in the presence of God." (Luke 1 : 19.) Michael is another, as he is ranked with Gabriel in the book of Daniel, and there pronounced one of the princes, even " the great prince " of the prophet's people. In the Apocryphal book of Tobit, Raphael is named as still another, where he announces himself, and says, " I am Raphael, one of the seven holy angels, which present the prayers of the saints, and which go in and out before the glory of the Holy One." Whether we take this book as inspired, as the Romanists do, or as not inspired, as the Protestants generally regard it, there is no matter touching this point. The passage referred to (Tob. 12 : 15) shows what the ancient people of God held for truth, and the representation harmonizes with the text and with the accepted books of Holy Scripture. The ancients believed that there are *seven presence angels*, and the Apocalypse ratifies that belief.*

These presence-angels are the highest and mightiest of created beings.

---

* The book of Enoch (chap. 20) has the following : " These are the names of the angels who watch. Uriel, one of the holy angels, who presides over clamour and terror ; Raphael, one of the holy angels, who presides over the spirits of men ; Raguel, one of the holy angels, who inflicts punishment on the world and the luminaries ; Michael, one of the holy angels, who, presiding over human virtue, commands the nations ; Sarakiel, one of the holy angels, who presides over the spirits of the children of men that transgress ; Gabriel, one of the holy angels, who presides over Ikesat, over paradise, and over the cherubim."

It is their privilege to " stand in the presence of God." They *stand ;* this is
the posture of service ; but standing *in the presence of God,* is to be above all
other servants. The seven Persian princes who " saw the king's face," were
the highest officers of the realm, and next to the monarch in rank and power.
(Esth. 1 : 14.) And what these princes were to the Persian kings, these
presence-angels are to God.

We thus get a glance into the economy of heaven. A democratic chaos
for the state, and a Laodicean herd for the Church, constitute the world's
ideal of perfection in these days. But the heavenly state is very different.
It is not a monotonous and lawless commonalty, but a complete organism,
in which each has his prescribed sphere and office, in orders towering above
orders, and princedoms over princedoms, till we reach the seven *archangels*
standing in the immediate presence of God, and holding place next to the
eternal throne itself.

And these sublimest ministers of God appear here as the prime executors
of the oncoming administrations. The Saviour Himself said : " In the end
of this world, the Son of man shall send forth his angels, and they shall gather
out of his kingdom all things that offend, and them which do iniquity, and
shall cast them into a furnace of fire." (Matt. 13 : 40–42.) And here John
beholds those angels—the glorious septemvirate of celestial archregents—
the mightiest and the highest creatures in the universe—presenting themselves for the momentous work.

" *And to them were given seven trumpets.*"—Trumpets are expressive instruments. The voice of the trumpet is the most significant voice known to the
Holy Scriptures. God Himself gave His ancient people very special directions
with regard to the use of the trumpet. It is itself described as *a cry*—a loud
and mighty cry—which related only to important occasions. The time for the
blowing of trumpets was always a time of moment—a time of solemnity—a
time for men to bestir themselves greatly in one way or another.

Trumpets connect with war. The command was : " If ye go to war in your
land against the enemy that oppresseth you, then ye shall blow an alarm with
the trumpets." Jeremiah cries : " O my soul, the sound of the trumpet, the
alarm of war ! " (Numb. 10 : 9 ; Jer. 4 : 19.)

Trumpets were for the convocation of the people, and the moving of the
camps of Israel. This is minutely prescribed in Numbers 8.

Trumpets proclaimed the great festivals. " Ye shall blow with the trumpets
over burnt-offerings, and over the sacrifice of your peace-offerings." " Ye
shall have a Sabbath, a memorial of blowing of trumpets, an holy convocation." " Thou shalt cause the trumpet of the Jubilee to sound, in the day of
atonement shall ye make the trumpet sound throughout the land." And so
" when the burnt-offering began, the song of the Lord began also with the
trumpets." (Numb. 10 : 10 ; Lev. 23 : 24 ; 25 : 9 ; 2 Chron. 29 : 27.)

Trumpets also related to the announcements of royalty. Zadok the priest
and Nathan the prophet were directed to anoint Solomon king over Israel,
and blow with the trumpet, and say, God save King Solomon. It is also
written : " They hasted greatly, . . . and blew with trumpets, saying,
Jehu is king." (Kings 1 : 34, 39 ; 2 Kings 9 : 13.)

Trumpets are also associated with the manifestation of the terrible majesty
and power of God. When the Almighty appeared on Mount Sinai, there was
" the voice of the trumpet exceeding loud ; so that all the people that was
in the camp trembled." And Amos says : " Shall a trumpet be blown in the
city, and the people not be afraid ? " (Ex. 19 : 16 ; Amos 3 : 6.)

Trumpets connect with the overthrow of the ungodly. It was at the
blowing of the trumpets that the walls of Jericho fell down, and the city was
given into the hands of Joshua. (Josh. 6 : 13–16.)

Trumpets also proclaimed the laying of the foundations of God's temple.
(Esdras 3 : 10.)

With these facts before us, we are already in a degree prepared to anticipate what these seven trumpets are to bring forth. Their number is the complete number, and we may expect from them everything to which trumpets stand related in the Scriptures. Are they related to war ? Then war is coming ; yea, " the battle of that great day of God Almighty." Are they for the calling of convocations and signals for motion ? Then we may look for great gatherings and mighty changes. Do they herald great solemnities and blessed feasts and sacrifices ? Then, may we anticipate the sublimest festivals, and victories, and jubilee, and burning up of the victims of sin, that the world has ever yet seen. Do they declare investiture with dominion and the commencement of a new reign ? Then may we look for the setting up of a new administration, and the opening of the reign of the true David, the greater than Solomon. Do they declare the presence of God in His awful majesty ? Then may we expect a revelation of Divine power and Godhead which shall fill heaven and earth with trembling. Do they bring the fall of the cities of the wicked and the destruction of their inhabitants ? Then we may look for the end of great Babylon and the sweeping of the dominion of Antichrist and all his confederates from the earth. Do they tell of the founding and building of the permanent temple of the Lord ? Then may we look for the incoming of that true tabernacle which the Lord pitched and not man, and of that firmly-founded city whose maker and builder is God. And all this accords entirely with what John subsequently describes as resultant from the sounding of these seven trumpets.

We thus also come upon an important fact, which is, for the most part, very strangely perverted. Writers on the Apocalypse generally treat it as if it depended for its imagery and materials upon the ancient Jewish regulations. They thus put the copy for the original, and deal with the original as if it were the copy. All the ancient regulations were nothing but copies and types. They were commanded to be made after some heavenly model, of which they were to be the remembrancers and prophecies. They were not the true—the real—but only earthly imitations of it. The true ideal is what John beholds in this book. These seven presence-angels, with their seven trumpets, are the true heavenly realities, with reference to which all the ancient laws relating to trumpets were ordained. What we here have, is not the work of John elaborating a dramatic poem out of the elements of the ancient ritual, but an Apocalypse of the great realities themselves, with reference to which those old appointments were constructed, as earthly pictures and mimic predictions. We go back to the ancient laws, and we there see reflected in earthly forms what John beholds in heavenly reality ; and we reverse the whole order and involve ourselves in inextricable confusion, when we take the images in his visions as mere earthly and Jewish drapery, and not rather as the very things from which those Jewish ceremonies took their existence and peculiarities. The Apocalypse is not a poem in Jewish dress, but the Jewish ceremonies were an earthly poem of the Apocalypse. Let this be understood, and much of the darkness hanging over the meaning of this book will at once disappear.

III. But, before these presence-angels sound their trumpets, " *another angel* " appears, and another scene intervenes, to which our attention must be given.

Many understand by this angel, the Lord Jesus himself—the Jehovah-Angel of the Old Testament, and the same referred to in the preceding chapter as the Sealer of the 144,000. In both instances the officer is called " *another angel*," which, whilst it associates him with angels as to ministry, seems to imply some Being very different from angels as to nature. This angel has a censer of gold, an implement belonging to the Holy of holies, and used only by the high priest ; which would seem to indicate our great High Priest that has passed into the heavens, Jesus the Son of God. This angel casts fire into the earth ; and Jesus says of Himself : " I came to cast fire into the earth ; and what could I wish if it were already kindled ? . . Suppose ye that I came to give peace in the earth ? I tell you nay, but rather division." (Luke 12 : 49–52.) This is in some sense realized in the course of the history and doings of the Church ; but we know that it is to be much more literally and terribly fulfilled in the day of judgment ; and here would seem to be its exact accomplishment. This angel offers the prayers of all the saints, and renders them savoury before God. Such an office is nowhere in the Scriptures assigned to angels proper, but is everywhere assigned to the Lord Jesus Christ.

There would seem to be strong reason, therefore, for supposing that this Angel is really the Jehovah-Angel, and none other than the Lord Jesus Christ, in His capacity of our great High Priest. Primasius says : " The Angel here is our Lord, by whom all our prayers have access to God (Eph. 2 : 18; 3 : 12), and therefore the Apostle says, through Him we offer sacrifices of praise to God continually (Heb. 13 : 15 ; 1 Pet. 2 : 5) ; and St. John says, He is our Advocate with the Father (1 John 2 : 1)." Wordsworth affirms that " this interpretation is sanctioned by other ancient interpreters, such as Augustine and Bede, and by Vitringa, Böhmer, and others, of later date ; " and that " Christ, in His human character and priestly office, may be called *another Angel*," as the high priest on the day of atonement is called *an angel* with reference to his ministrations, and as he believes Christ is called in chapters 10 : 1 ; 14 : 17 ; 18 : 1 ; 20 : 1. Cocceius was of the same opinion.

Neither does it overthrow this view, that the incenses offered up by this angel are represented as " *given to Him*." If the incenses here are to be taken as explained in chap. 5 : 8, that is, as the prayers themselves, of course they are *given to Him*, for he offers no prayers of saints which have not been put into His hands. And if it is the virtue of His Mediatorship that is to be understood by the incenses, there is still an important sense in which that is *given to Him*. It is given to Him in the sense of award, both by saints themselves, who credit and trust in Him as able to do for them, and by Sovereign Majesty, who adjudges Him entitled to exercise such offices and powers. Even all the glories of His Apocalypse are represented (chap. 1 : 1) as *given to Him*, though they are equally His own right, and the result of His personal obedience unto death, with His merits as our Advocate and Intercessor. It was no evidence that a champion in the ancient games had not lawfully and in his own person entitled himself to the honours of the victory, when the rightful judges and all Greece *gave him* those honours. It was rather a demonstration that he had justly merited and won them. And so, in the sense of judicial award, and general credit, confidence and acknowledgment, the intercessorial prerogatives and mediatorial earnings of Christ may be spoken of as *given to Him*. He glorified not himself to be made an high priest ; and the more excellent ministry of his mediatorship of the better covenant is everywhere spoken of as having been " obtained " by Him. (Heb. 5 : 5 ; 8 : 6.) All has really been *given to Him*—given to Him as the just due of His own perfect fulfilment of all righteousness—given to Him by eternal Deity and all saints. And such a giving to this Angel-Priest no more necessarily excludes him from being rightfully taken as the Christ, than the *giving* of the Spirit, or the *giving* of the kingdom, or the *giving* of the possession of the nations to the Saviour, proves that He is not the only begotten Son of God.

The object of the giving of these incenses was, " *that He might offer* [them] *for the prayers of all the saints*." Not *for* those prayers in the sense of *in their stead*, but in the sense of furthering them, benefiting them, and prospering them ; for the prayers themselves are included in the offering. Strictly rendered, he was to offer them *to* the prayers ; but ταῖς προσευχαῖς is a *dativus commodi*, and rather gives the sense of *in behalf of*—*with*—as a helper of their success. The idea is complex. There is an offering of incenses ; those incenses come to the prayers to enrich and forward them ; and the incenses imparted to the prayers are offered as the prayers. They are given *to* the prayers, and *with* the prayers, and *for* the prayers.

But why this offering just here, as the trumpets are about to be sounded ?

Many have taken it as denoting a state of much prayerfulness in the earthly Church about this time. But there is not a word said about an earthly church. Indeed, the Church proper is no longer on earth at the time to which these trumpets belong. There are still true worshippers of God on earth—the two olive trees—and those who refuse to adore the Beast; but their prayers cannot be taken for "the prayers of *all the saints*." The words are very comprehensive, and take in all the holy prayers ever offered.

We had an allusion to these precious treasures in chapter 5, where the account is given of the Living ones and Elders falling down before the Lamb, and holding up golden bowls full of incenses. Those incenses, like these of the text, were the prayers of the saints. There the saints themselves hold them up before the Lamb, as an adoring act of confidence that He was now about to enter upon their complete fulfilment, and as yet backstanding and waiting for an answer. Here *Christ* offers them, as the Great High Priest. He bears them in the golden censer, and perfumes them with the precious fragrance of His own meritorious favour and righteousness, and sanctifies them with the sacred fire, and presents them upon the golden altar before the throne of infinite Godhead. Not one of them is forgotten or lost. Those that came up when time was young, and those offered but yesterday, are all present and in hand. Jesus Himself is not ashamed of them, and handles them with holy care. He bears them in a heavenly vessel of gold, and presents them on the highest altar in the universe. He offers them as approved and indorsed by Himself, and for such acceptance that their fulfilment may no longer be delayed. He presents them *now*, because the fulness of the time has come for them to be brought into remembrance, seeing that all things are in final readiness to execute what is to satisfy them forever.

I have heretofore referred to the great burden of all holy prayer.* As put by Christ Himself into the lips and hearts of His people, it is : THY KINGDOM COME ! THY WILL BE DONE ON EARTH AS IT IS IN HEAVEN ! This is verily the sum and substance of all saintly supplication, the very crown and goal of all holy prayer. And for what purpose are those trumpets in the hands of the seven angels ? To what intent is this calling forward of such mighty ones to pour out blasts over the earth ? What is to be achieved by the sublime activities in which they stand ready to move ? What, but the revelation of the power and the glory of that very Kingdom, for the coming of which the saints have never ceased to pray ? What, but the enforcement of the reign of God where iniquity and usurpation now hold jubilee ? What, but the dethronement of sin, and death, and hell, and the setting up in their place of a heavenly order, in which God's will shall be done on earth as it is in heaven ?

Need any one ask, then, why this sublime offering of the prayers of all the saints is made just here, as the presence-angels are about to put their awful trumpets to their lips ? When prayers are to be answered, then is the time for them to be brought into remembrance. That which results from the sounding of those trumpets, is to fulfil what has been the great burden of the Church's prayers in all ages. Those prayers, therefore, have a most profound connection with the sounding of these mighty trumpets. And hence it is that they here come into view, and appear upon the golden altar of God.

Nor are they offered in vain. The ascension of their sweet vapour into the presence of God is equivalent to an announcement that they are heard. The coming up before God of the prayers and alms of Cornelius, was the good pleasure of God toward what thus ascended ; and the like ascent of the sweet vapour of these perfumed prayers is the token of a like approval and a like speedy answer. It is the effectual going up of the voices of them that cry day and night unto God. It is the signal that the time has come to avenge His own elect. And at once the mighty action begins.

"*And the Angel took the censer, and filled it out of the fire of the altar, and cast into the earth.*" The Saviour himself thus initiates the oncoming climax

* p. 118.

of the day of wrath. The people under the sixth seal thought the last and worst had come, but it was only the herald of still greater things which now begin.

Nor is it to be overlooked, that all this occurs in answer to the prayers of the saints. There are those who think meanly of prayer, and are always asking : " What profit should we have if we pray unto the Almighty ? " (Job 21 : 15.) The true answer is, " *much every way.*"

There is an eye that never sleeps
　　Beneath the wing of night ;
There is an ear that never shuts
　　When sink the beams of light.

There is an arm that never tires
　　When human strength gives way ;
There is a love that never fails
　　When earthly loves decay.

That eye is fixed on seraph throngs ;
　　That arm upholds the sky ;
That ear is filled with angel songs ;
　　That love is throned on high.

But there's a power which man can wield,
　　When mortal aid is vain,
That eye, that ear, that love to reach,
　　That listening ear to gain.

That power is PRAYER, which soars on high,
　　Through Jesus, to the throne ;
And moves the hand which moves the world,
　　To bring salvation down !

Here, prayer moves the Son of God—moves eternal Majesty upon His everlasting seat—sets the highest angels in motion—brings on the awful scenes of the day of judgment—influences the administrations in the heavens and induces wonders upon the earth.

And as these climaxes of judgment come in answer to " the prayers of *all the saints,*" the implication also is, that where there is no prayer there is no piety, no holiness, no salvation, and that people who do not wait, and long, and pray for the coming again of the Lord Jesus and this consummation are not saints, but belong to the population against whom these fiery revelations occur.

Fire is the great consumer. It always bespeaks wrath, torture, and destruction to the wicked. It tells of burning fury and the most dismal effects—even " vengeance upon them that know not God, and that obey not the Gospel of our Lord Jesus Christ." It is the common figure of divine terribleness toward the guilty—one of the great agents in the administrations of the great day—the chief torment of the lost. And when the sublime Priest-Angel of heaven turns His fire-filled censer on the earth, we have come to the day that shall burn as an oven, in the which all the proud and ungodly shall be as stubble to the devouring flames. (Mal. 4 : 1.)

This fire is taken from the altar. It is one of the fearful characteristics of God's gracious operations, that they breed and heighten the damnation of the disobedient and the unbelieving. It is not Adam's guilt, for there is full remedy in Christ against that. It is not the condemnation in which the Gospel finds them, for it comes with a full and everlasting reprieve. But here is the mischief, that when the great and costly salvation of God is carried to them they despise it, and make light of it, and go their way as if it were nonsense or nothing. It is not that their sins are too great for them to be saved, but because they tread under foot the Son of God, and count His sanctifying blood an unholy thing, and render despite to the Spirit of grace. Out of the very altar of sacrifice, therefore, comes their damnation. It is the saving word refused, which is a savour of death unto death in them that perish. The same fire which wafts the devotions of the obedient into the presence of God, kindles the hell of the unbelieving and the neglectful. Perdition is simply abused or perverted grace. It is the same censer, filled with the same ingredients, only turned downward in the case of those who believe not.

And when the glorious Angel of intercession emptied the fiery contents of his censer toward the earth, " *there followed thunderings, and lightnings, and voices, and an earthquake.*" These are the signs and instruments of God's judgments upon His foes. No age has ever been entirely without them, as no age has ever been without earnests and foretokens of the great day. But they mistake, who think to find the description fulfilled in events of the past, or in anything but the scenes which are to terminate the history of this present world. Indeed, it is the very climacteric of the day of judgment which is here betokened.

John perceives the awful effects before they have passed into actual fact on earth. *We* read and know things only from their outward symptoms, in or after their accomplishment. In heaven they read and know things from their inward principles, even before they have been wrought into historic fact. It is under the action of the trumpets that these thunderings, lightnings, voices, and convulsions are worked into the experiences of the earth and its inhabitants ; and it is only according to the interior view of them, from the heavenly standpoint, that the events to be achieved are thus summarily described. As the trumpets are sounded, and we come to consider the scenes they develop, we will see these thunderings, and lightnings, and voices, and convulsions, as they manifest themselves on the earthly theatre.

Meanwhile, I suggest just one thought more. It is in reference to the interest which holy beings take in these subjects of sacred prophecy. There is a very sublime picture, presented by the Apostle Peter in his first epistle, where he represents the ancient prophets as " inquiring and searching diligently " to understand " what, or what manner of time the Spirit of Christ, which was in them, did signify, when it testified beforehand the sufferings of Christ, and the glory that should follow ; " and the angels of heaven bending from their lofty thrones, desiring to look into these things. It is a masterly touch, to set forth the greatness, majesty, and glory of the Gospel, which makes us feel as we read, that here is a theme at once the wonder of the universe, and challenging the profoundest attention and study of man. It is an overwhelming vindication of any amount of absorbing captivation by the topics referred to. All agree to this, But what shall we say, then, for the themes with which the text stands connected ? Here is a subject which has engaged the devotions of " all the saints," and been the grand goal of all their holy desires since time began. Here are transactions which fill heaven with awe, and turn the songs of eternity into silence ! Here are administrations which call the seven archangels into action, and for looking after the results of which, the universe is spellbound and mute with solemn expectation ! Here are things, the mere prayers for which the Son of God holds in the golden censer, and offers on the golden altar, and sends up with awful solemnity into the presence of eternal Majesty ! Is not this, then, a subject to command and justify the holiest and profoundest interest, study, and attention of rational beings ! And yet there are people— men claiming to be Christians—leaders of religious thought—ministers ordained to teach the way of God truly—who have not hesitated to sneer at it as the theme of fools, the hobby of enthusiasts, or the plaything of religious idiots ! You may agree with them if you like. But, while I find these things treated with all soberness in the Scriptures, and blessing spoken from heaven upon those who give them devout and studious attention, and the Holy Ghost interpreting them as involving the highest hopes and prayers of " *all* the saints," and the whole celestial world becoming mute and motionless in the intensity of its interest as they unfold into fact, and prophets of God, and angels of glory, and Archangels of the Almighty's presence, and the blessed

Christ at the heavenly altar, and the universe of holy beings, occupied with heart and soul with reference to them, I must persist in a different judgment, and ask to be excused for believing that we have here, not only a legitimate and fitting theme for our devoutest study, but one as high and momentous as ever was presented to the contemplation of man, which grasps deep into everything dear to us for time or eternity, and which he who wilfully ignores, has reason to fear for his safety against the terrific plagues written in this book, and for the security of his part in the holy city.

May God, in mercy, save us from such dangerous unseemliness. Amen.

LECTURE EIGHTEENTH

PREPARATION OF THE ANGELS—ADJUSTMENT OF THE ORDER OF PROCEEDING—FIRST TRUMPET—A TEMPEST OF HAIL, FIRE, AND BLOOD—CONTRADICTORY VIEWS OF SYMBOLISTIC INTERPRETERS—NO CERTAINTY BUT IN THE LITERAL SENSE—SECOND TRUMPET—A METEOR STRIKES THE SEA, TURNS IT TO BLOOD, DESTROYS LIVING THINGS AND SHIPPING—A LITERAL PROPHECY—THIRD TRUMPET—A METEOR OR COMET FALLS ON THE EARTH, POISONS THE WATERS, AND CAUSES MANY TO PERISH—ALSO LITERAL—FOURTH TRUMPET—THE SUN, MOON, AND STARS OBSCURED—ALSO LITERAL.

REV. 8 : 6–12. (Revised Text.)—And the seven angels which had the seven trumpets prepared themselves that they might sound.

And the first sounded ; and there followed hail and fire mingled with blood, and it was cast into the earth ; and the third of the earth was burned, and the third of the trees was burned, and all green grass was burned.

And the second angel sounded ; and as it were a great mountain burning with fire was cast into the sea ; and the third of the sea became blood ; and the third of the creatures in the sea, the things which have lives [Gr. *souls*], died ; and the third of the ships was destroyed.

And the third angel sounded ; and there fell out of the heaven a great star, burning as a torch, and it fell upon a third of the rivers, and upon the springs of the waters ; and the name of the star is called wormwood ; and the third of the waters was turned into wormwood ; and many of men died from the waters, because they were made bitter.

And the fourth angel sounded ; and the third of the sun was smitten, and the third of the moon, and the third of the stars, so that the third of them should be darkened, and the day should not shine for the third of it, and the night likewise.

WE have reached a point in the history of the Apocalypse, at which everything stands in solemn readiness for those final blasts of judgment which bring the grand consummation. The last seal is broken. Heaven is in suspense to see the result. The prayers of all the saints have come up with acceptance before God, who has promised to avenge them. The coals and ashes of holy indignation have dropped from the golden censer to lodge upon the doomed world. In short, the time has come for the action of the great day to be hurried to its completion. May the Lord Almighty give us grace to contemplate the awful scenes foreshown, as becomes both the subject and ourselves !

I. THE PREPARATION.

" *And the seven angels which had the seven trumpets prepared themselves that they might sound.*"

Most of our apocalyptic interpreters tell us that " the angels preparing themselves to sound, signifies the difference in posture observable between one carelessly holding a trumpet by his side, and the bending of the arm, the erecting of the figure, the inflating of the lungs, and swelling of the lips and cheeks, as the trumpet is pressed firmly against the mouth." To me this appears a sorry way of dealing with grave records of such momentous things. It is plainly said that these angels *sounded* their trumpets. From this we know, in advance, that they lifted the instruments to their lips and blew into them. All such accidents of posture and gesture are already necessarily implied. Besides, many of these interpreters extend these trumpets over long series of years ; and if each angel put himself on a strain for a blast before either sounded, the last had his cheeks and lungs inflated very long before his turn came to sound ! We had better exercise a little consideration, and not make these solemn things ludicrous by the way we handle them. The rapt apostle had greater things to engage him than to be dwelling on such puerilities. There was occasion also for a more significant preparation.

Not all seven of these angels were to sound at once. Mighty events of varied character were also to be induced by their several soundings. It was necessary, therefore, that there should be some prearrangement, both as to the order of time for each to sound, and the particular class of results each one's sounding should control. Their soundings were not haphazard things ; neither were these sublime archangels mere machines, moving like puppets, only as they were moved by a superior will. No attentive reader can fail to observe a complete and forestudied system and order in these trumpets and their successive effects. No two of them are alike, and yet there is a gradual rising, one over the other, to the end. One touches the ground, the trees, and the green grass. Another touches the sea, the ships, and the creatures in the sea. A third touches the rivers and the springs of water. A fourth touches the sun, moon, and stars. A fifth breaks open the door of separation between earth and hell. A sixth unlooses the dreadful army of horses and horsemen, the seven thunders, and the mighty struggle and murder of the two witnesses. And the last brings on " the battle of the great day of God Almighty." There is a particular distinction between the first four and the last three ; and again between the last of the three and the two which immediately precede it.

To refer all this to mere accident, or to the artistic skill of the narrator of the events, is unreasonable. Such system and order do not come of nothing, and a faithful recorder must enter events as they occur. Great intelligence and prearrangement are manifest in the transactions themselves, apart from any art of the writer who describes them. Either, then, this was the work of the seven angels or that of the supreme Mind. And as we cannot conceive of such sublime beings as these seven archangels, going forward with the control of such mighty operations, without also exercising their own personal intelligence as to the manner of their proceeding ; when it is said that they " *prepared themselves that they might sound*," we are not to think of the mere mechanical accidents pertaining to the act of sounding a trumpet, but of a deliberative adjustment among themselves of the place and subject which each one was to take in the work.

We thus have a very significant hint respecting angelic ministrations, to wit : that the affairs of men and nations are much more under the influence of the thinking and deliberation of angels, and wear much more of the impress of angelic management, than we are accustomed to suppose. Even men, in the narrow spheres and powers assigned to mortals, have constant occasion to think, deliberate, consult, and judge. It is, therefore, reasonable to believe that angels, and particularly the seven archangels, in their high places and with their sublime intelligence, do also have need to confer, deliberate, and arrange for their proceedings, especially in cases so extraordinary as this. It was nothing less than the closing up of the affairs of a world that was here committed to them ; and they were all seven to be equally concerned in the tremendous administrations. The word ετοιμάζω, which is used to describe their ready-making, is also often employed to denote predeterminations of what is to be done, and the settling of appointments and designs before they are carried into effect. And it is but natural and just, and harmonizes best with the character of both the agents and the business assigned to them, to interpret their making of themselves ready as referring to their mutual adjustment of the method by which they would conduct the awful transactions.

II. The Sounding of the First Trumpet.

" *And the first sounded, and there followed hail and fire mingled with blood and it was cast into the earth ; and the third of the earth was burned, and the third of the trees was burned, and all green grass was burned.*"

Here is the first touch of what fell from the censer of the Priest-Angel. I take the language as it stands. This book does not give things veiled, but unveiled. It is the Apocalypse, the uncovering. The results here described are heralded by the sound of a trumpet ; what is published by a trumpet is no longer a secret. The phenomena are of a very stupendous sort ; but the actors are Archangels, the occasion is the day of judgment, and the business is the closing up of the history of a doomed world. In such a case we may well look for wonders. God has also declared His purpose to renew the miracles of Egypt, and to do " marvellous things " like unto what He did in the days of Israel's deliverance. (See Micah 7 : 15 ; Jer. 23 : 7, 8.) The plagues of Egypt were literal realities. They were miracles of judgment, such as have never been since on earth. And if it is the design of God to repeat them on a larger scale, or to do again what at all corresponds to that which He then did, the world has yet to witness just such scenes as are literally described under these trumpets. And " as it was in the day that Israel came up out of Egypt," so it is in what John beheld under the sounding of this first trumpet. Then " the Lord sent thunder and hail, and the fire ran along upon the ground ; and the Lord rained hail upon the land of Egypt. So there was *hail, and fire, mingled with the hail*, very grievous, such as there was none like it in all the land of Egypt, since it became a nation. And the hail smote throughout all the land of Egypt, all that was in the field, both man and beast ; and the hail *smote every herb of the field, and brake every tree of the field.*" (Ex. 9 : 23-28.) Here we have a corresponding visitation, only the fire is more destructive, and there is the further element of *blood* mingled with the fire and hail.

The whole picture is that of a tremendous tempest of hailstones, lightnings, and bloody products of the infuriated elements. Blood-red rains and blood-red snows are not unknown to the world. We occasionally hear of them. On the 17th of August, 1819, Captain Ross saw the mountains at Baffin's Bay covered for eight miles with blood-red snow, many feet in depth. Saussare found it on Mount St. Bernard, in 1778. Ramond found it on the Pyrenees, and Summerfield in Norway, and others have told of it in other places. So blood-rain has more than once fallen. It is recorded by Cicero, that word was brought to the Roman Senate, on one occasion, that it had *rained blood ;* also that the river Atratus had flowed with a bloody stream. (De Div. 2 : 27.) Slight falls of this kind have occurred in the Cape Verd Islands, at Lyons, at Genoa, and in the southwest of our own country, to the great alarm of the people of the vicinity. But whether the like of what John describes ever happened before or not, God has said, concerning the great day : " I will show wonders in heaven above, and signs in the earth beneath, *blood and fire.*" (Joel 2 : 30.) And the manner in which He will do it is here unveiled. A storm of hail, and fire, and bloody interminglings, shall fall upon and envelop the world.

The effects are correspondingly dreadful. At an earlier stage, under the sixth seal, the four angels at the four corners of the earth holding the four winds, were charged not to injure the earth, nor the trees, till the servants of God were sealed. That sealing being accomplished, the prohibition ceases, the spirit of storms is let loose, and the earth and the trees are hurt. Bloody hail and fire pour upon the world with such fury that the third of the earth is burned. Our English version says nothing of the burning of the earth. It speaks only of trees and grass. The best manuscripts specify the earth also. Modern critics agree that the omission is unwarranted. " *The third of the earth was burned* "—set on fire and charred by the fierce lightnings of heaven, and a corresponding destruction was, of course, wrought among buildings, flocks, herds, and human life.

" *The third* " is mentioned, not with rigid strictness, as absolutely just that proportion, but, as we would say in general terms, one-third of the earth was burned. And so also " *the third of the trees.*" The Egyptian plague " smote and brake *every* tree of the field ; " this destroys many more in the aggregate, because the visitation is so much more widespread, but it does not consume *all*. It carries fearful havoc among the forests, orchards, and timber-lands of the earth, but still the major part of the trees escape. Not so, however, with the grass and the more tender portions of vegetation. The Egyptian plague destroyed " *every herb of the field,*" and it is the same in this case. " *All green grass was burned."* A scene of distressing and far-reaching desolation is thus foreshown, in which a large portion of the earth's surface is charred with fire, many towns, cities, forests, and plantations reduced to ashes, every field and meadow stripped of its growing crops, and bloody and putrid blackness spread over all the smitten world.

But most interpreters object to the taking of this as a literal description. If their objection is valid, they must be able to show a different meaning, and one on which we may reasonably rest with greater certainty. If earth does not mean earth, then what does it mean ?   And if earth means earth, then the trees must mean trees, and the grass grass. If not, why not ? And if trees and grass do not mean trees and grass, the burden is upon those who so affirm to furnish the evidence of some other meaning.   But, alas, for such attempts !   Wordsworth says the trees mean princes and great men, and grass the glory and power of men.   Lord says the trees mean stronger men, and the grass the young, the feeble, and the aged. Hengstenberg and Williams say the trees mean great men, and the grass people generally.   Wetstein says the trees mean apostles and great doctors, and the grass common Christians. Durham says the earth means the visible Church, the trees what seems most strong in it, and the grass its lesser excellencies. The truth is, if *earth, trees,* and *grass* do not mean earth, trees, and grass, no man can tell what they mean. Letting go the literal signification of the record, we launch out upon an endless sea of sheer conjecture, turn the whole Apocalypse into an incomprehensible riddle, and force the conclusion that God was mistaken when He named it the lifting off of the veil ; nay, that, if it is a revelation, it has not yet become manifest what that revelation is, and never will, by the light which we now possess.

A large number of writers on this book agree, indeed, that the downfall of the Roman power in the West is at least the most prominent subject of the trumpets : and, as far as that downfall is included in the great day of judgment, and, as far as one judgment is a type of another, they are correct, but no further. Referring these foreshowings to the decline and fall of the Roman empire, there are not two expositors who concur as to the distribution of events under the several trumpets. Each has a different theory, and each finds the same particular predictions fulfilled in things the most diverse in character and the most widely separated in time. And if we must go to symbol and figure for the meaning, I find *one* theory about as respectable and well sustained as the other. It is mainly fancy and guesswork from first to last, as full of self-contradiction as destitute of solid foundation. Thus, Elliott, who has written with so much learning and pains on the subject, finds the fulfilment of this first trumpet in the wars of Alaric the Goth and Rhadagaisus the Vandal, against the Western Roman Empire. But this gives us *two* storms instead of the one which John beheld, and the blood of men on earth instead of the bloody substance which the record describes as falling from the sky, and fixes on events which suit as well for either of the first four trumpets instead of something as distinctive and peculiar as this trumpet is from all the rest. And so the thing works in every other instance. The law of departure from the direct sense of the record, is the law of uncertainty, of irreconcilable contradictions, of the substitution of human vagaries for the clear revelations of God, and there is no remedy for the chaos of opinions that obtains under it. As well might we look for the laws of symbolization to interpret the plagues of Egypt of the discovery and settlement of America, as to find such laws for the interpretation of the seals, trumpets, and vials of this book of anything but the great day of God Almighty. But, carrying them forward where they belong, and where God himself has so explicitly put them,—to that day beyond all other days of literal realities and astounding marvels,—there is no more hindrance to the literal acceptance of what is written here, than to such an acceptance of what is 'written concerning the life and deeds of Jesus, or concerning the acts of His apostles, whilst it gives us solid ground to stand

G

on, and involves us in no bewildering uncertainties and discomfiting self-contradictions.

I must, therefore, take these descriptions in the only really ascertainable sense of them, and insist that a mighty storm of hail and fire mingled with blood means a storm of hail and fire mingled with blood ; that earth, trees, and all green grass means earth, trees, and all green grass ; and that the burning, and scorching, and destruction means burning, scorching, and destruction. And, after wading through piles of volumes intended to prove and demonstrate the contrary, I come back to this, as fully persuaded, as I am convinced that the Bible is of God, that there can be no interpretation of the Apocalypse, as an intelligible revelation, on any other principle. There are, indeed, symbols and figures in it, as in all other portions of the Scriptures. But when they occur here, as in every other place, the distinct intimations to that effect are given ; and, in all other instances, we are to interpret precisely the same as in any other piece of serious writing intended for the instruction and enlightenment of men.

III. The Sounding of the Second Trumpet.

"*And the second angel sounded ; and, as it were, a great mountain burning with fire was cast into the sea ; and the third of the sea became blood ; and the third of the creatures in the sea, the things which had lives, died ; and the third of the ships was destroyed.*"

Here is one of the hints I speak of as indicating that a thing is not to be literally taken. The image of a burning mountain is before the writer. But it is not literally a mountain ; it is only something having the general appearance of a mountain ; and he plainly tells us so. He saw—ὡς—*as it were* a mountain. Of course, then, we are to take it, not as a real mountain, but as something resembling a mountain. A certain writer insists that the plague under this trumpet is not to be taken literally, because a mountain falling into the sea could never turn it into blood. But John does not say it was a mountain. He says that it was something that *looked like* a burning mountain. Exactly what it was, he could not better tell us, except that its effect upon the waters of the sea was, that it turned them into blood. An ordinary mountain would not do this ; but that falling, fiery mass, which had the appearance of a burning mountain, did it.

Some conceive of this fiery mass as a volcano, but neither is this the exact image. John says nothing of a mountain vomiting fire, but of a mountain burning with fire, which might be a volcanic mountain, or it might not. When God descended on Sinai, " the mountain burned with fire unto the heart of heaven, with darkness, clouds, and thick darkness " (Deut. 4 : 11) ; but there is no evidence that it was a volcanic eruption. The idea of John's language is rather that of a great mountainous mass of matter falling from the sky, clothed in seething, thundering, and flashing flames, and dashing into the ocean. The whole image is meteoric, rather than volcanic.

The plunging of this awful fiery mass into the sea, affects it wonderfully. It turns the waves to blood. And if any are disposed to doubt the possibility of such a thing, let them turn to the account of the exode of Israel from Egypt, where it is written that Moses " lifted up the rod, and smote the waters that were in the river, in the sight of Pharaoh, and in the sight of his servants, and *all the waters that were in the river were turned to blood.*" (Ex. 7 : 20.) In the Psalms also (105 : 29), it is written : " *He turned their waters into blood ;* " and again (78 : 44) : " *He turned their rivers into blood, and their floods,* that they could not drink." It was fresh water in that case, and it is sea or salt water in this ; but if God could work such changes by the staff of Moses, what is to hinder him from producing like changes, even on all the waters of the ocean, by means of this fiery mass, as it were a burning mountain ? And if the one was literal, as all admit, why not the other, although upon a mightier scale, corresponding to the momentousness of the great day ?

Suppose, however, that we follow the common course of expositors, and say that this whole matter is figurative or symbolical ; then what ? Some understand the mountain to mean heresy ; the sea, the Church with its baptismal waters ; its change to blood, the effect of deadly error ; the death of the fishes of the sea, the perdition of souls ; the destruction of the ships, the overthrow of churches. Others say the fiery mountain is Satan ; the sea, the nations ; its change into blood and the dying of the fishes, the persecution and slaughter of Christians ; the wreck of the ships, the extinction of congregations. Others tell us that this fiery mountain was Genseric with his Vandals, forced from their native seat by the Huns, and plunging through France and Spain into Africa, conquering the Carthaginians, settling themselves upon the conquered territory, and thence harassing the neighbouring islands and shores of the Mediterranean. Still others affirm that the sea is the sea of Galilee, figuratively considered ; the fiery mountain, Vespasian ; the fishes, the Jews ; the ships, the cities of Palestine. And again others interpret the picture of the overthrow of Jerusalem and the temple, and the dissolution of the Jewish polity ; the dying of the fishes, the relapses of men from Christianity to Gentilism ; the loss of the ships, the subversion of synagogues and churches. Nor is the list yet exhausted. To some, the sea is pure doctrine ; the mountain, aspiring prelates ; the fire, their ambition ; the discoloration of the waters, the introduction of false doctrine ; the fishes, the lower orders of ecclesiastics and monks ; the ships, the bearers of the Gospel. To others, the mountain is Rome ; its burning, the conflagration of that city by Alaric ; the destruction of the ships, the plunder of its wealth. Still others see in the record, a symbol of the ravages by Attila. And I only wonder that no one has discovered that it denotes the settlement of the Mormons in Salt Lake Territory ! The simple truth is, that if it does not mean what it says, as men ordinarily use language, no man can tell what it does mean ; and the opinion of one is just as good, and just as *bad*, as that of another.

I, therefore, take it as it is written, because there is no other way of taking it which yields any certain or reliable sense. What do we want with Vespasian, Alaric, Rhadagaisus, Attila, Genseric, Romans, Goths, Vandals, Arians, prelates, or the devil, when the inspired writer tells us it was a fiery meteoric mass,—an aerial mountain,—great and towering, precipitated from the atmosphere into the sea, as one of the great wonders of the day of judgment ? Men do but rave and trifle and undertake to make a Bible which God has not made, when they spend their time, and learning, and ingenuity trying to persuade themselves and the world that it was something else than John says it was.

This burning mass is plunged into " *the sea.*" It would seem as if some particular sea was meant. If so, most likely the Mediterranean Sea, around which the greatest recorded events of the world and of the Church have been enacted, and which is the central sea of all history, both sacred and profane. Its very name marks it as the *middle of the earth.* The result is, that the third of it becomes blood—poisonously bloody—so that a third of the living things in the sea perish.

It would seem, also, as if tempestuous commotion of the elements is to attend this awful precipitation. Both the vastness and the fiery condition of the mass ejected into the sea, naturally suggests such effects. Hence, " *the third of the ships was destroyed,*" burned, sunk, or dashed ashore.

And all this finds place also in some of the plain, old unsymbolic predictions concerning the day of the Lord. Fishes constitute one of God's precious gifts to man. They were among the principal food of Jesus, and were the subjects of some of His most marvellous miracles. And, in punishment of the sins of men, it is but reasonable to expect the fishes of the sea to be smitten, as well as the trees and the fruits of the earth. Hence, in foretelling the Divine judgments, Hosea said : " *The fishes of the sea also shall be taken away.*" (4 : 1–3.) So the Lord, also, said by Zephaniah (1 : 3), " I will consume the fowls of heaven, *and the fishes of the sea."* Isaiah further declares : " The day of the Lord of hosts shall be upon every one that is high and lofty. . . and upon *all the ships of Tarshish."* (Is. 2 : 16.) And here, under the second trumpet, the blessed John beholds exactly how these predictions are to be fulfilled.

IV. THE SOUNDING OF THE THIRD TRUMPET.

" And the third angel sounded, and there fell out of the heaven a great star, burning as a torch, and it fell upon the third of the rivers, and upon the springs of the waters ; and the name of the star is called Wormwood ; and the third of the waters was turned into wormwood ; and many of men died from the waters, because they were made bitter."

Here is another marvellous meteoric phenomenon ; perhaps a comet striking the earth. But nobody seems to be quite willing to take it for what John says it was. Interpreters tell us, that a *star* denotes an eminent teacher or angel of the Church. They refer us for proof of this, to the first chapter of this book. But there is one important link lacking in this argument, as applied to the case before us. There Christ himself says, that " the seven stars " beheld by the seer, denote " the angels of the seven churches ; " but here He says no such thing ; nor is there any proof that the Church is at all in question. This star falls out of heaven, but there is no evidence whatever that the Church is heaven. Besides, so great a star of the Church, in such lonely distinction, could only be Christ himself, who never falls out of the Church, whose name is not Wormwood, and who does not poison the fountains and rivers of the earth by His teachings. When the Scriptures tell us that a thing is a symbol, we are to take it as such ; but when they give no intimation that a thing is other than literal, there is no warrant for making a symbol or figure of it.

But, if this star denotes an apostate teacher, who is that teacher ? Some say Simon Magus, Menander, Cerinthus ; some, Manes ; some, Novatus ; some, Montanus ; some, Arius ; some, Pelagius ; some, Origen ; some, Mahomet ; and one with about as much reason as the other. Some, however, tell us that it does not mean an apostate teacher at all, but a warlike leader. Then, what one ? Grotius, Hammond, and Rosenmuller answer : Some actor in the Jewish war, as Eleazar, Josephus, or the like. Others answer, Genseric ; others Attila ; others, whole successions of bloody devastators ;— and nobody knows who ; for, with this mode of interpretation, the vision will fit one as well as the other.

If Attila, King of the Huns, is the star, as the leading modern expositors affirm, then there are some very important questions which yet remain to be solved. What was " the heaven " out of which he fell ? What was his fall ? How did he burn as a torch ? Are the Danube and the Rhine, along which he operated, " the third of the rivers ? " How did he embitter the fountains as distinct from the rivers, and make both fountains and rivers bitter like himself ? How was his name called Wormwood ? Were the deaths under him literal or spiritual deaths ? If literal, did they die of the bitterness of the waters ? And, if spiritual, did Attila produce any moral mortality among men ? O, the sloughs and bogs into which people plunge themselves when they let go the plain and direct sense of what is written ! Has not symbol and allegory been tried about long enough on these momentous plagues of the day of judgment ?

Apart from his stilted system of symbolization, Lord finds the description of the apostle very plain, and reproduces it in a way which well exhibits its literal import. " The star, obviously, was not a solid globe, but a thin, transparent meteor [or comet], which, as it swept along near the surface and sunk to the ground, still left the objects it enveloped perceptible to the apostle, and was soon absorbed by the waters and the earth. He beheld the rivers and fountains still running, discerned a change wrought in them by the meteor, and saw that it was the new element infused into them that rendered them deadly to many who drank of them."

A name is assigned to this meteor, not as though it had previously been known or should become known by this name, but in a way descriptive of its qualities and effects. Properly designated, " the name of the star is called Wormwood ; " or, according to some manuscripts, emphatically, " *the wormwood.*" Wormwood, or *absinthe*, is a bitter, intoxicating, and poisonous herb. Used freely, it produces convulsions, paralysis, and death. And this star is appropriately named " *the Absinthe*," as the embodiment of the very quintessence of all wormwood. It is bitterness itself—the poisonous bitterness of absinthe.

And this bitterness is communicated to whatever it touches. It falls upon the third of the rivers, and upon the springs of waters. It sinks into the earth and impregnates the fountains and the wells. Lord suggests that it falls upon the Alps, from whose melting glaciers so many rivers and fountains take their rise. At any rate, it touches the sources of many waters, and turns them into bitterness. Such a thing is by no means impossible. On the 21st of March, 1823, in one of the Aleutian Islands there was a great volcanic explosion, and, as one of the results, the river water assumed the colour of beer, and was so extremely bitter as to be unfit for use. God is at no loss for means to effect His ends. And if one meteor could turn the waters of the sea to blood, another may as readily turn the waters of the rivers and wells to the deadly bitterness of absinthe. Nay, something of this sort is indicated in the ancient prophecies, where we read : " Because they have forsaken my law which I set before them, and have not obeyed my voice, neither walked therein, but have walked after the imagination of their own heart, therefore, thus saith the Lord of hosts, the God of Israel : Behold, *I will feed them with wormwood, and give them water of gall to drink.*" (Jer. 9 : 13–15.) Even if this was figuratively fulfilled upon the apostate Jews, we are still warranted in counting on a more literal fulfilment in that great day which is to repeat and bring to their fullest consummation all the judgments that have ever gone before it.

The result of this embittering of the waters is fearful distress on account of the absence of wholesome drink, and great mortality among men.

V. The Sounding of the Fourth Trumpet.

" *And the fourth angel sounded, and the third of the sun was smitten, and the third of the moon, and the third of the stars, so that the third of them should be darkened, and the day should not shine the third of it, and the night likewise.*"

We have seen the judgments of God going forth on the land, with its trees and herbage—on the sea with its fishes and its ships—on the rivers and springs—and everywhere spreading disaster, suffering, and death. This trumpet carries us above, to portents and afflictions from the heavenly bodies. Jesus has told us, " there shall be signs in the sun, and in the moon, and in the stars " (Luke 21 : 25) ; and here John beholds some of them. We have had some of them before, but they increase and intensify as the end draws near. We shall see more of them hereafter.

But what are we to understand by the sun, moon, and stars ? Ask a child, and it will tell you ; but ask our Apocalyptic interpreters, and their answers are as various as their names, and all they have to say is nothing but loose conjecture and uncertainty. Grotius says they are the cities of Galilee, and the people of the Jews, destroyed by Vespasian. Hammond says the sun is the Jewish temple ; the moon, Jerusalem ; the stars, its population ; their obscuration, the taking of the city by Titus. Brightman says the sun is the Bible ; the moon, its doctrine ; the stars, the ministers of the Church ; their obscuration, the persecution of the African Church by the Vandals. Vitringa says the obscuration of the sun is the decay of the imperial government from Valens to the fall of Augustulus ; of the moon and stars, the false doctrines and corrupt manners of the patriarchs and bishops after the time of Constantine. Wordsworth sees in it " a prophecy of a great prevalence of errors, defections, apostasies, and confusions in Christendom, such as abounded in the seventh century." And Danbuz, Elliott, Lord, Cumming, Barnes, &c., consider it a picture of the subversion of the Western imperial government and its dependencies, and the setting up of the new rule of the Heruli under Odoacer. Will any one in his senses allow that all these can be true ? or that that can be a just way of dealing with the word of God, which gives us such wide-ranging diversity, and about equal reason for either theory ?

The application of this trumpet to Odoacer is the favourite modern way of disposing of it. Yet Barnes confessedly adopts it, only because the system on which he interprets the foregoing trumpets leaves him no other alternative, notwithstanding he cannot make the events and the prophecy correspond, except in the vaguest and most general manner. Lord embraces it because " there is *no other event* that in the slightest degree meets the conditions of the symbol." And so with the rest ; though, even as a symbol, this trumpet no more fits the case of Odoacer and the Heruli, than it fits the case of Vespasian or Titus, Napoleon Bonaparte or George Washington. Look at it. John beheld the third of the sun, moon, and stars smitten, and their light one-third diminished, whilst they retained their places, and for two-thirds continued the same as before ; but Odoacer made an utter end of the old imperial government of the West, and of all its dependencies, and set up an entirely new sun, moon, and stars in the political heavens. Here is a discrepancy which is eternally irreconcilable with the record, and which, without noting others, is fatal to the theory. And if the system of symbolic interpretation forces us to accept as the fulfilment of holy prediction what is so fundamentally at variance with it, then there remains but one rational alternative : either to surrender our warfare with rationalism and infidelity, or to renounce and denounce that symbolic system as inadequate and false, which it really is, even from foundation to summit. With all the great names by which it is adorned, I charge it, before God and men, with having obscured and sealed up from the view of the Church, some of the plainest and most important revelations from heaven, and hold it responsible for nearly all the uncertainty, doubt, and darkness which hang over this sublime and awful Apocalypse. And as surely as this Book is what God says it is, and as certainly as sun, moon, and stars mean sun, moon, and stars, just so surely this fourth trumpet no more refers to Odoacer, or any other men, events, or disasters of the past, than it does to the writers who have so applied it. It is a judgment scene of the great day that is foreshown, and it is a fearful and disastrous obscuration of the sources of light and heat to our world, so that sun, moon, and stars will shine with only the third of their force, disturbing the seasons, hindering the ripening of fruits and harvests, and filling the world with chilliness and sickening gloom. The same was prophesied by Isaiah (13 : 9), where it is said : " Behold, the day of the Lord cometh, cruel both with wrath and fierce anger, to lay the earth desolate ; and He shall destroy the sinners thereof out of it. For *the stars of heaven and the constellations thereof shall not give their light, the sun shall be darkened in his going forth, and the moon shall not cause her light to shine.* And I will punish the world for their evil, and the wicked for their iniquity ; and I will cause the arrogancy of the proud to cease, and will lay low the haughtiness of the terrible." (Compare Jer. 4 : 23, 28 ; Ezek. 32 : 7, 8 ; Joel 2 : 10, 30, 31 ; 3 : 15 ; Amos 5 : 20 ; Zeph. 1 : 14–16 ; Matt. 24 : 29.) Nor can we consider this unlikely or improbable, when we call to mind the plague of " thick darkness," for three days, which attended God's judgments upon Egypt.

Thus, then, we have the significance of the first four trumpets. The first angel sounds, and a fearful tempest of hail and fire, mingled with blood, follows. The third of the land is burned, and the third of the trees, and all green grass ;—a judgment upon the world for its wickednesses,

The second angel sounds, and a great meteoric mass, like unto a mountain burning with fire, is plunged into the sea, turning the third of its waters to blood, killing the third of all living things in the sea, and utterly destroying the third of the shipping on the sea ;—another sore judgment upon the guilty and God-defying children of men.

The third angel sounds, and a great starlike meteor falls out of the sky, blazing like a torch, and is absorbed by the earth and waters, embittering the third of the rivers, and the wells, and fountains, so that large portions of mankind die because of the poison it imparts to the waters ;—another sore judgment upon the wicked dwellers upon the earth.

The fourth angel sounds, and calamity befalls the luminaries of the sky. The sun, moon, and stars are one-third obscured, making the days' gloominess and the darkness of the nights still darker, with all the attendant distresses of such a beclouded and chilly state of things ;—a further judgment upon the generations of the unsanctified.

And yet these are only the preliminaries and preludes of still intenser woes to follow. Ah, yes ; sin has a voice that is heard in heaven. Though sentence against an evil work be not executed speedily, it will be executed at last. Jezebel may flourish in her iniquities for many years, but, finally, the horses trample her body in the streets, and the dogs of Jezreel gnaw and crunch her royal bones. Long was the old world left to drive its crimes, jeer at Noah's odd notions, and fling defiance into the face of God ; but presently the earth broke down beneath their feet, and their lifeless bodies dashed upon each other amid the waves of an ocean world ! The trampled law will assert its rightful honour, and Christ will not endure the smiting, taunts, and wrongs of Pilate's hall forever. And when these trumpets once give out their clangour, the vibrations will run through the universe, and everything created for human blessedness shall turn into a source of disaster and trouble to them that know not God and obey not the Gospel of Christ.

> Day of anger, day of wonder !
> When the world is driven asunder,
> Smote with fire, and blood, and thunder !

And will any one who hears these solemn things go away from the contemplation of them, not caring whether he is involved in these plagues or not ? There is now a free salvation from all of them offered through faith in Christ Jesus. Hid and housed in Him and His redeeming grace, not one of these calamities shall ever touch us. Who, then, can reconcile himself to retire from the exhibitions of this hour, without having his heart and mind made up, God being his Helper, never more to neglect or give over his devout endeavours to find the only shelter from the miseries of that terrible day ?

> King of Majesty tremendous,
> Who dost free salvation send us !
> Well of Mercy ! O befriend us.

LECTURE NINETEENTH

THE WOE-TRUMPETS—THE EAGLE IN MID-HEAVEN—CLASS TO WHICH HE BELONGS—MERCY IN JUDGMENT—THE FIFTH TRUMPET—THE FALLEN STAR—THE LOCUSTS FROM THE ABYSS—THEIR FORMS, INTELLIGENCE, AND TORMENTS—NOT JEWISH ZEALOTS—NOT GOTHS AND VANDALS—NOT ADHERENTS AND PROPAGATORS OF FALSE DOCTRINE—NOT THE LUTHERANS —NOT THE SARACENS—BELONG TO THE DAY OF THE LORD—HELL TORMENTS A REALITY.

REV. 8: 13, 9: 1–12. (Revised Text.)—And I beheld, and heard one eagle flying in mid-heaven, saying with a great voice, Woe, woe, woe, to the dwellers on the earth, by reason of the remaining voices of the trumpet of the three angels who are yet to sound.

And the fifth angel sounded, and I saw a star out of the heaven fallen into the earth ; and to him was given the key of the well-pit of the abyss ; and he opened the well-pit of the abyss ; and there came out of the well-pit smoke, as smoke of a great furnace ; and the sun was darkened, and the air, from the smoke of the well-pit. And out of the smoke came forth locusts into the earth ; and to them was given power, as the scorpions of the earth have power. And it was commanded them that they shall not injure the grass of the earth, nor any green thing, nor any tree, but only the men who have not the seal of God upon their foreheads. And it was given to them that they should not kill them, but that they shall be tormented five months ; and their torment [is] as the torment of a scorpion when he hath struck a man. And in those days the men shall seek death, and they shall not find it ; and they shall fervently desire to die, and death fleeth from them.

And the forms of the locusts [are] like unto horses prepared for war ; and on their heads as it were crowns like unto gold, and their faces as it were faces of men. And they had hair as the hair of women, and their teeth were as of lions. And they had breast-plates, as breast-plates of iron ; and the sound of their wings, as the sound of chariots of many horses running into battle. And they have tails like unto scorpions and stings ; and in their tails their power to injure the men five months. They have over them a king, the angel of the abyss, his name in Hebrew, Abaddon, and in the Greek he hath name Apollyon.

The one woe is past ; behold, there cometh yet two woes after these things.

FOUR trumpets have been considered. The three most distinguished ones yet remain. They have a special preface, consisting of a heavenly proclamation of woe, woe, woe to the dwellers on the earth. It is a pre-announcement of the general character of what is to come, and a merciful forewarning of the judgments which these remaining trumpets are to bring. It is from this that they have the name of woe-trumpets. Let us then look—

    I. AT THIS PRELIMINARY PROCLAMATION.

    II. AT THE NATURE OF THE FIRST WOE.

I. Our English version describes this proclamation as made by an *angel*. This is admitted to be an erroneous reading. It is not sustained by the best and oldest manuscripts. The Codex Sinaiticus, the Codex Alexandrinus, and the Codex Vaticanus, the very best and most reliable authorities on the true reading of the New Testament, have ἀετος, *eagle*, instead of ἀγγελος, *angel*. The Syriac has *eagle*. Griesbach, Scholz, Lachman, Van Ess, Hengstenberg, Stuart, Tischendorf, Tregelles, Wordsworth, Ewald, Alford, and the best critics in general, accept *eagle* as the proper and original reading. Bengel, a century and a half ago, wrote " the Italian version, and other most ancient authorities, widely separated from each other in age and clime, and in very great numbers, clearly vindicate the reading of ἀετου, *eagle*, from all suspicion of gloss." As this agent is in heaven and speaks intelligent words, it is easily to be seen how interpreters and transcribers, on the ground of congruity, might be tempted to read *angel* instead of *eagle ;* but, on the supposition that the original was *angel*, it is impossible to explain how the best, and the vast majority of ancient copies, came to have it *eagle*. I, therefore, take the true reading, and the only one critically defensible, to be *eagle*.

Are there, then, rapacious birds in heaven ? No ; nothing of the kind.

There are other eagles besides birds. The Saviour himself has spoken of them in more than one place. Speaking of the day of His future coming, He said to His disciples : " I tell you, in that night there shall be two men in one bed ; the one shall be taken, and the other shall be left. Two women shall be grinding together ; the one shall be taken, and the other left. Two men shall be in the field ; the one shall be taken, and the other left. And they answered and said unto him, Where [*whither*], Lord ? And he said unto them, Wheresoever the body is, *thither* will THE EAGLES be gathered together." (Luke 17 : 34–37.)

Here, then, those ready and watching saints, who are to be mysteriously conveyed away from the earth upon the first manifestation of the day of the Lord, are called *eagles*. We find them spoken of also in the Saviour's great prophetic discourse in Matt. 24 : 26–28, where He admonishes His people not to trouble or disturb themselves to find Him in the day of His coming, and not to heed those who shall say, Behold, He is here, or there ; " for," says He, " as the lightning cometh out of the east, and shineth even unto the west, so shall also the coming of the Son of man be ; for wheresoever the carcass [slain body] is, there will THE EAGLES be gathered together." Here, as Hilary observes, " He calls His saints *eagles*, soaring, as it were, to Him, the body, by a spiritual flight."

There are some who take these eagles to mean the Roman armies, which bore the eagle on their standards ; and consider the carcass to be the corrupt Jewish population and state which the Romans destroyed. But the whole face and intent of the passage, and the common voice of antiquity, and of the great reformers, unite in referring the description to Christ and His people, at the time of the second Advent. We are naturally repelled from the idea that Christ should be represented as a dead body, or that His meek followers should be likened to birds of prey. But when more carefully considered, there appears eminent propriety in the figure.

Jesus is the Saviour, most of all *by His death*. It is by His fall that we rise, and by His death that we live. " He that was dead " is one of His particular titles, though He is alive for evermore. He gave His flesh for the life of the world. His own word is : " Except ye eat the flesh of the Son of man, and drink his blood, ye have no life in you. Whoso eateth my flesh, and drinketh my blood, hath eternal life ; and I will raise him up at the last day : for my flesh is meat indeed, and my blood is drink indeed." (Jno. 6 : 53–55.)

He has also instituted a holy sacrament, concerning which He says : " Take, eat ; this is my body which is broken for you. Drink ; this is my blood which is shed for you and for many for the remission of sins." He is the Lamb " slain from the foundation of the world." He is, therefore, the true *slain body* on which all saints feed, to whom they are gathered in spirit, faith, and loving sympathy now, and to whom they shall be gathered in person hereafter, to see Him as He is, and to be with Him forever. And as saints have their life from the slain Christ, they are rightfully likened to the eagles which live on fallen bodies. They are eagles of faith. They feed on the body and blood of their Saviour, broken and shed for them.*

* " The congregated *eagles* are the assembly of saints and martyrs."—*Chrysostom*. " Christians are compared to eagles, because they partake in the royalty of Christ."—*Origen*. " Eagles are the saints whose youth is renewed like the eagles (Ps. 103 : 5), and who, according to the saying of Isaiah (40 : 31), mount up with wings as eagles, that they may ascend to Christ."—*Jerome*. " Christ's body crucified is that of which it is said : ' My flesh is meat indeed.' " (Jno. 6 : 55.) " The eagles, which fly on the wings of the Spirit, flock to this body. To this body the eagles are gathered who believe Christ to have come in the flesh." (1 Jno. 4 : 2.) " They fly to Him as to a dead body, because He *died* for us, so as all the saints fly to Christ wherever He is, and hereafter, as eagles, will be caught up to Him in the clouds"—*Augustine*. " As the eagles are gathered where the carcass is, so shall Christ's people be gathered where He is."—*Luther*.

As additional authorities on the same subject, we name Ambrose, Theophylact, Euthemius, Calvin, Brentius, Bullinger, Bucer, Gaulter, Beza, Pellican, Flacius, Musculus, Paræus, Piscater, Cocceius, Jansenius, Quesnel, Du Veil, Calovius, Suicer, Ravanell, Poole, Trapp, Cartwright, Pearce, Leigh, Andrewes, Wordsworth, &c.

But not all Christians are to the same extent, and so pre-eminently, *the eagles*. The eagle is a royal bird. It stands at the head of the feathered tribes, as the lion among beasts. There are also different orders and classes of saint-ship, as there are degrees of sanctity and spiritual attainment. When the Saviour first comes, according to His own word, He will take some and leave others—honour some servants, and cut off some other servants. And those who are " taken " while others are " left," are particularly and emphatically " *the eagles*." They are the heirs of royalty and dominion. They are to have crowns. They are to share in the official honours of eternity, as none but them-selves ever will. And the qualities of these are eminently the qualities of eagles.

Eagles are great watchers. They have a quick, clear, penetrating, and far-reaching vision. In this respect they excel all birds. It is almost impossible to surprise or deceive them. Audubon once placed himself in ambush to watch an eagle's nest. The parent birds were absent when he took his position. When the female returned, " ere she alighted she glanced her quick and piercing eye around, and instantly perceived her haunt had been discovered, and, dropping her prey, with a loud shriek communicated the alarm to her mate." And the eagle saints are those who are not taken unawares when the day of the Lord comes. That day is to come as a thief, with stealth, unob-served by the common world ; but it cannot surprise them. They are on the lookout for it. They have a clear and keen vision for all signs of its nearness, and they exercise that vision. They are ever on the watch, as commanded by the Lord. Whatever the duties in which they are engaged, both in their going out and in their coming in, they are never unmindful of what may at any time occur. They know their danger and they know their safety, and exercise a corresponding circumspection.

Eagles have elevated aspirations and instincts. They prefer the heights, both when they soar and when they rest. They make their homes among the most inaccessible crags, and excel all birds in their sublime ascensions. So eagle saints have their citizenship in heaven. They live in the world, but all their feelings, aims, affections, and desires are above it. Their greatest impulses are upward, ever upward. They love the higher atmosphere and the sublimer sunlight above the clouds and malarious mists and dangers of earthiness. They build their nests in the mountains of God, and prefer and long to be where they are never more annoyed with the vexations and dangers of this sordid world. .

Eagles are stronger of wing than other birds. Their swiftness and power are astonishing. So the eagle saints are distinguished by their vigour of faith and hope. They are particularly strong in those truths and promises which lift heavenward, anticipate the dawn of a sublimer economy, and sit " in heavenly places in Christ Jesus." Isaiah referred, in his day, to saints of these eminent qualities, and likens them to eagles, where he says : " They who wait for Jehovah, gain fresh strength, lift up their wings *as eagles*, run and are not weary, go forward and do not faint." (40 : 30, 31 ; *Delitzsch's Translation*.) And in Deuteronomy (32 : 11, 12), Jehovah is likened to a parent eagle, and His elect to young eagles, whom He feeds, and upbears, and teaches to fly and rise to himself.*

We thus identify a class of *eagles*, other than the rapacious birds denoted by this name ;—eagles that have voices, intelligence, and place in heaven.

* " This image, used in Exodus (19 : 4), is fully verified in Him who is called *the Great Eagle* (Rev. 12 : 14), and who bears His Church on eagle's wings through the wilderness of this world, and who ascended up into heaven with His young ones on His wings, and to whom, as their Parent, and their Life, and their Food, all true eagles of the Gospel, as His children, are gathered now on earth and will be gathered forever hereafter in heaven."— *Wordsworth in loc.*
" The comparison of Himself to *the hen* was adapted to the time of His first advent in humility. This latter reference to *the eagle* has relation to the time of His second advent in glory when the eagles of the Gospel will be gathered together where the body is."—*Ibid.*, on 2 Thess. 2 : 1.

These eagles are also in heaven before the judgments occur to which these trumpets refer. The Saviour himself, in Matt. 24, puts their gathering together where the body is, in advance of the sending forth of His angels with the great trumpet-sounding. When the sun is darkened, and the moon is obscured, and the stars fall, and the powers of the heavens are shaken, and the sign of the Son of Man appears, and all the tribes of the earth mourn ; these eagles are already where the Lord, on whom they live, is. John saw them there, among other images, under that of " *a flying eagle*," before the Lamb took the book or ever a seal was broken ; where also he heard them sing unto the Lamb : " Thou art worthy ; for Thou wert slain, and redeemedst us to God by Thy blood, out of every tribe, and tongue, and people, and nation, and Thou madest us unto our God, kings and priests, and we shall reign on the earth." (Rev. 4 : 5-10 ; 5 : 8-10.) And from among these was He whom John here beheld and heard flying in mid-heaven, saying with a great voice, " Woe, woe, woe, to the dwellers on the earth, by reason of the remaining voices of the trumpet of the three angels who are yet to sound."

The manner in which this eagle is spoken of, implies that there are others of the same class. The seer says : " I beheld and heard *one eagle* " thus flying and saying. This " *one eagle* " presupposes more eagles ; as " *one scribe*," in Matt. 8 : 19, presupposes more scribes ; as " *one voice* from the horns of the golden altar " (9 : 13) presupposes more voices ; as *" one mighty angel* " (19-21) presupposes more angels.

The Church of the first born is to have a part in the administrations of the judgment upon the guilty world. " Do ye not know that the saints shall judge the world ? " (1 Cor. 4 : 2.) Hence, when the first seals were broken, the voice of power was heard from the living ones. " *Go !* " And so here, " *one eagle* " has a mission which he executes between the sounding of the fourth and fifth trumpets, as the prelude to what the last three trumpets are to produce. Verily, we know not, and cannot half conceive what ministries and agencies of heavenly sublimity await us, if only we are faithful. We shall fly, like eagles, in mid-heaven, and mingle our voices with the trumpets of judgment, and fill offices of honour and celestial dignity among the transactions of archangels, as they go forth to close up the history of a rebellious world !

The precise manner in which this proclamation of the eagle is to reach men, is not stated. That it is to be heard on earth, I am quite sure. We can discern no reason why heaven should be thus specifically notified that the succeeding trumpets are woe-trumpets ; nor yet for the introduction of such a special agency to inform John that they were to be woe-trumpets. The results of the blowing of them would necessarily make this sufficiently manifest to him. The intention of the proclamation itself is evidently merciful. I take it as a heavenly signal, given in the midst of the ongoing of the scenes of the day of judgment, to apprise men of the terrible plagues next to be enacted, that those then living, who have not become utterly blind and deaf to sacred things, may take warning and seek refuge against the oncoming calamities. It is one of the principles of the Divine administrations, that mercy is remembered in the midst of wrath ; and, as long as there is any possibility of bringing men to a right mind, the opportunity for it is given. These three woe trumpets are to conclude the history of this world and to end forever this present economy. Hence, on the very eve of the end, and when the last awful visitations are about to fall upon the ungodly, still a mighty voice of warning goes forth from mid-heaven, that such as will heed it may prepare themselves, and cry for mercy before mercy is clean gone forever. God gives up the world to perdition with great reluctance. He has always said that He has no pleasure in the death of the wicked ; and we thus behold Him true to His word up to the last.

II. We come, then, to the first of these eagle-announced woes. The fifth trumpet brings it. It is quite different in character from the four preceding trumpets. All are blasts of judgment, and all belong to the great day of the

Lord ; but no two of them are alike except in this, that they all bring calamity and suffering to the wicked dwellers upon the earth.

Thus far the trumpets have blown only the objects of physical nature, and wrought their effects through disturbances in the material world. The first trumpet smote the land, the trees, and the grass. The second smote the waters of the sea, the fishes, and the ships. The third smote the fountains, wells, and rivers. And the fourth obscured and darkened the sources of light and heat to the world. From these several successive blasts great suffering and mortality result to the children of men. But the trumpet now before us goes beyond the physical world and calls into action quite other agencies. The doors of separation between the earth and the prison of evil spirits are opened, and mysterious and malignant tenants of the underworld are permitted to over-run the globe, and to inflict torture and woe upon its unsanctified inhabitants.

John hears the fifth angel sound, and beholds a fallen star in the earth. This is not a meteor like that which he beheld on the sounding of the third angel. He does not see the falling, but recognizes the star as a fallen one—*fallen*, he does not say when or how. This star is an intelligent agent, for things are distinctly ascribed to " him " which could not be said except of a living being. A key is given him. He takes that key. He uses it for the unlocking of a door, and he lets forth from their prison some of the tenants of the abyss. All this argues active and intelligent agency, and furnishes the Divine intimation that we are not to consider this star to be of the same kind as the star under the third trumpet. It is not a material but a spiritual star, and a fallen one—one fallen out of the heaven. We know of such spiritual and celestial stars. When the capstone of the grand pyramid of creation was laid, the Almighty himself hath declared that " the morning *stars* sang together, and all the sons of God shouted for joy." (Job. 38 : 4–7.) These were angelic beings. We know, also, that there are " *angels* which kept not their first estate, but left their own habitation." (Jude 6.) We read of " *the angels* that sinned," whom God did not spare. (2 Pet. 2 : 4.) These are of various orders and degrees, " principalities and powers." (Eph. 6 : 6 ; Col. 2 : 15.) Among them is one of pre-eminent dignity, the leader and prince of all the rest— " the great dragon, that old serpent, called the Devil and Satan." (Rev. 12 : 9.) Hence, we read of " the Devil and his angels." (Matt. 25 : 41.) Here, then, are *fallen stars* of a spiritual sort, and one of particular distinction and magnitude, answering to the description of the text. For the present they have possession of the aerial or heavenly spaces. (Eph. 6 : 12.) Satan is particularly described as " the prince of the power of the air." (Eph. 2 : 2.)* He is fallen morally, and fallen from the proper heaven of glory, and is even-tually to be entirely ejected from the heavenly places now occupied by him and his angels, previous to the great binding which is to shut him up in the abyss. The Saviour refers prophetically to this, where He says : " I beheld Satan as lightning fall from heaven." (Luke 10 : 18.) This ejectment, in its final completeness, is described by John in the twelfth chapter, where he speaks of " war in the heaven," and the ejection of " Satan and his angels " by Michael and his hosts. After that, these impure spirits have no more place in heaven forever. But, even after this precipitation from the aerial regions, their work on earth is continued for a time with augmented fierceness and wrath. There may also be a preliminary precipitation of Satan into the earth, previous to the great battle between him and Michael, to which the *fall* spoken of in the text may refer. It may be the result of a Divine force, or it may be a voluntary casting of himself into the earth for augmented mischief. At any rate, Satan is a fallen spiritual star, and John beholds him fallen into the earth with particular malignity, and bent on letting loose against men all

---

* Wordsworth has this note upon the place : " Satan and his angels, being cast down from heaven, but not being yet consigned to hell, have their empire in this lower air, and are therefore called the powers of the air and of darkness." The word οὐρανός is sometimes rendered *heaven* and sometimes *air*.

the evil powers which he can command. He also stands related to the inhabitants of the abyss as their chief lord, in a way which renders it congruous and fitting with all that we know of him, that we should see him in this " star out of the heaven fallen into the earth." Whatever the fall, whether moral or local, voluntary, or the result of force, it includes a will for mischief, and overflowing with malignity toward the children of men.

And because of the wickedness of the world, special powers are granted him. As people prefer the service of the devil, God allows them a full experience of his administrations. It has always been so. Because the nations before Christ, when they knew God, glorified Him not as God, neither were thankful, but became vain in their imaginations, and changed the truth of God into a lie ; He dropped the reins to them and gave them up to uncleanness, vile affections, and a reprobate mind, to be filled with all unrighteousness, and to receive in themselves that recompense of their error which was meet. (Rom. 1 : 19–32.) Because men receive not the truth and dislike it, God gives them what they love, and sends them strong delusions, that they may believe lies, and reap the reward of their perverse choice in its own line. And because men reject the Lordship of Christ for the lordship of Satan, God in judgment enlarges the powers of the lord of their preference that they may have the full benefit of the malignant will of their own chosen.

John beholds and describes how this is done. To this fallen star, he says " was given the key of the well-pit of the abyss." It was " *given* " to him, as all that Job had was *given* to the same fallen one, to do with it as he might list. Though Satan has great power, he is under bonds and limitations, beyond which he cannot go without permission. He is now allowed to employ his demons, but not to bring forth all the evil agencies who would fain serve him in his work of malignity. But, in the great day of judgment, and in augmentation of the punishments of the ungodly, he will be allowed to call into his service multitudes of evil beings now restrained and imprisoned in the under-world. Nor will he fail to use this power any more than he failed to exert his full liberty against Job. With the key to the well-pit of the abyss, he opens it, breaks down in part the wall of severance between earth and hell, and evokes a plague, such as the world has never before experienced.

Jehovah once said to Job : " Have the gates of Sheol been opened unto thee ? or hast thou seen the doors of the shadow of death ? " (37 : 17.) There are worlds of being and of darkness upon which man has never looked. There is a tenanted abyss of which the demons know, and concerning which they besought the Saviour that He would not send them into it.* It is a dark and horrible prison, in which many, many strange and evil things are shut up. Satan knows of that world, and would fain bring forth its malignant inhabitants into the earth if he only dared. At last, however, he receives permission to bring them, and the fifth trumpet gives the result.

As soon as the mouth of the pit is opened, a thick blackness issues from it like the black smoke of a great furnace—a blackness which fills the air and obscures the sun ; and out of the smoky blackness proceed living things, horrible in shape, malignant in disposition, and armed with power to afflict and torment men's bodies. John calls them *locusts ;* but they are supernatural, infernal, not earthly locusts. They neither consume nor injure any of the grass of the earth, or any green thing, or any tree. They do not appear to eat at all, though they have teeth like the teeth of lions. They are winged creatures, and their flight is noisy, sounding like chariots and horses rushing into battle. They seem to dwell mostly in the air and in the smoke and darkness. Neither is there any indication that they are capable of being caught or killed.

The forms of these creatures are particularly described. They are a sort of

---

* See Luke 8 : 27–31, upon which Doddridge remarks of the " abyss," that it is " the prison in which many of these fallen spirits are detained, and to which some, who may, like these, have been permitted for a while to range at large, are sometimes by Divine justice and power remanded."

infernal cherubim—antipodes of the Living ones conjoined with the heavenly throne. The horse, the man, the lion, the scorpion, are combined in them. Their general appearance is like horses caparisoned for battle. Their heads are surmounted by the semblance of crowns seemingly of gold. They have faces resembling the faces of men. They are hairy, with hair like women's hair. Their backs and breasts are encased as if with iron plates, after the manner of a Roman soldier, and they have tails of the size and shape of a scorpion. Their dimensions are not given. Scorpions vary in size ; some kinds are six inches in length. Figuring to ourselves then, an outline of body, the tail of which would correspond to the size and make of a large scorpion, we reach quite formidable proportions.

These horrible creatures have a certain degree of intelligence. Commands are addressed to them. They are able to distinguish between those who have the seal of the living God upon their foreheads and other people. They have a king whom they obey. Earthly locusts have no king (Prov. 30 : 27) ; but these have a king over them. This king is not Satan himself. Satan is, indeed, chief of all the powers of darkness, but he has archons and princes under him, with their own particular commands. It is Satan who opens the door for the egress of these hosts from the pit ; but their immediate king is one of Satan's angels—" the angel of the abyss."

This king has a descriptive name. It is given in Hebrew and in Greek, showing that this administration has to do with Jews and Gentiles. Christ is named *Jesus* because He is *the Saviour*. This king is named *Abaddon* in Hebrew, and *Apollyon* in Greek, because he is *a destroyer*—the opposite of saviour.

But the destructive power of these locusts is limited. As Satan was not allowed to touch Job's life, so these creatures are forbidden to kill men, and the sealed ones they are not permitted to touch at all. The extent of their power is to horrify and torment " the men who have not the seal of God upon their foreheads." They inflict their torment by means of stings, like the stings of scorpions. These stings are in their tails, which tails resemble scorpions. They have power " as the scorpions of the earth have power." They are not " of the earth," as scorpions are " of the earth." They are supernatural beings, but they have the capacity to injure and torture men which natural scorpions have.

The pain from the sting of a scorpion, though not generally fatal, is, perhaps, the intensest that any animal can inflict upon the human body. The insect itself is the most irascible and malignant that lives, and its poison is like itself. Of a boy stung in the foot by a scorpion, Laborde relates that, although of a race which bears everything with remarkable patience, he rolled on the ground, grinding his teeth, and foaming at the mouth. It was a long time before his complainings moderated, and even then he could make no use of his foot, which was greatly inflamed. And such is the nature of the torment which these locusts from the pit inflict. They are also difficult to be guarded against, if they can be warded off at all, because they fly where they please, dart through the air, and dwell in darkness.

The duration of this extraordinary plague is " *five months.*" No single generation of earthly locusts ever lasts so long. Twice is the period mentioned, as if the Holy Ghost would call special attention to it as marking the great severity of the plague. To be subjected to such intense anguish, and to have it endure for " five months," fills out a length and breadth of woe which only they who feel can fully know. Death itself would be preferable to such an existence. Willingly, also, would the sufferers of this torment resign life in preference to the continuance of it in such torture, if there were no inter- ference to prevent death. But there is such interference. Not only are the locusts forbidden to kill, but the people afflicted by them are hindered from dying. The statement is, that they shall " fervently desire to die," and " shall seek death ; " but the woeful peculiarity of " those days " is, that they cannot find death, and are obliged to live, whatever efforts they may make to escape from life. Perhaps these locusts themselves keep men from killing themselves. This trumpet accordingly introduces the very torments of hell upon the theatre of this present world.

Many, indeed, consider it mere fancy-work, fiction, and symbol, referring to events in the past history of the race and intended to describe quite other things than are thus literally depicted. But the account is given as an account of realities. There is no difficulty involved in the language employed. The grammatical sense is plain and obvious. Neither is there any intimation whatever of any other sense. And if any other sense was intended, there lives not a man who can tell, with any degree of certainty, what that other sense is. Many and great minds have laboured to make out an allegorical and historical interpretation of these locusts from the pit, but thus far, as Alford has justly remarked, only " an endless Babel " has been the result. Alford gives it up. Stuart gives it up. Hengstenberg gives it up. Vaughan gives it up. Others have given it up. And every candid man must give it up, on any scheme that will consistently interpret the Apocalypse as a whole, or preserve to the sacred records the credit and value which this book claims for its contents.— Observe the facts.

These locusts cannot mean the zealots who spread slaughter and devastation through Judea about the time of the fall of Jerusalem, as some have supposed, because those marauders killed people, whereas the locusts are forbidden to kill anyone. Those zealots had no king ; these locusts have a king. They were natural men ; these locusts come up out of the abyss. They had neither wings nor stings ; these locusts have both.

Neither do these locusts symbolize those nations of the North which ravaged Italy during the one hundred and fifty years from the invasion under Alaric to the capture of Rome by Totila, as others have supposed. Those invaders were not led by a single chief ; these locusts were. They killed men ; these locusts kill no one. They did not distinguish in their doings between any sealed or unsealed ones ; these locusts do thus distinguish. They did not refrain from harming the trees, grass, and products of the earth ; these locusts do thus refrain.

Nor yet do these locusts represent the adherents and propagators of false doctrines, as many have taught. Heresy is killing ; but these locusts are forbidden to kill. There never has been any system of error, whose abettors have run their course within " five months," by any method of computation yet devised ; or so stung and tormented the ungodly as to make them seek death for relief ; or so discriminated between God's sealed ones and the wicked, as to assail only the latter. Arius and his heresies have been named, also Popery and its falsities, also Mohammedanism and its abominations ; but, instead of being confined to " five months," or one hundred and fifty years, these have wrought for more than a thousand years, still work, and have never ceased to hurt and kill people of all classes, both literally and spiritually.

Neither does the description answer to Luther and the Lutherans, as Bellarmine and other Romish interpreters affirm. If Luther was the fallen star, who was the king over the Lutherans ? The locusts were to continue " five months," but the Lutherans have wrought now for more than three hundred and fifty years, and still are the particular grief of Papists, who, on this showing, have not the seal of God ! The locusts have stings to torment men ; the Lutherans have never been tormentors nor persecutors. They have done great things to release mankind from the tortures and inflictions of the papacy, but no people have ever so suffered from the Lutherans or their doctrines, as to seek death in order to escape their torments, without ability to find it. All the Protestant nations, and even many Romanists themselves, refer to the Lutheran Reformation with joy and thanksgiving, as one of the happiest enfranchisements of modern times. It was heaven-wide from this locust plague.*

* Compare pages 83, 84.

Nor yet will this vision apply, except in a very dim and imperfect way, to the mighty Saracenic invasion, in which so many moderns locate its fulfilment. If Mahomet was this star, it is impossible to show wherein he experienced the *fall* ascribed to this star. If he was the star, he was also the king of the powers he set in motion ; but the record plainly shows that the star and the king of the locusts are two distinct personages. If the cave of Hera was the mouth of the pit, the followers of Mahomet did not come out of that cave, as the locusts are said to come out of the abyss. If his flight from Mecca was his fall, then the pit was open and the smoke had begun to issue and breed locusts before the star's fall, which is again contrary to the record. If the smoke was Mahomet's false doctrines, then neither smoke nor locusts existed before the pit was opened, for the Arabians were not Mohammedans before Mahomet, but the vision represents the locusts as dwelling in the pit and in the smoke long ere the pit was opened or the smoke issued. It was after the smoke had already gone forth, and followers had been won, that Mahomet professed to have received *the key* from God ; he had therefore opened the pit before he got the key with which to open it ; neither was it ever pretended that this key of his was the key of hell. But this is not all.

The locusts were forbidden to touch any one upon whose forehead the seal of God was impressed ; but the wrath and fury of the Mohammedan hordes were directed mainly and above all against Christians and Christendom. The locusts were to torment all who had not the seal of God upon them ; but the Saracen invasion struck a very small part of the world outside of Christendom. The locusts were not allowed to take men's lives ; it was the work of Mohammedanism to kill both body and soul—the bodies of those who refused to accept it, and the souls of those who embraced it. It was the command of Mahomet to all his devotees, and delivered in the name of his god : " When ye encounter the unbelievers, strike off their heads, until ye have made a great slaughter among them. . . . As for the infidels, let them perish." (Koran 47.) So they slew 50,000 in one battle, and 150,000 in another, and spread death and slaughter whithersoever they went. Does this look like the absence of power to kill ? * The locusts were to do no injury to trees, crops, and vegetation. The Mohammedans destroyed with fire and sword the countries they invaded.† The locusts were so to torment men that they would seek to destroy their own lives, and yet should not be able to do it ; but neither of these things occurred under the Mohammedans. Men loved to live then as now, and fought to defend themselves, and paid tribute to be permitted to live, and could easily find death if they wished. The locusts were in shape like horses prepared for war ; Mohammedans had this appearance no more than any other armed hosts. The locusts wore seeming golden crowns; but " turbans of linen " very poorly meet the description, whilst, if the creatures are symbolical, the crowns are symbolical also. What, then, is the prophetic import of a turban ? The locusts had breastplates, which are said to be symbols of invulnerability ; but the Mohammedans were not invul-

---

* " I cannot forbear noticing the caprice of historical interpreters. On the command *not to kill* the men, &c., in verse 5, Elliott says, ' *i.e.*, not to annihilate them as a political Christian body.' If, then, the same rule of interpretation is to hold, the 6th verse must mean that the ' political Christian body ' will be so sorely beset by these Mohammedan locusts, that it will vehemently desire to be annihilated, and not find any way. For it surely cannot be allowed that *the killing of men* should be said of their annihilation as a political body in one verse, and their *desiring to die* in the next should be said of something totally different, and applicable to their individual misery. Is it in consequence of foreseeing this difficulty that Mr. Elliott has, as in the case of many important details in other places, omitted all consideration of this verse ?"—Alford *in loc.*

† Against this, the historical interpreters quote the command given to the Saracen army on the invasion of Syria : " *Destroy no palm-trees nor burn any fields of corn. Cut down no fruit-trees.*" But this was not the command of Mahomet or the Koran, but of Abubekr, and there is no instance of its repetition in all the Saracen wars. The command itself shows what was the general habit of these fanatical hordes ; besides, it excepted only palm and fruit trees, leaving other trees to be dealt with as inclination might prompt. It is simply absurd to speak of the Saracenic armies as having refrained from injuring trees and grass.

nerable ; they never went into battle without losing some of their number, and they were more than once defeated with great slaughter. The locusts have wings, and tails, and stings in their tails, and poison in their stings like the poison of scorpions ; but, in no respect was this true of the Mohammedans, any more than of any other conquering hordes. The locusts have power to operate only for the space of " five months "—on the year-day theory, one hundred and fifty years—but the warlike expeditions of the Saracens ranged through more than four hundred years, and their power is not yet taken away. The king of the locusts is named Abaddon and Apollyon, but neither of these was the name of the Moslem prophet, nor do they describe him any more than many others who have acted a like part in the world. Smoke may very well represent false doctrine, but what was the sun and air obscured by Mohammedanism, when those who see only Mohammedanism in this vision are obliged to consider the Christianity and churches which the Saracens overrun, as even worse than Islamism itself ? Besides, if Arabia, whence the Saracens came, is the well-pit of the abyss, as some seem to affirm, then it is into *Arabia* that the Devil is to be cast, and shut up, and sealed in, for the thousand years, if not also the place into which all the finally lost are to be consigned !

But apart from all this, God himself has named this book the book of " *The Apocalypse—the coming—of Jesus Christ."* John accordingly, also tells us that what he describes he saw *in the day of the Lord*—among the scenes and transactions of the great day of judgment as they were made to pass before him in vision. It is impossible, therefore, that this trumpet should refer to the past, unless the day of the Lord is passed and the judgment is over, and the Apocalypse of Jesus has already taken place.

We have seen that the seven Churches span the whole period, from the time of the apostle to the commencement of the day of Judgment. We have also had the declaration of the Saviour himself, that what else John saw and wrote in this book relates to a period of time *after* the Church period has passed. The seven trumpets come in under the breaking of the seventh seal, and the Church period is ended before *any of* the seals are broken. The Saracenic invasion occurred in the midst of the Church period. Hence, the locust-plague of the fifth trumpet cannot possibly be the Arabic irruption under Mahomet, unless an event can be both in the middle and at the end of the same period, at one and the same time. Judgments, indeed, prefigure each other, and every feature of the great consummation has its forerunners and preli-bations. And so there may have been a dim and inchoate likeness of this trumpet in the Saracenic scourge. But the height and fulness of it, and its only proper *fulfilment*, remains to be accomplished in the great day to come— the Day of the Lord—the period of Christ's unveiling—when it will be literally realized in all its horrible details.

Nay, more, it is clearly in evidence from the record itself, that all the occurrences under the sixth seal, and all that comes after the sixth seal, up to the events under the fifth trumpet, do really transpire within the natural earthly lifetime of the same persons. When these locusts issue from the pit, they find living among men certain people " who have the seal of God upon their foreheads," and whom they are not allowed to touch, because of that seal. It will not answer to jump at the conclusion that these were God's children in general, because it is specifically told us in a preceding chapter who they are. There is a definite number of them—144,000—and every one of them of Jewish blood. Their sealing occurs under the sixth seal. And here, under the fifth trumpet, they are yet on earth, among men, and as liable to the torture of the locusts as any others, but for the seal of the living God impressed upon their foreheads. They are not successors to the 144,000 sealed ones, for the work of sealing was finished before a single trumpet was blown, and the idea of succession is specifically excluded,first, by the definite-ness of their number, and second, by the declaration that " they are virgins."

We thus find *the same men* living under the fifth trumpet, who were already living under the sixth seal. The " five months " must accordingly mean *five months*, and not 150 years, and the locusts from the pit cannot be the Saracens, or anything else than what they are literally described to be. They are extraordinary and infernal agents, whom Satan is permitted to let loose upon the guilty world, as a part of the judgment of the great day. All the seals, trumpets, and vials of this book relate to that day. It is a day of miracle throughout—a day of wonders—a day of fierce and tormenting wrath. It is everywhere so described in the Scriptures. And we do greatly mistreat the records which God has given for our learning, if we allow the sceptical rationalizing of our own darkened hearts to persuade us that such supernatural things are impossible, and therefore must not be literally understood. On the same ground the whole doctrine of the judgment may be explained away and, every article of the distinctive Christian faith, until we have nothing left but a book of pre-eminent pretensions and equally pre-eminent obscurity, uncertainty, and emptiness.

It appears, then, that hell and hell-torments are not the mere fictions which some have pronounced them. Neither are they as remote from this present world as men often dream. There is a fiery abyss, with myriads of evil beings in it, malignant and horrible, and there is but a door between this world and that.* Heaven is just as near ; but heaven is above, and hell is beneath. Mortal man and his world lie between two mighty, opposite, spiritual spheres, both touching directly upon him, each operative to conform him to itself, and he predestined, as he yields to one or the other, to be conjoined eventually to the society on high, or to companionship with devils and all evil beings beneath. To doubt this, is to mistake concerning the most momentous things of our existence, and to have all our senses closed to the most startling realities of our lives. As we are heavenly in our inclinations and efforts, and open and yielding to things Divine, heaven opens to us, and spirits of heaven become our helpers, comforters, protectors, and guides ; and as we are devilish in our temper, unbelieving, defiant of God, and self-sufficient, the doors of separation between us and hell gradually yield, and the smoke of the pit gathers over us, and the spirits of perdition come forth to move among us and to do us mischief. And at the last, as the saints of God are taken up out of the world on the one side, the angels of hell with their malignity and torments are let in on the other.

People are prone to persuade themselves that this world of sense and time is all that we need be concerned about, and hence have no fears of an unseen world of evil, and no decided or active desire for the blessings of an unseen world of good. They live only for earth, not dreaming that this brief life is only the vestibule to worlds of mightier and eternal moment. Their houses are built by the very margin of hell, and yet they rest and feast in them without a feeling of insecurity or of danger. The flames of perdition clamour after them beneath the pavements on which they walk, but they have no sense of fear or serious apprehension. God and angels are ever busy to win their attention to the ways of safety, but they turn a deaf ear and drift along as they list, crying, Peace ! Peace ! And so will the wicked and the unbelieving go on, until ignored and offended Omnipotence gives over the power to Satan to let loose upon them these horrid beings from the abyss, under whose torment they will wish they never had lived at all, and vainly attempt to make their escape from what they once considered their chief and only good.

* King, in his *Morsels of Criticism*, after commenting on Is. 24 : 22 ; Ps. 69 : 15 ; Ezek. 26 : 20 ; 31 : 16 ; Is. 14 : 9 ; Numb. 16 : 33 ; Eph. 2 : 10 ; Ps. 28 : 1 ; 38 : 4 ; Job 17 : 16 ; Luke 8 : 31 ; 1 Pet. 3 : 18–20, &c., remarks : " Upon the whole, therefore, we may, consistently both with the words of Holy Scripture and with philosophical ideas, conclude, or at least suspect, if we do not venture to affirm, it that there is a place of habitation of, some kind or other, in the lowest depths, and in the heart of the earth, and that this place is indeed ἅδης, or *hell*." " *The abyss* cannot possibly mean *the sea*. . . . ἄβυσσος is by no means a word made use of in any of the Gospels for *the sea*."—Vol. II, pp. 373–404.

Friends and Brethren : The judgments of God are coming—they are coming. The agents for them are ready and at hand. They are to alight with awful severity upon all the rebellious and ungodly. They will not be delayed either till this life is over. They are coming in this present world. Men shall feel them while yet they stand upon their feet, and go on with their unbelief and earthiness. Hell is to be let in upon the living earth, and no human hand can stay its torments. And as the generations of the rebellious and the unsanctified complete their five months of horror and writhing under the scorpion stings of these infernal tormentors, the first woe will be fulfilled, whilst yet two other and more horrible ones follow.

God Almighty, in His mercy, save *us* from the evils of those days ! Amen.

LECTURE TWENTIETH

THE SIXTH TRUMPET—STATE OF SOCIETY AT THIS PERIOD—DEMON-WORSHIP—SPIRITUALISM
—REVIVAL OF IDOLATRY—HEATHENISH CONDITION OF MORALS—A PERIOD OF MURDER,
SORCERY, LEWDNESS, DISHONESTY—THE PARTICULAR JUDGMENT INDUCED—CRY FROM
THE HORNS OF THE ALTAR—THE FOUR EUPHRATEAN ANGELS—PLACE OF THEIR DETENTION
—SPIRIT HORSES—THEIR MEANS OF HARMING MEN—THEIR HAVOC WITH HUMAN LIFE—
HOW LONG THEY CONTINUE THEIR DESTRUCTIVE WORK—THE INTENT OF THIS WOE—NO
REFORMATION WROUGHT—THE FOLLY OF WAITING FOR JUDGMENTS TO BRING TO A BETTER
LIFE.

REV. 9 : 13–21. (Revised Text.) And the sixth angel sounded, and I heard one voice out of the four horns of the altar of gold [which is] before God, saying to the sixth angel, who had the trumpet : Loose the four angels which are bound upon [over or near] that great river Euphrates.

And there were loosed the four angels who had been made ready for the hour, and day, and month, and year, that they should kill the third of the men. And the number of the hosts of horse [was] two myriads of myriads ; I heard the number of them.

And thus saw I the horses in the vision, and them that sat on them : they have fiery, hyacinthine, and sulphureous coats of mail ; and the heads of the horses as it were heads of lions ; and out of their mouths issueth fire, and smoke, and sulphur.

From these three plagues were killed the third of the men, by the fire, and the smoke, and the sulphur, which issueth out of their mouths ; for the power of the horses is in their mouths, and in their tails ; for their tails [are] like serpents, having heads, and with them they injure.

And the rest of the men, who were not killed by these plagues, repented not from the works of their hands, that they should not worship the demons, and the idols of gold, and silver, and copper, and stone, and wood, which can neither see, nor hear, nor walk ; and they repented not out of their murders, nor out of their sorceries [or *use of drugs*], nor out of their fornication, nor out of their thefts.

THESE words describe one of the greatest and most terrific judgments we have thus far encountered.   In approaching its consideration, I propose to notice

I. THE STATE OF SOCIETY AT THE TIME.
II. THE NATURE OF THE JUDGMENT VISITED UPON IT.

The Apostle Paul assures us, that, as time advances toward its conclusion, " Evil men and seducers shall wax worse and worse, deceiving and being deceived." (2 Tim. 3 : 13.) I have also repeatedly quoted his startling description of the " perilous times " which will come " in the last days." (2 Tim. 3 : 1–5.) But Paul was not alone in these gloomy anticipations. Peter and Jude likewise speak of them. Nor were these statements without full warrant in the utterances of the Saviour himself, who particularly and often admonished his disciples, that the gigantic iniquities and sensualities of the days of Noah and of Lot, would repeat themselves as the end approached, and that the judgments of the great day would be pre-eminently deserved by the generation then living. It would, hence, be strange, if, in the visions of those terrible adjudications, we were to find no corresponding notices of the bad state of morals then prevailing. And when such notices are found, as in the words before us, it would be contrary to the tenor of the Scriptures on the subject, to take them as mere poetic exaggerations, or as anything other than a literal and true portraiture of the world at that time. Taking the words, then, as they have been written for our learning, we here have an account of the moral state of mankind in the period of the sixth trumpet.

1. *It is a period of abounding demon-worship.* What demons are, is to some extent an unsettled question. Justin Martyr, and some other Christian fathers, regarded them as the spirits of those giants who were born of the

sons of God and the daughters of men, in the days preceding the flood. John of Damascus, considered them the fallen angels. According to Plutarch, Hesiod, as he himself, held demons to be "the spirits of mortals when separated from their earthly bodies." Zoroaster, Thales, Pythagoras, Plato, and the heathen authors generally, viewed them as spiritual beings, intermediate between supreme Deity and mortals, and mostly the souls of heroes and distinguished persons who had departed this life. Lucian makes his dialogist ask : *What is man ?* Answer : *A mortal god. And what is a god ?* Answer : *An immortal man.* This gives the common heathen doctrine on the subject. Philo says, "The souls of dead men are called demons." The account which demons themselves mostly give of themselves, according to those who have most to do with them, is the same. Josephus gives it as the orthodox Jewish opinion, that demons are none other than the spirits of the wicked dead. With very few exceptions, the Christian fathers were of like opinion. Justin Martyr, Irenæus, Tertullian, Origen, Augustine, and the vast majority of early Christian writers, regarded demons as the souls or spirits of the unsanctified dead. And the burden of evidence and authority is to the effect, that *demons are the souls of dead men, particularly the spirits of those who bore a bad character in this life.**

It is acknowledged, both in Scripture and in the classics, that the "immortals" whom the heathen adored, were once men : and Paul assures us that the sacrifices of the Gentiles made to these "immortals," were sacrifices to demons, and that their sacred feasts were in honour of demons. (1 Cor. 10 : 20, 21.)† This would seem to give us scriptural authority for believing that demons are what the Jews and early Christians believed them to be. They are, at any rate, invisible spiritual beings, unholy in character, belonging to the kingdom of evil, and having a vicious and pernicious penchant to interfere in the affairs of mankind in the flesh. The Greeks often applied the name of demons to what they considered *good* spirits ; but the Scriptures always use the word with reference to unclean and wicked spirits only. There is no such thing known in the Bible as a good demon. The Scriptures everywhere distinguish demons from "the devil," Satan ; but our English translators continually call them "*devils*," a name which fitly describes them.

Among the Jews, in the Saviour's time, these wicked spirits incorporated themselves in the bodies of living men, intruding themselves between the soul and the nervous organism, getting possession of men's physical powers, measurably superseding the wills of those affected, so as to speak and act by means of human organs.

Among the Gentiles, many of the persons thus affected were accepted as inspired prophets and prophetesses ; and it had become a regular science to know how to induce such connections with demonic powers, and how, at option, to bring their influence to bear, whether for religious or for secular purposes.

There always have been ways of coming into communication with these unclean spirits, of consulting them, and securing their aid. Hence the scriptural allusions to those who have familiar spirits, enchanters, wizards, witches, magicians, soothsayers, diviners, necromancers, and the like. Long before the time of Moses, we read of consultations of the spirits of the dead, and the veneration of demons as helpers and guides, to whom it was the custom to resort. Special statutes were given against it in the laws of Moses, as great unfaithfulness and sin against God. The assumption all the way through is, that there was reality in what was pretended in these instances, and a very dangerous iniquity. The lying prophets whom Ahab followed to his ruin, were really inspired by wicked spirits. Paul encountered a girl at Philippi,

---

* See an argument on this subject elaborated in the *Lectures and Addresses* of Alexander Campbell, pp. 379–402.

† Compare Deuteronomy 18 : 10 ; 32 : 17 ; Leviticus 17 : 7, *et seq.* ; 2 Chronicles 11 : 15 ; Psalms 106–37.

whose keepers got great gain from her extraordinary powers resulting from being possessed of an evil spirit. He cast out the demon, and her peculiar power was gone, and Paul was thrust into prison for interfering with the men's business. This case explains the whole system of heathen oracles and mantology, as the heathen writers themselves explained it.

Modern spiritism, or so-called *spiritualism*, is but a revival of the same thing—a branch of the same iniquity. There doubtless is some reality in it ; and it is confessedly a system of intercourse with the dead, whose spirits are invoked in various forms and methods, to teach wisdom ; to dictate faith, religion, and life ; to comfort and help in trouble and necessity ; and to serve as saviours and as gods. It is demon-worship brought to life again. It claims to have vast multitudes of adherents, even among the baptized and nominally Christian. It is influencing whole communities of men and women, who are prepared to commit themselves body and soul, for time and eternity, into the care of these lying demon guides. It has made inroads upon people of all classes, and is received by many as a distinct and the only true religion. Its oracles are loud and hopeful in the prediction, that it will soon enlist to itself the governments and reigning classes of the whole world. The Word of God also forewarns, that it will be vastly successful. "The Spirit speaketh expressly, that in the latter times some shall depart from the faith, giving heed to seducing spirits, and doctrines of devils* speaking lies in hypocrisy, having their conscience seared with a hot iron, forbidding to marry, and commanding to abstain from meats." (1 Tim. 4 : 1–3.)† Instead of fearing, loving, and trusting in God above all things, people will bestow their loving confidence upon unclean spirits, invoking them for guidance, and placing religious dependence in their impious falsities. Having no relish for the saving Gospel of Christ, God will send them strong delusion, that they may believe a lie, and be visited with the damnation their perverseness deserves. And at the time this sixth trumpet sounds, the prevailing religion of the world will be this selfsame worship of demons, and following of demons' doctrines.

2. In connection with this demon-worship, will be *the revival of idolatry*. It is itself idolatry ; but, with it, idols of gold, and silver, and copper, and stone, and wood, which can neither see, nor hear, nor walk, will again command the genius of men for their construction, and be set up to please their demon-lords, to facilitate spiritual intercourse, and to help out the foul devotions of the infatuated people.

It may appear too disparaging to the understanding of this enlightened age, to entertain the possibility of a return to the ancient worship of images. People may feel insulted at the thought. But the way for it is opening, and the process to effect it is already going on. The minds of anti-christian religionists everywhere are fast relapsing into the old heathenish philosophies, and I know not what is to hinder their acceptance of the religions with which those philosophies are conjoined. Modifications of them may be made, to conform them somewhat to the requirements of an altered condition of the public mind and taste ; but idol-worship will again become, as it is even now becoming, the religion of some who claim to be among the most enlightened and the very illuminators of mankind. Socrates had his demon-guide, and Socrates

---

* Διδασκαλίαι δαιμονίων—*doctrines suggested by demons ;* doctrines engendered by the operation of evil spirits. The sense of this passage has been wrongly given by Mede and many others, in understanding the genitive as objective, as if it meant *doctrines concerning demons.* The true and only tenable exegesis is, not that men shall apostatize by accepting doctrines *about* demons, but that they will decline from the true mystery of godliness by taking into their confidence *doctrines which demons teach.*—*See Wordsworth, Alford, Conybeare and Howson, &c.*

† For an exposition of this text in its application to modern "*spiritualism,*" see *Prophetic Times,* vol. ii, pp. 158, 174, 185 ; vol. iii, pp. 14, 30, 46, 62, 75 ; vol. v, p. 134. On the general subject, see the author's monograph, entitled "*The Wonderful Confederation.*" Epiphanius, as given and translated by Mede (p. 637), thus paraphrases the passage : "Some shall apostatize from the sound doctrine, giving heed to fables and doctrines of demons ; for *they shall be worshippers of dead men, as they were worshipped in Israel.*"

approved idolatry ; and if men accept the Socratic philosophy in preference to the religion of the Bible, and submit to be taught by demons as their most trustworthy oracles, what is to prevent them from becoming philosophic idol-worshippers, especially if their spirit-friends should so dictate, and accompany those dictations with the power of working wonders. A little further on in this book, we read of a " false prophet," who teaches the dwellers upon earth to make *an image*, to which he gives the power of utterance, so that it both speaks and causes all who refuse to worship it to be put to death. (Rev. 13 : 14-16.)* All this is simply the culmination of the system already in vogue, showing a base, persecuting, and murderous idolatry, also the source and manner of its introduction. The symptoms and tendencies are even now strongly in this very direction. What is *Planchette*, but a household god to many, who resort to it as a means of spiritual communion, and speak to it, interrogate it, and reverently seek unto it, for light, consolation, and guidance ? What are the numerous and various inventions, constructed and constructing to please the spirits, and meant to serve as material forms and instruments through which the demon-gods are to manifest themselves, and hold communion with their devotees ? Is not much of the best science and mechanical skill of spiritualists now employed, in answer to spirit-bidding, fashioning implements for closer and easier commerce with these invisible powers ? Do not such machines and images of gold, and silver, and copper, and stone, and wood, already exist ? And are they not kept in devoted places as holy things, made the centres of circles of people gathered around them for intercourse with devils, as with the world of hope and blessedness, consulted with pious affection, and guarded and revered with all the awe, and sometimes tearful devotion with which the ancient heathen approached the oracles and images of their gods ? Only let all this grow and mature, in the line in which it has begun and is growing, and bald image-worship will soon live again in what claims to be the enlightened society of modern times, and men and women of boasted intelligence will everywhere be found paying their adorations at the shrines of devils, as to gods. And just this is one of the leading features of the time when the sixth trumpet sounds.

3. And corresponding with the heathen character of the dominant religion, will then be *a heathen state of morals also.*

Murder will be among the commonest of crimes. Sensual and selfish passion will make sad havoc of human life, with no serious thought about it on the part of the leaders of public sentiment. Fœticide, infanticide, homicide, and all forms of sin against human life, will characterize society, and be tolerated and passed as if no great harm were done. And well would it be for us, if such were not largely the state of things even now.

Sorceries, impure practices with evil agencies, and particularly with poisonous drugs, is also given as one of the dominant forms of vice and sin in those days. The word specially includes tampering with one's own or another's health, by means of drugs, potions, intoxications, and often with magical arts and incantations, the invocation of spiritual agencies, the putting under influences promotive of sins of impurity both bodily and spiritual. We have only to think of the use of alcoholic stimulants,† of opium, of tobacco, of the rage for cosmetics and medicaments to increase love attractions, of resorts to the pharmacopœia in connection with sensuality,—of the magical agents

---

* In describing these idols, in verse 20, John says that they " can neither *see*, nor *hear*, nor *walk* ; " but he specially refrains from saying that they cannot *speak*, or give out oracles ; for here he tells us that one at least *does speak*, so as to give intimation of the will of the gods who communicate through it. Grotius relates out of an ecclesiastical writer, that there was a statue of the notorious magician, Apollonius, which *spoke, being actuated by some assistant demon.*

† *Matheetees, Apocalypse Expounded*, says : " It is remarkable, that the sin of drunkenness is not among those here enumerated." He is entirely mistaken. The word φαρμακεία—the use of φάρμακα—directly embraces indulgence in intoxicating potions. It is a generic term including drunkenness among its leading species.

and treatments alleged to come from the spirit-world for the benefit of people in this,—of the thousand impositions in the way of medicines and remedial agents, encouraging mankind to recklessness in transgression with the hope of easily repairing the damages of nature's penalties,—of the growing prevalence of crime induced by these things, setting loose and stimulating to activity the vilest passions, which are eating out the moral sense of society,— for the beginnings of that moral degeneracy to which the seer here alludes as characteristic of the period when the sixth trumpet is sounded.

And interlinked with these sorceries, and reacting the one on the other, will also be the general subversion of marriage and its laws, and the deluging of society with the sins of fornication and adultery. The Apostle uses the word " fornication " alone, as embracing all forms of lewdness, but as if to intimate that marriage will then be hardly recognized any more. And already we hear the institution of legal wedlock denounced and condemned as tyrannical, and all rules, but those of affinity and desire, repudiated as unjust. Already, in some circles, we find the doctrines of *free love* put forth and defended in the name of right, a better religion, and a higher law. And it would be strange indeed, if the revival of the old heathen philosophies and religions, which justified, sanctioned, and sanctified promiscuous concubinage, did not also bring with it a revival of all these old heathen abominations. So also has the holy apostle written, that " in the last days . . . men shall be . . . *incontinent.*" And here the seer enumerates " fornication " as one of the out-standing features in the social character of those times.

And last in the catalogue stands the statement of general and abounding *dishonesty*, the obliteration of moral distinctions, the disregard of other's rights, and the practice of fraud, theft, and deceit wherever it is possible. Pollok makes his ancient bard of earth tell of a time, when

> ——" Blood trod upon the heels of Blood ;
> Revenge, in desperate mood, at midnight met
> Revenge ; War brayed to War, Deceit deceived
> Deceit, Lie cheated Lie, and Treachery
> Mined under Treachery, and Perjury
> Swore back go Perjury, and Blasphemy
> Arose with hideous Blasphemy, and Curse
> Loud answered Curse ; and drunkard, stumbling fell
> O'er drunkard fallen ; and husband husband met
> Returning each from other's bed defiled ;
> Thief stole from thief, and robber on the way
> Knocked robber down ; and Lewdness, Violence,
> And Hate, met Lewdness, Violence, and Hate.
> And Mercy, weary with beseeching, had
> Retired behind the sword of Justice, red
> With ultimate and unrepenting wrath."

And that time, with just this condition of things, will have come, when this sixth trumpet sounds. We need not wonder, therefore, that it brings a plague of horror and judgment upon mankind, exceeding all that we yet have had to contemplate.*

* " We may, a moment or two, compare the state of men at that time with former times, when the long-suffering of God was exhausted, and judgment burst forth.

" 1. This day is worse than the times of the flood. Then the earth was corrupt before God, and filled with violence. Here corruption of every kind, both between man and man, and man and the Most High, prevails ; and murders, the highest of the crimes of violence, are numerous. Besides this, there are idolatry and demon-worship, which are not named as existing before the flood. If then, even in that day, and despite of their few advantages, wrath broke out, overturning the usual course of things, how much more then !

" 2. Of the men of Sodom we read, that they were ' wicked, and sinners before the Lord exceedingly.' Sins of Sodom are here, and others superadded. If miracle avenged iniquity then, much more now !

" 3. Oppression, rising even to murder, sorcery, and idolatry, were found in Egypt. But other sins are found here. No marvel then, if plagues like those of Egypt overtake the world then !

" 4. Like to these were the sins of the nations of Canaan, when God commanded their

Notice then,

II. THE NATURE OF THIS VISITATION.

1. *It is evoked by a cry out of the four horns of the altar.* It comes from the immediate presence of God, and therefore with the sanction of God. The call itself is the common voice of all four of the horns of the altar, indicating the energy and the universality of the demand for vengeance, and of that vengeance itself. The call from the altar also reflects the character of a particular apostasy for which this invitation is sent. When there is a voice invocative of judgment, the locality of it expresses where the sin has been which is to be avenged. The voice that went up against Cain for the murder of his brother, cried from the ground which had received Abel's blood. The voice of woe to him that buildeth a town with blood, and establisheth a city by iniquity, comes from the stones and beams of the houses of that town and city. And when a call for retribution comes from the altar, it is because of some great crimes against that altar, and what connects with it. The united outcry of these golden horns tells of iniquity with special reference to them. They were not mere ornaments. God ordered them there to receive the blood of sacrifice for Israel's sins on the great day of atonement, and whensoever the whole people would seek to purge themselves from their transgressions. In these cases there went up from these golden horns the voice of blood, crying to God to spare. But here is a voice for the letting loose of the powers of judgment. The implication is that God's appointed way of forgiveness has been set aside ; that the Divine system of gracious atonement and salvation has been rejected and despised ; that the one propitiation provided of God has been abandoned and contemned ; that the great High Priest and only Mediator between God and man has been disowned, and thrust away to give place to other helpers ; that mankind in their guilt have blasphemously pronounced against God's plan of reconciliation ; and that the wickedness of earth has risen so high, especially in point of antagonism to the cross, and the doctrine of redemption by the blood of Jesus, that even the altar itself, which otherwise cries only for mercy, is forced into a cry for vengeance. It is terrible enough when *sin* cries to God against the transgressor ; but when the very altar, sin's only recourse, and the very horns of the altar, the sinner's only availing pleaders, unite in that cry, and utter it before God as their own, it is impossible to conceive an intenser density of gathering retribution, or a heavier surcharge of the enginery of the Almighty's judgments.

2. *The command issues to the Angel who sounds this trumpet.* This is further proof that these angel-trumpeters are of a superior order. Other angels are concerned, and yet this particular angel has binding and loosing power over them. The command itself, is the command of the contemned Saviour. It goes out from the presence of Almighty Sovereignty, and with its sanctions.

extermination by Israel. On them fell supernatural judgments, combined with the sword of the tribes.

" 5. The days of Ahab and Jezebel resemble these. Then was there murder of the righteous, and taking of his inheritance by fraud ; fornication, idolatry, and sorcery. Then fell the judgment of three and a half years' drought. Why should it not fall again on earth under like or greater sins ?

" 6. These are like the times of Israel and Judah, when Nebuchadnezzar sent and carried them away captives, destroying temple and city. Is it any wonder then, if the next chapter but one foretells judgment coming on both the temple and metropolis of Israel once more ? The type of the Assyrian came in Zedekiah's days ; but now that transgressors are come to the full, the great usurper appears.

" The world has heard the Gospel and refused it. Far greater is its responsibility in that day, than in any previous one. Far stouter and more deeply rooted is its attitude of resistance, than at any former time.

" Things are advancing with no slack pace towards this dismal consummation. Beneath the thin crust of formal Christianity, the germs of these trespassers here and there peep forth. Idolatry is putting forth its feelers ; and the giving heed to seducing spirits is already visible. On this basis all the other evils will establish themselves."—*The Apocalypse Expounded by Scripture,* vol. ii, pp. 438, 439.

But it is addressed to the angel. He obeys it as his Divine commission, and thus presides over the administration ushered in by his trumpet. He looses the imprisoned forces, and sets them free for action. And thus, from under his hand go forth the powers which smite the impious dwellers on the earth with terror, death, and torment.

3. *Other angels are the more direct executors of the woe.* Some have taken these to be good angels. I do not so regard them. Good angels are free, not bound. Good angels would not destroy men, except by special command of God ; but these had only to be *loosed,* and they at once rushed forth for slaughter, impelled to the dreadful business by their own malicious nature. But for their being bound, the implication is that they would have done the same all along. We also read of apostate angels whom God hath " delivered into chains of darkness, to be reserved unto the judgment of the great day." (2 Pet. 2 : 4 ; Jude 6.) This would seem to imply that, when the great day comes, they may perchance, for particular purposes, have their bonds relaxed. The common idea is that they are reserved for their own judgment ; but it may after all be for some one else's judgment. These woes all belong to the administrations of " the great day." This sixth trumpet is quite on the margin of the mighty consummation of all that day's proceedings. And if the record implies any such loosing of those everlasting chains, here is the place and time for it ; and what this trumpeter-angel did, would seem to be the very loosing referred to. They are not loosed for salvation—not loosed from their reservation unto eternal punishment,—but loosed from their restraint against inflicting death and torment upon men, and now in judgment permitted to act out their evil will upon earth's guilty inhabitants. They were bound in mercy to our race, and here they are let loose in wrath and judgment.

These bound angels " had been made ready for the hour, and day, and month, and year." How had they been made ready, except as fallen angels they had been put in chains, and held in constraint during all the preceding ages, with the foreknowledge and intent of their being loosed at this particular time, for this particular judgment ?

These angels are *four* in number. We know not how many kept not their first estate. There doubtless were very many, and not all of the same rank. Paul enumerates various classes of wicked agencies—the devil, chiefs, powers, world-lords, spirits of wickedness in the aerial regions. (Eph. 6 : 12.) These four are a particular four, " *the four.*" Either the wicked angels, then, are not all bound at one and the same place, or these four are to be regarded as specially distinguished from others in the relation they hold to the kingdom of evil. I infer that they are particular magnates in the realm of evil powers, with large commands and dependencies subject to them. The myriads of subordinate agents which their loosing brings into action, argues in this direction. Perhaps there are but four fallen angels of this particular rank, authority, and temper, with Satan as the chief of all. At any rate, the four evil angels here spoken of, are a particular four, confined to a particular place, held for a particular service, and representatives of myriad hosts, bound with their binding, loosed with their loosing, and acting their will the moment the bands of their forced inaction are taken off. Their number also indicates the universality of their operations.

A particular locality is named as the place of their detention : " *upon,*— ἐπὶ, *over, near, at,—that great river Euphrates.*" It was in this locality that the powers of evil made their first attempts against the human race. It was in this locality that the first murder was committed. It was in this region that the great apostasies, both before and after the flood, had their centres. It was in this region that Israel's most oppressive enemies resided, and that the Jews were compelled to drag out the long and weary years of their great captivity. It was in this region that the great oppressive world-powers took their commencement. It is the region where all this world's beginnings were made—where man first saw the light, first sinned, fell from his first estate, was banished from Paradise, and introduced all earth's miseries—where Satan first alighted upon our planet, won his first triumphs, and first set his foul agencies against man in operation. The Euphrates itself is one of the primeval rivers, and the only one we know of that remains. And there, where guilt came into the place of innocence, and Babylon supplanted Eden, and hell sent up its Upas instead of the Tree of Life, and death came in upon the children of men, these four fallen sons of light, with their evil hosts, rave in the bonds,* imposed in mercy, but, at the appointed hour, in wrath to be relaxed, that earth's blaspheming millions may feel what shall then have been so richly merited.

4. The moment the four bound angels are released from their constraint, *hosts of death-dealing cavalry overrun the earth.* There are such things as supernatural horses. Horses of fire took up Elijah into heaven. Horses and chariots of fire protected Elisha at Dothan. Heavenly horses and horsemen introduce the dominion of Christ, as described in a later chapter in this book. They are the forces which pertain to the celestial kingdom. And here John beholds troops of horse of like unearthly order, but pertaining to an opposite realm, *the infernal cavalry.* They are the powers of the four loosed angels, inbreathed with the spirit of death and destruction, and putting into execution their murderous and malignant will. As there are infernal *locusts*, so there are infernal *horses ;* and as the former were let forth to overrun the world with their torments under the fifth trumpet, so the latter are let forth to overrun the world with still more terrible inflictions under the sixth.

The number of these " hosts of horse " is enormous. Such a cavalcade in point of multitude, has never been marshalled on earth. John could not count them. No spectator could count them. They are as multitudinous as the Psalmist's chariots of God. (Ps. 68 : 17.) John " *heard* the number of them : " " two myriads of myriads," just two hundred millions, one-sixth as many as the present entire population of the globe ! This one particular should settle forever, that Turkish cavalry and the Moslem conquests are in no proper sense the subjects of this vision.

What the seer describes, he calls *horses*, while yet he says that they are not proper horses. Their heads are like lions' heads. Their tails are serpentine, *eels*, one of the fathers calls them, and terminate in heads like serpents' heads. They have riders, and yet the riders are parts of themselves, to whom no separate actions are ascribed. It is not the riders but *the horses* which do all the mischief. They are covered with coats of mail, the colours of which are the colours of fire, and hyacinthe, and sulphur, answering to the elements which they emit from their mouths. They do not eat, nor does it appear that they are capable of being wounded or killed. " Out of their mouths issueth fire, and smoke, and sulphur," the very elements of hell. Though leonine, they do not seize with their jaws, nor take flesh into their mouths, nor slay with teeth or claws. They stifle and destroy with their sooty, sulphureous, fiery breath—with " the fire, and the smoke, and the sulphur, which issueth

---

* It is an old Rabbinical tradition, dwelt upon by Heinrichs, that evil spirits are detained, and have their place in the deserts bordering on the Euphrates. This idea was doubtless derived from the Scriptures themselves. Isaiah represents Babylon as doomed to be the abode of *Ziim*, or evil spirits of the desert. The goat for Azazel, in the ceremonies of the great day of atonement, was always conveyed out into the wilderness. It is, indeed, not known what is meant by Azazel ; but the scape-goat was burdened with the sins of Israel, and sent to destruction ; which, in the oriental mind, would mean, to where the cursed spirits are. The Book of Enoch represents Azazel as an apostate angel, and says, " The Lord said to Raphael, bind Azazel hand and foot ; cast him into darkness ; and, opening *the desert in Dudael*, cast him in there." 10 : 6, 7. The Saviour himself says of the unclean spirit gone out of a man, that he " *walketh through dry* [desert] *places*, seeking rest and finding none ; " that is, as Liddell and Scott explain the word, in places " like the Delta of Egypt," " *and therefore in the East*," adds Green. The region of the Euphrates, above all, abounds with the sort of territory which the Jews regarded as the abode of evil spirits. Its topography and its history are such, that, if evil spirits are at all consigned to earthly spaces, as seems to be the case, it is just here that we would most naturally expect to find them in greatest numbers.

out of their mouths." Some say this means gunpowder, discharged from the muzzles of fire-arms and *cannon!* But, strange to say, when it comes to a following chapter, where it is recorded of the two prophesying witnesses, that "if any man will hurt them, fire proceedeth out of their mouth and devoureth their enemies," these interpreters at once drop gunpowder, and substitute prophetic denunciations and prayers ! If it is gunpowder in one place, it must be gunpowder in the other. But it is neither gunpowder nor prayers in either case, but simply what the holy seer says it is,—the elements of hell hurled upon the guilty while they still live in the flesh ; in the one case by the holy power of God direct, and in the other through the agency of malicious and infernal spirit-powers, which are permitted to put themselves forth in these horrid forms. Israel was once exhorted to consider that Egypt's horsemen were "flesh and not spirit ; " but here the case is reversed, and men have to do with horses and horsemen which are *spirit and not flesh.*＊

These agents have two means of harming men. They stifle and kill by what they belch forth from their mouths, and they hurt and injure with their snake-headed tails ; "for the power of the horses is in their mouths, and in their tails." As to what issues from their mouths, it would seem as if it were not always the same, but varying and alternating between fire, smoke, and sulphureous fumes ; either being fatal to human life. The fire would scorch and burn men to death, and the smoke or the sulphur would stifle and smother them. The three things are named as "three plagues," and the description is, that life is destroyed by each separately, as well as by the three conjointly.†
Hence, to meet one of these two hundred millions of infernal horses face to face, is certain death, either by burning or stifling. As to the serpentine tails, nothing is said of power to kill, but only of power to injure, to lame, maim, sting, or hurt.

The idea of serpentine tails suggests a capacity for lashing with painful and disabling strokes ; whilst the snake-heads at the ends suggest the additional capacity to bite and sting. At any rate, the tails of these horses are parts of the horses themselves, used by them as instruments of mischief, by which great suffering is inflicted. Yet Elliott, Barnes, and commentators of their class, see nothing in these appendages, but the tails cut from dead horses, dried, and hung on poles, which the Turks carry as standards ! Well may Alford remark, "I will venture to say, that a more self-condemnatory interpretation was never broached than this of the horsetails of the Pachas."

5. *Fearful havoc of human life is made by these infernal horses.* To say nothing of the dread and horror which their presence inspires, and the confusion which their advent strikes into every department of society, it is here written, that, by these horses, *one out of every three of the whole human family is killed*, destroyed from the face of the earth. It was a dreadful time for Egypt, when the destroying angel went through the land and smote down the first-born of every house. It evoked a cry from that guilty people, at which the world still trembles whenever the record is recited. But there, there could scarcely have been more than one in every ten ; whilst here one out of every three is killed. Suppose the population of the earth to consist of twelve hundred millions, this one visitation takes off four hundred millions— more than ten times as many as the entire population of the United States ! Nor would the mere numbers of the slain be so appalling, but for the dreadful manner in which they are put to death, and the awful dangers amid which the living are necessitated to do for the dead.

6. *The continuance of this plague is equally extraordinary.* The tormenting

---

＊ " We must not here think of earthly human horsemen."—*Ebrard in loc.*

† " We have here *three* destructive agencies, emphatically distinguished as *separate agencies*. It is first stated generally that the third part of men was destroyed by these three, and then, to prevent as it were a mistake, the three are again separately enumerated, each with its own article, *by the fire*, and *by the smoke*, and *by the brimstone*."—*T. K. Arnold.* Ebrard interprets the passage in the same way.

locusts continued for *five* months ; this, it would seem, is to continue for more than *thirteen.* " The hour, and day, and month, and year," noted by the seer, would seem most naturally intended to measure the exact duration of the plague. If so, it is to last one year, one month, one day, and one hour. The four specifications are given with a single article, which accordingly embraces them as a single period of time ; and the adding of these specifications together assigns to these operations just a day and an hour more than thirteen months.* Think of having to live amid such perils and such scenes, subject every moment to be horrified, smitten, stung, stifled and destroyed, for the space of three hundred and ninety-one days, with men, women, and children, associates and friends suffering and dying about you every day and every hour, killed by the visible monsters of hell, that throng about your path by day and about your dwelling at night ? The mere contemplation of it makes one's flesh chill with horror ! What then, must it be for those who experience it !

7. *The object of this woe is partly retributive and partly reformatory.* It belongs to the judicial administrations of the great day. It is God's terrific judgment upon the world, which has disowned allegiance to Him, and rejected the mediation of His Son. It is the righteous indignation of outraged justice which can no longer endure the superlative wickednesses of men. The trampled law of eternal right must assert its dignity. Christ cannot submit to the taunts, and thongs, and mockery of Pilate's hall forever. The blood of the covenant cannot be trampled under foot, and accounted an unholy thing, with unceasing impunity. There is a point over which the greatest forbearance and long-suffering dare not go, and at which mercy itself cries out for unsparing justice. And as these people, against all the light and warnings sent them, still drive on with their devil-worship, idolatry, murders, sorceries, lewdness, and dishonesties, until they have filled the measure of their guilt, and wearied out the very patience of indulgent God, the horses of hell are let loose upon them, to sweep one-third of them to speedy perdition.

And yet, in wrath God remembers mercy. He suffers only one-third of the race to fall a prey to this tremendous woe. Two-thirds of mankind He spares, not because they deserve to be spared, but that by means of their awful trials they might perchance be led to repent of their sins, and lay hold of salvation before it is clean gone forever. Ah, yes, the Lord is good and gracious, even in the severest of his visitations. He delighteth not in the death of the wicked, but would rather that they should turn from their evil ways and live.

But alas for those who continue in sin till trouble brings them to a better life ! Those content to give their good days to the devil's service, seldom come to reformation in their evil days. While the pressure of judgment is on them, they may cry, God have mercy ! and think to lead a different life ; but their vows and prayers vanish with their sorrows, and they are presently where they were before, only the more hardened in their iniquities. Thus was it in this case. The powers of hell had been let loose upon the guilty world. Times of danger, death, and horror, fell upon the people. The wrath of offended God flashed through the earth for thirteen months, until it seemed as if the entire race would be consumed. A plague unprecedented stripped the globe of one-third of its population, by a form of death giving visible demonstration of the truth of God's warnings to the wicked. There was left no room for any one any more to doubt the reality of hell, or his close proximity to it ; for hell had come in upon the earth ! And yet, " the rest of the men, who were not killed by these plagues, *repented not* from the works of their hands, that they should

---

* So Elliott conceives the meaning of the passage, aggregating together the hour, day, month, and year. There is a parallel instance in Daniel 12 : 7, where the Septuagint has εις καιρον, καιρους, και ημισυ καιρου ; *for a time, times, and half a time,* which is accepted as a chronological formula equivalent to the aggregated sum of the three specifications ; that is, a year, two years, and half a year added together, making twelve hundred and sixty days. So here we have the same εις followed by similar specifications of time, which, aggregated into one sum, make a period of thirteen months, one day, and one hour, during which this killing and injuring are to go on.

not worship the demons, and the idols of gold, and silver, and copper, and stone, and wood, which can neither see, nor hear, nor walk ; and *they repented not* out of their murders, nor out of their sorceries, nor out of their fornication, nor out of their thefts."

Such is depraved and infatuated human nature. " Though thou shouldest bray a fool in a mortar among wheat with a pestle, yet will not his foolishness depart from him." (Prov. 27 : 22.) If people will not listen in the days of peaceful opportunity, there remaineth very little hope for them. " If they hear not Moses and the prophets, neither will they be persuaded, though one rose from the dead." (Luke 16 : 31.)

LECTURE TWENTY-FIRST

REV. 10 : 1–11. (Revised Text.) And I saw another, a mighty angel descending out of the heaven, clothed about with a cloud, and the rainbow on his head, and his face as it were the sun, and his feet as it were pillars of fire, and having in his hand a little book [or roll] opened ; and he set his right foot upon the sea, but the left upon the land ; and he cried with a great voice even as a lion roareth ; and when he cried, the seven thunders uttered their voices ; and when the seven thunders spoke, I was about to write ; and I heard a voice out of the heaven saying, Seal up those things which the seven thunders spoke, and write them not.

And the angel whom I saw standing upon the sea and upon the land lifted up his right hand into the heaven, and sware by him that liveth for the ages of the ages, who created the heaven and the things in it, and the earth and the things in it, and the sea and the things in it, that there shall be no more delay ; but in the days of the voice of the seventh angel, when he shall sound, the mystery of God is [to be] fulfilled, even as he preached (glad tidings) to his servants the prophets.

And the voice which I heard out of the heaven [I heard] again speaking with me, and saying : Go, take the book [or roll] which is opened in the hand of the angel who standeth upon the sea and upon the land. And I went to the angel, saying to him, Give me the little book. And he saith to me, Take, and eat it, and it shall make bitter thy belly, but in thy mouth it shall be sweet as honey. And I took the little book out of the hand of the angel and ate it ; and it was in my mouth sweet as honey ; and as soon as I had eaten it, my belly was made bitter. And it was said to me, Thou must prophesy again upon peoples, and nations, and tongues, and kings many.

THIS part of the Apocalypse is sometimes treated as an episode, thrown between the second and third woe-trumpets, and having little or no relation to either. This is an error. We have still to deal with the blast of the sixth Trumpet. It is only in the fourteenth verse of the eleventh chapter, that we find the note of indication that the woe of the sixth Trumpet is accomplished. What now comes before us accordingly pertains to the sixth Trumpet, the same as the sealing of the 144,000, in chapter seven, pertained to the sixth Seal. It introduces new subjects and phases of the judgment administrations, but continues the same general narrative and burden found in what precedes and follows. God give us soberness of thought and earnestness of consideration, as we proceed to unfold what is here written for our learning !

We observe,

I. A VISION OF A VERY NOTABLE PERSON.

John writes, " *And I saw another, a mighty angel descending out of the heaven.*" This person I take to be the Lord Jesus himself. He is called an *Angel*, but there is nothing in that to prove him a created being. *Angel* is a title of office, not of nature. In the Old Testament the Son of God is continually described as the Jehovah-angel. We had a somewhat corresponding vision in the first chapter ; yet, he who there appeared, announced himself as the First and the Last, the Living One, who became dead and is alive forever. We had an account of an angel in the seventh chapter, and again in the eighth, whom there was reason to regard as none other than the Lord Jesus. We do know that he appears in the Apocalypse as a Lamb, as a Lion, and as an armed Warrior, and there is nothing to hinder his appearance also as an Angel.

This person is also very particularly distinguished from other angels who appear in these visions. He is not one of the four loosed from the Euphrates, nor one of the seven who sound the Trumpets, but quite " *another.*"

He is further described as " a *mighty* angel." This would seem to identify him as the " strong " Lord who judges Babylon, and the mighty One on whom God hath laid help, even Christ. When no more is said of an angel than simply that he is strong, or mighty, there is no reason to suspect anything but a created being, for all angels are powerful ; but when this quality is referred to as a mark of distinction among other high angels, and is conjoined with what does not properly belong to angels, it is to be taken as equivalent to Almightiness, and as meant to denote a being who is uncreated and divine.

The attire of this angel indicates Deity. John beholds him " *clothed about with a cloud.*" Wherever clouds are connected with glorious manifestations, there we find the presence of Divinity. If there is cloud, there is mystery ; and if there is mystery, there is suggestion of Deity. The Lord descended on Mount Sinai in *a thick cloud.* He appeared on the mercy-seat *in a cloud.* When Israel was delivered, " the Lord went before them by day *in a pillar of cloud.*" When the glory of the Lord filled the tabernacle, " *a cloud* covered the tent of the congregation." When God reproached Israel for their murmurings, " the glory of the Lord appeared *in the cloud.*" " The Lord said unto Moses, Lo, I come unto thee *in a thick cloud.*" The Psalmist gives it as the characteristic of the Almighty, that " *clouds and darkness* are round about him ; " that " he maketh *the clouds* his chariot : " and that about him are " *thick clouds.*" When the King of glory cometh in his divine majesty to judge the earth, the exclamation is : " Behold, he cometh *with clouds.*" Clouds, therefore, belong to the attire of Deity, particularly in his manifestations toward fallen men. They indicate his unapproachableness, his infinite majesty, his consuming power toward sin, which cannot live before his uncovered glory, and yet his drawing near to communicate with the dwellers upon earth. No mere angel is ever arrayed in such drapery, and the vision is that of the glorious Godman himself, in the midst of the grand administrations of judgment.

He has " *the rainbow on his head ; *" not *a* rainbow, but *the* rainbow. This is a further mark to show that he is not a created angel. We had this rainbow in the fourth chapter, where it is given as one of the grand appurtenances of the throne. It refers back to God's ancient covenant with the earth. It was originally ordained as God's mark in the cloud, and the sign of *His*, and no mere angel's covenant. We never read of any one surrounded with the rainbow, but the person is God. The clouds are indicative of Divine judgment, and storms, and rains, and floods of wrath ; and so the rainbow is indicative of Divine mercy in the midst of judgment, and a covenant of security to the believing, even though everything seem to be going to destruction. A garment of cloud, and a tiara of the iris, would, therefore, well befit the Saviour, in the administrations which we are now considering, but would in no manner of truth be suitable to a mere angel, however mighty.

" *And his face as it were the sun.*" This again identifies him as the same who appeared unto John in his first vision. It is there said of Him who walks in the midst of the golden candlesticks, that his countenance was " as the sun shineth in his strength." This luminousness of face is also one of the ascertained characteristics of Christ, in connection with the final revelation of his kingdom. Peter speaks of the appearance on the Mount of Transfiguration, as a foretaste and earnest of " the power and coming of our Lord Jesus Christ ; " and yet, in that sublime picture, the record is, " *his face did shine as the sun.*" It was thus that he appeared unto Saul of Tarsus, on his way to Damascus. (Acts 26 : 13.) And from the most ancient times, the prophets were accustomed to refer to him as the outbeaming glory of God—the very Sun of Righteousness.

" *And his feet as it were pillars of fire.*" These are manifestly the same feet beheld in the vision of the first chapter. There they dazzled the eyes of the seer, like fine brass melted and glowing in a furnace ; and they were the feet of Him who was dead, but is alive forevermore, and has the keys of death and of hell. There they presented an image of terrible pureness, and here they furnish an image of steadfast and consuming majesty, which no one can encounter and live. Nothing of the kind is ever affirmed of a created angel. We observe again,

II. A Notable Act of this Person.

" *And he set his right foot upon the sea, but the left upon the earth.*" This was a distinct and deliberate act, and is full of significance. To set one's foot in a place, expresses a purpose to take possession of that place. Jehovah said to Israel, " Every place whereon the soles of your feet shall tread shall be yours." (Deut. 11 : 24.) Abraham could not " set his foot on " any part of Palestine in this sense, inasmuch as God gave him none inheritance in it. And when this mighty Angel deliberately sets his right foot on the sea, and the left on the land, he thereby claims possession of it, and asserts his purpose to take it as his own, and to establish his occupancy and rule over it. It is an act befitting the character and office of Christ, but hardly a created angel. He is the rightful sovereign of sea and land. His taking of the sealed book from the hand of eternal majesty, and his breaking and destroying of its seals, proved and legitimated his right to the possession of the earth ; and here we have his assertion of that right, and his purpose to enforce it. Long has both sea and land been under the dominion of his enemies, but now he sets foot on each, and takes hold upon them as his own.

He does it also in a way which shows how useless it will be for his foes to resist him. Those feet are mighty columns of fire. Who can stand against columns of fire ? The image is one of invincible power and steadfastness, joined with consuming destruction to those who venture to withstand. Pillars are firm and mighty ; and pillars of fire are steadfastly irresistible ; and Christ plants his feet on sea and land " as pillars of fire." They are then immovable, and must needs consume all opposition.

And with the symbolic act, and as part of it, there is a corresponding utterance. " *He cried with a great voice, even as a lion roareth.*" It was not a cry of distress and fear, but a shout of power, and the herald of vengeance upon enemies and usurpers. We have already seen who it is that is called " the Lion from the tribe of Judah." Of old it was written, " The Lord shall roar out of Zion, and utter his voice from Jerusalem ; and the heavens and the earth shall shake." " The Lord shall roar from on high, and utter his voice from his holy habitation : he shall give a shout, as they that tread the grapes, against all the inhabitants of the earth. A noise shall come even to the ends of the earth : for the Lord hath a controversey with the nations, he will plead with all flesh, he will give them that are wicked to the sword." (Jer. 25 : 29–31.) And the great voice before us connects directly with these predictions. It is not the voice of a created angel, but the cry of the almighty Judge himself. As yet he is in his cloud, like the lion in his covert. But when he comes forth to set his feet upon the earth, the shout, like of those who tread the grapes, shall be given, and the winepress of the Divine fury shall be trodden. It is the cry for and the herald of the oncoming judgments of God ; and upon it follows,

III. A Notable Response from Heaven.

" *And when he cried, the seven thunders uttered their voices.*" Interpreters have been much tasked to tell what particular thunders are here meant. Seven times is thunder called " the voice of the Lord," in the 29th Psalm, and some pretend to find these seven thunders there, but what to make of them as thus found, they know not. Certain writers have spoken of "the thunders of the Vatican," and so some think they see these seven thunders in the bulls of the Popes against Luther and the Reformation ! But if we cannot find " the seven thunders " without resorts so remote and puerile, we might as well confess that we know nothing about them.

They are mentioned with the definite article. The force of this is that these are thunders of which the Apostle assumes that his readers already have some

H

knowledge. And if we will only go back in the record, we will find that we have heard of them before. In the vision of the fourth chapter, John saw " a rainbow " encircling the throne, and here he speaks of *that* rainbow (ἡ ἰρις) as upon the head of this mighty Angel. And in that same vision he beheld and said " out of the throne go forth lightnings, and voices, and *thunders.*" They are not specified as " *seven,*" but in the nature of the case, upon the principle on which the number seven is employed in this book, seven is their number. That is the number of dispensational completeness, and these thunders from the judgment throne are *the* thunders of the entire administration from that throne. They may, therefore, be very properly referred to as specifically " *the seven thunders.*" Some detonations of these same thunders were also remarked in the eighth chapter ; for, as the Priest-Angel turned the contents of his fire-filled censer upon the earth, " there followed *thunderings,* and lightnings, and voices."* They are the judgment thunders, and hence must proceed from the judgment throne, and everything attendant on that throne takes the characteristic number seven : " seven torches," " seven spirits of God," " seven seals," " seven angels," " seven trumpets," " seven vials ; " and for the same reason, and in the same sense, necessarily " seven thunders " of the Divine indignation.

The first readers of the Apocalypse, therefore, had no occasion to go to the 29th Psalm, nor yet to wait fifteen hundred years for the Pope's bulls against the Reformers, in order to find what thunders John here had in view. " The seven thunders " are the judgment thunders of the throne of God. And when the Lion from the tribe of Judah gives his roar, as on the eve of bounding forth upon the prey, these seven thunders utter themselves in full sympathy with the proceeding, and the righteous vengeance of the throne of eternal majesty vocalizes the sentences to be visited upon the guilty and still rebellious world. Verily, no created angel could thus evoke the seven thunders of the Almighty's wrath.

There is also a sort of personality ascribed to these thunders. It is amazing how everything takes animation, and becomes instinct with life, intelligence, and sympathy with the heavenly movements, in these awful processes. The very thunders have distinct articulation added to their terrific detonations. They speak ; they give forth intelligible utterances. John heard what they said ; and when the period to which he refers once comes, the dwellers on the earth will doubtless also hear and understand them. Thunder is an expression of the majesty of God, and of his wrath upon transgressors ; and the voices of these " seven thunders " were voices of consummated divine indignation to be launched upon the guilty world, though the seer was not permitted to record what they uttered.

At the beginning of these wonderful visions, he was commanded to write what he saw, and to make it known unto the churches. Therefore he says : " *When the seven thunders spoke, I was about to write : and I heard a voice out of the heaven saying, Seal up those things which the seven thunders spoke, and write them not.*" The command was absolute, and the holy apostle obeyed it. What the seven thunders said, is therefore unwritten and unknown, and must needs remain unknown, till, amid the ongoings of the judgment as here foreshown, they shall answer the great voice of the mighty Angel. And, until then, it is enough, and best, that the children of men should know no more upon this point than that there are such thunders ; that they have utterances to give in sympathy with the lion-cry of Christ when in the act of proceeding to take possession of the sea and land ; and that those voices, in all their terrific majesty, will be heard when the time comes. We observe,

IV. A NOTABLE DOCUMENT IN THE HAND OF THIS PERSON.

As the Angel proceeded to set his right foot upon the sea and his left upon the land, the Apostle saw " *in his hand a little book, or roll.*" This is a marked

* See page 187.

feature, and not without important significance. It is not the main thing in the vision, as Alford and some others have erroneously supposed, but it is an expressive accessory to the thrilling revelation.

The Apocalypse abounds with references to books and records of a remarkable character. The first verse of the fifth chapter disclosed to our view a very notable document, in connection with which all the interest, up to the chapter now before us, has arisen. We had a good deal to observe concerning that book, or roll, at the time. We were then constrained to look upon it as representing the title-deed of the inheritance, forfeited by man, and recovered by the Lamb.* We saw it lifted by that Lion-lamb, amid the adoring shouts of eternity, and one of its seals after another broken open, followed with miraculous commotions, which shook the earth from centre to circumference, and affected even the great orbs of immensity. When the last of the seals was broken, that book was still in the hands of Him who alone, in all the universe, was found worthy to take it, break its seals, or even to look upon it. The breaking of that seal introduced the seven trumpet-angels ; and then, for the time, we lost sight of the wonderful document around which all this interest and these wonders concentre. And as this mighty Angel can be none other than the self-same Lion-lamb who took the book from the hand of eternal majesty, why may not this roll in his hand be the same identical roll lifted from the throne? Some commentators have ridiculed the thought, but I take it to be a most reasonable supposition. If the book in the hand of this Angel be not the same book which the Lamb took from the throne in heaven, then that marvellous document, after all the wonderful interest and events created by it, most strangely and ingloriously disappears, and is never heard of any more forever. Such awe and exultation at its first appearance, and such mighty occurrences attending the mere opening of its seals, beget the expectation and belief, and indeed require, that we should hear of it again ; that it should not be so miserably hustled off the scene ; and that it should have an end befitting its character and its introduction into these visions. But an unaccountably sorry fate does it receive, if we are not to recognize it in the roll in the hand of this Angel.

It is said of the little book now before us that it was " opened." This implies that it had been shut, sealed ; and that what kept it shut, its seals, had been broken off ; all of which accords precisely with what we saw of the book taken by the Lamb.

Both documents were small rolls. They are both designated by the word βιβλιον, which is the diminutive of βιβλος. The one in the hand of the Angel is, also, by some manuscripts, called βιβλαριδιον ; but that is only another diminutive form of the same word, whilst all the best MSS., in one place or another, use precisely the same form of the word for the one which is used for the other.†

The nature of the case would also seem to call for the presence here of the same document which the Lamb had taken from the throne. The Angel is

* See pages 109-115, et seq.

† This little book is mentioned four times, and in the different MSS. and critical editions of the Apocalypse, is called βιβλιον, βιβλαριδιον, βιβλιδαριδιον ; all of which words are diminutives of βιβλος—different forms of the same word, about equal in signification.

In v. 2, the Codex Vaticanus, Cod. Coislinianus, two Codices of Stephens, Baroc. Cod. N. T., Sinaitic 5, Huntington 1, Pet. 2, and Matthaei, read βιβλιον, the same as in the case of the roll taken by the Lamb.

In v. 8, the Codex Alexandrinus, Cod. Basilianus, Cod. Ephraem, Cod. Coisln., Cod. Licestrensis, Aldine N. T., the Vulgate, Lachman, Tischendorf, Thiele, Bengel, Alford, and Tregelles, read βιβλιον.

In v. 9, the Codex Sinaiticus, Codex Basil, Cod. Coisln. Cod. Alexandrinus as corrected by original scribe, original Cod. Ephraem, the Vulgate, Bengel, Tyndale, read βιβλιον.

In v. 10, the Codex Vaticanus, Cod. Sinaiticus, Cod. Coisln., Baroc. Cod. N. T., Huntington 1, Card. Barbarini, Matthaei, the Vulgate, Tyndale, Bengel, &c., read βιβλιον.

And in each of these instances, where one MS. varies from another, or from itself, the word is either βιβλαριδιον, or βιβλιδαριδιον, neither of which can be said really to differ in sense from βιβλια.

engaged in the solemn and sublime act of formally claiming the possession of the earth. He needs his warrant for such an act. Redemption proceeds on a legal foundation. Christ as our Redeemer had to be made under the law. It was necessary that he should fulfil all righteousness. All his successes, triumphs, and exaltations were achieved on the basis of having meritoriously met and answered all demands of the law. He could neither rise from the dead, ascend to the right hand of the Father, propose free forgiveness to men, or dare to repossess man of the forfeited inheritance, except as he had satisfactorily atoned for all man's sins, and in himself meritoriously won and purchased all that he now or ever holds or claims for his redeemed. It was only as he was slain for mankind, and atoned for their unrighteousness, and thus overcame, that he was pronounced worthy to take the book, or open its seals, or act the *Goel* for those whose inheritance had been disponed away, and overrun by aliens. And so neither could he claim and take possession of the earth, and clear it of all foes and usurpers, except upon warrant from the law giving that right as the just due of his perfect righteousness. No man can claim land without showing that he holds his title-deed for it. No one can proceed to execute penalties even upon transgressors, without warrant from the government. And so our mighty *Goel* in proceeding to set his right foot on the sea, and his left on the land, claiming possession of the earth, and about to inflict extirpating punishments upon the rebels who infest it, holds in his hand the open title to it, worthily obtained from the right hand of eternal majesty, displays it to all observers as his warrant from the throne, and challenges the potencies of earth and hell to yield or perish ; whilst all the thunders of Almighty power utter themselves for his support.

The ultimate disposal made of this document is also such as to correspond with the character I have assigned to it, and to identify it as the same that was taken by the Lamb from the hand of sovereign majesty. John says, " *The voice which I heard out of the heaven* [*I heard*] *again speaking with me, and saying, Go, take the book* [or *roll*] *which is opened in the hand of the Angel who standeth upon the sea and upon the land. And I went to the Angel, saying to him, Give me the little book. And he saith to me, Take, and eat it. And I took the little book* [or *roll*] *out of the hand of the Angel, and ate it.*" Thus the history of this βιβλιον terminated. And for what does our blessed Redeemer take the book out of the right hand of eternal sovereignty ? Why does he appear in the court of heaven as a once slain Lamb that he may be accounted worthy to take the book and to open the seals thereof ? What indeed is the great object and intent of all his works and doings, whether on earth or in heaven, to procure rights, titles, and warrants from the throne ? Yea, what ? but that he may give and impart the same to his apostles and believing people, that they may take them, eat them, appropriate them, preach and prophesy them, live on them, and build themselves up with them unto eternal life ? There is no book like the roll which the Lamb takes from the right hand of the Sitter on the throne. It embodies in itself all the prophetic, priestly, and royal rights of Christ, in the attitude of our *Goel*, or Redeemer. It compasses the very spring and kernel of all sacred prophecy, all evangelic preaching, all true faith, all abiding hope. It is the eternal charter, from the right hand of eternal sovereignty, on which reposes the whole right, authority, work, kingdom, and dominion of Jesus, as the Lord and Saviour of men. And the grand intent and purpose of all that he has done in reference to that document, for which he has obtained it and freed it of its seals, and for which he holds it open in his hand as he proceeds to take possession of the earth is, that his people may have the benefit of it—that they may take it from his hand, feed on it, incorporate it with their inmost being, make it the subject of their hopes, their prophecies and their prayers, and in the strength and virtue of it live and reign with him forever. And if we have at all hit upon the nature of the document which John beheld upon the right hand of Him that sitteth upon the throne, the analogy of faith, and the whole congruity of things, come into play to establish and confirm the belief that this βιβλιον, or βιβλαριδιον, in the hand of the Angel, is the same book, and that the Angel who holds it is none other than the Lion from the tribe of Judah, the Root of David, the Lamb that was slain, the blessed Jesus.

The effect of this roll on the prophet likewise corresponds with the view we have taken of it. There is nothing sweeter than the Gospel to a willing and believing soul. The good things which Jesus has obtained for us from the Father, and especially the title to them, are so suitable to us that every child of God can exclaim with the Psalmist : " How sweet are Thy words to my taste ! Yea, sweeter than honey to the mouth ! " The victory of the Lamb over sin and death—the meritorious repurchase of our alienated inheritance— the acknowledged right, and power, and gracious promise of our Lord, to tread down Satan under our feet, and bring us into the goodly land of rest— all these are involved with the roll from the Saviour's hand, and are like living waters to the thirsty, and precious manna to the hungry. But,

> E'en the rapture of pardon is mingled with fears,
> And the cup of thanksgiving with penitent tears.

No one can truly eat the book, but he " must prophesy." Its power in us is to send on errands, lead through scenes, and charge with offices and duties, full of hardships, trials, and many a bitterness. The roll of God's word to Israel was in the mouth of Ezekiel " as honey for sweetness," but it carried him on a mission to which he " went in bitterness, in the heat of his spirit." It costs pains to be a full-souled believer, a faithful prophet, an unflinching candidate for an inheritance not seen as yet. And such dreadful " lamentation, and mourning, and woe," must come upon the unsanctified world before the precious charter Christ has obtained from the throne can go into full effect, that no true man can be other than sad when he contemplates it. So the book in John's mouth was " sweet as honey ; " but when he had eaten it " his belly was made bitter." To receive as his own, and as the food of his soul, these precious title-deeds of the blessed inheritance, thrilled him with joy and gladness ; but those scenes of blood and wrath to the dwellers upon the earth which must be enacted before the inheritance is reached—those hardships to the flesh in holding faithfully to the holy document—those conflicts, and contradictions of sinners, and harrowing contumelies, and trying dangers, and laborious toils, attendant upon honest prophesying of these things,—all combined to make the effects of the book bitter in his body, though so sweet to his taste. It is all perfectly natural and easily accounted for, just as I have taken it. Even Jesus wept on the very eve of triumph, and while the hosannas of final glory were already heralding their approach. But we have yet to observe,

V. A NOTABLE PROCLAMATION.

" And the Angel, whom I saw standing upon the sea and upon the land, lifted up his right hand into the heaven, and sware by Him that liveth for the ages of the ages, who created the heaven and the things in it, and the earth and the things in it, and the sea and the things in it, that there shall be no more delay ; but in the days of the voice of the seventh angel, when he shall sound, the mystery of God is [to be] fulfilled, even as he preached glad tidings to* his servants the prophets."

The Mystery of God is nothing more nor less than the final sum of all God's revelations and doings for the reinstatement of man into his lost inheritance. The fulfilment of this mystery is the final accomplishment of the last items of the Divine administrations which make up that sum—the ultimate realization of all the foreannouncements made to and by any and every one of God's prophets in all the ages—the Gospel of the kingdom of heaven at length merged into full and everlasting fruition of that kingdom—the consummation

---

* The word here is ευηγγελισε, from εναγγελιζω, to address with good tidings, to preach the Gospel, to declare, including in the declaration always glad tidings, particularly of salvation.

of all things. And concerning this consummation, sundry particulars are here observable.

(1.) It is true Gospel. What God has made known concerning it is glad tidings, good news, the proper evangely. People shake their heads, and say, that we are quite beside the Gospel, if not beside ourselves, when we preach about the second coming of Christ and the end of all things ; but this mighty Angel is of a different mind. Himself the very heart and soul and life of every-thing that is gospel, and apart from whose person, utterances, and work there is no gospel, He not only makes this consummation the one sole theme of, perhaps, the most majestic, solemn, and formal proclamation ever put upon record, but at the same time, and after the same manner, and as part of the same awful discourse, affirms, that the same was and is the prime subject of all God's inspirations of all His prophets. We, therefore, plant ourselves upon all the divinest of records, and upon the most authentic, direct, and solemn of all sacred utterances, and say, that he whose gospel drops and repudiates from its central themes the grand doctrine of the consummation of all things, as por-trayed in this Apocalypse, is not the true Gospel of God.

(2.) It is to be accomplished in the period of the seventh trumpet—" in the days of the seventh angel, when he shall sound." I say *period* of the seventh trumpet, for it spans a section of time, and its sounding is not over in an instant. The word is not *day*, but " *days ;* " as " the *days* of Abraham," " the *days* of David," " the *days* of youth," " the *days* " of Christ's sojourn on earth. The greatest events of time transpire under this trumpet, and it may overspan years. It is the grand climacteric of the Apocalypse, and so of these mysterious administrations of God. And " in the days " which it embraces, the whole Mystery of God shall be fulfilled, and everything foretold by the prophets consummated.

(3.) It will only come after long, repeated, and trying delay, if not on the part of God, yet in the estimates and expectations of His people. This is distinctly implied in the proclamation, the gist of which is to meet a feeling that the whole thing has receded so far into the distance as hardly to be any more within the bounds of sober credence. The idea is, that there has been delay, and repeated delay ; that time has intervened, and lengthened itself out to very suspicious proportions ; but that, notwithstanding, as God lives, and has made and controls all things, when once the period of the sixth trum-pet is reached, *there shall be no more delay.*

The Scriptures often allude to this postponement beyond all anticipation, and the temptation and ill effects of it upon men. Peter tells of people to whom the thing is put off so long, that they finally turn scoffers, and say, " Where is the promise of his coming ? for since the fathers fell asleep, all things continue as they were from the beginning ; " and in the same chapter he apologizes for the fact that the grand event is so long deferred. It is implied in the fact that some servants shall say, " The Lord delayeth his coming." The same is perceptible in the parable of the Ten Virgins. Even after the eagle-saints have been " taken," and the whole of remaining Christendom, having ascertained its place in the prophetic calendar, has been moved to go out as one man to meet the next great turn in the already present judgment-scenes, there is still such tarrying and delay, that all the animation and zeal upon the subject largely subside, and all sink into apathy and slumber with regard to it.

It is very true that the Scriptures nowhere definitely tell us when the time is. " Of that day and hour knoweth no man, no, not the angels of heaven." There is hence no warrant for any one, at any time since the blessed Saviour ascended, to put away into the distant future that day when judgment shall begin. The true attitude of the Church, and that to which all the representa-tions and admonitions of the Scriptures are framed, is to be looking and ready any day and every day for the coming of Christ to seize away his waiting and watching saints. But in faithfully assuming this attitude, and thus hoping and expecting the speedy fulfilment of what has been promised, the Church has been made to see one notable and quickening period after another pass away without bringing the consummation which was anticipated. Eve thought the promise on the point of fulfilment when Cain was born ; but He whom she was expecting was yet 4000 years away. When Simeon took the infant Saviour to his bosom and sung his exulting *Nunc demittis*, he supposed that the time for the consummation had arrived ; but it was only the preliminary advent that he had lived to witness. When John the Baptist thundered his rugged calls to repentance through the wildernesses of Judea, the joyous burden of his soul and preaching was, that now the Consummator was come with winnowing fan to make the final separation between the chaff and the wheat ; but what was most in his contemplation was yet a score of centuries off. The early Christians were lively in their expectations that yet in their day the standard of the coming One would be seen unfurled in the sky, and all their hopes be consummated ; but the days of the Apostles and of the apostolic fathers passed, and still " the Bridegroom tarried." Nearly every century, as it rolled, was designated as the one in which the Church might confidently count on being transferred from earth to heaven ; but each, like the one before it, came to an end, without bringing that more notable end on which our eyes are ever to be fixed. The Reformation, with the revival of the primitive faith, revived the primitive hope, that the great day must needs be very close at hand ; but the days of the Reformers passed, and all the days which they designated as those beyond which the day of judgment could not be delayed ; and yet the momentous period had not arrived. Many times within the past hundred years the attention of men has been called to particular dates as the times when this present world should end ; but they have all come and gone, as innocent of the great consummation as any that went before them. And although the Saviour may come any day, and our duty is to be looking for Him every day, it is still possible that all present prognostications on the subject may fail, as they have always failed ; that years and years of earnest and confident expectation may go by without bringing the Lord from heaven ; and that delay after delay, and ever-repeating prolongations of the time of waiting may intervene, till it becomes necessary for the preservation of the faith of God's people to hear the fresh edict from the lips of their Lord, that " *there shall be no more delay.*"

(4.) Though the coming of the final consummation be slow, *it will come.* There is not another truth in God's word that is so peculiarly authenticated. All the holy prophets since the world began have foretold it. All the evangelists and apostles have inwrought it in all their writings as one of the central and fixed things in the Divine purpose. Jesus himself has given us parable on parable, precept upon precept, and promise upon promise, all directed to this one thing. And God hath certified it to all men, in that He hath raised up Christ from the dead. But after all the rest of the canon of Inspiration was finished, another book was indited, making this its particular and specific theme ; and in that book is a particular vision, in which the mighty Judge himself appears, and gives forth the most intense and awful asseveration on the subject. With clouds for his garments and the rainbow for his crown—with his face shining as the sun and his feet glowing like pillars of fire—with a roll in his hand, lifted by his merit from the throne of infinite majesty, he stretches up his right hand into the sky, and *swears,*—swears by the Eternal—swears by the power which has given birth and being to all things,—that, in spite of all the mistakes, disappointments, delays, and consequent doubts upon the subject, what was made known to the prophets shall be, and that the time shall come when *there shall be no more delay !*

Shall we then have any doubt upon the subject ? Shall we allow the failure of men's figures and prognostications to shake our confidence or obscure our hope ? Shall we suffer the many and long delays that have occurred, or that ever may occur, to drive us into the scoffer's ranks ? True as the life of God—

certain as the Divine eternity—unfailing as the Power which made the worlds—immutable as the oath of Jesus—*the great consummating day will come*, when the whole Mystery of God shall be fulfilled. Unbelief, away! Misgiving, be thou buried in the depths of the sea! Doubt, be shamed into everlasting confusion! " Behold, He cometh with clouds, and every eye shall see Him, and they which pierced Him. Even so, Amen."

Holy One of heaven, have mercy upon us, and help us hold fast the profession of our faith without wavering ; for He is faithful that promised !

LECTURE TWENTY-SECOND

REV. II : I, 2. (Revised Text.) And there was given to me a reed like to a rod, saying, Rise, and measure the temple of God, and the altar, and those who worship in it. And the court which is outside the temple, cast out, and measure it not; for it is given to the Gentiles; and they shall trample the holy city forty and two months.

WE here come upon ground which has been very trying to expositors—the great battleground of conflicting systems, and the burial-ground of many a fond conceit and learned fancy. Alford has given it as his opinion that the chapter on which we now enter " is undoubtedly one of the most difficult in the whole Apocalypse." On all the prevalent theories for interpreting this Book, he is certainly right in this opinion, and the difficulties of which he complains must remain till those theories are abandoned, and another departure taken.

If we were to take a description of a horse-mill, and insist on expounding it as a description of a mill-horse, no matter what qualifications we might bring to the task, we would find ourselves continually beset with difficulties and embarrassments which we never could fully overcome. And just so it is with nearly all our commentaries on the Apocalypse. It is not learning, ability, research or ingenuity that is at fault, but an underlying misapprehension of the nature and intention of the record. It is a description of one thing, and they are all the while trying to make it quite another thing. It is an account of the wonders of " *The Lord's Day* "—the day of Judgment, and they propose to explain it of " *man's day* "—the day of the present dispensation. God gave it as " The Apocalypse of Jesus Christ," and they seek to interpret it as an apocalypse of human history. This is the great trouble. Nor is it to be wondered that the skin of the lion will not fit the ass, and that the ears of the inferior animal will stick out notwithstanding the most ingenious efforts to cover them.

It would, indeed, be affectation to pretend that there are no difficulties in the way of a satisfactory exposition of this Book, but I am well persuaded that the most of those encountered by our commentators, and which hinder thinking readers from seriously embracing their theories, are imported by themselves, in the primary mistake which wrests the record from its own proper subject, and applies it to another which is at best only remotely and inchoately embraced. Let it be fixed and settled that we here have to do with the scenes of miracle and judgment, and that this chapter relates to those grand and mysterious administrations by which Christ is to take possession of the earth and clear it of usurpers and enemies, and the way is open to understand all, so far as it is possible to comprehend such wonders beforehand.

It is evident that the events here narrated are of a piece with what was described in the preceding chapter, and follow directly from it. Concerning the relation between these two chapters, Dr. Elliott justly says, " The connection between what concludes the one, and what begins the other, appears to be as close as it well could be : seeing that the Angel who before addressed St. John still continues here to address him ; and the new injunction, Rise and measure, is but a sequel to His previous injunction, Thou must prophesy again."* We there saw the glorious Angel, which is Christ Himself, in the sublime attitude of taking possession of the earth, by setting His feet upon it, displaying in His hand the title-deed to it, and swearing that there should be no more delay. And what now comes before us must, therefore, relate to the same transaction, and to the time and occurrences in which the same is to be carried into effect. In other words, it describes to us the ongoing of the judgment, now rapidly moving to its climax.

The first thing in the process of this taking possession of the redeemed inheritance is indicated in the change made in the attitude of John. Having beheld the Angel, he is withdrawn from the position of a mere *seer* and made an *actor*. A voice from heaven directs him to take the document from the Angel's hand, to eat it, and so to make it his own by incorporating it with his very being ; whilst it is further announced to him : " Thou must prophesy again upon peoples, and nations, and tongues, and kings many." What did this mean ? John is not the only one who is to obtain the title to the inheritance. All the meek have it promised to them. Every true Christian is to share it. When the blessed *Goel* comes to give it to His redeemed ones, there will be many besides John to receive it. In what capacity then are we to contemplate this calling of John to take, eat, and have vested in him the title-deed to the inheritance ? Certainly not in his individual capacity ; for then none are ever to inherit but himself, as in him that title finds final lodgment.

It is a very common thing, in the delivery of sacred prophecies, for the individual prophet to act in himself what is meant to be understood of those whom he represents. " As remarked long since by Irenæus, the ancient prophets fulfilled their office of predicting, not merely in the verbal delivery of predictions, but by themselves seeing, hearing, or acting out the things *in type*, which were afterwards to be seen, heard, or acted out by others *in reality*—and this whether in real life, or perchance in vision. In all which cases they were to be considered, as they are called in Isaiah and in Zechariah, *mophthim ;* that is, figurative or *representative persons*."† And such a representative is St. John in the case before us. He acts the part in the apocalyptic scenes which pertains to the whole body to which he belongs. What is given him in the vision is to be understood as given them, and what he does and experiences is to be understood as done and experienced by them, when the vision becomes reality.

Nor can we be in any doubt as to the persons of whom he is thus the representative. He is an Apostle, and hence a divinely constituted representative of the Church. He is in heaven at the time, and so a representative of the Church thus shown to be in heaven at the time the vision is fulfilled, that is, of the resurrected, translated, and glorified saints. To the whole body of redeemed ones are we therefore to understand this giving of the title-deed of the inheritance to be ; in whom also it forever after inheres.

But as John receives and eats the little book as the representative of glorified saints, it is as the self-same representative of the self-same saints, that it is said to him : " *Thou must prophesy again*," and that it is further commanded him to " *Rise and measure the temple of God, and the altar, and those who worship in it*." And if so, then we have the key to the whole case, and there breaks in upon us a glorious light for the right interpretation of this otherwise very difficult passage.

To prophesy is not simply to foretell future events ; but to exercise the functions of a witness for God. In the verses following, the Two Witnesses get their name from their work, and that work is called *prophesying*. To declare the will and purpose of God, or to act as His ambassador and mouthpiece, is to fill the office of a prophet. Aaron was to be Moses' *prophet*, which is explained to mean that he should be a *spokesman* and a *mouth* for Moses. And

* Horæ Apocal. *in loc.*
† Elliott, *Horæ Apoc.* vol. I, p. 281.

so, to be the agent or instrument through which God utters Himself to men, whatever may be the nature or the subject of the utterance, is to prophesy. Such witnesses and mouth-pieces Jehovah has always upon earth. The whole Church is such a witness and prophet. In and through it the word of God ever sounds, and the mind and purpose of God ring out into the ears of the world ; and even principalities and powers in the heavenly places are being instructed by the Church. Every individual Christian is a confessor of the true God, in whose confession the will and purpose of God in Christ Jesus is testified and proclaimed. No one can become or continue a faithful Christian without this. In so far, then, every genuine Christian is a real prophet. Through him God speaks continually. His whole career on earth as a Christian confessor is a continuous *prophesying* against the wickedness of the world, of the necessity of godliness, and of the way of salvation in Christ. But even after the saints have gone from this world, they are still not yet done prophesying. As here said to John, they must *prophesy again*. After they have been " caught up together to meet the Lord in the air," and have " put on immortality," and the day of judgment has progressed to the second woe-trumpet, the Mighty Redeemer having delivered to them the recovered deed to the inheritance, new commissions issue ; and from being mere spectators of the ongoing judgment, they become actors in its administrations, and once more assume the office of witnesses for God. And what is involved in this *prophesying again*, together with its attendants and results, it is the object and intent of this chapter to set before us. Let us, therefore, approach it with due reverence and prayerfulness.

" *And there was given to me a reed like to a rod, saying, Rise, and measure the temple of God, and the altar, and those who worship in it. And the court which is outside cast out, and measure it not ; for it is given to the Gentiles : and they shall trample the holy city forty and two months.*"

These words set forth the initial processes of the actual taking possession of the earth by our triumphant Redeemer. Like the judgment-administrations as a whole, it is not a summary, but a gradual work. It certainly extends through years, and involves various particulars and stages. How, and where, and in what, the commencement is to be made, we may here learn.

A remarkable feature in the case is, that the glorified saints are the chief actors. It is John who receives the equipment and the commission, but in him, as was said, the glorified saints in general are included. This is true in every instance in which he is taken out of the position of a mere spectator and made an actor in what is narrated. His call and transfer to heaven, described in the fourth chapter, set forth the catching up into the aerial spaces all God's ready and waiting saints when once the time for the fulfilment of these wonders has come. And so his reception and eating of the little book, from the nature of the case, must be understood of the whole Church in heaven at the time these scenic representations become reality. So then likewise must we understand the prophesying again, and hence also the equipment and commission in the words in hand ; for they all necessarily go together as parts of each other, and must be accepted in one and the same way throughout. The giving and the command are to John, but only for the convenience of the description, whilst in the fulfilment they are to the whole body of glorified saints, for John here stands in place of the saints.

Nor need we be surprised at this, as if it were something foreign to the teachings of the Scriptures in general. Paul, in a plain and didactic epistle, says : " *Do ye not know that the saints shall judge the world ?* " (1 Cor. 6 : 2.) So also says the Psalmist : " Let the saints be joyful in glory : let them sing aloud upon their couches : let the high praises of God be in their mouth, and a two-edged sword in their hand ; to execute vengeance upon the heathen and punishments upon the people ; to bind their kings with chains, and their nobles with fetters of iron ; *to execute upon them the judgment written. This honour have all the saints.*" (Ps. 149 : 5-9.)

The office assigned in this particular instance, is the measuring of the temple and altar of God, and those who worship therein. *Measuring* is a judicial act—the laying down of lines and borders which are to mark and determine dimensions and boundaries. It is the sign of appropriation. When it is proposed to take possession, and to have things put to their purpose, men begin to measure. In the settlement of some new order, as beheld by Ezekiel, there is a great deal of measuring and marking out of portions and possessions. And so when the triumphant Redeemer is about to enter upon the inheritance, he gives command to measure. What is measured is from that moment His, and so designated by the measuring. What the lines of the measurement include, He acknowledges and claims ; and any indignity rendered toward it becomes a heinous sin against High Heaven. And what is outside of those lines, and not measured, is not acknowledged by Him, but is rejected, and held and treated as defiled.

The first things thus measured are the temple, the altar, and the worshippers in that temple. Peter says, " Judgment must begin at the house of God." The only house of God now on earth is the Church, the mystic temple, the spiritual house, constituted of all believers. At this house judgment begins by the sudden and miraculous catching away of God's waiting people to the sky, as we saw in the earlier chapters of this book.

But the Judgment-administrations have two sides. They consist of two series, and exhibit, so to speak, two different currents : the one the upward current, in which good and its representatives pass out of the world as if abandoning everything to utter perdition ; and the other the downward current, in which good and its representatives come again in victorious power to possess and hold everything. Each of these currents has its own particular beginning ; and, in both instances, the point of beginning is the most sacred point—the house or temple of God. But it is not the same house or temple in both instances. It is the mystic temple in the first, and it is a more literal temple in the second. When Christ once catches away to the heavenly spaces His ready and waiting saints, as described by St. Paul, the present Church ends. Fractions and inferior fragments of it may still float in the waves of the great tribulation and subsequently land on the shores of salvation, but without crowns, and only as the after-born, not as the first-born. And by the time the downward current of which I spoke sets in, the present Church, as such, will have been quite transferred to the regions above, and will constitute the *measurers* in the text, and not the object measured.

The measuring here commanded implies that what is measured had not, up to that time, been acknowledged on the part of Christ. This could not be true of the Church. The language is peculiarly Jewish. There is a fane, an altar, and a court of the Gentiles spoken of ; which accords with the ceremonial economy, but not with the Christian.* There is a " holy city " alluded to, which is given to the Gentiles to trample for a time, which carries us directly to Jerusalem, and indicates that we are here unmistakably on Jewish ground. There is no other city on earth so called in the Scriptures. In the account of the return from Babylon we read : " The people also cast lots to bring one of ten to dwell in *Jerusalem, the holy city*." (Neh. 11 : 1, 18.) Isaiah (52 : 1) calls out : " Put on thy beautiful garments, *O Jerusalem, the holy city*." In the account of the temptation it is recorded : " Then the devil taketh him up into *the holy city*, and setteth him on a pinnacle of the temple." (Matt. 4 : 5.) And even after its inhabitants had made themselves guilty of the innocent blood of Christ, the same language is still used ; for we read that " many of the saints which slept arose and came out of their graves after His resurrection and went into *the holy city*, and appeared to many." (Matt. 27 : 52, 53.) There is only one other " holy city " spoken of in all the Bible, to wit, the New Jerusalem ; but that never has been and never will be given

* Dr. A. Clarke, *in loc.* says : " This must refer to the temple of Jerusalem ; " though what to do with it he confesses he does not know.

to be trampled by the Gentiles. Some other " holy city " must then be meant. Many make it the Church ; but the Church has not only been measured, appropriated, acknowledged from the very beginning, but its untrue members have likewise been all the while rejected and unacknowledged, and just as really and conspicuously so before the Reformation as then or since. Incho- ately and secondarily, as a sort of shadow of the great substance, we may see some resemblances between these visions and the past history of the Church ; for the course of things conducting to the consummation takes the general outlines of that consummation ; but we have abundantly seen that this Book will not interpret on the mystical method, without most damaging prejudice to what belongs to a divine revelation, assuming to itself the pre-eminent importance and solemnity which this Book assumes. And so true and palpable is this, that the common Christian mind under its teachings, and the sorry acknowledgment of many of its most candid defenders, is, that this is a book of riddles and mysteries which it is not in the power of man to under- stand, and that nothing clear or solid is to be derived from it ;—nay, that Christians may now learn as much if not more, on the same subjects, by reading the infidel Gibbon, and a few writers on mediæval and subsequent history, than from the whole Apocalypse !* This is so damaging a confession for a Christian to make, that it wears the evidence on its face of some deep and radical mistake in the method of treatment which necessitates it. We cannot, therefore, take " the holy city " here as denoting the Church, but understand by it what the Scriptures always mean by the phrase, and interpret it with confidence of *Jerusalem*, to which alone the temple, with its altar and court of the Gentiles pertains.

What, then, is the implication, but that when this period is once reached, Jerusalem will have been largely repopulated by the children of its ancient inhabitants, its temple rebuilt, and its ancient worship restored. God is not yet done with the Jews as a distinct people. In their half-faith and " blindness in part," they will seek and find their way back to a revival of their ancient metropolis, temple, and ritual. Some of the most striking passages of holy Scripture assert this with a clearness and positiveness which no fair exegesis can ever set aside. The New Testament constantly assumes it. And when it is accomplished, as it certainly will be, Jerusalem will still be " the holy city," because of the consecration it of old received. The temple will also be in some sort God's temple, though at first unacknowledged and unappropriated by Christ. And among the worshippers will also be many true servants of God ; for already under the sixth seal we were called to contemplate a movement among the tribes of Israel by which 144,000 were marked as the Lord's, and singled out as the objects of His gracious protection. These still live on earth among men at the time to which the text refers ; for it is only as late as the transactions noted in the fourteenth chapter that they are found with the Lamb in glory. Nor will there be at that period a holier place or service on earth than this restored Jerusalem and temple. But with all, it will not till then receive the acknowledgment and appropriation of the glorious Messiah ; nor then entirely, nor at all without a strict *resurvey*, and the putting down of new lines, measurements, and boundaries from heaven.

Important changes are likewise indicated by this measuring. Where there is a new laying out of lines, the old is cast away, and things take a new shape. The same is indicated in the character of the rule or instrument of the measure- ment. In measuring the New Jerusalem, the instrument is a " golden reed." Here it is " *a reed like to a rod* "—a measuring implement, but having the prevailing aspect of an instrument of chastisement—hence indicative of an

* So, for example, Dr. A. Clarke, who prefaces his commentary on the Apocalypse with these words : " It is my firm opinion that the expositions of this book have done great disservice to religion. . . . In the words of Graserus : Mihi tota Apocalypsis valdè obscura videtur ; et talis, cujus explicatio *citra periculum*, vix queat tentaré. Fateor me hactenus in nullius Scripti Biblici lectione minus proficere, quam in hoc obscurissimo vaticinio."

afflictive, revolutionizing, measurement. There will, therefore, be rejections of some things, and additions of others. In other words, there will be a purging of the temple after the style of the proceeding of the Saviour when he took a scourge in his hand, and somewhat disturbed the business of the money-changers and them that sold doves. It is a measuring which is to proceed according to a rule which operates as a rod.

But the changes indicated are not arbitrary. The lines are all drawn by a fixed and heavenly rule, given for the purpose. It is called "*a reed.*" The original (κάλαμος) is the word which the Septuagint uses for the Hebrew word *Kaneh,* from which comes our ecclesiastical word *Canon,* both meaning *a rule,* particularly a rule of religious belief and duty. Hence the books of the Old and New Testaments are called *The Canon,* or *the canonical books,* seeing that they are the infallible Rule of all true faith and practice. This κάλαμος, therefore, is not to be associated so much with the idea of a frail reed shaken by every wind, as with the idea of a canon law, an inflexible rule, a divinely constituted directory. It does not mean our present Scriptures, as some expositors have represented ; for it is not THE *canon,* but A *canon*—not *the* Rule, but *a* Rule. For all the offices and duties pertaining to this life, the sacred Scriptures are the exclusive and supreme Rule ; but for the offices and duties of the " world to come," there will be other Rules, and another canon. The Scriptures have already been given to the saints. We have them complete, and our fathers have had the same for ages. The canon here in question is a new thing, first given at this stage in the ongoing Judgment, and given first to the glorified saints in heaven. The germs of it may indeed be embraced in our present Scriptures, as the germs of the New Testament were all contained in the Old, particularly as the Psalmist says the saints are " to execute *the Judgment written ;*" but still the new commission has also its new canon, not yet given, according to which this judicial measuring is to be done, and to which all the changes it brings will be conformed. The ancient Jews " received the law by the disposition of angels " (Acts 7 : 53) ; and it would seem that their descendants in the judgment time are to receive another canon " by the disposition of " glorified saints, in connection with the final fulfilment of that promise quoted by St. Paul : " Behold, the days come, saith the Lord, when I will make a new covenant with the house of Israel and with the hcuse of Judah : . . . for this is the covenant that I will make with the house of Israel after those days, saith the Lord ; I will put my laws into their mind, and write them in their hearts : and I will be to them a God, and they shall be to me a people ; and they shall not teach every man his neighbour, and every man his brother, saying, Know the Lord ; for all shall know me from the least to the greatest. For I will be merciful to their unrighteousness, and their sins and their iniquities will I remember no more." (Heb. 8 : 8–12. See Jer. 30 and 31, and Ezekiel 36.)

It appears, therefore, that, from the time of the measuring here described, there is again to be a true and divinely acknowledged temple of God upon earth, with an altar and worshippers set apart and marked off as the Lord's.

Some have given out the strange fancy that it is in heaven, and not on earth, and that it is only the outer court that is on earth. This is meant to avoid the difficulty created by the erroneous assumption that what is measured can never thereafter be defiled. But it is evidently a mistake. There is indeed a temple in heaven, as shown all through the Apocalypse ; but the temple, altar, and worshippers there, have all the while been acknowledged and appropriated as the Lord's, and required no new measurement to that effect at this late period ; and to apply the *rod* to people and things in heaven, argues a rather sorry appreciation of the holiness and happiness of that region. When the New Jerusalem is about to be entered and set apart as the glorious city of God and His saints, it is measured too, but with " a golden reed," not with one " *like to a rod.*" Besides, the outer court is rejected, and hence not acknowledged of God, which would leave us no temple of God at all upon

earth for " the captain of the robbers " to defile. And how can that be sacri-
legiously desecrated which God refuses to acknowledge and positively
disowns ? The great aggravation of the sin of Antichrist is, that he sets up an
idol in Jehovah's place, and turns God's true and acknowledged temple into a
house of murderous idolatry. There must, therefore, be a true temple of
God on earth, one which God acknowledges and claims as His, during the time
of Antichrist, which is immediately subsequent to this measuring.

The outer court of this temple is ordered to be rejected, and cast entirely
out of the measurement. The outer court is the court of the Gentiles, and this
fact is given as the reason for the rejection. The present dispensation began
with Jews exclusively ; and " in the regeneration " the new order on earth is
likewise to begin with Jews exclusively. And this casting out of the court of
the Gentiles because it is the court of the Gentiles, proves the present dispensation then at an end. Now Gentiles and Jews stand on the same level. The one
has no prerogatives or rights above the other. In the Church there is neither
Greek nor Jew, Barbarian, Scythian, bond nor free ; but all nationalities
and conditions in life yield to one common brotherhood and heirship. The
text, therefore, tells of a new order of things. New commissions issue, a new
canon comes into force, and the Jew is again in the foreground for the fathers'
sakes, and the Gentiles are thrust back. The mere presence of them in the
outer part of the temple causes it to be rejected and cast out of God's
acknowledgment.

From the very beginning of the admission of the Gentiles to fellow-heirship
with the seed of Jacob, the admonition of " the Apostle of the Gentiles " to
them was, and still is : " Be not high-minded, but fear ; for if God spared not
the natural branches, take heed lest he also spare not thee. Behold, therefore,
the goodness and severity of God : on them which fell, severity ; but toward
thee, goodness, if thou continue in his goodness : otherwise thou also shalt be
cut off. And they also, if they abide not in unbelief, shall be graffed in ; for
God is able to graff them in again. For if thou wert cut out of the olive-tree
which is wild by nature, and wert graffed contrary to nature into a good olive-
tree : how much more shall these, which be the natural branches, be graffed
into their own olive-tree ? For I would not, brethren, that you should be
ignorant of this mystery, lest ye should be wise in your own conceits, that
blindness in part is happened to Israel, *until the fulness of the Gentiles be come
in.*" (Rom. 11 : 21–25.) This is very remarkable language. It implies a
precariousness of our high calling in Christ Jesus which we would hardly
suspect, and which it is dangerous to overlook. It foreshows an end to the
favours now enjoyed by the Gentiles, and for the same causes that cast down
the Jews from their ancient pre-eminence in the Divine economy. It sets
forth that the existing depression of the Jew, and the exaltation of the Gentile
to equality with him, is only temporary, and must terminate. Yea, and in all
the Scriptures, there is a time contemplated, when the πληρωμα—*the full
complement*—of the Gentiles shall have come in, and things shall begin again
with the Jew at the head. And it is to the fulfilment of this mystery that the
text relates. The measurement of the temple, its altar, and its worshippers, is
the receiving again of the Jew, his regrafting upon the old theocratic root and
native olive-tree, and his re-establishment as the chosen of God among the
nations of the earth ; and the casting out of the court of the Gentiles, is the
diminishing, cutting off, and casting away of the Gentiles from their present
rank and privileges.

And when we consider the corruption, deterioration, and ever-increasing
apostasy of the present Church, from the time of the Apostles onward ;—
when we read in holy writ that in the last days the form of godliness shall be
found lingering over the utmost excesses of unrighteousness, the pure truth of
God be no longer tolerated by professed Christendom in its eagerness for
religious novelties and sensations, and faith have almost entirely evanished
from the earth ;—when we contemplate the prophetic pictures of the con-

summate heathenism and perversion of everything sacred and true which is to mark the closing periods of this dispensation ;—there is no room for wonder at the final command to cast out the unclean thing, whilst what follows begins again with the children of God's ancient people. It is the eternal law of things, that unfaithfulness brings judgment, and that if people do not appreciate and improve their privileges they must lose them. The Gentile Church apostatizes, and it dissolves, just as the Jewish Church before it.

But though God be again choosing Jerusalem and its temple as the place of His manifestation, and Israel for His earthly people, he does not yet defend either from all further disturbance and disaster. " Zion shall be redeemed with judgment, and they that return of her with righteousness." (Is. 1 : 27.)

" *They (the Gentiles) shall trample the holy city forty and two months ;* " not because of the superior holiness of these Gentiles, for in them wickedness comes to its highest earthly culmination, but God uses them for the chastisement of Israel, at the same time that he puts them in position to be themselves tormented and discomfited. He manifests their sin against His newly constituted people, that He may manifest the climax of His judgments against them, and require of them " the blood of all the prophets which was shed from the foundation of the world." They persecute the measured worshippers, desecrate the measured altar and temple, and set up an idol in the marked place of Jehovah, that the consummation of all plagues may fall upon them.

And here comes in a very important point to test the soundness of the spiritualistic interpretation ; to wit, the relation, in point of time, between the measuring of the temple and these forty-two months of the trampling of the holy city. Is there not every reason in the record for regarding the measuring as first performed, and the trampling as a sequel to it ? By no fair dealing with what is written can we put the trampling first and the measuring afterwards. But if the measuring precedes the trampling, or even synchronizes with it, then Popery and the Reformation cannot be the subject of the picture, as taught by our spiritualistic expositors. The Church cannot be at the same time both reclaimed from papal desecration and trodden down by it ; neither can its reformation from popish defilement precede the dominancy of such defilement. Yet one or the other of these must be true, if the measuring denotes the work of the Reformers, and the trampling the evils inflicted by the papacy. But as in the nature of things neither can be true, it follows that the Papacy and the Reformation are not here the subject, and many a splendid chapter of historic learning must pass for nothing, as regards the exposition of this prophecy. It is what is measured that suffers under the trampling, and the purged temple is again briefly defiled by the Gentiles. Nay, the measuring itself involves chastisement and trouble to those who are the subjects of it, such as cannot well be predicated of the Reformed Church. The reed with which it is done, is " *like to a rod ;* " and a *rod* (ῥάβδος) in the Apocalypse always denotes an instrument of chastisement. (See chapters 2 : 27 ; 12 : 5 ; 19 : 15.) It is likewise written of those then to be received into particular favour : " I will bring them through the fire, and will refine them as silver is refined, and will try them as gold is tried." (Zech. 13 : 9.) And the ordeal includes just such a spoliation of the holy city as is here described ; for God says He " will gather all nations (Gentiles) against Jerusalem to battle ; and the city shall be taken, and the houses rifled, and the women ravished ; and half the city shall go forth into captivity." (Zech. 14 : 1, 2.)

But the trouble, though sharp and severe, will not be perpetual, nor long ; for " then shall the Lord go forth, and fight against those nations (Gentiles) as when He fought in the day of battle. And his feet shall stand in that day on the Mount of Olives, which is before Jerusalem on the east " (Zech. 14 : 3, 4) ; and the great day of God Almighty will end it forever.

" *Forty and two months* " is the holy city to be trampled ; that is, three years and a half, no more, and no less. It is a literal city that is trampled and defiled ; it is a literal oppression and affliction that befalls it ; and so the months which compute the duration of the trouble are also literal months. These great chronological scaffoldings which men build around prophetic dates, is mere fancy-work—" wood, hay, and stubble "—nothing but rubbish and obscurations of the truth of God. When it is meant that we should take numbers and dates in some other way than as they read, He gives us intimation of it ; and in the absence of such divine hints, as in this case, there is no warrant for taking them any otherwise than as they stand written. " Forty and two months " are forty and two months, and not twelve hundred and sixty years.

The computation is given in " *months*," which is common in the Scriptures when troubles and afflictions are the subject. The beginning and duration of the flood is expressed in *months*. The ark was in the country of the Philistines seven *months*. The locusts torment men five *months*. And Jerusalem's last great trial is computed in *months*, as well as the term of the blasphemies of the Beast.

The number of the months is *forty-two*—six times the period that the ark was in captivity. Six is the number of evil, and seven of dispensational completion, and these are two marked factors of *forty-two ;* which would seem to signify a fulness or completion of the evil in those months. Israel in the wilderness had *forty-two* stations ; and the wicked youths slain by the bears for their mockery of Elisha were *forty-two*. The powerful monster who makes war with the saints, oppresses the nations, and blasphemes God, continues " *forty-two* months." And so the completion of Jerusalem's troubles is summed up in the same numbers and computation.

But ere the forty-two months are accomplished, there are yet many other things to come to pass, among the most marked of which is that *crux interpretum*, or rack of expositors—the history of *The Two Witnesses*. But what I have to say concerning these must be reserved for another occasion, when I hope to be able to identify them and their place in history without having to hunt up the obscure Waldenses, hidden away from the world like Chammoix in the Alps, or to lodge the true cause of God on earth for a dozen centuries with so variable, roving, and revolutionary a sect as the doubtful Paulikians, from whose history scarce a page survives which a true Christian can endorse as an untarnished testimony for God. Meanwhile, may the Lord add His blessing to what has been said, and cause it to be fruitful in bringing forth praises to His holy Name !

LECTURE TWENTY-THIRD

THE TWO WITNESSES—THEIR CONSPICUOUSNESS—THE ACCOUNT OF THEM DICTATED BY
CHRIST—THEIR NUMBER—THEIR PERSONALITY—THEIR INDIVIDUALITY—ARE SAINTS
FROM HEAVEN—DISTINCT FROM RESURRECTED AND GLORIFIED SAINTS—ENOCH AND
ELIJAH ANSWER TO THE DESCRIPTION—BEINGS FROM HEAVEN HAVE COME TO EARTH AND
DIED—THE PERSONAL RETURN OF ELIJAH AFFIRMED BY MALACHI, CHRIST, THE JEWS, THE
CHRISTIAN FATHERS—A TWOFOLD ELIJAH COMING—ANOTHER PROPHET TO ACCOMPANY
ELIJAH—ENOCH THAT PROPHET—BOTH ARE JUDGMENT-PROPHETS—THEIR CLOTHING—
HOW " THE TWO OLIVE TREES AND THE TWO LAMPS "—THEIR STANDING BEFORE THE LORD
OF THE EARTH.

REV. 11 : 3, 4. (Revised Text.) And I will give to my two witnesses, and they shall
prophesy a thousand two hundred and sixty days, clothed in sackcloth.
These are the two olive-trees and the two lamps, which stand before the Lord of the earth.

WHOEVER these witnesses may be, they are the most extraordinary of whom
there is any account. Many martyrs perish under the Beast (see chapters 13 :
15 ; 20 : 4) ; but none of them receive a tithe of the notice given to these two.
Antichrist himself, in all his despicable pre-eminence and vast dominions
does not more conspicuously stand out on the record than they. Nay, in all
the earth there are none to cope with him but them. He tramples the world
beneath his feet, and they alone are more formidable against him than all
other men besides. And this one simple fact is itself sufficient to shake and
overthrow forever many of the modern attempts to identify them. The priests
Ananus and Jesus at the time of Rome's siege of Jerusalem, Pope Sylvester
and Mena, Francis and Dominic, John Huss and Jerome of Prague, the
Waldenses and the Paulikians, in this view of the case, are not once to be
thought of.

These Witnesses are not presented to John in vision. They are described
to him by the glorious Angel, who is the Lord Jesus Himself. The account
we have of them is not John's account, as in most other instances in this book ;
but it is *Christ's* account, given in Christ's own words. But few interpreters
have remarked this, though a striking feature of the case, which shows that
we here have to do with something altogether extraordinary and special.*

The narrative is also somewhat anticipative. It brings together into one
compendious account the whole history, some of the details of which relate
to agencies and scenes which are only afterwards described in full. The Beast
who makes war with these Witnesses, and slays them, is not seen coming up
till we reach the thirteenth chapter. Their career accordingly reaches into
subsequent visions, and overspans scenes and events which remain to be
afterwards narrated. And the fact that the whole story of these Witnesses is
presented separately from everything else, in a different manner, and somewhat in advance of some of its connections, conclusively argues a peculiarity,
conspicuity, and extraordinariness in the matter, which cannot well be
exaggerated.

These Witnesses are *two* in number—δυσίν μάρτυσίν. This duality is three
times repeated, and is an essential part of the record. As stated by Alford,
" no interpretation can be right which does not retain and bring out this
dualism." Why two, we do not fully know. Both the law and the Gospel calls
for two witnesses to establish important truth. (Deut. 17 : 6 ; Matt. 18 : 16.)

---

* " From verse 3, to the sounding of the seventh trumpet, the matter is not exhibited in a
vision, but was dictated to John by an Angel personating Christ ; the observation whereof is
of no small consequence."—Joseph Mede, *Key of the Rev. in loc.*

God generally sets his heralds and witnesses in pairs, as Moses and Aaron, Caleb and Joshua, Zerubbabel and Jeshua, Peter and John, the twelve and the seventy, "two by two." And in the trying circumstances here described, two could better uphold and console each other than one, without companionship.

These witnesses are *persons*. Primasius says, though somewhat equivocally, " The Two Witnesses represent the Two Testaments preached by the Christian Church to the world," and Bede, and Bishop Andrews, and Melchior, and Affelman, and Croly, and Wordsworth, and some others, have taken this view. But it is altogether a mistaken view, necessitated by the embarrassment occasioned by wrong conceptions of the Apocalypse, rejected by the overwhelming majority of interpreters ancient and modern, and utterly irreconcilable with the text. It is not true that the Old and New Testaments are preached to the world only 1260 days, or years, and then end their testimony ; —that they are arrayed in sackcloth all the days they are preached ;—that fire issues out of their mouths and kills those who will to injure them ;—that there is no rain upon the earth during the days of their prophesying ;—that they have power over waters to convert them into blood, or at will to smite the earth with plagues ;—that they are capable of being killed by man ;—or that indignity can be offered them, being dead, by refusing to allow them to be put into a sepulchre. Yet all these things are affirmed of these Witnesses. Nor is either the Old or the New Testament ever called a μαρτυρ. Ten times do we find this word in the New Testament, and in every other place but this, no one questions that it denotes *persons*. In more than fifty places in the Old Testament, the corresponding Hebrew word denotes *persons* only. These Witnesses *prophesy*. This is the work of a *person*. More than one hundred times does this word (προφητευω) occur in the Bible, and never, except once by metonymy, but of *persons*. These Witnesses wear clothing of sackcloth, of which we read much in the Scriptures, but always of *persons*. They work miracles and execute judgments, but nothing of the sort is ever predicted of anything but personal agents. Not without the greatest violence to language and fact, therefore, can we regard these Witnesses as other than real persons. The conclusion may be very damaging to some men's cherished theories, but the integrity of God's word requires it, and it is impossible to escape it with any just regard to the laws of language and the nature of things.

These witnesses are *individuals*. No reader of the account, having no preconceived theory to defend, would ever think of taking them for bodies, or successions of people. All the early fathers, from whom we have any testimony on the subject, regarded them as two individual men. Two distinct and conspicuous bodies of witnesses for Christ, all prophesying in sackcloth through 1260 years, or even days, and all dying martyrs, as here represented, expositors have searched in vain to find in the history of the Christian ages. Such bodies of men, with such powers, and with such a history, have never existed. Modern writers have flattered themselves that they have found successions of people scattered through the middle ages, whom they would have us accept as The Two Witnesses of the text ; but they have been obliged to purchase their conclusions at the expense of explaining away every distinct feature of the record, doing violence to the facts of history, and super-exalting almost every species of obscure and even heretical sects and sectarists as God's only acknowledged prophets. This is by far too great a cost at which to accept a theory, which, even if true, would be totally unworthy of a place in so solemn and momentous a book as this Apocalypse. Good and able men have satisfied themselves with it ; but, on the same principles of interpretation, there is not a chapter in the Bible, nor a doctrine of our holy religion, which could not be totally explained away. By a happy inconsistency they do not so treat other portions of Scripture, or they would transmute the whole Revelation of God into uncertainty and emptiness. And whilst we give them credit for their learning, industry, and good intentions, and admit that a dim and imperfect correspondence to these Two Witnesses may perhaps be traced in the past history of the Church, yet, as we value the literal truth and certainty of the Divine Word, we cannot accept their expositions as exhaustive, or even as approximative to the revelation here given us.

WHO, THEN, ARE THESE TWO WITNESSES?

The connection in which the account of them is given, may serve to put us somewhat on the track of the right answer. These Witnesses come upon us suddenly, in the midst of the scenes of the judgment. The glorious Angel, which is Christ, is in the act of taking possession of the earth. New commissions have gone forth, which introduce the saints in heaven to new activities relating to the earth. In the person of John they are commanded to measure the temple, its altar, and the worshippers in it. And in connection with this command, and as part of the same address of the glorious Angel, the word is : " *And I will give to my Two Witnesses, and they shall prophesy a thousand two hundred and sixty days. These are the two olive-trees and the two lamps which stand before the Lord of the earth.*"

Now, as saints from heaven are to do the measuring, and the Two Witnesses are promised, in part at least, to accompany the measuring, would it not be natural to suppose *them* also to be some noted saints from heaven? Saints from heaven are in the field. These Witnesses fulfil their office in connection with a work assigned to those saints, and in some sort by way of co-operation or supplement of the same. Why should we then think of their being any other than also saints from heaven? Hence, with the whole body of the early Church, I take them to be none other than two such saints from heaven.

But a very marked and wide distinction is made between these Witnesses and the saints represented by John. Those are *measures*, these are *witnesses*. There is nothing said to show that the measures are known or visible to the people on the earth ; but these Witnesses prophesy and preach to men, and are seen, and heard, and known, and handled by them. There is no intimation that the measurers are the objects of persecution, affliction, or death ; but the Witnesses are hated, resisted, and finally killed. This difference indicates not only a difference of office and sphere, but also a difference in the form and susceptibility of being. The saints who have once died, and been resurrected and glorified, have put on immortality, and are no longer capable of death. " *Once* to die " is the lot appointed unto men ; and having paid that debt, bodily death hath no more power over them. And as these Two Witnesses die subsequent to their prophesying, we are driven to search for some saints in heaven, who never have died.

Nor will our search be a fruitless one. The Scriptures tell of two noted prophets, who have now been thousands of years in heaven, and who, for aught we know to the contrary, are just as capable of death and resurrection as ever ; especially if God has so arranged and intended. Need I say more plainly to whom I allude? They are so marvellously distinguished in the Scriptures from all others of the race, that it is at once suggested to the Christian mind who they are. They were, and still are, God's pre-eminent witnesses. They were God's most noted prophets while they sojourned upon earth, and, in the manner of their removal from among men, they are the only witnesses of the kind that God ever gave. One of them lived on the other side of the flood, " and was not, for God took him." The other was a Jew, of the degenerate times of Ahab and Jezebel, who " went up by a whirlwind into heaven." The one is ENOCH, the seventh from Adam ; the other is ELIJAH, the Tishbite.

It may strike the modern ear with some surprise to hear of these saints, or any saints, returning again to earth here to suffer and be killed. We live in a very materialistic and sceptical age ;—one slow to believe, and very unwilling to receive anything outside of the common round of human observation. People see things running on in one channel, and call it *Nature*, and will not hear of the possibility of any variation from it, though what they reject may really be no more unnatural than what they admit. They are so impressed with the uniformity and stability of things around them, though knowing almost nothing about them, that they give out with great confidence : " Since the fathers fell asleep all things continue as they were from the beginning of the creation " (2 Pet. 3 : 4), and ridicule the credulity of those who can listen to anything else. They forget how the Scriptures pronounce against such a temper, and foretell it as one of the marked symptoms of the last days, and warn us to beware of it as unspeakably dangerous with regard to the predicted wonders of the judgment time. We must, therefore, make due allowance for the sceptical spirit of our modern atmosphere, and not reject extraordinary truth simply because it strikes us as too extraordinary.

> There are more things in heaven and earth, Horatio,
> Than are dreamt of in your philosophy.

Neither is it so unheard of and improbable a thing after all, that beings from heaven should come to the earth, and suffer, and die, and rise again. An infinitely longer time than since the rapture of Enoch, had the blessed and adorable Son of God been in heaven ; yet he came to earth, suffered, *died*, and rose again. Even after His incarnation, on the mount with Peter, James, and John, he was as much arrayed in heavenly glory as Elijah who there appeared in converse with him ; yet, from that holy mount, and glory, and sublime transfiguration, he came down, and suffered, and *died*. Paul was once in heaven, caught up, he knew not how, and saw and heard things he dared not tell ; and yet, he came back, and preached, and suffered, and *died*. John was called up to heaven, to behold the wonders that are described in this Book ; yet he also returned, and suffered, and *died*. And if the eternal Son of God from the very throne of Deity, and the Son of Mary from the mount with Moses and Elijah in glory, and Paul in the third heaven, and John amid the wonders of the scenes he writes of in the Apocalypse, could and did come from thence to preach, and suffer, and *die*, what laws of things, or word of Revelation, can be produced to preclude the possibility of a like return, suffering and death on the part of Enoch and Elijah ? There are no such laws, and there is no such word.

But so marvellous a truth is not to be rested on mere likelihoods and probabilities. We must have something positive and decided for it, or dismiss it as a fancy. Something positive and decisive, however, we have.

Turning back to the ancient prophets, we find this word : " Behold, I will send my messenger, and he shall prepare the way before me : and the Lord, whom ye seek, shall suddenly come to his temple, even the messenger of the covenant, whom ye delight in : behold he shall come, saith the Lord of hosts. But who may abide the day of His coming ? And who shall stand when he appeareth ? for he is like a refiner's fire, and like fuller's soap : and he shall sit as a refiner and purifier of silver : and he shall purify the sons of Levi, and purge them as gold and silver, that they may offer unto the Lord an offering in righteousness. Then shall the offering of Judah and Jerusalem be pleasant unto the Lord, as in the days of old, and as in former years. And I will come near to you in judgment. . . . For, behold, the day cometh, that shall burn as an oven ; and all the proud, yea, and all that do wickedly, shall be stubble : and the day that cometh shall burn them up, saith the Lord of hosts, that it shall leave them neither root nor branch. . . . BEHOLD, I WILL SEND YOU ELIJAH THE PROPHET [the Septuagint, Arabic, and old Latin versions read ' *Elijah the Tishbite* '] *before the coming of the great and dreadful day of the Lord : and he shall turn the heart of the fathers to the children, and the heart of the children to their fathers, lest I come and smite the earth with a curse.*" (Mal. 3, 4.)

This is God's own word—the closing word of the Old Testament. It names Elijah the prophet, even Elijah the Tishbite, and says that God will send *him* again upon earth, to minister among men as the forerunner of the great and terrible day of the Lord—the day of the final overthrow of all the hosts of the wicked.

Here, then, we would seem to come upon solid Scriptural ground. If Elijah means Elijah, and the great and terrible day of the Lord is the day of Christ's final coming in judicial majesty to crush out Satan and his seed, there is no alternative left to believers in God's word, but to receive the doctrine that Elijah is to come again to prophesy and execute works of judgment upon earth, and just in that period of time to which the Apocalypse assigns these Two Witnesses. Whatever else may be compassed by the prediction, and in whatever narrower circles it may have been fulfilled, if words are not utterly deceitful, and certainty can at all be predicated of God's very specific promises, this prophecy cannot be considered fulfilled or accomplished in the past, nor until Elijah the Tishbite, *in propria persona*, returns again to the earth.

We accordingly find that the book of Ecclesiasticus (which the Roman Catholic Church receives as inspired, which the fathers and Reformers highly honoured, and which Protestants often have bound in their Bibles between the Old and New Testament), eulogizes Elijah and says, that he is anointed by God's order to appear again in the world, to rebuke evil, declare the impending judgment, reconcile the children of Jacob, rescue many, and make the way for the great and terrible day then about to break. (Chap. 48 : 1–11.) Hence also the ancient Jewish believers up to the time of Christ, as all strict Jews since, looked for the reappearance of Elijah in the flesh as the herald of the victorious Messiah. Arnold (in Ecclesiasticus 48 : 10) says : " It was the unanimous sense of the Jews, that Elias should first come himself in person before the Messiah, and restore all things." Their old Litany of the Hosannas celebrates this anticipation.* Their most honoured writers constantly refer to it.† Hence, too, the deputation to John the Baptist with the question : " *Art thou Elias ?* " (John 1 : 19, 20.) And hence the remark of the disciples to Christ : " *The Scribes say that Elias must first come.*" (Matt. 17 : 10.)

Some teach that this was a mistake—a mere Jewish notion. If so, it was a most extraordinary mistake. What was so devoutly accepted, taught, and believed by the holiest saints from Malachi to Christ, the theme of so many

* See Etheridge's *Targums on the Pentateuch*, I, 33, 34.

† " Pesiqta Rab., fol. 62, col. 1, speaks of it. Jalkuth Shimoni, fol. 53, col. 3, gives the same view : ' Elijah will come three days [years ?] before the Messiah ; ' quoted in *Eisenmeng. Entdeckt. Jud.*, II, p. 696. So the Talmund, Tract. Shabbath, fol. 118, col. 1 ; Rabbi Bechai, Shulcan Arba, fol. 5 ; col. 4 ; Jalkuth Shimoni in Mal., fol. 88, col. 4 ; each and all repeat the same sentiment, *Eisenm.*, *ut supra*, p. 712. Emek Hammelakh repeatedly declares the same thing ; quoted in *Eisenm.* II, 714, 715."—*Stuart in loc.*, II, 222.

" The passages from later Jews may be found collected in Frischmuth (*De Eliae Adventure*, Jena, 1659 ; reprinted in the *Thesaurus Antiquus*). In the Book *Chissuk Emunah* (Wagenseil's *Tela*, II, 318), Rabbi Isaac says, ' It is well known in the nation of Israel that the Messiah would not be manifested till Elias the prophet had come, as we find from this passage (in Malachi).' According to the *Schulchan Aruch* (in Frischmuth) the Jews were in the habit of remembering Elias every Sabbath, and praying that he might at length come and announce their redemption, which they regarded as the sole object of his coming. And Aben Ezra concludes his commentary on Malachi with the words, *Deus propter misericordiam suam vaticinium suam impleat, flnemque adventus illiu sacceleret.*"—Hengstenberg's *Christology of the Old Test.*, IV, 220.

" Indeed, the Jewish belief in the literal appearance of Elias as the herald of the Messiah was universal, and so universal does it continue to this hour, even after the lapse of eighteen centuries, that the Jews at their marriage feasts always place a chair and knife and fork for Elijah. They also set a chair for him at their passover feast, at which time they more especially look for him."—*Armageddon*, vol. i, p. 131.

" In the celebration of the Passover two large cups are filled with wine. One of these is taken by the master of the house, and a blessing pronounced. After this blessing the head of the family gives the cup to all those sitting around. He then brings forth the hidden cake, and distributes a piece to each. The second cup of wine, called ' *Elijah's cup*,' is then placed before him ; the door is opened, and a solemn pause of expectation ensues. It is at this moment that the Jews expect that the coming of Elijah will take place to announce the glad tidings that the Messiah is at hand. Well do I remember the interest with which, when a boy, I looked towards the door, hoping that Elijah might really enter ; for, notwithstanding the disappointment year after year, his arrival is still confidently expected."—*Herschell's Brief Sketch*, p. 61.

holy prayers and songs, and given out for the truth of God by the most eminent Christian fathers down to and inclusive of Jerome and Augustine, cannot safely be set down as a groundless conceit. We also have the highest Scriptural reasons for believing that it was not an empty notion, but a part of the true and abiding Revelation of God. Jesus Himself has affixed His own infallible authentication to it, and in such explicit terms that we can only wonder how people can speak so contemptuously of it as some writers who call themselves Christians.

On the mount of Christ's glorious Transfiguration Elijah appeared. The disciples saw him and knew him. And, as they were coming down from the mount, they asked the Master about this very point, alleging the doctrine of the scribes that " *Elias must first come*." And He answered and said unto them : " ELIAS TRULY SHALL FIRST COME, AND RESTORE ALL THINGS." (Matt. 17 : 11.) This passage is decisive. " The great Interpreter of prophecy gives right to that interpretation of the prophetic word which the scribes maintained," says Trench. It cannot refer to John the Baptist, for John was then dead, while every part of it specifically relates to *the future*. " Elias truly *shall* come,* and *shall* restore all things."† Besides, the restoration or " restitution of all things " (ἀποκαταστασις παντων), in the which it is affirmed that the coming Elias is to take part, is specifically referred by the Apostle Peter to the time of Christ's second coming. (Acts 3 : 19.) In all its terms and relations, therefore, we are compelled to accept this solemn declaration of the Saviour as looking to the future, and meant to set forth what yet awaited fulfilment. John the Baptist is here out of the question, unless indeed he is to come again. Dr. Stier has rightly said : " Whoever, in this answer of Christ, would explain away the manifest and striking confirmation of the fact that a coming of Elias was yet to take place, must do great violence to the words, and will never be able to restrain the future of their form and import so as to be applicable to John the Baptist."‡

But, it may be asked, Did not Christ say in the same connection, that Elias had come already, leaving it to be understood that He spoke of John the Baptist ? The answer is, Yes ; but in a way entirely distinct from the declaration we have just been considering. Elsewhere also he says of John : " If ye will receive [*it, him,* or something else] this is Elias, which was for to come." (Matt. 11 : 14.)§ This proves that there is a sense in which John the Baptist was Elias, but certainly not such a sense as that in which the Jews were expecting Elias, nor yet such a sense as that in which He declared, after John was dead : " *Elias truly shall first come and restore all things.*"** John was not

---

* The word here is ἐρχεται, which is indeed in the present tense, and might be read *cometh*, or *is coming*, which would still not admit of application to John, whose whole career was then in the past ; but it is a well-known rule in Greek composition to use the present tense when it is meant to emphasize the certainty of something still future, representing the thing in contemplation as actually commenced already. See Jelf's *Greek Grammar*, § 397, and Winer's *Idioms*, § 41,2. But, in the next clause, ἀποκαταστησει, which describes the work of the coming Elias, *is in the future*, and can by no means be applied to the work of John, which was then entirely in the past. Our translators have, therefore, rightly rendered it *shall come*.

† " Did John restore anything ? He restored nothing. He was the inspired rebuker of a country's sins, and he bade them prepare for the reception of that country's Lord ; but he literally restored nothing. And, therefore, this must apply to what shall be, and not to that which has already been."—Cumming, *in loc.*

‡ Words of the Lord Jesus, vol. ii, p. 368.

§ Our translators here have not been very happy in their rendering. Ἡλιας ὁ μελλων ἐρχεσθαι, does not mean *Elias which was for to come* in the exclusive sense that there could be no further coming of Elias more literally than in John the Baptist, but rather bears the intimation that a further coming is to be awaited. The literal translation would be, " He [in some sense] is *Elias who is about to come*." John had come and was then in prison, but the true, the literal Elias-coming is given as *future*.

** The apodosis (μεν, δε) in this passage is not between the two affirmations as to the truth of one and the falsity of the other, for both are given as true. There is no limitation or negation of the first clause by what is said in the second ; but the distinction indicated is, that one contemplates the Elias in one sense of the promise, *i.e.*, literally, and the other the literal Elias. This we are compelled to admit, or else he did not tell the truth ; for when the priests and Levites asked him, " *Art thou Elias ?* " he answered, " I AM NOT." (John 1 : 21.) And this clear and positive denial is further sustained by the facts (1) that he did not restore all things as was predicted of Elias, and (2) that the great and terrible day, which was to be ushered in immediately upon the finishing of the Elijah ministry, did not succeed the ministry of John, but is even yet future. Whilst, therefore, there is a sense of much importance in which John *was* Elias, there is another, more literal, and equally important sense, in which he was *not* Elias, and in which Elias is still to be expected, according to the Saviour's own word.

There was a twofold ministry embraced in the ancient promise to send Elijah, just as there was a twofold advent in the predictions concerning the Messiah. In neither case did the Old Testament clearly distinguish between these two, but viewed them both as if they were but one. And as the two *Messiah*-comings are widely separated in time, though belonging to one and the same work ; so there are two *Elijah*-comings, equally separated in time, and equally comprehended in the predictions. Hence, John, as the forerunner of Christ in the first advent, was Elias ; that is, he filled the Elijah place, operated in the Elijah spirit and energy, did for that occasion the Elijah work, and so far fulfilled the Elijah promise. As the angel said of him before he was born, he went before Christ " *in the spirit and power of Elias* " (Luke 1 : 15-17) ; which implies that he was not Elias himself. The Saviour could, therefore, truly say of him while living, " If ye will receive it, this is Elias which was for to come ; " and so likewise after he was dead, " Elias is come already, and they knew him not, but have done unto him whatsoever they listed." John the Baptist operated in the spirit and energy of Elias, and performed the Elijah mission for the first advent, and so far " *was Elias*," but, according to the word of the angel, only the *virtual*, and not the *literal* Elias. He could accordingly answer the Jews, who had in mind the literal Elias, that he was *not* Elias, while yet, in another respect, he *was* Elias. In him the prediction in Malachi concerning the sending of Elijah had a true and real fulfilment, but only a partial, germinant, preliminary fulfilment, whilst the highest and ultimate fulfilment respects another advent of the Messiah, and the coming of the literal Elijah as the herald of it.

Such also is the view which the fathers took of the matter ; and so they held and taught on the subject with great unanimity.

Justin Martyr says, " If Scripture compels you to admit two advents, shall we not allow that the word of God has proclaimed that Elijah shall be the precursor of the great and terrible day, that is, of His second advent ? Accordingly our Lord in His teachings proclaimed that this very thing would take place, saying, that Elijah would also come. And we know that this shall take

in another sense, *i.e.*, figuratively ; neither being at all inconsistent with the other. " Jesus answered and said unto them, Elias [μεν, on the one hand, in one respect] is coming first, and *shall* restore all things ; [δε, on the other hand, in another respect], I say unto you that Elias, is *come already*, and they knew him not." As Alford expresses it, " The *double* allusion is only the assertion that the Elias (in spirit and power) who foreran our Lord's first coming, was a partial fulfilment of the great prophecy which announces the *real Elias*, who is to forerun His greater and second coming," (*in loc.*) The Lord answers, not by hinting that the scribes were mistaken in their literal interpretation, but by intimating a double fulfilment of the promise. He asserts at once the partial fulfilment of it already, and its future accomplishment. The holding of both these views is absolutely necessary to render this passage intelligible.—*Govett on Rev.*, p. 158. Jesus declares the opinion of the scribes concerning the coming of Elias in person, according to Mal. 4 : 5, to be wholly correct, and defines the kind of labours in which he is to be engaged ; but intimates that one had already exercised for Him this office, one whom the scribes had put to death, one who had wrought in the spirit and power of Elias.—*Olshausen in loc.* " Jesus confirms the literal accuracy of the prophecy, showing that John was in truth what the angel Gabriel had announced he would be, *one coming in the spirit and power of Elias*, but not the predicted Restorer of all things, for he was the forerunner of the dissolution instead of the restoration of the Jewish polity and nation. But speaking in the future tense, he says, that Elias truly shall first come and restore all things."—*Armageddon*, I, 112.

place when our Lord Jesus Christ shall come in glory from heaven ; whose first manifestation the Spirit of God who was in Elijah preceded as herald in John."*

Hippolytus says, " As two advents of our Lord are indicated in the Scriptures, also two forerunners are indicated, the first was John, the son of Zacharias. He first fulfilled the course of forerunner. But since the Saviour is to be manifested again at the end of the world, it is matter of course that His forerunners must appear first, as He says by Malachi, I will send to you Elias the Tishbite before the day of the Lord, who shall come and proclaim the manifestation of Christ that is to be from heaven, and perform signs and wonders."†

So too *Origen :* " The vision upon the mountain in which Elias was seen, did not appear to agree with what the scribes had said : for it seemed Elias came not before Jesus, but after Him. They asked the question, therefore, supposing that the scribes had misled them. But to this the Saviour answers, *not contradicting the tradition about Elias,* but declaring that there was another coming of Elias before Christ, which had been unknown to the scribes."‡

Victorinus, Methodius, Cyprian, and *Lactantius* express the same belief and expectation that Elijah is yet to come in person.§

Chrysostom says, " As John was the forerunner of the first coming, so will Elias be the forerunner of the second coming "—" Christ called John Elias on account of his performing the same office."**

Theophylact says, " By saying that *Elias cometh*, He shows that he was not yet come ; *he will come* as a forerunner of the second advent, and will restore to the faith of Christ all the Jews who are open to persuasion." " If we will receive it, that is, if ye will understand it wisely (if we will not take it too literally), this [John] is he of whom the prophet Malachi spoke as the coming Elias ; for the forerunner and Elias perform the same service."**

Jerome writes, " Elias himself, who will truly come *in the body* at the second coming of Christ, has now come *in the spirit* through the medium of John the Baptist."**

And so the great *Augustine :* " It is a familiar theme in the conversation and heart of the faithful, that in the last days before the judgment the Jews shall believe in the true Christ by means of this great and admirable prophet Elias, who shall expound the law to them. For not without reason do we hope that before the coming of our Judge and Saviour Elias shall come."††

And so profoundly and universally was this belief rooted and grounded in the early Christian heart and teaching, that De la Cerda says, " All the ancient fathers have delivered it ; " and Huetius testifies, " It is the constant and most received opinion of the Church, and all the fathers ; " and Maldonatus declares, " It was always the most constant opinion of Christians that Elias was to come before the day of judgment ; "‡‡ and Bellarmine gives it as his belief that to reject this doctrine is, *vel haeresis vel haeresi proximus error*— either heresy, or error next thing to heresy.§§

And so likewise it was expected and believed, by both Jews and Christians, that the returned Elijah would be accompanied by some other great prophet of the olden time, who was almost uniformly believed to be *Enoch*. Hence the book of Ecclesiasticus (according to the rendering of Bossuet, who regarded it as inspired and canonical) sets forth that Enoch is to come again, turn the

* Dialogue with Trypho, cap. 49.
† Concerning Christ and Antichrist, 44, 45, 46.
‡ On Matt. 17 : 10 *seq.*
§ See Elliott's *Horæ Apoc.*, vol. iv. Appendix.
** See Suicer's *Thesaurus*, vol. i, p. 1317, art. 'Ηλιas, where the original quotations are given.
†† *De Civ. Dei*, 22 : 29.
‡‡ Quoted by Whitby on N. Test. Matt. 11 : 14.
§§ Quoted by Hengstenberg in *Christology*, iv. 223.
See this whole subject more fully discussed in *Armageddon*, by a Master of Arts of the University of Cambridge, vol. i, pp. 97–116 ; Gresswell *On the Parables*, vol. i, p. 153 *seq. ;* Homes's *Resurrection Revealed*, pp. 219–226.

hearts of the disobedient, and give repentance to the generations then living (Wisd. 44 : 16), after the same manner that it speaks of Elijah. Hence, when John the Baptist told the messengers of the Jews that he was not Elias, they immediately asked him the further question : " *Art thou that prophet ?* " and wondered who he could be if " not that Christ, nor Elias, *neither that prophet.*" (John 1 : 19–25.)

The apocryphal Gospels, Acts, &c., which, though we go not to them for doctrine, belong to the early literature of the Church, and hence are competent witnesses as to the opinions current among Christians at the time they were written, are also very positive and clear in the assertion, that *Enoch*, with Elijah, is to witness again upon earth. In the history of Joseph the carpenter, Jesus is represented as saying : " Enoch and Elias must, toward the end of time, return into the world and die, namely, in the day of commotion, terror, perplexity, and affliction ; for Antichrist will slay them." (Chap. 31.) So in the Gospel of Nicodemus, two old men are found living in their bodies in paradise, one of whom says : " I am Enoch, who was well-pleasing to God, and who was translated hither by Him ; and this is Elias the Tishbite ; and we are also to live until the end of the world ; and then we are to be sent by God to withstand Antichrist, and to be slain by him, and after three days to rise again, and to be snatched up in clouds to meet the Lord." (Chap. 9 alias 25.) So also in Revelation of John, a voice from heaven is represented as saying : " Three years shall those times be. . . . And then I shall send forth Enoch and Elias to convict him [Antichrist] ; and they shall show him to be a liar and deceiver ; and he shall kill them at the altar, as said the prophet." So also Tertullian (De Anima, 50) ; " Enoch was translated, and so was Elijah ; nor did they experience death ; it was deferred ; they are reserved for the suffering of death, that by their blood they may extinguish Antichrist." Arethas (on Rev. 11 : 13) declares the two Witnesses to be Enoch and Elijah, and claims that this was held with one accord in his day—*concorditer affirmatur.* Ephraem the Syrian, in quite another section of the Church, speaking of the Antichrist and the great day of judgment, says, " But, before these things, the merciful Lord will send Elijah the Tishbite, and with him Enoch, to teach religion to the human race : and they shall preach boldly to all men the knowledge of God, exhorting them not to believe in the tyrant through fear. They shall cry out and say, ' This is a deceiver, O ye men. Let none of you in any way believe him : for in a little while he will be utterly abolished. Behold, the Lord, the Holy One, cometh from heaven ! ' "[*] So also Ambrose, who reproves Victorinus for substituting the name of Jeremiah in the place of Enoch as the companion of Elijah in the last years of this present world. And scarcely, until after the first half of the Christian ages, do we hear of any other testimony on the subject. Whenever we hear of the last great Antichrist and the Witnesses who withstand him unto death, *Elijah and Enoch, Enoch and Elijah* are the names we hear from the lips of the most eminent teachers, bishops, apologists, and martyrs, from the time of the Apostles onward. Modern Christendom has wellnigh dropped these names from all such connections, as it has also wellnigh dropped most of the characteristics of primitive Christianity itself ; but nothing that it has substituted in place of these names can claim even a moiety either of the Scriptural or the traditional evidences, which still, in spite of everything, continue to proclaim *Enoch* and *Elijah* The Two Witnesses.[†]

It is also to be observed that these Witnesses are described as specially *Christ's* witnesses. He styles them by emphasis " MY two Witnesses "—not so much witnesses for Christ in general as the Mediator and Redeemer of men,

---

[*] Sermon on Antichrist. See Maitland's Apost. School of Proph. Interp., p. 218.

[†] LUTHER thus expresses himself on the subject : " The old opinion that Elias and Enoch are to come again in the time of Antichrist, is derived from the text where Christ says, *Elias truly shall first come and restore all things.* It has found place in all the books, and has spread itself through the entire Church. We have no controversy with those who entertain this old belief. They may even wait for a coming of Enoch and Elijah, if they will also

but the witnesses of Christ in the particular character and relations in which He was then speaking, namely, as the Mighty Judgment-Angel coming down from heaven, robed in clouds, His face like the sun, and His feet as pillars of fire, about to execute vengeance on His foes and Himself take possession of the earth. And of all men that have ever lived, Enoch and Elijah are *the judgment prophets*. This particular impress was upon their ministry from the very beginning.

As to Enoch, this characteristic is particularly emphasized. Milton sings of him, that he

> ——" spake much of right and wrong,
> Of Justice, of Religion, Truth, and Peace,
> And Judgment from above ; "

but from a higher inspiration than that of Milton we learn, that the grand substance of his faith, and preaching, and prophesying, was the last named. We do not know of a single other word that he ever uttered save on this theme of " Judgment from above." There is no evidence that he ever preached on any other subject. The all-absorbing, all-comprehending, as all-characterizing topic of his entire ministry, as attested by the New Testament, was this, that he prophesied, saying, " *Behold, the Lord cometh with ten thousand of his saints to execute judgment upon all, and to convict all that are ungodly among them of all their ungodly deeds which they have ungodly committed, and of all their hard speeches which ungodly sinners have spoken against Him.*" (Jude 14, 15.) He was, therefore, the great prophet of judgment before the flood, and hence one special witness of Christ in the specific character of the strong Angel coming down from heaven in the clouds to execute vengeance upon the guilty.

As to Elijah, he was also pre-eminently a messenger and prophet of judgment. The Book of Ecclesiasticus says of him, that he stood up as fire, and his word burned like a lamp ; he brought sore famine upon the guilty, and by his zeal he diminished their number, and brought kings to destruction, and anointed kings to take revenge. (Eccl. 48 : 1–8.) Words and works of death and portent to the wicked constituted the great outstanding characteristic of his whole prophetic career, interspersed with the power of resurrection. His spirit was not the evangelic, but the judgment spirit. That wild figure, that stern voice, those deeds of blood, that vehemence of judicial administration, which stand out in such startling relief from the pages of the old records concerning him, have become somewhat silvered over in the Christian's thoughts with the light of the Mount of Transfiguration ; but the fiery zeal, and destructive wrath, and rugged outline of the old prophet of woe and death to Ahab and Jezebel, Baal and Ashtaroth, is still the true and characteristic picture of Elijah, identifying him, of all others since his time, as a peculiar Witness and Messenger of the Judgment-Angel. We search in vain for any other two prophets so peculiarly, intensely, and characteristically *Judgment-prophets*, or that so specially take on the features of heralds and representatives of the coming of the mighty Judgment-Angel.

They are further said to be " *clothed with sackcloth.*" This also is significant. It shows that they are individuals, and not bodies of men extending through a dozen centuries. " It is hard to conceive how whole bodies of men and

permit us to regard it as only an opinion. It is also allowed to believe it possible to interpret the passages in Malachi and Ecclesiasticus as predicting that Elias shall come again."— *Walch's ed.*, vol. vii, col. 494.

" The whole question rests on this, whether the prophet Malachi is speaking of the second coming of the Lord at the end of the world, or of the first coming in the flesh and in the Gospel. If he is speaking of the day of judgment, then certainly Elias is to be looked for again ; for God cannot lie."—*Walch*, vol. xi, col. 140.

" What shall be said then of the coming again of Elias and Enoch to withstand Antichrist? I answer : concerning the coming again of Elias I hang between heaven and earth, and waver the more with reference to it, that I am of opinion he will not come bodily. I also do not contend hard against it. I let those believe it who are so minded. St. Augustine in one place says, that the coming of Elias and the Antichrist is clearly shown to Christians."— *Walch*, vol. xii, 208.

churches could thus be described. The principal symbolic interpreters have left out, or passed very slightly, this important particular. One does not see how bodies of men who lived like other men can be said to have prophesied *in sackcloth.*"* It also shows that we here have to do with another order of things, and not with the present Gospel dispensation. Neither the prophets, nor the children of the New Testament, come thus arrayed in the garb of judgment-times, calamity, and burdens of woe. When we put on Christ, it is not sackcloth we put on, nor is it the spirit of heaviness we enter into ; but a wedding garment has clothed us, a garment of praise has arrayed our Spirit. The wearing of sackcloth, and the sort of life which it betokens, befit not these years of grace and jubilee, and relate to other times and another ritual. The mention of it here is a distinct indication that the dispensation has changed. Assuming, however, that Elijah and Enoch are to be these witnesses, the description fits entirely to what is written concerning them in the past, and is just what we would expect in case of their return as heralds of the judgment.

Elijah, that prince of Hebrew prophets, with all his holy zeal, was a solitary and savage man, rough and shaggy as a lion, dwelling in the hills and caves and unfrequented ravines of Palestine, when not confronting thrones or hewing false prophets to pieces. The Bible tells of the girdle of skin he wore around his loins, and the hairy cloak in which he wrapped himself, to which it gives a name never applied to any garment but his, and shows at every point of reference to him what wild and ascetic austerity and severity marked his whole style of life, as he traced and trod the footprints of Jehovah, and surged hither and thither by the mighty inspiration of God, insulted and outraged by the idolatries of Israel, and the abominations of its kings.

Nor was it different with Enoch. The nature of the times in which he lived necessarily made him a man much like Elijah. Whatever else is couched in that pregnant statement that he " *walked with God,*" it tells of a life sequestered from that of other men, rugged, isolated, and singular. Walking with God, he did not walk with men. If we may at all credit the Book which bears his name, " he was wholly engaged with the holy ones, and with the watchers in his days ; "† only coming forth betimes to reprove the wicked world, and to sound forth upon unwilling ears the herald voice and midnight cry of coming judgment. And these two great prophets returned to earth again as they were of old, to reprove still greater sins and declare the forthcoming of still greater judgment, would give the exact outline of these Two Witnesses prophesying in sackcloth, and tormenting them that dwell upon the earth.

These Witnesses are furthermore " *the two olive trees and the two lamps which stand before the Lord of the earth.*" Who are the two olive-trees ? All agree that the allusion is to Zechariah's vision. (Zech. 4.) He saw " a candlestick all of gold, with a bowl upon the top of it, and his seven lamps thereon, and seven pipes to the seven lamps which are on the top of it ; *and two olive-trees by it, one upon the right side of the bowl, and the other upon the left side thereof.*" He asked, " *What are these two olive-trees upon the right side of the candlestick and upon the left thereof ?* " and again, " *What be these two olive-branches which through the two golden pipes empty the golden oil out of themselves ?* " The answer was, " *These are the two anointed ones [oil-children] that stand before the Lord of the whole earth.*"

What was the meaning of this vision ? The Angel gave it : " This is the word of the Lord unto Zerubbabel, saying, Not by might, nor by power, but by my Spirit saith the Lord of hosts." That is to say, it was a material image of the mysterious organism through which the heavenly potencies were coming forth to give success unto completion to the work in which Zerubbabel was then engaged. That work was the restoration of Jerusalem, its temple, its worship, and its system of ordinances—the type of the building of the

---

* Alford's N. T., *in loc.*
† The Book of Enoch, by Archbishop Laurence, 3d ed., p. 13.

spiritual temple of the Christian Church, and the pattern and prophecy of that final rebuilding and restoration when the times of the Gentiles are fulfilled. That candlestick of gold stands for the national Church of the Jews, and thence also for the Christian Church (see Rev. 1 : 20), whilst the two olive-trees— the anointed ones—standing between God and the people, were Zerubbabel the prince, and Jeshua the high priest. Hence, when Christ declares these apocalyptic Witnesses " *the two olive-trees*," the meaning is, that they are the Zerubbabel and Jeshua of the final restitution ;—great ministers of God corresponding to Zerubbabel and Jeshua of old, and occupying a similar position as the organs of heavenly potencies put forth for the occasion. The two olive-trees in the vision are two individual persons ; so then these two Witnesses are likewise two individual persons, for they *are* " *the two olive trees* " *for their day*, as Zerubbabel and Jeshua were in a former day.

But whilst they are " the two olive-trees " of their time, as viewed through the medium of Zechariah's vision, the whole order of things is changed from what it was in Zechariah's day, or what it is in the present Church-period. The golden candlestick, with its many conduits and multitudinous burners, is missing. All of that arrangement has disappeared.* The Church-period has ended. Gospel ministers are *stars ;* but these Witnesses are not *stars*. There are neither " stars " nor candlestick left in the time of these Witnesses. As the more direct and special messengers of God, like Zerubbabel and Jeshua, who gave out the golden oil into the golden bowl and candlestick, the two olive-trees remain ; but they are alone, with no golden organism of light-bearers to feed and supply. They are themselves the only lightbearers now for they are at once " the two olive-trees *and the two lamps*." This clearly demonstrates that the economy is a new one, whilst it at the same time singularly agrees with the two characters whom we take it to describe. Such a lone and self-supplying *lamp* was Enoch—the sole light-bearer to the old world, then on the eve of submersion in the great waters of judgment ; and such a lone and self-supplying *lamp* was Elijah to the nation of Israel, then in great darkness, and drawing near its great captivity. Many distinguished individual lightbearers have graced the several ages of time, but none of them so marked and conspicuous in self-standing loneness as these two. Never but once did the human race depend for a knowledge of God's purposes upon one mere man as it depended upon Enoch ; and never but once did the Hebrew faith hang upon one mere man, as it hung upon Elijah and his ministrations. He was himself " the chariot of Israel and the horsemen thereof." (2 Kings 2 : 12.) Looking through the world for two men pre-eminently entitled to the name of " *the two lamps*," we must inevitably settle upon Enoch and Elijah, who, as " *the two lamps*," are mysteriously preserved to come again for the illumination of still darker times, after the same style as of old.

" *Which stand before the Lord of the earth*." This is peculiar language, but exactly fitted to the same conclusions. " *Lord of the earth* " is not the Christian title of God ; for the Church, like Abraham in Canaan, is only a pilgrim and a sojourner here, and Satan is now the god of this world. The characteristic name of our God in the Gospel is, " *The Father of our Lord Jesus Christ*." Yet, when Israel was about to cross the Jordan, and to possess the promised land as a divine nation, God was called " *Lord of all the earth*." (Josh. 3 : 11–13.) When Jerusalem was conquered and its people carried away captive to Babylon, the Most High took the name of " *the God of heaven*." (Dan. 2 : 18, 28, 37, 44, &c.) When they came back to rebuild the temple, and repossess their land, and re-establish their holy state, God was again called " *the Lord of the whole earth*." (Zech. 4 : 14.) But when He is styled *Lord of the earth*,

---

* Concerning the absence of the candlestick here, Mede says : " I confess I am here at a *nonplus*, neither have I yet found out a reason of this difference, apt and evident enough." Had he located these Witnesses in the judgment-times, where alone they belong, he could have been at no such loss for an explanation.

the word is *Adon, Master*, and not *Jehovah*. It would, therefore, seem to be a theocratic title, having relation to a divine nationality and government upon the earth. If so, the occurrence of it here, again bespeaks the Jew in his own land, and Jerusalem and the temple rebuilt ; and proves that this part of the Apocalypse relates, not to the middle centuries of Christendom, as so many think, but to that time when the glorious Christ is taking forcible mastery of the earth, and setting up upon it His own visible supremacy and kingdom.

These two Witnesses " *stand before* the Lord of the earth." This standing before or in the presence of the Lord, or the king, ordinarily signifies the enjoyment of a near relation, acceptableness and authority, as the servants or officers of the Lord or king. But this is otherwise so clearly expressed and implied with regard to these Witnesses, that we are prompted to look for something more peculiar and characteristic in the phrase as here employed. If we keep to the strict reading of the text, this standing of the Witnesses before the Lord of the earth was already a matter of fact when the statement was given to John. It is not said that they *will* stand before the Lord in the time and office of their prophesying, but that they were *then*, while the Angel was speaking, *standing* before the Lord of the earth. To keep rigidly to the words then, these Witnesses were persons already living in the time of John, and hence not churches and bodies of men born centuries afterwards ;—living also a true bodily life, for still capable of bodily death, as shown from the killing of them by the Beast. But John's earthly contemporaries have all been dead for ages, and were all dead long before the time at which any one has located these two Witnesses. Being alive then in the time of John, and still living a bodily life susceptible of bodily death, and thus surviving all John's earthly contemporaries, they must have been living *in heaven*, having been taken thither without dying. This would also seem to be the more particular sense of the phrase " *standing before the Lord.*" When the Saviour exhorts to watchfulness and prayer, that we may be accounted worthy to escape the judgment sorrows, " *and to stand before the Son of man,*" what is it that He most of all proposes to us, but transference to the presence of Jesus in the heavenly spaces without the intervention of death ? And if so, why may not this standing of the two Witnesses before the Lord of the earth in the time of John, be taken as specially descriptive of a corresponding transfer and continuity of bodily existence bestowed upon them ? *Dying* is falling—ceasing to stand—becoming prostrate ; and, by just antithesis, standing is *living*—continuity of bodily life uninterrupted by death. And in this sense, to *stand* before the Lord must involve transfer to where the Lord is, without the suffering of death. If then these two Witnesses, destined to be murdered by the Beast, were standing before the Lord in uninterrupted bodily life at the time these words concerning them were spoken to John, who could they be but ENOCH and ELIJAH ? Of all men that have lived in heaven or on earth, these lone two answer to the description. They were still *standing* in the time of John, never having *fallen* under the power of death ; and they were *standing before the Lord of the earth*, having been miraculously conveyed away from among men into the mysterious heavens, where they still *stand* in waiting readiness to fulfil any commands of their Lord, even though it should be to return to the earth, here to repeat in increased intensity their great deeds of old, and have added to their crowns that of martyrdom also.

Thus, then, it would seem to me, that we have sufficiently identified these mysterious Witnesses, and also in strict accord with all the terms and surroundings of the record, without straining language or forcing history, as in every other interpretation that has been given. Other arguments lie couched in what further is revealed concerning them, which will be brought out when we reach the places. But I must close for the present, which I do in the words of Paul, written not without some relation to this very subject : " O the depth of the riches both of the wisdom and knowledge of God ! how unsearchable are his judgments, and his ways past finding out." (Rom. 11 : 33.)

LECTURE TWENTY-FOURTH

THE TWO WITNESSES CONTINUED—THEIR TIMES, NOT GOSPEL TIMES, EVIL TIMES, TIMES OF INTENSE SUPERNATURALISM, JUDGMENT TIMES—PROPHETS OF THE COMING JUDGE—EVINCE THE JUDGMENT SPIRIT—INFLICT GREAT PLAGUES—ARE RESTITUTIVE PROPHETS FOR JEWS AND GENTILES—PREVENT THE UTTER DESTRUCTION OF THE RACE—IMMORTAL TILL THEIR WORK IS DONE, FINALLY VANQUISHED AND SLAIN—REFUSED BURIAL—JOY OVER THEIR DEATH—THEIR RESURRECTION AND RECALL TO HEAVEN—THE EFFECT—A GREAT EARTHQUAKE—THOUSANDS DESTROYED—MIGHTY TERROR—CONCLUSION OF THE SUBJECT.

REV. 11 : 5-14. (Revised Text.) And if any one willeth to injure them, fire issueth out of their mouth, and devoureth their enemies ; and if any one willeth to injure them, thus must he be killed.

These have power to shut the heaven that rain may not fall during the days of their prophesying : and they have power upon the waters to turn them to blood, and to smite the earth with every plague as often as they will.

And when they shall have completed their testimony, the beast that cometh up out of the abyss shall make war with them, and overcome them, and kill them ; and their corpse [shall lie] upon the broad place of the great city, which is called spiritually Sodom and Egypt, where also their Lord was crucified. And [certain ones] from among the peoples and tribes and tongues and nations behold their corpse three days [and] half, and suffer not their corpses to be put into a sepulchre.

And they that dwell in the land rejoice upon them, and make merry, and shall send gifts to one another, because these two prophets tormented them that dwelt in the land.

And after the three days and half the spirit of life from God entered into them, and they stood upon their feet, and great fear fell upon those who beheld them.

And they heard a great voice out of the heaven saying to them, Come up hither. And they went up into the heaven in the cloud, and their enemies beheld them. And in that hour there happened a great earthquake, and the tenth of the city fell, and were killed by the earthquake seven thousand names of men ; and the remained became terrified and gave glory to the God of the heaven.

The second woe is past ; behold, the third woe cometh quickly.

I HAVE noted some of the reasons for the uniform belief of the early Church, that the Two Witnesses here spoken of are individual persons, and that they are none other than Enoch and Elijah, returned again to this world in its last evil days, according to other sacred prophecies and ancient beliefs. The subject is full of interest, and is far from having been exhausted. A number of important inquiries and circumstances remain to be considered ; and to these I now propose to direct attention.

Assuming that I have sufficiently identified these Witnesses as the returned Enoch and Elijah, I invite you to note more particularly, I. THEIR TIMES ; II. THEIR DOINGS ; III. THEIR END ; praying the God of prophecy to prosper the attempt to search out the mysteries of his holy Word, and to guide us into a right knowledge of the predications he has given for our learning.

I. As to the *Times* of these Witnesses quite a good deal has necessarily been anticipated in the preceding lecture ; but, that we may have the picture more fully before us, a few further observations are necessary.

1. *The times are not Gospel times.* There are indications of the presence of the Jew and his temple, but no traces whatever of the present Church. Though symbols, which in their original application embraced the Church, are referred to, they are modified and recast so as to eliminate from them what specially represented the Church. " The two olive trees " appear, but the golden candlestick is gone, and in its place is nothing but two lone lamps,—the two Witnesses themselves. Ministers of God are present, but their spirit and method are entirely different from what pertains to ministers of the Gospel in

the present dispensation. These witnesses kill, torment, deal out fiery judgments upon their enemies, and avenge and resent the very *wish* to injure them, even before it is outwardly manifested in act. This is not according to the Christian spirit, and very unlike the commands which are upon us now. We are not to avenge ourselves, not to render evil for evil, not to smite and kill our enemies, but to love them and do good to them, and to be " harmless as doves." Even Jesus himself, who had all power, refused to exercise it after the style of these Two Witnesses, and has given us commandment to follow his steps. He tells us that he came not to destroy men's lives, but to save them ; and in this spirit his servants have ever acted. Stephen is stoned, James is beheaded, Paul and Silas are beaten and imprisoned, Peter is crucified, Polycarp is burned, Antipas is put to death ; but neither of them resists, nor attempts to defend himself by miracle, or to avenge the wrong inflicted. But here are ministers of God of another order. " Fire issueth out of their mouth and devoureth their enemies ; and if any one willeth to injure them, thus must he be killed." The preaching of the Gospel is a thing of joy and gladness. " How beautiful upon the mountains are the feet of him that bringeth good tidings, that publisheth peace ; that bringeth good tidings of good, that publisheth salvation ! " (Is. 52 : 7.) But these Witnesses are arrayed in sackcloth, and their very garb betokens calamity and judgment. Nature itself is joyful over the course of the messengers of grace. The prophetic word was, " The mountains and the hills shall break forth before you into singing, and all the trees of the field shall clap their hands. Instead of the thorn shall come up the fir-tree, and instead of the brier shall come up the myrtle tree." (Is. 55 : 12, 13.) But here the heavens are shut up that no rain falls, the waters are turned to blood, the earth is smitten by many a plague, and they that dwell on it are tormented. " Peace on earth and good will toward men " is the keynote of the Gospel ; but the ministry of these Witnesses is one of the three great apocalyptic woes. It is simply impossible, therefore, to find place for these Witnesses as Gospel ministers of the present dispensation. They have quite another commission, and operate for quite other ends. They remind us rather of the old theocratic order, when Jeroboam's hand was withered by the unnamed " man of God " when put forth to lay hold on him, and fire from heaven consumed the soldiers of Ahaziah that came against Elijah on the hill.

2. *They are very evil times*—times of great affliction and sorrow for God's true ministers. This is signified by their habit. They gird themselves in sackcloth, as Jacob when he mourned for his son, as King David in his grief and abhorrence at the unjust killing of Abner, as Daniel when he came before the Lord to lament the sins of Israel, as Hezekiah when he heard the blasphemies and boasts of Sennacherib, and as the priests of God when the holy services of the temple were intercepted. The world is so full of malignant evil, that they cannot maintain a being in it without the power of miracle. Hell has incarnated itself upon earth. From the abyss has come up a mysterious Beast, to whom Satan gives power and authority as his chosen agent, whose mouth is open in blasphemies against God and His tabernacle, after whom all the world wonders, and whom the great mass of men worship and adore. War rages against the holy ones, and overcomes them, and kills even the fire-guarded Witnesses themselves, whilst the people congratulate each other and make merry over the death of God's most extraordinary prophets. Times there have often been for good men to sigh, and cry, and wrap themselves in the habiliments of lamentation and woe because of the wickedness and evils of the world, but none to compare with these times of the Two Witnesses.

3. *They are also times of intense supernaturalism and miracle.* All the ordinary laws of things are shaken and bent, like reeds in a swollen river ; and extraordinary agencies and results put themselves forth from all sides. Saints from heaven and potencies from hell are upon the scene, as never was the case to the same extent or in the same manner before. Here are Enoch

and Elijah, who so miraculously disappeared from the earth so many ages ago, again as miraculously moving and ministering among men, and breathing fire which devoureth those who will to injure them. They have power to shut heaven, so that no rain falls during all their ministry ; they have power over waters to turn them to blood ; and every species of plague is in their hands wherewith to smite the earth and torment its wicked inhabitants.

And a similar preternaturalism presents itself on the side of evil. When Moses comes to Pharaoh with his heavenly signs and wonders, hell's priests are there too with their perplexing mimicries and lying wonders. So here. Supernatural divine prophets appear, and they are at once confronted with a supernatural man from the abyss, and his false prophet at his right hand, doing great wonders, making fire come from the sky in the sight of men, deceiving them that dwell on the earth by those miracles which he had power to do, giving life and speech to an image, causing men to worship it, and all to be beheaded who will not conform to the detestable idolatry. " As Jannes and Jambres withstood Moses, so do these also resist the truth." The worst impieties of all ages shall concentrate in one. All the power of hell itself shall come into play upon earth. Such times the world has not yet seen. Indeed, human philosophy has become so wise as to banish from the range of possibility even the smaller variations from the ordinary course of nature which stand recorded of the past. But all such wisdom is folly. There is nothing permanent in nature. It is not true that " all things continue as they were from the beginning of the creation." Mighty changes and variations have occurred, and will yet occur. Nature's laws are not God, and are ever subject to modifications both from heaven and from hell. Satan could impoverish and sicken Job as Moses could afflict Pharaoh. Nay, here it stands written, from the lips of Him who is the Alpha and Omega, that there shall come times when spiritual potencies, good and bad, will show their activity on the earth, as if nature herself were about to be entirely superseded. Men are astounded, and hold back from believing when they read the doings of Abraham's God among the idols of Egypt, or in the camp of the pilgrim Hebrews. They hesitate, and talk of fiction, metaphor, superstitition, orientalism, exaggeration, when the life and deeds of Jesus are the theme. But their doubts about the supernatural, and all their grave science on the subject, shall yet be utterly confounded. Here are times indicated, which shall bring men on earth face to face with living powers from heaven and hell in the gigantic struggle of their last conflict, and fill the world with wonders, of which those in Egypt were but the dim foreshadows ;—times when that Devil, whose existence some count a mere myth, will put himself forth in things so marvellous that, if it were possible, the very elect would be deceived, whilst the deluded world gathers as one man to his worship as their God and Saviour. People may doubt, and shake their heads, and vaunt the sobrieties of their better philosophy ; but such will be the times of these Two Witnesses.

4. *The same will of course be judgment times*. We must not lose sight of the fact, that in all these wonders of the Apocalypse, we have to do with " the Day of the Lord," and the winding up of all the affairs of this present world. This is the one great theme, from the seven Epistles onward. Phase after phase, and act after act, of the drama of this world's ending have already passed before us, as we have gone forward with these expositions. In the preceding chapter we saw this selfsame speaker of the text, who is none other than Christ himself, setting his burning feet on sea and land, holding in his possession the open title to both, and swearing by the eternal Maker of all things that there should be no more delay. Between that oath and the completed mystery lay only these days of the Two Witnesses, and a little season beyond the finishing of their testimony. The days of the seventh angel, when he sounds, bring the consummation of the whole matter ; and that angel stands ready to sound the moment these Witnesses pass from the stage. Their times, therefore, belong to the period when judgment is hastening to its culmination.

I

The old prophecy also says that Elijah is to be sent immediately " before the coming of the great and dreadful day of the Lord ; " that is, immediately anterior to the outpouring of God's consuming wrath upon the wicked in its highest stress and fulness, while the woes of judgment are surging hither and thither through the world all ready for the final consummating act. And one of these Witnesses is Elijah. Their times are, therefore, the fearful times of the judgment.

II. We come, then, to note THEIR DOINGS OR WORK.

1. They are here presented in the special character of Witnesses—prophetic Witnesses. A witness is one who deposes to the truth, explains it, attests it. All the prophets were God's Witnesses. So were the Apostles, who so solemnly and convincingly testified to the Gospel and its facts. So, too, all the confessors of Christ, who gave up their lives rather than surrender their faith, are called *Martyrs, Witnesses*. And so even Christ himself is " the faithful and true Witness," because of what he taught and testified, sealing it with his blood. The character, therefore, under which these Two Witnesses are described, indicates the nature of their administrations. They are great messengers from God, sent into the world in its last dreadful extremity, to teach, explain, and attest His truth and purposes. As Enoch and Noah in the old world, as Moses before Pharaoh, as Jonah in Nineveh, as Elijah against Ahab and Jezebel, as John the Baptizer to Jerusalem and Herod, and as the Apostles in the world lying in sin, so are these Witnesses to the populations and powers of their day. They rebuke reigning iniquity, unmask Satan's falsities, insist upon the prompt repentance of sinners, and maintain righteousness over against apostasy and abounding wickedness. They *prophesy*, expound the Scriptures, demand obedience to God, point out the only way of escape from oncoming damnation, and labour to turn men from darkness to light and from the power of Satan unto God.

2. But they are not only prophetic Witnesses, but by emphasis the Witnesses of the Angel who is speaking to John, " *My* Witnesses." This is proof positive that the Angel is Christ himself. Angels are often God's ministers, but he has never sent and endowed prophets to be the servants and messengers of angels. Nor have angels anything going on in this world so as to have use for witnesses. And when engaged in doing for God and His Church, they are never recognized as other than fellow-servants and brother agents with prophets and apostles. (Rev. 22 : 9.) We everywhere read of prophets and witnesses of God and Christ, but nowhere do we read of prophets and preachers of angels. Yet, here are two of the most extraordinary prophetic Witnesses we know of, whom this Angel designates as emphatically *His* Witnesses. The same must, therefore, be Christ himself, and cannot, in the nature of things, be any other.

But this Angel is not Christ in His present office and attitude as our sin-bearer and intercessor ; but Christ as the mighty Judge and King, about to close up the whole history of this present world, having already set his burning feet upon it, and sworn by Him that liveth forever and ever that there shall be no more delay. And it is in this particular attitude and work that these Witnesses are by emphasis *His*. They are not Gospel ministers according to the present order ; for the Church period is past. They are extraordinary persons for an extraordinary work. They witness for Christ, not as the bleeding and pleading Lamb of God, but as the avenger of his elect, who is about to break his enemies with a rod of iron, and dash them in pieces like a potter's vessel. They are Judgment prophets sent to resist the gigantic blasphemies of the final Antichrist, give to the infatuated world its last awful warning, assure of the coming avalanche of destruction, and put into condition for deliverance a people to be carried over to that new and better order of things which is then to follow.

3. To this also agree the powers which they exercise. Everything is full of the spirit of judgment. " Fire issueth out of their mouth and devoureth

their enemies." Gospel ministers also have enemies, who often hate and persecute them unto death ; but they are not at liberty thus to defend themselves. These Witnesses live in other times. The Angel has placed his feet of fire upon the earth, and his Witnesses are armed with fire, with command to use it. They emit or breathe it from their mouths the same as the Euphratean horsemen. I can make nothing of the record except to take it literally as it is written. Nor do I find any difficulty in the way of such an acceptation. The horsemen were supernatural beings from hell, and the Two Witnesses are supernatural beings from heaven ; and, in either case, I know not why the thing may not be true to the exact letter. If we are to think of gunpowder in the case of the horsemen, we must do the same here, and set down these witnesses as a brace of sharp-shooters. We do, indeed, know of holy prophets using miraculous fire against the wicked, but I know of no case in which they carried rifles. Nor would it seem congruous for Enoch and Elijah, after having been these thousands of years in heaven, to go about the earth as holy messengers of God with each a breech-loader on his shoulder. They will need no such weapons. He who, after his brief sojourn in Sinai, could speak fire from heaven which consumed fifty soldiers at a time, and repeat the operation at will, certainly would be at no loss to speak killing fire upon his assailants, after having gone to heaven in a chariot of fire, and lived there amid the celestial splendours for thousands of years. And come now again into the world as God's great judgment-prophet, it befits the times, himself, and the Angel whose he is, to prove to the doomed world by the very breath of his mouth that the devouring wrath of the Almighty is fully kindled, and ready to break forth in fiery destruction to all who stand out against his messengers, or seek to destroy them.*

But these Witnesses not only have power and command to kill their assailants with fire, but otherwise to torment and afflict the wicked world. They breathe the law-spirit, and they execute law-penalties. Of old the threat upon apostasy was : " Thy heaven that is over thy head shall be brass, and the earth that is under thee shall be iron. The Lord shall make the rain of thy land powder and dust : from heaven shall it come down upon thee, until thou be destroyed." (Deut. 28 : 23, 24.) And now that the time has come for all God's threats to be executed, these messengers of his come to attest the true state of things, " *shut the heaven that rain may not fall during the days of their prophesying.*" When Elijah was the first time on earth, " he prayed earnestly that it might not rain : and it rained not on the earth by the space of three years and six months " (James 5 : 17, 18) ; and the same will be repeated when he comes again,—repeated in token of the presence and anger of the same sin-avenging Jehovah.† It is for the great sin of idol worship, trust in false gods, and sacrilegious desecration of God's temple, that this shutting off of rain is the special penalty. (Lev. 26 : 1, 19 ; Zech. 10 : 1, 2 ; Jer. 14 : 22 ; Hag. 1 : 9-11.) We thus see reflected something of the characteristics of the times of these Witnesses, and of the more specific aim of their prophetic endeavours. The shutting of the heaven tells of infamous idolatry, false confidence, and defilement of the temple, and the infliction of this particular chastisement by these Witnesses likewise tells of efforts on their part to set on foot again the true worship of Jehovah in his own chosen house.

---

* " And if any one willeth to injure them, thus [by fire] must be killed." Even the Beast from the abyss, who shall finally slay these witnesses, will be cast alive into the lake of fire (Rev. 19 : 20). So that everyone seeking to do them harm will be overwhelmed with the same element, first or last.

† Modern expositors, such as Elliott, Gill, and the historical school in general, can make nothing of this *drought* but a drought of doctrine, a famine of the word. This is the more remarkable, seeing that throughout the whole period of this absence of rain the most extraordinary prophets of all time are witnessing, and prophesying, and working miracles, so as to affect " peoples, and tribes, and tongues, and nations " with their faithful testimony. That is as much as to say, the very raingods themselves are here, and operating with unwonted power, but no rain comes ! If such interpretation means anything, it makes these Witnesses very *dry preachers.*

One of the great plagues which Moses brought upon Egypt was the turning of the waters into blood. It was an infliction particularly related to the bloody and oppressive tyranny which had been enacted against God's people. In like manner these Witnesses " have power upon the waters to turn them to blood." The thing having been done once, there is nothing to hinder it from being done again. And as oppression, persecution, and wholesale murder, were the particular forms of sin which brought this plague in the days of Moses, its recurrence here tells of similar transgression, and shows further against what the endeavours of these Witnesses are directed. They come to rebuke and resent the blasphemies of unprincipled power, the oppressions of assumed authority, the murders of persecuting government, attesting by the nature of their infliction the near coming of the Almighty to overwhelm these bloody tyrants and all their hosts forever. Nay, " to smite the earth with every plague, as often as they will," is the intrusted prerogative of these Witnesses, that they may prove how everything is in the hand of Him who sends them, and is now ready to be turned into enginery of irresistible destruction to those who still persist in their impieties.

4. These Witnesses are " the two olive-trees." This refers us back to Zachariah, where Zerubbabel and Jeshua appear as the two olive-trees. These were the two special ministers of God, the one a prince and the other a priest, who led the advance in Israel's return from the great captivity, stirred up the people to the rebuilding of Jerusalem and the temple, and restored again something of the old polity and worship to its ancient place. A still greater desolation has since come upon Israel for the rejection of Christ and his salvation. It is to continue " till the times of the Gentiles are fulfilled," and the present Church order has run its course. Then is to come another restoration, and a " restitution of all things," when God " will take the children of Israel from among the heathen, whither they be gone, and gather them on every side, and bring them into their own land, and will make them one nation in the land upon the mountains of Israel . . . and they shall dwell therein, even they, and their children, and their children's children forever ; and he will set his sanctuary in the midst of them for evermore." (Ezek. 36.) The time for this is everywhere given as the judgment time—somewhere about the period of these Two Witnesses. And if they are Zerubbabel and Jeshua in some sort over again, we thus have a very distinct light thrown upon the character of their work. They are to lead the restoration of fallen Israel. They are to go up with the vanguard to their ancient seat. They are to inaugurate the work of bringing back to the ancient worship God's long-rejected and afflicted people. They are to labour for the setting up again of the temple and the theocratic rule, and for the return of the smitten nation to its true God and Saviour King.

5. But all this is made still clearer when we connect with it the literal prophecies concerning the coming again of Elijah. We find those prophecies in the Old Testament and the New, from the servants, and from the Lord himself. It was the work of Elijah when he lived on earth to convince and lead back the apostate people to the God of their fathers, and with the spirit of judgment to testify against the heathen falsities which had taken possession of the nation. John the Baptizer, who came " in the spirit and power of Elias," fulfilled a like office, called the people to repentance, and by the threats of impending doom incited them to flee from the coming wrath, and put themselves in readiness for the Messiah King, even then standing unrecognized among them. And so Malachi tells us that, before the coming of the great and dreadful day of the Lord, Elijah the prophet will come, " and *he shall turn the heart of the fathers to the children, and the heart of the children to their fathers.*" (Mal. 4 : 5, 6.) So, too, the Saviour himself tells us that " Elias truly shall first come, *and restore all things.*" (Matt. 17 : 11.)*

---

* It is simply impossible, on any true principles of interpretation, to refer either of these passages simply and only, or in their true grammatical import, to John the Baptizer. They

We may not be able to tell the full meaning of these words ; but the reference is, above all, to the Jewish people. Malachi introduces the announcement of the coming again of " Elijah the prophet," with special command to remember " the law of Moses," and " the statutes " given through him in Horeb for all Israel. The " fathers " must needs be the heads of the Jewish race and economy, who first received God's Institutes, and best understood and observed them. The " children," then, must be their remoter descendants, contemplated as apostate and quite estranged from their holy ancestors. The turning and restoring must accordingly relate above all to the Jewish people, whatever minor relations it may have to the Gentiles. There is to be a bringing back of the branches that have been broken off, to be grafted again into their

had him in view, but only, so to speak, as a spiritual Elias, one who performed in some sort the Elias work for the first coming, but not the true and real Elias of the second coming. The observations of the learned Joseph Mede are here very forcible.

As to the prophecy given in the last chapter of Malachi, quoted by St. Mark, and by our Saviour, Matt. 11 : 14, he says : " It seems by Malachi himself to be applied, not only to the first coming of Christ, but also to his second coming to judgment. For in his last chapter, speaking of the coming of that day which shall burn like an oven, wherein all the proud, yea and all that do wickedly, shall be as stubble, and it shall burn them up, leaving neither root nor branch, and he addeth, ' Behold [saith the Lord], I will send you Elijah the prophet before the coming of that great and dreadful day of the Lord : and he shall turn [or restore] the heart of the fathers to the children, and the heart of the children to the fathers, lest I come and smite the earth with a curse.' If we will not admit the *day* here described to be the day of judgment, I know scarce any description of that day in the Old Testament but we may elude. For the phrase of *turning* (or, as I had rather translate it, *restoring*, as the LXX ἀποκαταστήσει) the heart of the fathers, &c., the meaning is, that this Elias should bring the refractory and unbelieving posterity of the Jewish nation to have the same heart and mind their holy fathers and progenitors had, who feared God and believed his promises, that so their fathers might as it were rejoice in them, and own them for their children : that is, he should convert them to the faith of that Christ whom their fathers hoped in and looked for ; lest continuing obstinate in their unbelief till the great day of Christ's second coming, they might perish along with the rest of the enemies of his kingdom. Therefore the son of Sirach, in his praise of Elias the Tishbite, paraphraseth this place after this manner : ' Who wast ordained (saith he) an ἔλεγχος or *type* [he should rather have said *a means of testing, confuting, reproving, convincing*, as in the presence of great presumption and false pretences and claims ; for this is the meaning of ἔλεγχω, and answers well to the office of a *Witness* as in the case before us], for the times to come, to pacify the wrath of the Lord's judgment before it break forth into fury, and to turn the heart of the father unto the son, and to restore the tribes of Israel.' (Ecclesiasticus 48 : 10.)

" For the better understanding of this we must know that the old prophets for the most part spake of the coming of Christ indefinitely and in general, without that distinction of first and second coming which we have more clearly learned in the Gospel. For this reason the prophets (except Daniel, who distinguisheth those comings, and the Gospel out of them) speak of the things which should be at the coming of Christ indefinitely and all together, which we, who are now more fully informed by the revelation of his Gospel of this distinction of a twofold coming, must apply each of them to its proper time : those things which befit the state of his first coming unto it, and such things as befit the state of his second coming unto the second : and that which befits both alike (as this of a harbinger or messenger), may be applied to both [one being viewed through the other].

" Matt. 17 : 10, 11, where his disciples immediately upon his transfiguration ask him, ' Why then say the Scribes that Elias must first come ? ' Our Saviour answers, ' *Elias truly shall first come*, καὶ ἀποκαταστήσει πάντα, *and shall restore all things*.' These words our Saviour spake when John Baptist was now beheaded, and yet speaks of a thing future, ἀποκαταστήσει πάντα, Elias *shall come, and shall restore* all things. How can this be spoken of John Baptist, unless he be to come again ? Besides, I cannot see how this *restoring of all things* can be verified of the ministry of John Baptist at the first coming of Christ, which continued but a very short time, and did no such thing as these words seem to imply ; for the *restoring of all things* belongs not to the first, but to the second coming of Christ, if we will believe St. Peter in his first sermon in the temple after Christ's ascension (Acts. 3 : 19, &c.), where he thus speaks unto the Jews : Repent (saith he) and be converted for the blotting out of your sins, that the times of refreshing may come from the presence of the Lord ; and that he may send Jesus Christ which before was preached unto you ; whom the heavens must receive until the times of the restitution of all things, which God hath spoken by the mouth of all his holy prophets since the world began. The word is the same ἀποκαταστάσεως πάντων. If the time of restoring all things be not till the second coming of Christ [as here proven], how could John Baptist restore all things at his first ? If the Master come not to restore all things till then, surely his harbinger, who is to prepare his way for restoring all things, is not to be looked for till then."—*Mede's Works*, I, 25, pp. 98, 99.

own native stock, purified, delivered, and settled after their old estates. And for this, among the rest, these Witnesses are sent, at least Elijah, whom we believe to be one of them. Hence the words of Augustine, that " it is a familiar theme in the conversation and heart of the faithful, that in the last days before the judgment the Jews shall believe in the true Christ by means of this great and admirable prophet Elias, who shall expound the law to them. For not without reason do we hope that before the coming of our Judge and Saviour Elias shall come, because we have good reason to believe that he is now alive. . . . When, therefore, he is come, he shall give a spiritual explanation of the law which the Jews at present understand carnally, and shall thus ' turn the heart of the fathers to the children.' . . . The meaning is, that the sons, that is the Jews, shall understand the law as the fathers, the prophets, and Moses himself among them, understood it. For the heart of the fathers shall be turned to the children, and the heart of the children to the fathers, when the children understand the law as the fathers did, and have the same sentiments."*

As John was sent " in the spirit and power of Elias," we may also see in his stirring mission an indication of what the work of the real Elias shall be. His office was, as declared by the Angel, " to turn the hearts of the fathers to the children, and the disobedient to the wisdom of the just, to make ready a people prepared for the Lord." (Luke 1 : 16, 17.) We know something of the thrilling power with which his voice rung out from the wilderness of Judea, assaulting the apostasies and sins of the nation, and demanding instant repentance and return to the ancient faith on pain of a speedy destruction. He was a bright and shining light in the midst of a perverse and crooked generation, turning " many of the children of Israel to the Lord their God," and making ready a people from among whom the Gospel derived its first adherents and the Church its apostolic leaders and princes. And thus, on the superior scale in which the original excels the picture, and the second Advent exceeds the first, will Elijah suddenly flash out the sharp messages of Jehovah in the last evil times, and draw forth from amid the incurable ungodliness a portion of the house of Jacob to become the centre of a new order in the final restoration.

6. And such an office with regard to the Jews on the part of Elijah, suggests and argues a corresponding office with regard to the Gentiles on the part of his fellow-Witness. Enoch was not a Jewish prophet. He lived and prophesied long before Moses and the law. It was through his ministry that a seed was prepared to survive the awful flood to become the heads and princes of the repeopled earth. The son of Sirach celebrates him as taken up alive to heaven, that he might be a token, teacher, witness, herald, of repentance to other generations.† Such a token and witness he was in his own degenerate times. Patristic poetry sings of him as the " signal ornament " of the patriarchal Church, who

> By counsel strove
> To recall peoples gone astray from God
> And following misdeed, while raves on earth
> The horde of robber renegades ;‡

and inspiration tells of the pungency and fire with which he prophesied of the fearful coming of the Lord to execute judgment upon all, and settle accounts with the wicked for all their hard speeches and ungodly deeds. (Jude 14, 15.) And as the future ministry of Elijah is to wear the same features as the first, only intensified and exalted, the same must also be true of Enoch, who comes with him as one of the Two Witnesses. His first mission was to the common

---

* *Civitate Dei*, xx, 629.

† Eccles. 44 : 16, on which Arnold remarks : " As we meet with no account in Scripture of Enoch's sinning or repentance, it seems better to understand ὑπόδειγμα μετανοίας ταῖς γενεαῖς of his exhorting the people that shall then be alive to a speedy repentance, to prepare for the approaching judgment, and to resist the power of Antichrist."—*Com. in loc.*

‡ *Five Books of Reply to Marcion*, III, 20. See Clarke's *Ante-Nicene Fathers*, xviii, p. 344.

world at large, then drawing toward its end in the flood ; and so will be his future mission at the end of this present world, to prepare a people from among the Gentiles also to survive the great day, even though many whom he recovers to obedience may meet the fate of holy martyrs under the bloody reign of Antichrist.

7. The work of these Witnesses is then a merciful work. Though they appear in judgment times, and evince the severity of the judgment spirit, dealing out plague and fire, lashing and harassing the impious Beast from the abyss, tormenting them that dwell on the earth, killing all who venture to harm them, and causing all nations to feel the disturbing effect of their presence, they are still messengers of mercy on an errand of good and grace. True, their ministry will not be more effectual than it was when they prophesied of old. Israel as a nation will not then be turned back from its apostasy, and the world will not be deterred from acknowledging and worshipping the Antichrist. Because men love not the truth, even miracle and judgment will not persuade them. (2 Thess. 2 : 9–12.) Still, the sending and ministrations of these Witnesses is an act of mercy in the midst of wrath, and accomplishes a gracious purpose. *Some* are rescued and saved. But for these supernatural messengers the whole race would yield to the Antichrist, and perish with him. It is that the earth may not be utterly swallowed up under the terrible ban of final judgment, that they are sent. This is specifically stated in connection with the promise of the coming again of Elijah. The word is, " I will send you Elijah the prophet . . . and he shall turn the heart of the fathers to the children, and the heart of the children to the fathers, *lest I come and smite the earth with a curse.*" (Mal. 4 : 6.) The Hebrew word here rendered *curse* denotes *utter destruction.* It is one of the most fearful words in use among the Jews, and was specially applied to the extermination of the Canaanites, whose cities were razed to their foundations, and their inhabitants utterly destroyed.* And this fate would befall the whole race but for the ministry of these Witnesses, and the gathering out of an elect remnant by their instrumentality, for which remnant's sake the desolating and all-consuming terrors of " the great and dreadful day of the Lord " are measurably pacified and softened. When Jerusalem fell, except those days of awful suffering had been shortened, none could possibly have survived ; " but for the elect's sake those days " were " shortened." (Matt. 24 : 21, 22.) And a corresponding modification in the stress of tribulation and ruin is to occur again in connection with the last awful catastrophe, by reason of what these Witnesses achieve.

III. Notice, then, WHAT BECOMES OF THEM. Their career, though illustrious, and crowded with miracle from beginning to end, is very brief. " They shall prophesy a thousand two hundred and sixty days "—*just three years and six months.* The mightiest of sacred ministries on earth have been the shortest.

1. These Witnesses are immortal till their work is done. How they are nourished, or whether they partake at all of earthly food, is not told us. Elijah was supernaturally fed when on earth the first time ; nor can much less be said of John, the spiritual Elias ; and there is no reason for doubting that it will be more eminently so when the true Elijah comes again. At any rate, nothing can harm these Witnesses till they " have completed their testimony." They that undertake to injure or interfere with them are instantly burned to death. No power of earth or hell can touch or bind them. There was a time when Elijah fled from the face of Jezebel, and Herod imprisoned John, and finally cut off his head. But there can be no intimidation, no imprisonment, no killing of these holy messengers till they have quite fulfilled all that they are sent to do.

2. When their work is finished they become vanquishable and are vanquished. " When they shall have completed their testimony, the Beast that

* See Henderson's *Minor Prophets, in loc. ;* also Newcome's *Minor Prophets, in loc.*

cometh up out of the abyss shall make war with them, and overcome them, and kill them." Whether in consequence of a withdrawal of their power of self-defence and the gradual wasting of their heavenly vigour, like the fading of the celestial halo from the face of Moses, or by an enlarged licence to hell to act out its murderous malignity, the potencies of the underworld eventually seize them and put them to death. What form of death they die is not described. The reference to crucifixion in verse 8 can hardly be applied to them. We know that beheading is the ordinary mode of execution under the Antichrist. (Rev. 20 : 4.) John, who was the spiritual Elias, was beheaded. And it is to be inferred that so these Witnesses are killed.

3. Their dead bodies are denied sepulture. Their corpses are exposed " upon the broad place of the great city, which is called spiritually Sodom and Egypt, where also their Lord was crucified." " It cannot be that a prophet perish out of Jerusalem " (Luke 13 : 33) ; and there these last great prophets, like their Lord before them, meet their end. Jerusalem is called a " great city ; "* and as there is another great earthly city spoken of in this book, the further mark is given, that it is the one " which is spiritually called Sodom and Egypt." The introduction of this word " spiritually " settles the literalness of the narrative. Only the names " Sodom and Egypt " are, to be spiritualized, or taken in a sense different from the letter. Men mistake God's mind, and pervert God's word, when they refuse to accept and interpret the Bible as it reads. When he means it to be taken otherwise, he gives us indication to that effect. Jerusalem is not Sodom ; and yet, " spiritually " considered, or Jerusalem in apostasy, is a Sodom, and is repeatedly so called by the prophets. (Is. 1 : 9, 10 ; 3 : 8, 9 ; Deut. 32 : 30–33 ; Jer. 23 : 14.) So also is it " spiritually " likened to an Egypt, because of its idolatries. (Ezek. 23 : 3, 4, 8, 19.) But to identify the place beyond mistake, it is further described as the city " where also their Lord was crucified," which was none other than the literal Jerusalem. The main description is a moral one, indicative of the ripeness of affairs for the great destruction that impends, but it is likewise local and geographic, to distinguish the city now in question from great Babylon, with which some improperly confound it. Everything betokens that we are here on Jewish soil, and have to do with the Jewish capital. And there, in the broad place of public concourse,† the dead bodies of these Witnesses are exposed. " And certain ones from among the peoples and tribes and tongues and nations behold their corpses three days and a half, and suffer not their corpses to be put into a sepulchre." This is so intense an outrage upon common decency and humanity, that it is full of significance here. Even to the worst of criminals the law awarded burial on the same day of their execution (Deut. 21 : 22, 23) ; but all law and right feeling is set at defiance with regard to these prophets of God. The exposure of their dead bodies tells of a most extraordinary malignity and spite, and attests the extraordinary potency and effectiveness of the objects of it. It shows at once a devilishness of unwonted intensity in the people, and a terribleness of efficiency in the Witnesses in provoking a fiendishness and resentment so monstrous and unrelenting that it could not be placated by their death, but continued to reek and vent itself upon their lifeless remains after they were dead.

4. Great joy is experienced over their death. " They that dwell in the land rejoice upon them, and make merry, and shall send gifts one to another." These Witnesses were a terrible dread and annoyance to the Beast and his

---

* Alford in loc. erroneously says that " Jerusalem is never called by this name." Nehemiah describes Jerusalem as a " city large and great." (7 : 3, 4.) Jeremiah, speaking of the desolation of Jerusalem, says, " They shall say every man to his neighbour, wherefore hath the Lord done thus unto this great city ? " (22 : 5, 8.) Compare chap. 21 : 10, " that great city, the holy Jerusalem."

† In 1 Esdras 9 : 83, we read of " the whole multitude coming together into the broad place of the holy porch toward the East." See also Jer. 5 : 1 ; 2 Chron. 32 : 6 ; 1 Kings 22 : 10.

adherents ; and many a sore torment had they occasioned to the wicked. Those torments were indeed but the earnests and precursors of far greater woes now ready to break forth. But so insane are Satan's dupes, that they count their redemption come, if only they can get rid of God's faithful ministers. Now that the two mighty Witnesses are dead, they dismiss all further fear, consider their greatest trouble at an end, and send presents and congratulations to each other, as upon some grand jubilee.*

5. Three days and a half the holy prophets lie in death, their corpses a public spectacle, their killing celebrated as a general benefaction. The days are literal days, not years. Corpses could not endure to be thus exposed for three and a half years. Three *years* and a half they prophesied, and three *days* and a half they lie under the power of death. It was long enough to prove the reality of their death, of which the representatives of the nations were so anxious to be perfectly assured.

6. But they do not remain dead. " After the three days and a half the spirit of life from God entered into them, and they stood upon their feet." The extraordinariness of the death and resurrection harmonizes well with the extraordinariness of the history of Enoch and Elijah throughout. Of old, they left the world as no other mortal ever did, and here they are resurrected in a band by themselves, and under circumstances quite differing from all other resurrections. Whilst their exposed corpses were being watched and guarded by men overjoyed at their destruction, those lifeless frames took vitality again. The spirit of life from God re-entered them, and they arose from their prostration, and stood upright, gazing round upon the terrified people who beheld them, and flashing a fresh and still deeper alarm into the guilty souls late so joyous over their death. " The triumph of the wicked is short ; " and the " great fear " which now " fell upon those who beheld them," was only the intenser because of the fiendish indignities which had since been added to the sum of previous crimes. Conscience is a fearful executioner. A very hell of plagues and torments instantly throngs the imaginations of these astounded spectators. They remember the power and terribleness of these Witnesses while they lived ; how the mere will to injure them was resented with sudden death ; and what revolting and distressing afflictions they had given forth upon the worshippers of the Beast. And now that organized and Satanic war, and veritable killing, and the baseness of the most malignant insults after the killing, had been perpetrated, what was to be apprehended from this their sudden resurrection ! But these holy messengers had completed their work on earth, and Jesus himself was now to be their avenger. No more devouring fire issues from their mouths, and no further plagues do they inflict. By the power of God life is restored to them, even a higher, more glorious, more indestructible life than that which was given them in their marvellous translation. They rise and stand upon their feet. Their enemies behold them. The reality of their resurrection is as manifest as was the reality of their death. The fiendish joy of the enemy is suddenly turned into overwhelming terror. Guilty consciences are now the prophets that torment the people. The Witnesses prophesy no more. They only stand up, and other fires seize their adversaries' souls.

7. Heaven immediately recalls them. They stood by Christ in their testimony, faithful unto death ; and Christ now rewards their fidelity, receives them to himself, and crowns them among his heavenly princes. " They heard a great voice out of heaven saying to them, Come up hither. And they went up into the heaven in the cloud, and their enemies beheld them." People who would not believe in the resurrection and ascension of Christ for their hope and consolation, are now compelled to witness the resurrection

* The joy over a reputed enemy's death, and refusal to bury him, have been man's modes of expressing enmity in all ages and countries. Thus it was at the death of Phocion, of Cleomanas, of Tiberius Gracchus, and others. Over John Huss, burnt at Constance, the Council held banquets, and testified their joy, as over enemies destroyed.—Matheetees, *in loc.*

and ascension of his last Witnesses, to their horror and dismay. The record is literal. As well might we think to do away with the literal reality of the death, resurrection, and ascension of Christ himself, as with the literal reality of the death, resurrection, and ascension of these Two Witnesses. Against their wishes and theories, many have been compelled to admit the inevitable literalness of " the first resurrection " in chapter 20 ; but much more clear, circumstantial, and certain is the literalness of the account of these Witnesses and their marvellous end. I therefore receive and hold it for a literal history.*

When Jesus ascended, and his friends stood gazing after him in tearful wonder and adoration, holy angels lingered by with words of promise and comfort. Here there is another gazing into heaven, as his prophets go up. But the gazers now are his murderous foes. Marvels follow here also ; but they are marvels of judgment. Not loving angels with words of consolation, but executioners of divine vengeance with signs of doom show their presence. " *In that hour there happened a great earthquake.*" It is a literal earthquake, for it overthrows buildings and kills men. " *The tenth of the city fell, and were killed by the earthquake seven thousand names of men.*" Earthquakes attended the death and resurrection of Jesus also, but we read of no deaths occasioned by them. Those were days of mercy and promise ; these are days of judgment. A tenth part of the city is thrown into ruins, and many people are slain. Seven thousand men are enumerated as killed by this earthquake.† The record says " *names* of men ; " but men's names stand for those who have them, and they have them in proportion as those names are in people's mouths. Hence many understand by it *men of name*, note, and distinction, being seven thousand in number. When Jesus said to the Church in Sardis (Rev. 3 : 4), " Thou hast a few *names* even in Sardis which have not defiled their garments ; " he meant *persons* in Sardis. So when the same Speaker here talks of *names* being killed by an earthquake, it is equally clear that the reference is to *persons*. Perhaps the phrase is meant to denote only men of name, but it certainly denotes *men*, of whom seven thousand perish from the earth. They would not allow burial to the slain Witnesses, and now they themselves are buried alive in the ruins of their own houses, and in hell forever.

We may well suppose that such a cluster of stunning marvels would not be without effect, even upon the hardened wretches of those evil times. Amazement, conviction, terror, strike in upon their guilty souls, and for the moment they acknowledge the hand of God and seem ready to repent. " *The remainder*," that is, those not destroyed with the seven thousand, " *became terrified and gave glory to God.*" To see those dreaded Witnesses come to life again, and go up in triumph to the sky, and, in the same hour, one house in every ten of the city fallen, seven thousand men of name killed by the disaster, and the world itself rocking as if in the throes of dissolution, was more than even their indurated hearts could bear. Against their will they are forced to the confession that God's almighty power is in it.

* Stuart *in loc.* says, " The whole scene is here a mere *symbol passing in vision before the eye of the seer.*" He is utterly mistaken. It is not a vision of the seer at all. John never saw the first particular in the case. The whole thing is a narration from the lips of the mighty angel simply taken down by John as an amanuensis. See chap. 10 : 11 ; 11 : 1–3. Stuart takes the earthquake and killing in verse 13 to be literal ; why not then the death, resurrection, and ascension of these witnesses in resentment of whose wrongs this judgment is inflicted ? He also is forced to admit the literalness of the resurrection in chap. 20 : 6 ; why not this ?

† Cocceius, Elliott, Cumming, Barnes, &c., understand that these thousands represent the Dutch provinces which were lost to the Papacy at the Reformation (!), that these " seven thousand names of men " denotes seven Dukes or Dukedoms (! !), and that this killing of them by the earthquake really describes the setting of them up in self-living independence (! ! !). A glorious theme for Christ's solemn revelation from heaven as a special message to his Churches in all time ! Well does old James Robertson remark to this : " If we explain prophecy in this way, we may bring ourselves under very great hardships. It is a very rude way of treating Scripture."

Bengel thinks we have token here of an ample conversion. He is evidently mistaken. Such a terror-extorted giving of glory to the God of heaven, bears not the marks of genuine penitence. Neither do we find it bringing forth fruits meet for repentance. The Beast goes on with his iniquities, and the masses continue to serve and adore him. When true repentance shows itself, judgment delays or lingers ; but there is no postponement here. The consternation of the survivors of the earthquake concludes the second woe ; but instantly the word is, " *Behold, the third Woe cometh quickly.*" And that third woe is the consummation of woes. We, therefore, do violence to the record to take this forced confession as evidence or token of revival and reformation.*
Pharaoh and his magicians smarting under the plagues of Moses, the Philistines under the sore afflictions which accompanied their profanation of the holy Ark, and the Roman centurion amid the signs that attended the death of Jesus, made similar acknowledgments, and gave utterance to similar convictions ; but in neither are we assured of any real conversion to God. Startling calamities and bitter afflictions sometimes turn men from their careless and wicked ways ; but the religion of fear and dread is never to be trusted. Remove the pressure, and things relapse into their former estate. These people were terror-stricken. Their alarm carried them captive for the moment. They saw and felt that Jehovah's hand was in these things, and confessed it. But their emotions were only transient, had no right seat in the heart, and brought forth no lasting fruits unto holiness. When the demons encountered Christ, they too were terrified, confessed his Deity, acknowledged his power, and stood aghast at his approaching judgments ; but no elements of change

* " That the words in themselves are capable of a *good* sense, *i.e.*, that they might well be employed to designate true repentance and conversion, is not to be denied. But that they do of *necessity* imply anything more than a temporary impression made by divine judgments, is plainly an erroneous assumption. The New Testament is full of the like idiom, when speaking of men according to external development made at a particular time, when they are deeply impressed by divine judgments, wonderful miracles, or powerful preaching. So Jesus was δοξαζόμενος by all in the Synagogue at Nazareth, and yet the same individuals who applauded him, soon led him forth to cast him down a precipice. See Luke 4 : 15, *seq.* So the whole multitude of Jews who had seen his miracles, on another occasion, are said ' to have been filled with fear, and to have glorified God.' Luke 5 : 26. The same thing for substance may be found in Luke 17 : 12–18 ; 23 : 47 ; 18 : 43 ; Matt. 9 : 8 ; 15 : 31 ; Acts 4 : 21. So Felix *trembled* at the preaching of Paul. Acts 24 : 25. Herod heard John *gladly* and did *many things* in consequence of it. Mark 6 : 20. The stony ground hearers *received the word with joy*, yet they soon became offended. Matt. 13 : 20, 21. Many of the Jews *believed* on Jesus, who nevertheless forsook him. John 2 : 23–25 ; 8 : 30, *seq.* Many *became disciples*, who soon left him. John 6 : 60–66. Simon Magus himself *believed*. Acts 8 : 13 ; Ps. 106 : 12. In all these, and many more texts of the like kind, it is easy to perceive that the sacred writers have merely said *what appeared to be matter of fact* from profession, or from temporary outward demeanour. We must consult the context, *i.e.*, the history of such cases, in order to know whether the *glory*, or *belief*, or *fear*, or *discipleship*, in question is genuine and permanent, or only temporary and apparent. The nature of the case before us shows that only a temporary fear and praising of God is connected with the present instance. . . . Indeed, when we view the whole case, either in the light of the general plan of the work, or in that of New Testament philological usage, we may well say that the cases are rare, at the present day, where an exegesis appears more arbitrary than in the present instance ; I mean the exegesis adopted here [by Bengel] and defended by Bleek, De Wette, and Ewald."—Moses Stuart *in loc.*
" It is said, Luke 5 : 26, ' they were all amazed, and glorified God.' This is spoken of the Scribes and Pharisees, upon the view of a miracle performed on a paralytic ; yet was there no religion in it. The same we find recorded of a very mixed multitude, convened at the funeral of the widow's son, whom Christ in their sight raised from the dead, Luke 7 : 16, ' there came fear on all, and they glorified God.' So that here we are under no necessity of understanding this as a sign of a hearty and entire conversion to God in this remnant ; though I shall not doubt but God might thereby work upon the hearts of some in a saving manner. *But there is no ground from this expression to think so of the whole herd ;* for God may be said to be glorified, in Scripture language, many a time when the person that does it is wanting in grace. God may be said to be glorified when his power is acknowledged in any emergency ; as the magicians said unto Pharaoh, ' This is the finger of God.' " Ex. 8 : 19.— James Robertson, Minister at Leuchars, *Exposition of the Revelation* (1730), p. 199.
" It is not to be understood of a real work of repentance."—James Durham, Minister in Glasgow (1680), *Com. on Rev.*, p. 826, *in loc.*

in their character were thereby betokened. And when men have sinned away their day of gracious visitation, fighting, killing, and glorying in the destruction of God's prophets, they are not likely to be suddenly transformed into saints by the constraints and terrors of the day of doom, though obliged to confess that it is the invincible God of heaven that is dealing with them.

Here, then, I conclude this review of the case of *The Two Witnesses*—their times, their doings, and their end. It is a marvellous history, hard for the rationalistic and materialistic temper of our day to receive, or to treat with respect. I am also well convinced that men will dispute and reject all such presentations of it till these Two Prophets themselves appear again ; and even then the dupes of Antichrist will still dispute and reject it to their everlasting perdition. But that will not alter the record which God has given, nor do away with the reality of what he has so solemnly foretold. I may perchance not apprehend the matter rightly ; but if I mistake, it is with the Bible in my hand, and following its statements just as the Holy Ghost has caused them to be written. If I have erred from the true meaning of the Sacred Word, it has not been from an intrusion of human fancy, reason, or philosophy, into the realm of inspiration, but from having dared to think that God knew how to say what he meant, and that he really means what he has said. If others are satisfied they understand the matter better, to the Master they and I must answer ; but with no clear conscience could I go before him, as things now address themselves to my understanding, were I to affirm anything at variance with what I here have said.

Nor is it a small satisfaction to me, to be able to say, that I have spoken in accord with the common teaching and belief of the Church of Christ and its greatest lights for ages next after the Apostles ;—with Justin, the noble Apologist and Martyr ;—with Hippolytus, the saint, bishop, and confuter of heresies ;—with Origen, the learned preceptor and annotator, who, with all his aberrations, was never charged with error for holding it to be a declaration of Christ that there is to be another coming of Elias ; with Victorinus, Methodius, Cyprian, and Lactantius ;—with Chrysostom of the golden mouth ;—with Jerome the great critic and scholar ;—and with Augustine the illustrious bishop and theologian. In such society it would seem hardly possible to go very far astray. To believe and teach what these with one accord have held and taught, can scarcely be in conflict with the faith, or with the duty and proprieties of a sober Christian teacher. And if with them I err, I may claim the same forgiveness by which they are excused and justified.

But I am not willing to believe that these saints, scholars, bishops, martyrs, and champions of the faith against the errors of their times, have all missed the sense and meaning of God's revelations on these points. Not on their authority, but on that of the same records which guided them, I follow in their track.

So, then, I must believe and teach, till better knowledge proves me in the wrong ; and,

> With faltering footsteps, I will journey on,
>   Watching the stars that roll the hours away,
> Till the faint light that guides me now is gone,
>   And, like another life, the glorious day
> Shall open o'er me from the empyrean height
> With warmth, and certainty, and boundless light.

LECTURE TWENTY-FIFTH

REV. 11 : 15–19. (Revised Text.) And the seventh angel sounded ; and there were great voices in the heaven, saying, The kingdom of the world is become our Lord's and his Christ's ; and he shall reign to the ages of the ages.

And the twenty-four elders which sit before God on their thrones, fell down upon their faces, and worshipped God, saying, We give to thee thanks, O Lord God the Almighty, who art and who wast [*and art to come*, is an addition without adequate authority here], because thou hast taken to thee thy great power, and shown Thyself King. The nations indeed were angry, and Thy indignation is come, and the time [*or season*] of the dead to be judged, and [the time or *season*] to give the reward to thy servants the prophets, and to the saints, and to them that fear thy name, the small and the great, and to destroy the destroyers of the earth.

And there was opened the temple of God in the heaven, and there was seen the ark of his covenant in his temple ; and there were [or, *ensued*] lightnings, and voices, and thunderings, and earthquake, and great hail.

WE here approach the grand climacteric of this world, and of the judgment-work of the Almighty One. The seventh angel, restrained so long from ushering in the final scenes which separate us from the glorious world to come, at length pours out his wondrous blast. It is the Last Trumpet, so often referred to by the sacred writers, and by the Saviour himself, as bringing with it the mightiest scenes and changes in the whole history of earth and time, that here sounds. And if there is anything in all the round of human thought to absorb, fix, and intensify interest and attention, we have it in this subject.

The particular passage we have now to consider, is only a synopsis of the matter—a rehearsal in brief of what is subsequently given in detail. It is an important point to remark, that the seventh trumpet does not sound merely for one instant or for one day. In that solemn oath of the cloud-robed Angel, which we were called to consider in chapter 10, and in which it was said that the fulfilling of the mystery of God should be finished at the sounding of the seventh angel, it is distinctly implied, that the sounding is continuous, and extends through a period of time. It is there said, that " in the *days* of the voice of the seventh angel, when he shall sound, the mystery of God is [to be] fulfilled." " Days " are included. What measure of " days," or how many of them, we are not told ; but a period of time is specifically indicated. In the case of the other woe trumpets, there is unmistakable continuity,—" five months " the one, and evidently no less a time in the other. And the presence of this distinct note of continuity here, taken along with the tremendousness of what turns out under this trumpet, is evidence enough that it is a mistake to confine this last and great woe trumpet to the few summary notations of the text, or to crowd it into an instant of time. From the plainly expressed character of the events, and from the oath of the Angel, we are sufficiently assured, that this seventh trumpet embraces everything involved in the completing of the whole mystery of God, up to the termination of all this judgment history. That fulfilment is certainly not accomplished without the seven vials of wrath, the harvest and vintage of the world, the manifestation of the great white throne, and the establishment of the new heavens and the new earth. In the nature of the case, that fulfilment overspans everything this side of the completed redemption ; and yet that fulfilment is most specifically located " in the days of the voice of the seventh angel, when he shall sound "

There is, therefore, no alternative, but to take the text as only synoptical of this trumpet—a sort of summary of its chief contents, the full details of which are subsequently described, and spread over a considerable period ;—an anticipative *programme*, so to speak, of the main elements and issue of the great drama, given out in advance of the more special narration of circumstantial particulars and related events.* In other words, we now have to do with a syllabus of the fulfilment or consummation of the mystery of God— with a prelusive sketch of the contents of the Last Trump, in which we may note :

I. The Symptoms which attend it.
II. The Items which it embraces.

And may He who sent His angel to disclose these wonders, open our eyes and hearts by His Holy Spirit, that we may rightly apprehend and ponder the same !

I. The symptoms which attend the sounding of the Last Trump are the most remarkable, the most numerous, and the most intense, both in heaven and on earth, that are anywhere detailed in the Scriptures. There were many mighty wonders attendant upon the deliverance of the chosen people from Egypt, and their planting in the promised land. In the air and in the waters, in the trees and in the rocks, in the clouds and in the dust, on animate and inanimate nature, there were manifestations that stand out among the greatest marvels of bygone time. At the birth, in the life, and at the death of Christ, there was also a great commotion, a stir among the angels, among the stars, among the elements, and among men both living and dead, which make up a history such as had never occurred before. And so when Jerusalem was finally destroyed, there were signs, and sounds, and voices, and portents, which have sent their report down through the ages, and which still oppress the breathing of men to hear about. But neither of these, nor all of them together, can at all approach the overwhelming intensity of the manifestations which attend the sounding of the Last Trump.

1. *Great voices in heaven utter themselves.* There is not only a stir and great activity excited there, but a great outcry, a giving forth of mighty intimations. Whose voices they are, is not here told us ; but there is tremendous commotion. Even eternity cannot keep quiet when this crisis comes. The inhabitants of glory have seen too much of earth, its behaviour toward God, and God's doings for it, not to be excited when the final termination is announced. Their silence breaks, and heaven rings with mighty voices.

What some of these voices are, we learn from the succeeding narrative. One is the voice, as the voice of many waters, and as a voice of great thunder, as the voice of harpers harping with their harps, and pouring forth a new song in the presence of the throne. Another is the voice of a mighty angel flying in midheaven, calling loud enough for every nation, and tribe, and tongue, and

---

* Bengel takes it as evident, " that chapter 12, from its very beginning, refers to the trumpet of the seventh angel ; for the voice which was heard immediately under the sound of that trumpet, chap. 11 : 15, respecting *the kingdom*, is repeated by Epitasis in chap. 12 : 10, with a remarkable increase of meaning ; nor can that by any means be placed before this trumpet." Bengel *in loc*. Even Hengstenberg, who, by his method of interpretation, makes a new beginning altogether with chap. 12, is forced to admit against himself, that " what we now, according to chap. 11 : 15–18, expect the appearance of the Lord, the final victory of God's kingdom, the resurrection of the dead, the last judgment, the glorification of the Church, all this is represented in verse 19 as having entered, but only by way of gentle indication ; for the seer would reserve the more particular delineation of the last things for a later part of the book, and by the enigmatical brevity with which he here treats them, would set expectation on the stretch regarding that more particular delineation in reserve." See his *Com. in loc*. Bengel was unquestionably right when he said that chapters 12–22 are but an *exergasia*, a further explanation or setting forth of the passage now before us.

people to hear.   Others are the voices of angels shouting the fall of great Babylon, and the fate of them that worship the Beast.   Another is a voice crying the blessedness of the dead.   Others again are the loud voices calling for the thrusting in of the sickle for the reaping of the harvest of the earth and the gathering of its clusters.   Still another is a great voice commanding the pouring out of the bowls of the wrath of God ;   and another a voice out of the temple, from the throne, crying, " It is done," and voices saying " Halleluia," " Amen," " Halleluia ; "   and still other voices, as it were the voice of a great multitude, and the voice of many waters, and as the voice of mighty thunderings, saying, Halleluia, because the Lord God Almighty reigneth.   And along with these are yet other great voices from the heavenly world, each in its place and all together combining to fill all the realm of God with intensest utterances.

When the Lamb took the book from the hand of the Sitter upon the throne, there was something of a corresponding commotion in the holy universe.   It was an act which included and looked to the consummation which the seventh trumpet brings ;   and all along the track of unfolding judgment, we find this same celestial interest and excitement continued, till, at the sounding of the last Trump, everything breaks out with cries, and shouts, and songs, and triumphings.

2. *The twenty-four Elders fall down upon their faces, and worship with sublimest thanks.*   When the mighty *Goel* took the book, they also fell down before the Lamb, and gave their solemn and adoring vote to his worthiness ; but here the prostration is still lowlier.   They not only fall into the posture of reverent adoration, but *" upon their faces ; "*   bury their immortal countenances in the pavement around the throne ;   by their very emotion hurled from their golden seats, overwhelmed and almost undone.   There they expressed their adoring sense of the Saviour's worthiness, exulting in the prospect of what was to result ;   but here they celebrate the whole issue reached, the blessed consummation come, the thing of hope for all these ages now translating into fact ;   and, crowned princes of heaven, and anointed coregents with the great Eternal as they are, they cannot contain themselves. Their glorified limbs sink under the weight of the contemplation ;   their heads bow down to the place of their feet ;   their whole being melts into one flux of overwhelming realization of what now is come, and the gush of their adoring soul-dissolving joy breaks like a sea of thankfulness against the throne.

Who these Elders are, I have elsewhere told.   They are the representatives of the first-born of the resurrection.   They are the seniors of the celestial congregation of the redeemed.   They are the ones accounted worthy to " escape " the sad scenes and tribulations of the judgment-time, taken away and hid in the pavilion of God while the anger of the Almighty sweeps the guilty world, and enthroned in heaven for their valiancy and faithfulness, when yet on earth.   They are already glorified, but that does not diminish their interest in the ongoing and completion of the same process in the case of others.   They have their golden crowns, but that does not withdraw their hearts and sympathies from those still in the graves, or from the still remaining fulfilment of all God's word.   There is no vanity and selfishness in heaven ;   no pride of privilege and place ;   no vaunting of authority.   The crowned Elders on their thrones are even more concerned over the conflicts still pending, and the victories yet to be achieved, than they were in those through which they had won their own crowns.   The destroyers of the earth were not yet destroyed. The great multitude of the dead had not yet been finally judged.   The mass of men had not yet been assigned their just deserts.   The reward had not yet fully come to the prophets and saints and fearers of God.   The divine righteousness and honour had not yet been fully vindicated.   The usurpation of Satan had not yet been overthrown.   The great redemption had not yet been fully wrought out into ultimate fact.   But the trumpet which brings all this was now ringing out its unmistakable notes, and not even these blessed kings could keep their seats, or restrain the outpouring of their hearts in grateful, adoring, and exultant thanks.*

3. *And the temple of God in heaven opened.* There is a heavenly temple and worship, from which the tabernacle and temple of the Jews was copied. When Jehovah directed the building of them, He said to Moses : " Look that thou make them after their pattern, which was showed thee in the mount " (Ex. 25 : 40) ; and the writer of the Epistle to the Hebrews calls them ὑποδείγματα, *copies* or likenesses of things in the heavens (9 : 23.) The heavenly and the earthly worship were once in close and manifest union. It was sin that divorced them, and separated between man and the divine, excluding him from the sacred communion of Paradise, and all but the consecrated priests from the sanctuary, and all but the high priest from the holy of holies in the Jewish tabernacle and temple, and even him, except once in a year, when alone he might enter it enveloped in clouds of incense. Sin has obscured and hidden from man the sacred and divine. It has repulsed heaven from his view and fellowship, with only a lingering ray left here and there, and even that so buried away as to be, for the most part, entirely unapproachable. Hence, when Christ paid the ransom-price for human sin, and introduced an availing righteousness for the race, and a new dispensation of mercy and grace received its foundation-stone, the veil of the temple rent, the way into the holiest opened, and the divine began to be visible and approachable again. And this opening of the temple in heaven at the last trumpet expresses the same idea. Knowledge and vision of heavenly things, and closer fellowship and intimacy between the worshippers on earth and the worshippers in heaven belong to the great consummation. As the Saviour has taught us to pray, then it is to be, " as in heaven so on earth." Oneness is again to be restored between the worship of both worlds. All this is shown in the twenty-first chapter, where the finished mystery is described. Hence, as this trumpet begins to sound, the mists begin to lift from sacred things, the excluding barriers give way, the seclusion yields to human gaze and approach, the veil withdraws, the holy begins to disclose itself again, and the temple of heaven opens.

4. And with that opening of the heavenly temple *the ark of God's covenant appears.* It is no unholy or profane exposure, but a hallowed symptom, setting forth still further the glory of the occasion. All the compacts of God with His people, and all His solemn promises to them, are in that ark. All His engagements, whether particular or general, are lodged and treasured there. In that sacred casket they have long been hidden away, as Jeremiah is said to have hidden the Jewish ark when the Chaldeans took Jerusalem.† But, though buried from view, it is not lost, and its holy contents have all been preserved. Not a promise is obsolete or dead. And now, at the ending of time,

* It is noticeable in this adoring thanksgiving that God is no longer addressed as ὁ ἐρχόμενος *who is to come.* The common text has this addition, but wholly without authority. All critics agree in rejecting it as an interpolation of some copyist who erroneously supposed that it should come in here the same as in chapter 1 : 4, 8. There He is called ὁ ἐρχόμενος because not yet manifested as He should be manifested for the great consummation ; but here it is already the time of the last trumpet, in which that manifestation is no longer future, but is already come. Hence, He is no longer addressed as the One who is to come, but as already in actual operation and present in that very respect in which He was previously ὁ ἐρχόμενος. So Bengel, who remarks : " Interpreters have long ago seen this." Ansbert says : " They do not here subjoin as they were accustomed, *and who art to come,* they speak of Him as already present." Haymo, who usually treads in the footprints of Ansbert, says : " It must be observed that he does not add, as before, *who art to come,* for they show Him already present in the judgment by which all these things are accomplished, and therefore they by no means speak of Him as yet to come." John Purvey, in his commentary, published with the preface of Luther, says : " He does not add the third clause, which he has usually added, namely, *and who is to come,* for this reason, that the prophet [rather the Elders] then saw God, as it were, already sitting in judgment."— BENGEL *in loc.*

† See 2 Maccabees 2 : 4–8.

that golden box reappears. As the Jews believed the old ark would be brought out again in the day of Israel's blessing, so the ark of God's covenant is now seen in the temple on high. A divine potency goes along with that ark. On earth the waters of Jordan rolled asunder beneath the shadow of it. The walls of Jericho fell down before it. The enemies of God were scattered where it set forward. The many thousands of Israel were in safety and blessedness where it rested. And its appearance here is a token of the recurrence of all these wonders, only on a completer, grander, and sublimer scale. It tells of the speedy fulfilment of all that God hath spoken, and the putting into living force of all that He has engaged to do. Whether as respects the seed of Abraham or the Gentiles, friends or enemies, the living or the dead, the Church or the world, blessing or punishment, all that the Almighty has covenanted is now to be fulfilled. And in token of this the ark, the sign and bearer of His promises, appears. There could all now see the pledge of God's remembrance of His holy covenant, and of His oath which he swore to Abraham, and of all that He hath spoken by the mouth of all His holy prophets since the world began.

5. *And lightnings, and voices, and thunderings, and earthquakes, and great hail ensued.* " The days of the voice of the seventh angel, when he shall sound," are terrible days ; days of sore scourgings and afflictions to the wicked dwellers on the earth, and the breaking forth upon them of sorrows which never end. When God revealed Himself on Sinai He charged the people to beware, lest He should break through upon them ; and now He is about to break through. The sky flashes with electric fires. Portentous voices ring out in stunning power. The air is filled with thunder. The earth trembles and quakes. The winds rush in noisy fury, and great hailstones fall upon the earth. Jehovah is now risen up from His place to punish the wicked. And as the ark of his covenant is revealed to give joy and hope to the parties to that covenant, lower nature is set in dread commotion to harbinger the bursting forth of His indignation upon his adversaries.

Such, then, are the predicted symptoms which attend the sounding of the Last Trump. Let us now look at—

II. THE ITEMS WHICH IT EMBRACES.

1. The first named is, *a radical change in the government of the world.* This is what all the great unidentified voices that first speak on the sounding of the seventh angel utter, as it is the sum of great consummation. The mighty administrators in the upper world exultantly proclaim, " *The kingdom* [not kingdoms, as the common reading is, but ἡ βασιλεία abstract—*the sovereignty*] *of the world* [τοῦ κόσμου—of the constituted order on the earth] *is become our Lord's and his Christ's ; and he shall reign to the ages of the ages.*" The tense of the expression is that peculiar to prophetic language, which fixes upon a result yet future, or only beginning to be, as if already accomplished. It is not until the scenes narrated in chapters 20 and 21 are fulfilled, that this change of sovereignty is finally completed ; but when God announces a thing, and especially when He proclaims Himself in motion to do a thing, it is the same to the heavenly orders as if it were already wrought out. The word of God is truth, and what it says is the same as fact and verity already, although not yet distributed out and located in present time. His word has virtue to make its contents present to those who really know Him. The seventh trumpet brings this change, and on the first tone of it all heaven sees and celebrates the work as already done, and the kingdom of the world become their Lord's and His Christ's.

Not yet has the sovereignty of this world become the Lord's. All earthly governments, principalities, and powers, from the beginning until now, are uniformly represented in the Scriptures as wild beasts, having no lawful owner, and full of destructive savageness and offensive uncleanness. A lion with eagle's wings, a bear crunching bones and flesh, a four-winged and four-headed leopard, a nondescript with many horns, dreadful and terrible and strong exceedingly, having great iron teeth to devour and break in pieces ; these are the prophetic symbols of the greatest and most lauded of them. Even the premiership of Daniel himself in one of them does not alter its general character. It is but folly and fanaticism for men to talk of Christian states and governments in this world. Christian and good men may be concerned in their administration, and Christian ideas may sometimes temper their enactments, but earthly states and governments themselves are not Christian, and in the nature of things cannot be. They are all the products of devastated nature's wilds, and full of savage nature's passions and ungodliness. Fix it as we may, such is the result. The best-planned institutions and the wisest laws are ever disappointing their framers. The very law which God Himself promulged from Sinai's thunder-shaken heights was " weak through the flesh," and did not serve to keep the Jewish commonwealth from like apostasy to that of other nationalities. To this hour there is nothing so great a desideratum among men as good and just government, nor another department in which the native evilness and God-antagonizing passions of men are so potent and defiant. True, the kingdom is by right the Lord's. All authority and power originates with Him and belongs to Him. Government is His own ordinance. But since the apostasy of the race to Satan's standard, usurpation, falsehood, and other powers than the rightful sovereign of men and nations, have held and directed the sway in this world. Many revolutions have been wrought, and men have laboured, and sacrificed, and bled, and died to achieve them, believing that now they would secure the precious boon for which the race has sighed and cried for ages ; but it was only the turning of the sick man on his bed, who keeps his pain however he may change his place. In our day especially people are looking and labouring for a grand jubilee of nations, shaped to popular rule, and compacted by common laws, interests, and creed, in which enlightened ideas shall be the king, and all the world be one ; but the result will be only a more horrible beast than any that preceded it, a leopard with bear's feet and a lion's mouth, full of heads and horns and names of blasphemy ; the very embodiment of hell, whose infamies so outrage High Heaven as to bring the great day of God Almighty upon the world. No, no ; your revolutions, and reforms, and progress of liberal ideas, and overturning of old creeds, and grand conventionalities in revision of the Decalogue, and internationalities for the redemption of the world without Christ, and glorious philosophies ruling out a personal God and exalting self and passion in His place, and all your glittering ideals to which to reconstruct society and relocate the highest interests of man, much as they may promise, and successfully as they may draw the heart and energy of the world after them, are but the nurslings of Satan's bosom in which this world lies, and the inspirations of his foul breath. Dream, and prate, and preach, and glory as men may, the devil is *de facto* the god and king of this world. His mantle may be often changed, and every day may exhibit a new garb, but the presiding genius within is still and always the devil, with all his pride, and malice, and spoliating falsities. And so it will go on, " wicked men and seducers waxing worse and worse," till the last trumpet sounds.

But then shall come another order ; not developed from below, but enforced with sudden and resistless power from above. *How*, we will see when we come to consider the details of the ensuing chapters. Meanwhile, however, the fact itself is sure to the exultant voices in heaven. God is king, and the sovereignty hath He given to His Son, Jesus Christ. And having given the world six thousand years in which to choose and settle upon its proper allegiance, and finding after all only an intenser and more malignant apostasy, He causes the final trump to sound, breaks in with His Almightiness, and enforces His rightful dominion. A kingdom comes which breaks in pieces, and consumes all other kingdoms, and stands forever. Laws are given to be changed no more. And the true Anointed reigns on earth in an empire of sinless, deathless life and peace, to the ages of the ages. The government is changed.

2. And closely connected with this change, and one of the things involved in it, is *the destruction of earth's destroyers*. This is announced in the thanksgiving of the Elders. The same word is used to denote Jehovah's act, that describes the character of those on whom the action is inflicted. What men and governments in this world sow, that shall they also reap. They that are a curse to the world, shall be accursed. The word (διαψθείρω) means to spoil, corrupt, ruin, make away with, kill, destroy ; and those who act in this line, shall be dealt with in the same line. Usurpers, liars, tyrants, persecutors, and murderers, who thus spoil God's world, shall be reacted upon by the violence of their own deeds, overwhelmed, and utterly put out of the way.

Peter gives it as one of the great objects to be achieved by the awful demonstrations of the day of the Lord, that then shall come " the perdition of ungodly men." That day shall find wickedness and confederation in iniquity ripened to the full. The very prince of hell shall then have incorporated himself personally in the government of the world, speaking through its heads, dictating its religion and its laws, controlling its trade, enforcing the worship of himself as God, cutting off the heads of those who dissent, filling the world with the worst of blasphemies, and compelling all that would live to receive the mark of allegiance to him. All existing nations on the prophetic earth shall have organically conjoined themselves with him as the representative of all authority and power, " and all that dwell upon the earth shall worship him." But when the seventh trumpet sounds, the end of this infamous confederation has come. Then the maddened nations shall suddenly be dashed to atoms, as a vessel of pottery struck with a rod of iron ; and their armies slain by the blasts of Jehovah, as the Syrians of old ; and the great beast that did rule them, and the deceiver that was with him, shall be cast alive into the lake of fire ; and great Babylon shall fall, as a millstone cast into the sea ; and the dragon shall be seized and shut up in his proper hell ; and death and the grave shall be extinguished ; and all the destroyers of the earth shall be destroyed ! O ! glorious riddance of our weary world, when " the Son of man shall send forth his angels, and they shall gather out of his kingdom all things that offend, and them which do iniquity, and shall cast them into a furnace of fire ! " (Matt. 13 : 41, 42.) Well may the enthroned Elders fall on their faces, and cry their thanks to the Lord Almighty for it.

3. And still another item in the grand schedule of the last trumpet is, *the judgment of the dead*. This also is recited in the thanksgiving of the Elders. When men die, and their bodies waste in the ground, it is not the end of them. Whatever may be their state meanwhile, they reappear again. John sees them, the small and the great, given up by the sea, and death, and hades, all standing before the great white throne, to be judged, every one of them, according to their works. There is to be a resurrection, even, of the wicked. They that put an end to their existence on earth, resolving not to live any more, must still live, and take the judgment and sentence of Heaven for all their deeds. Not one of all the race can escape it. And the time of the dead to be judged, is " in the days of the voice of the seventh angel."

This side the grave, full justice is never done ; and up to the great day, no one receives entirely all his deserts. That is reserved for the period of resurrection. Soul and body, having wrought together, shall reap together of what they have sown. Only the resurrection life is full retribution life. Incomplete and unequal are all the administrations here. Many a great criminal dies without having had his guilt so much as known, whilst perchance innocent ones have had to suffer for his sins. The wicked go unpunished, are even honoured in their crimes, and pass away with no experiences to mark how they stand in the estimate of God. Fortunes are made, and enjoyed, and respected, and their holders held in favourable esteem to the end of their days, every dime of which is stained with blood, corroded with crime, and marked with fraud, oppression, and soul-damning deeds of injustice. So marked and constant are the inequalities that occur, that even the holiest of men have often been tempted to despondency and doubt whether their faith and godliness are not after all a mistake. Nor is there any stay for the good man's confidence, or adequate justification of his course, but in the fact that the end of the matter is not in this world. Beyond is the theatre on which final settlement is to be made, and there is the invincible throne of inexorable justice. There shall all earth's wrongs be righted, all present inequalities adjusted, and the administrations of God forever vindicated. The dead have not gone beyond His reach. The grave does not cover them from His sight, nor bar them from His approach and power. Having escaped unpunished from this world, their just portion still awaits them in the next. People may call it fable and dream, and reason it an impossibility; but that will not alter it. And when the seventh angel sounds, there will be exultant thanksgivings in heaven, that " the time of the dead to be judged " is come.

4. And with this, yet one other point, *the giving of reward to the prophets, and the saints, and to them that fear God, the small and the great.* Piety and the fear of God are poor recommendations for the favours of this world. Our religion is the religion of the cross, and that cross has to be borne by all who are faithful and true. Nothing can abolish it—nothing can exempt from it. Since the days of Abel, whose confiding devotion and humble obedience to his God cost him his life, there has been no age, no nation, no realm or country on earth, where saintship and holiness have not subjected to losses, trials, and pains. The prophets all were persecuted and injured men, who lived martyr lives if they did not come to martyr deaths. For all these ages, the children of God have been children of affliction and sorrow. Some were tortured; others had trial of cruel mockings and scourgings, of bonds and imprisonments; some were stoned, sawn asunder, tempted, slain with the sword; some wandered about in sheepskins and goatskins, being destitute, afflicted, tormented, compelled to hide themselves in deserts, and in mountains, and in dens and caves of the earth. He that would come after Jesus must deny himself. He that would live godly in Christ Jesus must suffer persecution. There is no rest, no recompense, no hope for us here. For, if in this life only we have hope in Christ, we are of all men most miserable. But no Christian looks for his compensation in this present world. So long as he is in this tabernacle, he groans, being burdened, troubled on every side, distressed, perplexed, always bearing about in the body the dying of the Lord Jesus. And the only thing that reconciles to such a lot is, that God's servants " look not at the things which are seen, but at the things which are not seen." Glorious promises have come forth, and these the good have embraced, and are persuaded of them, and confess themselves strangers and pilgrims on the earth, looking for a better country, believing that God is a rewarder of them that diligently seek Him. And the realization of all these fond desires and blessed hopes belongs to the time of the seventh angel, when he shall sound. Piety may not pay as regards this world, but it will pay then. Not even the gift of a cup of water to the thirsty shall then go unrewarded; nor a loss, or pain, or labour of love, or pang of hardship, or tear of sorrow, incurred for Jesus or His truth's sake, fail of its just recompense. Rewards—rewards—for the wronged prophets, for the suffering saints, and for all that fear God, small and great, are in reserve. Jesus hath gone to make them ready. In heaven, in the counsel and purpose of God, in His covenant and promise, in His hand, secure from all peradventure, they are stored away. Faith sees them there, and waits for them with eager hope. And when the last trumpet sounds, they shall be given. Then shall Paul get his crown of righteousness, and all the apostles take their everlasting thrones. Then shall Daniel stand in his lot, and Moses possess the recompense to which he had respect, when he chose rather " to suffer affliction with the people of God, than to enjoy the pleasures of sin for a season." And every one that hath forsaken houses, or brethren, or sisters, or father, or mother, or wife, or children, or lands, for the sake of God and His Christ, shall receive an hundred fold, and shall inherit everlasting life.

No wonder, then, that the blessed Elders fall on their faces before God, and praise and thank Him with profoundest song, when the signal for so glorious a consummation sounds.

Nor is all this without the most intense moment to us. We are all concerned with that last trumpet's sound. Our sublimest eternal interests are wrapt up in what it is to bring. Big is it with the doom and destiny of everyone, and everything that is. Be our place, our state, our occupation what it may, our fate and lot, and every question, every doubt, shall then come to final settlement. Near or remote as those scenes may be, we shall all be in them, and take from thence the character of our forever. Believe it or not, we every one shall be there ; there as victims of the great day of Almighty wrath, as prisoners brought forth for final execution, or, as the friends and servants of Jesus, to be confessed, rewarded, and glorified by our blessed Lord.

And as we spend these swift-passing days, and conduct ourselves in this brief life, will be the character of our experience and portion then. Building on Jesus in humble faith and lowly steadfastness, we are safe, and our work is safe. Then may we sing, and exult, and give thanks with all the holy ones of heaven, as we see the day approaching. Then may we rejoice, and be exceeding glad, for great is the reward that we shall get. Otherwise there is no dreader sound than that of the Last Trump. And when we think of the millions of dead and living for whom it has no blessing, and of the utter destruction which it shall bring on them that know not God and obey not the Gospel, is there not reason for us all to be moved with fear, lest that day should come upon us unawares ? It will be too late then to remedy present mistakes, negligences, and omissions. If we are to meet that day with joy, and escape the horrors it brings to the unprepared, we must be getting ready now ; getting ready, by honest repentance of our sins, joining ourselves to Christ and His people, and with all our heart and energy seeking to be in accord with His word and will. Happy they, who, when the Last Trumpet sounds, shall be found in such a case !

> Jesus, do Thou mine eyes unseal,
>   And let them grow
> Quick to discern whate'er Thou dost reveal,
> So shall I be delivered from that woe,
>   Blindly to stray
> Through hopeless night, while all around is day.

LECTURE TWENTY-SIXTH

THE SUNCLAD WOMAN—NOT MARY—NOT JERUSALEM—THE CHURCH IN ITS ENTIRETY—HER WOMANLINESS—HER PREGNANCY—HER VICTORY—HER ROYALTY—HER TRAVAIL TO BRING FORTH.

REV. 12 : 1, 2. (Revised Text.) And a great sign was seen in the heaven, a woman clothed with the sun, and the moon under her feet, and on her head a crown of twelve stars, and, being with child, she crieth out, travailing and agonizing herself to bring forth.

THIS book of the Apocalypse is one of the most wonderful in the Sacred Scriptures. As the Bible among literature, so is this part of it among the inspired writings. Though it has had to fight its way in every age, and to struggle to maintain its place in the sacred canon, there is not another book in the volume of inspiration more strongly attested, or more fully authenticated. Its superscription, its historical statements, its catena of testimonies, and the nature of its contents, amply evidence its genuineness, and its divine original. Its imposing scenery, its grand similitudes, its pregnant maxims, its significant dialogues, its stirring exhortations, its glowing prayers, its evangelic songs, and its sublime doxologies, give to it all the majesty of the book of the mighty consummation, not of inspiration only, but of the grandest revealed plans and purposes of God. And if an inspired book at all, there is not another which so solemnly enforces itself upon the attention of the Churches, or that is compassed about with guards and penalties more explicit and severe. We must needs regard its author as an unaccountable boaster, if it is not the highest interest and duty of every earnest Christian to read and try to understand it, so as to take its momentous presentations in among the most settled and potent things by which to direct his way and fashion his expectations. Therefore, with a devout and able living divine beyond the sea, I would say " Join your prayers with mine, my brethren, that our resumption of the study of this Divine Book may be fruitful, not in curious speculation and intellectual gratification, but above and before all else, in the quickening of our Christian vigilance, and in the increase of our knowledge of God in His Son."

In the passage which we are now to consider, we have the picture of a marvellous Woman, clothed with the sun, and the moon under her feet, and on her head a crown of twelve stars, and she herself agitated and agonizing with the anxieties of parturition.

This, the Apostle tells us is *a sign*, σημεῖον, a word which he here uses for the first time in the Apocalypse, and which serves to show that the apparition is not simply a " *wonder,*" as our version has it, but a wonder intended to bring before us something beyond itself. I have repeatedly remarked, that when the Scriptures use figures or symbols, or speak in a way not intended to be taken literally, like all serious writings they always give some intimation of it, in one way or another. The text is a case in point. What is described, is said to be *a sign*, a representation or picture of something else—a symbol. And the fact that we are here told that this is *a sign*, goes far to prove that the Apocalypse in general is to be taken literally, except where indication to the contrary is given. It would be quite superfluous to tell us that this thing is a sign, and that certain things mean certain other things, except upon the assumption that whatever is not so labelled is to be taken just as it reads, a woman for a woman, a star for a star, a mountain for a mountain, and so on. But, whatever else is literal in this book, the case of this woman is not ; for the Apostle says it is *a sign*—a picture—a symbol of something else, which is the true subject of contemplation. He further tells us that it is " *a great sign.*" In itself it was something very imposing and sublime to the eye which beheld it. But the greatness cannot be well understood, except with reference to the thing signified. It was a *great* sign as indicating something great, remarkable, momentous. The whole picture is itself so marvellous and extraordinary as to necessitate the idea of something of the greatest excellence, conspicuity, and importance. And when it is yet added, that the sign is a " great " one, that to which it refers must needs be of the utmost consequence and consideration, and no trifling object or ordinary event can be admitted as fulfilling the majesty of such a picture.

This sign appeared " *in the heaven.*" But that does not seem to be of special significance. In the verses following, we read of another " sign," which appeared in the same place, whilst both the woman and the dragon are really as much on earth as in heaven. It is simply the scene of vision that is indicated. The seer is in the heavenly regions, and in those regions these signs appear, though relating to both earth and heaven.

A more important question is that respecting the object intended to be symbolized by this Woman. *Who is she, and what are we to understand by her ?* The answers returned by expositors are not in all cases the same.

Some are disposed to consider it the picture of the Virgin Mary giving birth to the blessed Saviour. Even Professor Stuart says, that no attentive reader can help thinking of the birth of Christ and the massacre of Bethlehem. But, much as we may think of it, and howsoever included, this cannot be the proper subject. If the Apostle had believed it a representative of Mary, he doubtless would have said so ; neither is it congruous thus mysteriously to give us the picture of one woman so superlatively exalted, in order to denote another woman so poor and lowly as Mary at the birth of our Lord. Nor was Mary ever clad and adorned as here set forth. She has also long since passed away from the earth, while this woman continues even until after the sounding of the last trumpet. When Christ was caught up to God, this Apocalypse was not yet written, nor for half a century after, whereas it was said at the time of the writing that it referred to things then still future.*

Others think that it means the City of Jerusalem. It has been said that there are only two women spoken of in this book, and that as the one is " that great city which reigneth over the kings of the earth," so the other is that city which spiritually is called Sodom and Egypt, where also our Lord was crucified. But it is as foreign to all Scripture diction, as it is contrary to the nature of things, for a material earthly city to take wings and fly away to the wilderness, and after 1260 days to return again.

A more common view, in which there is a more general agreement, is, that this woman somehow represents the Church, the body of God's professed people. It belongs to the ordinary Scripture imagery to speak of the Church under the figure of a woman, a spouse, a mother. We read of " the Daughter of Zion " as a personification of this kind under the Old Testament, and Paul speaks of the spiritual Jerusalem as " the mother of us all." The Canticles, which certainly are to be taken in a mystic sense, show how familiar such conceptions were to the Jews ; and the same sort of language is everywhere employed, in one form or another, in the New Testament. And when we contemplate all the splendid particulars respecting this woman, how she is assailed by Satan, and the destiny of the offspring she bears, there is hardly any room left for a doubt, that it is the collective body of the Church or people of God that we are to see in this picture.

But what Church, or the Church of what particular dispensation or era, or the Church in what particular aspect, is not so generally agreed. Some say it is the Old Testament Church, others that it is the Christian Church of the early centuries, persecuted by the heathen, agonizing for converts, and finally bringing forth the Emperor Constantine ; others, that it is the Latin Church

---

* See pp. 49 sq., 100 sq.

of a later period ; and others still, that it refers to the Church in yet other times, or the Church in general, without undertaking to find any one particular fulfilment for it.

In trying to come to a definite conclusion where there is so much irreconcilable diversity, it is necessary to bear in mind that we are here dealing with consummations. The Apocalypse is the Book and revealer of consummations ; and the seventh trumpet, under which this sign appears, above all, refers to the times and scenes in which everything runs to its final completion and end, and appears in its terminal culmination. It is the climax of the great judgment period, when all that has gone before comes to its full, and is finally disposed of. It would therefore harmonize best with the time, and with the character of the connected administrations, that any picture of the Church here introduced should embrace it in its largest fulness, as made up through all ages and dispensations, and as related to the great consummating events pertaining to the end.

So, then, I have been led to view and interpret this wonderful sign. It does not refer to the Jewish Church exclusively ; for that, apart from the Christian, never, to the same degree, possessed the majesty and glory which pertain to this woman. It is not the Christian Church exclusively ; for the man-child who is to rule the nations with the rod of iron must necessarily include the Lord Jesus as its Lord and head ; but he was born before the Christian Church, as such, had an existence. But the Church of the Old Testament and that of the New, are, after all, not so alien to each other. There is still an inner oneness between them never to be overlooked, which makes one a necessary part of the other, and which constitutes them the one Church of God, notwithstanding the differences of dispensations and outward form. Christian believers are children of faithful Abraham, and brethren of the ancient prophets, who were not perfect without us. Changes of external order and administration have occurred, and will perhaps occur again when the present age is consummated, but it is still the same Church of the living God. There has really been but one Church on earth, existing through all times and under all economies. And so we have here, as the symbol of it, this one glorious woman, in whom all its highest excellences and chief characteristics are summed up from the beginning even unto the great consummation, at which point, and with reference to the great occurrences of that time, it is here brought to our contemplation. It is the one only Church of God on earth, though its several parts have existed in succession—even the same which was patriarchal before Moses, Jewish before Christ, and Christian since Christ, here aggregately exhibited, that we may at one and the same view see it in its fulness, and particularly with reference to what is to happen it under the seventh and last trumpet.

It is wonderful also what a profound and complete view of the Church, in all its deepest peculiarities, excellences, office, and prospects, is here given in one single picture, at once as simple as it is sublime.

1. We have here the image of *a woman*. Woman was made out of Adam. A deep sleep fell upon him for the purpose, and out of that sleep woman came into being. From a rib out of his side was she builded. There was but one made, and Adam had none other. She was brought unto the man, and accepted and loved as bone of his bone and flesh of his flesh, and made one with him in the closest of all earthly relations. This is not only history, but also parable and prophecy. Paul is very particular to tell us that it is " a mystery," a sacred revelation set in historic facts, to show the character and relations of the Church. Adam was " the figure of Him that was to come." Christ is " the Second Adam." And the wife of the Second Adam is the Church, made out of Him by the hand and Spirit of God from that deep sleep of His for the sins of the world. It is but one, and beside it there is none other. It is Christ himself begotten in His people, and joined to Him in holy compact, service, fellowship, and love, so deep and close as to be really organic ; for

" we are members of his body, and of his flesh, and of his bones "—one with him as the branches with the vine—sharing each other's characteristics, estates, and destiny. And to say nothing of the feminine qualities as distinguished from the masculine, there is here the profoundest reason for the representation of the Church in the figure of a woman,—a pure, beautiful, sublime, and perfect woman. The Church is the woman, in her creation from the second Adam, in her naming after Christ, and in her receptivity, love, maternity, trusting dependence, beauty, and willing obedience. She is the betrothed of the Lord, His Bride, His Queen, partaker of His inmost love, and all His estate and kingdom, having her joy in Him and His in her. Nor is there another image known to man which more richly and truly sets forth that mystic body, which we recognize and identify in every age as the Church or people of God.

2. This woman is *in the way of motherhood*. This is the characteristic of the Church in every period of its existence, and with special reference to what is to be fulfilled when the last trumpet shall sound. She ever bears in her body the maturing germs of a mighty birth awaited in the future. There is one individual outward figure, but that figure incloses and carries within it an invisible seed, the royal sons of a royal sire. As seen and known to us, the Church is the assembly of God's called and chosen people, manifest in the fellowship and profession of the rites and signs of revealed religion. This assembly, however, embraces two classes, the truly elect and regenerate, whom God has begotten as His own children, and in whom the Church has its life-character as the congregation of saints, but along with them many nominal outward members, who are not God's children in living reality. It is quite manifest to those who look, that not all are saints who profess Christianity and observe its rites ; but who are the true members is not certainly known to us, but to God only. There is, therefore, a visible and an invisible Church—one woman, but compassing a hidden seed to be revealed hereafter. The invisible Church lies within the visible, and there is begotten, nourished, and borne, till the time comes for it to be brought forth. The visible Church is truly the Church, because the elect are in it, only it embraces some who are not of the elect. In it alone are God's true people to be found. There are the means and instruments through which saints are begotten and nurtured, and the Church collected, and its offices and administrations filled. Though it has many who are not really what they profess, and are not of the inner household of faith, it does not cease to be the true Church of God and the only mother of saints on that account. Their profession still is right, and the word and sacraments which they handle are still God's appointed means of grace and salvation. And it is the Church as one glorious whole, outward and inward, visible and invisible, that we are to see in this magnificent woman.

And there is much in the picture in this respect to teach us duty, and to support and encourage our faith. The Church is meant for the work of begetting and bearing saints. It is not for show but for fruitfulness,—for the carrying and bringing forth of a royal seed of God, to inherit His kingdom, and to rule and reign in the ages of eternity. In all places and in all time, this is her office. It is the one aim of all her equipments and all her high relations. Ministers and people forget their calling, pervert their mission, and take the attitude of hypocrites and usurpers, where this is not their one sole aim in all their ministrations and endeavours. And as they devote themselves, often in sadness and tears, to this their work and aim, it is a blessed thing to know that, wherever the Church is, this her mission is being fulfilled, however imperceptibly to human eyes. God's fact-picture of the Church is, that where she is found, she is at the same time burdened with a seed begotten of God, which is being nurtured from her own body for a glorious birth-hour when time reaches its close. The patriarchs and prophets were often discouraged in their privations and labours for God and His cause. The efforts of the faithful seemed ever to be coming to nought. The old world apostatized.

Noah's house degenerated into idolatry. Israel departed from Jehovah, and knew not the day of their gracious visitation. The Christian Institutes were soon alloyed, tainted, and soiled with the intermixtures of falsehood and heathenism. Again and again the true life of faith seemed to die out of the earth, leaving nothing but the corpse of godliness. And to this hour we are oft disheartened and desponding over the ill-success of our best and costliest efforts. The earnest messengers of God come weeping with Isaiah, that men will not believe their report. And when we look about us, the true servants of Jesus are as hard to find as grapes remaining after the vintage, whilst the man of sin takes possession of the very temple of God. But the Church lives nevertheless, and is ever " with child." With all the discouragements and defections, within her body, unseen to mortal eyes, the princes are maturing for the birth to celestial and eternal rulership. Blessed revelation which the dear Saviour thus sends us from heaven ! Why then should we despond or grow weary in our work ?

3. This woman is *magnificently arrayed*. It is sometimes decried as a woman's weakness that she is fond of beautiful attire, and has an irrepressible instinct for personal adornment. It is not a weakness, but an instrument of power. It is part of her God-given nature, as the original type and representative of the Church. She may abuse it, and fall into many silly mistakes and sins by reason of it, but it becomes her, and belongs to her proper womanliness to be as beautiful as possible; and to be as beautifully and appropriately arrayed as she honestly can. She owes it to herself, to her sex, to her husband, and to society. A slattern is a monstrosity to the Divine ideal. The Church is the truest and heavenliest woman, and she is splendidly arrayed. She is " clothed with the sun."

Of course, no mere creature, or any number of creatures, can be literally dressed with the sun. That sublime luminary cannot be worn as a garment. It is only a pictorial representation, which is to be figuratively understood. But it is a gorgeous and most expressive figure.

The sun is the fairest and most brilliant thing our eyes have ever seen. It is the great orb of brightness. To be clothed with it, one would needs be clothed with light. And so it is with the Church and the people of God. Jesus says, they are " the children of light " (Luke 16 : 8). It is the office and end of all God's merciful appointments " to turn men from darkness to light " (Acts 26 : 18). Of those whom the Apostles enrolled as members of the Church of Christ, it is written, " Ye were sometimes darkness, but now are ye light in the Lord " (Eph. 5 : 8). The Church has ever been an illuminated body. Its children are not of darkness, but of the day. God, who caused the light to shine out of darkness, hath shined into their hearts, to give the light of the knowledge of His own glory. They " walk in the light." They wear it about them as a garment. If there be any light in the Divine revelations, they have it as their constant possession. If there be any teaching and illumination of the Holy Ghost, they enjoy it. They are an instructed people, illuminated from on high. They are the truly wise. They have the true philosophy of things, and are the widest awake to the highest truth and wisdom. While others grope in darkness, they are arrayed in light.

The sun is at the same time the great light-giver. It radiates brightness as well as possesses it. Light streams forth from it as the illuminator of this whole sublunary world. And to be clothed with the sun, one must necessarily be a glorious dispenser of illumination. And such is the Church. Its members and ministers have been the brightest lights of the ages. It is the pillar and ground of the truth—the golden candlestick of God amid the abounding and otherwise sunless darkness of this alien world. It is constituted and ordained for the teaching of the nations, and the bearing of the light of heaven to the benighted souls of men. People can learn the way of truth only through its testimony and confession. Christ hath said of His people, " Ye are the light of the world " (Matt. 5 : 14). By them it is that the knowledge and joy of salvation are carried over the earth, and ministered unto the dwellers in darkness and the shadow of death. They are the dispensers of the light of God. It is a great and wonderful endowment and office ; but this treasure hath the Lord given to His Church. Oh, that His people may know and realize it !

The sun is likewise an orb of great excellence and purity. Nothing can diminish its glory, or taint its rays. To be clothed with it, is to be clothed with unsullied excellency. And so it is with the Church. It may have shabby members, but they are not really of it. Whatever may be the native corruption of men, or their entanglement with the errors and vices of an ungodly world, in becoming God's people they are washed, they are sanctified, they are justified, in the name of the Lord Jesus, and by the Spirit of our God. They are the purest and holiest of the race. They are the flower of mankind. They are the jewels of the Lord of hosts. They are saints, having put on the Lord Jesus Christ, who is " the Sun of Righteousness."

Light is the garment of God. It is the symbol of His own nature. And as all true people of His are " partakers of the divine nature," being begotten unto Him from above, they enter also into the same clothing. The Church is robed with the sun.

4. This woman is *victorious in her position*. She has " the moon under her feet." Needless is the perplexity which men have felt in ascertaining what we are here to understand by the moon. As the sun is the king of day, so the moon is the empress of night ; and hence a fit picture of the kingdom of darkness. And as to be clothed with the one is to be " light in the Lord," a glorious lightbearer to the world, a possessor of great excellence and purity ; so to tread the moon under foot is the image of victory over the powers of darkness, whether of nature, or aught else. And this is a blessed characteristic and honour of the Church. All her true members are conquerors. Not all have yet come to the final triumph. This is not a picture of the Church triumphant, for the woman is still the subject of persecution, compelled to fly into the wilderness for her life. But even now, all who have come to real standing and membership in the household of faith, must needs have gained certain victories, and attained to the character of conquerors. By whatever Divine helps and gratuities it has been achieved, they have vanquished their native ignorance and hatred of God. They have subdued their prejudices, and brought their bodies and passions under the sway of another and better dominion and discipline. They have risen in rebellion against the old bondage and have conquered it, and broken away from it, and by stern resolve through the grace of God have entered upon the field of self-mastery and independence. With some the battle still rages, and " there remaineth yet much land to be possessed." But they have not warred in vain. Some glorious vantage-grounds have been won. They have conquered so far, that if they will only stand firm, their final triumph is sure. On fields once held by Satan, they have succeeded in planting the banners of Jehovah. And from the heights they have already gained, they see the victory from afar, and realize it even now. The moon is under their feet.

And the same is equally true of the Church as a body. She is the child and hero of battles, sufferings and victories. It is the primordial condition of her being to fight, going forth " conquering and to conquer." Without having anything in this world, she has successfully made her way into it, in spite of all the antagonism and power of the devil, who has never ceased to assail and resist her with all the might of earth and all the craft and subtlety of hell. Without the show of conquest, and mostly in weakness and in pain, straitened betimes as if it were impossible for her to survive, she has moved on, through blood and fires, floods and wildernesses, never surrendering, never losing a jot of her character and office, and doing her work against all the powers arrayed against her. Kings have combined to exterminate her, tyrants have oppressed her, treason has been raised in her own bosom, children have betrayed her, friends have deserted her, prisons have closed upon her, despotism has stamped its feet upon her neck, men in power have taken pleasure in dashing her little ones against the walls and feeding their flesh to the beasts of the earth, and many a time have her foes sent up their congratulations to each other that at last she was effectually vanquished. But still she has lived on, like the bush of Moses, unharmed by the fires, gathering children as trophies from the ranks of her enemies, pushing her influence to the very throne of Satan, making mighty champions of truth out of the veriest sons of hell, penetrating into all the nations, and to-day still waves aloft the palm of ten thousand contests, singing her pæans of thanksgiving to her God, as when Miriam struck the cymbals on the Red Sea's further shore. Small, and weak, and feminine, and despised, and pursued by the great destroyer, and seemingly ever on the point of destruction, she has continued victorious through all, God himself turning her worst calamities to triumphs, and the very malice of her foes to her glory. The moon is under her feet.

5. Still further : this woman is *royal in rank and dignity*. Regal gems glitter about her brow. There is " on her head a crown "—a crown " of stars," —stars to the sacred number of completeness,—" twelve stars." Whatever the particular allusion may be, whether to patriarchs, or tribes, or apostles, or all of these, or to the totality of her teaching agency, there flashes forth from this the unmistakable idea of kinghood and authority ; yea, of celestial royalty and dominion. And this too is one of the sublime possessions of the Church. Christians are " a chosen generation, a *royal* priesthood." (1 Peter 2 : 9.) By anticipation at least, all who are washed from their sins in the blood of Jesus, are " *Kings* and priests unto God." (Rev. 1 : 6.) All who are called by the Gospel, are called to royal place and dignity, and in so far as they have made that calling sure, whatever be their earthly estate or place, they are anointed and sealed as lords and princes of the eternal realm. They are joint heirs with Him to whom all power in heaven and earth is given. Time only is needed to instate them in immortal thrones. Crowns are theirs and the glory of imperishable empire.

And if we take these " stars " in the crown of the Church as representative of her ministers and teachers, after the manner of " the seven stars " in the first chapter, her royal character is strikingly manifest. In the covenants and promises to the fathers, in the precepts of the law, in the revelations of the prophets, in the melody of the Psalms, in the wisdom of the Proverbs, in the records of the four Evangelists, together with the princely letters of the Apostles, there stands written a Royal Law, stamped with the signature of the Eternal, unalterable by any existing powers in earth or heaven, binding not only the bodies but also the souls and consciences of men, and enthroned forever in the Council Halls of Christendom. To monarchs at their coronations, to magistrates, and judges, and officers of state at their induction into office, to bishops, ministers, and teachers at their ordinations, to every witness coming to testify in the courts of justice, and to every man, woman, and child seeking recognition before the altar of God, it is solemnly delivered, and its mandates enjoined, as The One Supreme and unchangeable LAW, to which all must conform on pain of being denied of God, and of perishing eternally And as the possessor, guardian, and administrator of this Law and teaching, the Church attests her queenliness before all the earth. Herein she is even, already enthroned, judging men, and judging angels. People look with contempt upon the Church. They think her mean among the majesties of this world. They esteem her manner of life a letting down of man's proper dignity and consequence. They scorn her modesty and humility as effeminacy. But they are despising Jehovah's Queen. They are vaunting over a power which is charged with the decision of their own destiny. They are contemning the Mother of Eternity's Kings. They are making light of the sole mistress of the holy keys which bind and loose on earth, with the irresistible authority of the very throne of God. For the Church is a royal woman, crowned with the stars of heaven.

6. And she is *in travail to bring forth*. She is persecuted ; but these are not so much pains of persecution. The pains of persecution come upon her from without ; this anguish is from within. Persecution proceeds from the wicked, for the purpose of destruction ; this agony proceeds from a treasure of heavenly sons, and is a travail to produce. Persecution has its spring in hell's malignity ; this agonizing has its origin in the love, and faith, and hope of a pious maternity.

Friends and Brethren : There is a grand and glorious birthday on hand when once the seventh trumpet begins to sound,—a birthday foreshadowed by the seizing away from earth of Enoch and Elijah, and forepledged by the resurrection of Jesus Christ from the grave, and his sublime ascension to the right hand of the Father,—a birthday which Paul had in his eye when he wrote, " The trumpet shall sound, and the dead shall be raised incorruptible, and we shall be changed." (1 Cor. 15 : 52.) To that all the promises point. Of that the patriarchs were persuaded when they " confessed that they were strangers and pilgrims on the earth." (Heb. 11 : 13.) To that the twelve tribes under the law, instantly serving God day and night, hoped to come. (Acts 26 : 7.) For that the great Apostle of the Gentiles counted all his sacrifices and sufferings as nothing, and ever pressed, through stripes, and prisons, and losses, and privations, as the mark and prize of the high calling of God in Christ Jesus. (Phil. 3 : 4-14.) And, in all the ages, this is the grand birthhour for which the Church ever cries to God, and agonizes and strives. It is the goal of all her being. It is the pole-star of her hope, and faith, and labours. It is the opening of the consummation for which her inmost nature ever yearns. And the effort to bring her sons to that birth, is the travail and anxiety here portrayed.

For this present we are in heaviness and tribulation. Heaven is not in this world. Our inheritance is beyond, and only the resurrection can bring us to the full fruition of it. In the day of the seventh angel, when he shall begin to sound, the mystery of God shall be finished, and His saints come to that for which they look, and long, and cry out, in all these years of waiting. Think, then, what a time that will be when once the object of all these prayers, sufferings, and endeavours has at last been reached ! What, indeed, is all the glorious light, and victory, and royalty, and joy of faith and hope we now possess, compared with the fulness of joy which shall come with that glad consummation !

But we may not now anticipate. The subsequent portions of this book tell the blessed story. Till we come to them, we defer what more is to be said. We have seen enough to suffice us for the present. We have seen that God has a Church on earth. We have seen its features and characteristics as pictured by Himself. And blessed above all is the fact that it exists *for us*. It is, and lives, and agonizes thus, that we may be members of it and be nurtured and disciplined in it for the glories of immortal regency. And all this cheering light concerning it is given to draw us into it, here to steady and improve us in faith and duty, that we may be God's sons and daughters, and share the destiny of its children. God grant that none of us may fail of the transcendent honours !

> The Church—the Church—the holy Church—
> The Saviour's spotless Bride !
> Who doth not love her queenly form
> Above all earth beside !
> Be mine through life to live in her ;
> And, when the Lord shall call,
> To die in her, the Spouse of Christ,
> The Mother of us all.

REV. 12 : 3, 4. (Revised Text.) And there was seen another sign in the heaven, and behold, a great red dragon, having seven heads and ten horns, and upon his heads seven diadems. And his tail draweth along the third of the stars of the heaven, and cast them to the earth. And the dragon stands before the woman which is about to bring forth, that when she has brought forth he may devour her child.

PARALLEL with the history of the Church in this world, there runs another, of very great moment, and closely related to it. It is the history of a mighty antagonizing power with which the Church has ever to contend, and which is ever set to hinder her progress and destroy her hopes. Nor is it possible to have a complete view of the one without some corresponding account of the other. Hence, in connection with the apparition of the woman clothed with the sun, " there was seen another sign in the heaven," which is described to us in the text. It is " another *sign* "—σημεῖον, and therefore to be interpreted after the same manner as the preceding.

The image presented is that of " *a dragon* "—a sort of being better known to heraldry, fable, and fanciful art, than to natural history. In the book of Job (chap. 41) there is a description of some semi-marine animal, clad in a panoply of hard scales, " esteeming iron as straw, and brass as rotten wood, counting darts as stubble, and laughing at the shaking of a spear," setting at defiance all the power and courage of man. It is there called *Leviathan*, but the same, or some corresponding serpentine creature, is elsewhere identified as " *the dragon.*" (See Is. 27 : 1, and 74 : 13, 14.) Some think it the crocodile, others the whale, and others perhaps one of those gigantic reptiles whose remains are occasionally dug up out of the earth. Evidently we are to conceive of it as some terrible serpentine creature, inhabiting the estuaries of rivers, or the marshes and margins of the sea, clawed, and armed at every point, and delighting to attack, terrify, and devour. When Jeremiah would set forth the terrible voracity and oppression of Babylon, he assigned to it the characteristics of this beast, saying, " he hath swallowed me up *like a dragon.*" (Jer. 51 : 34.) Hence, it was given place on the escutcheon of Egypt, and adopted as one of the military ensigns of imperial Rome. The legions of the latter bore it aloft, with the winds whistling through its wide-open throat, causing it to hiss as if in a rage, while its tail dangled or floated in various folds to the breeze.

But while the picture here is in general that of a dragon, it is one altogether peculiar, and different from common dragons. It is " a *great* dragon," one in size and bulk vastly in excess of the ordinary idea, and with every dragon-feature hugely magnified. It is also of a peculiar colour, " *red* "—πυρρὸς, *fiery*, or *red as fire*. It has " *seven heads.*" Dragons ordinarily were assigned but one head ; but this is possessed of seven, and each head has on it a diadem or crown—" *upon his heads seven diadems.*" He is armed also with " *ten horns.*" And he has a most extraordinary " *tail*," which " *draweth along the third of the stars of the heaven.*" The image is most formidable and terrific. And the attitude is equally threatening and terrible. The monster confronts the Woman as a great and malignant destroyer, in determined readiness to devour her child the moment it is born.

What, then, are we to understand by this Dragon ? Who is he ? What is thus meant to be brought to our view ?

Fortunately on this point we can speak with entire confidence and certainty. The answer is given, in the ninth verse, by the inspired writer himself. We there read that " the great dragon " is none other than " *the old serpent, that is called the Devil and Satan, who seduceth* [or misleadeth] *the whole world.*" Whatever men's theories of the Apocalypse may be, they cannot go back of this statement. It is one of those divinely settled points by which the whole interpretation must accord, in order to be true. The Dragon, then, is not Egypt as such, nor Babylon, nor the Roman Empire, nor anything but what John here tells us it is, namely, the Devil, even Satan. So the early interpreters all taught and maintained. Even catechumens in the fifth century are addressed by their teacher as all-knowing, " that this dragon is the devil." He is not literally a dragon, as the Church is not literally a woman, but the Dragon here described is a divinely-given image or symbol of him.

And as we are now dealing with consummations, we are to take this image of the Devil in the same way in which we took the image of the Church ; that is, in his whole character, career, and manifestations, from the beginning up to the end of this present world, particularly with reference to the decisive occurrences under the last trumpet. As the sun-clad woman denotes the Church in its entirety with reference to the final termination, so this dragon denotes the devil in his entirety with reference to the same.

There is, then, *a Devil*. Of this the chapter before us is authoritative proof. If there were no other passages on the subject, this would be sufficient to settle the question. But we read of him from the very beginning. In the Pentateuch, in Job, in the Gospels, and in the Epistles there are the most direct allusions to him, his origin, his malignity, and his works. The Bible tells of evil spirits, and of Satan as the head of them. Reason is reluctant to receive such doctrine. It is one of the favourite resorts of Satan to try to persuade men that no such being as he exists. Some think it impossible for such an evil power to find place in the realm of almighty Goodness. But there is no greater difficulty in explaining or construing the existence of wicked angels than the existence of wicked and devilish men. The very nature of moral government implies and necessitates the possibility of evil. God never made an evil being ; but, having constituted moral agents, the ability to do wrong as well as good had to be in them. And with the ability to do wrong, there is nothing improbable in the doctrine that some have exercised that ability, perverted their being, and lost their character, standing and place as holy creatures. It is rather one of the unavoidable liabilities of such a constitution ; and without such a constitution God could not half be known as He is known, and the sublimest part of the universe would be nothing but a blank. Instead of being offended with God for having made it possible for evil to originate within his domain, and of finding fault with Him for allowing sin, we should rather be praising and blessing Him for those sublimities of moral being, to the existence of which the possibility of evil is necessarily incident. That evil exists is a plain and evident matter of fact. A man must have lost all perception not to see and admit it. It stares him in the face whithersoever he turns. He encounters it in others, and he feels it in himself. And if it is possible for men to be evil, it is just as possible and likely that other creatures, higher in the scale than we, likewise have among them some who are apostate and depraved. And if so, reason itself is sufficient to suggest the doctrine of some great leader and prince in evil, in exact accord with the Scripture teaching with regard to the Devil. At all events, Revelation tells us of a crafty and powerful spiritual being who was the cause of the fall of our first parents, who was the direct agent of Job's afflictions, who tempted and assailed Christ, and who is the head and soul of a great empire of evil, which has eaten its way into the glorious creation of God, drawing some of His sublimest works into peril and ruin. And with these teachings we can most safely abide, believing what our gracious Father in heaven has caused to be written for our learning, and ordering our thinking accordingly.

We could not but admire in our last the wonderful beauty and fulness with which the Church was portrayed to us in the sun-clad Woman. But no less remarkable and complete is the picture of Satan as sketched in this " great red dragon." The subject, of course, is not so inviting, but still it is very important. Let us look at it then with something of the care and solemnity which is called for by the circumstantial particularity with which God has caused it to be here introduced.

 1. When Moses was commanded to take up the serpent, into which his rod had been turned, he was told to " take it by *the tail*." (Ex. 4 : 4.) And this may be a very proper way to take hold of this Dragon, " the old serpent." His tail is certainly one of the most striking features in the picture, and with it very marvellous execution is done. It swings through heaven, coils about celestial principalities, and " draweth along the third of the stars."

These, however, are quite other stars from those in the crown of the Woman. Those were simply " stars," her coronal gems ; but these are " the stars of the heaven "—some particular stars. Neither are they literal stars, for the whole thing is a " *sign* "—a symbol. But we are not to think of " the body of pagan priests," as Adam Clarke would teach us ; nor of the apostasy of Licinius, as Elliott would have it ; nor yet of the princes and rulers of the world subdued to the Roman Empire, as Mede and Hengstenberg suggest. All this is far beneath the majesty and relations of the picture. Vitringa hit the truth much more successfully, when he spoke here of *the angels*. These are truly " the stars of the heaven." When God brought the world into being, we are told that " the morning *stars* sang together, and all the sons of God shouted for joy." (Job. 38 : 4–7.) These were the angelic hosts. They are fitly called *stars* by reason of their beauty and glory ; and they are pre-eminently " the stars of the heaven," as they pertain to heaven, and are the sublimest ornaments of the celestial world. Satan himself was once one of these stars, as we saw in chapter 9 : 1. Isaiah (14 : 12) alludes to this, where the exclamation is, " How art thou fallen from heaven, O Lucifer [literally, *day-star*], son of the morning ! "

Has there then been any calamity among the angelic hosts to answer the description before us ? The Scriptures distinctly tell us that there has. Jude (6) speaks of " angels which kept not their first estate [their principality], but left their own habitation." Peter refers to " the angels that sinned," whom " God spared not." (2 Pet. 2 : 4.) A time there has been when evil got in among these heavenly orders, infected many of these shining sons of light, soiled their robes, tarnished their crowns, silenced their songs, dislodged them from their glorious seats, and ate out of them every noble impulse and holy affection. How the sorrowful disaster came about, is suggested in various places, and distinctly indicated in the picture before us. Satan, one of the brightest and mightiest among them, was the cause and author of it all. Abusing his moral liberty, he dared to lift himself up against his Maker, and instituted a revolt against the throne and majesty of God. By his example, instigations, and persuasions, he infected others, imbued them with his spirit, and made them co-partners in his plot.

> By their aid, aspiring
> To set himself in glory, above his peers,
> He trusted to have equalled the Most High,
> And, with ambitious aim
> Against the throne and monarchy of God,
> Raised impious war in heaven and battle proud.

Here then was this dragon exerting his strength in the heaven, insinuating his coils about the sons of light, and drawing them along with his presumptuous cause. All these

> The Almighty Power
> Hurled headlong flaming from the ethereal sky,
> With hideous ruin and combustion down.

How many were thus involved is not told us. The text says that the terrible apostasy embraced " *the third* of the stars of the heaven." Many take this as significant only of a large proportion, without regard to any exact number. And so the meaning may be. But the statement itself is definite, and will bear the interpretation that just one-third of all the angelic host fell through that Satanic rebellion. Milton imagines a great multitude, greater than that which the north of Europe emptied out,

> When her barb'rous sons
> Came like a deluge on the south, and spread
> Beneath Gibraltar to the Lybian sands.

These were " *cast to the earth* "—not the literal earth, for we are contemplating " *a sign*," and we must interpret accordingly. Contrasted with the visible heavens, the earth is simply the lowest place—the ground—the base. For a star to be cast down to the earth, is to be plucked out and thrown down from its setting as a star. And so these rebel angels have been plucked from their places, dethroned and abased. Hence we read of them as " reserved in chains, under darkness, unto the judgment of the great day." (Jude 6.) Having failed voluntarily to keep to their proper place, they are now *kept* against their will, in the power and purpose of God, for a doom not yet fully executed. They lost their heavenly principality. In place of their starry brightness they are now darkness, which clings to them, as chains to a prisoner, and holds them for eternal punishment. They still roam at large, particularly about our earth, and in the atmosphere which surrounds it ; for the devil " goeth about " to do mischief. But, like tethered cattle, or chained dogs, their liberty is bounded, and they can go no further than that tether's length. And this is the casting down and disability which the picture before us symbolizes.

So much, then, for the *tail* of this dragon, his chief power, which draws along the third of the stars of heaven, and cast them to the earth.*

2. We advance now to his *heads and horns*, which look formidable enough ; for he has " seven " of the one, and " ten " of the other.

The head is the governing power, and implies rule. When crowned, it implies political rulership. These seven heads of the dragon are all crowned heads. He is an imperial personage. Each one of his heads has on it a diadem, indicating imperial rulership and autocratic administration. And just so far as these heads show themselves on earth, terrestrial magistracy and government are implied. The number of these crowned heads is *seven*, which is the number of dispensational fulness, the earthly complete number. Hence we have in these heads the symbol of the entire imperial government of this world from beginning to end, the universal secular dominion of the earth in all periods. They are seven heads, in the same sense that we read of " the *seven Spirits of God* "—a manifold unity. Daniel beheld the imperial authority of this world up to the great judgment day, under four successive beasts, and these several beasts together had also seven heads, to indicate the whole aggregate completeness of earthly empire.

We need not bother ourselves then about the seven hillocks on which the city of Rome was built ; nor about the seven administrations, or forms of dominion, or dynasties, which are said to have marked the history of the Roman Empire ; nor yet go on a search through the archives of the world to

---

* It is a strong confirmation of our correctness here, that the two verbs are in quite different tenses. The drawing, συρει, is in the *present*, denoting an action in continuity at the time John wrote, which is the fact with regard to Satan's influence over these fallen powers, but not the fact with regard to any other interpretation proposed. The *casting down*, εβαλεν, is in the *second aorist*, denoting an action past, as the deposition and dejection of the wicked angels is, and was at the apostle's time, a past event. Satan's drawing of them along with him began before their expulsion from heaven, and it continues long after, till now, and even under the last trumpet. To no other interpretation will the diction thus accurately fit.

K

find and identify seven successive imperial establishments to embrace the governmental history of time. However the facts in these cases may incidentally conform to the picture, it goes quite above and beyond all such arithmetical enumerations and trifling distinctions and details ; for trifling they are as compared with the mighty sweep of the subject. The number is the symbol of full completeness, which takes in all of its kind in the whole world-period. It is nothing more nor less than earth's political sovereignty, however and wherever put forth, from the beginning to the day of judgment, that is embraced in these crowned heads.

And they are the Devil's heads. All sovereignty is, indeed, of God ; but, in this world, Satan has usurped much of it. When he pointed out to Jesus " all the kingdoms of the world, and the glory of them," and offered them as a compromise and compensation to the blessed Christ if He would but " fall down and worship " him, it was not mere boast and false pretence. Three times the Saviour pronounces him " *The Prince of this world* " (John 12 : 31 ; 14 : 30 ; 16 : 11). Paul styles him the very " *god* of this world " (2 Cor. 4 : 4). The glorious ones in heaven are witnesses to us, that " the kingdom of the world " is not yet " our Lord's and His Christ's," nor will be till the last trumpet sounds, and the grand events under it are consummated. John testifies that " *the whole world lieth in the wicked one* " (1 John 5 : 19) ; that is, reposes in his bosom, as the source of its warmth and life, its lord and its resting-place. Its governments, therefore, above all, must be in his power, and pertain to his administration. Good elements, in a greater or less degree, may here and there be in them, and sometimes they may largely conform to what is right and true ; for God has not resigned His providence over the world ; but Satan has hold of them, and operates by them nevertheless. If now and then modified, so that his presence is not so conspicuous, and his influence repressed, it matters not. He is the great usurper, and one or the other of his numerous heads has been under and in every temporal crown that ever swayed the sceptre of sovereignty on earth, save only the Israelitish theocracy. So the Scriptures teach ; and hence the image before us presents him as wearing the diadems of all the dominions of this world. And through these world-powers he puts himself forth over against the kingdom of God.

Horns are the weapons of animals, their means of inflicting injury, their power for evil. As symbols, they do not so much represent rulership or dominion, as power to harm, wound, and afflict. The " four horns " in Zechariah's vision, were the powers which devastated Palestine, " scattered Judah," and injured, oppressed, and destroyed the people of God. (Zech. 1 : 18–21.) And such are the horns of this Dragon. The number of them is *ten*, the number of worldly completeness, especially in the line of worldly evil. All the tyrannies, oppressions, and hard inflictions that have tortured mankind, from the beginning to the end of them, are thus ascribed to Satan. They are his horns, with which he gores, and wounds, and scatters, and destroys. Every manifestation in the world, in the line of violent and oppressive injury or mischief, is from the Devil. And whatever the persons, combinations, or powers, whether governmental or otherwise, by which the damage is inflicted, they are the Devil's horns, which he has been using with mighty effect in every age, and is still using, and *will* use, till the great judgment sits, and he is put out of the way.

3. We look next at *his colour ;* for nothing in the description is without significance. This Dragon is " *red*," the hue of fire and blood. This was the colour of the horse whose rider was to take peace out of the earth, who carried the great sword of execution, and who filled the world with bloodshed and slaughter. (Rev. 6 : 4.) It is the colour of the apparel of the Almighty King, when he puts on his strength to crush out his enemies. (Is. 63 : 2–4 ; Rev. 19 : 11–15.) It tells of flaming heat, of intensity of fierceness, of bloody administrations. And this well describes the inmost nature of Satan, as everywhere portrayed. He is a fierce and murderous being, cruel, bloodthirsty, and ever

intent on destruction. Jesus says, " *He was a murderer from the beginning.*"
(John 8 : 44.) Peter warns all Christians against him, as one that walketh
about, as a roaring lion, seeking whom he may devour. (I Pet. 5 : 8.) He
is the Destroyer of both souls and bodies. He seduceth and misleadeth the
whole world, promising good and peace only that he may the more effectually
entrap and ruin. With what murderous malignity did he attack the innocence
of our first parents, and the heavenly purity of Jesus ! With what carnage and
misery has he overflooded the earth ! There has never been a murder, but he
caused it. There has never been a sanguinary war, but he instituted it. There
has never been a death-scene, but it is traceable to him. Every blight of
human happiness, every failure of human peace, every sorrow of human life,
has come from him. All the fiery passions that rankle in men, and break
forth in deeds of violence and blood, are his inspirations. Never a being has
been perverted from the beneficent object of its existence, never a soul has
lost its Creator's image or gone down to perdition, never a life has been
disabled or extinguished, never a heart has been broken or a wretchedness
enacted, of which he is not the primal cause. All graves, all tears, all mutila-
tions and dismemberments of earth's families, nations, or the race, are results
of his doings and malignity. And when we think of the blood that has been
shed, and the murders committed, since Cain raised his hand against his
brother's life ; how rapine, and plunder, and violence have disgraced and
tormented the world in every age ; what hellish devastations war alone has
wrought ; how human society has been continually spoliated and cursed with
intemperance, ignorance, uncleanness, and vice ; and remember that all
these, with all the calamities, misfortunes, and sufferings of time and eternity,
have their source in Satan, and are but outbirths, enactments or results of
his spirit ; how could a truer characterization be given of him, than that of a
monster, indyed with flames and blood ! He is *red*, for he is *the Satan, the
Devil, the Apollyon.*

4. Still another feature specially noted, is ·his *greatness*. He is a fierce,
malignant, and bloody monster, and a "*great*" one. But how shall we
get a right conception of what is thus portrayed ? Milton talks of him as
Titanian, long, and large, extending many a rood ; his shield, like the broad
circumference of the moon ; and his spear so great, that to it the tallest pine

> Hewn on Norwegian hills to be the mast
> Of some great admiral, were but a wand.

But, not in this way can we get a right idea of Satan's greatness. We must
lift our thoughts to much wider and mightier contemplations.

Looking out from this world into the depths of space about us, we see " an
outward, visible universe, studded with constellations of suns and their
attendant systems, circling in unmeasured orbits around an invisible and
omnipotent centre, which controls them all. Amazed and overwhelmed at these
stupendous displays of creative power, wisdom, and goodness, in adoring
ecstasy we inquire into the uses of these mighty orbs, which, in such untold
millions, diversify and adorn those undefined fields of ethereal beauty which
fill unbounded space. Reasoning from all our native analogies, and from the
scattering rays of supernal light that have reached our world, we must infer
that all these orbs are the mansions of social beings, of every conceivable
variety of intelligence, capacity, and employment, and that in organized
hierarchies, thrones, principalities, and lordships, they constitute each within
itself an independent world," though all together but so many members of the
one immense family of creation.

Now, in all these intellectual assemblages, spread over the immeasurable
area of universal being, there are but *two* distinct and essentially diverse
confederations—two empires, with two primal heads. On the one hand sits
the almighty and ineffable Jehovah, whose majesty transcends all human
thought or comprehension ; his being, eternal ; his nature, perfect ; his

throne, absolute ; to whom " every creature which is in the heaven, and on the earth, and under the earth, and upon the sea," in one form or another, is compelled to give the blessing, and the honour, and the glory, and the dominion, for the ages of the ages. But, on the other hand, stands a mimic god, a creature, indeed, and not at all beyond the Almighty's government and control, but one of the sublimest of angelic beings, a prince among the celestial hierarchies, set against God, seeking to overturn heaven, aiming to supplant the kingdom, authority, and rightful worship of the great Eternal, himself grasping for the reins of universal sovereignty. We tremble as we think of the awful daring. The ambition and adventure of earthly despots in setting out to conquer this world, is startling ; and because of what men have done towards accomplishing it, history calls them " *great*." Yet here is a being, who has adventured upon the exploit of conquering the universe, of wresting creation from its Maker ! Under the mysterious economy of God, he has also been enabled to make mighty strides towards the realization of his fell purposes. Principality after principality, in the celestial realms, succumbed, and fell in line beneath his banner. A third of the very stars of the heaven joined his cause, and followed in his train. The appointed lord and sovereign of the earth at the beginning was betrayed into his power, and all earth's naturally engendered children were made his born slaves and servants. And so there now exists a mighty confederation of evil, made up of angels and men, disembodied and in the flesh, numbering millions on millions of disloyal spirits, who burden our atmosphere, and overspread our planet with disorders, anarchy, misrule, darkness, gloom, sorrow, death, and ten thousand embitterments of existence, from which uncounted creatures sigh, and groan, and cry to be delivered ! Long ago, indeed, an effectual check was put upon the growth and sway of this impious coalition in heaven. Also, in the decrees of God, the unalterable determination stands, to uproot and destroy it utterly. But till the eternal Son of Deity undertook the case, not a potency in all the circle of created things could shake its hold upon this world of ours. Neither could He, without centuries on centuries of preliminary work, and then the resignation of His place in the Divine bosom, the conjoining of himself to human flesh and blood, and the enactment of an humiliation, as astounding to all heavenly intelligences as it was unparalleled in the history of things. No, nor even then without battle and conflicts so intense and horrible that they wrung even His mighty soul with anguish unspeakable, shook the fabric of His immortal being to the verge of annihilation, and put the very Lord of glory under the pangs, and bonds, and darkness of death and the grave ! And only when we have surveyed the dimensions of an empire so gigantic, and counted the cost at which alone its hold could be broken, are we in position to estimate the greatness of that fell spirit, who created it out of his own subtle deceit and unholy ambition, sits as its head giving force and direction to all its parts, and wields it with a genius and will inferior only to that of eternal uncreated Mind. Ah, yes, the Dragon is " *great*."

5. And yet one feature more is given in this picture, to wit, *his attitude and bearing toward the Church of God*. " The dragon stands before the woman which is about to bring forth, that when she has brought forth he may devour her child." How intensely does this sum up the whole history of the case in all the ages of time ! The Church and the Devil, the kingdom of heaven and the powers of darkness, have ever been the two great antagonizing forces on the earth. The one is the spirit of mercy, embodied in the work of man's deliverance ; the other is the spirit of malignity, going about to crush and kill every tendency, power, or prospect of man's salvation.

We go back to the beginning of the world, and contemplate the excellent sacrifice of Abel, " by which he obtained witness that he was righteous, God testifying of his gifts " as of an heir to a blessed immortality. But the Dragon is there, enraged that such a seed should come from among men. Envy, hate, and fratricide he stirs up in the sullen heart of Cain, till murder's hand is put forth for the first time in our world, and the meek and holy believer's blood is shed by his own brother, for no other reason than that in him was brought forth a child of eternal life and princehood.

With the seed of Abraham, Isaac, and Jacob was lodged the promise of spiritual sonship and glorious dominion. Out of them was to be developed a seed to redeem and rule the world. But as the time approached for them to take their place according to the covenant, lo, the claws of this same Dragon were upon them, clenching them tighter and tighter to keep them down, and giving forth imperial edicts for the slaughter of all their infant sons, to defeat what God had spoken. And through the whole national existence of that people, again and again, the heathen raged, and the people meditated mischief, and the kings of the earth set themselves, and the rulers took counsel together, against the Lord, and against His anointed, fulfilling ever more and more the great draconic image of the text, to prevent the Godchild's forthcoming to the rulership of the world.

We recur to Bethlehem, as the great Head and chief of all this divine seed appears. We hear the angels sing and the shepherds rejoice. We see the stars giving unusual indications, mighty sages of the far-off land coming to lay their royal treasures at his feet, and everything aglow with a sense of the wonderfulness of the event. But the Dragon is there, with rage inflamed, and eager to devour. In Herod he inquires, and plots, and sends his executioners to slay all the children in Bethlehem, and in all the coasts thereof, from two years old and under, to make doubly sure of reaching this child's life, and destroying this whole seed forever.

So has it also been in all succeeding time. While Jesus was going up and down among the villages of Palestine, fulfilling the prophecies and maturing God's plans for begetting a people for Himself, the earthly powers about him were ever prowling and plotting to destroy both him and his work, and finally seized him, killed him, and sealed up his mangled body in the sepulchre. When, by the Spirit of God, he rose again, and gave new commissions and endowments to his apostles, threatening and slaughter pursued them, and the sword, the cross, and the stake awaited them. Rome joined with Jerusalem in oppressing, banishing, and destroying them, and all who adhered to them. Emperors sported themselves with their sufferings, and edict after edict went forth from the throne of the world for their extermination. Ten mighty persecutions fell on Christians throughout all the jurisdiction of the Cæsars. The earth was repeatedly deluged in martyr blood. And what was it all but this seven-headed and ten-horned Dragon confronting the travailing woman, determined to make an end of her royal seed !

Nor was it essentially different after Paganism was dethroned, and the cross appeared upon the imperial banners. The tactics changed, but it was still the Dragon that wrought. Outward oppression was broken, but then came inward assaults, corruption, and decay. The sword of state for a while was sheathed, but then was drawn the more killing weapon of domineering heresy. Soon also the tiara became the imperial crown, the wearer of it the world's dictator, and kings and governments the slaves and menials of another Rome, robed in Christian symbols indeed, but at heart the Dragon still, with fagot, and bloody inquisition, and bans of terrible damnation, striving to enforce its blasphemous assumptions and soul-destroying lies. When the holy Reformers began again to shake the torch of evangelic truth to light the nations to their salvation, the Vatican thundered with its bulls, armies rallied for the onslaught, and massacres and butcheries filled many lands with the blood of God's confessors, or lighted them with flames to consume the bodies of the saints. And even to this day and hour, the old serpent lies coiled in the Church's path, and in the forms of a pretended superior science, a false philosophy, a perverted Gospel, and many an ugly persecution, still strikes, assails, and mightily struggles to crush the meek Galilean's power from the earth, and keep the God-child from his royal destiny and dominion.

So true is it, that "*The Dragon stands before the woman which is about to bring forth, that when she has brought forth he may devour her child.*"

Behold then, my friends, what a mysterious battle-field this world is. A contest here is waging which enlists and engages the mightiest powers that exist. It is the great and far-reaching conflict between good and evil, between truth and falsehood, between right and usurpation, between the Kingdom of God and the Empire of Satan, between Heaven and Hell—the great war of a divided universe, coming to final issue upon this little world of ours! It is largely silent and invisible. Though raging round us every hour, we perceive so little of it, that many doubt its reality. But its very hiddenness is evidence of its awful greatness. The little broils and disputes of a neighbourhood are loud, and thrust themselves on every ear, because they are confined to a level and limit within easy observation and comprehension ; but this conflict we can only know by divine Revelation, because it encompasses so much of eternity, and pertains to spiritual potencies under and behind the outward ongoing of things. The " noise of the captains," the " shouting," the rattle of arms, the boom of artillery, marking earthly battles, is but the fuss and ado pertaining to the local and circumscribed exhibits of man's doings. When it comes to a contest stretching through worlds and ages, and enlisting the greatest of invisible powers, the reach of human hearing and sight are necessarily far transcended, and the conflict is all the deeper and more tremendous because of its hiddenness and silence. But, whether conscious of it or not, such a mighty strife exists, and we ourselves are all parties to it, and combatants in it. If not of the glorious Woman, we are of the seven-headed and ten-horned Dragon, at war with her, her seed, and her God. Nor are any of us of the glorious Woman, who have not renounced Satan and all his works, and confessed ourselves to Christ in obedience to His Gospel. I ask not any of you to tell me to which side of this awful controversy you belong. The Word of God has settled that question. And from these holy oracles of truth I make it known to you this night, that if you have not yet enlisted under the banner of Emanuel, and at His altar sworn unfaltering allegiance to Him, you are under the Dragon's standard, serving his will, helping on his foul and murderous work, and on the way to share his destiny. God help every one in such a case to see it before it be forever too late ! Though involved in Satan's coils, it is not impossible yet to change sides ; but it must be done quickly, if ever. Hence, the very first question which we are bound to ask of those to whom we are to deliver the promise of salvation is : " *Do you renounce the Devil and all his works,—the vanities of the world and the sinful desires of the flesh ?* " And for those who decline to do this, now in the time of their probation, there is no hope, and no promise of eternal life.

LECTURE TWENTY-EIGHTH

THE MAN-CHILD—THE CONFUSION OF EXPOSITORS ON THE SUBJECT—LANDMARKS TO BE OBSERVED—THIS WOMAN AND CHILD THE VISIBLE AND INVISIBLE CHURCH—MANHOOD OF THIS CHILD—IS MEANT FOR RULERSHIP AND DOMINION—THE OBJECT OF SATAN'S PARTICULAR MALICE—THE BIRTH—THE GLORY OF THE CHRISTIAN CALLING.

REV. 12 : 5. (Revised text.) And she brought forth a son, a male [*neuter*, embracing either sex], who is to rule [*shepherdize*] all the nations with a rod of iron : and her child was caught away to God, and to his throne.

IN the discourses which last engaged our attention, we saw what is to be understood by the wonderful Woman clothed with the sun ; and likewise ascertained who the great red Dragon is that stands before her. But we are not quite done yet with either of them. This Woman was travailing and agonizing herself to bring forth, and really did bring forth, even in the face of the murderous Dragon. It remains, therefore, to inquire concerning this Child, the nature of the birth spoken of, and the results which followed ; remembering, of course, that we are still dealing with a symbolic picture, " *a sign.*"

In looking over the expositions that have been given of the matter, we encounter a strange and wide-ranging amount of conjecture and confusion. Some find the fulfilment in the birth of Christ ; some, in the birth and enthronement of Constantine, the great, the first Christian Emperor ; some, in the increase and growth of the Church in the period in which Constantine lived ; some, in the Christianization of the State under Constantine, and the nationalization of the Church in the Roman Empire. Others take this child to be " the Valenses and Albigenses as sequestered from the pure worshippers generally." Some even suppose it to be the Nicene Creed, the Church of Rome, or only a revitalized or repristinated Christianity in general, at some period in the times long past. Hengstenberg says, " The man-child denotes the manly, vigorous aftergrowth, or fresh growth of the people of God." Durham says, " It is *mystical Christ*, who in his members is brought to a flourishing condition, and his Church set at liberty from persecution, and some of her sons exalted to an honourable condition." Alford says, " The man-child is the Lord Jesus Christ, *and none other*." Elliott says, we are to see in it " a baptized emperor, the son of Christ's faithful Church, elevated to the whole empire, to an avowedly Christian throne." Robertson (of Leuchars) says, " This *Child* is a collective expression, and takes in the whole brood of the Church under Paganism, and in spite of its efforts to hinder the same." Adam Clarke affirms, " The man-child mentioned in this verse is the dynasty of Christian emperors, beginning with Constantine's public acknowledgment of his belief in the divinity of the Christian religion." " Matheetees " thinks, " The Child is the same body as the Great Multitude of chapter seven," which comes out of the great tribulation. Barnes says, " I understand the man-child here to refer to the Church in its increase under the Messiah, and the idea to be, that the Church was, at the time referred to, about to be enlarged, and that, though its increase was opposed, yet it was destined ultimately to assert a mild sway over all the world." By the *male son*, the editor of Lange *On the Apocalypse* understands " the 144,000 " referred to in chapters seven and fourteen. And so we might go on quoting the most divergent and contradictory interpretations, guesses and conceits, not one of which rests upon any self-consistent method for understanding this Book.

How, then, are we to bring ourselves through this labyrinth ? I answer, by simply following the straightforward, natural and self-indicated principles which have guided us in these expositions from the beginning. If these will not serve to bring us out with some good degree of satisfactoriness, it may as well be admitted first as last, that there are no means at present within the reach of man by which to arrive at any clear and assured understanding of what God here intended to make known to the Churches. Let us see, then, what these principles will do for us.

We have, I may venture to say, ascertained, that this image of the Woman clothed with the sun denotes the visible Church, the body of God's confessing people of all ages and dispensations. In one way or another, there is a some-what general agreement with Vaughan, from Hippolytus and other of the Fathers, that " the Woman clothed with the sun, and having on her head a crown of twelve stars, *is the Church of God ;* the Church, regarded as one whole from the days of Abraham, perhaps we may say, from the day of the Fall itself, under whatever dispensation placed, the patriarchal, the Israelite, or the Christian."*

It is also a most conspicuous particular in the description itself, that this mystic Woman is in the way of motherhood. Within her body, concealed from human view, but consciously to herself, there is a mystic seed, maturing for manifestation, to bring which to the birth is the one great object of his most intense anxieties.† This is one of the most marked and striking characteristics of the picture, and no application of it can be the true one which does not throughout answer to this travail and self-agonizing of the Church to bring forth this invisible seed into open day and proper life. The Woman being the entire Church, this seed, borne by her, and which she thus labours above all things safely to bring forth, cannot possibly be Constantine, or the State under him ; nor the Christians within that State ; nor the dynasty of the Christian Emperors of Rome ; nor the fresh growth of the people of God in those days ; nor the Valenses and Albigenses ; nor the 144,000 sealed ones ; nor the multitude out of the great tribulation ; nor the nationalized Church of the Roman Empire ; nor " the whole brood of the Church under Paganism ; " nor any local, individual, particular, fractional, temporary or incidental thing in the great sweep of the Church's history. The reason is manifest. None of these things were in the Church, consciously to her, through all ages and dispensations. Neither did either or all of them constitute the one great and pre-eminent thing on the bringing forth of which all the universal Church's desires, aims, efforts and intensest self-agonizings were concen-trated. Certainly, none of these things were present to the mind of the patriarchal and Jewish saints as the thing for which, above all else, they toiled and agonized ; nor yet to the apostles and the great body of the Christian Church ; no, not even in the particular times and localities to which these things relate. Never was the whole mind and energy of the Church thus anxiously preoccupied with any such bringings forth. And if the subject were not so sacred as to awe men from speaking out with regard to it as they do on other matters, they would laugh to scorn the floundering imbecilities which interpreters have shown in attempting to construe so definitely drawn a divine picture of the universal Church of God, with such trifles and local accidents of the ordinary history of earthly affairs, as are brought forward by Elliott, Faber, Clarke, Barnes, and the like. The declaring of Victoria the Empress of India, is not less the centre of the world's history, than these presentations of grave religious teachers are below the range of such a picture as that which God has here set before us of His universal Church.

---

* Lectures on Revelation of St. John, *in loc.*

† " The figurative phrases of *pregnancy* and *travailing in birth-throes* are applied, alike in ancient and modern languages, to the mind's full possession by any momentous truth or object of desire, and earnest longing to be delivered of it ; whether in the announcement of that truth, or accomplishment of that object. Of scriptural examples refer to Isaiah 26 : 17 ; 66 : 8, and Romans 8 : 22. Add Micah 5 : 3 ; Hos. 13 : 13 ; Psalms 7 ; 14 ; James 1 : 15 "—Elliott's *Horæ Apocalypticæ*, iii, p. 24.

Still another landmark in the case is, that the birth here spoken of is not consummated before the period of the end of this age. Whatever earnests of it may have preceded, it is not fully accomplished till the day of judgment comes. It is here placed under the seventh trumpet, and the seventh trumpet is the last, with which the whole history of this present world comes to an end. Accordingly, this child is unborn until the period of the end is reached. We cannot, therefore, legitimately understand it of anything in the past history of the Church, or of anything that comes to its maturity and is outwardly manifested, anterior to the judgment times. This one particular in the presentation, so clear and conspicuous that we dare by no means ignore it, of itself utterly sweeps away four-fifths of all the commentation on the subject, as irrelevant, unallowable, and only clouding the truth intended to be exhibited. Any and everything, of whatsoever kind or character, which is born, matured and outwardly manifested, prior to the day of judgment, is not, and cannot be, this man-child ; for he is not born, at least his birth is not fully accomplished, till the seventh trumpet sounds, and the end of the world is come.

With the way thus cleared, we are in position to inquire more directly, and to inform ourselves more surely, as to who this man-child is.

Let it be observed, then, first of all, that it is one of the accepted and necessary doctrines of common Christian Theology, that the Church of God exists, or is to be contemplated, in a twofold form : first, in the wide or general form of the whole congregation of those joined together in the confession of the Divine Word, and in the observance of the divine rites and ordinances ; and second, in the narrower form, which embraces only those who are true believers, and are really the children of God ; for " not all are Israel who are of Israel." In the one view, the Church is a visible body, made such by the having of an outward call of God, by joining in an external fellowship, and by the use of the outward means and instruments through which God collects and edifies His Church. This we call *the visible Church*, or the Church in that aspect of it in which it is recognizable by man, and becomes a subject of human history. It is the Church thus viewed, that is, the general congregation of God's confessing people, that is symbolized by this wonderful Woman. With this assembly, however, many are outwardly connected, whom the Holy Ghost has not regenerated, and who are not in reality the genuine children of God.   A very great difference therefore exists between such members, and those who have fully entered into their calling, and become partakers of that spiritual renewal and enlightenment which makes them truly the children and elect of God. Which of the outward members of the Church are thus truly regenerated, cannot be fully and certainly distinguished by us. They are *in* the visible Church, and they are also as visible as others, with respect to their outward calling, fellowship, and observance of the Divine ordinances ; but as to their inward estate and union with God, they are not certainly recognizable. The Church, as a visible body, knows that they are there ; but just who they are, it does not know, and cannot now surely determine. And this inner and narrower circle of the professed people of God, we call *the invisible Church ;* not because its members are not as visible as any others, nor yet as a Church separate and apart from the visible Church ; but with respect to that feature in their case, that we cannot now see and certainly decide as to the fact of their being of the regenerate and elect.

Here then is a great, broad, and necessary theological distinction, as deeply rooted in the nature of the case, as it is in the plain teachings of the Scriptures. It is approved and accepted by all parties, as true of the Church in all ages, and under all dispensations.

Now, if this Woman is the *visible* Church, who can that divine seed which she carries and nurtures within her body be, but just these genuine children of God, whose characteristics are yet hidden, and who are only to be manifested at the great day, to wit, the *invisible* Church ! Those who constitute the invisible Church are in the visible Church and for the present are still joined to the visible Church as a most important part thereof. They are her chief treasure. The visible Church exists for their begetment and nurture. **Where** she is, they are also. It is on their account she has all her trials, her anxieties, and her assaults of Satan. It is with them that she ever travails, and cries out, and agonizes herself, that they may be brought safely to birth and manifestation as the sons of God. The picture is as true and exact as it is beautiful, and as true of one age and dispensation as it is of another. Nor is there a single item in the whole case which does not go to strengthen the overpowering proof, that this is what we are to understand by this mystic Child. Look for a moment at a few additional particulars.

1. There is a peculiar manliness ascribed to this child. It is not only "*a man child*," as our English version renders the phrase, but more literally "*a son, a male*," or *a son who is a male*. There is special emphasis laid upon the masculinity. But this is in no way distinctive of Constantine. He was in no respect more conspicuously *a male*, or even in the higher sense *a man*, than many other notable sons of the Church. Moses, and David, and Solomon, and Daniel, and Zerubbabel, among the ancients, and Paul, and Peter, and Augustine, and Luther, and Gustavus Adolphus, among the men of our own dispensation, were in every respect as manly as he. Nay, the letter of the description is such as to prove that this child is collective and composite, the same as the mother, and likewise includes people of both sexes. The word (αρσεν) which means *male*, has the peculiarity of being in the neuter gender, and so applies to both men and women, and cannot apply to any one individual. We have a somewhat similar instance in 2 Tim. 3 : 6, where the apostle speaks of certain perverted religionists, "which creep into houses and lead captive silly women" (γυναικαρια), that is, silly women of the neuter gender, and so women, or womenish ones, of both sexes. Sex, however, is not so much the subject of this αρσεν as the higher qualities of manhood common to both men and women. Such forms of speech lose all propriety except when construed with the implication that a body of persons is meant, and that this body includes women as well as men, and men as well as women. But it is a body at the same time distinguished throughout with a special masculinity, which knows no sex ; that is, with the most manly of virtues, and the most vigorous and heroic of characteristics. This was not true of the Christians of the time of Constantine, of the Valenses, or of any other particular peoples who have been named in this connection, any more than of the genuine saints of God of any other time. Nay, we look in vain to the Christians of Constantine's day, or to those who lived under the dynasty of Christian Emperors after him, for exemplifications of this manliness at all special, or worthy to be compared with the heroism of the prophets, apostles, and martyrs which were before them, or with that of the great champions of the faith in more recent times. But if we understand here all God's saints, all who have been begotten of the Holy Ghost, of every age, then every letter of the narrative is realized to the full. Here are men and women, in multitudes upon multitudes, "of whom the world was not worthy," alike pervaded with the highest qualities of virtue, courage, self-denial and strength. They are all conquerors. They all have overcome the world, triumphed over the powers of darkness, won the race of faith, and through the grace of God possessed themselves of titles to everlasting crowns and honours. Their masculinity in these respects is unquestionable and most intense, whether they be men or women as to sex. Nor is this so true and characteristic of any people that have lived, or that shall live, as it is of the true children of God of all time. Here we find all the noblest and best of the race, and the embodiment of the highest virtue and wisdom that ever pulsated in the arteries of humanity. Here is the proper "*man* child," if ever there was or will be one upon earth.

2. This child "*is to rule [shepherdize] all the nations with a rod of iron*." He is to reign, with unrivalled and irresistible authority and power, over the world. He is to govern, discipline and control all the peoples of the earth, as a shepherd deals with his flock. To shepherdize with an iron sceptre, is to exercise a dominion which is inflexible, irrefragable, and that cannot be with-

stood.   Strength, absoluteness and perpetuity of rule, is unmistakably indicated ; and that rule is specifically said to be over " *all the nations.*"   It leaves none outside of it.   It is universal.   But none of this is strictly true, either of Constantine, or of the Christianized Roman Empire.   Neither is it true of any king or state, in favour with God, in any period, from the beginning of the world till now.   But it is true to the letter with respect to the regenerated and victorious children of God.   Every one whom grace has called, is called to be *a King.*   Every one redeemed by the blood of Jesus, and sanctified by the Holy Ghost, is the anointed heir of eternal regency.   From the days of the ancient prophets, the divine promise has been, that " the kingdom and dominion, and the greatness of the kingdom under the whole heaven, shall be given to the people of the saints of the Most High." (Dan. 7 : 27.) Nor was this a mere Jewish notion, clothed in Oriental extravagance.   It is spoken of in the New Testament in the plainest language.   In the last words of Christ, and uttered from heaven after his ascension, the promise rings out to and through the Church of Thyatira, " *He that overcometh, and keepeth my works unto the end, to him will I give power over the nations, and he shall rule them with a rod of iron ; as the vessels of a potter shall they be broken to shivers :* EVEN AS I RECEIVED OF MY FATHER." (Rev. 2 : 26, 27.)   Surely, the Roman State under Constantine was not the same as that glorious dominion given to the Saviour on account of his obedience unto death.   If it was, then many have been robbed of their share in this promise ; for it is made to every one that overcometh, and keepeth Christ's works to the end ; which is the fact with regard to all saints of all ages, many of whom lived before there was a Roman empire, and others have lived since that empire passed away.   How then could that promise have been fulfilled to these ! Moreover, that same " power over the nations," and shepherdizing with a sceptre of iron, is still held out as part of the hope and reward of every victor for God.   It must therefore be still future, and something different from a mere Christianized Cæsarian dominion, which at best a very few of God's people ever possessed.   Indeed there has never lived a manly saint, in any dispensation, who has not been called, anointed and predestined to the rulership here in question.   How then can it be Rome's emperorship !

Those who profess to find the fulfilment of this picture in the times long past, are still constrained to admit, that the language touching the official destiny of this child falls in precisely with the second Psalm.   And yet that Psalm refers particularly to the judgment time, and pre-eminently to Jesus Christ, that greatest Son, as well as Lord, of the Church, in whom and with whom all the blessed and holy who have part in " the first resurrection " shall " reign " and " judge " in a supernal and immortal administration, to which neither Constantine, nor the Valenses, nor any others ever yet attained.   The description fits to the true saints of God of every generation, with the glorified Jesus at their head ; but to none else.

3. This child is the special object of Satan's murderous malignity.   It is on the child's account that he assails the woman, takes his station before her, and stirs up all his power to hinder and destroy.   It is not so much she, as *the child,* that he is bent to devour.   But he was no more malignant towards Constantine, or the dynasty of Rome's Christian emperors, or any of the Christians of that era, than against the people of God in any other age.   The truth is that so-called Christian Rome has served his purposes about as well as Pagan Rome.   But here is something peculiar, special, and against which all the malice of hell is aroused and concentrated.   We can very well understand this, and the tremendous painting comes out in all its significance, when we see in this Child the universal body of God's saints.   To devour these, or to stop these from reaching the kingdom, is ever the one great malignant intent of the Dragon.   Their success is his defeat. Hence this intent of the unparalleled attempt to overwhelm them at the final extremity.   He might destroy Constantine, and destroy Constantine's empire, as he has destroyed it, and destroy any one particular class or company of Christian confessors or peoples,

and still the main object of his draconic enmity remain comparatively un-harmed. There still would be representatives of salvation left ; Christ would still have his army of saved ones ; and the main intent of infernal malice would not be reached. But if Satan could destroy the whole body of the redeemed, or at the last thwart their exaltation to the authority and dominion for which they are destined, this would be an accomplishment to answer to the awful significance of the picture. From the intensity and specialness of the Dragon's murderous intent, we may thus read the certainty of a momen-tousness about this Child which nothing can adequately explain, but the fact that it represents the whole regenerated purchase of the Saviour's blood.

So, then, I take this Man Child, and know not how else it can be taken without a miserable emasculation of the whole representation, emptying it of every significance at all up to the subject, or demanded by the circumstances.

But what, now, are we to understand by this Child's *Birth* ? for this is the crisis of the entire matter. All that precedes this looks to it, and all that comes after dates from it.

A man's birth is the most important event in his life. Everything that can come of him depends upon his being *born*. It is only by his birth that he comes into the possession of his own separate being. It is only by his birth that he begins to enter upon his proper life. Hence the birth of this child must needs be the chief event in all its history—the event on which its separate and proper existence as well as everything in its subsequent career depends. Without this birth it comes to nothing, and its entire being mis-carries. And if it is the invisible Church, the whole body of true saints, that is represented by the Child, then this birth must refer to the very greatest and most momentous occurrence in the whole history of the redeemed, even that on which their proper existence and glory depends. What is there, then, in the revelations of God with regard to all His regenerated children, to answer to so significant and striking a figure as that of *being born ?*

Remembering that it is under the seventh trumpet, which is the last trumpet, that this birth occurs, we are naturally conducted to the one only thing in all the everlasting career of God's saints to answer the description. But this one thing does answer it, and fills out every feature of it in absolute perfection.

Turn back to the Saviour's own great prophetic discourse, and see what he connects with this trumpet. The subject is His own coming and the end of the world. And we there read of mighty commotions in all the visible universe, and of the appearance of the sign of the Son of man in heaven ; whereupon it is said, " He shall send his angels *with a great sound of a trumpet, and they shall gather together his elect from the four winds, from one end of heaven to the other.*" (Matt. 24 : 29–31.)

Turn also to Paul's great chapter on the subject, and hear what he writes about it : " Behold, I show you a mystery ; we shall not all sleep, but we shall all be changed, in a moment, in the twinkling of an eye, at the last trump : *for the trumpet shall sound, and the dead shall be raised incorruptible, and we shall be changed.*" (1 Cor. 15 : 51, 52.)

Turn again to his still more specific statements to the Thessalonians : " The Lord himself shall descend from heaven with a shout, with the voice of the archangel, *and with the trump of God ; and the dead in Christ shall rise first ; then we which are alive and remain shall be caught up together with them in the clouds, to meet the Lord in the air.*" (1 Thess. 4 : 16, 17.)

Or turn to the Apocalyptist's account of the seventh trumpet, and to the summary of its contents as proclaimed in the song of the gold-crowned Elders : " And the seventh angel sounded, and there were great voices in heaven : We give Thee thanks, O Lord God Almighty, because Thou hast taken unto Thee Thy great power, and Thy wrath is come, *and the time of the dead, that they should be judged, and that Thou shouldest give reward unto Thy servants the prophets, and to the saints, and them that fear Thy Name, small and great.*" (Rev. 11 : 15–18.)

These passages are decisive. They each speak of the great trumpet of Judgment—the last trumpet, and tell us of glorious things then to be fulfilled. They tell of God's elect, small and great, from one end of heaven to the other, all gathered together for their rewards, the dead from their graves, and the living from their places wherever they are, and every one " *changed*," from corruption to incorruption, from dishonour to glory, from weakness to power, from earthly to heavenly, and all " together " caught up into the regions above, to meet their Lord in the heavens. The occasion is the grandest and most momentous in all their history. It involves the greatest change in all their experiences, the goal of the intensest anxieties and most agonizing endeavours that ever occupied the thoughts and energies of the saints, and the sublimest transition in the form of their being to which the Scriptures refer. It is their first entrance upon that proper life which till then is only a matter of promise and hope, toward which there is a growing indeed, but which only then becomes fruition. It is the great point to which everything that precedes looks, and from which all that succeeds dates its beginning. In a word, it is their great and glorious *Birth* into immortality and eternal life ; and the time of it is the time of the sounding of the last trump. Prior to then, the saints are indeed generated, begotten, quickened by the Holy Ghost, and full of prophetic yearning for what is beyond ; but they are not yet *born*. They are still invisible, hidden, inclosed, restrained, disabled. They do not yet know what they shall be. They pulsate with a heavenly life, but it remains for them to be set free, to be " brought forth," to be " delivered from the bondage of corruption into the glorious liberty of the children of God." And that deliverance is only consummated when the last trumpet sounds, bringing with it " the adoption " for which we groan, to wit, " the redemption of our body."

A birth is a manifestation, a bringing to the light, the making visible of what was before invisible. And so the Scriptures repeatedly speak of " the manifestation of the sons of God," which in this present order of things is expected and yearned after, but which only takes place in connection with the sounding of the last trump. (Rom. 8 : 19.) Malachi refers to that time when the Lord of hosts shall make up His jewels, and says, " Then shall ye discern between the righteous and the wicked, between him that serveth God and him that serveth Him not." (Mal. 3 : 17, 18.) Isaiah (25 : 7, 8) sings of a day when death shall be swallowed up of victory, and notes it as one of the glad concomitants, that then the covering shall be taken away. Paul, with unmistakable pointedness, writes to the Colossians (3 : 4) : " *When Christ, who is our life, shall appear, then shall ye also appear with him in glory.*" And hundreds of other passages, in all manner of forms, teach us how then for the first time it is to be demonstrated and shown who all are truly the regenerate children of God. Till then, this cannot be known with certainty. The child is as yet unborn ; but then it shall come to the light, the saints shall be revealed with their Redeemer, and the sons of God shall be manifested.

For the present the true congregation of God's ransomed ones is invisible, but it is " kept by the power of God through faith unto salvation *ready to be revealed in the last time.*" (1 Pet. 1 : 5.)

Here, then, is a most momentous Birth. It is the greatest birth of all time. It is a birth to be experienced by the very parties whom we take to be symbolized by this mystic Man-child. And it is a birth which reaches its completion just where God has placed the picture of it, to wit, under the last trumpet. It answers every feature of the symbol, and without the slightest straining of Scripture or of history. It comports with the proper dignity and importance of the subject. It corresponds perfectly with every item and implication in the wonderful painting. And it looks to me like an attempt to browbeat the Revelation of God, not to accept it as the true and proper thing here to be understood.

And yet, there is still one other particular in the text which would seem to make it impossible to get away from this interpretation. The instant this Man-child is born, it is " *caught away to God, and to His throne.*" We have just seen that it is the destiny of the saints to be *kings*. It is everywhere told us that they are to have crowns ; that they are to sit on thrones ; that they are to reign with Christ. Jesus says, " To him that overcometh will I grant to sit with me in my throne, even as I also overcame, and am set down with my Father in his throne." (Rev. 4 : 21.) On this point there can be no question. This throne is not an earthly throne, like Cæsar's, nor yet a mere moral influence, such as the saints already possess and wield : but a heavenly and divine throne, to which belongs a sceptre of iron, and a rulership which involves irresistible force and judical power, breaking to shivers whatsoever rises against it ; even the mighty throne of Jesus Christ in his glory, which all his people are to share with him. And *the time* for this sublime coronation and investiture of the saints is the time of resurrection, the time of the last trump, the time of the Revelation of Jesus Christ. When Paul gave out his last fare-well to the world, he said, " Henceforth there is laid up for me a crown of righteousness, which the Lord, the righteous Judge, shall give me *at that day*," the day of judgment, and not before. (2 Tim. 4 : 8.) Peter writes to " the elect through sanctification of the Spirit," and says to them, " *When the chief Shepherd shall appear*, ye shall receive a crown of glory that fadeth not away." (1 Pet. 5 : 4.) Daniel (7 : 26, 27) tells us specifically that *the time* when " the kingdom and dominion and the greatness of the kingdom " is given to the saints, is the time when " the judgment shall sit," even that great judgment under which the final antichrist is finally destroyed. And as the birth of this Man-child synchronizes with, or is instantly followed by his coronation and enthronement in heaven, and the time of that coronation is specifically defined to be the time of resurrection, it is simply impossible to locate this birth anywhere else than at the resurrection time. And if the birth is thus positively located in the resurrection time, what can it be but that very resurrection *change*, by which all the genuine saints of God have their full birth into immortality and exaltation to their immortal crowns ?

Nor does it at all militate against this view that some saints are raised, translated, or glorified in advance of others, and that the " change involved does not take place with the entire number at precisely the same instant." It is part of the Divine plan always to give forepledges and earnests of what is to come. There is in every instance some " first fruits " before the general harvest. So Christ was raised and glorified long in advance of the final redemption of his people, and many of the saints also arose with him. These were the preliminary specimens of what was to come long afterwards. So Enoch and Elijah were translated without tasting of death, as a sort of earnest of the promised translation of those who are alive and ready when Christ comes. All these are a part of the body denoted by the Man-child. They all belong to what is subsequently called " the first resurrection," to which " everything belongs that is raised to immortality before the last day."* And so we are taught, as Ambrose, and Luther, and Kromayer admit, that other particular resurrections and translations of certain eminent saints occur at intervals preceding the full completion of the glorified company. The very figure before us would indicate successive stages in the case. A birth is never so sudden a thing, but that some parts of the body appear before others. The picture is plainly meant to be a summary one. It is the symbol of the full consummation of the whole matter. In such a picture there is no occasion for the noting of minor distributions or details. It is enough to give the Birth and exalted destiny of the Child, without entering into the particulars of the presentations, which are sufficiently set forth in other places. And yet, even in so general and summary a picture, the fact, that not all belonging to the body come to the Birth at one and the same instant, is still not overlooked, nor precluded, but really involved.†

---

* Selnecker's *Exp. of the Rev. of St. John and the Prophet Daniel*, Jena, 1517 ; Rev. 20 : 5.
† We have had some of these earlier resurrections and translations of particular bands or companies, in the preceding portions of this book. One is given in the fourth and fifth chapters. (See pp. 96–105.) A translation of another special company is indicated

Behold, then, my friends, the dignity and glory of the Christian calling ! Having put on Christ, we belong to a fellowship, for which the sublimest things are reserved ! Living a life of faith on the Son of God, we are maturing for a wondrous accouchement ! These wrappings and disabilities of time are soon to give place to the liberty and blessedness of a glorious immortality ! Instead of these aches, and ills, and toils, and disabilities, and many anxieties, shall presently be the elastic vigour and untiring strength which we now see in the angels ! Instead of these doubts, and fears, and contests with evil in and around us, there shall be accomplished redemption, beyond all further vicissitude or danger ! And for these crosses shall come crowns of imperishable dominion with Jesus ! It amazes and confounds me when I attempt to survey the astounding changes that await the faithful. I am overwhelmed with the sublimities of exaltation and power which are set before the poor sinful children of men in the Revelations of God.

We are often disheartened with our hardships and trials, and begin to think it too hard a thing for us to be Christians. Nature is so weak and depraved ; there is such a burden in this incessant toil, and self-denial, and watchfulness, and prayer ; the way is so steep, and narrow, and difficult ; we are tempted again and again to give up. But when we think what the dear Lord has done for us, what glories he has set before us, what victories are to come to us, what princedoms and thrones in the great empire of eternity await us, and how sure is all if we only press on for the prize ; we have the profoundest reason to rejoice and give thanks every day that we live, that such opportunities have been vouchsafed us, were the sufferings even tenfold severer than they are.

Blessed be God, for His holy Church ! Blessed be God, that He has called us to be members of it ! Blessed be God, that every faithful one in it is on the way to a glorious birth-hour to immortal regency and power ! Only let us see to it, that we rightly appreciate our mercies, and give the diligence to make our calling and election sure. And " the God of all grace, who hath called us unto His eternal glory by Christ Jesus, after that ye have suffered awhile, make you perfect, stablish, strengthen, settle you. To whom be glory and dominion forever and ever. Amen."

> That clime is not this dull clime of ours ;
>   All, all is brightness there ;
> A sweeter influence breathes around its flowers,
>   And a far milder air.
> No calm below is like that calm above,
> No region here is like that realm of love ;
> Earth's softest spring ne'er shed so soft a light,
> Earth's brightest summer never shone so bright.
>
> Those dwellers there are not like these of earth,
>   No mortal stain they bear ;
> And yet they seem of kindred blood and birth,—
>   Whence, and how came they there ?
> Earth was their native soil, from sin and shame,
> Through tribulation they to glory came ;
> Bond-slaves delivered from sin's crushing load,
> Brands plucked from burning by the hand of God.

in chapter 7 : 9–17. (See p. 170 sq.) And so there is another in chapter 14, and perhaps still others, before the process is finished, and the whole body of the glorified completed, as beheld in chapter 20 : 4–6. All these, however, occur in the judgment period, and follow each other in such quick succession, that the more general passages on the subject take no special account of them, but grasp them into one and the same view. They are fully distinguishable only when we come to examine the Apocalyptic chart of the great fulfilment. Here, however, each comes in its proper order and place, though it is the whole of them together that makes up the Birth of the Man-child, and completes the glorious body of the Church of the first born in heaven. (Consult an article on the Successive Stages in the Removal of the Church, by Rev. E. E. Reinke, in *Prophetic Times*, vol. iv, pp. 56–63 ; also one by the author of these Lectures in the same volume, pp. 172–175.)

LECTURE TWENTY-NINTH

REV. 12 : 7–12. (Revised Text.) And there came to be war in the heaven : Michael and his angels warred with the Dragon ; and the Dragon warred and his angels, and they prevailed not, neither was even their place found any more in the heaven.

And the great Dragon was cast down, the Old Serpent, who is called the Devil and the Satan [adversary], he who seduceth [or *misleadeth*] the whole inhabited world : he was cast down into the earth, and his angels were cast down with him.

And I heard a great voice saying in the heaven, Now is come the salvation, the power, and the kingdom of our God, and the dominion of His Christ : for the accuser of our brethren is cast down who accuseth them before our God by day and by night. And they conquered him by reason of the blood of the Lamb, and by reason of the word of their testimony, and they loved not their life unto death. Therefore rejoice ye heavens, and ye that tabernacle in them.

FROM the earliest periods of the human race till now, its sublimest poets have occupied their sublimest numbers with pictures and descriptions of conflicts in the heavenly worlds, and battles of the gods. Contemporaneous with these dreams and songs, have also been the sneers and scoffs of the sceptic mind, ridiculing the idea, astonished that reasonable men should give entertainment to such fictions, no matter in what magniloquence arrayed. And it is

> Strange,
> At first, that angel should with angel war,
> And in fierce hosting meet, who wont to meet
> So oft in festivals of joy and love
> Unanimous, as sons of one great sire
> Hymning th' eternal Father.

But much as any one may be disposed to doubt and question, there is a background of solid reality in the case. Since Homer wrote, and Deborah and Barak sung of the stars fighting in their courses, there has been an increasing revelation of the spiritual economies, and in it accounts of conflict and war involving all beings in all worlds. Especially, in the great and wondrous outcome and consummation of the affairs pertaining to our race, a momentous collision in the heavenly spaces is foreannounced, in which the highest and mightiest of created beings are to be the combatants. The seer of Patmos, in rapport with the divine Spirit and prescience, was shown it, and by command of God has put it on record for the instruction of the Church, as a sober and settled part of Christian anticipation and eschatological theology. And here, among other stupendous visions of what is to come to pass hereafter, he has written it down for our learning, that " there came to be war in the heaven : Michael and his angels warred with the dragon ; and the dragon warred and his angels, and they prevailed not, nor was even their place found any more in the heaven. And the great dragon was cast down, the old serpent, who is called the devil and the Satan (or adversary), he who seduceth (or misleadeth) the whole inhabited world, he was cast down unto the earth, and his angels were cast down with him."

Some have supposed this to be a mere poetical and exaggerated account of certain moral conflicts in the history of the Church on earth. Some take the Dragon to mean the Pagan Roman Empire ; Michael, the Christian Roman Empire ; Heaven, the throne of the Roman Emperors ; and the war in Heaven, the different and opposing counsels of the adherents and supporters of the Pagan and Christian Roman Emperors. Others teach that we are not to understand it of any real transaction, but as a sort of summary of the prolonged antagonism between good and evil, which, to a lively poetic imagination, might seem *as if* the hidden principalities and powers were in actual war. But all such ideas pay very poor compliment to the inspiration claimed by the holy Apostle, to his capacity to write for the instruction of the Church, and to what he has by divine command put upon record as a veritable Revelation of the Lord Almighty. Having examined a long list of these symbolic and allegorical interpretations, and followed the processes by which their authors have tried to apply them, I have not found one which does not completely break down under the weight of its own cumbrous unfittingness. They each and all fail to explain the facts and relations of the record, and treat John as a half-demented sentimental old man, trying to make a grand poem out of a few dim anticipations touching the earthly fortunes of the Church, which could have been better told in one well-written chapter. They are, at best, the wild guesses of men who have never got hold of the real thread of the matter, whilst under the necessity of saying something. I take the holy Apostle as a fully inspired man. I take his Book, not as a crazy poem, but as a real *Revelation*. I take his visions to be exactly what the Angel actually showed him, all truly and faithfully written as he was divinely directed to write them, and not fabrications of his own brain, draped according to his own doting fancy. I take all his terms and statements literally, except where he gives plain intimation that they are to be otherwise taken. I locate all in the time and place in which he locates it, and in the order in which he gives it, conditioned with this one fundamental consideration, that the entire Book is intended to give to the Church an apocalyptic chart of the outcome and consummation of all history, in connection with the coming again of the Lord Jesus. Accordingly, I take the text as it stands, as the account of a real commotion in the aerial spaces,—a violent collision among immortals—a literal " *war in the heaven*,"—concerning which we are called to notice,

    I.   The Forces Marshalled ;

    II.   The Occasion of the Conflict ;

    III.   The Nature of the Battle ;

    IV.   The Issue of the Engagement.

May God help us to consider these particulars as the solemnity and momentousness of the subject deserves !

I. Let us look, then, at the Forces marshalled. These are specifically described. On the one side, " *Michael and his angels* " are the warriors ; on the other, " *the Dragon and his angels.*"

Who, then, is Michael ? Many answer, The Lord Jesus Christ, claiming that it would impinge upon the dignity and prerogatives of Christ to attribute all that is here implied to a mere angel, however exalted. But I do not find that those most inclined to this view are the most clear and decided in their recognition of the proper Deity of Christ. And though the Lord Jesus has His angels, there is nothing in that to prove that an archangel may not have angels as well. Satan has his angels, why may not Michael have them too ? What if the name does mean, *One like God ?* As a title of Christ, it would rather disprove than prove His proper Deity. There is also an unquestionable Godlikeness in all holy beings, which must be very exalted in those pre-eminent among the ministers of the throne. What if Michael is called a leader or prince of angels, and, by way of emphasis, " *the* archangel ? " We know from Daniel that there are other " chief princes " in the angelic world. Paul (1 Thess. 4 : 16) also refers to " *an archangel* " (see original) in a way which presupposes other archangels. The angel who communicated with Daniel calls Michael " *one of the chief princes*," which implies the existence of others of similar rank (Dan. 10 : 13). He also speaks of Michael as " holding with *him*," and not he with Michael, as the diction would be were Michael the same as The Son of God. What if he is " the great prince which standeth for the children of the prophet's people " in the time of their trouble ? Michael *is* a great prince, and one whom the Jews have always acknowledged, whilst they rejected and crucified Christ, and nationally refuse to have Him for their prince. What if the bruising of the serpent's head, and the destruction of the works of the devil, and the spoiling of Satan's goods, are ascribed to Christ ? Anything done by the agent is done by the principal ; and that Christ has appointed angels to minister to the heirs of salvation, and to execute such parts of the grand administration as may be appropriately assigned to them, is part of the clear teaching of the Scriptures. The war in this case is plainly in behalf of the child which the mystic woman brings forth, and the Head and front of that composite child is Christ Himself. As part of the body fought for, He is thus distinguished from " Michael and his angels " who do the fighting, just as Michael is distinguished from the Divine Son in the Book of Daniel. What if the establishment of the reign and dominion of Christ is the result of this war ? The general who conducts a campaign to victory is not therefore the king to whom the results of that success belong. In Christ's own explanation of some of these matters (Matt. 13) He says : " The Son of man shall send forth His angels, and *they* shall gather out of His kingdom all things that offend, and them which do iniquity ; " but He is no less the great Judge on that account, neither is the kingdom, and the power, and the glory a whit less His. " Michael the Archangel " was the disputant in the matter about " the body of Moses " (Jude 9) ; but it is there said of him that " *he durst not* bring against the devil a railing accusation, but said, The Lord rebuke thee." This shows a clear distinction between Michael and the Lord, as well as a law and restraint upon Michael which pertains only to a creature and a subject, and not to the almighty Son of God, who had not yet then become incarnate. Jesus could say, " Get thee behind me, Satan," but Michael dared not speak thus. Besides, " *Michael* " is everywhere used in the Scriptures as a proper name, the same as Gabriel, or Jesus, or John ; and occurring here the same as in all other places there would seem to be no more authority for making it mean the Lord Jesus than for making John mean Daniel, or Mary mean Martha. The Bible, indeed, abundantly speaks of the Angel of Jehovah, who plainly is none other than the only-begotten Son of God ; but there is no proof that this Jehovah-Angel is ever called Michael. And as the name here is *Michael*, I know not by what right any one can take it as meaning any other than Michael, the created archangel, who is not less than five times referred to by this name in the holy Scriptures.*

According to the Jewish teachings Michael is one of seven Archangels, and the chief of the seven. In this the Christian Church has ever been disposed to concur. Hence the Church references to " Michael and all angels." Hence also, in the highest of all the Christian services from the beginning, " with Angels and Archangels, and with all the company of heaven, we laud and magnify God's glorious Name." And as the very chief of all angels, though himself one of them, Michael would have " *his angels*," though no less God's, just as a

---

* " Michael is not to be identified with Christ, any more than any other of the great angels in this Book. Such identification here would confuse hopelessly the actors in this heavenly scene. Satan's being cast out of heaven to the earth is the result not of his contest with the Lord Himself, of which it is only an incident leading to a new phase, but of the appointed conflict with his faithful fellow-angels led on by the Archangel Michael."—Alford *in loc.* Bengel maintains the same view, and refers to Collado, Eglinus, Jonas Le Buy, Grotius, Cluver, Mede, Dimpelius, and others, as recognizing here the created angel named, and not a symbol of Christ.

general-in-chief has his aids, officers, and soldiers, who nevertheless all belong to the king. He would also thus be the proper one to stand at the head of the grand Army of heaven, when called out in force to put down " the Devil and his angels." All the holy angels, therefore, with " Michael the Archangel " as their chief, constitute the sublime forces on the one side, marshalled for this " battle of the gods."

Nor need we be at a loss to identify those on the opposite side. The Scriptures abundantly assure us of the existence of great spiritual powers and principalities ever arrayed against human welfare, and who are the enemies of God and all good. Paul (Eph. 6 : 11, 12) tells us that we are continually exposed to assaults, surprises, and dangers from an unseen and most subtle confederation of spiritual agents ; that there is a " devil," from whose " wiles " and agents we are in perpetual jeopardy ; that our contest is not only with blood and flesh, but with " the principalities, the powers, the sovereigns of this present darkness, the wicked spirits in the aerial regions ; " that there stands opposed to us, and to all good, a great malignant kingdom, a vast spiritual empire of evil. There are " angels which kept not their first estate, but left their own habitation " (Jude 6). God never made an evil being ; but He made angels, principalities, and powers capacitated for mighty joys and distinctions in His glorious domain, yet with free will, implied in the very creation of moral beings, which they could exercise for their everlasting weal or woe. Many have remained steadfast, to wit, " Michael and his angels." But some abode not in the truth, but revolted against the rule of Heaven, and became the unchanging enemies of God and His Kingdom. Among these is one of peculiar power and despicable pre-eminence, who drew his associates into his revolt, and ever stands as the head and leader of them. He is called *The Devil*, a name which the Scriptures, in the original, never use in the plural, and never apply to but one being. All others belonging to his wicked empire are " his angels," morally like him, but in place and position grouped around him, under his direction, agents of his imperial will. He is called " a prince," " the prince of this world," " the prince of the powers of the air," " the god of this world." And the same is here called " the great Dragon, the Old Serpent, the Satan, or Adversary, who seduceth or misleadeth the whole populated world." " The course of this world " is declared to be " according to " him. He, with his confederates, " rules in the darkness of this world," " blinding the eyes of them that believe not," " working in the children of disobedience," and leading men captive at his will. All apostates and false Christians are called his children, the tares of his sowing. The Man of sin, that Wicked, to whom the Scriptures impute such a terrible career of lawlessness and tyranny in the last period of the present world, is the incarnation of his spirit and evilness. The evil princes who had the sway over ancient Persia and Greece, and who withstood the good angels who communicated with Daniel, were his archons or world-lords, as Paul's word is. *Demons*,* whoever they may be, also belong to the empire of the Dragon, but they are of a lower order,—the plebeians of this detestable confederacy.

These, then, make up the opposing Forces in this battle.

II. Let us look now at the Occasion of the conflict. In the preceding verses we had the picture of a woman, glorious in her apparel, victorious in her position, royal in dignity, and travailing to bring forth a child destined to rule all nations. Before her stood the great red Dragon, bent upon devouring this child as soon as it should be born. We have seen, as Methodius also taught, that this woman represents the Church as a visible body, and the unborn child the invisible Church, which lies concealed in the visible, and consists of true saints only. We have further seen that the Birth to which the woman labours to bring the child, is the birth into immortality by resurrection and translation, otherwise called " the manifestation of the sons of God,"

* See my *Uriel*, pp. 237–240.

which occurs when " the Lord Himself shall descend from heaven with a shout, with the voice of the archangel, and with the trump of God, and the dead in Christ shall rise, and we which are alive and remain shall be caught up together with them in the clouds, to meet the Lord in the air," and to receive the promised crown of glory. And it is in immediate connection with this Birth of the man-child, and its being " caught away to God, and to His throne," that this " war in the heavens " comes on. Already in Daniel we are told that the time when Michael stands up for the sons of the prophet's people, is the time when everyone that is written in the book shall be delivered, —the time when many of them that sleep in the dust of the earth shall awake to everlasting life to shine as the firmament and the stars forever. It is this glorious exaltation of the saints that the devil and his angels have ever been most bent on defeating. For this they have been operating through all the ages, the Dragon ever standing before the travailing woman to destroy her seed. For this all the subtlety and power of hell are exerted, and are becoming the more intense as the resurrection time approaches. And no sooner are the graves of the saints about to open, and the true people of God to come forth into the honours and glories of immortality, than Satan stirs up all his power to prevent it, and thus arouses this commotion in heaven.

A prelude to this controversy, on a small scale, is referred to by Jude as occurring in connection with the body of Moses. There is reason to believe that Moses is not dead. He did indeed " die in the mount," according to the command of God ; but he was seen alive in the days of the Saviour on the mount of the Transfiguration, seen " *in glory*," and hence in resurrection life. He must therefore have been raised again from the state of death,—raised in advance of the general resurrection of the saints, as Enoch and Elijah were translated before the general translation of God's waiting and watching ones at the coming of the Lord. And if we are at all warranted in this belief, the dispute between the archangel Michael and the devil " about the body of Moses," was a contention about his resurrection, the one standing up for the recovery of that body from death, and the other resisting. Thus we have the precise parties named in the text, and a fierce contest over the same thing in one individual case, which we have here in the case of the saints in general. It was the resurrection and glorification of Moses which was the subject of collision then, and it is the resurrection and glorification of the saints in general which is the subject and occasion of the war here. It is Michael again, joined now by all his angels, that here stands up in behalf of the true people of God emerging into resurrection life and glory ; and it is the same Old Serpent, stirring up now all the power of his kingdom to hinder and prevent the sacred seed of faith from attaining their promised exaltation.

There is also every reason why the whole strength of the great adversary should be interposed to prevent this glorious coming forth of the children of God to immortal glory and power. With the dominion of death broken the whole empire of darkness breaks with it, the reign of hell is dissolved, and the victory of redemption is complete. With the curse of mortality and corruption thus swallowed up of life, the devil's sway is gone, his kingdom mutilated, and all his malignant hopes against the Church overwhelmed. To yield here without the most stubborn resistance would be to give up the aim of all his plans and endeavours since he first tempted man in Paradise, to let his whole empire collapse, to permit the chief power of his dominion to go by default. Hence his rallying of all his forces. Hence his most determined resistance just at this point. And hence this " war in the heaven."

III. Having thus identified the combatants and found the occasion of the conflict, we are also far on the way to a right apprehension of the Nature of the Battle. The beings engaged are all spiritual, and the region is " the heaven "—in the air—in the spaces above the earth. The battle therefore must needs be spiritual, and not physical. There is no taking of life—no killing—no bloodshed—no slaughter. Milton has ventured a description of it where he says :

Michael bid sound
Th' archangel trumpet : through the vast of heaven
It sounded, and the faithful armies rung
Hosanna to the Highest : nor stood at gaze
The adverse legions, nor less hideous joined
The horrid shock : now storming fury rose,
And clamour such as heard in heaven till now
Was never ; arms on armour clashing brayed
Horrible discord, and the madding wheels
Of brazen chariots raged ; dire was the noise
Of conflict ; overhead the dismal hiss
Of fiery darts in flaming volleys flew,
And flying vaulted either host with fire :
So under fiery cope together rushed
Both battles main, with ruinous assault
And inextinguishable rage ; all heaven
Resounded, and had earth been then, all earth
Had to her centre shook.

But Milton wrote from imagination, and drew his conceptions from earthly battlefields. True, all the strength of hell with heaven is measured ; but it is moral, intellectual, spiritual strength. The cannonading is thought, argument, subtle accusation, and defence. It is the war of mind with mind, of malignant and hellish intellect inflamed with desperate hate and anger against the intellect, reason, and right of heaven, a war which has its type rather in some tremendous forensic battle, where giants of the law dispute and contend, each intent on the victory. This is indicated in all the incidents and circumstances of the case. Satan appears here in his old character of the seducer and accuser, in which he has been for so long misleading and perverting the world, making the wrong seem right, and the right seem wrong, inciting to misjudgment, ruinous passion, and all the deadly consequences of moral and spiritual obliquity. As he appeared among the sons of God in the history concerning Job, sneering at the virtues of that man of God, insinuating the unreality and sordidness of his piety, and insisting that a fair trial would prove him nothing but a hypocrite ; so he appears with all his malignant forces in this case, accusing the saints, and God for proposing to do such sublime things for them, denying the reality of their virtues, the adequacy of the tests of their obedience and their right to be thus glorified.

Every saint of God embraced in this Man-Child was born a sinner, and by sin forfeited the favour of God and a blessed immortality. How can the Almighty be just and true to His nature, laws, and threatenings, and yet lift these people in honour and glory from their graves, receive them to His throne, and give them place in the heaven of His holy administrations ? Here is the devil's strong point, with which he ever assails men, and with which he here assails all the celestial powers. His line of battle is shown in the statement that he accuses the brethren, the saints, by day and by night. The great thunder of his tremendous cannonading is, that these people are not fit for and not worthy of such honours ; that God disowns His holiness, and casts dishonour on His throne by awarding to such a people such a portion and such a destiny ; that all reasonable being and intelligence is set at nought and outraged by such a proceeding. This is " the dismal hiss of fiery darts," flying " in flaming volleys," and vaulting either host. Accusation, accusation—keen, daring, deep, and clamorous accusation, subtly insinuated, and with infernal rancour hurled, is the artillery which belches forth with all the desperate energy of hell. This is further shown beyond mistake in the statement as to how he and his hosts are vanquished. The record says they overcame him by means of the blood of the Lamb and the word of their testimony, and their not having loved their lives to save them from death. Sinners indeed were all those who belong to the company of this mystic Child, and forever contrary is it to the nature and government of God to connive at sin, or to look with allowance upon iniquity ; but these people are not therefore without a maintainable cause. An ample atonement has been made. A Lamb has bled, whose meritorious blood, weighed in all the strictness of eternal right, by which the carping malignity of hell itself is silenced, covers the whole amplitude of their deficiencies, and cleanses away all account of their sins. " Who shall lay anything to the charge of God's elect ? It is God that justifieth. Who is he that condemneth ? It is Christ that died." " *Blood of the Lamb !* " This is the everlasting fortress of the saints ; and this stands foremost of all the means by which the accuser and his hosts are driven back. But, sheltered under this by faith in Him who died for them, there is also some claim and show for works. Justified and forgiven men, who have no hope but in their Saviour's merit, may still have title to some consideration and reward for their fidelities. Having given their word of testimony for the Lord that loved them, and stood firm to it against an adverse world, living martyr lives, or dying martyr deaths, cheerfully resigning all that man counts dear for the sake of the truth they confessed, God is not unjust to forget the work and labour of love they have shown towards His name in ministering to His people and His cause. And thus Michael and his angels, standing up for the Lord's saints, conquer the accuser and his hosts by reason of the blood of the Lamb, and the worthiness that appears in what they have done and sacrificed for Him. The means of the victory disclose the nature of the conflict.

But the sternness and tenacity with which every inch is contested, and the dreadfulness of the determination with which the resurrection and eternal rewards of the saints is withstood when Heaven thus comes to the fulfilment of its covenants and promises, necessarily involves a " horrid shock," and " storming fury," and bray of clashing and conflict, which even the genius of a Milton was incompetent to set forth. Michael and his angels war with the Dragon, because wickedly set to prevent the fulfilment of God's promises to His people ; and the Dragon wars, and his angels war ; and " madding wheels of brazen chariots rage," in the terribleness of a collision such as " in heaven till now was never."

IV. I now come to say a word or two about the Issue.

As we would expect from such a contest, the Dragon is defeated. With all his skilled generalship and energy, and all the desperate fury of his hosts, the effort is fruitless. " *They prevailed not.*" He might have known that this would be the result. But pride, depravity, and malice have wonderful power to blind the mind to reason and truth, and to give brazen hope even where there is not the slightest ground for hope. Satan has ever been so successful in the past, both in heaven among the angels, and on earth with the human race, and his proud daring is so unbounded, that he does not hesitate to believe that he can break even the decrees of Almightiness. So he attempts it. But every argument he urges is successfully met. Every accusation is answered. Every charge proved unfounded and false. He may deceive men, but he cannot impose his deceptions and subtleties on heaven. He cannot show a flaw in the foundations of God's covenant of eternal life to every true confessor of the Saviour's name. Every onset is adequately withstood. Every weapon he brings forth is shivered in his hands. Not all his own great genius, nor all the strength and determination of his hosts, is of any avail. The meritoriousness of the Blood of the Lamb is too much for him. The right and justice of reward to them who have stood to the faith even unto the giving up of life, are too mighty for him to overcome. He once drew with him a third of heaven, and succeeded in making himself " the god of this world ; " but daring now to think to thwart the good purpose of Omnipotence, he finds only

Joyless triumphals of his hoped success,
Ruin, and desperation, and dismay.

With his failure comes conviction as a murderous accuser, falsifier, and deceiver. Foiled at every point he stands revealed to all heaven in all the devilish baseness of his true character, and all his hosts as the ministers and abettors of Satanic falsehood and the most hellish malignity. Such convicts can no longer be tolerated in the vicinage of heaven. Stunned and effectually repulsed by the infallible merits of the blood of the Lamb, the celestial forces pursue him to an utter rout. Henceforward neither he nor his angels are any more to have the liberty of the heavenly spaces. Henceforward " their place is not found any more in the heaven." With his defeat and conviction eject-ment, complete ejectment, follows.

It may not be in every one's mind that the aerial regions, the air, the cloud-heavens, the spaces above the earth, are now the chief lurking-places of evil spirits. But so the Bible teaches. Paul says we wrestle not only with flesh and blood, but with principalities and powers, with *wicked spirits in high places*, literally " *in the heavens*," " in the aerial regions." (Eph. 6 : 12.) Hence also Satan is called " the prince of the power of the air," more literally, " the prince of *the aerial host*," meaning wicked spiritual powers dwelling in the aerial heavens. (Eph. 2 : 2.) Thus the Satanic confederation has its seat in the upper air—in the atmospheric heaven—in the spaces above and around our world. There they are permitted to have place up to the time of this war. But this base attempt results in their casting out and ejectment to the earth, preliminary to the shutting of them up in the fiery abyss. They not only fail to prevent the saints from reaching heaven, but displace themselves, with loss of power ever to return. To this also the Saviour had reference in his answer to his disciples when they came rejoicing that even the demons were subject to them. As the kingdom then was drawing sensibly near, this great result of its coming was even then preliminarily begun. And looking onward to the end He said, " I saw, or was beholding, Satan as lightning fall from heaven." And so the words of Isaiah in describing the great oppressor's fall, also reach forward to, and include what is first realized in its fulness in con-nection with this war in heaven : " How art thou fallen from heaven, O Lucifer, son of the morning ! " It is therefore *fact* and not costume—reality and not poetic drapery—that the Dragon and his angels, when this vision comes to fulfilment, are ejected from the spheres which they have held so long, and find place there no more for ever.*

And as a still further result, all heaven is filled with rejoicing. In mighty volume the triumphal song rings out : " Now is come the salvation, the power, and the kingdom of our God, and the dominion of His Christ ; for the accuser of our brethren, who accuseth them before our God by day and by night, is thrown down. Because of the blood of the Lamb, and of the word of their testimony, and of their not holding life too dear to be given up to death, he is overcome. Therefore rejoice, ye heavens, and ye that tabernacle in them ! " Full salvation does not come so long as Satan's accusations are not finally disposed of. The power of the kingdom of God has its chief revelation in the dethronement of the Dragon, first in the heart, and then in the heavenly places. This is salvation, and this is the power of the divine kingdom and the dominion of Christ, when Satan's hold is broken, when his foul sway is over-thrown, when he and his hosts are dislodged from their abodes, when he can no longer accuse and assail the saints or tyrannize over them. And when this great daring attempt to prevent their entrance into glory is vanquished, it is one of the gladdest events in time, and all holy beings thrill at the sight of its accomplishment. Verily, " there is joy in the presence of the angels of God over one sinner that repenteth ; " for it is the dislodgment of Satan from that

* " I would appeal in passing to the solemnity of the terms here used, and the particu-larity of the designation, and ask whether it is possible to understand this of the mere casting down of Paganism from the throne of the Roman empire ? whether the words themselves do not indicate their plain literal sense, as further illustrated by the song which follows ? "—ALFORD *in loc.*

heart. And when this great victory is achieved, and he and all his angels are forever cast out of all the upper localities, all heaven breaks forth with jubilations and sings with diapason power :

> Hail, Son of the Most High, heir of both worlds,
> Queller of Satan, on Thy glorious reign
> Now enter, hasting complete redemption !
> Thou didst defeat and down from heaven cast
> The false attempter of Thy Father's throne,
> And frustrated the conquest fraudulent ;
> He never more will dare to set his foot
> In Paradise to tempt : his snares are broke :
> A fairer Paradise is founded now
> For Adam and his chosen sons, whom Thou,
> A Saviour, comest down to re-instal,
> Where they shall dwell secure, from sorrow free,
> Of tempter and temptation without fear !

Such, then, is the story of this battle in the heaven.

Many cheering lessons, my friends, might we gather from this singular foreshowing ; but I cannot dwell on them now. Suffice it to say that we here may see what friendly and sympathetic interest is felt for us in heaven ; what mighty princes and courageous hosts stand ready there to espouse our cause and maintain our title to the glorious promises, when adverse powers assail, and prove too mighty for our feebleness ; what blessed hopes are guaranteed if only we trust in Jesus and His atoning blood, and continue true to our confession of His name, ready to die rather than disown Him as our only Lord and hope.

Take courage, then, O Christian, and gladly labour on. Heaven is on thy side. The object of thy fond aims shall yet be thine. The kingdom comes. The Saviour's meritorious blood shall bring thee through in spite of all thy weaknesses and lamented sins. Thy works and sacrifices for thy Lord shall not be forgotten. Satan's accusations shall yet drop powerless at thy feet. And with the exulting hosts that sing his fall shall thy place and portion be.

LECTURE THIRTIETH

THE FLIGHT OF THE WOMAN—THE CONDITION OF THE CHURCH AND THE WORLD AFTER THE REMOVAL OF THE MAN-CHILD—DEVILISM DEVELOPED TO THE FULL—HARD FATE OF THE "LEFT"—JERUSALEM THE CENTRE OF CONTEMPLATION—WHY THE WOMAN FLEES—WHITHER SHE FLIES—THE WATERS CAST AFTER HER—INCREASED RAGE OF THE DRAGON—TURNS UPON THE REMAINDER OF THE WOMAN'S SEED—REFLECTIONS FROM THE SUBJECT.

REV. 12 : 12–17. (Revised Text.) Woe to the earth and the sea ! because the devil is come down to you, having great wrath, because he knoweth that he hath but a short time.

And when the Dragon saw that he was cast down into the earth, he persecuted [or *pursued*] the woman which brought for the male [child]. And to the woman were given the two wings of the great eagle, that she might fly into the wilderness, to her place, where she is there nourished a time, times, and half a time, away from the face of the Serpent. And the Serpent cast from his mouth after the Woman water like a river, that he might cause her [to be] carried away by the river. And the earth helped the Woman ; yea, the earth opened her mouth and drank up the river which the Dragon cast forth from his mouth. And the Dragon was enraged against the Woman, and went away to make war with the remainder of her seed, who keep the commandments of God, and hold fast the testimony of Jesus.

THE ejectment of Satan from heaven lodged him upon the earth. This is the final cleansing of the heavenly spaces from his foul presence. His revolt began in heaven, and the effectual overthrow of his power commences there. The victory over evil follows the order in which it came into existence. The earth was the last conquest of the Devil, and he is thus cast to the earth, here to await his further doom.

We would think that so signal a defeat in the heaven would cure him of his malignity, at least induce him to refrain from any further attempts against God and His people. But he is hopelessly depraved, and nothing but absolute force can quell his devil nature. There is no cure for a being so totally perverted. And his ejectment from heaven and confinement to the earth only angers him the more, and calls forth increased violence, inducing a state of things by far the worst that this world ever experienced.

That which hinders the full revelation of devilism now is the Holy Spirit of God, embodied in his Church and people ; but that Spirit will not always strive with men. The birth of the Man-child into immortality takes out of the world the best material in it. Being made up of the truest and most devoted of God's saints, and being caught away to God, and to His throne, the earth is left minus the presence, prayers, activities, and moral forces of its holiest population. The removal of these faithful ones to their Lord is such a depletion of the spiritual power in earthly society, such a diminution of the salt of the earth and the light of the world, such a vacation of the most potent and active elements of good, as to give the field almost entirely to the Devil and his angels. And it is in punishment of the faithless and unbelieving ones " left," when the Man-child is caught up, that the Devil and all his are precipitated upon the earth, and circumscribed to it, here to act out the final scenes of his enraged malice, blasphemy, and spite. Hence, while heaven thrills with rejoicing over his defeat there, his ejectment to the earth commingles with the song of triumph a sad note of woe and pity for the dwellers here. *" Woe to the earth and the sea! because the devil is come down to you, having great wrath, because he knoweth that he hath but a short time."*

Everything in this record shows that it belongs to the very last years of this world's history. It is the judgment time ; for it is the time of resurrection and translation—of the seizing away of God's holy and prepared people to Him, and to His throne. It is the time of the sounding of the seventh or last trumpet, which in the progress of the visions has here already pealed forth its clarion proclamations that the time of the end has come. It is the time when the gold-crowned Elders are giving thanks to the Lord God Almighty that He has taken to Him His great power to assert His sway, to give reward unto His servants the prophets, the saints, and them that fear His name, and to destroy the corrupters of the earth. It is the time when the Devil himself is convinced, and swollen with unwonted rage and fury because he sees and knows that but a few brief years remain till his reign is over and the abyss is his prison-house. But this " short time " must be improved to the utmost. The text tells us that when the Dragon sees himself thus cast to the earth, he begins to stir himself for further mischief. Milton has not inaptly described the case, where he makes the arch-fiend address his prostrate confederates, saying :

> Princes and potentates,
> Warriors, the flower of heaven once yours, now lost !
> If such astonishment as this can seize
> Eternal spirits ; or have ye chosen this place,
> After the toil of battle, to repose
> Your wearied virtue, for the ease you find
> To slumber here, as in the vales of heaven ?
> Or in this abject posture have ye sworn
> T' adore the Conqueror, who now beholds
> Seraph and cherub rolling in the flood,
> With scattered arms and ensigns, till anon
> His swift pursuers from heaven's gates discern
> Th' advantage, and descending, tread us down
> Thus drooping, or with linked thunderbolts
> Transfix us to the bottom of the gulf ?
> Awake, arise, or be forever fallen !

We have seen that the mystic Woman, whose child is caught up to God and His throne, is the " sign " or symbol of the visible Church in its broadest sense, as an earthly and outward organization, the unborn Child being the invisible Church, in the narrower and truer sense of " the congregation of believers " those who are really begotten of God, and joined to Christ as the spiritual body of which He is the invisible Head. The bringing forth and catching away to heaven of the child, is not therefore the removal of the mother. She still continues on the earth, a visible body, though very greatly diminished and weakened by the birth and removal of the Child. This is very clearly exhibited in the vision ; for when the Man-child is brought forth, separated from her, and caught up to God and His throne, the seer still beholds her on earth, fleeing into the wilderness, where she has a place prepared of God, and where they nourish her a thousand two hundred and sixty days. The cause of her flight was not at first stated. The narrative was interrupted to relate the " war in the heaven," and the casting down of the Dragon and his angels. That being told, the narrative returns to the Woman and " the remainder of her seed," both of which are contemplated as still on the earth and the subjects of the Dragon's persecution. And so it is everywhere told us, that when the translation time comes, not all professed Christians will be " taken." The Saviour Himself has solemnly said, in so many words : " I tell you, in that night there shall be two in one bed ; the one shall be taken, and the other shall be left. Two shall be grinding together ; the one shall be taken and the other left. Two shall be in the field ; the one shall be taken and the other left." (Luke 17 : 34–36.) So again He speaks of professed servants of His, who say in their hearts, " My Lord delayeth His coming," and hence indulge themselves in uncharities, unwatchfulness, and worldly compliances, and so shall be overtaken in their unreadiness, *cut off* from the high honours of the faithful servants, and compelled to remain in the world to suffer here with hypocrites and unbelievers amid the sorrows of the great tribulation. (Matt. 24 : 42–51.) Hence, also, His special command to His people : " Watch ye, therefore, and pray always, that ye may be accounted worthy to escape all these things that shall come to pass, and to stand before the Son of man " (Luke 21 : 36) ; that is, be kept " from the hour of temptation which shall come upon all the world," after the waiting and ready saints have been " caught up to God and to His throne." (Rev. 3 : 10.) And those professed Christians who are " left " or " cut off " when the chosen ones are " taken," together with such as shall be recovered to a pious life and right faith amid the sorrows of the judgment time, will constitute the Woman and " the remainder of her seed " on earth, after the Man-child has made its ascension to glory.

And a hard time of it they will have. Then shall be " a time of distress, such as never was since there was a nation to that time." (Dan. 12 : 1.) " Then shall be great tribulation, such as was not from the beginning of the world to this time, no, nor ever shall be." (Matt. 24 : 21.) " For these be the days of vengeance, that all things which are written may be fulfilled." (Luke 21 : 22.)

First of all shall be the " weeping and gnashing of teeth "—the self-crimination and disappointment—at having lost the first honours of the kingdom, and at being compelled now to unlearn the mistaken philosophy and theology in which they trusted, and to begin again as little children to learn the truth which they so unreasonably sneered at, neglected, or denounced. And a very sore grief this will be to them. To have had the whole matter so plainly before them in God's Word, and yet not to have seen it ;—to have had so glorious a prize within their reach, and counted so hopefully on it, and now to find it lost and gone from them beyond recovery ;—to have grown grey, venerable, and mighty in learning, in wisdom, and in championship for the Gospel, and yet not to have learned the simple practical truth of waiting, watching, and keeping in readiness for the coming again of the Lord Jesus,— and forever deprived now of place in " the Church of the first-born," with nothing left to them but in sorrow and humiliation to make their way to the secondary places in eternity ;—these shall be among the scorpion stings which too many, alas, will then have to endure ! Had they but taken in what " watch the thief would come," they would have watched, and would not have suffered their house to be thus broken up.

Something of this, owing to a misapprehension which had been palmed upon them, was felt by the Thessalonian Christians in St. Paul's time. They were " shaken in mind," they were " troubled," they were in the deepest mental distress, because they were made to believe that the day of Christ (ενεστηκε) was then present, had arrived, was come ; that the resurrection was " past already ; " that the time for the rapture and glorification of the saints was here ; whilst the blessings, joys, and honours which they as Christians connected with it were not realized. In other words, they thought themselves " cut off " and " left." Just as they were previously disturbed and sorrowing over their deceased friends as possibly disabled for the joy and glory to be realized at the Lord's coming, which they were so eagerly expect-ing, so now they were filled with perturbation and alarm, under the tidings that Christ had come and had not taken them. It was a deep, terrible, and soul-agonizing distress,—one which called forth the apostle's sympathy, and all the energy of his great spirit and strongest words to roll off the load from their hearts. But when that day has once come in literal truth, and all half-Christians, self-deceivers, and unfaithful and unwatching ones, have it flashed upon them that they are " left," there will be a worse shaking than these Thessalonians felt, with no apostle to come with better tidings to their relief. And though a hope of salvation may still remain to them in case of a prompt and earnest repentance, still, the Saviour says, " there shall be weeping and gnashing of teeth."

But this is not the worst. The Man-child being " caught up to God and to His throne," the period of Satan's great anger comes, and hence the most terrible persecutions. The Hinderer being removed, " then shall that Wicked be revealed, whose coming is after the working of Satan with all power, and signs, and lying wonders, and with all deceivableness of unrighteousness." (2 Thess. 2 : 8–10.) Then the great Dragon rages, because he knoweth that he hath but a short time. He persecutes and pursues the Woman, as typified in the infamous proceedings of Antiochus Epiphanes in the Maccabean times. As the text clearly implies, and as more specifically set forth in the succeeding chapter, things shall be made so hot and oppressive to the Church that no Christians could live, except for the miraculous help of God. Weakened and depleted as the Woman is, she must flee, as of old time " it was told the king of Egypt that the people *fled*." The Dragon *pursues* her, as the avenger of blood while his heart was hot *pursued* the manslayer. The lament of Jeremiah will then reach its deepest pathos in the lips of God's people : " Our persecutors are swifter than the eagles of the heaven : they pursued us upon the mountains, they laid wait for us in the wilderness." (Lam. 4 : 19.) Then shall be the cry : " Plead my cause, O Lord, with them that strive with me : fight against them that fight against me. Take hold of shield and buckler, and stand up for mine help. Draw out also the spear, and stop the way against them that persecute me : say unto my soul, I am thy salvation. Let them be confounded and put to shame that seek after my life : let them be turned back and brought to confusion that devise my hurt. Let them be as chaff before the wind ; and let the Angel of the Lord chase them. Let their way be dark and slippery ; and let the Angel of the Lord persecute them. For without cause they have hid for me their net, in a pit which without cause they have digged for my soul. Let destruction come upon him at unawares ; and let his net that he hath hid catch himself : into that very destruction let him fall. O Lord, keep not silence : O Lord, be not far from me. Stir up thyself, and awake to my judgment, even unto my cause, my God and my Lord." (Ps. 35.) It is with reference to this very time that the Saviour himself says : " Except those days should be shortened, there should no flesh be saved ; but for the elect's sake those days shall be shortened." (Matt. 24 : 22.)

There can be no doubt that the centre of events and doings, as here contemplated, is Jerusalem. Already in the first part of the preceding chapter, we had the measuring of the temple, and its altar and worshippers, which presupposes their rebuilding, and God's taking possession of them again. This temple and altar, as Dr. Clarke admits, " must refer to the temple at Jerusalem." " *The holy city* " is named in connection as the locality, and the only earthly city so named in the Scriptures is Jerusalem. A partly Jewish and a partly Gentile population is distinctly recognized as having place in " the holy city " at that time. It is there that the Two Witnesses are slain and resurrected, even " where their Lord was crucified ; " and the ministry of the Two Witnesses is contemporaneous with " the Beast," who kills them. And it is under his domination that the persecution and flight of the Woman occurs. Jerusalem, then, is certainly the centre of the field of contemplation in the text, and the point from which the flight of the persecuted Woman takes place. As the flight of the Christians to Pella in the time of the Roman invasion eighteen hundred years ago was centrally from Jerusalem, so it will be again under the final " prince that shall come," armed with that same iron power, to overrun the temple court and to " trample the holy city forty and two months."

Why does the Woman fly ? Evidently because she cannot sustain herself or live without it. The persecution of the professed followers and worshippers of God is so severe and bloody as to compel them to fly in order to save their heads. It is the period of the dominion of the Beast as described in the chapter next succeeding ; and there we are told that as many as will not worship the image of the Beast shall be beheaded ; and that whosoever will not receive the mark of the Beast in the right hand or forehead, shall not be allowed to buy or sell. There will be no living under him without accepting him in the place of God and of Christ. And this Beast is the embodiment of the Dragon's rage against the Woman and such of her seed as still remains upon the earth. He has his power, and his seat, and his great authority from the Devil ; and the known worshippers of Jehovah must then fly or die ; there is no other help.   It is a dreadful strait ; but into it will all remaining Christians come when once the Hinderer is taken away, and the Man-child has been caught up to God. It was thus that Antiochus decreed that whosoever would not do according to his command, and totally abolish every vestige and observance of Jehovah's law should die (1 Macc. 1 : 41–50) ; and so, in yet fiercer vigour, shall it be under the Beast then.

But though such suffering and dread temptations and necessities come upon the unready ones after their more watchful and faithful brethren have entered the celestial apartments, they are not utterly forsaken. If true to their profession then God will help them by His own great power.

When Israel came out of Egypt God marvellously strengthened every muscle and invigorated every weakness. " There was not one feeble person amidst their tribes."   Not a foot swelled, and not even a garment or a shoe waxed old for forty years. And when they came to the wilderness of Sinai, where God spoke to them from the flaming mountain, He said : " Ye have seen how *I bore you on eagles' wings*, and brought you unto myself."   (Ex. 19 : 4.)   Again it was said : " As an eagle stirreth up her nest, fluttereth over her young, spreadeth abroad her wings, taketh them, *beareth them on her wings*, so the Lord alone did lead him." (Deut. 32 : 11, 12.)

And those same wings here appear again. " *And to the Woman were given the two wings of the great eagle*," that is, the special and direct help of God. In like miraculous manner the hand of the Lord was upon Elijah, enabling him to outrun the hasting chariot of King Ahab, even from Carmel to Jezreel. (1 Kings 18 : 46.)   The sore trial is not lifted off, but miraculous assistance is given according to the occasion.

But whither does the Woman fly ? When those wings were lent to Israel in the flight from the Dragon in Egypt they carried the people into the wilderness, even to Sinai.   And here we have " the wilderness " again, as well as the same eagle's wings, and that very same wilderness of Sinai.   Habakkuk, celebrating certain revelations of the Lord connecting with this very time, speaks of His coming from " Teman," the southern section of Idumea, and from " Mount Paran," which identifies with Sinai and its hills. (Hab. 3.)   It is here called " *her place* "—a place belonging to her which God hath prepared for her. And, remarkable enough, this was the locality to which Moses fled for security from the wrath of Pharaoh,—to which Israel fled from the tyranny and rage of the Egyptians,—to which Elijah betook himself for refuge from the wrath of the bloody Jezebel,—to which the faithful Jews retired from the persecutions of the Syrian kings in the Maccabean times. (1 Macc. 2 : 28–31.)   Having served as the place of shelter for God's faithful ones in so many instances, and on such marked occasions, it may well be called " *her place*,"—the one locality of all on earth prepared and consecrated as the desert asylum of God's persecuted people. It is further stated that there the woman is nourished. The idea is that of a miraculous feeding, and the past is prophecy of the future. It was there that God sent the manna to feed the fugitive thousands of Israel in the days of Moses. Elijah was miraculously fed by an angel, and received a meal from heaven, in the strength of which he went forty days, in his flight to this " mount of God."

The feeding of the Woman here, indicates the depth of her straits, and her utter helplessness in any resources of her own. She is in great need, and no amount of activity on her part can supply her with sustenance. But for some provision, answering to that made there for Israel of old, these poor distressed fugitives would all perish. But like the multitudes which followed Jesus into the desert place, she is fed in the wilderness ; and there she is nourished for three and a half years, the entire term of the persecuting dominion of the Beast, far away from the face of the serpent.   It is a sore thing to be chastised of the Lord ; but it is a blessed thought that He will not forsake those who cleave to Him, and that His grace shall be sufficient for them that meekly trust in Him.

But even in her mountain retreat the Dragon's enmity and rage against the Woman continue. He is bent on destroying her if he can.

When Pharaoh-Necho went up with his armies against Babylon, Jeremiah exclaimed : " Who is this that cometh up *like a flood, whose waters are moved as the rivers ?* Egypt riseth up like a flood, and *his waters* are moved like the rivers." (Jer. 46 : 7, 8.) When Nebuchadnezzar came with his Chaldean forces against Tyre and Sidon, the Lord said, " Behold, *waters* rise up out of the north, and shall be an overflowing flood, and shall overflow the land, and all that is therein ; then the men shall cry, and all the inhabitants of the land shall howl. At the noise of the stamping of hoofs of his strong horses, at the rushing of his chariots, and at the rumbling of his wheels, the fathers shall not look back to their children for feebleness of hands." (Jer. 47 : 2, 3.) And so here, John beheld, " *And the serpent cast from his mouth after the woman water like a river, that he might cause her [to be] carried away by the river.*" The interpretation is evident. Soldiers are despatched to assail and overwhelm her in her retreat, and to destroy her there where God is nourishing her. It is not " a flood," or a vast and universally devastating army, but " *water like a river*," a smaller expedition for one definite purpose, which keeps within its own track to the one end ; to wit, the destruction of these fugitives lodged in the wilderness. It was thus a detachment of the Syrian army was sent after the faithful fugitives in the time of the Maccabees. (1 Macc. 2 : 31–38.) But it is a force sufficient for its purpose, in all ordinary calculation. It is more than the Woman in her own strength could possibly withstand. It would sweep her away—quench her existence in blood—if no help came to her relief. But man's extremity is God's opportunity. What saith the record ? " *The earth helped the Woman ; yea, the earth opened her mouth and drank up the river which the Dragon cast forth from his mouth.*"

Exactly what sort of calamity befalls these armed forces of the Beast, we may not be able definitely to determine. When the hosts of Pharaoh, in mad pursuit of ancient Israel, were overwhelmed by the sea, the exulting song of Moses and his people was, " Who is like unto Thee, O Lord ! Thou stretchedst forth thy right hand, *the earth swallowed them.*" (Ex. 15 : 11, 12.) In this same wilderness, when God's anger was visited upon Korah, Dathan, and Abiram, for their rebellion against Moses and Aaron, " the ground clave asunder that was under them, and *the earth opened her mouth, and swallowed them up,* and their houses, and all the men that pertained unto Korah, and all their goods : they, and all that pertained to them, *went down alive into the pit,* and the earth closed upon them, and *they perished.*" (Numb. 16 : 31–33.) It is the region and time of miracle when this drinking up of the river which the Dragon sends against the woman occurs. It is the region and time when there is to be a renewal of wonders, " like as it was to Israel in the day that he came up out of the land of Egypt." (Is. 11 : 15, 16.) It is the region and time of great earthquakes and disturbances in the economy of nature. (Zech. 14 : 4 ; Luke 21 : 25, 26 ; Rev. 11 : 13, 19.) And there is reason to think that it is by some great and sudden rending of the earth that these pursuing hosts are arrested in their course, if not *en masse* buried up in the convulsion. At least, the object of their bloody expedition is thwarted. They fail to reach the Woman in her place of refuge. The very ground yawns to stop them in their hellish madness.

But though completely baffled in this attempt to destroy the Woman, the rage of the Dragon is not assuaged, but only burns the more fiercely. Compelled to desist from his attempt to destroy her, he turns about to seek after the lives of such remnants of her seed as may be elsewhere found. " His plans turn to dust in his mouth ; yet he is only angry, not penitent." Defeated beyond redress in this scheme, he abandons it ; but only to enter upon a further war with every fraction of humanity still within his reach which may be found adhering to the commandments of God or the testimony of Jesus.

Two classes appear to be referred to. Abraham was promised a twofold seed : an earthly, likened to the sands of the sea ; and a heavenly, likened to the stars of the sky. And from the beginning of the gospel there have always been two classes of believers : the Jewish and the Gentiles. So " the commandments of God " suggest to us God's older revelation by Moses, and the Law given through him : and " the testimony of Jesus " calls to mind the Christian profession. The allusion would, therefore, seem to be (1) to Jewish believers, the 144,000 of whom, described in chapter vii, are then still on the earth ; and (2) Gentile, servants of God who hold fast the confession of Christ over against the prevalent abominations of the time. These are now sought out with desperate hate, wherever they may be, and proceeded against with determination to conquer them to the worship of the Beast, or, failing in that, to cut off the heads of all who refuse to yield. This is also the time during which the Two Witnesses are prophesying ; and they, and those awakened by their witness, embracing both Jews and Gentiles, are specially noted in chapter 11 : 7, as those against whom the Beast shall make war, and overcome them, and kill them.

It is not the organized Church which is the object of this new outbreak of the Dragon's wrath ; for the Church as a visible body is in the wilderness beyond his grasp. According to the terms, this remaining portion of the Woman's seed consists rather of individual believers here and there, whose organic association with each other has been broken up, and who from the stress of the times no longer have their visible assemblies. Nevertheless, they are everywhere sought out, under the fell resolve to exterminate them from the earth.

The organs through which the Dragon puts forth all this bloody rage against the Woman and the remnants of her seed are described in the next chapter, and those that succeed it, where further details are given. I will not anticipate them here. At another time, God willing, I propose to enter upon them. Meanwhile, let us reflect a little over the subject-matter which has been engaging us to-night.

1. Note how dark is the outlook of the Church of Jesus with respect to this world ! We wonder betimes at the smallness of its success, and the hard struggle it ever has for its existence. But why should we wonder ? Think of the might of the Devil and his angels, of their malignity against it, and how deeply the whole world is in their possession. By reason of the depravity that is upon our race, every human being born is brought forth under Satan's dominion. We scarcely succeed in winning and training some to truth and holiness, till death comes and takes them away, leaving the same work to be gone over again and again continually, with the same result awaiting it every time. And while faithful ones are labouring, multitudes of their fellow-professors are a mere incubus on their exertions, hindering by their indifference and inconsistencies, whilst the great world continually opposes, and a universal depravity, inflamed of hell, perpetually fights against the calls and claims of heaven. Ever dreaming of victory to bring us the reign of righteousness and rest, we still find ourselves at the bottom of the hill, toiling to reach the unreachable summit. And how can we expect to ever it be otherwise as long as this present order of things lasts, seeing that Satan continues with ever-deepening malice and activity to the very end of the world, and that the last days are the wickedest and the worst ! All that we can do is to work on, like Paul, if that by any means we may " save some."

2. Note the true source of dislike and hatred to the Church. There be many who think more of anything on earth than of the Church. They may consider it well enough to have its services when they die, but whilst they live they only neglect and despise it, and are only offended and enraged when its claims are pressed. They forget that this is the very spirit of the devil. There is

nothing which Satan so much hates, which he so energetically opposes, which he persecutes to the end with such an unrelenting and undying rancour, or that he tries so hard to keep out of heaven and obliterate from the earth, as the Church. We are justly amazed at the intensity of his malice toward the mystic Woman and her seed, pursuing her with ever-increasing rage, even when God's judgments multiply upon him for it. And every one who dislikes, hates, or persecutes the Church and people of God, has in him the Devil's spirit, acts the Devil's will, and is one of the Devil's children.

3. Note what a lesson of rebuke and duty addresses itself to Christians from the Devil's example. He never rests from his murderous endeavours. He stops for no losses, succumbs to no adversities, desists for no hindrances, turns back from no encounters, and surrenders not even to the Almighty's judgments, so long as he has liberty to act or time in which to operate. His energy and activity increase the more as he sees and knows that his end is near. He does it out of wicked spite and mere evilness, and with no prospect but utter defeat and eternal damnation. And how should we, then, who claim to love God, and believe that everlasting crowns of glory and blessing are to be the reward of our fidelity, stand rebuked for our coldness in the presence of such an example ! His day runs from the beginning to the end of time, yet he works incessantly to its last hour. Our day is measured by a few brief years, half of which is spent in infancy and sleep, whilst the whole may at any moment end in death ; yet we fritter away our time and energies and opportunities as if no necessities were upon us, or as if we had no salvation to secure, no hell to escape, no God to serve, no heaven to win. Alas, alas, for such indifference ! Brethren, look at the untiring energy of Hell for destruction, and learn wisdom for eternal life.

4. Finally, note the pressing need there is to keep ourselves awake and in readiness for the coming of our Lord. Over and over we are told that He shall come as a thief in the night—when men think not—when many of His own servants are saying and believing that it is not possible that He should come in their day—when the great multitude is counting on nothing but peace and safety. The day and the hour knoweth no man. And if that day should come upon us unawares, and find us unprepared, even though we should not be finally lost, these presentations show that terrible experiences await us. No wonder that the beneficent and loving Jesus should make it one of his most constant and most urgent admonitions, to watch and pray that we come not into these dreadful tribulations. As we value our peace, let us not then be indifferent to things so solemn.

LECTURE THIRTY-FIRST

THE BEAST FROM THE SEA—THE DOCTRINE CONCERNING THE ANTICHRIST—THIS VISION A SYMBOL OF TEMPORAL SOVEREIGNTY IN ITS FINAL CONSUMMATION—AN INDIVIDUAL ADMINISTRATION EMBODIED IN ONE PARTICULAR MAN—A SUPERNATURAL PERSONAGE— HIS ATTRACTIVENESS AND GREATNESS—THE CONSUMMATE ANTAGONIST AND SUPPLANTER OF EVERYTHING DIVINE—HIS BLASPHEMY TOWARDS THEM THAT TABERNACLE IN THE HEAVEN—THE DEEP AND SOLEMN IMPORTANCE OF THESE FORESHOWINGS.

REV. 13 : 1–10. (Revised Text.) And I [some MSS. *he*, the Dragon] stood upon the sand of the sea ; and I saw a beast [or *wild beast*] coming up out of the sea, having ten horns and seven heads, and upon his horns ten diadems, and upon his heads names of blasphemy.

And the beast which I saw was like to a leopard [or *panther*], and his feet as of a bear, and his mouth as the mouth of a lion. And the Dragon gave him his power, and his throne, and great authority.

And (I saw) one of his heads as having been slain to death [killed], and the stroke of his death was healed ; and all the earth wondered after the beast. And they worshipped the Dragon because he gave the authority to the beast ; and they worshipped the beast saying, Who [is] like to the beast ! And who is able to war with him !

And a mouth was given him speaking great and blasphemous things ; and authority was given him to act for forty-two months.

And he opened his mouth for blasphemies towards God, to blaspheme His name, and His tabernacle, they which tabernacle in the heaven.

And it was given him to make war on the saints, and to overcome them, and authority was given him over every tribe, and people, and tongue, and nation. And all that dwell upon the earth shall (will) worship him,—[every one] whose name hath not been written, from the foundation of the world, in the book of life of the Lamb that hath been slain.

If any one hath an ear, let him hear. If any one [is] for captivity, into captivity he goeth ; if any one will kill with the sword, with the sword must he be killed.

Here is the patience and the faith of the saints.

THE Apostle John, writing to no particular Church, but in a general Epistle to a wide circle of churches, makes this remarkable statement : " *Little children, ye have heard that Antichrist shall come.*" (1 John 2 : 18.) Where and how had the Christians of his time thus heard about " the Antichrist," and become familiar with the fact of his coming ? The answer is, that this was a part of the common instruction given to God's people, both under the Old Testament and the New. It was distinct and prominent in the writings of the ancient prophets, and it was among the teachings of Christ, and those sent to preach and teach in His name. Even the light of the first promise of a coming Deliverer, had with it the dark adumbration of an antagonizing power to bruise His heel, and of a serpent brood to mass its strength against the mother's seed. And through all the ages of our world, there has been a Cain for every Abel, a Jannes and Jambres for every Moses and Aaron, a Babylon for every Jerusalem, a Herod for every John the Baptist, and a Nero for every going forth of God's consecrated apostles,—all the types and precursors of the ultimate heading up of all evil in one final foe, which is the Antichrist. Nor has it been possible for the teachers of God in any age to give full instruction touching the history of human salvation, without embracing in it the doctrine concerning this foul personage. It is part of the background of all Revelation, promise, and hope, given for the admonition and strengthening of God's people. And it is this Serpent seed, in its ultimate development, even THE MANIFESTED ANTICHRIST, whose portrait is given us in the chapter on which we now enter. May God help us to handle it with wisdom and soberness !

In the preceding chapter we were called to contemplate the great Dragon, the Old Serpent, his influence over our world, his perpetual malignity toward the saints, his casting out from the heavenly spaces at the glorification of the Church of the first-born, his great rage at being cast down into the earth, and his consequent determination to destroy all the people of God yet to be found among mortals. But Satan is a spirit, and cannot operate in the affairs of our world except through the minds, passions, and activities of men. He needs to embody himself in earthly agents, and to put himself forth in earthly organisms in order to accomplish his murderous will. And through the inspired seer, God here makes known to us what that organism is, and how the agency and domination of the enraged Dragon will be exerted in acting out his blasphemies deceits, and bloody spite. The subject is not a pleasant one, but it is an important one. It also has features so startling and extraordinary that many may be repelled, and led to treat it as a wild and foolish dream. Nevertheless, we all need to look at it, and to understand it. No one is safe in refusing to entertain it. And whether we are able to grasp it fully in all its particulars or not, it is here set forth for our learning, that we may know just how things will eventually turn out.

John " in the spirit," finds himself stationed on the sands of the sea,—that same great sea upon which Daniel beheld the winds striving in their fury. He beholds a monstrous Beast rising out of the troubled elements. He sees horns emerging, and the number of them is ten, and on each horn a diadem. He sees the heads which bear the horns, and these heads are seven, and on the heads are names of blasphemy. Presently the whole figure of the monster is before him. Its appearance is like a leopard or panther, but its feet are as the feet of a bear, and its mouth as the mouth of a lion. He saw also that the Beast had a throne, and power, and great authority. One of his heads showed marks of having been fatally wounded and slain, but the deathstroke was healed. He saw also the whole earth wondering after the Beast, amazed at its majesty and power, exclaiming at the impossibility of withstanding it, and celebrating its superiority to everything. He beheld, and the Beast was speaking great and blasphemous things against God, blaspheming His name, His tabernacle, even them that tabernacle in the heaven, assailing and overcoming the saints on earth, and wielding authority over every tribe, and people, and tongue, and nation. He saw also that all the dwellers upon earth, whose names are not written in the book of life of the Lamb slain, did worship this Beast. And for forty-two months the monster holds its place and enacts its resistless will. This is the picture. What are we to make of it? What does it mean? How are we to understand it?

1. My first remark on the subject is, that we here have a symbolic presentation of the political sovereignty of this world. The Beast has horns, and horns are the representatives of power. On these horns are diadems, and diadems are the badges of regal dominion. The Beast is said to possess power, a throne, and great authority. He makes war. He exercises dominion over tribes, and peoples, and tongues, and nations. He has control of buying and selling, and fixes the conditions on which they are carried on. He furnishes the power to slay every one who will not come under his regulations. All of which proves political sovereignty and imperial earthly dominion. He is a monstrous Beast, including in his composition the four beasts of Daniel. He comes out of the same agitated sea, and behaves as they behaved. From the interpreting angel we know that Daniel's four beasts denoted " four kings," or kingdoms, that arise upon earth. The identification thus becomes complete and unmistakable, that this monstrous Beast is meant to set before us an image of earthly sovereignty and dominion. And if any further evidence of this is demanded, it may be abundantly found in chapter 17 : 9–17, where the same Beast is further described, and the ten horns are interpreted to be " ten kings," together with other particulars, which identify the whole representation with this world's political sovereignty.

2. My second remark is, that we here are shown the world-power in its final consummation—the whole sum of it from the beginning to the end in one figure, as it will be in the last three and a half years of its existence. The duration of the dominancy of this Beast as such is explicitly given as forty-two months, or three and a half years ; and when he finally falls, as described in chapter 19, he goes into perdition and all this world's kings, armies, and administrations end forever. He is therefore the embodiment of this world's political sovereignty in its last phase, in the last years of its existence. Daniel's beasts were successive empires, the Babylonian, the Medo-Persian, the Græco-Macedonian, and the Roman. But the lion, the bear, the leopard, and the nameless ten-horned monster, each distinct there, are all united in one here. This Beast is therefore the consummation and embodiment of the whole world-power or political dominion from the beginning, as it presents itself at the final outcome. Nor do I know by what means this could be more definitely expressed than in the particulars and relations of this vision. " Every tribe, and people, and tongue, and nation," is included under the dominion of this Beast. There is no political sovereignty on earth during its administration but that embraced in its horns and heads. It is therefore the whole sum of it as then existing. And as there is nothing more of it left after this Beast's fall, it is clear that what is here shown us must needs be the entire political power of this world in its final outcome or consummation.

3. My third remark is, that this beast is an individual administration, embodied in one particular man. Though upheld by ten kings or governments they unite in making the Beast the one sole Arch Regent of their time.

Ever since the period of the Reformation until now, the battle of the commentators has hung heavy over the question whether this Beast is to be construed as an individual imperial *person*, or a mere system, power, government, or influence, having its life in a succession of agents or representatives. Some take one side and others the opposite. Both parties are largely in the right as to the fact, though the more common historical interpretation is greatly at fault in the manner in which it applies the fact. There can be no kingdom without a king, and no empire without an emperor ; neither can there be a king in fact without a kingdom. We cannot consistently speak of imperial power and dominion apart from a personal head which represents and embodies that power. A person is necessarily included in the conception, as well as an imperial dominion which that person holds and exercises. So far as the mere symbol is concerned, a succession of persons wielding the same authority might be embraced ; but it cannot be so in this case. The period of this Beast's dominancy is specifically limited to three and a half years, and there is no room for much of a succession in that space of time. The attempt to stretch out these 42 months into 1260 years is without warrant in the Scriptures ; and, if accepted, proves inadequate to any just application of the vision. It breaks down as to beginning, middle, and end. Try it as men will, it fails to reach the great day of final judgment, in which the dominion of this Beast so signally terminates.* The 42 months are 42 *months*, and the 1260 days are 1260 *days*, not years ; and the Beast, the measure of whose reign is thus limited, cannot stand for a series of successive sovereigns, but must be

---

* It is amazing to see the utter confusion to which those interpreters are reduced who take the 42 months or 1260 days as so many years. Joachim begins them with A.D.1, ending at A.D. 1260 ; Walter Brute makes them extend from A.D. 134 to 1394 ; Melancthon, from A.D. 660, or thereabouts, to 2000 ; Aretius, from 312–1572 ; Napier, from 316–1576 ; Brightman, from 304–1564 ; Artopæus, from 260–1520 ; Cocceius, from 292–1522 ; Fleming, from 606–1848 ; Daubuz, from 476–1736 ; Lowman, from 756–2016 ; Gill, from 606–1866 ; Frazer, from 756–1998 ; Galloway, from 606–1849 ; Cunningham, from 533–1792 ; Faber, from 606–1866 ; Frere, from 533–1792 ; Croley, from 533–1793 ; Woodhouse, from 622–1882 ; Fysh, from 727–1987 ; Habershon, from 584–1844 ; Elliott, from 529 to 608–1789 to 1868. This ought to be conclusive that by no possibility can any solid basis be found to rest on when the unwarranted assumption is admitted that these " 1260 days " mean 1260 *years*.

understood of one individual person.   And other particulars require the same
conclusion.   This Beast is worshipped as a god ; but people never worship an
empire as such ; neither do they make a succession of emperors into an object
of religious devotion.   The paying of divine homage to kings has been a
common thing in the world's history, but it has always been rendered to
individuals.   An image or statue of this Beast is set up, and the worship of it
demanded of all on pain of death ; but antiquity tells of no images or statues
of empires or dynasties set up for the religious reverence of subjects.   It has
always been the image or statue of the emperor, or the king ; and so it must
needs be in this instance.   This Beast also has a proper name,—a name
expressive of a particular number, and that number " a number of *a man ; "*
which cannot be conceived except on the idea of an individual person.   This
Beast is, by common consent, identical with " that Wicked," of which Paul
wrote to the Thessalonians ; but that monster instrument of Satan is called
" *that man of sin.*"   An apocalypse is also ascribed to him, the same as to
Christ, and various actions and position, nothing of which can be fairly
understood except as applied to *a person.*   This Beast is also clearly identifiable
with the wilful king of Daniel ; but that king is in every respect treated of as an
individual person, the same as Cyrus, Cambyses, Darius, Xerxes, or Alexander.
This beast is finally damned.   He goes into perdition, into the lake of fire,
where he continues to exist and suffer, after passing from this earthly scene
(chap. 17 : 11 ; 20 : 10), which cannot be true of systems of government.
We would therefore greatly err from the Scriptures, as well as from the
unanimous conviction and teaching of the early Church, were we to fail to
recognize in this Beast *a real person,* though one in whom the political power
of the world is finally concentrated and represented.*

* " The sense is not identical merely with a collective or abstract idea, that of Romanism
or Paganism, the Roman monarchy, and such like.   It is in the highest degree improbable
that that mode of expression would be applied if such a relation were meant as the weakening
of the Roman power by other nations, to which it has been repeatedly referred, or even by
Christianizing.   *The expressions appear natural only when they are explained of a definite
person.*"—Dr F. Bleek's *Lectures on the Apocalypse,* 1875, p. 92.
   " The representation given of Antichrist plainly describes him *as a person, as an individual.*
A stream of antichristian sentiment and conduct pervades the whole history of the world.
From this stream, in the last days, proceeds Antichrist, as the completed evil fruit ; it will
express itself in many individuals, but by all these *one personality* will be considered as the
centre of all their striving, and acknowledged as the master by whom they let themselves
be guided.   All great movements in the history of the world have definite personages for
pillars.   That the last and utmost development of evil will also attain to its centre *in a
personality,* has the analogy of history entirely in its favour.   That in Antichrist evil is
only to be conceived as an abstract clearly contradicts the teaching of the Scriptures."—
Olshausen, on 2 Thess. 2.
   " Taking the Bible as our guide, it seems strange that any other idea should be entertained of the Antichrist than that he will be *an individual human being.*   Endless as are the
passages referring to himself, his actings, and his end, they all, with one accord, so far as I
understand them, proclaim him to be an individual man.   All the attributes, circumstances,
as well as appellations of individual humanity, are addressed and ascribed to him.   He is
distinctly called, and declared to be, *a man,* ' that man of sin,' which itself, and in the absence
of any positive contradiction to it elsewhere in Scripture, ought to be conclusive.   In Rev.
13 : 18, he is called *a man.*   Also he is called ' the son of perdition,' as was Judas ; but Judas
was a man, and the inference is that such also will be his antitype.   John, speaking of *the*
Antichrist, says, ' Even now are there many antichrists.'   Who were these but Christ-
denying *men ?*   And who, then, or what would be *the* Antichrist yet to come but *a man*
too ?   Evidently the one to come was to be of the same nature as the ' many ' then already
come.   Christ was *a man,* a God-man, but still man, sin only excepted.   Then the Antichrist,
who is to appear as a false Christ, must needs be *a man* too, or how is it possible he could pass
himself off for Christ ?   Antichrist is described as a King, even as other kings.   Daniel
(7 : 24) teaches that ' ten kings arise ' and then ' another,' and that other, as verse 25
explains, undoubtedly is the Antichrist.   That Antichrist would be an individual man, was
never questioned in the first and purer ages of the Church.   The idea of a power or system,
or even series of individuals, being symbolized by the Man of Sin, was utterly unknown."
—Molyneux's *Lectures on Israel's Future,* 1860, pp. 68–70.
   " The old Fathers of the Church were for three centuries at least quite at one in understanding by ' the Man of Sin, the Son of Perdition, the Lawless One,' not a system of
falsehood and unrighteousness, nor a succession of individuals at the head of such a system,

4. My fourth remark is, that this Beast is a supernatural personage.   As a political power, he rises out of the convulsed sea of peoples, the same as world-powers in general ; but as a person, his origin is peculiar.   He is repeatedly described as " the Beast that cometh up *out of the abyss.*"   " The abyss " cannot mean less than the under-world, the world of lost spirits, the receptacle and abode of demons, otherwise called *hell*.   Ordinary men do not come from thence.   One who hails from that place must be either a dead man brought up again from the dead, or some evil spirit which takes possession of a living man. Many of the early Christians held and taught that the Emperor Nero is the Antichrist, and that he will return again to the earth, get possession of its empire, and enact all that is affirmed of the man of sin.*   They explained the passages referring to the matter to mean, either that Nero was not really dead, but in some mysterious way kept alive, presently to came upon the scene as this Beast ; or, that, being dead, he will be satanically resurrected for this purpose.   But even if not literally resurrected, he, or some other tenant of hell, might still fulfil the idea, after the style in which certain spirit-mediums claim to be animated and possessed, so as to think, speak, and act only as the will of the foreign spirit impels.   In either case, the Beast, as a person, is an extra-ordinary and supernatural being.   Nor can we adequately explain what else is said of him without assuming that such is the fact.

John tells us that he beheld one of the Beast's heads " as having been slain to death."   The expression is so strong, definite, and intensified, that nothing less can be grammatically made of it than that real death meant to be affirmed. It is further described as a sword-wound, " the stroke of his death," or a stroke which carries death to him who experiences it.   A man who has undergone physical death is therefore in contemplation. Whether he comes up again in literal bodily resurrection, or only by means of an obsession of some living man, we may not be able to decide.   Whatever the mode, it will be in effect the same as a resurrection.   The record is that his death-wound becomes effectually negatived, and so far healed, or made of non-effect, that, though dead, he enters again upon all the activities of life the same as if he never had been killed. Similar phraseology is used in this Book with regard to Christ, but all agree that it there means return to life by resurrection after a real bodily killing. How, then, can it mean less here ?   In the subsequent portions of the history this Beast is repeatedly spoken of as " he whose stroke of death was healed ; " " the beast which had the stroke of the sword, and *lived*," or became alive again,—" the beast that was, and is not, and *yet is*," or as the Codex Sinaiticus has it (*καὶ πάλιν πάρεσται*), *shall soon again be here*.   These expressions inevit-ably carry with them the notion of a violent and real death, and as real a return again to presence and activity on the earth.   Indeed, it seems to be this revivescence and remanifestation of one known to have been dead that

but, according to the most obvious and natural import of the language,—*some one man, the personal Antichrist*, the recipient of all Satan's energy, in whom Satan should, to so speak become incarnate, and thus bring to a decision the long-standing feud between himself and the Woman's seed. This ancient faith hath in it elements of truth which must be combined with the Protestant interpretation before we can get at the full import of this Divine Revelation."—DR. JOHN LILLIE's *Lectures on Thessalonians*, 1860, pp. 537, 538.

* Victorinus, *in loc.*, says : " Nero will be raised from the dead, appear again at Rome, persecute the Church once more, and finally be destroyed by the Messiah, coming in His glory, and being accompanied by the prophet Elijah."

Lactantius refers to this opinion, though not holding to it himself, that " Nero will come the precursor and forerunner of the Devil, coming to lay waste the earth."

Sulpicius Severus wrote : " Nero, the basest of men and even of monsters, was well worthy of being the first persecutor ; I know not whether he may be the last, since it is the current opinion of many that he is yet to come as Antichrist."

Augustine says : " What means the declaration, that the mystery of iniquity doth already work ? Some suppose it to be spoken of the Roman Emperor, and therefore Paul did not speak in plain words, although he always expected that what he said would be understood as applying to Nero, whose doings already appeared like those of Antichrist. Hence it was that some suspected that he would rise from the dead as Antichrist."— *Civit. Dei.*, xx, 19.

causes the universal wondering after this Beast. Be the explanation what it may, the implication strongly is, that this Beast is a man who once was living, who was fatally wounded, whose place was in the abyss of lost souls, who somehow comes forth from thence in convincing evidences of his real identity, and who, having been slain, returns again to take the lead in the activities and administrations upon earth, to the great wonder and astonishment of the whole world.

The source whence he derives his extraordinary character and power is clearly indicated. It is from no intervention of God in his behalf, though for the punishment of the godless world permitted. The record says : " The Dragon gave him his power, and his throne, and great authority." It is therefore by the Devil's power that he is thus revived, just as all demonism, necromancy, and witchcraft are of the Devil. When Christ was on earth, the Devil took him into an exceeding high mountain, and showed Him all the kingdoms of the world, and the glory of them, and said to Him : " All these things will I give thee, if thou wilt fall down and worship me." There certainly was supernaturalism here. The holy Jesus, indeed, spurned the offer ; but Satan eventually finds one to accept his conditions. This Beast is a worshipper of the Devil, and causes all under him to worship the Devil. In return, he gets what was proposed to Christ. The Devil makes over the infernal dominion into his hands, brings him again from the abyss, and constitutes him his great vice-regent in the sovereignty of the world. He thus becomes in some sense an incarnation of the Devil. Accordingly, it is written that his manifestation " is after the working of Satan, with all power and signs and lying wonders, and with all deceivableness of unrighteousness." (2 Thess. 2 : 9.) Unmistakably, then, we have here to do with a very extraordinary being— with a man altogether different from anything ever beheld in humanity before—with one who hails from the bottomless pit, endowed with all the energy and power of Satan himself.

5. My fifth remark is, that this " Man of Sin " will be an exceedingly attractive, fascinating, and bewitching personage. He draws upon himself the intensest admiration and homage of the world. John beheld, and " *all the world wondered after the Beast.*" Mankind are represented as so struck, captivated, and entranced by the contemplation of his wonderful qualities and powers, that they even render willing homage to the one who could give them so glorious a leader, and join in honouring and glorifying him as a very god of wisdom, power, daring, and ability. They can conceive of none like him, and celebrate his praise as the Invincible. The adoring cry is : " *Who is like to the Beast ? And who is able to war with him ?* " It cannot therefore be otherwise than that this man is supreme in whatever is admirable to the taste, judgment, and imagination of the world.

There has been much in the great empires of the past for men to wonder at and love. In Babylon was the golden majesty and splendour of sovereign rule, always so captivating to the souls of men. In Medo-Persia was the towering prowess and massive ponderousness of power, at which the world has ever stood in wondering awe. In Greece was the polish and elegance of intellect and art, combined with heroism for liberty, for which the human heart has ever been full of enthusiasm. And in Rome was the idea of justice, the iron strength of law and martial discipline, to which the nations still look with admiration. Conceive, then, the resistless attractiveness of these all combined in one, and attended with the results thereto pertaining. How would mankind even now idolize such an exhibition ? And how much the more if concentrated in an individual man, and he recognized and acknowledged as one of the great illustrious dead ? God means soon to manifest a man, even the Man who is His fellow, as the centre and channel of all majesty, wisdom, glory, and power. So Satan, as anti-God, glorifies with his glory the final Antichrist ; whilst men in their depravity and delusion rejoice in it, and cry their devoutest *vive le Roi* to his hell-derived majesty. Imagine all that has ministered to the glory of worldly empire in the ages past—the imposing array of intellect, knowledge, arts, and arms—the splendour of Oriental monarchs, the valour and grandeur of mighty heroes and conquerors—the eloquence, wisdom, and power of statesmen, orators, and poets, and all the varieties of mental accomplishment and external greatness united in one marvellous man, possessed of all the hitherto divided power and distributed attractions of all preceding times, and where is the soul, untaught of God, that would not run wild with enthusiastic adoration over him ?   Yet this is the sort of appeal which this Beast makes to the unsanctified millions of his time. Not as an instrument of terror, dismay, and horror is his revelation, but with all the blandishing allurements of the sublimest champion of human interests and greatness. Men will not fly from him, but love him, and delight and glory in him as the consummate sage and hero of all time. He will be the idol of the world. All kings will gladly yield him their thrones, and give their dominion to him ; and all the nations will think their millennium come in the splendour, and wisdom, and miraculous greatness of his teachings and his deeds.

In Nimrod's days, when the people combined to build a city, and a tower which should reach to heaven, and make themselves a name, lest they should be scattered abroad upon the earth, what was it but one grand ceremonial of worship to earthly greatness ? And if they could thus glory and sacrifice to the ambition and schemes of Nimrod, how much more to the wonderful Antichrist ? If the genius and exhibitions of such men as Cæsar, Charlemagne, Frederick, Napoleon, Voltaire, Mirabeau, Byron, and the like, have been able to delight the souls, fascinate the minds, and lead captive the wills of the children of disobedience, how can it be otherwise, when the glories of intellect and taste, of war and conquest, of miracle and majesty, of recovery from death, of mastery over all the mysterious forces of nature and spirit come forth in one sublime embodiment !

The very cities and regions over which this Beast rules will add to the fatal delusion of those times. Where, indeed, have the thoughts of men so fondly lingered as in Rome, in Greece, in Egypt, in Babylon, in Jerusalem ? All the associations of greatness, conquest, taste, learning, eloquence, art, and religion are mostly bound up with these places. And these are to rise up again under the Antichrist, as if from the world of death, whence he himself comes, mimicking the glories of the true restitution which the Son of God is then about to bring.

And to the natural impulses of the human heart will be added the unwonted instigations of the Devil himself operating behind and through all, influencing the hearts, and tongues, and energies of men. And so they will be deluded, bewitched, and rallied to the worship of the Beast, and to the acceptance of him as the true and only God.

6. My sixth remark is, that this Beast is the consummate antagonist and supplanter of everything Divine. He is exhibited in the vision as having " on his heads names of blasphemy." To the same effect it is added, that " a mouth was given him speaking great and blasphemous things,"—that " he opened his mouth for blasphemies towards God, to blaspheme His name, and His tabernacle, they which tabernacle in the heaven." The seven heads of the Beast are explained in chapter 17 to be " seven kings," or powers, five of which were fallen at the time, one of which then existed, and the seventh was not yet come. That is an allusion to a succession of imperial headships, of which the Antichrist is the consummation. It may refer either to the emperors of Rome, or to the successive great dominions of all time, the Roman emperorship being the one existing when the Apostle wrote. Taken in either way we have the key to something of the nature of the blasphemy which comes to its highest culmination in this Beast. Counting back from Rome as the sixth, we find five great empires,—the Grecian, Medo-Persian, Chaldean, Egyptian, and old Assyrian, and in every one of these the deification of the monarch, and the claiming and giving of divine honours to him was part of the common

piety of the state. Such was particularly the case with the emperors of Rome. Julius Cæsar took divine titles, accepted divine honours while he lived, and had temples erected to his worship after he was dead. Augustus Cæsar favoured the erection of temples for the worship of his uncle, and of others devoted to the worship of himself. At Angora the remains of one of these may still be seen, and on it the inscription : " *To the God Augustus.*" In the same locality there is an inscription, " To Marcus Aurelius, unconquered, august, pious, successful, by one most devoted to *his Godhead.*" Nero was styled *God* while he lived. Lamps have been found devoted to Domitian as " *our God and Lord.*" Nor can there be any question of the profession and award of Deity in the case of all the great heads of secular power from the beginning on. They all wore names of blasphemy. And these names of blasphemy are received by this Beast in augmented intensity and impiousness, and worn as of right his own. Daniel says of him : " He will exalt himself, and magnify himself above every god. He will speak marvellous things against the God of gods. He will not regard any god, for he will magnify himself above all." Paul says : " He opposeth and exalteth himself above all that is called God, or that is worshipped ; so that he as God sitteth in the temple of God, showing himself that he is God." (2 Thess. 2 : 4.) He is at once Anti-*God*, Anti-*Christ*, and Anti-*Spirit*, antagonizing each particular Person of the adorable Trinity, trampling on their claims, usurping their honours, putting himself into their place, and abolishing all worship and recognition of either.

As a necessary concomitant, he is a consummate persecutor. The Apostle in vision saw it " given him to make war with the saints, and to overcome them." It is he that wars with the Two Witnesses, and overcomes them, and kills them. (Chap. 11 : 7.) It is through him that Satan persecutes and pursues the Woman, and turns to make havoc of the remainder of her seed. It is under him that as many as will not worship his image shall be slain, and no one can either buy or sell without accepting his mark in hand or forehead as his slave and devotee. All this is set forth again and again in the Old Testament and the New.

A particular object of his blasphemies is " God's tabernacle, they which tabernacle in the heaven." This is a side-proof that our interpretation of the birth and rapture of the Man-child is correct. It will then be known and acknowledged that a resurrection and translation of saints has occurred. It will then be known and understood that they are in the pavilion cloud with the Lord in the heavenly spaces. (Ps. 27 : 5 ; 31 : 20.) Even the Beast, with all his setting aside, and ridicule of everything divine and sacred, is conscious of the presence of these glorified ones on high, and annoyed at thought of them. He speaks of them ; he acts with reference to them ; and he pours out his special blasphemies with regard to them. This is a necessity to him. The catching away to heaven of so many people of God must needs leave a deep impression behind it. The slain and abused bodies of the Two Witnesses are visibly revived, and taken up into the sky before the eyes of Antichrist's minions. This was a grand and most convincing evidence against him and all his infamous pretensions, a manifest token of his devilish falsity and approaching doom. And he needs above all to break it down, to cast discredit and dishonour upon it, and to root out the very idea if he can. Hence his particular railing and impatience with reference to this divine tent of the glorified ones, and his virulent blaspheming of those who tabernacle in it. The Dragon's wrath at the defeat of his efforts against these chosen ones is thus outwardly vented in this blasphemy of the Beast, and his bloody persecution of all on earth who dare to believe and hold contrary to his will. How blessed are they who through faith and watchfulness have been accounted worthy to escape his power by being caught up to God ere he is revealed !

7. My seventh and last remark, for the present, is, that Christians have great need to study and understand what is thus foreshown. There is appended

to the vision a special admonition and command : " *If any one hath an ear, let him hear.*" It is the same which the Great Divine Teacher has laid upon mankind with reference to the most vital things of His Gospel. It shows that something of the most intense and urgent importance is involved in these things, not only for theologians and scholars, but for every Christian—for all classes of men—for every one that hath an ear for the learning of divine truth. It shows that the predisposition will be, and is, to ignore and disregard this and such like subjects—to treat them as wild speculations—to pass them by as destitute of practical worth, if not as positively injurious. It shows that God's idea of the study of prophecy, and of the drawing from it of doctrine and admonition to condition our faith and shape our lives, is very different from that which many modern Christians inculcate. And it makes plain as language can tell, that it is the solemn and gracious will of heaven for every one to " mark, learn, and inwardly digest," for living practical use and effect, what is here foreshown of the character and doings of this Beast.

Nor is it difficult to see that the admonition to hear and understand this matter is rooted in the deepest practical necessities. Without a proper idea of the revelation of the final Antichrist, of the grievousness and abominations of his times, of his wonderful career and destiny, of the tribulations which his administrations will inflict, and of the offered privilege of being entirely saved from these awful trials, we cannot half fulfil the Saviour's commands to watch and pray for that salvation, and to aim at being accounted worthy to escape all these things. Without a proper knowledge of the subject treated in this vision, we cannot fully appreciate our Saviour, the offers He makes to us, the redemption He proposes, or the character of the administrations in which His kingdom comes. And particularly for those who are " left," and living on the earth at the time when this Beast comes into power, there is no security, hope, or consolation whatever, except as they understand these things and establish themselves upon them. It will be a time of such " deceivableness of unrighteousness," that if it were possible the very elect would be cheated out of their faith, and deluded to certain perdition. It will be a time of such awful pressure, that no one can maintain himself at all except as he is forewarned, forearmed, and entrenched in the fortifications provided in these revelations. For any one who holds fast to the name of Christ in those days there will be no alternative left but to recant, to accept the mark of the Beast, and go to inevitable perdition with him ; or be driven away into the mountains, the wilderness, the dens and caves of the earth. To hope for deliverance by the sword, or to take up arms against the Beast, can bring no relief ; for if any one will kill with the sword, with the sword must he perish. If any one is ready to accept flight or exile for his safety, into captivity he will have to go, with no pity for him, and no relaxation of the hard necessity. Even the Two miracle-girded Witnesses, who maintain themselves for a time, are eventually overcome and slain ; and no mortal can live where the Beast's power reaches, without letting go Christ for Antichrist.

Many a sore trial of their patience and faith have the saints of God experienced from the persecuting powers of this godless world ; but they will all be as nothing compared with the tribulations of these last evil days. Not under the Chaldean oppressions,—not under the Seleucid despots,—not under the bloody persecutions of the Cæsars,—not under the inquisitions of the Popes,—but " *here* is the patience and the faith of the saints." Under the Antichrist shall all true worshippers be tested and tried as never in all the ages before. Nor can any one hold out faithful then except he be posted and grounded beforehand in the divine teachings concerning the infernal character of the power which then reigns, the sure interference of Heaven for its speedy destruction, and the certain damnation of all who abet its blasphemies or accept its mark.

My dear friends, let me then add a word of solemn caution with regard to this subject. Having listened with so much patient attention to the imperfect sketch I have given, be careful that you do not go away and jest over it as nonsense and imbecility. Remember the words with which this Book of the Apocalypse opens : " Blessed is he who readeth, and those who hear the words of this prophecy, and observe the things which are written in it." Remember also what the holy Apostle appends to it when he says : " I testify unto every man that heareth the words of the prophecy of this Book, If any man shall add unto these things, God shall add unto him the plagues that are written in this Book ; and if any man shall take away from the words of the Book of this prophecy, God shall take away his part out of the Book of Life, and out of the Holy City, and from the things which are written in this Book." Mysterious and impossible as it may all seem to man's ordinary experience and reason, the thing is too overwhelmingly important and solemn to be ridiculed, or to be treated with indifference. Nor can any one tell how vitally his own security and salvation are wrapped up in right apprehensions of these very things. I therefore press the admonition which God Himself has affixed to this particular subject : " If any one hath an ear to hear, let him hear."

LECTURE THIRTY-SECOND

THE ANTICHRIST NOT ALONE—THE RELIGIOUS ELEMENT IN HUMAN SOCIETY—COUNTERFEIT OF THE ADORABLE TRINITY—COMMENTATORS ON THE BEAST FROM THE EARTH—AN INDIVIDUAL PERSON—HIS RISE OUT OF THE EARTH—PERHAPS JUDAS ISCARIOT—HIS TWO LAMB-LIKE HORNS—HIS DRAGON SPEECH—AT ONE WITH THE FIRST BEAST—A SUCCESSFUL OPERATOR—CAUSES "THE EARTH" TO WORSHIP THE BEAST—THE WEIRD ACCOUNT LITERALLY PROBABLE.

REV. 13 : 11, 12. (Revised Text.) And I saw another beast coming up out of the earth, and he had two horns like a lamb, and he was speaking as a dragon. And he exerciseth all the authority of the first beast in his presence, and causeth the earth and those that dwell in it to worship the first beast whose stroke of death was healed.

THE Antichrist, though an individual, is not alone. He not only has the ten sovereignties working into his hand with all "their power and strength," but he has a more intimate and more potent companion, hardly less remarkable than himself, duplicating his power, and without whom he could not be what he is.

When Pharaoh lifted himself up against Jehovah, and against God's two Witnesses, Moses and Aaron, the magicians were summoned as necessary helpers, to compete with their miracles, and to withstand their claims. When Balak, king of Moab, sought to destroy Israel, Balaam was in requisition to prophesy for the king as the arm of his success. When Dan, in marauding avarice, settled in Laish, he must needs have the Levite, son of Gershom, to set up a worship for him, though he had to steal both priest and gods. Absalom, the murderer and fratricide, plotting for his father's throne and life, and warring against God's anointed king, could do but little without Ahithophel to aid his treason, and further his parricidal schemes. Jeroboam, in revolt, found necessity for a new religious administration, with new gods and new observances, requiring priests and prophets to abet his wilfulness. Ahab, the seventh head of the line of Israel, could not have been Ahab except for Jezebel, with her herd of foreign priests. And thus the final Antichrist, of whom these were types and forerunners, cannot be the Antichrist without his great spiritual consociate and false prophet.

The religious element is one of the most powerful in humanity. Its great potency appears in all the history of mankind. It cannot be ignored, suppressed, or put aside. It may be misled and perverted, but its presence and power are inevitable wherever man is man. Nothing can securely stand against it. No other power can be sustained without its aid. True or false, human nature must have a religion. If the state does not provide one it must allow of it, and throw some sanction over it, or it kills itself. There can be no society, no kingdom, no commanding administration without it. Even the French Atheists, who pronounced against all traditional religion, and sought to abolish God, yet glided into one, carved images and idols of Liberty and Equality, offered incense to them, sung hymns to them, and knelt down before them in great civic ceremonials. Napoleon, who became the great military head of this revolution, held it as one of his maxims, that the state cannot live without a religion. Alison has told us how the Emperor, actuated by no spirit of oppression, by no jealousy of a rival authority, but out of what he viewed as essential to the solidity of his empire, sought to connect the Pope with his government, and to establish the See of Rome in close connection and subserviency to himself at Paris. And so the Antichrist, though opposing and exalting himself "above all that is called God, or that is worshipped," still finds it essential to have a religion. Christ is Prophet, Priest, and King ; and he who proposes to take His place, and to be the true Christ as against the incarnate Son of God, must needs fill out the same departments. To do this his Devil wisdom simply inverts the order, assigns to himself the central and all-conditioning position of absolute King, and accepts and adopts a grand religious establishment, whose head and centre is another great Beast, administering in the department of priesthood and prophecy.

The Eternal Power and Godhead is a Trinity. " The true Christian faith is this, that we worship one God in Trinity, and Trinity in Unity ; neither confounding the Persons, nor dividing the Substance. For there is one Person of the Father, another of the Son, and another of the Holy Ghost. But the Godhead of the Father, of the Son, and of the Holy Ghost, is all one, the glory equal, the majesty coeternal. Such as the Father is, such is the Son, and such is the Holy Ghost. The Father uncreate, the Son uncreate, and the Holy Ghost uncreate. The Father incomprehensible, the Son incomprehensible, and the Holy Ghost incomprehensible. The Father eternal, the Son eternal, and the Holy Ghost eternal. And yet they are not three Eternals, but one Eternal. Also there are not three incomprehensibles [or infinities], nor three uncreated ; but one Eternal, and one incomprehensible. So likewise the Father is Almighty, the Son Almighty, and the Holy Ghost Almighty ; and yet they are not three Almighties, but one Almighty. So the Father is God, the Son is God, and the Holy Ghost is God ; and yet they are not three Gods, but one God. So likewise the Father is Lord, the Son Lord, and the Holy Ghost Lord ; and yet not three Lords, but one Lord. For like as we are compelled by the Christian verity to acknowledge every Person by Himself to be God and Lord, so we are forbidden by the Christian religion to say, there be three Gods or three Lords. The Father is made of none, neither created nor begotten. The Son is of the Father alone, not made, nor created, but begotten. The Holy Ghost is of the Father and of the Son, neither made, nor created, nor begotten, but proceeding. So there is one Father, not three Fathers ; one Son, not three Sons ; one Holy Ghost, not three Holy Ghosts. And in this Trinity none is afore, or after other, none is greater or less than another ; but the whole three Persons are coeternal together, and coequal ; so that in all things, as aforesaid, the Unity in Trinity, and the Trinity in Unity is to be worshipped."

The truth of this holy doctrine is evinced and reflected in the copy of it which appears in the constitution of the Devil's grand system as the anti-God. The full embodiment of all evil in our world comes out in an infernal Trinity, the mimicry of eternal realities. First, is the unseen and hidden Father, the Dragon, that old serpent, the Devil. The next is the seven-headed and ten-horned Beast from the sea, " the Son of Perdition," begotten of the Devil, his earthly manifestation, who dies, and revives again, and reappears on earth after having been in the invisible world, as Christ, and is awarded the power and throne of his father the Devil. And to this comes a third, the two-horned Beast from the earth, who proceeds from the Dragon Father and Dragon Son, for his speech is the Dragon's speech, and " he exerciseth all the authority of the first Beast in his presence," carrying into living effect the Satanic will of both the father and the son. Thus we perceive three distinct personalities, the Devil, the Antichrist, and " The False Prophet ; " and these three are one,—one vital essence, one economy, and one administration. The Dragon sets up as the *anti-God ;* the ten-horned Beast, his son, is the *anti-Christ ;* and the two-horned Beast, proceeding from and operating in the interest of both, is the *anti-Holy Ghost.* And these three together are Hell's Trinity in Unity, the Devil's Unity in Trinity, as revealed and operative in our world, when iniquity has once come to the full.

At present we are to consider the third in this infamous Trinity, as exhibited in the vision before us. The Lord God of heaven and earth guide us into a right understanding of His truth !

The first, most direct, and most natural question on the subject is : *Who and what is this Beast, with two horns like a lamb ?* Carrying it to the leading commentators for solution, very confused and contradictory are the answers given. Out of some forty whom I could name, one-half say this Beast is the Pope, or the papacy, or the papal kingdom, or the Roman clergy, or the spiritual Roman Empire, or the various spiritual orders under the papacy ; whilst no one of them is able to define just exactly what he does mean ; for the theory falls so far short of the record that it is continually breaking down in the hands of its defenders. The other half give nearly as many different applications as there are writers. Sir Isaac Newton thinks the Greek Church is this Beast. Galloway thinks the French Republic is intended. Fysh thinks it means the Jesuits. Mulerius thinks it refers to the Roman theologians. Hengstenberg thinks it means the earthy, carnal wisdom, including the heathen philosophies, false doctrines, and the like. Waller says it is " the evil which arises in the Church of Christ." Stuart says it is the heathen priesthood. A nameless writer maintains that it is none other than the principle of the inductive philosophy, the mechanic arts, the mechanical forces. Gebhardt holds that witchcraft and soothsaying, the heathen religion as divination and magic, is meant. Whilst a large number of writers interpret both these Beasts, as well as the image which the second causes to be made to the first, as really one and the same thing, denoting only different aspects of the Romish Church, or the papal system.

To get anything solid out of such presentations is simply impossible. We must therefore abandon entirely the whole system of interpretation which results in such confusion and uncertainty, or conclude, with some, that nothing definitely ascertainable is contained in these prophecies ; in other words, that there is here no revelation at all. The fault has not been in the intentions, the learning, the earnestness, the diligence, or the candour of the men concerned, so much as in the unwarranted prepossessions, misconceptions, and defective methods by which they have approached what God has thus commanded to be written. In the simple straightforward way in which we have been contemplating this momentous Book, taking things as they are given, with all the mysteriousness of the contents difficulties have melted away as we approached them, and everything has come out in thorough self-consistency ; whilst the whole body of Holy Scripture takes on fresh illumination from the plain literal construction of what by special divine aid and direction the apostolic seer has put on record as the outcome of all. And by adhering to the same processes we may also reach some definite idea of what is intended to be foreshown in this vision of the second Beast.

One of the most embarrassing mistakes in the treatment of this vision is the assumption that we dare not here think of an individual person. But why not ? Every item in the record calls for individuality, as do all the relations of the subject. When Jesus told His disciples, " there shall arise false Christs, and false prophets, and shall show great signs and wonders, insomuch that if it were possible they shall deceive the very elect " (Matt. 24 : 24), everyone agrees that he referred to persons ; that is, to individual men, who should severally give themselves out as if they were Christ, or claim to be endowed with all wisdom and power to command the reverence and obedience of their fellows. But when the Saviour thus prophesied of the rise of false prophets, it is impossible to suppose that " the false prophet " which this second Beast is thrice declared to be (chaps. 16 : 13 ; 19 : 20 ; 20 : 10), was not embraced. He certainly is one of those many, nay, the impersonation of them all, as he is by emphasis " *The False Prophet*," as the first Beast is " *The Antichrist*." But being thus one of many whose individuality is conceded on all hands, he must also be of the same kind and nature with the rest ; that is, not a system, church, philosophy, school, corporation, order, or general spirit, but an individual person. Being a prophet, he must, of course, have a doctrine, a system which he puts forth, an economy which he seeks to sustain, and consociates and followers who operate with him ; but with whomsoever or whatsoever coalescing, confederated, or conjoined, he is not the False Prophet on their account, but in his own individual personality. All the prophets that have ever been, whether true or false, pagan, Jewish, or Christian, have been individual persons. And when it comes to " *The* False Prophet," the last and greatest of his class, the very consummation of all false prophets, we would do violence to all language or the use of terms, not to admit and recognize an individual personality. The Beast, as such, is not a person, but a symbol, which covers the whole economy and administration of the False Prophet ; yet, for that very reason, and above all, it includes a personal administrator, in whom the entire thing has its being and centre. It is also impossible for me to conceive how this False Prophet can be made the subject of divine punishments, be cast into the lake of fire, and be kept there in torment from age to age on account of his wickedness, as the record is (Rev. 19 : 20 ; 20 : 10), if he be not a true and real person. Do states, false churches, systems, hierarchies, and the like exist and suffer as such in hell ?

Prophecy and prophetic administration imply inspiration and miraculous power. In the case of true prophets the inspiration is from above, and the power from on high. This Beast is a *false* prophet, the consummation of all false prophets, and his inspiration and power must needs come from beneath. Hence he is represented as coming *up out of the earth*, as the first Beast comes *out of the sea*. If the sea in the one case means the political agitation of peoples, the earth in the other case represents what is more settled and firm in human thought and society. And so we find that the religious sentiments and systems have always been more firm and fixed than political sentiments. A prophet has to do with the religious element ; and the coming of this Beast out of the earth may refer to the evolution of his system out of the religions that have place among men, and the progress of human society with reference to beliefs and spiritual things. But this may not be the whole meaning.

There is a particular oppressor referred to in the tenth Psalm (ver. 15), who is described as " *The Man of the Earth*," and who meets his fate in the great judgment time. According to the uniform patristic application of this Psalm, the reference must be to one or the other of these Beasts ; but, as the first Beast is distinguished as the Beast from *the Sea*, and the second as the Beast from *the Earth*, this " Man of the Earth " must be this second Beast, if either. If so, his particular and emphatic characterization as " the Man of the Earth " so early as the days of David must mean something special and peculiar. The apparition to the witch of Endor came up " out of the earth " (1 Sam. 28 : 13). It was from the spirit-world, usually conceived of in the Scriptures as located under, or in the interior of the earth. Hence a recent writer, with whom I have often found good reason to agree, concludes that this Beast, as to his personality, is a man from the under-world, whom he identifies as Judas Iscariot, returned again to the activities of this world, either by Satanic resurrection, or by some form of obsession, something after the manner of the first Beast, whom he identifies as the Emperor Nero. This would harmonize with the fact that neither of these Beasts dies ; each goes down alive into the lake of fire (chap. 19 : 20). The startling character of the idea is also much relieved when we consider, as Hengstenberg observes, that the separation between earth and hell is at that time very slight, and the communication very easy. Even in the ordinary course of things, either heaven or hell, God or the Devil, spirits from above or spirits from beneath, are always in the background of all the spiritual and supernatural activities upon earth ; and very much more potent will be the putting forth of Hell in those last evil times, when everything pertaining to heaven is largely withdrawn, and all that remains in the earth is mostly abandoned for the time to the rule of the infernal powers. I should not wonder, therefore, if this would turn out to be the true interpretation, namely, that this coming up out of the earth means a coming from the under-world, and that this Man of the Earth, this Beast as to his personality, is, in one sense or another, that very Judas, " Son of Perdition," who betrayed his Lord.* He is at least a man, one who fills the office of a prophet in consociation with the first Beast, one possessed of supernatural powers, and one who has all his inspiration and miraculous potency from beneath, in contrast with that of true prophets, which is from above.

This second Beast has "*two horns like a lamb.*" Horns are the symbols of power ; but these horns have no diadems, and are like the horns of a gentle domestic animal. Political sovereignty, war, conquest, and the strength of military rule are therefore out of the question here. This Beast is a *Prophet*, a spiritual teacher, and not a king or warrior. His power has a certain softness and domesticity about it, which is sharply distinguished from the great, regal horns of the first Beast, although in reality of the same Wild Beast order, and belonging to the same Dragon brood.

What, then, are we to understand by these two lamblike horns, or the two-fold power of this Beast ? Here commentators have been at great loss, and have perpetrated some very absurd things to make their schemes tally with the record. But bearing in mind that the matter relates to a religion and a great religious establishment,—to the head centre of a universal spiritual teaching and worship,—I do not see that close thinkers should have much difficulty on this point.

Taking the whole history of all religions, true and false, from the beginning until now, and searching for the elements of their hold on men's minds, their power, it will be found to reside in two things, which, in the absence of better terms, we may call *naturalism* and *supernaturalism ;* that is, the presence of revelations, or what are accepted as revelations, from the superior powers, and held to be divine and binding ; or conclusions of natural conscience and reason, deemed sacredly obligatory because believed to be good and true. It is difficult to conceive on what other foundation a religion can rest ; and analysis will show that on one or the other of these, or on both combined, all religions do rest, and must rest. Here is the seat of their strength, their power,

* The considerations offered by this writer as favouring this opinion are, that the characteristics of " The False Prophet," as here offered to our notice, were typified in the former life of Judas. Does this beast exercise all the power of the first or kingly beast ? In his betrayal of Jesus Judas appears as leader of the band that took Jesus. He acts out the plans of the wicked Jews. They hated Christ, and he sold himself to them. Is the false prophet partly like a lamb, and partly like a dragon ? Judas meets Jesus with a kiss, and the salutation, " Hail, Master ; " while he says to His enemies, " Hold Him fast." He furthers the wish of the rulers of apostate Israel. He counsels them. He leads the way. He accomplishes their end for them. He professed great love for the poor, yet was influenced by thievish avarice. The false prophet presides over the worship of the empire of Antichrist. Judas was ordained an apostle of the Christian faith. Satan enters him, and he is made an apostle of the devil's son. The false prophet serves three and a half years, and that was the length of time Judas was hypocritically in the service of the Saviour. Does the false prophet do great wonders ? Judas was gifted with miraculous power, even though he was a devil, there is no intimation that it has been revoked, and because of this perhaps it was that Satan took possession of him for his own ulterior designs. Jesus sets him at the head of all unbelievers, as Peter at the head of believers, and said of him that he is a demon. Is the false prophet an instigator and patron of idolatry ? Judas was blindly and persistently covetous, and every " covetous man is an idolater." He was a suicide, like Ahithophel and Nero. He " went and hanged himself." The false prophet instituted a sign or mark for those who follow him ; so did Judas. " He gave them a sign " (Matt. 26 : 48). Parts of 109th Psalm are by inspiration applied to Judas, and the 6th verse must also apply to him : " Set thou a wicked man over him, and let Satan stand at his right hand." If he be the false prophet, the man of sin would be his superior, and Satan his great helper. The words as they stand have never yet been fulfilled ; this would fulfil them. There is something peculiar in the description of what became of Judas after death. He went " to his own place," as if reserved for some future time and work on the side of evil, as the Two Witnesses, Enoch and Elijah, on the side of good. He and the Man of Sin are the only two to whom the title of " *Son of Perdition* " is applied. This is not distinctive of them as going into perdition, for that is the common lot of multitudes of others. A son of perdition is rather one begotten and born of perdition, one that comes forth from hell, which would be most eminently true if they both are Satanically resurrected men, after having been in hell.— See *Apocalypse Expounded,* by Matheetees, *in loc.*

whether true or false, the horns by which they push their way to dominion over the hearts and lives of men. They are just *two*, and no more. As a religionist, therefore, this Beast-Prophet could have but two horns. But he *has* two horns, and hence both the two only powers in a religion ; therefore he is at once a naturalist and a supernaturalist,—a scientist and a spiritualist, —a Rationalist, yet asserting power above ordinary nature and in command of nature. In other words, he claims to be the bearer of the sum total of the Universal Wisdom, in which all reason and all revelation are fused into one great system, claimed to be the ultimatum of all truth, the sublime and absolute *Universeology*. And professing to have everything natural and super-natural thus solved and crystallized as the one eternal and perfect Wisdom, he must necessarily present himself as the one absolute apostle and teacher of all that ought to command the thought, faith, and obedience of man. The possession and exercise of the two horns of religious power certainly can mean nothing less than this.

The same helps to a right idea of the further particular concerning this Beast, to wit, that, though having but the two horns like a lamb, he yet speaks like a Dragon. He is lamblike in that he proposes to occupy only the mild, domestic, and inoffensive position of spiritual adviser. What more gentle and innocent than the counselling of people how to live and act, for the securement of their happiness ! But the words are like the Dragon, in that such professions and claims are in fact the assumption of absolute dominion over the minds, souls, consciences, and hearts of men, to bind them irrevocably, and to compel them to think and act only as he who makes them shall dictate and prescribe. Only to the eternal God belongs such a power ; and when claimed by a crea-ture, is, indeed, the speech of the Devil, the spirit of hell usurping the place and prerogatives of the Holy Ghost.

Hence, also, in so far as this Beast is able to maintain and enforce these prophetic claims, " he exerciseth all the authority of the first Beast." There is no more complete or exalted dominion under the sun than such a sway over the intellect and will of universal humanity. The first Beast, in all his imperial power, has no greater authority than the common acknowledgment of such claims would give. When this is exercised, all the authority of the first Beast is exercised. But the first Beast is quite willing that his hellish consociate should assert and press these claims ; for the two are but different Persons in the same infernal Trinity, the second witnessing to the first, as the Spirit witnesseth to the Son. It is all in the one interest of the Dragon, out of whom the whole administration comes, and it matters not through which of the Persons the Devil work is done, whether by the first Beast as imperial dictator, or by the second as the absolute spiritual adviser and teacher. Therefore the latter exerciseth all the authority of the former, " *in his presence*," with his approbation and consent, and as his consociate and prime minister.

It is not common for great impostors and powers in evil thus to agree. When Mahomet was ruling at Medina there arose another pretender of the same order with himself. The second proposed to make common cause between them, and wrote a letter to Mahomet which read : " From Moseilma, the prophet of Allah, to Mahomet, the prophet of Allah. Come now, let us make a partition of the world, and let half be thine, and half be mine." But Mahomet answered : " From Mahomet, the prophet of God, to Moseilma, *the Liar ;* " and there was nothing but hatred and war between them. When Napoleon, in the grandeur of his power, sought to avail himself of the authority and influence of the Pope, and to endow the pretended See of St. Peter with glory and honour as an instrument of imperial rule, the Pope answered him with a bull of excommunication. When certain vagabond Jews of Ephesus proposed to adorn and dignify themselves with the credit of casting out evil spirits in the Saviour's name the answer came : " Jesus I know, and Paul I know ; but who are ye ? And the man in whom the evil spirit was leaped on them, and overcame them, and prevailed against them, so that they fled out of that house naked and wounded." (Acts. 19 : 15, 16.) But between these last two outgrowths of hell there is a perfect understanding, harmony, and concord. It is Akiba and Barchocebas repeated on a mammoth scale—the Satanic mimicry of the sacred ministrations of the Holy Ghost to the Divine Saviour's cause.

And a most efficient minister does this False Prophet prove to be. Eight times it is written of him that " *he causeth.*" He is a successful executor. And what " he causeth " is the most extraordinary in all the history of false-hood and wickedness. The account is full and specific, and needs to be considered in detail.

First, we have the statement that " *he causeth the earth and those that dwell in it to worship the first beast, whose stroke of death was healed.*"

The meaning of " the earth," distinct from its inhabitants, some represent as a wordiness or pleonasm, meaning only all them that dwell upon the earth. But there is no proof that such is the fact. The Holy Ghost is not liable to load down His utterances with redundancies, as we in our infirmities often do. And I am always suspicious of that sort of exegesis which has occasion to throw out words and phrases from the divine records, as if they meant nothing. If there is any meaning to be attached to the particular statement that this Beast comes up " out of the earth," a corresponding significance must attach to the statement that " the earth," in contradistinction from the dwellers on it, is made to worship the Beast. It may be difficult for us to understand it, but we are not therefore to conclude that there is nothing in it.

If the coming of this Beast " out of the earth " means a coming from the place of depraved spirits, the worshipping ascribed to " the earth " may mean worship rendered by these evil spirits. The statement would then be, that this Beast first of all induces the tenants of the under-world to adore the great Son of perdition, who was wounded to death and became alive again. When it is said that " the whole earth wondered after the Beast," we can readily understand it to mean the inhabitants of the earth ; but when the earth is named separately along with its inhabitants, we can hardly be at liberty to construe it of the inhabitants only. Neither is it impossible for this great miracle-worker, who can cause fire to come down from heaven, and who has power to make an image speak, also to cause the rocks and hills, the woods and trees, the fountains and streams to give forth tokens of acknowledgment and reverence to the great, miraculous, Saviour-omnipotent claimed to be present in this marvellous man.

But, whatever the fact may be with regard to " the earth," there can be no question about " the dwellers in it." They are induced to accept the Beast as the Deity, and to worship him as God. In the first instance, when this man's great wonderfulness and power burst upon the view of the world, the astonishment, admiration, and celebration of him as the Invincible seems to have been spontaneous, a mere wild breaking forth and overflow of astounded popular feeling. But it was evidence of an impression in a direction of which the Devil could well avail himself for the better accomplishment of his ends. The second Beast accordingly appears as a sacred prophet to direct it, reduces it to a system, and enters upon the organization of a new religion, an infernal religion, of which he is the sublime oracle, and the Antichrist the supreme god.

The attempt proves a grand success. " *The earth and those that dwell in it worship the first Beast, whose stroke of death was healed.*" It seems like a fable from the land of dreams—like the wild story in Southey's Thalaba, in which the sorcerers

> Hasten to the inner cave,
> And all fall fearfully around the giant idol's feet,
> Seeking salvation from the power they served.

For here, almost, if not quite, as there, the picture is, that

> Where the sceptre in the idol's hand
> Touched the round altar, in its answering realm,
> Earth felt the stroke, and ocean rose in storms ;
> And ruining cities, shaken from their seats,
> Crushed all their inhabitants.
> His other arm was raised, and its spread palm
> Upbore the ocean weight,
> Whose naked waters arched the sanctuary,
> Sole prop and pillar he.

But, with all the weird strangeness of the record, the literal realization of it is neither impossible nor improbable. The consideration of the arguments and influences by which it is brought about we must reserve for another occasion, but we have only to recur to what *has* been to satisfy ourselves that there is nothing in it to which depraved human nature is not competent, and even predisposed and prone. Alexander was but a young man when he died, and never was more than a natural man ; yet he claimed and received divine honours as a god. Reading in Homer that the ancient heroes were sons of gods, he did not see that they were any better than himself, and hence began to think himself the son of Jupiter, and so announced to the priests, who oracularly proclaimed him such, and exhorted all inquirers to render to their victorious king the honours of a deity. The vile and infamous Antiochus Epiphanes was awarded an apotheosis, and assigned a place among the holy gods in the worship of Egypt. Herod, with all his baseness and his crimes, was hailed as a god, and took it as his due. (Acts 12 : 21–23.) Julius Cæsar was honoured as a god, and after his death many temples were raised and frequented for his worship. Statues, temples, altars, and trophies were consecrated to Augustus Cæsar. Tiberius rendered sacred homage to his statues, and also accepted similar honours to himself and his favourite, Sejanus. Trajan worshipped Nerva, and honoured him with a chief priest, with altars, and with sacred gifts. The younger Pliny proclaimed it as Trajan's due, that his statue should be cut in ivory, or cast in gold, and that the choicest victims should be sacrificed to his divinity. Caligula claimed to be a god, clothed himself with the acknowledged names of deity, assumed the attributes and ornaments of all the divinities, accepted temples, prayers, offerings, and sacrifices as pertaining to him, appointed a college of priests, consisting of all the richest men in Rome, to superintend the ceremonies of honour and worship to his sacred majesty. He even boasted that every nation of the earth, except the Jews, adored and worshipped him. The King of Parthia, kneeling before Nero, said to him : " You are my God, and I am come to adore you as I adore the sun. My destiny is to be determined by your supreme will ; " to which Nero replied : " I make you King of Armenia, that the whole universe may know it belongs to me to give or to take away crowns." Domitian filled the world with his statues, to which sacrifices were continually offered, and required that all letters written or published in his name should always begin, " Our Lord and God commands." And so common, universal, and stoutly demanded was this worship of the successors of the Cæsars, that the chief reason for the martyrdom of the Christians of their day was, that they would not sacrifice to the emperor as God.

It may be said that these were ancient, pagan, and benighted times, and that such abominations can never again be palmed upon mankind. But they were the times which produced our classics. The same has also occurred in later days, with far less reason or apology, and among those who claimed to be the most advanced and enlightened of mortals. How was it in the comparatively recent period of the French Revolution ? How was it with those world-renowned *savants*, whose boast was to dethrone the King of heaven as well as the monarchs of the earth ? Did they not sing halleluias to the busts of Marat and Lepelletier, not only in the streets of Paris and Brest, but in many of the churches all over France ? How came it that Robespierre was named and celebrated as a divinity, a superhuman being, "The New Messiah !" Can we blot out what Alison, and Lacretelle, and Thiers have written, that "Marat was universally deified," that the churches received his statues as objects of sacred regard, and that a new worship was everywhere set up in their honour ? Is it to be ignored how the foremost men of the nation, in state ceremony, conveyed a woman in grand procession to the Cathedral of Notre Dame, unveiled and kissed her before the high altar as the Goddess of Reason, and exhorted the multitude to cease trembling before the power-less thunders of the God of their fears, and "sacrifice only to such as this ?" Nay, at this very hour, there resides a man in the city of Rome, whom one-half of Christendom itself hails, honours, and adores as the Vicar of Jesus Christ, the Vicegerent of God upon earth, Infallible, and sole possessor of the Keys of heaven,—a man whom the greater festivals exhibit as a Divinity, borne along in solemn procession on the shoulders of consecrated priests, whilst sacred incense fumes before him, and blest peacocks' feathers full of eyes wave beside his moving throne, and every mortal on the street where he passes, uncovers, kneels, and silently adores ;—a man who, once a year, takes his seat upon the high altar of the sublimest church in Christendom, in the broad light of this favoured century, and there receives the adoration of the whole college of his most exalted subjects, who reverently bow amid chants, music, and burning lights to kiss the toe of "His Holiness !"

Let there come, then, a man from among the distinguished dead ; let him prove by signs evident that he is verily a great emperor returned to life again ; let him show the intelligence, the energy, the invincible power, and whatever else has made and marked the glory of the mighty, and let there come with him a great prophet to exercise all this power in the one direction of a new universal religion, advising and urging with eloquence and miracle, in the name of the absolute Wisdom, the worship and adoration of that man, as the only right worship in the universe ; and what is there in humanity to with-stand the appeal ! As surely as man is man, the same that he has hitherto been, it will and must be a grand success. As certain fact, the Saviour so anticipated, and says, that if it were possible to break Jehovah's promises, the very elect would be deceived.

There is, then, to be a new religion for our world, as scientists and reformers already claim and proclaim. It will also be a powerful and universal religion. It will ground itself in pretensions to the profoundest wisdom, intelligence, reason, truth, and progress. It will sway the earth, and carry with it all who are not written in the Lamb's book of life. It will be the final coronation of the progressivism of human perfectibility. But it will be a religion whose God is Antichrist, and whose sacraments are the seals of damnation, inevitable and eternal. God save us from unfaithfulness to His Gospel, that the "strong delusion" which leaves no hope may never touch any one who hears this warning of what is to come !

LECTURE THIRTY-THIRD

THE FALSE PROPHET CONTINUED—THE CONDITION OF THINGS WHEN HE COMES—HOW HE IMPOSES ON THE WORLD—MIRACLES TRUE AND FALSE—MAKING FIRE COME DOWN FROM HEAVEN—HIS ARGUMENT FROM THE SUPERNATURAL CHARACTER OF THE BEAST—THE IMAGE OF THE BEAST—ARGUMENTS FOR IT—THE CAUSING OF IT TO SPEAK—THE ADMINISTRATION COMPLETE—THE BLOODY TYRANNY—THE MARKING—THE HELPLESSNESS AND HOPELESSNESS OF MEN UNDER THE BEAST—WISDOM CONCERNING HIS NAME.

REV. 13 : 14–18. (Revised Text.) And he doeth great miracles, so that he even maketh fire come down from the heaven to the earth in the presence of men, and he deceiveth those that dwell on the earth by reason of the signs which it was given him to work in the presence of the beast, saying to those who dwell on the earth they should make an image to the beast, which had the stroke of the sword, and lived.

And it was given him to give spirit to the image of the beast, that the image of the beast should even speak, and should cause that as many as would not worship the image of the beast should be killed.

And he causeth all, the small and the great, and the rich and the poor, and the free and the bond to receive a mark [χάραγμα, *stamp* or *brand*] on their right hand, or on their forehead, that no one shall be able to buy or sell except he who has the mark, the name of the beast or the number of his name.

Here is the wisdom. Let him who hath understanding reckon the number of the beast ; for it is a number of a man, and the number of him is 666.

In the last Lecture we were engaged in considering the Beast from the earth, the False Prophet, the consociate and prime minister of the final Antichrist. We then saw something of his origin, his character, the sphere of his operations, the nature of his pretensions, and his success in introducing a new universal worship, or religion. But we did not then get through with him. It remains to be considered how he imposes on the world, and what oppressive and murderous use he makes of his power. The Lord help us to understand the matter truly !

Before proceeding directly to the subject it may be well to glance first at the antecedent state of things, by which the way is paved for his operations. No great movements or revolutions in human affairs ever come without preparative conditions and causes, some preliminary plantings which gradually mature until they ripen into the great ultimate results. It was so with the reformation wrought by Christ. It was so in the reformation which culminated in connection with the labours of Martin Luther. It has been so in science and philosophy. It has been so in every great political revolution. And when such gigantic changes and disasters come as foreshown in this chapter, they necessarily have had their roots in something which has gone before, of which they are the fruits, and which the nature of the times has served to favour and develop. Nor have the Scriptures failed to indicate various preliminary conditions and forerunners which serve to introduce the final false Christ and his abominations.

Speaking of the Man of Sin and his doings, Paul writes that that day shall not come, " *except there come a falling away first.*" There is then to be a general sinking from the true faith, and the substitution of human conceits, philosophies, and " science falsely so called," in the place of the divine verities, eating away the substance of true religion, and dissolving its hold on the hearts and minds of men. Such a terrible deceit could not be unless all society were first thoroughly corrupted. And so it will be. The Apostle says : "Know this, that in the last days perilous times shall come ; for men shall be lovers of their own selves, covetous, boasters, proud, blasphemers, disobedient to parents, unthankful, unholy, without natural affection, truce-breakers, false accusers, incontinent, fierce, despisers of those that are good, traitors, heady, highminded, lovers of pleasures more than lovers of God ; having a form of godliness, but denying the power thereof ; "—times " when they will not endure sound doctrine, but after their own lusts shall heap to themselves teachers, having itching ears ; and shall turn away their ears from the truth, and shall be turned unto fables." (2 Tim. 3 : 1–6 ; 4 : 3, 4.) Among the active causes of all this we are forewarned of a certain boastful and blatant scientism and naturalism which does not hesitate dogmatically to negative the doctrines of faith, and likewise of a demonic spiritualism, which denies that Jesus Christ has come, or is to come, in any literal sense, and sets up quite other revelations as the hope and dependence of the world. In so many words, it is affirmed " there shall come in the last days scoffers, walking after their own lusts, and saying [as a matter of doctrine and science], Where is the promise of His coming ? for since the fathers fell asleep, all things continue as they were from the beginning of the creation ; " and furthermore, " that in the latter times some [certain men] shall depart from the faith, giving heed to seducing spirits *and teachings of demons*, speaking lies in hypocrisy, forbidding to marry, and commanding to abstain from meats." (2 Pet. 3 : 3, 4 ; 1 Tim. 4 : 1–3.) As a necessary concomitant and result, we are further told of a perturbed, restless, and disabled condition in political affairs, a weakening of the laws, an unmanageableness of things of state and social order, making all the old formulæ and codes of none effect, and engulfing the whole world in a quagmire of confusion, from which there is no retreat, and whence the only prospect is of worse disaster ahead. The Saviour assures us that as before the flood " the earth was corrupt before God, and was filled with violence," justice and law having been supplanted by the base will of the corrupt multitude, *so* it shall be when the present world nears its end. (Matt. 24 : 37–39.) Besides, it is a time when the patience of God is about wearied out with the perverseness and inventions of the wicked,—when judgment has commenced,—when the One who hinders the revelation of the Man of Sin is taken away,—when the Holy Ghost, so long grieved and insulted, begins to withdraw from the world then approaching its doom,—when the holiest and best of earth's population is taken away, caught up to the heavenly pavilion,—when the very candlestick of sacred illumination is removed,—when they that love not the truth are given over, judically blinded, and allowed a loose rein to believe lies and hasten their own damnation,—when the doors of the abyss are unlocked, and the powers of perdition are given wider liberties,—and when Satan is angered to the intensest degree, because he knows that " he hath but a short time." And in this crisis and condition of things, when evil is ready to bloom forth in final maturity, and every form of it is confluent, and all that impeded it has wellnigh disappeared, the great embodiment of Hell's subtlety and deceit begins his ministry. The world, having rejected the Evangely of God, is therefore ripe and ready for the Gospel of the Devil, and his great Apostle comes.

Observe, then, in the next place, by what means this Prophet brings the world to his unholy cause.

We have seen what his pretensions are. We have seen that he has the two horns, *i.e.*, all the powers by which a religion, as such, makes its way upon the minds and hearts of men. We have seen that he presents himself as the bearer and interpreter of the absolute truth, the master and prophet of all that can rightfully demand the attention and obedience of any being. And what he thus professes and claims, he also proposes to prove and demonstrate, by exhibiting a supernatural control of all the forces and powers of Nature.

" *And he doeth great miracles. . . . And he deceiveth those that dwell on the earth by reason of the signs which it was given him to work in the presence of the Beast.*"

Miracles have ever been the chief evidence of the presence of what is worshipful and divine. It is by these especially that men's faith is begotten and controlled. It is by seeing and experiencing what is manifestly above and beyond all natural human power, and what cannot be accounted for on natural principles, that the human mind is forced to a conviction of the presence of some great and worshipful potency superior to Nature. It was by such demonstrations that Moses evidenced Jehovah's almightiness and his own legation as Jehovah's prophet, till the most inveterate unbelief was compelled to admit and confess that here was " the finger of God." It was one of the ways in which Jesus proved His Messiahship, and established for all ages that He is a teacher sent from God ; for, as Nicodemus said, no man could do the miracles which he did, except God were with him. Paul, in enumerating the powers by which he persuaded the Gentiles to faith in the Gospel, says, that it was in very deed the power of signs and wonders which Christ did by him in the power of the Holy Ghost, that he made his conquests. (Rom. 15 : 18.) And this arch-prophet of falsehood knows well how needful and mighty is the force of miracles to establish his credit, and to secure belief in his claims. The religion of God is a religion of miracles, and to make his infernal deception appear the only true and rightful religion, he needs to mimic and counterfeit all that supernaturalism on which the true faith reposes. To this, therefore, he sets himself, and becomes one of the greatest workers of signs and wonders the earth has ever seen.

Nor need we be surprised at this. There is a supernatural power which is *against* God and truth, as well as one *for* God and truth. A miracle, simply as a work of wonder, is not necessarily of God. There has always been a devilish supernaturalism in the world, running alongside of the supernaturalism of divine grace and salvation. " Aaron cast down his rod before Pharaoh and his servants, and it became a serpent." Here was divine miracle. But Pharaoh went and called his wise men and sorcerers, and " the magicians of Egypt also did in like manner with their enchantments ; for they cast down every man his rod, and they became serpents." Here was devil miracle, in imitation of the divine. In the same way the turning of the waters to blood was counterfeited, as also the plague of frogs. Only when it came to the creation of swarms of insect life, did the magicians give up, and admit that this was beyond their power. (See Exod., chaps. 7, 8 and 9.) So, again (in Deut. 13 : 1–5), God assumes and asserts that there may be supernatural revelations in behalf of idol worship ; for He gives it as a law for His people : " If there arise among you a prophet, or a dreamer of dreams, and giveth thee a sign or a wonder, and the sign or the wonder come to pass whereof he spoke unto thee, saying. Let us go after other gods, which thou hast not known, and let us serve them ; thou shalt not hearken unto the words of that prophet, or that dreamer of dreams ; for the Lord your God proveth you, to know whether ye love the Lord your God with all your heart and with all your soul." So the Saviour tells us that many will come up in the day of judgment, saying, " Lord, Lord, have we not prophesied in thy name, and in thy name cast out devils ? and in thy name have done many wonderful works (*all manner of miracles*) ?   And then I will profess unto them, I never knew you ; depart from me, ye that work iniquity." (Matt. 7 : 12, 23.) Of the " false Christs and false prophets " whom he foretold, he says they " *shall show great signs and wonders.*" (Matt. 24 : 24.) Paul says of Antichrist, and the doings in connection with him, that his " coming is after the working of Satan, with *all power, and signs, and lying wonders.*" (2 Thess. 2 : 9.) " Lying wonders " does not mean *unreal* wonders, mere trick, jugglery, and legerdemain ; but wonders *wrought for the support of lies*, that is, *devil miracles*. Mere pretended miracles have nothing of miraculous power ; but in this case the worker comes " *with all power.*" There is no emptiness or unreality about them. They are genuine miracles, wrought in the interests of Hell's falsehoods. The test of a miracle is its supernaturalness ; the test of its source, is the doctrine, end, or interest for which it is wrought. If in support of anything contrary to God and His revealed will and law, it is no less a miracle ; but in that case it is a work of the Devil ; for God cannot contradict himself. (See 1 John 4 : 1–3.) It is also plainly intimated in the Divine Word, that, in judgment upon the wicked world for its refusal of Christ, and its setting at naught of all the divine miracles, the present bonds and limitations of Satanic power will be relaxed, the Devil and his demons allowed freer range upon this planet, and those in love with falsehood and unrighteousness given over to delusions then so much stronger than ever before. (See 1 Kings 22 : 18, 22 ; 2 Chron. 18 : 18, 22 ; Isaiah 6 : 9, 10 ; Ezek. 14 : 9 ; Rom. 1 : 21, 25, 28 ; 2 Thess, 2 : 11, 12.) It is therefore in strict accord with all history and revelation, that the consummate False Prophet " *doeth great miracles*, and deceiveth those that dwell on the earth by reason of the signs which it was given him [permitted him of God] to work."

An example of these great miracles is described. The power of the False Prophet extends so far, " *that he even maketh fire come down from the heaven to the earth in the presence of men.*" It is useless to talk of trickery and mere sham in this case. Of the rebels, in chapter 20, it is said : " Fire came down from God out of heaven, and devoured them ; " and of the Two Witnesses it is said : " If any one willeth to injure them, fire issueth out of their mouth, and devoureth their enemies." (Chap. 11 : 5.) In both these instances we have literal fire ; for it consumes men ; and the same terms in this case must mean the same thing. Nor is it the first time Satan shows his power over the fire and lightnings of heaven. When God allowed him to assail and tempt Job, the report came : " The fire of God is fallen from heaven, and hath burned up the sheep and the servants, and consumed them." (Job 1 : 16.) It was Satan who directed and brought down that fire ; so then he is able to do again for his own great Prophet. There is also special reason why this particular miracle should be wrought at this time. The Two Witnesses showed this command over fire, and it was necessary to offset it by something of the same character. Besides, it was the test by which Elijah proposed to decide between the Godhead of Baal and Jehovah, insisting that " *the God that answereth by fire* " is to be accepted as the true God. And " the fire of the Lord fell " at the call of Elijah, and thus settled the question of Jehovah's Deity and majesty over against the impotent Baal. (1 Kings 18.) There needs therefore to be a meeting of that test on the part of this new Prophet, in order to make out his claim, as over against the God of the Bible. And as men refuse to abide by the *Jehovah*-answer by fire, this man is permitted to imitate that test, that it may appear how very ready and facile wicked people are to believe the Devil's miracles in preference to those of God.

Whether the fire in this case is allowed to be used for destruction, as it was in the ministry of Elijah, is not said ; but it certainly comes, and it comes " *in the presence of men* "—*men*, not babes, not idiots, not imbeciles. The subtle performer anticipates all suspicions of imposture, and provides against the possibility of having it said that it is nothing but a cheat, a mere piece of cunningly-devised pyrotechnics. When it comes to supernaturalism and miracle, people call for an open field, a fair test, the exclusion of every chance for collusion, and thorough care against deception by mechanical contrivances or a better knowledge than they have of nature's laws. The sceptical heart of man is jealous of miracles. But here every demand is met ; for the whole world is convinced, and all its science satisfied. Out of the open sky, on the broad plain, in the clear light of day, under the keen scrutiny of the keenest adepts of science, before the most competent of witnesses, this agent of perdition calls, and the fire comes and descends to the earth, attested as an unmistakable reality !

Every year, at Easter time, the Greek patriarch at Jerusalem goes through the farce of calling down fire from heaven, by which all the lamps of the Greek churches and shrines are lit for that year. Dean Stanley, from having been an eye-witness, has given a graphic account of the proceeding, and the terrific furore which attends it.* But there, the one who gets the fire is locked up alone in the darkness of a ceiled and covered vault, and no one sees the fire until it is put forth through an aperture at the top of the cell. No sensible person is deceived by it. It stands acknowledged a poor and disgraceful trick. It is not so in this case, for here every one's scruples are satisfied. The closest investigators and observers see and confess that the miracle is genuine, and are persuaded that the god of this man *is* divine, even on Elijah's test, though without doing full justice to Elijah's case.

Thus substantiating his own professions, this infernal Prophet points next to the supernatural character of the man whom he seeks to have adored. Hengstenberg agrees that the reason or ground on which the worship of the ten-horned Beast is solicited and urged, is the continually repeated and tremendously emphasized fact, that he was wounded to death, and that the stroke of his death was healed. With all his wonderful power, wisdom, and greatness, this is his sublimest personal characteristic ; and on this account the adoration of him is chiefly founded.

It is on account of Christ's obedience unto death and resurrection from the dead, that He has His place and glory, as the head of all power, and the object of worship, honour, and blessing. The songs of heaven are to " the Lamb *that was slain.*" The Antichrist is the mimic Christ ; and he must have honour too, because he died and is alive again. Though " Christ died for our sins, according to the Scriptures, and was buried, and rose again the third day, according to the Scriptures," and " showed Himself alive after His passion by many infallible proofs," and after forty days was visibly taken up into heaven, whence also He shed forth a regenerating and miraculous power, proving that He is forever exalted at the right hand of the Father almighty, worthy of the everlasting adoration of all creatures ; still the wicked world will not believe in Him, nor award Him the honour that is His due. But when the Antichrist comes, because he died of a sword-wound, and went to his fitting perdition, and reappears from out the abyss, it will be preached, and taught, and argued that he above all is worthy of the homage, credit, and worship of mankind ! And because a miracle-working prophet says so, and because they have the infernal Beast in his grand administrations before their eyes, they who could see no reason for hearkening to the miracle-working Apostles, listen, and are persuaded in favour of this new gospel, and agree that the foul monster shall be their Lord and only Deity !

And to make the infamous delusion the more easy and effective, this False Prophet avails himself further of the abomination which has been the besetting sin of the race, the great defilement of the ages. I cannot explain exactly what it is, but there has always been a peculiar witchery in the worship of idols. Even Aaron himself was persuaded to make a golden calf, and within hearing of the thunder of God's almightiness the people gathered themselves together, and paid willing homage to the similitude of an ox that eateth grass. This infernal messenger knows the advantage to be gained from this strange proneness of mankind, and therefore he counsels and directs, as the chosen method for giving due homage to the god, that " *they should make an image to the Beast which had the stroke of the sword, and lived.*" A statue was to be constructed ; and it was to be at once a statue " *to* the Beast," and " *of* the Beast,"—a material likeness of himself, set up in sacred honour of his majesty. Hengstenberg observes that *one* image is spoken of, " but in regard to the sense a multitude of images is meant." If so, this would give a sort of ubiquitous presence to the Beast, and would greatly facilitate his worship in all parts of his dominion. The vision, however, without excluding the idea of multiplication, contemplates but one original, which, according to other passages bearing on the subject, has its location at Jerusalem, and finds its way into the temple built for Jehovah, and is there set up as " the abomination

* Sinai and Palestine, pp. 464–470.

of desolation spoken of by Daniel the prophet." (Dan. 9 : 27 ; 11 : 45 ; Matt. 24 : 15 ; 2 Thess. 2 : 4.)

The worship of such a statue would be the worship of the Man himself, for this was the understanding and meaning of all image-worship. It is on this idea that Rome sanctions the veneration of images of Christ, the Virgin, and other saints. Chrysostom says : " When the images of the emperor are sent down and brought into a city, its rulers and multitude go out to meet them with carefulness and reverence, not honouring the tablet or the representation moulded in wax, but the standing of the emperor." Hence Basil says : " The image of the emperor is also called the emperor, because honour paid to the image passes to the original." " He that honours not the image, honours not the person represented." So also Athanasius says : " He who worshippeth the image, in it worshippeth the emperor ; for the image is his form and likeness." And so in all the history of ancient Rome, whatsoever was done to the statue of a god or man, was construed as done to him whose statue it was. The making of this image of and to the Beast is therefore a formulation of *the worship* of the Beast.

Nor is it difficult to trace what sort of arguments will be brought to bear for the making of this image. In the ages of great worldly glory and dominion statues were raised to the honour of the great of every class, but who of all the great ones of the earth is so great as the Antichrist ! Statues have ever been common for the commemoration of great events ; but what greater event and marvel has ever occurred than that in the history of this man, in that he was wounded to death, and yet is restored to life and activity, with far sublimer qualities than he possessed in his first life ? How much more worthy of memorialization this than the scar of Scipio, or the appearance of a star supposed to be miraculous which Octavianus commemorated on the conse-crated image of his imperial foster-father ? If the grand old Romans thus honoured their human emperors and benefactors, why withhold this veneration from one so evidently and eminently superhuman ? And who will there be among the proud sons of earth to stand out against such arguments ? The leaders of the apostate world will cheerfully acquiesce in the pre-eminent propriety of such a memorial, and an image of the beast, and to his sacred honour, is made and set up, particularly emphasizing his great characteristic, that he once was wounded to death, and that he has come back to life again with his death-wound healed.

But with the image constructed and in its place, another hellish wonder is wrought, perhaps the most marvellous of all the doings of this minister of perdition. " The idols of the heathen are silver and gold ; they have mouths, but *they speak not*." (Is. 35 : 15, 16.) But the powers of falsehood have by this time become mightier than of old. To the False Prophet it is given " *to give spirit to the image of the Beast, that the image of the Beast should even speak*." The unbelieving may laugh, and sneer, and say, " It is nonsense and impossi-bility." And so, indeed, it may be to them and their power. But, of old, it was written, " Woe to him that saith to the wood, *Awake !* to the dumb stone, *Arise, it shall teach*." (Hab. 2 : 19.) And here is the man who does it. For thus it stands recorded in the Revelation of God. And when it comes to pass, men will be only the more carried away by it, because of their previous unbelief of the possibility of anything of the sort. As God's word is true, and heaven and earth will sooner pass away than one jot or tittle of it go unfulfilled, *this thing will be done.* As the power of God restores breath and life to the Two Witnesses, so shall this arch magician have power to give animation and speech to this dead statue. And why not ? The infernal power which brings up a dead man from the abyss, and reinstates him in all the activities of a new life of wonder and greatness, certainly can be at no loss to make an image speak, and through its metallic mouth to give forth his oracles. Old Pagan and Christian writers have recorded instances in which the idols spake, and gave forth oracles. The papists affirm the same veritable truth concerning some of their images. The Hindoos to this day hold and maintain that a degree of life and supernatural power takes possession of their images when solemnly consecrated according to the prescribed ceremonies. And we are hardly warranted in declaring that it is all falsehood and misbelief. But if there be no truth or reality in these affirmations and beliefs, the thing will become literal fact under the ministrations of this son of perdition. This image *speaks ;* and the closest observation of all the science, wisdom, and scepticism of the time is satisfied of the fact. There will be no machinery, no collusion, no make-believe, no trick or deceit about it ; for the whole world is convinced. The image *speaks.* Oracles and commands come out of the dead metal. People may institute and apply what tests they please, and scrutinize with all the science the earth affords, but the result of all is the universal admission, that *the image does speak.* The Scriptures cannot be broken ; and John, in the spirit saw, and has written it down by command of God, that " *it was given the False Prophet to give spirit to the image of the Beast, that the image of the Beast should even speak.*" The Beast is supernatural ; the False Prophet is supernatural ; and the image, though made by man, likewise takes on of the supernatural ; and all the *savants* of the time agree and maintain that it is even so. They cannot help it. They cannot hold out against absolute demonstration.

Thus it is, then, that the False Prophet imposes on the world, wins credence to his professions and claims, and sways the public sentiment to the acknowledgment of a new divinity, demanding a new religion, whose vulgar abominations are thought but right and reasonable.

But with the grand machinery thus organized and completed in a Devil church united with a Devil state, the consummated Devil-rule goes into full effect. With the Beast systematically deified, an image set up and consecrated to his adoration, and the testimony, argument, and eloquence of a great miracle-working Prophet ringing through the world in his behalf, the Oracle speaks and the edicts issue—edicts from which we would think Pandemonium itself would recoil with horror. Behold, and see, the " Liberty, Equality, and Fraternity " which the unbelieving world so much adores, when once fully matured and put into universal command.

There be some in those days who cannot accept the new worship,—elect ones whom God has written in the Lamb's book of life, who cannot be deceived. There be Jews, with whose being it is ingrained never to accept the worship of an idol, and Christian believers, whom nothing can buy over to an abomination so foul and blasphemous. The voice of God's Two Witnesses is heard over against the grand speeches and miracles of the False Prophet, and some there be who take heed to its warnings, and keep themselves aloof from the terrible idolatry. But how do these fare at the hands of this sublimated embodiment of the supreme Reason and finished Progress of which it prates ? Where is the " Liberty, Equality, and Fraternity " for them ? From the mouth of the image, by the sanction of the great Prophet, and by the authority of the idolized Beast, the demand is, " *that as many as will not worship the image of the Beast shall be killed.*"

Abbé Barruel has told us about the worshippers of Liberty and Equality in France, how that on a great civic occasion at Brest, while the municipal officers, the justices of the peace, the tribunal, and the National Guards, were lying self-prostrated before a carved image of Mirabeau, some one whose conscience pricked him exclaimed : " Wretches, you are guilty of idolatry ! " but his voice being heard above the noise of drums and trumpets, the adorers of the idol at once cried out : " *Kneel down, or you shall die !* " But what was only mad impulse and sudden fury then, is finally framed into a great imperial enactment, into a sacred universal *law,* which admits of no exceptions and no exemptions. No one, of any class or race, is allowed to live under the dominion of these Beasts, if unwilling to conform to the worship they set up.

Hence the flight of the Woman into the wilderness, her miraculous help and defence, where the Beast endeavors in vain to overwhelm her.

Thus, in the name of Democracy and popular rights, comes absolute Dictatorship and Imperialism ; in the name of Freedom, comes complete and universal enslavement ; in the name of the better Reason, which tramples on religion and Revelation, comes a great consolidated system of gross idolatry ; in the name of a charitable Liberalism, which disdains allegiance to any creed, comes a bloody Despotism, which compels men to worship the base image of a baser man, *or die!* Here is one star in the crown of this world's boasted Progress.

But the religion of Christ has its holy Sacraments ;—its mark of baptismal consecration on the forehead, and its pledges of sacred fellowship and communion given into the hands. This god of the godless also travesties these. The subjects of Antichrist must show their allegiance and wear the badge of their infernal Lord. The False Prophet " *causeth all, the small and the great, and the rich and the poor, and the free and the bond, to receive a* χάραγμα, *a stamp or brand, on their right hand, or on their forehead.*" As masters in old time branded their slaves, and as owners of stock brand and mark their cattle, so are the people branded under the Antichrist. Declining the Baptism of Christ, they must take upon their bodies the sign and seal that they are sold and held as the goods and chattels of hell ! Money and place cannot buy them off. The rich and great are not exempted any more than the poor. The master must submit the same as the veriest slave. The ten kings themselves lie under the inexorable requirement.

The " mark " itself is at once a number and a name. The Apostle tells us what it is. As he gives it, it is made up of two Greek characters which stand for the name of Christ, with a third, the figure of a crooked serpent, put between them, χξς, the name of God's Messiah transformed into a Devil sacrament. This horrid sign must every one receive on one of the most conspicuous parts of the body, cut, stamped, or branded in, there to abide indelibly. No one may either " buy or sell " without this " mark," and all who do receive it take upon their bodies the token and seal of their damnation !

To believe on the Lord Jesus Christ, and to be baptized into His name, for the washing away of sin, and the securement of eternal life, is too much for some people. It is to them an humiliating nonsense, to which their superior dignity cannot stoop. But when the Devil-Messiah comes, in him they will believe and trust ; to him they will sell themselves, and to his branding-irons they will submit as helpless slaves and cattle, with no choice but to yield or die ; and yielding, to perish everlastingly. I say, *perish everlastingly*, for there is no more salvation for any one upon whom is this " mark." From heaven the clear, distinct, and awful sentence is : " If any man worship the Beast and his image, and receive his mark in his forehead, or in his hand, the same shall drink of the wine of the wrath of God, which is poured out without mixture into the cup of his indignation ; and he shall be tormented with fire and brimstone in the presence of the holy angels, and in the presence of the Lamb ; and the smoke of their torment ascendeth up for ever and ever ; and they have no rest day nor night, who worship the Beast and his image, *and whosoever receiveth the mark of his name.*" (Chap. 14 : 9–11.) This also proves that this Beast is not the Pope ; for not all under the Pope are lost. And it is just for the eternal ruin of such as will not accept the true and only Christ that this monster is permitted. People dislike the truth and refuse to obey the holy Gospel, and this minister of hell is allowed to make them the victims of his awful delusions that they may reap the fruits of their unbelief. And all is thus mercifully foreshown, that they may see and know to what a consummation their antichristian philosophies, beliefs, philanthropies, reforms, and proud self-will in sacred things is tending, and so learn righteousness before it is too late. God's Christ rejected is the opening of the soul to the Devil's Messiah, to the great impersonated lie of the universe, whose meretricious good is but the lure to infinite degradation and eternal death. And when men's dissatisfaction with the Lord's Christ and His institutes has worked itself out, and the seeds which it generates have come to their ripened fruits, they will find themselves in the position of slaves and cattle of a mighty tyrant, against whom they can do nothing but hold still, and receive upon their flesh the indelible seal of inevitable damnation.

Hence the peroration with which the vision closes. If men wish light, they can find it in these showings. If they wish to be wise, " here is wisdom." And if any one hath understanding, let him learn the number of the Beast and stand aloof. The arithmetic of it, and the hidden indication which it carries of the precise man who is to be the final Antichrist, need not concern us much. The endless guesses and experiments with which expositors have occupied themselves and their readers on this point can be of very little practical worth to us. When the monster comes, " the righteous shall understand." Our business is rather to reckon up the number of the Beast as to his moral identification. It is here that the chief stress falls, and where the greatest exposure lies. The figures 666 may spell *Nero Cæsar* in Hebrew, and " *the Latin,*" in Greek ; but whether this is certainly what the Spirit meant, no one can now tell ; neither would it help us if we knew. The wisdom here, as required by us, is the wisdom to detect and discern the antichristian badness, the ill principles which lay men open to Antichrist's power, the subtle atheism and unfaith by which people are betrayed into his hands. *Six* is the bad number, and when multiplied by tens and hundreds, it denotes evil in its greatest intensity and most disastrous manifestation. This number of the Beast's name thus gives his standing in the estimate of heaven, and fixes attention on that rather than on the numerical spelling of the name he bears on earth. If we can only know the principles pertaining to his badness ; if we can only have understanding to detect his spirit which already works so powerfully in so many specious forms about us, we shall have accomplished the most needful reckoning of the number of his name. And without this, we may be carrying his damning " mark " upon our souls, even whilst we think ourselves forearmed against his power by what we have discovered of the word by which his contemporaries designate him. The moral insight into his nature is the wisdom we require, rather than the orthography of the name by which he is called. In this, therefore, let us try to skill our souls, cleaving ever to our only Lord God, and His Son Jesus Christ our Saviour, in the meekness of a confiding faith and obedience, that no marks or stains of the Beast, or his abominations, even in spirit, may ever be found upon our souls.

LECTURE THIRTY-FOURTH

Rev. 14 : 1–13. (Revised Text.) And I saw, and behold, the Lamb standing on the mount Sion, and with Him an 144,000, having His name and His Father's name written on their foreheads.

And I heard a sound out of the heaven as a sound of many waters, and as a sound of great thunder : and the sound which I heard [was] as of harp-singers harping with their harps. And they sung a new song in the presence of the throne, and in the presence of the four Living Ones and the Elders : and no one was able to learn the song but the 144,000 who have been redeemed from the earth. These are they who were not defiled with women, for they are virgins ; these [are] they who follow the Lamb whithersoever He goeth ; these were redeemed from men, a first-fruit to God and to the Lamb ; and in their mouth was not found what is false ; they are blameless.

And I saw another angel flying in mid-heaven, having a Gospel everlasting to preach to [upon or over] those who dwell upon the earth and to [upon or over] every nation, and tribe, and tongue, and people, saying with a great voice, Fear God and give to Him glory, because the hour of His judgment is come : and worship Him who made the heaven, and the earth, and the sea and fountains of waters.

And there followed another, a second angel, saying, Fallen, fallen, the great Babylon which hath made all the nations drink from the wine of the wrath of her fornication.

And there followed them another angel, a third, saying with a great voice, If any one worship the beast and his image, and receive [the] mark on his forehead, or on his hand, even he shall drink of the wine of the wrath of God, which is mingled without dilution in the cup of His anger, and shall be tormented with fire and brimstone in the presence of the angels and in the presence of the Lamb : and the smoke of their torment goeth up to the ages of ages ; and they have no rest day or night, who worship the beast and his image, and whosoever receiveth the mark of his name.

Here is the patience of the saints who keep the commandments of God and the faith of Jesus. And I heard a voice out of the heaven saying, Write, Blessed are the dead who die in the Lord from henceforth : Yea, saith the Spirit, that they [may, in that they] shall rest out of their labours ; for their works follow with them.

THE blackest storms often give place to the loveliest sunsets. The winds and thunders exhaust themselves. The clouds empty and break. And from the calm heavens behind them comes a golden light, girthing the remaining fragments of gloom with chains of brightness, and overarching with the bow of promise the path along which the terrible tempest has just passed. Like this evening glory after the summer's gust, is the chapter on which we now enter. We have seen the coming of the Antichrist in all the frowning blackness of Satan's angry malice, and have shuddered at the awful shadow, distress, and darkness which he casts upon the world. We have seen what havoc he makes with human peace, and the base humiliation he brings upon the proud oaks and lofty cedars of the mountains of human conceit and self-will. We have felt the sickening shock of horror at the contemplation of his hellish power, his blasphemies, and his unparalleled tyranny. We have gazed upon the progress of the most disastrous storm hell's malignant wisdom can devise, or that is ever allowed to afflict our race. We have watched the thickening blackness of darkness amid which the indignation of God is poured upon the intoxicated nations which will not have Christ to rule over them. But now the scene begins to change. The reign of terror cannot last. God's merciful goodness cannot allow it long. The earth would dissolve under it if those days were not shortened, but for the elect's sake they are shortened. Three and a half years is the fulness of their duration. In heaven's count the tempest holds but for an " hour." And here already we begin to see the light breaking in from behind the clouds and darkness. Further details of what is to befall these terrible Beasts, their systems and their followers, remain to be looked at ; but the golden rays begin to show themselves. Where perdition has been holding grand jubilee of destruction, appear the symptoms of a better order. The still lingering gloom begins to show some gilding of its edges. And over the pathway of " the abomination of desolation " are seen the forming outlines of the arch of beauty, hope, and peace. In place of the horrid Beasts, the Lamb comes into view. In place of the blaspheming herd, the redeemed appear, with the name of the Father and the Son upon their shining brows. Voices from heaven, intoned with mighty joy, and attuned to golden harps, are heard in song,—" new song," fit to be sung before the throne and all/the celestial company. A first-fruit of a new beginning is waved before God. Successive angels cleave the air on outspread wing proclaiming messages of hope and patience to the faithful sufferers, and telling of the nearing deliverance. And the whole picture begins to look to the effectual and everlasting sweeping away of the horrible nightmare of a distressed and helpless world. The Holy Spirit of the Father and the Son assist us to a right understanding of what it all means !

I. *Who are these* 144,000 ? Some answer, they are representatively the true people of God of all ages—the symbol of the whole body of the sanctified and saved. Others say, they are the choice spirits of the congregation of the glorified, selected and honoured above all common Christians because of their pre-eminent qualities and abstinences on earth. Others tell us, they are the company of those who have remained true in faith under the errors and falsities of the Papacy. And still others say, they are none else than the assembly of the noble spirits who achieved the Reformation of the sixteenth century, and that their harp-notes and new song is " the harmony of the Reformed Confessions ! " I see not how it is possible for either of these interpretations to stand. Without entering upon the many points in which they severally fail to conform to the record, I may say, they all do violence to the consecutiveness and self-consistency of this Book, and defy all legitimate dealing with the particulars of the sacred description. We must find a better meaning, or give in that it is impossible to do anything more than *guess* at what the Lord intended to show us, whilst one guess is just as good and reliable as another. But God's Word is truth ; and therefore there must be truth in this presentation,—truth which will hold together with the rest of the Book, with the dignity of a divine prophecy so solemnly given, and with the grammatical sense of the words in which the account is presented. Nor do I know why candid and earnest men, but for their arbitrary and stilted theories, should be at a loss for an interpretation answering to the requirements. Let us look at the matter carefully, and see.

A considerate glance at the particulars of this vision will at once discover a direct and strong contrast having special relation to what went before in the preceding chapter. The account of the 144,000 is really only another side of what is related of the Beasts, the counterpart of the same history. Over against the wild and savage monster is a gentle and loving Lamb. Over against the confessors and worshippers of the Beast, having his mark, is the company of the Lamb's followers, having their mark, even the name of the Father and the Son written in their foreheads. Over against the Beast's moral system, which is nothing but harlotry, spiritual and literal, the worship of idols and the trampling under foot of all God's institutes, here is an opposing style of life and conformity—a virgin purity which refuses to be debauched by the prevailing fornication. Over against the slavery of those who sell themselves to the powers of perdition which then have command of the world, here is redemption from the earth and from man, a ransom out of the thraldom which holds others. Over against the new order of things set up by the Antichrist, these sing " a new song,"—a victory and glory never shared by any but them.   Over against the going of the Beasts and their dupes into perdition, there is here a going whithersoever the Lamb goeth.   Over against the doings in the presence of the Beast, under his patronage and authority, the doings here are in the presence of the Throne, and in the presence of the Living Ones and Elders, under the approval and counsels of heaven.   Everything in the mouth of the Beasts and all theirs, is *pseudos*, false, a lie ; the special character-istic of these is, that nothing *pseudos*, false, or a lie is found in their mouth. The Beast's number, and that by which he marks and numbers all his, is six sixes, the bad number intensified ; the number and numbering here is by twelves, the sacred number of completeness.   And in every item there is distinct allusion to things under the Beast, by way of contrast and opposition, proving that the account of these 144,000 is a counter-part of the same history, which can properly apply to none but persons who live contemporaneous with the Beast, and maintain themselves by divine grace in a course of life and profession over against him.

   But this is not the first time we hear of this 144,000.   Chapter seven told us of a body of people consisting of this precise number, of which we can hardly suppose two, unless specially instructed to that effect.   The fact urged by some that the company here is not introduced as " *the* 144,000," presents no grammatical reason for considering them distinct from the 144,000 there, as the best of Greek scholars agree.   The insertion of the article is needless where the identification is otherwise so clear, and would only tend to fix the emphasis at the wrong place.   Nor could the article, if inserted, make the indications of identity any stronger than they are.   This company is not so important as to call for the same sort of designation as when reference is made to " The Lamb," " The Living Ones," " The Elders," etc.   The number in Chapter VII is the same with the number here,—a number so remarkable and unique, that we must have very clear reasons for supposing that it does not refer to the same parties in both instances ; but no such reasons appear. There the 144,000 are presented as a select and special class of God's servants, chosen, marked, and set apart as none else, sealed by an angel with the seal of the living God.   So with the 144,000 here there is a special and peculiar isolation from all other classes of the saved.   They are distinct from the Living Ones, from the Elders, and from the multitude which no man can number ; and they are so unique and separate in their history, experience, and reward, that no one is able to learn or sing the song which they sing.   Those in Chapter VII were marked in their forehead with the seal of the living God ; these have that mark, even " the Lamb's name and His Father's name written on their foreheads."   Those were all Hebrews, chosen from the several tribes of undivided Israel ; and so it would seem to be with these.   They have on their foreheads the name of *the Father*, which is the Jewish mark.   They also have their place *on Mount Zion*, which though it may not mean the earthly hill, still connects with the seat of the palace and throne of David, Solomon, and all the Jewish kings.   Those sealed ones were to be supernaturally protected and preserved amid the plagues that followed ; and these appear as persons marvellously kept and sustained under the consummation of those plagues, the Antichrist.   The history of the 144,000 in Chapter VII is incomplete taken by itself.   No object or outcome of that sealing is anywhere stated, if not to be found in the passage before us.   The position these sealed ones were to hold, the relations they were to occupy as the specially chosen of their time, are all left untold if not told in this chapter.   Neither can we find adequate reason for the mention at all of that special sealing without some such contin-uation of the history as given here.   I accordingly conclude with entire confidence, that the 144,000 on Mount Zion are the identical 144,000 sealed ones spoken of in Chapter VII, with only this difference, that there we see them in their earthly relations and peculiar consecration ; and here we see them with their earthly career finished, and in the enjoyment of the heavenly award for their faithfulness.

And this fixes what must condition the whole interpretation of this Book, to wit, that from the opening of the sixth seal until after the sounding of the seventh trumpet, the third woe, and the revelation of the Man of sin, no more time elapses than the ordinary length of a human life ; for those who are already mature men, and capable of a sacred setting apart as witnesses for God when the sixth seal is broken, are still living and active under the reign of the Antichrist.   Alas, what a world of learned labour thus falls to the ground !

II. *What are the chief marks or characteristics of these* 144,000 ?   The first and foremost is that of a true and conspicuous confession.   They have the name of the Lamb and the name of His Father written on their foreheads. This is their public mark as against the mark of the worshippers of the Beast. There is nothing more honourable in God's sight than truth and faithfulness of confession.   " With the mouth confession is made unto salvation." (Rom. 10 : 10.)   The confession of these people is in opposition to the unbelieving Jew, who rejects and repudiates the Son ; and in opposition to the Antichrist, who denies both the Father and the Son.   As children of Abraham, they have embraced Christianity ; and as Christians, they take issue with the Beast, and persist in testifying against his blasphemous usurpations of the place of God and the only Saviour.

Another particular is their unworldliness.   Whilst most people in their day " dwell upon the earth," sit down upon it as their rest and choice, derive their chief comfort from it, these are " redeemed from the earth,"—withdrawn from it, bought away by the heavenly promises and the divine grace to live above it, independent of it, as no longer a part of it.   Also is it said that they are " redeemed from men,"—segregated entirely from the common course of the world, and removed from the ordinary fellowship of men.   Less than this the language concerning them can scarcely mean.   They are quite severed from the world in heart and life.

A third point is their pureness.   We are not to suppose with some that these 144,000 are all males who have never been married ; for there is no more impurity in marriage than in abstinence from marriage.   Celibacy is not the subject or virtue in this description, but *purity*, freedom from contamination by the corruptions which prevail in their time.   The reign of the Antichrist is the reign of harlotry, both literal and spiritual.   It is a time when chaste marriage is no more regarded than the worship of the true God.   But from all such defilements these people have kept themselves unspotted.   " they are virgins," in that they have lived chaste lives, both as to their faithfulness to God in their religion, and as to their pureness from all bodily lewdness.   The kingdom of heaven is likened to " ten virgins."   The object of Paul's ministry to the Corinthians was, that he might present them " as a chaste virgin to Christ."   And this is the sort of virginity attained and maintained by these people.

A further quality is their truthfulness.   " In their mouth was not found what is false."   There is a peculiar depth in John's conception of truth and its opposite falsehood.   Any one who fails to confess Christ in all the length and breadth of His nature and offices, any one who fails to live his profession or to show by his works what he speaks with his lips, is to him a liar.   The meaning here has the same deep significance.   It is a great thing for people to be careful about their conversation, always conforming their words to the reality of things.   To speak falsehood, to exercise a deceitful and untrustworthy tongue, is a devilish thing : for Satan is a liar and the father of lies.   These people were truthful in these respects, but had also a higher and profounder truthfulness. The times in which they live are the times of hell's worst lies,—times when the whole world has gone mad over lies,—times when the entire order of society is a lie,—times when men's religion is a lie,—times when their very god is a lie,— times when everything is pryed away from the foundation of truth by the dreadful leverage which perdition then possesses.   And it is over against all this that nothing false is found in their mouth.   They have the true faith ;

they hold to it with a true heart ; they exemplify it by a true manner of life.   They are the children of truth in the midst of a world of untruth.

III. *What, then, is their Reward ?*   Taking the last particular first, they stand approved, justified, and accepted before God.   " They are blameless." The added words, " before the throne of God," are not in the best manuscripts, and are dropped now by common consent as no part of the original.   They make no difference in the sense, for the blamelessness of these people must needs be a blamelessness before the throne ; but if the phrase be emphasized it might suggest a connection with the throne which does not here exist.   It is to be observed that these 144,000 are by no means the highest class of saints, as some have erroneously supposed.   They do not come into the congregation of the saved until after the highest orders of the saints have been caught up to God and to His throne.   The Living Ones are saints from the earth, for they sing the song of redemption by the blood of Christ.   So are also the Elders. But these are already in their heavenly glory wearing the crowns which Christ will give at that day, even before these people are sealed.   These 144,000 sing their song *in the presence of* the Living Ones and the gold-crowned Elders ; this expresses a lesser dignity.   Neither is there a word said about crowns for them. They sing in the presence of the throne, but they are not connected with it, as the Living Ones, nor seated on associated thrones, as the Elders.   They are not therefore of the highest orders of the saved and glorified.   There are many mansions in the Father's house many degrees in glory, and many ranks of saints as well as of angels.   There is such a thing as being saved with loss, such a thing as missing our crowns even though we may get to heaven.   There are also many " *virgins*," real virgins, who go and buy, and come at length with deficiencies repaired, but are in readiness too late to be admitted to the place and honour of the queen.   These 144,000 are virgins ; they come to glorious honour through their confession, purity, and devotion ; but they come in at a period when the Bride is already made up, and cannot be of the first and highest order of the glorified.   But still, they are approved and justified before God, which is in itself a great, high, and glorious attainment.   To stand before God approved and blameless from the midst of a condemned world,—a world given over to the powers of perdition by reason of its unbelief and sins,— a world which has become the theatre of all the consummated wickedness of the ages,—a world in which it is death to wear any badge or adhere to any profession contrary to the mark of the Antichrist, is an achievement of grace and faithfulness in which there may well be mighty exultation.

In the next place, they have a song which is peculiarly and exclusively their own.   Though not connected with the throne, as the Living Ones, nor crowned and seated as the Elders, they have a ground and subject of joy and praise which neither the Living Ones nor the Elders have ; nor is any one able to enter into that song except the 144,000.   None others ever fulfil just such a mission, as none others are ever sealed with the seal of the living God in the same way in which they were sealed.   None others ever have just such an experience, in such a world as that through which they come to glory. None others share with them in that particular administration of God which brings them away from the earth and men to their place on Mount Zion. Therefore, as angels cannot sing the song of the redeemed, never having been the subjects of redemption, so no other saints can sing the peculiar song of this 144,000.   They have a distinction and glory, a joy and blessedness, after all, in which none but themselves can ever share.

They stand with the Lamb on Mount Zion.   To be *with the Lamb*, as over against being with the Beast, is a perfection of blessing which no language can describe.   It is redemption.   It is victory.   It is eternal security and glory. To be with the Lamb *on Mount Zion* is a more special position and relation. It respects Jerusalem and the throne of David.   It will not meet the case to take Mount Zion here as simply " the heavenly Jerusalem ; " for that is not so distinctively the standing-place or point of occupation of these 144,000.   It

M

must take in some new and exalted order touching the earthly Jerusalem, the Jewish nationality, and that throne and Kingdom of David everywhere promised to be rebuilt and restored, never to fail any more.   The scene thus looks over into the new earth, to that time when " the ransomed of the Lord shall return, and come to Zion with songs and everlasting joy upon their heads, and shall obtain joy and gladness, and sorrow and sighing shall flee away " (Is. 35 : 10),—to that time when " they shall call Jerusalem the throne of the Lord, and all the nations shall be gathered unto it, to the name of the Lord, to Jerusalem " (Jer. 3 : 17),—to that time when " the Lord of Hosts shall reign in Mount Zion, and in Jerusalem, and before His ancients gloriously." (Is. 24 : 23.)   Glorious things are spoken of Jerusalem which have never yet been fulfilled.   On His holy hill of Zion God hath said that He will set up His King, even His Son, who shall rule all the nations. (Ps. 2.) The Lamb is yet to take possession of the city where He was crucified, there to fulfil what was written in Hebrew, Greek, and Latin over His head when He died.   And when that once comes to pass, these 144,000 are with Him, His near and particular associates in that particular relation and administration.

They are " a first-fruit to God and to the Lamb," not the first-fruit of all the saved, for the Living Ones and the Elders are in heavenly place and glory above and before them ; but a first-fruit of another and particular harvest ; the first-fruit from the Jewish field, in that new beginning with the Israelitish people for their fathers' sakes, which is to follow the ending of the present " times of the Gentiles."   What the Living Ones and Elders are to the Church universal these 144,000 are to the recovered, restored and redeemed children of Abraham, in that new order which is to come when the times of the Gentiles are fulfilled. They are all Jews.   They are brought to the confession of Christ, and sealed in their foreheads with the name of both the Father and the Son, during the time that the rest of their blood-kin are covenanting with and honouring the Antichrist as Messiah.   They are the particular witnesses for the Father and Son during those darkest days of Jacob's trouble.   And they take the first rank with Christ in His special relations and administrations in the final redemption of the Hebrew race.   For this they were extraordinarily sealed, and this is the reward of their faithfulness as against the lies and infamies of the Beast.   Hence, also, it pertains to their honour and blessedness to attend the Lamb whithersoever He goeth.   They are His heavenly suite and train in all His reign on Mount Zion.

IV. *What, now, of the Angel-Messages ?*   When Christ made His last entry into Jerusalem, and fault was found with the loud proclamations which were ringing to His praise as the Messiah-King, He answered : " If these should hold their peace, *the stones* would immediately cry out."   The truth of God and His claims *must* be spoken.   If men are silent, other things must become vocal to testify for Jehovah.   And when Antichrist succeeds in hushing up, or burying away in caves, mountains, and wildernesses all testimony for the Eternal One whom he seeks to abolish, the heavens speak, and the angels whom he cannot touch or slay become the preachers.   Mid-heaven is their pulpit, and all nations, tribes, tongues, and peoples are their auditors.   Hell may slay, imprison, and silence every human witness for God, but cannot chain the proclamation of His truth.   God's word cannot be bound.   It liveth and abideth forever.   It must be heard.

The First Message.—That an angel is the preacher here, is proof positive that the present dispensation is then past and changed.   Of old, Angels were employed for the giving of the Law, and in the Judgment time they are everywhere represented as again taking very conspicuous part in the divine administrations with regard to our world ; but in the dispensation under which we now are, the charge of preaching and witnessing for God, and the declaring of His Word, is the peculiar office of the Church.   It is a calling and office committed to men, to the chosen of our human race.   Angels are ministers to the heirs of salvation, but not in the sense of being the appointed public proclaimers and preachers of the Gospel. That is man's work, and man's peculiar honour, as things now are constituted. But here Angels are the preachers, with three or four distinct messages : one "having a Gospel everlasting ; " one proclaiming the doom of Babylon ; and one denouncing eternal damnation upon every worshipper of the Beast, or wearer of his mark. Of course, then, we have here another dispensation, a different order of things from that which now obtains. The same is also intimated in the features of the Word preached. It is no longer the meek and entreating voice, beseeching men to be reconciled to God, but a great thunder from the sky, demanding of the nations to Fear *the God*, as over against the false god whom they were adoring,—to Give glory to *Him*, instead of the infamous Beast whom they were glorifying,—to Worship *the Maker* of all things, as against the worship of him who can do no more than play his hellish tricks with the things that are made ; and all this *on the instant*, for the reason that " the hour of judgment *is come*."

Paul once said, if an angel from heaven preach unto you any other Gospel than that ye have received, let him be accursed. And when he so said, he spoke the very truth of God ; but it is the truth with special reference to the present dispensation, till the Church-period has come to its end in the day of judgment ; for here, when " the judgment *is come*," an angel from heaven preaches, and what he preaches is not " *the* everlasting Gospel " as the English version is, but " *a* Gospel everlasting." It is not indeed " another Gospel," for it is in inner substance the same old and everlasting Gospel, but now in the dress and features of a new order of things—the Gospel as its contents shape themselves in its addresses to the nations when " the hour of judgment is come," and the great final administrations are in hand.

Luther once said that he did not like this Book, because its spirit did not agree with his feelings as to the Gospel. He was right as to the fact. His great soul, permeated through and through with the very life and spirit of reconciliation in Christ Jesus as now preached to men, felt that here is something different, just as the Christian heart is disturbed by the imprecatory Psalms. But when we locate the matter rightly, and learn that here the Church-period has given place to the presence and ongoing of the day and hour of judgment, the whole matter clears up. Mercy towards the poor infatuated world still lingers in the very hour of wrath. In the heat and height of his indignation God still remembers it. Hence still something of a Gospel message sounds. And when there is no more voice on earth to speak it, an angel from heaven, uttering himself from the sky, proclaims to the guilty nations where they are, what has come, and what immediate revolution is needed, if they would not sink at once to everlasting destruction. It is *Gospel*, but it is the Gospel in the form it takes when the hour of judgment has set in. It is one of the very last calls of grace to an apostate world.

The Second Message.—With the hour of judgment comes the work of judgment. A colossal system of harlotry and corruption holds dominion over the nations. There is no country, no people, but is won to it, and intoxicated by it, and induced to cast off all the bonds of sacredness for the infamous delusions of the Antichrist and his false prophet. God has allowed it for the punishment of those who would not have Christ for their Lord, but now He will not allow it longer. Therefore another Angel comes with the proclamation: " *Fallen, fallen, the great Babylon, which hath made all the nations drink from the wine of the wrath of her fornication.*" The announcement is by anticipation as on the very eve of accomplishment, and as surely now to be fulfilled. The particulars are given in the seventeenth and eighteenth chapters. There also the explanation of the object of this announcement is given. It is mercy still struggling in the toils of judgment, if that by any means some may yet be snatched from the opening jaws of hell ; for there the further word is, " Come out of her, my people, that ye may have no fellowship with her sins, and that ye receive not of her plagues."

The Third Message.—And for the still more potent enforcement of this call a third Angel appears, preaching and crying with a great voice, that whosoever is found worshipping the Beast and his image, or has the Beast's mark on his forehead or on his hand, even he shall drink of the wine of the wrath of God which is mingled without dilution in the cup of His anger, and shall be tormented with fire and brimstone in the presence of the angels and in the presence of the Lamb, and the smoke of their torment ascends to the ages of ages, and they have no rest day and night ! It is an awful commination ; but these are times of awful guilt, infatuation, and wickedness. And when men are in such dangers, marching direct into the mouth of such a terrible perdition, it is a great mercy in God to make proclamation of it with all the force of an Angel's eloquence. The same is also for the wronged and suffering ones who feel the power of these terrible oppressors. It tells them how their awful griefs shall be avenged on their hellish persecutors. So, therefore, with mighty energy the Angel proclaims the eternal doom of the abettors of the Antichrist.

There be those who mock and jeer at the idea of an eternal hell for the wicked. Many are the jests they perpetrate at the expense of these preachers of fire and brimstone. But here a great and mighty Angel from heaven is the preacher, and his sermon from beginning to end is nothing but fire and brimstone, even everlasting burning and torment for all who take the mark of Antichrist ! Shall we believe our modern sentimental philosophers, or abide by the word of our God and of his holy angels ? Alas, alas, for the infatuated people who comfort themselves with the belief that perdition is a myth—the bugbear of antiquated superstition !

The Fourth Message.—There is no suffering for any class of God's people in any age, like the sufferings of those who remain faithful to God during the reign of the Antichrist. Here, at this particular time and juncture, is the patience or endurance of them that keep the commandments of God and the faith of Jesus. To come out of Babylon, and to stand aloof from its horrible harlotries, is a costly thing. It is equivalent to a voluntary coming forward to the state-block to have their heads chopped off. Therefore there is another proclamation from heaven for their special strengthening and consolation. Whether this word is also from an Angel we are not told ; but it is a message from glory and from God. And it is a sweet and blessed message. It is a message which John is specially commanded to write, that it may be in the minds and hearts of God's people of every age, and take away all fear from those who in this evil time are called to lay down their lives because they will not worship Antichrist. That message is : " *Blessed are the dead who die in the Lord from henceforth : Yea, saith the Spirit, that they may, in that they shall, rest out of their labours, for their works follow with them.*" This is true of all the saints of all ages, but it is pre-eminently and specially true of those who at this time lose their lives for their faithful obedience. It may look like calamity, but in comparison with the miseries of a life of faith under such a hellish despot, it is a blessedness. Death to a good man at any time is a greater beatitude than a disaster ; and when a life of truth and honour becomes so great a sorrow as at this time, it is a blessedness to have it ended. The implication is, that from this point on till death itself is vanquished, there is no more peace or comfort for a good man on earth, and therefore that no better thing can happen him than to die. When there is no more peace for us but in death, why should we wish to live ? When all hope for earth has faded out, why should we desire to remain in it ? When to open our mouths for Christ, or to bow the knee or speak a prayer to the God that made us, exposes to indignity and torture, why not welcome death, and account it good fortune to have the chance for such a release ? *Rest—Rest !* What would not those dupes of Antichrist finally give for *Rest !* But what they can never have, they that die in the Lord get through death. Like the worn mariner wearied out with his long and painful endurance of the tempests, dangers, and hardships of the sea, enters the calm port for which he steered so hard ;—like the soldier, scarred, mutilated, and sick of the miseries of deadly conflict, comes back from the field of blood to repose in the peace and security of his happy home ;—so do they rest out of their labours. And their works follow with them. The very hardships past make the peace the sweeter. Not a word of faithful testimony, not a tear of sympathy, not a sigh of prayer, not a gift of a cup of water in a disciple's name, shall fail in its contribution to the blessedness. Therefore it is written : " Blessed are the dead who die in the Lord from henceforth." And when violence, cruelty, and slaughter are the consequence of a life of truth and purity, the sooner it is over the greater the beatitude.

Here, then, is the comfort of the saints. Whatever they suffer, their peace is sure. Unable to live, death is their blessedness. Heaven speaks it. The Spirit confirms it. The apostles of God have written it. And from it springs a consolation—

> Which monarchs cannot grant, nor all the powers
> Of earth and hell confederate take away ;—
> A liberty which persecution, fraud,
> Oppression, prisons, have no power to bind.

LECTURE THIRTY-FIFTH

THE VISION OF THE HARVEST—A HARVEST OF WOE AND JUDGMENT—THE PARTICULARS OF
THE DESCRIPTION—THE ANGEL-CRY FOR THE SENDING OF THE SHARP SICKLE—THE REAP-
ING—THE VISION OF THE VINTAGE—THE ANGEL OUT OF THE TEMPLE—THE GREAT CRY
FROM THE ALTAR FOR THE SENDING OF THE SHARP SICKLE—THE GATHERING OF THE VINE
OF THE EARTH—THE TREADING OF THE WINE-PRESS.

REV. 14 : 14–16. (Revised Text.) And I saw and behold a white cloud, and upon the cloud is seated one like a son of man, having on his head a crown of gold, and in his hand a sharp sickle. And another angel came out of the temple, crying with a great voice to him that sat on the cloud, Send thy sickle, and reap ; because the time to reap is come, because the harvest of the earth is dried [dead ripe].

And he that sat on the cloud cast his sickle on the earth, and the earth was reaped.

And another angel came out of the temple which is in the heaven, he also having a sharp sickle. And another angel came out of the altar, he who hath power over the fire ; and he cried with a great cry to him who had the sharp sickle, saying, Send thy sharp sickle, and gather the clusters of the vine of the earth, because her grapes are fully ripe.

And the angel cast his sickle into the earth and gathered the vine of the earth, and cast [what he gathered] into the great wine-press of the wrath of God. And the wine-press was trodden outside of the city, and blood came forth out of the wine-press up to the bits of the horses, for a distance of a thousand six hundred stadia.

PROCLAMATION having gone forth that the hour of judgment is come, that great Babylon is on the brink of her fall, and that the damnation of every worshipper of the Beast is at hand, we find ourselves face to face with the last great administrations of divine wrath. And the nature and machinery of those administrations is the matter which now comes before us. The more specific details are given in the succeeding chapters, but a general summation is first presented in two visions, the Harvest and the Vintage, which, for awful brevity of narration and expressiveness of imagery, are perhaps the most wonderful in all this wonderful Book. God help us to consider them with reverent and believing hearts !

I. THE VISION OF THE HARVEST.

Some worthy expositors take this as a foreshowing of the final gathering home of the people of God. That the Scriptures often speak of such a harvest of the good seed of the Saviour's sowing there can be no question. John the Baptizer spoke of a time of threshing, when the Lord " will gather the wheat into His garner." (Luke 3 : 17.) The saviour commenced His heavenly instructions with an account of His sowing and husbandry, the harvest of which he said would be " the end of the age," when He " will say to the reapers, Gather the wheat into my barn." (Matt. 13.) He also said, " So is the kingdom of God, as if a man should cast seed into the ground, and should sleep and rise night and day, and the seed should spring and grow up, he knoweth not how ; for the earth bringeth forth fruit of herself ; first the blade, then the ear, after that the full corn in the ear. But when the fruit is brought forth, immediately he putteth in the sickle, because *the harvest* is come." (Mark 4 : 26–29.) But that this is the harvest foreshown in the text seems to me very improbable, if not entirely out of the question. According to the record up to this point, the great harvest of the good seed has already been reaped. The Living Ones, the Elders, the innumerable multitude, the Man-child, and the 144,000, all of whom are of the good seed, are in heaven before this reaping comes. This reaping is also immediately preceded by the gathering of a great company to glory, which is very unaccountably separated

358

from the harvest of saints directly to follow, if so we are to understand it. Ordinarily, indeed, we would think of harvest as a thing of gladness and blessing.   The Scriptures also speak of harvest as a great joy.   But it is the same with respect to the vintage, which all accept as here applying exclusively to the punishment of the wicked.   Any argument of that character bears as strongly against taking the vintage in the sense of a destruction as the taking of the harvest in that sense.

It must be remembered that evil has its harvest as well as good. There is a harvest of misery and woe,—a harvest for the gathering, binding, and burning of the tares,—as well as for the gathering of the wheat into the garner of heaven.   And this harvest of punishment has quite as prominent a place in the Scriptures as the harvest of the gathering home of the saints.   " Thus saith the Lord of hosts, the God of Israel ; the daughter of Babylon is like a threshing floor, it is time to thresh her ; yet a little while and the time of her *harvest* shall come."   (Jer. 51 : 33.)   Here is a harvest of judgment,—a harvest of woe to Babylon, and the harvest of the text follows as the direct consequence of the proclamation of great Babylon's fall.   Is it not, therefore, most naturally to be taken as the same in both cases ?   So again in Joel (3 : 11–16), looking to the very time and events with which we are here concerned, the word is : " Assemble yourselves, and come, all ye heathen, and gather yourselves together round about ; thither cause thy mighty ones to come down, O Lord.   Let the heathen be awakened, and come up to the valley of Jehoshaphat : for there will I sit to judge all the heathen round about. Put ye in the sickle, for *the harvest* is ripe : come, get you down, for the press is full, the vats overflow ; for their wickedness is great.   Multitudes, multitudes in the valley of decision : for the day of the Lord is near in the valley of decision.   The sun and the moon shall be darkened, and the stars shall withdraw their shining.   The Lord also shall roar out of Zion, and utter his voice from Jerusalem, and the heavens and the earth shall shake."   Here is both a harvest and a vintage ; the one like and part of the other, and both exclusively applicable to the destruction of the wicked.   This harvest and this vintage are unquestionably the same described in the text.   They belong to the same period of time, they are called for after the same manner, and for the same activities ; and they respect the same parties, whether as to the bearer of the sickle, the reapers, or the persons whom the reaping touches.   It seems to me impossible, therefore, rightfully to take this harvest as anything else than the final cutting off of the hosts of the wicked, the visitation upon them of the fruits of their sowing.   That harvest of which the 144,000 are a first-fruit is a very different matter from this.   That is a harvest of gathering to the Lamb on Mount Zion ; this is a gathering to the Valley of Jehoshaphat for destruction.   Verse 15 is a literal allusion to Isaiah 27 : 11, which refers to a scene of breaking and burning, and final withdrawal of all mercy.   The express mention of the sharpness of the sickle also shows that we have to do with a scene of judgment.   The mention of the cloud likewise points to a work of judgment, for wherever Christ appears on a cloud, the work immediately in hand is always a judgment.   The name of the Son of man also points in the same direction ; for it is as the Son of man that all judgment has been committed to Christ.   (Jno. 5 : 27.)   And such a contrast as would make only the vintage expressive of wrath and punishment, and the harvest one of a purely gracious character, has not a single trait or item of the account to support it.*
The harvest is simply one phase of a great final visitation upon the apostate

* Mede, Bishop Newton, Lowman, Doddridge, Bengel, Hengstenberg, Faber, Stuart, W. Robinson, William Jones, etc., agree that the *harvest* as well as the *vintage* here denotes a harvest of wrath. Mede well observes, " that the idea of harvest includes three things : the reaping of the corn, the gathering of it in, and the threshing of it ; whence it is made a type in Scripture of two direct opposites ; of *destruction*, when the reaping and the threshing are considered ; of *restitution and salvation* when the ingathering is considered."   It is here *the reaping* only.

world, of which the vintage is another phase.—Let us look at it, then, a little more particularly.

" *I saw, and behold a white cloud.*" From this we may be quite sure of what is coming. That cloud is the signal of the second advent of the Lord Jesus. When He ascended, " a cloud received him out of their sight ; " and at the same time it was told from heaven," This same Jesus, which is taken up from you into heaven, shall so come in like manner as ye have seen him go into heaven." (Acts 1.) The cloud took Him, and the cloud shall bring him. " They shall see the Son of man coming *in a cloud* with power and great glory." (Luke 21 : 27.) And what was thus predicted, the Apocalyptic seer here beholds fulfilling. That cloud is " *white*," like fire at its intensest heat, like the lightning itself, portending the purest as well as the hottest wrath towards the powers which have usurped the dominion of the earth.

" *On the cloud is seated one like a Son of man.*" No one else is here to be thought of but our blessed Lord Jesus. In John's first vision he saw, in the midst of the golden candlesticks, " One like to a Son of man ; " and that One said, " I am the First and the last, and the Living One ; and I became dead, and behold I am living for the ages of the ages ; and I have the keys of death and of hell." (Rev. 1 : 17.) It was the glorified Son of Mary there, and it is the same here. As the destroyer of the works of the Devil, and as the Judge of the quick and the dead, it belongs to Christ to reap the earth and to clear it of the hellish seed of the great enemy. The man of sin is to be destroyed only by the manifestation of the Saviour's presence. (2 Thess. 2 : 8.)

" *Having on his head a crown of gold.*" Daniel " saw in the night visions, and behold one like the Son of man came with the clouds of heaven, and came to the ancient of days, and there was given Him dominion, and glory, and a kingdom." (Dan. 7 : 13, 14.) It was the same Son of man, in the same cloud, settled in all the regal prerogatives of the same supreme dominion, and manifested for the same purpose of dispossessing and destroying the Beast. The sitting of Christ on the throne of His glory is for the judgment of the nations (Matt. 25 : 31, 32), and the taking to Him of His great power as the King is to destroy them that corrupt the earth, that He may set up in their place His own glorious dominion. (Rev. 11 : 17, 19 ; 19 : 16.)

And to this end, this heaven-crowned King holds " *in his hand a sharp sickle.*" There is nowhere such a description or holding forth of the instrument in any harvest scene referring to the gracious home-bringing of the good. The earth is to be cleared of its *ill* products now, therefore only a cutting implement is in hand, and so conspicuously displayed. The work is one of vengeance and sore judgment, therefore it is " sharp."

Thus seated in regal majesty, with His terrible instrument in hand for His appointed judicial work as the Son of man, there goes up to Him a mighty cry to send forth His sickle and reap, claiming that the time of the reaping has come, and that " the harvest of *the earth* " (not *the Church*) is dried to dead ripeness. This cry is from an angel, called " *another* angel," in allusion to those mentioned in verses 6, 8, 9. Some take it as the commission of the Father for Christ to proceed ; but that commission the great Harvester must already have had in order to take the position and equipment in which He here appears. It is not so much a commission as a *prayer*, a plea, an urgency. It does not come from the Father, but from the quarter of the afflictions and abominations calling for vengeance. This angel comes " *out of the temple ; *"—not " the temple which is in heaven," as in verse 17, or it would be so stated, but " the temple " as distinguished from " the temple which is in heaven ; " hence the temple on earth, referring either to the material temple re-built and recon-secrated, or the spiritual temple as made up of those who keep the command-ments of God and the faith of Jesus, or both ; that is, from the very point and place where the Antichrist has enacted his greatest enormities of wickedness. Abel's blood cried unto God from the ground. (Gen. 4 : 10.) The cry of Sodom's wickedness came up unto Jehovah. (Gen. 28 : 20, 21.) In like manner great Babylon's sins came up into heaven. (Rev. 18 : 5.) And this cry to the sitter on the cloud comes out of the earthly temple as the cry of righteous indignation at the abominations that are being done against that temple and its God, attesting the over-ripeness of the transgressors, and claiming the due judgment upon them, as the time has come.

The interests of God on earth are all more or less under the guardianship of angels. An angel had charge of the healing in Bethesda's pool, and angels have charge of God's temple too. The Archangel Michael presides over the affairs of the children of Daniel's people, and in the time of the Antichrist it is prophesied that he shall stand up for them. (Dan. 12 : 1.) And this angel-cry from the temple to the crowned, seated, and armed King of Judgment, to send His sickle and reap, is plainly connected with the administrations of these angel-helpers against oppression and oppressors. It shows us that when the time of judgment comes to the full, everything will be in a condition of one grand outcry for speedy vengeance. Iniquity will then have come to the full, to a thorough drying out of every modifying particle of immaturity, giving mighty argument for the loud outcry of every holy being for judgment to strike.

And as the cry is, the answer comes. "*He that sat on the cloud cast his sickle (ἐπὶ) on, or against, the earth, AND THE EARTH WAS REAPED.*" Tremendous words ! What an experience for the race of man is bound up in their awful brevity ! What plagues descend with that sharp sickle ! What a crash comes with its alighting upon a world now dead ripe for final judgment ! What powers and systems fall before it ! What sores and agonies it brings to them that bear the mark of the Beast and worship his image ! What pestilential putrescences it strikes into the sea whence that Beast rises, and into the rivers and fountains whence his subjects drink ! What new blazes of consuming heat it gives to the sun ! What torment it inflicts upon the throne of the Beast, and darkness and anguish upon his kingdom ! What cries, and thunders, and lightnings, and earthquakes, and hailstorms, and trembling of nations, and anxieties of men, it arouses into activity ! How does every upas growth give way before the sharp edge of that terrible sickle ! Just how much of this great Harvest pertains to the reaping, as distinguished from the vintage, we are not fully informed ; but it cuts from their foundations all the main sinews of the Antichrist. It includes all the disasters that come from the pouring out of the great bowls of wrath. It brings down great Babylon with a crash that fills the world with lamentations and horror. It strips the great Adulteress of all her pride and queenliness, and fills her with torment, and sorrow, and burning. It sinks all the riches and glories of a godless world into one common ruin, never to be brought up again. And of the two phases of those ministrations of the wrath of God which are to clear this planet of the products and representatives of rebellion against His Throne, this is one, and perhaps the most general and far-reaching of the two. When the seer says " *the earth has reaped,*" he tells of an amount of cutting down, divesture, and sorrowful sweeping away forever which the Scriptures describe as the termination of the whole present order of things ; for " the Harvest is the end of the world." (Matt. 13 : 39.) But it is nevertheless only one phase of the destruction which shall then be wrought. After the grain-harvest comes the grape-harvest. Accordingly we have.

II. THE VISION OF THE VINTAGE.

" Another angel " appears. He is " another " as a comer forth from the temple, and he is an " angel " with reference to his *mission*, not with reference to his nature ; for this angel is really the same as the Sitter on the white cloud. As to office, Christ is often represented as an angel, both in this Book and elsewhere. His very name, *Christ*, or *Messiah* implies as much. He is the One sent and appointed of the Father. In the Old Testament He is continually spoken of as the Jehovah—angel. In chapters 10 and 20 He appears as an angel. And in the very nature of the case we must here understand the Lord Himself, though in the character of an angel. The two images of the Harvest and the Vintage are too closely interconnected for us to assign one to Christ and the other to a created angel. The sharp sickle in the one is the same as in the other. The work is so great, and belongs so essentially to the mission and prerogatives of Christ, that it would trench upon the honour and appointment of Him to whom the Father hath committed all judgment, to refer it to a single ordinary angel. The destruction wrought is unquestionably the same which is more particularly described in the latter part of chapter 19 ; but there it is specifically assigned to the Lord Jesus himself. And so in Isaiah 63, the treader of the wine-press, corresponding to the picture here given, is none other than Christ. We would therefore involve ourselves in too many difficulties, not to admit that this *another messenger* is the same as the Sitter on the cloud.

He comes *" out of the temple which is in heaven ; "* the temple which is in heaven, as distinguished from the temple which is on earth. " The holy places made with hands are the figures of the true," fashioned after " the patterns of things in the heavens." (Heb. 10 : 23, 24.) It is in the heavenly temple that Christ now is, there appearing in the presence of God for us, as our great High Priest ; and out from thence He is to come when He comes the second time. (Heb. 10 : 24–28.) We have here reached the time appointed for the destroying of them that corrupt the earth. Hence the great commissioned One appears. He leaves His place in the temple which is in heaven, and stands ready, with sharp sickle in hand, for the work assigned. Where he stands is not said ; but the silence naturally carries us back to the white cloud.

Appearing with the sharp sickle, a great cry goes up to Him : *" Send thy sharp sickle and gather the clusters of the vine of the earth, because her grapes are fully ripe."* He who makes this cry is an angel who comes *" out of the altar,"* of course the earthly altar, or it would be otherwise stated, as in the preceding verse. This angel is " he who hath power over the fire." The altar-fire is the fire of divine justice ; the fire which ever burns against sin and sinners ; the fire which spares no victim, however innocent, when in the place and stead of transgressors ; the fire which ever cries out with mighty voice for the burning up of all rebels against God's righteous authority. There is a living spirit in charge of it ; and that spirit calls for vengeance against the Antichrist. The grapes in this case are the grapes of Sodom, " sour grapes," the clusters of wickedness ripened to the full. Such iniquities, blasphemies, tyrannies and systematic abominations, as the Antichrist develops, have no parallel on earth. In these all the depravities head up to their maturity. In these appears the consummation or final ripeness of the whole earth-growth and mystery of evil. The angel of the altar-fires is never so outraged as by this perfected vintage of earth's wickedness. Hence the loud and clamorous outcry for vengeance upon these clusters. The " grapes of gall " are " ripe." The time for cutting them has come. The Messenger with the sharp instrument is present. And the spirit of the justice-fires cries for the sickle to come in all its whetted sharpness. From under that altar had gone forth the plaint of murdered saints : " Until when, Thou Master, holy and true, dost Thou not judge and avenge our blood from them that dwell on the earth." (Rev. 6 : 10.) But now the very angel of the altar adds his mighty voice, and there can be no more delay.

" And the Angel cast His sickle into the earth, and gathered the vine of the earth." The vine of the earth is that which stands over against " the vine of heaven." The true vine is Christ, and Christians are the branches. " The vine of the earth " is Antichrist, and its branches are his adherents and followers. The saints are not of the earth, but born from above ; these are of the earth, born from the wisdom that is from below—the seed of the Devil's sowing—the children of the wicked one. The grapes of this vine of the earth are the

matured children of wickedness, and " their wine is the poison of dragons and the cruel venom of asps." (Deut. 32 : 32, 33.) They have by this time gone as far as, in the nature of things, they can go. They are *" fully ripe."* Hence the sharp sickle of the great judgment strikes, and the vine of the earth is cut, and its clusters gathered into the great wine-press of the wrath of God.

A more particular description of this gathering of the host of Antichrist into the wine-press, and the treading of it by the King of kings, and Lord of lords, is given in the latter part of chapters 16 and 19. It is in reality a war scene, the gathering of armies, the bringing together of the kings of the earth and of the whole world to the battle of the great day of God Almighty. It is for military purposes that they come, seduced, drawn, and impelled by unclean spirits that issue out of the mouth of the Dragon, out of the mouth of the Beast, and out of the mouth of the False Prophet. The region of their assemblage is the Holy Land. The various names denotive of the locality all circle around Jerusalem. *" Armageddon "* is the place named in the Apocalypse, which is the mount or city of Megiddo, or the great Esdraelon plain, " the Valley of Megiddo." That has ever been one of God's great battle-grounds for the judging of the armies of the wicked. There Jabin's hosts, with their 900 chariots of iron, were utterly overwhelmed by Jehovah's special interference. There the Midianites, and Amalekites, and children of the East were routed before Gideon's 300 men with pitchers and lamps. There Samson triumphed with his crude instrument over the might of the Philistines. There the ruddy son of Jesse met and slew the great Goliath, and opened a breach of destruction upon those who defied Israel's God. And it is but fitting that here should be the seat of the wine-press for the final crushing out of the mightier Jabin and Goliath of the last evil days. *" The Valley of Jehosaphat "* is named by Joel as the place which, geographically taken, denotes the immediate vicinity of Jerusalem, or else that part of Idumea where, by the special aid of heaven, Jehosaphat put down the rebellion of the Edomites. *" Bozrah "* is named by Isaiah as the place where the mighty Saviour treads the wine-press alone, and stains all His raiment with the blood of His foes. (Is. 34 : 6–8 ; 63 : 1–6.) The probabilities are that all these particular localities are included, and that a line of encamped forces shall extend from Bozrah, on the south-east, to Megiddo, on the north-west. And, singularly enough, this would measure exactly 1,600 *stadia*, the distance named in the text as that over which the blood from this great wine-press of Jehovah's anger flows. The same would also best realize Habakkuk's vision of the same scene, where he beheld, and " God came *from Teman*, and the Holy One *from Mount Paran.* His glory covered the heavens, and the earth was full of His praise. His brightness was as the light ; He had horns coming out of his hand ; and there was the hiding of His power. Before him went the pestilence, and burning coals went forth at his feet. He stood and measured the earth : He beheld, and drove asunder the nations ; and the everlasting mountains were scattered, the perpetual hills did bow. Thou didst march through the land of indignation ; thou didst thresh the heathen in anger. Thou wentest forth for the salvation of thy people, even for salvation with thine anointed ; Thou woundest the head out of the house of the wicked, by discovering the foundation unto the neck." (Hab. 3 : 3–16.)

The march of the terrific indignation of God on this occasion would, therefore, seem to be from the Sinaitic hills, crashing through Idumea, thundering by the walls of the holy city, and thence on to the great field of Esdraelon, where the chief stress of the awful pressure falls. Along this line will the main bodies of these assembled nations lie, eager, determined, and confident in the schemes that occupy them, not knowing that they are already in the great wine-press of the wrath of God. " Multitudes, multitudes," armies on armies, hosts on hosts, are there. The Beast is there ; the False Prophet is there ; and the kings, captains, mighty men, and drilled legions of all the nations in league with Antichrist are there ; all gathered into one great pen of slaughter.

" *And the wine-press was trodden.*" What strength have grapes against the weight and power of a man when he comes to set his feet upon them ? And the riper they are, the more helpless. They must needs be crushed, their existence destroyed, their life-blood poured out. And so with these " fully ripe " clusters, now gathered into the great wine-press of the wrath of God. No weapon they can raise, no resistance they can make, can avail them. The beast was hailed as the Invincible ; but his invincibility is nothing now. The False Phophet could make fire come down from heaven in the presence of men, but he can command no fires to withstand the lightnings of the angry and inexorable Judge. The heel of Omnipotence is upon them, and they can only break and sink beneath it.

Long ago had Jehovah spoken of this time and said : " Let the earth hear, and all that is therein ; the world, and all things that come forth of it. For the indignation of the Lord is upon all nations, and His fury upon all their armies ; He hath utterly destroyed them, He hath delivered them to the slaughter. Their slain also shall be cast out, and their stink shall come up out of their carcases, and the mountains shall be melted with their blood. And all the host of heaven shall be loosed, and the heavens shall be rolled together as a scroll ; and all their host shall fall down, as the leaf falleth off from the vine, and as a fallen fig from the fig-tree. For my sword shall be bathed in heaven : behold, it shall come down upon Idumea, and upon the people of my curse to judgment. For it is the day of the Lord's vengeance, and the year of recompenses for the controversy of Zion." (Is. 34 : 1–8.) But men would not hear, neither believe ; therefore, the sword of the Lord is filled with their blood. He cometh from Edom, with dyed garments from Bozrah, treading the wine-press alone, treading them down in His anger, trampling them in His fury, and staining all His raiment with their blood. " When they say, Peace and safety, then sudden destruction cometh upon them, and they cannot escape."

It is " *outside of the city* " that this treading of the wine-press takes place. " The city," mentioned thus absolutely, with no other note of identification, can be none other than " *the holy city*," the city of Jerusalem. The fact that this great judgment does not come within its gates, is evidence of its being " the holy city," the place owned of God the memorial of His salvation in the time of His fierce anger. Amid all the consuming wrath, the judgment stays outside the walls of Jerusalem. Within its holy enclosure is safety. And by some gracious interposition of Heaven, none of the doomed hosts of Antichrist are at this time inside of it. Has it become the possession of the 144,000 whom we saw on Mount Zion ? Has the Lamb by this time cleansed it with judgment as in Ezekiel's vision (chapter 9) ? Hath He already conse-crated and appropriated it as the intended metropolis of the new kingdom ? Has His wonder-working power come forth in such force in connection with the glorification of the 144,000, as then already to have started there an adminis-tration expelling the dominion of the Beast ? Joel says, Jehovah shall then utter His voice with power from Jerusalem. (Joel 3 : 17.) Has it not then already become the seat of His throne ? If so, this would explain why all these armies of the nations are there. Even apart from this, the implication is clear that these forces are gathered for war against the holy city, and against the Lamb. In the ordinary course of things there would be nothing in Jerusalem requiring or occasioning such a tremendous gathering of the kings and armies of the world. If, however, some visible presence of the heavenly kingdom about to take possession of the earth has there begun to display and assert itself ; if divine majesty, miracle and power have by this time taken hold, introducing a new rule and order, exhibiting the presence of the eternal reign of the Son of man, and manifesting the potencies of the world to come ; there is ample call and occasion for this mustering of all the powers of earth and hell.   Determined to crush it out, " the kings of the earth set themselves, and the rulers take counsel together, against the Lord, and against His anointed."   (Ps. 2 : 2.)   A power which could thus cleanse and clear the temple and city of everything contrary to God, and hold at bay all attempts of the unsanctified to enter, would be a thing wholly intolerable to Antichrist.   He who claims to be the only rightful object of human adoration, could not endure the presence of such temerity against his majesty.   If strength in earth and hell exists to subdue and crush it, that strength must be called forth.   And thus these kings and nations, with their armies, are convened.   It is meant to make sure of success.   They fill the land with their collected forces.   They mass themselves in line from Bozrah to Megiddo. They compass about the holy city.   But into it they dare not enter.   And when the wine-press of their destruction is trodden, it is " trodden *outside of the city*."   Before they are able to strike a blow, " the Lion of the tribe of Judah " is upon them in all the terribleness of His great exterminating judgment.

"*And blood came forth out of the wine-press up to the bits of the horses for a distance of* 1,600 *stadia !* "   A river of human blood 160 miles in length, and up to the bridles of the horses in depth, tells an awful story.   When the Romans destroyed Jerusalem, so great was the bloodshed that Josephus says the whole city ran down with the blood to such a degree that the fires of many of the houses were quenched by it.   When Sylla took Athens, Plutarch says the blood that was shed in the market-place alone covered all the ceramicus as far as Dipylus, and some testify that it ran through the gates and overflowed the suburbs.   Nor are we to think of any exaggeration or hyperbole in the very definite description of what John here saw as the consequence of the treading of this wine-press.   It is " *the great wine-press of the wrath of God.*" It is the last great consummate act of destruction which is to end this present world.   The masses on whom it is executed are " the kings of the earth and of the whole world, and their armies " (Rev. 16 : 14 ; 19 : 19), stationed in a line from Bozrah in Edom to Esdraelon in Galilee.   They are to be utterly consumed, so as to " leave them neither root nor branch." (Mal. 4 : 1.)   It is " the great and dreadful day of the Lord " about which all the prophets of all the ages have prophesied.   It is the result of the resentment and anger of Him who is Faithful and True, who in righteousness doth judge and make war, whose eyes are as fire, on whose head are the many crowns, whom all the armies of Heaven follow upon white horses, out of whose mouth goeth a sharp sword, and who " treadeth the wine-press of the fierceness and wrath of Almighty God."   And it must needs be all that John here states, a belt of blood from Bozrah to Esdraelon up to the horses' bridles in depth !   Isaiah says : " The land shall be drunk with blood, and its dust made fat with fatness, for it is the day of Jehovah's vengeance, the year of recompenses for the controversy against Zion."   (Is. 34 : 7, 8.)

Ah, yes ; men in their unbelief may laugh at the Almighty's threatenings. Because sentence against an evil work is not executed speedily, their hearts may be fully set in them to do evil.   And the proud rationalism of many may persuade them that God is too good and merciful ever to fulfil in any literal sense these sanguinary comminations.   But it will be no laughing matter then, no mystic fancy, no meaningless orientalism of the age of extravagant speech.   God hath set His own eternal seal to it, and said : " Seek ye out of the Book of the Lord, and read : no one of these things shall fail." (Is. 34 : 16.)   And yet people make light of it, and turn away to their sins and follies as if it were all nothing !

Child of Adam, hear, and be admonished now while salvation is so freely offered.   Be not deceived, for God is not mocked.   Those impieties of thine, those guilty sports and gaieties, will yet have to be confronted before the judgment seat.   Those gatherings in the gaming-hells and drink-shops of Satan, those sneers and witty jests at sacred things, those fiery lusts burning on the altars of carnal pleasure, are all written down in the account-books of eternity to be brought forth in the great day. That wicked profanation of thy Maker's name, that broken pledge, that unfulfilled vow to God and man, that scene of riot, that hidden going to the haunts of the profligate, all are noted for future settlement. The blood of wronged and murdered innocence will not always cry in vain. The wail of trampled helplessness will not be unheard forever. The mother who destroyed her babe, the clerk who dipped too deep in his employer's till, the enemy who set fire to his neighbour's goods or sought to blacken his good name, the boy who cursed his parents in secret, the spiteful slanderer and persecutor of God's ministers and people, and every despiser and neglecter of the great salvation, must each answer at the tribunal of eternal justice. And if clean repentance out of these and all such sins be not speedy and complete, there is no hope or mercy more. Before us stands the Angel with the sharp sickle for all the enemies of God, and beside Him is the great wine-press of destruction. Think, O man, O woman, how would you fare were He this night to strike! If not *in the city*, in reconciliation with the King, outside is only death and damnation, and nothing can make it different.

LECTURE THIRTY-SIXTH.

REV. 15 : 1–8. (Revised Text.) And I saw another sign in the heaven great and marvellous, seven angels having seven plagues, the last, because in them, the wrath of God was completed.

And I saw like to a sea of glass mingled with fire, and those who conquer from the beast, and from his image, and from the number of his name, standing on [over or by] the sea of glass, having harps of God. And they sing the song of Moses, servant of God, and the song of the Lamb, saying, Great and marvellous thy works, O Lord God, the Almighty, just and true thy ways, Thou the King of the nations : who shall not fear, O Lord, and glorify thy name ? because alone holy, because all the nations shall come and worship in thy presence, because thy judgments [righteous doings] have been made manifest.

And after these things I saw, and there was opened the temple of the tabernacle of the testimony in the heaven ; and there came forth the seven angels who had the seven plagues out of the temple, clothed in pure bright linen, and girdled about their breasts with golden girdles. And one from among the four Living Ones gave to the seven angels seven golden bowls full of the wrath of God, who liveth to the ages of the ages. And the temple was filled with the smoke from the glory of God, and from his power ; and no one could enter into the temple until the seven plagues of the seven angels were completed.

Rev. 16 : 1–11. (Revised Text.) And I heard a great voice saying to the seven angels, Go and pour out the seven bowls of the wrath of God into the earth.

And the first went forth, and poured out his bowl into the earth ; and there became a noisome and grievous sore upon the men who had the mark of the beast, and those who worshipped his image.

And the second poured out his bowl into the sea ; and it became blood as of one dead, and the things in the sea, and every soul of life, died.

And the third poured out his bowl into the rivers and the fountains of waters ; and they became blood. And I heard the angels of the waters saying, Righteous art thou, who art and who wast, holy One, because thou hast judged thus : because they have shed blood of saints and prophets, and thou hast given them blood to drink ; deserving are they. And I heard the altar saying, Yea, Lord God the Almighty, true and just are thy judgments.

And the fourth poured out his bowl on [or over] the sun ; and it was given to it to scorch men with fire. And the men were scorched with great scorching, and they blasphemed the name of the God, he who hath authority over these plagues ; and they repented not to give glory to him.

And the fifth poured out his bowl on [or over] the throne of the beast ; and his kingdom became darkened, and they bit their tongues from the pain, and they blasphemed the God of the heaven from their pain, and from their sores, and repented not out of their deeds.

THE accomplishment of the Harvest and the Vintage brings to the end of this present world. The next in succession would be the setting up of the eternal Kingdom, and the evolution of the new heavens and earth. But the Harvest and the Vintage do not adequately set forth all that we need to know about these closing scenes. Further particulars included in this momentous period require to be shown in order to complete the picture. The fate of the infernal Trinity,—the Dragon, the Beast, and the False Prophet,—and of what pertains to them, is to be more fully described before we come to the Millennium, the descent of the New Jerusalem, and the planting of God's Tabernacle with men. Hence the same ground covered by the visions of the Harvest and Vintage is traversed again and again with reference to particular objects and administrations. As we have four distinct Gospels to give us a full and accurate portraiture of the one glorious Saviour, so we have these several presentations with reference to one and the same momentous period of the end.   Each vision, however, has its own particular office, scope, and features, giving some special aspect or phase in the general sum of events. It is not mere repetition of the same thing, but the separate presentation of particular administrations or occurrences of which the whole is made up.

Chapters 15 and 16 belong together.   They form one whole, touching one important subject, to wit : the third or last *woe*.   The contents bear a close analogy to the conclusion of chapter 11, if they be not indeed the continuation and amplification of what was there summarily introduced ; for all these visions are very intimately related, both in general subject and time.   There the temple in heaven was opened, and lightning, voices, thunders, earthquake, and great hail followed.   Here the same temple is opened, and out of it issue seven angels, with the seven last plagues, who empty their bowls of the wrath of God in calamities upon the wicked world, culminating in the very things named as the result of the opening there.   There the Elders said that the nations were enraged, that God's wrath had come, and that the time to destroy them that corrupt the earth had been reached.   Here we are shown the pouring out of that wrath, its particular instruments, subjects, operations, and results.

John begins by telling of " another *sign* in the heaven."   In chapter 12 he told of two signs : the sign of the sun-clad Woman, and the sign of the great Red Dragon.   It is with reference to them that he calls this " *another* sign." Three signs were given to Moses, Gideon, Saul, and Elijah.   Three signs are mentioned in Matthew 24 as heralding the Lord's coming,—the sign of the Son of man in heaven, the putting forth of leaves by the withered fig-tree, and the lapse of the world into the condition in which it was at the time of the flood. And so we have here three signs.   The signs of the Woman and the Dragon, answer to the first and second chapters of Exodus ; the sign now before us, answers to the judgments which followed, through the ministry of Moses and Aaron.

This sign is " great and marvellous."   It is great, as involving so much more in range and intensity than anything of the kind that has ever been ; and it is marvellous, with reference to the unparalleled character of what it foretells. What it describes is altogether extraordinary, and on an astounding scale.   It is the consummation of marvels in this present world.   The sign itself is, " Seven Angels having seven plagues, the last ones, because in them the wrath of God was completed."   Signs of healing accompanied the preaching of the Gospel ; signs of death attend the end of the world.   Much of the Apocalypse treats of plagues—" the plagues that are written in this Book."   Those here signified are " *the last*," with reference to what happened to Egypt, or with reference to the judgments under the Seals and trumpets, or simply with reference to the particular end of things which they are to work.   They are visitations upon the living world—upon men in the flesh.   They have been named " the opening artillery of God, ere the shock of battle comes."   The seven Angels who bear them have been likened to priests of heaven, pouring out the drink-offerings of wine over the sacrifice ere it is slain and consumed.

But before proceeding to give the particulars of this great and marvellous " sign," the Seer interjects another vision, of a more gracious order, though connected with these outpourings of the plagues.   When the wicked are cut off, the righteous shall see it ; and when these plagues fall upon Antichrist and his hosts, those who through suffering and death keep clear of his worship and mark, are on high, singing, and harping, and giving glory to God and the Lamb, as stroke upon stroke from the heavenly temple smites their oppressors. John writes : " *I saw like to a sea of glass mingled with fire, and those who conquer out from the Beast, and from his image, and from the number of his name, standing on, over, or by the sea of glass, having harps of God.*"

This likeness to a sea of glass reminds of that " glassy sea " which spread

out before the throne in chapter 4.   If it is the same, it has become omi-
nously commingled now ; for there it was " like unto crystal " in clearness,
but here it is " mingled with fire." There it seemed to be a part of the economy
and pavement of the heaven ; here it appears rather as a mighty reservoir
of just judgments about to be precipitated upon the world below.   There it
looked like a sort of base on which the whole celestial establishment rested,
representing perhaps the purity, vastness, and strength of God's counsels, on
which all things depend ; here it does not seem to be the support of anything,
though the victors named may be over, by, or even on it.   It is probably
meant to symbolize the vastness, purity, justice and severity of the divine
counsels in those retributions about to fall upon the wicked.   It is best taken
as a sea of just judgments which are poured forth in the seven final plagues,
whilst in that regard at the same time a sea of blessed vindication and joy to
those faithful ones whom the Beast persecuted unto death.

The picture of these victorious ones standing on the shore of this sea,
holding harps of God, and singing the song of Moses, directly recalls the
rescued and victorious children of Israel on the further side of the Red Sea,
beholding the discomfiture of their foes, and singing and rejoicing in the
mighty accomplishments of the wonder-working Jehovah.   " Then sang
Moses and the children of Israel this song unto the Lord, and spake, saying, I
will sing unto the Lord, for He hath triumphed gloriously ; the horse and his
rider hath He thrown into the sea.   Who is like unto Thee, O Lord, among the
gods, who is like Thee, glorious in holiness, fearful in praises, doing wonders ? " (Ex. 15 : 1–11.)   And here the victors sing the song of Moses over
again, looking out upon another sea of judgment as its fiery waves dash upon
their oppressors.   Here, however, the song goes beyond that of Moses, and
takes in that of the Lamb as well, which is the song of victory over sin and
death, the song of justification and eternal life through the blood and triumph
of Jesus, whose dominion and right as the Lord of the nations are attested by
these mighty judgments.   Of old it was prophesied, that, when " the king "
for whom Tophet is ordained and prepared is smitten, the victory over him
shall be celebrated " with tabrets and harps " (Is. 30 : 32, 33) ; and here
John beholds the fulfilment. They stand by the sea of glass mingled with fire,
having harps of God, and they sing, saying, " Great and marvellous are Thy
works, O Lord God, the Almighty, just and true are Thy ways, Thou, the King
of the nations ! Who shall not fear, O Lord, and glorify Thy name, alone
holy ? because all the nations shall come and worship in Thy presence,
because Thy judgments have been made manifest ! "   When consuming
wrath falls on the servants of the false god, the true God's worshippers are
beyond the fiery sea, singing their adoration to their Deliverer. Having felt
the Dragon's wrath, they are joyously free and secure from the great wrath of
God. And their outlook is one of abiding blessedness. Verily, there is nothing
like being firm and true to what is right. Whatever it may cost for the time,
it will be amply recompensed in the great day.

With this statement concerning those whom the Beast and False Prophet
cannot conquer, the holy Apostle proceeds with what he began to tell about as
" another sign in the heaven "—the seven last plagues. He first describes the
heavenly economy of them, and then the execution of them, together with
their several effects. Let us follow him reverently.

He saw " *the temple of the tabernacle of the testimony in heaven opened.*"
This was the innermost part of the temple, the Temple of the temple, the
Holy of holies, the deepest centre of the dwelling-place and throne
of God.

The tables of stone, inscribed with the precepts of the Law, which God gave
to Moses, are called the " tables of testimony." These were commanded to
be put into the holy Ark, which thence was called " the Ark of the testimony."
This Ark had its place in the innermost and holiest department of the Tabernacle, which thus became the particular tent or " tabernacle of the testi-

mony." And this innermost shrine of the temple in heaven, John saw open, revealing, as stated, in chapter 11 : 19, the very ark itself, and indicating that all the hidden powers of eternity were now about to show themselves in active earthward administrations.

From the depth of this holiness issued *seven angels*. They are priest-angels, for they are clothed in pure bright linen, and girded about their breasts with golden girdles, which is the priest's dress. They appear as priests, because they come for the sacrificing of a great sacrifice to the offended holiness and justice of God. The girdle of the Jewish high priest was a mixture of blue, and purple, and scarlet, and fine-twined linen, along with the " gold " (Lev. 16 : 4) ; the girdles here are pure gold ; for the temple is higher, and the administration holier ; and the officiators belong to heaven, not earth.

" *And one from among the four Living Ones gave to the seven angels seven golden bowls full of the wrath of God.*" This is not the first time we hear of these Living Ones taking part in the actual administration of judgment. They are indeed glorified men ; but " do ye not know that the saints shall judge the world ? " (1 Cor. 6 : 2, 3.) When the horsemen of chapter 6 were sent forth, " one from among the four Living Ones " gave the command, as with a voice of thunder. Here a corresponding part of the same judgment work is to be executed, and the vessels containing the wrath of God are handed out by one of the same Living Ones. The vessels themselves were not *bottles*, as our English version would intimate, but shallow, pan-like, golden bowls, or censers, such as were used in the temple to hold the fire when incense was burned. They are priestly censers, as in chapter 8 : 5. That which gives vitality to the prayers of saints and sustains the Jehovah worship, at the same time carries the burning coals of judgment upon the wicked. That which seethes and smokes in these holy censers is God's punishment upon transgression, the consuming intolerance of His holiness toward sin and sinners. Seven of these bowls, full to the brim with the wrath of Him who liveth for the ages of the ages, are thus handed to the seven priest-angels to be poured upon the sacrifice preparatory to its final consumption. And terrible is the smoke of their burning.

When the first tabernacle was dedicated, a cloud filled it, and Moses was not able to enter into it because of the cloud of the glory of the Lord. (Ex. 40 : 34, 35.) When Solomon's temple was dedicated the cloud of the divine glory so filled the house that the priests could not stand to minister because of it. (1 Kings 8 : 10, 11.) It was *a cloud* then, veiling the insufferable brightness of that Jehovah-presence which it indicated ; but here is the day of the fierceness of divine wrath, and in place of the shadowing cloud is the lurid fiery smoke ;—the same which Isaiah saw (6 : 1-4) in his vision of the enthroned Jehovah. It fills the temple in heaven ; and so intense is the manifestation of the divine glory and power that no one, even of the sons of God, is able to enter until the filled censers have been quite emptied out upon the doomed world. And from the midst of these awful signs a great voice sounds, like the trumpet sounding from the smoke and fire on Mount Sinai, saying to the seven angels, " *Go, and pour out the seven bowls of the wrath of God into the earth.*"

Glancing now for a moment at some of the current interpretations of these seven last plagues, we cannot but wonder that any should consider all this tremendous and unparalleled ado in heaven to be for nothing more than a few petit events in the ordinary course of human history. Yet some gravely tell us that the first bowl is the French Revolution ; the second bowl, the naval wars of that Revolution ; the third bowl, the battles of Napoleon in Italy ; the fourth bowl, the tyranny and military oppression of Napoleon ; the fifth bowl, the calamities which befell the city of Rome and the Pope in consequence of the French Revolution ; the sixth bowl, the wane of the Turkish power, the return of the Jews to Palestine, and the subtle influences of infidelity, Popery and Puseyism ; and the seventh, some further war with

Romanism and disaster to the city of Rome. But can it be possible that God Almighty from His everlasting seat, the temple in heaven, all angels and holy ones on high, should thus be in new and unexampled commotion, with the mightiest of all celestial demonstrations, over nothing but a few occurrences in a small part of the smallest section of the globe, and those occurrences far less in meaning or moment than many others in other ages ! According to such interpretation mankind have been living for the last 100 years amid the extreme terrors of " the great and terrible day of the Lord " without ever knowing it ! yea, dreaming the while that we are happily gliding into the era of universal liberty and peace ! Are France and Italy *the earth !* Are half a dozen naval battles, scattered over a dozen years, and touching here and there a speck of sea hardly to be pointed out on a terrestrial globe, to be taken as the turning of the whole ocean to blood, by which everything that lives in the sea dies ! If Napoleon's artillery was the sunscorch of blasphemers, was not the blasphemy of the scorchers by far worse than the blasphemy of the scorched ! Alas for the worth of Revelation if this is the proper way of reading it !

The greatest plagues of judgment of which we read in the past were those poured out upon ancient Egypt. They were literal plagues, which happened according to the terms in which they are recorded. These seven last plagues are the consummation of God's judgment plagues, including in them all that have gone before, and rendering in final and intensest perfection what was previously rehearsed on a smaller scale, preliminary to the great performance. What the preparatory rehearsal was, that must the final rendering be. The last plagues must therefore be literal too. In what sense or degree, however, was the French Revolution, or the doings of Napoleon Bonaparte, a consummation of the plagues of Egypt ? Read, and ponder.

The first priest-angel " *poured out his bowl into the earth, and there became a grievous sore upon the men who had the mark of the Beast, and those who worship his image.*" Did none but Romanists suffer from the French Revolution and the military despotism which it evolved ? If so, this plague does not refer to that event ; for it touches only such as have the mark of the Beast. The sores of Lazarus at the rich man's gate were not Romish errors, nor French infidelity ; but the sore of this angel's outpouring is denoted by the same word which described the ailment of Lazarus. It is the Egyptian plague of ulcers intensified. Burnt earth was there scattered, " and it became a boil, breaking forth with blains, upon man and upon beast ; " and it was " upon the magicians, and upon all the Egyptians." (Ex. 19 : 8–12.) When Moses afterwards pronounced the curses of heaven upon those who disown God and throw off allegiance to Him, he said : " The Lord will smite thee with the botch of Egypt, and with the emerods, and with the scab, and with the itch, whereof thou canst not be healed. The Lord shall smite thee in the knees, and in the legs, with a sore botch that cannot be healed, from the sole of thy foot unto the top of thy head." (Deut. 28 : 15, 27, 35.) This has never yet been fulfilled ; but John here sees it fulfilled upon those who have cast off the worship of Jehovah for the worship and mark of the Antichrist.

" *And the second poured out his bowl into the sea ; and it became blood, as of one dead, and the things in the sea, every soul of life, died.*" So far as the naval battles of the French Revolution affected the sea, they killed nothing of the living things therein, but fattened them, and scarcely stained a single wave ; so far were they from turning all the ocean's waters into bloody clots. One of the plagues of Egypt was, that God " turned their waters into blood, and slew their fish." (Is. 105 : 30.) Under the second trumpet (chapter 8 : 8) the sea was affected, and the third of it was turned into blood. But here the whole sea is affected, and a change is wrought which makes all its waters like to the blood of one dead,—clotted, putrescent, and utterly destructive of the life of what lives in the sea. Hengstenberg and others say that we are here to think of " the shedding of blood in war ; " but there is not a word said about war ; and if living things in the sea mean human beings, peoples, nations, tribes, and tongues, this plague sweeps them all out of existence ; for every living thing in the sea dies of this blood. If it refers to war, it is a very anomalous war, for it leaves neither conquered nor conquerors, and the plagues which follow have no subjects on which to operate. Stuart holds that " a literal fulfilment is not to be sought after ; " but if it is not literal, then were not the plagues of Egypt literal, nor is any other sort of fulfilment possible ; and thus the tremendous record is rendered meaningless. I take it as it reads ; and if any dissent, on them is the burden of proving some other sense, and of reducing to agreement their mutually destructive notions as to what it does mean. Take it as God has caused it to be written, and there can be no disagreement ; take it in any other way, and the uncertainty is endless.

" *And the third poured out his bowl into the rivers and the fountains of waters ; and they became blood.*" When Moses stretched out his hand upon the waters of Egypt, upon their streams, upon their rivers, and upon all their pools of water, " all the waters that were in the river were turned to blood ; and the fish that were in the river died ; and the river stank, and the Egyptians could not drink of the water of the river ; and there was blood throughout all the land of Egypt." (Ex. 7 : 19–21.) And what thus happened with *one* river and *one* country, now occurs in all waters in all countries. Under the third trumpet (chap. 8 : 10, 11), a third of the rivers and water-springs became nauseous and noxious with bitterness ; but this plague touches them all, and turns them into blood, so that the hosts of Antichrist can find nothing to drink but blood. A more dreadful plague can hardly be imagined ; but it is just. "The angel of the waters," he who has the administration of this plague, is amazed at the greatness of the infliction, but breaks forth in celebration of the righteousness of Him who was, and is [now no longer *to come*, because already come], and praises Him for having thus judged. The punishment is full of horror ; but it is deserved. They shed the blood of saints and prophets, and it is due that now their only drink is blood. " Yea, Lord God the Almighty," answers the altar, " true and just are Thy judgments ! " When God once comes with His terrible awards upon the wicked, the righteousness of them will be so conspicuous, and the justice and truth of His administrations will be so clear and manifest, that it will not be in the power of any holy being to find a flaw, to raise a question, or to withhold the profoundest Amen. And when the earth refuses to yield any drink but blood to its apostate population, angels, and altar, and all heaven must confess and answer that it is just ; they deserve it.

" *And the fourth poured out his bowl* [here the preposition changes from εἰς to ἐπί] *on or over the sun ; and it was given to it [the sun] to scorch men [mankind] with fire. And the men were scorched with great scorching.*" This belongs to the predicted " signs in the sun." Under the fourth trumpet (chap. 8 : 12), the heavenly bodies were affected ; but in a different way from this. There the sun was one-third darkened ; here its power and heat are increased, till its rays become like flames. The sun exists and shines by God's command ; and He can make it scorch and torture, as well as cheer and warm. Moses and Malachi have spoken of that day as one that shall " *burn as an oven,*" when men shall be " devoured with burning heat." (Deut. 32 : 24 ; Mal. 4 : 1.) Here also belongs the fulfilment of Isaiah's words : " The earth mourneth and fadeth away, the world languisheth and fadeth away, the haughty people of the earth do languish ; because they have transgressed the laws, changed the ordinances, broken down the everlasting covenant, therefore hath the curse devoured the earth, and they that dwell therein are desolate ; therefore *the inhabitants of the earth are burned, and few men left.*" (Is. 24 : 4–13.) Some say, " It is not of the natural scorching of the sun's rays, and of the injurious effects flowing from it, such as excessive heats, drought, and famine, that we are here to think ; " but of what else can we think ? It is the sun that is smitten ; that smiting causes the emission of rays that scorch and burn to a degree that John says they are *fire ;* and to think of anything but scorching and consuming heat from the sun is simply to browbeat the words of inspiration. Men are scorched by an extraordinary power of the sun, oppressed, burned, killed by its fiery rays, smitten with sunstroke, overwhelmed with siroccos, suffocated with solar heat ; and yet we are not to think of the sun, or of any injurious effects from its burning rays ! O the havoc which men make of God's word to fit it to their faulty theories ! Here is one of the last plagues of " the great and terrible day of the Lord ; " and it is nothing less than God's glorious sunshine, intensified with fiery heat, so that it burns and scorches earth and man, decimating the inhabitants of city and country alike. Disastrous plague !

We would think that such a succession of ills would bring the most infatuated to their senses, and that there would come forth from all the world one loud repentant cry to God for mercy. We would think it impossible for people with souls in them to hold out against such exhibitions of angry Almightiness. But no ; they only blaspheme the name of the God having command of these plagues, and repent not to give glory to Him. They have all sold themselves to hell and received the sacrament and seal of it upon their bodies, and they only dare and sin on to their inevitable damnation.

Many are waiting for times of affliction and death to bring them to repentance and salvation ; but those who wilfully sin away their good days count in vain on something softening and remedial from the judgments of their despised and incensed Maker. The sun may scorch, and extort still further blasphemies, but it cannot change the stubborn heart, or burn into it the saving fear and love of God. Sin is a cancer, which, if left to run too long, can never more be cured. Another judgment-plague descends, but with no better effect.

" *The fifth Angel poured out his bowl on or over the throne of the Beast ; and his kingdom became darkened, and they bit their tongues from the pain, and they blasphemed the God of the heaven from their pain, and from their sores, and repented not out of their deeds.*" The effects of these judgments overlap each other. The sores of the first plague are still felt during the second and third, and even here under the fifth. This proves that these plagues all fall upon the people of one and the same generation, and hence dare not be extended through centuries. The Antichrist has but $3\frac{1}{2}$ years, and all seven of these last plagues fall upon him and his followers. Here his very throne is assailed, and his entire dominion is filled with darkness. The last but one of the Egyptian plagues was a plague of darkness. The Book of Wisdom (17 : 21) says : " Over them was spread a heavy night, an image of that darkness which should afterward receive them ; but yet were they unto themselves more grievous than the darkness." Here is a corresponding darkness, coextensive with the world-wide empire of this Beast. From the centre of his kingdom, even to its utmost limits, everything is darkened. Isaiah prophesied of this when he said, " Behold, *the darkness shall cover the earth, and gross darkness the people.*" (Is. 60 : 2.) Joel prophesied of it when he said : " The day of the Lord cometh, *a day of darkness and of gloominess, a day of clouds and thick darkness.*" " The sun shall be turned into darkness, and the moon into blood." (Joel 2 : 1, 2, 31.) Nahum prophesied of it when he said that the fierceness of God's anger shall be poured out like fire, and " *darkness* shall pursue His enemies." (Nah. 1 : 6, 8.) Our blessed Saviour prophesied of it when He declared : " In those days, after that tribulation, *the sun shall be darkened, and the moon shall not give her light, and the stars of heaven shall fall,*" failing in all their offices of light-givers. (Mark 13 : 24, 25.) And great are the miseries of that darkness ; for it causes those who feel it to bite their tongues by reason of the distress which it adds to all the rest of their torments. And is it nothing but the suppression of the monasteries and Romish clergy in France in 1789, and Napoleon's levies upon the revenues and seizure of the properties and person of a helpless old Pope ? Have all the prophets been thus stirred up by the Holy Ghost to tell the world of those few, limited, and temporary calamities incident to ordinary human ambition and war, that all men of all ages might stand in awe and fear God lest they should come under Napoleon's dealings with the papacy ? Would it not seem as if some shadows of this coming darkness were already upon the understandings of some of Christ's professed ministers ? God help them to the light, that they may repent out of their sad mistreatments of these great revelations, and give to Him the glory by doing just honour to His Holy Word !

The darkness which thus comes over the kingdom of the Beast must be literal, as that of Egypt was ; for that was the prelibation of this,—the pre-rehearsal of what is to come. If not literal, it is impossible for any man to tell us what it is. People may guess and reason, but that cannot fix the meaning of God's word. And to carry the theory of a mere " figurative representation " into all the sacred predictions which refer to it, can only spread this darkness upon some of the most momentous portions of divine revelation. It is at all events vastly better to risk mistake by clinging fast to the plain sense of what God has caused to be written for our learning, than to go floundering through a world of fancies, ever learning, but never able to come to the knowledge of the truth. And if in the great day of fulfilment, when God shall turn these prophecies into living realities, things should not turn out according to the terms used by the Holy Ghost, we shall be the more excusable for having clung to the record as it stands. In any event, our simple faith will be our best apology.

This darkening of the Beast's kingdom, added to the earlier inflictions, brings terrible distress. The description indicates the intensest writhings of anguish, the very madness of vexation and pain. The people who suffer these plagues bite their tongues, chew them, gnaw them, as their best diversion from their misery. Their tongues have spoken blasphemies, and they themselves thus punish them. Earth has become like hell for wickedness, and so it becomes like hell for darkness and torment,—nay, still further like hell, because there is no repentance in its inhabitants. Instead of cursing themselves for their impieties, they curse God as the offender, for thus interfering with their preferences and their peace. To the ulcers, the bloody waters, the sun-scorches, now comes this horrible darkness ; and a God of such administrations they disdain to honour, even under all their miseries. They will gnaw their tongues with pain and rage rather than speak a prayer of penitence to Him. Nothing but cursing and horrid denunciations will they utter. When they saw the two slain Witnesses come to life again and ascend to heaven, they were willing to own that the God of heaven is God, and to give Him something of His glory. But it was only a temporary reverence, which soon faded away. Here they are again compelled to acknowledge Him as " the God of heaven," but it is only to heap new blasphemies on His name.

Some talk of conversion in hell, and of an ultimate restoration of the wicked. Does this presentation look as if such a thing were possible ? If hell-torments can cure men of their wickedness, why are not these people subdued to penitence ? These are the outpourings of that very divine wrath which makes hell ; but where is the remedial impression, the turning from sin, the seeking for reconciliation ? And while sin lasts, hell must last. These people have rebelled until the very spirit of perdition has settled in upon their souls, and henceforth there is no more hope for them. Another bowl of wrath is poured out ; but its effect is the opening of the ways for the gathering of them together to the scene of slaughter ; and then follows the last, which lets loose upon them all the long-chained thunders of angered Omnipotence, overwhelming their works and lives in a sea of blood !

Many, my friends, are the pictures of God's judgments upon those who reject His Gospel, and refuse to have Him rule over them. A dreadful catalogue we have had before us to-night. But with how poor and feeble an interest do many regard these momentous revelations ! There is perhaps nothing which a sinner, or neglecter of God and his soul, so little expects, as the punishment of his sins. Of ungodliness in general, its sinfulness, its danger, and the certain judgment of God upon it, he can discourse with fluency and confidence. He has no doubt that God is a holy God, and will by no means spare those who fail to make their peace with Him. But when it comes to his own sins, negligence and disobedience, what thought or feeling has he of that awful accountability which in the abstract he so readily admits ? To what extent does he realize that *his* sins will find him out, or that *he* is the one in danger ? He listens ; he assents ; he hears with pleasure the array of reasoning about righteousness, temperance, and judgment to come ; he even admires the vivid and faithful preaching of the sure and terrible wrath of God upon transgressors ; and yet he goes on in his sins and disobedience, betimes a little disturbed, but soon recomposed in his impenitence, unconverted from his old ways, till the end comes, and he dies as he lived, unreconciled to God, unsanctified, and unsaved.

Have I thus hit upon the case of any one now listening to me ? Then let this subject be to you an effectual warning. Here is the laying open to your view of what must come upon the unbelieving wlord. Here is the sacred foreshowing of the end which awaits them that know not God, and obey not the Gospel of His Son. There is an indissoluble ligament which binds together impenitence in sin and inevitable damnation. Even the incense bowls of the holy altar are full of the'wrath of God for all despisers and neglecters of the great salvation. Angels of the heavenly temple stand girt in gold, prepared and ready to pour them out. And we need only listen with an attentive ear to hear the rustle and mutter of the dreadful thunder of those cataracts of God's indignation upon them that turn not from their sins. Have you never felt the sting and rankling poison in your soul, if not in your very bones, of some past transgressions of which you have made yourself guilty ? Has your conscience never smitten you, and made your sleep uneasy, and tinged your thinking with bitterness, for the sort of life you have been leading ? Is there not some conscious shame and sense of wretchedness going along with the indulgence even of those darling lusts and dislike of sacred things which you allow to have place in your heart ? And what is all this but the premonitory drops of that wrath of God which must presently come in great deluging showers ? O child of man, give heed, and turn, and fly, before the threatening avalanche of the Almighty's judgments comes ! And now, whilst this little feeling of anxiety and disturbance is upon you, let it not pass without a thorough change in all your ways ; lest the next time the feeling of compunction comes, it may find you amid the hopeless torments of eternal death.

LECTURE THIRTY-SEVENTH

THE SIXTH BOWL OF WRATH—THE EUPHRATES LITERALLY DRIED—THE UNCLEAN SPIRITS— THE ENTHUSIASM THEY AWAKEN—A SINGULAR NOTE OF WARNING—HARMAGEDDON— THE SEVENTH BOWL OF WRATH—ITS EFFECTS SYNOPTICALLY GIVEN—CONVULSIONS IN THE AIR—IN THE EARTH—TOPOGRAPHY OF JERUSALEM CHANGED—GREAT BABYLON REMEMBERED IN THE PRESENCE OF GOD—CONFIGURATION OF THE EARTH ALTERED—AN UNPRECEDENTED HAILSTORM—INVETERATE DEPRAVITY.

REV. 16 : 12–21. (Revised Text.) And the sixth poured out his bowl on [or *over*] the great river, the Euphrates ; and the water of it was dried up, that the way of the kings, they from the sunrising, might be prepared. And I saw out of the mouth of the dragon, out of the mouth of the beast, and out of the mouth of the false prophet three unclean spirits, like frogs ; for they are the spirits of demons, working miracles, which go forth on [or *over*] the kings of the whole habitable world, to gather them to the battle of the great day of God the Almighty. (Behold, I come as a thief ; blessed he that watcheth, and keepeth his garments, that he walk not naked, and they see his shame.) And they gathered them together to the place which is called in Hebrew Harmageddon.

And the seventh poured out his bowl on [or *over*] the air ; and there came forth a voice out of the temple from the throne, saying, *It is done.* And there became lightnings, and voices, and thunderings ; and there became a great earthquake, such as became not since there became a man on the earth, such an earthquake, so great. And the great city became into three parts, and the cities of the nations fell, and Babylon the great was remembered in the presence of God, to give to her the cup of the wine of the fierceness of his anger. And every island fled, and mountains w ere not found, and a great hail, like as a talent [in weight], fell out of the heaven on the men ; and the men blasphemed God on account of the plague of the hail, because the plague thereof is exceedingly great.

THE vision of the seven last plagues presents a distinct series of events, giving details of the last great afflictions which fall upon the world, then quite given over into the Devil's hands. Thus far we have briefly considered five of these disastrous outpourings from the golden bowls. Two more remain to engage our present attention. Let us not forget to look devoutly to God our Father to help us understand them.

" *And the sixth angel poured out his bowl on or over the great river Euphrates ; and the water of it was dried up, that the way of the kings, they from the sunrising, might be prepared.*" This must mean the literal river. The ulcers are literal ; the sea, streams, and watersprings, turned to a condition resembling blood are literal ; the heat and scorching from the sun are literal ; the darkness which covers the dominion of the Beast is literal ; and this must necessarily be literal too, whatever mysteriousness may be involved. The opening of a dry passage through the Red Sea, and through the Jordan, when Israel came out of Egypt and entered Canaan, were literal matters of fact ; and they were openings for judgments upon the wicked, as well as of help and favour to the Lord's chosen. The drying up of the tongue of the Egyptian sea prepared the way for the great and final destruction of the oppressive powers that sought Israel's ruin. The rolling back of Jordan's waters was likewise the preparation and opening for the fall of Jericho, and the overthrow of the Canaanitic confederations. And this drying up of the great river Euphrates is a corresponding event, to prepare the way for the more wonderful destruction to which the kings of the earth and their armies are gathered in the great day of God Almighty. Isaiah (11 : 15) refers to it where he says : "With His mighty wind shall he shake his hand over the river [evidently the Euphrates], and shall smite it in the seven streams, and make men go over dryshod." A recovery of certain remnants of the Jewish people is there connected with this miracle, " as it was to Israel in the day that he came up out of Egypt ; " but here, as there, one of the most marked things is the opening for and leading of the doomed powers to their destruction.   Zechariah refers to this, along with some of the preceding plagues, where he says : " He shall pass through the sea with affliction, and shall smite the waves in the sea, *and all the deeps in the river shall dry up*, and the pride of Assyria shall be brought down." (Zech. 10 : 11 ; see also Jer. 51 : 36.)   At the sounding of the sixth trumpet, the same great river was referred to as a bond or boundary to certain destructive powers, which were then let loose in dreadful inflictions upon the wicked populations of the earth.*   So here it is referred to as a barrier in the way of movements which terminate in fearful disaster to those who for unholy purposes avail themselves of its removal.

From time immemorial the Euphrates, with its tributaries, has been a great and formidable boundary between the peoples east of it and those west of it. It runs a distance of 1,800 miles, and is scarcely fordable anywhere or at any time.   It is from three to twelve hundred yards wide, and from ten to thirty feet in depth ; and most of the time it is still deeper and wider.   It was the boundary of the dominion of Solomon, and is repeatedly spoken of as the northeast limit of the lands promised to Israel.   (Gen. 15 : 18 ; Deut. 11 : 24 ; Josh. 1 : 4.)   Some think that Abraham is called a *Hebrew*, and all his descendants *Hebrews*, because he crossed this river, migrating from the further side of it to this. History frequently refers to the great hindrance the Euphrates has been to military movements ; and it has always been a line of separation between the peoples living east of it and those living west of it.   But in the time of the pouring out of the sixth bowl of judgment this river is to be mysteriously smitten and dried up, that the kings from the sunrising may have an easy passage for their armies in coming to join the great infernal crusade against the Lamb.   It looks like a gracious event, and a gracious aspect it has in some of the prophecies respecting it, for it also facilitates the return of certain remnants of the Israelitish people ; but as God's opening through the Red Sea proved a trap of destruction to the persecuting Egyptians, so will it be in this case to the kings from the sunrising.   Availing themselves of the easy passage thus afforded to come forth, they come to a scene of slaughter from which they never return.   It is the outpouring of a bowl of wrath which opens their way.   It is a judgment though it seems for the time to be a favour.

But the mere drying up of the river would not so much harm them were not other agencies at work, to induce them to make use of the facilities thus afforded.   The kings and armies of the world would not come together into Palestine were there not a very extraordinary influeuce to bring about the marvellous congregation.   Accordingly the rapt seer tells of a mysterious infernal ministry in the matter.   Not only does this sixth bowl of wrath dry up the Euphrates. It likewise evokes spirits of hell to incite, deceive, and persuade the nations to their ruin.   John says : " *I saw out of the mouth of the Dragon, and out of the mouth of the Beast, and out of the mouth of the False Prophet, three unclean spirits, like frogs ; for they are the spirits of demons, working miracles, which go forth on or over the kings of the whole habitable world, to gather them to the battle of the great day of God, the Almighty.*"

When the unexampled wickedness of Ahab was come to the full, and it was determined in heaven that an end should be made of him, " The Lord said : Who shall persuade Ahab, that he may go up and fall at Ramoth-Gilead ? And one said on this matter, and another said on that matter.   And there came forth a spirit, and stood before the Lord, and said : I will persuade him. And the Lord said unto him, Wherewith ? And he said : I will go forth, and I will be a lying spirit in the mouth of all his prophets.   And he said : Thou shalt persuade him, and prevail also ; go forth and do so."   So the Lord put a lying spirit in the mouth of all Ahab's prophets ; and he went up to Ramoth-Gilead, and was woundedˌbetween the joints of his harness,and was brought back

* Rev. 9 : 13–21. See pp. 217–222.

a dead man, and the dogs licked up his blood.   (1 Kings 22 : 19–38.)   A spirit of
hell was allowed to go forth to inflame and deceive him to his ruin. And so it is
in this case, only on a vastly greater scale, and with mightier demonstrations,
to persuade and deceive all the kings and governments of the earth to join in
an expedition which proves the most terribly disastrous of all the expeditions
ever undertaken by man.   In Ahab's case there was but one evil spirit ; here
are *three*, if indeed this definite number does not mean an indefinite multitude.
It is something of the plague of frogs repeated ; and then the number was
infinite.   By these demon spirits the cause of the Dragon, the Beast, and the
False Prophet, is furnished with a universal ministry.   They are sent out by
this infernal Trinity, issue from it, do its bidding, act for it and in its interest.
They have the power of working miracles, Satanic miracles, by which they
offset everything divinely supernatural, and persuade by their preaching,
oracles, and lying wonders, stirring up all the powers that be to unite in one
universal movement to suppress and exterminate the incoming kingdom and
power of the Lamb.

To tell exactly who and what these seducing devils are, and exactly how
they manage their infernal mission, may not be in our power.   It is not
necessary that we should have definite knowledge of that sort.   But this is
not the only place where their agency and successes are mentioned.   Paul tells
us that the Spirit speaketh expressly, that in the latter times seducing spirits
shall manifest themselves, even teaching demons, deceiving men with their
lies.   (1 Tim. 4 : 1, 2.)   They are spirits ; they are " unclean spirits ; " they
are " demon spirits ; " they are sent forth into activity by the Dragon Trinity ;
they are the elect agents to awaken the world to the attempt to abolish God
from the earth ; and they are frog-like in that they come forth out of the
pestiferous quagmires of the universe, do their work amid the world's evening
shadows, and creep, and croak, and defile, and fill the ears of the nations with
their noisy demonstrations, till they set all the kings and armies of the whole
earth in enthusiastic commotion for the final crushing out of the Lamb and
all His powers.   As in chapter 9, the seven Spirits of God and of Christ went
forth into all the earth to make up and gather together into one holy fellowship
the great congregation of the sanctified ; so these spirits of hell go forth upon
the kings and potentates of the world, to make up and gather together the
grand army of the Devil's worshippers.

Nor need we wonder at their success.   Those who will not hear and obey the
voice of God, are sure to be led captive by the Devil and his emissaries.   How
great was the stir, and how intense the enthusiasm, awakened throughout
Europe by the crusader craze set on foot by Peter the Hermit !   How were the
nations aroused and set on fire to recover the holy places from the dominion
of the Moslem !   What myriads rushed to arms, took the mark of the red cross
on their shoulders, and went forth as one man, never once calculating by what
means they should live, much less reach the expected victory !   And what
thus happened throughout Europe in reference to a campaign professedly *for*
Christ, may readily happen throughout the whole habitable world, when the
question of the sovereignty of the earth hangs upon the success or failure of
one last, grand, and universal engagement of battle.   It is in sacred irony of
the universal enthusiasm stirred up by these spirits, that Jehovah says by the
mouth of Joel (3 : 9–11) : " Proclaim ye this among the Gentiles ; prepare war ;
wake up the mighty men ; let all the men of war draw near ; let them come up.
Beat your ploughshares into swords, and your pruning hooks into spears ; let
the weak say, I am strong.   Assemble yourselves together round about ! "   The
divine taunt thus expressed reflects the character of the proceedings which it
scorns. The heathen are on fire with rage. The kings of the earth set themselves.
The rulers take counsel together against the Lord, and against His Anointed.
The cry is, Let us break their bands asunder, and cast away their cords from
us !   But He that sitteth in the heavens laughs, and the Lord hath them in
derision.   (Ps. 2 : 1–4.)

Just here, however, there breaks in a singular note of warning. Whilst the unclean spirits are successfully stirring up the kings of the whole habitable world and gathering them for the battle of the great day, John hears a voice, which says, " *Behold I come as a thief ; blessed he that watcheth, and keepeth his garments, that he walk not naked, and they see his shame.*" What means this strange announcement here ? It is plainly the voice of Jesus, and the word is like to that so often given to the Church with reference to His coming again ; but how does it apply here, after so many classes, including the great body of the saved, are already in heaven, with all their anxious watching past ? By referring to the vision interjected at the opening of this account of the seven last plagues, we may perhaps come upon the true explanation. There is a gathering of saints under these plagues, as well as a gathering of the armies of the apostate world. Those who live at the time of the Antichrist do not all worship him or his image. Some hold out to the last against the acknowledgment of Antichrist as God, and will not be marked with his number or his name. Most of them die martyrs to their faith, but they conquer all the blandishments and bloody persecutions of the Beast, unstained by his hellish abominations. In the preceding chapter we were furnished with an anticipative vision of their heavenly reward for their faithfulness. They ultimately stand by the sea of glass, having harps of God, and singing the song of Moses and the Lamb. John sees them there in glory and immortality. Their great characteristic is, that, having lived under the Beast, they conquered in all the terrible trials and temptations endured from him. Having thus reached their heavenly glory, there must have been a coming of Christ for them, a resurrection and translation for them, as there had been a resurrection and translation for other classes and companies at other periods and stages of these judgment administrations. The occurrence of the vision of their blessedness in connection with these last plagues indicates that it must be in among these outpourings that Jesus comes for them. When once the kings of the earth and their armies begin to gather for the great battle, the last act is close at hand, and the last of the Gospel age is reached. Somewhere about this time, then, Christ comes for this last band of the children of the resurrection, whether dead or yet living. Of course, it is a coming of the same kind and character as his coming for those saints who were taken earlier ; for it is the completion of that one coming for his people which is everywhere set forth. Here also, as in all other cases, nothing but a state of watchful readiness when the call comes can secure a share in the blessing. Though these people may have fought valiantly, if at the time they be not found steadfast and faithful at their posts, they must lose their reward. And failing in readiness at this last act of Christ's coming for His saints there would necessarily be entailed upon them a peculiar and irremediable nakedness. Whatever might be left for them on earth, it would strip them forever of all opportunity to share in any privileges or honours of the children of the resurrection. Hence this particular admonition interjected at this particular place. It is a note of indication that now at any moment Christ is about to call for such of His people as yet may be on earth. It is a note of instruction and direction to keep themselves in strictest readiness by watchful expectation and careful severance from the defiling abominations around them. And it is a note of warning that if found unready their nakedness and shame will be beyond remedy, as then the whole matter will be over, and the door of admission into the peculiar kingdom of the elect will be closed forever. There is a blessedness for them even down amid these last extremities of the judgment time ; but it can only be secured, as in every other case, by constant watchfulness, prayer, and readiness for the summons when it comes.

But, with this admonitory note from the Saviour, the narrative proceeds as if nothing had occurred. So few will be the number of saints remaining in those days, so obscure their condition, and so indifferent the world to what happens to them, that their sudden ereption to glory causes no interruption to the wild doings of the nations, and produces not even a ripple in the current of their movements. The mission of the unclean spirits effects its purpose. The whole world is in a furore of enthusiasm to conquer and dethrone the Lamb, and to crush out of the earth every vestige of His authority and power. From one end of the world to the other, everything is alive and bristling with this thought. The spirits of demons have so taught the nations, and they proceed accordingly. East, west, north, and south the call to battle sounds ; and kings, nations and armies are on the march—on the march to the scene of conflict—" *to the place which is called in Hebrew Harmageddon.*"

Where, then, is Harmageddon ? Some say it is the great Valley of the Mississippi. A few years ago some said it was Sebastopol, or the Crimea. Others think it is France. Whilst many take it as a mere ideal place, for an ideal assemblage, having no existence in fact. To such wild, contradictory, and mutually destructive notions are men driven when they once depart from the letter of what is written. *Harmageddon* means the Mount of Megiddo, which has also given its name to the great plain of Jezreel, which belts across the middle of the Holy Land, from the Mediterranean to the Jordan. The name is from a Hebrew root which means *to cut off, to slay ;* and a place of slaughter has Megiddo ever been. It is the great battlefield of the Old Testament between the Theocracy and its various enemies. In Deborah and Barak's time, " the kings came and fought, then fought the kings of Canaan in Taanach, *by the waters of Megiddo.*" (Judges 5 : 19.) When the good king Josiah fell before the archers of Pharaoh Necho, " he came to fight *in the valley of Megiddo.*" (2 Chron. 35 : 22–24.) And where God's king, in mortal flesh, thus fell a victim to the power of the heathen, there God's King, in resurrection glory, shall revenge himself on His enemies. Whether we take it as the mount or the valley, it makes no difference, for the mount and valley are counted as one, each belonging to the other. It was the valley in Josiah's fall, it is the mount in Messiah's victory. But with this gathering of the kings of the earth and their armies to this place this sixth bowl ends. It breaks off abruptly because it simply brings things into readiness for the final catastrophe, which only the seventh and final bowl brings forth.

" *And the seventh angel poured out his bowl on or over the air ; and there came forth a voice out of the temple from the throne, saying,* IT IS DONE." This tells us direct from the Judgment-seat itself that here the end is reached, and that with this outpouring the whole contents of the wrath of God upon this present world are exhausted. When Christ yielded up His life on the cross, He said : " IT IS FINISHED ! " The great sacrifice was complete. It was the ending up of all judgment upon them that believe, leaving nothing more of divine condemnation to come upon them. Here a similar word is given ; for it is the completion of another sacrifice, the ending up of all judgment on them that believe not, but leaving nothing more of probation, help, or hope for them.

The particular consequences of this seventh outpouring are more fully described in the chapters which follow ; but the commotions and disasters which it brings upon the earth are here stated in general, and they are without a parallel in the history of man.

" *And there became lightnings, and voices, and thunders.*" These are aerial convulsions. The contents of this bowl are poured upon the air, and the first impressions are in the air. The whole earth is to be affected, therefore the pouring is upon the most universal and all-inclosing element. There have been many atmospheric commotions during the progress of these judgment scenes, but here they reach their climax and consummation, fulfilling what so many of the prophets have spoken touching the changing and folding up of the heavens (Ps. 102 : 25, 26 ; Is. 51 : 6), the shaking of their powers (Matt. 24 : 29 ; Heb. 12 : 25), the passing of them with a great noise, and the dissolving of them with fire (2 Peter 3 : 10, 12). Speaking of this very time, when " the multitude of all the nations fight against Ariel," Isaiah says :

" The Lord of hosts shall visit with thunder, and with earthquake, and great noise, with storm and tempest, and the flame of devouring fire." (Is. 29 : 6.) Of the same did Asaph sing : " Our God shall come, and shall not keep silence, a fire shall devour before Him, and it shall be very tempestuous round about Him. He shall call to the heavens from above, and to the earth, that He may judge his people." (Ps. 50 : 3, 4.) A world is to be finally ended, and these are the signs and attendants from above. But below they are correspondingly terrible.

" *And there became a great earthquake, such as became not since there became a man on earth, such an earthquake, so great.*" Here is the fulfilment of what Isaiah prophesied concerning the arising of the Lord " to shake terribly the earth " (chapter 2 : 19, 21). Here is what Haggai wrote about, when he recorded the saying of the Lord of hosts : " Yet once, and I will shake the heavens, and the earth, and the sea, and the dry land ; and I will shake all nations " (chapter 2 : 3, 4). The full force of this earthquake, unprecedented in time for its extent and violence, is indicated in its effects. By reason of it, John says :

" *The great city became into three parts, and the cities of the nations fell.*" The great city here is Jerusalem, for it is specially distinguished from the cities of the Gentiles, which are entirely ruined. It is only partially destroyed, because now in part possessed and appropriated as the Lord's. (Rev. 11 : 1, 2.) At the resurrection and ascension of the Two Witnesses, there was a great earthquake, when the tenth of the city fell (chapter 11 : 12, 13). Here there is a greater earthquake, and a much vaster effect. This is the time when the Mount of Olives is to cleave in two from east to west, " and half of the mountain shall remove toward the north, and half of it toward the south," leaving a very great valley between the two parts. (Zech. 14 : 4.) Such an occurrence must necessarily affect the foundation and topography of the city itself. The earthquake rends it into three parts. The implication is, that great chasms divide it, and that great damage occurs to it. Zechariah tells of a trichotomy of the land at that time, in which two parts shall be cut off and die, and one part shall be left. (Zech. 13 : 8, 9.) If the same applies to the city, then this dividing of it into three parts effects the destruction of two parts, only one part remains standing. Three miraculous Witnesses appear there in those last years ; first Enoch and Elijah, and then at last Christ himself. Enoch and Elijah are put to death, but Christ is living forever. So the death of the two miraculous Witnesses is avenged on two-thirds of the city, and the one-third, which Christ has taken for His, remains standing, as His power and dominion stand. Multitudes of the population doubtless perish amid these terrible commotions ; but there is a refuge provided for those who acknowledge the Lord and call upon His name. (Zech. 13 : 9 ; 14 : 5.)

But the calamity to Jerusalem is not so great as the effect of this unprecedented earthquake upon the cities of the Gentiles. The great city is rent into fractions, but it does not utterly fall ; " the cities of the nations " are universally ruined. The whole earth is shaken terribly by this bowl of the wrath of God, and we are told of no city in all the world that escapes. Rome falls, and Paris falls, and London falls ; and wherever there are cities of the Gentiles they fall, shaken down, overwhelmed, or burnt up, under the terrible visitations of this great day of God Almighty. O the death and ruin which shall then be wrought ! It is the end of this present world, and this is the way it comes.

" *And Babylon the great was remembered in the presence of God to give to her the cup of the wine of the fierceness of His anger.*" The description and fate of great Babylon forms the subject of the next chapters. There are peculiarities of detail with reference to her which need to be more particularly set forth ; but here is the time and place in which all that befalls her occurs. There is a grade in the progress of this woe. Jerusalem is smitten, but only partially destroyed, because something of the sacred is there. Then the Gentile cities, which stand a remove deeper down in moral character, are entirely destroyed, for they all belong to the Beast. And then Great Babylon, standing at the base in the scale of guilt, is made to drink the bitterest draught of all, because she is the source and centre of the prevailing abominations.

And interlinked with the rest of the effects wrought by these convulsions of an ending world, the configuration of the earth is changed. John beheld : " *And every island fled, and mountains were not found.*" He does not say that islands ceased to be, or no mountains are to remain or exist afterwards ; but that there is to be a sudden recession of the islands from their present places, and that some mountains that now are shall entirely disappear. In other words, great portions of the earth as it now stands will be quite altered in their positions and relations. The globe itself is not to be annihilated. The matter of which it is composed is not to pass out of existence. But some of its elevations shall be depressed, and the present lines between sea and land shall be greatly altered, making ready for another climate, and for a better heavens and earth. What mountains shall sink, what shores be changed, and in what directions or to what extent the islands shall be moved we are not told. The facts alone are stated. There was something of this change under the sixth seal, as the effect of the great earthquake there beheld ; but that was little more than the mere loosing of the mountains and islands from their places. (Rev. 6 : 14.) Here there is an entire disappearance of some mountains, and a *fleeing, or running away from* their old places, on the part of the islands. That was the beginning of the change ; this is the consummation of it. Desolation comes to all that now is, and chaotic confusion to the whole face of the world. Looking down to this very period, and to these very occurrences, Jeremiah says (3 : 23–26) : " I beheld the earth, and lo, it was without form and void. I beheld the mountains, and lo, they trembled, and all the hills moved lightly,"—leaping and gliding from their places. " I beheld, and lo, the fruitful place was a wilderness, and all the cities thereof were broken down at the presence of the Lord, and by His fierce anger." And along with all the rest of these terrific and destructive convulsions comes also a most disastrous precipitation from the sky. John says : " *A great hail, like as a talent [in weight], fell out of the heaven on the men [or mankind].*" The Jewish talent for silver-weight was about 115 pounds, and that for weighing other things was about 135 pounds. The Egyptian talent was about 86 pounds, as also the Greek. Some make the Attic talent about 56 pounds, and a talent was used at Antioch which weighed about 390 pounds. Just which of these is meant we cannot say ; but taking the mean of all, or even the lightest, we have a weight equal to as much as a strong man can conveniently lift. Hail of a pound in weight is terribly destructive ; but this would give us hailstones as large as the blocks of ice which commerce wagons about our streets. Such masses falling upon houses would crash in the strongest of them, batter down walls, stave ships, and leave but few retreats of safety for human life on the surface of the world.*

The stones thrown by the Roman catapults against Jerusalem, Josephus says, were of the weight of a talent ; but these rugged ice masses, concreted

---

* Few persons can form a conception of the terrible character of a great hailstorm. Here is an account of one which occurred at Constantinople in the month of October, 1831, written by one who witnessed it :

" After an uncommonly sultry night, threatening clouds arose about six in the morning, and a noise, between thunder and tempest, and yet not to be compared to either, increased every moment, and the inhabitants of the capital, roused from their sleep, awaited with anxious expectation the issue of this threatening phenomenon. Their uncertainty was not of long duration ; lumps of ice as large as a man's foot, falling singly, and then like a thick shower of stones, which *destroyed everything with which they came in contact.* The oldest persons do not remember ever to have seen such hailstones. Some were picked up half an hour afterwards which weighed above a pound. This dreadful storm passed over Constantinople and along the Bosphorus, over Therapia, Bojukden, and Belgrade ; and the fairest, nay, the only hope of this beautiful and fertile tract, the vintage, just commenced, was in the troubled atmosphere on high, would necessarily come with more violence than Roman catapults could cast the same weight.   When the plague of hail fell upon Egypt, only such lives suffered as were exposed in the open fields and highways (Ex. 9 : 19).   But it will be infinitely worse when this great hail falls.   Think of the earthquake which lays men's abodes in ruins, driving them to the open plains, and then this terrific hail coming upon them where no shelter is !   What can they do ?   How must they be cut down by this dreadful artillery of the heavens !

> Day of anger ! Day of wonder !
> When the earth shall rend asunder,
> Smote with hail, and fire, and thunder !

But what is the moral effect ?   Do the people bend, and own their sins, and sue for Heaven's pity and forgiveness ? Alas for those in whom the spirit of hell has once taken firm root !   No one having the brand of Antichrist ever repents.   John beheld : " *And the men blasphemed God on account of the plague of the hail, because the plague thereof is exceedingly great.*"   Such obstinacy in sin and guilt was unknown when the world was younger.   When the hail-storm was heavy upon Egypt there was something of relenting.   Pharaoh confessed his sin, and asked Moses to intercede for him.   For the moment, at least, he agreed to let Israel go.   But here transgressors have come to the full.   They are dead-ripe for final judgment.   Antichrist has taught them to curse God and die ; and so they curse and blaspheme to the last, unsoftened and unchanged by all the terribleness of an oncoming perdition.   It is by these plagues that their earthly existence ends, with the whole economy of things to which they cling ; but their last words are curses, and their last breath is blasphemy.

Friends and brethren, I am at a loss at which to wonder most : whether at the severity of Almighty God upon the finally impenitent, or at the unconcern, neglect, and hardihood of men, who, with all this dreadful outcome before their eyes, still march calmly on in the very path which can have no other termination.   O how dreadful !   Retreat to the Lazar-house to refresh one's self with the groans and miseries of the wretched, a dance in the chamber of death, the singing of glees around the coffin of a beloved and honoured friend, the making of merry jests over the fresh grave of one's own dear mother, would not be half so unseemly, so unfeeling, and so insane, as to go on in a life of indifference and impenitence, with eyes open and ears informed of all the horrible consequences which must come of it !   There is but one explanation, —people do not half believe.   They profess to receive and honour the Bible, but they do not credit what it so plainly says.   They would feel indignant and resentful were we to call them infidels, and yet they are infidels.   They may not speak the infidel's creed, but they live it every day, and think well of themselves whilst they do it.   The inner temper of their souls—their spiritual tone—is infidel.   The practical spirit which influences and controls them is the infidel spirit, and accords with the infidel reasoning.   Either they do not think at all, and so reduce themselves to the level of the irrational brute ; or their thinking is secretly, if not confessedly, tinged with the suspicion that these mighty revelations are nothing but unsubstantial speculation or doubtful theory.   They have a deep persuasion of the certainty, regularity, and permanence of what they call natural laws, and have schooled themselves into such a trust and confidence and worship of Nature, that they see no need, or likelihood, or possibility of any other divinity or divine administrations. Thunder, lightning, tempests, plagues, pestilences, famines, earthquakes,

---

destroyed in a day ! Animals of all kinds, and even some persons, were *killed, an innumerable number are wounded, and the damage done to the houses is incalculable.* The force of the falling masses of ice was so great that they broke to atoms all the tiles on the roofs, and, like musket-balls, shattered planks."

What would it have been if the ice masses had been fifty or one hundred times larger ?

eclipses, comets, at which mankind once trembled as signs of God's angry interference with human affairs, they find so largely explainable on natural principles that they are slow to admit that God has anything to do with these things, or that He is able to use them as His weapons of judgment. They talk of God, but to them He is an impotent God. Consciously or unconsciously, their souls are thus in a condition of scepticism, which empties the Divine Word of all reality to them. They hear it, and see what it says, but have a lingering feeling that it cannot be true just as it reads, and so pass it by as a dead letter.

O ye people of earthly wisdom, be not deceived! Where there are such effective laws as you speak of, there must needs be an Almighty Lawgiver who made them and put them into force ; and He who could make them can also unmake them, and modify them as He pleases. Is efficient government any less the administration of sovereign power because it acts through great, settled, and well-known laws? Is His majesty disabled by having shown itself so great? What is more irrational than rationalism? Is God helpless to fulfil His word because He in Nature proves himself Almighty? Hath He made the blunder of binding His hands with His own Omnipotence? Such would seem to be the essence of some men's reasoning.

Be admonished then, dear hearer, and be not deluded to your ruin by the impertinent indifference and unwisdom of these evil times. Be sure that God is God, and that His Word must stand, though worlds dissolve. Now is your golden opportunity. You see what is the end that cometh. You see with what forbearance and mercy the threatened thunderstrokes of death are still held back, that men may hear and fear, and turn to Him and live. There is eternal security, if, with a true and honest heart, you will only believe what is written, and set your soul to obey and trust as He counsels and directs. It may cost you some sharp trials now, but it will bring you safety and salvation when the sceptical and blaspheming world goes down under the fierceness of His just anger. Overwhelmingly dreadful as the foreshowing is, there is no cause for despair if you will but take warning now. Only fix your trust in Jesus, and follow and obey Him in sincerity and in truth, and when His judgment strikes, it shall not harm you.

> Though mountains from their seats be hurled
> Down to the deep, and buried there,
> Convulsions shake the solid world,
> Our faith shall never yield to fear.

LECTURE THIRTY-EIGHTH

REV. 17 : 1-17. (Revised Text.) And there came one of the seven angels who had the seven bowls, and talked with me, saying, Hither, I will show thee the judgment of the great harlot that sitteth upon many waters, with whom the kings of the earth committed fornication, and the inhabitants of the earth were made drunk from the wine of her fornication.

And he bore me away in spirit into a wilderness, and I saw a woman sitting upon a scarlet beast, full of names of blasphemy, having seven heads and ten horns. And the woman was clothed in purple and scarlet, decked with gold and precious stone and pearls, having a cup of gold in her hand full of abominations and the unclean things of her and of the earth's fornication, and upon her forehead a name written, *Mystery, Babylon the great, the mother of the harlots and of the abominations of the earth.*

And I saw the woman drunken from the blood of the saints, and from the blood of martyrs [witnesses] of Jesus : and I wondered great wonder when I saw her.

And the angel said to me, Wherefore wonderest thou ? I will tell to thee the mystery of the woman, and of the beast that carrieth her, having the seven heads and ten horns.

The beast which thou sawest, was and is not, and is to ascend out of the abyss, and goeth into perdition : and they shall wonder who dwell upon the earth, whose names are not written upon the book of life from the foundation of the world, when they behold the beast because he was, and is not, and shall once more be here [or *come again*].

Here [is] the mind that hath wisdom : the seven heads are seven mountains where the woman sitteth upon them, and are seven kings ; the five are fallen, the one is, the other is not yet come, and when he shall come, he must continue a little time. And the beast that was and is not, even he is the eighth, and is out of the seven, and goeth into perdition.

And the ten horns which thou sawest are ten kings which have not yet received kingdom ; but they receive power as kings one hour with the beast. These have one mind, and give their power and authority to the beast. These shall make war with the Lamb, and the Lamb shall conquer them, because he is Lord of lords and King of kings, and they who are with him, called and chosen and faithful.

And he saith to me, The waters which thou sawest, where the harlot sitteth, are peoples and multitudes and nations and tongues. And the ten horns which thou sawest, and the beast, these shall hate the harlot, and shall make her desolate and naked, and shall eat her flesh, and shall burn her with fire. For God gave into their hearts to do his mind, and to make one mind, and to give their kingdom to the beast, until the words of God shall be fulfilled.

WE have already twice heard of Great Babylon, and calamity to her ; once in chapter 14 : 8, by anticipation ; and once in chapter 16 : 19, where her sins were said to have come into remembrance, and the cup of the fierceness of the wrath of God to have been administered to her. The particulars of that visitation, as well as the whole character and relations of this mystic personage, are given in the chapters upon which we now enter. As the first reference was somewhat anticipative, so these further accounts are somewhat retrogressive, and go back to exhibit in all its length and breadth what in the previous chapter was only synoptically stated.

The subject itself is one of great prominence in the Apocalypse, as in all the prophecies ; but it has proven about as difficult as it is conspicuous. On none of the current methods of treating this Book is it possible to come to any clear, consistent, and satisfying conclusions with regard to it. The body of preterist expositors have found themselves necessitated to take Great Babylon as meaning the city, the church, or the ecclesiastical system of Rome, not so much because the features of the record call for it, or really admit of it, when fairly dealt with, but because unable on their theory to do any better. That Rome and the Romish system are involved, may readily be admitted ; but that this is all, and that the sudden fall of Great Babylon is simply the fall of Romanism, or the utter destruction of the city of Rome, must be emphatically denied, if the inspired portraiture is to stand as it is written. If we cannot find more solid ground than that on which the Rome theory rests we must needs consign the whole subject to the department of doubt and uncertainty, and let all these tremendous foreshowings pass for nothing. Unite with me, then, dear friends, in praying God to open our understandings, that we may not fail to take in what He really intends that His people should see in these sacred visions.

The first thing which strikes me in the study of this subject, is one which I have nowhere seen duly noticed, namely: the evident correlation and contrast between the Woman here pictured and another Woman described in the twelfth chapter. There, " a great sign was seen in the heaven, *a Woman;* " here, it is remarked, " he bore me away in spirit into a wilderness, and I saw *a Woman.*" Both these Women are mothers; the first " brought forth a son, a male [*neuter,* embracing either sex], who is to rule all the nations ; " the second " is the mother of harlots and of the abominations of the earth." Both are splendidly dressed ; the first is " clothed with the sun." Her raiment is light from heaven. The second is " clothed in purple, and scarlet, decked with gold, and precious stone, and pearls." All her ornaments are from below, made up of things out of the earth and the sea. Both are very influential in their position ; the first has " the moon," the empress of night, the powers of darkness, " under her feet ; " the second " hath rule, or kingdom, upon the kings of the earth." Both are sufferers ; against the first is the Dragon, who stands watching to devour her child, and persecutes and pursues her, and drives her into the wilderness, and sends out a river to overwhelm her, and is at war with all her seed that he can find ; against the second are the ten kings, who ultimately hate her, and make her desolate and naked, and eat her flesh, and burn her with fire, whilst God in His strength judgeth her, and visits her with plague, death, and utter destruction. Both are very conspicuous, and fill a large space in the history of the world, and in all the administrations of divine providence and judgment. That they are counterparts of each other there can hardly be a reasonable doubt. The one is a pure woman, the other is a harlot. The first is hated by the powers on earth, the second is loved, flattered, and caressed by them. Where the one has sway, things are heavenly ; where the other lives, it is " wilderness." The one produces masculine nobility, which is ultimately caught away to God and to His throne ; the other produces effeminate impurity, which calls down the fierceness of the divine wrath. The one is sustained and helped by celestial wings ; the other is supported and carried by the Dragon power,—the Beast with the seven heads and ten horns. The one has a crown of twelve stars, wearing the patriarchs and apostles as her royal diadem ; the other has upon her forehead the name of the greatest destroyer and oppressor of the holy people, and is drunken with " the blood of prophets and of saints, and of all that have been slain upon the earth." The one finally comes out in a heavenly city, the New Jerusalem, made up of imperishable jewels, and arrayed in all the glory of God and the Lamb ; the other finally comes out in a city of this world's superlative admiration, which suddenly goes down forever under the intense wrath of Heaven, and becomes the habitation of demons, and a hold of every unclean spirit.

These two Women, thus related, and set over one against the other as opposites and rivals, must necessarily be interpreted in the same way. As Antichrist corresponds to Christ as a rival and antagonist of Christ, so Great Babylon corresponds to the Woman that bears the Man-child, as *her* rival and antagonist.

By recalling, therefore, who and what is meant by the first Woman, we will be in position to understand who and what is meant by the second.

Beyond question, the sun-clad Woman is God's great symbol of the visible

Church,—the Lamb's Wife,—the bone of His bone, and flesh of His flesh, fashioned out of His rifted side as the Second Adam, who fell into the deep sleep of death for that purpose. As Methodius taught, " The woman seen in heaven, clothed with the sun, and adorned with a crown of twelve stars, is, in the highest and strictest sense, our Mother. The prophets, considering what is spoken of her, call her Jerusalem, at other times The Bride, the Mount Sion, the Temple and Tabernacle of God." She is not the church of any one period or dispensation, but the entire Universal Church of all time, as Victorinus, the earliest commentator on this Book, held and affirmed, saying : " The Woman clothed with the sun, having the moon under her feet, is the Church of the Patriarchs, and of the Prophets, and of the holy Apostles "— that is, the Church from the days of Adam and Eve on to the last victory over the worship, name, and mark, of the final Antichrist. What then can this rival Woman be but the organized Antichurch, the pseudo-church, the Bride made out of Satan, the universal body and congregation of false-believers and false-worshippers ? As Christ has had a visible Church in all time, embodying the wisdom and spirit of heaven, and maintaining the confession of His truth and worship, so has the Devil had a corresponding following in all time, embodying the sensual and devilish wisdom and spirit, and maintaining the profession and teaching of Satan's lies. And as the first Woman denotes the one, so the second Woman denotes the other. The proofs of this will appear as we consider the particulars of the case.

1. One of the most characteristic features of this Woman is her *harlotry*. The Angel calls her " The Great Harlot," and she wears on her forehead as her name, " The mother of the harlots, and of the abominations of the earth." Harlotry is the standing symbol in the word of God for a debauched worship, idolatry, and false devotion. When people worship for God what is not God, or give their hearts to idols, or institute systems, doctrines, rites, or administrations, to take the place of what God has revealed and appointed, the Scriptures call it whoredom, adultery, fornication. (Jer. 3 : 6, 8, 9 ; Ez. 16 : 32 ; Hosea 1 and 2 ; Rev. 2 : 22.) The reasons are obvious. The breaking down of the divine laws and ordinances necessarily carries with it the dishonour of the marriage institution, and hence all supports of godly chastity and pureness. Accordingly all false religions are ever attended with lewdness, even in connection with their most honoured rites. The sacredness of marriage has no place in them. Besides, the very essence of the divine law is, that we love God our Lord with all the heart, mind, soul, and strength. This is Jehovah's due and requirement of all that live. Hence the bestowal of worshipful affection on any other object, or the putting of anything whatever in the place of the true God, is, in the very nature of the case, a great spiritual harlotry ; for it is the turning of the soul from the only legitimate object of its adoration, to take into its embrace what has no right to such room and place. And as this Woman is a *harlot*, " the great Harlot," and " the mother of the harlots and the abominations of the earth," she must needs be the great embodiment, source, and representative of all idolatry, false worship, and perversion of the word and institutes of God. This helps to determine her character as the rival and antagonist of the Woman clothed with the sun, and makes her the symbol of the universal body of the faithless, just as the sun-clad Woman is the symbol of the universal body and congregation of believers. She can by no means be Rome alone, whether Pagan or Papal, any more than the sun-clad Woman is the early Church alone, or Protestants alone. There were believers and saints in the 4,000 years before the Christian era, and so there were idolaters and perverters of the institutes of God in plentiful abundance before there were Popes or Roman emperors. And as the pure Woman is made up of the whole congregation of the faith*ful* from the beginning, so must this great Harlot be made up of all the faith*less* from the beginning.

2. This conclusion is rendered the more necessary by the name which this Woman has written upon her forehead. How could she be " the mother of the

harlots and of the abominations of the earth " if her existence does not date back to, and above all include, the great harlotries and abominations which preceded both the Popes and the Roman emperors ? Besides, we have here the motherhood of various harlots, or systems and economies of harlotry and abominations of the earth. If *Pagan* Rome is to be understood, that was but one individual system. If *Papal* Rome is to be understood, that again is but one individual system. The implication would thus be that the earth had no systems of harlotry or abominations but the one found in Pagan or Papal Rome, and this mother of the harlots would thus have no children to show ! The record is that she is herself the great original of all harlotries and abominations of the earth, that many others have sprung from her, and that all the harlotries of time have her for their primal representative and mother. The imagery, therefore, goes back to the beginnings, out of which all false systems, and false worships, and abominations of the earth have come.

3. Accordingly, also, we have in the very front of this Woman's name a designation which carries us back to the commencement of the whole ill-condition of things in this present world. Rome never was " Babylon " in the sense of being " the mother of the harlots and the abominations of the earth." Her place in the chart of time renders that impossible ; just as impossible as that some Sarah of to-day should be the mother of the patriarch Isaac, and so of the Jewish race. Neither was the Babylon of Nebuchadnezzar's day " the mother of the harlots and the abominations of the earth," and for the same reason. It comes too late. We must go further back, and much nearer to the landing of the Ark on Ararat, for such a beginning and motherhood. But when we search for it we find it, and find it under the very name which this mother of all harlots and abominations of the earth bears written on her forehead. The tenth and eleventh chapters of Genesis tell the story.

Turning to these chapters of national origins, we learn that *the beginning of the kingdom of Nimrod*, the grandson of Ham, *was Bab-el*, or BABYLON, in the land of Shinar, whither the then inhabitants of the earth, who were as yet of one language and one speech, journeyed together from the East. This implication is, that they came thither under the leadership of Nimrod, whose name means *a rebellious panther*, and that under him began that first great work of rebellion against God which brought the confusion of tongues, and inaugurated the original of all the subsequent harlotries and abominations of mankind. Against the command and known intent of the Almighty, it was there undertaken to " build a city and a tower whose top might reach unto heaven," and to make themselves a name that they might not be scattered abroad upon the face of the earth. It appears, also, that from the hunting and slaying of wild beasts, and with the armed forces grouped around him in that business, Nimrod betook himself to the subjugation and enslavement of men, compelling them into his service and daring schemes. Thus he " began to be a mighty one in the earth, the organizer of an arbitrary imperialism over against the patriarchal order and the divine institutes. The Arab records tell us that he was the first king, and thus the beginner of all kingcraft and tyranny which have since so much oppressed the world. It is said of him that he professed to have seen a golden crown in the sky, that he had one made like it, and that he put it on his own head, and thus claimed to rule in the name and as the earthly impersonation of the powers of the sky, either as Orion or the Sun.

The Bible says that it was further arranged for the people to make for themselves " *a name*,"—*a Sem*, token, sign, banner, ensign, or mark of confederation, fellowship, and organized unity, as an undivided people, lest they should become dispersed over the earth into separate societies. (Compare Jer. 13 : 11 ; 33 : 9 ; Ezek. 39 : 13 ; Zeph. 3 : 20.) Against God they had determined to hold together, and they wished to have a badge, standard, something by which they could be known, and in which they could all glory and rejoice as the centre and crown of their unity. That *Sem*, or *Sema*, was to be a mark of consolidated greatness, a loftiness and pride to them ; that is, in the language of the time, a *Sema-Rama*. Thus we have the name of the mythic *Semiramis*, the Dove-Goddess, which was the ensign of all the Assyrian princes, and which figures so largely as Ashtaroth, Astarte, the heavenly Aphrodite, and Venus. Semiramis is said to have been the wife of Nimrod ; so that the *Sem*, or token, of the Nimrodic confederation was probably the image of his wife, with a dove upon her head, with wings spread like the horns of the new moon. This, in the language of the time, would be called *Sema-Rama*, because the great *Sem*, name, or token, of the combination against being scattered abroad. The symbol of such a name or confederation would naturally and almost necessarily take the place of a god, and become the holy mother, the great heavenly protectress, the giver of greatness and prosperity to those rallying under it.

So again, Nimrod called his first and capital city *Bab-el*, which, in the language of the time, means *The Gate of God;* of course not the God of Noah and Shem, for the whole proceeding was in known and intended antagonism to the true God and His will and commands. Hebraistically, and by way of accommodation to the judgment which Jehovah there inflicted, *Babel* is made significant of *confusion* (Gen. II : 9), but in the original application of the name it means *The Gate of God*. Thus, in the very name of the place, we have the intimation and proof that these Nimrodic proceedings were not only the organization of a new and oppressive style of government, but with it, as an essential part of it, the inauguration of a new and idolatrous religion, the parent apostasy of the post-diluvian world.

The Bible says that Nimrod was *a mighty hunter before the Lord*. The Targum of Jonathan interprets this to mean that he was *a mighty rebel before the Lord, the mightiest rebel before the Lord that ever was in the earth*. The Jerusalem Targum reads it that he was *mighty in sin* before the Lord, a hunter of the sons of men, exhorting them to leave the judgments of Shem and adhere to the judgments of Nimrod. Hence it was the proverb concerning every notorious adventurer in wickedness and oppression, As the mighty Nimrod in rebellion and sin before God. Jarchi accordingly understands the record to be, that Nimrod was a most brazen offender, who did not fear or hesitate to withstand God to his very face. And every intimation concerning him shows that he was the Heaven-defying founder of a new system of rule and worship, instituting a government by brute force and earthly wisdom and policy, and a religion which quite abolished the true God, and set men to the adoration of the sun, moon, and stars, impersonated in himself, wife, relatives, and chief consociates, and represented in the idol standards of his kingdom.

It is a mistake to suppose that idolatry was the gradual growth of well-disposed but unenlightened human thinking. Its rise was sudden. It was conceived in intentional rebellion. It was the invention of a proud and tyrannous ambition at war with Jehovah's commands. It was brought into being to counteract the will and worship of the true and known God. It was the creature and handmaid of power for the deification of " the lust of the flesh, the lust of the eyes, and the pride of life " in the place of the Creator. And it originated with old Babylon, and Babylon's first king, the great rebel Nimrod, that very *Bar-Chus* (son of Cush), or *Bacchus*, who figures among the Greek and Roman gods as the great overflowing, enlivening, healing, and directing power. It is also a fact that all the Pagan mythologies and idolatrous devotions the world over, whatever their diversities, show a oneness of character, and an underlying likeness which proves that they are from one original source, and but modifications of one and the same primal invention, traceable to old Babylon and the Nimrodic plan to defeat the purposes of the God of Noah. The original design was thwarted by the confusion of tongues. Contrary to their oaths to the Dove-goddess of their standards, the people were obliged to disperse and leave off the building of their tower. But the charming novelties which Nimrod taught them were not lost. The seeds of the fascinating invention went with the dispersion, planting themselves in every new settlement, and growing ever fresh crops as the streams of humanity ran on amid the centuries, but ever reproducing the likeness of the original mother. Whatever changes or additions came, it still was old Babylon, which ever abides, potent through all the ages, and known to the judgment angels as " *Babylon the great, the mother of the harlots and of the abominations of the earth.*"

4. It is further said of this Woman that " the inhabitants of the earth were made drunk from the wine of her fornication." This is not true of Rome, Pagan or Papal ; for before and beyond either, the earth had a hundredfold more inhabitants untouched and uninfluenced by one or the other than ever were under the tutorage of both of them together. To talk of " the *Roman* earth " in such a description is worse than impertinence. " The inhabitants of the earth " are *the inhabitants of the earth*, and the people of the generations before Rome, and where Rome has never reached, as well as under Rome. The wine of old Babylon's fornication was a debauching system of idol worship and carnal self-exaltation, over against the revelations and institutes of Jehovah. It was already bottled and labelled before the first dispersion. It went with that dispersion into every country and nation under heaven. As a matter of fact, we find it to this day among all the nations of the earth, affecting if not controlling their thinking, their policies, their faith, and their worship. Not less than two-thirds of the population of the earth at this hour are Pagan idolaters, drivelling under the same old intoxication which came forth from Nimrod and Babylon ; whilst the great body of the other third is either Mohammedan, Catholic, Jewish, infidel, or adherents of some tainted and antichristian faith and worship. Nor is there a kingdom or government on the face of the whole earth at this hour which does not embody and exhibit more of the spirit and rebellion of Nimrod than of the spirit, commandments, and inculcations of God. All the kings of the earth and all the governments under heaven have more or less joined in the uncleanness and fornication of that same old Babylonian Harlot, who has defiled every spot and nook of the whole inhabited world, notwithstanding that God from the beginning set the seal of His wrath upon it. The Jewish whoredoms, and the Papal whoredoms, and the Mohammedan whoredoms, and the whoredoms of all perverted Christian religionists, though not entirely letting go the confession of the one only God, are still in essence the same old harlotry which first found place and embodiment on the banks of the Euphrates. It is the same old Babylon, and her harlot daughters, bearing rule or kingdom upon the dominions of the earth, and intoxicating the inhabitants thereof out of the wine of her fornication.

The cup held out is *golden*. To the sensual and carnal heart and imagination the world's religion and progress is something bright and glorious, the glittering fulness of good and blessing. But in that shining cup is only abomination and uncleanness—spiritual prostitution—nothing but spiritual prostitution.

The cup is *one ;* and in all the varied systems of false faith and false worship which taint our world there is held out and received but one and the same essence, and that essence is the harlotry of old Babylon. It is most direct in Paganism ; but it is in Mohammedanism, in Papalism, in the degenerate Catholicism of the Eastern churches, and in all the heretical isms, infidelities, and mere goodishnesses which afflict our Protestant Christianity as well. So true is it that Great Babylon, the mother of the harlots and of the abominations of the earth, hath made the inhabitants of the earth drunk with the wine of her fornication.

5. This Women is also herself drunken—" drunken from the blood of the saints, and from the blood of the martyrs or witnesses of Jesus." " In her was found the blood of prophets, and of saints, and all that have been slain [as martyrs] upon the earth." This is proof positive that the Great Harlot is not Papal Rome only, for all *the prophets* were dead hundreds of years before the rise of the Papacy ; and myriads on myriads of God's true people died as martyrs to the faith ere ever there was a Pope or a Papal hierarchy. The same

is proof positive that she is not Pagan Rome alone ; for the old prophets were dead or gone before either Cæsar lived, or ever Romulus was born ; and great hosts of martyrs suffered before Rome was at all. Drunken as the Romish power made itself upon the blood of the witnesses of Jesus, Roman government is not chargeable with the shedding of *all* the martyr blood that has flowed upon the earth. It is, however, very certain, and beyond dispute, that all the persecution and slaying of saints, and prophets, and witnesses for God that have ever occurred upon earth, past or present, ancient or modern, stand charged against the mystic kingdom of idolaters, false religionists, and such as accepted fellowship with spiritual harlotry. Persecution of God's prophets or people is itself a mark and evidence of spiritual whoredom. It shows alienation from God and His true worship. And wherever such presentation finds place, or saints are sacrificed for their faith, there this great Harlot is in living and visible force and presence, whether among Pagans or Jews, Mohammedans or Christians, Catholics or Protestants. It is the old Nimrod over again, tyrannously enforcing his murderous will against the will and commands of God.

6. Again, this mystic Woman sits upon many waters, which waters the angel says " are peoples, and multitudes, and nations, and tongues." There is a vastness and universality in these terms, and in the extent of these symbolic waters, which ill accords with the extent of the Papal dominion. Though extending over many peoples, multitudes, nations, and tongues, there are many many more peoples, and far greater multitudes, and numbers of nations, and tongues, over which the hierarchy of Rome has no control, whose interest and sympathy she does not possess, and on whom she cannot lean for support. So with regard to Pagan Rome, there were peoples, and multitudes, and nations, and tongues, never within the territory of the Cæsars, and many indeed of whom the Cæsars had no knowledge. Giving the words the latitude which properly belongs to such a description as this, the masses of the earth's population, not only of one period, but of all periods since nations came into being, would seem to be the conception. And it is only when we understand this mystic Harlot as the whole body of organized alienation from God, as in heathenism, false religion, and spiritual prostitution, that we find an object coextensive in time and territory with the " peoples, and multitudes, and nations, and tongues," which make up the seat, dependence, and support of this great Harlot. At one period or another she has been found sitting on every people, and nation, and tongue, since the tongues or multitudes of men have been sundered.

7. John further saw this Woman sitting upon a scarlet Beast, full of names of blasphemy, having seven heads and ten horns. This Beast is the same described in chapter 13. He is referred to here, not so much to make us better acquainted with him, as to give us a full understanding of the Great Harlot and her relationships. The " wisdom " or inner sense and meaning of the presentation is, that " the seven heads are seven mountains, where the Woman sitteth upon them, and are seven kings." These are the words which are supposed to fix the application of the picture to the city of Rome, as Rome is called a city of seven hills. But a flimsier basis for such a controlling and all-conditioning conclusion is perhaps nowhere to be found. The seven *hills* of the city of Rome, to begin with, are not *mountains*, as every one who has been there can testify ; and if they were, they are not more characteristic of the situation of Rome than the seven hills are characteristic of Jerusalem. But the taking of them as literal hills or mountains at all is founded upon a total misreading of the angel's words.

A *mountain*, or prominent elevation on the surface of the earth, is one of the common scriptural images, symbols, or representatives of a kingdom, regal dominion, empire, or established authority. So David, speaking of the vicissitudes which he experienced as the king of Israel, says : " Lord, by Thy favour Thou didst make *my mountain* to stand strong "—margin, " settled strength for *my mountain* ;" meaning his kingdom and dominion. (Ps. 30 ;

7.) So the Lord in His threat against the throne and power of Babylon said : " I am against thee, O destroying *mountain*, which destroyest all the earth ; and I will stretch out mine hand upon thee, and will roll thee down from the rocks, and will make thee a burnt *mountain*." (Jer. 51 : 25.) So the kingdom of the Messiah is likened to " a stone, which became a great *mountain*, and filled the whole earth." (Dan. 2 : 35.) And this is exactly the sense in which the angel uses the word here, as he himself tells us. He does not say " the seven heads are seven mountains, where the Woman sitteth upon them," and there leave off ; but he adds immediately, " *and they are seven kings*," or *personified kingdoms*. The mountains, then, are not piles of material rocks and earth at all, but royal or imperial powers, declared to be such by the angel himself. The description, therefore, so far from fixing the application to the Papacy, or to the city of Rome, decisively settles that it cannot possibly apply to either, for neither has seven such mountains. The late Albert Barnes has written in his *Notes* that " all respectable interpreters agree that it refers to Rome ; either Pagan, Christian, or Papal." Of course he is one of the " respectable interpreters," but then he should be able to tell which of the objects he names it is, for it cannot be all three. Most people assign Dr. E. W. Hengstenberg, the great Berlin professor, a place among " respectable interpreters," but Hengstenberg says Rome cannot possibly be meant by these seven heads. The angel says they are seven regal mountains, seven kings, seven great ruling powers. Rome Papal cannot be meant, for Rome Papal has no such count of seven regal powers. Rome Christian cannot be meant, for Rome Christian, as distinguished from Rome Papal, never support- ed and carried the great Harlot in any possible sense, and could not without ceasing to be Christian. Rome Pagan cannot be meant, for Rome Pagan ceased with the conversion of the throne, and no count of emperors or kings can be found in it to " respectably " fill out the angels' description. The succession of the forms of administration, enumerated as *Kings, Consuls, Dictators, Decemvirs, Military Tribunes*, and *Emperors*, were not seven kings or regal mountains. Prior to the empire most of these administrations were less than anthills in the history of the world, and furnished rather slender ponies for the great purple-clad and pearl-decked mother of harlots to ride on in her majesty. Rome surely comes into the count of these seven moun- tains of empire ; but to make Rome the whole seven, including also the eighth, requires a good deal more " respectability " of interpretation in that line than has thus far appeared. Barnes is sure the whole thing applies to Rome because this Woman " hath rule or kingdom upon the kings of the earth, and there was no other empire on the earth to which this could be properly applied." But this assumes that the Woman is an empire, for which there is not a particle of evidence. The Woman is *not* an empire any more than the Church of Christ is an empire. She rides upon empires, kings, and powers of the world, and inspires, leads, and controls them ; but she herself is not one of them, and is above all of them so that they court her, and are bewitched and governed by her—governed, not with the reins of empire, but with the lure of her fornication. This Woman is longer-lived than any one empire. We have seen that she began with Nimrod, bears the name of Babylon, and is not destroyed until the day of judgment. The seven imperial mountains on which she rides must therefore fill up the whole interval ; or there was a time, and the most of her history, when she did not ride at all, which is not the fact. Seven is itself the number of fulness, which includes the whole of its kind. The reference here is to kings, to mountains of temporal dominion, to empires. It must therefore take in all of them. And when men once get over their " respectability," and rise to the height and range of the interpreting angel's view of things, they will have no difficulty in identifying the mountains, or the times to which they belong.

Of these seven regal mountains, John was told " *the five are fallen*," dead, passed away, their day over ; " *the one is*," that is, was standing, at that moment, was then in sway and power ; " *the other is not yet come, and when he shall come, he must continue a little time.*" What regal mountain, then, was in power at the time John wrote ? There can be no question on that point ; it was the Roman empire. Thus, then, we ascertain and identify the sixth in the list, which shows what sort of *kings* the angel meant. Of the same class with this, and belonging to the same category, there are five others—five which had then already run their course and passed away. But what five imperial mountains like Rome had been and gone, up to that time ? Is history so obscure as not to tell us with unmistakable certainty ? Preceding Rome the world had but five great names or nationalities answering to imperial Rome, and those scarce a schoolboy ought to miss. They are Greece, Persia, Babylon, Assyria, and Egypt ; no more, and no less. And these all were imperial powers like Rome. Here, then, are six of these regal mountains; the seventh is not yet come. When it comes it is to endure but a short time. This implies that each of the others continues a long time ; and so, again, could not mean the dictators, decemvirs, and military tribunes of the early history of Rome, for some of them lasted but a year or two. Thus, then, by the clearest, most direct, and most natural signification of the words of the record, we are brought to the identification of these seven mountain kings as the seven great world-powers, which stretch from the beginning of our present world to the end of it. Daniel makes the number less ; but he started with his own times, and looked only down the stream. Here the account looks backward as well as forward. That which is first in Daniel is the third here, and that which is the sixth here is the fourth in Daniel. Only in the commencing point is there any difference. The visions of Daniel and the visions of John are from the same Divine Mind, and they perfectly harmonize, only that the latest are the amplest.

By these seven great powers then, filling up the whole interval of this world's history, this great Harlot is said to be carried. On these she rides, according to the vision. It is not upon one alone, nor upon any particular number of them, but upon all of them, the whole seven-headed Beast, that she sits. These seven powers, each and all, support the Woman as their joy and pride ; and she accepts and uses them, and sways their administrations, and rides in glory by means of them. They are her devotees, lovers, and most humble servants ; and she is their patronizing and most noble lady, with a mutuality of favours and inter-communion belonging to her designation. This is the picture as explained by the angel. But, to say that the Romish Papacy was thus carried, nurtured, and sustained by the ancient empires of Greece, Persia, Babylon, Assyria, and Egypt, would be a great lie on history. It was not so. In the nature of things it could not be so. By no means then can this Harlot be the Papacy alone, as maintained by all "*respectable* interpreters." Furthermore, it is a matter of fact, that as surely as Rome in John's day, and Greece, Persia, Babylon, Assyria, and Egypt, before Rome, existed and bore sway on earth as regal mountains, so surely and conspicuously were they each and all ridden by this great Harlot. They were each and all the lovers, supporters, and defenders of organized falsehood in religion, the patrons of idolatry, the foster friends of all manner of spiritual harlotry. Nimrod, the hunter of the sons of men and author of despotic government, established his idolatrous inventions as the crown and glory of his empire, and intertwined the worship of idols with the standards of his power. It was the same with Egypt whose colossal remains, unfading paintings, and mummy scrolls confirm the Scripture portraitures of her disgusting devotions, and tell how the priests of these abominations were honoured by the throne, of which they were the chief advisers. It was so with Assyria, as the recent exhumations of Nineveh abundantly attest. It was so with the Babylon of Nebuchadnezzar, as Daniel, who lived amid it all, has written. It was so with Persia, as her various records all declare. It was so with Greece, as her own most cherished poets sung, her mightiest orators proclaimed, and all her venerated artists and historians have set forth. It was so with Rome, as all her widespread monuments still show, and all the Christian testimonies, with her own, render clear and manifest as the sun. And it will be so with the last, which is yet to come, as declared in the apocalyptic foreshowings, and in all the prophecies in the Book of God upon the subject. It requires but a glance at history to see that spiritual harlotry has ever been the particular pet and delight of all the Beast-powers of time. If ever the worship and requirements of the true God won their respect and patronage, they soon corrupted it to their own selfish and ambitious ends, or never were easy until freed from the felt restraint.

True religion and an uncorrupted Church have never suited the representatives of power, or pleased them long. Dragon agencies are ill at ease without some form of Dragon worship. Only what will dignify, if not deify, lust and selfishness, is in accord with their spirit. They simply favour and honour their own when they favour and cherish the base Woman. Her gaudiness and pomp, her gaiety and ready compliances, her ennoblement of " the lust of the flesh, the lust of the eyes, and the pride of life," enamour them, and make them glad to bear her on their shoulders. It is a sad commentary on humanity, but it is the truth, that all the great world-powers, from first to last, are the paramours and props of the Harlot Woman. Government is indeed a thing of God, instituted for human good, necessary to man, and invested with rights from the eternal throne ; but Satan has ever known too well how to pervert it to his own base ends. And so the mountains of worldly power have ever served him as grand homes for his adulteress Bride.

What else remains of the story must wait for another occasion. God help us all to keep ourselves from idols !

LECTURE THIRTY-NINTH

GREAT BABYLON CONTINUED—THE WILDERNESS IN WHICH SHE APPEARS—HER TWOFOLD-
NESS, IN MYSTERY AND AS A CITY—SHALL THE CITY OF BABYLON BE RESTORED—PROPHE-
CIES OF HER ABSOLUTE OBLITERATION NOT YET FULFILLED—PROPHECIES WHICH
SEEM TO REQUIRE HER RESTORATION—ZECHARIAH'S EPHAH—HER FEATURES AND FALL
TOUCHING THIS QUESTION—REASONABLENESS OF THE IDEA.

REV. 17: 18. (Revised Text.) And the Woman whom thou sawest, is the great city
which hath rule [kingdom] upon the kings of the earth.

WHEN John was taken to see " the judgment of the Great Harlot," he was
borne " into a wilderness." This description of her dwelling-place is very
expressive. Where spiritual harlotry occupies the place of the true worship of
God, there is desolation. There may be riches and worldly glory, as here.
There may be the fulness of power and dominion ; there may be purple, and
scarlet, and gold, and gems of stone, and pearls, and drink from golden cups ;
there may be luxuries, sumptuous living, pomp, display, and everything to
delight the sensual heart ; and yet, where the word, worship, and institutes
of God are trampled underfoot, it is wilderness. Some set great store
on general education, on the achievements of science, on the progress of man
in his material and social interests, on the success of reforms in government
and laws, on the universal spread of liberty, equality, and fraternity, wrought
out by the diffusion of intelligence and right reason. Those claiming to be
leaders in this line of thought are everywhere full of prognostications of a
great and glorious condition of humanity to be achieved by the new ideas over
against what they consider the old nonsense, superstition, and ignorance,
which, as they say, have too long held dominion. And in proportion to the
confidence and zeal in these hopes is the averseness to the Bible and its
teachings, or any such way of receiving it as takes it for what it says. Indeed
the Church, its doctrines and confessions, are ignored, sneered at, and more
and more resisted and set aside, as the particular impediment to the
true interests of man, and the worst hindrances to human progress and
blessedness. But the Scriptures have anticipated this, and tell us that so
things will go on until the world believes itself wiser than its reputed Maker.
And when the gospel of the sensual and devilish wisdom has once won its
way to victory, as it surely will ; when the atheistic materialism to which so
many are betaking themselves has attained its bloom ; and when the ten
thousand goodishnesses for which so large a portion of the professed Church
is selling its birthright have brought forth their inevitable fruits, the result
will be a universal *wilderness*, with nothing but a monster Beast from the abyss
for government, a hell-inspired self-will for law, and the uncleannesses of a
gaudy Harlot for paradise. And this is the world in its final outcome, when
Antichrist reigns and Great Babylon reaches its full development. The true
people of God will then have been removed to the heavenly pavilion, or killed
off by the powers of a blaspheming persecution. According to the prophet's
figure, they will have become as scarce on earth as the remaining grapes after
the vintage has been gathered. The Living Ones will have reached their
places in connection with the celestial throne. The Elders will have obtained
their crowns and golden seats. The numberless multitude will have taken its
stand before the throne of God. The salt of the earth and the light of the
world will have been mostly withdrawn. And whatever of accumulated
wealth, gorgeousness, luxury, or perfected human civilization may remain,

what can this habitation of mortals be but one great moral wilderness and desolation, where the powers are full of blasphemy, and the accredited worship is abomination ?   Such, at least, is the pictured scene of things to which the Apostolic Seer was carried to see the Great Harlot and the end that awaits her.

When John beheld the Woman, he was much astonished.   He tells us himself that he " wondered great wonder."   When the Beast first displayed himself all the world wondered after the Beast.   (Chap. 13 : 3.)   But that was a wonder of admiration ; this is a wonder of perplexed horror.   He had had a view of that Beast before.   He had beheld and described his heads and horns.   He had seen the wounding to death and the healing from the wound, and how men were carried captive by the marvel.   But he experienced no such astonishment as here.   But he had seen and described the glorious Woman, whose mystic child was caught up to God and to His throne.   Could it be that this was the same Woman,—the Bride of Heaven transformed into such a character, with such names on her forehead, and thus associated with the Son of Perdition ?   God had once exclaimed over the defections of Jerusalem, " How is the faithful city become an harlot ! "   (Isa. 1 : 21.) Was John to understand a similar transformation here ?   This was the seat of his amazed horror and bewilderment.   But the angel at once interposed to relieve him.   The Beast is the same which he saw before, but the Woman is not.   And the Beast is here seen in the fulness of his development.   No colour was noticed on his first rise ; but by this time he has developed his bloody hue by his slaughter of the saints.   Then he had names of blasphemy on his heads ; by this time he is full of them all over.   There his infernal origin did not so fully appear ; by this time he has demonstrated that he comes up out of the abyss.   His seven heads were there left in mystery ; here they are explained, and his true history and relations indicated.   There his ten horns were noted ; but only here is it told that they are ten contemporaneous kings, who arise contemporaneously with the Beast, and who colleague with him in one mind and policy, and give their power and authority to him, and join with him and each other in desolating and devouring the Woman whom at first they carried in affection, and finally make war against the Lamb in a contest for the sovereignty of the world.   The Woman is a new and different object.   The first was the mother of saints ; this is the mother of harlots and of the abominations of the earth, first organized in the rebellion of Nimrod, and the gaudy but unclean rider upon all the great mountains of world-power from the beginning, for whose special delectation all the martyr blood that ever flowed has been shed, and who is here shown for the purpose of exhibiting her end.

There is a twofoldness of the judgment upon this great Harlot.   Not only is her fall mentioned twice, and each time with a double fall ; but two sorts of visitation, and seemingly at different times, are here described.   At first the Beast carries the Woman ; but the angel says that the ten horns, in connection with him, eventually " hate the Harlot, and make her desolate and naked, and shall eat her flesh, and burn her with fire."   In the next chapter, however, there is a different picture, and her final ruin takes the form of a sudden and complete overthrow of a great city, over which these same kings lament and mourn.   These two different presentations are owing to the two different aspects in which the Woman is contemplated.   In chapter 17 we have the picture of Great Babylon *in mystery* only, in which she has various centres and forms at different times, and presents herself in a variety of ways. The last forms of Babylon *in mystery* are those which the ten kings with the Beast attack and destroy.   How this comes about is plain enough.   The two great Beasts, as we have seen, set up an entirely new religion upon earth,—a religion which they insist on making as universal as their own dominion, and so must needs make war on all existing religions, true or false.   The record is, that they will not permit anyone to live under them who will not conform to their new worship, nor allow anyone to buy or sell without first accepting their hellish sacrament or mark.   Hence every form of existing worship then upon earth, be it Romanism, Mohammedanism, degenerate Protestantism, or any other species of false worship, it will come under the ban of this great infernal confederation.   Whatever riches or possessions they may have will be confiscated.   Their temples, cathedrals, mosques, institutions, and treasure-depositories, will be rifled, stripped, burned to the ground, and all their owners turned out in perfect nakedness ; and any of them daring to resist, or refusing to conform to the new worship of the Beast and his image, will be put to the sword.   All this is necessarily implied in what was shown of the doings of the False Prophet, and what occurs under his administrations ; but it is here independently stated as part of " the judgment of the Great Harlot."   This is the first part of her final calamities.

But Great Babylon in final revelation is also *a local city*.   As a system, its essential principle is alienation of soul from God, and so whatever is developed from the carnal wisdom, either against or in the place of the true worship. But as the sun-clad Woman develops into a heavenly city, the new Jerusalem embodying all the ultimate glories pertaining to the spiritual wisdom and the true devotion, so the Great Harlot also develops into an earthly city, embodying all the completed temporal results of the sensual wisdom and the ultimate bloom of human apostasy.   Hence her final overthrow sums up in the fall and destruction of a great, rich, and powerful city.   Hence, also, the angel says : " The Woman whom thou sawest is *the great city* which hath rule upon the kings of the earth."   It is the same Woman which, as a system of false worship, rode all the governments and powers of earth, but which makes its final presentation in the form of a literal city.

Some think only an ideal city is meant, but nearly all interpreters, however diverse their ways of looking at these visions, agree that we must here understand a real city.   Most of them say it is the city of Rome ; some say it is Jerusalem ; and a few say it is the island of England, which they take as the great centre of an unclean system of union between Church and State.   My own impressions are that a literal city is contemplated in the vision, but that we must look for it in a different region of the world.   However much Rome, Jerusalem, or states having national churches may be involved, they do not, and it is hard to see how they possibly can, fill out the picture of this final Babylon.   The realization is yet in the future, and we cannot speak with confidence as to how matters will eventuate ; but there seems to be reason for the belief that the literal Babylon will be restored, and that we are to look to the coming up again of that primal city for the fulfilment of what is here foreshown.   The mention of such a thing may seem like a wild dream, and appear to clash with some of the prophecies touching the irrecoverable destruction of ancient Babylon.   But let us look a little at the subject, and endeavour to construe the Scriptures as they are, and not according to the loose impressions which have found currency as if they were settled truths.

First of all, it seems to be pretty clear that the ancient predictions concerning the utter destruction of Babylon have never yet been entirely fulfilled. Isaiah gives the sentence upon Babylon, in which he says that her destruction shall come suddenly from the hand of the Almighty, that her glory and beauty shall be " as when God overthrew Sodom and Gomorrah," never more to be inhabited, nor dwelt in from generation to generation ;   and that the Arabian shall never again pitch tent there, nor shepherds make their fold there. (See Isaiah 13.)   So again it was said to Jeremiah, " Babylon shall become heaps, a dwelling-place for dragons, an astonishment, and an hissing, without an inhabitant."   At the same time he directed Seraiah to take the manuscript of this prophecy, after reading it, bind a stone to it, cast it into the midst of Euphrates, and say, " Thus shall Babylon sink, and shall not rise from the evil that I will bring upon her." (Jer. 51.)   That all this has been in large measure strikingly fulfilled must be admitted. It is part of the evidence of the truth of God's word. And if it all belongs to the past, it is equally certain that Babylon never can be restored. Two facts, however, appear, which go very far to prove that these predictions do not belong exclusively to the past, but await further fulfilment. The one is, that Isaiah locates the destruction of which he speaks in "*the day of the Lord.*" (Is. 13 : 6.) That day, in literal fulness, has not yet come. The world has witnessed many earnests and prelibations of it, but that day proper is still in the future, and only comes when Christ himself shall come again. And if the utter destruction thus suddenly to come upon Babylon belongs to "the day of the Lord," she must again revive in order to become the subject of it. The other fact is that Babylon, in all the deep calamities and desolations which have come upon her, never yet experienced all that has been thus prophesied. When did Babylon ever fall with so complete a fall, or meet with such an utter obliteration from the earth, "as when God over-threw Sodom and Gomorrah ? " Sodom and Gomorrah were completely blotted out. But this has never yet been the case with Babylon. Such was not its fate when the Medes and Persians seized it from the hands of the infamous Belshazzar, for they made it one of their royal cities. In the time of Alexander it still stood, and was the chosen capital of the Græco-Macedonian empire, the second city of Alexander's dominions, where he himself lived and died. It continued to be a populous place under the Syrian kings, who succeeded Alexander in the rule over it. In the time of the apostles it was still a populous place, for both Peter and Bartholomew preached the Gospel there, and there Peter wrote his first Epistle. As late as A.D. 250, there was a Christian church there, and an influential bishopric for many years thereafter. Five hundred years after Christ there were Jewish academies there, who issued the celebrated Babylonian Talmud. Here, then, was a lengthening out of the existence of Babylon as a populated city for more than a thousand years subsequent to the taking of it by Cyrus. And even to this present hour there is a city in the middle of the area occupied by old Babylon containing 10,000 people, and which pays to its governor a revenue of 342,000 Turkish piastres, more than $17,000, a year. Shepherds do make their folds there, as testified by all modern travellers, and the Arabians do pitch their tents there. It is not an utter desolation without inhabitant, and never has been since Nimrod laid its first foundations. The sentence upon Babylon is therefore not yet fulfilled, and cannot be unless that city comes up again into something of its former consequence.

In the next place, there are Scripture prophecies which I am at a loss to understand except upon the theory that Babylon will be restored, become a great commercial centre, and be the last of this world's great centres to go down under the terrific visitations of the day of the Lord.

What is the world's common symbol for commerce, the accepted picture to represent it ? I have asked this question, and looked to verify the answer. In general I have found it to be an ornamented coin, weight, measure, or bowl of the scales, bearing a representation of the power that authorizes it, and a figure of a woman on each side,—one surrounded with the implements of navigation looking to the sea, and the other surrounded with the implements of trade, husbandry, and transportation looking toward the land,—the two mutually supporting what is between them, whilst above are the wings of some vigorous bird, to indicate the far-reaching flights of what is thus pictured to the eye and imagination. Nor would it be easy to improve on this. It has been evolved in the course of ages, and the whole modern world, so far as I know, has set the seal of its approval upon it as the accepted emblem of commerce. But it is the same that was shown to the prophet Zechariah 500 years before the commencement of the Christian era. Just at the time when he sees the great flying roll of the curse of God going forth over the face of the whole earth to cut off transgressors, he beholds an *ephah*, the common bushel measure, and *a talent of lead*, the flat rounded weight used in the calculation of tonnage, put upon the mouth or top of the bushel measure, whilst on each side of it was a woman, having wings " like the wings of a stork," with the winds in their wings ; and they two lifted up the ephah between earth and heaven to bear it away. Besides, in the midst of the united measure and weight was another woman called *Wickedness*, the Lawless Woman, answering to the Great Harlot of these chapters. The prophet wondered what it all meant, and asked the angel in converse with him what these intended to do with the measure and weight inclosing the Woman of Wickedness. The angel said : *" To build it an house in the land of Shinar ; and it shall be established and set there upon her own base."* (Zech. 5 : 1–11.)

Now this joined measure and weight, with the two winged women bearing them, and the winds in their wings, is unquestionably a symbol of *commerce ;* not so much as it was then, but as it was to become in the period verging on the end, and as it has become in our day. The building of a house for it, and the establishment and settling of it upon its own base, can mean nothing less than the creation for it of a great independent centre, with its own ruler, king, or government. The place of this house is specifically stated to be *" the land of Shinar."* What that land is we can have no difficulty in ascertaining. When the people in Nimrod's time journeyed from the East they found a plain in the land of *Shinar* and dwelt there, and there built the city called Babel, or Babylon. (Gen. 11 : 2–9.) When Nebuchadnezzar, king of Babylon, invaded Palestine, it is said that he took Jehoiakim, and part of the vessels of the house of God, and carried them *" into the land of Shinar,"* that is, Babylon. (Dan. 1 : 1, 2.) " The land of Shinar," then, is Babylon ; and in this Shinar the angel said this *commerce,* borne by the favouring winds on mighty wings, was to be established and settled on its own base.

This prophecy was delivered subsequent to the Babylonish captivity, and at least half a lifetime after Babylon had been conquered by the Medes and Persians. It certainly has never yet been fulfilled according to its terms. By the connection in which it is given, its fulfilment belongs to the time when the great curse of God upon the wicked goes forth over all the face of the earth ; that is, in the great judgment period. By the indications thus given as to time, and by the whole contents of the foreshowing, its accomplishment belongs to the future, and necessarily includes the revival of old Babylon as a great commercial centre, standing independent of all other powers, and exercising its own peculiar dominion over the governments of the earth. And this is all the more confirmed in that it exhibits the Woman of Wickedness, the Great Harlot, ensconced in it, as the great spirit which pervades the whole.

It is also distinctly prophesied that Babylon shall be the very last of the powers of the earth compelled to drink of the cup of the divine wrath in the great day of the Lord. That cup is to go around to all the nations and potencies of this world, to " all the kings of the north, far and near, one with another, and all the kingdoms of the world which are upon the face of the earth ; *and the king of Sheshack shall drink after them."* (Jer. 25 : 17–26.) All the Jewish interpreters agree that *Sheshack* is only another name for *Babylon,* and so, in another place, Babylon is called " the hindermost of the nations," because thus belated in the judgment which is to make her " a wilderness, a dry land, a desert," so as to be " wholly desolate," and " no more inhabited forever." (Jer. 50 : 12, 13, 35–40.) Thus far Babylon has been *the foremost* of the nations in experience of the judgments of God, and cannot possibly to " *the hindermost,"* as thus described, except as rebuilt and become once more a great centre of independent power existing at the time when the final day of vengeance comes.

Furthermore, it seems to me impossible to do justice to the description which John here gives of the features and fall of the Great City which he was called to contemplate, except on the supposition of such a revival of the old Chaldean metropolis.

The name itself is a tower of strength to the idea. There is no great city,

Babylon, now ; nor has there been for many ages. Nor is there any other great city on the face of the earth that answers to the picture, or that is at all likely ever to answer to it on any possibilities that can be imagined. And yet the name of this great city is *Babylon*—Babylon living and ruling over the kings and nations of the earth when the day of judgment reaches its consummation. It is not Babylon in mystery, but simply " the great city Babylon, the mighty city ; " and there is no intimation whatever that this city of Babylon does not mean the city of Babylon. By what right then are we to think of any other city than that which has been known by this name ever since Nimrod lived ?

The city here described is pre-eminently, if not exclusively, a commercial city,—a great commercial city,—a mart of nations. There is nothing military, nothing ecclesiastical, nothing educational, alluded to in the account ; everything is *commercial*, or merged into the one idea of exchange, trade, and what relates to mercantile aims and accumulations. Ships, merchants, commodities, are the main subjects of the description. And when this city falls, it is " the merchants of the earth " that " mourn and weep over her," and with them such as are most concerned with commerce,—" every ship-master, and everyone who goeth by sea, and sailors, and as many as trade by sea," for " all who had ships in the sea were made rich from her costliness." The lamentation is of the same character as that over the fall of Tyre (Ezek. 26 : 15–18), and we know that Tyre was the great mercantile metropolis of its time ; therefore this city must also be a corresponding commercial centre. It cannot, therefore, be Rome, for Rome never was a great centre of commerce. In all the Bible we never read of " a ship of Rome," or of one sailing *from* or *to* Rome. It cannot be Paris for similar reasons. It might be London, New York, or San Francisco, but there is nothing whatever in the account to fix the picture on either of them, whilst none of them could become so independent of all government but its own, as indicated in this case. The land of Shinar is named as the locality in the old prophets, and the particular city of that land, in its own proper name, is given by John as the subject of what he describes. And such is the location of that city politically, geographically, and in all the qualities of accessibility, commercial facilities, remoteness from interferences of Church or state, and yet centralness with regard to the general trade of the whole world, as to point it out above any other known as the elect spot for just what is predicted of this great city.

Even apart from the direct Scriptural prophecies and implications on the subject, the prospect is as they represent. The whole world is rapidly developing a system of things which, in the ordinary working of human affairs, must inevitably result in something of the kind. In what, indeed, does the mightiest and furthest reaching power on earth now already centre ? A power which looms up in all lands, far above all individual or combined powers of Church, or state, or caste, or creed ? What is it that to-day monopolizes nearly all legislation, dictates international treaties, governs the conferences of kings for the regulation of the balance of power, builds railways, cuts ship-canals, sends forth steamer-lines to the ends of the earth, unwinds electric wires across continents, under the seas, and around the world, employs thousands of engineers, subsidizes the press, tells the state of the markets of the world yesterday that everyone may know how to move to-day, and has her living organizations in every land and city, interlinked with each other, and coming daily into closer and closer combination, so that no great government under the sun can any longer move or act against her will, or without her concurrence and consent ? Think for a moment, for there is such a power ; a power that is everywhere clamouring for a common code, a common currency, common weights and measures ; and which is not likely to be silenced or to stop till it has secured a common centre on its own independent basis, whence to dictate to all countries and to exercise its own peculiar rule on all the kings and nations of the earth. That power is COMMERCE ; the power of the ephah and the talent—the power borne by the winged women, the one with her hand on the sea and the other with her hand on the land,—the power which even in its present dismemberment is mightier than any pope, any throne, any government, or any other one human power on the face of the globe. Let it go on as it has been going, and will go, in spite of everything that earth can interpose to hinder, dissolving every tie of nationality, every bond of family or kindred, every principle of right and religion which it cannot bend and render subservient to its own ends and interests ; and the time must come when it will settle itself down somewhere on its own independent base, and where Judaism and Heathenism, Romanism and Protestantism, Mohammedanism and Boodhism, and every distinction of nationality,—English, German, French, Italian, Greek, Turk, Hindoo, Arab, Chinee, Japanee, or what not,—shall be sunk in one great universal fellowship and kingdom of *commerce.*

And when it once comes to that, as there is every prospect that it will, for Providence in judgment for the greed and covetousness of men will prosper it, filling the wings of the women with the winds of heaven, where on earth is the spot so suited to the purpose as that where the first city this side the flood was built ? There is the great navigable river, emptying out into the open sea, whose waters lave every country and island most filled with the treasures of the far East.* From thence there are almost level avenues for railway lines to Egypt, Smyrna, and Constantinople, connecting with Vienna, Paris, and London, for some of which the Turkish Sultan, it is said, has granted Firman, and which Western Europe in its own defence will presently be compelled to construct. There could all the great mercantile combinations unite in one common centre, with no other power on earth to interfere with them. All the considerations which bear on the question speak for old Babylon.

And with a world-wide commercial organization thus established on its own independent base, with the great mercantile houses of England and her colonies, of the Americas, of the other countries lining the Mediterranean, of the maritime and monetary centres everywhere, represented in corresponding houses there ; with the ships, and passengers in ships, congregating in and about the Euphrates as the central exchange of the world ; and with the gold-kings, money-lords, and merchant princes of the earth, thus combined without regard to creeds or nationalities in the one great interest of regulating and managing the commerce of the globe, it is easy to see how every feature in the Apocalyptic picture of Babylon would be filled out. Her merchants would thus be the great men of the earth. Her chief purchases would necessarily be as here described : (1) the most precious and valuable metals ; (2) the costliest articles of clothing, ornaments, and display ; (3) the most rare and sumptuous of furniture and materials for it ; (4) precious aromatics, spices, and ointments ; (5) the finest of eatables ; (6) the most luxurious of equipages, chariots, and horses ; and (7) slaves and attendants necessary to the maintenance of the style and grandeur going along with such wealth, consequence, and power. The city would thus literally be " clothed in fine linen, and purple, and scarlet, and decked with gold, and precious stone, and pearl," creating a market for the skill and most excellent products of the whole world, enriching artisans, ship-masters, ship-owners, ship-senders, and all the traders in these things in all nations. Kings of the earth would thus naturally find it their interest and their delight to be on good terms and friendliest intimacies with a power so much wider and greater than their own. Governments would have to throw their influence in its favour, legislate out of the way what it wishes away, direct their policies according to its desires, and make war and conclude peace as it dictates, as is even now already largely the case, for commerce is the law-maker of the world. The purse-strings of the

---

* G. Rawlinson, in his notes on *Herodotus*, says, with General Chesney's *Euphrat. Expedition*, that the Euphrates " is navigable without any serious interruption from Samosata to the sea, nearly 1,200 miles ; " that from Busrah to the sea it is on an average 30 feet deep and 1,200 yards wide, and at Babylon it averages 15 feet in depth and 200 yards in width.

nations would thus be in the hands of a universal independent power, whose ban would be worse than the Pope's edicts of excommunication in the Middle Ages ; and to make war with it would be to make war against the allied world. All the kings of the earth would thus necessarily become participant in everything belonging to the system, the very organization of which is the utter negation of all distinctive creeds, and the complete abrogation of all religious and moral laws which stand in the way of its purposes.

And thus also the old harlotry would necessarily be the chief spirit of the whole thing. Zealous and earnest worship there would needs be, but a worship concentrated upon the ephah and the talent ; a worship which makes temples of banks, and warehouses, and exchanges, and pleasure-parks ; a worship not of the sun, or moon, or stars, or emperors, or popes, but of pounds, and francs, and piastres, and dollars ; the worship of greed, and epicurean luxury ; the worship of Mammon perfected, and overriding and supplanting all other devotions ; the perpetuation and crown of the great moral defilement of the ages, only taking to the souls' embrace and into the place of God the meaner object which the divine word stigmatizes as " filthy lucre." Covetousness is idolatry, and a form of it which is the root of all evil ; and here will be covetousness, deep-wrapped in the embracing arms of its god, and dazing and defiling the world with the glory and grandeur of its abominations.

Such would Babylon be under the suppositions to which I have alluded, and such is the Great Babylon of these chapters in its final outcome. Is it not reasonable, therefore, to believe that this is the way in which this prophetic description is to be realized ?

Besides, it would be a strange thing if Babylon were to be the only exception to the general revival and renewal which is to come to the long desolations of the East in general. Egypt, long the basest of the kingdoms, is rapidly coming up again, and is everywhere presented as prominent in the time when Christ comes to take the sovereignty of the earth. The English occupation of Cyprus must give strong impulse to the rebuilding of the mighty cities which once had place upon and around that island. Tyre and its associated cities, and Antioch, and Damascus, and Tadmor, and Nineveh, and all the ancient localities, are becoming more and more the objects of interest to the Western peoples and powers, and plans for the revival of some of them, including especially old Babylon, have been put forth with eloquence and received with favour.*

* In 1857 a work was published in London, entitled *Memoir of the Euphrates Valley Route to India, with Official Correspondence and Maps*, by W. P. Andrew, F.R.G.S., etc. After a large circulation the same was enlarged, and published in a volume, entitled *The Scinde Railway and its Relations to the Euphrates Valley and other Routes to India*. This enlargement and republication of the work was undertaken, on the considerations stated in the preface, viz., that " it is believed to be *essential*, not only to the vital interests of this country (England) in the East, and the well-being of Turkey, but to the peace and progress of the world, to establish, with as little delay as possible, steam and telegraphic communication, *via* the Euphrates, between England and India ; " and " to indicate to statesmen the political power, to the philanthropist the enlightenment, and to the merchant the profit that would of necessity accrue from re-establishing this highway of forgotten empires and ancient commerce."

The author of this book recounts the many and glowing histories which cluster around the Euphrates and its tributary, the Tigris ; points out the extraordinary capabilities of the country, and adds : " Every way, commercially, historically, and politically, the Euphrates Valley route is a grand scheme, and must affect immediately the commerce, and, in some measure, the destinies of our race ; and that depends not on a thorough traffic, but holds within its own confines the elements of a great prosperity.

" Why have the governments and peoples of the West combined to uphold the Sultan in the possession of Constantinople ? And why has he who thought fit to menace that position met with the armed opposition of Europe ? Because the passage from the Mediterranean to the Black Sea is of so much importance that whatever European power might become master of it would domineer over all the rest, and destroy that balance which the whole world is interested in preserving. Establish then, at another and far more extensive point of the Ottoman Empire, a similar and yet more important position ; make the Valley of the Euphrates *the highway of the commercial world*, and you would restore millions of unproductive acres to the revenue, bring thousands of merely vassal tribes within the pale

Jerusalem, we know, is to be rebuilt and re-established as a great national and religious centre, of a very numerous, rich, and powerful people. And when Israel with its wealth and commercial energy begins to rally again around its old metropolis, the Euphrates will again be needed as much as Germany needs the Danube, Egypt the Nile, or London the Thames ; whilst the prodigious fertility of its great alluvial plains, and the unbounded riches of nature which there spring up almost unbidden to the hand that would gather them, and a ready progress of opulence that would realize the wonder-working power of Aladdin's lamp, cannot fail to arrest and command the sharp-sighted covetousness of the human heart. How, then, are we to suppose it possible that Babylon will not also come up again with the rest of these Eastern schemes and renovations ? Already a walled town there exists, taking in both sides of the river, as old Babylon did. It is encircled with villages, and approached through an outspread country dotted with beautiful groves of date-trees, forming a broad and verdant colonnade to a growing city. That city, strangely enough, also bears the name of *Rest* (Hillah), as if inviting the wide-wandering tribes of an apostate world to come back to the bosom of the old mother, there to plant and erect the final tower of their finished greatness.

I conclude, then, that such a great commercial city, different from all that now exist, will yet be, and that it will be old Babylon rebuilt. When the New Jerusalem, the Lamb's Wife, comes down out of heaven from God, there is every intimation that it will be stationed over the old Jerusalem. And when the wisdom, progress, and harlotries of this world come to their final culmination and embodiment in Great Babylon, there is corresponding reason to believe that it will be centralized upon the very spot where it first started, and meet its ultimate doom in the selfsame locality in which it was born.

But the description of that doom, its character, and its results, must be

of order and fair tribute, and create in the East another immovable seat of power for the great powers of Europe."

So, also, an article in *Colburn's Monthly*, quoted by this author, says : " England and France, and even other nations, appear now called to great works, which throw into the shade the most striking deeds of history. Among these works of the future it appears that the opening of the Euphrates Valley, and *the restoration of Syria and Mesopotamia, of Assyria and Babylonia*, stands first in rank. Such a proceeding, by multiplying and strengthening the ties by which people of all climates, of all races, of all beliefs, are united to Great Britain and France, would connect forever the general prosperity of nations with the happiness of those countries, their security with their power, and their independence with their liberty."

Mr. Andrew further says : " Amongst the numerous administrations of a wise and merciful design of Providence, it is not unreasonable to believe that the opening of the valleys of the Euphrates and the Tigris, and *the resuscitation of the great nations of antiquity*, are amongst the events designed to minister to the growing wants and improvements of the human race. . . . It is not too much to say that there is no existing or projected railroads that can for a moment compare, in point of interest and importance, with that of the Euphrates Valley. It brings two quarters of the globe into juxtaposition, and three continents,—Europe, Asia, and Australia,—into co-relation. It binds the vast population of Hindustan by an iron link with the people of Europe ; it inevitably entails the colonization and civilization of the great valleys of the Euphrates and Tigris, *the resuscitation in modern shape of Babylon and Nineveh*, and the reawakening of Ctesiphon and Bagdad of old."

In the *Life of Sir C. Napier*, vol. iv, p. 70, there is given an extract from his journal, in which he writes : " Civilization was travelling west in Alexander's time, but now how changed is the drama ! More than 2,000 years have passed, and civilization arises on the rear of barbarism ; we English have seized the baggage, are following up our blow, *and in a few years shall be at Babylon, a revived empire !* We shall go slowly, but *one hundred years will see us at Babylon !* " This was written fifty years ago.

A letter written at Mosul (Nineveh), February 26th, 1854, and published in the *New York Tribune*, says : " There is but little soil in the world like that of the valleys of the Tigris and the Euphrates. . . . It is among the possibilities that a railway will ere long be built from Antioch to Seleucia along the Orontes, across Mesopotamia to Mosul, and thence down to Bagdad and Busrah,—the second short route to India. If this part of Turkey should fall into the hands of England, there is no doubt that such a road would be speedily constructed. *The line has been surveyed.* These barren fields are too rich always to remain idle. ITS TIME HAS NEARLY COME ! "

All these statements are quite apart from what many are too prone to call mere prophetic speculations.

deferred for another occasion. I can only ask you now to think over what has been presented, and not to be envious at the prosperity of the wicked. Let the gold, and the silver, and the scarlet, and the purple, and the fine linen, be to those who make them their God. We have quite another Saviour, and quite another calling. They that worship these things shall lose them, and perish with them ; but they who, for the kingdom of heaven's sake, deny themselves and refuse to be beguiled and swayed by the deceitful glitter and sumptuous allurements of wealth and fortune, shall live to enjoy a far sublimer estate,— one which shall never fade away. Yet a little while, and they shall come forth in a city whose gates are pearl and its streets gold, themselves as pure as the gates through which they pass, and as excellent and glorious as the streets on which they tread ; immortal parts of a new and everlasting system of God, when Babylon has gone down into perdition, as a millstone cast into the midst of the sea.

REV. 18 : 1–8. (Revised Text.) After these things I saw another angel coming down out of the heaven, having great authority, and the earth was lighted up from his glory. And he cried with mighty voice, saying, Fallen, fallen Babylon the great, and become a habitation of demons, and a hold of every unclean spirit, and a hold of every unclean and hated bird ; because of the wrath of her fornication all the nations have fallen, and the kings of the earth committed fornication with her, and the merchants of the earth became rich out of the power of her wantonness.

And I heard another voice out of the heaven, saying, Come out of her, my people, that ye may have no fellowship in her sins, and that ye receive not of her plagues ; because her sins have been builded together as far as the heaven, and God hath remembered her iniquities. Reward to her even as she rewarded, and double double according to her works ; in the cup which she mixed, mix for her double ; insomuch as she glorified herself and was wanton, to that proportion give to her torment and grief ; because she saith in her heart, I sit a queen and am not a widow, and shall see no mourning ; therefore in one day shall come her plagues, death, and mourning, and famine, and with fire shall she be burnt, because strong the Lord who hath judged her.

HAVING already consumed two evenings in our endeavours to identify and understand what is meant by Great Babylon, we come now to the consideration of her final fall.

But before proceeding directly to that subject, it may be well first to relieve a perplexity into which some may have fallen by reason of what I have said concerning the restoration of the literal city of Babylon.

When we speak of the day of the Lord, or the judgment period, many have the notion that it is but one day, or a very brief space of time. They are consequently led to wonder how we can speak of the impending nearness of that day, and yet look for the rebuilding of a great city then to be destroyed. The difficulty, however, does not lie in the nature of the things, but in the popular misapprehensions of what the day of the Lord means, and the length of the period which it covers. The mistake is in taking the day of the Lord, or the coming again of our Saviour, as if one particular moment of time, and one single event or scene were to be understood. What the Scriptures describe as the day of the Lord, and the second coming of Christ, is no more limited to a single event or moment of time than was the day of his first coming, which extended over more than thirty years, and embraced various stages and successive presentations. If we take the prophecies concerning the first advent, we find it impossible to apply them to any one day, year, or scene, in the evangelic history. Micah said that Christ should " *come* " out of Bethlehem (Ephratah), but Hosea said that he would *come* " out of Egypt." Malachi said that he should " suddenly *come* to his temple," and Zechariah that he would *come* to Zion " riding upon an ass, upon a colt the foal of an ass ; " whilst, according to Isaiah, " the land of Zebulun and the land of Naphtali " were to see the " great light." All these presentations were his coming. He did *come* when he was born at Bethlehem ; he did *come* out of Egypt ; he did *come* when he announced himself at Nazareth ; he did *come* as a great light among the people of Northern Galilee ; he did *come* riding into Jerusalem on the ass ; he did *come* suddenly to his temple when he twice drove out the money-changers ; and he *came* when he reappeared after his resurrection. Each one of these particular incidents is alike called his *coming;* but they were only so many separate presentations, at different dates, extending through a period of thirty-three years, all of which together are required to make up the first advent as a whole. And just as it was then, so it will be again. The second coming, like the first, is complex and distributive, extending through a variety of successive and diverse scenes, stages, events, and manifestations, requiring as many, if not still more, years. Just what length of time will intervene between the first and sudden catching away of the watching and ready saints, and the final overthrow of Babylon and Antichrist, we may not be able precisely to determine ; but I am fully persuaded that it will be a goodly number of years. Antichrist reigns for a full week of years,— that is seven years,—three and a half as the friend and patron of the Israel-itish people, and three and a half as the great Beast. (Dan. 10 : 27 ; Rev. 11 : 2 ; 12 : 6.) But the Antichrist is not revealed until after the Hinderer is taken away ; who is only taken away when the saints are removed, the removal of whom is the taking away of the Hinderer. The Antichrist does not appear at all amid the scenes of the Apocalypse until after the seven seals have been opened, and six of the succeeding trumpets have been sounded. How many years those seals and the six trumpets may consume we are not informed, but we have every reason to believe that they may be counted by tens, if not by scores, subsequent to the opening of the door in the heaven and the taking up of the saints, which is the first act in the great drama. The space occupied in narrating what occurs under the seals and trumpets would indicate this. The long waiting of the Ten Virgins for the coming of the Bride-groom, which is subsequent to the first translation, indicates the same thing. Forty years, at least, perhaps a whole jubilee period of fifty years, or even a full seventy years, answering to the period during which the judgment was upon Israel for its sins, are likely to be embraced in what the Scriptures call the day of the Lord, and the second coming and revelation of Jesus Christ.

Supposing, then, that Babylon should not even begin to be rebuilt until after the day of the Lord has commenced in the rapture of the eagle-saints (Luke 17 : 34–37 ; 1 Thess. 4 : 14–17 ; Rev. 4 : 1), there still would be ample time for it to come up in all the grandeur and force indicated before the great acts of destruction in which that day reaches its consummation. Much can be accomplished in forty, fifty, or seventy years.

A few years ago I was the guest of a man, scarcely older than myself, who was already grown, and secretary of a frontier trading company, before the first dwelling was built of what is now the great and powerful city of Chicago. And if the rich merchants, money-kings, and great mercantile organizations of the world were to unite for the establishment of such a centre of wealth, influence, and trade, as the foreshowings are respecting great Babylon, with the treasures, facilities, and energies that would at once be brought to bear, a much shorter time would be required to realize all that has been foretold, even if nothing special were to occur to hasten the project. But the indications are that there will be special providences in its favour. Zechariah saw the winds of heaven filling the wings and favouring the flight of the two women bearing the ephah to its house in the land of Shinar. It will then be the midst of the judgment time, when great and startling events are to succeed each other in quick succession, when things will move under other and mightier impulses than now, and when God in the administrations of His wrath upon nations and systems will hurry them on to the destructions which await them, or so give them over to the spirits and powers of hell because of their unbelief, that the most wonderful changes and achievements will go forward with a celerity of which we now have no conception. And even if the great day of the Lord should break in upon the world this night, it would not at all embarrass the idea, or prevent the possibility of the restoration of old Babylon in all the magnificence and power ascribed to her in these chapters. The time would still be ample for it all.

But it is with the *fall* of Babylon, and not with the time and incidents of her restoration from present depression that we are now concerned. God help us to understand it as we should !

A glorious being from heaven appears. To John he seems like an angel, but quite " another " from the one who was showing him these things. This angel does not speak from heaven, but comes down out of the heaven. He comes also with " great authority." There is reason to believe that it is Christ himself whom we are to see in this angel ; for the Father " hath given him authority to execute judgment, because he is the Son of Man." (Jno. 5 : 27.) When Satan was cast out of heaven the celestial worshippers celebrated this ἐουσία, authority, dominion, or power, as the particular possession of Christ, who is appointed to " put down all rule and all authority and power." (Cor. 15 : 24.) It is said that " *the earth was lighted up from his glory.*" Such language is nowhere used concerning created angels, but is quite common to all the prophets with regard to our Divine King and Saviour. The Psalmist (72 : 18, 19) blesses the glorious name of the Lord God of Israel, and speaks of a scene in which " the whole earth is filled with his glory." Isaiah (6 : 1-3), in his vision of the enthroned Messiah, heard the seraphim cry, " The whole earth is full of his glory." Ezekiel (43 : 2) beheld the glory of the God of Israel coming from the way of the East, and says : " His voice was like the noise of many waters [answering to the ' mighty voice ' here], and the earth shined with his glory." The garment of Jehovah is light, and such intense luminousness everywhere attaches to what is divine ; whilst the enlightening of things by the glory of God and the Lamb is specially spoken of in these visions. (Rev. 21 : 23 ; 22 : 25.) We are not likely to be mistaken, then, in taking this angel for the Lord Jesus himself, and the more so as the remembrance of Great Babylon to give to her the cup of the wine of the fierceness of divine wrath is specially said to be " *in the presence of God,*" as if God in Christ were then manifested and personally revealed upon the earth. (Chap. 16 : 19.)

From this glorious being the word goes forth in tremendous power : " *Fallen Fallen, Babylon the Great.*" It is not simply the word of information as to what has been or what is to be, but the word which effects what it describes,— the word which brings Great Babylon down, and makes it " a habitation of demons, and a hold of every unclean spirit, and a hold of every unclean and hateful bird." The twice-repeated word describes two separate parts or stages of the fall, answering to the two aspects in which Babylon is contemplated, referring first to Babylon in mystery, as *a system* or spirit of false worship, and second to Babylon as *a city*, in which this system or spirit is finally embodied. The thrice-repeated cry of " woe, woe, woe," in chapter 8 : 13, meant three distinct woes, as the subsequent account makes plain ; and so here, the twice-repeated " fallen, fallen," means two distinct falls. The first fall, or the fall of Babylon in mystery, is accomplished through the agency of the Beast in confederation with the ten kings (chap. 17 : 16, 17), which occurs soon after the Antichrist is fully revealed ; but after the denudation and burning which they inflict, she is represented as still existing as a city, who sits as a boastful queen, promising herself an immortality of worldly glory, and from which certain people are called out that they may not share her doom. Two falls are thus inevitably implied, and the last is more than three years after the first ; for the reign of the Beast is three and one-half years, and the setting up of the enforced worship of his image, and hence the first great Babylonian disaster occurs at the beginning of those years, whilst the final catastrophe occurs at the pouring out of the last bowl of wrath, which sweeps the Beast as well as Great Babylon to perdition.

But before the mighty word of this glorious angel goes into full effect upon the final Babylon, a voice from heaven says : " *Come out of her, my people, that ye may have no fellowship in her sins, and that ye receive not of her plagues."* It seems that there will be children of Abraham among the population of the final Babylon, for wherever there is great trade and banking we may expect to find Jews, and these are the people to whom this call is made. If the glorious angel is Christ, it is the Father who here speaks, and who now again acknowledges Israel as his earthly people. The New Testament Church is here out of the question. Every divinely acknowledged part of that has been by this time taken, and is with the Lord Jesus in heaven. But the times of the Gentiles being fulfilled, the *Lo Ammi* (not my people) is reversed with regard to Israel, and this is the time when the Spirit comes upon them again, and they are recovered to life and salvation. Jeremiah (50 : 4–9) writes : " In those days, and in that time [the very time of the threatened destruction of Babylon], saith the Lord, *the children of Israel* shall come, *they and the children of Judah together*, going and weeping ; they shall go and seek the Lord their God. They shall ask the way to Zion with their faces thitherward, saying, Come, let us join ourselves to the Lord in a perpetual covenant that shall not be forgotten. My people hath been lost sheep ; their shepherds have caused them to go astray, they have turned them away on the mountains ; they have gone from mountain to hill, they have forgotten their resting-place. All that found them have devoured them ; and their adversaries said, We offend not, because they have sinned against the Lord, the habitation of justice, even the Lord, the hope of their fathers." And in immediate connection with this description the command is : " *Remove out of the midst of Babylon, and go forth out of the land of the Chaldeans*, and be as the he goats before the flocks." " *Flee out of the midst of Babylon, and deliver every man his soul ; be not cut off in her iniquity ;* for this is the time of the Lord's vengeance ; he will render unto her a recompense " (51 : 6). " *My people, go ye out of the midst of her*, and deliver ye every man his soul from the fierce anger of the Lord " (verse 45). " *Though Babylon should mount up to heaven, and though she should fortify the height of her strength, yet from me shall the spoiler come unto her, saith the Lord* " (53). " And I will make drunk her princes, and her wise men, her captains, and her rulers, and her mighty men : and they shall sleep a perpetual sleep, and not awake, saith the King whose name is Lord of hosts " (57). Thus beautifully and unmistakably do the records of the ancient prophet explain what the Apocalyptic seer was shown. The merciful providence of God has by this time again taken hold on the long-rejected children of Israel and Judah, and such of them as are in Babylon are divinely warned of what is coming, and brought away from the impending destruction, as Lot was called out of doomed Sodom (Gen. 19 : 15–22), and as the people in Moses' time were called to get them up from the tents of Dathan and Abiram in the day that judgment came upon these rebels (Numb. 16 : 23–26).

The particular calamities which then break forth are described as *death, mourning, famine, and burning with fire.* Both the calling out of those who are not to share Babylon's doom, and the nature of these inflictions immediately following, prove that a literal city is meant. Part of the trouble is also of just such a character as to fall in with the idea, and so to prove that that city is Babylon, and that the drying up of the waters of the Euphrates under the sixth bowl of wrath is a literal occurrence. Terrible mortality and famine would be the natural and inevitable result of the failure of that river to a city built upon it, and so dependent on its waters. All her shipping would thus be disabled. All the fertility of her gardens and surrounding country would be turned to dust and barrenness. The exposed and stagnant filth of so great a river, together with the decaying vegetation for the space of nearly 2,000 miles, would be a source of deadly pestilence, which no skill or power of man could abate or stay. With such a plague over all the place all helpers would fear to approach, their markets would be unsupplied, their communication with the rest of the world, already so largely emptied and desolated by the march of the kings with their armies to the scene of battle against the Lamb, would be without avail. And thus black death and helpless want would stalk through every street, and highway, and lane, and alley, of the whole city, and fill all the region round about with unexampled suffering, mourning, and horror.

And amid it all comes the great unprecedented earthquake, by which the cities of the nations are thrown down. Fires break forth, and there is no water to extinguish them, and no hands to apply it if it were to be found. The whole city burns to ashes, and all its population with it, " as when God overthrew Sodom and Gomorrah," making the very land vitreous round about.

Thus would be fulfilled what Isaiah sung : " Come down, and sit in the dust, O virgin daughter of Babylon ; sit on the ground ; there is no throne, O daughter of the Chaldeans ; for thou shalt no more be called tender and delicate. Sit thou silent, and get thee into darkness, O daughter of the Chaldeans ; for thou shalt no more be called, the lady of kingdoms. Thou saidst, ' I shall be a lady forever,' so that thou didst not lay these things to thy heart, neither didst remember the latter end of it. Therefore hear now this, thou that art given to pleasures, that dwellest carelessly, that sayest in thine heart, ' I am, and none else beside me ; I shall not sit as a widow, neither shall I know the loss of children ; ' these two things shall come to thee in a moment, in one day, the loss of children and widowhood ; they shall come upon thee in their perfection, for the multitudes of thy services, and for the great abundance of thine enchantments. For thou hast trusted in thy wickedness ; thou hast said, ' None seeth me.' Thy wisdom and thy knowledge, it has perverted thee ; and thou hast said in thine heart, ' I am, and none else beside me.' Therefore shall evil come upon thee ; and thou shalt not know from whence it riseth ; and mischief shall fall upon thee ; thou shalt not be able to put it off ; and desolation shall come upon thee suddenly, which thou shalt not know. Stand now with thine enchantments, and with the multitude of thy sorceries, wherein thou hast laboured from thy youth ; if so be thou shalt be able to profit, if so be thou mayest prevail. Thou art wearied in the multitude of thy counsels. Let now the astrologers, the star-gazers, the monthly prognosticators, stand up, and save thee from these things that shall come upon thee. Behold, they shall be as stubble ; the fire shall burn them ; they shall not deliver themselves from the power of the flame." (Isa. 47 : 1–15.)

Babylon burned Jerusalem and the temple of God, and her end is a conflagration, which leaves nothing of her. As the Lord said by Jeremiah, so it cometh to pass : " I will render unto Babylon, and to all the inhabitants of Chaldea, all their evil that they have done in Zion." (Jer. 51 : 24.) The voice from the heaven says that her iniquities come into remembrance. So long a time had passed since the early wickednesses of Babylon that it might seem as if Jehovah had forgotten them, or never meant to recall them to mind ; but the last Babylon is but the final outgrowth of the same principles and spirit which animated the first, and is so interiorly identified with that same old apostasy that all the old offences come forward again with the new, and help to inflame the final vengeance ; just as the full punishment of the sin of Israel respecting the golden calf is not yet over (Ex. 32 : 34), and as all the martyr blood of all the ages still cries to be further avenged.

In connection with these final plagues upon Babylon the voice from heaven says : " *Render to her even as she rewarded, and double [the] double according to her works ; in the cup which she mixed, mix for her double ; insomuch as she glorified herself and was wanton, to that proportion give to her torment and grief.*" Some take this as a commission to returning the house of Israel, which is to become a cup of trembling and a burdensome stone to the people round about in connection with these events ; but I do not so understand it. Israel will at that time be so enclosed, and under the heel of the great beast, as to be quite disabled from such an office until Christ himself has gone forth to avenge them of their enemies. Besides, the final judgment upon Great Babylon is so miraculous and direct from heaven, that mere earthly agents have but little to do with it, if anything. There is also another and far mightier class of operators in the infliction of these great judgments. Angels are concerned, and the descended Son of God himself. But there are others in addition to these, and taking part with them in these administrations. Among the promises to the overcomers out of the seven churches, was one that they should have authority over the nations, and rule or judge them with a rod of iron, *and break them to shivers as a vessel of pottery is dashed to pieces* (Rev. 2 : 26, 27). Of old it was sung of the saints in glory, that, with the praises of God in their mouth, and a two-edged sword in their hand, they should *execute vengeance upon the nations*, even punishments upon the people, to bind their kings with chains, and their nobles with fetters of iron, *to execute upon them the judgment that is written.* " This honour have all the saints." (Ps. 149 : 5–9.) Paul reminded the Corinthians, as if indignant at their low appreciation of the Christian calling : " *Do ye not know that the saints shall judge the world?*" (1 Cor. 6 : 2.) Of the mystic man-child caught up to God and to his throne, the record was that he should rule or shepherdize all the nations with a rod of iron. (Rev. 12 : 5.) When the Beast and the False Prophet, and their allied kings and armies perish at Harmageddon, the saint-armies of heaven, robed in fine linen, and riding on white horses, are those taking part in the terrible vengeance then to be executed. (Rev. 19 : 11–21.) And it would be strange, indeed, if in the rendition of final judgment upon Babylon, which sends a thrill of joy through all the holy universe, they were to have neither place nor part. To these, then, and to all the avenging powers of heaven, are we to consider this direction and commission to be addressed.

In the days of mercy and forbearance God is not strict to mark iniquity, or to punish it at once according to its deserts. There is much that he winks at and suffers to pass for the present. But it is all written in his book, and when the final recompense comes there is no more sparing. As the sinner has measured, so it will be measured to him again. It is an awful thought, but true, that by the ills and wrongs which people do on earth they are themselves setting the gauge or measure by which they are to have judgment dealt to them at the last.

The language here might seem to imply that God meant to double up vengeance upon Babylon without proportion to her deservings ; but a more attentive consideration shows that such is not the case. God is always just, and the duplication and intensifying of the torment and grief still has a righteous rule underlying it. The judgment is to be double, and double double ; but it is to be " *as she rewarded*,"—" *according to her works*,"—a cup of mixture such as she herself gave, doubled because her administration was only half of her iniquity. There may be great self-sins, over and above the sins against rights and peace of others. And such are here charged against Babylon, even blasphemy, self-honour, self-security, wantonness, and the deification of wealth and luxury. For these, as well as for the cup of uncleanness and oppression given by her to others, the cup is doubled to her. Her real evilness is double, and she must drink her own cup double. She is herself double, being both *a system* of abominations, and *a city* of abominations ; and what is visited upon the one is repeated or duplicated on the other.

The result of all this is that Great Babylon will be blotted from the earth, " as in the day when God overthrew Sodom and Gomorrah," and so fulfil to the letter all that the old prophets have spoken. The symbolic act which Jeremiah commanded Seraiah to perform at Babylon to signify the utter extinction that was to come upon her (Jer. 51 : 63, 64), John beholds repeated in a still more striking form : " *A mighty angel took up a stone, as a great millstone, and cast [it] into the sea, saying, Thus with a bound shall the great city Babylon be cast down, and shall not be found any more.*"

When Jesus was upon the earth, he said : " Whoso shall offend one of these little ones which believe in me, it were better for him that a millstone were hanged about his neck, and that he were drowned in the depth of the sea." (Matt. 18 : 6.) But who or what is a greater stumbling-block to the believers in God, and to the faith of Jehovah's humble worshippers, than Great Babylon ! In every form in which she has existed, and through all the ages, in all the world, she has been holding up the golden cup of her abominations wherewith she has intoxicated and demented the nations, and filled the whole earth with spiritual madness. Therefore, to her neck the stone is hanged, and into the depths she is cast, descending with still increasing speed toward the seething abyss of everlasting fires.

Babylon is a region full of bitumen. The mortar of its buildings from the beginning was not clay, but bituminous slime. All the earth around it is, therefore, full of inflammable material, as was the vale of Siddim before the conflagration of the cities of the plain, which was " full of slime-pits," so that when the fiery judgment of God descended, and it began to rain " brimstone and fire out of heaven," the thunderbolts ignited the oil-springs, and naphtha, and petroleum, and bituminous wells, till " all the land of the plain glowed and burned as a furnace," sinking as the burning went on, and swallowing up the doomed cities in a literal " lake of fire," which has left nothing but a dead sea and everlasting desolation where they stood. With corresponding conditions of the ground, and the ancient prophets assuring us that " the beauty of the Chaldees' excellency shall be *as when God overthrew Sodom and Gomorrah*" (Is. 13 : 19 ; Jer. 49 : 18 ; 50 : 40), we may readily infer something of the nature of the fires amid which Great Babylon is to find her perdition. First is the drying up of her waters, as God said by the mouth of Jeremiah, " I will dry up her sea, and make her springs dry " (Jer. 51 : 36) ; then the consequent death-plague, mourning, and famine ; and then the fires which run over her, and around her, and under her, feeding on the parched and pitchy ground, and sinking the whole region into a charred and igneous desolation, never again to be inhabited. Nimrod called it, " *The Gate of God*," and lo, it proves *the mouth of hell*, where the unclean spirits throng, and the very filth of the universe finds its hold ! The world's greatest power was concentrated there, which all the kings of the earth were delighted to court and serve ; but " in one hour " all her greatness, might, and majesty, come to nought. She was a mart for the nations, enriching multitudes on land and sea, but in one day the harvest of her soul's desire is gone, and all her bright and dainty things perished, with no one left to buy or enjoy them any more. She had " great riches," and was " clothed in fine linen, and purple, and scarlet, and decked with gold, and precious stone, and pearl," but not a scrap or fragment of all her costliness and treasure is left. She was the very paradise of musicians, harp-singers, and flute-players, and trumpeters ; for these are always a great feature and one of the chief glories of a rich, gay, luxurious, and worldly city ; but every note is silenced, and no voice of song, or dance, or opera, is ever heard there again. The finest artists and artisans of the world, of every order, had found there a very Golconda, but in one hour their glorious elysium is gone, and they and their works with it. It was the centre of the grandest and most noted of bridals, and the sublime resort of grand bridal tours, but with one stroke of heaven's judgment every sound of joy is hushed, " and the voice of bridegroom and bride " ceases to be heard there any more.

When the curse upon Jerusalem was spoken, it was that " the voice of mirth, and the voice of gladness, the voice of the bridegroom, and the voice of the bride," should cease from her streets (Jer. 7 : 34) ; but it was at the same time added that God would " restore the captivity of the land, as at the first," and that, in the place of the threatened desolation, there should yet again be " the voice of joy, and the voice of gladness, the voice of the bridegroom, and the voice of the bride, the voice of them that shall say, Praise the Lord of hosts ; for the Lord is good ; for his mercy endureth forever." (Je1.

33 : 10, 11.) But in the case of Great Babylon there is to be no recovery, no restoration. There shall be no remnant left to rebuild it, no workman to lift up tool to reconstruct it, no mills to sound there any more, no light of candle or token of joyous civilization to shine again amid its darkness ; but it shall be " a habitation of demons, and a hold of every unclean spirit, and a hold of every unclean and hated bird ; " and " it shall be no more inhabited forever, neither shall it be dwelt in from generation to generation." (Jer. 50 : 39, 40.)

So great a judgment argues gigantic crimes. Glance a moment then at these, that we may learn to stand in awe and " have no fellowship in her sins ; " for it does not require that we should live in Babylon when she fails in order to be involved in her perdition. Every place is Babylon to them that have her spirit and exhibit her iniquities, and the same judgment awaits them.

To the credit of Babylon's worldly greatness, but also as a marked ingredient of what procures her doom, it is said : " *Thy merchants were the great men of the earth.*" Most people would see no crime in that. What harm is there in buying and selling and getting gain, and in making the weight of fortune felt according to its greatness ? Nothing, indeed, if no wrong spirit is under it, and no wrong principles animate the accumulation, or control its management when it is made. But, the son of Sirach hath truly said : " As a nail sticketh fast between the joinings of stones, so doth sin stick close between buying and selling." (Ecclesiasticus 17 : 2.) And commerce is certainly indicated as the chief vehicle, support, and embodiment of the great defiling wickedness of the last days. In the bushel measure, and under the weighing talent, sits the Woman whom the angel says is *Wickedness*. Nor should it be thought strange that commerce, and the machinery connected therewith, should supply the formative principles of a great and godless apostasy. Is there a prominent country now on earth in which commerce does not rule, or where things are not all being determined by commercial principles, ideas, and interests ? " Have we heard nothing respecting the wondrous results expected from commerce in making nations happy, in bringing men together in ties of amity and brotherhood, in developing the resources of the earth, in making nations conscious of their mutual dependence on each other, and so effecting, by the suggestions of self-interest, a result which the Gospel (it is said) has failed to accomplish. These and suchlike sayings are continually being sounded in our ears. Nor can we say that they are altogether untrue, or that there is no wisdom in them." (B. W. Newton.) But who that looks with an attentive eye but can see in it the coming forth of a wisdom which is not from above, but which savours of him who said to Jesus, " All these things will I give thee, if thou wilt fall down and worship me." Commerce is not necessarily sinful. Exchange on just and right principles may be a thing of beneficence and good, involving nothing against God or his truth. But the tendency is otherwise. The disposition is to concentration and consolidation on selfish principles for selfish ends. The struggle is continually more and more to monopolize, to crush out rivalry and competition, and to enter into world-wide combinations to seize first one interest and then another, till everything is finally swallowed up in one great centralized aristocracy of unbounded wealth, to which all the kings and governments on the earth must truckle. In our day an association of merchants has commanded the riches of the Indian seas, dragged along with it the armies and legislation of England to effect its ends, and enriched itself at the sacrifice of innocent blood, national treasure, and every honourable principle, whilst the good Queen Victoria, helpless in its hands, must submit in royal gratitude to bear for it the title of the Empress of India ! The eloquence of a Burke, in sentences which shall never die, has given a tongue to a few of the abominations which have accompanied those administrations ; but not a moiety of them has been told, as they have added stain upon stain to the escutcheon of England, and dishonoured the whole Anglo-Saxon race.

This is but one instance, and one belonging to the babyhood of these great commercial combinations ;   what then may we not expect when these privileged associations, which control the local exchanges, money markets, and commercial affairs of the nations, have fully consolidated, and a great, united, money aristocracy, takes command of the commerce of the world ? These would indeed be " the great men of the earth," and their rule would be the rule of the earth.

But what sort of a rule would it necessarily be ? Would it be God's kingdom come, and God's will done, on earth as it is in heaven ? So the arguments and oratory of the priests of that interest would seem to say. But, is it so ? Can it possibly be so ? Look at the root-principle of these commercial compacts. Co-equality of man with man is to them the greatest absurdity. What right, or place, or standing, can a man who has no money have in them ? Wealth is the only ticket of admission, and for that all seats are absolutely reserved. But who would ever think of going among these money-lords and bourse-kings to find saints of God ! There are some rich men from whose hearts the Holy Ghost has not been choked out ; but " how hardly shall they that have riches enter the kingdom of God ? It is easier for a camel to go through the needle's eye, than for a rich man to enter into the kingdom of God." (Mark 10 : 23–25.) It has become an axiom that " corporations have no souls," and upon this all great moneyed corporations act, though the men who constitute them will find out a different doctrine when they come to the day of judgment. And when it comes to these great and ever magnifying commercial compacts and interests, there is not a law of God or man which is not compelled to yield if found in the way. Protestant and Papist, Pagan and Jew, Mohammedan and Infidel, believer and unbeliever, Bible, Talmud, Vedas, Shasters, Koran, and Book of Mormon, are all alike, and stand in these organizations on one and the same footing, provided only that there is power of wealth to aid and direct the one great scramble for the world's trade and riches. If the question were ever pressed in these circles, *What is truth ?* it would be hooted and laughed to scorn. The cry would be, " What have we to do with that ?   Let every one quietly enjoy his own opinions.   Give each a share, not only in the protection of the government, but in its fostering and sustaining care, for the office of government is to minister for the governed, not to concern itself with the laws and revelations of God."   Accordingly, also, the greatest mercantile government on earth, England, Protestant England, which claims to maintain the only true church, and hails all her sovereigns as " Defenders of the Faith," at the dictation and demand of secular and commercial interests makes her appropriations to Romish institutions, salaries Roman priests and professors, advances Jews to her highest offices, expends her blood and treasure to sustain the tottering existence of the deadly curse of Mohammedan dominion, pensions Brahmin nobles, and pays and pampers Pagan priests.   And such is the tendency and bearing of legislation in general, and from the same causes.   Governments are in the hands of commerce and the money-kings ; and commerce knows no God but gold, and no law but self-interest and worldly gain.   Church is nothing, State is nothing, creed is nothing, Bible is nothing, Sunday is nothing, religious scruples are nothing, conscience is nothing, everything is practically nothing, except as it can be turned or used to the one great end of accumulation and wealth.   To make common cause with all classes of men, to honour Mohammedan festivals and Jewish rites alike with those commanded by the one only rightful King of the world, to pay Hindoo and Romish priests, to endow their seminaries, and to give aid and comfort to their idolatries with all Christian institutes,—which is now not only being done, but advocated and defended on the ground that this is the only rightful sphere of government, and these the only principles on which the true progress of humanity depends,—is already the incipient dethronement of all positive truth, the turning of it into a lie, or into a mere ideal thing without claims upon the human soul ; the systematic inauguration of a latitudinarian infidelity, removing human society into many degrees of greater distance from God than ever it has been in all the ages. And when once the earth has come to acknowledge the representatives and embodiments of such a system of ideas and rule as its true and only " *great men*," there lies couched in this one simple statement a whole world of iniquitous apostasy, which well deserves the doom which makes an end of Great Babylon. Yes, commerce will yet have an account to settle, at which the world shall shake.

Another ingredient in the cup of Babylon's doom, is her bewitching sorcery, by which she leads all the nations astray. Some understand by this that she is to be the great patron and head centre of spiritism and necromancy. Magicians constituted an integral part of the state officials there in Daniel's time, and it is quite likely that a goodly share of her wisdom, and policy, and influence, will come from familiar intercourse with demons and their unclean teachings. But it does not seem to me that this touches the nerve of what is here called her sorcery. The great preponderating idea which runs through the whole description, is that of *commercial* greatness, success, and power ; and the potent and contaminating sorcery must be something which is naturally construable with this,—some bewitching attractiveness going along with a mercantile system, and drawing after it the admiration and sympathy of the world. Meretricious allurement, gathering around it the homage of governments and kings, is the idea. And it is in Great Babylon's management to ennoble her chief aims and spirit that we are to find her witchery.

It is hardly possible to separate traffic, and especially great commercial combinations and schemes, from *covetousness*, which is idolatry. But naked covetousness is not attractive. Even the natural heart is repelled by it, and is ready to condemn and denounce it. When the possession of wealth is made the final end, when it is treasured in the coffer and not expended, or when means disreputable are adopted for its attainment, the pursuit of riches is regarded with disdain. The acquisition, under such circumstances, is connected with what is so repulsive to pride, and taste, and respectabilities which hold in approved society, that it meets only with frowns and disfavour. To array it in honourable garb, to dignify it, to make it appear good and praiseworthy, so that men may love, bless, and follow it as something noble and beneficent,—this is what calls for the magician's wand and the wizard's power. And here it is that Great Babylon's delusive witchery comes in. If a godless and unscrupulous commerce can be made to appear as the great and only availing civilizer, if it can show its end to be, not only the welfare of individuals, but the prosperity of nations and peoples ; if its office is the development of the resources of the whole earth, and for that end visits every land and traverses every sea ; if it is really the great stimulant to intellectual effort, the helper of science, the procurer and disseminator of all useful wisdom and intelligence, the rewarder of inventive genius and engineering skill, the self-sacrificing handmaid of all social, moral, and legislative improvement ; if it is not the mere possession of wealth for its own sake, but to secure the beneficent power, and influence and glory to result from its wise and proper employment that makes up the end and aim of its endeavours, then will the ugliness of avarice be voided, bitter will have been made sweet, and all attendant deflections from right and truth swallowed up in the grandeur, and beauty, and beneficences of its purposes. The demon of covetousness would then have become an angel of light. A halo of glory would encircle its head. Nations would hail its undertakings, admire its enterprise, and praise its wonderful benignity. The arts and the sciences, the museums and the universities, would lay their chaplets at its feet. Kings and governments would cheerfully become its nurses and patrons. Religions would be glad to bestow upon it their prayers and benedictions. The apostles and prophets of this world's progress would clap their hands and shout over its success. And myriads would celebrate its triumph as the ushering in of the long-dreamed millennium.

And here is the sorcery with which Great Babylon leads all the nations astray. Linking the false doctrines of human progress and perfectibility to the worst of passions, she lures the world to her support, and makes mankind the willing slave of her base idolatry.   And already, from pulpit and platform, from philosopher and political economist, from orator and poet, are we compelled to hear just these very glorifications of the cupidities of man as the forerunner, if not the instrument, of this world's regeneration.   Alas, for such philosophy and such hopes ! What estimate God puts upon them may be learned from what he has revealed of the doom of Babylon.   It is *sorcery*, the penalty for which is death.   (Ex. 22 : 18.)

I can mention now but one more particular in the count of Great Babylon's sins, and that is her presumptuous self-glorification, conceit, and arrogance. She has no rights of kingdom from God or man, and yet she presumes to bear rule over all the kings of the earth, to dictate their policies, to fashion their laws, and to be their protector and redeemer.   She acknowledges no God, no Christ, no Holy Ghost, and yet proposes to do for the world what she assumes to be beyond the power of the institutes and administrations of heaven.   She makes no claims to sacred prophecy, acknowledges no sacred books, and glories in being entirely secular in her sphere and aims, and yet presumes to teach the nations the ways and means of their highest prosperity and redemption, and to realize for them their sublimest peace and good.   She is but human in her derivation, her principles and her power, and purely earthly in her dependence her treasures, and her glory ; yet she presumes to think herself invincible, immortal, and forever sufficient in her own possessions against all adversity. *" She saith in her heart, I sit a queen, and am not a widow, and shall see no mourning."*   She thus exalts herself over the Church of God, in which all that is divine on earth resides, and where the preaching has ever been about divine sonship, and kinghood, and a glorious kingdom, but to which no dominion has ever come.   The saints are to reign ; but while the Devil reigns their kingdom is in abeyance, and Babylon taunts them and congratulates herself with having in reality what they have only in empty promise.   They do not reign ; she sits a queen.   While Christ is away the Church is in widowhood ; her husband is absent.   All her hope is in his return.   Babylon boasts that she experiences no such privation.   She is no widow.   Her lovers are plenteous.   Her joy is full.   She claims to have in fruition what the Church has in mere expectation. The people of God have perpetual sorrow and trial on earth.   Like their Lord, they are poor, despised, persecuted, with scarce a place to lay their heads in peace from their enemies.   Great Babylon glories in being far above a condition so mean, or vicissitudes so afflicting.   She is rich ; she is mighty ; she hath all her necessary goods secure ; she is not the one to see mourning.   Thus she vaunts, professes, and glorifies herself.   Though the world from the beginning is crowded with monuments of the wrath of heaven upon every such spirit, and though through all the long gallery of ages the voice comes echoing down, *" They that walk in pride God is able to abase,"* she heeds not the lesson, and defies all judgment.   Hence Jehovah writes it once more in larger letters, drawn with the black cinders of her own eternal desolation, that all the universe may read and tremble.

Friends, let *us* learn the lesson.   It is to this end that all these things have been written.   Participation in Great Babylon's sins must needs bring Great Babylon's doom, be the offender who or where he may. And to but little avail will we have considered this subject if it does not serve to imprint upon our souls at least this one eternal truth of God, that *" whosoever exalteth himself shall be abased ; and he that humbleth himself shall be exalted."*   (Luke 14 : 11.)

LECTURE FORTY-FIRST

SEQUENCES OF THE FALL OF BABYLON—THE WAILS OF ROYALTY—THE WAILS OF THE MERCHANTS—THE WAILS OF OTHER CLASSES—HEAVEN'S GLADNESS—THE SAINTS, APOSTLES, AND PROPHETS AVENGED—THE DOUBLE HALLELUIA—THE AMEN—FURTHER ITEMS OF THE JOY—THE TAKING OF THE KINGDOM—BLESSEDNESS OF THE RULE OF GOD.

Rev. 18 : 9–24. (Revised Text.) And shall wail and mourn over her the kings of the earth, who committed fornication with her, when they see the smoke of her burning, standing afar off through the fear of her torment, saying, Alas, alas (woe, woe), the great city Babylon, the mighty city ! because in one hour came thy judgment.

And the merchants of the earth weep and mourn over her because no one buyeth their merchandise [or *ship's freight*] any more,—merchandise of gold, and of silver, and of precious stone, and of pearl, and of fine linen, and of purple, and of silk, and of scarlet, and all thyne [or *citron*] wood, and every article of ivory, and every article of most costly wood, and of brass, and of iron, and of marble ; and cinnamon, and amomum, and odours, and ointment, and frankincense, and wine, and oil, and fine meal, and wheat, and cattle, and sheep ; and [merchandise] of horses, and of chariots, and of bodies and souls of men. And thy harvest of the soul's desire has departed from thee, and all dainty things and bright things have perished from thee, and they shall not find them any more. The merchants of these things, who were made rich from her, shall stand afar off through the fear of her torment, weeping and mourning, saying, Alas, alas (woe, woe), the great city which was clothed in fine linen, and purple, and scarlet, and decked with gold, and precious stone, and pearl, because in one hour such great riches hath been desolated.

And every shipmaster, and everyone who goeth by sea, and sailors, and as many as trade by sea, stood afar off and cried out when they saw the smoke of her burning, saying, What is like to the great city ! And they cast heaped-up earth upon their heads, and cried out, weeping and mourning, saying, Alas, alas (woe, woe), the great city by which all who had ships in the sea were made rich from her costliness [or *treasures*], because in one hour she hath been desolated !

Rejoice over her, O heaven, and saints, and apostles, and prophets, because God hath judged your judgment out of her.

And one, a mighty angel, took up a stone, as a great millstone, and cast [it] into the sea, saying, Thus with a bound shall the great city Babylon be cast down, and shall not be found any more. And the sound of harpers, and musicians, and flute-players, and trumpeters shall not be heard in thee any more, and every artisan of every art shall not be found in thee any more ; and sound of the millstone shall not be heard in thee any more ; and light of a candle shall not shine in thee any more ; and the voice of the bridegroom and bride shall not be heard in thee any more ; because thy merchants were the great men of the earth ; because by thy sorcery all the nations were led astray.

And in her was found the blood of prophets, and of saints, and of all that have been slain upon the earth.

Rev. 19 : 1–6. (Revised Text.) After these things I heard as a great voice of much multitude in the heaven, saying, Alleluia, the salvation, and the glory, and the power, of our God, because true and righteous his judgments, because he judged the great harlot that corrupted the earth with her fornication, and avenged the blood of his servants out of her hand. And a second time they say, Alleluia ; and her smoke goeth up for the ages of the ages.

And the twenty-four Elders and the four Living Ones fell down and worshipped the God the sitter upon the throne, saying, Amen, Alleluia.

And a voice came out from the throne, saying, Praise our God all his servants, those that fear him, the small and the great.

And I heard as a voice of much multitude, and as a voice of many waters, and as a voice of mighty thunders, saying, Alleluia, because the Lord God the All-Ruler hath assumed the kingdom.

THE fall of Great Babylon is one of the most marvellous events of time.   More is said about it in the Scriptures than perhaps any one great secular occurrence. And when it comes to pass the whole universe is thrilled at the sight.   But the emotions are not all of the same kind.   Two worlds are concerned, and in nothing are they more sharply in contrast than the manner in which they are respectively affected by the dreadful catastrophe.   Great Babylon does not mean the world, as some have erroneously supposed ; for there is still a world of unsanctified people left to mourn and lament over her after she is no more. And great is the lamentation and terror which her destruction calls forth.   Let us look at it for a moment and see to what sudden disappointment and helplessness the schemes of human progress and development are leading.   Just when the wisdom, and reforms, and utilitarian philosophies of apostate man have wrought themselves out, and their glorious fruits are being realized, the strong hand of judgment strikes, and all is confounded and blasted in an hour. And the terribleness of the disaster may be read from the lamentation which ensues.

First of all the apostolic Seer hears the wailings of royalty and dominion. " The Kings of the earth wail and mourn."   They were all in close affinity with Babylon.   They had lent themselves to her bewitching schemes and policy.   They were enamoured with the enriching and glorifying power of her greatness.   They had given their influence and favours to her, and consented to be the willing ministers to her wantonness.   She was their particular love, in whom was their chief delight, and on whom they were glad to lavish their treasures. And when she falls, the main artery of earth's glory is cut, and every government feels its life-blood ebbing away.   They contemplate the smoke of her burning with horror.   They stand afar off in dread of her torment, alarmed and terrified at the consequences of her ruin.   They leaned upon her mightiness, but the strong staff is now stricken from their hands.   The mightier power of judgment is before them, and they tremble before its disastrous strokes. They show no penitence, but *Alas, alas,—woe, woe,—*is the note of outcry from every capital when it is seen and known that Babylon is no more.

Next come " the merchants of the earth," full of tears and grief over the sudden collapse of their enriching trade.   It was promised that the wand of the sorceress would give prosperity to nations, and that as commerce ruled all people would be blest by its administrations ; and a great tidal wave of mercantile thrift and glory is indicated as having come over the world by this grand unification.   There never was so great a market or so brisk a trade as that which grows up with the revival and restoration of Babylon.   The whole world becomes alive with traffic in " merchandise of gold, and of silver, and of precious stone, and of pearl, and of fine linen, and of purple, and of silk, and of scarlet, and all thyne or citron wood, and every article of ivory, and every article of most costly wood, and of brass, and of iron, and of marble ; and cinnamon, and amomum [a precious preparation from an Asiatic shrub], and odours, and ointment, and frankincense, and wine, and oil, and fine meal, and wheat, and cattle, and sheep ; and merchandise of horses, and of chariots, and of bodies and souls of men."   Never before was there such a demand for these things, and for all things dainty and goodly, as when the house of the Ephah is built in the land of Shinar, and that Ephah is settled there upon its own base. " The merchants of these things " the world over never before experienced so great a harvest, and double up riches on riches with a rapidity which seems like miracle. Everything looks like secure and perfect triumph for earth's wisdom and inventions.   But all at once this mighty commerce stops, and all its wheels stand still.   The mercantile circles of the whole earth are stricken with consternation.   Every counting-room becomes a place of mourning.   The great traders all weep and mourn, not so much for Babylon's sufferings, for man's sympathy for man shall then have been eaten away by the common sordidness ; nor yet for their great sins, for the day of repentance is then over for them.   The centre of their distress is that *their market is gone,* that " no one buyeth their merchandise any more," that " in one hour such great riches hath been desolated," that the scorching of the great city's torment reaches them even at the remotest distances.   *Alas, alas,—woe, woe,—*is the cry that comes from all their warehouses and homes.

But there is a third and still larger class of mourners.   Great firms have more employés than heads, and very many are dependent on them for

o

occupation and livelihood.   Shipmasters, and seagoers, and sailors, and as many as trade by sea, with all their helpers and crews, also have their harvest out of this great and enriching Babylonian traffic.   And these still more sorely feel the calamity of its sudden interruption.   Therefore, from them also comes the cry of lamentation when they behold the smoke of Babylon's burning. And so bitter is the realization of the calamity to them, that " they cast heaped-up earth upon their heads and cry out, weeping and mourning, saying, *Alas, alas,—woe, woe,*—the great city by which all who had ships in the sea were made rich from her costly treasures ! "

Thus, from every throne on earth, and from every power behind the throne, from every seat of trade, and every city,—from every continent, every island, every sea, and every ship that plies upon the sea,—comes forth the voice of woe and irremediable disaster.   It is a triple voice, each part of which is double.   It is the evil six complete.   It is the inconsolable lament of all the potencies and activities of earth, exhibiting another star in the crown of this world's wisdom and progress.

But whilst the chorus of lamentation, disappointment, and terror is upon the earth, a grand jubilation fills the sky.   As this world's great ones, and rich ones, and dependent ones cry *Woe, woe,* over Great Babylon's fall, all the peoples on high pour out their mightiest *Halleluias.*   No sooner has the harlot city gone down amid her judgment fires, than a voice springs up spontaneous over all the holy universe : " *Rejoice over her, O heaven, and saints, and apostles, and prophets, because God hath judged your judgment out of her.*"

For all the ages had God's messengers and people been protesting, prophesying, and declaiming against these worldly philosophies, systems, hopes, and spirit.   It lies in the very nature and essence of the profession of all saints to " renounce the Devil and all his works, the vanities of the world, and the sinful desires of the flesh."   No one in any age can have place among God's holy ones without this.   As Noah by his faith, so the children of God in all time, by the very act of becoming God's children, " condemn the world," and give judgment against its wisdom, its principles, its spirit, and its hopes.   So, too, all the teachings of the apostles, all the holy messages of the prophets, and all the sermons of God's faithful ministers the world over.   What, indeed, has been the great controversy ever since the race begun, but that between revelation and the sensual wisdom, between the system of God's salvation and that which men propose to work out for themselves, between the bringing up of the world on principles of human progress and the only redemption through faith in Christ Jesus ?   And between these two there is an inherent, irreconcilable, and eternal antagonism.   That which makes and marks the saints, the apostles, and the prophets, is at perpetual variance with what characterizes and animates all the rest of the world, condemns it, and ever pronounces and prophesies against it.   Thus far, however, as respects this world, the saints, apostles, and prophets have had the worst of it.   Always in the minority, the world at large has never listened to them, never agreed with them, never consented to accept their system, never sympathized with their hopes, never respected their profession. They depreciate its interests too much. They are too severe on its principles.   They are in the way of its liberties. They would draw a cowl over its joys.   They would disable its beneficent progress.   They are *pessimists*, who shut off all blessed outcome from its philosophies and efforts touching the amelioration of the condition of the race. In a word, they are intolerable to the world, a poor croaking set, fit only to be killed off by the hand of power where they are too persistent and loud, and unfit at best to receive respectful attention.   If the world can find a Balaam, ready to compromise himself for gold, to bless it for a price, and to speak God's benediction on its lusts and passions, him it will honour, and to him will Balak's nobles come ; but for the Elijahs, Isaiahs, Jeremiahs, Peters, and Pauls, their fate has ever been to be mocked, scourged, imprisoned, stoned, sawn asunder, slain with the sword, nailed to the cross, thrown to wild beasts, or compelled to seek asylum in deserts, mountains, and dens and caves of the earth, being destitute, tormented, afflicted, because they condemn the godless world, its Ahabs, its Jezebels, its Herods, and its sins. Compared with the great mass of mankind, the true Church has always been a " little flock," toiling with difficulties, opposition, and hatred, and never able to make effective headway against the powers holding sway over the race. Now and then the course of history seemed on the point of justifying her principles and profession, but then came internal defections, setting her back again, and almost extinguishing her being. And so it will be unto the end. So far as this present world is concerned, the general verdict of mankind, sustained by the great current of human history for 6,000 years, is against the faith and testimonies of the saints, apostles, and prophets of God. To the general population of the earth their profession stands branded as mere hallucination and lies. But at last their vindication comes. When the vaunted wisdom, and progress, and experiments of unregenerate man are consummated, and there is nothing to show from it but a valley of burning cinders and desolation, with the whole earth from highest kings to meanest subjects howling in helpless lamentations, terror, and despair, history will have added its seal to all that saints, apostles, and prophets have said and maintained. Then will their judgment have been judged out of that world which despised and persecuted them, and spurned their hated *pessimism* for more flattering philosophies. Then will their renunciation of this world and its delusive hopes be justified by the ruin of its most cherished greatness. Then will the false verdict under which they have lain and suffered for sixty centuries be reversed in the living facts, of which they never ceased to tell and prophesy. Now they have sorrow, and can only weep and lament, whilst the world rejoices and sets them at naught ; but then the sorrow and joy will exchange places, and the sorrow of the one be turned to joy, and the joy of the other to enduring lamentation.

It is in answer to this call for heaven, saints, apostles, and prophets to rejoice, that the sublime outbursts described in this chapter occur. John listens and looks, and sounds fall on his ears, and sights pass before his eyes, which stir and affect him more deeply than anything he yet had seen or heard since the first vision.

First of all he hears " a great voice of much multitude in heaven, saying, *Alleluia.*" Here, for the first time in the New Testament, we come upon one of the most admirable words of praise ever made known on earth. It is the same that occurs so often in the most exultant of the Hebrew Psalms. Anselm of Canterbury, considers it an angelic word, which cannot be fully reproduced in any language of man, and concurs with Augustine that the feeling and saying of it embodies all the blessedness of heaven. The Apocrypha (Tobit 13 : 21) gives it as among the great glories of the New Jerusalem that all the streets shall say, *Alleluia.* And this word John hears sounding from the sky,

> Loud as from numbers without number,
> Sweet as from blest voices uttering joy.

It is one of the very highest acknowledgments and celebrations of God. Where it is understandingly sung there is at once the profoundest adoration and the most exultant joy. And this is the feeling and experience in the heaven when the proud system of this world's apostate wisdom and glory falls.

We are not told precisely from whom this voice comes. It may be from the souls under the altar who waited so long to be avenged. It may be from that multitude which no man could number who come out of the great tribulation. It may be, but not so likely, from the host of holy angels who had been ministering for all these ages for what is then being realized. It may be from the 144,000 remembering the terribleness of the Antichristian severities they suffered, whose acclaim is elsewhere compared to mighty thunder. (Chap. 14 : 2.) But whoever the particular parties may be, it is the voice of a multitudinous company of people in the heaven, and it is the voice of exultant adoration, celebrating " *the salvation, and the glory, and the power of our God.*" Thus, what the kings, merchants, and shippers on earth mourn and lament as destruction, is celebrated in heaven as divine " salvation." What is considered nothing but woe here is praised as divine glory there. And what is here regarded as the unmaking of all that earth called mighty is sung there as the very triumph of divine goodness. Heaven's estimate of things is widely different from that entertained by this world. The object of earth's fondest love and delight is the object of God's intensest wrath. That which men most work for, and most fondly serve, is that which God most severely judges. And that which the great ones most deplore is the very thing which evokes the sublimest heavenly Halleluias.

The destruction of Great Babylon is an illustrious exbihition of the truth and righteousness of the divine administrations. Often it would seem as if God had forgotten his word, or quite abandoned the earth, so great is the prosperity of the wicked, the triumph of injustice, the wrongs and afflictions which those who most honour him suffer. But it is not so. He is true. His ways are just. Everything will come out fully equalized at the last. And here is a signal demonstration of the fact. The godless wisdom and pride of men are left to work themselves out to the full, but when the harvest is ripe the sweep of the sharp sickle of judgment comes against it and it suddenly falls, and all its just deservings it gets. The harlot has her day ; but then comes her night with never a star of hope to rise upon her any more. She is permitted to lure, delude, and debauch the world, because men preferred her abominations to the truth and kingdom of God ; but only that her judgment may be the more conspicuous, and her destruction the more signal and complete. And the Halleluia of eternity is all the louder and more intense because her judgment comes as it does. Ah, yes, God's ways are right ; his judgments are true and righteous. Perplexing and trying as they may be for the time, our Halleluias will be all the deeper and the sweeter by reason of what we may now deplore. Nay, they will be double then, by reason of the darkness now ; for " a second time they say, *Alleluia.*"

And what the unnamed heavenly multitude so exultantly express, the twenty-four Elders and the four Living Ones equally feel and endorse. They even prostrate themselves in profoundest adoration, and " worship the God, the sitter upon the throne, saying, *Amen, Alleluia.*"

And here we meet with another of those peculiarly sacred and expressive words, reasonably supposed to have had their origin in heaven. From our first meeting with it in the Scriptures (Numb. 5 : 22) to the concluding word of this Book, we find it used as the special word of holy acquiescence and sacred ratification. It was constantly on the lips of the Saviour in his most solemn enunciations. It is the sealing word to all the Gospels and Epistles. It is not an oath, yet it has much of the solemnity and force of an oath. It contains no adjuration or appeal, yet it authenticates, confirms, binds, seals, and pledges to the truth of that to which it is affixed. It is not an imprecation upon him who utters it, but it is a tying up and giving over of his whole being and life to what he thus acknowledges and confirms. When placed at the end of an utterance or act of devotion, as placed by the Saviour at the end of the prayer he propounded as our model and form, it has the office of an under-writing or subscription, carrying the hearty consent and confidence of the worshipper with what has gone before. It is the word of fervency and soul-earnestness by which every utterance is grasped up again, and renewedly laid before God, as the full and ardent desire of our hearts, and as that which our souls most feel and most sacredly rest in. And so it is in the case now before us. The Elders and the Living Ones hear the triumphant celebration of the salvation, and the glory, and the power of our God, as sounded forth in the great voice of the much multitude, and feel the convictions and emotions of their own souls so completely expressed that they adoringly bow down and sacredly make it their own. All heaven is of one mind and of one soul.

Therefore the self-prostrated Elders and Living Ones answer the Halleluias of the unnamed host with a third *Halleluia*, prefaced with the *Amen*, which makes the other two theirs also.

But this triple utterance of exultant praise and celebration of the salvation glory, and power of our God, is still further urged on by a voice that comes out from the throne itself, saying, " *Praise our God, all his servants, those that fear him, the small and the great.*"

We are not told whose voice this is.   Some take as the voice of Christ, who is elsewhere said to be " in the midst of the throne." (7 : 17.)   If it is his voice, he thus recognizes the Father as his God, as he did in the days of his earthly life, and at the same time owns all the glorified as his associates.   But whether it is Christ's voice or not, it is the voice of the throne, a voice having authority to command and lead off in further exultation for the marvellous things then being accomplished.   Nor is it unlikely that the Saviour himself leads in the praise enjoined.   So the promise runs in Psalm xxii : "I will declare thy name unto my brethren ; in the midst of the congregation *will I praise thee*.   Ye that fear the Lord, praise him.   *My praise* shall be of thee in the great congregation ; *I will pay my vows before them that fear him.*"

The subject of the praise here called for seems to look two ways, embracing the judgment just executed, and new glories about to be realized, of which that judgment is the pledge and inauguration.   The voice which gave the first and second *Halleluias* was the voice of a vast heavenly multitude.   The *Amen* and third *Halleluia* were from the Elders and the Living Ones.   These all centre in the display of divine truth, justice, and almightiness in the judgment of Great Babylon, and the avenging of the blood of the saints out of her hand. If there be any other servants and fearers of God, great or small, they are also called to join in the exulting praises for the same.   But as response comes to this admonition from the throne, the songs take in other subjects, and seem to embrace all that is described in the latter part of the chapter.   The *Halleluia* which now comes with redoubled power and majesty celebrates the assumption of the kingdom by the Lord God, which would seem to imply that the victory in the battle of the great day is included.   The marriage of the Lamb, the readiness and array of the Bride, and the blessedness of those who are called to the marriage banquet are likewise recounted, which can hardly be taken as coincident with the fall of Babylon.   A point would, therefore, seem to be indicated in this call, from which the contemplation is both backward to Babylon's overthrow and forward to the fall of the Beast, and the contemplation of the Church's blessedness in her Lord ; the main stress gravitating now toward what follows the judgment on Babylon.

No sooner does the voice from the throne give command for praise than John " heard as a voice of much multitude, and as a voice of many waters, and as a voice of mighty thunders, saying, *Alleluia, because the Lord God the All-Ruler hath assumed the kingdom.*"   This is a mightier *Halleluia* than either of the preceding.   It refers also to an ampler subject.   The judgment of Great Babylon demonstrated, indeed, that God is mighty, and that he is the All-Ruler. It also showed a potent taking up and enforcement of his sovereign and righteous authority.   But what was thus shown in one aspect and relation is at once followed out to a much wider and more direct assumption of active rule and sovereignty.   When the seventh trumpet was sounded a great voice anticipatively exclaimed : " *The kingdom of the world* [not kingdoms, as some versions and unsupported copies read, but ἡ βασιλεία του κοσμου, as all the great manuscripts have it, rendered by Wickliffe, the Rheims version, the old Vulgate, and the still older Syriac, *the kingdom of the world*], *is become our Lord's and his Christ's.*"   The kingdom of the world means the political sovereignty of the world, the rulership of the world, the kingly dominion or government of the world, the same which is now exercised by the potentates and authorities of the earth.   And this kingdom of the world, this sovereignty this rule, this power of making and enforcing the laws regulating human society, the great voice said was then about to pass into the hands of the Lord. It does not mean the leavening of existing governments with Christian principles, the spiritual conversion of countries and empires, leaving them in existence, and simply Christianizing them so as to exhibit something of Christ's spirit in their administrations ; but the total displacement of all this world's sovereigns and governments, the taking of all dominion and authority out of their hands, and the putting of it in the hands of Christ, as the true and only King of the world. And the actual assumption of this rulership of the earth in the place and stead of existing governments and lordships is what the song of praise to God here so mightily celebrates. " As a voice of much multitude, as a voice of many waters, and as a voice of mighty thunders." comes forth the grand " *Alleluia, because the Lord God, the All-Ruler, hath assumed the kingdom ;* " that is, has himself entered upon the actual administration of the sovereignty and government of the world.

The fall of Great Babylon heralds and begins the political regeneration of the earth.

And well may the tide of holy exaltation swell to its sublimest height over such an actuality. What is the crown and consummation of that prayer which the Lord Jesus put upon the lips and into the hearts of all his followers when he said, pray, " *Thy kingdom come ?* " Does it mean no more than that our own hearts may be thoroughly subdued to our Maker, purged of idolatry and lust, purified by the Holy Ghost, and filled with all pureness, heavenly knowledge, devotion, obedience, and grace ? That might be, and yet the earth be crushed with misrule, tyranny, corruption, and oppression. Does it mean simply that the Church may be ever dear and faithful to God, its ministers multiplied, its membership increased, its Scriptures distributed, its faith kept pure, its sacraments observed, its defections healed, its weaknesses removed, its success augmented, and all its members blessed with all spiritual riches in Christ Jesus ? That might all be and the world still be to her a valley of Baca, a Bochim, a wilderness of sorrow and hardship. Does it mean only the removal of what hinders the preaching and belief of the Gospel, or the progress of faith and piety in the individual and in the world ? That might also be and still God's kingdom be no nearer than it is at present. When Isaiah prophesied of Christ, he said : " *The government* shall be upon his shoulder ; of the increase of his *government and peace* there shall be no end, *upon the throne of David, and upon his kingdom,* to order it, and to establish it with judgment and justice." (Is. 9 : 6, 7.) When the Holy Ghost explained the meaning of the all-crushing stone in Nebuchadnezzar's dream, which broke to atoms the whole statue of worldly power and dominion, took its place, and filled the whole earth, the word was, This is the kingdom which the God of heaven shall set up, which shall break in pieces and consume all other kingdoms and it shall stand forever. (Dan. 3 : 32–45.) When Daniel was beholding till " the judgment was set and the books opened," he saw in the night visions, like to the Son of Man, brought before the Ancient of days, " and there was given him dominion, and glory, *and a kingdom,* that all people, nations, and languages should serve him," even " *the kingdom, and dominion, and the greatness of the kingdom under the whole heaven,*" " *an everlasting kingdom.*" (Dan. 7.) When Gabriel announced to Mary the child to be born of her, he said : " He shall be great, and shall be called the Son of the Highest, and the Lord shall give unto him *the throne* of his father David, and he shall *reign* over the house of Jacob forever, and of *his kingdom* there shall be no end." (Luke 1 : 26–33.) When he himself was among men, because some " thought that the kingdom of God should immediately appear," he spake a parable, and said that the matter is as a nobleman going " into a far country to receive for himself *a kingdom,* and to return," meanwhile entrusting to his servants certain possessions with which to trade and occupy till he should come. (Luke 19 : 11–13.) And so again he said : " When the Son of Man shall come in his glory, and all the holy angels with him, *then shall he sit in the throne of his glory."* (Matt. 25 : 31.)   All these and many like passages treat of that very *kingdom,* for the coming of which all are commanded to pray.   Nor can they be explained according to their plan and pointed terms without taking in the coming again of Christ to reckon with his servants, to take the rule out of the hands of those who have usurped dominion over the earth, to dethrone Satan and all his agents, and to reign from sea to sea, the only rightful *King* of the world.   And thus, when Great Babylon falls, it will be God's kingdom come, as it never yet has come, and the burden of the prayer of all these weary ages answered.

This assumption of the rule of the world will likewise bring with it the great desideratum of the race.   When Adam was in Eden God was king.   In the days of Israel's greatest triumph it was the same.   And until the original Theocracy is restored, and the powers of heaven again take the rulership and control of the nations, there is no peace, no right order for man.   There is no earthly blessing like that of good, wise, and righteous government ; but there is no such government outside of the government of the Father and the Son.   Some are better than others, but none are satisfactory.   Men have experimented with power for 6,000 years, and yet there is no department in which there is more disability, corruption, and unsatisfactoriness than in the administrations of government.   There is nothing of which all people so much complain, or have so much cause to complain, as of the manner in which their political affairs are managed and administered.   Those who live on government patronage and plunder are enthusiastic enough in behalf of what they call their country, and consider it piety to eulogize the instrument which pampers their greed and passions ; but the helpless multitude is left to sigh and cry in vain over the abominations that are done.   The best governments man has ever tried have invariably disappointed their founders, and proven themselves too weak or too strong, too concentrated or too dissevered, and in one way or another have turned into instruments of injustice, ambition, selfishness, and affliction.   The demonstration of the ages is, that " that which is crooked cannot be made straight, and that which is wanting cannot be numbered."   So true is this that one has said, with a pathos that shows how deep the conviction was, " I know no safe depository of power among mortal men for the purposes of government.   Tyranny and oppression, in Church and State, under every form of government,—social, civil, ecclesiastical, monarchical, aristocratical, or democratic,— have, sooner or later, characterized the governments of the earth, and have done so from the beginning."   Bad government is doubtless better than no government.   In the nature of things we must have government of some sort.   Because of the worse ills of anarchy we take the lesser afflictions of government in such forms as we can get it.   But what right-thinking and right-feeling man is not outraged every day at the injustice, maladministration, perversion, and abominations that go along with every government of man ?   So it ever has been, and so it ever will be while "man's day" lasts. "The kingdom is the Lord's," and till he comes and assumes it there will be disappointment, misrule, revolution, and incurable trouble in all human calculations and affairs.   Nothing but the sway and reign of heaven can redeem this fallen world out of the pestilential morasses of its incompetent and oppressive governments.   But there is an All-Ruler who will yet assume the kingdom, and give the race the reign of blessedness.   " He shall come down like rain upon the mown grass, as showers that water the earth.   In his days shall the righteous flourish, and abundance of peace so long as the moon endureth.   He shall have dominion also from sea to sea, and from the river unto the ends of the earth.   They that dwell in the wilderness shall bow before him, and his enemies shall lick the dust.   All kings shall fall down before him ; all nations shall serve him.   For he shall deliver the needy when he crieth, the poor also, and him that hath no helper.   He shall redeem their soul from deceit and violence, and precious shall their blood be in his sight.   He shall live, and to him shall be given of the gold of Sheba ; prayer also shall be made for him continually, and daily shall he be praised. His name shall endure forever, and men shall be blessed in him. All nations shall call him blessed."

Thus flowed the glorious numbers from David's prophetic harp, telling of the All-Ruler's assumption of the kingdom, and exulting in it, until the royal singer's soul fired up into the very *Alleluia* of the text, crying, " *Blessed be his glorious name forever ! and let the whole earth be filled with his glory. Amen, and Amen."* Human utterance could go no higher. The mountain summit of the promised blessedness was reached. And there the prayers of David, the son of Jesse, ended. (Ps. 72.)

We thus begin to see something of the dawn and character of those better times to come when once the mystery of God is finished. Tyrants, despots, and faithless and burdensome governments shall then be no more. Like wild beasts, full of savage instinct for blood and oppression, have the world-powers roamed and ravaged the earth, treading down the nations, their will the only law, the good and happiness of men the furthest from their hearts. But it will be otherwise then. "The Lord shall be king over all the earth," and therein is the signal and pledge of the dominion of right and everlasting peace. Wars shall be no more. Injustice and unequal laws shall be done away. Enemies will be powerless. Men will then have their standing according to their moral worth. The salvation of God will be nigh to them that fear him. Truth shall spring out of the earth, and righteousness shall look down from heaven. And sorrow and sighing shall flee away. Therefore the voice of eternal right is, " *Praise our God, all his servants, those that fear him, the small and the great,"* and from all the holy universe comes the song, in volume like the sea, in strength like the thunder, " ALLELUIA, BECAUSE THE LORD GOD THE ALL-RULER HATH ASSUMED THE KINGDOM."

LECTURE FORTY-SECOND

REV. 19 : 7–10. (Revised Text.) Let us rejoice and exult, and we will give the glory to him, because is come the marriage of the Lamb, and his wife [the Woman] prepared herself. And it was given to her that she should clothe herself in fine linen, bright pure ; for The fine linen is the righteousnesses of the saints.

And he saith to me, Write, Blessed they who have been called to the supper of the marriage of the Lamb. And he saith to me, These are the true words of God.

And I fell down before his feet to worship him. And he said, Take heed, no ; I am a fellow-servant of thee and of thy brethren that have the witness of Jesus ; worship God ; for the witness of Jesus is the spirit of the prophecy.

THE fall of Great Babylon lifts a heavy load from the hearts of all the holy universe. The day and reign of apostate man then reach their final close. The hopes and prayers of faith, and all the gracious prophecies and promises of God, then come to the goal of their fulfilment. Earth's true, invincible, and eternal king then takes the sovereignty, never again to pass it into other hands. The heavenly worlds understand it, and pour forth their mightiest exultations. And thick and thronging are the subjects of joy which now crowd upon their enraptured attention. Among the rest is one singled out with special interest and delight. Whilst the song of *Halleluia* swells to the dimensions of mighty thunders, because the Lord God the All-Ruler hath assumed the kingdom, a call goes forth, " *Let us rejoice and exult, and we will give the glory to him, because is come The Marriage of the Lamb.*" The Harlot swept away, the faithful Woman comes to her rightful honours. The betrothed, so long waiting amid privation, persecution, and contempt, now becomes a Bride. The time of her marriage has at length arrived, and the grand nuptial banquet begins. And that marriage and that banquet are what we are now to consider. God help us to understand it, and to rejoice ourselves in the contemplation !

Expositors generally have taken it for granted that this marriage is so familiar to the readers of holy Scripture, and so well understood, as to need no explanation. Perhaps had they attempted to set forth in definite form what they pass as so plain, they would have found the task less easy than they thought. Though the subject is common to both Testaments, there is not another of equal prominence and worth upon which so little direct attention has been bestowed by modern divines, or upon which clear ideas are so scarce. In my study of it, question after question has come up, even with regard to some of the most essential points, which I find it very hard to answer satisfactorily. And if others have found it so plain and easy as to render the explanation of it a work of supererogation, they would have relieved me much, as well as an almost total blank in our theologies with regard to one of the most frequently recurring subjects of Holy Writ, if they had condescended to record the results of their examinations. As it is, we must examine for ourselves.

I. *Who is the Bridegroom ?* On this point, fortunately, there is not much room for misunderstanding. It is " The Lamb," the blessed Saviour, who gave himself to death as a sacrifice for our sins, and is alive and living forever. It is the everlasting Son of the Father made incarnate for our salvation, and in his twofold nature exalted, glorified, and enthroned in eternal majesty. And yet it may be a question whether, in his character and marriage as *The*

Lamb, everything is to be understood to which the Scriptures refer under the figure of man's marriage to God ; whether there is not some particular and special intimacy or relationship meant to be set forth in this case ; whether it respects the Jewish people only, or Christian people only, or all saints alike. The Old Testament Church is everywhere represented as betrothed to God as a candidate for a glorious union with him in due time. (Isa. 14 : 1–8 ; Ezek. 16 : 7 seq. ; Hos. 2 : 19 seq.) It is the same with regard to the New Testament Church. Christ represents himself as the Bridegroom. (Matt. 9 : 15.) He speaks of the kingdom of heaven being " like unto a certain king which made a marriage for his son," and those called by the Gospel as " bidden to the marriage." (Matt. 22 : 1–13.) He speaks often of the judgment time as the coming of the Bridegroom for his Bride. (Matt. 25 : 1–10.) John the Baptist spoke of Christ as the Bridegroom, and of himself as " the friend of the Bridegroom, which standeth and heareth him, and rejoiceth greatly because of the Bridegroom's voice." (Jno. 3 : 29.) Paul speaks of those whom he begat in the Gospel as espoused to one husband, whom he desired to present as a chaste virgin to Christ. (2 Cor. 11 : 2.) Earthly marriage is likewise spoken of as a mystery, significant of Christ's relation to his Church. (Eph. 5 : 23–32.) All this proves, as clearly as may be, that in the economy of grace and redemption our blessed Saviour takes the character and relation of a Bridegroom or Husband to his people, of one class or another, and that a great and blessed union between himself and them remains to be celebrated. Whether the marriage in each case is precisely one and the same thing, or respects the same identical parties, it is equally certain that it is *The Lamb*,—the glorified Lord Jesus Christ,—who is here contemplated as the Bridegroom and Husband.

II. *Who is the Bride ?* Upon first blush the answer would be, the Lord's true and faithful people, all who by faith and obedience were affianced to him, and continued faithful to the end. In a general way this answer may be accepted as the truth, but in a narrower and closer view of things it cannot be taken as strictly and absolutely correct.

The 45th Psalm unmistakably refers to this subject. The qualities and doings of the King, come forth from the ivory palaces, are there described with great vigour and animation. But there is also the Queen, the King's Bride, standing on his right hand, in gold of Ophir, and all glorious within. It is said of her that " she shall be brought unto the King in raiment of needle-work." But, besides the Queen, the King's Bride, there is another blessed company, who are also to enter with rejoicing into the King's palace, and to share the light of his countenance. They are called " the virgins," the " companions," associates, and bosom friends of the Queen, but plainly distinct from the Queen herself. They do not go with her when she is taken, but " follow her,"—come after her,—and are " brought unto the King " at a subsequent time, and in quite another capacity from that of the Queen and Bride. All of them belong to the general congregation of the saved. All of them are made forever happy in their Lord, the King. But the Queen is one class, and " the virgins her companions that follow her," are another class.

So, too, in the Song of Solomon (6 : 8–9), we read of queens, concubines, and virgins, whom the fathers, for the most part, understood as referring to the various classes which make up the Church as a whole. Theodoret, and some others, have held that these are not to be taken as representing the true people of God ; but why then are they called by names so descriptive of the King's most intimate associates and household ? Or how could they have that devout and admiring sympathy with the Bride, blessing and praising her as they do, if not of the same general fellowship with her ? Some narrow Churchmen see here the various sects which stand opposed to what they consider the Church ; but opposition and secession are not significant of admiration and blessing, and if these queens, etc., be of the household of faith in any sense, their relation to the King, in the very nature of the terms, must be true and real. The oldest Christian interpretation, and that which is best sustained, sees in them none but genuine believers, but of different degrees of honour and nearness to their Lord ; in which case, again, not all have the Bride's place.

So the parable of the Ten Virgins tells of a coming Bridegroom, and of friends of the Bride going out, as in ancient custom, to meet and welcome him, and to go in with him to the marriage ; but where is the Bride ? Both the connection and the terms of this parable imply that she is then already within the Father's house, there awaiting the coming of the Bridegroom, whilst these her friends go out to meet him,—not in hope of becoming his Bride, but of having the blessedness of going in with him to the marriage. As a matter of fact, distinctly stated, the day of the Lord has already commenced when the kingdom of heaven assumes the precise shape here indicated. In the verses preceding, the Saviour spoke of the gathering of certain eagle saints to that body on which they live, of the mysterious taking of some, while others are left, and of the sadness of being cut off from the high privileges and honours of that first class ; and it is " *then*," he says, only *then*, that matters take the shape described in the parable. Those who are " *taken* " before " then " are people of pre-eminent saintship and watchful preparedness. (Comp. Luke 17 : 33–37 ; 21 : 34–36.) They correspond to the Bride, whilst the wise virgins come after, not being ready when the Bride was taken. Nay, it is the removal of these waiting and ready ones which awakens the intense adventism of those that are " left," and serves as the means of bringing at least half of them in as guests and witnesses of the marriage. The " left " know now that Christ is presently to come as the Bridegroom, on his way to join his Bride. To be ready for that Bridegroom coming, that they may go in with him to the marriage, is now the one great thought. In all ordinary custom—to which the allusion is—the going in would be the going into the Father's house where the Bride already is, arrayed and ready for her coming Lord.

To say nothing, then, of the place and fate of the five unwise virgins, this parable, taken in its connections, inevitably implies that not all of those who finally get to heaven are of that class which actually constitutes the Bride of Christ, however related to that Bride.

It is also the common doctrine of the Scriptures that there are great diversities in the portions awarded to the saints. There are some greatest and some least in the kingdom of heaven. There are some who shall be first and some who shall be last. There are some who get crowns, and there are some who get none. There are some who are assigned dominion over ten cities, some over five, and some who lose all reward, and are saved only " so as by fire." The four Living Ones, and the four-and-twenty Elders, are the representatives of men saved from the earth. They sing the song of redemption by the blood of Christ. But they are in heaven, crowned, glorified, and installed in blessed priesthoods and kinghoods in advance of the vast multitude whose rewards are far inferior. Diversities so great are incompatible with the peculiar honours and regality of the wife of a king.

Besides, princesses and queens, above all on occasions of their marriage, always have their associates, companions, maids of honour, attendants, suites, and friends, who, in a general way, are counted with them as making one and the same company, but who in fact are very distinct in honour and privilege from those on whom they find it their happiness to attend. Just as the Bridegroom comes not alone, but with attendants, companions, and a long train of rejoicing ones who make up his party, the whole of whom together are called the Bridegroom's coming, whilst, strictly speaking, there is a wide difference between him and those with him ; so it is on the side of the Bride. She has her companions and attendants too,—" virgins which follow her." They make up her company and train. In coming to wed her the Bridegroom comes also into near and close relation to them. To a blessed degree they share the Bride's honours. And in general terms we must include them when we speak of the Bride, although, in strict language, they are not all the

Bride. The Bride has relations to the Bridegroom which belong to her alone, and it is only because of her and their association and companionship with her, and not because they are the Bride in actual fact, that the whole company of the saved Church of God is contemplated as the Lamb's Wife.

Hence, also, the angel directed John to write, " Blessed they who have been called to the supper of the marriage of the Lamb." It is the wider and the more general blessedness of the occasion that the seer was thus to attest. If all the saved were actually the Bride, it would have been enough, and more to the point, to say, " Blessed they that are called to be the Wife of the Lamb." But there is a blessedness of being called to witness his marriage, and a blessedness of participation with the bridal company in the marriage banquet, as well as a more special blessedness of being the actual Bride of the Lamb. The call is indeed to make up the Bride. It is out of these called ones that the Bride is chosen. But the choosing of the Bride does not, therefore, exclude the rest of the company from the honours and privileges of the marriage supper, or from companionship with the Lamb and his Wife. The blessedness of the marriage supper is much wider than that of becoming the Bride, though the Bride has honour and nearness to the Lord which belong to her only. Hence the writing was to be, not simply " Blessed they that are called to be the Wife of the Lamb," but " blessed they who are called to the supper of the marriage of the Lamb,"—called as in the parable of the marriage of the king's son, which call includes the opportunity to become the Bride as well as happy guests.

In this sense also am I constrained to take the subsequent showing of " the Bride, the Lamb's Wife," " that great city, the holy Jerusalem, descending out of the heaven from God." It is called the Bride, because it embraces the Bride, and because it is the Bride's everlasting home and residence. But for the very reason that it is the home and residence of the Lamb's Wife, it must include her retinue, her companions, and her attendants, who share the glory with her, but who are not strictly the Bride herself. In general terms the whole city, as made up of those who inhabit it, including all the saved up to the time of the resurrection of all saints, is the Bride, the Lamb's Wife, because all that are there pertain to her company, fill out the grandeur and glory of her estate, and share immensely in it ; albeit, some are there who, in a narrower and more particular discrimination, are not actually the Bride.

III. *What is the making of Herself ready ?* The allusion seems to be to something of the same sort with the putting on of the wedding garment, of which so much is made in the parable of the marriage of the king's son. (Matt. 22 : 1-14.) There one of the guests was found without a wedding garment, and for that deficiency was put away from the happy company amid shame and sorrow. But in this case the Bride " prepared herself. And it was given to her that she should clothe herself in fine linen,—bright, pure,—for the fine linen is the righteousnesses of the saints." Thus it is said in Isaiah (61 : 10), " I will greatly rejoice in the Lord, my soul shall be joyful in my God ; for he hath clothed me with the garments of salvation, he hath covered me with the robe of righteousness, as a bridegroom decketh himself with ornaments, and as a bride adorneth herself with jewels." Thus, also, when the seer saw the holy city coming down from God out of heaven, she was " prepared as a bride adorned for her husband." (21 : 2.) The excellencies in which the Bride here arrays herself are described as the finest linen, of the intensest purity and lustre ; but it is at the same time a spiritual linen, which is " the righteousnesses of the saints."

Three things appear in the notice of this ready-making. (1) There is self-activity on the part of the Bride to prepare herself. (2) There is gratuity and bestowment, putting what is requisite at her command. And (3) she is receptive and obedient in making the intended use of what is given her. The description evidently takes in the whole previous career of those who make up the Bride. The preparation refers not only to something that is done at this time, but also to what has been in the course of doing all along, and now comes to its fruit and award. The coming to Christ, the learning of him, the espousal to him in holy confession, and justification by faith in his blood and merit, are unquestionably included.   Paul was aiming at this very preparedness and honour of the Bride of the Lamb, and counted all temporal possessions as nothing, and exerted himself in every way to be fit for it. But that fitness, he tells us, was his being found not having his own righteousness, which is of the law,—a mere show of human works,—but having that righteousness which is through faith of Christ, the righteousness which is of God by faith. (Phil. 3 : 8–14.) But the righteous acts and good works of the justified are also included.   The word is in the plural—" the righteousn*es*s of the saints." Some call it the plurality of dignity, and make nothing special of it. Others say it is the distributive plural, in allusion to the many who have it. But parallel instances are wanting to sustain either of these theories. It distinctly implies that the saints have more than one righteousness, as the Scriptures elsewhere teach.

There is a righteousness of justification, and a righteousness of life and sanctification. There is a righteousness which is the free gift of God in Christ Jesus, and a righteousness of man's own active obedience to God's ordinances and commands.   True, saints have both ; a righteousness by imputation through faith without works, and a righteousness which is the fruit of faith, consisting of works springing from and wrought in faith.   And both enter into that adornment of the Bride wherein she maketh herself ready. She is clothed with the fine and shining linen of " the *righteousnesses* of the saints," the righteousness of a free justification by faith in her Lord who died for her, and the righteousness of a life of earnest, active, and grateful devotion to make herself meet and worthy for so good and gracious a Husband. (Comp. Luke 20 : 35 ; 21 : 36 ; Eph. 4 : 1 ; Col. 1 : 10 ; Rev. 3 : 4.)

But it is not certain that the clothing of herself in these righteousnesses is all that is embraced in the Bride's preparation for the wedding. That is the part of her ready-making as respects this life ; but who knows what else remains for her to do after this life is over, or what practical activities remain for the saints between the moment of their removal to immortality and the heavenly solemnities which are shadowed to us under the idea of the marriage of the Lamb ? Heaven is no more a scene of quiescence than earth. There is history in the career of saints after they leave this world as well as in it, and far greater and sublimer history than pertains to them here. And who knows into what grand activities the people of God are ushered when their mortality is swallowed up of life ? or with what preparations they may then be called to busy themselves for the sublime events and ceremonies that lie before them in their instalment into the relations and dignities of their everlasting estate ? The celestial population seem to know of ready-making in heaven, which comes after the ready-making on earth, which is to them a subject of glad rejoicing, and of new and special giving of glory to God. But just what it is, or exactly to what it relates, we must content ourselves not to know till the time for it comes.

IV. *What is the Marriage ?* Here again we must be satisfied with very imperfect information. John did not see the marriage, neither was it explained to him. He only heard the heavenly rejoicing that the time for it had come, that the Bride had prepared herself, and that he was to declare the blessedness of those who are called to the banquet then to be spread. That the marriage and the supper are not one and the same thing, the nature of the case, as well as the manner in which they are referred to, would seem to make evident. The marriage is accompanied with a becoming feast, but the feast is one thing and the marriage is another, though occurring at the same time and most intimately correlated.

It is curious to observe how various are the notions which interpreters have given of this marriage of the Lamb. Beza, Robertson (of Leuchars), Clarke, and others are confident that it refers to a happy condition of the Church in this world, when " whole contemporary churches are in covenant with Christ in a most upright manner." It is supposed by these that when the Church becomes more pure in her doctrines, more pious in her experiences, and more righteous in her conduct than ever she has yet been, this whole showing will be exhausted. Accordingly, the Bride of Christ would be nothing but the Christians of one particular generation, and the Living Ones, and Elders, and the multitude which no man can number, and the 144,000 sealed ones, and other classes which this Book shows to be in heaven before the marriage of the Lamb is announced, have no part nor lot in it. Fuller and William Jones see the whole picture fulfilled in a fancied Millennium on earth, " when Jews and Gentiles from every nation under heaven shall be brought to believe in Jesus, and led to confess him as their true Messiah, Saviour, and King ; " which likewise cuts off all those who have lived and faithfully served Christ in all the long ages prior to the thousand years, and equally vacates the whole marriage idea as contrasted with the already existing union between Christ and his people. Hengstenberg thinks that " we are here beyond the thousand years, beyond the last victory over God and Magog," though he thus makes the people in heaven say it *is come* a thousand years before it does come. Some refer it to the taking again of the seed of Abraham to be God's peculiar people, after the present church period has reached its termination. This would well accord with a variety of Scripture passages otherwise obscure, but it does not meet some of the main features of the case. If at all in the contemplation, it cannot be more than an earthly and inferior correspondence of the chief thing, which must relate to heaven, for when the Bride was shown to John he beheld her in the form of a glorious city coming down from God out of heaven, proving that her marriage must needs have been in heaven. Vaughan speaks of the marriage as " the ideal concourse and combination of the blessed company of all faithful people on their entrance into their rest." This would seem to accord with the presentations as to time and place, but tells nothing as to what the marriage itself is. Düsterdieck understands it to be " Christ's distribution of the eternal reward of grace to his faithful ones, who then enter with him into the full glory of the heavenly life ; " which may be true enough in general, for the marriage is surely the result, award, and consummation of grace toward the Bride ; but it still leaves us in the region of mist and darkness as to any difference between the marriage and the judgment. The translator of Lange (*in loc.*) comes closer to the truth when he represents the marriage as " the union of the whole body of the saints with a personally present Christ in glory and government—the establishment of the kingdom." As the writer of *The Apocalypse Expounded* says, " It is a scene taking place in the heaven, after the resurrection of the saints, and ere Jesus and his risen ones are manifested to the earth, as heaven is not opened till the marriage has occurred." The blessedness of it is not inaptly described by Lange to be " the reciprocal operation of a spiritual fellowship of love." It is Christ in the character of the Lamb, the mighty *Goel*, formally acknowledging and taking to himself as copartners of his throne, dominion, and glory, all those chosen ones who have been faithful to their betrothal, and appear at last in the spotless and shining apparel of the righteousnesses of the saints, thenceforward to be with him, reign with him, and share with him in all his grand inheritance, forever.

Just what the ceremony of this marriage is we are nowhere told. Some have thought that it is the first opening of the city of God, the New Jerusalem, to the footsteps of the redeemed. Jesus says that he is now preparing a place for us. The ancient saints looked for a city whose maker and builder is God. That city John saw and describes in a subsequent chapter. That city was shown him as the Bride, the Lamb's Wife, so called on account of those who inhabit and dwell in it. The placing of the redeemed with their Redeemer in that sublime and eternal home necessarily involves some befitting formality.

Nor is it far-fetched to connect that first formal entrance into that illustrious heaven-built city with the ceremonial of what is described as the marriage of the Lamb. When the sacred tabernacle was first opened and used it was with great solemnities, which God himself prescribed, and in the observance of which there was also a marked coming together of God and his people. By visible manifestations of Deity a point of union and communion was then and there established between man and Jehovah, so direct and close that the holy prophet could say of Israel, " Thy Maker is thy Husband." And the fact that God so ordered and honoured the occasion is ample warrant for taking it as the type of a corresponding formality in the heavens, answering to the coming together of the Lamb and his affianced people for the first time in that glorious city, which even the great voice from the throne calls " THE TABER-NACLE OF GOD." (Chap. 21 : 2, 3.)

V. *What is the Marriage Supper ?* Contrary to all congruity, many take it as about one and the same with the marriage itself. Marriage is the establish-ment of relationship and status ; a marriage feast is the refreshment, the eating, and drinking, and general social joy on the part of those attending upon a marriage. First the Bridegroom comes, next the marriage is solem-nized, and then the assembled company is invited to the special repast provided for the occasion. And so in this case. The Bridegroom appears, the marriage takes place, and then the grand banquet ensues ; so that the supper is a different thing from the marriage, though following immediately upon it.

Everywhere in the Scriptures do we hear of this feast. As in the matter of the marriage, something of it is to be enjoyed already in this life. There is a supper of Gospel blessings of which we may now partake. But as the actual marriage occurs in heaven subsequent to the resurrection, so also the fulness of the Gospel supper is deferred till then. Isaiah (25 : 6–9) sung of a feast of fat things, of wines on the lees, of fat things full of marrow, of wines on the lees well refined, which the Lord of Hosts is to make. The feast of Gospel blessings is doubtless included ; but it is a feast whose glorious fulness is beyond the grave. A chief part of its glory is that then " death is swallowed up in victory," tears are all wiped away by Jehovah's hand, the disabilities and hardships of his people are gone, and the shout is, " Lo, this is our God ; we have waited for him ; we will be glad and rejoice in his salvation." Of that same feast the Saviour spoke when he said to his disciples, " I will not drink henceforth of this fruit of the vine until that day when I drink it new with you in my Father's kingdom." (Matt. 26 : 29.) So, also, when he had finished the paschal supper, and said, " I will not any more eat thereof until it be fulfilled in the kingdom of God." (Luke 22 : 16.) As Melchisedek, king of righteous-ness, and king of peace, brought forth bread and wine to Abraham returning from the scenes of judgment upon the marauding kings, so will he whom Melchisedek typified spread before his victorious people the precious viands of a heavenly banquet, of which our holy Lord's supper is the constant prophecy and foretaste.

Of what that supper shall consist we cannot yet know. The Scriptures speak of bread of heaven and angel's food, and the Saviour tells of eating and drinking there. He who supplied the wedding at Cana, and fed the thousands in the wilderness, and furnished the little dinner to his worn disciples as they came up from the sea of toil to the shore trodden by his glorified feet, can be at no loss to make good every word, and letter, and allusion which the Scriptures contain with reference to that high festival. The angels know some-thing about it, and the angel told John that it will be a blessed thing to be there. " Write," said the heavenly voice, " write, *Blessed they who have been called to the supper of the marriage of the Lamb.*"

VI. *Who, then, are the Guests ?* Chief of all who sit down to the marriage banquets on earth are the bridegroom and the bride. It is in honour of their union that the feast is held, and to them is assigned the most conspicuous place. This is a genuine marriage feast, the antitype of all the marriage feasts of time, and this particular feature cannot be wanting there. In the after chapters we are told that the Lamb is the light of the golden house in which it is held. He, therefore, is there in unveiled glory, the observed, the adored, the sublimest joy of all. And where he is there his bride is also, for they are united now, never to be separated any more. She is there in all her perfected loveliness, " not having spot, or wrinkle, or any such thing," but " all glorious within," and enfolded in her garments of needle-work, and gold, and in the faultless and radiant linen of the righteousnesses of the saints. There also are " the virgins, her companions that follow her," and make up her sublime and glorious train. And whosoever, in any age, in any land, of any language, of any tribe, has heard of the promised seed of the woman, and believed in him, and listened to the calls and promises of God, and directed his heart and pilgrim steps for that blest city, shall likewise be there. Whether as bride or guest, the whole Church of the first-born, from Adam down to the last martyr under the Antichrist, shall be there, radiant in that redemption for which they hoped and suffered. The quaint old hymn says truly :

There be prudent Prophets all,
    The Apostles six and six,
The glorious Martyrs in a row,
    And Confessors betwixt.
There doth the crew of righteous men
    And nations all consist ;
Young men and maids that here on earth
    Their pleasures did resist.

The sheep and lambs that hardly 'scaped
    The snare of death and hell,
Triumph in joy eternally,
    Whereof no tongue can tell ;
And though the glory of each one
    Doth differ in degree,
Yet is the joy of all alike
    And common certainly.

There David stands, with harp in hand,
    As master of the choir ;
A thousand times that man were blessed
    That might his music hear.
There Mary sings " Magnificat,"
    With tunes surpassing sweet ;
And all the virgins bear their part,
    Singing about her feet.

" Te Deum," doth St. Ambrose sing,
    St. Austin doth the same ;
Old Simeon and Zacharie
    Anew their songs inflame.
There Magdalene hath left her moan,
    And cheerfully doth sing,
With all blest saints whose harmony
    Through every street doth ring.

And in that holy company
    May you and I find place,
Through worth of him who died for us,
    And through his glorious grace ;
With Cherubim and Seraphim,
    And hosts of ransomed men,
To sing our praises to The Lamb,
    And add our glad *Amen.*

VII. *What authority have we for all this ?* There be those who count it all a dream, a pleasant fancy, a sweet hallucination, by which enthusiastic souls impose upon themselves. And if it were, why deny to poor, sorrowing, and afflicted humanity its consoling radiance ? Be it a mere conceit, is not the

race the happier and the better for believing it ? But no, it is not delusion.
The very blessedness which it diffuses through the souls that take it to their
thoughts is a voucher for its heavenly reality. The holy being who told of it
to the seer propounds it as the sum of all sacred revelations, and says, " *These
are the true words of God.*"

Ah, yes ; there is a Lamb, once slain, now risen and glorified, moving serene
and mighty amid the principalities of eternity, himself the highest of them all,
to whom all believers stand betrothed and plighted, preparing and waiting
for a wedding day to come, when they shall be joined to him in fellowship,
glory, and dominion forever. There is a city of gold, and light, and jewels for
God's people, building for these many ages, and now near its readiness for their
everlasting habitation. There is in store a banquet when once the honoured
Bride sets foot upon its golden streets, the call to which, if heeded, is man's
superlative blessedness. Room for doubt, is none ; for " *these are the true
words of God.*"

The revelation to John was overpowering. It so thrilled upon his soul, and
so stimulated his sense of grateful wonder and adoration, that he fell down
before the angel's feet to worship him. It was an error to offer such honour to
a fellow-servant with himself, and the same was promptly checked ; but
it helps to tell the entrancing magnificence of the final portion of the saints—
the overwhelming majesty of the glory to come when the Bridegroom comes.
It bends the soul in awe even toward the messengers who tell of it.   It is
more than heart of flesh can well stand up under, even in prospect. What
then will be the actual realization ? A holy apostle falls upon his face in
adoration when he hears of it, and the glorified in heaven cry, " Let us rejoice
and exult, and we will give the glory to God," when the time for it arrives.

What then, O man, O woman, is the state and feeling of your heart concerning it ? To you has come the call to the supper of the marriage of the
Lamb ; what is the response you have made to it ? To you is offered the
wedding garment to appear there in honour and glory ; have you accepted it,
and put it on, and kept its purity unsoiled ? The cry has long been ringing
in your ears, " Behold, the Bridegroom cometh ! " Are your loins girded
about, your lights burning, and ye yourselves like unto those who wait for
their Lord ? Five virgins once set out to reach that festival, but when they
came " *the door was shut.*" They knew what was required ; but the Bridegroom came, and this was the consequence of their unreadiness. God forbid
that this should be your experience !

> Wake, awake, for night is flying,
> The watchmen on the heights are crying ;
>   Awake, Jerusalem, at last !
> Midnight hears the welcome voices,
> And at the thrilling cry rejoices ;
>   Come forth, ye virgins, night is past !
>   The Bridegroom comes, awake,
>   Your lamps with gladness take ;
>   Halleluia !
> And for His marriage feast prepare,
> For ye must go to meet Him there.

REV. 19 : 11–21. (Revised Text.) And I saw the heaven opened, and behold a white horse, and one seated upon him, Faithful and True, and in righteousness he judgeth and warreth ; his eyes flame of fire, and on his head many diadems, having a name written which no one knoweth but himself, and clothed in vesture dipped [or *stained*] with blood, and his name is called THE WORD OF GOD. And the armies, the ones in the heaven were following him on white horses, clothed in fine linen, white, pure. And out of his mouth proceedeth a sharp sword, that with it he may smite the nations ; and HE shall rule [or *shepherdize*] them with a rod of iron ; and HE treadeth the winepress of the wine of the anger of the wrath of the God, the All-Ruler. And he hath upon his vesture, even upon his thigh a name written, KING OF KINGS AND LORD OF LORDS.

And I saw a certain angel standing in the sun, and he cried with a great voice, saying to all the fowls that fly in mid-heaven, Hither, be gathered together to the great supper of God, that ye may eat flesh of kings, and flesh of captains of thousands, and flesh of mighty men, and flesh of horses, and of those that sit on them, and flesh of all [classes], both free and bond, and small and great.

And I saw the beast, and the kings of the earth, and his armies, gathered together to make the battle with the sitter upon the horse, and with his army. And the beast was taken, and with him the false prophet who wrought the miracles in his presence with which he deceived those who received the mark of the beast and those who worship his image ; these two were cast alive into the lake of fire which burneth with brimstone ; and the rest were slain with the sword of the sitter on the horse, which (sword) proceedeth out of his mouth ; and the fowls were filled from their flesh.

THE marriage of the Lamb, and the grand banquet which attends it, are speedily followed with the closing scene of this present world. It is a scene of war and blood. It is the battle of the great day of God Almighty. It is the coming forth of the powers of eternity to take forcible possession of the earth. It finds all the confederated kingdoms of man mustered in rebellion against the anointed and rightful sovereign of the earth. A collision ensues, which is the most wonderful that ever occurs under heaven. And the result is a victory for the right, which is to be forever. The description is one of the grandest contained in these Revelations. In proceeding to contemplate it four things are to be considered :

    I.   THE MIGHTY CONQUEROR.

    II.   THE HOSTS WHICH FOLLOW HIM.

    III.   THE ARMIES HE ENCOUNTERS.

    IV.   THE COMPLETENESS OF HIS TRIUMPH.

God help us to take in these particulars to our edification and spiritual profit.

I.

The sublime Hero of the scene is none other than our ever blessed Lord Jesus. His name is not given, but the marks and inscriptions which he bears, and all that is said of him, infallibly identify him as that same Jesus who went up into heaven from the summit of Mt. Olivet, and whose holy feet are to stand again on these self-same heights.

He comes forth out of heaven. For this purpose John saw it opened. When Jesus came up from the waters of baptism, " the heavens were open unto him," and the Spirit descended upon him, and a voice from the empyrean depths said, " This is my beloved Son, in whom I am well pleased." (Matt. 3 : 16.) When Stephen was martyred he saw " the heavens opened, and the Son of Man standing on the right hand of God." (Acts. 7 : 55.) When Jesus was on earth he promised his disciples that they should see the heaven opened. (Jno. 1 : 51.) At the beginning of these visions John beheld a door opened in the heaven, and through that opening he was called up, while all was closed to the general mass of men. (Rev. 4 : 1.) But here was quite a different opening from any that has occurred or will occur till then. This is that rending of the heaven for the glorious Epiphany of Christ with his people, to which the Scriptures refer so much. For, as we believe that " he ascended into heaven, and sitteth on the right hand of God the Father Almighty," so we believe that " from thence he shall come to judge the quick and the dead." So the Lamb, being married now, leaves the Father house and comes forth to take possession of what is peculiarly his own.

He rides upon a white horse. This horse tells of royalty, judgment, and war. His white colour tells of righteousness and justice. Light is the robe of divine majesty, and *white* is the colour that most attaches to Christ in all these judgment scenes. When the first seal broke he rode a white horse ; when the great harvest is reaped he sits upon a white cloud ; and at the end of the thousand years he sits upon a white throne ; and so here he is seated on the white steed of battle, for " in righteousness doth he make war." In the day of his humiliation he rode but once—when he came to the Jewish nation as its anointed king. But he then rode upon an ass, a colt, the foal of an ass. Then he was the meek and lowly one ; but here the little domestic animal is exchanged for the martial charger, for this is another and mightier coming as the King of the World, " just and having salvation." In his majesty he rides prosperously, because of truth, and meekness, and righteousness.

He is Faithful and True. This presents him in sharp contrast with those whom he cometh to judge and destroy. The Dragon is the deceiver ; the Beast is the False Christ ; his companion is the False Prophet, and the great confederacy is made up of false worshippers. These are to be handled now, and it is the embodiment of all faithfulness and truth that comes to deal with them. There is then no hope for them, for if justice be done them they have no show whatever. The worst thing that can happen to some is to give them what they deserve. But greatly do these attributes exalt this Hero. They lift him far above the level of humanity. They bespeak almightiness and essential Godhead. (Comp. chaps. 3 : 7 ; 6 : 10 ; 15 : 3 ; 16 : 7.) They cannot be predicated of any mere man. " Cursed be the man that trusteth in man." There is too much deceit and treachery in human nature for it to be always and implicitly trusted. (Com. Ps. 72 : 9 ; 116 : 11 ; 118 : 8 ; Jer. 17 : 5.) But here is one who is absolutely true and faithful. It is not in him to be or to prove unreliable. Though all men be liars, he is true, and cannot disappoint.

In righteousness he judgeth and warreth. In the letter to the Laodiceans he was " the Faithful and True *Witness*," reproving and instructing his friends ; here he is the Faithful and True *Warrior and Judge*, for the punishment of his enemies. Heaven cannot be at peace with iniquity, and justice cannot be at amity with falsehood and rebellion. When sin is once incorrigible, and incurable by remedial measures, it must be put down by force of arms. Mercy slighted and abused brings the executioner. The world banded together in arms against its true Sovereign brings against it the sword of insulted majesty. Not as human kings and nations war,—out of covetousness, pride, and an ambition for selfish greatness and dominion,—but in absolute justice and right, and in strictest accord with every holy principle and every holy interest he now unsheaths and wields the sword of infinite power. Dreadful is the carnage which follows, but no one can ever say that it is not precisely what was merited and demanded. The powers of judging and making war are often separated in earthly sovereignties, but it is only a conventional separation. They necessarily go together after all. Wherever there is war there is first a judgment made or entertained against those upon whom it is made, or in behalf of those whom it is to benefit. The general in the field is simply the sheriff and hangman of the court. And Christ is both judge and executioner, all powers in one, and all exercised in righteousness. To the Church he is the High Priest, with girdle and ephod, stars and lamps, the minister of righteousness unto salvation. To the world in armed rebellion he is the mounted Warrior, the minister of righteousness unto destruction ; but in both and always " Jesus Christ The Righteous."

His eyes flame of fire. To judge rightly he must see through and through, search all depths, look beneath all masks, penetrate all darkness, and try everything to its ultimate residuum. Hence this flaming vision, which likewise tells of the fierceness of his wrath against his enemies. There is often something wonderfully luminous, penetrating, overawing, in the human eye. Men have been killed by the look of kings. It is like the living intellect made visible, which seems to read all secrets at a glance, and before which the beholder cowers. It is this infinitely intensified, flashing like a sword of fire from the visual orbs, that the holy apostle here beheld in this Warrior Judge. It is an eye-flame of Omniscient perception and out-breaking indignation and wrath, which seizes and unmans the foe before he feels the sword.

On His head many diadems. He is not only Judge and General, but at the same time the King himself. When David conquered the Ammonites, he put the crown of the vanquished king on his own head, in addition to the crown he already had. (2 Sam. 12 : 30.) When Ptolemy entered Antioch, he set two crowns upon his head, the crown of Asia and the crown of Egypt. (1 Macc. 11 : 13.) The Popes wear a triple crown, emblematic of three sovereignties united in one. The Dragon has *seven* diadems on his seven heads, as the possessor of the seven great world-powers (chap. 12 : 3). The Beast has *ten* diadems on his ten horns, as combining ten sovereignties. (Chap. 13 : 1.) In all these cases, the accumulation of crowns expresses accumulated victory and dominion. It is the same in this case. Christ comes against the Beast and his confederates as the conqueror on many fields, the winner of many mighty battles, the holder of many sovereignties secured by his prowess and power. He comes as the One anointed and endowed of heaven with all the sovereignties of the earth as his rightful due and possession. When he came as the mighty Angel, with the little book in his hand as his title to the earth, the *rainbow* was on his head (chap. 10) ; but he then came in mercy and promise to his own. He comes now as the Warrior, Judge, and King against combined usurpers in arms, against those who dispute his right to the dominion purchased with his blood, and he puts on all his royal rights.

He has an unknowable Name. John saw it written, and was awed with its splendour ; but it was too much for him, or any other man, to understand or know. Jesus once said, " No man knoweth the Son but the Father " (Matt. 11 : 27) ; and here he appears in all those unrevealed and unknowable wonders, which connect him with incomprehensible Godhead. The Beast is full of names, great, high, and awful names ; but they are false names— " names of blasphemy." This Warrior, Judge, and King has a name ineffable and unknowable, but it is a true and rightful name,—a name of reality, " which is above every name." We do not yet know all the majesty of attributes or being which belong to our sublime Saviour ; and when he comes forth out of heaven for the war upon the Beast, he will come in vast unknowableness of greatness,—in heights of majesty and glory, " which no one knoweth but himself." (Comp. Judges 13 : 18 ; Rev. 2 : 17.)

Clothed in vesture dipped or stained with blood. Some are embarrassed, that the blood should here appear upon Christ's garments before the engagement begins, and so talk of anticipation. It is a needless perplexity, although these bloodstains are certainly not from his own blood. They have no reference whatever to his having died upon the cross. They are stains from the blood of enemies slain,—enemies previously vanquished,—and so the marks of a veteran in battle. This conquering Hero is not now for the first time to try his capacities for war. Who but he was it that " cut Rahab and wounded the Dragon ? " Who but he was it that fought for Israel " in the days of Joshua, when opposing kings with kings were put to the sword and all their armies ? " Who but he was it that " fought from heaven " against the kings of Canaan in Taanach by the waters of Megiddo, when " the stars in their courses fought against Sisera ? " Who but he was the vanquisher of the six great blasphemous world-powers already dead and gone? And as the seventh, and last, and worst of all is now to be overwhelmed, and the same almighty Conqueror comes forth to execute the doom, he properly comes in the same garments worn and stained on so many battlefields, indicating that he comes in the same capacity, for the same ends, and with the same invincible power, as in other judgments upon his enemies. That red apparel, and those garments like one that treadeth the vinefat, are at once the memorials of the past, and the prophecies of what is now to be consummated upon these last confederates against his kingdom.

His Name is called THE WORD OF GOD. This is one of the pre-eminent designations of the Son of God, who became incarnate in Jesus Christ. " By the Word of the Lord were the heavens made." (Ps. 33 : 6.) " In the beginning was the Word, and the Word was with God, and the Word was God. All things were made by him. And the Word was made flesh, and dwelt among us, and we beheld his glory, the glory as of the only begotten of the Father, full of grace and truth " (Jno. 1 : 1–14.) He is the Word of God—the Logos—as the true and only expression of the eternal Godhead, as the great subject and substance of the written Word, as the accomplishment and fulfiller of the written Word, and the very expression and revelation of the Father, the same as words express the thoughts of the heart.

Out of his mouth proceedeth a sharp sword, that with it he may smite the nations. Some take this as " the sword of the Spirit, which is the Word of God ; " but that is an instrument of mercy and salvation ; this is an instrument of wrath and destruction. It is "sharp" like the sickle, and fulfils the same office. It is the word of almighty justice. It proceeds out of his mouth. So Isaiah (11 : 4) said, " He shall smite the earth with the rod of his mouth, and with the breath of his lips shall he slay the wicked."   This shows the ease with which he accomplishes his purpose. He speaks, and it is done. He commands, and it is accomplished. Something of this was preintimated when the armed mob came forth against him in Gethsemane. " When Jesus spake to them, I am he, they went backward, and fell to the ground." (Jno. 18 : 5.) If so mild an utterance prostrated his enemies then, what will it be when he girds and crowns himself for the " battle of the great day of God Almighty "—when he comes with all the cavalcade of heaven to tread the winepress of the fierceness of Jehovah's anger ? " The Word of God is quick, and powerful, and sharper than any two-edged sword, piercing even to the dividing asunder of soul and spirit, and of the joints and marrow " (Heb. 4 : 12) ; and when that Word goes forth in execution of Almighty wrath upon those in arms against his throne, what a flow of blood, and wilting of life, and tornado of deadly disaster must it work !

And he hath upon his vesture, even upon his thigh a name written, KING OF KINGS AND LORD OF LORDS. Thus the Psalmist in anticipation sung, " Gird thy sword upon thy thigh, O most Mighty." (Ps. 45 : 3.) It is on his thigh that the warrior carries his sword ; but here the sword proceeds from the mouth, and hence in its place is a name representing it ; for the Psalmist defines the sword in this case as his glory and majesty. The sword stands for authority and the right to punish rebels and evildoers. It tells of the majesty and dominion of him who bears it. And the authority, majesty and dominion of Christ is this, that he is " *King of kings and Lord of lords,*" now no longer in mere theory or appointment, but in present assertion, armed to enforce his rights. For ages the government of the world had been in other hands. Beasts held the sword and reigned. They have ever abused it against him and his people. And now they have confederated with Hell to hold it even against the forces of Omnipotence. Dreadful miscalculation ! The Lion of the tribe of Judah comes to meet them. He comes in the claim and majesty of the sharp sword of the King over all these kings and Lord over all these lordly ones. On his thigh is the name of his authority—the sword name of his sovereignty. And woe to the powers that now think to withstand him. " The Lord shall swallow them up in His wrath, and the fire shall devour them." (Ps. 21 : 19.)

Such, then, is the mighty Hero who comes forth from the opened heavens to fight this " battle of the great day of God Almighty." Let us look next at the HOSTS WHICH FOLLOW HIM.

II.

When the Lord Jesus is revealed from heaven, in flaming fire taking vengeance upon them that know not God and that obey not the Gospel, he does not come alone. He is married now, and his Bride is with him. Even before the flood, Enoch prophesied of this epiphany of the promised One, and said, " Behold the Lord cometh with ten thousand of his saints to execute judgment upon all." (Jude 14, 15.) They are with him now, therefore they must have been taken before. John saw, and writes, " *The armies, the ones in the heaven, were following him.*" Christ is the Head and Leader, and he goes before ; his saints follow in his train. The promise from the beginning was, that the seed of the woman should bruise the serpent's head, and here it is emphasized that " He himself treadeth the winepress of the wine of the anger of the wrath of the God, the All-Ruler." He himself is the Great Hero and Conqueror in this battle. But he is " Jehovah of hosts." He has many under his command. The armies of the sky are his, and he brings them with him, even " the called and chosen, and faithful." (Chap. 17 : 14.)

On white horses. The great Captain is mounted, and they are mounted too. He comes as the Warrior, Judge, and King, and they share with him in the same character. They are warrior judges and kings with him. In chapter 9, we were introduced to cavalry from the under world, of spirit horses from beneath ; why not then celestial horses also ? Horses and chariots of fire protected Elisha at Dothan. Horses of fire took up Elijah into heaven. And heavenly horses bring the saints from heaven when they come with their great Leader for the final subjugation of the world to his authority. It is up to the bridle-bits of these horses that the blood in that battle is to flow. (Chap. 14 : 20.) These horses are all white, the same as the Great Captain rides. Everything is in harmony. The riders all are royal and righteous ones, and the same is expressed in the colour of their horses.

Whether literal horses are to be understood, it is not necessary to inquire. Power is an abstract quality, incapable of being seen with the eye. It must put on shape in order to become visible. It is best shown in living forms. So we had to do with symbolic horses in chapter eleven. But here the whole character of the showing is different. This opening of the heaven, the coming forth of Christ with his heavenly armies to the battle which ensues, the destruction which is wrought, the victory which is won, and the kingdom which is set up, is so essentially literal in each particular, that it is hard to find room in the record for any other conclusion than that the horses are as literal as the sitters on them. They are at least the pictures of holy power bearing the King and his hosts to battle and victory over literal armies. There was reality in the powers which carried up Elijah, and there is reality in the powers on which these heavenly armies ride forth to the battle of the great day ; and I know not why these powers should not be in the form of real horses, of the character of the world to which they belong. " The four Spirits of the heavens, which go forth from standing before the Lord of all the earth," were shown to Zechariah (6 : 8) as horses, drawing four chariots ; and I know not why we may not here understand the same or similar " spirits of the heavens," put forth in similar forms. Habakkuk (3 : 8), referring to this very scene, addresses the Lord, and says, " *Thou didst ride upon thine horses, thy chariots of salvation.*" There are " chariots of God ; " and so there must be horses of God. It is never safe to explain away what may have in it a momentous literal reality, even though it may be very different from anything we know of. At any rate, the armies of heaven, as they here appear, are all cavalry.

" *Clothed in fine linen, white, pure.*" The fine linen was explained in the verses preceding. It is " the righteousness of the saints." Therefore these armies are saints, and not angels, as some have supposed. Those who share the kingdom with Christ are everywhere called " the righteous," and these have the apparel of the righteous, even that with which it was given the Bride to be clothed. Long ago, referring to this very scene, the Psalmist (58 : 10, 11) sung, " The righteous shall rejoice when he seeth the vengeance : he shall wash his feet in the blood of the wicked ; so that a man shall say, verily there is a reward for the righteous : verily He is a God that judgeth in the earth." They reign with the mighty Conqueror after the battle ; and so they share in the battle and triumph which bring the Kingdom. " Do ye not know that the saints shall judge the world ? " (1 Cor. 6 : 2.)

They wear no armour. They are immortal, and cannot be hurt ; and they are not the executors of this vengeance. It is Christ's own personal victory, in accordance with the Apostolic declaration, that " for this purpose the Son of God was manifested, that *he* might destroy the works of the Devil." (1 Jno. 3 : 8.) He bears the only sword, and he alone uses it. He treadeth the wine press *alone.* Those who accompany him in the scene of conflict therefore need no weapons. The sword of the great Captain is enough. Their defence is in him, and their victory is in him. They follow up the achievements of his sword. They ride through the blood it causes to flow. They " wash their feet in " it, for it is up to the horses' bridles. But it is *David* who slays Goliath, and the hosts of God's Israel have only to follow up the mighty triumph, shouting their songs along the path of the victory. When the wicked are cut off, they shall see it ; they shall diligently consider the place of the wicked, and it shall not be ; but the meek shall inherit the earth, and delight themselves in the abundance of peace. (Ps. 37 : 10, 11, 34.) BUT WHO ARE THE ARMIES ENCOUNTERED ?

III.

Here we are left in no doubt. John says, " *I saw the Beast, and the kings of the earth, and his armies, gathered together to make the battle with the Sitter upon the horse, and with his army.*" How they were gathered, we were told in what occurred under the pouring out of the sixth bowl of wrath (chap. 16 : 12–16.) Devil agents working devil miracles, were brought into requisition. They went forth " unto the kings of the earth, even of the whole world, to gather them to the battle of that great day of God Almighty." It was through these devil oracles that they learned of Christ's coming to unseat and destroy them ; and by these devil miracles they were led to believe themselves competent to withstand all the armies of the heaven. Therefore they agreed to try it, and to defeat all these Jehovah purposes of ill to their usurped dominion and blasphemous pretensions. Had they not a supernatural and immortal leader in the Beast, that was not but is again present ? Had they not with him a great supernatural and equally immortal Prophet, who knew everything, who had power over the forces of nature, who could even command fire from heaven and give spirit to a metallic image ? Would not these additional miracle-working spirits be their efficient helpers ? If they made no effort, no resistance, what hope was there for them ? Was not the Beast God, " above all that is called God ? " Had eternity anything that could harm or vanquish such powers ? Had not every soldier in their armies learned how to strengthen and sustain himself by spirit influences far above unaided human ability ?

Let the Rider on the white horse come ;—let him be supported by myriads of his white-robed cavalry on their white horses ;—if he did work miracles in his lifetime, neither he nor his followers ever wrought such as those which the potencies now urging them to armed resistance had shown. The struggle might be a hard one, but a combined and energetic effort would surely be successful. So they were taught ; so they reasoned ; so they believed. *"Strong delusion "* was upon them " that they should believe a lie, that they all might be damned." (2 Thess. 2 : 9–12.) So they all with one accord, went zealously into a great hell-indited and hell-sealed compact and confederation, to make battle with the Lamb, the Sitter on the horse, and his army.

We may wonder how rational men could be carried with one impulse into an attempt so daring and so absurd ; but when people put the truth from them, and submit themselves to the Devil's lead, what is there of delusion and absurdity into which they are not liable to be carried ? How many among us comfort and assure themselves in their selfishness and sins with the belief that either there is no God, or that he is too good and merciful to fulfil his threatenings upon transgressors ? To this there needs to be added only one step more, to defy his judgments, and with that goes pledge of battle and declaration of war with his Omnipotence. And the final outcome of this world's wisdom, unbelief, and repudiation of the rule and government of Jesus Christ, is the assembly of all the kings and armies, and captains of thousands, and mighty men, and men of all ranks and classes, upon the hills and valleys of Palestine, from Idumea to Esdraelon, equipped, resolved, eager, and confident of success, to meet the Son of God and his army in hostile collision, to decide by dreadful battle whether they or he shall have the sovereignty in the earth. Every one that denies Christ, is on the way to defy Christ, and to take up arms for the Usurper to conquer Christ. Every one who refuses to be baptized into Christ, and objects to the oath of allegiance to Christ, is a fit subject for the branding irons and infamous mark of the Antichrist ; and when that is once impressed, there is no more recession from this gathering together to fight Christ, and to be dashed to destruction against his invincible throne. And when Hell's emissaries come, with all their marvel of word and deed to encourage the enemies of God to join, assemble, strike,. and have the world forever to themselves, deluded mortals are persuaded, and march their armies to that field of blood from which there is no more return. " The heathen rage, and the people imagine a vain thing. The kings of the earth set themselves, and the rulers take counsel together against the Lord, and against his anointed, saying, Let us break their bands asunder, and cast away their cords from us." (Ps. 2 : 1–3.) Never was there a more wicked or more disastrous madness. But when men cut loose from the bonds of obligation to their Maker, there is no limit to the delusions to which they expose themselves, and no enormity of daring or wickedness into which they are not liable to be betrayed, thinking it the true wisdom. And thus the kings of the earth and their armies gather toward Jerusalem, to conquer the Son of God, and to crush out his rule and Kingdom for ever. WHAT, THEN, IS THE RESULT ?

IV.

One of the most awful expressions in the Word of God, is that which the Psalmist utters with regard to these enraged and deluded kings, and this their expedition, where he says, " *He that sitteth in the heavens shall laugh : the Lord shall have them in derision.*" (Ps. 2 : 4.) That laugh of God, who shall fathom it ! How shall we even begin to tell its dread significance ! From the depths of his eternal being, he so loved the world, as to give his co-eternal and only begotten Son for it. No gift was too precious in his sight, no sacrifice too great, to be made for its redemption. For six thousand years he has been ordering his gracious Providence in heaven and earth for its recovery from sin and death. His prophets and his Son have laboured, wept and died, and the ministries of his sublimest servants have been unceasingly employed, to bring it to salvation. But now he *laughs !* What failure of love, what exhaustion of grace, what emptying of the sea of his infinite mercies, what decay and with-drawal of all kindly interest and affection must have occurred that there should be this laugh ! The demonstrations of these confederates with the Beast are tremendous. The whole world moves with one heart, one aim, with all its genius and power concentrated on one end, and with all the potencies of Hell to nerve and help and guide it. Never before was there such a combina-tion of forces, natural and supernatural, directed with such skill, or animated with so daring and resolved a spirit. Yet, Jehovah *laughs !* What an infini-tude of majesty and sovereign contempt does he thus express ? The rebels are confident. They believe their leader invincible. They are sure of powers to handle all nature's forces. They have no question about being able to cope with mortals or immortals, with men or gods. They despise alike the names and the sword of Him who rides the white horse, and all his heavenly cavalry. They deem themselves ready and equal for any emergency of battle even with him who calls himself Almighty. But God *laughs !* Oh, the disappoint-ment and destruction which that laugh portends !

An angel stationed in the sun anticipates the coming result. With a great voice he cries to all the birds of prey that fly in mid-heaven to come to a supper on the flesh of kings, captains, mighty men, horses and their riders, free and bond, small and great. This tells already an awful story. It tells of the greatest of men made food for the vultures ;—of kings and leaders, strong and confident, devoured on the field, with no one to bury them ;—of those who thought to conquer Heaven's anointed King rendered helpless even against the timid birds ;—of vaunting gods of nature turned into its cast off and most dishonoured dregs. And what is thus foreintimated soon becomes reality. The Great Conqueror bows the heavens and comes down. He rides upon the cherub horse, and flies upon the wings of the wind. Smoke goes up from his nostrils, and devouring fire out of his mouth. He moves amid storms and darkness, from which the lightnings hurl their bolts, and hailstones mingle with the fire. He roars out of Zion, and utters his voice from Jerusalem, till the heavens and the earth shake. He dashes forth in the fury of his in-censed greatness amid clouds, and fire, and pillars of smoke. The sun frowns. The day is neither light nor dark. The mountains melt and cleave asunder at his presence. The hills bound from their seats and skip like lambs. The waters are dislodged from their channels. The sea rolls back with howling trepidation. The sky is rent and folds upon itself like a collapsed tent. It is the day for executing an armed world,—a world in covenant with Hell to overthrow the authority and throne of God,—and everything in terrified Nature joins to signalize the deserved vengeance. So the Scriptures everywhere represent. John saw it, but does not describe it. He only tells the result he beheld.

And the Beast was taken. The great Judgment strikes the head and leader first. He is not a system ; or he would not fall till the myriads of his supporters fall. He is a *person*, as truly as his Captor is a person. He is distinct from his armies, as Christ is distinct from his ; or he could not be taken in advance of his armies. He is the living god and confidence of all his hosts, and all this war is for his glory ; therefore the assault is first made upon him. He is a supernatural being, a man resurrected from the dead by the Devil's power, and seemingly incapable of corporeal death ; for he is not slain. No sword smites him. He does not die. In contradistinction from all save his com-panion, the False Prophet, it is specifically stated that he is simply " *taken* "—taken " *alive*," and " *cast alive* into the lake of fire." His worshippers held him to be invincible. They asked in the utmost confidence and triumph, Who is like unto the Beast ? Who can war with him ? But, without the strik-ing of a blow, and with all his worshippers in arms around him, he is " *taken*," captured as a lion seizes his prey, dragged away from the field as a helpless prisoner. With all his power, greatness, and resurrection-vigour and immunity from death, he is " taken." With greater ease than the Jewish mob took the unresisting Jesus, the Sitter on the white horse catches him away from the very centre of his hosts. All the resistance he makes is the same as if it were not. He cannot help himself, and all his armies cannot help him. He must go whither his mighty Captor would take him. Tophet gets its own. And into the lake of fire he sinks to rise no more.

And with him the False Prophet who wrought the miracles in his presence. This is no warrior ; but still a main author of this culminated wickedness of the nations. From him, together with the Dragon and the first Beast, went forth the miracle-working spirits who wrought this terrible deception, and stirred up the world to this war. By his instigations were these armies equipped and gathered to the dread attempt to vanquish the Son of God. He caused men to adore the Beast, and he shares the Beast's fate. He is no system, no abstraction, no succession, no mere ideal figure, but a person. He is not slain ; he does not die ; he seems like the Antichrist incapable of death. But he is " taken," as the Beast was taken, made a captive, and hurried away to the same seething prison. All his miraculous power cannot save him. All his boasted wisdom cannot help him. All the armies of the world cannot rescue him from the grasp of the Sitter on the white horse.

The two great leaders gone, short work is made with their followers. A few awful words tell the story. They are mortals all, and there is no salvation for them. In terrible brevity, the Seer records what came to pass. " *And the rest were slain with the sword of the Sitter on the horse, which sword proceeded out of his mouth ;* AND THE FOWLS WERE FILLED FROM THEIR FLESH." Such a feast of death was, perhaps, never before seen.

Long ago had the holy prophets sung of this Mighty One, and this his triumph. As the Psalmist foresaw, his arrows are sharp in the heart of the King's enemies, whereby the people fall under him. (Ps. 45 : 5.) He sends out his arrows, and scattereth them ; and shoots out lightnings, and discomfits them. (Ps. 18 : 14.) He marches through the land in indignation ; he threshes the heathen in anger. (Hab. 3 : 12.) All the strength of the nations is dashed to fragments before him, like pottery struck with an iron rod. (Ps. 2 : 9.) The stone from the eternal mountain falls on the great statue of this world's power, and it is ground to powder, never again to be regathered. (Dan. 2 : 35 ; Matt. 22 : 44.) The victory of the Sitter on the white horse is complete !

And He shall rule or shepherdize them with an iron rod. With many a severe judgment on the survivors of that day, the Conqueror now assumes the dominion. With their heads and armies destroyed in the winepress of the wine of the anger of the wrath of the God the All-Ruler, he now sends forth the new law from Jerusalem. After the sword of destruction, comes the rod of correction and reorganization. The world now gets a new Master, a King whose eternal right it is to reign, and whom they must at once obey or die. The shepherdizing rod of iron, is the administration which follows up the battle, gathers the populations of the earth into their proper flocks, assigns them their laws and rulers, and allows of no more disobedience.

Thus ends this present world. Thus comes in the final reign and kingdom of the Prince of Peace. It only remains to tell the Devil's fate, and then come the glorious pictures of the other side of this " great and terrible day of the Lord."

I only add, that our contemplations to-night will fail of their end, if they do not serve to teach us, and to write it indelibly upon our hearts, that rebellion against God is death ;—that no weapon formed against Jehovah can prosper ;—that those who will not have Christ to rule over them must perish ! Though the wicked should wield the power of archangels, they cannot withstand the punitive majesty of the Warrior Judge and King who rides upon the white horse. His sword is mightier than Satan, mightier than the Beast deemed invincible, mightier than the command of infernal miracle over nature's laws, mightier than all the forces of earth and hell combined. And that sword is pledged to drink the life-blood of all who neglect his mercy, despise his laws, and stand out against his authority. All may seem well and promising now. People may indulge their unbelief and passions during these days of forbearance and grace, and see no disadvantages growing out of it. They may get angry at our earnestness, and account us croakers and fools when we put before them the demands and threatenings of the Almighty. But " *woe to him that striveth with his Maker !* " There is a deluge of bottled fury yet to be poured out on them that refuse to know God, and on the families that call not on his name, from which there is no escape, and from whose burning and tempestuous surges there is no deliverance. God help us to be wise, that we come not into that sea of death !

> Righteous Judge of retribution,
> Grant thy gift of absolution,
> Ere that day's dread execution !

LECTURE FORTY-FOURTH

THE BINDING OF SATAN—HIS FOUR NAMES—THE ANGEL WHO APPREHENDS HIM—A LITERAL TRANSACTION—THE ECONOMY OF THE UNDERWORLD—THE WORD "HELL," SHEOL, HADES—CHRIST'S DESCENT INTO HELL—HADES NO LONGER THE ABODE OF DEPARTED SAINTS—"ABADDON," THE ABYSS—TARTARUS—GEHENNA—THE BEAST AND FALSE PROPHET IN GEHENNA—SATAN IMPRISONED IN THE ABYSS—OBJECT OF HIS IMPRISONMENT —SATAN NOT BOUND AT THE COMMENCEMENT OF THE CHRISTIAN ERA, NOR AT THE CONVERSION OF CONSTANTINE, IS LOOSE NOW.

REV. 20 : 1–3. (Revised Text.) And I saw an angel coming down out of the heaven, having the key of the abyss, and a great chain in [or *resting upon*] his hand. And he laid hold on the dragon, the old serpent, which is the devil, and satan, and bound him a thousand years, and cast him into the abyss, and locked and sealed [it] upon him, that he should not lead astray the nations any more until the thousand years be accomplished : after these he must be loosed a little time.

THE issue of the battle of the Great Day goes beyond the disaster to those found in arms against the Sitter on the white horse. There is another and still greater power back of those armies, by whose instigation this war was undertaken, by whose influence these kings and mighty ones with their troops were deceived into the fatal idea of conquering the King of kings and Lord of lords, and by whose malignant cunning they were marched into the winepress of the wrath of God. The judgment, therefore, proceeds to deal with this chief culprit.

He is called by four names, the same that were given him in chapter 12 : 9. The Sitter on the white horse also had four names ; and as in his case, so here, the names describe the being who wears them. He is called "*the Dragon.*" This is his designation with particular reference to his connection with earthly sovereignties and his administrations through the political world-powers, which, up to this great day, are continually contemplated in the Scriptures as the Dragon powers. But when these kings and their armies fall, the Dragon power ceases. Though the same evil spirit comes up again after the thousand years, he comes with only two of his four names, and not as "the Dragon ;" for he never again gets possession of the sovereignty of the earth. Christ and his saints reign on the earth from this time forth forever ; so that whoever those may be whom Satan then deceives and brings into rebellion, they are not the governors, kings, and rulers of the earth. They are from its distant corners, not its great central administrations. He is the Dragon now, as he ever has been since the days of Nimrod, and as he ever will be till the confederated kings of the earth meet their final fall at Harmageddon ; and he is "the Dragon " with particular reference to the relation which he holds to this world's political powers.

He is further called "*the Old Serpent ;*"—"old" in allusion to the fact that he has been in existence since the beginning of human history ; and "*the Serpent*" in allusion to his subtlety, his crooked and deceiving ways, his subtle poisons, and his deadly malignity. It was as the serpent that he beguiled our first parents and seduced them into sin and death. It is as the serpent that he deceives souls, insinuates false doctrine, unbelief, and presumption into the human heart, corrupts the purity of the Church, and deludes men with a false and perverted wisdom. It refers, particularly, to his subtle temptations of the good. Since the days of Adam's innocence in Eden, and on to the glorious Epiphany of his great Conqueror, he fulfils this particular designation ; but it does not appear that he ever comes up again in that

precise capacity. The good are thenceforward beyond the power of temptation, and the deception by which he finally brings Gog and Magog against the
citadel of the saints does not seem to be of the sort which he now practises as
" the old Serpent." He is still the same evil spirit as to his individuality, but
his particular serpentine manifestation seems to cease with the present order
of things, the same as his Draconic manifestation. Only as " *the Devil and
Satan* " does he reappear at the end of the thousand years.

The word *Devil* means a slanderer, a calumniator, a malignant liar ; and
this has been one of this evil spirit's chief characteristics from the beginning.
His first suggestions to Eve were full of base aspersions cast upon God, and
burdened with all manner of ruinous falsehood.   Hence the Saviour says :
" He was a murderer from the beginning, and abode not in the truth ; when
he speaketh a lie, he speaketh of his own ; for he is a liar, and the father of
it." (Jno. 8 : 44.) This is his essential character, the same everywhere and
always.   And as a murderous liar, calumniator, slanderer, and author of
malignant untruth, he comes up again subsequent to the thousand years.
The lie is his deepest nature, and it is that which makes him in bad pre-
eminence " *the Devil.*"

Satan means an adversary, an accuser. It is a Hebrew word simply transferred. It is mostly used as a proper name of some great spirit of evil. It is
used in this sense about forty times in the Scriptures. It denotes one who
lies in wait to entrap, to oppose, to disable, to bring under condemnation or
into disaster. And such the evil one has ever shown himself. So he accused
and opposed God at the beginning. So he accused Job and sought to destroy
his peace. So he assailed Christ, questioning his divine Sonship and power,
if not proven to him as he chose to dictate. And so he is the adversary of all
the children of God, and still stands as their accuser before God, even when
the time comes for their birth to immortal glory. In this character he also
reappears after the thousand years, stirs up enmity to God's holy people,
and instigates an attack upon their citadel.

It is in all these particular aspects that this great spirit of evil was concerned
in bringing about this war against the Sitter on the white horse and his army.
It was first and principally as " the Dragon," operating with and through the
political powers ; for he gave the Beast his power, throne, and great authority,
and sent the lying spirits to influence the kings of the earth in this fatal
business. It was next as " the Old Serpent," beguiling, deceiving, and leading
into the wickedest unbelief and false faith.   It was furthermore as " the
Devil," calumniating and blaspheming God and Christ, all true worship, and
all rightful divine authority. And it was finally as " Satan," the malignant
adversary and opponent of God and all good, disputing his right to reign, and
bent on defeating his becoming the King of the earth.   And as this great
spirit was thus the life and soul of all this tremendous rebellion against the
Son of God, the anointed All-Ruler, it was impossible that he should be
permitted to escape, or to remain at liberty, when the Warrior King and
Judge comes forth to enforce his royal rights.

We accordingly read of an Angel from heaven advancing to dispose of this
old, malignant, and subtle Deceiver. Who this Angel is, we are not told. The
particulars would seem to indicate, as many able commentators have concluded, that he is the Lord Jesus Christ himself. It was Christ who, in the
first vision, claimed to have " the Keys of Hades and of Death," which
would most naturally seem to include " the Key of the Abyss," which this
Angel possesses. The whole achievement of this victory is also so emphatically
ascribed to the Saviour himself, that it would seem incongruous, if not conflicting, to make the arrest of the chief of all this dreadful antagonism the
work of a created Angel. The mere fact of the angelic appearance argues
nothing against its being Christ himself, for we have seen him appearing
several times already in the character of an Angel. (Comp. chap. 10 : 1–7 ;
14 : 18, 19 ; 18 : 1.) When he comes to vanquish and destroy armies, it is

fitting that he should appear as a mighty Warrior ; but when he appears for
the seizure and binding of a fallen angel, it is equally fitting that he should
appear as an Angel.   His appearances continually vary according to the
work to be done, and all things considered, we would most naturally expect
that this particular act would be done in the character of an Angel.   The
point is of no great consequence either way ; for it is still the act of Christ,
and part of his victory, whether done by himself or by a created angel.   It was
Michael the Archangel who fought Satan in the battle in heaven (chap. 12 :
7), but that was rather a *forensic* contest.   This is a different work, the grasping
of the Devil's person, the chaining of him, and the casting of him into prison.
This Angel possesses the Key of the Abyss, and carries a great chain.   He
lays hold on the Dragon, the Old Serpent, which is the Devil and Satan,
binds him with the chain, casts him into the Abyss, and locks and seals him
in, that he may no more delude the nations for a thousand years.

Is this a literal transaction ?   Certainly it is.   The battle is literal ;   the
taking of the Beast and the False Prophet is literal ;   the slaying of the kings
and their armies is literal ;   Satan is literal ;   and his binding must be equally
literal.   It will not resolve itself into anything else, and fit to the connections
or the terms.   Some have asked, with an air of triumph, How can a chain of
iron or brass bind a spirit, and that spirit an archangel ?   But the record does
not say that it is a chain of iron, or brass, or steel, or any other material of
earthly chains.   It is a chain of divine make, as the sword that proceeds from
the mouth of the Son of God.   It is a spirit-chain, as the horses of the celestial
army are spirit-horses.   It is a chain of a character that can bind spirit and
fetter angels.   Jude tells of such chains, actually holding now (Jude 6), and
which not even the angels can break.   What they are made of, and how they
serve to bind the freedom of spiritual natures, it is not for us to know or show ;
but they are not therefore any less real and literal chains.   Figures, tropes, and
shadows cannot bind anybody, unless it be some commentators, who seem to
be hopelessly entangled in them.   The abyss is a reality, and the chain is also
a reality, or it is not what inspiration says it is.   It is called " a *great* chain ; "
and " great " it must be to hold and confine the great Red Dragon.   But it is
adequate to its purpose.   Heaven makes no miscalculations.   It is fastened
on the limbs of the old monster.   He cannot resist it, nor shake it off.
Archangel as he is, he is compelled to submit, bound as a helpless prisoner, and
violently cast into his dungeon, there to lie in his fetters for a decade of
centuries.

The place into which Satan is cast is called ἄβυσσος, *the Abyss*.   This is a
different place from that into which the Beast and the False Prophet are cast.
They were thrown into " the lake of fire which burneth with brimstone."
The Devil, after the thousand years, is also cast into that same burning
lake (chap. 19: 10) ; but here he is cast into " *the Abyss*," whence the
Beast came (chap. 17 : 8), and also the terrible plague of the spirit-locusts.
(Chap. 9 : 1–3.)

The question thus arises, What is the difference between " the Abyss " and
" the lake of fire ? " I might answer truly, that " the lake of fire " is the final
Hell, the place of the eternal punishment of the damned ; whilst " the Abyss "
is a sort of fore-hell, a prison in which evil spirits are detained prior to their
final judgment.   The relation between the two is much like that of the county
gaol in which accused criminals are detained prior to their sentence, and the
state penitentiary to which they are assigned for final punishment.   But, as
the question calls up the whole economy of the underworld, about which the
Scriptures tell us more than is generally suspected or understood, it may be
proper and desirable to look a little deeper into the matter.

In general, people have very dim, confused and inadequate ideas with
regard to the whole unseen world.   This is owing in part to the reserve of the
Scriptures on the subject, but more particularly to the obscuration of what is
revealed by the faulty manner in which our English translators, though

generally so correct, have dealt with the words and phrases of the sacred writers referring to this particular subject, begetting erroneous impressions, which reappear in our theological systems. Thus the word *Hell*, which in the Saxon vocabulary means simply the covered or unseen place, is used as the equivalent of words of very different signification, whilst those for which it is properly the equivalent are frequently rendered by other words which carry the mind quite aside from the real meaning. And so again, in popular language, the word *Hell* is carried away from its etymological signification, and made to stand for the place of final punishment, with which all other terms referring to the hidden abodes of wicked spirits are again confounded, whilst some of the original terms for which it is made to stand do not refer to the place of final punishment at all. The whole matter has thus become most sadly confused, involving in that confusion the article of the Creed respecting Christ's descent into Hell, and urgently needing to be unravelled and set right according to the true ideas of Revelation and of the early Church.

There is a word used sixty-five times in the original Hebrew of the Old Testament, which our English translators in thirty-one instances render *Hell*, in thirty-one instances *Grave*, and in three instances *the pit*. That word is *Sheol*, uniformly rendered *Hades* in the Greek of the Old Testament, and wherever the New Testament quotes the passages in which it occurs. By common consent the Greek word *Hades* is the exact equivalent of the Hebrew *Sheol*. It occurs eleven times in the New Testament, and always in the same sense as the Old Testament *Sheol*. To all intents and purposes, therefore, Sheol and Hades denote one and the same thing. But Sheol or Hades is never used to denote the Hell of final punishment. Neither is it ever used to denote the mere receptacle of the body after death, the grave. Nor yet is it ever used to denote the mere state of being dead as to the body ; and still less to denote *the pit* or *Abyss* as such. A careful inventory of all the passages conclusively proves that Sheol or Hades is the name of *a place* in the unseen world, altogether distinct from the Hell of final punishment or the Heaven of final glory. Its true and only meaning is " *the place of departed spirits,*"—the receptacle of souls which have left the body.* To this place all departed spirits, good and bad, up to the time of the resurrection of Christ, went. In it there was a department for the good, called *Paradise* by the Saviour on the cross, and another department for the bad. Thus both the rich man and Lazarus went to Hades when they died ; for the word is, " *in Hades* he lifted up his eyes, and seeth Abraham afar off and Lazarus in his bosom." Lazarus was then in Hades too, as well as Abraham ; and the only difference between them and Dives was, that the good were separated from the bad by an impassable gulf, and that Lazarus was comforted and Dives tormented.† So the dying Saviour told the penitent malefactor that they would yet that day be together *in Paradise ;* that is, in the more favourable part of Hades. There they were neither in Heaven proper, nor in Hell proper ; but simply in *Hades*. To this *Hades* all departed spirits went, the good with the good, and the bad with

---

* " Translating the word *Hades*, according to its etymology and its use among the Greeks, it is rendered an invisible place, which was all that Homer intended when he said the souls of his brave heroes were hurried, by the Trojan war, into Hades, where he exhibits them celebrating the Elysian games. The fathers, therefore, condemn the language of our translation (of the New Testament), and in the article of what is called the Apostles' Creed, which says Christ descended into *Hell*, misleading the vulgar by an English word, which *now* conveys an idea not contained in the original. This is so well known as to require no argument ; but so little regarded as to demand repeated protest."—*Bennett's Theology of the Early Christian Church*, pp. 323, 324.

" I cannot give a better periphrasis of it (the word *Hades*) than by translating it, *that invisible place where the souls that leave their bodies live*, whether it be a place of bliss or torment. In this sense it is taken in Scripture, the Apocrypha, Fathers, yea, and in heathenish authors too. And as for the Latin *inferi*, it is often taken in the same sense, and mostly used to express *Hades*."—*Beveridge on the XXXIX Arts.*, pp. 115, 116.

† " Lazarus in *Hades* obtained comfort in Abraham's bosom ; the rich man, on the other hand, the torment of flame."—*Tertullian, De Idol.* 13.

the bad.   There was comfort there for the pious, and privation and torment for the wicked ; and they of the one part could not pass over to the other part ; but still they could see and converse with each other, and none of them were yet in their final happiness or misery.   Even at the best, it was not a place to be coveted.   With all the blessed release which it brought to pious sufferers, and the good promise it bespoke of something better for them at the resurrection, the Scriptures everywhere describe it as a sombre world,—a place of detention and waiting even for the best.   There is nothing ever said about going up to it, or of full compensation there for works of piety and deeds of love.   The ancient saints drew satisfaction from the thought of being gathered to their fathers, and of resting there with the holy dead ; but never as enjoying there the bright presence of God and the society of angels.   All the higher and better recompenses to which they looked, they invariably connected with the resurrection, and located quite beyond the Hadean world.   It is to the Paradise side of this Hades that the Saviour and the penitent thief went when they died, as all the pious dead up to that time.

But this going of Christ into the place of departed spirits with the penitent thief was not the descent into Hades of which the Creed speaks.   By virtue of having died, Christ thus became an inmate of Hades, just as all other good men who had died before him ; whilst the descent into Hades, of which the Creed speaks, was part of his active redemption work, and the beginning of his exaltation as the successful Redeemer, which wrought a great change in Hades itself, and in the whole condition of the pious dead from that time on.   His dead body having been requickened and glorified by his divine power, recalling his departed soul to it, even before he reappeared on earth, he went to Hades, not as a subject of death, but as the Conqueror of death, heralding his victory to the spirits therein detained (I Pet. 3 : 18, 19), and actually bringing out with him all faithful souls, even resurrecting many of them.   (Matt. 27 : 52, 53 ; Ps. 68 : 18.)   It is with special reference to this, that he announced himself to John, in the first vision, as having " the Keys of Death and of Hades."   Paradise now is no longer in Hades, but above, in the heavens, where its inmates enjoy a far more blessed portion than was ever enjoyed in Hades.   Christ " led captivity captive " when he made his triumphant descent into Hades of which the Creed speaks, and no true believer now ever goes to Hades.   Christ said of his Church, that the gates of Hades should never prevail against it ; that is, it should never close on any true members of his Church.   Paul, in triumphant exultation over the portion of believers now, exclaims : " O Death where is thy sting ?   *O Hades, where is thy victory ?* "

The " grave " holds the victory now just as it ever has done, but Hades does not ; and the victory of which the Apostle speaks and gives thanks is a victory over Hades, not over the " *grave* " as our translators have put it.   Hence our Confession says, " Christ descended into Hades, *and abolished it for all believers.*"   (*Formula of Con.*)*   Hades now is, therefore, the receptacle of

---

* Speaking of the several opinions concerning the descent of Christ into Hades, and the efficacy of it, Bishop Pearson makes this observation : " Of those who did believe the name of *Hades* to belong to that general place which comprehended all the souls of men, as well those who died in the favour of God as those who departed in their sins, some of them thought that Christ descended to that place of *Hades*, where the souls of all the faithful, from the death of the righteous Abel to the death of Christ, were detained ; and there dissolving all the power by which they were detained below, translated them into a far more glorious place, and estated them in a condition far more happy in the heavens above."   Pearson did not himself accept this view, which is so evidently that of the Scriptures, still he adds this testimony concerning it : " This is the opinion generally received in the schools, and delivered as the sense of the Church of God in all ages ; but though it were not so general as the schoolmen would persuade us, yet it is certain that many of the fathers did so understand it."   He then quotes Eusebius, Cyril, Ambrose, and Jerome in evidence of this fact.

The same author quotes Justin Martyr, Irenæus, Tertullian, Hillary, Gregory of Nyssa, and others, as holding and teaching that the souls of believers do not enter heaven immediately upon their death, but go into the bosom of Abraham, into Paradise, where the patriarchs and prophets are, where they all remain till the time of the resurrection, when first they get their crowns, and enter upon the fulness of their blessedness.   But the place

only such departed spirits as have no share in Christ's redemption,—a mere prison of bad and unbelieving souls, who there pine over their crimes, awaiting the day of judgment, when all in Hades, and Hades itself, shall be cast into the Hell of final punishment. (Chap. 20 : 14.) Sheol or Hades then is not *Hell*, except in the old and now obsolete sense of *the covered place*, the hidden temporary receptacle of departed spirits, into which *all* departed souls formerly went at death, but since Christ's resurrection only the bad and unbelieving go.*

The Old Testament speaks of another place in the underworld, called in Hebrew *Abaddon* (Greek *Apoleia*), which our English Bible renders *destruction*. Thus we read " Hades is naked before him, and *Abaddon* hath no covering." (Job 26 : 6.) " *Abaddon* and death say, We have heard the fame thereof." (Job 28 : 22.) " It is a fire that consumeth to *Abaddon*." (Job 31 : 12.) " Shall thy loving kindness be declared in the grave, or thy faithfulness in *Abaddon* ? " (Ps. 88 : 12.) " Hades and *Abaddon* are ever before the Lord." (Prov. 15 : 11.) " Hades and *Abaddon* are never full." (Prov. 27 : 20.) Abaddon thus connects with Sheol or Hades, but is a deeper, darker, and a more wretched place. " The pit of the Abyss," referred to in chapter 9 : 1–3, and from which came the plague of spirit-locusts, seems to identify with this Hebrew Abaddon ; for the angel of this pit, and the King over these locusts, has a name " which in the Hebrew tongue is *Abaddon*, but in the Greek tongue hath his name Apollyon." Nine times do we read of this *Abyss* in the New Testament. The demons, whom Christ cast out of the wretched man of Gadara, besought the Saviour not to command them into *the Abyss*. (Luke 8 : 26–31.) Paul says that our faith needs not to inquire " Who shall descend into *the Abyss*, that is, to bring Christ up again from among the dead " (Rom. 10 : 7), as if he were only one of the more powerful of these demons. Thus also the great Beast, the Antichrist, cometh up out of *the Abyss* (Rev. 11 : 7 ; 17 : 8.) Abaddon and the Abyss would therefore seem to be the abode of demons, a sort of deeper pit beneath Hades, where the wickeder and baser spirits of dead men, and other foul spirits of the lower orders, are for the most part held as melancholy prisoners till the day of final judgment. It is a place intermediate between Hades and the final Hell, as Paradise is now a sort of intermediate place between Hades and the final Heaven. It is a remove below Hades, as Paradise is now a remove above Hades.

It does not appear that fallen angels now have their place in Hades. The Lucifer of whom Isaiah (14 : 15) speaks as having been " brought down to *Hades* " is explained (verse 4) to be the king of Babylon, and so a bad man, and not an angel. Fallen angels are never said to be in Hades. The place of their present detention is described by quite another name. Thus Peter tells us that " God spared not the angels that sinned, but cast them down to *Tartarus*, and delivered them into chains of darkness to be reserved unto

where departed saints now are, or go at their death, is plainly no longer in *Hades ;* for when Paul in vision was taken to behold that place, the action or motion which took him to it from the earth is described as an *ascent*,—" he was caught *up to Paradise* " (2 Cor. 12 : 4),— whereas the action or motion describing the entrance into *Hades*, even for the saints, is everywhere represented as a *descent*. Not only is it declared that Korah and his company " *went down* alive into Hades," or Sheol, but Jacob said, " I will *go down* into Hades unto my son." (Gen. 37 : 35.) So also Samuel, after his death, and in his rest, said, " Why hast thou disquieted me to *bring me up ?* " (1 Sam. 28 : 15.) And so of Jesus, when he went to that place, it is said he " *descended* into the lower parts of the earth." (Eph. 4 : 9.) Paradise then was below in Hades ; now, since the resurrection of Christ, it is above, in the heavenly regions, and no longer in Hades. Thus Basil, Cyprian, and Ambrose speak of Paradise now as a place of rest *in heaven*, in which the pious are, but still not in heaven, in the same way as they shall be after the resurrection.

* From these representations of the economy of the underworld, which are the result of a more matured study of the whole subject, some obvious modifications are required to the statements made previously, which were written some fourteen years prior to the writing of this Lecture. I then believed that all departed souls went to Hades, whereas, it is now plain to me that, since the resurrection of Christ, none of the souls of the saints ever go there, as they did previously. When a man has learned better, it is due that he should be allowed to correct himself.

P

judgment." (2 Pet. 2 : 4.) Our translators also call Tartarus *Hell*, as if Tartarus, Hades, the Abyss, and the final lake of fire were all one and the same thing. The truth is, that they are each distinct and separate, though all departments of the underworld.

The burning lake is the only true *Apoleia*, perdition, destruction, second death, or the final *Hell*. It too has its own proper name. It is called *Tophet* in the Old Testament. (Is. 30 : 33 ; Jer. 7 : 31, 32.) In the New it is twelve times called *Gehenna*, which, in the Greek, is the same as Tophet in Hebrew. From denoting a place of horrible burning on earth, it came to be used to denote the place of final punishment. Our translators have uniformly translated Gehenna by the word *Hell*. But Gehenna is altogether a different Hell from Sheol, Hades, the Abyss, or Tartarus. Thus the Saviour says, that whosoever indulges malignant and devilish spite towards his brother " shall be in danger of *Gehenna* fire " (Matt. 5 : 22) ; that it is much better to sacrifice a right eye or a right hand in this world than that " the whole body should be cast into *Gehenna* " (Matt. 5 : 29, 30) ; that we are not to fear them which kill the body, but rather to fear him " who is able to destroy both soul and body in *Gehenna* (Matt. 10 : 28) ; and that " it is better to enter into life with one eye, than having two eyes to be cast into *Gehenna* fire." (Matt. 18 : 9.) Thus also he denounces the hypocritical Pharisees as the candidates for " the greater damnation," the " children of *Gehenna* " (Matt. 23 : 14, 15), and asks them, " How can ye escape the damnation of *Gehenna* ? " (Matt. 23 : 33.) This Tophet or Gehenna, as will be seen at once, is something different from Hades, Tartarus, or the Abyss. It is manifestly the same which John here calls "*the lake of fire which burneth with brimstone*," and into which the Beast, the False Prophet, Satan, Death, Hades, and whosoever is not found written in the book of life, are finally cast, and swallowed up forever ; that is, it is the ultimate Hell of full punishment.

Into this final Hell no one has yet ever entered. It is " prepared for the Devil and his angels ; " but none of them is there now. The first persons that ever go into this place are the Beast and the False Prophet, at the time of the battle of the great day of God Almighty. (Chap. 19 : 20.) The next to get into it is Satan himself, more than a thousand years afterwards (chap. 20 : 10), where the Beast and the False Prophet are represented as still alive and suffering at the time when he is cast in with them. And then follows the casting of all the wicked, along with Death and Hades. (Chap. 20 : 14, 15.)

It is not a little surprising that things should come out so clearly from the original Scriptures, and that there should be such confusion on the subject in the popular mind, and even in our theologies. But in the light of what I have thus briefly indicated, any one can readily see the consistency and propriety of all these terms and references touching the underworld, and what is meant by the different places from which or to which these infernal actors either come or go. The Beast is from the Abyss, the under-pit of Hades, as twice distinctly stated. The False Prophet, his companion and prime minister, is doubtless from the same place. Under the fifth Trumpet, " the Key of the Abyss " was given to the fallen star, which is none other than Satan, and he unlocks the Abyss for the bringing up of the spirit-locusts, and then for the bringing forth in Satanic resurrection from thence these two great instruments of his malice and deception, the Beast and the False Prophet. It is not in the Devil's power thus to resurrect any one from the Abyss now ; but in the ongoing of the judgment, and for the greater punishment of the unbelieving, the power is given him to do it, and he does it. He is allowed to have " the Key," and he uses it, unlocks the Abyss, and brings forth again into the activities of life the two ablest of his particular servants. They go through with their blasphemous and dreadful work in judgment upon the world for its unbelief. And when the end comes, they are at once cast into the final Hell, the very first that ever try those awful fires, which they so richly deserve. The kings and armies whom they deceive into this presumptuous war are mortal men, who are simply

" slain,"—*killed*,—and so turned into Hades, there, with the wicked dead, to await the judgment at the end of the thousand years, when they all shall be brought forth together, and assigned their place in the same final Hell of the burning lake.　The old Serpent, the Devil, who has been at the back of it all, is arrested and imprisoned.　But there is still a reason in the divine purposes why he should not yet be finally disposed of ; therefore he is not yet cast into the burning lake of ultimate perdition.　Nevertheless, he is chained as to his power, and locked and sealed up as to his place, in that under-pit of Hades, where only the foulest and basest of spirits are,—in the Abyss whence he brought up the two Beasts and their demon helpers,—there to writhe in his helplessness till the thousand years are fulfilled.

The particular object of this binding and imprisonment of Satan is not so much for his due punishment, as for the temporary restraint and prevention of his deceptions of men.　It is specially stated to be, " *that he should not lead astray the nations any more until the thousand years be accomplished.*"　Ruinous deception is the Devil's trade and all false ones and deceivers are his apprentices and children.　The truth is ever against him ; therefore falsehood is his particular recourse and instrument.　But naked falsehood is only repulsive.　What we know to be a lie cannot command our respect.　" In vain is the net spread in the sight of any bird."　There is in the very framework of the soul an impossibility of feeling toward known falsehood the same as if it were truth.　The structure of our being revolts against it.　Untruth can only gain credence and acceptance by being so disguised as to appear to be the truth.　Falsehood can have no power over us until we are led to believe and conclude that it is the truth.　And this deluding of men, getting them to accept and follow lies and false hopes, under the persuasion that they are accepting and following truth, is the great work and business of Satan in every age.　From this work and business he never rests so long as he has the liberty to act.　In this work and business he has been engaged from the beginning.　And in this work and business he is engaged now ; for his binding and imprisonment do not occur until after " the Battle of the great Day of God Almighty," and that battle has not yet come off.

Some assume and teach that this binding and imprisonment of Satan occurred at the opening of the Christian dispensation, and point to the miracles wrought by the Apostles and early Christians, the silencing of the Pagan oracles, and the onward march of the Church to political victory over Paganism, as the evidence of it.　But then the inspired Peter was all wrong ; for he sent out a general Epistle to all Christians, in which he wrote : " Your adversary the Devil, as a roaring lion, *walketh about*, seeking whom he may devour."　(1 Pet. 5 : 8.)

Others assume and teach that this binding and imprisonment of Satan occurred at the conversion of Constantine and the consequent triumph of Christianity over Pagan Rome.　But that event was followed by a millennium of corruption and apostasy for the Church, and of darkness and barbarism for the world, far worse than had occurred during the thousand years before ; whilst the termination of the thousand years after Constantine brought a period the brightest in evangelic purity and activity, and the most triumphant for truth and constitutional liberty, that has ever been since Constantine occupied the imperial throne.

Still others assume and teach that, to whatever date we are to refer this binding and imprisonment of Satan, he is bound now, because imperialism in government has been wellnigh banished from the earth, and hierarchism in the Church is quite disabled from its old dominion, and general intelligence and freedom are becoming the common possession of the race.　I wonder that there should be sane men who can come to such a conclusion.　If ever there was a time when the Devil was loose, active and potent in human affairs, *that time is now*, in the days in which we live.　The Devil's dominion is the enthronement of error, falsehood, deception, lies, and moral rottenness ; and when was this dominion ever more patent than in these years of the existing generation ? The Devil bound ! And yet the people who claim to be most enlightened, and occupy the very top waves of modern progress, do not hesitate to give out that it is with them a matter of serious doubt whether there is a God, a Providence, a soul to live after this life, anything eternal but matter, any Lord but Nature, any retribution but what natural laws administer in this world, any principles of morality but expediency, and scout all idea of a personal incarnation of Diety, of atonement by divine sacrifice, of justification by faith in the merits of a substitute, of any coming again of Christ as King to judge the world and reign in righteousness. We look abroad upon society in general, and what do we see ? Reverence, that great balance-wheel in the economies of life, scarcely exists any more ; oaths are nothing ; good faith is scarce as grapes after the vintage ; and all moral bonds are trampled down without compunction under the heels of greed, and lust, and deified selfishness. Falsities and treacheries confront us unblushingly at every point. People not only make falsehoods, speak falsehoods, print falsehoods, and believe falsehoods ; but they eat them, and drink them, and wear them, and act them, and live them, and make them one of the great elements of their being. One-half, at least, of all that the eye can see, or the ear hear, or the hands touch, or the tongue taste, is bogus, counterfeit, pinchbeck, shoddy, or some hash or other of untruth. A man cannot move, or open his eyes, without encountering falsehood and lies. In business, in politics, in social life, in professions, and even in what passes for religion, such untruthfulness reigns, that he who would be true scarcely knows any more whom to trust, what to believe, how to move, or by what means to keep his footing, amid the ever-increasing flood of unreality and deception. And yet the Devil is bound ! Do I colour the picture too deeply ? Look, consider, and see for yourselves. Is not the world full of people, many of them your neighbours and personal acquaint-ances, some of them under your own roofs, in your own homes,—people with their apostles, male and female, on the rostrum everywhere with applauding crowds around them,—people to whom the Church is a lie ; the ministers of the Gospel, a fraud ; the sacraments, absurdity ; prayer, a weak delusion ; the Bible, a dull record of superannuated beliefs ; special providence, an impossibility ; a personal God or Devil, a superstitious conceit ; moral accountability to a future judgment, a thing to be laughed at ; society, marriage, and the body of our laws, mere faulty conventionalities ; government a mere device of the ambitious and self-seeking ; immortality, a mere fiction ; and even life itself, something of an impertinent imposition, or a mere freak of mother Nature ! And with such ideas afloat, and swaying the hearts and minds of the multitude as the new Gospel of advanced thought and human progress, *what is truth ? Where* is it ? On what are we to rest ? How find a foundation to build on for anything ? To such a philosophy, what is not a lie, a perversion, a delusion, a superstition, a cheat ? And, on the other hand, if our Gospel be true ; if what the Bible says of God, and Christ, and the nature and destiny of man, is indeed reality ; was there ever a more subtle, more specious, more potent, more Satanic deception and misleading of the race, than that which the wiseacres and savants of our time would thus palm upon our world ? And yet the Devil is bound ! By what eccentricity of the human intellect, or freak of human intelligence, or stultification of man's common-sense, could such all-revolutionizing and infernal falsehood find place on earth, and pass current for the true and higher wisdom, but for the living presence and effective operations of that old Deceiver who cheated our first parents out of Paradise, beguiled the early world to its destruction in Noah's flood, and is now engaged preparing the way for his favourite son to captivate all the great powers of the earth to their inevitable damnation !

No, no, my friends ; the Devil, that old Serpent, is not bound. He is loose. He ranges at large, with his ten thousand emissaries, all the more active and earnest in his Satanic schemes as he seeth that his time is short. He has his nests and conventicles in every city, town, and hamlet all over the world, labelled with all sorts of attractive and misleading names.   Clubs, institutes, circles, societies, conventions, lyceums, and a thousand private coteries, under show of investigating science, improving knowledge, inquiring into truth, and cultivating the mind, free from the disturbing influences of sect, religion, tradition, and old fogy notions,—these are among the common machinery through which he instils his deceits and subtle poisons.   A broader philosophy, a more compliant church, a more active humanity disdaining dogmas and positive creeds, a larger liberality to take every one for a child of God who refrains from denouncing the devilish atheisms and heresies of the times,— these are the flags he hangs out for the rallying of his unsuspecting dupes. And see how he induces men and women to usurp ministerial functions without ministerial responsibilities, and gives them power on the plea of breaking down denominationalism and making better saints without any church at all ; how he prostitutes the pulpits to entertaining sensationalisms, defying all sense and sacred decency, or narrows them down to sweet platitudes which serve to bury the true Gospel from those whom it was meant to save,—and how he stirs up Christian ministers of place and influence to say and make believe that all this attention to sacred prophecy is nothing but a stupid craze, that the holy writers never meant just what they said, and that all these ill-bodings touching the destiny of this present world are but the croakings of birds that love to fly in storms !   And yet he is bound !   O, ye people, on your way to the nearing judgment of the great Day, " Be not deceived ; God is not mocked."   You may be sincere, but that is not enough.   Eve thought she was innocent and safe when she took the Devil's recommendation of the forbidden fruit ; but her trustful confidence did not excuse her.   No delusion can serve to justify before God.   No tricks or disguises can impose on him.   He will be true though that truth should make every man a liar.   His old and everlasting Word must stand till every jot and tittle of it be fulfilled.   The existence of a Devil is not a myth, but an awful reality, and to his doings and destiny we have other relations than that of mere spectators.   His dread power over those who will not have Christ as their Saviour is not a nightmare fancy, or the dream of a disordered mental digestion, but a thing of living fact.   And these solemn and momentous Revelations are Jehovah's finger boards, set up in mercy along the path of human life, to point out the places of danger and the way of safety.   To despise, neglect, or disregard them is not a characteristic of wisdom.   To refuse to note and heed them, is to try the insane experiment of seeing how near you can graze the brink of perdition, and yet win the credit of not tumbling in.   Can you be wiser than God who made you?   Then mark the signals he has given, and follow them implicitly.

REV. 20 : 4–5. (Revised Text.) And I saw thrones, and they sat upon them, and judgment [the power of judging] was given to them.

And (I saw) the souls of them who had been beheaded on account of the testimony of
Jesus, and on account of the word of God, and [of those] who did not worship the beast nor
yet his image, and did not receive the mark on [their] forehead and on their hand ; and they
lived (= lived again) and reigned with the Christ a thousand years.

The rest of the dead ones lived not (*again*) until the thousand years be completed ; this
[being] the resurrection the first.

A RICH and magnificent revelation here comes before us.   Beautiful and
blessed contemplations would it also afford were it not for the noise and dust
of controversy which surrounds it.   Unfortunately it has become a battle-
ground of opposing schemes, not only of the interpretation of the Apocalypse,
but of the whole outcome of God's promises and man's redemption.   A war of
the theologians has hung upon it for centuries.   Hence it is seldom treated
otherwise than polemically, or with partisan bias.   Nor is it possible to touch
it at all without entering in some degree into the deep and far-reaching
controversy which here comes to its intensest and final tug.   It is a great pity
that it is so.   The effect is disastrous in many directions.   It turns multitudes
from looking at the subject.   It creates suspicions of any doctrines that seem to
depend on the passage in question.   It induces numbers to accept the
unwarranted conclusion that the whole thing is so mysterious, incomprehensible, and dark, that no light or spiritual edification is to be gained from it.   It
has led disputants into inventions, assertions, and ways of dealing with the
Divine Word, which, if consistently followed out, would undermine every
distinctive doctrine of Inspiration.   Nor is there, perhaps, another section of
holy Scripture the consideration of which so much needs the aid and guidance
of the Holy Ghost to keep the inquirer in balance and temper, to look and see
with unprejudiced eyes, and to form conclusions with sound and conscientious
regard to what has been written for our learning.   God help us in our handling
of the subject that we may rightly conceive, embrace, and rest on his own
everlasting truth !

I.

The first point to which I direct attention, and one too much overlooked, is
the connection of these presentations with the scenes and statements of the
preceding chapter.   We there saw the heaven opened, and the Lord of lords
and King of kings, with his risen and glorified saints, coming forth to meet the
Beast and his confederated kings and their armies in dreadful battle.   The
result was the taking and casting of the Beast and the False Prophet alive into
the final Hell, the slaying of the rest with the sword, and the chaining and
locking up of Satan in the prison of the Abyss.   But, in connection with these
administrations, it was said of the Sitter on the white horse, as it was said of
the Manchild in chap. 12 : 5, " *And he shall rule or shepherdize the nations with
a rod of iron.*" (Chap. 19 : 15.)   The repetition of this declaration renders it
particularly significant, and calls for our special attention.   The numerous
references to it in the Scriptures assign to it every element of a special
dispensation.

That it does not refer only, if at all, to the calamities inflicted on the Beast and his armies is clearly evident from the record.   The instrument of that infliction was not *a rod*, but is twice stated to be *the sharp sword*, proceeding from the mouth of the Sitter upon the white horse.   The effect in that instance was slaughter and death ; but *shepherdizing*, with whatever severity of judgment and invincible force, is not the taking of life.   The word ποιμαινω occurs often in the New Testament, but always in the sense of *feeding, tending, directing, and helping*, with a view to preservation, not destruction.   Thus Christ was fore-announced by the Father, as " a Governor that *shall shepherdize* (margin, *feed*) my people Israel."   (Matt. 2 : 6.)   So Christ speaks of one " having a servant ploughing or *feeding cattle*," literally, *shepherdizing*. (Luke 17 : 17.)   So his command to Peter was, " *Feed* (*shepherdize*) my sheep."   (Jno. 21 : 16.)   And so Paul said to the Elders at Miletum, " *Feed* (*shepherdize*) the Church of God."   (Acts 20 : 28 ; also 1 Pet. 5 : 2.)   In all these instances the word is used to express a gracious and merciful proceeding, the very contrary of slaughter and destruction.   And when it is here said of the King of kings that he (ποιμανεῖ) *shall shepherdize* the nations, even though it be " with an iron rod," we would do great violence to the word to interpret it of the slaying of the armies of the Antichrist.

Besides, this *shepherdizing* is a dealing with " *the nations* " as such ; whilst the subjects of the destruction at Harmageddon are not " the nations " as such but " the kings of the earth and their armies."   Kings may fall, and armies in the field of battle be destroyed, and the nations, or peoples to which they belong, still continue to exist.   The defeat and capture of Napoleon at Sedan did not extinguish the French people, or even the French nationality.   Had he and every French soldier perished on that field, France would still have remained ; though the conqueror might have followed up the victory, and given to the French quite other laws and institutions, and organized them under a new rule for an entirely new life.   In that case he would have done to and for the French something of what is implied in these terms as done to all nations by the Conqueror of the Beast and his armies.   The kings fall, and their armies are clean swept away, making an utter end of the Dragon dominion upon the earth ; but then comes the rod of iron in the hands of the Conqueror, to *shepherdize*, provide for, and put into new and better order, the home-peoples out from among whom these armies went into the disastrous field.   The battle of the Great Day of God Almighty is one thing ; the shepherdizing with the rod is another.   The two are closely connected.   They are both judgment administrations.   The one is the sequel to the other.   But they are wholly different in their immediate subjects, character, and results.   The one is temporary, the other is continuous.   The sword comes first, and strikes down the enemy in the field ; and then follows the shepherdizing with the rod of discipline and new rule over the peoples whose kings and armies are no more. The two together fulfil what is stated in Psalm 2 : 5–12, Isaiah 11, and Matt. 25 : 31–46, where the same rod power and shepherdizing are further described.

The Shepherdizer is the same who conquers in the battle with the Beast and his confederate kings.   He is the All-Ruler, and it is his power and dominion which are thus enforced with justice and with judgment.   But his army of glorified saints accompanies him. They follow him in his victorious treading down of his armed enemies.   They ride through the blood of his foes up to the horses' bridles.   They pursue the triumph with him.   And particularly in this shepherdizing with the rod of iron, the Scriptures everywhere assign *to them* a conspicuous share.   Hence the Psalmist sung ; " Let the saints be joyful in glory ; let them sing aloud upon their beds (resting-places).   Let the high praises of God be in their mouth, and a two-edged sword in their hand, *to execute vengeance upon the heathen, and punishments upon the people ; to bind their kings with chains, and their nobles with fetters of iron ; to execute upon them the judgment written :* THIS HONOUR HAVE ALL HIS SAINTS."   (Ps. 149.)

The same as also very pointedly declared by the Saviour himself.   To his twelve Apostles he said, that when he should sit in the throne of his glory, they also should " *sit upon twelve thrones, judging the twelve tribes of Israel.*" (Matt. 19 : 28.)   In the address to the Church at Thyatira, he said :　" He that overcometh, and he that keepeth my works unto the end, to him will I give *authority over the nations, and he shall shepherdize them with a rod of iron ; as a vessel of earthenware shall they be broken to shivers* AS I ALSO RECEIVED OF MY FATHER."　(Rev. 2 : 26, 27.)　If there were not another passage on the subject, this alone would be decisive of the point, that this shepherdizing of the nations is shared in by the saints in resurrection glory.　But there are other passages.　(See Dan. 7 : 26, 27 ; 1 Cor. 6 : 2, 3 ; Rev. 3 : 21.)　One particularly to the point is that in which it is said of the *Manchild*, born into immortality, and caught away to God and his throne, that he shall " *shepherdize all the nations with a rod of iron.*"　(Rev. 12 : 5.)　We have seen that this Manchild is a figure or symbol of the true Church, with Christ at its head, and that the birth and catching away to God is the resurrection and glorification of the saints with their Lord.*　No other consistent interpretation of that marvellous " sign " is at all possible.　And yet, to that Manchild, after its removal to glory, is assigned this very shepherdizing of the nations.

It is therefore scripturally certain that this ruling or shepherdizing with the rod of iron, which follows up the destruction of the armies of the Antichrist, is a thing in which the glorified saints have a very conspicuous part.

Where, then, in the apocalyptic chart do we find this very particular administration but in the grand vision now before us ?　As I have been led to view things, we have here the picture of the victorious Christ, with his enthroned and glorified saints, in the rule or shepherdizing of all the nations with a rod of iron, the same which is celebrated by the Psalmist, promised by Christ, and so distinctly affirmed in the description of the Manchild, as well as in the account of the coming forth of the Sitter on the white horse.

II.

With this view of the connection and *scope* of this vision, we pass to the more direct consideration of its presentations, every item of which goes to prove that this is the natural, true, and necessary conception of the whole matter.

John saw " *thrones.*"　Judicial or regal administrations imply seats of authority.　The Sitter on the white horse came *crowned.*　His shepherdizing of the nations is in his character as conquering King.　It is therefore, in its very nature, an administration of sovereign authority.　The saints share with him in it, as we have seen.　Hence the need for thrones, or royal seats, for these sovereign shepherdizers.　Daniel speaks of these same thrones.　He saw them set, and the going forth of authority from them, which is further described as the authority of one like a Son of man, to whom was given " dominion, glory, and a kingdom, that all people, nations, and languages should serve him."　(Dan. 7 : 9-14.)　They are the same of which the Saviour spoke to his twelve Apostles, and concerning which he has promised, " To him that overcometh will I give to sit with me on my throne, as I also overcame and sat down with my Father on his throne."　(Rev. 3 : 21.)

These are not empty seats.　John says : " *They sat upon them.*"　Who " *they* " are, seems to have troubled commentators to determine.　Some say " they " are the martyrs ; some say " they " are the spirits or disembodied souls of the martyrs ; some say " they " are the *principles* of the martyrs ; some say " they " are the men of that generation quickened from the death of sin and raised up to eminent zeal, saintship, and influence while yet living in mortal flesh ; some say " they " simply represent a more potent dominion of Christianity, the sway of the Gospel over the nations ; and some are entirely at a loss to say who " they " are.　But there must be something funda-

* See Lectures XXVI and XXVIII.

mentally wrong in men's theories of the Apocalypse as a whole, or they could not here be in such straits of uncertainty.

Surely the sitters on these thrones are those to whom this implied judicio-regal authority is everywhere promised. Nor are the passages few in which those promises are given. In the text itself it is expressly said that these sitters upon these thrones are " *priests of God and of Christ, and reign with him,*"—" *reign with Christ.*" But what attentive reader of the Bible does not know that God's chosen and anointed kings and priests are none other than his true and faithful people ? In the opening of this Book, John spoke of himself and fellow-Christians,—all who are freed from sin by Christ's blood,—as those whom God hath made kings and priests. (Chap. 1 : 5, 6.) The Living Ones and the Elders gave glory to the Lamb for making them " *kings and priests of God,*" destined to " reign on the earth." Who are they but glorified men, redeemed unto God by the blood of the Lamb " out of every tribe, and tongue, and people, and nation ? " (Rev. 5 : 9, 10.) These king-priests must therefore be God's ransomed people ; Peter pronounces his fellow-Christians " a chosen generation, a *royal priesthood,*" who, " when the *chief Shepherd* shall appear," for this shepherdizing of the nations, " shall receive a glorious crown." (1 Pet. 2 : 9 ; 5 : 4.)

To what did he thus refer but these very dignities, and to the true people of God as the inheritors of them ? Daniel, in vision, saw the judgment sit, and the dominion of the Beast taken away by the mighty power of God, and declares that then " *the Kingdom and dominion, and the greatness of the Kingdom under the whole heaven, shall be given to the people of the saints of the Most High.*" (Dan. 7 : 26, 27.) What did he mean but the very thing here beheld by John, and that the sitters on these thrones are the saints of God ? Paul wrote of " *a crown,*" for which he strove, which is to be the possession of all " good soldiers of Jesus Christ," and which the Lord, the righteous judge, would give him " at that day," and " unto *all them that love his appearing.*" (2 Tim. 2 : 3–5 ; 4 : 7, 8.) And so the Saviour himself exhorts his " little flock " not to fear, as it is the Father's good pleasure to give *them* the kingdom (Luke 12 : 32), enjoins upon his disciples to hold fast that no one take *their crown* (Rev. 3 : 11), and promises every faithful and good servant to " make him *ruler over all his goods* " (Matt. 24 : 46, 47). Is it also an inevitable principle, that the conquerors take the dominion ? The Sitter on the white horse conquers in the Battle of the Great Day, and by virtue of that triumph he becomes the Supreme King. But with him through all the mighty engagement were his glorified saints, in white apparel, on white horses, indicative of their character of associate *governors and judges.* (Judges 5 : 10.) With him in the fight, they are with him in the victory, and share the sovereignty which that victory secures. He conquers, and therefore reigns ; *they* conquer with him, and there-fore *they* " reign with him." Thus the sitters on these thrones are none other than Christ's saints whom John saw following their Lord when he came forth to make an end of the antichristian domination, and inaugurate his own shepherdizing of the nations.

Their sitting upon these thrones is not an empty show. As Christ's taking of the sovereignty of the earth is a sublime reality, so must that of his victorious people's participation in it also be. Nor are we left to gather this by mere inference. John says expressly that " *judgment was given to them,*"—κρῖμα,—*the act or power of judging,* including the forming of sentences and the execution of the same, as in Matt. 7 : 2 ; 19 : 28 ; Jno. 9 : 39 ; Rom. 2 : 2, 3 ; 1 Cor. 6 : 7. That is, as Alford remarks, " they were constituted judges." The work of shepherdizing the nations with a rod of iron necessarily involves intrust-ment with discretionary power to act ; and this is the office and power here said to be given to these sitters on these thrones.* The " judgment " which

---

* " The word κρῖμα in this clause may be interpreted as applying to the supervision or making of statutes, ordinances, arrangements, etc., by those who are in a superior station. This seems to many to be the most easy and natural construction."—Stuart, *in loc.*

they thus receive is otherwise expressed when it is said of them that they
"*reign*." The possession of the judging power is most intimately conjoined
with sovereignty, or the office of reigning. Thus "David *reigned* over all
Israel ; and David *executed judgment and justice* unto all the people." (2
Sam. 8 : 15.) Thus the Queen of Sheba said to Solomon : " The Lord made
thee *king*, to do judgment and justice." (1 Kings 10 : 9.) They are enthroned
kings and priests, and they are thus endowed with the prerogatives of the
regal office. They are to reign. They are to exercise the royal functions.
Therefore they get the power of judging and of executing judgment and justice,
which is the very office of the shepherdizing promised to the victorious
children of God, and so emphatically set forth in what was said of the particular destiny of the Manchild. Up to this time it is a matter of promise and
hope, but here it is made a matter of possession and actual fact,—a thing
finally reached and realized.

Once it was the fate of believers to be judged by the ungodly world-powers.
Jesus told his followers that they should be brought before councils, governors, and kings, and that time would come when men would think it a holy
thing to adjudge them worthy of stripes, imprisonment, and death. So Paul
stood before the courts of earth, saying : " *I stand and am judged*." But man's
day has a limit, and then comes another order, when, as Mary sung, God
" shall put down the mighty from their seats," and " exalt them of low
degree,"—when the Pauls shall be the royal judges, and the Felixes, and
Festuses, and Agrippas, and Cæsars, then in place, shall be obliged to accept
the sentences of heavenly justice from God's immortal potentates, who
once stood helpless at earth's tribunals ; for so it is written, " the saints shall
judge the world " (1 Cor. 6 : 2), and " shall take the Kingdom, and possess
the Kingdom forever, even forever and ever " (Dan. 7 : 18) ; and Christ, the
victorious All-Ruler, according to his promise, will " give them *authority
over the nations*, to shepherdize them with a rod of iron " (Rev. 2 : 26, 27),
invincibly and effectually.

Among those who suffer the greatest penalties and privations for their
faith are the holy martyrs and those who hold out faithful under the dreadful
Antichrist. When a man lays down his life for his Lord, he surrenders all that
he can surrender, and lets go what all the instincts of humanity lead one to
cling to to the last. Human law knows no heavier penalty than the taking of
a man's life ; and when this is accepted, rather than deny the Saviour or his
Word, the common world, as well as Christianity, takes it as the sublimest
testimony a man can give of his devotion. And when people consent to suffer
nakedness, banishment, and death, rather than make themselves guilty of an
act of homage to the Antichrist, it is a demonstration of steadfastness as
great as it is possible to furnish. Hence there is a somewhat special vision
vouchsafed to the Apocalyptic seer to indicate the rewards of such fidelities.
Not only does he behold the sitters on the thrones in general, and the giving
of judicial and royal authority to the body of the saints as a whole, but he is
particularly shown that the martyrs, and those who worship not the Beast,
are surely among them. Thus he tells us :

" *And (I saw) the souls of them who had been beheaded on account of the
testimony of Jesus, and on account of the word of God, and [of those] who did not
worship the beast nor yet his image, and did not receive the mark on [their] forehead and on their hand ; and they lived (= lived again) and reigned with the
Christ.*"

Whilst the body of the saints in general participate in these rewards, it is
thus shown that the martyrs in particular, together with the faithful ones of
the last evil time, are specially included. The martyrs and the faithful ones
under the Beast are not different parties from the sitters on the thrones, but
special classes specifically included. A somewhat parallel presentation occurs
in chapter 1 : 7, where it is said of the Saviour at his great Epiphany, that
" every eye shall see him, and they which pierced him." The meaning is not

that " they which pierced him " form a separate class apart from " every eye," but that even those who slew Christ shall also be among those denoted by " every eye," and that they too shall look upon him. It deserved to be thus noted specially that the murderers of Christ will have to confront him, as well as men in general ; and so here it deserved to be noted specially that the holy martyrs, and the faithful ones under the Antichrist, have their part and place with the sitters upon the thrones, and that they particularly are among those who reign with Christ.

Special notice of the martyrs in their disembodied state was taken in chapter 6 : 9. They were not enthroned then, but in depression, anxious for their final vindication. The record says : " When he opened the fifth seal, I saw beneath the altar the souls of those that had been slain on account of the Word of God, and on account of the testimony which they held fast : and they cried with a great voice, saying, Until when, thou Master, the holy and true, dost thou not judge and avenge our blood from them that dwell on the earth. And there was given to each of them a white robe, and it was said to them that they should rest yet a little time, until their fellow-servants also, and their brethren, shall have been completed, who are about to be slain as also they themselves had been." The very parties there spoken of are here specified as among the sitters upon the thrones ; to wit, the martyrs then under the altar, their fellow-servants who were subsequently to fall because of their refusal to worship the Beast. A necessity was thus begotten for some subsequent notice of them in connection with the final outcome for which they were told to wait. That notice we have in the text, which notice takes its special character from the previous allusion to these particular parties, and the implied promise given them, not as over against the sitters on the thrones, or as the only sitters there, but as specially included among them. It is a gracious note of testimony from heaven to the greatest sufferers for Christ that, when it comes to the inheritance of the Kingdom and the reigning of the saints with their Lord, they are to be specially considered. Having laid down their lives for their faith, or having held out faithfully against the horrible deceptions and persecutions of the Antichrist, the assurance is, that they particularly shall be among these priests of God and of Christ, to share in his sublime dominion. Though in the ashes before, they are to live again for this very purpose.

Some stumble at the word *souls* (ψυχὰς), by which these martyrs are denoted, as if that introduced a peculiarity determinative of the whole character and interpretation of the vision. But it is nothing but a metaphysical quibble, by which to obscure and get rid of a plain doctrine of the Word of God which some do not like. It is a sufficient answer to say, that one of the common uses of this word in the New Testament is to denote individual beings, and persons in the body, rather than spirits of men out of the body. So the converts on the day of Pentecost are called " about three thousand *souls ;* " and Jacob and his kindred who went down into Egypt are spoken of as " threescore and fifteen *souls ;* " and those sailing with Paul in the ship were " two hundred threescore and sixteen *souls ;* " and in the ark with Noah " eight *souls* were saved." In such passages disembodied souls are out of the question. Indeed, one of the rarest uses of the word by the sacred writers, if ever so used, is that which confines its meaning to the designation of that part of man capable of existence apart from the body. More commonly, it means corporeal life as distinguished from corporeal death. And as respects principles, or a mere moral influence, there is no instance in all the Word of God of its use in that sense. That the word *souls*, in John's vision of the martyrs beneath the altar, means *persons dead as to their bodies*, is very evident, not, however, from the meaning of the word, but from the accompanying statement that the *souls* he saw were people *slain* on account of their faith. He sees the same people, persons, *souls*, here ; but this time ἔζησαν—"*they lived again.*"* As mere souls separate from the body, they never were dead. John saw them, and heard them speaking, and beheld them invested in white robes, and recognized them as still living and waiting, though dead as to their bodies. The *living again* in which he now sees them, must therefore be a living in that in which they were dead when he first saw them, that is, *corporeally dead.* There is a resurrection of *the bodies* of dead men, but there is no such thing as the resurrection of *the spirits* of dead men. For *living* men there may be a spiritual resurrection from the death-state of sin, but there is no such spiritual resurrection for *dead* men. John had seen these " souls " under death as to their bodies, but here as "*living again ; *" of course, living now in that in which they were dead then ; that is, *in corporeal resurrection,* for as to their spirit life they had not been dead.†

So far, then, from this word *souls* introducing an element requiring the exclusion of any thought of literal corporeal resurrection, it the rather proves that we cannot possibly understand any other sort of resurrection. That of which their martyrdom deprived them, their *living again* restores to them ; hence, necessarily, corporeal resurrection,—the only resurrection of which martyrs are capable. Spiritual resurrection is out of the question, for they were spiritually resurrected before they became martyrs, and could not be holy martyrs without it. Mere influential resurrection is equally out of the question, for their living again is to possess the rewards of martyrdom, which would be a mere farce in any case not involving a literal personal resurrection. What reward is it to a man under the altar who has lost his head for his fidelity, that somebody else after him shows the same fidelity ! What compensation was it to Paul for his execution at Rome, that Constantine some centuries after sat on the throne of the Cæsars, and inscribed the sign of the Cross upon his banners ! Such a result was indeed worth sacrifice to achieve ; but that achievement was nothing of a personal reward to Paul. The souls under the altar knew there were men of their own faith and spirit on the earth, who should be as true to God as they had been ; but that was no compensation to them, and did not keep them from crying with a great voice : " Until when, thou Master, the holy and true, dost thou not judge and avenge our Blood ! " Besides, the Scriptures everywhere place the recompenses of the sacrifices and devotions of the saints "*at the resurrection of the just.*" (Luke 14 : 14.) Neither, martyrs nor saints get their rewards till then. (2 Tim.

* " I argue from the Greek text that the *souls* must in this instance be a synecdoche for *the persons,* and that the *living again* must signify the union of body and soul. For first in the passage ' which, or who, had not worshipped the Beast,' the word *which* (οιτινες) is in the masculine gender, whereas *souls,* which is the antecedent to it, is feminine. So also, ' the rest of the dead ' (οἱ λοιποι) is in the masculine, in antithetical opposition to those that were beheaded, των πεπελεκισμενων."—Dr. N. Holmes's *Resurrection Revealed,* p. 58.

† " How can we avoid coming to the conclusion that ἔζησαν here must mean *reviving* or *rising from the dead ?* The use of ζάω elsewhere in the Apocalypse shows very plainly that it may mean *revived, lived again,* in reference to the body which had been dead. Thus the Saviour speaks of himself, in Rev. 2 : 8, as being he who had been *dead,* καὶ ἔζησε, *and had revived, lived again,* after the death of the body. Thus, too, it is said of the Beast (Rev. 13 : 14) which had the deadly wound of the sword, that ἔζησε, *it revived.* Thus also it is said, the rest of the dead οὐκ ἔζησαν, *lived not again.* Surely the writer does not mean that Christians of lower rank, or the wicked, have no existence at all after the death of the body."—Stuart *in loc.*

" It does not mean that they lived *spiritually,* for so they did before, and whilst they bore their testimony to Christ and against Antichrist previous to their death ; nor *in their successors,* for it would not be just and reasonable that *they* should be beheaded for their witness of Christ and his word, and *others* should live and reign with Christ in their room and stead. Nor is this to be understood of their living in their souls, for so they live in their separate state ; the soul never dies ; God is not the God of the dead, but of the living. But the sense is, that they *lived again,* as in verse 5 ; they lived corporeally ; their souls lived in their bodies, their bodies being raised again, and reunited to their souls ; their whole persons lived, or the souls of them that were beheaded lived ; that is, their bodies lived again, the soul being sometimes put for their body ; and this is called the first resurrection in the next verse."— Dr. John Gill *in loc.*

4 : 8 ; 1 Pet. 1 : 7, 8 ; 5 : 4.) The compensations of the saints must there-fore wait till " the resurrection of the just." But here we have the rewards of God's faithful witnesses ; therefore the resurrection spoken of can be none other than a literal and real resurrection, the same which is set forth in all the Scriptures as the great hope of all saints.

So likewise the antithesis between the living again of these " souls " and the non-living again of " the rest of the dead till the thousand years be completed," evidences that the resurrection spoken of is a literal resurrection. The deadness of this " remainder of the dead " certainly is a bodily deadness ; otherwise there are to be no conversions on earth for full a thousand years. Their living again at the completion of the thousand years is a bodily resurrec-tion ; for they come up out of the sea, out of death, out of Hades, where they could not have been without being corporeally dead. John says expressly that they are " *the dead, the great and the small*," and that they thus live again, in a state of recovery from death and Hades, for the purpose of receiv-ing their final doom. If this does not signify a literal resurrection of them at the end of the thousand years, there is no way of proving that there ever will be a literal resurrection for anybody. But if their living again at the termi-nation of the thousand years is a literal resurrection, then their non-living again during those thousand years must be a state of literal corporeal dead-ness. And if their non-living again till the thousand years are accomplished is a continuation in a state of corporeal death, then the living again of those to whom they stand correlated as " the remainder of the dead " must be a literal corporeal resurrection also.* There is no escape from this argument. As Alford well says, " If in a passage where *two resurrections* are mentioned, where certain ' souls ' live again at the first, and ' the rest of the dead ' live again only at the end of a specified period after the first,—if in such a passage the *first resurrection* may be understood to mean spiritual rising with Christ, while the *second* means *literal* rising from the grave ; then there is an end of all significance in language, and Scripture is wiped out as a definite testimony to anything. If the first resurrection is spiritual, then so is the second ; but if the second is literal, then so is the first, which, in common with the whole primitive Church and many of the best modern expositors, I do maintain, and receive as an article of faith and hope." (*Gr. Test.* in loc.)

Furthermore, it is inwoven and implied in every particular in the presenta-tion concerning these sitters on these thrones, that the scene to them is a post-resurrection scene.

In chapter 11 : 18, it was adoringly said by the holy Elders, that the time of the sounding of the seventh trumpet is the time or season for judging the dead, to give reward to the servants of God, the prophets, the saints, and them that fear his name, the small and the great. The description before us belongs to the season of the sounding of the seventh trumpet, which terminates at this point a thousand years before another resurrection of any sort occurs. Either then this sets forth the reward given to the servants, prophets, and saints of God, inclusive of their resurrection, or these holy Elders were alto-gether mistaken and misinformed, and John was in error in recording what they said as true.

Paul says, that when Christ, who is our life, shall appear, *then* shall his people appear with him in glory. (Col. 3 : 4.) But here Christ has appeared. The heaven has opened, and he has come forth as triumphant King of kings and Lord of lords, crowned with all his many diadems, consigning the Beast and the False Prophet to final perdition, striking their assembled armies dead, and locking up the Devil in the Abyss. Where, then, are his people who

---

* " In the phrases *first* resurrection, and *second*, a discrepancy as to *time* is implied. Any great change from a degraded and wretched condition, temporal or spiritual, may indeed be figuratively called a *resurrection, a restoration to life, i.e.,* to happiness ; but it would be out of the question to name it a *first* resurrection. This implies of necessity a comparison with a *second*, in which the first must be like the second in *kind*."—Stuart *in loc.*

are to be revealed with him in resurrection glory when these things come to pass, if these sitters upon these thrones be not they?

These enthroned ones have had their judgment and obtained reward; otherwise they could not be thus enthroned, for enthronement is reward. But the time of such reward of the saints is the time of their resurrection, and not before; therefore, these enthroned ones must here be in their resurrected and glorified estate.

They occupy thrones, and they reign; therefore they must have received their crowns; but the saints are not crowned till the chief Shepherd appears, and they have been recalled from their graves (2 Tim. 4: 8; 1 Pet. 5: 4); therefore, again, these crowned ones must here be in their resurrected condition.

They are kings and priests, they reign, they are enthroned as royal judges and potentates, they share with Christ in his judging and shepherdizing of the nations: but it is only to those who have overcome, and been crowned by the great Judge of all as victors,—to the Manchild born into immortality and caught up to God and his throne,—that this power over the nations thus to rule or shepherdize is given. (Rev. 2: 26, 27; 12: 5.) How, then, can these enthroned and reigning ones be any other than resurrected saints, in possession of post-resurrection rewards and glory? I wonder at the strange obtuseness of candid and sensible men, that they should have the slightest question on the subject. Either human theorizings are more authoritative than God's positive revelations, or those are all wrong who refuse to take these sitters on these thrones as the resurrected and glorified saints.

And still the evidence is not exhausted. There is a word in the record which makes the matter doubly sure. This whole presentation concerning the lifting and placing of these enthroned ones in their royal seats to live and reign with Christ for a thousand years, John pronounces "*The Resurrection*"—"*The Resurrection the First.*" The word *Resurrection* (ἀνάστασις) is never once used in the New Testament, except to denote the coming up again of the fallen body from the grave. It occurs more than forty times, and always in this one, uniform, and exclusive sense. Yet the emplacement of these people in these sublime seats is called their ἀνάστασις—their *Resurrection*. Nay, more, the Holy Ghost calls it ἡ ἀναστασις, emphatically *the Resurrection*, partly in its relation to a second, and partly with reference to its own transcendent pre-eminence, as the particular object of our highest Christian hopes. How men, who profess loyalty to the Scriptures, and hold themselves in conscience bound to the Word of God, can get over such facts, and reduce the whole picture of this glorious enthronement of the saints, to what they call "special respect to their principles, their memory, and their character" rendered by mortal men, or to a mere revival of the martyr spirit and faith in times of glory for the Church on earth when there is no more room for martyrs, is utterly beyond my comprehension. It upturns all acknowledged principles of interpretation from their very foundations. It opens the door for the explaining away of every distinctive feature of the Christian faith. And it turns all the great promises of God and hopes of his Church into mist, dimness, and dreamy nothing. If these thrones, this royal judgeship, this reigning with Christ, this thousand years' dominion and rulership, this lifting of the holy martyrs including prophets and apostles into seats of sovereignty and shepherdizing of the nations, do not belong to the awards which only the Resurrection can bring, it is simply impossible to find any solid basis in God's Word for any special doctrine of our faith which we claim to derive from that source.

Look at it, my friends. The Bible tells us unmistakably that the illustrious apostles do not get their thrones till "the regeneration when the Son of man shall sit upon the throne of his glory" (Matt. 19: 28); and yet men would teach us that some of their disciples in the flesh shall sit on exactly such thrones, and reign with Christ as his kings and priests for a thousand years,

" *as if they were apostles raised from the dead,*" whilst yet those apostles themselves are all the while still sleeping unrewarded in their graves ! The holy martyrs we know do not get their recompense till " the resurrection of the just ; " and yet we are to accept it as the revelation of God, that mortal men, who are not martyrs at all, and have no chance of becoming martyrs, ascend martyr thrones, and sit and reign with Christ as kings for ten centuries, " *as if they were martyrs raised from the dead,*" whilst the martyrs themselves are meanwhile left in the ashes beneath the altar, crying, How long, O Lord, how long ! Apart from all the linguistic and exegetical arguments which stand out against such notions, as a continent against the sea, the very absurdity of the implications ought to be enough to satisfy every one that such anomalies certainly cannot belong to the administrations of a just and holy God.

But I cannot go further into the subject to-night. Believing that I have contributed something toward a right understanding of this much-abused passage of the divine revelation, I close with the single remark : How sublime and glorious is the portion which remains for God's true people ! Here are thrones to last a thousand years, and forever, and they are to occupy them. Here is sovereignty and judicial rule over the nations, and they are to exercise and wield it along with their victorious Redeemer and King. Here are a thousand years of glorious life over against a thousand years in the sombre abodes of Hades,—a life which they are to possess and enjoy forever free from all fear or power of " the second death." What is beyond will appear as we come to the concluding chapters ; but this alone presents a prospect and honour for the saints well worth a life of suffering and trial, and for which life itself is not too dear a price.

LECTURE FORTY-SIXTH

THE FIRST RESURRECTION—A RESURRECTION OF SAINTS ONLY—TAKES PLACE IN SUCCESSIVE STAGES—NOT DESCRIBED IN ANY ONE VISION—INTRODUCES A WONDERFUL CHANGE IN THE EARTH'S HISTORY—PROMOTES ITS SUBJECTS TO A TRANSCENDENT DIGNITY AND GLORY.

REV. 20 : 6. (Revised Text.) Blessed and holy he that hath part in the resurrection the first ! Over these the second death has no power, but they shall be priests of the God and of the Christ, and reign with him a thousand years.

My conviction is clear and positive that the resurrection here spoken of is the resurrection of the saints from their graves, in the sense of the Nicene Creed, where it is confessed : " I look for the Resurrection of the dead, and the life of the world to come." With the distinguished Dean of Canterbury, Dr. Alford, to whose critical labours the Christian world is much indebted, " I cannot consent to distort words from their plain sense and chronological place in the prophecy, on account of any considerations of difficulty, or any rise of abuses which this doctrine may bring with it." With Paul, " I can do nothing against the truth, but for the truth." (2 Cor. 13 : 8.) The word here rendered *Resurrection* is more than forty times used in the New Testament and four times in the Apocrypha, and always in the one only sense of a rising again of the body after it has fallen under the power of death. The emphasizing of it as *The Resurrection* cannot, with any degree of propriety, be understood of any mere metaphorical or symbolic rising. The placing of it as *the first* in a category of two resurrections, the second of which is specifically stated to be the literal rising again of such as were not raised in the first, fixes the sense to be a literal resurrection. What it describes is located in the time of the judging of the dead and the giving of reward to the saints, for which recovery from their graves is a pre-requisite. It exalts to an office of judging, shepherdizing, and reigning, the same which is elsewhere dependent upon the final victory and the complete redemption of the whole man. All the rewards, dignities, and honours promised to saints at and after the resurrection, are necessarily included in what is assigned to those who share in this resurrection. All the connections and surroundings, antecedent and consequent, and the impossibility of consistently adjusting it to the rest of the Apocalypse or the Scriptures in general on any other supposition, combine to show that the reference is and must be to persons in resurrection life and glory. I am also perfectly sure, that any candid critic, set to work to make out an honest list of the men of the first three centuries of the Church who believed in a literal resurrection of saints a thousand years before the resurrection of the wicked, would find in this chapter the most ample and cogent reasons for placing the Apostle John among them. I cannot, therefore, but take it as the true meaning and intent of the Holy Ghost, that we should here understand a real and literal resurrection of saints and martyrs from their graves.

Who partake in it ? is the question suggested and answered in the text now before us, concerning which I remark :

1. *It is a resurrection of saints only*. They that have part in it are " blessed and holy." Whether the reference be to the qualifications for it, or to what it brings, or to both, the result is the same, that none but true members of Christ are in this resurrection ; for none but such are " blessed and holy." Neither in this life, nor in that which is to come, can an unbeliever, a wicked or profane person, be reckoned with the " blessed and holy ; " but every one that hath part in this resurrection is " blessed and holy."

Many have the idea that there is but ōne resurrection for all men, good and bad alike. It is also true that " as in Adam all die, even so in Christ shall all be made alive." (1 Cor. 15 : 22.) But it is immediately added, " *every man in his own order.*" It is not a summary thing, all at once, and the same in all cases. The resurrection of the wicked is in no respect identical with that of the saints, except that it will be a recall to some sort of corporeal life. There is a " resurrection of life," and there is a " resurrection of damnation " (Jno. 5 : 29) ; and it is impossible that these should be one and the same. There is a " resurrection of the just,"—" a better resurrection,"—a resurrection out from among the dead (ἐξανάστασις ἐκ νεκρῶν), for which great zeal and devotion are requisite (Luke 14 : 14 ; Heb. 11 : 35 ; Phil. 3 : 10, 11),— which is everywhere emphasized and distinguished from another, more general, and less desirable. As it is " the resurrection of the just," the unjust have no share in it. As it is a resurrection from among the dead ones, it is necessarily *eclectic*, raising some, and leaving others, and so interposing a difference as to *time*, which distinguishes the resurrection of some as in advance of the resurrection of the rest. Hence the Scriptures continually draw a line of distinction between the resurrection of the good and the resurrection of the bad ; and when the two are mentioned together, the resurrection of the good is always mentioned first. Hence, in the celebration of the standing up again of the congregation of the righteous, the Psalmist is particular to say that sinners shall *not stand up* with them. (Ps. 1 : 5.) Thus Paul also assured the Thessalonians that " *the dead in Christ shall rise first.*" (1 Thess. 4 : 16.) If we understand this " first " as over against the translation of living saints, as some take it, or as over against the resurrection of the dead *not in Christ*, as Professor Stuart claims the meaning to be, it is all the same. The declaration is that only " *the dead in Christ* " are partakers of this resurrection ; and if there is this difference in time between " the resurrection of the dead in Christ " and the translation of the living " in Christ," all the more surely will there be a still wider difference in time between the rising of " the dead in Christ " and the rising of the dead *not* in Christ, who are altogether excluded from those who are said to rise *first*. It is not true, therefore, that we go contrary to the analogy of Scripture when we construe " the first resurrection," in which only the blessed and holy have part, as a literal resurrection of the saints, occurring long before and apart from the resurrection of the non-blessed.*

2. *It is a resurrection which takes place in different stages*, and not all at one and the same time. Paul tells us expressly that there is an " *order* " in it,

---

* " There is a general impression that the belief in the First Resurrection at a different time from that of the general resurrection rests solely on this passage. (Rev. 20 : 6.) But this is a great mistake. Omitting the passages from the Old Testament Scriptures, sustained by the promises of which the ancient worthies suffered and served God in hope of ' a better resurrection ' (Heb. 11 : 35), our Lord makes a distinction between the resurrection which some shall be accounted worthy to obtain, and some not. (Luke 20 : 3, 5.) St. Paul says there is a resurrection ' *out from among the dead* ' (ἐξαναστασις), to attain which he strove with all his might as the prize to be gained. (Phil. 3 : 11.) He also expressly tells us, that while as in Adam all die, so in Christ shall all be made alive ; yet it shall not be all at once. (1 Cor. 15 : 22–24.) It is to be remarked, that wherever the resurrection of Christ, or his people, is spoken of in Scripture, it is a ' resurrection *from*, or *from among*, the dead ; ' and wherever the general resurrection is spoken of, it is the ' resurrection *of* the dead.' This distinction, though preserved in many instances in the English translation, is too frequently omitted ; but in the Greek the one is always coupled with the preposition, ἐκ *out of* or *from among*, and the other is without the preposition ; and in the Vulgate it is rendered by *à mortuis* ; or *ex mortuis*, as distinct from *resurrectio mortuorum*. In Rom. 8 : 11, ' the spirit of him that raised up Jesus from the dead,' it is ἐκ νεκρῶν, à *mortuis*. So in Rom. 10 : 7 ; Eph. 1 : 20 ; Heb. 3 : 20 ; 1 Pet. 1 : 3, 21. So Lazarus was raised ἐκ νεκρῶν. (Jno. 12 : 1, 9.) Our Lord, in his reply to the Sadducees, made the distinction between the general resurrection of the dead and the resurrection which some should be accounted worthy to obtain. (Luke 20 : 34, 35.) St. Paul, when he spoke of a resurrection to which he strove and agonized to attain (Phil. 3 : 8, 11), as if one preposition was not enough to indicate or emphasize his meaning, uses it doubled, τὴν ἐξαναστασις τὴν ἐκ νεκρῶν, ad *resurrectionem, quæ est ex mortuis*—the special or eclectic resurrection, *that one from among the dead*."—Consult M. Stuart on the Apocalypse, vol. ii, pp. 474–490.

which brings up some at one time, and others at other times. It starts with "Christ the first fruits;" *afterwards* they that are Christ's at his coming; *then* (still later) the end, "completion, or last." (1 Cor. 15 : 23, 24.) Christ's resurrection was also attended with the resurrection of others. The Gospel says: "The graves were opened, and many bodies of the saints which slept arose, and came out of the graves after his resurrection, and went into the holy city." (Matt. 27 : 52, 53.) This, Selnecker, one of the authors of the *Formula Concordiæ*, says "places and parcels out the resurrection of those who are raised to eternal life before the general resurrection at the last day; and the meaning properly is, that not only those of whom the Evangelist is writing become alive again, but also others, as Luther and Ambrose have written, and that such resurrections occur at various times throughout the whole period or dispensation of the New Testament, even up to the final day." These various particular resurrections he also calls "The First Resurrection, to which," he says, "belongs everything raised up again to eternal life before the final day."*

This statement agrees also with what we have found in the course of our exposition of this Book. In chapter 4, immediately following the sentences to the Churches, John saw a door open in the heaven, through which he was called to come up. That door and ascension indicate a resurrection and rapture of saints (answering to 1 Thess. 5 : 16, 17); for John immediately beheld Living Ones and Elders in glory. They were saints from earth, for they sing of being redeemed by Christ's blood "out of every kindred, and tongue, and tribe, and people." They are in resurrection life, for they are enthroned and crowned; and no saints are crowned till "the resurrection of the just." They correspond to "the Eagles" gathered together where the body they live on is, who are thus sheltered in the heavenly pavilion from the sorrows of the great tribulation. (Matt. 24 : 27, 28; Luke 17 : 34-37; 21 : 34-36; Rev. 3 : 10.) They are already in heaven, before ever a seal is broken, a trumpet sounded, or a bowl of wrath emptied.

Further on, in chapter 7, under the sixth seal, a great multitude was seen, also in heaven, clothed with white robes, and bearing palms of victory. John beheld them with the Living Ones and Elders, but distinct from them, and then just arrived. Whence they came, is asked and explained. They come "out of the great tribulation,"—a tribulation from which the Elders or seniors in heaven were saved altogether, being "accounted worthy to escape all these things." They answer to the wise virgins, who were not ready when the watchful and far-sighted Eagles were "taken," but who, in sorrow and mortification, had now repented out of their misbeliefs, taken up the lamps of a better confession, and gone out in true advent faith to meet the Bridegroom, thus washing their robes and making them white in the blood of the Lamb, securing a heavenly portion indeed, but with certain losses, and at a period subsequent to the taking up of the Elders and Living Ones.

So at a still later period, even after the revelation of the blasphemous Beast, two great Witnesses appear, whom he finally slays. Three days and a half their bodies lie unburied. But, at the end of that time they come to life again, stand on their feet, and ascend to heaven in sight of their enemies. Whether any of their disciples are taken up with them, as might reasonably be inferred, or whether they alone are raised at this time, here is certainly another special or particular resurrection which goes to make up the company of the "blessed and holy."

Yet further on, in chapter 14, still another special company appears, quite distinct from any thus far named, consisting of 144,000, "redeemed from the earth" and "from among men," singing a new song of their own, and joined with the Lamb to follow him whithersoever he goeth. They certainly belong to "the children of the resurrection," to the congregation of God's glorified

* *Exp. of Rev. and Daniel*, Gena, 1567. See also Danhauer. Kromayer's *Elenchticus in Aug. Conf.*, 501-2, and Lange's *Ap. Licht, u. Recht.* 179.

saints ; but the season of their inbringing is not the same as that of the others referred to.

So, in connection with the gathering of the kings and their armies at Harmageddon, there is a note of indication that other saints were then on the eve of being taken (chap. 16: 15) ; whilst here in the vision of the whole body finally made up, some are described as having lived in the very last days of the Antichrist, yet did not worship him or receive his mark ; indicating that the first resurrection is not finally complete until the very last period of of the Man of sin.

It is thus clear and manifest, even to the extent of demonstration itself, that the First Resurrection is not one summary event, but is made up of various resurrections and translations at different times, beginning with the resurrection of Christ, who is the head and front of " the resurrection of the just," and receiving its last additions somewhere about the final overthrow of the Beast and his armies.

3. *It is a Resurrection which as a whole is nowhere pictorially described.* As it does not occur all at once, it is not fully given in any one vision, as in the case of " the rest of the dead." The nearest to such a scenic presentation is that given in chapter 12, in the picture of the birth of the Manchild, which is immediately caught up to God and to his throne. That birth and ascension is the pictorial " sign " of the bringing forth of all " the Church of the first-born " into eternal life and resurrection glory, which began in the resurrection and ascension of Christ himself, and which reaches its completion when the last martyr under the Beast attains his final blessedness. But even there, no circumstantial details appear, except the malignant and murderous attempt of the Dragon to prevent it. It is quite too varied and diverse in its several sections, and in the different parts which the blessed and holy have in it, for any one picture adequately to represent it. Hence there is no such picture. What John here sees and describes is not so much the scene of its occurrence as the body of its subjects, the estate to which it brings them, the blessedness and honour with which it clothes and endows them. He beholds who and what they are that have part in it ; but when, how, or in connection with what times, formalities, and surroundings they are made to live again, he does not here see or state, as in the case of those who live not again till the thousand years are ended. The reason is, that the subject is not capable of it, because so parcelled out in various particular scenes, relating to different classes and times, and with very diverse circumstances and attendant facts.

It is not so with " the rest of the dead." As none of them share in the First Resurrection, so none of them belong to " the blessed and holy." They are all of the one general class of the non-saved. The reading in the Codex Sinaiticus is, that they are all κατεκρίθησαν—*condemned.*

The book of life is opened and searched from end to end, but there is no account of any name of any one of them being found there. Leaving out the Beast and the False Prophet, who are then already in the lake of fire, they are all resurrected together. They all have their judgment at one and the same time, and all meet the same fate. One picture can readily give the whole scene, with all the circumstances and particulars. And so it is given, in connection with the great white throne. But, in the nature of the case, thus it could not be with " the resurrection of the just." Nor does Christ ever mount a throne of judgment toward his Church and people. They are his familiar servants, friends, and brethren. Leaving the world, he leaves them to occupy for him, and in his name. The Kingdom he gets is not against them, but for them, that they may share it with him. They are of the King's party and household. When he comes, he comes, according to the Parables, first to one, and then to another, and so in succession, advancing each band of faithful and good servants to their reward one after another, " every man in his own order." He meets and rewards the best first, and so descends from class to class, as from time to time, till the whole body of his redeemed ones is made up in all its variety of orders and degrees, according to fidelity to his word and service.

4. *The completion of this Resurrection introduces a wonderful change in the earth's history.* It is the breaking through of an immortal power ;—a power which sweeps away, as chaff before the wind, the whole economy of mortal and Dragon rule, and thrusts to death and Hades every one found rising up or stiffening himself against it ;—a power which shears the Old Serpent of his strength, binds him with a great chain, locks and seals him up in the Abyss, pulls down all his works, tears off and clears away all his hoary falsehoods, which have been oppressing, deceiving, misleading, and swaying the world to its destruction for so many ages ;—a power which gives to the nations new, just, and righteous laws, in the administration of immortal rulers, whose good and holy commands men must obey or die ;—a power which cuts at once the cords of life for every dissembling Ananias and Sapphira, blasts every Nadab and Abihu that ventures to offer strange fire before the Lord, consigns to death and burning every Achan that covets the Babylonish garment or wedge of gold which God hath pronounced accursed, and causeth the earth to open her mouth and swallow up on the spot every Korah, Dathan, and Abiram that dares to open his mouth against the authority of the holy princes whom Jehovah hath ordained ;—a power which grasps hold of the plethoric fortunes accumulated in meanness and oppression and held in greedy avarice for the pampering of lust and pride, hewing them down in righteousness and scattering them in restitutions to those out of whom they have been so uncharitably and dishonestly ground and wrung ;—a power which goes forth in vindication of the worthy poor, the oppressed, the weak, the friendless, and the downtrodden, the righting of their cause, the maintenance of their just claims, and the enforcement of truth and brotherhood between man and man ;—a power which lifts the mask from deceit, pretence, and false show, puts each one in his true place according to what he really is, gives credit only where credit is due, stamps an effectual condemnation on all false weights and measures, and tries everything and everybody in the balances of a strict and invincible justice. I think of the coming in of that power, —of the havoc it must needs make in the whole order of things,—of the confusion it will cause in the depraved cabinets, and courts, and legislatures of the world,—of the revolution it must work in business customs, in corporation managements, in political manipulations, in mercantile and manufacturing frauds, in the lies and hollownesses which pervade social life,—of the changes it must bring into churches, into pulpits, into pews, into worship, into schools, into the newspapers, into book-making and book-reading, into thinking and philosophy, and into all the schemes, enterprises, judgments, pursuits, and doings of men,—of how it will affect literature, art, science, architecture, eating, drinking, sleeping, working, recreating,—of what it must do concerning playhouses, and rumshops, and gambling hells, and the unhallowed gains by which great masses of people have their living and keep themselves up in the world. And as I thus begin to realize in imagination what the irresistible enforcement of a true and righteous administration in all these directions and relations necessarily implies, I can see why the Book of God describes it as a shepherdizing *with a rod of iron*, and calls it a breaking like the dashing to pieces of an article of pottery. Think of the sudden collapse of all the haunts of sin, the rooting out of the nests and nurseries of iniquity, the clearing away of the marshes and bogs of crime, where every style of damning pestilence is bred, and the changes that must hence come ;—think of the summary abolition of all infamous cliques, combinations, and rings,— political rings, whisky rings, municipal rings, state rings, railroad rings, mercantile rings, communistic rings, oath-bound society rings, and a thousand kinds of other rings,—all the children of wickedness, hindering just law, suppressing moral right, crippling honest industry, subsidizing legislation, corrupting the Press, robbing the public treasuries, eating up the gains of

honourable occupation, perverting public sentiment, spotting and exorcising men who cannot be made the tools of party, transmuting selfish greed and expediency into principle, razeeing the dominion of virtue and intelligence, subordinating the common weal to individual aggrandisement, and setting all righteous administration at defiance ;—think of the universal and invincible dragging forth to divine justice of every blatant infidel, perjurer, liar, profane swearer, drunkard, drunkard-maker, whoremonger, hypocrite, slanderer, trickster, cheat, thief, murderer, trader in uncleanness, truce-breaker, traitor, miser, oppressor of the poor, bribe-taking legislator, time-serving preacher, mal-practitioner, babe-destroyer, friend-robber, office-usurper, peace-disturber, and life-embitterer ;—think of the instantaneous going forth into all the world of a divine and unerring force, which cannot be turned or avoided, but which hews down every fruitless tree, purges away all chaff from every floor, negatives all unrighteous laws, overwhelms all unrighteous traffic, destroys all unrighteous coalitions, burns up every nest of infamy and sin, ferrets out all concealed wickedness, exposes and punishes all empty pretence, makes an end of all unholy business, and puts an effectual stop to all base fashions, all silly conceits, all questionable customs, and all the hollow shams and corrupt show and fastidiousness of what calls itself society, transferring the dominion of the almighty dollar to Almighty Right, and reducing everything in human life, pursuits, manners, and professions to the standard of rigid truth and justice ;—think of the tremendous revolution, in all that the eye can see, the ear hear, the hand touch, the heart feel, or earthly being realize, that must needs attend the putting into living practical force of such an administration,—the high it must make low, the famous it must make infamous, the rich it must make poor, the mighty it must make powerless, the loud it must sink to oblivion, the admired and worshipped it must turn to disgrace and abhorrence, and the despised and contemned poor it must lift into place and respectability,—the different impulse under which every wheel must then turn, every shuttle move, every hammer strike, every foot step, every mind calculate, and every heart beat ;—the change that must come over the houses we enter, over the streets we walk, over the people we meet, over the words we pronounce, over the food we eat, over the air we breathe, over the sunlight of the day, over the repose of night, over the spirit of our waking hours and the very dreams of our slumbers, and over all the elements, relations, activities, and experiences which go to make up what we call *life ;*—think, I say, of all this tremendous revolution, and conceive it going into invincible effect, unchangeably, without compromise, at once, and forever ; and you may begin to have some idea of the alteration which *The First Resurrection* is to introduce into the history of our earth. For this, and nothing less than this, is the meaning of this sitting upon thrones, receiving power of judgment, shepherdizing the nations, and reigning on the earth, on the part of these blessed and holy immortals.

And a good thing it will be for the nations when that day comes. There can be nothing better than God's law. There can be nothing more just, more reasonable, more thoroughly or wisely adapted to all the well-being of man and the highest wholesomeness of human society. All the blessedness in the universe is built upon it. All that is needed for the establishment of a holy and happy order is for men to obey that law, for it to be put in living force, for it to be incarnated in the feelings, actions and lives of men. And this is what is to be effected when " the children of the resurrection " get their crowns, and go into power, with Christ the All-Ruler at their head. They are to shepherdize, and deal with the nations, and with all that make up the nations, as unerring and immortal kings and priests, to direct, instruct, and feed them with all the loving care of angels, but with " a rod of iron " in their hands to enforce docility, obedience, and unreserved surrender to all the laws and requirements of the Lord God Almighty. And under this reign shall be fulfilled what the prophets have prophesied, and sung in golden numbers, about the peace and blessedness which is in reserve for this sin-hurt and long down-trodden inheritance of man. You may call it Judaism, if you like ; you may sneer at it as fantastical conceit ; you may denounce it as a carnal dream ; you may brand it as heresy ; but it is nevertheless the truth of God, to which you, and I, and all men, are inexorably bound ; and which has every prospect of becoming experimental fact before the century approaching has passed away. I hail its coming, and I bid it welcome, as the great hope and regeneration of our depraved and misgoverned world.

5. *The completion of this Resurrection promotes the subjects of it to a transcendent glory.* Saintship means honour. It is not so in this present world. The greatest of the Apostles, with all his great achievements and sublime experiences, was compelled to say, " If in this life only we have hope in Christ, we are of all men the most miserable." (1 Cor. 15 : 19.) The great Master of all told his disciples from the beginning, " If ye were of the world, the world would love his own ; but because ye are not of the world, but I have chosen you out of the world, therefore the world hateth you." (Jno. 15 : 19.) The unregenerate heart does not like the Gospel philosophy and the Gospel requirements ; and whilst it continues unregenerate, it has no favours for those who defend and live it, and insist on its acceptance as the only hope for man. Hence the history of the Church, wherever it has been truest, purest, and most itself, is a *Book of Martyrs.* But " the resurrection of the just " brings the people of God their compensation. " *Blessed and holy is he that hath part in the Resurrection the First ! Over these the Second Death has no power, but they shall be priests of the God and of the Christ, and reign with him a thousand years.*" Analyse a little the exultant statement.

First of all, they are partakers of *resurrection,* the first resurrection, the blessed resurrection. Not all of them actually suffer death. Such of them as are alive, and remaining, and ready, when the time comes, are " caught up," translated, carried off into the resurrection life, without dying at all. But the translation in those instances is the equivalent of the resurrection. It is the same change to incorruption and immortality, not from the grave indeed, but from mortal life, and so is included in the one term, which means, that, to all of them alike, a power is vouchsafed which strikes from every one of them forever every vestige of the old slavery to corruption, death, or mortal disability. Mere living again, great and wonderful as that is, is the smallest part of the matter. By the prophets, by Christ, and by the apostles, some were recalled to life, resuscitated, made to live again after they were dead, and yet died again as men ordinarily die, the same as if they had never been recalled from death. The living again in this case involves a far " better resurrection," even the renewal of the whole corporeal being, refashioned to a heavenly model, with heavenly qualities, and to a vastly sublimer life than ever was enjoyed before ;—a *resurrection,* in which corruption puts on incorruption, dishonour puts on glory, weakness puts on power, and the earthy body becomes a spirit body, lifted quite out of the sphere of the earthly life, and over which neither the first death nor the second has any further power. Having been " accounted worthy to attain that world," they " neither marry nor are given in marriage ; neither can they die any more ; for they are *equal unto the angels ;* and are the children of God, being the children of the resurrection." (Luke 20 : 35, 36.)

They are *holy.* They were holy in their lives and aims while they lived in the flesh. They had " the testimony of Jesus " and " the word of God," and confessed it over against a gainsaying world, and held it fast against persecution and death, and willingly suffered the loss of all things, counting them but refuse and offal, rather than let go their confession and hope in Christ Jesus. They were the salt of the earth and the light of the world, the golden candlesticks of eternal truth in the realm of abounding sin and darkness, yet never content with that to which they had attained, but ever reaching forth unto still higher and better things, and, like the Olympian racers, pressed toward the mark for the prize of the high calling of God. Reviled, persecuted, evil spoken of, and accounted the very offscourings of the world, because of their faith, devotion, and self-sacrifice for their Saviour and his cause, they resented not, but counted it all joy, and were exceeding glad, sure that it was working for them a far more exceeding and an eternal weight of glory. Many of them were tortured, not accepting deliverance, that they might obtain the better resurrection ; and others had trial of cruel mockings and scourgings, of bonds and imprisonments, were stoned, sawn asunder, tempted, slain with the sword, wandered about in sheepskins and goatskins, being destitute, afflicted, tormented, of whom the world was not worthy. But consecrated and set apart to God as his servants and lightbearers in their earthly lifetime, they are a hundredfold holier now. Released forever from the deathworking law in their fleshly members, their whole being has come under the power of a complete and untemptable sanctification, which sets them apart and consecrates them to a sublime and unapproachable holiness, to which dwellers in the flesh must stand in greater awe than ever was called for in the sublimest of earthly kings or the most sacred of Jewish high-priests ; —a holiness which inspires while it awes, which attracts while it reproves and condemns, and which lifts and assures those whom it strikes with humiliation and dread. When Isaiah saw the Lord sitting upon his Almighty throne, and the seraphim with covered faces round about him saying, Holy, Holy, Holy, is the Lord God of Sabaoth, he fell down and cried, " Woe is me ! for I am undone ; because I am a man of unclean lips, and dwell among a people of unclean lips." (Is. 6 : 1–5.) And something of this same awful holiness is then to appear in the immortal king-priests of this resurrection, before which men and angels will veil their eyes in reverence ; for in them and through them God will set his glory among the nations, and all the earth shall be filled with it. (Ezek. 29 : 21 ; Is. 6 : 3.) There is a great and awful majesty of consecration in a true child of God even while living and walking here in the flesh. To the outward eye and carnal view there is but little that is special. The thoughtful brow, the sober mien, the dignified behaviour, the reserved and careful utterance, the keeping aloof from the world's wild pleasures and gaieties, and the solemn regard for holy names and holy things, along with a calm and firm confession of the truth as it is in Jesus, is about all that can be externally noticed. But his name is in the books of heaven. He is there enrolled as a celestial citizen and prince. The angels are ministers and servants to him. He is allied by regeneration to the blood-royal of eternity. He is marked with the name and sacrament of the King eternal, immortal, and invisible. He has upon him an unction from the Holy One, consecrating him for transfiguration to supernal principality. He is brother and joint-heir with Him who sits enthroned at the right hand of eternal Majesty, and who is presently to be revealed as the King of kings and Lord of lords. The very ground on which he treads takes on sacredness from his presence. The Holy Ghost dwells in his body, breathes in his breath, walks in his steps, and speaks in his words. Through that Saviour in whom he trusts, he is already in a measure a divine man, partaker of the divine nature. All of which shall be made complete, manifest, and visible when he comes forth in the sublime sanctity of the First Resurrection ; for " *blessed and holy is he that hath part in the Resurrection the First.*"

Further, *they have very exalted place and occupation.* John saw them seated on thrones. He beheld them endowed with judgeship. He pronounces them kings and priests. They share in the administrations of government. They reign with Christ. Their business is to shepherdize nations. These things all tell of official relations and prerogatives. They are not mere names and empty titles. The saints know no sinecures. No meaningless ceremonials or hollow designations find place in heaven. Nothing is there but substantial realities. The children of the resurrection are no sham kings, and no mock judges, but everything which these high titles and offices imply. They are not co-regents and co-shepherdizers with Christ, without being and doing what such words import and express. The dignity is transcendently exalted, but it is all real ;

and the reality of the offices necessitates the reality of the activities which pertain to them. I said that saintship means honour ; but saint honour means *duty, activity, work,* not idleness, not quiescence. There is no heaven for laziness ; much less is heaven made up of it. Not for parade badges, but for corresponding services, do the children of this resurrection get their dignities. As kings, they are to fill the places and do the work of kings. As judges, they are to judge and administer justice. As priest-regents, they are charged with the cares and duties of royal priesthood. They not only have the name and place of sovereigns, but they *reign,* as truly and really as ever Saul, or David, or Solomon *reigned.* The end of their salvation is not to sit on clouds and sing psalms, or to luxuriate in the idle bliss of an eternal languor or ecstasy. They are redeemed and glorified for sublime offices and the work pertaining to those offices. The life of Christ in heaven is an intensely busy life. He is administering the Kingdom of the universe. When the present dispensation ends he will deliver up that Kingdom to the Father, and enter upon a new and particular administration of his own, in which the children of the resurrection are to be joined with him, as angels are now associated with him in the administration of the Kingdom of the Father, yea, in a still closer union. The work to be done is the shepherdizing of the nations with a rod of iron,—the following up of the victory of the great day of God Almighty, putting in force the rule of eternal right and justice where the blasting rule of the Dragon has so perverted things and held disastrous sway for so many ages. For this they have their thrones. For this judgment is put into their hands. For this they are lifted high above all the infirmities of mortal life. For this they are perfected in holiness and invested with such divine and awful consecration. And in this they have their honour and their blessedness. Through their completed redemption in Christ Jesus they come into such full harmony with the mind and will of God, and into such living consociation with their Redeemer, as to know no higher dignity or joy than to fill out the great administration of reducing the mortal survivors of the awful day to divine order, and to employ their immortal energies in tutoring the race from which they have sprung, till returned to that Paradise from which it has been in exile for 6,000 years.

These are quite different ideas from those usually entertained about heaven. People spiritualize and explain away the great things of God's Revelation until the whole matter evaporates in their hands, and the true Christian hope vanishes into insipidity and nothingness. They make ado about getting to heaven, but have lost all understanding of what it means. All the singing, and longing, and fond anticipation on the subject really amounts to very little more than a going to see Jesus, to meet some departed friends, and to make the acquaintance of some distinguished people who once lived. Crowns are sometimes alluded to, but they are only fancy crowns, glittering shadows, empty dreams, badges without corresponding dignities, administrations without subjects, thrones to which nobody is amenable. They talk of rest ; but rest is not heaven, any more than sleep is life. And the impossibility of finding realities with which to fill up the scriptural images and descriptions of the final portion of the redeemed, on the part of those who spiritualize the First Resurrection, is ample evidence of their tremendous mistake. They, in effect, abolish everything that makes heaven heaven, and all their pictures of futurity are simply the taking of God's ransomed kings into a world of shadows, to find their eternal bliss and ever-growing greatness in the languor of songs, or the dreamy joys of an endless spiritual intoxication, all as impossible as it is uninviting to rational natures, or to beings invested with immortal powers. No, the joys and honours of the children of the resurrection are, that they are made kings and priests unto God and Christ, installed and endowed as immortal benefactors of the nations upon the earth, the unerring lords, rulers, and invincible shepherds, of a renewing and renewed world, the everlasting guides, judges, and potentates of a redeemed race. So the word before us is ; and to this outcome all the promises in the Book of God are fitted.

LECTURE FORTY-SEVENTH

REV. 20 : 7–15. (Revised Text.) And when the thousand years are completed, Satan shall be loosed out of his prison, and shall go out to lead astray the nations which are in the four corners of the earth, Gog and Magog, to gather them together into war, of whom the number (of them) as the sand of the sea.

And they went up on the breadth of the earth [or *land*], and encompassed the citadel of the saints and the beloved city. And there came down fire out of the heaven, and devoured them. And the Devil, who leadeth them astray, was cast into the lake of fire and brimstone, where also the Beast and the False Prophet [are], and shall be tormented day and night to the ages of the ages.

And I saw a great white throne, and the one sitting upon it, from the face of whom fled the earth and the heaven, and place was not found for them.

And I saw the dead ones the great and the small standing in the presence of the throne, and books [or *rolls*] were opened, and another book [or *roll*] which is [that] of the life ; and the dead ones were judged out of the things written in the books according to the works of them.

And the sea gave the dead ones in it, and Death and Hades gave the dead ones in them, and they were judged [Codex Sin. *were condemned*] every one according to their works.

And Death and Hades were cast into the lake of fire. This is the death the second, the lake of fire.

And if anyone was not found written in the book [or *roll*] of the life, he was cast into the lake of fire.

THE reign of Christ and his glorified saints is a reign on or over the earth. It is a shepherdizing of " the nations," and " nations " belong to the race of man in the flesh. The Living Ones and Elders sung of being made kings and priests unto God, and proclaimed themselves thus ordained to " *reign on the earth.*" (Chap. 5 : 10.)

This reign is to last a thousand years, a millennium, a chiliad. Any thousand years is a millennium ; but because of the peculiarities and pre-eminence of this particular thousand years, it has come to be called *The Millennium*, about which there is much unfounded oratory and empty song.

The prevailing modern doctrine is, that the world is to progress, and is progressing, toward a golden age of wisdom, righteousness, liberty, and peace, when error, false worship, vice, wickedness, oppression, and all anti-christian-ism, will be effectually eradicated, and all nations and peoples brought under the sway of a purified and all-governing Christianity ; that this is to be accomplished by the gradual advancement of civilization, science, reforms, political revolutions, the spread of liberality, beneficence, and Christian principles, and the revival of the churches in devotion and missionary zeal, helped by increased measures of the Spirit of God and such providential directions of human affairs as may augment the efficiency of the appliances we now have ; and that this is the consummation for which all Christians are to look, labour, and pray, as the glorious outcome of this world's history. This men call *The Millennium*, and about this they dream, and sing, and preach. You will find it in nearly all the popular teachings of our times, just as I have stated it. That it involves some dim elements of truth, may be admitted ; but they are so sadly disfigured and overlaid as to make out of them a system of very faulty philosophy, manipulated into an article of faith, wholly unknown to the Church in the first thousand years of its existence, and as much an invention of man as the Romish dogmas of the immaculate conception and the Pope's infallibility. It is certainly not taught in any respectable creed in Christendom. It is not to be found in any of the Church's books of devotion, liturgies, hymnals, or accepted songs, for the first fifteen centuries, including the period of its greatest purity and faithfulness. All the great confessions, either by implication or direct specification, are adverse to it, and unconstruable with it. The old theologians, such as Luther, Melanchthon, Calvin, Knox, Hutter, Hunnins, Quenstedt, and even the Wesleys, are against it. Daniel Whitby, who died in 1726, by whom mainly it was brought into vogue, offered it to the consideration of the learned as only an *hypothesis*, which he considered *new* in his day. And the Scriptures everywhere, on every principle of just interpretation, negative and contradict it. The Church, in its very name and divine designation, is an *Ecclesia*, a body called out from the rest of mankind, with the majority ever outside of itself. By every saying and foreshowing of the Saviour, it lies under the cross for the whole period of its earthly career, and from that state is never lifted this side of the resurrection. The tares and the wheat occupy the same field, and both grow together till the harvest, which is the end of the age, the termination of the present dispensation. Everywhere the last days are painted as the worst days, and men as waxing worse and worse till the end comes. And all the precepts and admonitions divinely given to the Church with reference to the coming again of the Lord Jesus, are such as to render it impossible for them to be kept by any people of any generation believing that a thousand years would have to pass before that coming could take place. I therefore arraign all such teaching as full of chiliastic error, and as one of those subtle, plausible, but delusive insinuations of the great deceiver, by which God's people are beguiled from the truth to his ruinous lies.

I. Notice then the Scriptural teachings with regard to what is called the Millennium.

1. It is a period of "a thousand years," dating from the overthrow of the Beast and his confederates, in the battle of the great day of God Almighty, the casting of him and the False Prophet into the lake of fire, and the binding and locking up of Satan in the Abyss. I understand these to be literal years, the same as all other dates given in this Book. The year-day interpreters, to be consistent with themselves, must needs lengthen out this period to at least three hundred and sixty thousand years, which is a most astonishing elongation of the "*little while*" and the "*quickly*" in which Christ promised that he would come again.

2. These thousand years begin only after this present world, αιων, age or, dispensation is closed. The intent of the Church period is stated to be the gathering together of an elect, the taking out of a people for the name of the Lord, the development and qualification of a particular number of the human family to be Christ's immortal king-priests. That object being attained, all the present arrangements terminate. There is not a command to preach, make disciples, baptize, observe the Eucharistic supper, or anything else peculiar to the Church, which is not limited in its own specific terms to the coming again of Christ to avenge his people, and judge his enemies. Such a coming was shown us before the introduction of these thousand years ; but no such coming is shown us at their termination. A fiery judgment is there, and a great white throne of terrific adjudication upon the unholy dead, but not a word about any coming of Christ either for or with his people, any gathering together of his elect, any taking of the eagle watchers to where he is, any coming as he was seen going up from Mount Olivet, or any *coming* whatever. The fact that the saints appear on thrones, in the blessedness and holiness of resurrection life and glory, at the beginning of this period, and that they reign through it, demonstrated that Christ's coming to raise his saints to glory, give them their rewards, and thus end this dispensation, has then already taken

place.   This Millennium, therefore, lies altogether on the further side of that occurrence ; and the present Church, so far from finding earthly blooming time in it, does not get into it at all, except in the immortal kinghoods and priest-hoods of the children of the resurrection.

3. The so-called Millennium brings with it an altogether different dispensation from that under which we now live.   During the whole course of the present order of things, Satan is loose and active in his work of leading astray ; but he is bound, locked up in the Abyss, and not allowed to enter the world at all, either personally, or with any of his agents, for all this thousand years.   The great work and office of the Church now is to preach the Gospel to every creature, and to witness for Christ to an adverse and gain-saying world ; but there is not one word said about any such office in mortal hands during all that long period.   In its stead, however, there is to be a shepherdizing of the nations with a rod of iron, an authoritative and invincible administration of right and justice on the part of immortal king-priests, and a potent disciplining of men and nations far beyond anything which the mere preaching of the Gospel ever has wrought or ever was intended to do for earthly society.   Now the sovereignty of the earth is in the hands of the Dragon, moulded by his influence, and not at all under the command of saints ; but then it is to be exclusively in the hands of the Lord of lords and his immortal king-priests.   Now we can only beseech men in Christ's stead to be reconciled to God ; then they will be compelled to take the instructions given them, to serve with fear and rejoice with trembling, to kiss, give the required adoration to the Son, or perish from the way.   (Ps. 2 : 10–12.)   Now it is left to men's option to serve God or not, with nothing to interfere with their choice but the judgment to come ; then they will be obliged to accept and obey his laws, or be smitten and blasted on the spot.

The present is the period of God's mercy and long-suffering ; that will be the period of prompt and rigid administration, when sentence against an evil work will be executed speedily.   Now the dutiful and obedient are obliged to suffer, to endure manifold wrongs, and to wait for their reward till the resurrection of the just ; but " then shall the righteous flourish " in proportion to their righteousness, and they " shall go forth and grow up as calves of the stall," " and the work of righteousness shall be peace, and the effect of righteousness, quietness and assurance for ever." (Is. 32 : 17.)   Now it is a hard and self-sacrificing thing to be a saint, justly made hard because of the transcendent dignity and glory to be gained ; but then the difficulty and hardship will be on the other side, so that people can scarcely help being what they ought to be, and sin will be embarrassed with greater disadvantages than a life of faith has ever been.   Thus, in every particular, the dispensation of things will then be wholly changed from what it is now.

4. The general condition of the earth, and man upon it, will then also be vastly improved.   We cannot speak with definiteness ; but all the intimations show that this whole terrestrial economy will then be far on in the process of that " regeneration " and renewal of which the Saviour speaks (Matt. 19 : 28), and in which " the creation "—" the whole creation "—" shall be delivered from the bandage of corruption into the glorious liberty of the children of God." (Rom. 8 : 21, 22.)   Great and mighty changes in the configuration of the earth were shown in the visions of the judgment-time preceding this thousand years, —changes in the relations of sea and land,—changes in the mountains, hills, and islands,—changes in the atmospheric heavens,—changes in the sun, moon, and stars,—changes which must needs alter the whole climate, fruitfulness, and habitability of the earth.   As it is the time when " God shall judge the people righteously and govern [shepherdize] the nations upon earth," so it is the time when " the earth shall yield her increase," and when the nations shall " be glad and sing for joy." (Ps. 77.)   As it is the time when " the Lord bindeth up the breach of his people," so it is the time when " rivers and streams of waters shall be upon every high mountain and every hill," and " the increase

of the earth shall be fat and plenteous," and " the light of the moon shall be as the light of the sun, and the light of the sun shall be sevenfold, as the light of seven days." (Isaiah 30 : 18–26.) The physical condition of man will be greatly ameliorated. " The inhabitant shall not say, I am sick." (Is. 33 : 24.) Life will be wonderfully prolonged. " There shall be no more thence an infant of days, nor an old man that hath not filled his days." One dying at the age of a hundred years will die so young only as a judgment for sin, and will be accounted as having died a child at that great age. The days of a man are to be as the days of a tree, as in the antediluvian world. (See Isaiah 65 : 20–23.) Indeed we read of no deaths during this thousand years, except those which occur by reason of transgression and disobedience. The population of the world will have been greatly thinned down by the various judgments, removals, and plagues which precede this Millennium ; but " instead of the fathers shall be the children, who may be made princes in all the earth " (Ps. 45 : 16) ; and a blessed and happy fruitfulness shall be upon the race of humanity, as well as in the whole system of nature, so that by the end of the thousand years, even the remote corners of the world will be able to muster people as multitudinous as the sands of the sea. It will not yet be the eternal state, called " the new earth," in which there is no more sin, nor death, nor curse, nor tears ; but it will be a mighty stride toward it, and the stage next to it. The mental, moral, social, and political condition of the people who then live will necessarily be like heaven itself, compared with the order of things which now prevails ; for they shall be shepherded by Jesus and his immortal co-regents, and " the deaf shall hear the words of the book, and the eyes of the blind shall see out of obscurity and darkness ; the meek also shall increase their joy in the Lord, and the poor among men shall rejoice in the Holy One of Israel" (Is. 29 : 18, 19) ; " and wisdom and knowledge shall be the stability of the times and the strength of salvations." (Is. 33 : 6.)

5. The ending of this period will not be the ending of the blessedness which it introduces. The years terminate, but what it begins to realize of the new heavens and earth abides. What marks the end of the thousand years, and distinguishes it from the years that succeed, is not a cessation of the heavenly order that has been established. Christ and his saints do not then cease to reign over the nations. Men do not cease to live in the flesh. The kingdom come does not then recede, or cease to be the same enduring and everlasting kingdom. The earth is not disturbed in that wherein it has advanced toward its complete " regeneration." But that which marks the end of the thousand years, and divides it off from the eternal state which follows, is the letting of Satan loose again for a little time, the testing of the loyalty and devotion of the nations which have experienced these high favours, the rebellion of Gog and Magog, the destruction of the rebels by fire from heaven, the casting of Satan into the final hell, the calling up of all the wicked dead to judgment and final doom, and the putting forth of what further touches are requisite to complete " the restitution of all things."

II. Notice then more particularly what immediately follows this thousand years.

1. *The Devil is let loose.* He who lets him loose is, of course, the same who bound him, and sealed him in the prison of the Abyss. God uses even the wickedest of beings, and overrules the worst depravity, to his own good and gracious ends. He allows Satan liberty, and denies him liberty, and gives him liberty again, not because the Devil or the Devil's malice is necessary to him, but to show his power to bring good out of evil, to make even the worst of creatures praise him, and to turn their very wickedness to the furtherance of the purposes they would fain defeat.

It seems like a great pity, after the world has rested for a thousand years, that this arch-enemy of its peace should again be let loose upon it. But there seems to be some sort of necessity for it. The statement to John was, that

" he *must* be loosed a little time." (V. 3.) Some interest of righteousness and moral government renders it proper that he should be allowed this last limited freedom.   If for nothing else, it is not unimportant that he should have this opportunity to prove how little an imprisonment of a thousand years had served to change him, or reform his malignity.   Even the Devil is granted a final trial to make a better record to himself, if so minded.   But neither judgment nor mercy has the least effect.   He is, and remains to the last, the same depraved and wicked being, and employs even the little time of freedom before he is cast into perdition in tempting, seducing, and deceiving the happy and peaceful world.   Perhaps, too, it was necessary for the millennial nations to be taught that, even after having been so far redeemed as to live a thousand years of holy obedience, they still are unable to stand without the special help and grace of Almighty God.   At any rate, this brief period of Satan's last freedom proves, that he is still Satan, and that man is still man, after a thousand years of bonds and imprisonment for the one, and a thousand years' experience of next thing to Paradise for the other ; the Devil being just as eager to tempt and deceive, and man liable to be tempted and deceived. Nor can it be of small account to the after ages, or for the generations to whom it is foretold, that the full demonstration of these facts should be made before things are finally settled into the eternal state.   Hence Satan is let loose for a little time.

2. *He seduces Gog and Magog into rebellion.*   He does not send forth this time to " the kings of the earth," for there are then no mortal kings to be led astray, but he goes direct to the people, insinuates his malice against the rule under which the King of kings has placed the nations, and seeks to persuade them into an attempt to overthrow it.   To those who dwell in the outskirts and darker places of the earth, he wends his sullen way.   He made his first attempt in Eden by assailing the weaker and more compliant vessel ; and this is his method in his last.

Just who Gog and Magog are we may not be able to tell.   A thousand years of uninterrupted peace and prosperity are likely to make great changes in the distribution and locations of peoples.   But the allusion to the " corners of the earth " as the regions whence these rebels come, sufficiently indicates that they are among the hindermost of peoples and the least advanced and cultured among the millennial nations.   It has taken more than a thousand years to develop the civilization which marks the better portions of the present population of the globe ; and a thousand years, even of millennial tutelage, would not avail to bring up the darker and more degraded sections to a very exalted height.   And among these ruder peoples Satan finds the pliant materials for a new and last revolt.   Jerome and Theodoret identify Gog and Magog with " the Scythian nations, fierce and innumerable, who live beyond the Caucasus and the lake Mæotis, and near the Caspian Sea, and spread out even onward to India."   The Koran does the same, and represents them as barbarians of the North, who are somehow restrained until the last period of the world, when they are to swarm forth toward the South in some great predatory irruption, only to be hurled into Gehenna fire.   It is doubtful whether we can get beyond this by any ethnic or geographic inquiries in the present state of human knowledge.   It is also questionable whether this post-millennial Gog and Magog are the same described by Ezekiel. (37 : 1–14.) They may be the same, or the one may be the type of the other ; but in either case the reference is to peoples lying outside of the more civilized world, among whom the old Devil influence lingers longest, and hence the most susceptible to these new instigations. At least Satan succeeds in rendering them dissatisfied with the holy rule of God's glorified saints, and induces them to believe that that they can successfully throw it off and crush it out, as the deluded kings under the Antichrist were persuaded a thousand years before.   How he does this we are not told ; but under him they come forth in swarming myriads, enter the same holy land, and compass about the citadel of the saints and the beloved city, in the vain hope of wresting the dominion from its immortal possessors.

3. *A terrible disaster ensues.* A madder thing than Gog and Magog's attempt was never undertaken upon earth. It is simply a march into the jaws of death, for no rebellion against the kings who then hold the reins of government can be tolerated. The insane war is quickly terminated. One brief sentence tells the fearful story : " *There came down fire out of the heaven and devoured them.*" When Israel was encamped in the wilderness, a guard of Levites was set about the tabernacle, and the command to them was : " *The stranger that cometh nigh shall be put to death.*" (Numb. 1 : 51.) So a guard of immortal king-priests keep the ways to the throne and temple of Jehovah in that day, and the presumptuous dupes of Satan's last deception who dare to approach with hostile intent, are instantly hurled to a fiery destruction. Not a man of them escapes.

4. *Satan meets his final perdition.* He was imprisoned in the Abyss before ; but he is now " cast into the lake of fire and brimstone, where also the Beast and the False Prophet [are]." When the Saviour was on earth, he discoursed to his disciples about an " everlasting fire, prepared for the Devil and his angels." (Matt. 25 : 41.) This is it ; and this is the time when he for whom it is prepared first feels those terrific flames.

Thus ends the last rebellion ever seen upon this planet,—the last sin, and the last deaths, that ever occur in this dwelling-place of man.

III. Notice now what happens to " the rest of the dead," who did not have part in the first resurrection.

1. *A great white throne appears.* A similar throne was beheld by John at the commencement of the great judgments which precede the Millennium. (Rev. 4 : 2-6.) That was set in the heaven ; where this is set we are not told. That had a rainbow over it, to indicate fulfilment of covenant promises ; this is naked, for it has no hopes to offer, no covenant of good to fulfil. Out of that proceeded lightnings, thunders, and voices, indicative of revolutionary judgments upon the living world ; to this nothing is ascribed but *greatness* and *whiteness*, indicative of immeasurable power, and of pure, complete, unmingled, and invincible justice. There is no more probation on the part of those against whom its adjudications issue, and hence no further threatenings of coming judgment, as in lightnings and thunder. Around that first throne were sub-thrones, occupied by associate judges, and with it were conjoined Living Ones, taking part in the administrations, for they are varied and mingled, both as to kinds and subjects, and many find occupation in them ; here the throne is one only, for the administration is of but one kind, summary, direct, and having respect to but one class. Seven burning torches, representing the seven Spirits of God, were with that throne, because its adjudications were to be partly gracious and remedial, as well as retributive, toward those with whom it dealt ; this is accompanied with nothing gracious, for its dispensations are purely retributive, and only damning to what they strike. That throne had before it a glassy sea, pure and crystalline, like a grand celestial pavement, indicative of a place of blessed heavenly refuge, for it was about to exalt many to glory ; here there is no celestial landing-place, no platform of heavenly peace, for it has no salvations to dispense. In connection with the first throne there was singing, joyful exultation, the giving of mighty praises to God and the Lamb, for it was the setting in of an administration which was to bring saints to their consummated redemption and rewards ; here there is not a song, not a voice of gladness, not a note of exultation, for it is simply and only the administration of retributive justice, which consigns the unsanctified to their final perdition, and which has nothing whatever of gladness about it.

The presentations in both instances correspond to the proceedings issuing from them, and the one helps to explain the other. Indeed they are counterparts of one another,—the right hand administrations and the left hand administrations, the morning and the evening, of the great Day of Judgment viewed as a whole.

2. *This throne has an awful Occupant.* Of course it is the same beheld in the first instance. There is no name, no figure, no shape, in either case ; but only an awful, mysterious, and composed presence, which can be nothing less than the One, unnamable, indescribable, eternal Godhead. If it were the Lord Jesus Christ, simply as the God-man, he would appear in some definite form, as in every other instance. He is indeed the Judge, to whom all judgment is committed, and he does the judging in this instance ; but he does it under and in the presence of the enthroned Godhead of the Father, the Son, and the Holy Ghost, and not as the absolute and eternal King over all things. In the first instance, the Sitter on the throne had a particular appearance,—an appearance like to a jasper and a sardine stone, a reddish, crystalline brilliancy, like pure and smokeless flames, attractive even in its awfulness ; here there is nothing but the naked presence of almightiness, so dreadful that the very earth and heavens seem to flee into nothingness before it. The earth and heaven do not literally fly away and disappear. Similar language was used in chapter 6 : 14 ; but the earth still continued afterwards. And here, in the subsequent verses, the sea is still in its place ; and in the next chapters nations are still found inhabiting the earth. (21 : 24 ; 22 : 2.) It is simply the intensification of the description of the awfulness and majesty of the Sitter upon the throne that is thus expressed, signifying that almightiness by which all the creations and changes in the universe are effected, and who here assumes his eternal power to dispose of his enemies forever, and to put the last finishing touches upon the great *re-genesis* of things. And this infinite, repellent awfulness is a further indication that there is absolutely nothing of hope for those objects on which the adjudication now falls.

3. *A resurrection occurs.* No trumpet is sounded ; for the sounding of the trumpet is for those in covenant with the King, as his armies and friends ; but these are not his people nor his friends. There is simply the going forth of eternal power, into the sea, into the graves, into Hades, into all the depositories of the souls and bodies of the unholy dead, and all the vast multitudes in them suddenly stand in the presence of the throne. Not one of them that ever lived and died, from the beginning of the world till then, save and except the Beast and the False Prophet, but is in that unblest congregation. "The great and the small," the big sinners and the little sinners, rulers and subjects, nobles and plebeians, the learned and the ignorant, the refined and the vulgar, the civilized and the barbarous, emperors and beggars, all alike are there. We read of no white robes, no spotless linen, no palms, nothing but naked sinners, before the naked majesty of enthroned Almightiness, awaiting their eternal doom.

4. *Books are opened.* Heaven keeps record of all the deeds of men, and of all the thoughts and feelings under which they act. Myriads of human beings have lived and died of whom the world knows nothing ; but the lives they lived, the deeds they wrought, the thoughts and tempers they indulged, still stand written where the memory of them cannot perish. Not a human being has ever breathed earth's atmosphere whose career is not traced at full length in the books of eternity. Yes, O man ! O woman ! whoever you may be, your biography is written. An unerring hand has recorded every item, with every secret thing. There is not an ill thought, a mean act, a scene of wrong in all your history, a dirty transaction, a filthiness of speech, or a base feeling that ever found entertainment in your heart, but is there described in bold hand, by its true name, and set down to your account, to be then brought forth for final settlement, if not clean blotted out through faith in Christ's blood before this present life of yours is ended. And if no other books are to be thought of, the book of your own conscience, and the book of God's remembrance, will then and there attest your every misdeed and ill-desert. Think,

ye that fear not God, and make nothing of trampling his laws, how your case will stand when those books are opened !

But there is " *another book, which is that of the life,*"—the roll-book of the regenerate in Christ Jesus,—the register of the washed and sanctified through faith in his redeeming blood. This must needs be opened too ; for many there be whose lives are fair and honest, who spend their days in conscientious purity, who live and die in the persuasion that they have fulfilled all the requirements of virtue, but who have never experienced the regenerating power of the new creation, who have never felt the need of atonement by the propitiation of a crucified Saviour, and who have disdained to build on the merit and righteousness of the one only Mediator as the sole hope of diseased and guilty humanity. Exalted as they may have been in their own goodness and morality, they have not believed on the only begotten Son of God, and therefore have not life, and so are not written in the book of life. The records of their own deeds is therefore not enough for the determination of their proper place and standing. Men may appear well in these, and still not be prepared to pass the final inquisition. There is another and still mightier question in the case, and that is whether they have come to a regenerate and spiritual life through faith in Christ Jesus. Therefore the book of life must be opened too, and its testimony brought into the decision. If the name of any one is not on that roll, no matter how virtuously and honestly he may have lived, there is no help for him ; for only "he that believeth on the Son hath everlasting life." (Jno. 3 : 36.)

5. But *judgment is given as the works have been.* There is just gradation in the sorrows of the lost, as well as in the rewards of the righteous. If there is anything in any case to modify the guilt of sinners, or in any measure to palliate their deficiencies and crimes, the plain intimation is that every just allowance shall be made. Though all the finally condemned go into one place, they do not all alike feel the same pains, or sink to the same depths in those dreadful flames. But the mildest hell is nevertheless *hell*, and quite too intolerable for any sane being to be content to make experiment of it.

The judgment of these people according to these books is, in each instance, a judgment of condemnation, whether to the lesser or the greater damnation. There is no account of the name of any one of them being found in the book of life ; " and if any one was not found written in the book of the life, he was cast into the lake of fire." Not one of them is adjudged place with the " blessed and holy," or his resurrection would not have been deferred till now. And the Codex Sinaiticus, one of the very oldest and best of the ancient manuscripts of the New Testament, here reads : " The sea gave the dead ones in it, and Death and Hades gave the dead ones in them, and THEY WERE CONDEMNED, EVERY ONE, *according to their deeds.*"

6. And *sentence is followed with immediate execution.* When the Beast and the False Prophet were taken, they " were cast alive into the lake of fire which burneth with brimstone." (Chap. 19 : 20.) A thousand years afterwards, when Satan proved himself the same deceiver he always was, he " was cast into the lake of fire and brimstone." And into that same "lake of fire" all the condemned ones in this judgment are hurled. What that " lake of fire " is I cannot tell, I do not know, and I pray God that I may never find out. That it is a *place*, everything said about it proves. People in corporeal life, as these condemned ones are, must needs have locality. That it is a place of woe, pain, and dreadful torment, is specifically stated, and is the chief idea in every image of the description. What God adjudges a just punishment for the wickedness of the great head of all evil, for having ruined many of the sublimest creatures in heaven, and for the mischiefs, impieties, and desolations wrought in our world by more than six thousand years' unremitted exertions against the peace of man and the gracious purposes of God, certainly must involve a length, and breadth, and depth, and height of misery at which the universe may well stand aghast. He who understands it best, calls it " a lake of fire and brimstone,"

and I do not know what mortal man can tell us better.   If perchance it be not material fire, or the brimstone which feeds it be not the article which commerce handles, it still is fire of some sort, fed with its proper fuel,—*fire* which can take hold on body and spirit,—*fire* which preys on the whole being, whether clothed with corporeity or not,—*fire* kindled and kept alive by almighty justice, and a great lake of it, commensurate with the infinite holiness of an infinite law.   It is called " *The Second Death.*"   Hence some think it means extinction of existence, annihilation, a cremation of body and spirit, which leaves no ashes after it.   But the Beast and the False Prophet were in that death for more than a thousand years, and at the end of that time the implication seems to be that they are still alive.   Concerning those who are compelled to make proof of that death, the specific statement is, " *they shall be tormented day and night, to the ages of the ages.*"   This does not look like either annihilation or final restoration.   Nor is Death an extinction of all existence.   The first death is a killing of the body, a mutilation of the being, but not an extinction of it.   If death is the equivalent of annihilation, then these resurrected ones are condemned and punished for the crimes and defects of some other beings than themselves, and are not the people who did what is written in these books. The first death is a terrible mutilation and degradation, especially to a wicked man ;   though not a blotting out of his being and identity.   " The Second Death " must needs be still more terrible and disastrous, for it is a more inward fret ;   but not therefore a reduction to absolute nothingness.   Angels are regarded in all theology as immortal by inherent constitution ;   yet wicked angels are under the horrors of this Second Death.   The children of the better resurrection are " *as the angels of God ;* " so these partakers of the " resurrection of damnation " are *as the Devil and his angels.*   If " the lake of fire " is not annihilation to one, so neither is it to the other.   But it is Death, and it is torment ;   and there is every reason to believe that it is eternal.   It is " to the ages of the ages."   Confirmed depravity cannot be cured where no means of grace are ;   neither can those cease to sin whose whole nature has been turned to sin.   And if there can be no end of the sinning, how can there be an end of the suffering ?   Remorse cannot die out of a spirit ever conscious of its self-imposed damnation !   Therefore, " *their worm dieth not, and the fire is not quenched.*"   (Mark 9 : 44, 48.)

And Death and Hades, here viewed as if they were personal beings, share the same fate.   They, of course, cease to be.   There is nothing more of temporal death or of the place of departed spirits after this.   They are not personal beings, hence their casting into " the lake of fire " is the end of them ; but, conceived of as persons, they are consigned to exactly the same eternal punishment with the other wicked. They are the products of sin, and they share the doom of what produced them.   And thus, in an ever-burning Hell, from which there is no more deliverance, all the enemies of God and his Christ find themselves at last.

And now, in the presence of these awful verities, what shall I say to those who know it all, yet go deliberately on in ways which can have no outcome but this Second Death ?   I look at them, and think ;   and the terribleness of their hallucination paralyses my utterance.   I would fain arouse them to their better senses ;   but when I speak my intensest words seem but ashes in my mouth in comparison with the alarum for which their situation calls.

Ho, ye unbelieving men,—ye dishonest men,—ye profane men,—ye lewd men and women,—ye slaves of lust and appetite,—ye scoffers at the truth of God,—" *How can ye escape the damnation of hell ?* "   (Matt. 23 : 33.)   Ye men of business,—ye whose souls are absorbed with the pursuit of gain,—ye people of wealth without riches toward God,—ye passengers on the voyage of life, without prayer, without Church relations, without concern for your immortal good, your God, or the eternity before you,—hear : " *Hell hath enlarged herself, and opened her mouth without measure, and your glory, and your multitude, and your pomp, and your rejoicing, shall descend into it !* "   (Is. 5 : 14.) Ye almost

Q

Christians, lingering these many years on the margin of the Kingdom, looking in through the gates, but never quite ready to enter them, intending but never performing, often wishing but still postponing, hoping but without right to hope,—the appeal is to you : "*How shall ye escape if ye neglect so great salvation ?*" (Heb. 2 : 2–4.) And ye who call yourselves Christians but have forgotten your covenant promises,—ye Terahs and Lot's wives, who have started out of the place of sin and death but hesitate halfway, and stay to look back,—ye baptized Elymases, and Judases, and Balaams, who, through covetousness and feigned words make merchandise of the grace of God,—see ye not that "*your judgment now of a long time lingereth not, and your damnation slumbereth not !*" (2 Pet. 2 : 3.) And if there be any one oblivious or indifferent toward these great matters,—asleep amidst the dashing waves of coming retribution,—the message is to you : "*What meanest thou, O sleeper ? Arise, call upon thy God, if so be that God shall think upon thee, that thou perish not !*" (Jno. 1 : 6.) For if any one be not found written in the Book of Life, he must be swallowed up by the Lake of Fire.

LECTURE FORTY-EIGHTH

PERPETUITY OF THE EARTH AND THE RACE OF MAN—"END OF THE WORLD" NOT THE EXTINCTION OF THE EARTH—CONTINUOUS GENERATIONS—THE REDEEMED WORLD—THE SCENE OF IT—THE BLESSEDNESS OF IT—THE OCCUPANTS OF IT.

Rev. 21 : 1–8. (Revised Text.) And I saw heaven new and earth new : for the first heaven and the first earth are gone, and the sea no longer is.

And I saw the city, the holy, new Jerusalem coming down out of the heaven from God, prepared as a bride adorned for her husband.

And I heard a great voice out of the throne, saying, Behold, the Tabernacle of God, with the men [or *mankind*], and he shall tabernacle with them, and they shall be his people, and he, the God with them, shall be their God.

And God shall wipe away every tear from their eyes ; and death shall no longer be, neither sorrow, neither crying, neither pain, shall any longer be ; because the first things are gone.

And the Sitter upon the throne said, Behold, new I make everything. And he saith, Write, because these words are faithful and true.

And he said to me, They are accomplished. I am the Alpha and Omega, the Beginning and the End. I to him that thirsteth will give out of the fountain of the water of the life freely. He that overcometh shall inherit these things ; and I will be God to him, and he shall be son to me ; but the cowardly, and unbelieving, and polluted, and murderous, and fornicators, and sorcerers, and idolaters, and all the false, their part [shall inherit] in the lake burning with fire and brimstone, which is the death the second.

HUMANITY was created and constituted a self-multiplying order of existence, —*a race*,—to which this earth was given as its theatre, possession, and happy home. God created man in his own image ; male and female created he them, and said to them, Be fruitful, and multiply, and replenish the earth, and subdue it, and have dominion over it. When sin first touched man, it found him thus constituted and domiciled. Had the spoliations of sin never disturbed him, humanity, as a race, must needs have run on forever, and been the happy possessor of the earth forever. Anything else would be a contravention and nullification of the beneficent Creator's intent and constitution with regard to his creature man. Meanwhile came the fall, through the Serpent's malignity ; and then a promise of redemption by the Seed of the woman. If the nature of the fall was to destroy the existence of man as a race, and to dispossess him of his habitation and mastery of the earth, the nature and effect of the redemption must necessarily involve the restitution and perpetuation of the race, as such, and its rehabilitation as the happy possessor of the earth ; for if the redemption does not go as far as the consequences of sin, it is a misnomer, and fails to be redemption. The salvation of any number of individuals, if the race is stopped and disinherited, is not the redemption of what fell, but only the gathering up of a few splinters, whilst the primordial jewel is shattered and destroyed, and Satan's mischief goes further than Christ's restoration.

I therefore hold it to be a necessary and integral part of the Scriptural doctrine of human redemption, that our race, as a self-multiplying order of beings, will never cease either to exist or to possess the earth.

There is a notion, bred from the morbid imagination of the Middle Ages, which has given birth to many a wild poetic dream, which has much influenced the translators of our English Bible, which has unduly tainted religious oratory, song, and even sober theology, and which still lingers in the popular mind as if it were an article of the settled Christian creed, that the time is coming when everything that is, except spiritual natures, shall utterly cease to be, the earth consume and disappear, the whole solar and sidereal system collapse, and the entire physical universe vanish into nothingness.   How this can be, how it is to be harmonized with the promises and revealed purposes of God, wherein it exalts the perfections of the Deity, there is not the least effort to show.   The thing is magniloquently asserted, and that is quite enough for some people's faith, though sense, reason, and Revelation be alike outraged.

There is indeed to be an " *end of the world.*"   The Bible often refers to it. But men mistake when they suppose *the world* spoken of in such passages to be the earth as a planet.   Three different words have our translators rendered " *world :* "   γη, which means the earth proper, the ground, this material orb which we inhabit ; κοσμος, which means what constitutes the inhabitableness, the ornamentation, beauty, cultivation, external order, *fashion* of the world, but not the substance of the earth as a terraqueous globe ; and αιων, which is used more than one hundred times in the New Testament, but always with reference to *time,* duration, eras, dispensations,—a stage or state marking any particular period, long or short, past, present, or future,—the course of things in any given instance, rather than the earth or any theatre on which it ,is realized.   It may be earth or heaven, time or eternity, a material or an immaterial world, it is all the same as to the meaning of the word αιων, which denotes simply the time-measure and characteristics of that particular period or state to which it is applied.*   And this is the word used in all those passages which speak of " the end of *the world.*"   It is not the end of *the earth,* but the end of a particular time, age, condition, or order of things, with the underlying thought of other orders of things, and perpetual continuity in other forms and ages.   *Æons* end, times change, the fashion of the world passeth away,—but there is no instance in all the Book of God which assigns an absolute termination to the existence of the earth as one of the planets, or any other of the great sisterhood of material orbs.

So in those passages which speak of the *passing away* of the earth and heavens (see Matt. 5 : 18, 24, 34, 35 ; Mark 13 : 30, 31 ; Luke 16 : 17, 21, 33 ; 2 Pet. 3 : 10 ; Rev. 21 : 1), the original word is never one which signifies termination of existence, but παρερχομαι, which is a verb of very wide and general meaning, such as *to go* or *come* to a person, place, or point ; *to pass,* as a man through a bath, or a ship through the sea ; to pass from one place or condition to another, to arrive at, to go through ; to go into, to come forward as if to speak or serve. As to time, it means going into the past, as events or a state of things once present giving place to other events and another state of things.   That it implies great changes when applied to the earth and heavens is very evident ; but that it ever means annihilation, or the passing of things *out of being,* there is no clear instance either in the Scriptures or in classic Greek to prove.   The main idea is *transition* not extinction.

Some texts, particularly as they appear in our English Bible, express this change very strongly, as where the earth and heavens are spoken of as *perishing,* being *dissolved, flying away* (Is. 34 : 4 ; 54 : 10 ; Rev. 6 : 14 ; 20 : 10) ; but the connections show that the meaning is not cessation of being, but simply

---

* " The word αιων appears originally to have denoted *the life which hastes away in the breathing of our breath, life as transitory,* then the *course of life,* in general, *life in its temporal form*—*an age* or generation—*a space of time, course of time, time as moving,*—time so far as history is accomplished in it.   It always includes a reference to the *life, filling time,* or a space of time, as *sœculum* denotes the time in which life passes."—Cremer's *Biblico-Theological Lexicon of New Testament.*

" Κοσμος is the world, *mundus,* in its wide extention ; αιων, the age, *sœculum,* the present world, in its distinguishing character, its course, and the estimate to be formed of it."—James Bryce in Bengel's *Gnomon,* Eph. 2 : 2.

" Αιων in its primary sense signifies *time,* short or long, in unbroken duration ; essentially time as the condition under which things exist, and the measure of their existence.   All that floating mass of thoughts, opinions, maxims, speculations, hopes, impulses, aims, at any time current in the world, which it is impossible to seize and accurately define, but which constitute a most real and effective power, being the moral or immoral atmosphere which at every moment of our lives we inhale, again inevitably to exhale,—all this is included in the αιων."—Trench's *Synonyms of New Testament,* second series, pp. 38–40.   It therefore refers to something altogether different from the substance of the earth as a planet.

the termination or dissolution of the present condition of them to give place to a new and better condition. At least one such *perishing* of the earth has already occurred. Peter, speaking of the earth and heavens of Noah's time, says : " *The world that then was being overflowed with water,* PERISHED." (2 Pet. 3 : 5, 6.) But what was it that *perished?* Not the earth as a planet, certainly ; but simply the mass of the people, and the condition of things which then existed, whilst the earth and race continued, and have continued till now. Equally strong expressions are used with regard to the destruction or passing away of the old in the case of one born again to newness of life in Christ Jesus ; but no one therefore supposes that the bringing of a man from Satan to God is the annihilation of him. It is simply the change of his condition and relations. And so in the case of the earth and heavens ; for the same word which describes the change in the individual man is used to describe the change to be wrought in the material world. It is *regeneration*—παλιγγενεσια—in both instances (Matt. 29 : 28; Tit. 3 : 5), and therefore not the putting out of existence in either case. The *dissolving* of which Peter is made to speak, is really a deliverance rather than a destruction. The word he uses is the same which the Saviour employs where he says of the colt, " *Loose* him ; " and of Lazarus when he came forth with his death-wrappings, " *Loose* him, and let him go ; " and of the four angels bound at the Euphrates, " *Loose* them ; " and of the Devil, " He must be *loosed* a little season." It is the same word which John the Baptist used when he spoke of his unworthiness to *unloose* the Saviour's shoestrings, and which Paul used when he spoke of being " *loosed* from a wife." It is simply absurd to attempt to build a doctrine of annihilation on a word which admits of such applications. The teaching of the Scriptures is, that the creation is at present in a state of captivity, tied down, bound, " not willing, but by reason of him who hath subjected the same in hope ; " and the *dissolving* of all these things, of which Peter speaks, is not the destruction of them, but the breaking of their bonds, *the loosing of them*, the setting of them free again to become what they were originally meant to be, their deliverance. (Compare Romans 8 : 19–23.) And as to the *flying* or *passing away*, of which John speaks, a total disappearance of all the material worlds from the universe is not at all the idea ; for he tells us that he afterwards saw " *the sea* " giving up its dead, the New Jerusalem coming down " *out of the heaven*," the Tabernacle of God established among men, and " nations " still living and being healed by the leaves of the Tree of Life.

Great changes in the whole physical condition of the earth and its surrounding heaven are everywhere indicated ; but the idea of the extinction of the material universe amid " the wreck of matter and the crush of worlds," is nothing but a vulgar conceit, without a particle of foundation in nature, reason, or Scripture.* Things have no more tendency to annihilation than nothing has a tendency to creation. There is no evidence that a single atom of matter has ever been annihilated, whence analogy would infer that such a thing is not at all in the will or purpose of God. On the contrary, the teaching of Revelation is, that " one generation passeth away, and another generation

---

* The subject of the perpetuity of the earth was under consideration in a clerical association some years ago, when one of the members pronounced all such ideas wholly *unscriptural*, and said the word of God is full of passages which prove that the earth is to be utterly destroyed, so that it will no more be. He was pressed to point out even one. He then referred to Psalm 46 : 2 : " Therefore will we not fear, *though the earth be removed*." This, he said, proved conclusively that the earth is to pass away altogether. He was asked to read a little further, when he gave the parallelism, " *and though the mountains be carried into the midst of the sea*." To which the remark was somewhat facetiously, but very effectively, made, " Brother, that don't appear to be anything more than *a large landslide*." The positive objector had no more passages to produce.

Dr. J. Pye Smith, in his *Geology and Revelation* (p. 161), says : " I cannot but feel astonished that any serious and intelligent man should have his mind fettered with the common—I might call it the vulgar—notion of a proper destruction of the earth. I confess myself unable to find any evidence for it in nature, reason, or Scripture."

cometh ; but *The Earth abideth forever."* (Ecc. 1 : 4 ; Ps. 15 : 5 ; 119 : 90.) Whatever new cataclysms or disasters are yet to befall this planet, we are assured that they will not be as destructive even as Noah's flood ; for God covenanted then, and said : *" I will not again curse the ground any more for man's sake, neither will I again smite any more every living thing, as I have done."* (Gen. 8 : 21, 22.) It is specifically promised that " the meek shall inherit the earth," and that " the righteous shall dwell in it forever." (Matt. 5 : 5 ; Ps. 37 : 9, 11, 29 ; Is. 60 : 21 ; Rom. 4 : 13.) And if the righteous are to inhabit it forever, it must exist forever. The kingdom of which Daniel prophesied is to be an everlasting kingdom, which shall stand forever. That kingdom is located " under the whole heaven," and takes in among its subjects " peoples, nations, and languages," and has its seat upon the earth. (Dan. 2 : 44 ; 7 : 14, 27.) But if the earth is to have an indestructible kingdom, it must itself be indestructible. John describes the sovereignty of this world as finally assumed by the Lord, even Christ, who is to hold and exercise it to the ages of the ages. (Rev. 11 : 15.) But how can Christ reign forever in a world which is presently to cease to be ? God has specifically and repeatedly coven- anted and promised a certain portion of the earth to a certain people for " an everlasting possession " (Gen. 48), in which they are to " dwell, even they, and their children, and their children's children, *forever* " (Ezek. 37 : 25), and not cease from being a nation before him forever. (Jer. 31 : 36.) How can this be fulfilled if the earth is to be annihilated ?

There is also a peculiar consecration upon the earth which makes it revolt- ing to think of its being handed over to oblivion. The footsteps of the Son of God upon its soil, the breathing of its atmosphere by his lungs, the saturation of its mould with his sweat, and tears, and blood, the wearing of its dust upon his sacred person, the warming of its fluids in his arteries, ought to be enough to satisfy us that neither the Devil nor destruction shall ever possess it. It is the place where God's only begotten Son was born and reared, and where he taught, and slept, and suffered, and died. It is the territory on which Divine Love and Mercy have poured out the costliest sacrifice the universe has ever known. It is the chosen theatre of the most momentous deeds that ever attracted the adoring interest of angels. It has furnished the death-place, the grave, the scene of the bruising and the triumph of Jesus Christ. And how can it ever be delivered over to everlasting nothingness ? Perish what may, a world so consecrated can never be blotted out, or cease to be one of the most cherished orbs in God's great creation.

And with the continuity and redemption of the earth, goes the perpetuation and redemption of *the race.* For why is the one continued if not for the other ? As surely as " the earth abideth forever," so surely shall there be eternal generations upon it. Paul speaks with all boldness of " *the generations of the age of the ages."* (Eph. 3 : 21.) After the termination of the present Æon, he contemplates many more Æons, even an Æon of Æons ; and those inter- minable years he fills up with generations and generations. The covenant which God made with Noah, and all living things, the sign and seal of which still appears in almost every summer shower, is, by its own terms, unending in duration ; but that duration is at the same time described as filled in with *unceasing generations.* (Gen. 8 : 22, 23 ; 9 : 8–16.) Joel tells of generations and generations for Jerusalem through all that " *forever* " in which cleansed and ransomed Judah is to dwell in the covenanted land. (Joel 3 : 20, 21 ; Ezek. 37 : 25, 26.) Eternal generations were certainly provided for when humanity was originally constituted and made the possessor and lord of earth ; eternal generations certainly would have been the effect of God's constitution and commands had sin not come in to interfere with the wonder- ful creation ; and as surely as Christ's redemption-work is commensurate with the ruinous effects of the fall, *eternal generations* must necessarily be. Earth and multiplying man upon it surely would never have passed from living fact into mere legend had sin never come in. Much less, then, can they now pass into mere legend, since the new and more costly expenditures of redeeming love have been superadded to the original gifts of creative wisdom and beneficence.

We thus reach the underlying foundations and background of the sublime presentations of the text. The Apostle here beholds the final redemption of our earth and race, the restitution of all things accomplished, the damages, disorders and spoliations of sin repaired, the glorious picture of The Redeemed World.

I. OBSERVE THE SCENE OF THAT WORLD.

" *Heaven new ;* "—not blotted out ; not swept into nothingness ; but retouched, changed, renovated, cleansed, and brightened up from all its old disorders and imperfections. The heaven over us now is very charming and beneficent. How beautiful and blessed the never-ceasing procession of sun, and moon, and stars, and clouds, and seasons, and days, and nights, and showers, intermingled as they are with heat and cold, storm and calm, gloom and brightness ! This old garment of things is still full of rejoicing, and glory, and scenes and themes to touch, inspire, and lift, and discipline, and make glad the heart. What, then, will that new investment be, to which it is to give place ! We cannot describe the meteorology of that new heaven ; but it will be a heaven which no more robes itself in angry tempests and menacing blackness ; nor ever flashes with the thunderbolts of wrath ; nor casts forth plagues of hail ; nor rains down fiery judgment ; nor gives lurking-place to the Devil and his angels ; nor is disfigured with dread portents ; nor is subject to commotions breeding terror and disaster to the dwellers under them. We often look at the blue sky that arches over us, at the rosy morning's welcome to the king of day, at the high noon's flood of brightness, at the mellow glories of the setting sun, at the solemn midnight lit all over with its twinkling star-gems, and we are thrilled with the perfection and beauty of Jehovah's works. What, then, shall it be when the great Architect, set to do honour to the love and faithfulness of his only begotten Son, shall put forth his hand upon it the second time, to renew it in a fresh and eternal splendour !

" *And Earth new.* " The earth now is full of ailments and disorders, and in deep captivity to corruption, yet it has much attractiveness. Most men would prefer to stay in it forever, if they could. Ah, this homestead of our fathers for so many generations, carpeted with green and flowers, waving with pleasant harvests and shady trees, girded with glorious mountains, gushing with water-springs, gladdened with laughing brooks, ribboned with rivers that wind in beauty about the rocky promontories, varied with endless hills and valleys, and girthed about with the crystal girdle of the ruffled seas,—these numerous zones, and continents, and islands,—these youthful springtimes bursting out with myriad life under all their dewy steps,—these blazing summer glories,—these gorgeous mellow autumns,—these winters, with their snowy vestments, and glazed streams, and glowing firesides,—and living Nature in its ten thousand forms, singing, and dancing, and shouting, and frisking, and rejoicing all around us,—what pictures, and memories, and histories, and legends, and experiences have we here, to warm our hearts, and stir our souls, and wake our tongues, and put fire and enthusiasm into our thoughts, and words, and deeds ! But this is only the old earth in its soiled and work-day garb, where the miseries of a deep, dark, and universal apostasy from God holds sway. Think, then, what its regeneration must bring !—an earth which no longer smarts and smokes under the curse of sin,—an earth which needs no more to be torn with hooks and irons to make it yield its fruits,—an earth where thorns and thistles no longer infest the ground, nor serpents hiss among the flowers, nor savage beasts lay in ambush to devour,—an earth whose sod is never cut with graves, whose soil is never moistened with tears or saturated with human blood, whose fields are never blasted with unpropitious seasons, whose atmosphere never gives wings to the seeds of plague and death, whose ways are never lined with funeral processions, or blocked up with armed men on their way to war,—an earth whose hills ever flow with salvation, and whose valleys know only the sweetness of Jehovah's smiles,—an earth from end to end, and from centre to utmost verge, clothed with the eternal blessedness of Paradise Restored !

And the Sea new, for I take the specification of it here the same as in the third commandment, where it is said, " In six days the Lord made heaven and earth, *the sea,* and all that in them is." (Ex. 20 : 11 ; also Rev. 10 : 6.) It is not mentioned to indicate for it a different fate from that of heaven and earth, but because it is so conspicuous and peculiar a part of them. The sea is not heaven, neither is it earth ; hence in God's enumeration of the first creation-work he mentions heaven, earth, *and sea ;* and so in the new creation-work, we have again heaven, earth, *and sea.* It is the literal sea, just as the heaven and the earth are literal ; but the non-existence affirmed of it is the same that is affirmed of the first heaven and the first earth. In other words, it undergoes the same *Palingenesia* which they undergo, and comes forth *a new sea,* the same as the old heaven and earth come forth a new heaven and earth. There is renewal, but no annihilation.

Some say there was no sea in the pristine condition of the world, and hence none will be in the finally redeemed world. But they are mistaken in both instances. The first chapter of Genesis tells of the formation of *the seas* contemporaneously with the formation of *the dry land.* (Gen. 1 : 9, 10.) When the flood came we are told that " all the fountains of *the great deep* were broken up," and that " *the sea* broke forth." (Gen. 7 : 11 ; Job 38 : 8.) There must then have been a sea from the beginning. It existed when Adam was in Paradise, as well as since Noah came out of the ark. And so there will be a sea in the new world, the same as a new heaven and a new earth. If not, this is the only passage in all the word of God that tells us anything to the contrary. We read of a river in the new earth, as of rivers in the original Paradise ; and where there are rivers there are seas. When Christ the cloud-robed Angel (chap. 10) set his feet on the earth in the solemn act of claiming and appropriating it as his own, " He set his right foot *upon the sea,*" and thus claimed and appropriated *it* the same as he claimed and appropriated the ground.* Many passages also which refer to Israel and the kingdom of God in the blessed times to come, distinctly speak of *the sea* as being turned in their favour, and as taking part in the general acclaim over the ultimate accomplishment of the mystery of God. (See Is. 42 : 10 ; 60 : 5, 9 ; Ps. 24 : 2 ; 96 : 11 ; 98 : 6, 7 ; 2 Chron. 16 : 32 ; Rev. 5 : 13.) When the time to which the text refers arrives the present sea " *no longer is,*" just as the first heaven and the first earth " *are gone.*" There is no more left of the one than of the other, but likewise no less. Just as much of the sea as of the earth abideth forever. The *Re-Genesis* touches both alike, just as the first Genesis. As there is a renewed eternal heaven and earth, so there is a renewed eternal sea also, for one is a part of the other. Then, however, it will be no longer a thing of danger and dread, but only of beauty, joy, and blessing. Some of the old Rabbins taught that, in the new world of Messiah, men shall be able to walk the surface of the sea with equal ease that they now walk the earth. Nor is this unlikely ; for the Saviour, as a man, walked on the sea, and did not sink ; and so did Peter also, until his faith and courage failed him. The regeneration is the making of Christ's miracles universal. The miracles of Christ were the pre-intimations and beginning of the great Regeneration to come, and the new creation is simply those miracles carried out into universal effect. Why not then also this with regard to the sea ? At any rate it will be subdued and rebegotten to Him who maketh *all things new,* and become a joy and service without being as now an unmanageable and dangerous hindrance and barrier. People only misread the text, and load themselves with endless perplexities, when they interpret it to mean the total abolition of all seas. As the *old sea*

---

* See page 223.

it is abolished, just as the old heavens and earth ; but, as in their case, it is an abolition which eventuates in a more congenial sea, even a *new sea*.

A new City. Occasion will offer to consider this when we come to the special vision of it in the after portions of the chapter ; but it here presents itself as the crown of the regenerated world. It is called by the old Hebrew name of *Jerusalem* ('Ιερουσαλήμ), and not by the Grecized name of the earthly city ('Ιεροσυλυμα). If the heaven, the earth, and the sea be literal, then certainly must this also be a literal city. The harlot Woman was finally developed and embodied in a literal city, and it is the same with the true Woman. It is the Bride, the Lamb's Wife, who appears in this new city for eternal blessedness, as the old Adulteress appeared in the new Babylon for everlasting destruction. That was man's glory proudly lifting itself in defiance of heaven ; this is the Lamb's glory, graciously descending in benediction to the earth. That was the consummation of this world's progress, and its end ; this is the consummation of the achievements of divine grace, and its memorial forever.

It is a *new* city, one which never appeared before, one of which all other cities are but the poor pre-intimations, and one as compared with which all present cities will sink out of mind and memory. It is new in its materials, in its size, in its location, in its style, in its permanence, in its moral purity, and in everything characteristic of it. It is heaven-built ; jewelled in its foundations, walls, and streets ; perfected in everything that is charming and beautiful, " as a bride adorned for her husband ; " lighting the nations with its brilliancy, itself ever luminous with the glory of God and the Lamb ; the true " Eternal City ; "—the imperishable palace of the immortal kings of the ages.

II. Observe the Blessedness of that World.

There is a long list of negations, telling the ills from which it brings relief.

Every tear is wiped away. He who dries them off is God himself. Human hands are poor at drying tears. If they succeed in removing one set, others come which they cannot wipe away. Earthly power, however good and kind, cannot go far in the binding up of broken hearts. Only the hand that made the spirit can reach the deep sources of its sorrows, or dry up the streams that issue from them. The springs of grief yield to no other potency. But then his loving Almightiness shall wipe every tear. " As one whom his mother comforteth, so will I comfort you, and ye shall be comforted," saith the Lord. " *Every tear*," for they be many ;—tears of misfortune and poverty, such as Job and Lazarus wept ;—tears of bereaved affection, such as Mary, and Martha, and the widow of Nain shed ;—tears of sympathy and mercy, such as Jeremiah and Jesus wept over the sins and calamities of Jerusalem ;—tears of persecuted innocence, tears of contrition and penitence for faults and crimes against the goodness and majesty of heaven ;—tears of disappointment and neglect ;—tears of yearning for what cannot now be ours ;—these, and whatever others ever course the cheeks of mortals, shall then be dried forever.

Death no longer exists. O the reign of death ! Whom has it not touched ! What circle has it not invaded ! What home has it never entered !

> There is no flock, however watched and tended,
> But one dead lamb is there !
> There is no fireside howsoe'er defended,
> But hath one vacant chair.

Around our churches lie our graveyards, and all the highways are lined with cemeteries and depositories of the dead. We can scarcely open our eyes without seeing the gloomy hearse, the funeral procession, the undertaker's warehouse, the shop full of mourning goods, or the stonecutter chiselling epitaphs. Every newspaper we pick up has its obituary lists, and every week brings forth its bills of mortality. On the right hand, on the left hand, before us, behind us, around us, beneath us, in all seasons, in all climes, everywhere, is death. We ourselves are only waiting, not knowing what day or hour we shall fall beneath its stroke. Physicians are sent forth by hundreds and thousands every year from our colleges and universities, and myriads of hands are ever busy collecting and preparing medicines for the sick ; and yet there is no check, no restraint, to the career and reign of death ! But, at length, an end to his fell dominion comes. The time will be when death itself shall die ; not by the power of man, not by mortal skill or earthly medicines, but by the great redemption of God. When the sunlight of the new Genesis dawns upon this stricken world, the grand thanksgiving shall ring out over every zone, from the equator to the poles, that " *Death is swallowed up in victory.*" Never another dying-bed shall then be seen again. Never another grave shall then be dug. For " *death shall no longer be.*"

Sorrow then ceases. Thousandfold are the heartaches and the griefs which now beset and torment the children of men. Choose what path of life we will, we cannot escape them. They follow us like our shadow. Bright as the lives of some may seem, each heart knoweth its own bitterness. Martyrs suffer where no faggots or flames are visible. But there is a boundary line over which no sorrows ever pass,—the line which divides between the new earth and this. There hearts no longer bleed in secret ; there the cold shadows never again fall on sensitive souls ; there the killing frosts no more settle on the springing plants or blooming flowers of human peace. Christ drank the cup of sorrow for our world, and it will be found empty then.

And all crying shall be hushed. Sore complaining is the commonest sound on earth. It is often without just cause ; but there is no stoicism from which it is never wrung. Man comes into the world with a cry, and goes out of it with a groan, and all between is more or less intoned with helpless wailing. The cry of pain and passion—the cry of fear and strife—the cry of wrong and oppression—the cry of want, and harm, and danger—the cry of torn affection and blasted hopes—the cry of weariness and disability—the cry of suffering and of death—the cry of a thousand unnamed distresses—how it vibrates on every breeze in every land ! But the Halleluias of the renewed world will drown out the voice of woe forever.

Neither shall pain any more be. O the racking torments to which these mortal bodies are exposed ! O the ills, and aches, and sharp distresses which come upon us through these earthly tenements ! But they shall come no more when the new world comes.

These are blessed exemptions, but there is greater good.

Life is there,—life that is life,—life in its highest fulness and noblest activities and associations,—eternal life,—for all who tread the soil and breathe the air of that new world. "The water of life" flows there free and plenteous for each and all. What that water is, is more than we can tell ; but it is a water of freshness, purity, and cleansing,—a water that slakes all thirst,—a water that revives against all symptoms of age or decay. Though years heap on years, and centuries on centuries, and cycles on cycles, never shall they dry up the moisture of immortal youth and beauty which those blessed waters give. They are the life-waters which gladden eternity, and which make eternally glad.

A soul-satisfying worship is there. The children of men there join in sublime fellowship with heaven ; for it is " on earth as it is in heaven." The Tabernacle of God, with Deity visible and approachable, as when Adam talked with his Maker as a friend and companion, shall be there, with its living oracles of unveiled truth, and assemblies of the sons of God into which Satan can no more insinuate his foul presence, or introduce a doubt, or jar, or imperfection in the flow of unsullied adoration.

And with it all is *the possession of God* himself. Jehovah is the highest good, the sum of all good. Union and intercommunion with him, the possession of him, is the crown of human blessedness and glory. To have God with us as our God, to know him, and see him, and enjoy him as our own, is the very height and coronal of all human attainment and possession—the focal point of all the promises—the fruition of the sublimest hopes. In this eternal life reaches its acme and fullest bloom.   In this man reaches the superlative of glory ; for in it he *inherits all things*. Such then and so transcendent is the blessedness of the new world, never more to end.

III. OBSERVE THE OCCUPANTS AND POSSESSORS OF THAT WORLD.

Not the " *cowardly* " who shrink from the conflict with sin, ashamed or afraid to avow and maintain their faith in God and his Christ ;—not the " *un-believing,*" who set at nought the testimonies of their Maker, scorn to trust for salvation in the merits of a crucified Saviour, and will not have Christ to rule over them ;—not the " *polluted,*" who basely degrade themselves with their uncleanness, bestiality, and abominations ;—not the " *murderers,*" whether such by outward act or inward malice ;—not "*fornicators,*" whether of the body or the cherished lust of the soul ;—not " *sorcerers,*" practitioners in the black arts, conjurers, necromancers, and seekers and exercisers of powers such as God has forbidden ;—not " *idolaters,*" whether in the form of pagan worship, or the giving of the heart to covetousness, selfishness, Mammon, or what is not God ;—nor any *false ones*, who make, or love, or act lies ;—for " *the cowardly, and unbelieving, and polluted, and murderers, and fornicators, and sorcerers, and idolaters, and all the false, their part* [*shall inherit*] *in the lake burning with fire and brimstone, which is the second death.*" Not one of all such characters ever comes into the new heaven and earth.

But all saints are there—the Church of the first-born—the holy people of God from Abel to the last martyr under the Antichrist. Jehovah has had a people in every age,—a people called out from the world, marked with holy signs, pervaded with a holy spirit,—a people signalized as pilgrims and strangers on the earth ever seeking for a firmly founded and continuing city whose maker and builder is God. Such were the patriarchs of the early ages, who saw the promises, and embraced them, and lived on earth as citizens of another and heavenly country.   Such were the prophets, who prophesied beforehand of the sufferings of Christ and the glory that should follow, and searched and inquired into those blessed things which the angels also desired to look into. Such were those in the first centuries of the Church who held fast the name of Jesus, and denied not their faith in him even amid the roaring flames, and when the blood of his confessors flowed like water. Such were those who sighed and cried through the gloom of the Middle Ages, like souls under the altar, and those who afterwards shook the torch of Jehovah's truth afresh to light the modern nations into life. And such are those in every land, of every tongue, of every age, who show by their lives and testimony that they seek a city yet to come. All these are there, not in flesh and blood, not returned to an earthy corporeal life, but in resurrection transfiguration, made like to the angels, like to their Redeemer now in glory, and having their home-place and palace in the Golden City for which they looked, and wrought, and waited, and suffered when one earth.   These are there, as occupants of the new heavens, the dwellers in the new city, the sublime and heavenly kings and priests of the eternal nations and generations.

And the still ongoing race redeemed is there. Many can think of none but glorified saints in this grand picture ; but the terms of the record will not construe with that idea. The glorified saints all belong to the celestial city, and have their home and residence in it. That city is the Tabernacle of God which comes down out of the heaven. Yet when it comes, a great voice out of the throne says : " Behold, The Tabernacle of God [is] *with the men,* [*with mankind*], and he shall tabernacle *with them, and they shall be his people, and he, the God with them, shall be their God.*" Who then are these to whom the Tabernacle of God comes, and with whom it dwells ? Who are these people distinct from it, and whom it is to enlighten and bless ? Who can they be, if not the nations of the ongoing race, dwelling in the new earth in the flesh ? They are redeemed now, holy, innocent, undying, and the Lord's people forever ; but only the Church of the after-born, and not of the first-born. Jesus, in Matthew 25, describes a judgment of " *the nations*," when, as a shepherd, he shall divide the sheep from the goats, and when the sheep "nations" shall be set on his right hand, and " go into life everlasting," whilst the goat " nations " go " into everlasting fire prepared for the devil and his angels." So, in the next chapter, we read of these same sheep " nations " walking by means of the light and aid of this celestial city (chap. 21 : 24), but quite distinct from the royal Church of the first-born, which is the New Jerusalem, the Lamb's Wife. Likewise the whole analogy of the Scriptures, from first to last, bears along with it this implication. There is not a word which asserts any purpose of God to terminate the perpetuity of humanity as an ever-expanding race. It was constituted and given command for unending perpetuity before sin touched it. If it fails to go on forever, it can only be in consequence of the introduction of sin. But there has been promised and constituted a Redeemer to ransom it from all captivity to sin and corruption. And if his redemption does not go far enough to exempt the ongoing race from being finally extinguished, then it is not redemption, and the Destroyer beats out the Almighty Redeemer. There is no escape from this alternative if we do not allow that the race of man as a race continues in the new earth, and there realizes its complete and final recovery from all the effects and ill consequences of the fall. Ransomed nations in the flesh are therefore among the occupants of the new earth, and the blessed and happy dwellers in it, as Adam and Eve dwelt in Paradise. The Sitter on the throne saith, " *Behold, new I make everything.*" That *everything* includes heaven, earth, and sea, and by necessary implication, had we no other proofs, the race of humanity is also included as a subject of the great Re-Genesis. Hence said the Almighty to Isaiah, " Behold, I create new heavens and a new earth. Be ye glad and rejoice forever in that which I create. And they shall build houses and inhabit them ; and they shall plant vineyards and eat the fruit of them. They shall not labour in vain, nor bring forth for trouble ; for they are the seed of the blessed of the Lord, and their offspring with them." (Is. 65 : 17–25.)

Men may think we dream when we thus propose to read God's word as it is written ; but he has anticipated all their rationalizing and scepticism. The Sitter upon the throne saith, " WRITE, BECAUSE THESE WORDS ARE FAITHFUL AND TRUE." There can be no mistake about it. God knew how to say what he meant, and he knew the meaning of what he did say. And to that which he has said, he affixes his own infallible seal, that the words are " faithful and true." Here, then, let us rest till their fulfilment comes.

LECTURE FORTY-NINTH

THE NEW JERUSALEM—MATERIALISM IN THE REVELATIONS OF THE FUTURE—A LITERAL CITY—HOW THE BRIDE OF THE LAMB—ITS DERIVATION—ITS LOCATION—ITS SPLENDOUR—ITS AMPLITUDE—ITS SYSTEM OF ILLUMINATION—ITS LACK OF A TEMPLE—ITS RELATION TO THE WORLD AT LARGE—ITS SUPERLATIVE HOLINESS.

REV. 21 : 9–27. (Revised Text.) And there came one of the seven angels which had the seven bowls full of the seven last plagues, and he talked with me, saying, Hither, I will show thee the Bride, the Wife of the Lamb.

And he carried me away in the spirit on to a mountain great and high, and showed me the holy city Jerusalem coming down out of the heaven from God, having the glory of God ; her brightness like a stone most precious, as a jasper stone, crystal-clear ; having a wall great and high, having twelve gates, and at the gates twelve angels, and names written thereon, which are the names of the twelve tribes of the sons of Israel ; from the east three gates, and from the north three gates, and from the south three gates, and from the west three gates. And the wall of the city having twelve foundation-stones, and on them twelve names of the twelve apostles of the Lamb.

And he that spoke with me had a measure, a golden reed, that he might measure the city, and her gates, and her walls.

And the city lieth four-square, and her length is as great as her breadth.

And he measured the city with the reed to the extent of twelve thousand stadia. The length, and the breadth, and the height of it are equal.

And he measured her wall [height] of a hundred forty-four cubits, measure of a man, which is of an angel.

And the construction of her wall jasper, and the city pure gold, like to clear glass.

The foundation-stones of the wall of the city adorned with every precious stone. The first foundation-stone, jasper, the second, sapphire ; the third, chalcedony ; the fourth, emerald ; the fifth, sardonyx ; the sixth, sardius, the seventh, chrysolyte ; the eighth, beryl ; the ninth, topaz ; the tenth, chrisoprasus ; the eleventh, jacinth ; the twelfth, amethyst.

And the twelve gates twelve pearls, each one of the gates separately was out of one pearl.

And the street of the city pure gold as transparent glass.

And a temple I saw not in it ; for the Lord God the All-Ruler and the Lamb is its temple.

And the city hath not need of the sun, nor of the moon, that they should illumine it ; for the glory of God lighted it, and the Lamb the lamp of it, and the nations shall walk by means of the light of it. And the kings of the earth bring their glory to [or *into*] it. And its gates shall not be shut by day, for night shall not be there. And they shall bring the glory and the reverence of the nations to [or *into*] it.

And there shall not enter into it anything common [or *unclean*], nor he that doeth abomination and falsehood, but only they that are written in the book [or *roll*] of the life of the Lamb.

ONE of the most remarkable paradoxes of the Church of our times is its abhorrence of materiality in connection with the Kingdom of Christ and the eternal future, whilst practically up to its ears in materialism and earthiness. Were one of the old Christians of the Apostolic age to revisit the world to take a look at our modern Christianity, I think he would be greatly puzzled to understand how, under the guise of spirituality, the whole Church is permeated and loaded down with carnal philosophies, hopes, and aims. Remembering the sublime simplicity of the ancient times, when the Church was set, like a golden circlet, on the head of the King of Glory, in contact everywhere with Divinity, he would be amazed to see how that circlet has been divorced from its original setting, stained with the flesh, and pushed into the morasses and bogs of this world, whilst earthly glories—crowns, mitres, tiaras, wealth, and secular consequence—are looked to and worshipped everywhere as the insignia of what in sad mockery is called a " spiritual " kingdom ! Would he not wonder to find Christians locating their most orthodox rejoicing in monarchs, in popes, patriarchs, bishops, sect leaders, numbers, luxurious arts, boastful speeches, worldly orators, secular education, march of intellect, and a fancied progress toward a " spiritual " millennium of mere secularism, to merge at last into an empty and impossible heaven ! And venturing to inquire of some of our popular preachers, whether this is thought to be the proper waiting for the Lord from heaven,—the way to pray " Thy kingdom come,"—the method by which to realize the blessed consummation when it shall be " on earth as it is in heaven,"—the holding fast of the characteristic and animating patriarchal hope of a celestial city which Christ has gone to build and to bring down out of the heaven as the eternal residence of his enthroned saints,—what would be his surprise to get for answer : " Sir, you are labouring under a delusion,—the kingdom was set up 1,800 years ago, —the speedy coming again of Christ in person to reign on earth is a carnal idea, long since exploded, and held only by a few eccentric people who cannot rise to a conception of the true spirituality of the Bible ;—and as to the heavenly Jerusalem, why that is only a gorgeous Oriental symbol of the beautiful church state which you see all around you. The glory of Christianity is to keep abreast with the times, to press popular education, to create machinery to reach and elevate the masses, to follow up the conquests of arms with Bibles and missionaries, schools and civilization, to purify and influence legislation, to improve society by gradual reforms and general enlightenment, to win for the Church the patronage of the rich and great, and so to progress till the whole earth shall rest in the embrace of a worldwide ' spiritual ' kingdom (located here in Satan's lap !) to last for indefinite ages ! " With a groan over his inability to rise to such a philosophy, I can fancy the ancient saint gladly returning to his grave, to sleep in honest earth till that resurrection on which *his* hopes were fixed, rather than hear any further about a " spirituality " so carnal, and a Christianity so doubtful and earthy.

A spiritualized earthiness is simply a white-washed sepulchre ; and an incorporeal and immaterial eternity for man, is equally aside from the teachings of God's Word. No wonder that professed believers of our day are anxious to put off getting into the heaven they believe in as long as the doctor's skill can keep them out of it, and finally agree to go only as a last despairing resort. It has no substance, no reality, for the soul to take hold on. It is nothing but a world of shadows, of mist, of dim visions of blessedness, with which it is impossible for a being who is not mere spirit, and never will be mere spirit, who knows only to live in a body and shall live forever in a body, to feel any fellowship or sympathy.

But such are not the ideas of our futurity which the Bible holds out to our faith and hope. Did men but learn to know the difference between a Paradise of sense and a Paradise of sensuality, the truth of God would not suffer in men's hands as it does, and their souls would not suffer as they do for something solid to anchor to amid the anxious perturbations of life and death. Did men but rid themselves of the old heresy that matter means sin, and learn to know and feel that there was a material universe before sin was, and that a material universe will live on when sin shall have been clean washed away from the entire face of it, they would be in better position both to understand and to enjoy the fore-announcements of the futurity of the saints which God has given for their consolation amid these earthly vicissitudes and falsities. Says one of the greatest of Scottish preachers : " There is much of the innocent, and much of the inspiring, and much to affect and elevate the heart in the scenes and contemplations of materiality,—and we do hail the information, that, after the loosening of the present framework, it will again be varied and decked out anew in all the graces of its unfading verdure, and of its unbounded variety,—that in addition to our direct personal view of the Deity, when he comes down to tabernacle with men, we shall also have the reflection of him in a lovely mirror of his own workmanship,—and that instead of being transported to some abode of dimness and mystery, so remote from human experience as to be beyond all comprehension, we shall walk forever in a land replenished with those sensible delights, and those sensible glories, which, we doubt not, will lie most profusely scattered over the ' new heavens and new earth.' We are now walking on a terrestrial surface, not more compact, perhaps, than the one we shall hereafter walk upon ; and are now wearing terrestrial bodies, not firmer and more solid, perhaps, than those we shall hereafter wear. It is not by working any change upon them that we could realize, to any extent, our future heaven. The spirituality of our future state lies not in the kind of substance which is to compose its framework, but in the character of those who people it. There will be a firm earth, as we have at present, and a heaven stretched over it, as we have at present ; and it is not by the absence of these, but by the absence of sin, that the abodes of immortality will be characterized." (Chalmers.)

The New Jerusalem, which we now come to consider, is in the line of these ideas. It stands in antithesis to the final Babylon. John is called by one of the same particular angels, in precisely the same way, to be shown it as he was called to be shown the great Harlot. (See chap. 17.) The world and all its activities and achievements is made up of two opposing sides,—the side of the heavenly, the good, the blessed, and the side of the earthy, sensual, and devilish,—the true and the false,—the things which gravitate toward eternal life, and the things which gravitate toward destruction and the second death,—the kingdom of heaven, and the kingdom of the devil. These two are at present intermingled, and are differently situated toward each other at different periods, the one often hard to be distinguished from the other. But everything on either side has an affinity for its own, and is true to its own ; so that, in the progress of time, each side becomes more and more itself, developed and consolidated, until the two antagonistic influences, tendencies, and parties crystallize to their true spirit, and finally come out in two opposite cities ; the one of the earth and from the earth, and the other of heaven and from the heaven ; the one for everlasting extinguishment under the wrath of God, and the other for eternal illumination with his unveiled presence and glory. Whatever, therefore, may be the run of our ideas of the one, the same must hold good of the other also ; for what Great Babylon is on the side of the bad, this New Jerusalem is on the side of the good ; for they are counterparts of each other, and each is the ultimate consummation of that to which it relates.

The Apostle had already seen this city " coming down out of the heaven from God ; " but he saw it only at a distance, and without that particular spiritual transport which was necessary to enable him to see it so as to describe it. God meant that we should have as clear and thorough an outlook upon the ultimate crown on the side of grace and salvation, as he has given us of the ultimate crown and end of the sensual wisdom and the man-wrought progress ; and hence this angel comes to show John the Bride, the Lamb's Wife, in her final condition and domicile, and in all the magnificence of her eternal glory. And whatever tabernacle of God, or congregating of true worshippers, or seat or character of Divine economies, constitutions, or manifestations, have been graciously vouchsafed to men, as individuals, nationalities, or churches, from the foundation of the world to this time, is here shown in its final consummation, completeness, and eternal reality.

That a real City as well as a perfected moral system is here to be understood, I see not how we can otherwise conclude. Great Babylon, to which it stands as the exact antithesis, came out finally in a real and universally potent city ; so, therefore, must this. All the elements of a city are indicated. It has specific dimensions. It has foundations, walls, gates, and streets. It has guards outside and inhabitants within, both distinct from what characterizes it as a real construction. It is called a city—" *The Holy City.*" It is named as a city, " *The Holy Jerusalem.*" It is called " The *New* Jerusalem," as over against an *old* Jerusalem, which was a material city. Among the highest promises to the saints of all ages was the promise of a special place and economy answering to a heavenly city, and which is continually referred to as an enduring and God-built city. Abraham " looked for *a city* which hath foundations, whose maker and builder is God." (Heb. 11 : 10.) Of all the ancient saints it is written, that " God hath prepared for them *a city*." (Heb. 11 : 16.) Jesus assured the disciples from whom he was about to be separated, " I go to prepare *a place* for you. And if I go and prepare *a place* for you, I will come again, and receive you unto myself ; that where I am there ye may be also." (Jno. 14 : 2, 3.) Hence the Apostle, in the name of all Christians of his day, said, " Here we have no *continuing city*, but we seek *one to come*." (Heb. 13 : 14.) Hence also it is given as one of the great exaltations of true believers, even here on earth, that they " are come unto *the city* of the living God, the heavenly Jerusalem " (Heb. 12 : 22) ; not indeed as to actual possession as yet, but as having attained to title to it and to citizenship in it by faith, hope, and sure anticipation. And whatever difficulty we may have in taking it in, or in reconciling it to our prepossessions, I do not see how we can be just and fair to God's Word, and the faith of the saints of former ages, and not see and admit that we here have to do, not with a mere ideal and fantastic city, but with a true, real, God-built city, substantial and eternal ; albeit there has never been another like it.

The angel calls it " *the Bride, the Lamb's Wife.*" The heavenly city is Christ's Bride, not on account of what makes it a city, but on account of the sanctified and glorified ones who inhabit it. Without the saints, whose home and residence it is, it would not be the Lamb's Wife ; and yet it is the Lamb's Wife in a sense which does not exclude the foundations, walls, gates, streets and constructions which contribute to make it a city. Mere edifices and avenues do not make a city ; neither does a mere congregation or multitude of people make a city. You cannot have a living city without people to inhabit it ; and you cannot have a city without the edifices and avenues arranged in some fixed shape for the accommodation of those who make up its population. It is the two together, and the order in which the parts are severally disposed, the animate with the inanimate, which constitute a city. And whilst this holy Jerusalem is the Bride and Wife of Christ with reference to its holy occupants, it is still those occupants as disposed and arranged in that city. So that the city as a city, as well as its people as a people, even the whole taken together, is embraced in what the angel calls " the Bride, the Lamb's Wife," as she finally appears in her eternal form and completeness.

The description which the Apostle gives us of this city, though very brief, is very magnificent, and presents a picture which almost blinds us with its brightness. It is not necessary that I should enter upon a discussion of the numerous details. They can be found more or less accurately given in almost any respectable commentary on the Apocalypse. Only to a few of its broader and more important features do I invite attention at present, with a few brief remarks on each.

1. *Its Derivation.*—John sees it " coming down out of heaven from God." It is of celestial origin. It is the direct product of Almighty power and wisdom. He who made the worlds is the Maker of this illustrious city. No mortal hand is ever employed upon its construction. The saints are all God's workmanship. They are all begotten of his Spirit, and shaped and fashioned into living stones from the dark quarries of a fallen world, and transfigured from glory to glory by the gracious operations of his hand. They reach their heavenly character and places through his own direct agency and influence. And he who makes, prepares, and places them, makes, prepares, and places their sublime habitation also. It is elsewhere said, in so many words, that the maker and builder of this city is God. (Heb. 11 : 10.) It has no architect, no workmen, but himself. He who by his Spirit garnished the heavens, erects and fashions the New Jerusalem.

2. *Its Location.*—This is not specifically told, but the record is not without some hints. John sees it coming down out of heaven. The idea is that it comes close to the earth, and is intended to have a near relation to the earth ; but it is nowhere said that it ever alights on the earth, or ever becomes part of its material fabric. Though coming into the vicinity of the earth, it is always

spoken of as the " Jerusalem which is *Above*." (Gal. 4 : 26.) The nations on the earth " walk by means of its light," which implies that it is *over* them. John could only get a near view of it by being spiritually transported to the top of " a mountain great and high," like the greatest altitudes of the Alps or the Himalayas. The prophecies also speak of a future Jerusalem as set at the tops of the mountains, and exalted over the hills. (Is. 2 : 2.) If a final exaltation of the earthly Jerusalem is contemplated in such passages, the language still is borrowed from something higher, in which alone its literal import can be realized, and hence includes more especially the " Jerusalem which is above," of which the earthly Jerusalem is the type. The probabilities are that it will stand high over Palestine, and perhaps stationary, as the earth revolves under it, not so high as not to be in ample view of all the dwellers of the earth, and not so low as not to throw its illumination upon all nations and countries, and upon at least half the earth at a time. Something like what the pillar of cloud and fire were to the tribes of Israel when they came up out of Egypt, shall the relation and location of this glorious city be, with reference to the generations of men in the new earth.

3. *Its Splendour.*—Here the specifications are numerous and transcendant, as we would expect in a city erected and ornamented by Jehovah, and coming forth direct from the heavens. Everything built by God's direction is the very best and most splendid of its kind. So was the ship in which Noah was saved ; so was the Great Pyramid, of which there is reason to believe that it was built by divine direction ; * and so were the Jewish Tabernacle and Temple. Much rather then would it be so in a " Great City," built with his own hands, and intended as the sublime crown of the most marvellous of all his glorious works. And as we would expect, so the description is.

Earthly cities are often very magnificent and charming ; but if we take our stand on some high point from which to look down upon them, we can see nothing but irregular heaps of human habitations and buildings, mostly involved in a mist of fumes and smoke, having but a dim light of their own ; dusty, dingy, and by no means the most beautiful objects on which the eye can rest. It is very different with this heavenly city. It is as clean, and pure, and bright as a transparent icicle in the sunshine. John describes it as " having the glory of God." *Glory* is brightness, lustre, splendour. The glory of God, or that in which God is arrayed, that which most bespeaks and characterizes Deity, is *Light ;* for " God is light," and in him is no darkness at all. And this city has, and is invested with, the glory, light, brightness, and radiating splendour of God. That brightness as it flashed on Saul of Tarsus on the road to Damascus, surpassed the radiance of the noonday sun of Syria. The very intensity of its brilliancy struck him blind. And this brightness the New Jerusalem has, only with its sharpness when manifested against sin and sinners softened, for there are no more sinners, and no wrath. Hence the brightness is like a most precious *jasper stone.* A jasper stone is wavy with the various colours of the rainbow ; but it is opaque. This city has this jasper appearance, but without the opacity. It is " like a most precious jasper stone *crystal-clear*," perfectly transparent, like a diamond or rock-crystal. So pure, so bright, so soft, is the luminous and divine splendour in which this whole city is arrayed.

It has " a wall great and high," which is not only like jasper, but which is built of jasper itself. And that wall stands on twelve foundation-stones, and each of those twelve immense stones is a separate and distinct jewel in itself. There are certain substances in nature, found in very small fragments, which are so scarce, rare, beautiful, and enduring that they are called gems, or precious stones ; so precious that the prices of them are almost fabulous, and hence they are used almost exclusively for rich and costly ornament. Twelve kinds of these, each a vast, apportioned, and solid mass, make up the foundations on which the jasper walls of this city are built. Through these

* See my volume, *A Miracle in Stone.*

walls are twelve openings or gateways, with twelve gates ; and each of these twelve gates is made of one solid pearl.

From these gates inward there are as many main streetways, and all the streetway is gold,—gold in perfect purity, such as cannot be reached by any earthly refinement,—gold with a peculiar heavenly quality beyond what is ever seen in our gold,—*transparent gold* like the most perfect glass. Men have built some very grand cities, the houses of which they have constructed of all manner of costly stones, granite, marble, and other solid productions of the earth, dressed, and polished, and ornamented to degrees of great excellence. But there is one part of every such city which they are satisfied to have of inferior material, only so that it is even and smooth ; namely, the part which is trodden under every one's feet. It therefore gives a very high touch to the splendour of this celestial city that its very streets are pure transparent gold.

And the city itself is of the same material,—nothing but "*pure gold like to clear glass.*" It is a true *crystal palace*, made of nothing but transparent gold. An object is thus presented, the splendour of which far outshines the most sublime creations of which the human imagination ever dreamed.

4. *Its Amplitude.*—There is no stint or meanness in God's creations. When he set himself to the making of worlds, he filled up an immeasurable space with them. He brought them forth in numbers without number, of grades upon grades, from the moons which play around the planets to luminous masses beyond any power of man to commensurate their enormous magnitude. When he created angels he added myriads on myriads, and orders on orders, till all earthly arithmetic is lost in the counting of them. When he started the human race it was on a career of multiplication to which we can set no limit. When he began the glorious work of redemption, and commenced the taking out and fashioning of a people to become the companions of his only begotten Son and co-regents with their Redeemer, these pictures of the final outcome tell of great multitudinous hosts, in numbers like the sands of the seashore. And the city he builds for them is of corresponding dimensions.

Starting from the centre of our own city, though perhaps the largest in extent on this continent, we can travel but a few miles till we get beyond its built-up limits ; and its breadth is but slight compared with its length. But the golden city for which the Church of the first-born is taught to look as its eternal home, is 1,500 *miles square;* for 12,000 *stadia* make 1,500 miles. John saw it measured, and this was the measure of it, just as wide as it is long, and just as high as it is wide ; for the " length and the breadth and the height of it are equal." Here would be streets over streets, and stories over stories, up, up, up, to the height of 1,500 miles, and each street 1,500 miles long. Thus this city is a solid cube of golden constructions, 1,500 miles every way. The base of it would stretch from furthest Maine to furthest Florida, and from the shore of the Atlantic to Colorado. It would cover all Britain, Ireland, France, Spain, Italy, Germany, Austria, Prussia, European Turkey, and half of European Russia, taken together ! Great was the City of Nineveh, so great that Jonah had only *begun* to enter it after a day's journey. How long then would it take a man to explore this city of gold, whose every street is one-fifth the length of the diameter of the earth, and the number of whose main avenues, though a mile above each other, and a mile apart, would not be less than eight millions ! " Stupendous magnitude ! Alexandria is said by Josephus to have had a length of 30 stadia, and a width of not less than 10 stadia. According to the same, the circuit of Jerusalem is defined by 33 stadia ; that of Thebes, according to Dicæarchus, by 43 stadia ; that of Nineveh, according to Diodorus Siculus, by 400 stadia. Herodotus, in his first book, says that Babylon had 120 stadia in each side, and 480 stadia in each circuit, and that its wall was 50 cubits thick and 200 cubits high. This is 12,000 stadia every way. All the cities in the world are mere villages in comparison with the New Jerusalem." (Bengel, *in loc.*) Even the jasper wall which surrounds it is higher than the highest of our church spires. Earth has no foundations on which such a city could be set, to say nothing of the materials of which it is built ; therefore it comes forth out of the heaven from God, and has its place above the tops of the mountains.

It has ever been an anxious question to believing souls, what proportion of the people who have lived, or now live, are likely to reach this blessed city. Men came to the Saviour when on earth, inquiring, " Lord, are there few that be saved ? " It is a complex question which could not be made profitably clear to those who put it, and it has nowhere been directly answered. It is better that we should be about making our own salvation sure, than speculating about the number who finally get to heaven. But the picture here placed before us casts a light upon the inquiry, as exalting to the grace of God as it is encouraging to those who really wish to be saved. This golden city has not been built in all this amplitude and magnificence of proportions for mere empty show. God did not create the earth in vain ; " he formed it to be inhabited." (Is. 45: 18.) Much rather, then, would he not lavish all this glory and splendour upon the Eternal City, without knowing that enough out of the family of man would embrace his salvation to fill and people it. And the population to fill and occupy a city 1,500 miles long, and broad, and high, allowing the amplest room and space for each individual, family, tribe, and tongue, and nation, would necessarily mount up to myriads on myriads, who sing the songs and taste the joys of the redemption that is in Christ Jesus. Amplitude—amplitude of numbers, as well as glorious accommodations—is unmistakably signified, in whatever way we contemplate the astonishing picture.

5. *Its System of Illumination.*—What is a city without light ! And what is more difficult of management in utilizing city spaces than the arrangements for light ! Fortunately no gas trusts are needed in the New Jerusalem, nor light of the sun, nor light of the moon. It is itself a grand prism of inherent light, the Light of God and the Lamb, which illuminates at once the eyes of the body and of the soul, and shines not only on the objects without but on the understandings within, making everything light in the Lord. The glory of God's brightness envelops it like an unclouded halo, permeates it, and radiates through it and from it so that there is not a dark or obscure place about it. It shines like a new sun, inside and out, sending abroad its rays over all the earth, and into the depths of space, making our planet seem to distant worlds as if suddenly transformed into a brilliant luminary, whose brightness never wanes.   And that shining is not from any material combustion,—not from any consumption of fuel that needs to be replaced as one supply burns out ; for it is the uncreated light of Him who is light, dispensed by and through the Lamb as the everlasting Lamp, to the home, and hearts, and understandings, of his glorified saints. When Paul and Silas lay wounded and bound in the inner dungeon of the prison of Philippi, they still had sacred light which enabled them to beguile the night-watches with happy songs. When Paul was on his way to Damascus, a light brighter than the sun at noon shone round about him, irradiating his whole being with new sights and understanding, and making his soul and body ever afterwards light in the Lord. When Moses came down from the mount of his communion with God, his face was so luminous that his brethren could not endure to look upon it. He was in such close fellowship with light that he became informed with light, and came to the camp as a very lamp of God, glowing with the glory of God. On the Mount of Transfiguration that same light streamed forth from all the body and raiment of the blessed Jesus. And with reference to the very time when this city comes into being and place, Isaiah says, " the moon shall be ashamed and the sun confounded,"—ashamed because of the out-beaming glory which then shall appear in the New Jerusalem, leaving no more need for them to shine in it, since the glory of God lights it, and the Lamb is the light thereof.

6. *Its Lack of a Temple.*—" A Temple," says the seer, " I saw not in it." What a vacuum it could create in every earthly city if its temples were taken away ! What would ancient Jerusalem have been without its Temple ? How much does the fame and glory of the most renowned of cities, ancient and modern, rest on their Temples ! Strip them of these and what would be their nakedness ! But it is no privation to the New Jerusalem that there is no Temple in it. Nay, it is one of its sublimest peculiarities. Not that worship is then to cease. Not that communion with the eternal Spirit and Source of all things is no longer to exist. While God and holy beings live, their loving adoration of him cannot cease, nor acts of worship be discontinued. But then and there the worship and communion will no longer be through symbols, veils, and intermediate ceremonials, which now are needed to help the soul to divine fellowship. Deity will then have come forth from behind all veils, all mediating sacraments, all previous barriers and hidings because of the infirmities of the flesh or the weaknesses of undeveloped spirituality. Himself will be the Temple thereof. The glorious worshippers there hold direct communion with his manifested glory, which encompasses them and all their city alike. As consecrated high priests they will then have come into the holiest of all, into the very cloud of God's overshadowing glory, which is at once their covering, their Temple, their God.

When Jesus walked with his disciples on earth, wherever he was they had a Temple. In the mountains and wildernesses of retirement, in the midst of the street concourse, on the heights where he was transfigured, in the upper room where they ate with him the paschal supper, along the way to Emmaus, on the shores of Galilee, on the Mount of Ascension, wherever his divine presence, power, and goodness spoke its " Peace be unto you," was a Temple to them. What an encumbrance and detraction would have been Aaron's garments, and Aaron's breastplate, and Aaron's ceremonials of inquiry and worship, when they had with them " God manifest in the flesh," on whose bosom they could lay their heads, whose cheeks they could kiss, whose feet they could bathe with their tears, whose words they could hear, and whose gracious services and benedictions they could at all times command ! What need of Solomon's Temple had they, when the embodied Shechinah himself, in ever-approachable form, was with them by day and by night, their brother, their master, their everlasting friend ! And when the saints in immortal glory dwell within the enclosing light of the unveiled presence of God and the Lamb, as his Bride and Wife, what more need have they of Temple, or outward ceremonial, to commune with Deity, or to have fellowship with the Father and the Son ! God and the Lamb are then themselves the Temple, and the intervention of any other Temple would be a disability, a clog, and a going back from the sublime exaltation which the saints there reach and enjoy. Hence John saw no Temple in that city, " for the Lord God, the All-Ruler, and the Lamb is its Temple." The worship there is immediate and direct.

7. *Its Relation to the World at Large.*—Of old, the song of the Psalmist was : " Beautiful for situation, the joy of the whole earth, is Mount Zion, the City of the Great King." (Ps. 48 : 2.) In every land into which the Jewish people wandered, there was a glad thrill upon their souls when they remembered Jerusalem. Night and morning they knelt down with their faces thitherward to chant the praises of Him who there dwelt between the Cherubim ; and year by year the pilgrim bands went up from all lands, with gladness of heart, and lute, and song, unto the mountain of the Lord, to the Mighty One of Israel. Thither came the tribes of the Lord, unto the Testimony of Israel, to give thanks unto the Name of the Lord ; for there were set the thrones of judgment, the thrones of the house of David. (Ps. 122.) Out of Zion went the law, and the Word of the Lord from Jerusalem. We cannot look back upon those times, even now, without a degree of fascination which draws like a magnet upon every feeling of the heart. And what was then realized on a small and feeble scale, in the case of one people, is to be the universal exper-

ience with regard to this blessed city. It is to be the centre and illuminator of the world.

" *The nations shall walk by means of the light of it.*" Spiritual illumination for the soul, as well as glorious light for the eyes,—the light of truth and righteousness, and the light of Life for all wants, personal, social, and national, in the redeemed family of man,—shall go forth from that sublime city ; and " the nations " shall walk in that light. Their polity, their religion, and all that goes to make up for them an economy of Edenic blessedness, shall come forth from that sublime metropolis. Their kings, their judges, their priests, their loving guides, their Saviour, their only Lord God, are there, visible to their eyes, and ever present to their hearts and minds. What never yet has been upon this earth, a really holy nation, will then be found wherever man is found, and all people shall be the people of the Lord. Men talk of *Christian nations ;* but, in all this dwelling-place of man, from the beginning until now, there is nothing of the sort to answer to the phrase. There is no such thing, and there never will be, till the New Earth appears, and the New Jerusalem comes into the view of men. But then, all nations, as nations, shall be sanctified and holy ; for they shall walk in the light of the Eternal City of the Eternal King. That City, raised aloft, and filled with the Spirit and glory of God and the Lamb, will be the illumination and the great glory of the world, the centre of supremest interest,—the joy of the waking thoughts and the sleeping dreams of all the children of men.

" *And the kings of the earth bring their glory and honour to* (or *into*) *it.*" The Kings will then be Christ and his glorified saints. These will reside in this city, and whatever pertains to them as kings will have its centre and seat there. Their glory as kings, their authority and their thrones, will all go to honour, dignify, and distinguish this city. And if by " kings *of the earth* " we are to understand sub-kings belonging to unglorified humanity, the statement implies that the homage and gratitude of earthly royalty will then devote everything of greatness and glory that it possesses to the service and honour of that city.

" *And they shall bring the glory and reverence of the nations to* (or *into*) *it.*" All the honour the world can give will be given to that city. All nations, as one man, shall then be happy worshippers, and all devotion shall concentre in the New Jerusalem. All eyes, all ears, shall be turned to it. And all the honour that men can render, and all the delight the human heart can feel, will flow forever to that high tabernacle, whose gates are never shut, and where no night is ever known.

8. *Its superlative Holiness.*—" Holy, Holy, Holy, is the Lord God of hosts," cried the six-winged Seraphim ; and where that God is, only what is holy can find place. This is " the mountain of his Holiness," the city where his glory dwells ; therefore no common or unclean thing can ever enter it, nor any one that doeth abomination, or worketh what is false. "*Holy things for holy people,*" was the announcement given out by the Church for many ages whenever about to present the mystery of the holy Supper ; and a similar word forever flames around those gates of pearl. The city is ample ; it is magnificent ; and there is place within it for every one ready and willing to become its denizen ; but it is " *holy,*" and no one can ever set foot upon its golden streets who is not enrolled in the book of life of the Lamb. Sinners may come there, yes ; for sinners it was made ; but only for such as are cleansed in the proffered bath of regeneration, by the washing of water and the word. No place is there for them that believe not in Jesus, and submit not themselves to his saving righteousness. No place is there for them that say, " Lord, Lord," but do not the things which he has commanded. And if any love their sins better than God's salvation, the New Jerusalem is not for them. It is for those only whose names, through faith and sanctification of the Spirit, have been written in the Lamb's book of life.

Such, then, in brief, is that holy City which has been glittering in the imaginations and the songs of God's people, in every age and under all dispensation.

Its foundations by their colours speak of grace, mercy, and God's sure covenant earthward. Its gates of pearl speak of righteousness, obedience, and the heart set on the precious things of the divine kingdom, as the medium of transit from earth to glory. Its cubic form, and its streets and constructions of purest gold, proclaim it the embodiment of all perfection, the supremest seat of the supremest saintship. And within those immortal gates, in the very presence and company of God and the Lamb, surrounded with light, riches, and splendours beyond all that human thought can estimate, amid the liberties, securities, and perfections of the highest of all the material creations of gracious Omnipotence, as the jewelled link between the Eternal Father and his redeemed earthly family, and with a strength that walks unshaken under all the exceeding and eternal weight of glory, the Church of the first-born, the Bride and Wife of Christ, shall live and reign with him, day without end, for the ages of the ages.

> Exult, O dust and ashes,
> 　Thy God shall be thy part !
> His only, His forever,
> 　Thou shalt be and thou art !

LECTURE FIFTIETH

THE NEW JERUSALEM CONTINUED—A MORE INWARD VIEW—THE WONDERFUL RIVER—THE TREE OF LIFE—THE CURSE REPEALED—THE EVERLASTING THRONE—THE ETERNAL BLESSEDNESS.

REV. 22 : 1–5. (Revised Text.) And he showed me a river of water of life clear as crystal, coming forth out of the throne of God and the Lamb. In the midst of the street of it [the city] and on either side of the river, tree of life producing twelve fruits [or *kinds of fruit*], according to each month yielding its fruit, and the leaves of the tree unto healing of the nations. And every curse [or *accursed thing*], shall not be any more ; and the Throne of God and of the Lamb shall be in it, and his servants shall serve him, and they shall see his face, and the name of him [shall be] upon their foreheads ; and night shall not be any more, and they shall not have need of lamp and light, because the Lord God shall shine upon them, and they shall reign to the ages of the ages.

THE Apostle here continues his description of the New Jerusalem, and for this reason these verses should not have been separated from the section which precedes them. They relate to the same subject, and have nothing to mark them from what has gone before, except that they refer more to the interior of the heavenly city. The description throughout is rather external than internal. John saw from the outside, and from a distance ; and his account is necessarily more occupied with what the city is to those who contemplate it from without, than with what it is in itself or to those who have their homes in its " many mansions." The reason may be that it is not possible for us to form right conceptions of things so much above and beyond all present experiences. When Paul recovered from his trance-vision of Paradise, and the third heaven, he said that it was not permitted him to tell the transcendent things which he saw and heard. And so John is not brought to such a view of the sublime palace of the saints as to tell us all about its internal economy. Yet, what was shown him, as narrated in these verses, relate more to the inside, than what we had before us a week ago. To these more inner particulars, then, let us direct our thoughts, humbly looking to God to aid us to form right impressions of his glorious revelations.

It is due to remark that we here have the final touches in the picture of the eternal future. These verses give us the furthest and fullest outlook into the everlasting economies. Precious, therefore, should it be to us. With what deep and anxious attention should we dwell on every intimation, and cherish every image ! Even when about to leave off contemplating some noted earthly picture, we always turn to take a last impression to carry with us as we depart. How much rather, then, should we incline our energies to get a clear idea of these richest and fullest delineations of that ultimate home to which we aspire, beyond which there is no further knowledge to be had till we come to take up our everlasting residence there !

Very noteworthy also is it that these last glimpses of a finished Redemption end up with the same images with which the first chapter of human history begun. All worlds move in circles ; and the grand march of God's providence with man moves in one immense round. It starts with Paradise, and thence moves out through strange and untried paths, until it has fulfilled its grand revolution by coming back to the point from which it started ; not indeed to repeat itself, but thenceforward to rest forever in the results of that wonderful experiment. Genesis is the Book of beginnings ; the Revelation is the Book of the endings of what was then begun ; and the last laps back again upon the first, and welds the two ends of the history into the golden ring of eternity.

There was a time of innocence, and then came a long and dreary time of the absence of innocence ; and here we are shown the time of innocence returned, to depart no more. Nor is it without the most cheering significance, that in the account of the final consummation we again come upon a group of objects answering to the most conspicuous and fondly remembered in all the bright story of the original opening of the world.

I. The Apostle begins by telling us of a wonderful River.

One of the gladdest things on earth is water. There is nothing in all the world so precious to the eye and imagination of the inhabitant of the dry, burning and thirsty East, as a plentiful supply of bright, pure, and living water. Paradise itself was not complete without it. Hence "a river went out of Eden to water the garden ; and from thence it was parted and became into four heads," rolling their bright currents over golden sands and sparkling gems (Gen. 2 : 10–12), as if meant to water and gladden all the earth. "A city without water would be a most disconsolate and unpleasant thing ; therefore we see cities at the greatest pains to provide themselves with water, and those are reckoned the best which are the most happily watered. It is one of the great excellencies of Ezekiel's city, that it has a river ever deepening as it flows." (Ezek. 47 : 3.) And so the New Jerusalem is not without its plentiful supply of living waters. Of the angel who came to show him this great metropolis of the saints, John says : "*And he showed me a river of water of life, bright as crystal, coming forth out of the throne of God and of the Lamb.*"

With whatever tenacity the interpreters of this Book cling to the notion that waters, in prophetic language, always mean peoples, they give it up when it comes to this river. Peoples do not issue from the throne of God. But what to make of this water they hardly know. Some make it Baptism. Some make it saving knowledge, flowing out from God over all the habitable world. Some make it the grace of God through the preaching of Christ crucified. Some make it the giving of peace to the perturbed nations. Some make it " the renewing and sanctifying influences by which the nations are to be imbued with spiritual life." Some make it a mere Oriental image of abounding happiness and plenty. And many who even see in the description a picture of Paradise regained, are still so fettered down to the present world, that they cannot get on with it above or beyond what is purely earthy. Why cannot men see and read that it does not belong to the earth at all, nor to any earthly people, or any earthly good. There is not a word said to show that these waters in this particular form ever touch the earth, or any dwellers on the earth. The river is a heavenly river, and belongs to a heavenly city, and is for the use and joy of a heavenly people. Its waters are literal waters, of a nature and quality answering to that of the golden city to which they belong. Man on earth never knew such waters, as men on earth never knew such a city ; but the city is a sublime reality,—the home and residence of the Lamb and his glorious Bride,—and these waters are a corresponding reality. Of old, the Psalmist sung, " There is a river, the streams whereof shall make glad the city of God, the holy place of the tabernacles of the Most High " (Ps. 46 : 4), " the river of God's pleasures," where they that put their trust under the shadow of his wings shall be abundantly satisfied with the fatness of his dwelling-place, even at the headspring of life, amid visions of light in the pavilion of his glory. (Ps. 36 : 7–9.) Heaven is not a place of dust and drought. It has its glad water-spring and ever-flowing river, issuing direct from the eternal throne, whose crystal clearness cannot be defiled. There flow the immortal waters, for the joy of glorified natures, bright with the light of God, and filling all with life-cheer as immortal as themselves.

These waters are called " water of life coming forth out of the throne." They are the issuing life of the throne, as the city itself is the embodiment of God's glory. The throne is the throne of the Lamb, in whom is the eternal Godhead. The Father reigns in and through the Son, and this is the reviving and all-animating life and spirit of all this embodiment of Deity in that

sublime city.   It is the Holy Ghost for that celestial Tabernacle, as God and
the Lamb are the Temple of it. It is the divine emanation from the Father and
the Son which fills and cheers and forever rejoices the dwellers in that place.
These waters also come to the inhabitants of the earth, and refresh and bless
them too, as these celestial king-priests have to do with the people of the earth ;
but they reach the earthly population in other forms, and not in the form of
this voluminous river.   In this form they belong to the Holy City alone.
Only these saints in glory come to the throne, and share its life and administration ; and for them alone is the crystal river which issues from it.   It is the
Spirit of glory which they drink and embody ; and it is for their pleasure and
blessedness, as to no other class of the human family.   Yet we are not without
something of those waters in the saving administrations of the Holy Ghost,
even now, and the dwellers in the New Earth shall have more of them than we
have ; but neither now nor then can those living in the flesh have them
in anything of the unmingled purity, heavenliness, and glorious fulness
with which they flow forever in the New Jerusalem.   In the first
Eden, "there went up a mist from the earth, and watered the whole face
of the ground." (Gen. 2 : 6.)   There was a watering through an earthly
medium.   And in some such mediate way these waters come to the Church
now, and will come still more plenteously to the nations when this Great City
comes to its place.   But in the Holy City they roll as a river, through no
secondary medium, and give forth their exhaustless blessedness direct from
the throne of God and the Lamb.

The Jordan is often spoken of as a sacred river, and many sacred memories
connect with it.   Palestine's penitent thousands there flocked to the wild
Baptizer, and sought in that stream to wash away their sins.   Thither the
Saviour himself came, to receive upon his spotless person those same
consecrating waters.   But Jordan is the symbol of earthly, not heavenly life.
Bright and beautiful in its cradle, it laughs away its merry morning amid the
flowery fields of Hulêh ; then plunges with the recklessness of youth into the
tangled breaks and muddy marshes of Merom ; and thence it issues full-grown,
like earnest manhood with its noisy bustle, dashing along till it quiets into a
picture of life's sober midday in the placid Lake of Genesareth.   Thence its
course is down, down, like the declivities of age, sinking lower and lower amid
doublings and windings innumerable, until it finally reaches the sea of death,
where there is no remedy but to breathe itself out upon the thin air, and vanish
in the clouds.   Like human life, it is mostly a turbid and clouded stream.
This, however, is a different river, and betokens a very different life.   It rises
from no dark caves of earth.   It does not grow from additions from without.
It has no windings, no stagnations, no obstructions, no clouds, no muddiness,
no rising and falling, no sea of death, no precipitations of earthiness, no
evaporations to deadly asphalt and salt.   The life it symbolizes, and is, and
gives, is divine life, the life of the throne of God and of the Lamb, the life that
rolls forth in highest fulness from its living source, pellucid as the city which it
supplies, and as unfailing and all-gladdening as the Spirit of holiness itself.
O the blessedness of the eyes that see and the people who enjoy this river of
God—these crystal waters of eternal life.

II. In the next place the Apostle tells us of a wonderful Tree.

What is more beautiful than trees ?   What a charm they add to our world !
What a joy they are to the monotony of a city !   How did the fancy of the
Greek poets revel in the hanging gardens and artificial forest scenery with
which the king of Babylon adorned his imperial city to gratify his Median
queen !   There trees twelve feet in circumference, fifty feet in height, grew on
mounds of masonry, nodding like woods on their mountains, and still defying
the wastes of time in the days of Quintus Curtius.   The first Eden had its glad
and glorious trees, "the tree of life also in the midst of the garden."
(Gen. 2 : 9.)   It was not one individual tree, but a particular tree as to its
kind, as we speak of " the apple " or " the oak," denoting a species of which

there are many specimens. It has the name of the Tree of Life, because man in innocence was to keep and preserve his life by eating of its fruits. It was the symbol and support of eternal life, both for body and for soul. And it is one of the special joys and provisions of the New Jerusalem that it is supplied with this same tree, in the same multitudinous sense, fulfilling something of the same offices. " *In the midst of the street of the city, and on either side of the river*," John saw " *the Tree of Life* [in numerous specimens] *producing twelve fruits* [or kinds of fruit], *according to each month yielding its fruit ; and the leaves of the tree unto the healing of the nations.*"

In Ezekiel's visions of the renewed earthly Jerusalem, a similar presentation is made. There a river issues from the sanctuary and runs down into the sea, of which the angel said, " By the river, upon the bank thereof, on this side and on that side, shall grow all trees for meat, whose leaf shall not fade, neither shall the fruit thereof be consumed : it shall bring forth new fruit according to his months ; because their waters issue out of the sanctuary ; and the fruit thereof shall be for meat, and the leaf thereof for medicine." (Ezek. 47 : 12.) But that relates to an order of things on earth, which comes into being during the thousand years. What John describes is the order of things in the heavenly Jerusalem, which comes into existence only after the thousand years have passed away. But the one has its model in the other, the earthly is a picture of the heavenly. The trees in both cases line the river ; but in the earthly order they are outside of the city ; and though bread trees, they are not the Tree of Life. The heavenly River issues not from the sanctuary but from the throne. It does not flow to the sea, but through the avenues and streets of the city. From the grand centre of the whole establishment it seems to flow through the midst of all the streets in the city ; that is through every street. And both sides of it are lined with the Tree of Life ; so that all the myriad mansions of the New Jerusalem thus open upon the Tree and the River of Life.

These trees, like the River whose sides they line, are first of all for the joy and blessedness of the dwellers in the Holy City, to beautify their eternal home, and to minister to their happiness. They are fruit-bearing trees, yielding their products every month, and each month a new variety.

It is sometimes asked whether the glorified saints are to eat in heaven? We may safely answer that *they can eat*, although under no need to eat ; just as we can enjoy a rose, and yet not suffer from its absence. The Saviour after his glorious resurrection did eat, even of the coarse food of mortals. The angels did eat of Sarah's cakes and of Abraham's dressed calf. (Gen. 18 : 6–8.) There is also much that is moral and spiritual in eating. It was by eating that the fall and all its consequences came into the world. All the holy appointments of God in the old economy had eating connected with them. The highest impartation of Christ and his salvation to his people on earth is done in connection with a sacred eating and drinking. The Saviour several times refers to eating and drinking in the kingdom of glory. He again and again likens the whole provision of grace to a banquet, a feast. One of the most emphasized scenes of the future, to which this Apocalypse refers, is *a supper*, even the supper of the marriage of the Lamb. And so the implication here is that there will be eating in this Eternal City, the eating of fruits, the eating of the monthly products of the Tree of Life. The inhabitants there drink Life-water, and they eat Life-fruits.

The eating of the fruit of the Tree of Life in the first Paradise was the sacrament of fellowship with life, a commemoration, pledge, support, and participation of life eternal, for soul and body. Hence sin cut off man from it ; and all the ordinances and ministries of grace since that time are meant for his recovery and readmission to that Tree. Hence also the promise was given to the Church of Ephesus, " To him that overcometh will I give to eat of the Tree of Life, which is in the Paradise of my God." (Rev. 2 : 7.) And so again, " Blessed they who wash their robes, that they may have right to the Tree of Life." (Rev. 22 : 14.) Like the golden table of shewbread which ever stood in the ancient Tabernacle and Temple for the priests to eat, so the Tree of Life stands in all the golden streets of the New Jerusalem, with its monthly fruit for the immortal king-priests of heaven. And whether they need it for the support of their undecaying immortality or not, it is everywhere presented as one of the most precious privileges of God's glorified saints. We cannot suppose that they ever hunger or thirst in that high realm, or that there is ever any waste in their immortal energies needing recuperation from physical digestion ; but still the participation of these Life-fruits bespeaks a communion with Life, the joy of which exceeds all present comprehension.

But these trees are for a still further purpose. The leaves of them are for the healing of the nations. As the fruits add to the joys of heaven, the leaves add to the joys of earth. Who gathers them, and how they are applied, and what the healing is which they are to work, is not told us, and it is vain to attempt to be wise above what is written. But " nations " are then to be who eat not of these fruits, though benefited by the leaves in connection with which the fruits are produced. Two classes of people are thus distinctly recognized in the new heaven and earth ;—a class in glory who get the fruits of the Tree of Life, and a class in the estate of " nations " who get the leaves ; but, whether fruits or leaves, a great and glorious blessing. As there will always be need for the ministrations of these celestial king-priests to those dwelling on the earth so will those ministrations also bring them the healing leaves from the Tree of Life. As the Life-waters are not wholly shut up in the city, but descend in a form to men on the earth ; so the Life-tree, in a form, yields its benefits to them too. The meaning is not that the nations are full of sicknesses and ailments ; for these remains of the curse are gone then, though it may be from the virtue of these leaves. The meaning rather is the preservation of health and comfort, and not that maladies then exist to be removed. The Life-leaves are for the conservation and augmentation of Life-blessedness of men on earth, as the Life-fruits are for the joy of the saints in heaven.

III. The Apostle further informs us that there all sin and its ill consequences will no more be.

The first Paradise was glorious ; but with all its blessedness, sin entered it, and the curse came, under which earth and man have been labouring and sighing for six thousand years. Hence, with all the transcendent glory described by the Apostle, the question might still be open as to its permanence, —whether sin might not again insinuate itself, with its ever-attending spoliations. Man once had a happy and unabridged right to the Tree of Life, but lost it ; and that Tree, and all the Garden in which it grew, evanished from him, and left the world smoking under the tokens of Jehovah's anger. The curse came. It came upon man himself and all his seed. It came upon innocent nature with which he stood connected. It came upon the very ground on his account. Might not the same happen again, even to Paradise regained ? Therefore the special assurance is here inserted, that " *every curse, or accursed thing, shall not be any more.*" The relief from it is to be an eternal relief. Its disappearance from all this scene of things is to be an everlasting disappearance. The glory and blessedness will never again give place to darkness, sin, and death.

I do not fancy that the freedom of man redeemed will be any more constrained than it was when man first sinned ; but the victory having been fairly achieved, under far mightier trials, by the second Adam, the Tempter will be restrained, a training and experience will then be upon the redeemed which will stand like a wall between them and danger, and the love and appreciation of what has been so dearly purchased will be so intense and high after all these ages of the reign of sin and death that they will never consent for anything to let it go. Holy angels stand fast in their blessedness forever, not because they are less free to sin than were those who kept not their first estate ; but because, having stood the test, the whole momentum of their moral being moves only toward what is true and good, and so they never fall.   And such shall be the security of man redeemed. Stationed on the high vantage-ground of a victory won through pain and suffering, and made strong in the unfailing helps and mercies of his God, there will be no more fuel left in him for sin to kindle, and no more curse or danger to him forever.

Being innocent, man ate of the tree of knowledge of good and evil, and learned to know *evil*. For all these weary ages he has been tasting and experiencing the bitterness of evil. Through the redemption that is in Christ Jesus, they that believe in him come to know *good ;* and knowing good, there will be no more turning of their hearts from it, and hence no more sinning and no more curse. And man being finally and permanently redeemed, everything that has been disordered, disabled, or cursed for man's sake, shall also be permanently delivered. (Rom. 8 : 9–23.)

When God pronounced judgment upon the sins committed in the first Paradise, " Unto the woman he said, I will greatly multiply thy sorrow and thy conception ; in sorrow shalt thou bring forth children ; and thy desire shall be to thy husband, and he shall rule over thee." (Gen. 3 : 15.) All this was imposed as penalty and curse, peculiar to her who " was first in transgression." But here the assurance is that it will be completely lifted off, and be no more. (Com. 1 Tim. 2 : 15.) " And unto Adam he said, Because thou hast hearkened to the voice of thy wife, and hast eaten of the tree, of which I commanded thee, saying, Thou shalt not eat of it ; cursed is the ground for thy sake ; in sorrow shalt thou eat of it all the days of thy life ; thorns also and thistles shall it bring forth to thee ; and thou shalt eat the herb of the field ; in the sweat of thy face shalt thou eat bread, till thou return unto the ground ; for out of it wast thou taken : for dust thou art, and unto dust shalt thou return." (Gen. 3 : 17–19.) Here was penalty and curse, whose potent condemnation has been binding and afflicting earth and man from that day to this. It affects all the elements man touches, and the whole order of things amid which he lives. It affects what he eats and what he drinks, the air he breathes and the ground on which he walks. It affects all the growths of nature in all its sublunary kingdoms, and conditions the seasons and the sea. It has opened the avenues of disease, calamity, and death, till the earth is no longer habitable for man, except for a few brief years. Everywhere, on everything, we read and have it flashed upon us, that man is a sinner ; that a fearful condemnation hangs over him ; that a curse for his sin is festering in all that pertains to him and his dwelling-place. But it is not incurable. The remedy may be long in taking effect, but it is provided,—provided in Jesus Christ, his achievements as the second Adam, and his sovereign power and purpose to destroy all the works of the devil, and to subdue all things to himself. The first note that John heard coming forth from the Throne when the final judgment was over, was, "BEHOLD, NEW I MAKE EVERYTHING." (Rev. 21: 5.) And the effect of that renewal is further stated in the text to be, that every curse shall cease to exist. Not of the holy city alone can this be said ; for there the curse never was. It is a word which applies above all to the place where the curse has been. It was upon woman, and man, and earth, and the economy of things on the earth, that the sentence was put ; and from them therefore must be its cessation. Nor do we go beyond the necessary implications of this divine assurance when we read from its massive terms that this whole scene of earthly life, where sin and death have reigned so long, will yet come up out of all its desolations ; that the very blessedness of Paradise shall revisit all its hills and vales ; and that throughout this nether world, disordered, cut with graves, and full of miseries, that goal of the prayer our Lord has taught us shall be realized, when it shall be " *on earth as it is in heaven.*"

IV. The Apostle tells us also of a glorious throne.

There is a central throne of the universe where Christ now sits and reigns with the Eternal Father. The dominion which he there holds as " head over all things for the Church," he is to deliver up when the time for the great consummation arrives. He is now with the Father on his throne, but there is another throne peculiarly his own, which he will then take, and on which his glorified people shall reign with him, as he now reigns with the Father. (Compare 1 Cor. 15 : 24-28, and Rev. 3 : 21.)   This throne is in the New Jerusalem.   It is " the throne of God," as Christ is God ; and it is " the throne of the Lamb," in that it is held and occupied as the result of Christ's achievement as a sacrifice for sin, and in his particular character as the world's Saviour and Redeemer.   It is the throne of God as the Lamb, the All-Ruler, who once was slain, but lives again, and here is to reign with his glorified saints to the ages of the ages.

There is something peculiar about these thrones.   In the first three chapters of this Book, Christ appears in the sanctuary, walking amid the golden lamp-stands, noting and pronouncing upon his Churches.   There no throne is visible, for the Church is only the kingdom in process of formation, answering to the period of Israel's pilgrimage in the wilderness.   In the succeeding chapters a throne appears; but with surroundings indicative of a special dispensation with regard to the old earth, partly retributive and partly remedial.   It is the throne of the judgment period which holds only during " the day of the Lord," in which Christ is engaged in enforcing the principles of his Kingdom and his claims by visitations of successive judgments upon the world ; answering to the reign of the Judges, when the Ark and its accompaniments were yet in the movable and temporary tabernacle, and the kingdom was not yet established.   With the Halleluias over the fall of Babylon, this particular throne disappears, and we see only the thrones of the Shepherdizers, who for a time rule the nations with a rod of iron ; answering to the warlike reign of David, when the preparations for the Temple were making.   The last rebellion, typified by that enacted by Absalom against his father, having been put down, the " Great White Throne " appears, the final judgment throne, with no signs of blessing, consigning all the unholy dead to their final doom. And then comes the Holy City and the full establishment of the Kingdom of peace, answering to the illustrious reign of the wise and peaceful Solomon, when the Temple took its place on Mount Moriah, and there " was neither adversary nor evil."   In the Holy City the throne then takes its position, as the final throne of God and the Lamb with reference to the earth and man.   It is a single throne, the seat and centre of all the authority and power ever thenceforward put forth for the regulation and government of human affairs. And its occupants, and the only administrants of its dominion, are God, the Lamb, and his glorified saints.   " *And they shall reign to the ages of the ages.*" No more faulty politics, no more false religion, no more rabble rule or oppressive tyranny, shall then be any more.   For the reign of righteousness has come, and it will fail no more forever.

V. Finally, the Apostle tells us of the condition of things under this administration.

He has already given us something on this point.   He has told us of the directness of communion with God in that Blessed City,—of the centre of light, interest, attraction, and holy reverence which it will be to the whole earth,—of the joyful obedience with which the nations will walk in its light,—of the health which is to go forth from its immortal trees,—of the endless and unintermitting light of God and the Lamb which shall be in it ;—but he adds still other items as instructed by the angel.

" *His servants shall serve him.*"   In general the servants of a king are his subjects.   So taken, there is in this affirmation a picture of universal obedience and loving devotion ;—no more sin, no more rebellion, no more forgetfulness or neglect of the claims or word of the Eternal King.   All life is to be permeated and transfigured with the most complete and happy accord with the divine will, which then is done " on earth as it is in heaven."   The prophecies are everywhere full of the most glowing pictures on this point.   Even the bells or bridles of the horses shall be Holiness unto the Lord, and the commonest utensils in the houses and kitchens of mankind shall take on a sacredness like that of the consecrated vessels of the temple itself. (Zech. 14 : 20, 21.) For the glory of the Lord shall cover the earth as the waters cover the sea. It will be the abounding element in which everything is bathed.

But the servants of a king, in a more particular sense, are his immediate attendants, those who are in waiting upon the throne, and who act as its agents and representatives. Hence, when the Queen of Sheba saw " the sitting of Solomon's *servants*, and the attendance of his ministers and their apparel, and his cup-bearers," she said : " Happy are thy men, happy are *these thy servants which stand continually before thee*." (I Kings 10 : 5, 8.) So Solomon made hewers of wood and drawers of water of some of his subjects, but others he made " men of war, and *his servants*, and his princes, and his captains, and rulers of his chariots and his horsemen." (I Kings 9 : 22.) So the priests, the prophets, the ministers of the Word, and such as hold official rank and place in the divine economies, are more especially called *the servants* of God. Such are all the members of the Church of the first-born, the elect, the citizens of the heavenly Jerusalem, the sharers in the administration of that holy kingdom. And of these especially is this word spoken. It tells of the very highest honour and dignity, of the closest intimacy with eternal power and authority, of the most inward nearness and participation in the administration of divine government. But it tells also of mighty activities and responsible duties. It shows us most clearly that the heaven of the glorified saints is not one of idleness. They have something more to do than to sing, and worship, and enjoy. Indeed the perfection of worship is service, activity for God, the doing of the will of God. And this is to be one of the highest characteristics of the heaven of the saints. They are to do work, heavenly work, the highest kind of work, the execution and administration of the will and bidding of the throne of eternity, the work of the high officials who stand nearest to the throne, and through whom the throne expresses itself. Like " the seven *princes* of Persia and Media which *saw the king's face*, and which *sat first in the kingdom* " (Esth. 1 : 14), so these " *servants* shall serve him, and *they shall see his face, and the name of him shall be upon their foreheads*."

The Jewish high priest, when fully arrayed as the officer and agent of Jehovah, in addition to his mitre, had a plate of burnished gold upon his brow, on which was engraved the great Name of that almighty Being for whom he served. These dwellers in the New Jerusalem are all priests then, as well as kings, and so they have the tokens of their sublime office and consecration on their foreheads. The name of their King and God is there, to tell of their dignity, their office, and the transcendent authority and glory of him for whom they officiate. In the courts of kings, the most honoured servants and favourites wear badges and marks in token of the king's confidence, favour, and affection. The noble knights have their ribbons ; and those whom the king delighteth to honour have their chains of gold about their necks, their rosettes, their indications of standing with their sovereign. So these all have the Name of the All-Ruling Lamb upon their foreheads, showing exaltation, honour, and blessedness of the very highest degree. They are the enthroned princes of the eternal realm, the servants of the Supreme God, the very organs and expressions of the everlasting Throne.

Again it is said that " night shall not be any more." The repetition of this particular, emphasizes it as a very special and a very glorious blessing. The light of God and the Lamb shall be so full, glorious, and abiding, that night no longer can exist in that city. Its inhabitants need no shutting off of day to give them sleep. They are independent of all material orbs or their revolutions. Of course, this statement does not apply to " the nations " on the earth. The succession of day and night existed before Adam fell, and he needed the repose of night even in his innocence. He lived in an earthly body, and that body needed sleep. We also have the positive statement that he did sleep, even before he sinned. Likewise those who then live in the flesh, will need sleep, and their seasons of repose. Hence, the covenant with Noah was, that, " while the earth remaineth, day and night shall not cease." (Gen. 8 : 22.) But in the home of the glorified saints there will be no more night. Darkness of all orders, physical, mental, and moral, shall have no place there. As the glory of the Shekinah ever glowed in the Holy of Holies, so shall the Jehovah brightness ever illuminate the heavenly Jerusalem, and all its inhabitants shall themselves be light ; for they " shall shine as the brightness of the firmament, and as the stars forever and ever." (Dan. 12 : 3.)

" *And they shall reign to the ages of the ages.*" Not for the thousand years only, but forever shall their glory and dominion last. This tells at once their eternal dignity, and the eternal perpetuity of men in the flesh. If they are to be kings forever, they must have subjects forever ; and their subjects, whom they shepherdize, over whom they rule, and for whom they hold the dominion, are everywhere described as " *the nations* "—" all people, languages, and nations under the whole heaven." (Rev. 2 : 26 ; 12 : 5 ; 22 : 1 ; 24 : 26 ; Dan. 7 : 14, 27 ; Matt. 19 : 28, 29 ; 1 Cor. 6 : 2.) Either, then, their kingdom must come to an end for want of subjects, or nations, peoples, and men on the earth must continue in the flesh, as Adam and Eve before the fall. But these glorified ones are to " reign to the ages of the ages," and their " kingdom is an everlasting kingdom ; " and as they cannot reign without subjects, so nations on earth must last coequally with their regency. Both their office, and the activities in which their sublimest happiness is located, must fail them, if the nations over whom their rule is, ever cease to be. They neither marry, nor are given in marriage ; for they are as the angels of God ; but their subjects are of a different order, and their dominion and glory shall grow forever, by the ceaseless augmentation of the number of their subjects throughout unending generations.

Such is the final picture set before us in these wonderful prophecies and foreshowings of the purposes of our God. Such are the fore-intimations of that new heavens and earth wherein eternal righteousness dwells. And such are the glimpses which our gracious Saviour has given us of the dignities and blessedness to which we are called by his Gospel.

See, then, my friends, how very high our calling is. And shall we not value, cherish, and improve it ? Shall we throw away our chance for such an eternal home ? Shall we slight the offers and opportunities of blessedness like this ? Let fortunes pass ; let friendships be forfeited ; let earthly comforts go unenjoyed ; cast honours, titles, crowns, empires to the wolves and bats ; but let not the privilege go by of becoming an immortal king and co-regent with the Lamb in the Golden City of the New Jerusalem.

> Rise, my soul, and stretch thy wings,
>   Thy better portion trace ;
> Rise from transitory things
>   Toward heaven, thy native place.
>
> Sun, and moon, and stars decay,
>   Time shall soon this earth remove ;
> Rise, my soul, and haste away
>   To seats prepared above !

LECTURE FIFTY-FIRST

LAST SECTION OF THE BOOK—CERTAINTY OF THESE REVELATIONS—THE REPEATED BENE-
DICTION UPON THOSE WHO TREASURE THEM—EFFECT OF THEM ON THE APOSTLE—THE
DIRECTION TO HIM WHAT TO DO WITH THEM—AN ARGUMENT FOR THE SAME—THE CON-
DITION ON WHICH THE BEATITUDES OF THIS BOOK ARE TO BE ENJOYED—A PARTICULAR
WASHING OF ROBES.

Rev. 22 : 6–15. (Revised Text.) And he said to me, These words [are] faithful and true
and the Lord the God of the spirits of the prophets sent his angel to show to his servants
what things must come to pass shortly.

And behold, I come quickly : blessed he that keepeth the words of the prophecy of this
book.

And I, John [was] hearing and seeing these things. And when I had heard and seen, I
fell down to worship before the feet of the angel who showed me these things. And he saith
to me, See, no ; I am fellow-servant of thee and of thy brethren the prophets, and of those
who keep the words of this book : worship God.

And he saith to me, Seal not up the words of the prophecy of this book ; the time is near.
Let the unjust one do injustice more and more, and the filthy [or *polluted*] one defile [or *do
pollution*] more and more, and the righteous one do righteousness more and more, and the
holy one sanctify more and more.

Behold, I come quickly, and my reward with me, to give to each as his work is, I the
Alpha and the Omega. First and Last, the Beginning and the End. Blessed they that wash
their robes that they may [in that they shall] have the power over the tree of life, and enter
by the gates into the city. Excluded [or *outside are*] the dogs, and the sorcerers, and the
fornicators, and the murderers, and the idolaters, and every one loving or making a lie
[or, *what is false*].

We come now to the last section of this wonderful Book—the Epilogue—the
closing remarks. The Grand Panorama of an ending and renewing world has
reached the point where everything enters upon the eternal state, and we are
now to take leave of the wonderful exhibit. We have seen the Church in its
universality and varied historic continuity from the days of the Apostle down
to the time when Christ shall come for his people, and how he will end its
career by taking one here and another there, and leaving the rest, because
of their unreadiness to taste the sorrows of the great Tribulation. With the
judgment thus begun at the house of God, we have seen it roll along through
the breaking of seals, the sounding of trumpets, and the pouring out of bowls
of wrath, in ever-varying scenes of miracle and wonder, towards saints and
sinners, the living and the dead. We have seen the Antichrist coming up from
his abyss, captivating the world, running his course of unexampled blasphemy,
and sinking forever in his deserved perdition. We have seen the final doings of
Satan, in heaven and earth, his arrest and imprisonment, his short loosing, and
his final consignment, with all his, to the lake of fire. We have seen the thrones
of the shepherdizers of the nations, the breaking down of all rebellion, and the
coming forth into the living world of the eternal principles of righteousness.
We have seen the shaking of the old heavens and earth, and the same passed
through the throes of the long-expected Regeneration. We have seen the
crowned princes of the first resurrection wedded to the All-Ruling Lamb, and
led into the golden city of their hopes. We have seen the New Jerusalem come
down out of heaven from God ; Sin, Death, Hades, and the curse swept into
Gehenna ; the Tabernacle of God taking its place among men ; redemption
complete ; Paradise regained ; and the nations of the earth in Edenic peace
and glory setting out under their immortal kings for an eternity of uninterrupted blessedness. And it only remains now to give a few closing particulars
with reference to these momentous Revelations, that men may attend to them

with that reverence and faith which of right belongs to them. May God help us to hear, learn, and inwardly digest them to our abiding consolation !

I. The first thing we are called on to note is, their absolute truth and certainty.   There is nothing in which the difference of the Scriptures from all other teachings is more manifest than in the positiveness and authority with which they deliver themselves on all subjects, even where reason can tell us nothing, and where the presentations are so marvellous as to stagger belief. When the Saviour was on earth, he spake with such clearness and simplicity, and with such knowing majesty and commanding mastery of all wisdom that men who heard him were amazed, forgot all other authorities, and hasted away in awe, saying, " *Never man spake like this man.*"   And so it is in all the word of inspiration.   Even where angels would scarce dare to tread, it enters with perfect freedom, as upon its own home domain, and declares itself with all that assured certainty which belongs only to Omniscience.   Even with regard to all the astounding and seemingly impossible wonders of this Book, the absolute truth of every jot and tittle is guaranteed with the abounding fulness of the completest knowledge of everything involved.   In case of some of the most wonderful of these presentations, the word to John was, "*Write, because these words are faithful and true.*"   And so here, with regard to all the contents of the Book, it was said to the Seer, " *These words [are] faithful and true.*"

Thrice is it repeated, that these presentations are faithful and true (19 : 9 21 : 5 ; 22 : 6) ; and twice is it affirmed that these showings are all from God. In the opening of the Book it is said, that he " sent his angel to his servant John " for the purpose of making these revelations, and here at the conclusion, we have it repeated, that " *the Lord the God of the spirits of the prophets sent his angel to show to his servants what things* MUST *come to pass.*"   Nay more, Christ himself adds special personal testimony to the fact : " I, JESUS, *sent my angel to testify to you these things.*"   Thus the very God of all inspiration, and of all inspired men, reiterates and affirms the highest authority for all that is herein written.

Either, then, this Book is nothing but a base and blasphemous forgery, unworthy of the slightest respect of men, and specially unworthy of a place in the Sacred Canon ; or it is one of the most directly inspired and authoritative writings ever given. But a forgery it cannot be. All the Churches named in its first chapters, from the earliest periods succeeding the time of its writing, with one accord, accepted and honoured it as from their beloved Apostolic Father. Papias, Bishop of Hieropolis, a disciple of St. John, a colleague of the Seven Angels of these Churches, and who gave much attention to the collection of all the memorable sayings and works of the Apostles, accepted and honoured this Book as the genuine production of this venerable Apostle. Nor is there another Book in the New Testament whose genuineness and inspiration were more clearly and strongly attested on its first appearance, and for the three half-centuries next following.   Augustine and the Latin Council unquestionably had good and sufficient reason for classing it with the most sacred apostolic records, and the Church in general for regarding it as a Book of prophecy " from Christ's own divine, omniscient, and eternal Spirit."** And if it really is the Lord Jesus who speaks to us in this Book, there is nothing in all the Canon of Scripture which he more pointedly attests, more solemnly guards, or more urgently presses upon the study and devout regard of all who would be his disciples. People may account us crazy for giving so much attention to it, and laugh at our credulity for daring to believe that it means what it says ; but better be accounted possessed, as Christ himself was considered, and be pronounced beside ourselves and mad, after the manner of Paul, than to take our lot with Pharisees, and Festuses, and Agrippas, and Galios. If we err in this, we err with the goodly fellowship of the saints, with the noble army of the martyrs, in the society of many great and good and wise in many ages and nations. And if it should finally turn out that we have

* See p. 21.

R

been beguiling ourselves with dreams, they still give us the most consistent philosophy of Providence, and the most comforting solutions of life's mysteries whilst our pretensionless submission to what seems most surely to be our Creator's word and will may serve us best when we come to answer at his judgment-seat. We believe that it is God who tells us, " *these words are faithful and true ;* " therefore we so take them, and build our faith upon them, and testify them to all the world.

II. A second particular to be noted in this Epilogue is the repetition of the benediction upon those who treasure what is written in this Book. In the opening verses the inspired writer said: " Blessed he who readeth, and those who hear the words of the prophecy, and observe the things which are written in it." But here the Saviour himself, even he whose nearing Apocalypse these records were given to describe, says, in a voice uttered from his glorious throne in heaven, " *Blessed he that keepeth the words of the prophecy of this Book.*" All this is additional to the seven times repeated admonition, " *He that hath an ear, let him hear what the Spirit saith unto the Churches.*" Is there another Book in the holy Canon so intense, so emphatic, so constant, so full from end to end, in its expressions of the good to be gained and the ill to be avoided by the hearing and learning of its own particular presentations ? It is precisely as if the Saviour knew and foresaw, as he certainly did, what neglect, prejudice, and mistreatment this Book would encounter in the later ages of the Church, and how it and the students of it, and especially the believers in its wonderful descriptions, would be ridiculed, avoided, and put aside, as not in the line of proper and wholesome edification. And how will some of these pious scorners, whom Christ has set and ordained to feed his sheep and give them meat in due season, feel and fare, when from the judgment-seat he shall say : " Sirs, I gave you the complete chart of my promised Apocalypse ; I caused it to be made as plain as words and visions can make anything of the sort ; I told you over and over of the momentous importance of studying, treasuring, and making known to the Churches what I thus sent my angel and my beloved disciple to show you ; and yet you have held it to be a crazy Book, one which either finds or leaves crazy those who study it, and have not believed my word, nor taught it to my people, nor allowed it to speak in the appointed Lectionaries, and have only sought to explain away its momentous import into a little dim foreshowing of a few ages of ordinary earthly history ! Was this the way for good servants of their Lord to act ? Was this being faithful stewards of the mysteries of God ? Was this the way to treat what I have been at such pains to give, and pointed you to with so much solemnity, and promised to reward your study of it with such special benedictions ? " Alas, alas, what answer will they make ? Will they say that it was too difficult a Book for them to understand ? This would only be adding insult to their unfaithfulness. Dare we suppose that the merciful Jesus would hang his benedictions so high as to be beyond the reach of those to whom they are so graciously proposed ? Would he mock us by suspending his offered blessings on terms beyond our power ? Yet this is the charge men bring against their Redeemer when they think to plead the incomprehensibility of this Book for their neglect and practical rejection of it. The very propounding of these blessings and rewards is God's own seal to the possibility of understanding this Book equally with any other part of Scripture. Would he, the God of truth, lie to us ? Would he, the God of mercy, mock us ? Would he who gave his life for us, and ever lives and ministers in heaven and earth for our enlightenment and salvation, give us a Book to tell us of the outcome of all his gracious operations, command us to note its words, to believe and treasure its contents, and promise us a special blessedness in so doing, if what he has thus put into our hands is not at all within the limits of our comprehension and successful mastery ? Does not everything that we know of the dear God above us rise up to condemn all such thoughts as slanderous of heaven, and blasphemy against our precious Saviour's goodness ? Therefore these very benedictions pronounce against the common notion that this Book is too difficult for ordinary Christians, and rebuke all who despise and avoid it. If it is anything, these proffered blessings are more than a divine justification for all the time and pains which we have been bestowing upon it, and for accepting, believing, holding, and testifying as the very truth of God all that we have found herein written.   Let men estimate us and our work as they please, we have here the unmistakable authority of heaven for it, that this Apocalypse is capable of being understood; that its presentations are among the most momentous in all the Word of God ; and that the highest blessedness of believers is wrapped up with the learning and keeping of what is pictured to us in it. And if Christians would rise to the true comfort of their faith,—if they would possess themselves of a right philosophy of God's purposes and providence,—if they would be guarded against the greatest dangers and most subtle deceptions of the Old Serpent,— if they would really know what Redemption means, and what the height and glory of their calling is,—let them not despise or neglect this crowning Book of the New Testament, but study its pages, take its statements as they read, get its stupendous visions into their understandings, treasure its words in their hearts, and believe and know that it is comprehensible for all who are really willing to be instructed in these mighty things. If we wait till they are fulfilled, it will then be too late to get the blessing which the reading, hearing, and keeping of what is said concerning them is to bestow. It is in our understanding of them before they come to pass that the blessedness lies ; for when once Christ comes in the scenes of his Apocalypse, the time to begin to put ourselves in readiness for it will be past. We must understand beforehand, as this record was meant to advise us beforehand, or it will be useless to think of getting ourselves in position when once these momentous scenes become accomplished realities. By all that is sacred, therefore, let us beware how we treat this Book, and the showings which it contains, remembering this word of the Lord Jesus, spoken to us from heaven : " *Blessed he that keepeth the words of the prophecy of this Book.*"*

III. Another particular to be noticed is, the effect which these showings had upon the Apostle at the time. So wonderful were the revelations, and so wonderful was the knowledge and understanding of the angel which communicated these things, that John was filled with the profoundest adoration. Twice he fell down before the feet of the angel to worship him. He meant no idolatry ; but so wonderful in wisdom and intelligence was his heavenly guide, and so transcendent were the things shown, that he could not but think that it was God himself. The presentations all along were such as to make it hard to distinguish whether it was God himself speaking, or whether it was through a created messenger that he spoke. And in this instance particularly, it certainly was the Lord Jesus whom he heard say, " Behold I come quickly ; " and not distinguishing between him who spoke, and the messenger through whom he spoke, John " fell down before the feet of the angel." This clearly shows that the holy Apostles held Christ to be a worshipful being, and that he was none other than true God as well as true man. John knew that it was and must be Christ who spoke, and his instant adoration was meant for Christ, therefore he held Christ to be adorable God. The only mistake was that he did not at the moment perceive that it was a created angel speaking for Christ, and not Christ himself in the form of an angel. Even the best and holiest of men may make mistakes from their human impulses, as Moses when he broke the tables of the Law, and Peter when he avoided the Gentile Christians at Antioch. But

---

* Old James Robertson, in issuing his book on the Revelation in 1730, made this remark : " Some are not ashamed directly to flout at, and spit contempt upon these that meddle with the exposition of this Prophecy ; which is an indirect battering of a great part of God's word. Thus Dr. South, in one of his sermons, affirms, that none but a madman will meddle with the Revelation ; or, if he has wits at the beginning, before he has done they will be cracked. And Davies, a Welsh bombastic barrister, has the impudence to insult a learned and reverend prelate, yet alive, because he consumed two full years and more on this Prophecy." But we can afford to let men sneer when we have the sure benediction of God.

innocent mistakes, and those which result from the truest and devoutest intentions, may be very injurious, and need to be promptly corrected. There was danger here of a double sin, one on the part of John in giving worship to the angel instead of Christ, and one on the part of the angel in accepting worship which belongs only to Deity. But John was in doubt, which the angel had not, and therefore it belonged to the angel in truth and fidelity to John, as well as to God and himself, to correct John's mistake on the spot. The Devil solicits adoration, but holy angels repel it as a detraction from Jehovah. Hence, when John fell down to worship before this holy angel's feet, promptly came the word," *Take heed, no ; I am fellow-servant of thee and of thy brethren the prophets, and of those who keep the words of this Book ! worship God.*" The misapprehension being dispelled, the Apostle of course desisted. The incident shows that no saint or angel worship can have the approval of heaven. If it was wrong to worship this glorious heavenly messenger, in and through whom came forth the very voice of Jesus, how can it be right to worship and pray to the Virgin Mary, to whom is assigned no such dignity or office ? The impulse and intention may be devout and good ; but it is a great mistake, and we take the side of heaven and holy angels when we say to those who do it : " See, no, no ; you do greatly err ; you are taking Christ's honour from him and bestowing it upon his human mother or friends ; worship God, for it is written, ' Him only shalt thou serve.' "

But whilst this incident brings out the fact that the best of men may mistake, even out of the holiest motives, it also brings out the more important facts, that John fully believed all these revelations, that he was most profoundly convinced that they were from God, that angels also treasure them as the great divine lights touching what is to be, and that John is recognized in heaven as a genuine prophet. The angel calls him a fellow-servant with himself, the same as the whole brotherhood of sacred prophets. Mistaken as he was for the moment in not distinguishing his heavenly guide from his Lord, he yet was duly illuminated as a prophet, and still had the office and inspiration of God for the understanding of these mysteries, and the making of them known to the Churches. Angels have often been commissioned to disclose to men important sacred truths. It was an angel who was thus employed in acquainting Ezekiel and Daniel with many of the most important features of their wonderful prophecies ; and so it was in the giving of these particulars of the Apocalypse to John. In this respect angels are prophets too, and prophetically minister to the heirs of salvation. Not only as servants of God are they the fellow-servants of the prophets ; but they also become fellow-prophets when engaged in communicating a knowledge of the divine mind and purposes to men. And in this fellowship of servants of the same Lord, and of service in making known divine things, John is here acknowledged as a co-partner with the angel himself. What he writes us, therefore, is true prophecy, and demands to be received as such.

IV. A further particular here to be noted is the direction to John what to do with these revelations. Whether from Christ direct, or through the angel whom Christ sent to show him these things, command was given him : " *Seal not up the words of the prophecy of this Book.*" Some take this as antithetical to the command given Daniel with regard to his prophecies. (Dan. 8 : 26 ; 12 : 4, 9.) But that is plainly a mistake. There is no reference whatever to Daniel. Besides, the direction given to Daniel was the very reverse of what is thus assumed.* The true antithesis is the command with regard to what the seven thunders uttered, as referred to in chapter 10 : 4. From the beginning of these marvellous experiences John was directed to write what he saw and heard, and to make the same known to the Churches. So, " when the seven thunders spoke," he " was about to write ; " but a voice from heaven said, " *Seal up those things which the seven thunders spoke, and write them not.*" The *sealing* enjoined stands over against writing and making known, and hence is

* See my *Voices from Babylon*, pp. 304-306.

quite a different sealing from that which was commanded Daniel. John was to bury up the thing in his own breast, not to write it, not to make it known at all. But what he was not to do respecting the utterances of the seven thunders, he was to do with reference to all other " words of the prophecy of this Book." He was not to seal them up ; that is, not to conceal them, but to record them, to make them known, to publish them to the Churches.

Not from any self-will on his part, therefore, have these Apocalyptic records been put before us ; but by direct command of our God and Saviour. They constitute his last and crowning legacy to his Church and people. They are written by his appointment and command. They are put into our hands by the specific direction of eternal power and Godhead. They are therefore God's word to us. And if he commanded the writing of them, I cannot see how men are to excuse themselves from the reading and study of them ; or how any Christian can think lightly of them, or put them from him as of no practical worth, and yet retain his holy faithfulness to the plain will and inculcations of our blessed Lord and Judge. O, my friends, let us beware how we neglect or despise a Book upon which God Almighty has laid so much stress, urgency, and importance. If John had sealed it up, or failed to lay it before us as it is, he would have forfeited his place and standing as an apostle of Christ ; how, then, can we think our duty discharged, or the provisions for our highest blessedness duly accepted and used, if we pass it by as a dead letter, or make it to us as if it had never been ?

V. Again, there is added here a very singular argument. It is not easy to give the exact literal sense of the peculiarly constructed phraseology ; but taking the whole connection and bearing of the passage, it may perhaps be best rendered, " *Let the unjust one do injustice more and more, and the filthy one defile more and more, and the righteous one do righteousness more and more, and the holy one sanctify more and more.*" Many take the statement as referring to the eternal fixedness of character, both for the bad and good, when once these Apocalyptic scenes have been fulfilled. It is indeed a great truth, that a time comes to every one when the seal of permanence is set upon the spiritual condition, rendering the unjust one unjust forever, and the righteous one righteous forever. The same is also involved in this statement. But it is hardly to be taken as the main thought. The meaning has immediate reference to the non-sealing, that is, the writing and publication of " the words of the prophecy of this Book," and the nearness of the time of their fulfilment. The direct bearing of the statement is that of an argument for the writing and publishing of these revelations, and the holding of them up to the view of all men, over against the non-effect or ill effect they may have upon the wicked and unbelieving, or upon the Antichrist and his adherents, who is emphatically the unjust and unclean one. Though " wicked men and seducers shall wax worse and worse," and even wrest what is herein predicted of them as if it were a licence for their wickedness or a fixing of it by an irresistible necessity, and so are only the more encouraged and urged on in their injustice and abominations ; still, this is not to prevent the freest and fullest proclamation of the whole truth. Let the unjust one be the more confirmed in his unbelief and wickedness ;—let the filthy one go on in his idolatries and moral defilement with all the greater hardihood and blasphemy ;—that is not to restrain the making known of what shall come to pass. If it accelerates the antichristian development, and the wicked are only the more indurated in their wickedness, let it so be. Though the sun breed pestilence and death in the morasses, and only hasten putrefaction in what is lifeless and rotten, it must not therefore be blotted from the heavens, or hindered from shining into our world. There is another side to the question. If it is an ill thing to what is ill, the life of what is living requires it. Believers must be forewarned and forearmed, or they too will be deceived and perish. And if the wicked are made the wickeder, the righteous and holy will be the holier, and without it cannot be defended and kept as they need to be. Therefore, let not this holy book be

sealed up, nor its grand prophecies shut off from the fullest record and the most
unreserved proclamation. There is always a twofold effect from the preaching
of the divine word. It is quick and powerful, and never leaves men where it
finds them. It either makes them better, or it makes them worse. It if does
not absolve, it the more condemns. If it does not soften to penitence,
it hardens in iniquity. If it is not a savour of life unto life, it is a savour
of death unto death. And, unfortunately for the great masses of its
hearers, it is an instrument of damnation rather than of salvation.
Particularly is this true with regard to the foreshowings of prophecy
as set forth in this Book. For the most gracious purposes have these revelations been given. They come to us freighted with spiritual blessing, light, and
confirmation. They are the very things, in God's estimate, for the setting of
believers right in their conceptions, lives, hopes, and aims, and for shielding
them against perils from which it is next thing to impossible otherwise to
escape. And yet there is the strangest unwillingness to believe or receive them
as they stand written. Even good men are offended at them, denounce them,
ridicule them, explain them away, do anything with them but admit them
into their belief and expectations of the future. I doubt not, that this Apocalypse has been and will be the rock on which many a one's salvation is wrecked
by reason of the offence taken at its presentations. To the savants and scientists of this world, there is no part of all the Scriptures which seems so absurd
and impossible. They can get on with everything else a thousandfold better
than with the outlines of the future which this Book gives. To their philosophy
it is the very consummation of nonsense. And if this is the scheme and outcome of the Gospel system, they will have none of it. They know better.
They have got beyond all such puerilities. They would not swallow such things
for their lives, and scorn to take for divine what embraces them as the
consummation of this world. Their sneers, contempt, and blasphemy nowhere
rise to such a pitch as when they are asked to accept and believe that this
Book is of God, and means what it says. And all the more so shall the temper
be as the sensual and devilish wisdom matures, develops, and exhibits its
proud knowledge and mastery of the material elements. But the truth of God
must be spoken nevertheless. Let the unjust one do injustice all the more ;
let the filthy one defile himself all the more ; let the offence, and the stumbling,
and the scepticism, and the scorning, and the blasphemy, and the condemnation be aggravated by it as they may, " the words of the prophecy of this
Book " must not be sealed up. There are some elect ones whom it will benefit,
enlighten, and save from the toils of the Old Deceiver. There are righteous
ones whom it will establish and secure in their righteousness. And there are
some consecrated ones whom it will the more set apart for God and the more
intensify in their devotion and their ready-making to join their Lord and
Master in the Golden City of the New Jerusalem. Though the wicked shall
do wickedly, and none of the wicked shall understand, yet the wise shall
understand, and for them the Book is necessary.

VI. One particular more in this Epilogue is all that I can notice to-night.
It is a particular which the oldest and best manuscripts and all the most
competent critics agree in giving in a different form from that in which it
stands in our English Bibles. It relates to the conditions and qualifications
upon which the beatitudes of this Book are suspended. Our English version
reads, " Blessed are they that do his commandments, that they may have
right to the tree of life, and may enter in through the gates into the city."
The now better-established reading, to which all consent, literally rendered,
is : " *Blessed they that wash their robes, that they may [in that day shall] have
the power over the tree of life, and enter by the gates into the city.*"* The meaning
is not essentially different ; but the true reading cuts out the possibility of a

* See the Codex Sinaiticus, Codex Alexandrinus, the Vulgate, the Ethiopic, and some
Armenian copies, Lachmann, Buttmann, Ewald, Thiele, Tregelles, Alford, Wordsworth,
and all the great authorities.

legalistic interpretation, gives to the passage its genuine evangelic flavour, and conforms its imagery to what was previously said in this Book with reference to what brought the great multitude out of the great tribulation. (Chap. 7 : 14.)

Washing, or cleansing, is the great qualification for heaven,—" the washing of water by the word " (Eph. 5 : 26),—" the washing of regeneration " (Tit. 3 : 5),—cleansing by the blood of Jesus Christ (1 John 1 : 7). There is no doing or keeping of commandments that can save us without this. (Eph. 2 : 8, 9.) Hence Paul speaks of the Corinthian Christians as " washed, sanctified, justified in the name of the Lord Jesus, and by the Spirit of our God " (1 Cor. 6 : 11) ; and John ascribes glory and dominion to the Lord Jesus for having washed [freed] us from our sins in His own blood (Rev. 1 : 5) ; and the writer of the Epistle to the Hebrews speaks of our drawing near to the holiest of all, " having our hearts sprinkled from an evil conscience, and our bodies washed with pure water " as the high priest of old (Heb. 10 : 22). Nor can we ever hope to enter the Holy City, or eat of its fruits, or taste of its blessedness, without this spiritual washing from all the filthinesses of the flesh and of the spirit. " The dogs, or unclean ones, and the sorcerers, and the fornicators, and the murderers, and the idolaters, and every one loving and making a lie [or what is false]," are all excluded from that pure and holy habitation. And whoever hath good hope of seeing and being with Christ in heaven, " purifieth himself even as he is pure." (1 John 3 : 2, 3.)

But the washing of which the text speaks, whilst presupposing and including this general cleansing, is something more special. It is a washing of *garments* or *robes*. It has reference to habit in particular, in addition to the nature in general. One's clothes are reckoned with himself. They are an outside part of him, but that which marks the form, order, or habit in which he bears himself. There is something moral and spiritual in clothes. They express much of the inward taste and character. They come between us and society, to a large extent represent us to society, and react again on our inner consciousness, moral sense, and state of mind and heart. We cannot always judge one from the clothes he wears, but we cannot help the effect which clothes have upon our judgment of people. They tell a story of the wearers of them. And if any one is habitually filthy, slovenly, unclean, and untidy in his garments, it is a blur upon him, a repugnance, a thing to make his presence unwelcome and undesirable in respectable company. When it comes to agreeable social recognition and intercourse, clean clothes are associated with a right heart, a right mind, and a right feeling. Anything short of this is an offence and a disqualification. Hence the Scriptural figure of keeping one's garments and washing one's robes, as a spiritual requirement for the society of heaven. He that hath not on " a wedding garment " is cast out, and not permitted to have place at the supper-table of the king. We must therefore distinguish this washing of robes and cleanness of apparel from the spiritual and more inward washing of the man in general.

What, then, is this particular washing of garments ? This question I have nowhere seen answered ; and yet it needs to be answered, and can be answered. Nor need we be surprised if it should turn out to have direct reference to the main subject of this Apocalypse. The chief honours of the kingdom at Christ's coming are everywhere connected with a looking and waiting for that coming, and the earnest and loving direction of our hearts and hopes to it as the great goal of our faith. Thus we read, " Unto *them that look for him* shall he appear the second time without sin unto salvation." (Heb. 9 : 28.) " The grace of God that bringeth salvation hath appeared, teaching us that denying ungodliness and fleshly lusts, we should live soberly, righteously, and godly in this present world, *looking for that blessed hope, even the glorious appearing of the great God and our Saviour Jesus Christ.*" (Tit. 2 : 11–13.) " There is laid up for me a crown of righteousness, which the Lord the righteous Judge shall give me at that day ; and not to me only, but unto *all them also that love His appearing."* (2 Tim. 4 : 8.) " Ye turned to God from idols to serve the living and true God, *and to wait for his Son from heaven."* (1 Thess. 1 : 9, 10.) It appears from this, and suchlike passages, that the attitude of looking, waiting, watching, and constant stretching forth of the heart, for the coming again of the Lord Jesus in his great Apocalypse, is the proper Christian habit, and that we put our prospects in peril where this habit is not cherished and kept as the very spirit and life of our faith. And the putting of ourselves in this attitude, and the cultivation of this habit, is what I take to be the particular washing and keeping of our garments to which the Scriptures so frequently refer. It is the general washing in the blood of Christ carried out into the habit of the soul toward his promised return.

An example of this particular washing and whitening of the Christian's robes is given us in the case of the great multitude which comes out of the great Tribulation. (Rev. 7 : 9–14.) What was the particular defect and trouble which brought them into that tribulation ? Why were they not in the company of those who were kept from that " hour of trial " and already crowned in heaven before the great tribulation set in ? The Saviour himself, in Matthew 24 : 42–51, and elsewhere, gives the explanation. They would not believe that Christ could come in their lifetime. They did not watch and keep themselves in readiness for his return. They said, " My Lord delayeth his coming ; " and began to smite their fellow-servants, to run with the common world around them, to eat and drink with the drunken, and did not keep themselves girded as servants that wait for their Lord. Hence they were not ready when their Lord came, and for that reason were cut off from the exalted favours of the waiting and ready ones, and compelled to feel the weight of the afflictions which then fall in judgment upon the godless world. And this was the having of soiled garments, unwashed robes, which had to be made white to fit them for place in the society of heaven. A great multitude of them get to heaven afterwards, because they wash their robes and make them clean in the blood of the Lamb. And that washing, as we learn from the Parable of the Ten Virgins, is the bringing of themselves to a true advent faith and habit.

So again, in Rev. 16 : 15, this same keeping of garments is specifically connected with a state or habit of watching and being in readiness for the impending advent of the Lord Jesus Christ. " Behold, I come as a thief ; blessed is he that watcheth and *keepeth his garments."*

It is therefore clear to me that this washing of robes and keeping of garments relates to the attitude and habit of looking for the coming of Christ, and keeping in constant expectation and readiness for it as an impending event. And the blessedness of access to and power over the Tree of Life, and of entrance by the gates of pearl into the Golden City, is here made to depend on this very washing of our robes and keeping of our garments. What a lesson for those who despise the advent teachings and make light of the doctrine of the certain and speedy coming of the Lord ! Brethren, as you hope to walk those golden streets, and eat of those immortal fruits, see to it that you have your garments clean and " your loins girded about like unto men waiting for their Lord."

> Watch ! 'tis your Lord's command ;
>   And while we speak, He's near.
> Mark the first signal of His Hand,
>   And ready all appear.
>
> O happy servant he,
>   In such a pasture found !
> *He* shall his Lord with rapture see,
>   And be with honour crowned.

LECTURE FIFTY-SECOND

END OF THE BOOK—CHARACTER AND MAJESTY OF CHRIST—TIME FOR FULFILLING THESE WONDERS—HOW WE ARE TO BE AFFECTED TOWARD THEM—GUARDS ABOUT WHAT IS WRITTEN—CHRIST'S OWN SUMMATION OF THE CONTENTS OF THE BOOK—THE ATTITUDE OF THE CHURCH—CONCLUSION.

REV. 22 : 16–21. (Revised Text.) I Jesus sent my angel to testify to you these things upon [or, *over*] the churches. I am the Root and the race [or, *Offspring*] of David, the bright, the morning star.

And the Spirit and the Bride say, Come. And let him who heareth say, Come. And let him who is athirst come. He who willeth let him take water of life freely [or, *as a gift*].

I testify to every one who heareth the words of the prophecy of this book, If any one add [or, *shall have added*] to [or, *upon*] them, God shall add to [or, *upon*] him the plagues which are written in this book ; and if any one shall take away from the words of the book of this prophecy, God shall take away his part from the tree of life and the holy City which are written in this book.

He who testifieth these things saith, Yea, I come quickly.

Amen, Come, Lord Jesus.

The grace of the Lord Jesus [be] with all the saints.

EVERY attentive reader will observe how much the conclusion of this Book is like its beginning. Its derivation from God, the signifying of it by the angel, the seeing, hearing, and writing of it by John, the blessing upon those who give due attention to it, the nearness of the time for the fulfilment of what is described, the solemn authentication from Christ, the titles by which he describes himself, and even the personal expressions of John, recur in the Epilogue, almost the same as in the Prologue. Much, therefore, which would here be in place has already been anticipated in the opening Lectures in this course. And after what was said a week ago, there remain but a few points more upon which to remark in bringing this exposition to a close.

I. The first of these points relates to the character and majesty of Christ.

Before he was born, the angel said to Joseph, " Call his name JESUS, for he shall save his people from their sins." (Matt. 1 : 21.) This name was given him ; and this name he still owns in heaven. He says : " *I, Jesus*, sent my angel to testify to you these things." It is as our Saviour that he has given these revelations, and it is as our Saviour that he will fulfil them. It is part of his salvation work—the great superstructure of which his first coming was the foundation—the bloom and fruitage of what was then planted. As Jesus, *Saviour*, he was spoken of by the ancient prophets ; as Jesus, *Saviour*, he was born into our world ; as Jesus, *Saviour*, he died, rose again, and ascended into heaven ; as Jesus, *Saviour*, he sent the Holy Ghost, and ever liveth to intercede for us ; and as Jesus, *Saviour*, he sent his angel to signify these things, and will come again to fulfil them.

But, in claiming that *he* sent this angel, he at the same time claims to be the sovereign of all sacred wisdom and truth. In verse 6 it was said that " the Lord, the God of the spirits of the prophets," sent this angel ; and here he says, " I, JESUS," sent him—sent him as " *my angel.*" He thus identifies himself with the eternal source of all inspiration—with the very Lord God Almighty. He is not only a *Saviour*, but " a great one." What he thus does, and proposes to do, and tells the churches that he will do, he does, not as a mere man, not as a mere prophet and high priest, but as the possessor of all prerogatives and powers of Godhead—as the Lord God of angels, and the Lord God of the spirits of all prophets. There is no place for the Arian heresy in this Book. Whilst he is ever JESUS, born of the Virgin Mary, and the Lamb that was slain, he is nevertheless the ever-living JEHOVAH, true God as well as true man, whom all the principalities of heaven worship even as the Lamb, to whom " the blessing, and the honour, and the glory, and the dominion, for the ages of the ages," is to be ascribed.

Nor are these the only titles under which he here presents himself. He who says " Behold, I come quickly, and my reward with me to give to each as his work is," further adds, " *I, the Alpha and the Omega, First and Last, the Beginning and the End.*" Three times does he take to himself this designation. (Chap. 1: 8; 21: 6; 22: 13.) Of these three expressions, the first is symbolic, signifying the same relation to the universe which the first and last letters of the alphabet bear to the whole series of letters ; the second is the same in signification, and is the Old Testament designation of God, even that by which he encourages confidence in the promises and predictions given through the prophets (Is. 41: 4; 44: 6; 48: 12) ; and the third emphasizes the same thought only in a more philosophic style. The three together are among the most profound and intense denotations of the eternity, the immutability, the almightiness, the omniscience, and the faithfulness of Deity. In thus appropriating them to himself, the Lord Jesus claims to be the eternal One, from whom all being proceeds, and to whom all being tends and returns,—the source and the end of all history,—he who called the world into existence, presides over all its changes, and brings it to its consummation according to his own will. He thus sets himself before our faith as he who originated all things, who knows equally all that has happened and that will happen, and who is the ever-living and unchanging Administrator of all that is or can be, so that what he makes known as yet to take place may be accepted and relied on with perfect confidence, as rooted and grounded in the eternal Wisdom and Almightiness. He must therefore be very God of very God, the coequal and co-eternal Son of the Father. And in this character he makes and engages to perform whatever is predicted in the prophecies of this Book.

And still further does he describe himself in relation to these revelations. Sending his angel to testify these things for the churches, he declares, " *I am the Root and the offspring of David, the bright, the morning Star.*" The duality of his nature, as at once both God and man, is here affirmed. As God, he is the Root or origination of David,—he who gave David being and place, and out of whom David was raised up, even David's Lord ; and as man, he is the offspring of David, David's son, one born of the house and lineage of David. (Matt. 22: 43.) He is the Kernel in the Kernel of the ancient Theocracy, at once the source and blossom of it,—the Jehovah which induced it, at length revealed as its product,—the object of Old Testament adoration incarnated as the great promised One of the seed of Abraham, of the house of David. Hence the additional statement, that he is " *the bright and morning Star.*" The covetous prophet, Balaam, impelled by the Spirit contrary to his wishes, prophesied of a star to come out of Jacob, and a sceptre to rise out of Israel, with which should be the dominion. (Numb. 24: 17–19.) That star, now come to its full brightness, and ushering in the morning of the eternal blessedness, Christ here claims to be. And as the Godman risen out of Jacob, and possessed of all authority and dominion, he gives forth these revelations, and pledges to fulfil them. He thus teaches us what a sublime Lord and Saviour we have, and what is the foundation on which we may count that he will fulfil all the wonders of this Apocalypse.

II. A second of these remaining points relates to the time when these things shall come to pass.

One cannot but be impressed with the constantly repeated expressions touching the nearness of these occurrences. In the very opening verses the note was sounded, " *The time is near.*" The same is heard throughout all that followed. And here, in the conclusion of all, the same is reiterated, over and over, that these things " *must come to pass shortly.*" Three times the Saviour says, " *Behold, I come quickly.*" And the voice which commanded the seer not to seal up what he heard and saw, also adds, " *The time is near.*" Nor is it here· alone, but throughout the New Testament in general, that such expressions are used. Everywhere is the promised Apocalypse of the Lord Jesus represented as close at hand, liable to occur at any time. The impression thus made upon the early Christians was, that Christ might come at any day or hour, even in their own lifetime. Exactly when he would come, was nowhere told them. According to the Saviour's word, it was not for them to know the times or the seasons, which the Father hath put in his own power. (Acts I : 6, 7.) Nay, from that time to the present, and for all time till the promise itself comes to be fulfilled, the saying of Christ has held, and must hold, " Of that day and hour knoweth no man, no, not the angels of heaven, but my Father only." (Matt. 24 : 36.) It was useless, therefore, for them, and will continue to be useless for any one, to attempt to ascertain or determine, how long it will be till Christ shall come again, or how soon all these things shall be accomplished. When once they begin to come to pass, men will be able to tell where they are, and to know that the time has arrived ; but, till then, they must needs remain in ignorance. All the instruction which we have upon the subject is, that what is foreshown will certainly come to pass ; and that, from the beginning until the fulfilment commences, we are to be in constant expectation of it any year, any day, any hour ; to which the ever-present and ever-intensifying signs, together with the multiplied precepts of the holy Scriptures, continually admonish us. Well has Archer Butler said, " To seek to penetrate more closely into these awful secrets is vain. A sacred obscurity envelops them. The cloud that shrouded the actual presence of God on the mercy-seat, shrouds still his expected presence on the throne of judgment. It is a purposed obscurity, and most salutary and useful obscurity, a wise and merciful denial of knowledge. In this matter it is his gracious will to be the perpetual subject of watchfulness, expectation, conjecture, fear, desire,— but no more. To cherish anticipation, he has permitted gleams of light to cross the darkness ; to baffle presumption, he has made them *only* gleams. He has harmonized with consummate skill, every part of his revelation to produce this general result ;—now speaking as if a few seasons more were to herald the new heaven and the new earth, now as if his days were thousands of years ; at one moment whispering into the ear of his disciple, as if ready to be revealed, at another retreating into the depth of infinite ages. It is his purpose thus to live in our faith and hope, remote yet near, pledged to no moment, possible at any ; worshipped not with the consternation of a near, or the indifference of a distant certainty, but with the anxious vigilance that awaits a contingency ever at hand. This, the deep devotion of watchfulness, humility, and awe, he who knows us best knows to be the fittest posture for our spirits ; therefore does he preserve the salutary suspense that ensures it, and therefore will he determine his advent to no definite day in the calendar of eternity."

But the much-emphasized fact, put forth with all these promises and pre- dictions of his return, that the interval between us and their accomplishment dare never be extended in our estimate, and is always represented as brief,— so brief that we never know but that another year, or month, or week, or day may reveal to us our coming Lord,—ought not to be without the most quick- ening effect upon our hearts and devotions. Certainly, what we are so solemnly told is " near," and " must shortly come to pass," we are at no liberty to postpone, or to think yet far away. And especially now, that eighteen hundred years of that "shortly" have passed, and that every symptom of the close proximity of the end is so manifest, should we beware of thinking that years and ages are yet to intervene before our Lord's coming can occur. Ever, as the Church moves on through time, and above all in the days in which we live, the next thing for every Christian to be looking for in this world is the coming of Christ to fulfil what is written in this Book. The Bible tells of nothing between us and that Day.

III. A third of these remaining points relates to the proper spiritual affection toward the speedy accomplishment of these holy predictions.

The Apocalypse of Christ is the coming or revelation of Christ in the scenes and achievements which are here described. But it is not made known to us as a thing of cold and barren speculation. It is the living outcome of all our faith and hope as Christians. It is a thing to which every proper Christian impulse necessarily goes out. There can be no genuine Christianity, no true and living sympathy with what we profess to believe, if there be no going forth of the soul to what is thus set before us. This is here expressed with a depth and intensity which should not fail to impress every serious heart.

First of all, the Holy Ghost himself calls for the Apocalypse of Christ. " The Spirit says, *Come ;* " that is, *Come thou ;* as an answer made to the announcement of the preceding verse. So the Syriac version, and all sound interpreters. When the promise of the Paraclete, the Spirit of truth, was given, Christ said : " He will guide you into all truth : and *he will show you things to come.*" (John 16 : 13.) Descending upon the Church always to abide with it, that Spirit has ever been active and operative in and through the Church. And in all these gracious operations there is a direct and constant reference to these things to come, to make them known, to awaken and nurture faith in them, and to prepare men to become partakers in their blessedness. In all these operations there is therefore a constant looking and yearning for the fulfilment of what is thus to come, and hence an unceasing calling of the Holy Ghost to the bright and morning star to come, as promised and foreshown,—to consummate the great work by that Apocalypse to which all prophecy, all faith, all hope, and all the operative graces of the Spirit have reference. In other words, it is the very spirit, soul, and aim of divine grace to bring the great consummation, which comes alone through the coming of Christ. In the inspiration of prophets and apostles, in the regeneration and sanctification of men, and in all the appointments, endowments, and labours of the Church, in so far as the Holy Ghost is potent and active in them, there is one unceasing call and pleading for that return of the Godman, by whose coming again all things are to be completed and the whole work finished up. Two things, therefore, are thus certified to us ; first, that there is no true and saving religion—no piety originating from and resting in the Spirit of God—which does not anxiously move toward and centre on Christ and his promised Apocalypse ; and second, that the fulfilment of these predictions is absolutely certain, in that the operations of the Holy Ghost in the Church are all conditioned to and ever calling for the bright and morning star to come.

And what the Spirit looks to and calls for is repeated in the spiritual consciousness of the Bride. The Bride is not the Church outwardly taken ; for not all who have connection with the Church as a visible body shall be everlastingly joined with the Lamb. None are the Bride but those who in living inward fact are joined to Christ as the branches are joined to the vine. Only those who are spiritually in Christ, " members of his body, of his flesh, and of his bones " (Eph. 5 : 30), are his Bride. And it is here given as a characteristic of the Bride, that she re-echoes and embodies the call of the Spirit, even the call for the bright and morning star to come. When men forget to think of the coming again of the Lord Jesus in his great Apocalypse,—when they cease to look and long for that as the crown and goal of their faith and hope,—when they make light of it, and treat it as a fable, and regard all concern about it as fanaticism,—they show and prove that they do not belong to that elect body of God's saints which constitutes the Bride of the Lamb ; for the deepest heart-voice of the Bride, with that of the Spirit itself, is, " Come, Lord Jesus ; come as thou hast promised and foreshown ; come quickly." Taking all the precepts and inculcations of the sacred Scriptures with regard to Christ's return, it becomes a plain and evident impossibility for people to be true and obedient followers of the Gospel, and not to look, and watch, and long, and pray, and make it a great point in all their religious activity and devotion to be ready for the glorious coming of the great God and our Saviour Jesus Christ. The Apostles and early Christians were all alive to this subject beyond everything else in Christianity. It was their life, their inspiration, the pole-star of their faith and hope. It was the thing which most marked them, set them apart from the world, and was their great distinguishing spirit, as compared with other people. And if it is not so with Christians now, it is because they have sunk away from the original life of their religion, and lost their proper fellowship with the true and only Bride of the Lamb ; for the voice of the Bride to her Lord continually is, " *Come.*" Nor can she be in the spirit and life of a true Bride without having this feeling ever living in her soul, and permeating her whole being. Destined for Christ, and having her chief joy and salvation in him and what he is ordained to accomplish for his people, she cannot but go out with all zeal and fervency for his revelation, or she ceases in soul from her character as his Bride.

And what the Spirit and the Bride say, every one that heareth is to say, and must learn to say, if ever he is to become partaker in these glorious things. The hearer is he who is made acquainted with these great purposes of God, and is informed of what is in reserve for God's true people. But his hearing will profit him nothing if it does not awaken his soul, kindle his desires, and draw him to devout longing and endeavour to possess and realize these things for himself. Nor is he rightly awake and appreciative to what he hears, so long as he does not care whether Christ is to come again or not, or does not centre his soul upon what can only come with Christ's glorious Apocalypse. Therefore the word here is, " *Let him who heareth say, Come.*" Redemption lies in that coming ; and if men do not learn to desire it, they do not yet desire the redemption that is in Christ Jesus, and are not yet true and believing hearers. For all effectual hearing of the Gospel must come to fervent and loving desire and prayer for Christ to fulfil all his plan and purposes of grace.

And from this emphatic and all-pervading looking and yearning of everything Christian for the Apocalypse of Christ, the call for it widens and deepens into an invitation and incentive to all who desire eternal blessedness, and to all who have any mind or appetite for the waters of life. " *And let him who is athirst come. He who willeth let him take the water of life freely.*" The meaning is, that the waters of life, as they flow in the New Jerusalem, which comes not till Christ comes, are to be had without money and without price ; but that those who thirst for those waters are to join with the company and call of those who thus yearn for the blessed consummation. If any one is athirst for these waters, or has a mind and appetite for them, the word is, " *Let him come.*" Come *whither,* come *to what ?* Come into fellowship with the Spirit, the Bride, and every believing hearer of their testimony, in yearning, and looking, and praying for the coming of the Lord to fulfil what he has promised, and this Book describes. Everything in grace is moving and looking to that ; and if any are athirst for God's living waters, or if any have a will to partake of them, this is the way to get them. No price is set upon them. They are free as the air to every one who would have them. But the free partaking of them is by faith in Christ, by seizing hold upon his promises to his Church, and by joining the cry of the Spirit, the yearning of the Bride, and the soul of all right hope, in " looking for and hasting unto the coming of the day of God," even the glorious Apocalypse of the blessed Christ.

IV. Accordingly there is presented still another point with reference to the preservation of what is set forth in this Book. It is the Book of the outcomes of all the operations of God in our world. It is the great Redeemer's own fore-showing to his people how and wherein all their faith in him and all their expectations as true believers are to reach their final goal. There is therefore no more important sacred Book, none more necessary to regulate the beliefs and anticipations of Christian people with regard to the future. To tamper with it, is to tamper with the divinely given chart of the most momentous things in the destiny of Christ and his Church and people. And hence, with a solemnity that we nowhere else encounter, and with a stringency the most intense in all the word of God, the Saviour himself, from his throne in heaven, says : " *I testify to every one who heareth the words of the prophecy of this Book, If any one add* [or *shall have added*] *to or upon them, God shall add to or upon him the plagues which are written in this Book ; and if anyone shall take away from the words of the Book of this prophecy, God shall take away his part from the tree of life and the holy City which are written in this Book.*"

As if this Book were itself the Tree of Life which it describes, here are the Cherubim with flaming sword turning every way to guard and protect it. To Israel, in the days of Moses, God said, " Ye shall not add unto the word that I command you, neither shall ye diminish from it." (Deut. 4 : 2.) At a later period the wise man said, " Every word of God is pure. Add thou not unto his words lest he reprove thee, and thou be found a liar." (Prov. 30 : 5, 6.) But here the warning and prohibitions are far more intense, and the penalties terrible in the extreme. To mutilate this Book, to take from or to add to what it describes as the course and outcome of the divine purposes, is simply to forfeit salvation itself. Could this be if we did not here have the very kernel and consummation of all that prophets have written, and in which grace and salvation have their chief significance and crown ? Would God affix the profoundest sanctions of eternity to a dim outline of a little mixed history of this world, which three-fourths of its readers never knew or could understand, and which might never have been revealed at all without any appreciable damage to the piety or to the hopes of God's people in any age ? The very absurdity of the thought is demonstration that this Book is something infinitely higher, more solemn, and more essential than the vast mass of modern exposition makes it. No man can be lost or saved simply on account of his receiving or rejecting what the historical interpreters set forth as the chief meaning of the Apocalypse. On their theory, the whole Book might be sunk in eternal oblivion, and still no serious damage result to the faith of the Church, or men's calculations for the future. But in the estimate of God, he who adds to or takes from what it presents, disables all right conception of the system of redemption, and inflicts an injury so great that he who does it need never hope for salvation. How important, therefore, how precious in the eye of heaven, how necessary to the right instruction of God's people, how vital to the proper Christian faith and hope are the unmutilated and unchanged foreshowings which this Book was given to set forth !

The penalty upon every corrupter of these records also helps to fix and establish the right interpretation of them. " Plagues " constitute one of the prominent subjects ; and those " plagues " are to be laid upon each hearer who involves himself in the guilt of adding to or diminishing the contents of this Book. They must therefore be literal " plagues," such as can be laid upon separate individuals, and not mere symbols of disturbances of nations, shakings of empires, calamities to systems, and revolutions in governments. Such " plagues " are incapable of being imposed upon individual men, and individual men are contemplated in this anathema. Except, therefore, where otherwise indicated, " the plagues which are written in this Book " are contemplated by Christ himself as literal " plagues ; " and we have simply followed his mind in so explaining them. Just what particular plagues are covered by the threat, we may not be able to determine ; but what the wicked suffer, the same is to be the portion of him who dares to abridge or augment the contents of these records. And when we consider how unbelief despises this Book and its philosophy of things,—how a self-wise and rationalistic latitudinarianism neglects it, ridicules all serious attention to it, and empties it of all respectable meaning and worth,—how a presumptuous criticism disables it with wild and stilted theories of poetry and symbolization,—and how even Christian men fight against the admission of its clear teachings when allowed to speak for themselves,—what are we to conclude, but that in these very things we have the sowing for the whole harvest of plagues written in this Book ?

O, my friends, it is a fearful thing to suppress or stultify the word of God, and above all " the words of the prophecy of this Book." To put forth for truth what is not the truth,—to denounce as error, condemn, repudiate, or emasculate what God himself hath set his seal to as his mind and purpose, is one of those high crimes, not only against God, but against the souls of men, which cannot go unpunished. With an honest and ever-prayerful heart, and with these solemn and awful warnings ever before my eyes, I have endeavoured to ascertain and indicate in these Lectures what our gracious Lord and Master has been so particular to make known and defend. If I have read into this Book anything which he has not put there, or read out of it anything which he has put there, with the profoundest sorrow would I recant, and willingly burn up the books in which such mischievous wickedness is contained. If I have in anything gone beyond the limits of due subjection to what is written, or curtailed in any way the depth and measure of what Jesus by his angel has signified for the learning of the Churches, I need not the condemnation of men to heap upon me the burden of censure which I deserve. If feebleness, or rashness, or overweening confidence in my own understanding has distorted anything, I can only deplore the fault, and pray God to send a man more competent to unfold to us the mighty truths which here stand written. According to the grace and light given me, have I spoken. And before God, angels, and men, I am compelled to protest, especially, against all that modern interpretation which dwarfs this Book into an overwrought and indeterminate showing of a few meagre chapters of the Church's history this side the day of judgment. If I err, God forgive me ! If I am right, God bless my feeble testimony ! In either case, God speed his everlasting truth !

V. Yet one other point remains to be noticed. It is Christ's own final summation of the contents of this Book. From the beginning we were told that it was given to show the Apocalypse of Jesus Christ. The whole series of visions fit together as so many successive acts and administrations in the closing up of this present world, and the introduction of the eternal order, according to God's eternal purpose. And so here, in the last words of the Book, the Saviour himself sums up the all-comprehending substance of the whole in this one brief sentence : " *He who testifieth these things saith,* YEA, I COME QUICKLY."

Who that has ever looked carefully into the subject, but has been struck with the towering prominence which the Scriptures everywhere assign to the coming again of the Lord Jesus ? The New Testament has more references to this particular topic than it has pages. Of all the seven or eight thousand verses of which it is composed, one out of every twenty-five points forward with eager gesture to the appearing again of the Lord Jesus. Again and again it is set forth as the great hope of the Church. There is not a Christian grace or virtue for the enforcement of which appeal is not made to it. Nor is there another subject upon which more stress is laid in all the Word of God. To many, indeed, it is anything but welcome. There be even professing Christians who would rather not hear about it, and who, if they could have their way, would erase it from the Creed, and silence all preaching concerning it. But the religion of such is much aside from the Scriptures, and occasion is urgent for them to bestir themselves to re-examine and relay their foundations. *Christian faith and hope have no outcome but in the glorious Apocalypse of Jesus.* And only when we come to understand that the coming again of Christ is the fulfilment of the things described in this Book, can we appreciate why so much is referred to that coming, and why the venerable Apostle should here, at the end of his Book, bow his hoary head, and say, and write, his solemn " *Amen. Even so come, Lord Jesus.*"

The truth is, my friends, that there is no greater or gladder promise in all the Book of God, than this last word of Jesus to his people, " *Yea, I come quickly.*" It is the promise of promises—the crown and consummation of all promise—the coronation of all evangelic hopes—the sum of all prophecy and

prayer. Nature and grace alike proclaim a glorified Messiah, come again from
heaven in his almightiness, as indispensable to complete their appointed
course. Nature calls for him thus to come, to rectify her unwilling disorders,
to repair her shattered structures, to restore her oppressed energies, to vindicate her voice of conscience long despised, her sublime testimony to the
Creator so long questioned and overlooked. But grace sends forth a still
mightier call. If the whole creation groans and travails together in pain for
the manifestation of the sons of God, how much more those sons of God
themselves !

And why should not this be our spirit ? Compare the sordidness of this
world with the crystal purity and splendour of the New Jerusalem. Think
of the dust, and dearth, and soil and toil of earth, in comparison with that
River and Tree of Life which refresh, and adorn, and satisfy the dwellers
in those eternal mansions. Consider the ill mixtures, defects, wearinesses,
vexations, darkness, and disabilities of life here, alongside of the perfections
and sublimities which mark the society and estate of those who walk those
streets of gold. Why should we wish to suffer, and toil, and sigh amid the
miseries of a scene like this, when such a city of unchanging blessedness throws
open its gates of pearl for our admission ? Are we so in love with aches, and
ills, and wrongs, and disappointments, and treacheries, and diseases, and
death-beds, and graves, and torments and temptations of Satan, as not to be
willing to be done with them forever ? With what ardour, then, and delight,
and enthusiastic joy, should we embrace this word of our Saviour, " *Yea,
I come quickly !* " Have we no mind for the realization of that precious
" liberty of the children of God,"—no wish to behold our lowliness glorified
in the glory of the Man of Nazareth,—no longing to have our humble labours
recognized and approved by our enthroned Redeemer,—no appreciation of
the vindication of our persevering faith, of the consummation of our hopes
and prayers, of the brightening of our love and charity into rewards eternal
and infinite ? Ah, yes ; everything in and about us, in the weakness of man
and in the working of God, yearns and calls and prophesies for the coming
again of Jesus,—everything but the cold, unfeeling, unsanctified heart of
man ! But there, alas, no voice is heard going forth to bid the Lord of salvation welcome ! People's hearts are inured to the world's corruptions, and how
can they hail an immortality of meekness, simplicity, and love ? Men's spirits
are habituated to seek unholy ends by means still more unholy, and how can
they endure the bringing in of everlasting righteousness ? Their calculations,
hopes, and aims are bounded to things of time and sense, and how can they
regard otherwise than with terror so complete a change as that when he who
now rules behind a mass of permitted evils visibly assumes the reins of
universal dominion ? Of course all such are ill at ease with our doctrines, and
well may tremble, and call to rocks and mountains to cover and hide them
from the discomfiture and sorrow which Christ's Apocalypse must bring to
souls so earthy. But let all God's saints hold fast the blessed hope, and lift
up their heads as they see the time approaching. What is there to command
our fondest joy, our gladdest anticipation, if not this coming day of our completed happiness and finished redemption ?

Fiction has painted the picture of a maiden whose lover left her for a voyage
to the Holy Land, promising on his return to make her his beloved bride.
Many told her that she would never see him again. But she believed his word,
and evening by evening she went down to the lonely shore, and kindled there
a beacon-light in sight of the roaring waves, to hail and welcome the returning
ship which was to bring again her betrothed. And by that watchfire she took
her stand each night, praying to the winds to hasten on the sluggish sails,
that he who was everything to her might come. Even so that blessed Lord,
who has loved us unto death, has gone away to the mysterious Holy Land
of heaven, promising on his return to make us his happy and eternal Bride.
Some say that he has gone forever, and that here we shall never see him

more. But his last word was, " *Yea, I come quickly.*" And on the dark and misty beach sloping out into the eternal sea, each true believer stands by the love-lit fire, looking, and waiting, and praying and hoping for the fulfilment of his word, in nothing gladder than in his pledge and promise, and calling ever from the soul of sacred love, " EVEN SO COME, LORD JESUS." And some of these nights, while the world is busy with its gay frivolities, and laughing at the maiden on the shore, a form shall rise over the surging waves, as once on Galilee, to vindicate forever all this watching and devotion, and bring to the faithful and constant heart a joy, and glory, and triumph which never more shall end.

To bring listless and uninstructed souls believingly and intelligently to the position and attitude of that maiden, is the intent of this Book, and of these Lectures upon it. And if by these long studies any hearers are brought to such love-waiting and watching on these dark shores of time, with thanks and praises to Him from whom has come the grace, and with heart and soul set in confident expectation of the speedy fulfilment of the wonders we have been contemplating, I am content to take my leave of these labours.

" *The grace of the Lord Jesus be with all the saints.*"

AMEN.

S

INDEX

The figures refer to the pages, and the letter n to the footnotes.

A.

Abaddon, king of the locusts, 206 ; as a place, 449.

Abyss, the, opened by Satan, 205–210 ; place of, 210, n ; differs from "lake of fire," 446.

Adam of St. Victor, quoted, 106, n.

Advent, Second, of Christ, 30–32, 73, 74 ; brings honours to the redeemed, 74 ; near at hand, 96, 97 ; 522, 523 ; gradual, 235 ; extending through a variety of scenes, 405, 406 ; how we are to await the, 524, 525 ; attitude of the church toward, 527–529 ; signs accompanying, 31 ; delay of, 230, 231 ; certainty of, 231, 232 ; visible, 31, 434–437.

Air, convulsions in, during the seventh plague, 380.

Alford, quoted ; on Elijah, 247, n ; on the locusts, 208, n ; on the first Resurrection, 461, 464.

Alleluia, 419–421.

Amen, 420.

Andreas, quoted, 76.

Angel, the one sent to John, 19 ; the mighty, of the sixth trumpet, 223, 224 ; act of, 225 ; book in hand of, 226–229 ; proclamation of, 229, 230 ; the Euphratean, 218, 219.

Angels, the seven, of God's presence, 182, 183 ; prepare to sound the trumpets, 190, 191 ; the first sounds, 191–194 ; the second, 194–196 ; the third, 196, 197 ; the fourth, 197–199 ; the fifth, 203–211 ; the sixth, 212–222 ; the seventh, with the golden bowls of wrath, 370–374, 376–382.

Angels, orders of, 182, 183 ; ministrations of, 191 ; evil, 204, 449 ; direct executors of the woes at sounding of sixth trumpet, 218, 219.

Angels, of the churches, 51, 52.

Angel-messages of Rev. 14 : 1–13, 354 ; the first, 354–355 ; the second, 355 ; the third, 356 ; the fourth, 356.

Antichrist, the, 321, 322 ; the beast from the sea, 322 ; the embodiment of political sovereignty, 322 ; one particular man, 323, 324, n ; reigns 42 months, 323, 373, 406 ; the "Man of Sin," 324 ; the same as the wilful king of Daniel, 324 ; or supernatural personage, 325 ; his attractiveness and greatness, 326, 327 ; the antagonist of everything divine, 327, 328 ; the consummate persecutor, 328 ;

the great blasphemer, 328 ; the importance of the doctrine concerning, 328–330 ; not alone, 331 ; assisted by the second beast, 331, 336, 337 ; image of, set up, 345 ; caused to speak, 345, 346 ; worshipped, 345, 346 ; all branded with the mark of, 347 ; number of, 348 ; plagues visited upon, 373 ; church of, 387–391.

Ἀποκάλυψις, pref. vi, 16, 17.

Apocalypse, the, some object to study of, pref. v, vi ; of Jesus, meaning of, 16, 17 ; pref. vi. ; value of study of, 22, 23 ; truth of, 513, 514 ; in relation to the churches on earth, 35–86 ; difficulties of the current method of interpreting, 233, 234 ; blessings accompanying study of, 514, 515, 525, 526 ; Christ's summation of the contents of, 527.

Apocryphal gospels, quoted, 250.

Apollyon, 206.

Apostles, the twelve, shall sit on twelve thrones, 456.

Archangels, the seven, 182, 183.

Ark of the covenant, 272, 273.

Armageddon, 363 ; place of, 380.

Army of Satan, 439, 440 ; slaying of, 442 ; birds invited to the slaughter, 442.

Asia, country of, 26.

Athanasian creed, quoted, 332.

Auberlen, quoted, 96.

Augustine, quoted, on Elijah, 249.

Augsburg Confession, 83, 84.

Azazel, goat for, 219, n.

B.

Babylon, the great, drinks the cup of wrath, 381 ; a difficult subject, 385 ; not Rome alone, 385, 386, 388 ; the church of Antichrist, 387 ; characteristics of, 387–391 ; connected with the primal apostasy after the flood, 388, 389 ; her twofoldness, in mystery and as a city, 396, 397 ; the city of, shall be restored, 397, 398, 405, 406 ; prophecies of her absolute obliteration not yet fulfilled, 398, 399 ; prophecies which seem to require her restoration, 399–404; modern testimonies, 402, n, 403, n, fall of, 407 ; twofold, 407 ; heralds the political regeneration of the earth, 422–424 ; the people called out of, 408 ; calamities visited upon, 408–412 ; causes of